The Humanities in Contemporary Life

EDITED BY

Robert F. Davidson
University of Florida

Sarah Herndon
Florida State University

J. Russell Reaver
Florida State University

William Ruff
University of Florida

The Humanities In Contemporary Life

HOLT, RINEHART AND WINSTON, NEW YORK

Library of Congress Catalog Card Number: 60-6177

21744-0310

Printed in the United States of America

April, 1961

CONTENTS

Part Three

THE WORLD OF INTUITIVE THOUGHT

ILLUSTRATIONS

Following Page 96

Following Page 112

Following Page 272

Following Page 496

INTRODUCTION

There are many ways of interpreting the spirit of the age in which we live. One can analyze the political and social conflicts of our times; one can describe the influence of the sciences which have profoundly altered our existence; or one can emphasize the historical forces that brought the modern world into being. Yet there is a sense in which none of these quite catches the spirit and the pulse of contemporary life. The forces that have shaped modern civilization have also produced a new view of the nature of man and of the character of life itself.

For many thoughtful men and women today, the moral and religious convictions which our ancestors once took for granted have been seriously weakened by what Walter Lippmann aptly terms "the acids of modernity." These ancestors of ours were entirely sure of their own importance in the universe; we have lost that confidence. We tend to live from day to day with little sense of an enduring purpose and meaning in life; we are not sure where we are going—or why. Some the ablest contemporary thinkers doubt whether man has any great significance or life any enduring worth. This critical point of view has found widespread expression in the characteristic literature, philosophy, and art of our age; indeed it is in these three areas that the nature of such a view of life is most clearly to be seen. The humanities when rightly interpreted are not removed from the pulse of life, but are a vital part and expression of it.

No one can live fully and intelligently until he has in some measure made the great cultural achievements of mankind his own, and this aim is an important one in the study of the humanities. But to meet successfully the conflicting demands of modern life, we must also understand clearly the issues that face us today. We must be familiar with the changes that have taken place in the traditional view of human nature and human destiny, and must work out for ourselves—if we can—a satisfying philosophy to give life direction and purpose. The selections included in this volume are designed not only to clarify the role of the humanities in our age but also to make some contribution to this larger need of the human spirit.

Plan of the Book

No attempt will be made to survey all aspects of contemporary life as these are at present interpreted in literature, philosophy, art, and music. Such a task would be impossible in one volume and of questionable worth even if possible. We have made an effort instead to integrate our material around certain crucial aspects of the life and thought of our day, to select works in which these concerns are unmistakably reflected, and to relate the material selected to the experience and problems of young men and women of college age.

The anthology proper is divided into three major sections. Each opens with two general essays which clarify the central issue of that section and provide necessary background for its thoughtful consideration. The first section, "Man in Contemporary Society," is designed to show how the humanities are conditioned by the social forces of our age and to portray the underlying spirit of these social forces. It is as impossible to write as it is to live in a social vacuum. The literature, the philosophy, the art, and even the music, of our generation reflect the character of contemporary life just as surely and just as plainly as the thought and life of the Middle Ages reflected an "Age of Faith" or the outlook of the seventeenth and eighteenth centuries reflected an "Age of Reason."

The second section, "The Impact of Scientific Thought," deals with what many have taken to be *the* major influence upon human life in the contemporary world. If today some of us are less enthusiastic than we should be about what science is doing for mankind, we are certainly none the less responsible for understanding the kind of influence scientists have had in shaping the contemporary mind.

The third section, "The World of Intuitive Thought," gives the other side of the picture. The writers represented here share the conviction that no matter how vigorously we try to direct life by reason and scientific thought, forces beyond our conscious control—instinct, passion, ambition, the will to power, the ideals of religion—do in fact determine human conduct. It is in this connection that we must find meaning and purpose to life—if it is to be found at all. *Anti-intellectualism* and *existentialism* are two terms that suggest the issues raised in this section, issues that are fundamental to the life and thought of our age and that are reflected clearly in the most characteristic contemporary literature, philosophy, and art.

Without question a major concern of our age is to discover values that are enduring and meaningful enough to give to human life the purpose and significance it must have to rise above the animal instincts of survival and reproduction. This is likewise, of course, our most difficult problem; but it is a problem that higher education cannot evade. Our schools and colleges must make a contribution at this level to the insights of their students or they will fail to meet one of their gravest social responsibilities. Hence the final section, "The Search for Values in Contemporary Life," contains half a dozen significant attempts to deal with this issue. If any one of these provides an answer that will enable a student to face the perplexities and the opportunities of contemporary life with new courage, insight, or strength of conviction, then this section will have served its function well.

Principles of Order

The anthology includes fiction, poetry, autobiography, letters, dialogues, and critical essays. We have in general selected material written during the past hundred years, but we have concentrated on the twentieth century, because we find that a contemporary voice usually speaks more directly to college freshmen and sophomores who are just beginning their study of the humanities. We have tried to choose authors of standing in their respective fields who write in a fashion that students such as these will find both understandable and provocative. Poems and short stories are reprinted in their entirety; to abridge these would do violence to the creator's artistic concept. But an essay, a letter, or an autobiographical sketch is a different matter. It is often possible to extract the main point from a number of additional inferences and examples without doing injustice to the thought of the author.

Aim

If we were to select a single motto for the anthology it could well come from Mill's essay *On Liberty:* "He who knows only his own side of the case, knows little of that." We are much interested in stimulating students to think for themselves about the more important issues that concern us all today; we are not interested in trying to force anyone to think as we do about these things. A study of the material included here will provide some genuine understanding of the literature, philosophy, art, and music of our times. But such a study, we believe, can do more than develop a person's appreciation and enjoyment of the humanities; it can also deepen his understanding of issues of living about which he is already being forced to make important decisions. His sense of values can become surer; his insight and his criticism of the superficial, more penetrating. If he considers thoughtfully the ideas presented here, he can come away with a greater ability to make for himself a life that has depth and richness, enlarged understanding, and appreciation. This we take to be the major purpose of a study of the humanities.

October 1959

R. F. D.
S. H.
J. R. R.
W. R.

Part One

MAN IN CONTEMPORARY SOCIETY

1. Social Orientation in Philosophy
2. Social Idealism as Religion
3. The Social Significance of Architecture
4. Painting as Social Protest
5. Social Concern in Literature
6. Nationalism in Music

THE POINT OF VIEW

THE RAPID DEVELOPMENT of the social sciences during the past hundred years is evidence enough of the increasing social awareness of twentieth-century Americans. A century ago history was cultural; geography, physical; economics and politics were branches of philosophy, and sociology and psychology nonexistent. Now these are all full-fledged "social sciences," and the increasing professional curricula of our universities are largely based upon them.

More and more we recognize the needs of social groups rather than of individuals—labor, agriculture, teen-agers, management, education, white-collar workers, the suburbanites. Our most pressing problems are social: the high cost of living, social security, education, defense, mental health, transportation, segregation. In all these the important consideration is not the behavior and achievement of the individual but the needs of social groups. Frequently we forget the well-adjusted teen-ager for the delinquent, the mentally balanced for the pathological, and the exceptional child for the average, and we feel that when we have taken care of group needs we have little further responsibility for the individual. It is up to him to adjust. Even minorities have become "groups."

The Humanities and the Social Sciences

It is important, therefore, to understand the relationship of the humanities to our social problems and interests. In some ways the humanities may seem to be in conflict with the social sciences. In the social sciences the individual is easily lost in the group. In the humanities the individual artist or thinker is of primary importance; he is valuable mainly for the uniqueness of his ideas and expression. Moreover, the study of the humanities is as a rule the study of individual men and women rather than the study of types or groups. Understanding of individual experience comes from direct contact with a work of art rather than from generalizations and abstractions based on statistical data. Hence a study of the humanities complements and supplements the social studies; it takes both to give us mature insight into human life.

More important, however, than this difference between the humanities and the social sciences is the pervasive influence of social forces on our philosophy, our religion, our literature, our music, and our visual art. Our sense of values is largely shaped by the social consciousness of our time. We do not always like to admit the extent to which we have left behind the individualistic ideals of an older frontier way of life and have become a highly complex, highly socialized society. In order that we may better understand the social orientation of contemporary thought and its effect upon the humanities, this section of the anthology is devoted to a consideration of "man in contemporary society."

We include here various interpretations of man and his role in society, but particularly those confronting us in America today. Some selections deal with the greatest contemporary threat to our American way of life, that of communism. Others are concerned with certain aspects of our own complex industrial and social life. These two are not unrelated. A new kind of collectivism seems to be replacing the traditional American faith in individualism. David Riesman and William H. Whyte, Jr., recently startled the reading public with their analysis of this aspect of contemporary life and we use their analysis as our point of departure. For an understanding of our traditional democratic view of liberty and individual rights we go back to John Stuart Mill's classic essay, *On Liberty*. But it is essential also that we recognize the influence of the communist philosophy upon the outlook of the world today. Lenin, one of the major leaders of the Russian movement, has presented in his *State and Revolution* the essential communist philosophy of our day in a nontechnical fashion; we include a brief selection from this book. For a thoughtful analysis of the twentieth-century conflict of communist and democratic ideals we turn to the columnist Walter Lippmann.

The religious dimension of this conflict must also be better understood. A selection by Crane Brinton outlines the religious character of Marxism, and Arthur Koestler in explaining his rejection of communism makes it clear that the power of this revolutionary philosophy over men's minds is really similar to that of a religion. Finally Will Herberg points to the danger that in America we may be substituting for faith in God a kind of vague faith in our own political and social system.

Social Awareness in the Arts

Every artist is deeply affected by the ideals, problems, frustrations, and anxieties of the society in which he works. In our own time we see expressions of this in many ways. One of the major problems of our industrial society has been the development of great cities. As technology has taken hold of these cities, the architects and social engineers have been called in to plan for a better esthetic and practical use of metropolitan centers. In contrast to these developments in city planning and architecture, where the artist, technologist, and social scientist have worked together constructively, the socially aware painter of the nineteenth and twentieth centuries has, for the most part, employed his art as a protest against the *status quo*. Thus Honoré Daumier's social and political caricatures satirized the various types of French character with remarkable effectiveness. In *Guernica* Pablo Picasso, the most versatile and influential contemporary painter, expressed a bitter hatred for modern warfare unparalleled anywhere else in art. In Mexico Diégo Rivera has used mural painting as direct propaganda for his revolutionary ideas and in a strong essay he has argued that art is always an instrument of social message.

The poets and novelists of the late nineteenth and early twentieth centuries have been equally aware of social issues, but are quite diverse in their points of view. Walt Whitman, for example, considered himself the "poet of democracy" and championed many of the social ideals of nineteenth-century America. Carl Sandburg, a generation later, realized more fully an ambition similar to Whitman's: to go up and down the land reading his poetry for the average American. Robert Frost portrays human relationships in a constructive spirit, while Robinson Jeffers, on the contrary, expresses throughout his poems an active and complete pessimism about modern civilization. Among novelists the most ambitious history of our era comes from John Dos Passos, whose "hero" in *U.S.A.* is really American society, the dominant force in the lives of its people. Lionel Trilling, on the other hand, in his fiction as well as criticism effectively reasserts moral values and emphasizes personal responsibility.

While it is impossible for music to express directly a social awareness or social protest, "nationalism" has been one of the important trends in music for the past hundred years. Smetana in Bohemia (Czechoslovakia), Sibelius in Finland, Shostakovitch in Russia, and Aaron Copland in America are well-known composers who have made effective use of distinctly national themes or folk music.

David Riesman

In 1950, with two collaborators, Reuel Denney and Nathan Glazer, David Riesman published The Lonely Crowd: A Study of the Changing American Character, *the result of a research project undertaken for the Yale University Committee on National Policy. To the average reader Riesman is best known for his share in this book, which has sold more than 70,000 copies in a paperback edition and has given contemporary American society a new and widely discussed description of itself. The major thesis of* The Lonely Crowd *is that a fundamental change has been taking place in the character of the American people; where formerly men whose character was "inner-directed" dominated our society, now the tendency is toward the dominance of the "other-directed" individual. This position Riesman undertakes to clarify and support by a broad psychological and sociological study of American life.*

Born in Philadelphia in 1909, Riesman graduated from Harvard University in 1931 with a major in biochemistry and a Phi Beta Kappa key, and received his LL.B. at the Harvard Law School in 1934. After serving as law clerk to Supreme Court Justice Louis Brandeis, he entered the private practice of law in Boston. From 1937 to 1941 he was a professor of law at the University of Buffalo. A few years later, however, he became deputy assistant district attorney of New York County and then shortly thereafter gave up law as a career, taking a position with the Sperry Gyroscope Company on Long Island. Perhaps it was from his experience at Sperry that he conceived the analogy of the gyroscope for the internal mechanism of the "inner-directed" man. In 1946 he resumed his academic career, accepting a position as associate professor of social sciences at the University of Chicago where he is now professor of sociology. In addition to The Lonely Crowd *Riesman has published* Faces in the Crowd *(1952) with Glazer,* Thorstein Veblen: A Critical Interpretation *(1953),* Individualism Reconsidered and Other Essays *(1954), and* Constraint and Variety in American Education *(1956).*

While The Lonely Crowd *has been an influential book, it has also been the subject of much controversy in social science circles. Riesman has not been afraid to deviate from accepted theories, and his critics find in his work strong speculative and imaginative interpretations of social change which do not always seem strictly "scientific." Nevertheless, Riesman was one of fifteen writers, artists, and composers to receive an award of $1000 each by the American Academy and National Institute of Arts and Letters in 1954; and to the general public* The Lonely Crowd *has seemed a true description of our own society. The selection we reprint from this book summarizes the basic changes that Riesman sees at work in American character today.*

THE CHANGING AMERICAN CHARACTER

I speak of the American in the singular, as if there were not millions of them, north and south, east and west, of both sexes, of all ages, and of various races, professions, and religions. Of course the one American I speak of is mythical; but to speak in parables is inevitable in such a subject, and it is perhaps as well to do so frankly.

SANTAYANA, *Character and Opinion in the United States*

THIS IS A BOOK about social character and about the differences in social character between men of different regions, eras, and groups. It considers the ways in which different social character types, once they are formed at the knee of society, are then deployed in the work, play, politics, and child-rearing activities of society. More particularly, it is about the way in which one kind of social character, which dominated America in the nineteenth century, is gradually being replaced by a social character of quite a different sort. Just why this happened; how it happened; what are its consequences in some major areas of life: this is the subject of this book.

But just what do we mean when we speak of "social character"? We do not speak of "personality," which in current social psychology is used to denote the total self, with its inherited temperaments and talents, its biological as well as psychological components, its evanescent as well as more or less permanent attributes. Nor even do we speak of "character" as such, which, in one of its contemporary uses, refers to only a part of personality—that part which is formed not by heredity but by experience (not that it is any simple matter to draw a line between the two): Character, in this sense, is the more or less permanent socially and historically conditioned organization of an individual's drives and satisfactions—the kind of "set" with which he approaches the world and people.

"Social character" is that part of "character" which is shared among significant social groups and which, as most contemporary social scientists define it, is the product of the experience of these groups. The notion of social character permits us to speak, as I do throughout this book, of the character of classes, groups, regions, and nations.

I do not plan to argue over the many ambiguities of the concept of social character—whether it may properly be ascribed to experience rather than to heredity; whether there is any empirical proof that it really exists; whether it is "more important" than the elements of character and personality that bind all people everywhere in the world together, or those other elements of character and personality that separate each individual from every other, even the closest. The assumption that a social character exists has always been a more or less invisible premise of ordinary parlance and is becoming today a more or less visible premise of the social sciences. It will consequently be familiar under one name or another to any of my readers who are acquainted with the writings of Erich Fromm, Abram Kardiner, Ruth Benedict, Margaret Mead, Geoffrey Gorer, Karen Horney, and many others who have written about social character in general, or the social character of different people and different times.

Most of these writers assume—as I do—that the years of childhood are of great importance in molding character. Most of them agree—as I do—that these early years cannot be seen in isolation from the structure of society, which affects the parents who raise the children, as well as the children directly. My collaborators and I base ourselves on this broad platform of agreement, and do not plan to discuss in what way these writers differ from each other and we from them.

I. *Character and Society*

What is the relation between social character and society? How is it that every society seems to get, more or less, the social character it "needs"? Erich Fromm succinctly suggests the line along which this connection between society and character training may be sought: "In order that any society may function well, its members must acquire the kind of character which makes them want to act in the way they have to act as members of the society or of a special class within it. They have to desire what objectively is *necessary* for them to do. *Outer force* is replaced by *inner compulsion,* and by the particular kind of human energy which is channeled into character traits."

Thus, the link between character and society—certainly not the only one, but one of the most significant, and the one I choose to emphasize in this discussion—is to be found in the way in which society ensures some degree of conformity from the individuals who make it up. In each society, such a mode of ensuring conformity is built into the child, and then either encouraged or frustrated in later adult experience. (No society, it would appear, is quite prescient enough to ensure that the mode of conformity it has inculcated will satisfy those subject to it in every stage of life.) I shall use the term "mode of conformity" interchangeably with the term "social character"—though certainly conformity is not all of social character: "mode of creativity" is as much a part of it. However, while societies and individuals may live well enough—if rather boringly—without creativity, it is not likely that they can live without some mode of conformity—even be it one of rebellion.

One of the categories I make use of is taken from demography, the science that deals with birth rates and death rates, with the absolute and relative numbers of people in a society, and their distribution by age, sex, and other variables, for I tentatively seek to link certain social and characterological developments, as cause and effect, with certain population shifts in Western society since the Middle Ages.

It would be very surprising if variations in the basic conditions of reproduction, livelihood, and survival chances, that is, in the supply of and demand for human beings, with all it implies in change of the spacing of people, the size of markets, the role of children, the society's feeling of vitality or senescence, and many other intangibles, failed to influence character. My thesis is, in fact, that each of these three different phases on the population curve appears to be occupied by a society that enforces conformity and molds social character in a definably different way.

The society of high growth potential develops in its typical members a social character whose conformity is insured by their tendency to follow tradition; these I shall term *tradition-directed* people and the society in which they live a *society dependent on tradition-direction.*

The society of transitional population growth develops in its typical members a social character whose conformity is insured by their tendency to acquire early in life an internalized set of goals. These I shall term *inner-directed* people and the society in which they live a *society dependent on inner-direction.*

Finally, the society of incipient population decline develops in its typical members a social character whose conformity is insured by their tendency to be sensitized to the expectations and preferences of others. These I shall term *other-directed* people and the society in which they live one *dependent on other-direction.*

Let me point out, however, before embarking on a description of these three "ideal types" of character and society, that I am not concerned here with making the detailed analysis that would be necessary before one could prove that a link exists between population phase and character type. Rather, the theory of the curve of population provides me with a kind of shorthand for referring to the myriad institutional elements that are also—though usually more heatedly—symbolized by such words as "industrialism," "folk society," "monopoly capitalism," "urbanization," "rationalization," and so on. Hence when I speak here of transitional growth or incipient decline of population in conjunction with shifts in character and conformity, these phrases should not be taken as magical and comprehensive explanations.

II. *The Lonely Crowd*

Bearing these qualifications in mind, it seems appropriate to treat contemporary metropolitan America as our illustration of a society—so far, perhaps, the only illustration—in which other-direction is the dominant mode of insuring conformity. It would be premature, however, to say that it is already the dominant mode in America as a whole. But since the other-directed types are to be found among the young, in the larger cities, and among the upper income groups, we may assume that, unless present trends are reversed, the hegemony of other-direction lies not far off.

If we wanted to cast our social character types into social class molds, we could say that inner-direction is the typical character of the "old" middle class—the banker, the tradesman, the small entrepreneur, the technically oriented engineer, etc.—while other-direction is becoming the typical character of the "new" middle class—the bureaucrat, the salaried employee in business, etc. Many of the economic factors associated with the recent growth of the "new" middle class are well known. They have been discussed by James Burnham, Colin Clark, Peter Drucker, and others. There is a decline in the numbers and in the proportion of the working population engaged in production and extraction—agriculture, heavy industry, heavy transport—and an increase in the numbers and the proportion engaged in white-collar work, and the service trades. People who are literate, educated, and provided with the necessities of life by an ever more efficient machine industry and agriculture, turn increasingly to the "tertiary" economic realm. The service industries prosper among the people as a whole and no longer only in court circles.

These developments lead, for large numbers of people, to changes in paths to success and to the requirement of more "socialized" behavior both for success and for marital and personal adaptation. Connected with such changes are changes in the family and in child-rearing practices. In the smaller families of urban life, and with the spread of "permissive" child care to ever wider strata of the population, there is a relaxation of older patterns of discipline. Under these newer patterns the peer group (the group of one's associates of the same age and class) becomes much more important to the child, while the parents make him feel guilty not so much about the violation of inner standards as about failure to be popular or otherwise to manage his relations with these other children. Moreover, the pressures of the school and the peer group are reinforced and continued—in a manner whose inner paradoxes I shall discuss later—by the mass media: movies, radio, comics, and popular culture media generally. Under these conditions types of character emerge that we shall here term other-directed.

What is common to all the other-directed people is that their contemporaries are the source of direction for the individual—either those known to him or those with whom he is indirectly acquainted, through friends and through the mass media. This source is of course "internalized" in the sense that dependence on it for guidance in life is implanted early. The goals toward which the other-directed person strives shift with that guidance: it is only the process of striving itself and the process of paying close attention to the signals from others that remain unaltered throughout life. This mode of keeping in touch with others permits a close behavioral conformity, not through drill in behavior itself, as in the tradition-directed character, but rather through an exceptional sensitivity to the actions and wishes of others.

It is perhaps an insatiable force of this psychological need for approval that differentiates people of the metropolitan, American upper middle class, whom we regard as other-directed, from very similar types that have appeared in capital cities and among other classes in previous historical periods, whether in Imperial Canton, in eighteenth- and nineteenth-century Europe, or in ancient Athens, Alexandria, or Rome. In all these groups fashion not only ruled as a substitute for morals and customs, but it was a rapidly changing fashion that held sway. It could do so because, although the mass media were in their infancy, the group corresponding to the American upper middle class was comparably small and the elite structure was extremely reverberant. It can be argued, for example, that a copy of *The Spectator* covered its potential readership more thoroughly in the late eighteenth century than *The New Yorker* covers its readership today. In eighteenth- and nineteenth-century English, French, and Russian novels, we find portraits of the sort of people who operated in the upper reaches of bureaucracy and had to be prepared for rapid changes of signals. Stepan Arkadyevitch Oblonsky in *Anna Karenina* is one of the more likeable and less opportunistic examples, especially striking because of the way Tolstoy contrasts him with Levin, a moralizing, inner-directed person. At any dinner party Stepan manifests exceptional social skills; his political skills as described in the following quotation are also highly social:

> Stepan Arkadyevitch took in and read a liberal newspaper, not an extreme one, but one advocating the views held by the majority. And in spite of the fact that science, art, and politics had no special interest for him, he firmly held those views on all subjects which were held by the majority and by his paper, and he only changed them when the majority changed them—or, more strictly speaking, he did not change them, but they imperceptively changed of themselves within him.
>
> Stepan Arkadyevitch had not chosen his political opinions or his views; these political opinions and views had come to him of themselves, just as he did not choose the shapes of his hats or coats, but simply took those that were being worn. And for him, living in a certain society—owing to the need, ordinarily developed at years of discretion, for some degree of mental activity—to have views was just as indispensable as to have a hat. If there was a reason for his preferring liberal to conservative views, which were held also by many of his circle, it arose not from his considering liberalism more rational, but from its being in closer accord with his manner of life. . . . And so liberalism had become a habit of Stepan Arkadyevitch's, and he liked his newspaper, as he did his cigar after dinner, for the slight fog it diffused in his brain.

Stepan, while his good-natured gregariousness makes him seem like a modern middle-class American, is not fully other-directed. This gregariousness alone, without a certain sensitivity to others as individuals and as a source of direction, is not the identifying trait. Just so, we must differentiate the nineteenth-century American, gregarious and subservient to public opinion though he was found to be by Tocqueville, Bryce, and others, from the other-directed American as he emerges today, an American who in his character is more capable of and more interested in maintaining responsive contact with others both at work and at play.

III. *The Three Types Compared*

One way to see the structural differences between the three types is to see the differences in emotional sanction or control in each type.

The tradition-directed person feels the impact of his culture as a unit, but it is nevertheless mediated through the specific, small number of individuals with whom he is in daily contact. These expect of him not so much that he be a certain type of person but that he behave in the approved way. Consequently the sanction for behavior tends to be the fear of being *shamed*.

The inner-directed person has early incorporated a psychic gyroscope which is set going by his parents and can receive signals later on from other authorities who resemble his parents. He goes through life less independent than he seems, obeying this internal piloting. Getting off course, whether in response to inner impulses or to the fluctuating voices of contemporaries, may lead to the feeling of *guilt*.

Since the direction to be taken in life has been learned in the privacy of the home from a small number of guides and since principles, rather than details of behavior, are internalized, the inner-directed person is capable of great stability. Especially so when it turns out that his fellows have gyroscopes too, spinning at the same speed and set in the same direction. But many inner-directed individuals can remain stable even when the reinforcement of social approval is not available—as in the upright life of the stock Englishman isolated in the tropics.

Contrasted with such a type as this, the other-directed person learns to respond to signals from a far wider circle than is constituted by his parents. The family is no longer a closely knit unit to which he belongs but merely part of a wider social environment to which he early becomes attentive. In these respects the other-directed person resembles the tradition-directed person: both live in a group milieu and lack the inner-directed person's capacity to go it alone. The nature of this group milieu, however, differs radically in the two cases. The other-directed person is cosmopolitan. For him the border between the familiar and the strange—a border clearly marked in the societies depending on tradition-direction—has broken down. As the family continuously absorbs the strange and so reshapes itself, so the strange becomes familiar. While the inner-directed person could be "at home abroad" by virtue of his relative insensitivity to others, the other-directed person is, in a sense, at home everywhere and nowhere, capable of a rapid if sometimes superficial intimacy with and response to everyone.

The tradition-directed person takes his signals from others, but they come in a cultural monotone; he needs no complex receiving equipment to pick them up. The other-directed person must be able to receive signals from far and near; the sources are many, the changes rapid. What can be internalized, then, is not a code of behavior but the elaborate equipment needed to attend to such messages and occasionally to participate in their circulation. As against guilt-and-shame controls, though of course these survive, one prime psychological lever of the other-directed person is a diffuse anxiety. This control equipment, instead of being like a gyroscope, is like a radar.

IV. *The Characterological Struggle*

We can picture the last few hundred years of Western history in terms of a gradual succession to dominance of each of the later two types. The tradition-directed type gives way to the inner-directed, and the inner-directed gives way to the other-directed. Shifts in type of society and type of character do not, of course, occur all at once. Just as within a given culture one may find groups representing all phases of the population curve, so, too, we may find a variety of characterological adaptations to each particular phase. This mixture is made even more various by the migration of peoples, by imperialism, and by other historical developments that constantly throw together people of different character structures, people who "date," metaphorically, from different points on the population curve.

These character types, like geological or archaeological strata, pile one on top of the other, with outcroppings of submerged types here and there. A cross section of society at any given time reveals the earlier as well as the later character types, the earlier changed through the pressure of being submerged by the later. Tradition-direction seems to be dominant in Latin America, agricultural southern Europe, in Asia and Africa. Inner-directed types seem to be dominant in rural and small-town United States and Canada, in northwestern Europe, and to a degree in Central Europe. One notices an energetic campaign to introduce the inner-directed pattern in eastern Europe, in Turkey, and in parts of Asia. And one notices the beginnings of dominance by other-directed types in the metropolitan centers of the United States and, more doubtfully, their emergence in the big cities of northwestern Europe. This last and newest type is spreading outward into areas where inner-direction still prevails, just as the latter is spreading into unconquered areas where tradition-directed types still hang on.

Such a view may help us to understand American character structures. In America it is still possible to find southern rural groups, Negro and poor white, in the phase of high growth potential—and it is here that we look for the remnants of tradition-directed types. Similarly, immigrants to America who came from rural and small-town areas in Europe carried their fertility rates and character patterns with them to our major cities as well as to the countryside. In some cases these people were and are forced to make, in one lifetime, the jump from a society in which tradition-direction was the dominant mode of insuring conformity to one in which other-direction is the dominant mode. More frequently the jump is made in two generations; the peasant is converted to inner-directed ways; his children then make the jump to other-direction.

Studies of American Indians provide analogies for some of the things that may happen when an older character type is under pressure from a newer one. Among Sioux reservation children, as described by Erik H. Erikson, there seem to be two reactions to white culture: one is resentful resistance, the other is what might be termed "compliant resistance." The behavior of the former seems, to the white educator, incorrigible; of the latter, almost too ingratiating, too angelic. In both cases, because he has at least the tacit approval of his parents and other Sioux adults, the child preserves something of the Sioux character and tradition whether or not he yields overtly to the whites. The conflict, however, drains the child of emotional energy; often he appears to be lazy. Both the resistant and the seemingly compliant are apathetic toward the white culture and white politics.

I think that there are millions of inner-directed Americans who reject in similar fashion the values that emanate from the growing dominance of other-directed types. Their resentment may be conscious and vocal. As with the Sioux, this resentment is culturally supported both by the old timers and by the long historical past which is present to all in rural and small-town areas. This past is carried in the tales of the old men and the editorials of the rural press, not yet blotted out by urban sights and sounds. Hence, the resentment can express itself and win local victories over the representatives of other-directed types. Nevertheless, the "moralizers," as we will later term them, do not feel secure—the weight of the urban world outside is against them—and their resentment hardens until these residual inner-directed persons are scarcely more than caricatures of their characterological ancestors in the days of their dominance.

A second locus of resistance and resentment is to be found among the vanishing tradition-directed migrants to America, migrants both from American colonies: Puerto Rico, the deep South, and previously the Philippines, and from Mexico, Italy, and the Orient. Here it is more difficult to find cultural support for one's resistance to the enforced change of signals called "Americanization." The southern poor white or the poor Negro who moves North does not have to learn a new language, but he is usually about as deracinated as are the migrants from abroad. The costume and manners of the zoot-suiter were a pathetic example of the effort to combine smooth urban ways with a resentful refusal to be completely overwhelmed by the inner-directed norms, that are still the official culture of the city public schools.

A similar type of resentment is to be found among miners, lumberjacks, ranch hands, and some urban factory workers. As in many other societies, the active dislike of these workers for the dominant culture is coupled with a feeling of manly contempt for smooth or soft city ways. These men have their own cocky legends as the Sioux have stories of the cowboy as well as of their own belligerent past. We must ask to what extent all these groups may be dying out, like their Sioux counterparts, as other-direction spreads down the class ladder and beyond the metropolitan areas. In the absence of a home base, a reservation, these people have their choice, if indeed there be a choice, between homelessness and rapid acculturation to other-directed values.

William H. Whyte, Jr.

The Lonely Crowd *defines the new type emerging in American society today as "other-directed," that is, dominated by the standards and values of other individuals of comparable age, class, and status. Influenced by Riesman's ideas, William H. Whyte, Jr., one of the editors of* Fortune, *carries this notion of other-directedness considerably further in his provocative book,* The Organization Man *(1956). There is, Whyte points out, a deep conflict in values at the center of midcentury American life; our traditional Protestant ethic with its strong faith in individualism no longer fits the kind of group life that middle-class Americans must lead in contemporary society. The most striking phenomenon in modern America is the growing domination of the Organization. This is true not only in the complex business corporation but also in education, the church, research foundations, medicine—indeed wherever the Institution has become central and men are valued according to their loyalty to it. Whyte does not mean to be satirical, though in many places his book sounds like satire; he is entirely serious in his protest against the insidious tyranny of the Organization.*

Whyte's career has followed the general pattern of many able young men of his generation. Born in West Chester, Pennsylvania, in 1917, he graduated cum laude *from Princeton in 1939. After two years with the Vick Chemical Company he entered the United States Marine Corps at the outset of World War II, fought through the entire Guadalcanal campaign, and was discharged as a captain. In 1946 he joined the* Fortune *staff where he has been an editor since 1951. He belongs to a group of postwar editors and writers who have been articulate and often controversial. Much of the material in* The Organization Man *first appeared in* Fortune *articles.*

In 1952 Whyte published Is Anybody Listening? *a satire on modern communications, also largely taken from articles which had appeared in* Fortune. *In 1953 he received the Benjamin Franklin Writing Award and in 1957 the Liberty and Justice Book award.*

The selection we reprint from The Organization Man *describes the way of life that many young Americans are now leading and many college students are likely to lead in the near future, and discusses the social ethic which Whyte believes has largely replaced the traditional Protestant ethic in contemporary America. While he sees no real solution to the present situation, Whyte urges that we recognize the dangers in it and fight continually against complete submission of the individual to the demands of group cooperation.*

THE ORGANIZATION MAN

1. *The Social Ethic*

THIS BOOK is about the organization man. If the term is vague, it is because I can think of no other way to describe the people I am talking about. They are not the workers, nor are they the white-collar people in the usual, clerk sense of the word. These people only work for The Organization. The ones I am talking about *belong* to it as well. They are the ones of our middle class who have left home, spiritually as well as physically, to take the vows of organization life, and it is they who are the mind and soul of our great self-perpetuating institutions. Only a few are top managers or ever will be. In a system that makes such hazy terminology as "junior executive" psychologically necessary, they are of the staff as much as the line, and most are destined to live poised in a middle area that still awaits a satisfactory euphemism. But they are the dominant members of our society nonetheless. They have not joined together into a recognizable elite—our country does not stand still long enough for that—but it is from their ranks that are coming most of the first and second echelons of our leadership, and it is their values which will set the American temper.

The corporation man is the most conspicuous example, but he is only one, for the collectivization so visible in the corporation has affected almost every field of work. Blood brother to the business trainee off to join Du Pont is the seminary student who will end up in the church hierarchy, the doctor headed for the corporate clinic, the physics Ph.D. in a government laboratory, the intellectual on the foundation-sponsored team project, the engineering graduate in the huge drafting room at Lockheed, the young apprentice in a Wall Street law factory.

They are all, as they so often put it, in the same boat. Listen to them talk to each other over the front lawns of their suburbia and you cannot help but be struck by how well they grasp the common denominators which bind them. Whatever the differences in their organization ties, it is the common problems of collective work that dominate their attentions, and when the Du Pont man talks to the research chemist or the chemist to the army man, it is these problems that are uppermost. The word *collective* most of them can't bring themselves to use—except to describe foreign countries or organizations they don't work for—but they are keenly aware of how much more deeply beholden they are to organization than were their elders. They are wry about it, to be sure; they talk of the "treadmill," the "rat race," of the inability to control one's direction. But they have no great sense of plight; between themselves and organization they believe they see an ultimate harmony and, more than most elders recognize, they are building an ideology that will vouchsafe this trust.

It is the growth of this ideology, and its practical effects, that is the thread I wish to follow in this book. America has paid much attention to the economic and political consequences of big organizations—the concentration of power in large corporations, for example, the political power of the civil-service bureaucracies, the possible emergence of a managerial hierarchy that might dominate the rest of us. These are proper concerns, but no less important is the personal impact that organization life has had on the individuals within it. A collision has been taking place—indeed, hundreds of thousands of them—and in the aggregate they have been producing what I believe is a major shift in American ideology.

Officially, we are a people who hold to the Protestant Ethic. Because of the denominational implications of the term many would deny its relevance to them, but let them eulogize the American Dream, however, and they virtually define the Protestant Ethic. Whatever the embroidery, there is almost always the thought that pursuit of individual salvation through hard work, thrift, and competitive struggle is the heart of the American achievement.

But the harsh facts of organization life simply do not jibe with these precepts. This conflict is certainly not a peculiarly American development. In their own countries such Europeans as Max Weber and Durkheim many years ago foretold the change, and though Europeans now like to see their troubles as an American export, the problems they speak of stem from a bureaucratization of society that has affected every Western country.

It is in America, however, that the contrast between the old ethic and current reality has been most apparent—and most poignant. Of all peoples it is we who have led in the public worship of individualism. One hundred years ago de Tocqueville was noting that though our special genius—and failing—lay in cooperative action, we talked more than others of personal independence and freedom. We kept on, and as late as the twenties, when big organization was long since a fact, affirmed the old faith as if nothing had really changed at all.

Today many still try, and it is the members of the kind of organization most responsible for the change, the corporation, who try the hardest. It is the corporation man whose institutional ads protest so much that Americans speak up in town meeting, that Americans are the best inventors because Americans don't care that other people scoff, that Americans are the best soldiers because they have so much initiative and native ingenuity, that the boy selling papers on the street corner is the prototype of our business society. Collectivism? He abhors it, and when he makes his ritualistic attack on Welfare Statism, it is in terms of a Protestant Ethic undefiled by change—the sacredness of property, the enervating effect of security, the virtues of thrift, of hard work and independence. Thanks be, he says, that there are some people left—e.g., businessmen—to defend the American Dream.

He is not being hypocritical, only compulsive. He honestly wants to believe he follows the tenets he extols, and if he extols them so frequently it is, perhaps, to shut out a nagging suspicion that he, too, the last defender of the faith, is no longer pure. Only by using the language of individualism to describe the collective can he stave off the thought that he himself is in a collective as pervading as any ever dreamed of by the reformers, the intellectuals, and the utopian visionaries he so regularly warns against.

The older generation may still convince themselves; the younger generation does not. When a young man says that to make a living these days you must do what somebody else wants you to do, he states it not only as a fact of life that must be accepted but as an inherently good proposition. If the American Dream deprecates this for him, it is the American Dream that is going to have to give, whatever its more elderly guardians may think. People grow restive with a mythology that is too distant from the way things actually are, and as more and more lives have been encompassed by the organization way of life, the pressures for an accompanying ideological shift have been mounting. The pressures of the group, the frustrations of individual creativity, the anonymity of achievement: are these defects to struggle against—or are they virtues in disguise? The organization man seeks a redefinition of his place on earth—a faith that will satisfy him that what he must endure has a deeper meaning than appears on the surface. He needs, in short, something that will do for him what the Protestant Ethic did once. And slowly, almost imperceptibly, a body of thought has been coalescing that does that.

I am going to call it a Social Ethic. With reason it could be called an organization ethic, or a bureaucratic ethic; more than anything else it rationalizes the organization's demands for fealty and gives those who offer it wholeheartedly a sense of dedication in doing so—*in extremis*, you might say, it converts what would seem in other times a bill of no rights into a restatement of individualism.

But there is a real moral imperative behind it, and whether one inclines to its beliefs or not he must acknowledge that this moral basis, not mere expediency, is the source of its power. Nor is it simply an opiate for those who must work in big organizations. The search for a secular faith that it represents can be found throughout our society—and among those who swear they would never set foot in a corporation or a government bureau. Though it has its greatest applicability to the organization man, its ideological underpinnings have been provided not by the organization man but by intellectuals he knows little of and toward whom, indeed, he tends to be rather suspicious.

Any groove of abstraction, Whitehead once remarked, is bound to be an inadequate way of describing reality, and so with the concept of the Social Ethic. It is an attempt to illustrate an underlying consistency in what in actuality is by no means an orderly system of thought. No one says, "I believe in the social ethic," and though many would subscribe wholeheartedly to the separate ideas that make it up, these ideas have yet to be put together in the final, harmonious synthesis. But the unity is there.

In looking at what might seem dissimilar aspects of organization society, it is this unity I wish to underscore. The "professionalization" of the manager, for example, and the drive for a more practical education are parts of the same phenomenon; just as the student now feels technique more vital than content, so the trainee believes managing an end in itself, an *expertise* relatively independent of the content of what is being managed. And the reasons are the same. So too in other sectors of our society; for all the differences in particulars, dominant is a growing accommodation to the needs of society—and a growing urge to justify it.

Let me now define my terms. By social ethic I mean that contemporary body of thought which makes morally legitimate the pressures of society against the individual. Its major propositions are three: a belief in the group as the source of creativity; a belief in "belongingness" as the ultimate need of the individual; and a belief in the application of science to achieve the belongingness.

In subsequent chapters I will explore these ideas more thoroughly, but for the moment I think the gist can be paraphrased thus: Man exists as a unit of society. Of himself, he is isolated, meaningless; only as he collaborates with others does he become worthwhile, for by sublimating himself in the group, he helps produce a whole that is greater than the sum of its parts. There should be, then, no conflict between man and society. What we think are conflicts are misunderstandings, breakdowns in communication. By applying the methods of science to human relations we can eliminate these obstacles to consensus and create an equilibrium in which society's needs and the needs of the individual are one and the same.

Essentially, it is a utopian faith. Superficially, it seems dedicated to the practical problems of organization life, and its proponents often use the word *hard* (versus *soft*) to describe their approach. But it is the long-range promise that animates its followers, for it relates techniques to the vision of a finite, achievable harmony. It is quite reminiscent of the beliefs of utopian communities of the 1840's. As in the Owen communities, there is the same idea that man's character is decided, almost irretrievably, by his environment. As in the Fourier communities, there is the same faith that there need be no conflict between the individual's aspirations and the community's wishes, because it is the natural order of things that the two be synonymous.

Like the utopian communities, it interprets society in a fairly narrow, immediate sense. One can believe man has a social obligation and that the individual must ultimately contribute to the community without believing that group harmony is the test of it. In the Social Ethic I am describing, however, man's obligation is in the here and now; his duty is not so much to the community in a broad sense but to the actual, physical one about him, and the idea that in isolation from it—or active rebellion against it—he might eventually discharge the greater service is little considered. In practice, those who most eagerly subscribe to the Social Ethic worry very little over the long-range problems of society. It is not that they don't care but rather that they tend to assume that the ends of organization and morality coincide, and on such matters as social welfare they give their proxy to the organization.

II. *A Generation of Bureaucrats*

When I was a college senior in 1939, we used to sing a plaintive song about going out into the "cold, cold world." It wasn't really so very cold then, but we did enjoy meditating on the fraughtness of it all. It was a big break we were facing, we told ourselves, and those of us who were going to try our luck in the commercial world could be patronizing toward those who were going on to graduate work or academic life. We were taking the leap.

Seniors still sing the song, but somehow the old note of portent is gone. There is no leap left to take. The union between the world of organization and the college has been so cemented that today's seniors can see a continuity between the college and the life thereafter that we never did. Come graduation, they do not go outside to a hostile world; they transfer.

For the senior who is headed for the corporation it is almost as if it were part of one master scheme. The locale shifts; the training continues, for at the same time that the colleges have been changing their curriculum to suit the corporation, the corporation has responded by setting up its own campuses and classrooms. By now the two have been so well molded that it's difficult to tell where one leaves off and the other begins.

The descent, every spring, of the corporations' recruiters has now become a built-in feature of campus life. If the college is large and its placement director efficient, the processing operation is visibly impressive. I have never been able to erase from my mind the memory of an ordinary day at Purdue's placement center. It is probably the largest and most effective placement operation in the country, yet, much as in a well-run group clinic, there seemed hardly any activity. In the main room some students were quietly studying company literature arranged on the tables for them; others were checking the interview timetables to find what recruiter they would see and to which cubicle he was assigned; at the central filing desk college employees were sorting the hundreds of names of men who had registered for placement. Except for a murmur from the row of cubicles there was little to indicate that scores of young men were, every hour on the half hour, making the decisions that would determine their whole future life.

Someone from a less organized era might conclude that the standardization of this machinery—and the standardized future it portends—would repel students. It does not. For the median senior this is the optimum future; it meshes so closely with his own aspirations that it is almost as if the corporation was planned in response to an attitude poll.

Because they are the largest single group, the corporation-bound seniors are the most visible manifestation of their generation's values. But in essentials their contemporaries headed for other occupations respond to the same urges. The lawyers, the doctors, the scientists—their occupations are also subject to the same centralization, the same trend to group work and to bureaucratization. And so are the young men who will enter them. Whatever their many differences, in one great respect they are all of a piece; more than any generation in memory, theirs will be a generation of bureaucrats.

They are, above all, conservative. Their inclination to accept the status quo does not necessarily mean that in the historic sweep of ideas they are conservative—in the more classical sense of conservatism, it could be argued that the seniors will be, in effect if not by design, agents of revolution. But this is a matter we must leave to later historians. For the immediate present, at any rate, what ideological ferment college men exhibit is not in the direction of basic change.

This shows most clearly in their attitude toward politics. It used to be axiomatic that young men moved to the left end of the spectrum in revolt against their fathers and then, as the years went on, moved slowly to the right. . . . If the seniors do any moving, however, it will be from dead center. Liberal groups have almost disappeared from the campus, and what few remain are anemic. There has been no noticeable activity at the other end of the spectrum either. When William Buckley Jr. produced *God and Man at Yale*, some people thought this signaled the emergence of a strong right-wing movement among the young men. The militancy, however, has not proved particularly contagious; when the

McCarthy issue roused and divided their elders, undergraduates seemed somewhat bored with it all.

Their conservatism is passive. No cause seizes them, and nothing so exuberant or willfully iconoclastic as the Veterans of Future Wars has reappeared. There are Democrats and Republicans, and at election time there is the usual flurry of rallies, but in comparison with the agitation of the thirties no one seems to care too much one way or the other. There has been personal unrest—the suspense over the prospect of military service assures this—but it rarely gets resolved into a thought-out protest. Come spring and students may start whacking each other over the head or roughing up the townees and thereby cause a rush of concern over the wild younger generation. But there is no real revolution in them, and the next day they likely as not will be found with their feet firmly on the ground in the recruiters' cubicles. Some observers attribute the disinterest to fear. I heard one instructor tell his colleagues that in his politics classes he warned students to keep their noses clean. "I tell them," he said, "that they'd better realize that what they say might be held against them, especially when we get to the part about Marx and Engels. Someday in the future they might find their comments bounced back at them in an investigation."

The advice, as his colleagues retorted, was outrageously unnecessary. The last thing students can be accused of now is dangerous discussion; they are not interested in the kind of big questions that stimulate heresy and whatever the subject—the corporation, government, religion—students grow restive if the talk tarries on the philosophical. Most are interested in the philosophical only to the extent of finding out what the accepted view is in order that they may accept it and get on to the practical matters. This spares the bystander from the lofty bulling and the elaborate pose of unorthodoxy that my contemporaries often used to affect, but it does make for a rather stringent utilitarianism.

In judging a college generation, one usually bases his judgment on how much it varies from one's own, and presumably superior, class, and I must confess that I find myself tempted to do so. Yet I do not think my generation has any license to damn the acquiescence of seniors as a weakening of intellectual fiber. It is easy for us to forget that if earlier generations were less content with society, there was a great deal less to be contented about. In the intervening years the economy has changed enormously, and even in retrospect the senior can hardly be expected to share former discontents. Society is not out of joint for him, and if he acquiesces it is not out of fear that he does so. He does not want to rebel against the status quo because he really likes it—and his elders, it might be added, are not suggesting anything bold and new to rebel for.

Perhaps contemporaryism would be a better word than conservatism to describe their posture. The present, more than the past, is their model; while they share the characteristic American faith in the future also, they see it as more of same. As they paraphrase what they are now reading about America, they argue that at last we have got it. The big questions are all settled; we know the direction, and while many minor details remain to be cleared up, we can be pretty sure of enjoying a wonderful upward rise.

III. *The New Suburbia*

I now turn to organization man at home —and, I hope, some clues as to where he is going. In these next chapters I am going to examine him in the communities that have become his dormitories—the great package suburbs that have sprung up outside our cities since the war. They are fascinating institutions in their own right, and here and there I will detour into aspects of them that are tangential to my main theme. What I wish to concentrate on, however, is the way in which they reflect the values of the organization man—and of the next generation to come.

They are communities made in his image. There are other kinds of people there, too, and for many a resident the curving superblocks of suburbia are the end of a long road from the city wards to middle-class respectability. But it is the young organization man who is dominant. More than others, it is he who organizes the committees, runs the schools, selects the ministers, fights the developers, makes the speeches, and sets the styles.

It is a communal way of life, and the residents are well aware of it. They are of many minds how to describe it. Sometimes they lean to analogies like the frontier, or the early colonial settlements. Other times they are a little more wry: "sorority house with kids," a projection of dormitory life into adulthood, or, slightly better, a lay version of Army post life. But no matter how sharp the coinages—"a womb with a view," "a Russia, only with money"—it is a way of life they find suited to their wants, their needs, and their times. They are not unwitting pawns—educated to be more aware of social trends than their forebears, they discuss their situations with considerable sophistication; at times, the way they casually toss out words like "permissive" and "kid-centered," it almost seems as if everyone was his own resident sociologist.

In part, these communities are a product of the great expansion of the middle class, for the new suburbs have become a mecca for thousands of young people moving up and out of city wards. It is not these people, however, who are dominant. In his wanderings, the organization man has found in the new suburbs an ideal way station. He is the one who is most quick to move out, but as soon as he does another replaces him, and then another. It is he who sets the tone, and if he is as uncertain as any in keeping up with the Joneses, it is because he *is* the Joneses.

Park Forest, the community I studied most intensively, has its unique features, but its most salient characteristic is that it is virtually a controlled sample of organization people. As elsewhere, there are other kinds of people too, and for many a newcomer from the city such communities are an education in middle-class values. What might be called the modal man, however, is a twenty-five to thirty-five-year-old white-collar organization man with a wife, a salary between $6000 and $7000, one child, and another on the way.

If one wishes to study the next generation of organization men, a pretty good form chart is the record of how the younger ones handle their problems when they are away from their elders. Because they are jammed into such propinquity with one another in their new suburbia, everything they do carries a certain degree of exaggeration: the schools are a little more modern than elsewhere, the politics a little more intense, and most certainly the social life is a lot more social. Abnormal? Or the portent of a new normality? The values of Park Forest, one gets the feeling, are harbingers of the way it's going to be.

This kind of suburbia is a natural phenomenon. They bear a resemblance to such utopian ventures as the Oneida community or the Fourier settlements, but where earlier utopias were an expression of revolt and idealism, the new suburbs are a response to social and economic realities. Park Forest, for example, was set up, quite simply, to make money, lots and lots of it.

Looking at the real-estate situation right after the war, a group of Chicago businessmen saw that there was a huge population of young veterans, but little available housing suitable for young people with (1) children, (2) expectations of transfer, (3) a taste for good living, (4) not too much money. Why not, the group figured, build an entire new community from scratch for these people? The group, incorporated as American Community Builders, bought up 2400 acres in the cornland thirty miles south of Chicago and brought in a remarkable man, former Federal Public Housing Commissioner Philip Klutznick, as president.

When the doors were thrown open in 1948 the rental courts were islands in a sea of mud, but the young people came streaming out of Chicago. The first wave of colonists was heavy with academic and professional people—the place, it appeared, had an extraordinary affinity for Ph.D.'s. Since Chicago is one of the great business-training grounds of the U. S., however, another kind of affinity proved even stronger: poised at the nexus of America's junior-executive migration, Park Forest quickly became a haven for the organization man. Out came trainees for the big corporations, research chemists with the AEC, captains and majors with the Fifth Army, airline pilots, FBI men—in total, a cross section of almost every kind of organization man in America.

Why the attraction? Since I am going to emphasize some of the nonmaterial factors let me at once put first things first. The people who went to Park Forest went there because it was the best housing for the money. . . . The space for the money, the amenities not elsewhere available, and, most important, the fact that it was so well set up for children have been in most cases the dominant factors.

Park Foresters, in short, went there for quite rational, and eminently sensible, reasons. Once there, however, they created something over and above the original bargain. Together, they developed a social atmosphere of striking vigor, and while it might have been as one to ten with the more material attractions, it was to be a significant extra. The developers were quick to recognize it. At first they had advertised Park Forest as housing. Now they began advertising happiness. They retained an advertising agency, Weiss and Geller, famed as the most motivation-minded of all agencies, and after a bout of depth interviews and psychiatric panel discussions, the ads began belting away at the overtones of Park Forest more than the homes themselves.

Here's the way they went:

> You *Belong*
> in PARK FOREST!
> The moment you come to our town you know:
> You're welcome
> You're part of a big group
> You can live in a friendly small town instead of a lonely big city.
> You can have friends who want you—and you can enjoy being with them.
> Come out. Find out about the spirit of Park Forest.
>
> —*Ad for Park Forest Homes, Inc., November 8, 1952*

The ads are quite right. Let's take, for example, a couple we shall call Dot and Charlie Adams. Charlie, a corporation trainee, is uprooted from the Newark office, arrives at Apartment 8, Court M-12. It's a hell of a day—the kids are crying, Dot is half sick with exhaustion, and the movers won't be finished till late.

But soon, because M-12 is a "happy" court, the neighbors will come over and introduce themselves. In an almost inordinate display of decency, some will help them unpack, and around suppertime two of the girls will come over with a hot casserole and another with a percolator full of hot coffee. Within a few days the children will have found playmates, Dot will be *Kaffeeklatsching* and sunbathing with the girls like an old-timer, and Charlie, who finds that Ed Robey in Apartment 5 went through officers' training school with him, will be enrolled in the Court Poker Club. The Adamses are, in a word, *in*—and someday soon, when another new couple, dazed and hungry, moves in, the Adamses will make their thanks by helping them to be likewise.

In the court, they find, their relationships with others transcend mere neighborliness. Except for the monastic orders and the family itself, there is probably no other social institution in the U. S. in which there is such a communal sharing of property. Except for the $200 or $300 put aside for the next baby, few of the transients have as yet been able to accumulate much capital or earthly possessions, and so they share to make the best of it. One lawn mower (with each man doing his allotted stint) may do for the whole court. For the wives there may be a baby-sitting "bank" (i.e., when one wife baby-sits for another she is credited with the time, and when she wishes to draw on it one of the wives who has a debit to repay will sit for her). To hoard possessions is frowned upon; books, silverware, and tea services are constantly rotated, and the children feel free to use one another's bikes and toys without asking. "We laughed at first at how the Marxist society had finally arrived," one executive says, "but I think the real analogy is to the pioneers."

But the court social life, important as it is in rooting the transient, is only part of the acclimation. Before long Charlie Adams may feel the urge to shoot out a few extra roots here and there and, having normal joining instincts, may think a mild involvement in some community wide organization just the thing. When the matter is bruited to him he may be tentative—nothing strenuous, understand, awfully busy with company work; just want to help out a little. Instantaneously, or no longer than it takes one person to telephone another, the news is abroad. Charlie will never be quite the same again.

He has plunged into a hotbed of Participation. With sixty-six adult organizations and a population turnover that makes each one of them insatiable for new members, Park Forest probably swallows up more civic energy per hundred people than any other community in the country. Every minute from 7:00 A.M. to 10:00 P.M. some organization is meeting somewhere. Looking through the picture windows of one of the community buildings one typical night I saw: on the top floor, the church choir rehearsing; the Explorer Scouts (waiting for a quorum to plan next week's hike); world politics discussion group (to discuss what causes war; a second discussion group was to meet on a different evening to take up American foreign policy). Bottom floor: school board meeting (to talk over interior decoration of the new school); an organizing committee to organize a new organization (the Protestant Men's Club); Husanwif Club (to watch slides on safety rules for children).

The participation, as I have remarked, is often participation for the sake of it, and sometimes one is tempted to apply H. G. Well's description of the town of Bromstead—"a dull, useless boiling up of human activities, an immense clustering of futilities." But this would miss an important point. In a community where there are real issues—schools to be built, segregation problems—its residents are immersed in the main stream of life, not insulated. If they appear stimulated over and above the call of community necessity, this itself is evidence of how very much they seek ties more meaningful than those of bridge and canasta and bowling.

For no one is this quest more important than the organization man. One of the dangers in the transient life is that these young people, because they must move about so frequently, will more and more identify their total destiny with one particular organization. For society as well as for themselves, the organization transients need to multiply their allegiances—to the church, to community, and the like. These additional allegiances provoke no great ideological conflicts with the office, certainly, but they do turn the executive away from complete preoccupation with one encompassing organization. Places like Park Forest do not solve this problem—The Organization will still come first—but they do ameliorate it.

IV. *Conclusion*

Here, finally, is the apotheosis of the Social Ethic. Some might summarize the suburban temper in different terms—pragmatism, perhaps, or utilitarianism—and their intonation would depend on their own outlook. But the dominant motif is unmistakable. Not just as something expedient, but as something right, the organization transients have put social usefulness at the core of their beliefs. Adaptation has become more than a necessity; in a life in which everything changes, it has become almost a constant.

Since I am using suburbia as a vehicle to bring together many strands, it can be asked if it is fair to generalize from such places to organization man in general. Suburbs like Park Forest are not typical places—even as lodging for organization people—and it is obvious that in degree many of the pressures there are peculiar to such places. No matter how stanch an individualist you might be, if you have to live in such close union with others, the sheer instinct of survival, let alone good sense, is likely, at the time, to make you emphasize the extroverted side of your nature. The suburbanites' group-mindedness, it could be argued, is merely a passing phase, an expedient dictated by necessity and not by any inner impulse.

But I am not talking about overt behavior; I am talking about values, and the suburbanites themselves provide evidence that their values are a great deal more than a function of the physical environment. That they respond to the pressure of the court or the tight-knit block is not so significant. They have to. What is significant is how they feel about these pressures—and how, ideally, they think a person should feel about them.

Their children, for example. In building the school system the suburbanites have had to face the question, and if the passing-phase explanation were correct, we could find the answer in the kind of well-roundedness they ask for. In deciding what the children needed most to learn, or least, parents might reason that since the children were already so well instructed by the environment in social skills the schools should teach them not to overcompensate. For the sake of mental health, if nothing else, it would follow that the schools would emphasize the more neglected, inner aspect of the child to the end that personality development be truly balanced. In this light, the more asocial, intellectual disciplines could be utilized as highly pragmatic tools—not to mention any utility their content might have.

But this, we know, is not the way the great majority of parents feel. They do not wish the great cycle of which they are a part reversed, but intensified. It is an age of group action, they well agree, and skilled as they are in the ways of group living, it is a source of pride to them, rather than concern, that their children may be even more so. As some parents point out, they themselves have had to learn adjustment the hard way, without the benefit of an education anywhere near as contemporary, or socially conscious, as that the schools are now offering. If they have made their adjustments as successfully as they have, they wonder, how much more successfully may their children when they come of age?

But where is the boat going? No one seems to have the faintest idea; nor, for that matter, do they see much point in even raising the question. Once people liked to think, at least, that they were in control of their destinies, but few of the younger organization people cherish such notions. Most see themselves as objects more acted upon than acting—and their future, therefore, determined as much by the system as by themselves.

In a word, they *accept*, and if we do not find this comforting at least we should recognize that it would be odd if they did not feel this confidence. For them society has in fact been good—very, very good—for there has been a succession of fairly beneficent environments: college, the paternalistic, if not always pleasant, military life, then, perhaps, graduate work through the G. I. Bill of Rights, a corporation apprenticeship during a period of industrial expansion and high prosperity, and, for some, the camaraderie of communities like Park Forest. The system, they instinctively conclude, is essentially benevolent.

No one should begrudge them the prosperity that has helped make them feel this way. If we have to have problems, after all, the adversities of good times are as worthy as any to have to worry about. Nor should we regard the emphasis on cooperation as a reversal of our national character. When the suburbanites speak of re-establishing the spirit of the frontier communities, there is a truth in their analogy. Our country was born as a series of highly communal enterprises, and though the individualist may have opened the frontier, it was the cooperative who settled it. So throughout our history. Our national genius has always lain in our adaptability, in our distrust of dogma and doctrine, in our regard for the opinion of others, and in this respect the organization people are true products of the American past. "The more equal social conditions become," de Tocqueville, no friend of conformity, presciently observed, "the more men display this reciprocal disposition to oblige each other."

And there is the crux. When de Tocqueville wrote this a century ago it was the double-edge nature of this disposition that haunted him. He understood its virtue; he was an aristocrat and he confessed that he missed the excellence of the few in the good of the many, but he saw clearly that our egalitarianism and our ease of social cooperation were the great fruits of democracy. We could not sustain these virtues without suffering their defects. But could we keep them in balance? De Tocqueville made a prophecy. If America ever destroyed its genius it would be by intensifying the social virtues at the expense of others, by making the individual come to regard himself as a hostage to prevailing opinion, by creating, in sum, a tyranny of the majority.

And this is what the organization man is doing. He is doing it for what he feels are good reasons, but this only makes the tyranny more powerful, not less. At the very time when the pressures of our highly organized society make so stringent a demand on the individual, he is himself compounding the impact. He is not only other-directed, to borrow David Reisman's concept, he is articulating a philosophy which tells him it is right to be that way.

My charge against the Social Ethic, then,

is on precisely the grounds of contemporary usefulness it so venerates. It is not, I submit, suited to the needs of "modern man," but is instead reinforcing precisely that which least needs to be emphasized, and at the expense of that which does. Here is my bill of particulars.

It is redundant. In some societies individualism has been carried to such extremes as to endanger the society itself, and there exist today examples of individualism corrupted into a narrow egoism which prevents effective cooperation. This is a danger, there is no question of that. But is it today as pressing a danger as the obverse—a climate which inhibits individual initiative and imagination, and the courage to exercise it against group opinion? Society is itself an education in the extrovert values, and I think it can be rightfully argued that rarely has there been a society which has preached them so hard. No man is an island unto himself, but how John Donne would writhe to hear how often, and for what reasons, the thought is so tiresomely repeated.

It is premature. To preach technique before content, the skills of getting along isolated from why and to what end the getting along is for, does not produce maturity. It produces a sort of permanent prematurity, and this is true not only of the child being taught life adjustment but of the organization man being taught well-roundedness. This is a sterile concept, and those who believe that they have mastered human relations can blind themselves to the true bases of cooperation. People don't cooperate just to cooperate; they cooperate for substantive reasons, to achieve certain goals, and unless these are comprehended the little manipulations for morale, team spirit, and such are fruitless.

And they can be worse than fruitless. Held up as the end-all of organization leadership, the skills of human relations easily tempt the new administrator into the practice of a tyranny more subtle and more pervasive than that which he means to supplant. No one wants to see the old authoritarian return, but at least it could be said of him that what he wanted primarily from you was your sweat. The new man wants your soul.

It is delusory. It is easy to fight obvious tyranny; it is not easy to fight benevolence, and few things are more calculated to rob the individual of his defenses than the idea that his interests and those of society can be wholly compatible. The good society is the one in which they are most compatible, but they never can be completely so, and one who lets The Organization be the judge ultimately sacrifices himself. Like the good society, the good organization encourages individual expression, and many have done so. But there always remains some conflict between the individual and The Organization. Is The Organization to be the arbiter? The Organization will look to its own interests, but it will look to the individual's *only as The Organization interprets them.*

It is static. Organization of itself has no dynamic. The dynamic is in the individual and thus he must not only question how The Organization interprets his interests, he must question how it interprets its own. The bold new plan he feels is necessary, for example. He cannot trust that The Organization will recognize this. Most probably, it will not. It is the nature of a new idea to confound current consensus—even the mildly new idea. It might be patently in order, but, unfortunately, the group has a vested interest in its miseries as well as its pleasures, and irrational as this may be, many a member of organization life can recall instances where the group clung to known disadvantages rather than risk the anarchies of change.

It is self-destructive. The quest for normalcy, as we have seen in suburbia, is one of the great breeders of neuroses, and the Social Ethic only serves to exacerbate them. What is normalcy? We practice a great mutual deception. Everyone knows that they themselves are different—that they are shy in company, perhaps, or dislike many things most people seem to like—but they are not sure that other people are different too. Like the norms of personality testing, they see about them the sum of efforts of people like themselves to seem as normal as others and possibly a little more so. It is hard enough to learn to live with our inadequacies, and we need not make ourselves more miserable by a spurious ideal of middle-class adjustment. Adjustment to what? Nobody really knows—and the tragedy is that they don't realize that the so-confident-seeming other people don't know either.

1

SOCIAL ORIENTATION IN PHILOSOPHY

John Stuart Mill

"The pursuit of happiness" is a phrase with which Americans are well acquainted. Thomas Jefferson, when writing the Declaration of Independence, laid it down as one of the primary goals of the new American experiment in democracy. We have lived so long with this assumption that most of us now take it for granted that government should be aimed at the general welfare, the happiness of all men. The principle that the rightness of an action is measured by the amount of happiness or pleasure it causes was vigorously defended by John Stuart Mill in an essay on Utilitarianism. In his famous essay, On Liberty, Mill carefully analyzed another basic principle of democratic philosophy. This essay is cited whenever there is any serious discussion of the meaning of liberty; a generous selection from it is included here. The insight Mill brought to the question from his own rich experience should prove helpful to all thoughtful students today in view of the present danger to our traditional freedoms.

Born in England in 1806, Mill gave promise of unusual distinction early in life. At the age of three he began a study of Greek and in the next few years read more Greek works than are usually required today for a college degree in classical languages. At eight he took up the study of Latin, and soon went through all the usual authors. At twelve he set out to master logic and at thirteen the principles of political economy. But Mill was no armchair philosopher. He went to work for the East India Company when he was seventeen; at twenty-two he was handling details of the administration of the company's vast empire in India; at fifty he was one of its top officials. Despite these exacting business responsibilities, he nevertheless found time to write numerous articles for liberal magazines and several solid books as well. His System of Logic (1843) and Principles of Political Economy (1848) were standard works for decades. His essay On Liberty appeared in 1859, the essay on Utilitarianism in 1863.

In 1865, when nearly sixty, Mill was elected to Parliament. He agreed to run only if he were not required to make any campaign speeches or to pay others to speak in his behalf; it was also understood that if he were elected he would ignore local interests in order to *concentrate on national problems among which he included women's suffrage. One politician is said to have remarked that the Almighty Himself could not win office on those conditions —yet Mill won. The last years of his life were spent in further writing, though at a more leisurely pace. He died in 1873.*

ON LIBERTY

The grand, leading principle, towards which every argument unfolded in these pages directly converges, is the absolute and essential importance of human development in its richest diversity.

WILHELM VON HUMBOLDT, *Sphere and Duties of Government*

THE SUBJECT of this Essay is not the so-called Liberty of the Will so unfortunately opposed to the misnamed doctrine of Philosophical Necessity; but Civil, or Social Liberty: the nature and limits of the power which can be legitimately exercised by society over the individual. A question seldom stated, and hardly ever discussed, in general terms, but which profoundly influences the practical controversies of the age by its latent presence, and is likely soon to make itself recognized as the vital question of the future. It is so far from being new, that, in a certain sense, it has divided mankind, almost from the remotest ages; but in the stage of progress into which the more civilised portions of the species have now entered, it presents itself under new conditions, and requires a different and more fundamental treatment.

I

The object of this Essay is to assert one very simple principle, as entitled to govern absolutely the dealings of society with the individual in the way of compulsion and control, whether the means used be physical force in the form of legal penalties, or the moral coercion of public opinion. That principle is, that the sole end for which mankind are warranted, individually or collectively, in interfering with the liberty of action of any of their number, is self-protection. That the only purpose for which power can be rightfully exercised over any member of a civilised community, against his will, is to prevent harm to others. His own good, either physical or moral, is not a sufficient warrant. He cannot rightfully be compelled to do or forbear because it will be better for him to do so, because it will make him happier, because, in the opinions of others, to do so would be wise, or even right. These are good reasons for remonstrating with him, or reasoning with him, or persuading him, or entreating him, but not for compelling him, or visiting him with any evil in case he does otherwise. To justify that, the conduct from which it is desired to deter him must be calculated to produce evil to some one else. The only part of the conduct of any one, for which he is amenable to society, is that which concerns others. In the part which merely concerns himself, his independence is, of right, absolute. Over himself, over his own body and mind, the individual is sovereign.

It is, perhaps hardly necessary to say that this doctrine is meant to apply only to human beings in the maturity of their faculties. We are not speaking of children, or

[From John Stuart Mill, *On Liberty*, Ch. II (abridged) with brief passages from Chs. I, III, and V.]

of young persons below the age which the law may fix as that of manhood or womanhood. Those who are still in a state to require being taken care of by others, must be protected against their own actions as well as against external injury. For the same reason, we may leave out of consideration those backward states of society in which the race itself may be considered as in its nonage. The early difficulties in the way of spontaneous progress are so great, that there is seldom any choice of means for overcoming them; and a ruler full of the spirit of improvement is warranted in the use of any expedients that will attain an end, perhaps otherwise unattainable. Despotism is a legitimate mode of government in dealing with barbarians, provided the end be their improvement, and the means justified by actually effecting that end. Liberty, as a principle, has no application to any state of things anterior to the time when mankind have become capable of being improved by free and equal discussion. Until then, there is nothing for them but implicit obedience to an Akbar or a Charlemagne, if they are so fortunate as to find one. But as soon as mankind have attained the capacity of being guided to their own improvement by conviction or persuasion (a period long since reached in all nations with whom we need here concern ourselves), compulsion, either in the direct form or in that of pains and penalties for non-compliance, is no longer admissible as a means to their own good, and justifiable only for the security of others.

It is proper to state that I forego any advantage which could be derived to my argument from the idea of abstract right, as a thing independent of utility. I regard utility as the ultimate appeal on all ethical questions; but it must be utility in the largest sense, grounded on the permanent interests of a man, as a progressive being. Those interests, I contend, authorise the subjection of individual spontaneity to external control, only in respect to those actions of each, which concern the interest of other people. If any one does an act hurtful to others, there is a *prima facie* case for punishing him, by law, or, where legal penalties are not safely applicable, by general disapprobation. There are also many positive acts for the benefit of others, which he may rightfully be compelled to perform; such as to give evidence in a court of justice; to bear his fair share in the common defence, or in any other joint work necessary to the interest of the society of which he enjoys the protection; and to perform certain acts of individual beneficence, such as saving a fellow-creature's life, or interposing to protect the defenceless against ill-usage, things which whenever it is obviously a man's duty to do, he may rightfully be made responsible to society for not doing.

But there is a sphere of action in which society, as distinguished from the individual, has, if any, only an indirect interest; comprehending all that portion of a person's life and conduct which affects only himself, or if it also affects others, only with their free, voluntary, and undeceived consent and participation. When I say only himself, I mean directly, and in the first instance; for whatever affects himself, may affect others through himself; and the objection which may be grounded on this contingency, will receive consideration in the sequel. This, then, is the appropriate region of human liberty. It comprises, first, the inward domain of consciousness; demanding liberty of conscience in the most comprehensive sense; liberty of thought and feeling; absolute freedom of opinion and sentiment on all subjects, practical or speculative, scientific, moral, or theological. The liberty of expressing and publishing opinions may seem to fall under a different principle, since it belongs to that part of the conduct of an individual which concerns other people; but, being almost of as much importance as the liberty of thought itself, and resting in great part on the same reasons, is practically inseparable from it. Secondly, the principle requires liberty of tastes and pursuits; of framing the plan of our life to suit our own character; of doing as we like, subject to such consequences as may follow: without impediment from our fellow-creatures, so long as what we do does not harm them, even though they should think our conduct foolish, perverse, or wrong. Thirdly, from this liberty of each individual, follows the liberty, within the same limits, of combination among individuals; freedom to unite, for any purpose not involving harm to others: the persons combining being supposed to be of full age, and not forced or deceived.

No society in which these liberties are not, on the whole, respected, is free, whatever may be its form of government; and none is completely free in which they do not exist absolute and unqualified. The only freedom which deserves the name, is that of pursuing our own good in our own way, so long as we do not attempt to deprive others of theirs, or impede their efforts to obtain it. Each is the proper guardian of his own health, whether bodily, or mental and spiritual. Mankind are greater gainers by suffering each other to live as seems good to themselves, than by compelling each to live as seems good to the rest.

II

The time, it is to be hoped, is gone by, when any defence would be necessary of the "liberty of the press" as one of the securities against corrupt or tyrannical government. No argument, we may suppose, can now be needed, against permitting a legislature or an executive, not identified in interest with the people, to prescribe opinions to them, and determine what doctrines or what arguments they shall be allowed to hear. This aspect of the question, besides, has been so often and so triumphantly enforced by preceding writers, that it needs not be specially insisted on in this place, . . . and, speaking generally, it is not, in constitutional countries, to be apprehended, that the government, whether completely responsible to the people or not, will often attempt to control the expression of opinion, except when in doing so it makes itself the organ of the general intolerance of the public. Let us suppose, therefore, that the government is entirely at one with the people, and never thinks of exerting any power of coercion unless in agreement with what it conceives to be their voice. But I deny the right of the people to exercise such coercion, either by themselves or by their government. The power itself is illegitimate. The best government has no more title to it than the worst. It is as noxious, or more noxious, when exerted in accordance with public opinion, than when in opposition to it. If all mankind minus one were of one opinion, and only one person were of the contrary opinion, mankind would be no more justified in silencing that one person, than he, if he had the power, would be justified in silencing mankind. Were an opinion a personal possession of no value except to the owner; if to be obstructed in the enjoyment of it were simply a private injury, it would make some difference whether the injury was inflicted only on a few persons or on many. But the peculiar evil of silencing the expression of an opinion is, that it is robbing the human race; posterity as well as the existing generation; those who dissent from the opinion, still more than those who hold it. If the opinion is right, they are deprived of the opportunity of exchanging error for truth: if wrong, they lose, what is almost as great a benefit, the clearer perception and livelier impression of truth, produced by its collision with error.

It is necessary to consider separately these two hypotheses, each of which has a distinct branch of the argument corresponding to it. We can never be sure that the opinion we are endeavoring to stifle is a false opinion; and if we were sure, stifling it would be an evil still.

First: the opinion which it is attempted to suppress by authority may possibly be true. Those who desire to suppress it, of course deny its truth; but they are not infallible. They have no authority to decide the question for all mankind, and exclude every other person from the means of judging. To refuse a hearing to an opinion, because they are sure that it is false, is to assume that *their* certainty is the same thing as *absolute* certainty. All silencing of discussion is an assumption of infallibility. Its condemnation may be allowed to rest on this common argument, not the worse for being common.

Unfortunately for the good sense of mankind, the fact of their fallibility is far from carrying the weight in their practical judgment which is always allowed to it in theory; for while every one well knows himself to be fallible, few think it necessary to take any precautions against their own fallibility, or admit the supposition that any opinion, of which they feel very certain, may be one of the examples of the error to which they acknowledge themselves to be liable. Absolute princes, or others who are accustomed to unlimited deference, usually feel this complete confidence in their own opinions on nearly all subjects. People more happily situated, who sometimes hear their opinions disputed, and are not wholly unused to be set right when they are wrong, place the same unbounded reliance only on such of their opinions as are shared by all who surround them, or to whom they habitually defer; for in proportion to a man's want of confidence in his own solitary judgment, does he usually repose, with implicit trust, on the infallibility of "the world" in general. And the world, to each individual, means the part of it with which he comes in contact; his party, his sect, his church, his class of society; the man may be called, by comparison, almost liberal and large-minded to whom it means anything so comprehensive as his own country or his own age. Nor is his faith in this collective authority at all shaken by his being aware that other ages, countries, sects, churches, classes, and parties have thought, and even now think, the exact reverse. He devolves upon his own world the responsibility of being in the right against the dissentient worlds of other people; and it never troubles him that mere accident has decided which of these numerous worlds is the object of his reliance, and that the same causes which make him a Churchman in London, would have made him a Buddhist, or a Confucian in Pekin. Yet it is as evident in itself, as any amount of argument can make it, that ages are no more infallible than individuals; every age having held many opinions which subsequent ages have deemed not only false but absurd; and it is as certain that many opinions now general will be rejected by future ages, as it is that many, once general, are rejected by the present.

The objection likely to be made to this argument would probably take some such form as the following. There is no greater assumption of infallibility in forbidding the propagation of error, than in any other thing which is done by public authority on its own judgment and responsibility. Judgment is given to men that they may use it. Because it may be used erroneously, are men to be told that they ought not to use it at all? To prohibit what they think pernicious, is not claiming exemption from error, but fulfilling the duty incumbent on them, although fallible, of acting on their conscientious conviction. If we were never to act on our opinions, because those opinions may be wrong, we should leave all our interests uncared for, and all our duties unperformed. An objection which applies to all conduct can be no valid objection to any conduct in particular. It is the duty of governments, and of individuals, to form the truest opinions they can; to form carefully, and never impose them upon others unless they are quite sure of being right. But when they are sure (such reasoners may say), it is not conscientiousness but cowardice to shrink from acting on their opinions, and allow doctrines which they honestly think dangerous to the welfare of mankind, either in this life or in another, to be scattered abroad without restraint, because other people, in less enlightened times, have persecuted opinions now believed to be true. Let us take care, it may be said, not to make the same mistake: but governments and nations have made mistakes in other things, which are not denied to be fit subjects for the exercise of authority: they have laid on bad taxes, made unjust wars, ought we therefore to lay on no taxes, make no wars? Men, and governments, must act to the best of their ability. There is no such thing as absolute certainty, but there is assurance sufficient for the purposes of human life. We may, and must, assume our opinion to be true for the guidance of our own conduct: and it is assuming no more when we forbid bad men to pervert society by the propagation of opinions which we regard as false and pernicious.

I answer, that it is assuming very much more. There is the greatest difference between presuming an opinion to be true, because, with every opportunity for contesting it, it has not been refuted, and assuming its truth for the purpose of not permitting its refutation. Complete liberty of contradicting and disproving our opinion is the very condition which justifies us in assuming its truth for purposes of action; and on no other terms can a being with human faculties have any rational assurance of being right.

When we consider either the history of opinion, or the ordinary conduct of human life, to what is it to be ascribed that the one and the other are no worse than they are? Not certainly to the inherent force of the human understanding; for, on any matter not self-evident, there are ninety-nine persons totally incapable of judging of it for one who is capable; and the capacity of the hundredth person is only comparative; for the majority of the eminent men of every past generation held many opinions now known to be erroneous, and did or approved numerous things which no one will now justify. Why is it, then, that there is on the whole a preponderance among mankind of rational opinions and rational conduct? If there really is this preponderance—which there must be unless human affairs are, and have always been, in an almost desperate state—it is owing to a quality of the human mind, the source of everything respectable in man either as an intellectual or as a moral being, namely, that his errors are corrigible. He is capable of rectifying his mistakes, by discussion and experience. Not by experience alone. There must be discussion, to show how experience is to be interpreted. Wrong opinions and practices gradually yield to fact and argument; but facts and arguments, to produce any effect on the mind, must be brought before it. Very few facts are able to tell their own story, without comments to bring out their meaning. The whole strength and value, then, of human judgment, depending on the one property, that it can be set right when it is wrong, reliance can be placed on it only when the means of setting it right are kept constantly at hand. In the case of any person whose judgment is really deserving of confidence, how has it become so? Because he has kept his mind open to criticism on his opinions and conduct. Because it has been his practice to listen to all that could be said against him; to profit by as much of it as was just, and expound to himself, and upon occasion to others, the fallacy of what was fallacious. Because he has felt, that the only way in which a human being can make some approach to knowing the whole of a subject, is by hearing what can be said about it by persons of every variety of opinion, and studying all modes in which it can be looked at by every character of mind. No wise man ever acquired his wisdom in any mode but this; nor is it in the nature of human intellect to become wise in any other manner. The steady habit of correcting and completing his own opinion by collating it with those of others, so far from causing doubt and hesitation carrying it into practice, is the only stable foundation for a just reliance on it: for, being cognizant of all that can, at least obviously, be said against him, and having taken up his position against all gainsayers—knowing that he has sought for objections and difficulties, instead of avoiding them, and has shut out no light which can be thrown upon the subject from any quarter—he has a right to think his judgment better than that of any person, or any multitude, who have not gone through a similar process.

It is not too much to require that what the wisest of mankind, those who are best entitled to trust their own judgment, find necessary to warrant their relying on it, should be submitted to by that miscellaneous collection of a few wise and many foolish individuals, called the public.

I must be permitted to observe, that it is not the feeling sure of a doctrine (be it what it may) which I call an assumption of infallibility. It is the undertaking to decide that question *for others,* without allowing them to hear what can be said on the contrary side. And I denounce and reprobate this pretension not the less, if put forth on the side of my most solemn convictions. However positive any one's persuasion may be, not only of the falsity but of the pernicious consequences—not only of the pernicious consequences, but (to adopt expressions which I altogether condemn) the immorality and impiety of an opinion; yet if, in pursuance of that private judgment, though backed by the public judgment of his country or his contemporaries, he prevents the opinion from being heard in its defense, he assumes infallibility. And so far from the assumption being less objectionable or less dangerous because the opinion is called immoral or impious, this is the case of all others in which it is most fatal. These are exactly the occasions on which the men of one generation commit those dreadful mistakes which excite the astonishment and horror of posterity. It is among such that we find the instances memorable in history, when the arm of the law has been employed to root out the best men and the noblest doctrines; with deplorable success as to the men, though some of the doctrines have survived to be (as if in mockery) involved in defense of similar conduct towards those who dissent from *them,* or from their received interpretation.

Mankind can hardly be too often reminded, that there was once a man named Socrates, between whom and the legal authorities and public opinion of his time there took place a memorable collision. Born in an age and country abounding in individual greatness, this man has been handed down to us by those who best knew him and the age, as the most virtuous man in it; while we know him as the head and prototype of all subsequent teachers of virtue, the source equally of the lofty inspiration of Plato and the judicious utilitarianism of Aristotle, "*i maëstri di color che sanno,*" the two headsprings of ethical as of all other philosophy. This acknowledged master of all the eminent thinkers who have since lived—whose fame, still growing after more than two thousand years, all but outweighs the whole remainder of the names which make his native city illustrious —was put to death by his countrymen, after a judicial conviction, for impiety and immorality. Impiety, in denying the gods recognized by the State; indeed his accuser asserted (see the "Apologia") that he believed in no gods at all. Immorality, in being, by his doctrines and instructions, a "corrupter of youth." Of these charges the tribunal, there is every ground for believing, honestly found him guilty, and condemned the man who probably of all then born had deserved least of mankind to be put to death as a criminal.

To pass from this to the only other instance of judicial iniquity, the mention of which, after the condemnation of Socrates, would not be an anti-climax: the event which took place on Calvary rather more than eighteen hundred years ago. The man who left on the memory of those who witnessed his life and conversation such an impression of his moral grandeur that eighteen subsequent centuries have done homage to him as the Almighty in person, was ignominiously put to death, as what? As a blasphemer. Men did not merely mistake their benefactor; they mistook him for the exact contrary of what he was, and treated him as that prodigy of impiety which they themselves are now held to be for their treatment of him. The feelings with which mankind now regard these lamentable transactions, especially the later of the two, render them extremely unjust in their judgment of the unhappy actors. These were, to all appearance, not bad men —not worse than men commonly are, but rather the contrary; men who possessed in a full, or somewhat more than a full measure, the religious, moral and patriotic feelings of their time and people: the very kind of men who, in all times, our own included, have every chance of passing through life blameless and respected. The high-priest who rent his garments when the words were prounounced, which, according to all the ideas of his country, constituted the blackest guilt, was in all probability quite as sincere in his horror and indignation as the generality of respectable and pious men now are in the religious and moral sentiments they profess; and most of those who now shudder at his conduct, if they had lived in his time, and been born Jews, would have acted precisely as he did. Orthodox Christians who are tempted to think that those who stoned to death the first martyrs must have been worse men than they themselves are, ought to remember that one of those persecutors was Saint Paul.

Let us add one more example, the most striking of all, if the impressiveness of an error is measured by the wisdom and virtue of him who falls into it. If ever any one, possessed of power, had grounds for thinking himself the best and most enlightened among his contemporaries, it was the Emperor Marcus Aurelius. Absolute monarch of the whole civilized world, he preserved through life not only the most unblemished justice, but what was less to be expected from his Stoical breeding, the tenderest heart. The few failings which are attributed to him were all on the side of indulgence: while his writings, the highest ethical product of the ancient mind, differ scarcely perceptibly, if they differ at all, from the most characteristic teachings of Christ. This man, a better Christian in all but the dogmatic sense of the word than almost any of the ostensibly Christian sovereigns who have since reigned, persecuted Christianity. Placed at the summit of all the previous attainments of humanity, with an open, unfettered intellect, and a character which led him of himself to embody in his moral writings the Christian ideal, he yet failed to see that Christianity was to be a good and not an evil to the world, with his duties to which he was so deeply penetrated. Existing society he knew to be in a deplorable state. But such as it was, he saw, or thought he saw, that it was held together, and prevented from being worse, by belief and reverence of the received divinities. As a ruler of mankind, he deemed it his duty not to suffer society to fall in pieces; and saw not how, if its existing ties were removed, any others could be formed which could again knit it together. The new religion openly aimed at dissolving these ties: unless, therefore, it was his duty to adopt that religion, it seemed to be his duty to put it down. Inasmuch then as the theology of Christianity did not appear to him true or of divine origin; inasmuch as this strange history of a crucified God was not credible to him, and a system which purported to rest entirely upon a foundation to him so wholly unbelievable, could not be foreseen by him to be that renovating agency which, after all abatements, it has in fact proved to be; the gentlest and most amiable of philosophers and rulers, under a solemn sense of duty, authorized the persecution of Christianity. To my mind this is one of the tragical facts in all history. It is a bitter thought, how different a thing the Christianity of the world might have been, if the Christian faith had been adopted as the religion of the empire under the auspices of Marcus Aurelius instead of those of Constantine. But it would be equally unjust to him and false to truth to deny, that no one plea which can be urged for punishing anti-Christian teaching was wanting to Marcus Aurelius for punishing, as he did, the propagation of Christianity. No Christian more firmly believes that Atheism is false, and tends to the dissolution of society, than Marcus Aurelius believed the same things of Christianity; he who, of all men then living, might have been thought the most capable of appreciating it. Unless any one who approves of punishment for the promulgation of opinions, flatters himself that he is a wiser and better man than Marcus Aurelius—more deeply versed in the wisdom of his time, more elevated in his intellect above it—more earnest in his search for truth, or more single-minded in his devotion to it when found; let him abstain from that assumption of the joint infallibility of himself and the multitude, which the great Antoninus made with so unfortunate a result.

III

Let us now pass to the second division of the argument, and dismissing the supposition that any of the received opinions may be false, let us assume them to be true, and examine into the worth of the manner in which they are likely to be held, when their truth is not freely and openly canvassed. However unwillingly a person who has a strong opinion may admit the possibility that his opinion may be false, he ought to be moved by the consideration that, however true it may be, if it is not fully, frequently, and fearlessly discussed, it will be held as a dead dogma, not a living truth.

There is a class of persons (happily not quite so numerous as formerly) who think it enough if a person assents undoubtingly to what they think true, though he has no knowledge whatever of the grounds of the opinion, and could not make a tenable defense of it against the most superficial objections. Such persons, if they can once get their creed taught from authority, naturally think that no good, and some harm, comes of its being allowed to be questioned. Where their influence prevails, they make it nearly impossible for the received opinion to be rejected wisely and considerately, though it may still be rejected rashly and ignorantly; for to shut out discussion entirely is seldom possible, and when it once gets in, beliefs not grounded on conviction are apt to give way before the slightest semblance of an argument. Waiving, however, this possibility—assuming that the true opinion abides in the mind, but abides as a prejudice, a belief independent of, and proof against, argument—this is not the way in which truth ought to be held by a rational being. This is not knowing the truth. Truth, thus held, is but one superstition the more, accidentally clinging to the words which enunciate a truth.

If the cultivation of the understanding consists in one thing more than another, it is surely in learning the grounds of one's own opinions. Whatever people believe, on subjects on which it is of the first importance to believe rightly, they ought to be able to defend against at least the common objections. But, some one may say, "Let them be *taught* the grounds of their opinions. It does not follow that opinions must be merely parroted because they are never heard controverted. Persons who learn geometry do not simply commit the theorems to memory, but understand and learn likewise the demonstrations; and it would be absurd to say that they remain ignorant of the grounds of geometrical truths, because they never hear any one deny, and attempt to disprove them." Undoubtedly: and such teaching suffices on a subject like mathematics, where there is nothing at all to be said on the wrong side of the question. The peculiarity of the evidence of mathematical truths is that all the argument is on one side. There are no objections, and no answers to objections. But on every subject on which difference of opinion is possible, the truth depends on a balance to be struck between two sets of conflicting reasons. Even in natural philosophy, there is always some other explanation possible of the same facts; some geocentric theory instead of heliocentric, some phlogiston instead of oxygen; and it has to be shown why that other theory cannot be the true one; and until this is shown, and until we know how it is shown, we do not understand the grounds of our opinion. But when we turn to subjects infinitely more complicated, to morals, religion, politics, social relations, and the business of life, three-fourths of the arguments for every disputed opinion consist in dispelling the appearances which favor some opinion different from it. The greatest orator, save one, of antiquity, has left it on record that he always studied his adversary's case with as great, if not still greater, intensity than even his own. What Cicero practised as the means of forensic success requires to be imitated by all who study any subject in order to arrive at the truth. He who knows only his own side of the case, knows little of that. His reasons may be good, and no one may have been able to refute them. But if he is equally unable to refute the reasons on the opposite side; if he does not so much as know what they are, he has no ground for preferring either opinion.

Nor is it enough that he should hear the arguments of adversaries from his own teachers, presented as they state them, and accompanied by what they offer as refutations. That is not the way to do justice to the arguments, or bring them into real contact with his own mind. He must be able to hear them from persons who actually believe them; who defend them in earnest, and do their very utmost for them. He must know them in their most plausible and persuasive form; he must feel the whole force of the difficulty which the true view of the subject has to encounter and dispose of; else he will never really possess himself of the portion of truth which meets and removes that difficulty. Ninety-nine in a hundred of what are called educated men are in this condition; even of those who can argue fluently for their opinions. Their conclusion may be true, but it might be false for anything they know: they have never thrown themselves into the mental position of those who think differently from them, and considered what such persons may have to say; and consequently they do not, in any proper sense of the word, know the doctrine which they themselves profess. They do not know those parts of it which explain and justify the remainder; the considerations which show that a fact which seemingly conflicts with another is reconcilable with it, or that, of two apparently strong reasons, one and not the other ought to be preferred. All that part of the truth which turns the scale, and decides the judgment of a completely informed mind, they are strangers to; nor is it ever really known, but to those who have attended equally and impartially to both sides, and endeavored to see the reasons of both in the strongest light. So essential is this discipline to a real understanding of moral and human subjects, that if opponents of all important truths do not exist, it is indispensable to imagine them, and supply them with the strongest arguments which the most skilful devil's advocate can conjure up.

To what an extent doctrines intrinsically fitted to make the deepest impression upon the mind may remain in it as dead beliefs, without being ever realized in the imagination, the feelings, or the understanding, is exemplified by the manner in which the majority of believers hold the doctrines of Christianity. By Christianity I here mean what is accounted such by all churches and sects—the maxims and precepts contained in the New Testament. These are considered sacred, and accepted as laws, by all professing Christians. Yet it is scarcely too much to say that not one Christian in a thousand guides or tests his individual conduct by reference to those laws. The standard to which he does refer it, is the custom of his nation, his class, or his religious profession. He has thus, on the one hand, a collection of ethical maxims, which he believes to have been vouchsafed to him by infallible wisdom as rules for his government; and on the other a set of every-day judgments and practices, which go a certain length with some of those maxims, not so great a length with others, stand in direct opposition to some, and are, on the whole, a compromise between the Christian creed and the interests and suggestions of worldly life. To the first of these standards he gives his homage; to the other his real allegiance. All Christians believe that the blessed are the poor and humble, and those who are ill-used by the world; that it is easier for a camel to pass through the eye of a needle than for a rich man to enter the kingdom of heaven; that they should judge not, lest they be judged; that they should swear not at all; that they should love their neighbour as themselves; that if one take their cloak, they should give him their coat also; that they should take no thought for the morrow; that if they would be perfect they should sell all that they have and give it to the poor. They are not insincere when they say that they believe these things. They do believe them, as people believe what they have always heard lauded and never discussed. But in the sense of that living belief which regulates conduct, they believe these doctrines just up to the point to which it is usual to act upon them. The doctrines in their integrity are serviceable to pelt adversaries with; and it is understood that they are to be put forward (when possible) as the reasons for whatever people do that they think laudable. But any one who reminded them that the maxims require an infinity of things which they never even think of doing, would gain nothing but to be classed among those very unpopular characters who affect to be better than other people. The doctrines have no hold on ordinary believers—are not a power in their minds. They have an habitual respect for the sound of them, but no feeling which spreads from the words to the things signified, and forces the mind to take *them* in, and make them conform to the formula.

Now we may be well assured that the case was not thus, but far otherwise, with the early Christians. Had it been thus, Christianity never would have expanded from an obscure sect of the despised Hebrews into the religion of the Roman empire. When their enemies said, "See how these Christians love one another" (a remark not likely to be made by anybody now), they assuredly had a much livelier feeling of the meaning of their creed than they have ever had since. And to this cause, probably, it is chiefly owing that Christianity now makes so little progress in extending its domain, and after eighteen centuries is still nearly confined to Europeans and the descendants of Europeans. Even with the strictly religious, who are much in earnest about their doctrines, and attach a greater amount of meaning to many of them than people in general, it commonly happens that the part which is thus comparatively active in their minds is that which was made by Calvin, or Knox, or some such person much nearer in character to themselves. The sayings of Christ coexist passively in their minds, producing hardly any effect beyond what is caused by mere listening to words so amiable and bland. There are many reasons, doubtless, why doctrines which are the badge of a sect retain more of their vitality than those common to all recognized sects, and why more pains are taken by teachers to keep their meaning alive; but one reason certainly is, that the peculiar doctrines are more questioned, and have to be oftener defended against open gain-sayers. Both teachers and learners go to sleep at their post, as soon as there is no enemy in the field.

IV

It still remains to speak of one of the principal causes which make diversity of opinion advantageous, and will continue to do so until mankind shall have entered a stage of intellectual advancement which at present seems at an incalculable distance. We have hitherto considered only two possibilities: that the received opinion may be false, and some other opinion, consequently, true; or that, the received opinion being true, a conflict with the opposite error is essential to a clear apprehension and deep feeling of its truth. But there is a commoner case than either of these; when the conflicting doctrines, instead of being one true and the other false, share the truth between them; and the nonconforming opinion is needed to supply the remainder of the truth, of which the received doctrine embodies only a part. Popular opinions, on subjects not palpable to sense, are often true, but seldom or never the whole truth. They are a part of the truth; sometimes a greater, sometimes a smaller part, but exaggerated, distorted, and disjointed from the truths by which they ought to be accompanied and limited. Heretical opinions, on the other hand, are generally some of these suppressed and neglected truths, bursting the bonds which kept them down, and either seeking reconciliation with the truth contained in the common opinion, or fronting it as enemies, and setting themselves up, with similar exclusiveness, as the whole truth. The latter case is hitherto the most frequent, as, in the human mind, one-sidedness has always been the rule, and many-sidedness the exception. Hence, even in revolutions of opinion, one part of the truth usually sets while another rises. Even progress, which ought to superadd, for the most part only substitutes, one partial and incomplete truth for another; improvement consisting chiefly in this, that the new fragment of truth is more wanted, more adapted to the needs of the time, than that which it displaces. Such being the partial character of prevailing opinions, even when resting on a true foundation, every opinion which embodies somewhat of the portion of truth which the common opinion omits, ought to be considered precious, with whatever amount of error and confusion that truth may be blended. No sober judge of human affairs will feel bound to be indignant because those who force on our notice truths which we should otherwise have overlooked, overlook some of those which we see. Rather, he will think that so long as popular truth is one-sided, it is more desirable than otherwise that unpopular truth should have one-sided assertors too; such being usually the most energetic, and the most likely to compel reluctant attention to the fragment of wisdom which they proclaim as if it were the whole.

In politics, it is almost a commonplace, that a party of order or stability, and a party of progress or reform, are both necessary elements of a healthy state of political life; until the one or the other shall have so enlarged its mental grasp as to be a party equally of order and of progress, knowing and distinguishing what is fit to be preserved from what ought to be swept away. Each of these modes of thinking derives its utility from the deficiencies of the other; but it is in a great measure the opposition of the other that keeps each within the limits of reason and sanity. Unless opinions favorable to democracy and to aristocracy, to property and to equality, to cooperation and to competition, to luxury and to abstinence, to sociality and individuality, to liberty and discipline, and all the other standing antagonisms of practical life, are expressed with equal freedom, and enforced and defended with equal talent and energy, there is no chance of both elements obtaining their due; one scale is sure to go up, and the other down. Truth, in the great practical concerns of life, is so much a question of the reconciling and combining of opposites, that very few have minds sufficiently capacious and impartial to make the adjustment with an approach to correctness, and it has to be made by the rough process of a struggle between combatants fighting under hostile banners. On any of the great open questions just enumerated, if either of the two opinions has a better claim than the other, not merely to be tolerated, but to be encouraged and countenanced, it is the one which happens at the particular time and place to be in a minority. That is the opinion which, for the time being, represents the neglected interests, the side of human well-being which is in danger of obtaining less than its share. I am aware that there is not, in this country, any intolerance of differences of opinion on most of these topics. They are adduced to show, by admitted and multiplied examples, the universality of the fact, that only through diversity of opinion is there, in the existing state of human intellect, a chance of fair play to all sides of the truth. When there are persons to be found who form an exception to the apparent unanimity of the world on any subject, even if the world is in the right, it is always probable that dissentients have something worth hearing to say for themselves, and that truth would lose something by their silence.

. . . . .

We have now recognized the necessity to the mental well-being of mankind (on which all their other well-being depends) of freedom of opinion, and freedom of the expression of opinion, on four distinct grounds; which we will now briefly recapitulate.

First, if any opinion is compelled to silence, that opinion may, for aught we certainly know, be true. To deny this is to assume our own infallibility.

Secondly, though the silenced opinion be an error, it may, and very commonly does, contain a portion of truth; and since the general or prevailing opinion on any subject is rarely or never the whole truth, it is only by the collision of adverse opinions that the remainder of the truth has any chance of being supplied.

Thirdly, even if the received opinion be not only true, but the whole truth; unless it is suffered to be, and actually is, vigorously and earnestly contested, it will, by most of those who receive it, be held in the manner of a prejudice, with little comprehension or feeling, of its rational grounds. And not only this, but, fourthly, the meaning of the doctrine itself will be in danger of being lost, or enfeebled, and deprived of its vital effect on the character and conduct; the dogma becoming a mere formal profession, inefficacious for good, but cumbering the ground, and preventing the growth of any real and heartfelt conviction, from reason or personal experience.

V

Such being the reasons which make it imperative that human beings should be free to form opinions, and to express their opinions without reserve; and such the baneful consequences to the intellectual, and through that to the moral nature of man, unless this liberty is either conceded, or asserted in spite of prohibition; let us next examine whether the same reasons do not require that men should be free to act upon their opinions—to carry these out in their lives, without hindrance, either physical or moral, from their fellowmen, so long as it is at their own risk and peril. This last proviso is of course indispensable. No one pretends that actions should be as free as opinions. On the contrary, even opinions lose their immunity when the circumstances in which they are expressed are such as to constitute their expression a positive instigation to some mischievous act. An opinion that corn-dealers are starvers of the poor, or that private property is robbery, ought to be unmolested when simply circulated through the press, but may justly incur punishment when delivered orally to an excited mob assembled before the house of a corn-dealer, or when handed about among the same mob in the form of a placard. Acts, of whatever kind, which, without justifiable cause, do harm to others, may be, and in the more important cases absolutely require to be, controlled by the unfavorable sentiments, and, when needful, by the active interference of mankind. The liberty of the individual must be thus far limited; he must not make himself a nuisance to other people. But if he refrains from molesting others in what concerns them, and merely acts according to his own inclination and judgment in things which concern himself, the same reasons which show that opinion should be free, prove also that he should be allowed, without molestation, to carry his opinions into practice at his own cost.

In maintaining this principle, the greatest difficulty to be encountered does not lie in the appreciation of means towards an acknowledged end, but in the indifference of persons in general to the end itself. If it were felt that the free development of individuality is one of the leading essentials of well-being; that it is not only a coordinate element with all that is designated by the terms civilization, instruction, education, culture, but is itself a necessary part and condition of all those things; there would be no danger that liberty should be undervalued, and the adjustment of the boundaries between it and social control would present no extraordinary difficulty. But the evil is, that individual spontaneity is hardly recognized by the common modes of thinking as having any intrinsic worth, or deserving any regard on its own account. The majority, being satisfied with the ways of mankind as they now are (for it is they who make them what they are), cannot comprehend why those ways should not be good enough for everybody.

Few persons, out of Germany, even comprehend the meaning of the doctrine which Wilhelm von Humboldt, so eminent both as a *savant* and as a politician, made the text of a treatise—that "the end of man, or that which is prescribed by the eternal or immutable dictates of reason, and not suggested by vague and transient desires, is the highest and most harmonious development of his powers to a complete and consistent whole;" that, therefore, the object "towards which every human being must ceaselessly direct his efforts, and on which especially those who design to influence their fellow-men must ever keep their eyes, is the individuality of power and development;" that for this there are two requisites, "freedom, and variety of situation;" and that from the union of these arise "individual vigor and manifold diversity," which combine themselves in "originality." [1]

VI

The principles asserted in these pages must be more generally admitted as the basis for discussion of details, before a consistent application of them to all the various departments of government and morals can be attempted with any prospect of advantage. The few observations I propose to make on questions of detail are designed to illustrate the principles, rather than to follow them out to their consequences. I offer, not so much applications, as specimens of application; which may serve to bring into greater clearness the meaning and limits of the two maxims which together form the entire doctrine of this Essay, and to assist the judgment in holding the balance between them, in the cases where it appears doubtful which of them is applicable to the case.

The maxims are, first, that the individual is not accountable to society for his actions, in so far as these concern the interests of no person but himself. Advice, instruction, persuasion, and avoidance by other people if thought necessary by them for their own good, are the only measures by which society can justifiably express its dislike or disapprobation of his conduct. Secondly, that for such actions as are prejudicial to the interests of others, the individual is accountable, and may be subjected either to social or to legal punishment, if society is of opinion that the one or the other is requisite for its protection.

In the first place, it must by no means be supposed, because damage, or probability of damage, to the interests of others, can alone justify the interference of society, that therefore it always does justify such interference. In many cases, an individual, in pursuing a legitimate object, necessarily and therefore legitimately causes pain or loss to others, or intercepts a good which they had a reasonable hope of obtaining. Such oppositions of interest between individuals often arise from bad social institutions. Whoever succeeds in an overcrowded profession, or in a competitive examination; whoever is preferred to another in any contest for an object which both desire, reaps benefit from the loss of others, from their wasted exertion and their disappointment. But it is, by common admission, better for

[1] *The Sphere and Duties of Government*, from the German of Baron Wilhelm von Humboldt, pp. 11-13.

the general interest of mankind, that persons should pursue their objects undeterred by this sort of consequences. In other words, society admits no right, either legal or moral, in the disappointed competitors to immunity from this kind of suffering; and feels called on to interfere, only when means of success have been employed which it is contrary to the general interest to permit—namely, fraud or treachery, and force.

It is one of the undisputed functions of government to take precautions against crime before it has been committed, as well as to detect and punish it afterwards. The preventive function of government, however, is far more liable to be abused, to the prejudice of liberty, than the punitory function; for there is hardly any part of the legitimate freedom of action of a human being which would not admit of being represented, and fairly too, as increasing the facilities for some form or other of delinquency. Nevertheless, if a public authority, or even a private person, sees any one evidently preparing to commit a crime, they are not bound to look on inactive until the crime is committed, but may interfere to prevent it. If poisons were never bought or used for any purpose except the commission of murder it would be right to prohibit their manufacture and sale. They may, however, be wanted not only for innocent but for useful purposes, and restrictions cannot be imposed in the one case without operating in the other. Again, it is a proper office of public authority to guard against accidents. If either a public officer or any one else saw a person attempting to cross a bridge which has been ascertained to be unsafe, and there were no time to warn him of his danger, they might seize him and turn him back, without any real infringement of his liberty; for liberty consists in doing what one desires, and he does not desire to fall into the river. Nevertheless, when there is not a certainty, but only a danger of mischief, no one but the person himself can judge of the sufficiency of the motive which may prompt him to incur the risk: in this case, therefore (unless he is a child, or delirious, or in some state of excitement or absorption incompatible with the full use of the reflecting faculty), he ought, I conceive, to be only warned of the danger; not forcibly prevented from exposing himself to it.

I have reserved for the last place a large class of questions respecting the limits of government interference, which, though closely connected with the subject of this Essay, do not, in strictness, belong to it. These are cases in which the reasons against interference do not turn upon the principle of liberty: the question is not about restraining the actions of individuals, but about helping them; it is asked whether the government should do, or cause to be done, something for their benefit, instead of leaving it to be done by themselves, individually or in voluntary combination.

The objection to government interference, when it is not such as to involve infringement of liberty, may be of three kinds.

The first is, when the thing to be done is likely to be better done by individuals than by the government. Speaking generally, there is no one so fit to conduct any business, or to determine how or by whom it shall be conducted, as those who are personally interested in it. The principle condemns the interferences, once so common, of the legislature, or the officers of government, with the ordinary processes of industry. But this part of the subject has been sufficiently enlarged upon by political economists, and is not particularly related to the principles of this Essay.

The second objection is more nearly allied to our subject. In many cases, though individuals may not do the particular thing so well, on the average, as the officers of government, it is nevertheless desirable that it should be done by them, rather than by the government, as a means to their own mental education—a mode of strengthening their active faculties, exercising their judgment, and giving them a familiar knowledge of the subjects with which they are thus left to deal. This is a principal, though not the sole, recommendation of jury trial (in cases not political); of free and popular local and municipal institutions; of the conduct of industrial and philanthropic enterprises by voluntary associations.

The third and most cogent reason for restricting the interference of government is the great evil of adding unnecessarily to its power. Every function superadded to those already exercised by the government causes its influence over hopes and fears to be more widely diffused, and converts, more and more, the active and ambitious part of the public into hangers-on of the government, or of some party which aims at becoming the government. If the roads, the railways, the banks, the insurance offices, the great joint-stock companies, the universities, and the public charities, were all of them branches of the government; if, in addition, the municipal corporations and local boards, with all that now devolves on them, became departments of the central administration; if the employees of all these different enterprises were appointed and paid by the government, and looked to the government for every rise in life; not all the freedom of the press and popular constitution of the legislature would make this or any other country free otherwise than in name. And the evil would be greater, the more efficiently and scientifically the administrative machinery was constructed—the more skilful the arrangements for obtaining the best qualified hands and heads with which to work it.

If every part of the business of society which required organized concert, or large and comprehensive views, were in the hands of the government, and if government offices were universally filled by the ablest men, all the enlarged culture and practised intelligence in the country, except the purely speculative, would be concentrated in a numerous bureaucracy, to whom alone the rest of the community would look for all things: the multitude for direction and dictation in all they had to do; the able and aspiring for personal advancement. To be admitted into the ranks of this bureaucracy, and when admitted, to rise therein, would be the sole objects of ambition. Under this regime, not only is the outside public ill-qualified, for want of practical experience, to criticize or check the mode of operation of the bureaucracy, but even if the accidents of despotic or the natural working of popular institutions occasionally raise to the summit a ruler or rulers of reforming inclinations, no reform can be effected which is contrary to the interest of the bureaucracy. Such is the melancholy condition of the Russian empire, as shown in the accounts of those who have had sufficient opportunity of observation. The Czar himself is powerless against the bureaucratic body; he can send any one of them to Siberia, but he cannot govern without them, or against their will. On every decree of his they have a tacit veto, by merely refraining from carrying it into effect.

A government cannot have too much of the kind of activity which does not impede, but aids and stimulates, individual exertion and development. The mischief begins when, instead of calling forth the activity and powers of individuals and bodies, it substitutes its own activity for theirs; when, instead of informing, advising, and, upon occasion, denouncing, it makes them work in fetters, or bids them stand aside and does their work instead of them. The worth of a State, in the long run, is the worth of the individuals composing it; and a State which postpones the interests of *their* mental expansion and elevation to a little more of administrative skill, or of that semblance of it which practice gives, in the details of business; a State which dwarfs its men, in order that they may be more docile instruments in its hands even for beneficial purposes—will find that with small men no great thing can really be accomplished; and that the perfection of machinery to which it has sacrificed everything will in the end avail it nothing, for want of the vital power which, in order that the machine might work more smoothly, it has preferred to banish.

V. I. Lenin

One of our major responsibilities as intelligent American citizens today is to understand communism more clearly. Vladimir Ilich Lenin (1870-1924) was the dominant figure in the revolution that led to the overthrow of the czarist regime in Russia and the establishment of the present communist dictatorship. To this cause Lenin devoted his life. He participated in the abortive revolution of 1905; he was several times imprisoned for revolutionary activities and twice sent to Siberia. His brother was executed for plotting the assassination of Alexander III, and Lenin himself was forced to live in exile, first in Germany and England and later in Switzerland. During these years in exile he devoted all his efforts toward hastening the revolution in Russia, spending his time largely in study and propagandistic activity.

The widespread inefficiency and corruption of the czarist regime became clear during World War I. In 1917 the Russian war effort collapsed, and internal revolution broke out in Russia. With the help of the Germans, who permitted him to cross Central Europe in a sealed railroad car, Lenin returned to Russia in February 1917. He set to work at once to break the provisional democratic government under Alexander Kerensky, which had come to power in March of that year, and to establish his own Communist government.

In November 1917 the Communist party under Lenin's leadership seized control by force and managed to establish itself in power. Lenin at once set up a dictatorship with himself at the head and for five years he directed its activities with great skill and surprising success. His physical collapse in 1922 and death in 1924 gave Stalin the opportunity to seize control of the government and paved the way for the more recent political developments in Russia.

Lenin was a prolific writer and his works, along with those of Marx, are still regarded as a sort of Communist gospel. The State and Revolution, *perhaps his most influential book, was written in 1917, largely as a reply to the less radical socialists in Europe who wanted to establish a socialist regime gradually and peacefully rather than by revolution. In the selection from this work included here, we find the kind of attack upon democracy in a capitalistic society which advocates of communism generally employ, together with Lenin's argument that communism will have a greater appeal to the masses than democracy. The selection provides valuable information for understanding the social philosophy of communism. When* The State and Revolution *was first published, intellectuals in this country laughed at it, as later they laughed at Hitler's* Mein Kampf. *Both books proved to be accurate predictions of coming events, well worth the careful study of all who seek to oppose the destructive forces they describe.*

THE STATE AND REVOLUTION

The Transition from Capitalism to Communism

MARX WRITES:

> Between capitalist and Communist society lies the period of the revolutionary transformation of the one into the other. There corresponds to this also a political transition period in which the state can be nothing but the *revolutionary dictatorship of the proletariat.*

Marx bases this conclusion on an analysis of the role played by the proletariat in modern capitalist society, on the data concerning the development of this society, and on the irreconcilability of the antagonistic interests of the proletariat and the *bourgeoisie.*

Earlier the question was put in this way: in order to achieve its emancipation, the proletariat must overthrow the *bourgeoisie,* conquer political power and establish its revolutionary dictatorship.

Now the question is put somewhat differently: the transition from capitalist society—which is developing towards Communism—to a Communist society is impossible without a "political transition period," and the state in this period can only be the revolutionary dictatorship of the proletariat.

What, then, is the relation of this dictatorship to democracy?

We have seen that *The Communist Manifesto* simply places the two ideas side by side: "to raise the proletariat to the position of all the ruling class" and "to win the battle of democracy." On the basis of all that has been said above, it is possible to determine more precisely how democracy changes in the transition from capitalism to Communism.

In capitalist society, under the conditions most favorable to its development, we have more or less complete democracy in the democratic republic. But this democracy is always restricted by the narrow framework of capitalist exploitation, and consequently always remains, in reality, a democracy for the minority, only for the possessing classes, only for the rich. Freedom in capitalist society always remains about the same as it was in the ancient Greek republics: freedom for the slave-owners. Owing to the conditions of capitalist exploitation the modern wage-slaves are so crushed by want and poverty that "they cannot be bothered with democracy," "they cannot be bothered with politics"; in the ordinary peaceful course of events the majority of the population is debarred from participating in social and political life.

Democracy for an insignificant minority, democracy for the rich—that is the democracy of capitalist society. If we look more closely into the mechanism of capitalist democracy, everywhere, in the "petty"—so-called petty—details of the suffrage (residential qualification, exclusion of women, etc.), in the technique of the representative institutions, in the actual obstacles to the right of assembly (public buildings are not for "beggars"!), in the purely capitalist organization of the daily press, etc., etc.—we see restriction after restriction upon democracy. These restrictions, exceptions, exclusions, obstacles for the poor, seem slight, especially in the eyes of one who has never known want himself and has never been in close contact with the oppressed classes in their mass life (and nine-tenths if not

[From V. I. Lenin, *The State and Revolution,* Ch. V. Reprinted from *The Essentials of Lenin,* Vol. II, London, Lawrence and Wishart, 1947. By permission of the publishers.]

ninety-nine hundredths, of the bourgeois publicists and politicians are of this category); but in their sum total these restrictions exclude and squeeze out the poor from politics, from taking an active part in democracy.

Marx grasped this *essence* of capitalist democracy splendidly, when, in analyzing the experience of the Commune, he said that the oppressed are allowed once every few years to decide which particular representatives of the oppressing class should represent and repress them in parliament!

But from this capitalist democracy—inevitably narrow, tacitly repelling the poor, and therefore hypocritical and false to the core—forward development does not proceed simply, directly and smoothly to "greater and greater democracy," as the liberal professors and petty-bourgeois opportunists would have us believe. No, forward development, *i.e.*, towards Communism, proceeds through the dictatorship of the proletariat, and cannot do otherwise, for the *resistance* of the capitalist exploiters cannot be *broken* by anyone else or in any other way.

But the dictatorship of the proletariat, *i.e.*, the organization of the vanguard of the oppressed as the ruling class for the purpose of crushing the oppressors, cannot result merely in an expansion of democracy. *Simultaneously* with an immense expansion of democracy, which *for the first time* becomes democracy for the poor, democracy for the people, and not democracy for the rich, the dictatorship of the proletariat imposes a series of restrictions on the freedom of the oppressors, the exploiters, the capitalists. We must crush them in order to free humanity from wage-slavery; their resistance must be broken by force; it is clear that where there is suppression, where there is coercion, there is no freedom and no democracy.

Democracy for the vast majority of the people, and suppression by force, *i.e.*, exclusion from democracy, of the exploiters and oppressors of the people—this is the change democracy undergoes during the *transition* from capitalism to Communism.

Only in Communist society, when the resistance of the capitalists has been completely broken, when the capitalists have disappeared, when there are no classes (*i.e.*, when there is no difference between the members of society as regards their relation to the social means of production), *only* then does "the state . . . cease to exist," and it "*becomes possible to speak of freedom.*" Only then will really complete democracy, democracy without any exceptions, be possible and be realized. And only then will democracy begin to *wither away*, owing to the simple fact that, freed from capitalist slavery, from the untold horrors, savagery, absurdities and infamies of capitalist exploitation, people will gradually *become accustomed* to observing the elementary rules of social intercourse that have been known for centuries and repeated for thousands of years in all copybook maxims; they will become accustomed to observing them without force, without compulsion, without subordination, *without the special apparatus* for compulsion which is called the state.

The expression "*the state withers away*" is very well chosen, for it indicates both the gradual and the spontaneous nature of the process. Only habit can, and undoubtedly will, have such an effect; for we see around us millions of times how readily people become accustomed to observing the necessary rules of social intercourse if there is no exploitation, if there is nothing that causes indignation, nothing that calls forth protest and revolt or evokes the necessity for *suppression*.

Thus in capitalist society we have a democracy that is curtailed, wretched, false; a democracy only for the rich, for the minority. The dictatorship of the proletariat, the period of transition to Communism, will for the first time create democracy for the people, for the majority, in addition to the necessary suppression of the minority—the exploiters. Communism alone is capable of giving really complete democracy, and the more complete it is the more quickly will it become unnecessary and wither away of itself.

In other words: under capitalism we have a state in the proper sense of the word, that is, a special machine for the suppression of one class by another, and of the majority by the minority at that. Naturally, the successful discharge of such a task as the systematic suppression of the exploited majority by the exploiting minority calls for the greatest ferocity and savagery in the work of suppression, it calls for seas of blood through which mankind has to wade in slavery, serfdom and wage labor.

Furthermore, during the transition from capitalism to Communism suppression is *still* necessary; but it is now the suppression of the exploiting minority by the exploited majority. A special apparatus, a special machine for suppression, the "state," is *still* necessary, but this is now a transitory state; it is no longer a state in the proper sense; for the suppression of the minority of exploiters by the majority of the wage-slaves of *yesterday* is comparatively so easy, simple and natural a task that it will entail far less bloodshed than the suppression of the risings of slaves, serfs or wage laborers, and it will cost mankind far less. And it is compatible with the extension of democracy to such an overwhelming majority of the population that the need for a *special machine* of suppression will begin to disappear. The exploiters are naturally unable to suppress the people without a very complex machine for performing this task; but *the people* can suppress the exploiters even with a very simple "machine," almost without a "machine," without a special apparatus, by the simple *organization of the armed masses* (such as the Soviets of Workers' and Soldiers' Deputies, we may remark, running ahead a little).

Finally, only Communism makes the state absolutely unnecessary, for there is *nobody* to be suppressed—"nobody" in the sense of a *class*, in the sense of a systematic struggle against a definite section of the population. We are not utopians, and we do not in the least deny the possibility and inevitability of excesses on the part of *individual persons*, or the need to suppress *such* excesses. But, in the first place, no special machine, no special apparatus of repression is needed for this; this will be done by the armed people itself, as simply and readily as any crowd of civilized people, even in modern society, parts two people who are fighting, or interferes to prevent a woman from being assaulted. And secondly, we know that the fundamental social cause of excesses, which consist of violating the rules of social intercourse, is the exploitation of the masses, their want and their poverty. With the removal of this chief cause, excesses will inevitably begin to "*wither away.*" We do not know how quickly and in what order, but we know that they will wither away. With their withering away the state *will also wither away.*

Without indulging in utopias, Marx defined more fully what can be defined *now* regarding this future, namely, the difference between the lower and higher phases (degrees, stages) of Communist society.

The First Phase of Communist Society

In the *Critique of the Gotha Program*, Marx goes into some detail to disprove Lassalle's idea that under Socialism the worker will receive the "undiminished" or "whole proceeds of his labor." Marx shows that from the whole of the social labor of society it is necessary to deduct a reserve fund, a fund for the expansion of production, for the replacement of "used up" machinery, and so on; then, also, from the means of consumption must be deducted a fund for the costs of administration, for schools, hospitals, homes for the aged, and so on.

Instead of Lassalle's hazy, obscure, general phrase ("the whole proceeds of his labor to the worker") Marx makes a sober estimate of exactly how Socialist society will have to manage its affairs. Marx proceeds to make a *concrete* analysis of the conditions of life of a society in which there will be no capitalism, and says:

> What we have to deal with here (in analyzing the program of the workers' party) is a Communist society, not as it has *developed* on its own foundations, but, on the contrary, as it *emerges* from capitalist society; which is thus in every respect, economically, morally and intellectually, still stamped with the birthmarks of the old society from whose womb it emerges.

And it is this Communist society—a society which has just come into the world out of the womb of capitalism and which, in every respect, bears the birthmarks of the old society—that Marx terms the "first," or lower, phase of Communist society.

The means of production are no longer the private property of individuals. The means of production belong to the whole of society. Every member of society, performing a certain part of the socially-necessary labor, receives a certificate from society to the effect that he has done such and such an amount of work. And with this certificate he draws from the social stock of means of consumption a corresponding quantity of products. After deduction of the amount of labor which goes to the public fund, every worker, therefore, receives from society as much as he has given it.

"Equality" apparently reigns supreme.

But when Lassalle, having such a social order in view (usually called Socialism, but termed by Marx the first phase of Communism), speaks of this as "equitable distribution," and says that this is "the equal right" of "all members of society" to "equal proceeds of labor," he is mistaken, and Marx exposes his error.

"Equal right," says Marx, we indeed have here; but it is *still* a "bourgeois right," which, like every right, *presupposes inequality*. Every right is an application of an *equal* standard to *different* people who in fact are not alike, are not equal to one another; that is why "equal right" is really a violation of equality and an injustice. As a matter of fact, every man, having performed as much social labor as another, receives an equal share of the social product (after the above-mentioned deductions).

But people are not alike: one is strong, another is weak; one is married, another is not; one has more children, another has less, and so on. And the conclusion Marx draws is:

> . . . With an equal output, and hence an equal share in the social consumption fund, one will in fact receive more than another, one will be richer than another, and so on. To avoid all these defects, right, instead of being equal, would have to be unequal. . . .

Hence, the first phase of Communism cannot yet produce justice and equality; differences, and unjust differences, in wealth will still exist, but the *exploitation* of man by man will have become impossible, because it will be impossible to seize the *means of production*, the factories, machines, land, etc., as private property. In smashing Lassalle's petty-bourgeois, confused phrases about "equality" and "justice" *in general*, Marx shows the course of *development* of Communist society, which at first is *compelled* to abolish *only* the "injustice" of the means of production having been seized by private individuals, and which cannot at once abolish the other injustice, which consists in the distribution of articles of consumption "according to the amount of labor performed" (and not according to needs).

The vulgar economists, including the bourgeois professors and also "our" Tugan-Baranovsky, constantly reproach the Socialists with forgetting the inequality of people and with "dreaming" of abolishing this inequality. Such a reproach, as we see, only proves the extreme ignorance of Messieurs the Bourgeois Ideologists.

Marx not only scrupulously takes into account the inevitable inequality of men but he also takes into account the fact that the mere conversion of the means of production into the common property of the whole of society (usually called "Socialism") *does not remove* the defects of distribution and the inequality of "bourgeois right" which *continue to prevail* as long as products are divided "according to the amount of labor performed." Continuing, Marx says:

> But these defects are inevitable in the first phase of Communist society as it is when it has just emerged after prolonged birth pangs from capitalist society. Right can never be higher than the economic structure of society, and the cultural development thereby determined.

And so, in the first phase of Communist society (usually called Socialism) "Bourgeois right" is *not* abolished in its entirety, but only in part, only in proportion to the economic transformation so far attained, *i.e.*, only in respect of the means of production. "Bourgeois right" recognizes them as the private property of individuals. Socialism converts them into *common* property. *To that extent*—and to that extent alone—"bourgeois right" disappears.

However, it continues to exist as far as its other part is concerned; it continues to exist in the capacity of regulator (determining factor) in the distribution of products and the allotment of labor among the members of society. The Socialist principle: "He who does not work, neither shall he eat," is *already* realized; the other Socialist principle: "An equal amount of products of an equal amount of labor," is also *already* realized. But this is not yet Communism, and it does not yet abolish "bourgeois right," which gives to unequal individuals, in return for an unequal (actually unequal) amount of labor, an equal amount of products.

This is a "defect," says Marx, but it is unavoidable in the first phase of Communism; for if we are not to indulge in utopianism, we must not think that having overthrown capitalism people will at once learn to work for society *without any standard of right*; and indeed the abolition of capitalism *does not immediately* create the economic premises for *such* a change.

And there is as yet no other standard than that of "bourgeois right." To this extent, therefore, there is still need for a state, which, while safeguarding the public ownership of the means of production would safeguard equality of labor and equality in the distribution of products.

The state withers away in so far as there are no longer any capitalists, any classes, and, consequently, no *class* can be *suppressed*.

But the state has not yet completely withered away, since there still remains the safeguarding of "bourgeois right," which sanctifies actual inequality. For the complete withering away of the state complete Communism is necessary.

The Higher Phase of Communist Society

Marx continues:

> In a higher phase of Communist society, after the enslaving subordination of individuals under division of labor, and therewith also the antithesis between mental and physical labor, has vanished; after labor, from a mere means of

life, has itself become the prime necessity of life; after the productive forces have also increased with the all-round development of the individual, and all the springs of cooperative wealth flow more abundantly—only then can the narrow horizon of bourgeois right be fully left behind and society inscribe on its banners: From each according to his ability, to each according to his needs!

Only now can we appreciate to the full the correctness of Engels' remarks in which he mercilessly ridiculed the absurdity of combining the words "freedom" and "state." While the state exists there is no freedom. When there will be freedom, there will be no state.

The economic basis for the complete withering away of the state is such a high stage of development of Communism that the antithesis between mental and physical labor disappears, that is to say, when one of the principal sources of modern *social* inequality disappears—a source, moreover, which cannot be removed immediately by the mere conversion of the means of production into public property, by the mere expropriation of the capitalists.

This expropriation will facilitate an enormous development of productive forces. And seeing how capitalism is already *retarding* this development to an incredible degree, seeing how much progress could be achieved even on the basis of the present level of modern technique, we are entitled to say with the fullest confidence that the expropriation of the capitalists will inevitably result in an enormous development of the productive forces of human society. But how rapidly this development will proceed, how soon it will reach the point of breaking away from the division of labor, of removing the antithesis between mental and physical labor, or transforming labor into "the prime necessity of life"—we do not and *cannot* know.

That is why we are entitled to speak only of the inevitable withering away of the state, emphasizing the protracted nature of this process and its dependence upon the rapidity of development of the *higher phase* of Communism, and leaving question of length of time, or the concrete forms of the withering away, quite open, because there is *no* material for an answer to these questions.

The state will be able to wither away completely when society applies the rule: "From each according to his ability, to each according to his needs," *i.e.*, when people have become so accustomed to observing the fundamental rules of social intercourse and when their labor is so productive that they will voluntarily work *according to their ability*. "The narrow horizon of bourgeois right," which compels one to calculate with the stringency of a Shylock whether one has not worked half an hour more than another, whether one is not getting less pay than another—this narrow horizon will then be left behind. There will be no need for society to regulate the quantity of products to be distributed to each; each will take freely "according to his needs."

From the bourgeois point of view, it is easy to declare that such a social order is "a pure utopia" and to sneer at the Socialists for promising everyone the right to receive from society, without any control of the labor of the individual citizen, any quantity of truffles, automobiles, pianos, etc. Even now, most bourgeois "savants" confine themselves to sneering in this way, thereby displaying at once their ignorance and their mercenary defence of capitalism.

Ignorance—for it has never entered the head of any Socialist to "promise" that the higher phase of the development of Communism will arrive; but the great Socialists, in *foreseeing* its arrival, presuppose not the present productivity of labor *and not the present* ordinary run of people, who, like the seminary students in Pomyalovsky's stories,* are capable of damaging the stocks of social wealth "just for fun" and of demanding the impossible.

Until the "higher" phase of Communism arrives, the Socialists demand the *strictest* control by society *and by the state* of the measure of labor and the measure of consumption; but this control must *start* with the expropriation of the capitalists, with the establishment of workers' control over the capitalists, and must be carried out not by a state of bureaucrats, but by a state of *armed* workers.

The mercenary defence of capitalism by the bourgeois ideologists (and their hangers-on, like Messrs. Tsereteli, Chernov and Co.) lies in their *substituting* controversies and discussions about the distant future for the essential and imperative questions of *present-day* policy, *viz.*, the expropriation of the capitalists, the conversion of *all* citizens into workers and employees of *one* huge "syndicate"—the whole state—and the complete subordination of the whole of the work of this syndicate to the really democratic state, *the state of the Soviets of Workers' and Soldiers' Deputies.*

In reality, when a learned professor, and following him the philistine, and following him Messrs. Tsereteli and Chernov, talk of the unreasonable utopias, of the demagogic promises of the Bolsheviks, of the impossibility of "introducing" Socialism, it is the higher stage or phase of Communism they have in mind, which no one has ever promised or even thought to "introduce," because generally speaking it cannot be "introduced."

And this brings us to the question of the scientific difference between Socialism and Communism, which Engels touched on in his above-quoted argument about the incorrectness of the name "Social-Democrat." The political difference between the first, or lower, and the higher phase of Communism will in time, probably, be tremendous; but it would be ridiculous to take cognizance of this difference now, under capitalism, and only isolated anarchists, perhaps, could invest it with primary importance.

But the scientific difference between Socialism and Communism is clear. What is usually called Socialism was termed by Marx the "first" or lower phase of Communist society. In so far as the means of production become *common* property, the word "Communism" is also applicable here, providing we do not forget that it is not complete Communism. The great significance of Marx's explanations is that here, too, he consistently applies materialist dialectics, the doctrine of development, and regards Communism as something which develops *out of* capitalism. Instead of scholastically invented, "concocted" definitions and fruitless disputes about words (what is Socialism? what is Communism?), Marx gives an analysis of what may be called the stages in the economic ripeness of Communism.

In its first phase, or first stage, Communism *cannot* as yet be fully ripe economically and entirely free from traditions and traces of capitalism. Hence, the interesting phenomenon that Communism in its first phase retains "the narrow horizon of *bourgeois* right." Of course, bourgeois right in regard to the distribution of articles of *consumption* inevitably presupposes the existence of the *bourgeois state,* for right is nothing without an apparatus capable of *enforcing* the observance of the standards of right.

Consequently, not only bourgeois right, but even the bourgeois state for a certain time remains under Communism, without the *bourgeoisie!*

* The reference here is to N. Pomyalovsky's *Sketches of Seminary Life,* in which this Russian novelist exposed the absurd system of education and the brutal customs that held sway in the Russian theological schools in the 1850s and 1860s.—*Ed.*

This may sound like a paradox or simply a dialectical puzzle, of which Marxism is often accused by people who do not take the slightest trouble to study its extraordinarily profound content.

But as a matter of fact, remnants of the old surviving in the new confront us in life at every step, both in nature and in society. And Marx did not arbitrarily insert a scrap of "bourgeois" right into Communism, but indicated what is economically and politically inevitable in a society emerging *from the womb* of capitalism.

Democracy is of great importance to the working class in its struggle for emancipation from the capitalists. But democracy is by no means a boundary that must not be overstepped; it is only one of the stages on the road from feudalism to capitalism, and from capitalism to Communism.

Democracy means equality. The great significance of the proletariat's struggle for equality and the significance of equality as a slogan will be clear if we correctly interpret it as meaning the abolition of *classes*. But democracy means only *formal* equality. And as soon as equality is obtained for all members of society *in relation* to the ownership of the means of production, that is, equality of labor and equality of wages, humanity will inevitably be confronted with the question of going beyond formal equality to real equality, *i.e.*, to applying the rule, "from each according to his ability, to each according to his needs." By what stages, by what practical measures humanity will proceed to this higher aim—we do not and cannot know. But it is important to realize how infinitely mendacious is the ordinary bourgeois conception of Socialism as something lifeless, petrified, fixed once for all, whereas in reality *only* under Socialism will a rapid, genuine, really mass forward movement, embracing first the *majority* and then the whole of the population, commence in all spheres of social and personal life.

Democracy is a form of state, one of its varieties. Consequently, it, like every state, on the one hand represents the organized, systematic application of force against persons; but on the other hand it signifies the formal recognition of the equality of all citizens, the equal right of all to determine the structure and administration of the state. This, in turn, is connected with the fact that, at a certain stage in the development of democracy, it first rallies the proletariat as the revolutionary class against capitalism, and enables it to crush, smash to atoms, wipe off the face of the earth the bourgeois, even the republican bourgeois, state machine, the standing army, the police and bureaucracy, and to substitute for them a *more* democratic state machine, but a state machine nevertheless, in the shape of the armed masses of workers who are being transformed into a universal people's militia.

Here "quantity is transformed into quality"; *such* a degree of democracy implies overstepping the boundaries of bourgeois society, the beginning of its Socialist reconstruction. If indeed, *all* take part in the administration of the state, capitalism cannot retain its hold. And the development of capitalism, in turn, itself creates the *premises* that really *enable* "all" to take part in the administration of the state. Some of the premises are: universal literacy, which is already achieved in a number of the most advanced capitalist countries, then the "training and disciplining" of millions of workers by the huge, complex, socialized apparatus of the post-office, railways, big factories, large-scale commerce, banking, etc., etc.

Given these *economic* premises it is quite possible, after the overthrow of the capitalists and bureaucrats, to proceed immediately, overnight, to supersede them in the *control* of production and distribution in the work of *keeping account* of labor and products by the armed workers, by the whole of the armed population. (The question of control and accounting must not be confused with the question of the scientifically trained staff of engineers, agronomists and so on. These gentlemen are working today and obey the capitalists; they will work even better to-morrow and obey the armed workers.)

Accounting and control — that is the *main* thing required for the "setting up" and correct functioning of the *first phase* of Communist society. *All* citizens are transformed into the salaried employees of the state, which consists of the armed workers. *All* citizens become employees and workers of a *single* national state "syndicate." All that is required is that they should work equally—do their proper share of work—and get paid equally. The accounting and control necessary for this have been simplified by capitalism to an extreme and reduced to the extraordinarily simple operations—which any literate person can perform—of checking and recording, knowledge of the four rules of arithmetic, and issuing receipts.

When the *majority* of the people begin independently and everywhere to keep such accounts and maintain such control over the capitalists (now converted into employees) and over the intellectual gentry who preserve their capitalist habits, this control will really become universal, general, national; and there will be no way of getting away from it, there will be "nowhere to go."

The whole of society will have become a single office and a single factory, with equality of labor and equality of pay.

But this "factory" discipline, which the proletariat will extend to the whole of society after the defeat of the capitalists and the overthrow of the exploiters, is by no means our ideal, or our ultimate goal. It is but a necessary *step* for the purpose of thoroughly purging society of all the hideousness and foulness of capitalist exploitation, *and for further* progress.

From the moment all members of society, or even only the vast majority, have learned to administer the state *themselves*, have taken this business into their own hands, have "set up" control over the insignificant minority of capitalists, over the gentry who wish to preserve their capitalist habits, and over the workers who have been profoundly corrupted by capitalism—from this moment the need for government begins to disappear altogether. The more complete democracy, the nearer the moment approaches when it becomes unnecessary. The more democratic the "state" which consists of the armed workers, and which is "no longer a state in the proper sense of the word," the more rapidly does *every form* of the state begin to wither away.

For when *all* have learned to administer and actually do administer social production independently, independently keep accounts and exercise control over the idlers, the gentlefolk, the swindlers and similar "guardians of capitalist traditions," the escape from this national accounting and control will inevitably become so incredibly difficult, such a rare exception, and will probably be accompanied by such swift and severe punishment (for the armed workers are practical men and not sentimental intellectuals, and they will scarcely allow anyone to trifle with them), that very soon the *necessity* of observing the simple, fundamental rules of human intercourse will become a *habit*.

And then the door will be wide open for the transition from the first phase of Communist society to its higher phase, and with it to the complete withering away of the state.

Walter Lippmann

It is not easy to classify Walter Lippmann in terms of the usual political and social distinctions. Is he liberal or conservative? Both terms are used in America today in a complimentary as well as a derogatory sense. Actually the liberal and the conservative are often further apart psychologically than ideologically, and Lippmann illustrates how close together they sometimes come. An early book of his, A Preface to Politics *(1913), was widely hailed by the young liberals a generation ago; his more recent work,* The Good Society, *is frequently cited as the ablest available defense of our free-enterprise economy. In recent years Lippmann's position has become increasingly difficult to label. Some critics denounce him for selling out to big business; others consider him one of the most important liberals of this generation. Still others support him because they believe him to be a powerful champion of capitalism.*

In public affairs Lippmann has been a familiar figure in this country for almost forty years. Born in 1889 in New York City, he was the only child of a well-to-do manufacturer and had all the privileges of private schooling, Harvard University, and travel in Europe. His first work as a journalist, however, was an investigation of corruption in big business and politics. A few years later he took an active part in founding the New Republic, *an outstanding American journal of liberal opinion, and he was originally hired by the* New York Herald Tribune *to provide a liberal comment that would offset the newspaper's conservative point of view. He is best known to most Americans through his syndicated column "Today and Tomorrow," a thoughtful commentary on contemporary political life carried for many years in major newspapers throughout the country. He has also expressed his views in seventeen influential books on politics, morals, economics, and social life.*

In addition to his career as a journalist Lippmann has had some practical experience in government: at the outbreak of World War I he served as Assistant Secretary of State for a brief period and helped prepare data for the Paris Peace Conference at the end of the war. During World War II he was a stanch friend of Great Britain and a supporter of closer American cooperation with British war aims. The Good Society *(1937), from which our selection on "The Pursuit of Liberty" is taken, grew out of problems raised by the conflict of democracy with fascism and communism in the 1930s.*

Obviously John Stuart Mill, the major champion of liberty in the nineteenth century, does not provide a twentieth-century philosophy of democracy. Eloquent as are Mill's arguments in behalf of democratic ideals, his purpose is to show the advantages of freedom, not the disadvantages of the totalitarian state. What are the arguments for the good society conceived in democratic rather than communist terms? It is this problem to which Lippmann addresses himself in the present selection.

THE PURSUIT OF LIBERTY

1. *A Human Affirmation*

Of the development of liberty we have . . . seen only the beginnings: the emancipation even of Englishmen, let alone mankind, was not completed in 1859 when Mill wrote his essay *On Liberty*. At best the foundation for the advancement of liberty had been laid in a few countries. But the advance itself has no visible end. Always there will remain to be liquidated subtler privileges and immunities; always there will remain to be checked the refinements of violence, fraud, intrigue, and conspiracy by which men bedevil themselves and their fellows. The ideal of a society in which all are equally free of all arbitrary coercion is a receding goal. From each new plateau in the ascent higher levels become visible.

If we scrutinize the progress of human emancipation, it appears to consist largely in a series of restraints upon the exercise of power by men over men. The organized liberty of mankind is established by laws and usages which seek to limit coercive authority, traditional prerogatives, vested rights and all manner of predatory, violent, fraudulent dealing among men.

But though in practice the organization of liberty is achieved largely by restraints and denials, these bounds have been set upon arbitrary power by men who had to be free, by men who would rather have been dead than submit to it any longer. Now men have not staked their fortunes and their lives simply because it was irrational that their kings and their lords and masters should have so much power: the pursuit of liberty has not been inspired by a pedantic, a doctrinaire, an ideological predilection. Men have rebelled against arbitrary power because they collided with it in their work and in the enjoyment of their faculties. So while the constitutional means to liberty are in the main a series of negatives raised against the powerful, the pursuit of liberty is a great affirmation inspired by the positive energies of the human race.

Once we have discerned the character of these energies, we cannot but recognize that they are inexhaustible and irresistible. By virtue of these energies mankind will, because it must, seek its happiness, not by submitting to providential authority but by organizing its liberty. Those energies we must affirm once more as we call upon men to resist and overcome the great reaction of our times.

2. *The Will to Be Free*

When the Inquisitors summoned Galileo before them, they told him he must not find that the earth revolves around the sun. Galileo had been observing the heavens through a telescope: he had become convinced that the evidence warranted his conclusion. But the Inquisitors did not look through the telescope. They knew all about astronomy from reading the Bible. So against Galileo's telescope the Inquisitors employed another instrument: the rack. And by the rack, which could inflict pain on the astronomer's body, they undertook to cure the astronomer of his scientific error. Thus they prohibited the exploration of the heavens by the exercise of their physical power.

But the rack is not an instrument for exploring the heavens. A concentration camp is not a political seminar. Burning men at the stake is not a mode of religious revelation. Firing squads are not commissions for observing and analyzing the economic situation. Censorship is not testimony and argument. As regards the intrinsic issues, these exercises of power are nothing but senseless interference, sheer brute irrelevance like the incursion of a herd of wild asses. What Galileo needed was the criticism of other astronomers: what he suffered was the meddling of powerful ignoramuses. Galileo was unfree to be an astronomer because these ignoramuses insisted on weighting the scales with the terror of prisons, torture chambers, and the stake; he had to take his astronomy from men who had never studied it.

The movement which drives human life forward is exemplified by Galileo's impulse to explore the heavens. The forces which hold mankind back, pinned to the ignorance they happen to be in, are exemplified by the Inquisitors insisting that the preponderant force and not the preponderant evidence shall determine whether the sun is the center of our solar system. Thus we may think of the creative, the productive, and the adaptive energies of mankind as struggling to release themselves from the entanglements and perversions, the exploitation and the smothering, the parasitism and the obfuscation and the discouragement of aggressive, acquisitive, dogmatic, and arbitrary impulses. Men are moved to plant, but the seeds bear fruit with difficulty, so rank are the weeds which choke them. The cutting back of the weeds, the clearing of little spaces in which good things can grow, has been the task of human emancipation. Its method is to restrain arbitrariness. But its object is to disengage the human spirit in order that it may flourish.

Thus liberalism, which in its moral essence is a challenge to all arbitrariness, to all who would use the rack rather than the telescope, is not itself the substantive principle of the good life. The substantive principle is in Galileo's curiosity and his genius; in fostering and protecting curiosity and genius, liberalism is the guardian principle of the good life. It stakes its hopes upon the human spirit released from and purged of all arbitrariness. It does not say what such a spirit can or will or ought to make of men's lives. For men have never yet known but a little of such freedom. And they cannot hope to imagine what they have never yet known. But they have known enough of freedom to know that the arbitrary power of men over men is parasitical, that it perverts, that it sterilizes and corrupts.

Though liberalism has often been identified with indifference, inaction, and nonresistance, it should now be evident that this is mere confusion. A doctrine which is opposed to all arbitrariness must mean the determination to resist arbitrariness, to check it, to cut it down, to crush it, wherever and whenever it appears. It cannot mean, for example, that in the seventeenth century the King was under God and the law, but that in the nineteenth century the owners of property were not, that in the twentieth century majorities, pluralities, mobs, or dictators are not, under God and the law. For liberalism all arbitrary power is evil. It matters not what are the titles or the pretensions or the promises of arbitrary power. It must be resisted and brought under control.

So liberalism is not quietism and weak government. That is the corruption of liberalism. In its vigorous periods liberalism has always meant rebellion against oppression and a determination to police aggression and acquisitiveness. Liberalism, therefore, is not the doctrine of laissez faire, let her rip, and the devil take the hindmost. It does not envisage the demobilization of the police, the repeal of the laws, the disestablishment of legislatures and courts. On the contrary, the effective liberals have always been concerned with the development of the law, with the definition of rights and duties, with the organizing of constitutions, with the absorption of all power to coerce in the hands of duly constituted authorities, with the liquidation or regulation of all kinds of private and petty powers within the community. For the liberal, as distinguished from the anarchist, holds that mere unrestraint does not give the freedom of a voluntary society, that unrestraint merely inaugurates a competitive struggle in which the ruthless will exploit the rest. He insists that the promise of a voluntary life can be realized only as the law is strong enough to restrain aggressors at home and abroad.

But in the liberal view the reward for restraining the aggressor is that the creative and productive faculties can then begin to work. Suppose that Galileo had been able to study the heavens without having at any time to consider whether he would be punished for his conclusions. Suppose that he had needed only to argue with the theologians and to debate with other astronomers. Suppose that his opponents and his critics had been unable to invoke the threats of prison and the rack, or even of ostracism and the muttering of the mob. Suppose that his relations with his contemporaries had been purged of all the irrelevance of arbitrary power, that he had felt that if he was wrong his only punishment would be the knowledge that he had been wrong. Suppose that those who opposed him could have thrown into the scales only the immaterial weight of tradition, experience, observation, and dialectic. Is there any question that in such a community Galileo's faculties would have been enhanced, that others would have been encouraged to use theirs, that immense energy devoted to the coercive enforcement of a particular dogma would have been available in the search for the truest cosmology?

The essence of the matter is that arbitrariness is a disturbing intrusion in the creative life of mankind. It may be a mere annoyance, like the buzzing of a fly around the nose of a philosopher; or it may be like a great catastrophe, say an earthquake, which stops his work by bringing down the house around his ears. We can appreciate the real energy of freedom if we think of men, working, studying, collaborating, but beset by conquerors, exploiters, adventurers —by men who do not work, but appropriate the work of others; who do not produce, but take tolls; who do not invent, but impose prejudices; who do not create, but coerce those who do. The pursuit of liberty is the affirmation of those who produce the really good things of life.

When a Galileo is coerced by a more powerful but a more ignorant inquisitor, his scientific genius is arbitrarily leveled down to the obscurantism of his masters. It is only by freeing him from the bondage of authority that his superiority as an observer and thinker can be exercised. In our time there are governments which enforce an official culture by exile, proscription, the axe, firing squads, castor oil, and imprisonment in concentration camps: they are using arbitrary force to reduce scholars and artists, and in fact the whole population, to the cultural level of the dominant politicians. The opinion of unqualified men is artificially, by the mere arbitrary intervention of the police, made to prevail over the opinion of men who are specially gifted and have labored to qualify themselves.

The same kind of obscurantism results from the exercise of all privileges. The man who has built himself a castle above the highway in order that he may exact a toll from the merchants on their way to market acquires wealth not by producing it but by seizing it. His predatory incursions arbitrarily yield the returns which would otherwise go to invention, industry, and thrift. But for his castle and his armed hands he would be poorer than the passing merchant whom he despoils; because he is more powerful but is unrestrained, he reaps a greater reward from highway robbery than other men can make by producing wealth. Thus the ideal of equal rights for all and special privileges for none is inseparable from the pursuit of liberty. A free society is one in which inequalities in the condition of men, in their rewards, and in their social status do not arise out of extrinsic and artificial causes—out of the physical power to coerce, out of legal privilege, out of special prerogative, or out of fraud, sharp practice, necessitous bargaining.

This is no forcible leveling of men to a uniform condition of life. That is the tyrant's way. The libertarian does not demand that all the runners in the race must keep in step and finish together; he asks that they start from scratch and that none shall be permitted to elbow his rival off the track. Then the winner will be the best runner. The winner will not be the competitor who wangled a handicap from the judges, or obtained an advantage which had nothing to do with his ability to run the race. Manifestly, the liberal conception of equality does not promise to make all men equal in riches, influence, honor, and wisdom. On the contrary, its promise is that as the extrinsic inequalities imposed by prerogative and privilege are reduced, the intrinsic superiorities will assert themselves.

This, I believe, is the insight at the heart of the liberal conception of society. I am only too well aware of how imperfectly I have understood it, how imprecisely I have been able to put it into words. But I think it is not misleading to say that some such dim but pregnant apprehension as this has been hammered out on the anvil of long experience, that it is no abstract and *a priori* speculation arrived at in the eighteenth century and declared to mankind by William Ewart Gladstone, but that it is much older, has its roots in centuries of confused struggle with all manner of censorship and inquisition, prerogative and privilege.

In those struggles men gradually perceive that they must disengage creative and productive labor and the friendly adaptability of men to one another from the exactions and interferences of the predatory, acquisitive, parasitic, prejudicial, domineering, and irrational elements of human life. This is the "obvious and simple system of natural liberty" which the classic liberals discerned. Though their history was wrong when they adopted the naive belief that this natural order prevailed in the childhood of the race, though they greatly underestimated the length and the complexity of the struggle, their insight was true and their hearts were in the right place.

We must not deny the prophet because he speaks in parables and ephemeral myths: the classic liberals arrived at a profound and enduring insight into the difference between the real and the factitious in human affairs. They were on the side of Galileo because by protecting Galileo the knowledge of astronomy is advanced. They knew that to find truth is to add to the real values of human existence. They were against the Inquisitors because they knew that astronomy cannot be advanced by imprisoning astronomers, or by compelling them to obtain a license from the secret police and the minister of propaganda.

The ultimate concern of the liberal is with the enhancement of real values by men who actually observe, reason, meditate, invent, dig, construct—seeking to arrange the world to satisfy human demands. To this end the laws, constitutions, bills of rights, courts, and social philosophies are but the means which allow creative labor to proceed without arbitrary interference.

Thus the challenge to oppression arises from the productive energies of men. The movement toward human emancipation is the rebellion of those who plant and till, dig and make, invent and construct, explore and understand; they cannot work and reap their rewards until they have subdued those who exploit and throttle and dominate their productive labors. Men withdrawn into an ivory tower can be indifferent to oppression and can come to terms with it; but those who must earn their living in the sweat of their brows cannot be indifferent, nor those who have the instinct of workmanship, or are curious and must understand the world and their destiny in it.

Among them the liberators have found their followers—among rebellious slaves, serfs demanding land and peace, merchants crying out against the robber barons, small men resisting the monopolists, industrial workers demanding recognition and status and equality of bargaining power, among artists and men of science and educators and parents crying out against the conscription of all they have created.

Their impulse to create has been their impulse to be free. And as they create it becomes more and more necessary that they should be free. For as men work, and perfect their work by invention and skill, they lift themselves out of the primitive condition in which they lead a meager and self-sufficing existence. The improvement of their skill, the development of their special aptitudes, the use of their particular opportunities, result in the specialization of their labor. Because they do the work they are able to do, they are no longer self-sufficing and must live by the exchange of their products. They enter into the economy of the division of labor.

The division of labor was not invented by economists; it was not invented by the inventors of machinery and steam railroads. The division of labor in an exchange economy is implied in the very essence of productive labor itself. In order that Galileo might study the heavens it was not sufficient that the Inquisitors should let him alone; it was necessary that someone else should grow the food he ate and make the clothes he wore and grind the lenses through which he observed the heavens. He had to be liberated not only from the oppression of arbitrary authority but from the sterile drudgery of a self-sufficient existence. And because by the division of labor he was liberated from the drudgery, he was able to be an astronomer who necessarily rebelled against authority.

Thus the connection between liberty and the industrial revolution is organic. The impulse to create and the impulse to be free are cumulative: each is to the other both cause and effect. Because men wish to work they insist on freedom from arbitrary interference; because they are free, they work by a division of labor which requires the freedom of certain and equal rights.

This is the reason why all the conceptions which constitute the testament of liberty have been evolved in great societies that have lived by extensive and complicated commerce. They come to us from the Graeco-Roman society, from the merchant cities of the Renaissance, from western Europe, from England, France, the Netherlands, and Italy, from the peoples who first emerged from self-sufficiency and had to establish a common law in which their transactions could be secure. It is no accident that it was the Athenians, living by commerce, rather than the Spartans living by exploitation and war, who conceived the good life; or that the Romans who traded all over the known world should have understood the necessity for law; or that the nation of shopkeepers was the mother of parliaments; or that Yankee traders in Boston fomented the American Revolution and the abolition of slavery. For among a people living by a primitive undifferentiated economy under routine and in isolation, the necessity for constitutional liberty does not exist and can scarcely be conceived.

3. *On Designing a New Society*

This truth our contemporary authoritarians, whether of the left or of the right, have failed to grasp. They look upon the great sprawling complex of transactions by which mankind lives, seeing that these transactions are in large part still unregulated by law, and that therefore there is much confusion and injustice, they have turned their backs upon the task of regulation by law and have beguiled themselves with the notion that they can plan this economy systematically and administer it rationally. The exact contrary is the truth. The modern economy is perhaps the least systematic of any that has ever existed. It is world-wide, formless, vast, complicated, and, owing to technological progress, in constant change. For that reason it is incapable of being conceived as a system, or of being replaced by another system, or of being managed as an administrative unit.

The hankering for schemes and systems and comprehensive organization is the wistfulness of an immature philosophy which has not come to terms with reality, no less when the conservators of vested interests would stabilize the modern economy in status quo by protective laws and monopolistic schemes than when the revolutionist makes blueprints of a world composed of planning national economies "coordinated" by a world-planning authority. Neither takes any more account of reality than if he were studying landscape architecture with a view to making a formal garden out of the Brazilian jungle.

For the greater the society, the higher and more variable the standards of life, the more diversified the energies of its people for invention, enterprise, and adaptation, the more certain it is that the social order cannot be planned *ex cathedra* or governed by administrative command. We live in such an immensely diversified civilization that the only intelligible criterion which political thinkers can entertain in regard to it, the only feasible goal which statesmen can set themselves in governing it, is to reconcile the conflicts which spring from this diversity. They cannot hope to comprehend it as a system. For it is not a system. They cannot hope to plan and direct it. For it is not an organization. They can hope only to dispense lawful justice among individuals and associations where their interests conflict, to mitigate the violence of conflict and competition by seeking to make lawful justice more and more equitable.

It requires much virtue to do that well. There must be a strong desire to be just. There must be a growing capacity to be just. There must be discernment and sympathy in estimating the particular claims of divergent interests. There must be moral standards which discourage the quest of privilege and the exercise of arbitrary power. There must be resolution and valor to resist oppression and tyranny. There must be patience and tolerance and kindness in hearing claims, in argument, in negotiation, and in reconciliation.

But these are human virtues; though they are high, they are within the attainable limits of human nature as we know it. They actually exist. Men do have these virtues, all but the most hopelessly degenerate, in some degree. We know that they can be increased. When we talk about them we are talking about virtues that have affected the course of actual history, about virtues that some men have practised more than other men, and no man sufficiently, but enough men in great enough degree to have given mankind here and there and for varying periods of time the intimations of a Good Society.

But the virtues that are required for the overhead administration of a civilization are superhuman; they are attributes of providence and not of mortal men. It is true that there have been benevolent despots and that for a little while in a particular place they have made possible a better life than their subjects were able to achieve without the rule of a firm and authoritative guardian. And no doubt it is still true that a community which does not have the essential discipline of liberty can choose only among alternative disciplines by authority. But if a community must have such a guardian, then it must resign itself to living a simple regimented existence, must entertain no hopes of the high and diversified standard of life which the division of labor and modern technology make possible. For despots cannot be found who could plan, organize, and direct a complex economy.

To do that would require a comprehensive understanding of the life and the labor and the purposes of hundreds of millions of persons, the gift of prophesying their behavior and omnipotence to control it. These faculties no man has ever possessed. When in theorizing we unwittingly postulate such faculties, we are resting our hopes on a conception of human nature which has no warrant whatever in any actual experience. The collectivist planners are not talking about the human race but about some other breed conceived in their dreams. They postulate qualities of intelligence and of virtue so unlike those which men possess that it would be just as intelligible to make plans for a society in which human beings were born equipped to fly like the angels, to feed on the fragrance of the summer breezes, and endowed with all possible knowledge.

Thus while the liberal philosophy is concerned with the reform of the laws in order to adapt them to the changing needs and standards of the dynamic economy, while the agenda of reform are long and varied, no one must look to liberalism for a harmonious scheme of social reconstruction. The Good Society has no architectural design. There are no blueprints. There is no mold in which human life is to be shaped. Indeed, to expect the blueprint of such a mold is a mode of thinking against which the liberal temper is a constant protest.

To design a personal plan for a new society is a pleasant form of madness; it is in imagination to play at being God and Caesar to the human race. Any such plan must implicitly assume that the visionary or someone else might find the power, or might persuade the masses to give him the power, to shape society to the plan; all such general plans of social reconstruction are merely the rationalization of the will to power. For that reason they are the subjective beginnings of fanaticism and tyranny. In these utopias the best is the enemy of the good, the heart's desire betrays the interests of man. To think in terms of a new scheme for a whole society is to use the idiom of authority, to approach affairs from the underlying premise that they can be shaped and directed as an overhead control, that social relations can be fabricated according to a master plan drawn up by a supreme architect.

The supreme architect, who begins as a visionary, becomes a fanatic, and ends as a despot. For no one can be the supreme architect of society without employing a supreme despot to execute the design. So if men are to seek freedom from the arbitrary dominion of men over men, they must not entertain fantasies of the future in which they play at being the dictators of civilization. It is the bad habit of an undisciplined imagination. The descent from fantasy to fanaticism is easy. Real dictators raised to power by the fanatics who adore them are only too likely to adopt the fantasy to justify their lust for power.

On the other hand, reasonable and civilized people who would like to make the best of the situation before them, but have no ambition for, or expectation of, the power to reshape a whole society, get no help from these architectural designs. The blueprint, be it as grandiose a work of genius as Plato's *Republic*, cannot hope to fit the specific situation. No *a priori* reasoning can anticipate the precise formulae which will reconcile the infinitely varied interests of men. The reconciliation has to be achieved by the treatment of specific issues and the solution will appear only after the claims and the evidence have been examined and fairly judged. Thus in Plato's great scheme each man was assigned his station and his duties; any architectural plan is necessarily based on the same presumption. But Plato's scheme worked only in Plato's imagination, never in the real world. No such scheme can ever work in the real world. For the scheme implies that men will remain content in the station which the visionary has assigned to them. To formulate such plans is not to design a society for real men. It is to re-create men to fit the design. For in real life men rest content in their station only if their interests have been successfully reconciled: failing that, they do not fit the design until they have been dosed with castor oil, put in concentration camps, or exiled to Siberia.

That is why the testament of liberty does not contain the project of a new social order. It adumbrates a way of life in which men seek to reconcile their interests by perfecting the rules of justice. No scheme which promises to obliterate the differences of interest can be deduced from it, no architectural design of society in which all human problems have been resolved. There is no plan of the future: there is, on the contrary, the conviction that the future must have the shape that human energies, purged in so far as possible of arbitrariness, will give it. Compared with the elegant and harmonious schemes which are propounded by the theoretical advocates of capitalism, communism, fascism, it must seem intellectually unsatisfying, and I can well imagine that many will feel about the liberal society as Emma Darwin felt when she wrote about the *Descent of Man*, "I think it will be very interesting, but that I shall dislike it very much as again putting God further off."

But though it must seem an insufficient ideal both to those who wish to exercise authority and to those who feel the need of leaning upon authority, it is the only practicable ideal of government in the Great Society. When huge masses of men have become dependent upon one another through the division of labor in countless, infinitely complex transactions, their activities cannot be planned and directed by public officials.

Thus it is true that the liberal state is not to be conceived as an earthly providence administering civilization. That is the essence of the matter. To the liberal mind the notion that men can authoritatively plan and impose a good life upon a great society is ignorant, impertinent, and pretentious. It can be entertained only by men who do not realize the infinite variety of human purposes, who do not appreciate the potentialities of human effort, or by men who do not choose to respect them.

The liberal state is to be conceived as the protector of equal rights by dispensing justice among individuals. It seeks to protect men against arbitrariness, not arbitrarily to direct them. Its ideal is a fraternal association among free and equal men. To the initiative of individuals, secure in their rights and accountable to others who have equal rights, liberalism entrusts the shaping of the human destiny. It offers no encouragement to those who dream of what they could make of the world if they possessed supreme power. In the testament of liberty these ambitions have been assessed: the record of all the Caesars from Alexander to Adolf is visible. The world has known many societies in which each man had his station, his duties, and his ordained destiny, and the record shows that it is beyond the understanding of men to know all human needs, to appreciate all human possibilities, to imagine all human ends, to shape all human relations.

Yet if the ambitions of liberalism are more modest than those of authority, its promise is greater. It relies upon the development of the latent faculties of all men, shaped by their free transactions with one another. Liberalism commits the destiny of civilization, not to a few finite politicians here and there, but to the whole genius of mankind. This is a grander vision than that of those who would be Caesar and would set themselves up as little tin gods over men. It is a hope engendered in the human heart during the long ages in which the slowly emerging impulses of civilization, beset by barbarism, have struggled to be free.

2

SOCIAL IDEALISM AS RELIGION

Crane Brinton

It is essential for us not only to understand our own democratic ideals and philosophy of life but also to see clearly why communism appeals to other peoples. Included in this section of the anthology, therefore, are two selections that examine the religious dimensions of the communist way of life. During the past hundred years many writers have expressed their religion in social terms, in programs for social betterment, and in visions of an ideal society. As the social consequences of the Industrial Revolution became increasingly apparent in the nineteenth century, men like Charles Kingsley in England tried in vain to arouse the conscience of Christians to the plight of their less fortunate fellows. In the early twentieth century religious liberals in America under the inspiration of Walter Rauschenbusch made the "social gospel" the heart of Christianity and re-emphasized the responsibility of the Christian church for the ills of the social order. Until World War II most Western expressions of religious idealism were in the framework of Christianity or Judaism. Recently, however, we have been confronted with a new program of social reform that has acquired all the attributes of religion.

Only with considerable difficulty do Americans realize how much of the power of communism in the world today derives from the religious character of its tenets and the religious fervor with which it is promoted. The brief selection that we reprint from Ideas and Men *by Crane Brinton shows clearly how Marxism, especially as it has been worked out in Soviet Russia, has become one of the most powerful forms of religious commitment in the world today. This selection suggests that the dream of a good society may be actively pursued by those whose conviction seems to pervert all our own traditional ideas of right and wrong.*

Crane Brinton, McLean Professor of Ancient and Modern History at Harvard University, is a recognized authority on the French Revolution and on intellectual history. Born in 1898, Brinton attended Harvard and later, as a Rhodes scholar, studied at Oxford University. Returning to this country in 1923, he was appointed instructor in history at Harvard where he has taught ever since. His controversial Anatomy of Revolution *(1938), in which he suggested some brilliant and incisive analogies among four major revolutions, earned him a place among the philosophers of history. Becoming increasingly interested in the history of ideas, he published an able study of Friedrich Nietzsche a few years later and in 1950 a more popular history of Western thought,* Ideas and Men, *from which the present selection is taken. This volume, originally written for the general education program at Harvard, has been widely read; it is available in part in an inexpensive paperbound edition entitled* The Shaping of the Modern Mind.

MARXISM AS A RELIGION

IF YOU FEEL that the term "religion" should be limited to systems of belief that maintain the existence of a God, or gods, or spirits, or at any rate something *immaterial, supernatural,* then you have already been thrown off the track by our comparing national patriotism with religion. In this book [*Ideas and Men*] we have applied terms taken from our Western religious history to any organized and articulate set of beliefs about the Big Questions—right and wrong, human happiness, the order of the universe, and so on—which for the believer did at least two things: gave him intellectual orientation in this world (that is, answered his questions) and gave him emotional participation in a group through ritual and other forms of common action. In such terms Marxism, especially as it has been worked out in Russia, is one of the most active forms of religion in the world today, and one that all educated persons must make some effort to understand.

Marxism clearly fulfills one of the simple requirements of a religion: It has its sacred books, its authoritative scripture—in the orthodox tradition the writings of Marx and Engels with the comments, exegesis, and additions brought by Lenin and, to a much less important extent, Stalin. It has also its heresies, of which the most important goes back to the nineteenth-century "revisionist" movement associated first of all with the name of Eduard Bernstein, and which substituted for the *violent* revolution and subsequent dictatorship of the proletariat of orthodox Marxism the *gradual* achievement of social and economic democracy (equality) by legal political action. There are many other Marxist splinter-groups or heresies, for which we cannot here find space. The existence of such heresies is not necessarily, however, a sign of weakness of the movement; indeed, if one thinks of the rise of Christianity, it is possible that these heresies are an indication of vitality in Marxism, of a continuing intellectual fermentation that is a sign of life rather than of decay and dispersion.

We must here concentrate on the orthodox form of the doctrine. Now Marx's great work is *Das Kapital,* which is in form a treatise on economics. Obviously, however, even *Das Kapital* is no narrowly professional study of economic theory, but a philosophy of history, a system of sociology, and a program for political action. Together with the rest of the accepted canon, it gives a rather more complete and systematic cosmology than any *single* work in the orthodox democratic tradition of the Enlightenment. Marxism is a *tighter, neater* thing than conventional democracy.

The movement [Marx] founded has come to power in a great state, and his followers, though somewhat split by heresies, are strong in many parts of Western society. Marxism is one of the religions—or if that word is too strong for you, one of the great clusters of guiding principles—that compete today for the loyalties of Western man.

The Marxist God is the omnipotent if impersonal force of dialectical materialism. Like the gods of other advanced religions, dialectical materialism is omnipotent. The Marxists themselves do not hesitate to use the word *determinism,* with all its overtones of St. Augustine and Calvin. For them the overtones are those of science. This system, they insist, is a scientific one, which is why it must be true. Theirs is not, to an outsider, the science of the laboratory and the clinic, but a hypostasized science that does for them what the hypostasized science of Newton did for the eighteenth-century philosophers. That is, it gives them the comforting assurance that they have the key to the universe.

Dialectical materialism, then, will for the Marxist bring about the inevitable world revolution of the proletariat. It will bring that about in spite of anything the capitalists can do; indeed, the more the capitalist, following the course of action dictated to him by the means of production under which he works, behaves like a capitalist, the quicker will come the proletarian victory. The Rockefellers and the Morgans are doing just what dialectical materialism wants them to do. This does not apparently make the Marxist feel any more kindly toward them and their like. Nor does the certainty that the stars in their courses are working for the inevitable triumph of the proletariat make the Marxist a fatalist. We have already seen that for the Calvinist the certainty that God's will must prevail seems to make the believer all the more ready to go out into the world and fight to help God's will to prevail; and we have noted that for the Calvinist there is always the saving uncertainty that the individual human worm, even though he is a good member of the church of Calvin, may not really *know* God's will. For the Marxist there is not even this remnant of Christian humility to provide some logical support for his actual conduct as a fighter for the right as he sees it. The Marxist—and Marx himself—knows absolutely that dialectical materialism will do its work in the foreordained way. But one does not see the convinced Marxist sitting back and letting dialectical materialism do its work without him. On the contrary, he is an ardent propagandist, an ethical meliorist, a man who to judge by his conduct believes that his own efforts can make a difference in human behavior. Once more, we can only note that metaphysical belief in determinism seems for the Marxist as for the Calvinist he so much resembles quite consonant with a psychological belief in free will.

To continue with our religious parallel: The Marxist heaven, as we have already noted, is the classless society, a state men can achieve here on earth, and which has in common with the eschatologies of other advanced religions the concept of a state of things where no human desires will be frustrated. It is true that the Marxist prides himself on his materialism, and believes that in the classless societies all *decent* human appetites will be satisfied; he would deny indignantly that his paradise has anything in common with that mystical and among intellectual Christians predominant concept of heaven as a place in which *all* appetites are overcome, extinguished, spiritually sublimated. Yet the classless society is no gross place, no place for the kind of sensual delights the Marxist associates with the vulgar capitalist ideal. Indeed, there is, in almost the common acceptance of the term, a *puritanical* aspect of Marxism: the Marxist is as scornful as any Calvinist of the merely Epicurean side of life, of vulgar, gross pleasures and even more of their aristocratic refinements. Marx himself is a moralist, as indignant at the crassness and injustices of an industrial society as Carlyle or Ruskin. The Marxist tries hard to save a positive aspect of his heaven, to insist that in the classless society men will compete and make progress as good children of our culture should; but what really strikes one in the Marxist as in other heavens is the ideal of absence of conflict and frustration, of the extinction of desire.

The notion of the revolution and the dictatorship of the proletariat can be taken as roughly a parallel to the Christian notion of a day of judgment. Again there is the obvious difference that the Marxist believes his saving catastrophe will be brought about by "natural" rather than by supernatural forces. For the Marxist the state of grace, the thing that marks off the faithful from the heathen, is simply the ability to see the universe in Marxist terms, "scientific" terms as the Marxist would put it. His Marx is the rationalist Messiah set over the spiritual—and to the Marxist, of course, false—Messiah, Christ.

Again as in most religious bodies, this awareness of belonging, of *knowing the truth*, of having the inner light, is balanced by performance of certain symbolic acts that bind the believer to the whole body of the faithful. In other words, the Marxist has his works as well as his faith: He reads his Marxist holy books, he goes to meetings, he has his party card and his party duties. He has a clue to everything, an answer to all his questions. There should be nothing surprising to an informed outsider that in Communist Russia there is Marxist music, Marxist history, and even Marxist biology.

It is probably true that there is no clear Marxist equivalent for the kind of religious experience that for the Christian is focused in the word *conscience*. One whole aspect of Christianity, as we have noted in an earlier chapter, centers on the plight of the individual soul of sinful man in its willful struggle with God; Christianity is a highly individualistic faith with a highly individualistic concept of salvation. Marxism is committed to the notion that the true fulfillment of the individual is, not of course in mere ant- or beelike automatic participation in the social whole, but at least in a thorough identification of the individual with the whole collectivity. Marxism is a collectivist faith, and its notion of individual salvation cannot be very closely paralleled in Christianity. Yet the Marxist has a conscience, and however ill the notion fits with dialectic materialism, can suffer the tortures of conscience. This you will see readily enough in the hero of Arthur Koestler's *Darkness at Noon;* and if you take the trouble to look into his career, you will see it in Mr. Koestler himself.

In pure theory—or in Marxist theology at its highest level—Marx and Engels did the great work. Though Soviet practice has canonized Lenin and Stalin as having made essential additions to the main body of Marxist beliefs, to an outsider their importance seems rather as organizers than as thinkers. Marxism has not yet combined the thinker and the doer as successfully as they were combined in St. Paul. Lenin indeed, faced with the fact that the wicked capitalist nations of the West seemed in the early years of the twentieth century to be prospering, that at any rate they were not going on the rocks quite as Marx had predicted, added to the Marxist analysis a corollary to the effect that having reached the limit of exploiting their own citizens English and other Western capitalists had postponed the evil day by colonial imperialism, by exploiting the rest of the world. But this in itself was, according to Lenin, a confirmation of Marx; imperialism was the inevitable overripeness of capitalism, the last stage before the revolution of the proletariat.

Arthur Koestler

The religious appeal of communism that Crane Brinton describes in the preceding selection is apparent also in recent stories by Communist writers who have lost their earlier faith and have been disillusioned with the gods of Marx and Lenin. A number of such writers—both men and women—have been publishing accounts of the way in which the Communist party at first commanded their complete devotion, then slowly betrayed all their best instincts. Arthur Koestler is one of the clearest thinkers and ablest writers in this important group of contemporary authors.

Koestler was born in Budapest in 1905. His father was Hungarian, his mother Viennese. Until World War I, the family was comfortably well off, but in September 1914 their resources, like those of most other middle-class Europeans, were swept away. Koestler's father never recovered from this experience, and in 1919 the family moved to Vienna, where they lived in straitened circumstances. During these years, Koestler gained at first hand a knowledge of social tension and anxiety. On December 31, 1931, he joined the Communist party. Later he spent a year in Russia and there saw a new side of communism. In 1936 he went to Spain as a Communist newspaper correspondent. In 1938, disillusioned by what he had learned of Communist theory and practice, he resigned from the party. Making his home in England, Koestler has devoted himself in recent years to writing and lecturing.

As he explains in an autobiographical essay, published in Richard Crossman's The God That Failed *(1949) and reprinted here in part, Koestler lost his faith in the capitalist system when his family in Hungary lost its fortune during World War I; he lost his faith in the German Republic before the coming of Hitler; then, ever so slowly, he lost his faith in the ability of the German Communist party to fight Hitler, and finally gave up hope for the party even in Russia. Koestler has told this story on many different occasions and in many different ways. Our selection from* The God That Failed *is the first account of his experiences written in straightforward autobiographical form. He has also written a brilliant novel about communism in Russia, called* Darkness at Noon *(1941), which was adapted for the stage a few years ago by Sidney Kingsley.*

As suggested above, Koestler has a principal theme—disillusionment with communism —that runs through all his books. Spanish Testament *(1937) shows mistakes made by the Communists in their conflict with France during the Spanish Revolution; a widely read essay,* The Yogi and the Commissar *(1945), is a provocative analysis of the dilemma of the consistent Communist;* Insight and Outlook *(1949) states more directly Koestler's own philosophy. Probably no other popular writer today has given us so clear a picture of the underlying principles of the Communist philosophy of life and its ultimate inadequacies.*

THE GOD THAT FAILED

A FAITH IS not acquired by reasoning. One does not fall in love with a woman, or enter the womb of a church, as a result of logical persuasion. Reason may defend an act of faith—but only after the act has been committed, and the man committed to the act.

Persuasion may play a part in a man's conversion; but only the part of bringing to its full and conscious climax a process which has been maturing in regions where no persuasion can penetrate. A faith is not acquired; it grows like a tree. Its crown points to the sky; its roots grow downward into the past and are nourished by the dark sap of the ancestral humus.

From the psychologist's point of view, there is little difference between a revolutionary and a traditionalist faith. All true faith is uncompromising, radical, purist; hence the true traditionalist is always a revolutionary zealot in conflict with pharisaian society, with the lukewarm corrupters of the creed. And vice versa: the revolutionary's Utopia, which in appearance represents a complete break with the past, is always modeled on some image of the lost Paradise, of a legendary Golden Age. The classless Communist society, according to Marx and Engels, was to be a revival, at the end of the dialectical spiral, of the primitive Communist society which stood at its beginning. Thus all true faith involves a revolt against the believer's social environment, and the projection into the future of an ideal derived from the remote past. All Utopias are fed from the sources of mythology; the social engineer's blueprints are merely revised editions of the ancient text.

Devotion to pure Utopia, and revolt against a polluted society, are thus the two poles which provide the tension of all militant creeds. To ask which of the two makes the current flow—attraction by the ideal or repulsion by the social environment—is to ask the old question about the hen and the egg. To the psychiatrist, both the craving for Utopia and the rebellion against the status quo are symptoms of social maladjustment. To the social reformer, both are symptoms of a healthy rational attitude. The psychiatrist is apt to forget that smooth adjustment to a deformed society creates deformed individuals. The reformer is equally apt to forget that hatred, even of the objectively hateful, does not produce that charity and justice on which a utopian society must be based.

Thus each of the two attitudes, the sociologist's and the psychologist's, reflects a half-truth. It is true that the case history of most revolutionaries and reformers reveals a neurotic conflict with family or society. But this only proves, to paraphrase Marx, that a moribund society creates its own morbid gravediggers.

It is also true that in the face of revolting injustice the only honorable attitude is to revolt, and to leave introspection for better times. But if we survey history and compare the lofty aims, in the name of which revolutions were started, and the sorry end to which they came, we see again and again how a polluted civilization pollutes its own revolutionary offspring.

Fitting the two half-truths—the sociologist's and the psychologist's—together, we conclude that if on the one hand oversensitivity to social injustice and obsessional craving for Utopia are signs of neurotic maladjustment, society may, on the other hand, reach a state of decay where the neurotic rebel causes more joy in heaven than the sane executive who orders pigs to be drowned under the eyes of starving men. This in fact was the state of our civilization when, in December 1931, at the age of twenty-six, I joined the Communist party of Germany.

I became converted because I was ripe for it and lived in a disintegrating society thirsting for faith. But the day when I was given my party card was merely the climax of a development which had started long before I had read about the drowned pigs or heard the names of Marx and Lenin. Its roots reach back into childhood; and though each of us, comrades of the Pink Decade, had individual roots with different twists in them, we are products of, by and large, the same generation and cultural climate. It is this unity underlying diversity which makes me hope that my story is worth telling.

I was born in 1905 in Budapest; we lived there till 1919, when we moved to Vienna. Until the First World War we were comfortably off, a typical Continental middle-middle-class family: my father was the Hungarian representative of some old-established British and German textile manufacturers. In September 1914, this form of existence, like so many others, came to an abrupt end; my father never found his feet again. He embarked on a number of ventures which became the more fantastic the more he lost self-confidence in a changed world. He opened a factory for radioactive soap; he backed several crank inventions (everlasting electric bulbs, self-heating bed bricks, and the like); and finally lost the remains of his capital in the Austrian inflation of the early twenties. I left home at twenty-one, and from that day became the only financial support of my parents.

At the age of nine, when our middle-class idyl collapsed, I had suddenly become conscious of the economic Facts of Life. As an only child, I continued to be pampered by my parents; but, well aware of the family crisis, and torn by pity for my father, who was of a generous and somewhat childlike disposition, I suffered a pang of guilt whenever they bought me books or toys. This continued later on, when every suit I bought for myself meant so much less to send home. Simultaneously, I developed a strong dislike of the obviously rich; not because they could afford to buy things (envy plays a much smaller part in social conflict than is generally assumed) but because they were able to do so without a guilty conscience. Thus I projected a personal predicament onto the structure of society at large.

It was certainly a tortuous way of acquiring a social conscience. But precisely because of the intimate nature of the conflict, the faith which grew out of it became an equally intimate part of my self. It did not, for some years, crystallize into a political creed; at first it took the form of a mawkishly sentimental attitude. Every contact with people poorer than myself was unbearable—the boy at school who had no gloves and red chilblains on his fingers, the former traveling salesman of my father's reduced to cadging occasional meals—all of them were additions to the load of guilt on my back. The analyst would have no difficulty in showing that the roots of this guilt complex go deeper than the crisis in our household budget; but if he were to dig even deeper, piercing through the individual layers of the case, he would strike the archetypal pattern which has produced millions of particular variations on the same theme—"Woe, for they chant to the sound of harps and anoint themselves, but are not grieved for the affliction of the people."

Thus sensitized by a personal conflict, I was ripe for the shock of learning that wheat was burned, fruit artificially spoiled, and pigs drowned in the depression years to keep prices up and enable fat capitalists to chant to the sound of harps, while Europe trembled under the torn boots of hunger-marchers and my father hid frayed cuffs under the table. The frayed cuffs and drowned pigs blended into one emotional explosion, as the fuse of the archetype was touched off. We sang the *Internationale*, but the words might as well have been the older ones: "Woe to the shepherds who feed themselves, but feed not their flocks."

In other respects, too, the story is more typical than it seems. A considerable proportion of the middle classes in central Europe was, like ourselves, ruined by the inflation of the twenties. It was the beginning of Europe's decline. This disintegration of the middle strata of society started the fatal process of polarization which continues to this day. The pauperized bourgeois became rebels of the Right or Left. Those who refused to admit that they had become *déclassé*, who clung to the empty shell of gentility, joined the Nazis and found comfort in blaming their fate on Versailles and the Jews. Many did not even have that consolation; they lived on pointlessly, like a great black swarm of tired winterflies crawling over the dim windows of Europe, members of a class displaced by history.

I was ripe to be converted, as a result of my personal case history; thousands of other members of the intelligentsia and the middle classes of my generation were ripe for it, by virtue of other personal case histories; but, however much these differed from case to case, they had a common denominator: the rapid disintegration of moral values, of the pre-1914 pattern of life in postwar Europe, and the simultaneous lure of the new revelation which had come from the East.

I joined the Party (which to this day remains "the" Party for all of us who once belonged to it) in 1931, at the beginning of that short-lived period of optimism, of that abortive spiritual renaissance, later known as the Pink Decade. The stars of that treacherous dawn were Barbusse, Romain Rolland, Gide, and Malraux in France; Piscator, Becher, Renn, Brecht, Eisler, Säghers in Germany; Auden, Isherwood, Spender in England; Dos Passos, Upton Sinclair, Steinbeck in the United States. (Of course, not all of them were members of the Communist party.) The cultural atmosphere was saturated with Progressive Writers' congresses, experimental theaters, committees for peace and against Fascism, societies for cultural relations with the USSR, Russian films, and avant-garde magazines. It looked indeed as if the Western world, convulsed by the aftermath of war, scourged by inflation, depression, unemployment and the absence of a faith to live for, was at last going to

> Clear from the head
> the masses of impressive rubbish;
> Rally the lost and trembling
> forces of the will,
> Gather them up and
> let them loose upon the earth,
> Till they construct at last
> a human justice.
>
> —AUDEN

The new star of Bethlehem had risen in the East; and for a modest sum, Intourist was prepared to allow you a short and well-focused glimpse of the Promised Land.

I lived at that time in Berlin. For the last five years, I had been working for the Ullstein chain of newspapers—first as a foreign correspondent in Palestine and the Middle East, then in Paris. Finally, in 1930, I joined the editorial staff in the Berlin "House."

My transfer from the Paris office to the Berlin house was due to an article I wrote on the occasion of the award of the Nobel prize for physics to the Prince de Broglie. My bosses decided that I had a knack for popularizing science (I had been a student of science in Vienna) and offered me the job of Science Editor of the *Vossiche* and adviser on matters scientific to the rest of the Ullstein publications. I arrived in Berlin on the fateful day of September 14, 1930—the day of the Reichstag election in which the National Socialist [Nazi] party, in one mighty leap, increased the number of its deputies from 4 to 107. The Communists had also registered important gains; the democratic parties of the Center were crushed. It was the beginning of the end of Weimar; the situation was epitomized in the title of Knickerbocker's best-seller: *Germany—Fascist or Soviet?* Obviously there was no "third alternative."

I did my job, writing about electrons, chromosomes, rocket ships, Neanderthal men, spiral nebulae, and the universe at large; but the pressure of events increased rapidly. With one third of its wage earners unemployed, Germany lived in a state of latent civil war, and if one wasn't prepared to be swept along as a passive victim by the approaching hurricane it became imperative to take sides. Stresemann's party was dead. The Socialists pursued a policy of opportunist compromise. Even by a process of pure elimination, the Communists, with the mighty Soviet Union behind them, seemed the only force capable of resisting the onrush of the primitive horde with its swastika totem. But it was not by a process of elimination that I became a Communist. Tired of electrons and wave mechanics, I began for the first time to read Marx, Engels, and Lenin in earnest. By the time I had finished with *Feuerbach* and *State and Revolution*, something had clicked in my brain which shook me like a mental explosion. To say that one had "seen the light" is a poor description of the mental rapture which only the convert knows (regardless of what faith he has been converted to). The new light seems to pour from all directions across the skull; the whole universe falls into pattern like the stray pieces of a jigsaw puzzle assembled by magic at one stroke. There is now an answer to every question, doubts and conflicts are a matter of the tortured past—a past already remote, when one had lived in dismal ignorance in the tasteless, colorless world of those who *don't know*. Nothing henceforth can disturb the convert's inner peace and serenity—except the occasional fear of losing faith again, losing thereby what alone makes life worth living, and falling back into the outer darkness, where there is wailing and gnashing of teeth. This may explain how Communists, with eyes to see and brains to think with, can still act in subjective *bona fides*, anno Domini 1949. At all times and in all creeds only a minority has been capable of courting excommunication and committing emotional hara-kiri in the name of an abstract truth.

In the late summer of 1932 my Soviet visa was granted at last. I obtained it on the strength of an invitation from the International Organization of Revolutionary Writers to tour the country and write a book about it. This was to be called *The Soviet Land Through Bourgeois Eyes*. The idea was to describe how Mr. K., a bourgeois reporter with strong anti-Soviet prejudices, is gradually converted by seeing the results of Socialist Reconstruction during the first Five Year Plan, and ends as Comrade K.

I left for the USSR six months before Hitler came to power in Germany, armed with a recommendation to Comrade Gopner, at that time head of the *Agitprop*, EKKI (Executive Committee of the Communist International), in Moscow. The EKKI, in its turn, provided me with a so-called "strong" letter asking all Soviet authorities to help me to accomplish my mission "as a delegate of the Revolutionary Proletarian Writers of Germany."

A letter of this kind carries in Soviet Russia the weight of a decree. It enabled me to travel unhampered all over the country without a guide, to obtain railway tickets without queuing, sleeping accommodations in government Guest Houses, and food in restaurants reserved for civil servants. It further enabled me to pay for my travels, with several thousand rubles left over at the end of my stay. The procedure was as follows.

When I arrived in a provincial capital, say in Tiflis, I went to the local Writers' Federation, where I produced my Comintern letter. The Secretary of the Federation thereupon arranged the usual banquets and meetings with the political leaders and members of the intelligentsia of the town, appointed somebody to look after me, and put me in touch with the editor of the local literary magazine and the director of the State Publishing Trust—in this case the Trust of the Georgian Soviet Republic. The editor of the magazine declared that it had been for many years his dearest wish to publish a story by me. I handed him a copy of a story published some time ago in Germany; and the same day a check for two or three thousand rubles was sent to my hotel. The director of the State Publishing Trust asked for the privilege of publishing a Georgian translation of the book I was going to write; I signed a printed agreement form and was sent another check for three or four thousand rubles. (The salary of the average wage earner was at that time 130 rubles per month.) I thus sold the same short story to eight or ten different literary magazines from Leningrad to Tashkent, and sold the Russian, German, Ukranian, Georgian, and Armenian rights of my unwritten book against advance payments which amounted to a small fortune. And as I did all this with official encouragement, and as other writers did the same, I could wholeheartedly confirm that Soviet Russia was the writer's paradise and that nowhere else in the world was the creative artist better paid or held in higher esteem. Human nature being what it is, it never occurred to me that my contracts and cash advances had been granted not on the strength of my literary reputation, but for reasons of a different nature.

At that time I had not published a single book; my name was completely unknown to those who paid ready cash for a story they had not read and a book that was not written. They were civil servants, acting on instructions. In a country where all publications are state-owned, editors, publishers, and literary critics become *ipso facto* part of the civil service. They will make or break a writer according to orders received: the publishers, by printing vast editions of his new book or by pulping all his previous works; the critics, by calling him a new Tolstoy or a depraved cosmopolitan vermin, or both within an interval of a few months.

The average visiting foreign author knows little about all this; and the little which his intuition makes him guess, his vanity will quickly make him forget. The people whom he meets at banquets and parties seem to know his works by heart; he would have to be a masochist, with a touch of persecution mania, to assume that they have been specially briefed for the occasion. The Central State Publishing Trust offers him a contract for his next book and an advance covering the royalties on a sale of 150,000 copies. If he is very honest, the honored guest will mention with a blush that this is about fifteen times the number of copies on whose expected sale the cash advances of well-known European writers are calculated. But that, the director points out to him with a smile, is the practice of capitalist publishers. In the Soviet Union all publishing enterprises are owned by the People, and the average Soviet citizen buys 231.57 percent more books than the average American; at the end of the second Five Year Plan this quotient will reach and outstrip

365 percent. So it is only natural that honored writers in the Soviet Union, instead of living in garrets as in capitalist countries, own two-room flats with a lavatory all their own, not to mention motorcars and summer *datchas*. Our visitor is slightly nettled by being suspected of living in a garret; but this, he reassures himself, is petty-bourgeois vanity. He signs the contract and a few days later leaves for home, where he will declare that nowhere else in the world is the creative artist held in higher esteem, etc., etc. Though he can't take his rubles with him, as they are not convertible into foreign currency, he can buy some quite decent Bokhara carpets and leave the rest in the State Bank in Moscow; it is a pleasant feeling to have a nest egg in the Socialist sixth of the earth. In exceptional cases the State Publishing Trust is even authorized to convert part of the sum into the author's home currency and to send it to him in monthly installments. I know of two famous exiled German authors in France who for years drew monthly royalty checks of this kind, though one of them never had a book published in Russia. Both were passionate and lucid critics of democratic corruption; neither of them has ever written a word of criticism against the Soviet regime. I do not mean that they have been bribed; we are not concerned here with such crude machinations, but with the dialectics of the unconscious—with that subtle inner voice which whispers that in the capitalist world publishers are sharks who don't care a damn what you write as long as your books sell, whereas your Soviet publishers are the Soviet People, justifiably resentful of any criticism of their free country.

Russia is indeed the artist's Paradise—but alas a Paradise of forbidden trees guarded by peak-capped angels with flaming swords.

I stayed in the Soviet Union for one year, half of which I spent traveling, the other half in Kharkov and Moscow, writing my book. A German edition of it was actually published in Kharkov, under a changed title. The Russian, Georgian, Armenian, etc. editions have, as far as I know, never seen the light.

My travels led me through the industrial centers along the Volga; then southward through the Ukraine and across the Transcaucasian Republics—Georgia, Armenia, and Azerbaijan—to Baku; across the Caspian and through the Central Asiatic Republics—Turkmenistan and Uzbekistan—down to the Afghan frontier; then, via Tashkent and across Kazakstan, back to Moscow. What I saw and experienced came as a shock—but a shock with a delayed-action effect, as it were. My party education had equipped my mind with such elaborate shock-absorbing buffers and elastic defenses that everything seen and heard became automatically transformed to fit the preconceived pattern.

I spoke Russian fairly fluently but, though I traveled alone, I had little occasion to practice it on people other than official acquaintances; the ordinary Soviet citizen knows that to be seen talking to a foreigner is as unhealthy as touching a leper. Those who did talk to me, in restaurants and railway compartments, used the stereotyped clichés of *Pravda* editorials; one might have thought they were reciting conversation pieces from a phrase book. All this I registered with approval: it was a healthy sign of revolutionary discipline and Bolshevik vigilance. I saw the ravages of the famine of 1932-1933 in the Ukraine: hordes of families in rags begging at the railway stations, the women lifting up to the compartment window their starving brats which—with drumstick limbs, big cadaverous heads, puffed bellies—looked like embryos out of alcohol bottles; the old men with frostbitten toes sticking out of torn slippers. I was told that these were kulaks who had resisted the collectivization of the land and I accepted the explanation; they were enemies of the people who preferred begging to work. The maid in the Hotel Regina in Kharkov fainted from hunger while doing my room; the manager explained that she was fresh from the countryside and through a technical hitch had not yet been issued her ration cards; I accepted the technical hitch.

I could not help noticing the Asiatic backwardness of life; the apathy of the crowds in the streets, tramways, and railway stations; the incredible housing conditions which make all industrial towns appear one vast slum (two or three couples sharing one room divided by sheets hanging from washing lines); the starvation rations handed out by the cooperatives; or the fact that the price of one kilogram of butter on the free market equaled the average worker's monthly wage, the price of a pair of shoes two months' wages. Living standards were low, but under the czarist regime they had been even lower. The working classes in the capitalist countries were better off than in the Soviet Union, but that was a static comparison: for here the level was steadily rising, there steadily falling. At the end of the second Five Year Plan the two levels would be equalized; until that time all comparisons were misleading and bad for the Soviet people's morale. Accordingly, I not only accepted the famine as inevitable, but also the necessity of the ban on foreign travel, foreign newspapers and books, and the dissemination of a grotesquely distorted picture of life in the capitalist world. At first I was shocked when after a lecture I was asked questions like these: "When you left the bourgeois press was your ration card withdrawn and were you kicked out at once from your room?" "What is the average number per day of French working class families starving to death (a) in rural areas, (b) in the towns?" "By what means have our comrades in the West succeeded in temporarily staving off the war of intervention which the finance-capitalists are preparing with the aid of the Social Fascist traitors of the working class?" The questions were always painstakingly formulated in neo-Russian Djugashwilese. After a while I found them quite natural. There was always a small element of truth in them—this had, of course, been exaggerated and simplified according to the accepted technique of propaganda; but propaganda was indispensable for the survival of the Soviet Union, surrounded by a hostile world.

The necessary lie, the necessary slander; the necessary intimidation of the masses to preserve them from shortsighted errors; the necessary liquidation of oppositional groups and hostile classes; the necessary sacrifice of a whole generation in the interest of the next—it may all sound monstrous and yet it was so easy to accept while rolling along a single track of faith. It had all happened before, in the history of the medieval churches, in Byzantium, in the hothouses of mystic sects; but the mental world of the drug addict is difficult to explain to the outsider who has never entered the magic circle and never played Wonderland croquet with himself.

I left Soviet Russia in the autumn of 1933; yet I stayed in the Party for another four and a half years, until the early spring of 1938. My faith had been badly shaken, but thanks to the elastic shock absorbers, I was slow in becoming conscious of the damage. A number of external events and inner rationalizations helped me to carry on and delay the final crack-up.

While I was in Russia, Hitler had come

to power in Germany; so, in the autumn of 1933 I joined my Party friends in the Paris exile. The whole Red Block, with the exception of those caught by the Gestapo, was now reassembled here, in the little hotels of the Left Bank. The next five years were for me years of near-starvation compensated by hectic political activity. Its center and motor was Willi Münzenberg, head of the *Agitprop* for Western Europe and Germany. He was a short, stocky man of proletarian origin; a magnetic personality of immense driving power and a hard, seductive charm. He broke with the Comintern in 1938, six months after myself, and was murdered in the summer of 1940 under the usual lurid and mysterious circumstances; as usual in such cases, the murderers are unknown and there are only indirect clues, all pointing in one direction like magnetic needles to the pole.

On July 18, 1936, General Franco staged his *coup d'état*. I went to see Willi and asked him to help me to join the Spanish Republican army; this was before the international brigades were formed. I had brought my passport along; it was a Hungarian passport. Willi looked at it absentmindedly; as an inveterate propagandist he was not enthusiastic about writers wasting their time digging trenches. In the passport was my press card as a Paris Correspondent of the *Pester Lloyd*. I had never written a word for the *Pester Lloyd*, but every self-respecting Hungarian *émigré* in Paris was equipped with a press card from one Budapest paper or another, to obtain occasional free theater and movie tickets. Willi's eyes suddenly brightened; he had an idea.

"Why don't you make a trip to Franco's headquarters for the *Pester Lloyd?*" he suggested. "Hungary is a semi-fascist country; they will welcome you with open arms."

I too thought it was an excellent idea, but there were some hitches. Firstly, the *Pester Lloyd* would never agree to sending me; but then why bother to inform them of my going? In the muddle of a civil war, nobody was likely to take the trouble to check my accreditation. Secondly, other foreign correspondents might think it fishy that a poor Hungarian paper was sending a special correspondent to Spain. That difficulty too was overcome. I had friends on the *News Chronicle* in London; the *News Chronicle* was violently anti-Franco and stood no chance of having a staff correspondent of its own admitted to rebel territory; so the foreign editor gladly agreed that I should act as his special correspondent provided that I ever got into Franco Spain.

I did get in, via Lisbon to Seville, but my sojourn was short. On the second day in Seville, what was then Franco's headquarters, I was recognized and denounced as a Communist; but thanks to the incredible Spanish muddle, managed to get out in the nick of time via Gibraltar. Even during that short visit, however, I had seen the German pilots and German airplanes of Franco's army; I published the facts in the *News Chronicle* and in a pamphlet, and thereby incurred the special hostility of the Franco regime. Accordingly, when I was captured six months later, as a correspondent with the Republican army, by Franco's troops, I was convinced that to be shot without unpleasant preliminaries was the best I could hope for.

I spent four months in Spanish prisons, in Málaga and Seville, most of the time in solitary confinement and most of the time convinced that I was going to be shot. When, in June 1937, thanks to the intervention of the British Government, I was unexpectedly set free, my hair had not grayed and my features had not changed and I had not developed religious mania; but I had made the acquaintance of a different kind of reality, which had altered my outlook and values, and altered them so profoundly and unconsciously that during the first days of freedom I was not even aware of it. The experiences responsible for this change were fear, pity, and a third one, more difficult to describe. Fear, not of death, but of torture and humiliation and the more unpleasant forms of dying—my companion of patio exercises, Garcia Atadell, was garroted shortly after my liberation. Pity for the little Andalusian and Catalan peasants whom I heard crying and calling for their *madres* when they were led out at night to face the firing squad; and finally, a condition of mind usually referred to in terms borrowed from the vocabulary of mysticism, which would present itself at unexpected moments and induce a state of inner peace which I have known neither before nor since.

The lesson taught by this type of experience, when put into words, always appears under the dowdy guise of perennial commonplaces: that man is a reality, mankind an abstraction; that men cannot be treated as units in operations of political arithmetic because they behave like the symbols for zero and the infinite, which dislocate all mathematical operations; that the end justifies the means only within very narrow limits; that ethics is not a function of social utility, and charity not a petty-bourgeois sentiment but the gravitational force which keeps civilization in its orbit. Nothing can sound more flatfooted than such verbalizations of a knowledge which is not of a verbal nature; yet every single one of these trivial statements was incompatible with the Communist faith which I held.

If this story was fiction, it would end here; the chief character, having undergone a spiritual conversion, takes leave of his comrades of yesterday and goes his own way with a serene smile. But when I was liberated I did not know that I had ceased to be a Communist. The first thing I did after the Guardia Civil put me across the frontier at Gibraltar was to send a cable to the Party. It started with the line from Schiller, "*Seid umschlungen, Millionen*"—"I embrace thee, ye millions." And, even more strange, I added the words "am cured of all belly-aches"—"belly-ache" being our slang expression for qualms about the party line.

It was a short euphoria. I spent three quiet months with friends in England, writing a book on Spain; then, after a short trip to the Middle East for the *News Chronicle*, which offered no points of friction with the Party, the conflict began. There was nothing dramatic about it. I made a lecture tour through England for the Left Book Club; whenever a questioner, in the predominantly Communist audiences, asked for details about the treasonable activities of the POUM—an independent Left-Wing splinter group of Trotskyite leanings in Spain, whom the party accused of being "agents of Franco"—I answered that their fractional policy might be bad for the cause, but that they were certainly not traitors. Surprisingly enough, I got away with that; the British CP was notoriously lax in denouncing deviations to higher quarters.

Then I learned that, in the Russian mass purges, my brother-in-law and two of my closest friends had been arrested. My brother-in-law, Dr. Ernst Ascher, was a doctor who worked at a state hospital in the Volga German Republic. Though a member of the German CP, he was politically naïve and indifferent. The accusation against him, as I later learned, was that he was a saboteur who had injected syphilis into his patients, that he had demoralized the people by pretending that venereal diseases were incurable, and thirdly, as a matter of course, that he was the agent of a foreign power. He has never been heard of since his arrest twelve years ago.

The other two were Alex Weissberg and his wife Eva. Alex, a physicist, was employed at the Ukrainian Institute for Physics and Technology (UFTI); I had known them both for many years and had stayed with them in Kharkov. He was arrested in 1937 on the charge (as I learned much later) of having hired twenty bandits to ambush Stalin and Kaganovitch on the next hunting trip in the Caucasus. He refused to sign a confession, was kept in various prisons for three years, then, after the Ribbentrop-Molotov Pact, was handed over by the GPU to the Gestapo, in 1940, at Brest Litovsk, together with a hundred-odd other Austrian, German, and Hungarian Communists. He survived the Gestapo, took part in the Warsaw revolt, and has written a book which will shortly be available to English readers.

Alex' wife Eva was a ceramist; she was arrested about a year before Alex and was at first accused of having inserted swastikas into the pattern on the teacups which she designed for mass production; then, of having hidden under her bed two pistols which were to serve to kill Stalin at the next party congress. She spent eighteen months in the Lubianka, where the GPU tried to brief her as a repentant sinner for the Bukharin show trial. She cut her veins, was saved, and was released shortly afterwards thanks to the extraordinary exertions of the Austrian Consul in Moscow, who happened to be a friend of her mother.

I met Eva after she had been released and expelled from Russia, in the spring of 1938. Her experiences in Russian prisons, and particularly of the GPU's methods of obtaining confessions, provided me with part of the material for *Darkness at Noon.* I promised her to do what I could to save Alex. Albert Einstein had already intervened on his behalf; so I wrote a carefully worded cable to Stalin, for which I obtained the signatures of the three French Nobel prize physicists, Perrin, Langevin, and Joliot-Curie. The cable, a copy of which was sent to State Attorney Vishinsky, requested that the charges against Weissberg, if any, be made public, and that he be given a public trial. It is characteristic that although both Langevin and Joliot-Curie were Soviet sympathizers who shortly afterward became members of the Party, they obviously did not set great store by the methods of Soviet justice—for, though they had never heard of Alex before, and knew me only slightly, they at once took it for granted that he was innocent.

The moral of this story is that Joliot-Curie, and the rest of our nuclear Marxists cannot claim starry-eyed ignorance of the goings on in Russia. They know in detail the case history of colleagues, loyal servants of the Soviet Union, arrested on grotesque charges, held for years without trial, and delivered to the Gestapo. They further know that these cases are not exceptional; reliable, secondhand reports of hundreds of similar cases in Russian academic circles are available to them. And the same is true of all Communists or fellow-traveling authors, journalists, and other intellectuals. Every single one of us knows of at least one friend who perished in the Arctic subcontinent of forced labor camps, was shot as a spy, or vanished without trace. How our voices boomed with righteous indignation, denouncing flaws in the procedure of justice in our comfortable democracies; and how silent we were when our comrades, without trial or conviction, were liquidated in the Socialist sixth of the earth. Each of us carries a skeleton in the cupboard of his conscience; added together they would form galleries of bones more labyrinthine than the Paris catacombs.

At no time and in no country have more revolutionaries been killed and reduced to slavery than in Soviet Russia. To one who himself for seven years found excuses for every stupidity and crime committed under the Marxist banner, the spectacle of these dialectical tight-rope acts of self-deception, performed by men of good will and intelligence, is more disheartening than the barbarities committed by the simple in spirit. Having experienced the almost unlimited possibilities of mental acrobatism on that tightrope stretched across one's conscience, I know how much stretching it takes to make that elastic rope snap.

The end came as a curious anticlimax. Some time during the spring of 1938, I had to give a talk on Spain to the German Emigré Writers' Association in Paris. Before the talk, a representative of the Party asked me to insert a passage denouncing the POUM as agents of Franco; I refused. He shrugged, and asked me whether I would care to show him the text of my speech and "to discuss it informally." I refused. The meeting took place in the hall of the Société des Industries Francaises in the Place St. Germain des Près, before an audience of two or three hundred refugee intellectuals, half of them Communists. I knew it was my last public appearance as a member of the Party. The theme of the speech was the situation in Spain; it contained not a single word of criticism of the Party or of Russia. But it contained three phrases, deliberately chosen because to normal people they were platitudes, to Communists a declaration of war. The first was: "No movement, party, or person can claim the privilege of infallibility." The second was: "Appeasing the enemy is as foolish as persecuting the friend who pursues your own aim by a different road." The third was a quotation from Thomas Mann: "A harmful truth is better than a useful lie."

That settled it. When I had finished, the non-Communist half of the audience applauded, the Communist half sat in heavy silence, most of them with folded arms. This was not done by order, but as a spontaneous reaction to those fatal commonplaces. You might as well have told a Nazi audience that all men are born equal regardless of race and creed.

A few days later I wrote my letter of resignation to the Central Committee of the Party.

Will Herberg

An able sociological study of the three great religious groups in this country was published in 1955 under the title Protestant—Catholic—Jew. *This book by Will Herberg is a penetrating analysis of the relation between our traditional religious values and contemporary American social and political ideals.*

Herberg was born in 1906 and educated at Columbia University where he received both his undergraduate and graduate degrees. He is known for his work in areas not frequently associated: labor and religion. For a number of years he directed research for a large American Federation of Labor union; more recently his major interest has been in historical theology and social philosophy. Herberg has lectured widely and published frequent articles on social, political, and religious subjects; his book Judaism and Modern Man *(1951) was termed "a milestone in American religious thought" by Reinhold Niebuhr. In 1956 Herberg went to Drew University as professor of Judaic studies and social philosophy.*

The selection we reprint from Protestant—Catholic—Jew *includes a thoughtful discussion of the "religious situation" in America today—with particular reference to the way in which popular American religion is being largely reshaped by our strong commitment to the American way of life. The paradox that faces every thoughtful foreigner who visits our country—"pervasive secularism amid mounting religiosity"—creates the problem for which Herberg seeks to find an explanation. His discussion of the "American way of life" shows particular insight. In Herberg's opinion this is not a vague and meaningless phrase, as some critics claim, but rather "an organic statement of ideas, values, and beliefs" that are genuinely operating in the lives of most Americans—and he gives us the kind of concrete analysis of its meaning that we all need to clarify our thinking. He is unhappy, it is true, to see the American way of life replace our traditional Hebrew-Christian faith as the "common religion of Americans," but this is because he has a high opinion of the worth of religion, not a low opinion of the American way of life. One need not be as certain as Herberg that democracy and social idealism are replacing the traditional faiths in America to recognize that his indictment of the popular revival of religion today raises some serious questions.*

DEMOCRACY AS THE COMMON FAITH OF AMERICA

1. *Religion in America: The Problem*

THE RELIGIOUS SITUATION in the United States today confronts us with a perplexing problem. "The fact of a religious revival in America cannot be gainsaid," Barbara Ward noted in her recent *Report to Europe on America*. "We did not need the evidence of polls or church attendance to confirm what we could so easily observe—the walls of new churches rising in town and countryside wherever we went." Miss Ward's impression is fully borne out by the available evidence. Whether we judge by religious identification, church membership, or church attendance, whether we go by the best-seller lists, the mass media, or the writings of intellectuals, the conclusion is the same: there is every sign of a notable "turn to religion" among the American people today.

And yet, writing not much before Miss Ward's visit, a perceptive historian of America noted that at the mid-twentieth century, "the trend toward secularism in ideas was not reversed." Professor [Oscar] Handlin could find as much evidence for his conclusion as Miss Ward for hers, though the secularism to which he referred is not something that can be pointed out as obviously as Miss Ward's evidences of a religious revival. The secularism dominating the American consciousness is not an overt philosophy; it is an underlying, often unconscious, orientation of life and thought. Because it is so pervasive and omnipresent, it is hard to put one's finger on it. Yet perhaps something of what it implies may be suggested by a startling contrast. When Ignazio Silone, the Italian writer and Socialist, was asked what he felt to be the "most important date in universal history," he replied unhesitatingly: "The twenty-fifth of December in the year zero." But when nearly thirty outstanding Americans were asked not long ago to rate the hundred most significant events in history, first place was given to Columbus' discovery of America, while Christ, His birth or crucifixion, came fourteenth, tied with the discovery of x-rays and the Wright brothers' first plane flight. Silone is no orthodox Christian, yet it is evident that he takes his Christianity seriously in a way that the eminent American historians, educators, and journalists, who forgot all about Christ in listing significant events in history, obviously do not. The secularism that pervades the American consciousness is essentially of this kind: it is thinking and living in terms of a framework of reality and value remote from the religious beliefs simultaneously professed.

In the five years from 1949 to 1953 the distribution of Scripture in the United States increased 140 percent, reaching an all-time high of 9,726,391 volumes a year. People were apparently buying and distributing the Bible at an unprecedented rate. Furthermore, over four fifths of adult Americans said they believed the Bible to be the "revealed word of God" rather than merely a "great piece of literature." Yet when these same Americans were asked to give the "names of the first four books of the New Testament of the Bible, that is, the first four gospels," 53 percent could not name even one. The Bible can hardly be said to enter into the life and thought of Americans quite as much as their views on its divine inspiration and their eagerness to buy and distribute it might suggest.

This is at least part of the picture presented by religion in contemporary America: Christians flocking to church, yet forgetting all about Christ when it comes to naming the most significant events in history; men and women valuing the Bible as revelation, purchasing and distributing it by the millions, yet apparently seldom reading it themselves. Every aspect of contemporary religious life reflects this paradox—pervasive secularism amid mounting religiosity, "the strengthening of the religious structure in spite of increasing secularization." The influx of members into the churches and the increased readiness of Americans to identify themselves in religious terms certainly appear to stand in contrast to the way Americans seem to think and feel about matters central to the faiths they profess.

The paradox is there, and it would be misleading to try to get rid of it by suppressing one or the other side of the apparent contradiction. It will not do to brush aside the evidences of religious revival by writing off the new religiousness as little more than shallow emotionalism, "escapism," or mere pretense. The people who join the churches, take part in church activities, send their children to church schools, and gladly identify themselves in religious terms are not fools or hypocrites. They are honest, intelligent people who take their religion quite seriously. Of that there cannot be much doubt.

Nor, on the other hand, can there be much doubt that, by and large, the religion which actually prevails among Americans today has lost much of its authentic Christian (or Jewish) content. Even when they are thinking, feeling, and acting religiously, their thinking, feeling, and acting do not bear an unequivocal relation to the faiths they profess. Americans think, feel, and act in terms quite obviously secularist at the very time that they exhibit every sign of a widespread religious revival. It is this secularism of a religious people, this religiousness in a secularist framework, that constitutes the problem posed by the contemporary religious situation in America.

It is the thesis of the present work that both the religiousness and the secularism of the American people derive from very much the same sources, and that both become more intelligible when seen against the background of certain deep-going sociological processes that have transformed the face of the American people in the course of the past generation. The distinctive character of American religiosity, so perplexing at first sight in its contradictions and discrepancies, becomes somewhat more intelligible when so interpreted, and the entire religious situation is viewed in its essential relation to the inner development of American society. American religion and American society would seem to be so closely interrelated as to make it virtually impossible to understand either without reference to the other.

II. *The Religion of Americans and American Religion*

"Every functioning society," Robin M. Williams, Jr. points out, "has to an important degree a *common* religion. The possession of a common set of ideas, rituals, and symbols can supply an overarching sense of unity even in a society riddled with conflicts." What is this "common religion" of American society, the "common set of ideas, rituals, and symbols" that give it its "overarching sense of unity"? Williams provides us with a further clue when he suggests that "men are always likely to be intolerant of opposition to their central ultimate values." What are these "central ultimate values" about which Americans are "intolerant"? No one who knows anything about the religious situation in this country would be likely to suggest that the things Americans are "intolerant" about are the beliefs, standards, or teachings of the religions they "officially" acknowledge as theirs. Americans are proud of their tolerance in matters of religion: one is expected to "believe in God," but otherwise religion is not supposed to be a ground of "discrimination." This is, no doubt, admirable, but is it not "at least in part, a sign that the crucial values of the system are no longer couched in a religious framework"?

What, then, is the "framework" in which they *are* couched? What, to return to our original question, is the "common religion" of the American people, as it may be inferred not only from their words but also from their behavior?

It seems to me that a realistic appraisal of the values, ideas, and behavior of the American people leads to the conclusion that Americans, by and large, do have their "common religion" and that that "religion" is the system familiarly known as the American Way of Life. It is the American Way of Life that supplies American society with an "overarching sense of unity" amid conflict. It is the American Way of Life about which Americans are admittedly and unashamedly "intolerant." It is the American Way of Life that provides the framework in terms of which the crucial values of American existence are couched. By every realistic criterion the American Way of Life is the operative faith of the American people.

It would be the crudest kind of misunderstanding to dismiss the American Way of Life as no more than a political formula or propagandist slogan, or to regard it as simply an expression of the "materialistic" impulses of the American people. Americans are "materialistic," no doubt, but surely not more so than other people, than the French peasant or petty bourgeois, for example. All such labels are irrelevant, if not meaningless. The American Way of Life is, at bottom, a spiritual structure, a structure of ideas and ideals, of aspirations and values, of beliefs and standards; it synthesizes all that commends itself to the

American as the right, the good, and the true in actual life. It embraces such seemingly incongruous elements as sanitary plumbing and freedom of opportunity, Coca-Cola and an intense faith in education—all felt as moral questions relating to the proper way of life. The very expression "way of life" points to its religious essence, for one's ultimate, over-all way of life is one's religion.

The American Way of Life is, of course, conceived as the corporate "way" of the American people, but it has its implications for the American as an individual as well. It is something really operative in his actual life. When in the *Ladies' Home Journal* poll, Americans were asked "to look within [themselves] and state honestly whether [they] thought [they] really obeyed the law of love under certain special conditions," 90 percent said yes and 5 percent no when the one to be "loved" was a person belonging to a different religion; 80 percent said yes and 12 percent no when it was the case of a member of a different race; 78 percent said yes and 10 percent no when it concerned a business competitor—but only 27 percent said yes and 57 percent no in the case of "a member of a political party that you think is dangerous," while 25 percent said yes and 63 percent said no when it concerned an enemy of the nation. These figures are most illuminating, first because of the incredible self-assurance they reveal with which the average American believes he fulfills the "impossible" law of love, but also because of the light they cast on the differential impact of the violation of this law on the American conscience. For it is obvious that the figures reflect not so much the actual behavior of the American people—no people on earth ever loved their neighbors as themselves as much as the American people say they do—as how seriously Americans take transgressions against the law of love in various cases. Americans feel they *ought* to love their fellow men despite differences of race or creed or business interest; that is what the American Way of Life emphatically prescribes. But the American Way of Life almost explicitly sanctions hating a member of a "dangerous" political party (the Communist party is obviously meant here) or an enemy of one's country, and therefore an overwhelming majority avow their hate. In both situations, while the Jewish-Christian law of love is formally acknowledged, the truly operative factor is the value system embodied in the American Way of Life. Where the American Way of Life approves of love of one's fellow man, most Americans confidently assert that they practice such love; where the American Way of Life disapproves, the great mass of Americans do not hesitate to confess that they do not practice it, and apparently feel very little guilt for their failure. No better pragmatic test as to what the operative religion of the American people actually is could be desired.

1

What is this American Way of Life that we have said constitutes the "common religion" of American society? An adequate description and analysis of what is implied in this phrase still remains to be attempted, and certainly it will not be ventured here; but some indications may not be out of place.

If the American Way of Life had to be defined in one word, "democracy" would undoubtedly be the word, but democracy in a peculiarly American sense. On its political side it means the Constitution; on its economic side, "free enterprise"; on its social side, an equalitarianism which is not only compatible with but indeed actually implies vigorous economic competition and high mobility. Spiritually, the American Way of Life is best expressed in a certain kind of "idealism" which has come to be recognized as characteristically American. It is a faith that has its symbols and its rituals, its holidays and its liturgy, its saints and its sancta; and it is a faith that every American, to the degree that he is an American, knows and understands.

The American Way of Life is individualistic, dynamic, pragmatic. It affirms the supreme value and dignity of the individual; it stresses incessant activity on his part, for he is never to rest but is always to be striving to "get ahead"; it defines an ethic of self-reliance, merit, and character, and judges by achievement: "deeds, not creeds" are what count. The American Way of life is humanitarian, "forward looking," optimistic. Americans are easily the most generous and philanthropic people in the world, in terms of their ready and unstinting response to suffering anywhere on the globe. The American believes in progress, in self-improvement, and quite fanatically in education. But above all, the American is idealistic. Americans cannot go on making money or achieving worldly success simply on its own merits; such "materialistic" things must, in the American mind, be justified in "higher" terms, in terms of "service" or "stewardship" or "general welfare." Because Americans are so idealistic, they tend to confuse espousing an ideal with fulfilling it and are always tempted to regard themselves as good as the ideals they entertain: hence the amazingly high valuation most Americans quite sincerely place on their own virtue. And because they are so idealistic, Americans tend to be moralistic: they are inclined to see all issues as plain and simple, black and white, issues of morality. Every struggle in which they are seriously engaged becomes a "crusade." To Mr. Eisenhower, who in many ways exemplifies American religion in a particularly representative way, the second world war was a "crusade" (as was the first to Woodrow Wilson); so was his campaign for the Presidency ("I am engaged in a crusade . . . to substitute good government for what we most earnestly believe has been bad government"); and so is his administration—a "battle" for the republic against "godless Communism" abroad and against "corruption and materialism" at home. It was Woodrow Wilson who once said, "Sometimes people call me an idealist. Well, that is the way I know I'm an American; America is the most idealistic nation in the world"; Eisenhower was but saying the same thing when he solemnly affirmed: "The things that make us proud to be Americans are of the soul and of the spirit."

2

The American Way of Life as the "common faith" of American society has coexisted for some centuries with the historic faiths of the American people, and the two have influenced each other in many profound and subtle ways. The influence has been complex and reciprocal, to the point where causal priority becomes impossible to assign if indeed it does not become altogether meaningless. From the very beginning the American Way of Life was shaped by the contours of American Protestantism; it may, indeed, best be understood as a kind of secularized Puritanism, a Puritanism without transcendence, without sense of sin or judgment. The Puritan's vision of a new "Promised Land" in the wilderness of the New World has become, as we have suggested, the American's deep sense of the newness and uniqueness of things in the Western Hemisphere. The Puritan's sense of vocation and "inner-worldly asceticism" can still be detected in the American's gospel of action and service, and his consciousness of high responsibility before God in the American's "idealism."

The reciprocal action of the American Way of Life in shaping and reshaping the historic faiths of Christianity and Judaism on American soil is perhaps more readily discerned. By and large, we may say that these historic religions have all tended to become "Americanized" under the pervasive influence of the American environment. This "Americanization" has been the product not so much of conscious direction as of a "diffuse convergence" operating spontaneously in the context of the totality of American life. What it has brought, however, is none the less clear: "religious groupings throughout [American] society [have been] stamped with recognizably 'American' qualities," to an extent indeed where foreign observers sometimes find the various American religions more like each other than they are like their European counterparts.

Under the influence of the American environment the historic Jewish and Christian faiths have tended to become secularized in the sense of becoming integrated as parts within a larger whole defined by the American Way of Life. "There is a marked tendency, "Williams writes in his discussion of the relations of religion to other institutions in the United States, "to regard religion as a good because it is useful in furthering other major values—in other words, to reverse the ends-means relation implied in the conception of religion as an ultimate value." In this reversal the Christian and Jewish faiths tend to be prized because they help promote ideals and standards that all Americans are expected to share on a deeper level than merely "official" religion. Insofar as any reference is made to the God in whom all Americans "believe" and of whom the "official" religions speak, it is primarily as sanction and underpinning for the supreme values of the faith embodied in the American Way of Life. Secularization of religion could hardly go further.

It is hardly necessary to continue this analysis much farther along these general lines. The optimism, moralism, and idealism of Jewish and Christian faith in America are plain evidence of the profound effect of the American outlook on American religion. Indeed, such evidence is amply provided by any tabulation of the distinctive features of religion in America, and needs no special emphasis at this point.

What is perhaps of crucial importance, and requires a more detailed examination, is the new attitude toward religion and the new conception of the church that have emerged in America.

Americans believe in religion in a way that perhaps no other people do. It may indeed be said that the primary religious affirmation of the American people, in harmony with the American Way of Life, is that religion is a "good thing," a supremely "good thing," for the individual and the community. And "religion" here means not so much any particular religion, but religion as such. "Our government makes no sense," President Eisenhower recently declared, "unless it is founded in a deeply felt religious faith—*and I don't care what it is*" (emphasis added). In saying this, the President was saying something that almost any American could understand and approve, but which must seem like a deplorable heresy to the European churchmen. Every American could understand, first, that Mr. Eisenhower's apparent indifferentism ("and I don't care what it is") was not indifferentism at all, but the expression of the conviction that at bottom the "three great faiths" were really "saying the same thing" in affirming the "spiritual ideals" and "moral values" of the American Way of Life. Every American, moreover, could understand that what Mr. Eisenhower was emphasizing so vehemently was the indispensability of religion as the foundation of society. This is one aspect of what Americans mean when they say that they "believe in religion."

It must be remembered that in America the variety and multiplicity of churches did not, as in Europe, come with the breakdown of a single established national church; in America, taking the nation as a whole, the variety and multiplicity of churches was almost the original condition and coeval with the emergence of the new society. In America religious pluralism is thus not merely a historical and political fact; it is, in the mind of the American, the primordial condition of things, an essential aspect of the American Way of Life, and therefore in itself an aspect of religious belief. Americans, in other words, believe that the plurality of religious groups is a proper and legitimate condition. However much he may be attached to his own church, however dimly he may regard the beliefs and practices of other churches, the American tends to feel rather strongly that total religious uniformity, even with his own church benefiting thereby, would be something undesirable and wrong, indeed scarcely conceivable. Pluralism of religions and churches is something quite axiomatic to the American. This feeling, more than anything else, is the foundation of the American doctrine of the "separation of church and state," for it is the heart of this doctrine that the government may not do anything that implies the pre-eminence or superior legitimacy of one church over another.

So firmly entrenched is this denominational idea in the mind of the American that even American Catholics have come to think in such terms; theologically the Catholic Church of course continues to regard itself as the one true church, but in their actual social attitudes American Catholics, hardly less than American Protestants or Jews, tend to think of their church as a denomination existing side by side with other denominations in a pluralistic harmony that is felt to be somehow of the texture of American life.

The denominational idea is fundamental to American thinking about religion, but it is not the last word. Americans think of their various churches as denominations, but they also feel that somehow the denominations fall into larger wholes which we have called religious communities. This kind of denominational aggregation is, of course, something that pertains primarily to Protestantism and to a lesser degree to Judaism; both have more or less organized denominations which, taken together, form the religious communities. Catholicism, on the other hand, has no such overt inner divisions, but American Catholics readily understand the phenomenon when they see it among Protestants and Jews. Denominations are felt to be somehow a matter of individual preference, and movement between denominations is not uncommon; the religious community, on the other hand, is taken as something more objective and given, something in which, by and large, one is born, lives and dies, something that (to recall our earlier analysis) identifies and defines one's position in American society. Since the religious community in its present form is a recent social emergent, its relations to the denominations properly so-called are still relatively fluid and undefined but the main lines of development would seem to be fairly clear.

When the plurality of denominations comprehended in religious communities is seen from the standpoint of the "common faith" of American society, what emerges is the conception of the three "communions"—Protestantism, Catholicism, Judaism—as three diverse, but equally legitimate, equally American, expressions of an over-all American religion, standing for essentially the same "moral ideals" and "spiritual values." This conception, whatever may be thought of it theologically, is in fact held, though hardly in explicit form, by many devout and religiously sophisticated Americans. It would seem to be the obvious meaning of the title, *The Religions of Democracy*, given to a recent authoritative statement of the Protestant, Catholic, and Jewish positions. "Democracy" apparently has its religions which fall under it as species fall under the genus of which they are part. And in this usage "democracy" is obviously a synonym for the American Way of Life.

3

THE SOCIAL SIGNIFICANCE OF ARCHITECTURE

Herbert Muller

No other art form rests so solidly upon a social basis as architecture. Its main purpose is to satisfy some social purpose: religious worship, entertainment, business, industry, or family life. In architecture both methods of construction and principles of design are determined to a large extent by function; great public buildings have always been structures where people have lived, worked, worshipped, or played together; and the city has been the place where great architecture has developed: the Parthenon in Athens, Solomon's Temple in Jerusalem, the Hagia Sophia in Constantinople, St. Peter's in Rome, the modern skyscraper in New York.

In the brief selection that we reprint from The Uses of the Past, *Herbert Muller describes the city as not only the center of civilization but the very source of its greatest achievement. Modern civilization is primarily industrial and urban, and the problems of the modern city have been produced by increasing industrialism and technological developments. Muller mentions most of the problems that are involved in city planning: the elimination of the slums, the growth of the suburb, the congestion of traffic, decentralization, and defense in a possible atomic war. By showing so clearly the significance of the city for a study of the humanities, Muller gives us a sound starting point from which to consider the relationship between city planning and human values.*

Herbert Muller is not an architect, a city planner, or even a sociologist; he is a professor of English at Purdue University. His earlier and later books deal with literary criticism: Modern Fiction *(1937),* Science and Criticism *(1943),* The Spirit of Tragedy *(1956). In* The Uses of the Past *(1952), however, Muller applied his liberal, humanistic, and critical approach to a study of past societies in order to find useful insights into our present conflict with totalitarianism. He is especially interested in treating more intelligently the confusion in our social philosophy produced by this conflict. A later selection from* The Uses of the Past *(see pp. 590-599 below) presents in some detail the thoughtful philosophy of history underlying this provocative book together with the personal philosophy to which Muller has been led through his study of literature and history.*

THE CITY AS CENTER AND SYMBOL

AMONG THE LITERARY tendencies of recent years has been the revolt against the City. The emancipated young writers of the twenties who scorned Main Street and the Bible Belt, flocking to Chicago or New York in search of freedom, art, and life, are now fleeing the city and celebrating the free, wholesome life of the village. This is an old story. The city has always bred a contempt for the peasant—the "villein," the hayseed, the yokel—and then bred weariness and disenchantment, a wistful idealization of the pastoral life. The modern industrial city has indeed blasted the landscape as has no other, achieving a unique drabness and ugliness; but for congestion, filth, noise, and mongrel disorder it is hardly worse than ancient Rome, medieval Paris, or Elizabethan London. And always we read the same complaints, of the vulgarity, the artificiality, the immorality and irreligion, the physical and spiritual squalor, the soullessness—the age-old follies and vices of Babylon, which in every age seem new. So the story is true, as far as it goes. The city is always vain and wicked enough to provoke the prophet of doom. "Wail, O inhabitants of the Mortar!"

Yet the old story is also superficial and vain—if we value civilization itself. *Civilization* means literally the making of cities and city life, and it is literally impossible without them. The village world has been relatively stable (at least until the Industrial Revolution) because of its inertia; what energy was left over from the labor of supporting life was spent in maintaining the ancient rites and customs, or resisting the new-fangled ones coming from without. The rise of the city has been the historic sign of a society on the march; it stimulated further adventure by bringing people together, pooling their efforts, promoting change by exchange, enlarging the world through contact with other peoples and cities. The great city became the center of unrest and disorder because it remained the center of creative activity. In time the poet or the philosopher might flee to the village (or more often the villa), but his very understanding and appreciation of nature were a product of the city; his work was inspired by it, addressed to it, circulated and preserved by it. Without London and Boston Thoreau could have had no Walden, or no spiritual interests to take there. Although civilization has always rested on the labor of the village world, its history is the history of Babylon, Jerusalem, Athens, Rome, Constantinople, Paris, London.

Even religion owes its highest achievements to the city. Simply because the village is conservative, orthodox, and pious, while the city is given to heresy and unrest, the higher religions have grown up in the cities. Thus Jesus, the Galilean, went to Jerusalem to enact the climactic scenes of his failure and his triumph. His Apostles spread the gospel in the cities of the Roman Empire. The first great churches were established in the great cities of Ephesus, Antioch, Alexandria, and Rome, which among other things were famous for their mobs, their luxury, and their vice. The bulk of the early converts to Christianity came from the despised city rabble. The last to be converted were the peasants or "pagani" —who in the backward sections of Christendom still worship pagan deities, under the guise of patron saints. The village remains the stronghold of the old-time religion, which may not be good enough for the future.

Hence we might discount somewhat the notorious evils of city life—the life that has always attracted the more ardent, enterprising spirits from the countryside. Its popularity is not due simply to the inducements of the big money. It is doubtful whether the ordinary city dweller is more grasping than the French peasant, say, or even the sturdy New Englander. Nor are his morals necessarily lower than the countryman's (apart from the later's rude mode of education in the facts of life). As Morris Cohen observed, the stabler *mores* of the village do not permit the freedom that may be abused in the city; yet stability is not the *summum bonum* and freedom is essential if morality is to be rational and responsible. Traditionalists are likely to deplore city life because they have something of the attitude of the small-town moralist.

The basic truth, however, is that the city is a symbol of both the best and the worst in civilization, and all the risks of its bold presumptions. It is open to a much wider world than the village, and walled off from the natural world; by its variety, bustle, and commotion it stirs new interests and aspirations, and weakens old faiths and natural pieties. As the political capital, the seat of rule and misrule, it launches the national adventures in statesmanship and conquest, and loses the victories or squanders the spoils. As the social capital, it is the school of grace, urbanity, intrigue, and frivolity, the arts of living and of living on others. As the cultural capital, the marketplace of ideas, it is the birthplace of new movements in art thought, which may mean regeneration or degeneration.

In the modern world the terms of this problem have been at once magnified and altered. All past societies were predominantly agricultural and rural. Even in the Greco-Roman world, which was conspicuously a city world, the bulk of the population were still peasants. Modern civilization is predominantly industrial and urban. The great majority of Americans live in or about the city; the big, sprawling, fast-growing city—Chicago, Cleveland, Detroit—is the most distinctive product of the Industrial Revolution. At the same time, industrialism has been radically transforming the ancient village world. Main Street has undergone a remarkable change within a generation, and is no longer isolated from the city, physically or spiritually; the hayseed or yokel survives only in the backwoods or on the vaudeville stage. And city life itself is being altered by the growth of the suburb. New means of transportation, in particular the automobile, have enabled increasing numbers to combine the advantages of the city with some of the advantages of the village. With this have come efforts at city planning and decentralization, which are still in their infancy but are potentially revolutionary.

In any event, it seems plain that the city is here to stay, at least as long as our civilization, even though it may have to go underground in the atomic age. The Southern agrarians of yesteryear, with their glorification of the gentleman farmer and the dignity of the life of the soil, were playing a variation on an ancient theme, in the usual minor key and to the usual negligible effect. We may hope to beautify the city, to eliminate its slums, to quarantine its worst diseases, to bring the country into it, to facilitate escape from it. Nevertheless, it remains indispensable to both the cultural and the commercial life of civilization.

Henry S. Churchill

Henry S. Churchill, a distinguished member of a group of civic-minded and socially conscious urban architects, was born in Chicago in 1893 and educated at Cornell University. He became a practicing architect in 1923, and since World War II has been particularly interested in city planning. As a member of the Architect's Advisory Committee of the federal Public Housing Authority, he has had an opportunity to influence political thinking about public housing, and as a private consultant he has done much to improve community planning in a number of American cities. His New York firm, Churchill Fulmer Associates, was for years one of the better known consultants in city planning. Less active at present, Churchill makes his home in Philadelphia.

Churchill believes that the city itself is an art form in which the over-all design enhances the architecture of individual buildings, giving them proper scale and relationship. He sees the design of a city as three dimensional; it is more than a two-dimensional ground plan and must always be people-oriented: a place where human beings live and work. Where politics and pure commercialism gain control, these human values are destroyed, as seen so clearly in the history of Philadelphia and Washington recounted here.

Like Herbert Muller, Churchill is well aware of the continuity of the social forces that bring about changes in the modern city, and he is also certain that we can learn a great deal from past civilizations about the forces at work in our own society. In the present selection he shows the essential relation, both social and esthetic, between a city and the kind of civilization that produces it. Old Peking, medieval Venice, Litchfield, Connecticut, and Williamsburg, Virginia, are among the cities he discusses. When they were built, these cities were eminently practical, but beautiful too. They are superb examples of the precept that in city planning form must follow function.

Although not primarily a writer, Churchill has expressed his strong convictions about architecture and city planning in numerous essays and professional journals. In The City Is the People *(1941) he brought together various essays that show his grasp of the whole problem of urban planning: its historical development, its present status, its future possibilities, and the social and human values involved. Our selection, taken from various parts of this volume, presents the larger humanistic scope of Churchill's ideas. As one reads this selection, it becomes increasingly evident that we are concerned here with an issue that properly belongs in a study of the humanities. Perhaps nowhere else do we find so clear an integration of the various aspects of modern life.*

THE CITY IS THE PEOPLE

1. *Antecedents*

WE ARE ON the threshold of a crucial era of change in the urban way of life. Vast disintegrating and destructive forces are loose in the world; but also, almost for the first time, there is a common consciousness that these forces can be turned to the constructive uses of the community. We are seeking new physical urban settings just as we are seeking new social and economic patterns.

[From Henry S. Churchill, *The City Is the People*, New York, Reynal and Hitchcock.

There is endless talk of "urban redevelopment," and "master planning," and "stopping the spread of blight," and "the process of decentralization." There is little understanding of the processes at work, of the historical continuity of our urbanism. "The more things change, the more they remain the same." The forces for change are relentless, the human aspirations remain the same. New forces are at work, which are incomprehensible except in terms of the past, if only for contrast, and are perhaps unpredictable on any score. The inability to predict should not make us fear understanding, rather it should make us seek it, for if we are to replan our cities we must know what it is that changes and why.

1

All the ancient cities were surrounded by walls for defense. The extent of the walls differed, depending on the type of site and the degree of power and wealth of the city, just as the material varied with the place, baked mud, fine brick, good stone, sometimes the palisaded fence. In hill towns the hill top was always the strong point, the sacred place. The lord spiritual or temporal lived there and the people clustered around his stronghold. If the city grew great and strong, the walls were enlarged: Athens, Rome, Toledo are cases in point.

On the hill or on the plain, dominated by church or by castle, the wall was the determining factor of the city plan. It made crowded living a necessity, except for a few of the rich and powerful. The restricted number of gates set the street pattern; this pattern was designed to make penetration difficult even if the gates were battered down. The streets were planned with off-sets, they were not intended to go directly from gate to gate or to the center of the city or the strong place. Often these irregularities led to space relations of charm and beauty. They invited three-dimensional groupings of subtlety, sudden conclusions of form of great power.

Peking is one of the great city plans,* a unit of manifold variety of parts, a pattern as intricate as the design of an ancient bronze, and as well ordered and composed. Peking was planned for Kubla Khan in the middle of the thirteenth century, and Marco Polo has left a highly ornate and vivid account of it, as strange and ornate as Coleridge's dream. He was enormously impressed, as well he might be, for in his day nothing like it existed in Europe. The basic order and good sense of its layout has persisted, although a good deal of the grandeur and orderliness has succumbed to time and war. Here is the superblock—the main thoroughfares making traffic-free islands of dwellings, infinite variety within a rectilinear frame. Here too is great monumentality—the long and splendid approach, through the gates of the Chinese city, flanked by the Temples of Heaven and Earth, to the gates of the Tartar City, and on in increasing splendor to the Forbidden City, the Palace of the Emperor, and the final climax of the great altar on the highest point. Peking was designed in three dimensions—the two-storied palaces, the towers, the gates, all placed for definite effect, their gold tiles shining over the dull roofs of the ordinary one-story houses.

The medieval cities were full of drama—you stepped from the dark of the filthy side street, the houses almost touching overhead, into the wider main street, and there, ahead but not head on, was the spire of the cathedral; before you reached it, the market square opened for you, or around a corner was the guild hall. In Venice† you came from a dingy alley out under an archway into the Piazza San Marco suddenly, or else the approach was from the sea, marked from afar by the exclamation point of the

* See Figure 1.
† See Figure 2.

Campanile, the great Byzantine gem of San Marco itself scarcely to be seen until approached by foot, shielded by the side-way approach through the Piazzetta, heralded by the Palace of the Doges. The eye never grows weary, the spirit never flags, as one walks in Perugia or Rothenberg, Salamanca, Salisbury, or Bourges; and this is not because of the architecture alone, but because the plan enhances the architecture, gives it scale and relationship, dramatizes it, and places new values and new accents on it. There was always emphasis, focus, even in the meanest villages dominated by the meanest lords. . . . It was not by accident that as society outgrew the central donjon and replaced it by the central church, that the church took the high place. Great care was taken that nothing should compete with it. The walls and towers of defense, the mansions of the rich, the lesser places of worship, the mass of houses, all were carefully subordinated to the climax.

2

None of the cities of America were medieval, none were ever walled in, in the sense that Carcassonne was walled. From the beginning our cities were open cities, mercantile cities, free cities. Defense was only incidental, wooden palisades against the Indians.

For this reason the colonial towns show a pattern quite different from anything to be found in Europe. It is true that New Amsterdam and Charleston showed vestigial traces of the European defense pattern, but Wall Street soon became a name and the bastions of Charleston didn't last long.

In the North, except for the coastal cities, the economy was primarily agricultural, the social life limited and simple. The emphasis was on a correct attitude towards God and a shrewd one toward your neighbor, the right to own land and to share in political activity and, gradually, to enrich life by education and the acquisition of goods from England and the Orient. The plans of all these cities centered around the common; beyond that, old roads and topography influenced their layout most.

The small towns, particularly the "hill towns," developed a quite different esthetic, of which Litchfield, Connecticut, is a superb but by no means isolated example. Litchfield was founded in 1720 as an offshoot of Hartford. It was planned. There were sixty parcels of fifteen acres each, and the purchasers drew lots for their choice. The minister and the schoolmaster were assigned twenty additional acres each. These splendid sites had an average street frontage of about five hundred feet; the main streets were three hundred and forty feet and two hundred and sixty-four feet wide, with deep grass borders and elm trees on each side, a stately setting. The houses, of course, were all one-family homes, starting modestly enough and growing into exquisite examples of wood architecture. Each house was a single thing, to be seen as such, with its trees, its white fences, its garden. The fifteen acres were eventually subdivided, but Litchfield itself did not grow so large as to lose its sense of space. It is this conception of the individual house on its own lot, unrelated except in spirit to the neighbors, that is the essence of the American city plan, however perverted it became.

In the South, things were somewhat different. Instead of a democratic, farming organization, it was aristocratic, tenant, and plantation-owning. The focus was not on the town meeting and the church, but on the governor and his little house of Lords, and the church was the Church of England. This difference is apparent in a different emphasis in the plan of cities. The southern tradition, in the main, derived from the tradition of the great baronial park and the formality associated with the aristocratic court. Williamsburg shows this clearly, with its fine axis closed by the Capitol at one end and the College of William and Mary at the other, its carefully placed Governor's Palace on a strong but minor axis, and the studied relation of the secondary streets and open spaces.* It is a plan of exquisite relationships, a miniature, humanly scaled "grand plan." What happened to it between colonial times and the recent restoration is an example of all that has been wrong with our civil development. The main street was cluttered with shacks and shops, filling stations and roadside stands, without regard to building lines or order; the back streets deteriorated and the properties were subdivided and built upon without control. Fortunately the basic framework was so strong and fine that it was possible to restore it, and although the restoration may have its elements of preciousness, nevertheless it brought back to us the finest example of small-town planning this country has produced.

Philadelphia† was another story; Penn was shrewd and sharp, and he saw in the broad reaches of the Delaware the great outlet of his principality. He (or rather his surveyor, Thomas Holme) laid out the City of Brotherly Love stretching from the Delaware to the Schuylkill in a hard rectangular pattern, the first of our gridiron cities, the first laid out with a cold eye for speculative profit. The blocks were large, about 400 feet square, and the streets, with the exception of Market and Broad, were none too wide. The blocks proved unwieldy, there was too much inaccessible center land, and they were eventually split down the middle by alleys, which have been a detriment to the city ever since. The plan is quite unimaginative, but it was prophetic. Every block was just as good as any other, except, of course, for the commercial advantage of the Delaware frontage. The city was divided by Broad and Market, at right angles to each other, with a little park or "square" in each quadrant, and a good-sized one at the intersection. The latter provided the only possible focal point anywhere, and so was sensibly chosen, eventually, for the site of the city hall. Philadelphia has, of course, more than justified Penn's foresight and faith in its industrial and commercial importance; it still suffers, as a place in which to live or work, from the aridity of his plan.

Here comment must be made on what is the most famous of all our city plans, that of Washington, D. C.,* which, as everyone knows, was the creation of Major L'Enfant, with the assistance of one of the first great surveyors and speculators, Washington himself.

Basically the plan of Washington is alien to America. The idea of a new capital city was only agreed upon after Philadelphia and other places had been found politically unacceptable. Jefferson probably understood only too well how little either Philadelphia or New York had to offer in the way of satisfactory physical setting. Philadelphia today proves how right he was; and New York by the end of the Revolution was already sprouting germs of the 1811 plan in the 10th Ward—the present Lower East Side approximately—and in the suburb of Greenwich Village. Jefferson was enamoured of Paris—Paris, even then the city of regal vistas, the candles on the straight lines of chestnut trees lighting the way in spring for processions and stately equipages. He probably knew, too, that in the ancient side streets the mass of people lived in dank and festering squalor. For Jefferson the new capital of the New World was to be all avenues and vistas and no slums; for General Washington and the boys it was to

* See Figure 3.
† See Figure 4.

* See Figure 5.

be all profit. Neither expectation was fulfilled.

Considering that the site was a political compromise, that it was largely a malarial swamp, palmed off on the federal government by astute speculators, L'Enfant's conception was truly magnificent and far seeing. How far seeing it was is clear when it is understood that for well over a hundred years it was not only unrealized but seemed unrealizable. For over a century Washington was a lot of muddy, unpaved streets; even Pennsylvania Avenue was sparsely lined by squalid shacks and dingy business buildings. The Mall was full of the Pennsylvania Railroad, the Capitol stood in splendid isolation on the Hill, and what there was of the city clustered around the executive end of the town—the White House, State, and Treasury—spreading out along Sixteenth Street, overflowing eventually into Massachusetts Avenue and along Rock Creek.

All this was contrary to L'Enfant's idea. He thought the Capitol would be the center, with natural residential growth on the high land. He faced the Capitol that way. But fancy speculation in land, together with the social pull of the executive mansion, turned the city around. It is only in recent years that the plan has been filled out in all its quadrants.

L'Enfant's original plan had many virtues some of which were modified in Ellicott's revision. Ellicott was a surveyor under L'Enfant, the "practical" man probably, and it is his version of the plan, both published and executed, which is often confused with L'Enfant's. Aside from the famous diagonal avenue-rectilinear street pattern, L'Enfant's great idea was the Capitol—Potomac axis, with the executive mansion on a shorter subaxis at right angles to it, much like the plan of Williamsburg. Unlike the Williamsburg scheme, he further connected the Capitol and the executive mansion along the third side of the triangle by Pennsylvania Avenue. It was a grandiose plan, completely lacking in scale and impossible of visual success. Nevertheless, it was a unified conception until Andrew Jackson ruined it by placing the Treasury directly across the Avenue. This was the crowning point of the civic ignominy of the civically debased nineteenth century; at no other point in the history of urbanism could such a structure as the White House have been flanked by such things as Treasury and State.

Still more serious was the failure to develop any fine focus of national activity together with an appropriate architectural setting. The lack of focus was not remedied by the famous Macmillan Commission, which, under Theodore Roosevelt, was given the task of rescuing the L'Enfant plan from the neglect and spoilation of the intervening years. It did do an essential and important job of getting the railroad out of the Mall, thus restoring some measure of integrity to that vast space, and redrafting the plan to provide not only for the exigencies of the Union Station, but also working out new sites for public improvements, the Tidal Basin, the Memorial Bridge between Washington and Arlington, and other such monumental features. It failed, understandably, to overcome the essential lack of scale in the original plan. The lining of buildings on each side of the Mall is ineffective; the width is too great. It is too long and cannot be held together the way the Champs Élysées is held together and terminated by the Arc de Triomphe at one end and the Louvre at the other. The Capitol, moreover, fails completely as a focus from any angle, and the other government buildings, the Senate and House offices, for which it is the dominating structure on paper are without relation to it in fact.

Downtown, the development of the Triangle, an inadequate space stuffed with pompous building by pompous architects, is neither functional nor monumental. From the civic art point of view it is simply terrible. There is no architectural emphasis nor architectural unity. The columnar treatment of the buildings is merely dull, and as each building is slightly different, the unity of Bath or the Rue de Rivoli is not achieved either. The enormous concentration of clerical workers in a small space, without any provision for parking in proportion to their numbers, is inexcusable. Although the Macmillan Commission could not have foreseen this need, its plan could have been modified as the need became evident. It is not only in wartime that Washington lacks organization, the lack is inherent in its diffuse and unfocused plan, the impossibility of making its two-dimensional grandeur apparent as three-dimensional reality.

II. *Problems and Trends*

The problems which need to be resolved in the remaking of our cities are complex, and particularly so in a democracy where full play is given to the many counter currents of special interests which are its life blood. There have been no examples of city replanning in the few democratically governed states of the past, so that we today must guide ourselves not by the precedent of Nero, Sixtus V, and Haussmann, but by the method of trial, error, and reconciliation.

Basically our difficulties are physical, due to too rapid growth and to extraordinary industrial and scientific developments in the last hundred and fifty years. A hundred and fifty years ago—five short generations—the total population of the United Kingdom was only 15,200,000, of London 959,000, of Paris 553,000, of New York City 60,000. In 1942 the count was United Kingdom, 47,889,000; Greater London, 8,200,000; Greater Paris, 4,900,000; New York City (the five boroughs), 7,455,000. It is not to be wondered that the problems of physical planning are immense and unsolved. Nor have economics, law, or the quasi-sciences of sociology and government kept abreast of the times, and their failure to do so complicates and delays physical action in city replanning.

The specific problems which cities face vary, of course, from city to city, but nevertheless there is a broad pattern common to three categories of cities, which roughly may be classified as the small city, the big city, and the megalopolis. These problems are of three kinds: physical, economic, social, and each centers around three major factors: (1) habitation, working facilities, traffic; (2) land values, service costs, taxation; (3) child raising, health and recreation, social satisfactions.

1

Physical problems are, as has been said, an inheritance of unregulated, overoptimistic, and speculative growth. The older residential portions of the city suffer from overcrowding of the land and lack of organized open spaces for common or private use. In many instances this is not the result of too high densities of population so much as just plain bad use of land—too many streets, too many alleys, too much building coverage, not enough playground. The gridiron pattern contributes to this, with its lack of differentiation between traffic needs of various intensity and speed and its failure to provide satisfactory variation in sites and locations for different uses of land. In New York City, for instance, 35.55 percent of the land is in streets, whereas 25 percent would be fully sufficient. In Chicago, the great depth of the standard block forced deep, narrow building lots and back alleys.

At the same time, vast areas of the business portion of most cities are empty—devoted to parking lots, or to a solitary "dining car," or to junk yards. Stores are empty, loft buildings are deserted.

The actual working facilities are also important. The industrial plants of many cities are obsolete, so are a great part of the business and commercial structures. Consider any "Main Street," the stores have had their faces lifted by "modern" fronts, but the second, third (and often more) stories above are run down and dingy. There is, everywhere, too much business area. One can name principal streets in almost any city, Camden's Broadway, Cleveland's Euclid, Buffalo's Delaware, Main Street anywhere, vast sections of New York, Philadelphia, Boston.

The skyscraper fad also did much harm to the business centers of cities. Aside from the extreme examples, few of which have paid their way (according to the Urban Land Institute there are about five hundred buildings over twenty stories in height in the United States, none of which has been successful financially), the crop of lesser skyscrapers has brought financial disaster to the surrounding properties.

Integration of work and living rarely exists. In general, the present zoning laws, designed to "protect" high-class residential neighborhoods, prevent any adequate attempts at solving the problem. Such zoning is designed to keep land uses in separate categories by progressive exclusion—that is, starting from an undifferentiated area permitting any use, various classes of industry, business, etc., are excluded until the Simon-pure single-family-house district is reached. Under this system of classification, which usually calls for rigid and inflexible mapping, it is very difficult to plan integrated neighborhoods or communities.

Lack of integration is responsible for a good part of the traffic difficulties which beset city and nation—difficulties in the movement of people and of goods. This problem has been the one most vigorously attacked everywhere, but the attack has been without much effect because the basic plan has been untouched. The traffic planner who takes traffic counts and then recommends a series of street widenings and lights and intersection remodelings is like a doctor who takes bloodcounts and then recommends an old-fashioned bleeding as a remedy for arteriosclerosis. Solution must be by way of complete diagnosis; railroads, markets, docks, airports, congested areas, and recreational areas must be brought into some kind of proper relation with each other, the lines of future growth plotted, and controls put into effect. The design of streets and highways does not make sense unless the land use along them, and at their terminations, is strictly regulated to suit the type and kind of traffic for which they are designed.

The coming of the cheap car, the subsidizing of the automobile business through the building of vast networks of paved roads—first macadam, then concrete, first two lanes, then three, then four or more—made the accommodation of this traffic a naturally primary concern of cities and towns. Streets were widened, bypasses provided, municipal parking lots established. All to no avail, because the problem was only partially thought through. The new arteries immediately became choked, because the secondary routes were deemed unsatisfactory or difficult by the traveling public, and because the easier it was made to get some place else, the more people wanted to go. "Sunday driving" as a phenomenon can be explained rationally only one way—the places people live in are so unpleasant almost any discomfort of hot and crowded roads seems better, their recreational opportunities and inner resources are so slight and so poor that movement of any kind any place is at least one degree more tolerable than "staying put."

Trucking also brought new problems. In the cities loading and unloading created congestion in industrial areas, just as parking clogged circulation in business districts. In the small towns the trucks created a monstrous hazard, particularly in "one street" towns and villages which had grown naturally along a highway. The towns could, and did, institute some measure of police control, but the villages became mere points on a high speedway. In both cases, once pleasant and often beautiful residential sections were ruined. Tourist cabins, tourist homes, "motels," filling stations, cheap eating places and roadside stands took the place of the once decent homes and of the old trees that were ruthlessly cut down to provide an additional traffic lane.

The airplane is bringing new problems. Where should airfields be located in relation to residential areas, industry and other shipping facilities such as railroad freight yards? As yet there are no clear answers indicated, because the airplane is in the process of development, and we do not know what the future will bring. All that can be done is to provide facilities for the immediate present, knowing full well that mistakes will be made of the same kind that were made in the early days of the railroads. The plane of today bears the same relation to the plane of tomorrow that the locomotive of the 1850s bore to the electric or diesel giant of today. The early railroads brought problems of noise, smoke, and danger at crossings which have only been eliminated as technical developments have been made and capital invested. The airplane of today is insufferably noisy and the landing fields required are too big in proportion to the commerce. Nevertheless, the situation must be met as it exists, even if it proves to be all wrong in twenty years. Physical planning cannot anticipate unprecedented developments in other technics.

2

In the broad sense, neither physical nor economic planning has any meaning except in reference to social objectives. These objectives are, or should be, a city in which children can be raised and educated to become healthy, decent human beings; in which it is possible to earn a "living wage" with reasonable prospects of security; in which the amenities of life, social intercourse, amusement, recreation, and cultural advantages are procurable. It is not an Utopian ideal, by any means—many towns in the past and some in the present have approached it. The fact is, most people do not want a great deal of anything, nor have they fancy standards. A clean house, with room for family life, and privacy, a bit of ground for the children, or adequate community playgrounds; a good school; a steady job that will feed, house, clothe, and doctor the family; the neighborhood movie, bowling alley, saloon; and the libraries, museums, theaters, or what not somewhere in the center of things. That is for the everyday living of the backbone of the city; the bright lights, the crowds, the tension of the market place, the intensity of metropolitan life with its luxury are only centers, not their reality. They may be what attract people to the big show of the big metropolis; they are what makes the little man puff out his chest and call his cousin from Littleburg a hick; they are what brings in the tourists and wastrels, but they are not what keeps a city going, and certainly not the towns.

The opportunity to exchange work, merchandise, and ideas, these are primary to the concept of a city. It is the scale on

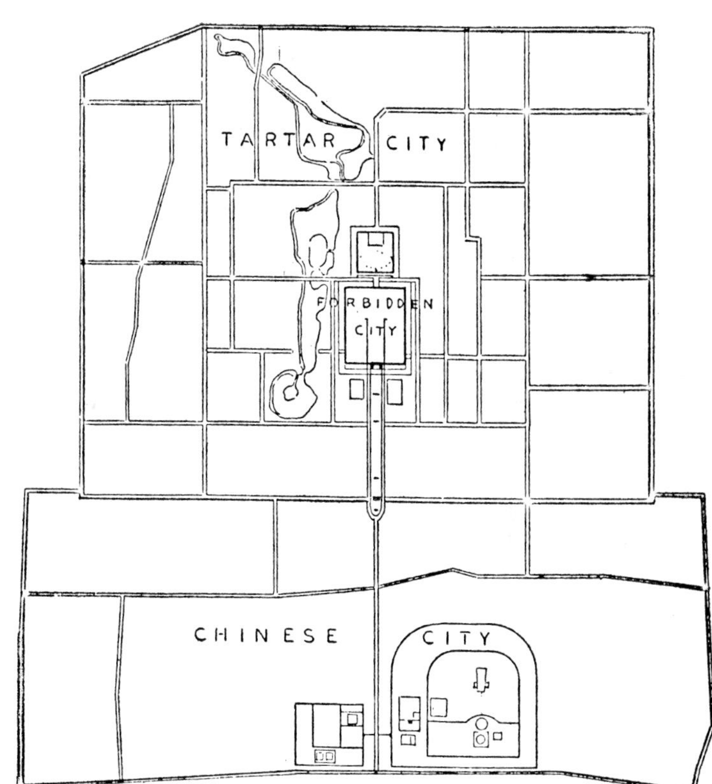

1 (*right*). Peking, plan of en-city showing main streets and approach.

2 (*below*). Piazza San Marco, ice.

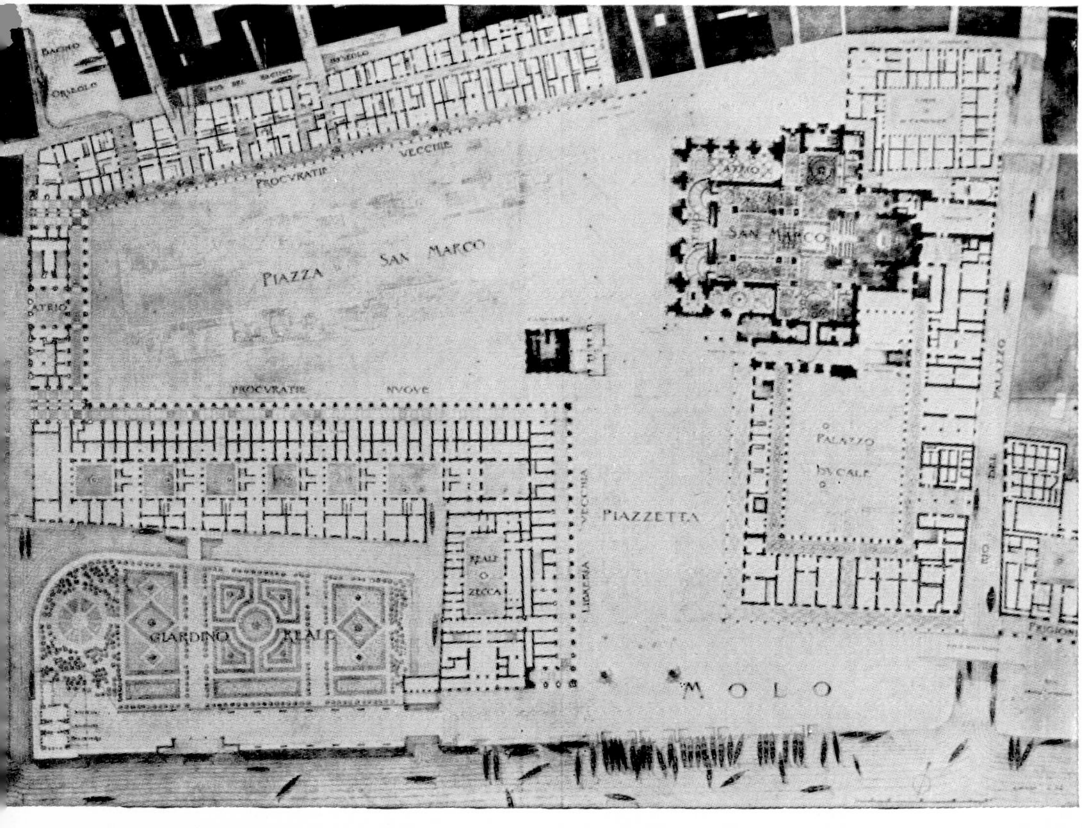

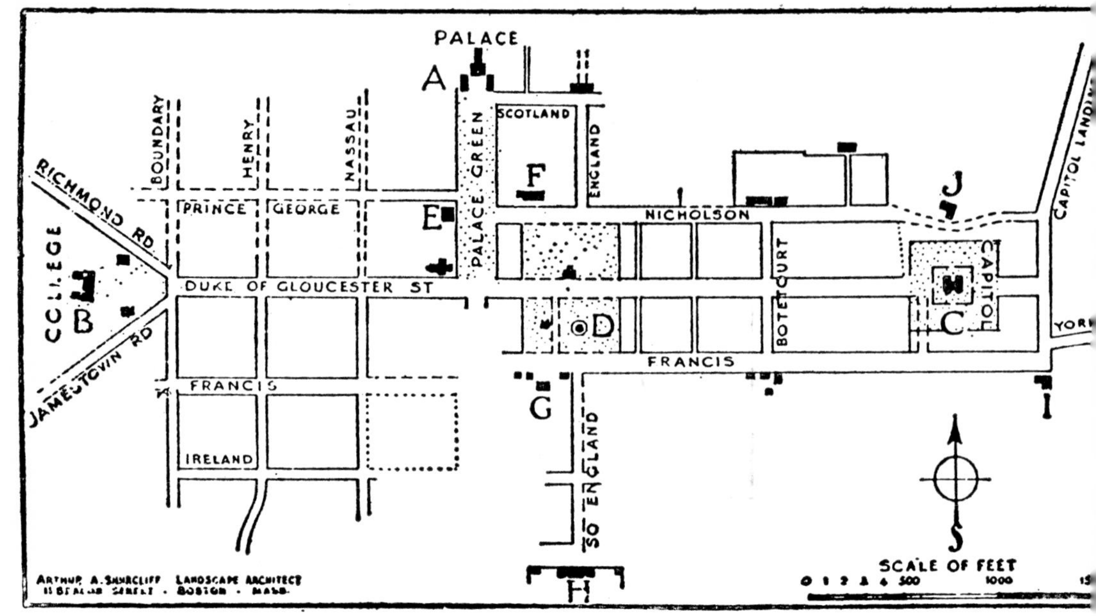

Fig. 3 (*above*). Williamsburg, Virginia, plan. The Grand Plan scaled down to human livin

Fig. 4 (*below*). Philadelphia, the Holme plan of 1683.

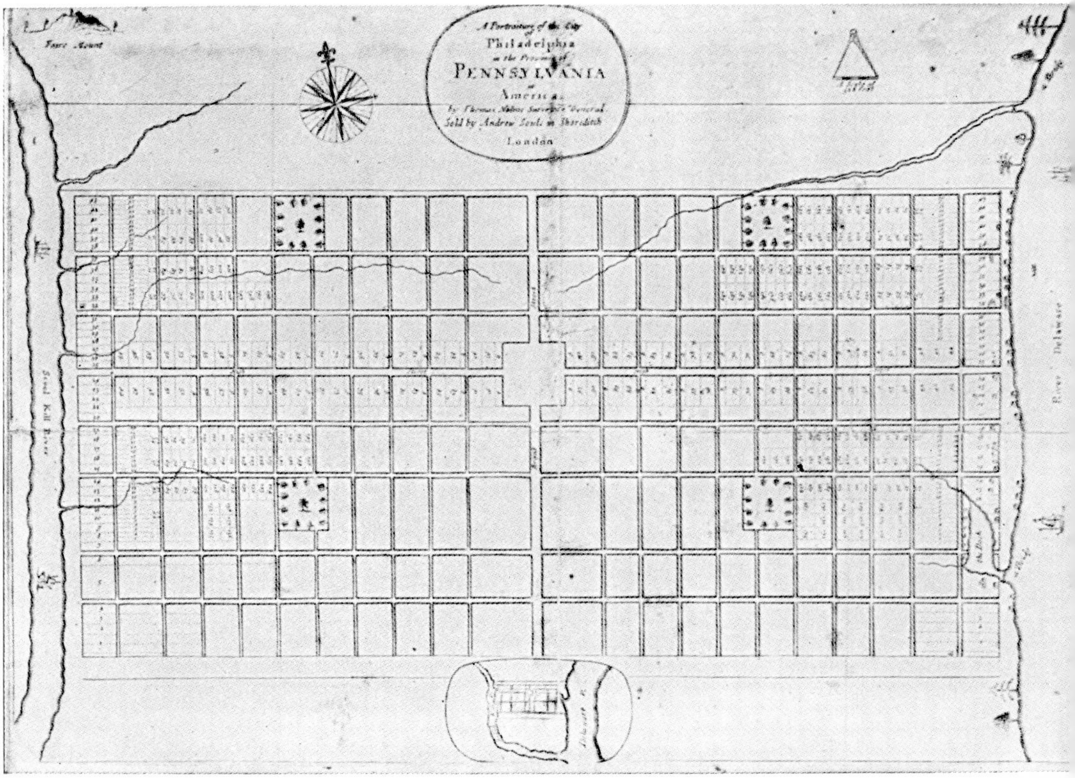

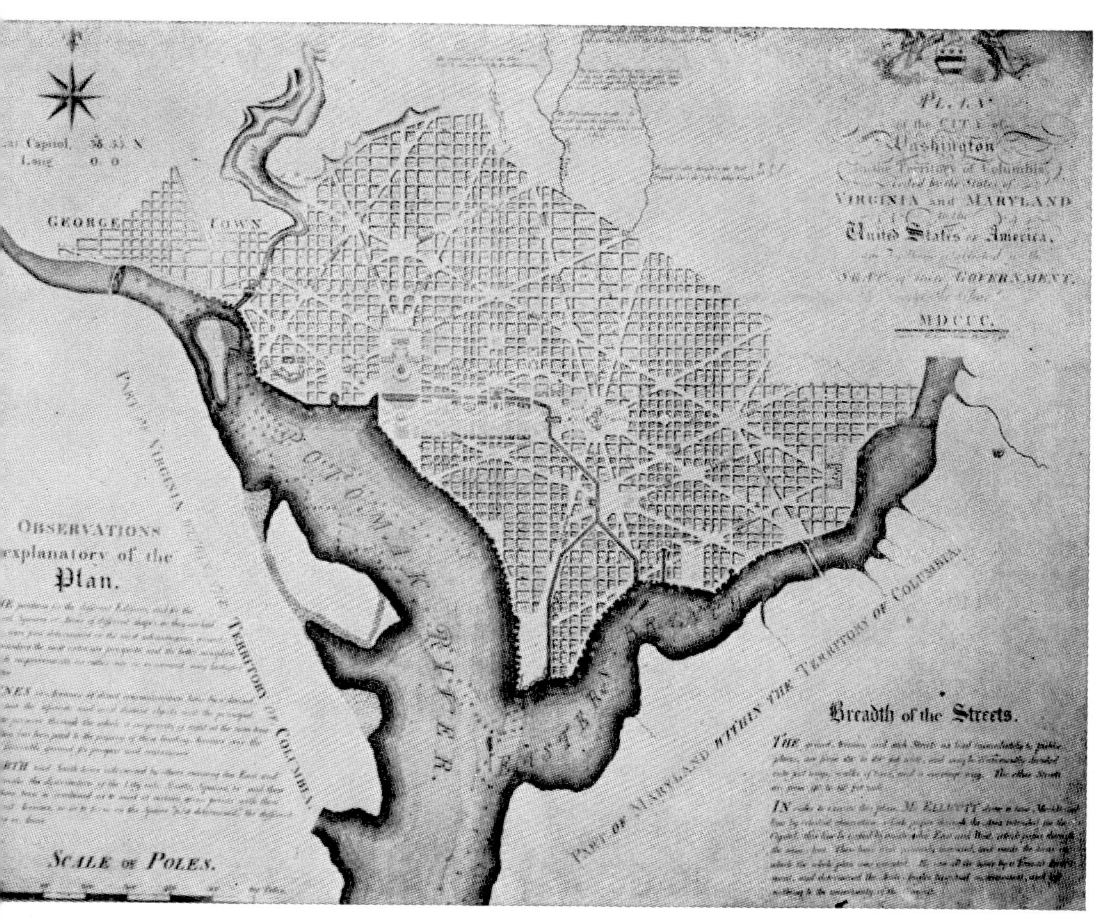

FIG. 5. Washington, D. C., 1800, the Ellicott version of the L'Enfant plan.

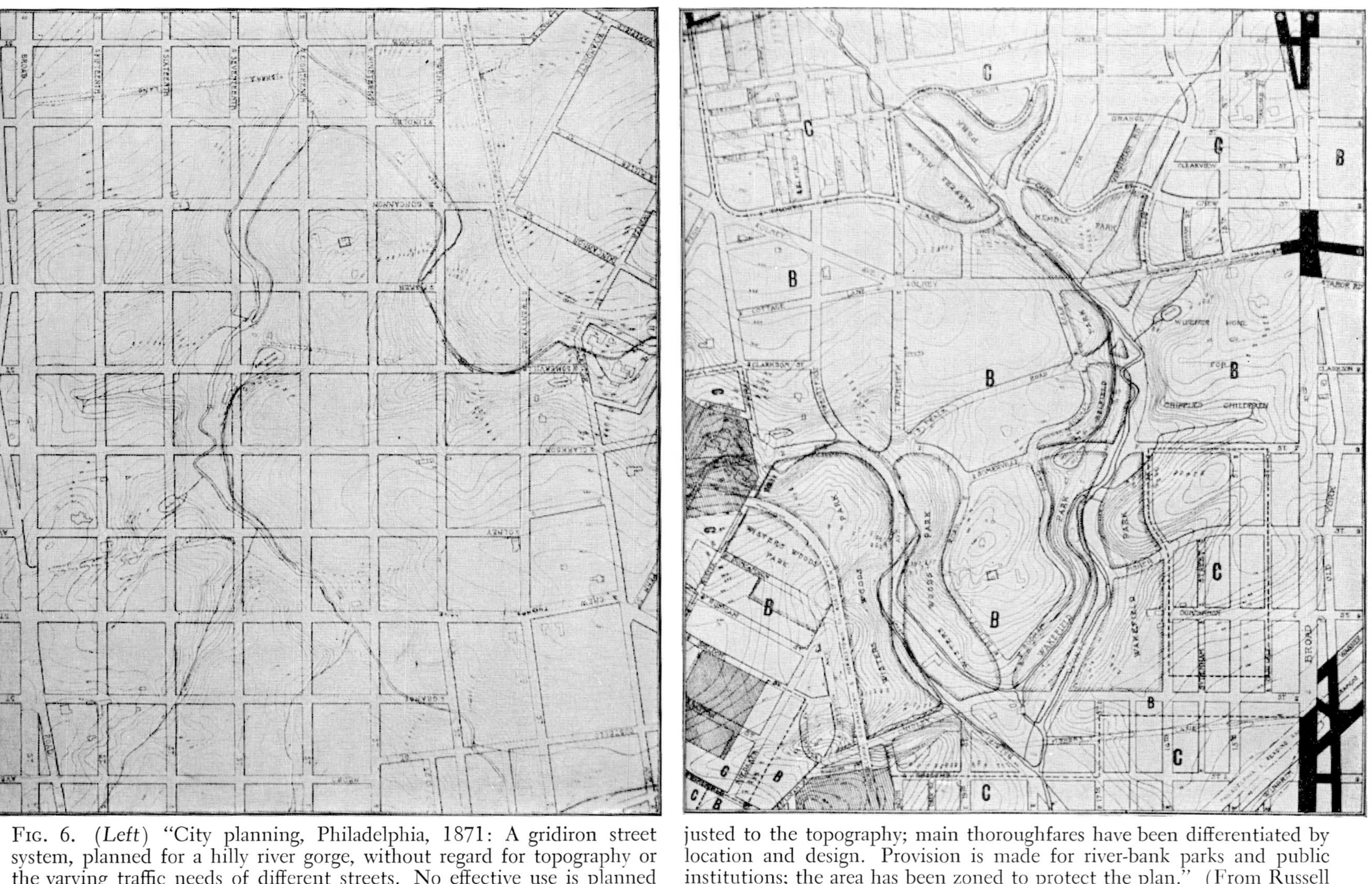

FIG. 6. (*Left*) "City planning, Philadelphia, 1871: A gridiron street system, planned for a hilly river gorge, without regard for topography or the varying traffic needs of different streets. No effective use is planned for the stream banks; some of the streets could not possibly be built." justed to the topography; main thoroughfares have been differentiated by location and design. Provision is made for river-bank parks and public institutions; the area has been zoned to protect the plan." (From Russell Van Nost Black, *Plans for the Small American City* as reprinted in *The*

which these things are humanly possible that has been lost sight of, and which must be restored.

Nor, in considering the social aspects, problems and objectives of the city should its esthetic qualities be forgotten. It is fashionable to sneer at the City Beautiful, it is fashionable to talk about city planning in terms of the cold, hard facts of economic impossibilities, in terms of pseudoscientific approaches to density or to cost of services, or in terms of fatuous assumptions derived from highly dubious surveys. The planner or architect who whispers about doing something merely because it would be beautiful and delightful simply sticks his neck right under the knife.

There is no use evading the question. Our cities, any and all, are at best glorifications of the ungracious. The gridiron plan will permit of nothing else, and the "civic centers" are mere agglomerations of diverse buildings. Separately beautiful buildings, unrelated spacially, do not make a beautiful city nor a beautiful civic center. One need only look at Foley Square in New York to see the truth of this dictum—it is the most revolting ugly public "square" in the world, and probably the most expensive. Copley Square in Boston is another example, though of a different order. There the contrast and interest in McKim's Library and Richardson's Trinity Church are damaged by the dull fronts of the Huntington Avenue stores and houses and by the incongruous mass of the Copley Plaza Hotel. Washington, which had opportunities, has been botched by the incompetence of the architectural profession in civic art. Philadelphia, New York since 1811, Cleveland, Denver, Los Angeles, Chicago, Fort Wayne, all those designed for speculation in land, never had a chance.

That the difference between the beautiful and the ugly, the delightful and the squalid, the varied and the monotonous, has important psychological effect is a commonplace, except in the field of city planning. If it be not quoting the Devil for Scripture, Nietzsche has written: "All that is ugly weakens and afflicts man. It reminds him of deterioration, of danger, of impotence. He actually suffers loss of power by it. The effect of ugliness can be measured by the dynamometer. Whenever man is depressed, he has a sense of the proximity of something ugly. His sense of power, his will to power, his courage, his pride—they decrease with the ugly, they increase with the beautiful." All his words have been confirmed by the more solemn, if no more convincing, studies of Ph.D.'s. But to date there has not been any study of the relation of physical monotony and positive squalor to crime, nor of the subconscious effect upon civic pride of mere loveliness of environment. When a beautiful parkway or an esthetically satisfying subdivision comes into being, ninety-nine times out of a hundred it is, as the movies say, purely coincidental.

The purposeful esthetic qualities of medieval towns have been described; every traveler is aware of them, and calls them "picturesque," mistakenly. The Piazza San Marco, the Plaza Major of Salamanca, the Places de la Cathedrale of innumerable French towns—Albi, Bourges, Chartres—the market places of England and Belgium, these are deliberate, dynamic designs. And later, when the Renaissance brought back the concept of static symmetry, the great axial plans opened on a mountain, the sea, a fine colonnade or building, or groups of buildings, or else when long and extended the avenue itself became the view, the trees closing in always beyond, until at the end of long travel a turn or a closure of permanency brought it to an end. The minor axes were carefully proportioned and the buildings were meticulously studied for placing, form and height. In other words, it was three-dimensional and consequently architectural planning. In typical gridiron planning the axis has degenerated into a series of parallel lines without emphasis, leading to a garbage dump, a slum, or an empty space.

This does not mean one must have either the "grand plan" or the sinusoidal street. It merely means taking care and thought in relation to topography: giving variety in the type and size of street, whether arterial highway, business thoroughfare, straight or curved or dead-end residential street; seeing that there is uniformity of architecture and planting within the confines of each, permitting variation from street to street; that open places and public structures are placed with an eye for their effect on their surroundings and each other. It means, above all, three-dimensional thinking. The ground plan of a city, no matter how fine, is completely meaningless to the person walking through it unless it is also expressed in the third dimension. The ground plan controls only the great general movements of people and things; the particular development of the particular street or square is what makes the city pleasant or unpleasant, and this means not so much control of the architecture of individual buildings as it does control of bulk, skyline, and placing.

It must become part of the social aspect of city replanning that the esthetic of it, the relation of spaces to each other and to the buildings that form the spaces, is admitted to be as important to health and welfare as sewers and playgrounds. *

3

Actually, the cities face two great planning problems: how to restore livability and financial soundness to their cores; how to develop the peripheral land so as to maintain a sound balance with the centers and prevent overexpansion and undue neighborhood obsolescence. [See Fig. 6.]

There has been emerging, in recent years, a theory of planning which has something of a common denominator for both urban redevelopment and peripheral expansion. This is the "neighborhood unit," which is much bruited about. The term has pretty well lacked definition, and is used indiscriminately for a *physical* neighborhood, a *social* neighborhood, a *school* neighborhood, and an *administrative* neighborhood. It rarely occurs that all of these are identical. . . . Perhaps the word "neighborhood" is an unfortunate one because of its connotations and overtones. "Planning area" would have been better for it could include, without cavil, industrial areas, business areas, residential areas, or mixtures of them. The true, social neighborhood would be a subarea within the larger one. The ideal planning area might be set up as a political-educational unit, in which the voting district (for the local legislative body), the school district, police and fire precinct, census tract, health district, and other administrative elements would be coterminous and delimited by through traffic routes, parkways, or natural geographic features. The French *arrondissement* is something of the sort, and the English idea of "precinct planning" is similar.

Many, if not all cities, have some universally recognized "neighborhoods." These are natural "planning areas" and should be retained. The County of London plan shows how such areas are being made use of in the proposed replanning of Greater London. The application of planning area control to the peripheries of cities and to subdivisions both within the city limits and in adjoining counties would do much to prevent a repetition of the damage done by uncontrolled development after World War I.

* Incidentally, why are all city playgrounds so drear and bleak, so bald, wobegone, and desolate? They are as bare and functional as the inside of a toilet bowl.

The neighborhoods, or living areas, within the planning areas, should be of the latest type—free from through traffic, arranged for the easy use of their inhabitants for getting children to school and letting them play, for access to shopping, and with facilities for the proper functioning of democratic government by public meetings, and democratic recreation in parks and playgrounds, and with facilities for the enjoyment of such things as music, books, and other hobbies for those who want them either as audience or as participant.

Nor is there any reason why these developments should be as drab and generally unhappy as we are accustomed to seeing them. The location and general type and scale of groups of public structures—schools, shops, service and municipal buildings, churches, and so on—should be predetermined and rigorously controlled. In the case of very important squares the height of adjacent structures within sight-lines should carefully and definitely be determined. In closely built-up sections, some control of dwellings also might be desirable, again not as to architectural "style," but as to general broad requirements of scale and relation to the street and, in the case of row houses, material. As has been pointed out again and again, monotony is not a function of repetition only, but of disorder. An example of how this can be avoided and pleasant variety achieved at no cost at all is shown in the plan of the World War I town of Hilton, Virginia. Other well-known examples of variety through careful study of the street plan and the relation of structures are Hampstead Garden Suburb by Sir Raymond Unwin, and Römerstadt by Ernst May. There are many others, of course.

4

Finally, there is the greatest of all centrifugal pressures—defense against warfare from the air. The destruction of cities in the present war is only a prelude to the destruction that will be possible in World War III. The only possible protection is scattering of industry, buildings, people. This is of a piece with the other forces making for decentralization. True, there are some "industrial designers" who foresee cities of tunnels and caves, air-conditioned, efficiently lighted, violet-rayed, sprayed with the faint nostalgic scent of automobile exhausts and pervaded by soft music, and inspiring oratory from loud speakers. Interurban communication, when physically necessary, will be either by rocket planes into the carefully blacked-out empyrean, or by traveling a hundred miles an hour over express roads which will be completely enclosed by glass block and controlled by radar. Somehow, the dispersion pattern seems easier although less romantic.

It seems probable, in the light of the various forces at work, that the forms of cities may undergo radical changes which will be more far reaching in nature than any they have undergone in the long historical past. This will not, of course, be true for all cities, any more than it has been for many of the most ancient ones now still existing. There are cities which are many hundreds of years old which are virtually unchanged. People live and die in them and the daily routines of life go on much as they did when the world was new and all. This is not true and cannot be true of cities whose reason for being is the industrial technology of the modern world. Nor is there any city so remote as to be outside the current of world war. They must change to meet the new facts that face them. What is so difficult, what makes adjustment so difficult and planning so imperative, is the rate of change. The world of flight and electronics is upon us, and there is little time for the honored process of evolution. Our future is a revolutionary one, and it must be planned revolution or it will be confusion, if not chaos.

There have been a good many attempts to reveal the form of the future city. Most of these have failed to take into consideration the persistence of the past or the tenacity of human habit. And yet since as Blake has said, "Everything possible to be believed is an image of truth," it will be well to pause and consider.

There is Le Corbusier's belief that life will be mechanized on a completely rational basis: "La Ville Radieuse," the stately rows of skyscrapers, the well-organized open spaces, the direct lines of communication, the dehumanizing of existence, the complete lack of humor characteristic of the authoritarian process. The Radiant City would be splendid and heartless, the lights Kleig lights, the radiance that of false dawn. Yet in part it is a viable concept—there is no reason why the skyscraper should be scrapped because it has been abused; it provides a way of life, and Le Corbusier has shown the possibilities of achieving it if anyone cares for it.

There is Frank Lloyd Wright's Broadacre City, the belief of a man who believes in democracy the way Jefferson believed in it. It roots back into the oldest American tradition—a house and a substantial piece of land for everyone who wants it. Privacy and neighborliness, elbow room and easy access to the communal needs and facilities, exquisite organization, beauty beyond our desert. Perhaps it is because he has expressed so clearly and simply the average American's dream that his concept has been so mocked by the high priests. Yet it most surely is an image of truth, Keats' as well as Blake's.

It is not the purpose of this book to forecast form. Form follows function, as Louis Sullivan said, and the form may have many expressions. It does not concern us here whether the form of the tree that gives the shade is that of oak or maple or elm; the essential function with which we are concerned is the function of the city as a place in which people live.

Russell Lynes

In our discussion of the city, attention has been given thus far to the relation of building to building, to the three-dimensional aspect of the city as an architectural form, and to the problems of city planning. For a fuller view of the social significance of architecture, private houses and their contents should be examined and the taste of their owners noted. What better place to look for this aspect of architecture is there than in "suburbia," the home of the "organization man," where the fads and fashion in American taste are freely expressed! In The Tastemakers *Russell Lynes has done just such a study. This book is a popular history of American taste, with particular emphasis upon the place of art in American life. Lynes is impressed by the fantastic complexity and diversity of American taste, its frequent high artistic quality, its conspicuous waste, and its mass mediocrity. The selection, "Suburbia in Excelsis," which we reprint from Lynes' book, traces with whimsical detachment the mushroom growth of the suburbs in the twenties; the rise of modernism in architecture with its new concept of the way man ought to live; the mass-produced, single-class communities of the forties, and the final emergence of the ranch house as the current fashion. Modern advertising, the motion pictures, and the automobile industries, as well as the decentralized city or "suburbia in excelsis," have helped to produce this era of corpo-*

rate taste with its resultant stratification which Lynes classifies as Highbrow, Lowbrow, Middlebrow.

Lynes is an editor and popular writer rather than a professional art critic, architect, or city planner. His purpose in writing is primaily to amuse and to stimulate thought. A New Englander, born in Great Barrington, Massachusetts, in 1910, his education marks him as a highbrow, according to his own scheme. He spent five years at the Cathedral Choir School in New York and was graduated from a New England private school and from Yale. Since 1944 he has been with Harpers, first as assistant editor and later managing editor. The Tastemakers *was originally published in 1949 as* Highbrow, Lowbrow, Middlebrow *and re-edited in 1955 with the present title. Lynes is the author also of* Snobs *(1950) and* Guests *(1951).*

SUBURBIA IN EXCELSIS

I

HEAVEN KNOWS what Mrs. Trollope would have thought of the suburbs of the 1920s; they were like nothing under the sky that she knew in America a century before. They were, indeed, quite unlike anything that had ever existed anywhere. As a woman who believed strongly in the virtue of a neatly stratified society, she would have been at a loss to know where to pigeonhole what was to all intents and purposes a brand-new kind of landed gentry. Many of them were only slightly landed and they were gentry in an American sense that Mrs. Trollope had not been able to understand or countenance. They were gentry simply because they were free Americans. The only wealth and position that they had inherited was the tradition of equality, but now they had land instead of landlords.

The weedlike growth of the suburbs was more than just a geographical shift by hundreds of thousands of people from the hot and cluttered pavements of the city to the nearby spaces which, if they were not exactly open, were at least ajar. It was a major upheaval in the social and cultural structure of the nation and in the patterns of the lives of millions of families. America had been long divided into cities and towns and rural areas, and those who lived in the cities and towns did the business and those in the rural areas managed and tilled the soil and tended the cattle. With the arrival of the suburbs came a whole new class of people who lived in the country, where they produced nothing but floral borders and privet hedges and children; they commuted to the cities to do their business. "Their hearts and their treasure," said Agnes Rogers, "are twenty miles apart."

Busy new islands of civilization appeared where there had been dumps and marshes and potato fields. Little sleeping towns that had had many of the aspects of communities hundreds of miles from a metropolis were astonished to wake up and find themselves all but incorporated into the city limits, with populations that doubled and tripled in a decade. What had once been a small cluster of village stores suddenly turned into a flourishing main street with movie theaters and specialty shops, with chain stores that offered overwhelming competition to small merchants, with rows of filling stations, and cars, mostly driven by women, bumper to bumper clogging the thoroughfare. By day the suburbs were nearly deserted by men, who had gone to the city, and the community, its culture and its climate, became a woman's world. In the suburbs a man's home is his wife's castle.

The exodus to the suburbs was a . . . middle-class revolution, and never has there been a revolution so bloodless in so many different senses of the word. It was a movement in which the virtues of stability, conformity, and reasonableness were paramount, in which education, healthful recreation, and community service were not steps to the good life but the good life itself. To those concerned with the level of the public taste it seemed to offer great promise. It seemed to indicate that Americans were going to settle down and thereby give the roots of culture a chance to grow and take firm hold. For another thing the suburbs seemed to offer a place where individual tastes might have a decent chance to develop, and where children could be raised without either the onus of rural provincialism or the oppressiveness of the crowded city. Perhaps the new member of the landed gentry had only a five-room house on a quarter acre of land and even on that there was a heavy mortgage, but at least he was not the tenant of a great holder of metropolitan real estate. A man who owns his own home is likely to be a great deal more concerned with the taste that it betrays than a man who pays rent. A home owner's home is nobody's fault but his own.

From the relatively short perspective of thirty years the houses that were built in the suburbs in the early and mid-twenties, and in which a great many people are still living, may seem strangely out of keeping with the new architectural ideas that were bubbling then to the surface, but they do not seem in the least inexplicable. There is certainly nothing odd in the behavior of the new small landowner who builds or buys a house that is a smaller version of what the wealthier landowner has built for himself. The country house from the time that Hunt introduced the doctrine of "adaptation" has been entirely that; it was a chateau or a chalet, it was a Dutch burgher's house or a steam-heated version of a Spanish hacienda. When the new suburbanite moved out of the city to build his house on a small plot of land the models that were suggested to him by the *Ladies' Home Journal* and *House Beautiful* were modest versions of the houses that sat at the ends of long driveways behind high hedges. The picturesque again came into fashion, as it had in the sixties and seventies of the previous century, and what did it matter if a six-room chateau that had a slate roof and a turret and was built of granite let almost no light into its living and bed rooms through the leaded glass of tiny windows? What did it matter that one's neighbor just across the privet hedge lived in a doll's version of an English country house, half-timbered and stuccoed, with the second floor projecting out slightly over the first to make a "charming irregularity"?

It was in the twenties that the "antiques craze" turned every old farmhouse and barn into a potential treasure trove, and aged maple beds and corner cupboards, spinning wheels and cobblers' benches, chests of drawers and blanket chests became the apples of a million eyes. Never has so much old paint been scraped off so much old furniture in order, as collectors said, "to get down to the original wood." Hundreds of houses on back roads and highways in New England were turned into furniture and bibelot shops. Pewter that the family had put away when they could afford china, and luster candlesticks that had been forgotten when they could buy brass or silver came out of the attic or the cold-cupboard to be proudly displayed and sold for gratifying prices to avid collectors. There was hardly a suburban housewife who didn't harbor a secret "little" dealer in a "darling little shop" (or shoppe) to which she would not risk taking even her closest friends. Affluent collectors began to buy entire paneled rooms and build homes to go around them; others built exact replicas of seventeenth-century houses, some even going so far as to scorn electricity and bathrooms. Husbands became experts in antiquing modern copies of old pieces with dirt and linseed oil so that they might not be out of character with the "authentic pieces." John Marquand describes a barn in *Wickford Point* that was done over into a dwelling and in which there was genuine fire-proofed hay sticking out of the loft. (Mr. Marquand himself in the thirties bought a seventeenth-century house in West Newbury, Massachusetts, which he intended to move in its entirety to his place on Kent's Island in Newbury; the expense, however, was prohibitive.)

"Personality" became a word more and more frequently connected with the house and its decorations. Downing had said in his day: "Much of the character of every man may be read in his house," but the somewhat ominous tone of voice was missing in the thirties of this century. Personality and the early American craze became inescapable. Even Childs restaurants, once famous for their white-tiled walls, business-like appearance, and chefs in the front windows making griddle cakes, began to redecorate either in the Early American elegant style, or the tavern style, or the Spanish manner. Alice Foote McDougall made a fortune out of suburban ladies who looked upon her restaurants, bristling with ancestral gewgaws, as the acme of the quaint and the picturesque.

The concern with expressing personality in architecture and decoration was by no means limited to the suburban home. Even our great universities spent millions upon millions of dollars trying to dress up for what they thought their role. Harvard with money from the Harkness family suddenly began to erect tremendous dormitories (called "houses") in the Georgian manner, each of which looked, as one architect said, "like a lot of New England public libraries with a town hall on top." At Yale the architect James Gamble Rogers turned to the English university tradition and built in a style known as "collegiate Gothic," with the result that undergraduates learned to live in a moat-surrounded building behind tiny leaded window panes and to disport themselves on lawns beneath soaring Gothic towers. There was a city ordinance in New Haven that all buildings facing on the Harkness Quadrangle must be in a sympathetic style of Gothic, and clothing stores and little restaurants were housed in stone-gabled buildings with arched doorways. College presidents and trustees rummaged around in the past, uncertain just what the personalities of their institutions were or how best to express them and give them substance. It was, indeed, a time when America in general was more confused about who and what it was than it had ever been before.

II

From another quarter a new wind had begun to blow, quietly at first and then with increasing velocity until it reached the full cry of a hurricane. It was the wind of "modernism," and for the most part suburban America was content to batten down its doors and windows and ride out the storm. As we look at the suburbs now, about thirty years after the wind first began to blow, we can distinguish some traces of the storm but not as many as one might expect. At first glance the effect seems slight indeed, and considering the intensity of the attack that was leveled at American architecture by those who were promoting the International Style, as it was called, as the *summum bonum*, there are only a few scattered buildings to show where the attack was successful. The real consequences, however, are less spectacular than the few "machines for living" that were built in the late twenties and thirties. The wind blew a good deal of fancy work out of a good many homes and planted in them new and simpler furniture. It provided architects, even those who believed in what they called "traditional styles," with a good many new words in their architectural vocabulary that they were quick to combine into clichés. It simplified and "streamlined" the kitchen, making surfaces smooth and cupboards often flush and hidden; it did not necessarily make the kitchen a more efficient workroom. It increased the size of living-room windows until they became known as "glass areas." But more important than these superficial changes and many others of the same nature, it eventually took the heart out of the "adaptation" movement, out of the archaeological search for styles, and laid the ghost of Richard Morris Hunt, which had stalked the land for more than half a century.

There is no need for us to trace the rise of the "Modern Movement" from its nineteenth-century origins, from H. H. Richardson and Louis Sullivan, from the beginnings of styles based on "tension" instead of on "thrust," but without chauvinism it can be said that much of it started in America, was transplanted to Europe, and was brought back to this country in the 1920s as a European idea. In the American public mind it didn't become a "movement" or a cause at all until after the depression of the thirties was well under way. The influence of the Museum of Modern Art was a prime factor in spreading the gospel of the new architecture. When the museum was founded in 1929 with money given by four or five wealthy patrons including Mrs. John D. Rockefeller, Jr., and Miss Lizzie Bliss, it devoted itself entirely to exhibitions of paintings. By 1931 its young director, Alfred H. Barr, Jr., who had wanted to have a department of architecture from the start, enlisted the help of two friends, both in their twenties, Philip Johnson, who later became an architect, and Henry-Russell Hitchcock, now one of America's most distinguished architectural historians, and architecture and industrial design became an active concern of the museum. In the spring of 1932 they held their first exhibition of buildings by the men who are now considered the old masters of Modern architecture: Le Corbusier, Mies van der Rohe, Gropius, J. J. P. Oud, Frank Lloyd Wright, and some others. The public reaction was sufficiently violent to cause a considerable amount of argument and a good many columns of publicity in magazines and newspapers. It was Alfred Barr who invented the name of the International Style, and it was in the catalogue of that exhibition that the term "functionalism" (actually used in a derogatory sense) was first publicized.

Modern was a good deal more than just a method of building with reinforced concrete in a manner in which the forms, to use the language of its own arguments, expressed the function and the materials. It was more than just a "flat-chested" style, as Frank Lloyd Wright called it, or as the Museum of Modern Art said, a new system based on building "in terms of *volume* of space enclosed by planes or surfaces—as opposed to mass and solidity." It was a new concept of the way men, if they were sensible, rational beings ought to live, and the concept had not only a structural but also a social morality built into it. Modern was said to be *honest*, whereas "adaptation" was dishonest; the *truth* of architecture was to be found in the new style, not, as the adapters had so fervently believed, in the slow accretion of architectural knowledge over the ages.

The International Style quickly came to be identified in most people's minds with a phrase coined by Le Corbusier, one of the progenitors and practitioners of the new style. He insisted that a house should be "a machine for living." The idea was enough to send the shivers down the backs of most Americans, as well as most Germans and most Frenchmen. Isolated buildings were built by adventurous souls, but the style caught on nowhere as a fad. It did, however, fire the imaginations of young architects with a zeal as intemperate as that with which Hunt had fired an earlier generation with the glories of the Beaux Arts. A new battle of the styles was on.

The reason why this new style (unlike many that had been presented to Americans before) did not catch on tells as much about the people who rejected it as about the style itself. It arrived in all its pristine, chaste, and essentially puritan simplicity at a moment when, as we have noted, a great many Americans were moving to the suburbs to adopt a new way of life. But simplicity was not what they wanted—least of all simplicity with a machine-made look. To nearly everyone "functional" architecture was identified with the factory or with the office—with the skyscrapers that were built in such profusion in the decade before the depression, and the industrial plants that were all business and very little humanity. "Own your own home!" a slogan so familiar in the twenties as to be almost meaningless, sometimes meant a new house in an established suburb, sometimes a house in a "development" or a "subdivision." But in those days, unlike the mass-produced houses of almost identical shape and style that we have seen rising near all big cities in the last six or seven years, a home-of-one's-own meant a house different from one's neighbor's. Often the difference was merely in an architectural slip cover that went over the plan. Taste was a quality to be carefully strained, and the court of appeal on all such matters was first a peek into your neighbor's window and then a careful study of the women's magazines. In the latter the housewife would find an occasional "modern" house or interior which the editors presented in order to show they were up to date, and she was likely to find conventional interiors or a style popularly known as "modernistic."

"Modernistic" was the bane of the existence of those who were seriously trying to promote "modern." It was, in effect, a sort of jazz-age version of a classic style. The simple rectangles and curves of the Modern were squeezed into oblique angles; mirrors and wall brackets became spiked and askew and were often made of blue glass; modernistic furniture was typified by the bookcase that stepped up like a skyscraper and was capped with a copy of an African mask, or a piece of copper beaten into a bas-relief of a draped female. Fireplaces were surrounded by metal moldings, sometimes combinations of brass and steel in angular abstract patterns or conventionalized flowers. It was, in some respects, a decorator's interpretation of the Duchamps and Picassos of the Armory Show plus the influence of Greenwich Village bohemianism where people sat on poufs and Ottomans and burned incense and used long, tapering cigarette holders. As a style, modernistic was far more urban than suburban and it caught on less firmly in people's houses than it did in hotels such as the new Waldorf-Astoria in New York and in the lobbies of such skyscrapers as the Chrysler Building and the Empire State.

The collapse of the stock market in October 1929 did not change the essential complexion of taste overnight, but taste went ghastly pale and stayed that way for nearly a decade. Private building slowed down to a lethargic shuffle; skyscrapers that were on their way up when the crash came found themselves half-empty towers, ghostly symbols of a recently unbridled optimism. An architecture such as America had never seen in the environs of its great cities grew up in deserted lots and near dumps—shacks of discarded packing boxes and advertising signs, of odd pieces of rusted corrugated iron and broken fence slats. They were called Hoovervilles, and they were the disgrace of the nation. But it was disgrace and hardship that gave the style known as Modern its chance. It was a social architecture, an architecture of reform with dreams of a better society built into its esthetic doctrine. When the planners who were desperately trying to cope with the famous "third of a nation," ill-housed and ill-fed, began to devise ways of relieving the desperate housing situation, it was natural that they should turn to this simple new architecture for their inspiration. Government projects like Greenbelt, Maryland, were conceived in the new, flat-roofed, and "functional" style, and city planners worked with architects in an attempt to create communities that someday might serve as models to private builders. Towns like Roosevelt, New Jersey, not far from Princeton, were built all at once—single-storied houses, flat-roofed, and with walls of glass; there were housing projects on the outskirts of many cities—most of which looked like clusters of brick or concrete boxes with holes punched in them at regular intervals. They were singularly lacking in the promise of joy, but they were happier than the slums.

If Modern had failed to make more than a slight and official dent on domestic architecture, it had, by the end of the thirties, caught on and firmly established itself in a good many other nooks and crannies of life. Not only was some department-store furniture beginning to assume the squared-off clichés of functionalism but designers had gone on a spree of streamlining from which they have yet to return. Everything from toasters to refrigerators, from vacuum cleaners to orange-juice squeezers became wind-resistant. The new profession of industrial design was coming into its own, and "machine art" was like American antiques a decade before, enshrined in a museum in 1934. At the Museum of Modern Art, bearing springs, dentists' x-ray units, electric waffle irons, alarm clocks, cash registers, and any number of other "useful objects" were put on pedestals under spotlights. Modern became almost mandatory for the design of up-to-date shops and gas stations; even roadside diners cast off their old Pullman-car look and emerged gleaming with glass brick and aluminum and furnished with chairs made of bent chromium tubing.

III

If the Second World War implanted any single architectural idea more firmly than any other in people's minds it was that of impermanence and makeshift. Wartime housing was slapped together with haste and a modicum of attention to style. Temporary buildings—as houses for factory workers, as government offices, as military installations—were the rule rather than the exception, and tens of thousands of families lived in that perfect symbol of American mobility, the trailer. Whether, if there had been no war, Modern would have emerged during the forties as the characteristic architecture of America is scarcely worth speculating about. The fact was that the war left a housing crisis. Another fact was that people were glad to live in anything, even

Quonset huts. Conversion from war to peace played some odd tricks on taste, but it did not greatly change it.

It was a time of dreams; almost anything that anybody could suggest that might actually get a house built was worth considering. Apartments were not to be had except occasionally by bribing an agent or a superintendent or by watching the obituary columns and getting your bid in before the body was buried. People who owned houses wanted twice or three times what they had paid for them a year or so earlier. It looked like a moment when a great many people, having to build from scratch and with GI loans to help them, might almost create an architectural renaissance. Books on how to plan a house, how to get a good architect, how to be Modern or advanced poured onto the market. R. H. Macy and Company held an exhibition of "Homes America wants"; the designs were originally made for *Good Housekeeping* and the decorations were "created by the magazine's decorating staff under the supervision of Dorothy Draper." At the Museum of Modern Art there was an exhibition called "Tomorrow's Small House"—ten scale models of houses designed at the behest of the *Ladies' Home Journal.* The Museum said, "A million and a quarter new dwellings will be needed each year after the war, a challenge without precedent in American building history."

Good Housekeeping's guess was better than the *Ladies' Home Journal*'s; they claimed that people set great store by "sentiment" and that they would want the "exterior to be a contemporary treatment of some familiar architectural style, the interior to be the ultimate in modern convenience." One of the houses that *Good Housekeeping* had selected was described in *The New York Times*: "The most inviting, if not the most practical for this locality, is probably the ranch house planned by Allen G. Siple of Beverly Hills, Calif." It is doubtful if even the editors of *Good Housekeeping* had any idea what was going to happen to the ranch house in the next decade.

Something else, however, happened first, something that was to establish a brand-new suburban pattern that even contemporary critics of our culture looked upon with wide-eyed dismay. Hundreds and then thousands of almost identical houses began to spread out over a 1400-acre tract of land on Long Island. In 1945 William J. Levitt started to build Levittown, and by 1948 he was putting up houses at the rate of 150 a week until he had completed 6000 of them. Now, as I write this five years later, there are 70,000 people in Levittown. Eric Larrabee said in *Harper's*: "His [Levitt's] house is the model-T equivalent of the rose-covered cottage—or Cape Coddage, as someone has called it. It is meant to look like the Little Home of One's Own that was a subsidiary myth of the American Dream long before Charlie Chaplin put it into 'Modern Times'." Levittown is not alone; Lakewood, a suburb of Los Angeles, is even larger than Levittown, and Park Forest, thirty miles south of Chicago, now is approaching a population of 30,000. Not even the federal government, that insures mortgages on the houses in these new mass-produced suburbs, knows how many such developments there are, but as Harry Henderson, who has made a study of the way people live in them, has written, "One can safely assume that their combined population totals several million people."

The quality of these mass-produced communities that distinguishes them from the suburbs of the twenties and thirties is that their populations are highly mobile and they are almost entirely inhabited by families in the same age and income groups. They are, in effect, single-class communities where there is no living on the wrong side of the tracks, and any spiritual tracks that there may be are not determined by income or background or promise; they are determined by personality.

"The standardized house," wrote Harry Henderson in *Harper's* in November 1953, "creates an emphasis on interior decorating. Most people try hard to achieve 'something different.' In hundreds of houses I never saw two interiors that matched—and I saw my first tiger-striped wallpaper. (The only item that is endlessly repeated is a brass skillet hung on a red brick wall.) Yet two styles predominate: Early American and Modern. . . . Taste levels are high. My interviews with wives revealed that their models and ideas came primarily from pictures of rooms in national magazines. Nobody copies an entire room, but they take different items from different pictures."

Here was something new in the attitude of the suburbs. True, "approval insurance" had long been basic to the housewife's exercise of her taste or her adaptation of the taste of the magazines, and "something different" is merely a play on the old theme of expressing one's personality. What was new was that there was no ladder in the suburban community that one might climb conscientiously, hoping one day to reach the top rungs. One does not move up in a one-class suburb; one moves out—to another suburb where the houses and the lawns are bigger, the trees older and taller, and the atmosphere is one of permanence not transience. Eventually the families that prosper will presumably arrive in the old, established suburbs—not the ones so close to the metropolis that they have been all but absorbed into it, but those like Winnetka or Pasadena or Montclair. There the top levels of corporate management, the corporation lawyers, the consultants to industry live in spacious houses set back from the same street on which lower but aspiring management lives in smaller replicas of the big houses. There the taste of Elsie de Wolfe, and her successors to positions of eminence in the field of decoration, hold sway—chic but styleless elegance, luxuriousness with an air, comfort without daring or distinction.

But less and less do the tastes of the relatively poor and the relatively well-to-do seem to differ in the ways in which they are expressed, and there is no better example of this unity of taste than the ubiquitous ranch house. It has become the standard new suburban dwelling in the suburbs of New York as of Boston, of Chicago as of Cincinnati or Seattle or, of course, Los Angeles. It varies in price from the least expensive (around $7000) to any amount a man can afford. In a single suburb of Chicago, for example, you can buy ranch houses that cost $10,000 or $65,000 just a few hundred yards apart, and the expensive one will be merely a larger, more carefully built, and more completely gadgeted version of the former. Stylistically they are sired by the same California notion of the good life. They are all one-story cottages with gently sloping roofs and outsized picture windows. Some (the expensive ones) are long and some are U shaped with patios; some have a slight touch of the Cape Cod cottage, some have Spanish Colonial touches, some have "dropped" living rooms and "split levels," but somehow the romantic appeal of the West is built into all of them. The suburban ranches are often a quarter of an acre or less, and the view from the picture window is of another picture window. The pervasive Western spirit of the open range and the barbecue, of sunshine and leisure is nonetheless nationwide. For the nostalgic pleasures of exhuming the early American past, this generation has substituted the romantic dream of the prairie. The enchantment of Paul Revere, hero and silversmith, has been displaced by Hopalong, and the American architectural tradition of making things seem to be what they are not has found a new expression.

This ironing out of regional differences in taste does not mean that America has come to be a place where everyone likes exactly the same things, as the pages upon pages of different styles of furniture in the Sears catalogue bear witness. It means several other things. It means that our highly mobile suburban population take their tastes with them, rub them against new friends and absorb new tastes at the same time they are depositing their old ones in the new community. It means that styles and fads and tastes travel faster than they used to—through the movies, through magazines with circulations in the several millions, through radio and TV. The time lag between the introduction of a new style and its popularization has been narrowed down as communications media feel impelled to provide their audiences constantly with something new and different.

But what does it mean in progress of taste? Is the national taste any better now than it was in the 1890s? Is it any better than it was when Edward Bok spread the *Ladies' Home Journal* houses across the country at the same time that Wilson, The Bungalow Man, was marketing the precursor of the ranch house, and the Portland Cement companies were promoting the Age of Concrete? It is a question that each reader will answer first in terms of his own home and the homes of his friends. "On the whole," he will say, "I think taste has improved." But then he will look beyond his own immediate circle at the tastes of millions of people he does not know, and he will say, "On second thought, I'm not so sure."

4

PAINTING AS SOCIAL PROTEST

Honoré Daumier

Probably no major artist has reached so wide and varied a public as Honoré Daumier did through his thousands of published lithographs depicting the social life and character of France during the mid-nineteenth century. His art is as rich in human warmth as it is in scorn for sham and hypocrisy of all kinds, and he has few peers in the ability to compress in a few suggestive lines the temper, the character, and the heart beat of a society. In its portrayal of essential humanity stripped of all irrelevancies, his work demonstrates convincingly that an art of social protest can also realize the esthetic ideal of classic art.

Daumier was born in 1808 in Marseilles of relatively poor parents. After trying to earn his living first as a bailiff's errand boy and then as a bookseller's clerk, he found his real talent in lithography, a new technique of printing. In 1832 he joined the staff of a new journal, La Caricature, *a periodical intended to satirize the government and French society of that day. For drawing a caricature of King Louis Phillipe as Gargantua, Daumier spent six months in prison at Ste. Pélagie. Following his imprisonment he published a series of political caricatures culminating in the famous* Legislative Body *and the* Rue Transnonain, *which portrayed the results of a civilian massacre in Lyon. When censorship laws stopped his political satires, he turned to the bourgeoisie, the law, and the social mores of his time as subjects for pictorial ridicule. A list of his lithographed plates compiled in 1904 numbered nearly four thousand.*

Lithography is both an art and a method of printing. Developed in the eighteenth century, it had its greatest vogue in France soon after 1800. Its chief value at the time was the possibility of reproducing in large quantity drawings which closely resembled the originals. The artist draws with a greasy substance, usually a special crayon or ink, on a special type of stone or metal. It is a very direct kind of art, for as the drawing is done, the artist can see the exact value of each line and an unusually accurate reproduction is possible. Daumier is one of the recognized masters in the field of lithography. In his later years, however, he associated more with painters and did a number of well-known pictures, some on Biblical as well as social subjects and a famous series on Don Quixote. In 1878, a year before his death, he exhibited his work in Paris.

Elizabeth Luther Cary (1871-1936), from whose book on Daumier the present selec-

tion is taken, was art editor of The New York Times *from 1908 until her death. The first individual delegated by the* Times *to cover art news exclusively, she reviewed current art exhibitions for the* Times, *wrote on all aspects of art, lectured widely, and published three important books,* The Art of William Blake *(1907),* Honoré Daumier *(1907), and* Artists Past and Present *(1908).*

HONORÉ DAUMIER: *Social and Political Caricatures*

IF WE CARE to look upon the France of the past century through eyes that note not merely the surface view, but types, characteristics, deep-seated principles, unconscious tendencies, with a clear appreciation of their values and relations, we cannot do better than turn page by page a collection of Daumier's drawings, if by good fortune such may have fallen in our way. The chances are that our social and political ruminations will, however, be somewhat disturbed, and at times overwhelmed, by the extraordinary beauty of the art thus unfolded. Whether we are contemplating a Bohemian of the Paris streets, an amateur of art, a barrister, a bourgeois family, or a statesman, we are confronted by the same magnificent vitality of line, the same exquisite modulations of light and shade, the same massive structure and clear definition of form. The artist's sense of sheer fun, his willingness to lash political opponents, his discerning eye for temperamental and moral traits, unquestionably are elements in our enjoyment; but nothing counts as much as the esthetic charm. By this Daumier's art ranks with that of the masters, and conclusively demonstrates, if demonstration were needed, that the "subject" and the "literary" interest of a picture as little impair as improve its pictorial value.

Honoré Daumier was born at Marseilles on the twenty-sixth of February 1808 and by the time he was twenty-one had commenced his career as a lithographer. His education in art had been, apparently, of the slenderest description, but had been supplemented by long strolls through the galleries of the Louvre, especially in the department of antiques, where, no doubt, classic simplicity and breadth had their effect upon his vision, enabling him, after the fashion of great art, to perceive these qualities in the world of multitudinous detail surrounding him. Chance brought him into relations with a lithographer who taught him his trade, and by the time he was twenty-one he was working, for the most part anonymously, for a publisher by the name of Béliard, and presently for Ricourt, Hautecoeur-Martinet, and, most important of all, for Charles Philipon and the house of Aubert.

It is difficult to recognize in his beginnings the presage of his robust genius. He notes expression and detail, but is feebly uncertain in his composition, and his lights and shadows are scattered over the space like a brood of frightened chickens without organization or intention. In the admirable *catalogue raisonné* of the lithographs, edited by MM. Hazard and Delteil, the earliest know lithograph is tentatively ascribed to 1829. This represents a fatuous old man (Mayeux) seated between two ambiguous charmers who are plying him with champagne. In the background is a maid leaving the room with a bottle and a plate in her

[From Elizabeth L. Cary, *Honoré Daumier, Social and Political Caricatures*, New York, G. P. Putnam's Sons, 1907.]

hands. The drawing is weak and indeterminate, and the values are practically non-existent so far as any logical relation between them is concerned; yet the picture manages to convey the artist's meaning with singular directness.

The following year the political weekly entitled *La Caricature* was founded by Philipon with the artistic collaboration of Daumier, Grandville, Despéret, Monnier, Decamps, Raffet, Traviès, Bouquet, Benjamin Roubaud, and others. From the beginning of 1832 Daumier played an active part in connection with this publication, contributing to it from first to last no fewer than a hundred lithographs. The earlier ones were signed with the pseudonym, *Rogelin*, and were without especial distinction of execution. One, signed H. Daumier, published prior to August 30th, 1832, and entitled *Gargantua* represents Louis-Philippe seated on his throne and swallowing bags of coin which have been extracted from the poor by his ministers, and which are carried by Lilliputian personages up a plank that stretches from the ground to his mouth. At the foot of the plank is a crowd of miserable men and women handing over their money. About the throne are fat little favorites gathering up peerages, decorations, commissions, and the like, into which the enforced offerings have been converted. Here still the drawing is to the last degree immature, the only suggestion conveyed by it of the later richness and solidity of Daumier's work appearing in the good round contour of Louis-Philippe's heavy body, pendent over his small legs. The satiric intention, however, was sufficient to throw the artist into prison, where he remained from September 1832 to February 1833 accumulating, apparently, a fine store of antipathies toward judges, juries, and barristers that were to form the basis of a remarkable series of drawings and a few paintings in which his genius reaches its highwater mark. For two and a half years after his release—until *La Caricature* was stopped by the restriction of the liberty of the press—he produced work in which a certain ferocity of moral conviction and ardent youthful vengeance against social evils, found expression in blacks and whites and greys marshalled and ordered for his artistic purposes with the firmest authority. He was now in full possession of his instrument and able to support his intellectual idea with his ripened craftsmanship.

II

A composition directly reflecting Daumier's own experience is the lithograph entitled *Souvenir de Ste. Pélagie** and published in *Charivari* for the 14th of March 1834. It shows two young men and one old man in a prison cell. One of the younger men is reading to his companion from the *Tribune*. The coarse furnishings of the cell are shown in detail. The three men are said by Champfleury to be Daumier's companions in captivity, Lerouge, the engraver, Landon, the lawyer, and Masse, the writer of romance. The light and shade of the picture are sharply contrasted, the shining white jacket of the standing figure and the illumined wall back of the other giving an effect of great brilliancy to the whole. The modelling, however, is still a little soft, and lacks the decisive simplicity of other works even of the same year. One of these, which we reproduce, is well-known, *Rue Transnonain, Le 15 Avril, 1834.*† In this powerful composition we see what Mr. McCall defines as Daumier's "grand and elemental" style, which he says, is exercised upon trivial matter, but which in this instance is devoted to a subject that no critic, French or British, could condemn as "trivial." The scene is laid in one of the little side streets

* See Figure 7.
† See Figure 8.

. 7 (*right*). HONORÉ DAUMIER: *uvenir de Ste. Pelagie*, 1834. urtesy of The Metropolitan Mu-m of Art, Gift of Arthur Sachs, 23.

. 8 (*below*). HONORÉ DAUMIER: *Transnonain, Le 15 Avril, 1834*. urtesy of The Metropolitan Mu-m of Art, Rogers Fund, 1920.

D.

FIG. 9. HONORÉ DAUMIER: *Le Ventre Legislatif*, 1834. Courtesy of The Metropolitan Museum Art, Rogers Fund, 1920.

10 (*right*). HONORÉ DAUMIER: *Three* *yers.* Phillips Collection, Washington, C.

11 (*below*). HONORÉ DAUMIER: *The* *ising,* c. 1860. Phillips Collection, shington, D. C.

FIG. 12. HONORÉ DAUMIER: *The Laundress,* c. 1863. Courtesy of The Metropolitan Museum of Art, Bequest of Lizzie P. Bliss, 1931.

FIG. 13. PABLO PICASSO: *Minotauromachy*, 1935. Collection Museum of Modern Art, New York.

FIG. 14 (*left*). PABLO PICA *Horse's Head*, study for *Guer* 1937. On loan to The Museur Modern Art, New York, from artist.

FIG. 15 (*below*). PABLO PICA Composition study for *Guer* 1937. On loan to The Museur Modern Art, New York, from artist.

:. 16 (*above*). PABLO PICASSO: *ernica,* 1937. On loan to The ıseum of Modern Art, New rk, from the artist.

:. 17 (*right*). PABLO PICASSO: *ernica,* 1937. Installation pho- raph at the Spanish Pavilion, celona. On loan to The Muse- of Modern Art, New York, m the artist.

Fig. 18. DIEGO RIVERA: *Night of the Poor*, 1923-1928. Ministry of Education. Photo courtesy of Institute of Fine Arts, Mexico City.

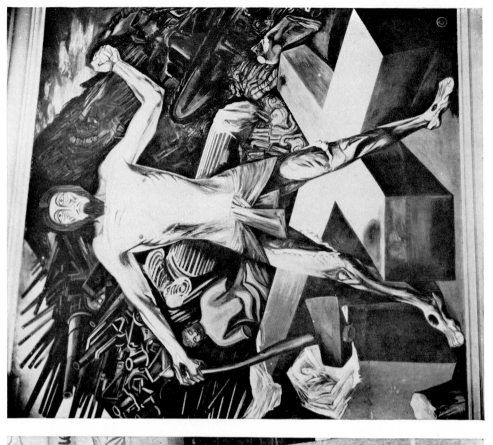

Fig. 19. JOSÉ OROZCO: *Christ and His Cross*, 1932. Baker Library. By permission of Dartmouth College.

of the Saint-Martin quarter which are inhabited by workmen, and which were invaded by furious soldiery on one of the days of insurrection. A room has been entered, the furniture overturned, and the occupants slaughtered. Daumier has chosen the moment following the massacre. A deadly silence seems to pervade the place depicted. On the floor is lying a workman in a bloodstained shirt; under him a young child who has been crushed by his fall; at the right is an old man, and, in the background, near the door, a woman, both dead. The horror of such material is obviated for us only by the serene nobility of the method. Daumier is nowhere more completely the detached artist deeply moved by his subject, but unforgetful of the esthetic rights of his art. As in the *Souvenir de Ste. Pélagie* he is as little as possible the satirist. The human situation has revealed its tragedy to him, and he treats it without exaggeration or whimsicality, and with a breadth and sombre splendor of style that accords with its significance.

The *Rue Transnonain* drawing belongs to a set of five drawings, furnished by Daumier for a collection called *L'Association Mensuelle* which Philipon published. Another of the set is the famous one entitled *Le Ventre Legislatif*,* in which thirty-five of the ministers and deputies of the Center of 1834 are represented. It is a composition that seems to summarize Daumier's achievement in that divination of character upon which the success of the caricaturist must inevitably depend. The field abounded with types to which his pencil fitted itself as if by conscious compatibility. Louis-Philippe's reign was one in which Marseillaise fervor could find enough to condemn, and the people by whom he was surrounded lent themselves readily to the sarcasm of critics; especially of those critics who had in their own veins the fiery blood of Southern France; and to whom incessant compromise and the contradiction of high ideals by debased practices was fuel for an ever-burning flame of moral ardor in the cause of liberty.

As the historian of the bourgeois government Daumier has much to say to the student of French politics. Against the apostles of moderation and profitable peace he launched the arrows of his wit, not too sharply pointed, but none the less capable of inflicting ugly wounds. In the caricatures of this period much of the effect is due to the masterly psychological portraiture which interprets, without misrepresentation and even without any extraordinary emphasis, the inner qualities and moral features of the subject, precisely as the outer features are modeled with a terrible truth far more to be feared than the grossest exaggeration. It is interesting to recall that many of these portraits were made from little colored clay models, in which Daumier revealed himself as to sculpture born, and nourished the tendency to be found in all his early work, the tendency to suggest high relief and to place an excessive emphasis upon what Mr. Berenson calls the "tactile values."

Of these clay models M. Geoffroy (writing in *L'Art et les Artistes* for June 1905) says thirty-eight are in existence. Champfleury in this article is quoted as saying that Daumier was present at the sessions of the Chamber of Peers, a bit of clay in his hand, and modeled his portraits from life, using them later as the basis for his lithographs. M. Geoffroy-Dechaume, on the other hand, speaks of his making the little busts not "from life," but *immediately after* leaving the Chamber of Deputies, which, of course, would make them memory studies. Whatever the method, and with an observation so acute and a memory so retentive as Daumier's, such distinctions matter little, he arrived at a result in which the salient

* See Figure 9.

characteristics of his subjects were raised to the *n*th power without overwhelming their natural appearance. M. Geoffroy, whose privilege it has been to study the clay models at first hand, says of them, as they now appear in their damaged condition, with remnants of color still clinging to them:

> Here in these glass cases, this exhibition of little busts is particularly vengeful. It suggests a massacre in which genius has not once missed its mark. Certain resemblances, even, might be put aside and certain identifications, without lessening the general appalling effect. No doubt it is interesting to see Persil, the Attorney-General with his straight sharp obstinate profile; Delessert, the *préfet*, with his bit of a nose and his baboon mouth; Jacques Le Févre, the banker, with his face like a knife-blade; Dubois d'Anger, the deputy and president of the Court of Assizes, with his flesh, his thick neck and shoulders, and his chubby face; Chevandier, the deputy, with the double twist of his forelock and his trumpet nose; d'Argout, minister, his chin poised on his cravat, his mouth and eyes artful, and his enormous nose like the beak of a *toucan;* Odier, banker and deputy, old, with a concentrated expression, his long white hair falling over his collar; Dupin the elder, president of the Chamber, all mouth, a huge mouth which pushes forward, fleshy and gaping, the lower part of the face heavy and surmounted by a low forehead with a pointed skull flanked by two vast ears; and Gady, judge at Versailles, and Ganneron, deputy and candle merchant, and Lecomte, and Delort, general and deputy—I follow, for the most part, the labels edited by Champfleury.
>
> But I insist that the individual portrait is outrun and that we find ourselves here in the presence of human types, of forms and expressions which have such an interest as to make unnecessary the putting of a name to the masks. Caricature it may be, but a caricature that gives its value to the dominant truth by these enormous noses, these minute noses, these apologies for noses, these hollow or drooping cheeks, these pointed or blunt skulls, these tightly pressed or open mouths, these thin or thick lips which look in or pour forth their secrets, these thin or harsh smiles, these fat smiles, these grins that deform the entire physiognomy by their frightful bitterness, these heavy chins which hang over their white cravats, these bits of white or black whisker which frame red or yellow countenances, these pallid, puffed, or emaciated faces, these eyes with red lids and encircled with greenish rings, these round humid eyes that leap from their sockets and seem about to roll down the cheeks. Many of these visages make one think of animals that growl, that grunt, that chew their cud, and that sleep, or of sick birds that weary on their perch. In truth they appear to be undergoing tortures, a prey to torments gnawed by suffering, convulsed with grief. Moral maladies are added to physical defects, and their faces express with unusual violence their characteristic pretentiousness, self-importance, meanness, ill-temper: they are old beaux, sly accomplices, bourgeois burlesques, cruel ogres. And in spite of all there is good-nature and kindliness in Daumier's pitiless talent. He is ferocious, and he has the air of being so for fun. One certainly laughs, but the ferocity remains.

In the lithographs founded upon these models the good nature is more apparent than the ferocity. It was all very well to manipulate his bits of clay sufficiently to throw into violent relief the dominating feature of the physiognomy observed, but when it came to making a picture, the spirit of art swayed [Daumier] as the spirit of satire could not, and the bitterness of his clay caricatures melted into the tenderness of closely related values, the beauty of fathomless shadows and caressing half-tones, the dignity of finely composed masses and free sweeping contours. Nevertheless, it is in this series of portraits of judges and lawyers that Daumier lays bare his ideal of justice and honesty with most force. His barristers* delivering their arguments with shallow fury and conspicuous vanity arouse in one's mind an inevitable fervor of sympathy with dignity and quietude and candor. His judges, half-asleep or eager for the hour of release, inattentive or pompous, inspire not only a disgust for characters so unresponsive to high demands upon them, but also a more definite respect for the opposite type, fortunately known to most of us.

* See Figure 10.

III

When we arrive at the work undertaken in a gayer frame of mind with a more obvious joy in the pictorial possibilities of the scene, we find the lithograph chalk more frequently indulging in the extravagance of grotesque. In such a series as that of *Les Beaux Jours de la Vie,* that of *Types Parisiens,* or that of *Voyage en Chine,* there are occasional noses, mouths, or eyebrows for which one can find no parallel in commonplace experience. Even here, however, it is impossible to observe one after another of the drawings without discovering a type that is not as familiar as the street through which one daily passes. An astute French critic recently pointed out that Daumier frequently expressed his ideal by showing forms of ugliness that call up in contrast a mental vision of classic charm; that he emphasized his love of righteousness by holding vice up to ridicule; his love of integrity by setting forth the vulgarity of deception, and so on. This adroit analysis is certainly quite justified as far as it goes, and Daumier's passion for beauty is plausibly inferred from his keen eye for departures from it in our debased human physique. I recall a drawing belonging to the series called *Histoire Ancienne* in which *le beau Narcisse* is kneeling on the bank of a stream, regarding with delight his reflection in the water. The scrawny limbs, the awkward attitude, the large bullet head crowned with flowers, contradict all the features attributed to the classic conception. The figure is the cleverest of parodies, and has the hateful quality of the parody, in that it imposes itself upon the original, which henceforth we can see only in company with its distorted shadow. Daumier in this instance has yielded to a temptation altogether rare with him. He has brought the sordid real in contrast with the imagined ideal without displaying the esthetic possibilities of the former. His forms are cramped and his light and shade are distracted. In general, however, he exhausts every resource of reality from which esthetic pleasure may be drawn, and his opulent supple line plays gaily over the most commonplace subjects, secure in its power to extract from them homage to the esthetic ideal.

Nevertheless, if in our appreciation of his sunny good nature and of his readiness to clothe a ridiculous situation with all the charm of which his art is capable, we are oblivious of his well-defined intellectual attitude toward the small people of the world, we shall go far out of our path. His studies of bourgeois homes and bourgeois characters show clearly enough his detachment from their limited views and egoistic interests. The petty domain of a family without large ambitions or general ideas, without standards or measures of value, becomes under his scrutiny a laughable and also a more or less contemptible affair. He shows us with remorseless implication the complacency of mediocre citizens with their property, their pride in their stupid children, their satisfaction in their little fêtes and little occupations, their willingness to let the personal horizon everywhere shut out the wider view. In one of the lithographs a crowd of these good dull people are looking at the blossom of a night-blooming cereus, the extraordinary attributes of which are loudly proclaimed to them by a showman. In the craning heads, in the gaping mouths, in the vacant eyes, in the forced self-conscious wonder and admiration of the group we read without difficulty how superficial their sentiment is, how largely composed of a vulgar curiosity and desire merely to plume themselves upon having seen something that all the world does not see every day. For shams, innocent as they may be, Daumier has nothing but a scathing comment. His honest pencil unveils the foolish pretense and by the simple act seems to place the artist on that high plane of mental aristocracy where to be consciously superior or consciously exclusive is to be an alien.

This instruction by suggestion in the values of the social order betrays upon Daumier's part a finer instinct for social relations than that which he commonly is credited. Bourgeois and bohemian—so far as the latter is the inevitable state of the French artist—he may have been, but he was also to a degree patrician in his ultimate criticisms. Without the taste for languid figures that gives to Gavarni's subjects a look of physical elegance, he separates with greater precision the qualities that depend upon external and those that depend upon inner delicacy. The democratic tendency which inspired his love of liberty and his scorn of those who assailed it openly or in secret was a deep-rooted sentiment, too vital and too intense to satisfy itself with the affectation of freedom implied by unrestrained manners. While for the most part he follows the tendency analyzed by M. Gaultier and displays his appreciation of the mellifluous charm clinging to a social order founded upon high traditions and guarded seclusion by revealing the shuffle and clatter of a too-democratic publicity, he is capable, as we see in the drawing just described, of penetrating the very temple of aristocracy, and making its stillness, its exclusiveness, its fastidious felicity, apparent, without changing his own style or pitch of expressiveness with a quietness equal to that of his subject and, too, with a feeling for the exquisite unsurpassed by any of his contemporaries.

When we turn to the subjects drawn from his own profession, it is interesting to note how his comic spirit sharpens. The air of good nature that softens the most caustic of his comments upon the world without drops as he enters his own domain. He unveils with a quite ferocious glee the pretentiousness of ignorant amateurs and casual buyers, and the stupidity of the vast public who throng the picture galleries. He depicts a sale at the Hotel Drouot with a crowd of eager bidders wisely inspecting an undecipherable canvas; he reproduces the flattered countenances of *bons bourgeois* who behold themselves in effigy on the walls of the salon and feel their money to have been well spent, the shrewder features of the patron who buys a second-hand portrait to have it touched up into his own likeness at a reduced rate, the haughty expression of the influential critic who passes through the galleries, notebook in hand, the indignant gesture of the Philistine who cannot be forced to admire a picture of Courbet. The logical visitor to exhibitions who wishes to know why the woman in Manet's picture of the year is called Olympia, and decides that it is the cat that bears the name; the conscientious visitor who discovers merits in dubious canvases by the aid of a magnifying glass; the ardent lover of art who turns hastily away from the entrance door of the exhibition on finding that he has hit upon a payday; the self-sufficient visitor who finds fault with composition and color with an air of authority —these appear in his lithographs clearly and coldly defined. On the other hand he is not less ready to put before us the painter who allows himself to take pleasure in ignorant praise, the painter who is content to copy fellow-artists in place of nature, and the one who panders to the vanity of his sitter.

IV

It would be plausible to say, in spite of the instances noted of subtle characterization and refined implication, that the examples of Daumier's art, chosen almost at random from the four thousand or so described in the catalogue, show, after all, as a whole, no supremely original vision, that the morals are for the most part commonplace, and that the wit is obvious. They are made, it is easy to see, for the every-day public. They represent familiar scenes and figures in a way to claim immediate recognition if not immediately to convey their intellectual message—that is the *sine qua non* of the caricaturist's trade. Even if they have the subtlety of feeling that is claimed for them they have a bluntness and completeness of expression that contrasts sharply with the abstract outline of a *Caran d'Ache*. They come into the presence of more modern caricature as the burly form of an elderly farmer might enter a dapper society of some one of the great cities of the world. They have about them an atmosphere of incorrigible innocence and solid worth that is not of modernity or for that matter of any time or place, that is purely an individual envelope. For the most part they are jovial and outspoken, they have mental energy and a spontaneous exuberance. They are not mysterious or alluring. They are oftener gay than sad. They are always agreeably confidential, taking the observer into their secret at once and assuring him that he knows all there is to know. But they are nevertheless, like Joey Bagstock, sly—deep and sly in their wealth of reserve quality. They wear their plainness on their sleeve, resembling some old miser who goes about in homespun with a pot full of gold in his cellar. They are perfectly exemplified in the story told of Daumier himself by Champfleury, who says that he once passed an entire night with a body of national guards who failed to have the least suspicion that their companion was a dangerous observer upon whom nothing was lost. Beneath the bonhomie of his large, free style, his magnificent simplicity are hidden treasures of observation for the assiduous student who frequents the lithographs in a sympathetic mood.

As one follows Daumier's work with reference to its artistic development from his early and feeble drawings through the magisterial portraits of Louis-Philippe's reign to the more varied record of passing events and social types, one perceives a steady growth of the quality least often found in connection with a monumental style—the sense of movement. In all the later lithographs nothing is more salient than this. The energy of motion is in every line of the men and women and children, of the dogs and cats and horses—nothing is fixed or posed, everything is ready to shift and change as in a Japanese drawing of the Ukiyo-ye school. In the later work, too, there is a closer relation than in the earlier between the shadows or lights and the middle tones. The whites are not less white—Daumier has to the end a fondness for broad patches of the pure unsullied ground of white paper which gleams in a shirt front, a nightcap, a blouse, a tablecloth, an apron, or a broad stretch of blank wall; but the greys are higher in key as they approach the highest light and where the proportion of dark is greatest in a drawing there is more of the low-toned grey, so that the forms are relieved with less violence against their background. In the modeling of flesh there is a finer sense of the variations of surface, the local color of different parts of the face also receives a singularly exact translation into terms of black and white; the texture of fabrics, of glass and wood, of hair and fur, are differentiated with a closer precision, and especially the envelope of air becomes more pervasively felt. In a word, as Daumier continued practicing his art with the spontaneity and freedom required of a contributor to the daily press he became more and more an artist—the world appealed to him more and more on its purely pictorial side. In 1860, according to the current tradition, he decided to quit *Charivari* and abandon lithography for painting; but according to a statement made by Philippe Burty and transcribed by M. Delteil, he became at this time unpopular with the magazines which formerly had relied upon his support and *Charivari* declined to renew its contract with him. Whatever the exact cause, he did at this period turn to painting and produced watercolors and oils as remarkable in their kind as his drawings in theirs. I have seen the originals of only a few of these paintings, but the ones owned by Mr. Cyrus J. Lawrence of New York, Sir William van Horne of Montreal, and Mr. John G. Johnson of Philadelphia are of an authority, a homogeneity, and an amplitude of style sufficient to prove his place among the masters of painting. The more we study him the more we realize that his simplicity of workmanship is made up of many contributions from sources of great variety; his simplicity of character is perhaps the unifying element that made even his rich perception of the incongruous a beneficent tool in his hands rather than a destructive weapon.

Pablo Pícasso

Picasso is probably the outstanding creative artist of our time, and he is certainly the most influential. His career illustrates the entire history of modern art. He has mastered every style and participated in every art movement in the twentieth century. In many he has been the leader. Today at seventy-seven he seems to be as full of creative force as he was at twenty. In his home on the Mediterranean coast he paints, engraves, sculpts, and makes pottery with all the zest and love of life he has aways shown.

About twenty years ago a dramatic event in the Spanish Civil War led Picasso to do a group of paintings and engraving with a strong social message. He was an active Spanish Loyalist at the time and was commissioned to do a mural in 1937 that would portray the horrors of an air attack by the fascists upon the small Spanish village of Guernica. His surrealist-cubist painting by this name (on exhibit at The Modern Museum of Art in New York) is one of the most striking and widely discussed examples of contemporary art as social protest.

Born in Malaga, Spain, in 1881, Picasso did his first drawings at ten. When he was fourteen the family moved to Barcelona, where he had his first exhibition at the age of sixteen. In 1900 he went to Paris to study art and thereafter France has generally been his home. His life is easily divided into periods; during the first, his Blue Period *(1901-1904), he was influenced by the French impressionists and by the unhappy circumstances of his own life; in his* Rose Period *(1905-1906), he turned to light subjects—harlequins, circus clowns, traveling actors—and softer colors. In 1906 he met Matisse and for two or three years he fell under the spell of the new primitivism. In 1909 under the influence of Cézanne he developed, with Braque, the cubist technique and principles which he practiced till 1923. Cubism and Picasso's contribution to that movement are discussed more fully in later selections* *(see pp. 298-301 and 311-312).*

The description and analysis of his Guernica *in the following selection is reprinted from* The Challenge of Modern Art *(1949) by Allen Leepa, a member of the art faculty at Michigan State University. Professor Leepa was born in New York in 1919, studied at the American Art School and Art Students League in New York, and at the Sorbonne and Grande Chaumière, in Paris. He holds academic degrees from Columbia University, is a member of the Committee on Art Education of the Museum of Modern Art, and has exhibited paintings in Philadelphia, Birmingham, Detroit, and Madison, Wisconsin. In* The Challenge of Modern Art *Leepa discusses the important painters and movements of our own time; his chapter on* Guernica *indicates the kind of analysis upon which an adequate understanding of a painting is based.*

PICASSO'S GUERNICA

In the panel on which I am working, which I shall call Guernica, and in all of my recent works of art, I clearly express my abhorrence of the military caste which has sunk Spain in an ocean of pain and death . . .[1]

I

PABLO PICASSO, one of the leading modern painters of the twentieth century, made this statement in May 1937 while working on his now famous Guernica mural. This mural is as meaningful today as it was in 1937, for it speaks a language symbolic of our times. The Guernica mural was commissioned by the Spanish Republican government during the Civil War in Spain in 1937, for display in the Paris Exposition of that year. Picasso felt so strongly about the theme and worked so energetically that the mural was completed in little more than a month. Though he had been commissioned in January, it was not until May 1, two days after the Basque town of Guernica was destroyed by German bombers flying for General Franco, that he began work on this mural. [See Figs. 14-17.]

The mural may be interpreted in many ways. Basically, it expresses an abhorrence for war and serves a double purpose, stating symbolically, at one level, the destruction that violence and brutality cause; and, on another level, either the triumph of the people of Spain over reactionary forces, or the method by which brutality may be eliminated in society.

The picture is constructed symmetrically in three parts: a triangular form in the center, and a verticality of forms on either side. At the left is a complex of forms consisting of a woman holding a lifeless baby, fitting into the curving form of a bull. In the middle section a horse, pierced by a spear, is standing with its head stretched upward. To the right of the horse are two women. The upper one is leaning from a window, and only her head and an outstretched arm holding a lamp are visible. The lower, kneeling woman is part of the right side of the large triangle in the center of the picture, in the left corner of which is the head and outstretched arm of a prostrate warrior. At the right of the picture is a figure with arms stretched upward.

We see figures in agony, such as the woman with the child, the disembowelled horse pierced with a spear, and the helpless figure at the far right, while other figures are terrified, concerned, or bewildered. The dismembered forms, the number of sharp angles, and the staccato rhythm of separate and contrasted shapes contribute to the effect of destruction. All of the forms are involved in this mass of destruction, except the bull which stands alone, emphasized by the large expanse of dark area surrounding it. It is the most composed and majestic figure in the mural, turned away from the

[1] *Picasso: Fifty Years of His Art*, by Alfred H. Barr, Jr., The Museum of Modern Art, 1946, p. 202.

scene, looking quietly out of the picture at the spectator.

The actions of the figures and animals take place in a stage or barnlike enclosure lit by an electric bulb, illuminating the forms below and casting sharp shadows on forms while leaving other areas of the picture in comparative darkness. The preponderance of shadowy black forms contributes a sense of drama to the whole. This is furthered by the elimination of color, for the painting is done only in black, white, and gray.

What does all of this mean? What has the artist been trying to say? Two interpretations suggest themselves, one based on Picasso's statement of 1945 which he in part contradicts at a later date, and another suggested by the mural itself. These are determined by whether the bull symbolizes brutality and the horse humanity, or whether the bull represents the Spanish republic and the horse, military force. This mural may have more than one meaning and the artist may have had such a double intent when creating this work. (There seems to be a basic meaning running through both interpretations, however, for the woman holding the light may represent both the need and the triumph of liberty and truth, since she is apparently a symbolic counterpart of our own statue of liberty.) The most important factor for each person to determine for himself is whether the meaning for him is convincingly created, for above and beyond the literal meaning in a work of art are the creative ones. The artist's imagined conception in his work is part of the created form, which in turn gives vitality to literary meanings and at the same time creates its own content.

The statement by Picasso on which one interpretation of Guernica can be based was made in March 1945, shortly after the liberation of Paris during World War II. It was made in reply to questions on *Guernica:*

> No, the bull is not fascism, but it is brutality and darkness . . . the horse represents the people . . . the Guernica mural is symbolic . . . allegoric. That's the reason I used the horse, the bull, and so on. The mural is for the definite expression and solution of a problem and that is why I used symbolism."[2]

The use of the bull and horse brings to mind the Spanish bullfight arena in which the horse is the helpless victim of the ferocious bull. While the bull stands independent and undisturbed at the left of the mural the horse is badly mutilated and in apparent agony. It is enmeshed in a large triangular shape along with the slain warrior and the kneeling woman. It is as if these three figures are victims together. At the left the screaming woman immediately below the bull is contrasted with the feeling of superiority and brutality of the bull.

The symbolism of the woman trying futilely to illuminate the scene by holding a primitive light, might possibly be that old-fashioned ideas and feelings are not enough to solve the problem. She is helpless to do anything, as if kindness and humaneness alone are insufficient. Coupled with this idea is the significance of the texture of the mutilated horse in the center of the picture, which might be thought of as newsprint and could symbolize propaganda which confuses and misinforms humanity. This is a very broad interpretation of the meaning of the texture, for its main function may have been intended merely as a visual one. Yet, whether the texture is interpreted to be newsprint or not, the meaning nevertheless seems the same: the woman holding the light symbolizes liberty. The horse, representing the people violently struggling to free itself of entanglement, represents ignorance, propaganda, or the regressive forces in society, which hold the

[2] *Ibid.*

people down. The violent struggle of the figures is held within the framework of a symmetrical design structure. It is as if, no matter how vigorously the figures struggle in agony, they are held by forces that they cannot overcome.

If we follow through the interpretation that ignorance blinds the people, the implication would then be that people need further education, further enlightenment so as not to be victims of their own stupidity which finally destroys them. Man has not been able to help himself against evil forces any more than the horse can save himself from the bull. A vicious circle is represented; the solution is not through human kindness, but through enlightenment. The individual is so highly propagandized that he does not know what is good for him, and will continue to be a victim of destructive forces until he liberates himself.

A second interpretation, and one which seems to be more completely substantiated by the mural itself, is possible. The bull may represent the Spanish Republic triumphant over military force symbolized by the horse. The facts that appear to support this idea are the following: the traditional meaning of the bullfight to the Spanish people, for whom the bull represents all that is courageous and noble; the apparent animistic function of the spear in the horse's body placed there, it would seem, by Picasso himself; the light held by the woman directly above the head of the horse, as if to symbolize freedom; and the slain warrior holding a sword which could represent military force.

In 1947, in reply to questions again submitted to him, Picasso stated:

> But, this bull is a bull, this horse is a horse. There is also a sort of bird, a chicken or a pigeon, I no longer remember, on the table. This chicken is a chicken. Of course, these are symbols . . . but it is not necessary that the painter create them, these symbols, otherwise it would be better for him to write just what one wants to say, instead of painting it. It is necessary that the public, the spectators, see in the horse, in the bull, symbols that they interpret as they understand them. There are animals: these are massacred animals. That is all, for me; let the public see what it wants to see.[3]

This reply would seem paradoxical in view of his earlier answer if it were not for the fact, as he has indicated on numerous occasions, that he strongly believes art should not be described, analyzed, or taught, but should be experienced directly by the observer. Too often intellectual analysis becomes a substitute for the meaning which only the work of art itself possesses as experience. Art loses its meaning and becomes something else. Possibly because of the abhorrence of this intellectualization of an art work, and possibly because the work itself may have several meanings, Picasso prefers to throw the interpretation of Guernica back on the spectator—who must after all discover and experience it for himself. An additional consideration is that the artist, unknown to himself, expresses unconscious feelings and ideas, giving to his work both direct and indirect meanings. The bull, for example, which Picasso insists does not represent fascism, but only brutality, and which can also be interpreted to stand for the Spanish republic, has a pointed ear which resembles an emblem worn on the military hat of Benito Mussolini's Italian fascists.

The bullfight in the Spanish culture symbolizes the tragic in life; it stands for life and death, passion, virility, and courage. In the ring man tests his skill, cunning, and bravery against the strength and courage of

[3] This statement by Pablo Picasso was made in response to the following question submitted to him by Mr. Alfred H. Barr, Jr., director of The Museum of Modern Art, through Mr. Henry Kahnweiler of the Galerie Louise Leiris in Paris on May 29, 1947: "Does the bull represent the triumphant Spanish people or does it represent brutality, more specifically the nationalism of the Franco government?"

the bull; there is a battle to death between the bull and man. The bull in Spanish culture represents the most courageous and powerful of beasts and, therefore, a worthy opponent of man. The horse, on the other hand, in contrast to our own idealized concept of him as the noblest of beasts, is considered a weak animal suitable for goring by the bull.

From the first inception of *Guernica,* as revealed in the early sketches, the woman who is holding the light and the bull are the triumphant forces. They are not in conflict, as in Picasso's earlier etching, *Minotauromachy,* in which a man with the head of a bull seeks to shield himself from a light held by a child [Fig. 13]. Rather, both the Spanish republic and justice, represented by the bull and the woman, are triumphant. It seems reasonable to assume that they both stand for a similar purpose, with the bull perhaps not only representing the Spanish republic, but strength as well.

The horse is pierced by a spear, yet there is no figure in the picture that placed it there. The slain warrior is holding a broken sword, not the remnants of a shattered spear. The horse seems to be an animistic object, which Picasso has himself pierced as if magically to destroy it. The slain warrior, representing the military caste of Spain, is holding a military, rather than a bullfighter's sword. He is underneath the horse, completely vanquished, with his only means of defense, his sword, shattered.

To further support the idea that the horse represents the forces of evil, possibly the military caste itself, which is vanquished by liberty and justice—in several sketches for the mural the woman leaning from a window holds her light triumphantly *directly above* the horse.

Picasso, as a Spaniard, has both a conscious and subconscious relation to the events in Spain. Symbolism in a painting is both conscious and subconscious in origin. And the conscious symbols have strong affinity to subconscious forces. The strong emotional feeling attracted to the symbols can be attributed in part to their subconscious appeal to the artist and the spectator.

II

The sketches leading up to *Guernica* give us some insight into how the work developed. The first sketch, *Guernica—Composition Study I,* is only the roughest schematic representation of his idea. Interesting to note is that the space direction into the third dimension is diagonal toward the left, which is similar to the final sketch on the mural itself, before painting. The planes creating this movement are parallel to the surface of the canvas and form the structural basis of the picture. *Guernica—Composition Study II* shows two scenes, the upper again representing the same feeling as the first sketch, while the lower shows individual forms for the first time definitely delineated, with emphasis on a more linear surface relationship of forms. *Guernica—Composition Study III* seems to substantiate this space idea, for forms are based on imaginative, rhythmic line relationships, emphasizing the flatness of the canvas. In the next two composition studies which are more complete, done on May 1st and May 2d, Picasso has more clearly indicated how the symbols were to be used. The comprehensive composition study done on May 9th has a greater number of forms than before; there is a greater sense of destruction, a stagelike space, and a combination of abstract and realistic forms: light and dark are used, and the whole has taken on a dramatic, deathlike, and wholly destructive effect [Fig. 15].

While Picasso was making compositional sketches, and even after he had put a preliminary drawing on his canvas, *Guernica, 1st state May 11,* he created numerous sketches of isolated elements in the mural. For example, the compositional study, *Hand with Broken Sword,* shows the slain warrior's hand, which very expressively conveys, even in this detail, the agony of the soldier. Figures are twisted out of position, clasping the sword handle; and the whole is simply and powerfully designed. *Woman with Dead Child,* a sketch done on May 28 while the mural was in progress, very expressively creates the suffering of the woman holding the child, who is pierced by an arrow. The compositional design is very different from that finally evolved for the woman and child under the bull in the mural. The creative and emotional vitality of the artist can be realized in this sketch and in the way he works out his feelings, constantly changing his forms and trying to express his emotions as powerfully as possible. Picasso did not copy either of these sketches in the mural. They served rather as means of projecting his feeling, as if he needed these drawings for purposes of exploring and intensifying them, perhaps at the same time helping himself become more fully acquainted with the potential expression his subject matter would suggest.

In the first drawing that was placed on the canvas the space structure moves diagonally to the left into depth, at the same time that an imaginary frontal plane has been created. Abstract structural planes help to create this frontal plane, and help bring the forms in depth back to the surface. Compare this preliminary stage of *Guernica* with the last painting and notice how the whole has changed. In the final painting the scene takes place indoors, the bull has been represented at the far left, the horse's head is placed high, and the head of the slain warrior is placed toward the edge of the picture. Notice, too, how forms have been altered as a result of the change in the artist's conception and the method of execution. In the final painting the abstract planes now become emphasized. In developing this picture, Picasso worked in large areas of black, white, and grey, some of which changed along with the shapes already drawn. At the same time entirely new ones developed. Here the artist has worked with an over-all plan but constantly changed and developed and enlarged on it.

III

In analyzing the two- and three-dimensional movements of the mural we find that the numerous forms comprising the large triangular shape in the middle of the picture direct the three-dimensional space diagonally into depth from left to right in a counterclockwise direction. The forms closest to the spectator are below the horse and it is through these that we are led into the picture. The slain warrior, horse and light triangular plane to the right of the horse, create the diagonal space movement into depth. The counterclockwise movement is created by the plane cutting across the body of the horse, by its tail, by its head, by the arm clutching the sword, by the kneeling woman, by the light triangular plane, and by the woman holding the light. To balance the space movements one against the other, the horse's head directs space forward from right to left, while the arm directs space forward from left to right. The edge of the light plane cutting across the horse's body from the man's head at the left to the base of the horse's neck, shifts down and right at an angle, and is opposed by a movement up and to the left directed by the position of the horse's head, the lamp, and the electric bulb.

In the left portion of the mural, the circular movement of the figures of the bull, woman and child depends upon the interlocking and opposing movements based on the directions of the light masses, the linear directions of the edges of the forms, and the directions of areas behind and between the forms. At the right the figure of the man balances the tripart design.

This mural was created to convey a message. How well does it succeed, and to whom is this message directed? Picasso could have made his forms more realistic as he did in *Minotauromachy*, yet he chose in the final version of the work to keep them semiabstract. Apparently he felt that this way of presenting his work better served his purpose. The mural has a cartoonlike quality. A cartoon serves to present a forceful message, and its forms represent persons and ideas, and are often distorted; it is quite often symbolic and its message is direct and simple. But while using cartoonlike forms, Picasso presents a message that is complex, though direct. At the same time the clarity of the objects as realistic forms is subordinated to design and abstract planes. One is forced to search for the meaning of the images and symbols used at the same time that attention is focused on the vehicle of communication. The relation between the two, the nature and importance of contemporary art and perhaps the very important relation between esthetic experience and the world in which we live is emphasized. Because there is not a very simple literary interpretation of *Guernica* it cannot be easily pigeonholed into one of the accepted concepts and thereby easily forgotten. Rather, it offers a challenge. Apparently it is the very meanings accepted so readily by many persons that Picasso wants to challenge. And it is to those who will make the effort to understand its message that the mural addresses itself. But even more important than its message is the creative concept of the work. Does it convey strong emotional meanings? Is it a vital statement by a contemporary artist? Does it seem to embody the crisis and tempo of the present-day world? Does it live as a creative work of art? These are the questions that you must determine for yourself. Perhaps you will find that the answers to them depend more on the emotional meanings that the mural has for you than on its literal meanings. If so, new directions in the *experiencing* of art may suggest themselves to you.

Diego Rivera

Among other ways the social outlook of our day has found expression in the rebirth of mural painting. Murals are paintings that do not hang on a wall in a frame but form part of the wall itself. With its close dependence on architecture, mural painting tends naturally toward epic breadth, objectivity, and collective appeal. As a rule, in order to be effective a mural must be direct and simple. Complexity and subtlety endanger its appeal. If it is a part of a public building, it must appeal to the public directly rather than to art lovers and critics only. Social criticism, nationalism, and the glorification of a nation's historic roots in folklore and legend are interwoven in the subject matter of many modern murals. Mural art, therefore, is essentially an "idea art," and, whether we agree or disagree with the concept thus expressed, no medium offers a better opportunity to study the interrelationship between social message or propaganda and visual form. Among contemporary painters the work of Diego Rivera and of José Orozco, influential Mexican muralists, provide the clearest example of this relationship.

Rivera was born in Guanajuato, a small town in western Mexico, in 1886. Like a number of contemporary painters, composers, and writers, he first tried to find inspiration in the great international centers of culture. During his years in Paris, his "cubist period," his work showed little originality. His great talent and superb draftsmanship made it easy for him to follow any style that took his fancy, and for a time he was a diligent student and imitator of Picasso and Braque, influential artists only a few years older than Rivera himself. Only after his return to Mexico in 1922 did Rivera really "find himself." He abandoned the idea of art for art's sake and instead of painting abstractions began to work in a style that looked simple and illustrative. He used a great deal of symbolism, but his symbols were always easily understood. The oppression of the Indians by the Spaniards and the contrast between the wealthy and the poor were problems that impressed him deeply.

These issues gave Rivera's painting from the outset the character of social message and even of propaganda, for he expressed his radical political views explicitly in the subjects he painted. In this country, he worked under the sponsorship of two wealthy men, John D. Rockefeller, Jr., and Edsel Ford, and in both instances his murals caused violent controversy. The Rockefeller Center murals in New York were destroyed by order of the outraged representatives of the Rockefeller family; the murals at the Detroit Institute of Arts still stand intact. Many of the important public buildings in Mexico also contain murals done by Rivera, and even there frequent controversy has resulted from his painting. He died in 1958.

Few great artists have been as vocal as Rivera in explaining what they were attempting to do. An article of his included here, "The Revolutionary Spirit in Modern Art," makes it clear that for him idea and visual form are inseparable and art is always an instrument of social message. [See also Figs. 18 and 19.]

THE REVOLUTIONARY SPIRIT IN MODERN ART

I

ART is a social creation. It manifests a division in accordance with the division of social classes. There is a bourgeois art, there is a revolutionary art, there is a peasant art. The proletariat produces art of struggle but no class can produce a class art until it has reached the highest point of its development. The bourgeoisie reached its zenith in the French Revolution and thereafter created art expressive of itself. When the proletariat in its turn really begins to produce its art, it will be after the proletarian dictatorship has fulfilled its mission, liquidated all class differences, and produced a classless society. The art of the future, therefore, will not be proletarian but Communist. During the course of its development, however, and even after it has come into power, the proletariat must not refuse the best technical devices of bourgeois art, just as it uses bourgeois technical equipment in the form of cannon, machine guns, and steam turbines.

Such artists as Daumier and Courbet in the nineteenth century were able to reveal their revolutionary spirit in spite of their bourgeois environment. Honoré Daumier was a forthright fighter, expressing in his pictures the revolutionary movement of the nineteenth century, the movement that produced the Communist Manifesto. Daumier was revolutionary both in expression and in ideological content. In order to say what he wanted to say, he developed a new technique. When he was not actually painting an anecdote of revolutionary char-

[Reprinted from *Modern Quarterly*, Autumn 1932.]

acter, but was merely drawing a woman carrying clothes or a man seated at a table eating, he was nevertheless creating art of a definitely revolutionary character. Daumier developed a drastic technique identified with revolutionary feeling, so that his form, his method, his technique always expressed that feeling. For example, if we take his famous laundress,* we find that he has painted her with neither the eye of a literary man nor with that of a photographer. Daumier saw his laundress through class-conscious eyes. He was aware of her connection with life and labor. In the vibration of his lines, in the quantity and quality of color which he projected upon the canvas, we see a creation directly contrary and opposed to the creations of bourgeois conservative art. The position of each object, the effects of light in the picture, all such things express the personality in its complete connection with its surroundings and with life. The laundress is not only a laundress leaving the river bank, burdened with her load of clothes and dragging a child behind her; she is, at one and the same time, the expression of the weariness of labor and the tragedy of proletarian motherhood. Thus we see, weighing upon her, the heavy burdens of her position as woman and the heavy burdens of her position as laborer; in the background we discern the houses of Paris, both aristocratic and bourgeois. In a fraction of a second, a person, unless he be blind, can see in the figure of this laundress not only a figure but a whole connection with life and labor and the times in which she lives. In other paintings of Daumier are depicted scenes of the actual class struggle, but whether he is portraying the class struggle or not, in both types of painting we can regard him as a revolutionary artist. He is so not because he was of proletarian extraction, for he was not. He did not come from a factory, he was not of a working-class family; his origin was bourgeois, he worked for the bourgeois papers, selling his drawings to them. Nevertheless, he was able to create art which was an efficacious weapon in the revolutionary struggle, just as Marx and Engels despite their bourgeois origin were able to write works which serve as basis for the development of the proletarian revolutionary movement.

The important fact to note is that the man who is truly a thinker, or the painter who is truly an artist, cannot, at a given historical moment, take any but a position in accordance with the revolutionary development of his own time. The social struggle is the richest, the most intense, and the most plastic subject which an artist can choose. Therefore, one who is born to be an artist can certainly not be insensible to such developments. When I say born to be an artist, I refer to the constitution or make-up of his eyes, of his nervous system, of his sensibility, and of his brains. The artist is a direct product of life. He is an apparatus born to be the receptor, the condenser, the transmitter, and the reflector of the aspirations, the desires, and the hopes of his age. At times, the artist serves to condense and transmit the desires of millions of proletarians; at times, he serves as the condenser and transmitter only for small strata of the intellectuals or small layers of the *bourgeoisie*. We can establish it as a basic fact that the importance of an artist can be measured directly by the size of the multitudes whose aspirations and whose life he serves to condense and translate.

The typical theory of nineteenth-century bourgeois esthetic criticism, namely "art for art's sake," is an indirect affirmation of the fact which I have just stressed. According to this theory, the best art is the so-called "art for art's sake," or "pure" art. One of its characteristics is that it can be appreciated only by a very limited number of

* See Figure 12.

superior persons. It is implied thereby that only those few superior persons are capable of appreciating that art; and since it is a superior function it necessarily implies the fact that there are very few superior persons in society. This artistic theory which pretends to be apolitical has really an enormous political content—the implication of the superiority of the few. Further, this theory serves to discredit the use of art as a revolutionary weapon and serves to affirm that all art which has a theme, a social content, is bad art. It serves, moreover, to limit the possessors of art, to make art into a kind of stock-exchange commodity manufactured by the artist, bought and sold on the stock exchange, subject to the speculative rise and fall which any commercialized thing is subject to in stock-exchange manipulations. At the same time, this theory creates a legend which envelops art, the legend of its intangible, sacrosanct, and mysterious character which makes art aloof and inaccessible to the masses. European painting throughout the nineteenth century had this general aspect. The revolutionary painters are to be regarded as heroic exceptions. Since art is a product that nourishes human beings it is subject to the action of the law of supply and demand just as in any other product necessary to life. In the nineteenth century the proletariat was in no position to make an effective economic demand for art products. The demand was all on the part of the bourgeois. It can be only as a striking and heroic exception, therefore, that art of a revolutionary character can be produced under the circumstances of bourgeois demand.

II

At present art has a very definite and important role to play in the class struggle. It is definitely useful to the proletariat. There is great need for artistic expression of the revolutionary movement. Art has the advantage of speaking a language that can easily be understood by the workers and peasants of all lands. A Chinese peasant or worker can understand a revolutionary painting much more readily and easily than he can understand a book written in English. He needs no translator. That is precisely the advantage of revolutionary art. A revolutionary painting takes far less time and it says far more than a lecture does.

Since the proletariat has need of art, it is necessary that the proletariat take possession of art to serve as a weapon in the class struggle. To take possession or control of art, it is necessary that the proletariat carry on the struggle on two fronts. On one front is a struggle against the production of bourgeois art,—and when I say struggle I mean struggle in every sense—and on the other is a struggle to develop the ability of the proletariat to produce its own art. It is necessary for the proletariat to learn to make use of beauty in order to live better. It ought to develop its sensibilities, and learn to enjoy and make use of the works of art which the *bourgeoisie*, because of special advantages of training, has produced. Nor should the proletariat wait for some painter of good will or good intentions to come to them from the *bourgeoisie*; it is time that the proletariat develop artists from their own midst. By the collaboration of the artists who have come out of the proletariat and those who sympathize and are in alliance with the proletariat, there should be created an art which is definitely and in every way superior to the art which is produced by the artists of the *bourgeoisie*.

Such a task is the program of the Soviet Union today. Before the Russian Revolution, many artists from Russia, including those who were leading figures in the Russian revolutionary movement, had long discussions in their exile in Paris over the question as to what should be the true nature of revolutionary art. I had the opportunity to take part, at various times, in those discussions. The best theorizers in those discussions, misunderstanding the doctrine of Marx which they sought to apply, came to the conclusion that revolutionary art ought to take the best art that the *bourgeoisie* had developed and bring that art directly to the revolutionary masses. Each of the artists was certain that his own type of art was the best that the *bourgeoisie* had produced. Those artists who had the greatest development of collective spirit, those who had grouped themselves around various "isms," such as cubism and futurism, were convinced that their particular group was creating the art which would become the art of the revolutionary proletariat as soon as they were able to bring that particular "ism," that particular school of art, to the proletariat. I ventured to disagree with them, maintaining that while it was necessary to utilize the innumerable technical developments which bourgeois art had developed, we had to use them in the same way that the Soviet Union utilizes the machine technique that the *bourgeoisie* has developed. The Soviet Union takes the best technical development and machinery of the *bourgeoisie* and adapts it to the needs and special conditions of the new proletarian regime; in art, I contended, we must also use the most advanced technical achievements of bourgeois art but must adapt them to the need of the proletariat so as to create an art which by its clarity, by its accessibility, and by its relation to the new order, should be adapted to the needs of the proletarian revolution and the proletarian regime. But I could not insist upon their accepting my opinion, for, up to the time of that discussion, I had not created anything which in any way differed fundamentally from the type of art that my comrades were creating. I had arrived at my conclusion in the following manner: I had seen the failure and defeat of the Mexican revolution of 1919, a defeat which I became convinced was the result of a lack of theoretical understanding on the part of the Mexican proletariat and peasantry. I left Mexico when the counterrevolution was developing under Madero, deciding to go to Europe to get the theoretical understanding and the technical development in art which I thought was to be found there.

The Russian comrades returned from Paris to Russia immediately after the Revolution, taking with them the most advanced technique in painting which they had learned in Paris. They did their best and created works of considerable beauty, utilizing all the technique which they had learned. They carried on a truly heroic struggle to make that art accessible to the Russian masses. They worked under conditions of famine, the strain of revolution and counterrevolution, and all the material and economic difficulties imaginable, yet they failed completely in their attempts to persuade the masses to accept cubism, or futurism, or constructivism as the art of the proletariat. Extended discussions of the whole problem arose in Russia. Those discussions and the confusion resulting from the rejection of modern art gave an opportunity to the bad painters to take advantage of the situation. The academic painters, the worst painters who had survived from the old regime in Russia, soon provided competition on a normal grand scale. Pictures inspired by the new tendencies of the most advanced European schools were exhibited side by side with the works of the worst academic schools of Russia. Unfortunately, those that won the applause of the public were not the new painters and the new European schools but the old and bad academic painters. Strangely enough, it seems to me, it was not the modernistic painters but the masses of the Russian people who were correct in the controversy. Their vote showed not that they considered the academic painters as the painters of the proletariat, but that the art of the proletariat must not be a hermetic art, an art inaccessible except to those who have developed and undergone an elaborate esthetic preparation. The art of the proletariat has to be an art that is warm and clear and strong. It was not that the proletariat of Russia was telling these artists: "You are too modern for us." What it said was: "You are not modern enough to be artists of the proletarian revolution." The revolution and its theory, dialectical materialism, have no use for art of the ivory-tower variety. They have need of an art which is as full of content as the proletarian revolution itself, as clear and forthright as the theory of the proletarian revolution.

III

In Russia there exists the art of the people, namely peasant art. It is an art rooted in the soil. In its colors, its materials, and its force it is perfectly adapted to the environment out of which it is born. It represents the production of art with the simplest resources and in the least costly form. For these reasons it will be of great utility to the proletariat in developing its own art. The better Russian painters working directly after the Revolution should have recognized this and then built upon it, for the proletariat, so closely akin to the peasant in many ways, would have been able to understand this art. Instead of this the academic artists, intrinsically reactionary, were able to get control of the situation. Reaction in art is not merely a matter of theme. A painter who conserves and uses the worst technique of bourgeois art is a reactionary artist, even though he may use this technique to paint such a subject as the death of Lenin or the red flag on the barricades. In the same fashion, an engineer engaged in the construction of a dam with the purpose of irrigating Russian soil would be reactionary if he were to utilize the bourgeois procedures of the beginning of the nineteenth century. In that case he would be reactionary; he would be guilty of a crime against the Soviet Union, even though he were trying to construct a dam for the purpose of irrigation.

The Russian theater was safe from the bankruptcy which Russian painting suffered. It was in direct contact with the masses, and, therefore, has developed into the best theater that the world knows today. Bit by bit, the theater has attracted to it painters, sculptors, and, of course, actors, dancers, musicians. Everyone in the Soviet Union who has any talent for art is being attracted to the theater as a fusion of arts. In proportion with the progress made in the construction of socialism in the Soviet Union, artists are turning more and more to the theater for expression and the masses are coming closer and closer to the theater as an "expression of their life." The result is that the other arts are languishing and Russia is producing less and less of the type of art which, in the rest of Europe, serves as shares on the stock exchange.

Mural art is the most significant art for the proletariat. In Russia mural paintings are projected on the walls of clubs, of union headquarters, and even on the walls of the factories. But Russian workers came to me and declared that in their houses they would prefer having landscapes and still-lives, which would bring them a feeling of restfulness. But the easel picture is an object of luxury, quite beyond the means of the proletariat. I told my fellow artists in Russia that they should sell their paintings to the workers at low prices, give them to them if necessary. After all, the government was supplying the colors, the canvas, and the material necessary for painting, so that artists could have sold their work at low prices. The majority, however, preferred to wait for the annual purchase of paintings made by the Commissariat of Education when pictures were, and still are, bought for five hundred rubles each.

I did not feel that I had the right to insist upon my viewpoint until I had created something of the type of art I was talking about. Therefore, in 1921, instead of going to Russia where I had been invited by the Commissariat of Education, I went to Mexico to attempt to create some of the art that I had been exalting. This effort of mine had in it something of the flavor of adventure because, in Mexico, there was a proletarian regime. There was in power at that time, a fraction of the *bourgeoisie* that had need of demagogy as a weapon in maintaining itself in power. It gave us walls, and we Mexican artists painted subjects of a revolutionary character. We painted, in fact, what we pleased, even including a certain number of paintings which were certainly communistic in character. Our task was first to develop and remake mural paintings in the direction of the needs of the proletariat, and, second, to note the effect that such mural painting might have upon the proletarians and peasants in Mexico, so painting would be an effective instrument of the proletariat in power. But let me note also another fact. In Mexico there existed an old tradition, a popular art tradition much older and much more splendid than even the peasant art of Russia. This art is of a truly magnificent character. The colonial rulers of Mexico, like those of the United States, had despised that ancient art tradition which existed there, but they failed to destroy it completely. With this art as background, I became the first revolutionary painter in Mexico. The paintings served to attract many young painters, painters who had not yet developed sufficient social consciousness. We formed a painters' union and began to cover the walls of buildings in Mexico with revolutionary art. At the same time we revolutionized the methods of teaching drawing and art to children with the result that the children of Mexico began producing artistic works in the course of their elementary school development.

As a result of these things, when, in 1927, I was again invited to go to Moscow, I felt that I could go as we Mexicans had some experience which might help Soviet Russia. I ought to remark at this point that among the painters in Mexico, thanks to the development of the new methods of teaching painting in the schools of the workers, there developed various working-class painters of great merit, among them Maximo Patcheco, whom I considered the best mural painter in Mexico.

The experience which I tried to offer to the Russian painters was brought to Russia at a moment of intense controversy. In spite of the fact that it was a poor time for artistic discussion and development, Corrolla, the comrade who was formerly in charge of Agitprop work, organized a group, "October," to discuss and make use of the Mexican artistic experiments. I was asked to paint by the metallurgical workers who wanted me to paint the walls in their club, the Dynamo Club on the Leningrad Chaussée. Soon, however, owing to differences not of an esthetic but of a political character, I was instructed to return to Mexico to take part in the "election campaign beginning there." A few months after my return to Mexico I was expelled from the party. Since then, I have remained in a position which is characteristically Mexican, namely that of the guerilla fighter. I could not receive my munitions from the party because my party had expelled me; neither could I acquire them through my personal funds because I haven't any. I took them and will continue to take them, as the guerilla fighter must, from the enemy. Therefore, I take the munitions from the hands of the *bourgeoisie*. My munitions are the walls, the colors, and the money necessary to feed myself so that I may continue to work. On the walls of the *bourgeoisie*, painting cannot always have as fighting an aspect as it could on the walls, let us say, of a revolutionary school. The guerilla fighter sometimes can derail a train, sometimes blow up a bridge, but sometimes he can only cut a few telegraph wires. Each time he does what he can. Whether important or insignificant, his action is always within the revolutionary line. The guerilla fighter is always ready, at the time of amnesty, to return to the ranks and become a simple soldier like everybody else.

IV

And now we come to the question of propaganda. All painters have been propagandists or else they have not been painters. Giotto was a propagandist of the spirit of Christian charity, the weapon of the Franciscan monks of his time against feudal oppression. Breughel was a propagandist of the struggle of the Dutch artisan petty *bourgeoisie* against feudal oppression. Every artist who has been worth anything in art has been such a propagandist. The familiar accusation that propaganda ruins art finds its source in bourgeois prejudice. Naturally enough the *bourgeoisie* does not want art employed for the sake of revolution. It does not want ideals in art because its own ideals cannot any longer serve as artistic inspiration. It does not want feelings because its own feelings cannot any longer serve as artistic inspiration. Art and thought and feeling must be hostile to the *bourgeoisie* today. Every strong artist has a head and a heart. Every strong artist has been a propagandist. I want to be a propagandist and I want to be nothing else. I want to be a propagandist of communism and I want to be it in all that I can think, in all that I can speak, in all that I can write, and in all that I can paint. I want to use my art as a weapon.

For the real development on a grand scale of revolutionary art in America, it is necessary to have a situation where all unite in a single party of the proletariat and are in a position to take over the public buildings, public resources, and the wealth of the country. Only then can there develop a genuine revolutionary art. The fact that the *bourgeoisie* is in a state of degeneration and depends for its art on the art of Europe indicates that there cannot be a development of genuine American art, except in so far as the proletariat is able to create it. In order to be good art, art in this country must be revolutionary art, art of the proletariat, or it will not be good art at all.

5

SOCIAL CONCERN IN LITERATURE

Walt Whitman

The poetry of Walt Whitman reflects clearly and directly the American national ideals of the nineteenth century—the dream that European immigrants might find new hope and freedom in the West; the desire to realize in this nation the democratic ideals of liberty, equality, and brotherhood; the belief that here was a new frontier for decadent Europe. In both poetic form and idea Whitman considered himself a part of democracy. He praised it often and vigorously; it seemed to him almost a religion. But for Whitman democracy was not primarily a matter of government or politics; he based his theory of democracy on comradeship, on the meeting of kindred spirits, on the opportunity America offered its young men and young women, whom he greatly admired, to grow to full stature and to lead the world to a community of nations.

Born on Long Island in 1819 in what was then open country, Whitman lived in Brooklyn when it still had the atmosphere of a small town and worked in New York as it grew to be a great city. When he wrote about different aspects of American life, he nearly always spoke from experience. At various times he was a carpenter, a school teacher, a reporter, and a newspaper editor. He worked in Washington as a clerk in the Indian Bureau of the Department of the Interior until dismissed for writing Leaves of Grass, *which was then considered an indecent book. His last years were spent in retirement at Camden, New Jersey, where he died in 1892. The fame he openly desired during his life came to him belatedly in the twentieth century.*

Leaves of Grass *is Whitman's major book of verse. It first appeared as a slim volume in 1855, and Whitman spent the rest of his life amplifying and revising it. In all, eleven editions were published, each larger than the one before. Emerson and others hailed the first collection but were shocked and repelled by some of the franker poems in the second. Whitman's poetry does not seem to us today so revolutionary as it did to his contemporaries. He freed himself completely from the restrictions of traditional metrical forms, however, and worked out a technique of his own, utilizing free organic rhythm, parallelism, various repetitive devices, and a large and indiscriminate vocabulary drawn from all levels of linguistic usage.*

It is ironic that for the most part he has never been widely accepted by the common people whose cause he wished to champion. On the contrary, especially in America, he has been admired chiefly in intellectual circles. His great fame and influence as a writer in practically every country of the world, however, is evidence of the wide appeal of his poetic message. Both the spirit and the form of this message are apparent in the three poems we include here.

I HEAR AMERICA SINGING

I hear America singing, the varied carols I hear,
Those of mechanics, each one singing his as it should be blithe and strong,
The carpenter singing his as he measures his plank or beam,
The mason singing his as he makes ready for work, or leaves off work,
The boatman singing what belongs to him in his boat, the deck-hand singing on the steamboat deck,
The shoemaker singing as he sits on his bench, the hatter singing as he stands,
The wood-cutter's song, the ploughboy's on his way in the morning or at noon intermission or at sundown,
The delicious singing of the mother, or of the young wife at work, or of the girl sewing or washing,
Each singing what belongs to him or her and to none else,
The day what belongs to the day—at night the party of young fellows, robust, friendly,
Singing with open mouths their strong melodious songs.

PIONEERS! O PIONEERS!

Come my tan-faced children,
Follow well in order, get your weapons ready,
Have you your pistols? have you your sharp-edged axes?
Pioneers! O pioneers!

For we cannot tarry here,
We must march my darlings, we must bear the brunt of danger,
We the youthful sinewy races, all the rest on us depend,
Pioneers! O pioneers!

O you youths, Western youths,
So impatient, full of action, full of manly pride and friendship,
Plain I see you Western youths, see you tramping with the foremost,
Pioneers! O pioneers!

Have the elder races halted?
Do they droop and end their lesson, wearied over there beyond the seas?
We take up the task eternal, and the burden and the lesson,
Pioneers! O pioneers!

All the past we leave behind,
We debouch upon a newer mightier world, varied world,
Fresh and strong the world we seize, world of labor and the march,
Pioneers! O pioneers!

We detachments steady throwing,
Down the edges, through the passes, up the mountains steep,
Conquering, holding, daring, venturing as we go the unknown ways,
Pioneers! O pioneers!

We primeval forests felling,
We the rivers stemming, vexing we and piercing deep the mines within,
We the surface broad surveying, we the virgin soil upheaving,
Pioneers! O pioneers!

Colorado men are we,
From the peaks gigantic, from the great sierras and the high plateaus,
From the mine and from the gully, from the hunting trail we come,
Pioneers! O pioneers!

From Nebraska, from Arkansas,
Central inland race are we, from Missouri, with the continental blood intervein'd,
All the hands of comrades clasping, all the Southern, all the Northern,
Pioneers! O pioneers!

O resistless restless race!
O beloved race in all! O my breast aches with tender love for all!
O I mourn and yet exult, I am rapt with love for all,
Pioneers! O pioneers!

Raise the mighty mother mistress,
Waving high the delicate mistress, over all the starry mistress, (bend your heads all)
Raise the fang'd and warlike mistress, stern, impassive, weapon'd mistress,
Pioneers! O pioneers!

See my children, resolute children,
By those swarms upon our rear we must never yield or falter,
Ages back in ghostly millions frowning there behind us urging,
Pioneers! O pioneers!

On and on the compact ranks,
With accessions ever waiting, with the places of the dead quickly fill'd,
Through the battle, through defeat, moving yet and never stopping,
Pioneers! O pioneers!

O to die advancing on!
Are there some of us to droop and die? has the hour come?
Then upon the march we fittest die, soon and sure the gap is fill'd,
Pioneers! O pioneers!

All the pulses of the world,
Falling in they beat for us, with the Western movement beat,
Holding single or together, steady moving to the front, all for us,
Pioneers! O pioneers!

Life's involv'd and varied pageants,
All the forms and shows, all the workmen at their work,
All the seamen and the landsmen, all the masters with their slaves,
Pioneers! O pioneers!

All the hapless silent lovers,
All the prisoners in the prisons, all the righteous and the wicked,
All the joyous, all the sorrowing, all the living, all the dying,
Pioneers! O pioneers!

I too with my soul and body,
We, a curious trio, picking, wandering on our way,
Through these shores amid the shadows, with the apparitions pressing,
Pioneers! O pioneers!

Lo, the darting bowling orb!
Lo, the brother orbs around, all the clustering suns and planets,
All the dazzling days, all the mystic nights with dreams,
Pioneers! O pioneers!

These are of us, they are with us,
All for primal needed work, while the followers there in embryo wait behind,
We to-day's procession heading, we the route for travel clearing,
Pioneers! O pioneers!

O you daughters of the West!
O you young and elder daughters! O you mothers and you wives!
Never must you be divided, in our ranks you move united,
Pioneers! O pioneers!

Minstrels latent on the prairies!
(Shrouded bards of other lands, you may rest, you have done your work,)
Soon I hear you coming warbling, soon you rise and tramp amid us,
Pioneers! O pioneers!

Not for delectations sweet,
Not the cushion and the slipper, not the peaceful and the studious,
Not the riches safe and palling, not for us the tame enjoyment,
Pioneers! O pioneers!

Do the feasters gluttonous feast?
Do the corpulent sleepers sleep? have they lock'd and bolted doors?
Still be ours the diet hard, and the blanket on the ground,
Pioneers! O pioneers!

Has the night descended?
Was the road of late so toilsome? did we stop discouraged nodding on our way?
Yet a passing hour I yield you in your tracks to pause oblivious,
Pioneers! O pioneers!

Till with sound of trumpet,
Far, far off the daybreak call—hark! how loud and clear I hear it wind,
Swift! to the head of the army!—swift! spring to your places,
Pioneers! O pioneers!

YEARS OF THE MODERN

Years of the modern! years of the unperform'd!
Your horizon rises, I see it parting away for more august dramas,
I see not America only, not only Liberty's nation but other nations preparing,
I see tremendous entrances and exits, new combinations, the solidarity of races,
I see that force advancing with irresistible power on the world's stage,
(Have the old forces, the old wars, played their parts? are the acts suitable to them closed?)
I see Freedom, completely arm'd and victorious and very haughty, with Law on one side and Peace on the other,
A stupendous trio all issuing forth against the idea of caste;
What historic denouements are these we so rapidly approach?
I see men marching and countermarching by swift millions,
I see the frontiers and boundaries of the old aristocracies broken,
I see landmarks of European kings removed,
I see this day the People beginning their landmarks, (all others give way;)
Never were such sharp questions ask'd as this day,

Never was average man, his soul, more energetic, more like a God,
Lo, how he urges and urges, leaving the masses no rest!
His daring foot is on land and sea everywhere, he colonizes the Pacific, the archipelagoes,
With the steamship, the electric telegraph, the newspaper, the wholesale engines of war,
With these and the world-spreading factories he interlinks all geography, all lands;
What whispers are these O lands, running ahead of you, passing under the seas?
Are all nations communing? is there to be but one heart to the globe?
Is humanity forming en-masse? for lo, tyrants tremble, crowns grow dim,
The earth, restive, confronts a new era, perhaps a general divine war,
No one knows what will happen next, such portents fill the days and nights;
Years prophetical! the space ahead as I walk, as I vainly try to pierce it, is full of phantoms,
Unborn deeds, things soon to be, project their shapes around me,
This incredible rush and heat, this strange ecstatic fever of dreams O years!
Your dreams O years, how they penetrate through me! (I know not whether I sleep or wake;)
The perform'd America and Europe grow dim, retiring in shadow behind me,
The unperform'd, more gigantic than ever, advance, advance upon me.

Carl Sandburg

One might almost say that Carl Sandburg was born with a passionate love of humanity and a powerful imagination. His early life filled him with a revolutionary urge to help bring about the millennium in America. Although he had no particular program for eliminating the evils of an industrial society, he mounted the soapbox as a young man to condemn the injustices he so keenly felt and he participated in various ways in the labor movement before World War I. In 1914 his poem Chicago *won the Levinson Award given by* Poetry *magazine for the "best poem written by a citizen of the United States during the year," and two years later, with the publication of* Chicago Poems, *his fame as a poet was established. From then on he published steadily. In 1927 he collected an anthology of folk songs,* The American Songbag; *in 1936 his poem,* The People, Yes, *paid an epic tribute to American democracy.*

Abraham Lincoln came to symbolize for Sandburg the highest ideals of American democracy, and the major achievement of his life has been his Lincoln biography. In 1940 he won the Pulitzer prize for this monumental six-volume work which came out in two parts, The Prairie Years *in 1926,* The War Years *in 1939. The work of a painstaking scholar, his biography is the work also of an artist and skilled craftsman; it shows poetic feeling rare in a scholarly study.*

Born in Galesburg, Illinois, in 1878, Sandburg belongs to the first generation of modern American poets. Like Whitman, whom he resembles in many ways, he had a wide experience in the common walks of American life and developed a great devotion to ordinary men and women. At thirteen he left school to take a job on a milk wagon; he worked as porter in a barbershop, scene-shifter in a theatre, and trucker in a brick kiln, then traveled west from Galesburg to successive jobs building railroads, washing dishes, and harvesting wheat. During the Spanish-American War he fought in Puerto Rico and with his mustering-out pay entered Lombard College in Galesburg, where he spent three or four years without actually graduating. Here he had his first taste of literary activity and sharpened his desire to improve social and economic conditions for the working man.

In later years Sandburg read his poetry to enthusiastic audiences the length and breadth of the land. With his "songbag" and guitar he thought of himself as a kind of contemporary American bard. He writes in free verse; his language is full of slang and jargon of every kind; but his poems have caught the rhythm of the American vernacular and this rhythm is determined by ordinary speech rather than by any set metrical pattern. The poem reprinted here is typical of his style and is widely known. It shows Sandburg's hatred of hypocrisy, his championship of the underdog, his relish for the vernacular and the whole panorama of American life.

THE SINS OF KALAMAZOO

The sins of Kalamazoo are neither scarlet nor crimson.
The sins of Kalamazoo are a convict gray, a dishwater
drab.
And the people who sin the sins of Kalamazoo are
neither scarlet nor crimson.
They run to drabs and grays—and some of them sing
they shall be washed whiter than snow—and
some: We should worry.

Yes, Kalamazoo is a spot on the map
And the passenger trains stop there
And the factory smokestacks smoke
And the grocery stores are open Saturday nights
And the streets are free for citizens who vote
And inhabitants counted in the census.
Saturday night is the big night.
Listen with your ears on a Saturday night in
Kalamazoo
And say to yourself: I hear America, I hear,
what do I hear?

Main street there runs through the middle of the town
And there is a dirty postoffice
And a dirty city hall
And a dirty railroad station
And the United States flag cries, cries the Stars and
Stripes to the four winds on Lincoln's birthday
and the Fourth of July.

Kalamazoo kisses a hand to something far off.
Kalamazoo calls to a long horizon, to a shivering silver
angel, to a creeping mystic what-is-it.
"We're here because we're here," is the song of Kalamazoo.
"We don't know where we're going but we're on our
way," are the words.
There are hound dogs of bronze on the public square,
hound dogs looking far beyond the public square.

Sweethearts there in Kalamazoo
Go to the general delivery window of the postoffice
And speak their names and ask for letters
And ask again, "Are you sure there is nothing for me?
I wish you'd look again—there must be a letter for
me."

And sweethearts go to the city hall
And tell their names and say, "We want a license."
And they go to an installment house and buy a bed on
time and a clock.
And the children grow up asking each other, "What
can we do to kill time?"

They grow up and go to the railroad station and buy
tickets for Texas, Pennsylvania, Alaska,
"Kalamazoo is all right," they say. "But I want to
see the world."
And when they have looked the world over they come
back saying it is all like Kalamazoo.

The trains come in from the east and toot for the
crossings,
And buzz away to the peach country and Chicago to
the west
Or they come from the west and shoot on to the Battle
Creek breakfast bazaars
And the speedbug heavens of Detroit.

"I hear America, I hear, *what* do I hear?"
Said a loafer lagging along on the sidewalks of Kal-
amazoo,
Lagging along and asking questions, reading signs.

Oh yes, there is a town named Kalamazoo,
A spot on the map where the trains hesitate.

I saw the sign of a five and ten cent store there
And the Standard Oil Company and the International
Harvester
And a graveyard and a ball grounds
And a short order counter where a man can get a
stack of wheats
And a pool hall where a rounder leered confidential
like and said:
"Lookin' for a quiet game?"

The loafer lagged along and asked,
"Do you make guitars here?
Do you make boxes the singing wood winds ask to
sleep in?
Do you rig up strings the singing wood winds sift over
and sing low?"
The answer: "We manufacture musical instruments
here."

Here I saw churches with steeples like hatpins,
Undertaking rooms with sample coffins in the show
window
And signs everywhere satisfaction is guaranteed,
Shooting galleries where men kill imitation pigeons,
And there were doctors for the sick,
And lawyers for people waiting in jail,
And a dog catcher and a superintendent of streets,
And telephones, water-works, trolley cars,
And newspapers with a splatter of telegrams from
sister cities of Kalamazoo the round world over.

And the loafer lagging along said:
Kalamazoo, you ain't in a class by yourself;
I seen you before in a lot of places.
If you are nuts America is nuts.
And lagging along he said bitterly:
Before I came to Kalamazoo I was silent.
Now I am gabby, God help me, I am gabby.

Kalamazoo, both of us will do a fadeaway.
I will be carried out feet first
And time and the rain will chew you to dust
And the winds blow you away.
And an old, old mother will lay a green moss cover
on my bones
And a green moss cover on the stones of your post
office and city hall.

Best of all
I have loved your kiddies playing run-sheep-run
And cutting their initials on the ball ground fence.
They knew every time I fooled them who was fooled
  and how.

Best of all
I have loved the red gold smoke of your sunsets;
I have loved a moon with a ring around it
Floating over your public square;
I have loved the white dawn frost of early winter
  silver
And purple over your railroad tracks and lumber
  yards.

The wishing heart of you I loved, Kalamazoo.
I sang bye-lo, bye-lo to your dreams.
I sang bye-lo to your hopes and songs.
I wished to God there were hound dogs of bronze on
  your public square,
Hound dogs with bronze paws looking to a long horizon
  with a shivering silver angel,
  a creeping mystic what-is-it.

Robert Frost

Robert Frost is today the most widely read American poet. On March 24, 1950, the United States Senate unanimously adopted a resolution honoring Mr. Frost on his 75th birthday. His poetry has been popular in a way unusual among twentieth-century poets. Not only has he been recognized by the critics of our age but he has spoken to the common man as Whitman wished to speak but was never quite able to. Perhaps the apparent simplicity of Frost's subjects and his use of traditional poetic form and ordinary speech have helped him to gain a wide audience. In a sense all his poems have social implications because he is primarily concerned with our relationships to each other as human beings. Frost is largely unaffected, however, by the technological revolution of our age and his poetry is always remote from urban life. A number of his poems are dramatic monologues in a rural setting using country activities and country experiences to portray basic human reactions. The two poems included here indicate clearly this concern with the problems of human life in its social setting.

It seems strange that Frost, who so completely belongs to New England, should have been born in San Francisco (in 1875). His father hated New England, however, and had fled from it as far as possible; but after his death in 1884, Frost's mother returned to their New England home in Lawrence, Massachusetts, with her son and daughter. The poet, then, grew up and was educated in the land of his ancestors. Although he spent a year at Dartmouth College and two years at Harvard, Frost never completed his college work nor did he find his vocation in life easily. As a young man, he tried various trades and was successively a country schoolteacher, a cobbler, an editor of a small-town newspaper, and finally a farmer. Perhaps his most complete failure was as a farmer.

Frost had been writing poems all this time but American publishers and critics gave him little encouragement. His career as a poet did not begin until 1912, when he was thirty-eight. He emigrated to England that year and gave himself completely to writing poetry amid the companionship of congenial fellow poets. Three years later he returned to the United States and began publishing a succession of slender books of verse, among them Mountain Interval *(1916),* West Running Brook *(1928),* A Further Range *(1939), and* A Witness Tree *(1943). In recent years several editions of his collected poems have also appeared. In 1920 Frost received a Pulitzer prize; since that time he has lectured and read his poems to a wide audience and has had numerous honors bestowed upon him including honorary degrees from both Dartmouth and Harvard. One of his best-known achievements has been the founding of the Breadloaf School for writers at Middlebury, Vermont.*

MENDING WALL

Something there is that doesn't love a wall,
That sends the frozen-ground-swell under it,
And spills the upper boulders in the sun;
And makes gaps even two can pass abreast.
The work of hunters is another thing:
I have come after them and made repair
Where they have left not one stone on a stone,
But they would have the rabbit out of hiding,
To please the yelping dogs. The gaps I mean,
No one has seen them made or heard them made,
But at spring mending-time we find them there.
I let my neighbour know beyond the hill;
And on a day we meet to walk the line
And set the wall between us once again.
We keep the wall between us as we go.
To each the boulders that have fallen to each.
And some are loaves and some so nearly balls
We have to use a spell to make them balance:
"Stay where you are until our backs are turned!"
We wear our fingers rough with handling them.
Oh, just another kind of out-door game,
One on a side. It comes to little more:
There where it is we do not need the wall:
He is all pine and I am apple orchard.
My apple trees will never get across
And eat the cones under his pines, I tell him.
He only says, "Good fences make good neighbours."
Spring is the mischief in me, and I wonder

If I could put a notion in his head:
"*Why* do they make good neighbours? Isn't it
Where there are cows? But here there are no cows.
Before I built a wall I'd ask to know
What I was walling in or walling out,
And to whom I was like to give offence.
Something there is that doesn't love a wall,
That wants it down." I could say "Elves" to him,
But it's not elves exactly, and I'd rather
He said it for himself. I see him there
Bringing a stone grasped firmly by the top
In each hand, like an old-stone savage armed.
He moves in darkness as it seems to me,
Not of woods only and the shade of trees.
He will not go behind his father's saying
And he likes having thought of it so well
He says again, "Good fences make good neighbours."

TWO TRAMPS IN MUD TIME

Out of the mud two strangers came
And caught me splitting wood in the yard.
And one of them put me off my aim
By hailing cheerily 'Hit them hard!'
I knew pretty well why he dropped behind
And let the other go on a way.
I knew pretty well what he had in mind:
He wanted to take my job for pay.

Good blocks of beech it was I split,
As large around as the chopping block;
And every piece I squarely hit
Fell splinterless as a cloven rock.
The blows that a life of self-control
Spares to strike for the common good
That day, giving a loose to my soul,
I spent on the unimportant wood.

The sun was warm but the wind was chill.
You know how it is with an April day
When the sun is out and the wind is still,
You're one month on in the middle of May.
But if you so much as dare to speak,

A cloud comes over the sunlit arch,
A wind comes off a frozen peak,
And you're two months back in the middle of March.

A bluebird comes tenderly up to alight
And fronts the wind to unruffle a plume
His song so pitched as not to excite
A single flower as yet to bloom.
It is snowing a flake: and he half knew
Winter was only playing possum.
Except in color he isn't blue,
But he wouldn's advise a thing to blossom.

The water for which we may have to look
In summertime with a witching-wand,
In every wheelrut's now a brook,
In every print of a hoof a pond.
Be glad of water, but don't forget
The lurking frost in the earth beneath
That will steal forth after the sun is set
And show on the water its crystal teeth.

The time when most I loved my task
These two must make me love it more
By coming with what they came to ask.
You'd think I never had felt before
The weight of an ax-head poised aloft,
The grip on earth of outspread feet.
The life of muscles rocking soft
And smooth and moist in vernal heat.

Out of the woods two hulking tramps
(From sleeping God knows where last night,
But not long since in the lumber camps).
They thought all chopping was theirs of right.
Men of the woods and lumberjacks,
They judged me by their appropriate tool.
Except as a fellow handled an ax,
They had no way of knowing a fool.

Nothing on either side was said.
They knew they had but to stay their stay
And all their logic would fill my head:
As that I had no right to play
With what was another man's work for gain.

My right might be love but theirs was need.
And where the two exist in twain
Theirs was the better right—agreed.

But yield who will to their separation,
My object in living is to unite
My avocation and my vocation
As my two eyes make one in sight.
Only where love and need are one,
And the work is play for mortal stakes,
Is the deed ever really done
For Heaven and the future's sakes.

Robinson Jeffers

The poetry of Robinson Jeffers is permeated by a negative view of life and a pessimism about man and society. As Jeffers sees it, civilization is doomed; man appears to be a dying race, and perhaps this is a good thing. Men are blind and cruel, and humanity suffers because materialism has crushed all natural feeling. These convictions derive, at least in part, from the world view of nineteenth-century science, the two world wars of our century, and the austerities of the particular portion of the California coast where Jeffers makes his home. In the preface to The Double Axe *he defines his philosophical attitude as "inhumanism, a shifting of emphasis from man to not-man." In this view Jeffers seems like a philosophical descendant of the German philosopher, Nietzsche. Although his style is rather prosaic, bare and austere, it is strong and powerful. His favorite symbols are the hawk, the horse, and stone; here he finds independence and serenity in contrast to man's self-seeking passion and violence.*

In 1914 Jeffers received a legacy which enabled him to retire as a kind of hermit poet to the stone Tor House, built with his own hands on the California Coast at Point Sur, Carmel. Since then he has been associated with this piece of wild and rocky coastline, although he is not a native Californian. He was born in Pittsburgh, Pennsylvania, in 1887, the son of a well-to-do doctor. His early education was at private schools in Switzerland and Germany, but he completed his college work at Occidental College in Los Angeles, where he was a mile runner and champion swimmer, and did graduate work in English and then in medicine at the University of Southern California. After some further study at Zürich he abandoned medicine and studied forestry at the University of Washington. In the end nothing but poetry really satisfied him. It is easy to see in his poetry, however, the reflection of his various experiences, his powerful physique, his study of science, and his interest in the wilder aspects of nature.

Jeffers' first book of poems, Flagons and Apples, *appeared in 1912.* Tamar and Other Poems *(1924),* Roan Stallion *(1925), and* Cawdor and Other Poems *(1928) were widely acclaimed, but later volumes such as* The Double Axe *(1948) and* Hungerfield *(1954) repelled even his admirers by their nihilistic philosophy, isolationism, and aggressive pessimism. His name became widely known when he freely adapted Euripides'* Medea *for a successful Broadway production by Judith Anderson in 1947. But critics generally agreed that the power of Miss Anderson's acting overshadowed the play, which was too violent to be tragic.*

SHINE, REPUBLIC

The quality of these trees, green height;
of the sky, shining; of water, a clear flow;
of the rock, hardness
And reticence: each is noble in its quality
The love of freedom has been the quality of
Western man.

There is a stubborn torch that flames from Marathon
to Concord, its dangerous beauty
binding three ages
Into one time; the waves of barbarism
and civilization have eclipsed but have never
quenched it.

For the Greeks the love of beauty, for Rome
of ruling; for the present age the passionate
love of discovery;
But in one noble passion we are one; and
Washington, Luther, Tacitus, Aeschylus,
one kind of man.

And you, America, that passion made you. You
were not born to prosperity, you were born
to love freedom.
You did not say "en masse," you said "independence."
But we cannot have all the luxuries
and freedom also.

Freedom is poor and laborious; that torch is not
safe but hungry, and often requires blood
for its fuel.
You will tame it against it burn too clearly, you
will hood it like a kept hawk,
you will perch it on the wrist of Caesar.

But keep the tradition, conserve the forms,
the observances, keep the spot sore. Be great,
carve deep your heel-marks.
The states of the next age will no doubt remember
you, and edge their love of freedom
with contempt of luxury.

SHINE, PERISHING REPUBLIC

While this America settles in the mould of its vulgarity,
heavily thickening to empire,
And protest, only a bubble in the molten mass, pops and
sighs out, and the mass hardens,

I sadly smiling remember that the flower fades to make
fruit, the fruit rots to make earth.
Out of the mother; and through the spring exultances, ripeness and decadence; and home to the mother.

You making haste on decay: not blameworthy; life is good,
be it stubbornly long or suddenly
A mortal splendor: meteors are not needed less than mountains: shine, perishing republic.

But for my children, I would have them keep their distance
from the thickening center; corruption
Never has been compulsory, when the cities lie at the
monster's feet there are left the mountains.

And boys, be in nothing so moderate as in love of man, a
clever servant, insufferable master.
There is the trap that catches noblest spirits, that caught—
they say—God, when he walked on earth.

APOLOGY FOR BAD DREAMS

I

In the purple light, heavy with redwood, the slopes drop
seaward,
Headlong convexities of forest, drawn in together to the
steep ravine. Below, on the sea-cliff,
A lonely clearing; a little field of corn by the streamside; a
roof under spared trees. Then the ocean
Like a great stone someone has cut to a sharp edge and
polished to shining. Beyond it, the fountain
And furnace of incredible light flowing up from the sunk
sun. In the little clearing a woman

Is punishing a horse; she had tied the halter to a sapling at
the edge of the wood, but when the great whip
Clung to the flanks the creature kicked so hard she feared
he would snap the halter; she called from the house
The young man her son; who fetched a chain tie-rope, they
working together
Noosed the small rusty links round the horse's tongue
And tied him by the swollen tongue to the tree.
Seen from this height they are shrunk to insect size,
Out of all human relation. You cannot distinguish
The blood dripping from where the chain is fastened,
The beast shuddering; but the thrust neck and the legs
Far apart. You can see the whip fall on the flanks . . .
The gesture of the arm. You cannot see the face of the woman.
The enormous light beats up out of the west across the cloud-
bars of the trade-wind. The ocean
Darkens, the high clouds brighten, the hills darken together.
Unbridled and unbelievable beauty
Covers the evening world . . . not covers, grows apparent out
of it, as Venus down there grows out
From the lit sky. What said the prophet? "I create good:
and I create evil: I am the Lord."

II

This coast crying out for tragedy like all beautiful places,
(The quiet ones ask for quieter suffering: but here the
granite cliff the gaunt cypresses crown
Demands what victim? The dykes of red lava and black
what Titan? The hills like pointed flames
Beyond Soberanes, the terrible peaks of the bare hills under
the sun, what immolation?)
This coast crying out for tragedy like all beautiful places:
and like the passionate spirit of humanity
Pain for its bread: God's, many victims', the painful deaths,
the horrible transfigurements: I said in my heart,
"Better invent than suffer: imagine victims
Lest your own flesh be chosen the agonist, or you
Martyr some creature to the beauty of the place." And I said,
"Burn sacrifices once a year to magic
Horror away from the house, this little house here
You have built over the ocean with your own hands
Beside the standing boulders; for what are we,
The beast that walks upright, with speaking lips
And little hair, to think we should always be fed,
Sheltered, intact, and self-controlled? We sooner more liable

Than the other animals. Pain and terror, the insanities of
desire; not accidents but essential,
And crowd up from the core." I imagined victims for those
wolves, I made them phantoms to follow,
They have hunted the phantoms and missed the house. It
is not good to forget over what gulfs the spirit
Of the beauty of humanity, the petal of a lost flower blown
seaward by the night-wind, floats to its quietness.

III

Boulders blunted like an old bear's teeth break up from the
headland; below them
All the soil is thick with shells, the tide-rock feasts of a dead
people.
Here the granite flanks are scarred with ancient fire, the
ghosts of the tribe
Crouch in the nights beside the ghost of a fire, they try to
remember the sunlight,
Light has died out of their skies. These have paid something
for the future
Luck of the country, while we living keep old griefs in
memory: though God's
Envy is not a likely fountain of ruin, to forget evils calls
down
Sudden reminders from the cloud: remembered deaths be
our redeemers;
Imagined victims our salvation: white as the half moon at
midnight
Someone flamelike passed me, saying, "I am Tamar Cauldwell,
I have my desire,"
Then the voice of the sea returned, when she had gone by,
the stars to their towers.
. . . Beautiful country burn again, Point Pinos down to the
Sur Rivers
Burn as before with bitter wonders, land and ocean and the
Carmel water.

IV

He brays humanity in a mortar to bring the savor
From the bruised root: a man having bad dreams, who invents
victims, is only the ape of that God.
He washes it out with tears and many waters, calcines it
with fire in the red crucible,

Deforms it, makes it horrible to itself: the spirit flies out and
 stands naked, he sees the spirit,
He takes it in the naked ecstasy; it breaks in his hand, the
 atom is broken, the power that massed it
Cries to the power that moves the stars, "I have come home
 to myself, behold me.
I bruised myself in the flint mortar and burnt me
In the red shell, I tortured myself, I flew forth,
Stood naked of myself and broke me in fragments,
And here am I moving the stars that are me."
I have seen these ways of God: I know of no reason
For fire and change and torture and the old returnings.
He being sufficient might be still. I think they admit no
 reason; they are the ways of my love.
Unmeasured power, incredible passion, enormous craft: no
 thought apparent but burns darkly
Smothered with its own smoke in the human brain-vault:
 no thought outside: a certain measure in phenomena:
The fountains of the boiling stars, the flowers on the fore-
 land, the ever-returning roses of dawn.

John Dos Passos

John Roderigo Dos Passos belongs to a generation whose views about society were conditioned by military service in World War I. Born in 1896 in Chicago, he was the son of a well-to-do father of Portuguese descent; as a boy he traveled with his family in Mexico, Belgium, and England, attended an exclusive preparatory school, and was graduated from Harvard in 1916, just in time to be plunged into World War I. After the war he traveled widely in Spain and the Near East, and recorded his experiences in Orient Express *(1921). His first important novel,* Three Soldiers *(1921), portrays with stark realism the tragic effect of war upon three soldiers of divergent backgrounds. Four years later in* Manhattan Transfer *Dos Passos gave an impressionistic portrait of New York City in the mid-twenties, with its rush and confusion and its shattering impact upon people from every walk of life. The trilogy* U.S.A.*, from which our selections are taken, was first published as three separate novels,* The 42nd Parallel *(1930),* 1919 *(1931), and* The Big Money *(1936).*

During these years Dos Passos became involved with various radical groups in an effort to express his championship of the underdog and his active opposition to injustice of various kinds. He was arrested and briefly jailed, along with Edna St. Vincent Millay and the communist Michael Gold, when he participated in a picket line on behalf of Sacco and Vanzetti. However, like many other idealistic Americans he suffered a disillusionment over leftist philosophy in the late thirties and has since then become actively anticommunist. In recent years he has lived quietly on Cape Cod and in Westmoreland County, Virginia, writing at a leisurely pace.

Dos Passos' U.S.A. *is unique in its method and form. A broad panorama of American life from the early 1900s through the Great Depression of the 1930s, it is at once a portrait and a criticism. Although there are numerous characters who pass in and out of the scenes and whose lives become intertwined, the real hero is Society. Modern life, as Dos Passos sees it, is more collective than individual; people are basically neither heroes nor villains but are largely controlled by the drift of society.*

The narrative parts of U.S.A. are interspersed with certain documentary materials: Sections called "Newsreels" are made up of bits of speeches, headlines, and popular songs, handled impressionistically. These are selected to evoke the mood of an era. Sections called "The Camera Eye" give semi-autobiographic impressions presented in a stream-of-consciousness style. These represent Dos Passos himself. The most direct parts of the novel, from which the present selections are taken, may be called "Biographies." They give brief accounts of well-known public figures and emphasize some of the most important social issues of the era. The style here is a variety of free verse with broken lines to indicate poetic stress.

U.S.A.

THE YOUNG MAN walks fast by himself through the crowd that thins into the night streets; feet are tired from hours of walking; eyes greedy for warm curve of faces, answering flicker of eyes, the set of a head, the lift of a shoulder, the way hands spread and clench; blood tingles with wants; mind is a beehive of hopes buzzing and stinging; muscles ache for the knowledge of jobs, for the roadmender's pick and shovel work, the fisherman's knack with a hook when he hauls on the slithery net from the rail of the lurching trawler, the swing of the bridgeman's arms as he slings down the whitehot rivet, the engineer's slow grip wise on the throttle, the dirtfarmer's use of his whole body when, whoaing the mules, he yanks the plow from the furrow. The young man walks by himself searching through the crowd with greedy eyes, greedy ears taut to hear, by himself, alone.

The streets are empty. People have packed into subways, climbed into streetcars and buses; in the stations they've scampered for suburban trains; they've filtered into lodgings and tenements, gone up in elevators into apartmenthouses. In a showwindow two sallow windowdressers in their shirtsleeves are bringing out a dummy girl in a red evening dress, at a corner welders in masks lean into sheets of blue flame repairing a cartrack, a few drunk bums shamble along, a sad streetwalker fidgets under an arclight. From the river comes the deep rumbling whistle of a steamboat leaving dock. A tug hoots far away.

The young man walks by himself, fast but not fast enough, far but not far enough (faces slide out of sight, talk trails into tattered scraps, footsteps tap fainter in alleys); he must catch the last subway, the streetcar, the bus, run up the gangplanks of all the steamboats, register at all the hotels, work in the cities, answer the want-ads, learn the trades, take up the jobs, live in all the boardinghouses, sleep in all the beds. One bed is not enough, one job is not enough, one life is not enough. At night, head swimming with wants, he walks by himself alone.

No job, no woman, no house, no city.

Only the ears busy to catch the speech are not alone; the ears are caught tight, linked tight by the tendrils of phrased words, the turn of a joke, the sing-song fade of a story, the gruff fall of a sentence; linking tendrils of speech twine through the city blocks, spread over pavements, grow out along broad parked avenues, speed with the trucks leaving on their long night runs over roaring highways, whisper down sandy byroads past worn-out farms, joining up cities and filling stations, roundhouses, steamboats, planes groping along airways; words call out on mountain pastures, drift slow down rivers widening to the sea and the hushed beaches.

It was not in the long walks through jostling crowds at night that he was less alone, or in the training camp at Allentown, or in the day on the docks at Seattle, or in the empty reek of Washington City hot boyhood summer nights, or in the meal on Market Street, or in the swim off the red rocks at San Diego, or in the bed full of fleas in New Orleans, or in the cold razor-wind off the lake, or in the gray faces trembling in the grind of gears in the street under Michigan Avenue, or in the smokers of limited expresstrains, or walking across country, or riding up the dry mountain canyons, or the night without a sleeping-bag among frozen beartracks in the Yellowstone, or canoeing Sundays on the Quinnipiac;

but in his mother's words telling about longago, in his father's telling about when I was a boy, in the kidding stories of uncles, in the lies the kids told at school, the hired man's yarns, the tall tales the doughboys told after taps;

it was the speech that clung to the ears, the link that tingled in the blood; U. S. A.

U. S. A. is the slice of a continent. U. S. A. is a group of holding companies, some aggregations of trade unions, a set of laws bound in calf, radio network, a chain of moving picture theatres, a column of stock-quotations rubbed out and written in by a Western Union boy on a blackboard, a publiclibrary full of old newspapers and dogeared historybooks with protests scrawled on the margins in pencil. U. S. A. is the world's greatest rivervalley fringed with mountains and hills, U. S. A. is a set of bigmouthed officials with too many bank-accounts. U. S. A. is a lot of men buried in their uniforms in Arlington Cemetery. U. S. A. is the letters at the end of an address when you are away from home. But mostly U. S. A. is the speech of the people.

MEESTER VEELSON

The year that Buchanan was elected president Thomas Woodrow Wilson

was born to a presbyterian minister's daughter

in the manse at Staunton in the valley of Virginia; it was the old Scotch-Irish stock; the father was a presbyterian minister too and a teacher of rhetoric in theological seminaries; the Wilsons lived in a universe of words linked into an incontrovertible firmament by two centuries of calvinist divines,

God was the Word

and the Word was God.

Dr. Wilson was a man of standing who loved his home and his children and good books and his wife and correct syntax and talked to God every day at family prayers;

[From John Dos Passos, U.S.A. Boston, Houghton Mifflin Company.]

he brought his sons up
between the bible and the dictionary.
The years of the Civil War
the years of fife and drum and platoon-fire and proclamations
the Wilsons lived in Augusta, Georgia; Tommy was a backward child, didn't learn his letters till he was nine, but when he learned to read his favorite reading was Parson Weems'
Life of Washington.

In 1870 Dr. Wilson was called to the Theological Seminary at Columbia, South Carolina; Tommy attended Davidson college,
where he developed a good tenor voice;
then he went to Princeton and became a debater and editor of the *Princetonian.* His first published article in the Nassau Literary Magazine was an appreciation of Bismarck.

Afterwards he studied law at the University of Virginia; young Wilson wanted to be a Great Man, like Gladstone and the eighteenth century English parliamentarians; he wanted to hold the packed benches spellbound in the cause of Truth; but law-practice irked him; he was more at home in the booky air of libraries, lecturerooms, college chapel, it was a relief to leave his law-practice at Atlanta and take a Historical Fellowship at Johns Hopkins; there he wrote *Congressional Government.*

At twentynine he married a girl with a taste for painting (while he was courting her he coached her in how to use the broad "a") and got a job at Bryn Mawr teaching the girls History and Political Economy. When he got his Ph.D. from Johns Hopkins he moved to a professorship at Wesleyan, wrote articles, started a History of the United States,
spoke out for Truth Reform Responsible Government Democracy from the lecture platform, climbed all the steps of a brilliant university career; in 1901 the trustees of Princeton offered him the presidency;
he plunged into reforming the university, made violent friends and enemies, set the campus by the ears,
and the American people began to find on the front pages
the name of Woodrow Wilson.

In 1909 he made addresses on Lincoln and Robert E. Lee
and in 1910
the democratic bosses of New Jersey, hardpressed by muckrakers and reformers, got the bright idea of offering the nomination for governor to the stainless college president who attracted such large audiences
by publicly championing Right.

When Mr. Wilson addressed the Trenton Convention that nominated him for governor he confessed his belief in the common man, (the smalltown bosses and the wardheelers looked at each other and scratched their heads); he went on, his voice growing firmer:
that is the man by whose judgment I for one wish to be guided, so that as the tasks multiply, and as the days come when all will feel confusion and dismay, we may lift up our eyes to the hills out of these dark valleys where the crags of special privilege overshadow and darken our path, to where the sun gleams through the great passage in the broken cliffs, the sun of God,
the sun meant to regenerate men,
the sun meant to liberate them from their passion and despair and lift us to those uplands which are the promised land of every man who desires liberty and achievement.

The smalltown bosses and the wardheelers looked at each other and scratched their heads; then they cheered; Wilson fooled the wiseacres and doublecrossed the bosses, was elected by a huge plurality;

so he left Princeton only half reformed to be Governor of New Jersey,

and became reconciled with Bryan

at the Jackson Day dinner: when Bryan remarked, "I of course knew that you were not with me in my position on the currency," Mr. Wilson replied, "All I can say, Mr. Bryan, is that you are a great big man."

He was introduced to Colonel House,

that amateur Merlin of politics who was spinning his webs at the Hotel Gotham

and at the convention in Baltimore the next July the upshot of the puppetshow staged for sweating delegates by Hearst and House behind the scenes, and Bryan booming in the corridors with a handkerchief over his wilted collar, was that Woodrow Wilson was nominated for the presidency.

The bolt of the Progressives in Chicago from Taft to T.R. made his election sure;

so he left the State of New Jersey half-reformed

(pitiless publicity was the slogan of the Shadow Lawn Campaign)

and went to the White House

our twentyeighth president.

While Woodrow Wilson drove up Pennsylvania Avenue beside Taft the great buttertub, who as president had been genially undoing T. R.'s reactionary efforts to put business under the control of the government,

J. Pierpont Morgan sat playing solitaire in his back office on Wall Street, smoking twenty black cigars a day, cursing the follies of democracy.

Wilson flayed the interests and branded privilege refused to recognize Huerta and sent the militia to the Rio Grande

to assume a policy of watchful waiting. He published *The New Freedom* and delivered his messages to Congress in person, like a college president addressing the faculty and students. At Mobile he said:

I wish to take this occasion to say that the United States will never again seek one additional foot of territory by conquest;

and he landed the marines at Vera Cruz.

We are witnessing a renaissance of public spirit, a reawakening of sober opinion, a revival of the power of the people the beginning of an age of thoughtful reconstruction . . .

but the world had started spinning round Sarajevo.

First it was *neutrality in thought and deed,* then *too proud to fight* when the *Lusitania* sinking and the danger to the Morgan loans and the stories of the British and French propagandists set all the financial centers in the East bawling for war, but the suction of the drumbeat and the guns was too strong; the best people took their fashions from Paris and their broad "a's" from London, and T.R. and the House of Morgan.

Five months after his reelection on the slogan *He kept us out of war,* Wilson pushed the Armed Ship Bill through congress and declared that a state of war existed between the United States and the Central Powers:

Force without stint or limit, force to the utmost.

Wilson became the state (war is the health of the state), Washington his Versailles, manned the socialized government with dollar a year men out of the great corporations and ran the big parade

of men munitions groceries mules and trucks to France. Five million men stood at attention outside of their tarpaper barracks every sundown while they played *The Star Spangled Banner*.

War brought the eight hour day, women's votes, prohibition, compulsory arbitration, high wages, high rates of interest, cost plus contracts and the luxury of being a Gold Star Mother.

If you objected to making the world safe for cost plus democracy you went to jail with Debs.

Almost too soon the show was over, Prince Max of Baden was pleading for the Fourteen Points, Foch was occupying the bridgeheads on the Rhine and the Kaiser out of breath ran for the train down the platform at Potsdam wearing a silk hat and some say false whiskers.

With the help of *Almighty God, Right, Truth, Justice, Freedom, Democracy, the Selfdetermination of Nations, No indemnities no annexations,*

and Cuban sugar and Caucasian manganese and Northwestern wheat and Dixie cotton, the British blockade, General Pershing, the taxicabs of Paris and the seventyfive gun

we won the war.

On December 4th, 1918, Woodrow Wilson, the first president to leave the territory of the United States during his presidency, sailed for France on board the *George Washington*,

the most powerful man in the world.

In Europe they knew what gas smelt like and the sweet sick stench of bodies buried too shallow and the grey look of the skin of starved children; they read in the papers that Meester Veelson was for peace and freedom and canned goods and butter and sugar;

he landed at Brest with his staff of experts and publicists after a rough trip on the *George Washington*.

La France héroïque was there with the speeches, the singing schoolchildren, the mayors in their red sashes. (Did Meester Veelson see the gendarmes at Brest beating back the demonstration of dockyard workers who came to meet him with red flags?)

At the station in Paris he stepped from the train onto a wide red carpet that led him, between rows of potted palms, silk hats, legions of honor, decorated busts of uniforms, frockcoats, rosettes, boutonnières, to a Rolls Royce. (Did Meester Veelson see the women in black, the cripples in their little carts, the pale anxious faces along the streets, did he hear the terrible anguish of the cheers as they hurried him and his new wife to the hôtel de Mûrat, where in rooms full of brocade, gilt clocks, Buhl cabinets and ormolu cupids the presidential suite had been prepared?)

While the experts were organizing the procedure of the peace conference, spreading green baize on the tables, arranging the protocols,

the Wilsons took a tour to see for themselves: the day after Christmas they were entertained at Buckingham Palace; at Newyears they called on the pope and on the microscopic Italian king at the Quirinal. (Did Meester Veelson know that in the peasants' wargrimed houses along the Brenta and the Piave they were burning candles in front of his picture cut out of the illustrated papers?) (Did Meester Veelson know that the people of Europe spelled a challenge to oppression out of the Fourteen Points as centuries before they had spelled a challenge to oppression out of the ninetyfive articles Martin Luther nailed to the churchdoor in Wittenberg?)

January 18, 1919, in the midst of serried uniforms, cocked hats and gold braid, decorations, epaulettes, orders of merit and knighthood, the High Contracting Parties, the allied and associated powers met in the

Salon de l'Horloge at the quai d'Orsay to dictate the peace,

but the grand assembly of the peace conference was too public a place to make peace in

so the High Contracting Parties

formed the Council of Ten, went into the Gobelin Room and, surrounded by Ruben's History of Marie de Medici,

began to dictate the peace.

But the Council of Ten was too public a place to make peace in

so they formed the Council of Four.

Orlando went home in a huff

and then there were three:

Clemenceau,

Lloyd George,

Woodrow Wilson.

Three old men shuffling the pack,

dealing out the cards:

the Rhineland, Danzig, the Polish corridor, the Ruhr, self determination of small nations, the Saar, League of Nations, mandates, the Mespot, Freedom of the Seas, Transjordania, Shantung, Fiume and the Island of Yap:

machine gun fire and arson

starvation, lice, cholera, typhus;

oil was trumps.

Woodrow Wilson believed in his father's God

so he told the parishioners in the little Lowther Street Congregational church where his grandfather had preached in Carlisle in Scotland, a day so chilly that the newspaper men sitting in the old pews all had to keep their overcoats on.

On April 7th he ordered the *George Washington* to be held at Brest with steam up ready to take the American delegation home:

but he didn't go.

On April 19 sharper Clemenceau and sharper Lloyd George got him into their little cosy threecard-game they called the Council of Four.

On June 28th the Treaty of Versailles was ready

and Wilson had to go back home to explain to the politicians who'd been ganging up on him meanwhile in the Senate and House and to sober public opinion and to his father's God how he'd let himself be trimmed and how far he'd made the world safe

for democracy and the New Freedom.

From the day he landed in Hoboken he had his back to the wall of the White House, talking to save his faith in words, talking to save his faith in the League of Nations, talking to save his faith in himself, in his father's God.

He strained every nerve of his body and brain, every agency of the government he had under his control; (if anybody disagreed he was a crook or a red; no pardon for Debs).

In Seattle the wobblies whose leaders were in jail, in Seattle the wobblies whose leaders had been lynched, who'd been shot down like dogs, in Seattle the wobblies lined four blocks as Wilson passed, stood silent with their arms folded staring at the great liberal as he was hurried past in his car, huddled in his overcoat, haggard with fatigue, one side of his face twitching. The men in overalls, the workingstiffs let him pass in silence after all the other blocks of handclapping and patriotic cheers.

In Pueblo, Colorado, he was a grey man hardly able to stand, one side of his face twitching:

Now that the mists of this great question have cleared away, I believe that men will see the Truth, eye for eye and face to face. There is one thing the American People always rise to and extend their hand to, that is, the truth of justice and of liberty and of peace. We have accepted that truth and we are going to be led by it, and it is going to lead us, and through us the world, out into pastures of quietness and peace such as the world never dreamed of before.

That was his last speech;

on the train to Wichita he had a stroke. He gave up the speaking tour that was to sweep the country for the League of Nations. After that he was a ruined paralyzed man barely able to speak;

the day he gave up the presidency to Harding the joint committee of the Senate and House appointed Henry Cabot Lodge, his lifelong enemy, to make the formal call at the executive office in the capitol and ask the formal question whether the president had any message for the congress assembled in joint session;

Wilson managed to get to his feet, lifting himself painfully by the two arms of the chair. "Senator Lodge, I have no further communication to make, thank you . . . Good morning," he said.

In 1924 on February 3rd he died.

TIN LIZZIE

"Mr. Ford the Automobileer," the featurewriter wrote in 1900,

"*Mr. Ford the automobileer began by giving his steed three or four sharp jerks with the lever at the righthand side of the seat; that is, he pulled the lever up and down sharply in order, as he said, to mix air with gasoline and drive the charge into the exploding cylinder . . . . Mr. Ford slipped a small electric switch handle and there followed a puff, puff, puff. . . . The puffing of the machine assumed a higher key. She was flying along about eight miles an hour. The ruts in the road were deep, but the machine certainly went with a dreamlike smoothness. There was none of the bumping common even to a streetcar. . . . By this time the boulevard had been reached, and the automobileer, letting a lever fall a little, let her out. Whiz! She picked up speed with infinite rapidity. As she ran on there was a clattering behind, the new noise of the automobile.*

For twenty years or more,

ever since he'd left his father's farm when he was sixteen to get a job in a Detroit machineshop, Henry Ford had been nuts about machinery. First it was watches, then he designed a steamtractor, then he built a horseless carriage with an engine adapted from the Otto gasengine he'd read about in *The World of Science*, then a mechanical buggy with a onecylinder fourcycle motor, that would run forward but not back;

at last, in ninetyeight, he felt he was far enough along to risk throwing up his job with the Detroit Edison Company, where he'd worked his way up from night fireman to chief engineer, to put all his time into working on a new gasoline engine,

(in the late eighties he'd met Edison at a meeting of electriclight employees in Atlantic City. He'd gone up to Edison after Edison had delivered an address and asked him if he thought gasoline was practical as a motor fuel. Edison had said yes. If Edison said it, it was true. Edison was the great admiration of Henry Ford's life);

and in driving his mechanical buggy, sitting there at the lever jauntily dressed in a tightbuttoned jacket and a high collar and a derby hat, back and forth over the level illpaved streets of Detroit,

scaring the big brewery horses and the skinny trotting horses and the sleekrumped pacers with the motor's loud explosions,

looking for men scatterbrained enough to invest money in a factory for building automobiles.

He was the eldest son of an Irish immigrant who during the Civil War had married the daughter of a prosperous Pennsylvania Dutch farmer and settled down to farming near Dearborn in Wayne County, Michigan;

like plenty of other Americans, young Henry grew up hating the endless sogging through the mud about the chores, the hauling and pitching manure, the kerosene lamps to clean, the irk and sweat and solitude of the farm.

He was a slender, active youngster, a good skater, clever with his hands; what he liked was to tend the machinery and let the others do the heavy work. His mother had told him not to drink, smoke, gamble or go into debt, and he never did.

When he was in his early twenties his father tried to get him back from Detroit, where he was working as mechanic and repairman for the Drydock Engine Company that built engines for steamboats, by giving him forty acres of land.

Young Henry, built himself an uptodate square white dwelling house with a false mansard roof and married and settled down on the farm,

but he let the hired men do the farming;

he bought himself a buzzsaw and rented a stationary engine and cut the timber off the woodlots.

He was a thrifty young man who never drank or smoked or gambled or coveted his neighbors' wife, but he couldn't stand living on the farm.

He moved to Detroit, and in the brick barn behind his house tinkered for years in his spare time with a mechanical buggy that would be light enough to run over the clayey wagonroads of Wayne County, Michigan.

By 1900 he had a practicable car to promote.

He was forty years old before the Ford Motor Company was started and production began to move.

Speed was the first thing the early automobile manufacturers went after. Races advertised the makes of cars.

Henry Ford himself hung up several records at the track at Grosse Pointe and on the ice on Lake St. Clair. In his 999 he did the mile in thirtynine and fourfifths seconds.

But it had always been his custom to hire others to do the heavy work. The speed he was busy with was speed in production, the records records in efficient output. He hired Barney Oldfield, a stunt bicyclerider from Salt Lake City, to do the racing for him.

Henry Ford had ideas about other things than the designing of motors, carburetors, magnetos, jigs and fixtures, punches and dies; he had ideas about sales,

that the big money was in economical quantity production, quick turnover, cheap interchangeable easilyreplaced standardized parts;

it wasn't until 1909, after years of arguing with his partners, that Ford put out the first Model T.

Henry Ford was right.

That season he sold more than ten thousand tin lizzies, ten years later he was selling almost a million a year.

In these years the Taylor Plan was stirring up plantmanagers and manufacturers all over the country. Efficiency was the word. The same ingenuity that went into improving the performance of a machine could go to improving the performance of the workmen producing the machine.

In 1913 they established the assemblyline at Ford's. That season the profits were something like twentyfive million dollars, but they had trouble in keeping the men on the job, machinists didn't seem to like it at Ford's.

Henry Ford had ideas about other things than production.

He was the largest automobile manufacturer in the world; he paid high wages; maybe if the steady workers thought they were getting a cut (a very small cut) in the profits, it would give trained men an inducement to stick to their jobs,

wellpaid workers might save enough money to buy a tin lizzie; the first day Ford's announced that cleancut properlymarried American workers who wanted jobs had a chance to make five bucks a day (of course it turned out that there were strings to it; always there were strings to it)

such an enormous crowd waited outside the Highland Park plant

all through the zero January night

that there was a riot when the gates were opened; cops broke heads, jobhunters threw bricks; property, Henry Ford's own property, was destroyed. The company dicks had to turn on the firehose to beat back the crowd.

The American Plan; automotive prosperity seeping down from above; it turned out there were strings to it.

But that five dollars a day
paid to good, clean American workmen
who didn't drink or smoke cigarettes or read or think,
and who didn't commit adultery
and whose wives didn't take in boarders,
made America once more the Yukon of the sweated workers of the world;
made all the tin lizzies and the automotive age, and incidentally,
made Henry Ford the automobileer, the admirer of Edison, the birdlover, the great American of his time.

But Henry Ford had ideas about other things besides assemblylines and the livinghabits of his employees. He was full of ideas. Instead of going to the city to make his fortune, here was a country boy who'd made his fortune by bringing the city out to the farm. The precepts he'd learned out of McGuffey's Reader, his mother's prejudices and preconceptions, he had preserved clean and unworn as freshprinted bills in the safe in a bank.

He wanted people to know about his ideas, so he bought the *Dearborn Independent* and started a campaign against cigarettesmoking.

When war broke out in Europe, he had ideas about that too. (Suspicion of armymen and soldiering were part of the midwest farm tradition, like thrift, stickativeness, temperance and sharp practice in money matters.) Any intelligent American mechanic could see that if the Europeans hadn't been a lot of ignorant underpaid foreigners who drank, smoked, were loose about women and wasteful in their methods of production, the war could never have happened.

When Rosika Schwimmer broke through the stockade of secretaries and servicemen who surrounded Henry Ford and suggested to him that he could stop the war,

he said sure they'd hire a ship and go over and get the boys out of the trenches by Christmas.

He hired a steamboat, the *Oscar II*, and filled it up with pacifists and socialworkers,

to go over to explain to the princelings of Europe

that what they were doing was vicious and silly.

It wasn't his fault that Poor Richard's commonsense no longer rules the world and that most of the pacifists were nuts,

goofy with headlines.

When William Jennings Bryan went over to Hoboken to see him off, somebody handed William Jennings Bryan a squirrel in a cage; William Jennings Bryan made a speech with the squirrel under his arm. Henry Ford threw American Beauty roses to the crowd. The band played *I Didn't Raise My Boy to Be a Soldier*. Practical jokers let loose more squirrels. An eloping couple was married by a platoon of ministers in the saloon, and Mr. Zero, the flophouse humanitarian, who reached the dock too late to sail,

dove into the North River and swam after the boat.

The *Oscar II* was described as a floating Chautauqua; Henry Ford said it felt like a middlewestern village, but by the time they reached Christiansand in Norway, the reporters had kidded him so that he had gotten cold feet and gone to bed. The world was too crazy outside of Wayne County, Michigan. Mrs. Ford and the management sent an Episcopal dean after him who brought him home under wraps,

and the pacifists had to speechify without him.

Two years later Ford's was manufacturing munitions, Eagle boats; Henry Ford was planning oneman tanks, and oneman submarines like the one tried out in the Revolutionary War. He announced to the press that he'd turn over his war profits to the government,

but there's no record that he ever did.

One thing he brought back from his trip was the Protocols of the Elders of Zion. He started a campaign to enlighten the world in the *Dearborn Independent*; the Jews were why the world wasn't like Wayne County, Michigan, in the old horse and buggy days;

the Jews had started the war, Bolshevism, Darwinism, Marxism, Nietzsche, short skirts and lipstick. They were behind Wall Street and the international bankers, and the whiteslave traffic and the movies and the Supreme Court and ragtime and the illegal liquor business.

Henry Ford denounced the Jews and ran for senator and sued the *Chicago Tribune* for libel,

and was the laughingstock of the kept metropolitan press;

but when the metropolitan bankers tried to horn in on his business

he thoroughly outsmarted them.

In 1918 he had borrowed on notes to buy out his minority stockholders for the picayune sum of seventy-five million dollars.

In February, 1920, he needed cash to pay off some of these notes that were coming due. A banker is supposed to have called on him and offered him every facility if the bankers' representative could be a member of the board of directors. Henry Ford handed the banker his hat,

and went about raising the money in his own way:

he shipped every car and part he had in his plant to his dealers and demanded immediate cash payment. Let the other fellow do the borrowing had always been a cardinal principle. He shut down production and canceled all orders from the supplyfirms. Many dealers were ruined, many supplyfirms failed, but when he reopened his plant,

he owned it absolutely,

the way a man owns an unmortgaged farm with the taxes paid up.

In 1922 there started the Ford boom for President (high wages, waterpower, industry scattered to the small towns) that was skillfully pricked behind the scenes

by another crackerbarrel philosopher,

Calvin Coolidge;

but in 1922 Henry Ford sold one million three hundred and thirtytwo thousand two hundred and nine tin lizzies; he was the richest man in the world.

Good roads had followed the narrow ruts made in the mud by the Model T. The great automotive boom was on. At Ford's production was improving all the time; less waste, more spotters, strawbosses, stoolpigeons (fifteen minutes for lunch, three minutes to go to the toilet, the Taylorized speedup everywhere, reach under, adjust washer, screw down bolt, shove in cotterpin, reachunder adjustwasher, screwdown bolt, reachunderadjustscrewdownreachunderadjust until every ounce of life was sucked off into production and at night the workmen went home grey shaking husks).

Ford owned every detail of the process from the ore in the hills until the car rolled off the end of the assemblyline under its own power, the plants were rationalized to the last tenthousandth of an inch as measured by the Johansen scale;

in 1926 the production cycle was reduced to eightyone hours from the ore in the mine to the finished salable car proceeding under its own power,

but the Model T was obsolete.

New Era prosperity and the American Plan

(there were strings to it, always there were strings to it)

had killed Tin Lizzie.

Ford's was just one of many automobile plants.

When the stockmarket bubble burst,

Mr. Ford the crackerbarrel philosopher said jubilantly,

"I told you so.

Serves you right for gambling and getting in debt.

The country is sound."

But when the country on cracked shoes, in frayed trousers, belt tightened over hollow bellies,

idle hands cracked and chapped with the cold of that coldest March day of 1932,

started marching from Detroit to Dearborn, asking for work and the American Plan, all they could think of at Ford's was machineguns.

The country was sound, but they mowed the marchers down.

They shot four of them dead.

Henry Ford as an old man

is a passionate antiquarian,

(lives besieged on his father's farm embedded in an estate of thousands of millionaire acres, protected by an army of servicemen, secretaries, secret agents, dicks under orders of an English exprizefighter,

always afraid of the feet in broken shoes on the roads, afraid the gangs will kidnap his grandchildren,

that a crank will shoot him,

that Change and the idle hands out of work will break through the gates and the high fences;

protected by a private army against

the new America of starved children and hollow bellies and cracked shoes stamping on souplines,

that has swallowed up the old thrifty farmlands

of Wayne County, Michigan,

as if they had never been).

Henry Ford as an old man

is a passionate antiquarian.

He rebuilt his father's farmhouse and put it back exactly in the state he remembered it in as a boy. He built a village of museums for buggies, sleighs, coaches, old plows, waterwheels, obsolete models of motorcars. He scoured the country for fiddlers to play old-fashioned squaredances.

Even old taverns he bought and put back into their original shape, as well as Thomas Edison's early laboratories.

When he bought the Wayside Inn near Sudbury, Massachusetts, he had the new highway where the newmodel cars roared and slithered and hissed oilily past (*the new noise of the automobile*),

moved away from the door,
put back the old bad road,
so that everything might be
the way it used to be,
in the days of horses and buggies.

ARCHITECT

A muggy day in late spring in eighteen eightyseven a tall youngster of eighteen with fine eyes and a handsome arrogant way of carrying his head arrived in Chicago with seven dollars left in his pocket from buying his ticket from Madison with some cash he'd got by pawning Plutarch's *Lives*, a Gibbon's *Decline and Fall of the Roman Empire* and an old furcollared coat.

Before leaving home to make himself a career in an architect's office (there was no architecture course at Wisconsin to clutter his mind with stale Beaux Arts drawing) the youngster had seen the dome of the new State Capitol in Madison collapse on account of bad rubblework in the piers, some thieving contractors' skimping materials to save the politicians their rakeoff, and perhaps a trifling but deadly error in the architect's plans;

he never forgot the roar of burst masonry, the flying plaster, the soaring dustcloud, the mashed bodies of the dead and dying being carried out, set faces livid with plasterdust.

Walking round downtown Chicago, crossing and recrossing the bridges over the Chicago River in the jingle and clatter of traffic, the rattle of vans and loaded wagons and the stamping of big drayhorses and hooting of towboats with barges and the rumbling whistle of lakesteamers waiting for the draw,

he thought of the great continent stretching a thousand miles east and south and north, three thousand miles west, and everywhere, at mineheads, on the shores of newlydredged harbors, along watercourses, at the intersections of railroads, sprouting

shacks roundhouses tipples grainelevators stores warehouses tenements, great houses for the wealthy set in broad treeshaded lawns, domed statehouses on hills, hotels churches operahouses auditoriums.

He walked with long eager steps

towards the untrammeled future opening in every direction for a young man who'd keep his hands to his work and his wits sharp to invent.

The same day he landed a job in an architect's office.

Frank Lloyd Wright was the grandson of a Welsh hatter and preacher who'd settled in a rich Wisconsin valley, Spring Valley, and raised a big family of farmers and preachers and schoolteachers there. Wright's father was a preacher too, restless illadjusted Newenglander who studied medicine, preached in a Baptist church in Weymouth,

[From John Dos Passos, *U.S.A.* Boston, Houghton Mifflin Company. Copyright 1930, 1937, 1958, by John Dos Passos. Reprinted by permission of the author.]

Massachusetts, and then as a Unitarian in the middle west, taught music, read Sanskrit and finally walked out on his family.

Young Wright was born on his grandfather's farm, went to school in Weymouth and Madison, worked summers on a farm of his uncle's in Wisconsin.

His training in architecture was the reading of Viollet le Duc, the apostle of the thirteenth century and of the pure structural mathematics of gothic stonemasonry, and the seven years he worked with Louis Sullivan in the office of Adler and Sullivan in Chicago. (It was Louis Sullivan who, after Richardson, invented whatever was invented in nineteenthcentury architecture in America).

When Frank Lloyd Wright left Sullivan he had already launched a distinctive style, prairie architecture. In Oak Park he built broad suburban dwellings for rich men that were the first buildings to break the hold on American builders' minds of centuries of pastward routine, of the wornout capital and plinth and pediment dragged through the centuries from the Acropolis, and the jaded traditional stencils of Roman masonry, the halfobliterated Palladian copybooks.

Frank Lloyd Wright was cutting out a new avenue that led towards the swift constructions in glassbricks and steel

foreshadowed today.

Delightedly he reached out for the new materials, steel in tension, glass, concrete, the million new metals and alloys.

The son and grandson of preachers, he became a preacher in blueprints,

projecting constructions in the American future instead of the European past.

Inventor of plans,

plotter of tomorrow's girderwork phrases,

he preaches to the young men coming of age in the time of oppression, cooped up by the plasterboard partitions of finance routine, their lives and plans made poor by feudal levies of parasite money standing astride every process to shake down progress for the cutting of coupons:

The properly citified citizen has become a broker, dealing chiefly in human frailties or the ideas and inventions of others, a puller of levers, a presser of buttons of vicarious power, his by way of machine craft . . . and over beside him and beneath him, even in his heart as he sleeps, is the taximeter of rent, in some form to goad this anxious consumer's unceasing struggle for or against more or less merciful or merciless money increment.

To the young men who spend their days and nights drafting the plans for new *rented aggregates of rented cells upended on hard pavements,*

he preaches

the horizons of his boyhood,

a future that is not the rise of a few points in a hundred selected stocks, or an increase in carloadings, or a multiplication of credit in the bank or a rise in the rate on callmoney,

but a new clean construction, from the ground up, based on uses and needs,

towards the American future instead of towards the painsmeared past of Europe and Asia. Usonia he calls the broad teeming band of his new nation across the enormous continent between Atlantic and Pacific. He preaches a project for Usonia:

It is easy to realize how the complexity of crude utilitarian construction in the mechanical infancy of our growth, like the crude scaffolding for some noble building, did violence to the landscape. . . . The crude purpose of pioneering days has been accomplished. The scaffolding may be taken down and the true work, the culture of a civilization, may appear.

Like the life of many a preacher, prophet, exhorter, Frank Lloyd Wright's life has been stormy. He has raised children, had rows with wives, overstepped boundaries, got into difficulties with the law, divorce-courts, bankruptcy, always the yellow press yapping at his heels, his misfortunes yelled out in headlines in the evening papers: affairs with women, the nightmare horror of the burning of his house in Wisconsin.

By curious irony

the building that is most completely his is the Imperial Hotel in Tokyo that was one of the few structures to come unharmed through the earthquake of 1923 (the day the cable came telling him that the building had stood saving so many hundreds of lives he writes was one of his happiest days)

and it was reading in German that most first Americans learned of his work.

His life has been full of arrogant projects unaccomplished. (How often does the preacher hear his voice echo back hollow from the empty hall, the draftsman watch the dust fuzz over the carefullycontrived plans, the architect see the rolledup blueprints curl yellowing and brittle in the filingcabinet.)

Twice he's rebuilt the house where he works in his grandfather's valley in Wisconsin after fires and disasters that would have smashed most men forever.

He works in Wisconsin,

an erect spare whitehaired man, his sons are architects, apprentices from all over the world come to work with him,

drafting the new city (he calls it Broadacre City).

Near and Far are beaten (to imagine the new city you must blot out every ingrained habit of the past, build a nation from the ground up with the new tools). For the architect there are only uses:

the incredible multiplication of functions, strength and tension in metal,

the dynamo, the electric coil, radio, the photo-electric cell, the internalcombustion motor,

glass

concrete;

and needs. (Tell us, doctors of philosophy, what are the needs of a man. At least a man needs to be notjailed notafraid nothungry notcold not without love, not a worker for a power he has never seen

that cares nothing for the uses and needs of a man or a woman or a child.)

Building a building is building the lives of the workers and dwellers in the building.

The buildings determine civilization as the cells in the honeycomb the functions of bees.

Perhaps in spite of himself the arrogant draftsman, the dilettante in concrete, the bohemian artist for wealthy ladies desiring to pay for prominence with the startling elaboration of their homes has been forced by the logic of uses and needs, by the lifelong struggle against the dragging undertow of money in mortmain,

to draft plans that demand for their fulfillment a new life;

only in freedom can we build the Usonian city. His plans are coming to life. His blueprints, as once Walt Whitman's words, stir the young men:—

Frank Lloyd Wright,

patriarch of the new building,

not without honor except in his own country.

Lionel Trilling

Lionel Trilling, American critic, scholar, and writer of fiction, was born in 1905 in New York City. He attended the city public schools, graduated from Columbia College, and has spent most of his adult life studying and teaching at Columbia University, where he is now professor of English and comparative literature. He began publishing in 1925 and over the years has written a succession of short stories, essays, and reviews for periodicals like The Nation, The New Republic, The New York Times, The Partisan Review, *and* The Kenyon Review. *He has been a member of the advisory board of the last two magazines, and with John Crowe Ransom and F. O. Matthieson he helped organize the experimental Kenyon School of Letters, located first at Kenyon College, later at Indiana University. His connection with both the controversial leftwing* Partisan Review *and the more academic* Kenyon Review *is evidence of the undogmatic kind of liberalism he advocates.*

Trilling is perhaps best known as a literary critic and scholar, but he does not hesitate to deal with moral and social issues. His books include studies of Matthew Arnold (1939) and E. M. Forster (1943), a collection of more popular essays, The Liberal Imagination *(1950), and* Freud and the Crisis of Our Culture *(1955). His first novel,* The Middle of the Journey, *published in 1947, is a story based upon the moral dilemma of an America faced by the menace of communism from without and the problem of liberals and former Communists within. As a novel of ideas, it was well received by the critics, who admired not only Trilling's literary skill but his courage in attempting such a book at that time. Although often characterized as a left-of-center intellectual, Trilling, like Herbert Muller and Walter Lippmann, is best labeled simply as a "liberal," and for that reason is often assailed from both right and left.*

In his story The Other Margaret, *which we include here, he shows a keen awareness of social problems, yet he is clearly committed to the humanistic tradition with its emphasis upon a personal responsibility for many of the ills of society. To a critic whose orientation is almost entirely social, Trilling may seem to back away from the more controversial issues. But his recognition of individual moral responsibility provides a needed balance for the revolutionary fervor of modern social reformers.*

THE OTHER MARGARET

Mark Jennings stood the picture up on the wide counter and he and Stephen Elwin stepped back and looked at it. It was one of Rouault's kings. A person looking at it for the first time might find it repellent, even brutal or cruel. It was full of rude blacks that might seem barbarically untidy.

But the two men knew the picture well. They looked at it in silence. The admiration they were sharing made a community between them which at their age was rare, for they had both passed forty. Jennings waited for Elwin to speak first—they were friends but Elwin was the customer. Besides, the frame had been designed by Jennings and in buying a reproduced picture the frame is of great importance, accounting for more than half the cost. Elwin had bought the picture some weeks before but he was seeing it framed for the first time.

Elwin said, "The frame is very good, Mark. It's perfect." He was a rather tall man with an attractive, competent face. He touched the frame curiously with the tip of his forefinger.

Jennings replied in a judicious tone, as if it were not his own good taste but that of a very gifted apprentice of his. "*I* think so," he said. And he too touched the frame, but intimately, rubbing briskly up and down one moulding with an artisan's possessive thumb, putting an unneeded last touch. He explained that considerations of color and proportion made the frame right for the picture. He spoke as if these were simple rules anyone might find in a book.

The king, blackbearded and crowned, faced in profile to the left. He had a fierce quality that had modulated, but not softened, to authority. One could feel of him—it was the reason why Elwin had bought the picture—that he had passed beyond ordinary matters of personality and was worthy of the crown he was wearing. Yet he was human and tragic. He was not unlike the sculptured kings of Chartres. In his right hand he held a spray of flowers.

"Is he a favorite of yours?" Elwin said. He did not know whether he meant the king or the king's painter. Indeed, as he asked the question, it seemed to him that he had assumed that the painter was this archaic personage himself. He had never imagined the painter painting the canvas with a brush. It was the beginning of a new thought about the picture.

Jennings answered with a modified version of the Latin gesture of esteem, a single decisive shake of his lifted hand, thumb and forefinger touching in a circle.

Elwin acknowledged the answer with a nod but said nothing. He did not want Jennings' admiration, even though he had asked for it. Jennings would naturally give as much admiration to most of the fine pictures in fine reproduction with which his shop was filled. At that moment, Elwin was not interested in admiration or in art. But he liked what Jennings next said.

"It will give you a lot of satisfaction," Jennings said. It was exactly as if he had just sold Elwin a suit or a pair of shoes.

Elwin said, "Yes," a little hesitatingly, only politely agreeing, not committing himself in the matter of his money's worth until it should be proved.

From behind the partition that made Jennings' little office they had been hearing a man talking on the telephone. Now the conversation ended and a young soldier, a second lieutenant, came out into the shop. Jennings said to him, "Did the call get through?" and the young man said, "Oh yes, after some difficulty. It was eighty-five cents. Let me pay you for it." "Oh nonsense," said Jennings, and took him by the arm and quickly introduced him to Elwin as a cousin of his wife's. The young man offered Elwin the hand that had been reaching into his pocket and said, "I'm glad to meet you, sir."

He said it very nicely, with the niceness that new young officers are likely to have. Pleased with themselves, they are certain that everyone will be nice to them. This young man's gold bar did a good deal for him, did perhaps more than rank ought to have to do for a man. He was not really much of a person. Yet Elwin, meeting him, felt the familiar emotion in which he could not distinguish guilt from envy. He knew it well, knew how to control it and it did not diminish, not much, the sense of holiday he was having. The holiday was made by his leaving his office a little early. He published scientific books in a small but successful way and the war had made a great pressure of work for him, but he had left his office early when Jennings phoned that the picture was back from the framer's.

The young lieutenant was looking at the picture. He so clearly did not like it that Jennings said quickly, "Mr. Elwin's just bought it."

The lieutenant regarded the picture thoughtfully. "Very nice," he said, with an enthusiastic and insincere shake of his head. He did not want to spoil things for Jennings by undermining the confidence of the customer. Elwin looked from the king to the lieutenant and back to the king. It was perfectly polite, only as if he had looked at the young man to hear his opinion more clearly and then had examined again the thing they were talking about.

But Jennings understood the movement of Elwin's glance, for when the lieutenant had shaken hands and left the shop, Jennings said stoutly, "He's a good kid."

"Yes he is," Elwin said serenely.

"It's funny seeing him an officer. He used to be against anything like that. But he was glad to go—he said he did not want to miss sharing the experience of his generation."

"A lot of them say that," Elwin had heard it often from the young men, the clever ones. Someone had started it and all the young men with the semi-political views said it. Their reasons for saying it were various. Elwin liked some of the reasons and disliked the others, but whether he liked the reasons or not, he never heard the phrase without a twinge of envy. Now it comforted him to think that this man with the black beard and the flower had done his fighting without any remarks about experience and generations.

The idea of age and death did not present itself to Elwin in any horrifying way. It had first come to him in the form of a sentence from one of Hazlitt's essays. The sentence was, "No young man believes he shall ever die," and the words had come to him suddenly from the past, part of an elaborate recollection of a scene at high school. When he looked up the quotation, he found that he had remembered it with perfect accuracy, down to that very *shall* which struck his modern ear as odd and even ungrammatical. The memory had begun with the winter sunlight coming through the dirty windows of the classroom. Then there was the color, texture and smell of varnished wood. But these details were only pointing to the teacher himself and what he was saying. He was a Mr. Baxter, a heron-like man, esteemed as brilliant and eccentric, what some students called "a real person." Suddenly Mr. Baxter in a loud voice had uttered that sentence of Hazlitt's. He held the book in his hand but did not read from it. "No young man believes he shall ever die," he said, just as if he had thought of it himself.

It had been very startling to hear him say that, and this effect was of course just what the teacher wanted. It was the opening sentence of an essay called "On the Feeling of Immortality in Youth," and to Baxter it was important that the class should see what a bold and captivating way it was to begin an essay, how it was exactly as if someone had suddenly said the words, not written them after thought.

The chalky familiar classroom had been glorified by this moment of Mr. Baxter's. So many things had been said in the room, but here was one thing that had been said which was true. It was true in two ways. For Mr. Baxter it was true that no *young* man believes he shall ever die, but Mr. Baxter was not exactly a young man. For Stephen Elwin it was true that he would never die—he was scarcely even a young man yet, still only a boy. Between the student and the teacher the great difference was that the student would never die. Stephen Elwin had pitied Mr. Baxter and had been proud of himself. And mixed with the boy's feeling of immortality was a boy's pleasure at being involved with ideas which were not only solemn but complicated, for Mr. Baxter's mortality should have denied, but actually did not deny, the immortality that Stephen felt.

The Hazlitt sentence, once it had been remembered, had not left Elwin. Every now and then, sometimes just as he was falling asleep, sometimes just as he was waking up, sometimes right in the middle of anything at all, the sentence and the full awareness of what it meant would come to him. It felt like an internal explosion. It was not, however, an explosion of force but rather an explosion of light. It was not without pain but it was not wholly painful.

With the picture neatly wrapped in heavy brown paper, Elwin walked down Madison Avenue. It was still early. On a sudden impulse he walked west at 60th Street. Usually he came home by taxi but this evening he thought of the Fifth Avenue bus, for some reason remembering that it was officially called a "coach" and that his father had spoken of it so, and had sometimes even referred to it as a "stage." The "coach" that he signaled was of the old kind, open wooden deck, platform at the rear, stairs connecting platform and deck with a big architectural curve. He saw it with surprise and affection. He had supposed that this model of bus had long been out of service and as he hailed it his mind sought for and found a word long unused. "DeDion," he said, pleased at having found it. "DeDion Bouton."

He pronounced it *Deedeeon,* the way he and his friends had said it in 1917 when they had discussed the fine and powerful motors from Europe that were then being used for the buses. Some of them had been Fiats, but the most powerful of all were said to be the DeDions from France. No one knew the authority for this superlative judgment but boys finding a pleasure in firm opinions did not care. Elwin remembered the special note in his friends' voices as they spoke of the DeDions. They talked about the great Mediterranean motors with a respect that was not only technical but historical. There had never been more than a few of the DeDions in America. Even in 1917 they were no longer being imported and the boys thought of them as old and rare.

Elwin took his seat inside the bus, at the rear. As suddenly as the name DeDion, it came to him how the open deck had once been a deck indeed—how, as sometimes the only passenger braving the weather up there, he had been the captain of the adventure, facing into the cold wind, even into the snow or rain, stoic, assailed but unmoved by the elements, inhaling health, fortitude and growth, for he had a boy's certainty that the more he endured, the stronger he would become. And when he had learned to board the bus and alight from it while it was still moving—"board" and "alight" were words the company used in its notices—how far advanced in life he had felt. So many landmarks of Elwin's boyhood in the city had vanished but this shabby bus had endured since the days when it had taken him daily to school.

At 82nd Street the bus stopped for a red light. A boy stood at the curb near the iron stanchion that bore the bus-stop sign. He clutched something in his hand. It must have been a coin, for he said to the conductor, "Mister, how much does it cost to ride on this bus?"

Elwin could not be sure of the boy's age, but he was perhaps twelve, Elwin's own age when he had been touched by his friends' elegiac discussions of the DeDions. The boy was not alone, he had a friend with him, and to see this friend, clearly a follower, was to understand the quality of the chief. The subaltern was a boy like any other, but the face of his leader was alight with the power of mind and a great urgency. Perhaps he was only late and in a hurry, but in any case the urgency illuminated his remarkable face.

The conductor did not answer the question.

"Mister," the boy said again, "how much does it cost to ride on this bus?"

His friend stood by, sharing passively in the question but saying nothing. They did not dare "board" until they knew whether or not their resources were sufficient.

The boy was dressed sturdily enough, perhaps for a boy of his age he was even well dressed. But he had been on the town or in the park most of the afternoon, or perhaps he had been one of those boys who, half in awe, half in rowdy levity, troop incessantly through the Egyptian rooms of the Museum, repeatedly entering and emerging from and entering again the narrow slits of the grave vaults. His knickerbockers were sliding at the knees and his effort to control a drop at his nose further compromised but by no means destroyed his dignity. He had the clear cheeks and well-shaped head of a carefully reared child, but he seemed too far from home at this hour quite to be the child of very careful parents. There was an air about him which suggested that he had learned to expect at least a little resistance from the world and that he was ready to meet it.

The conductor did not reply to the second question. He had taken a large black wallet of imitation leather from some cranny of the rear platform and was making marks with a pencil on the cardboard trip-sheet it contained. He was an old man.

"Mister," said the boy again, and his voice, though tense, was reasonable. It was the very spirit of reasonableness. "Mister, how much does it cost to ride on this bus? A nickel or a dime?"

The conductor elaborately lifted his eyes from his record. He looked at the boy not hostilely nor yet quite facetiously, but with a certain quiet air of satisfaction. "What do you want to know for?" he said.

Elwin wanted to lower the window to tell the boy it was a dime. But he had waited too long. The conductor put his hand on the bell-button and gave the driver the signal. The light changed and the bus began to move.

"Mister!" the boy shouted. He may have been late to his supper but it was not this urgency that made his voice go up so loud and high. "For God's sake, mister!"

He of course did not bring in God by way of appeal. There was no longer any hope of his getting an answer. It was rather an expostulation with the unreasonable, the most passionate thing imaginable. Elwin looked back and saw the boy's hatred still following the conductor and, naturally, not only the conductor but the whole bus.

The conductor had now the modest look of a person who has just delivered a rebuke which was not only deserved but witty.

Well, Elwin thought, he is an old man and his pride is somewhere involved. Perhaps it was only that he could not at the moment bring himself to answer a question.

But he believed that in the past it could not have happened. When he was a boy the conductor might have said, "What do you want to know for?"—boys must always be teased a little by men. But the teasing would have stopped in time for him to board the bus. The bus was peculiarly safe. The people who rode in it and paid a dime after they had taken their seats were known to be nicer than the people who rode in the subway for a nickel which they paid before admission. It was the first public conveyance to which "nervous" parents entrusted their children—the conductors were known for their almost paternal kindness. For example, if you found on your trip to school that you had forgotten your money, the conductor would not fail to quiet the fear of authority that clutched your guilty heart. But this old man had outlived his fatherhood, which had once extended to all the bus-world of children. His own sons and daughters by now would have grown and gone and given him the usual causes for bitterness.

The old man's foolish triumph was something that must be understood. Elwin tried to know the weariness and sense of final loss that moved the old conductor to stand on that small dignity of his. He at once brought into consideration the conditions of life of the old man, especially the lack of all the advantages that he himself had had—the gentle rearing and the good education that made a man like Stephen Elwin answerable for all his actions. It had long been the habit of Elwin's mind to raise considerations of just this sort whenever he had reason to be annoyed with anyone who was not more powerful than himself.

But now, strangely, although the habit was in force, it did not check his anger. It was bewildering that he should feel anger at a poor ignorant man, a working man. It was the first time in his life that he had ever felt so. It shamed him. And he was the more bewildered and ashamed when he understood, as he did, that he was just as angry at the boy as at the old man. He was seeing the boy full grown and the self-pity and hatred taking root beside the urgency and power. The conductor and the boy were links in the great chain of the world's rage.

Clearly it was an unreasoning thing to feel. It was not what a wise man would feel. At this time in his life Stephen Elwin had the wish to be wise. He had never known a wise man. The very word sounded like something in a tale read to children. But the occasion for courage had passed. By courage Elwin meant something very simple, an unbending resistance of spirit under extreme physical difficulties. It was a boy's notion, but it had stayed with Elwin through most of his life, through his business and his pleasure, and nothing that he had ever done had given him the proof that he wanted. And now that the chance for that was gone—he was forty-one years old—it seemed to him that perhaps to be wise was almost as manly a thing as to be brave.

Two wars had passed Elwin by. For one he was too young, for the other too old, though by no means, of course, old. Had it not been for the war, and the consideration of age it so ruthlessly raised, the recollection of the sentence from Hazlitt would no doubt have been delayed by several years, and so too would the impulse to which it had given rise, the desire to have "wisdom." More and more in the last few months, Elwin had been able to experience the sensation of being wise, for it was indeed a sensation, a feeling of stamina, poise and illumination.

He was puzzled and unhappy as he "alighted" from the bus at 92nd Street. It seemed to him a great failure that his knowledge of death and his having reached the years of wisdom—they were the same thing—had not prevented him from feeling anger at an old man and a boy. It then occurred to him to think that perhaps he had felt his anger not in despite of wisdom but because of it. It was a disturbing, even a horrifying, fancy. Yet as he walked the two blocks to his home, he could not help recurring to it, with what was, as he had to see, a certain gratification.

In his pleasant living-room in his comfortable chair, Stephen Elwin watched his daughter as she mixed the drink he usually had before dinner. She was thirteen. About a month ago she had made this her job, almost her duty, and she performed it with an unspeakable seriousness. She measured out the whiskey and poured it into the tumbler. With the ice-tongs she reached the ice gently into the bottom of the glass so that there would not be the least splash of whiskey. She opened the bottle of soda. Holding up the glass for her father's inspection, she poured the soda slowly, ready to stop at her father's word. Elwin cried "Whoa!" and at the word he thought that his daughter had reached the stage of her growth where she did indeed look like a well-bred pony.

Now Margaret was searching for the stirring-spoon. But she had forgotten to put it on the tray with all the other paraphernalia and she gave a little cry of vexation and went to fetch it. Elwin did not tell her not to bother, that it did not matter if the drink was not stirred. He understood that this business had to proceed with a ceremonial completeness.

Margaret returned with the stirring-spoon. She stirred the highball and the soda foamed up. She waited until it subsided, meanwhile shaking the spoon dry over the glass with three precise little shakes. She handed her father the drink and put a coaster on the table by his chair. She watched while he took his first sip. He had taken the whole responsibility for the proportion of soda to whiskey. Still, she wanted to be told that she had made the drink just right. Elwin said, "Fine. Just right," and Margaret tried not to show the absurd pleasure she felt.

For this ritual of Margaret's there were, as Elwin guessed, several motives. The honor of her home required that her father not make his own highball in the pantry and bring it out to drink in his chair, not after she had begun to take notice that in the homes of some of her schoolmates, every evening and not only at dinner-parties, a servant brought in, quite as a matter of course, a large tray of drinking equipment. But Margaret had other reasons than snobbishness—Elwin thought that she needed to establish a "custom," not only for now but for the future, against the time when she could say to her children, "And every night before dinner it was the *custom* in our family for me to make my father a drink." He supposed that this ritual of the drink was Margaret's first traffic with the future. It seemed to him that to know a thing like this about his daughter was one of the products of what could be called wisdom and he thought with irony but also with pleasure of his becoming a dim but necessary figure in Margaret's story of the past.

"I bought a picture today," Elwin said.

Margaret cocked an eye at him, as if to say, "Are you on the loose again?" She said, "What is it? Did you bring it home?"

"Oh just a reproduction, a Rouault."

"Rouault?" she said. She shook her head decisively. "Don't know him." It quite settled Rouault for the moment.

"Don't know him?"

"Never heard of him."

"Well, take a look at it—it's over there."

She untied the string and took off the paper and sat there on the big hassock, her feet far out in front of her, holding the great king at arm's length. It was to Elwin strange and funny, this confrontation of the black, calm, tragic king and this blonde child in her sweater and skirt, in her moccasin shoes. She became abstracted and withdrawn in her scrutiny of the picture. Then, Elwin, seeing the breadth and brightness of her brow, the steady intelligence of her gaze, understood that there was really no comic disproportion. What was funny was the equality. The young lieutenant had been quite neutralized by the picture. Even Mark Jennings had been a little diminished by it. But Margaret, with her grave, luminous brow, was able to meet it head on. And not in agreement either.

"You don't like it?" Elwin said.

She looked from the picture to him and said, "I don't think so."

She said it softly but it was pretty positive. She herself painted and she was in a very simple relation to pictures. She rose and placed the picture on the sofa as if to give it another chance in a different position and a better light. She stood at a distance and looked at it and Elwin stood behind her to get the same view of it that she had. He put his hand on her shoulder. After a moment she looked up at him and smiled. "I don't really *like* it," she said. The modulation of her voice was not apology, but simply a gesture of making room for another opinion. She did not think it was important whether she liked or disliked the picture. It said something to her that was not in her experience or that she did not want in her experience. Liking the picture would have given her pleasure. She got no pleasure from not liking it. It seemed to Elwin that in the little shake of her head, in her tone and smile, there was a quality, really monumental, by which he could explain his anger at the old conductor and the boy and forgive himself for having had it.

When Lucy Elwin came in, her face was flushed from the stove and she had a look of triumphant anticipation. She shamelessly communicated this to her family. "It's going to be ver-ry good," she said, not as if she were promising them a fine dinner, rather as if she were threatening them with a grim fate. She meant that her dinner was going to be so very good that if they did not extravagantly admire it, if they merely took it for granted, they would be made to feel sorry. "It will be ready in about ten minutes," she said. "Are you very hungry?"

"Just enough," Elwin said. "Are you tired?" For his wife had stretched out in the armchair and put back her head. She slouched with her long legs at full length, her skirt a little disordered, one ankle laid on the other. Her eyes being closed made her complicated face look simple and she seemed young and self-indulgent, like a girl who escapes from the embarrassment of herself into a broody trance. It was an attitude that had lately become frequent with Margaret.

Lucy Elwin said, "Yes, a little tired. But really, you know, I'd almost rather do the work myself than have that Margaret around."

She spoke with her eyes still closed, and so she did not see her daughter stiffen. But Elwin did. He knew that it was not because Margaret thought that her mother meant her but because of the feelings she had for the other Margaret, the maid. The other Margaret, as so often, had not come to work that day.

Margaret had mixed a drink for her mother and now she was standing beside Lucy's chair, waiting with exaggerated patience for Lucy to open her eyes. She said, "Here's your drink, Mother!"

She said it as if she had waited quite long enough, using the lumpish, martyred, unsuccessful irony of thirteen, her eyebrows very weary, the expression of her mouth very dry. Lucy opened her eyes and sat up straight in her chair. She took the drink from Margaret and smiled. "Thank you, dear," she said. For the moment it was as if Margaret were the mother, full of rectitude and manners and Lucy the careless daughter.

That Lucy was being careless even her husband felt. No one could say of their Negro maid, the other Margaret, that she was a pleasant person. Even Elwin would have to admit to a sense of strain in her presence. But surely Lucy took too passionate a notice of her. Elwin felt that this was not in keeping with his wife's nature. But no, that was really not so. It was often disquieting to Elwin, the willingness that Lucy had to get angry even with simple people when she thought they were not behaving well. And lately she had been full of stories about the nasty and insulted temper that was being shown by the people one daily dealt with. Only yesterday, for example, there had been her story of the soda-fountain man who made a point of mopping and puttering and changing the position of pieces of pie and only after he had shown his indifference and independence would take your order. Elwin had to balance against the notice his wife took of such things the deep, literal, almost childish way she spoke of them, the innocence of her passion. But this particular story of the soda-fountain clerk had really distressed him, actually embarrassing him for Lucy, and he had pointed out to her how frequent such stories had become. She had simply stared at him, the fact was so very clear. "Why, it's the war," she said. "People are just much meaner since the war." And when his rebuke had moved on to the matter of the maid Margaret, Lucy had said in the most matter-of-fact way, "Why, she just hates us." And she had shocked Elwin by giving, just like any middle-class housewife, a list of all the precious things Margaret had broken. "And observe," Lucy had said, "that never once has she broken anything cheap or ordinary, only the things I've pointed out to her that needed care."

Elwin had to admit that the list made a case. Still, even if the number of the green Wedgwood coffee cups had been much diminished, cups for which Elwin himself had a special fondness, and even if the Persian bowl had been dropped and the glass urn they had brought from Sweden had been cracked in the sink, they must surely not talk of such things. The very costliness of the objects which proved Margaret's animosity, the very affection which the Elwins felt for them, made the whole situation impossible to consider.

Lucy must indeed have been unaware of how deeply her husband resisted her carelessness in these matters and of what her daughter was now feeling. Otherwise she would not have begun her story, her eyes narrowing in anger at the recollection, "Oh, such a rotten thing happened on the way home on the bus."

It was Elwin who had had the thing happen on the bus, not quite "rotten" but sufficiently disturbing, and he was startled, as if his wife's consciousness had in some way become mixed up with his own in a clairvoyant experience. And this feeling was not diminished as Lucy told her story about a young woman who had asked the conductor a question. It was a simple, ordinary question, Lucy said, about what street one transferred at. The conductor at first had not answered, and then, when he came around again and the question was asked again, he looked at the young woman—"looked her straight in the face," Lucy said—and had replied in a loud voice, "Vot deed you shay?"

"*Mother!*" cried Margaret. Her voice was all absolute childish horror.

Elwin at once saw what was happening, but Lucy, absorbed in what she had experienced, only said mildly, "What's the matter, dear?"

"Mother!" Margaret grieved, "you mustn't do that." Her face was quite aghast and she was standing stiff with actual fright.

"Why, do what, Margaret?" said Lucy. She was troubled for her daughter but entirely bewildered.

"Make fun of—fun of—" But Margaret could not say say it.

"Of Jews?" said Elwin in a loud, firm, downright voice.

Margaret nodded miserably. Elwin said with enough sharpness, "Margaret, whatever makes you think that Lucy is making fun of Jews? She is simply repeating—"

"Oh," Margaret cried, her face a silly little moon of gratitude and relief. "Oh," she said happily, "what the woman said to the conductor!"

"No, Margaret. How absurd!" Lucy cried. "*Not* what the woman said to the conductor. What the conductor said to the woman."

Margaret just sat there glowering with silence and anger.

Elwin said to Margaret with a pedagogic clearness and patience, "The conductor was making fun of the woman for being Jewish."

"Not at all," Lucy said, beginning to be a little tried by so much misunderstanding. "Not at all, she wasn't Jewish at all. He was insulting her by pretending that she was Jewish."

Margaret had only one question to ask. "The *conductor?*" she cried with desperate emphasis.

And when Lucy said that it was indeed the conductor, Margaret said nothing, but shrugged her shoulders in an elaborate way and made with her hands a large grimace of despairing incomprehension. She was dismissing the grownups by this pantomime, appealing beyond all their sad nonsense to her own world of sure right reason. In that world one knew where one was, one knew that to say things about Jews was bad and that working men were good. And *therefore*.

Elwin, whose awareness was all aroused, wondered in tender amusement what his daughter would have felt if she had known that her gesture, which she had drawn from the large available stock of the folk-culture of children, had originally been a satiric mimicry of a puzzled shrugging Jew. The Margaret who, only a few minutes before, had looked at the picture with him and had seemed, almost, to be teaching him something. Now he had to teach her. "That isn't a very pretty gesture," he said. "And what, please, is so difficult about Lucy's story? Don't you believe it?"

A mistake, as he saw at once. Margaret was standing there trapped—no, she did not believe it, but she did not dare say so. Elwin corrected himself and gave her her chance. "Do you think Lucy didn't hear right?"

Margaret nodded eagerly, humbly glad to take the way out that was being offered her.

"We studied the transit system," she said by way of explanation. "We made a study of it." She stopped. Elwin knew how her argument ran, but she herself was not entirely sure of it. She said tentatively, by way of a beginning. "They are underpaid."

Lucy was being really irresponsible, Elwin thought, for she said in an abstracted tone, as if she were musing on the early clues of an interesting scientific generalization, "They hate *women*—it's women they're always rude to. Never to men." Margaret's face flushed, and her eyes darkened at this new expression of her mother's moral obtuseness, and Elwin felt a quick impatience with his daughter's sensitivity—it seemed suddenly to have taken on a pedantic air. But he was annoyed with Lucy, too, who ought surely to be more aware of what her daughter was feeling. No doubt he was the more annoyed because his own incident of the bus was untold and would remain untold. But it was Lucy who saved the situation she had created. She suddenly remembered the kitchen. She hurried out, then came back, caught Margaret by the arm in a bustle of haste and said, "Come and hurl the salad." This was a famous new joke in the family. Elwin had made it, Margaret loved it. It had reference to a "tossed green salad" on a pretentious restaurant menu. Of the salad, when it was served to them in all its wiltedness, Elwin had said that apparently it needed to be more than tossed, it needed to be hurled.

And so all at once the family was restored, a family with a family joke. Margaret stood there grinning in the embarrassment of the voluptuous pleasure she felt at happiness returned. But she must have been very angry with her mother, for she came back and pulled Elwin's head down and whispered into his ear where he would be able to find and inspect the presents she had for Lucy's birthday next week.

He was to look for two things. In the top left-hand drawer of Margaret's desk he would find the "bought present" and on the shelf in the clothes closet he would find the "made present." The bought present was a wallet, a beautiful green wallet, so clearly expensive that Elwin understood why his daughter had had to tease him for money to supplement her savings, and so adult in its expensiveness that he had to understand how inexorably she was growing up.

The made present was also green, a green lamb, large enough to have to be held in two hands, with black feet and wide black eyes. The eyes stared out with a great charming question to the world, expressing the comic grace of the lamb's awkwardness. Elwin wondered if Margaret had been at all aware of how much the lamb was a self-portrait. When Elwin, some two years before, had listened to his daughter playing her first full piece on the recorder, he had thought that nothing could be more wonderful than the impervious gravity of her face as her eyes focused on the bell of the instrument and on the music-book while she blew her tune in a daze of concentration; yet only a few months later, when she had progressed so far as to be up to airs from Mozart, she had been able, in the very midst of a roulade, with her fingers moving fast, to glance up at him with a twinkling, sidelong look, her mouth puckering in a smile as she kept her lips pursed, amused by the music, amused by the frank excess of its ornamentation and by her own virtuosity. For Elwin the smile was the expression of gay and conscious life, of life innocently aware of itself and fond of itself, and, although there was something painful in having to make the admission, it was even more endearing than Margaret's earlier gravity. Life aware of itself seemed so much more life.

His daughter's room was full of life. His own old microscope stood on Margaret's desk and around it was a litter of slides and of the various objects from which she had been cutting sections, a prune and a dried apricot, a sliver of wood, a piece of cheese and what seemed to be a cockroach. There were tools for carving wood and for cutting linoleum blocks. The books were beginning to be too many for the small bookshelf, starting with *The Little Family* and going on to his own soiled copy of *The Light That Failed* that Margaret had unearthed. There was her easel and on one wall was a print of Picasso's trapeze people in flight, like fierce flames, and on another wall one of Benton's righteous stylizations, both at home, knowing nothing of their antagonism to each other. The dolls were no longer so much to the fore as they once were, but they were still about, and so was the elaborate doll's house which contained in precise miniature, accumulated over years, almost every object of daily living, tiny skillets, lamps, cups, kettles, packaged groceries. Surrounded by all that his daughter made and did and read, Elwin could not understand how she found the time. And then, on the thought of what time could be to a child, there came to him with more painful illumination than usual, the recurrent sentence. "No young man believes he shall ever die." And he stood contemplating the room with a kind of desolation of love for it.

Margaret burst in suddenly as if she were running away from something—as indeed she was, for her eyes blazed with the anger she was fleeing. She flung herself on the bed, ignoring her father's presence.

"Margaret, what's the matter?" Elwin said.

But she did not answer.

"Margaret!" There was the note of discipline in his voice. "Tell me what the matter is."

She was not crying, but her face, when she lifted it from the pillow, was red and swollen. "It's mother," she said. "The way she talked to Margaret."

"To Margaret? Has Margaret come?"

"Yes, she came." The tone implied: through flood and fire. "And mother—oh!" She broke off and shook her head in a rather histrionic expression of how impossible it was to tell what her mother had done.

"What did she say that was so terrible?"

"She said—she said, 'Look here—' " But Margaret could not go on.

Lucy strode into the room with quite as much impulse as Margaret had and with eyes blazing quite as fiercely as her daughter's. "Look here, Margaret," she said. "I've quite enough trouble with that Margaret without your nonsense. Nobody is being exploited in this house and nobody is being bullied and I'm not going to have you making situations about nothing. I'm sure your Miss Hoxie is very sweet and nice, but you seem to have got your ideas from her all mixed up. You weren't that way about Millie when she was with us. As a matter of fact," Lucy said with remorseless irony, "you were often not at all nice to her."

Margaret had not heard the end of Lucy's speech. At the mention of Miss Hoxie in the tone that Lucy has used—"your Miss Hoxie"—at the sacred name of her teacher blasphemously uttered, she looked at her mother with the horror of seeing her now in her true terrible colors. The last bond between them had snapped at this attack upon her heart's best loyalty.

But Lucy was taking no account of finer feelings. She closed the door and said firmly, "Now look here, the simple fact is that Margaret is a thoroughly disagreeable person, a nasty, mean person."

"Oh, she is not," Margaret wailed. And then, despite all her passion, the simple fact broke in upon her irresistibly. Elwin's heart quite melted as he saw her confront the fact and struggle with it. For the fact was as Lucy had stated it, and he himself at that moment had to realize it. And it was wonderful to see that Margaret's mind, whatever the inclination of her will, was unable to resist a fact. But the mind that had momentarily deserted her will, came quickly again to its help. "She's not responsible," she said desperately. "It's not her fault. She couldn't help it. Society—" But at that big word she halted, unable to handle it. "We can't blame her," she said defiantly but a little lamely.

At that moment Lucy saw the green clay lamb that Elwin was still holding. She rushed to it and took it and cried, "Margaret, is this yours? I've never seen it, why didn't you show it to me?"

It was, of course, a decided point for Margaret that her birthday surprise was spoiled. She sat there looking dry and indifferent amid the ruins of family custom. Elwin said, "It's a birthday present for you, Lucy. You weren't supposed to see it," and their glances met briefly. He had been a little treacherous, for he could have managed to put the lamb out of sight, but some craftiness, not entirely conscious, had suggested its usefulness for peace.

"It's so *lovely*," Lucy said. "Is it really for me?"

Margaret had to acknowledge that it was, but with an elaborate ungraciousness from her bruised and empty heart. Her mother might have the gift, meaningless as it now was. But Lucy was in a flood of thanks and praise impossible to withstand—it was lovely, she said, to have a gift in advance of her birthday, it was something she had always wanted as a child and had never been able to induce her parents to allow, that she should have one, just one, of her presents before the others, and the lamb itself was simply beautiful, quite the nicest thing Margaret had ever made. "Oh, I love it," she said, stroking its face and then its rump. "Why darling!" she cried, "it looks exactly like you!" And Margaret had to submit to the child's pain at seeing the eminence of grief and grievance swept away. But at last, carried beyond the vacant moment when the forgiving and forgiven feeling had not yet come, she sat there in an embarrassed glow, beaming shyly as her mother kissed her and said quietly and finally, "Thank you."

When they were in the dining-room, all three of them feeling chastened and purged, Lucy said, "I must have it here by my place." And she put the lamb by her at the table, touching its cheek affectionately.

The dinner that Lucy had cooked was served by the other Margaret. She was a tall, rather light colored girl, with a genteel manner and eyebrows that were now kept very high. As she presented the casserole to Lucy, she looked far off into a distance and stood a little too far away for convenience. Lucy sat there with the serving spoon and fork in her hand and then said, "Come a little closer, Margaret." Margaret Elwin sat rigid, watching. Margaret the maid edged a little closer and continued her gaze. She moved to serve Elwin but Lucy said, "It's Margaret you serve next." Her tone was a little dry. Margaret Elwin flushed and looked mortified. It had been a matter of some satisfaction that she was now of an age to be served at table just after her mother, but she hated to have a point made of it if Margaret objected, and Margaret did seem to object and would not accept the reassuring smile that was being offered her over the casserole.

In the interval between the serving of the casserole and the serving of the salad that had once that evening made the family peace, Margaret held her parents with a stern and desperate eye. But she was unable to suppress a glance her mother sent to her father, a glance that had in it a touch of mild triumph. And her father did not this time fortify himself against it. The odds were terribly against her and she looked from one to the other and said in an intense whisper, "It's not her fault. She's not responsible."

"Why not?" Elwin asked.

It was his voice that made the question baffling to Margaret. She did not answer, or try to. It was not merely that the question was, for the moment, beyond her powers. Nor was it that she was puzzled because her father had seemed to change sides. But she was touched by the sense, so little formulated, so fleeting as scarcely to establish itself in her memory, that something other than the question, or the problem itself, was involved here. She barely perceived, yet she did perceive, her mother's quick glance at her father under lowered lids. It was something more than a glance of surprise. Neither Margaret nor Lucy, of course, knew anything about the sentence from Hazlitt. But this was one of the moments when the sentence had occurred to Elwin and with it the explosion of light. And his wife and daughter had heard the event in his voice. For Elwin an illumination, but a dark illumination, was thrown around the matter that concerned them. It seemed to him—not suddenly, for it had been advancing in his mind for some hours now—that in the aspect of his knowledge of death, all men were equal in their responsibility. The two bus conductors, Lucy's and his own, the boy with his face contorted in rational rage against the injustice he suffered, Margaret the maid with her genteel malice—all of them, quite as much as he himself, bore their own blame. Exemption was not given by age or youth, or sex, or color, or condition of life. It was the sense of this that made his voice so strange at his own dinner-table, as if it came not merely from another place but another time.

"Why not?" he said again. "Why not, Margaret?"

Margaret looked at her father's face and tried to answer. She seriously marshalled her thoughts and, as always, the sight of his daughter actually thinking touched Elwin profoundly. "It's because—because society didn't give her a chance," she said slowly. "She has a handicap. Because she's colored. She has to struggle so hard—against prejudice. It's so *hard* for her."

"It's true," Elwin said. "It's very hard for her. But it's hard for Millie too." Millie had been with the Elwins for nearly seven years. Some months ago she had left them to nurse a dying sister in the South.

Margaret of course knew what her father meant, that Millie, despite "society," was warm and good and capable. Her answer was quick, too quick. "Oh, Millie has a slave-psychology," she said loftily.

Really, Elwin thought, Miss Hoxie went too far. He felt a kind of disgust that a child should have been given such a phrase to use. It was a good school, he approved of its theory; but it must not give Margaret such things to say. He wondered if Margaret had submitted the question of Millie to Miss Hoxie. If she had, and if this was the answer she had been given, his daughter had been, yes, corrupted. He said, "You should not say such things about Millie. She is a good loyal person and you haven't any right to say she is not."

"Loyal!" said Margaret in triumph. "Loyal!"

"Why, yes. To her sister in Alabama, Margaret, just as much as to us. Is it what you call slave-psychology to be loyal to your own sister?"

But Margaret was not to be put down. She kept in mind the main point, which was not Millie but the other Margaret.

"I notice," she said defiantly, "that when Millie sends you parts of the money you lent her, you take it all right."

Poor child, she had fumbled, and Elwin laid his hand on hers on the table. "But Margaret! Of course I do," he said. "If I didn't, wouldn't that be slave-psychology? Millie would feel very lowered if I didn't take it."

"But she can't afford it," Margaret insisted.

"No, she can't afford it."

"Well then!" and she confronted the oppressor in her father.

"But she can't afford not to. She needs it for her pride. She needs to think of herself as a person who pays her debts, as a responsible person."

"I wonder," Lucy said, "I wonder how Millie is. Poor thing!" She was not being irrelevant. She was successful in bringing her husband up short. Yes, all that his "wisdom" had done was to lead him to defeat his daughter in argument. And defeat made Margaret stupid and obstinate. She said, "Well, anyway, it's not Margaret's fault," and sat sulking.

Had he been truly the wise man he wanted to be, he would have been able to explain, to Margaret and himself, the nature of the double truth. As much as Margaret, he believed that "society is responsible." He believed the other truth too. He felt rather tired, as if the little debate with Margaret had been more momentous than he understood. Yet wisdom, a small measure of it, did seem to come. It came suddenly, as no doubt was the way of moments of wisdom, and he perceived what stupidly he had not understood earlier, that it was not the other Margaret but herself that his Margaret was grieving for, that in her foolish and passionate argument, with the foolish phrases derived from the admired Miss Hoxie, she was defending herself from her own impending responsibility. Poor thing, she saw it moving toward her through the air at a great rate, and she did not want it. Naturally enough, she did not want it. And he, for what reason he did not know, was forcing it upon her.

He understood why, Lucy, when they had risen from the table, made quiet haste to put her arm around Margaret's shoulders as they went into the living-room.

They were sitting in the living-room, a rather silent family for the moment, when the other Margaret stood in the doorway. "You may as well know," she said, "that I'm through here." And she added, "I've had enough."

There was a little cry, as of horror, from Margaret. She looked at her parents with a bitter and tragic triumph. Lucy said shortly, "Very well, Margaret. Just finish up and I'll pay you." The quick acceptance took the maid aback. Angrier than before, she turned abruptly back into the dining room.

For the third time that evening, Margaret Elwin sat in wretched isolation. Her father did not watch her, but he knew what she felt. She had been told *she* might go, never to return. She saw the great and frightening world before her. It was after all possible so to offend her parents that this expulsion would follow. Elwin rose to get a cigarette from the table near the sofa on which Margaret sat and he passed his hand over her bright hair. The picture of the king with the flower in his hand was in the other corner of the sofa.

It was as Elwin's hand was on his daughter's head that they heard the crash, and Elwin felt under his hand how Margaret's body experienced a kind of convulsion. He turned and saw Lucy already at the door of the dining room, while there on the floor, in many pieces, as if it had fallen with force, lay the smashed green lamb, more white clay showing than green glaze. Lucy stooped down to the fragments, examining them, delicately turning them over one by one, as if already estimating the possibility of mending.

The maid Margaret stood there, a napkin in her hand clutched to her breast. All the genteel contempt had left her face. She looked only frightened, as if something was now, at last, going to be done to her. For her, almost more than for his own Margaret, Elwin felt sad. He said, "It's all right, Margaret. Don't worry, it's all right." It was a foolish and weak thing to say. It was not all right, and Lucy was still crouching, heartbroken, over the pieces. But he had had to say it, weak and foolish as it was.

"Ah, darling, don't feel too bad," Lucy said to her daughter as she came back into the living-room, tenderly holding the smashed thing in her hand.

But Margaret did not answer or even hear. She was staring into the dining-room with wide, fixed eyes. "She meant to do it," she said. "She *meant* to do it."

"Oh, no," Lucy said in her most matter-of-fact voice. "Oh, no, dear. It was just an accident."

"She meant to do it, she meant to do it." And then Margaret said, "I saw her." She alone had been facing into the dining-room and could have seen. "I saw her—with the napkin. She made a movement," and Margaret made a movement, "like this . . ."

Over her head her parents' eyes met. They knew that they could only offer the feeble lying of parents to a child. But they were determined to continue. "Oh, no," Elwin said, "it just happened." And he wondered if the king, within his line of vision as he stood there trying to comfort his daughter, would ever return to the old, fine, tragic power, for at the moment he seemed only quaint, extravagant and beside the point.

"She meant to. She didn't like me. She hated me," and the great sobs began to come. But Elwin knew that it was not because the other Margaret hated her that his Margaret wept, but because she had with her own eyes seen the actual possibility of what she herself might do, the insupportable fact of her own moral life. She was weeping bitterly now, her whole body shaking with the deepest of sobs, and she found refuge in a corner of the sofa, hiding her head from her parents. She had drawn up her knees, making herself as tight and inaccessible as she could, and Elwin, to comfort her, sat on what little space she allowed him on the sofa beside her, stroking her burrowing head and her heaving back, quite unable, whatever he might have hoped and wanted, to give her any better help than that.

6

NATIONALISM IN MUSIC

Friedrich Smetana

Every work of art is conditioned by a triple relationship—to the art itself, to the artist, and to the audience or public. A poem, painting, or musical composition is what it is because of a long tradition of art to which it belongs; at the same time it is the direct creative expression of an individual poet, painter, or musician; and both these factors may also be modified by the particular public for which the work is designed. Where there is social awareness in the art of music, it is this third factor that explains it—the public for whom the music is composed and performed.

In the nineteenth century the movement known as musical nationalism was perhaps the most obvious expression of such social consciousness. Romanticists idealized folk material in all the arts, and the political events of the time encouraged national movements. Especially in the countries where there had been little art music before the nineteenth century, such as Russia, Bohemia (Czechoslovakia), and Scandinavia, the leading musicians emphasized folk music and themes drawn from national history and legend. Composers attempted to speak directly to the native public and to inspire patriotic feelings. In some cases the purpose was to arouse the desire for political freedom from foreign domination; in others it was simply the encouragement of national loyalty. Important figures such as Moussorgsky, Smetana, Dvořák, and Grieg belong in this movement. In Germany, France, and Italy, all of which had a long tradition of art music, national characteristics had always been evident, but nineteenth-century musicians found a ready audience for the more specific use of folk themes and national myths and legends. In Germany Wagner is an especially good example of this trend.

Near the middle of the nineteenth century Bohemia, then a part of the Austrian Empire but since 1918 known as Czechoslovakia, made a strong bid for independence. The movement achieved nothing politically except some relaxation of Austrian controls, but the political resentments of the time and a strong desire to break away from the cultural dominance of Germany led to a flowering of a Czech school of music under the leadership of Friedrich Smetana.

Smetana was born in 1824, the seventh child and first boy in the family of a fiddle-

playing, music-loving village brewer. The boy seems to have been something of a child prodigy; he made his first public appearance as a pianist at the age of six and he began to compose at eight. Although the father was proud of these musical gifts, he was opposed to a musical career for his son. In the gymnasium (high school), first at Prague, then at Pilsen, Friedrich was torn between his duty to his schoolwork and his love of music. Eventually his father gave him twenty florins and washed his hands of him; Smetana went to Prague to try to make a living from music. For a time he was employed in the family of Count Thun as resident music master, a post which ended with his involvement in the abortive revolution of 1848. As one of the Bohemian patriots, he found it necessary to take a post abroad and became director of a Philharmonic Society in Sweden for five years.

In 1859, Italy freed herself from Hapsburg domination and the Austrians somewhat relaxed their iron-handed control over the Czechs. The result was a great stirring in the political, social, and artistic life of Prague. Smetana returned and assumed leadership in the movement for a national theater and a national Philharmonic Society. He dreamed of an art that would be truly Czech in spirit but at the same time universal in appeal. His greatest contributions to this ideal were his operas, of which the Bartered Bride *is his finest and best known. In 1874, at fifty, Smetana became totally deaf. In that year of misfortune he composed the cycle of symphonic poems entitled* My Country (Ma Vlast)*. Ten years later he suffered a severe loss of mental powers and died soon afterward, in 1884.*

In Czechoslovakia his music became the center of a truly national cult and stimulated the national rebirth which took place after World War I and which ended so disastrously when the Communists took control of the country in 1948. Never greatly interested in abstract music, Smetana was attracted by the symphonic or tone poem, which introduces a dramatic quality into instrumental music by utilizing associations taken from some episode in life or literature. The Moldau (Vltava)*, one of his best-known and most popular works of this sort, is discussed in some detail in the selection reprinted here from* A Listener's Anthology *by Lillian Baldwin.*

VLTAVA—THE RIVER

IN HIS magnificent work, *My Country*, Smetana has shown us nationalism at its best. The proud patriot speaks even in the title, and the music itself is one long celebration of the beauty and glory of Bohemia. But Smetana was too ambitious for Bohemian music to be content with mere musical Bohemianism. He dreamed of a Czech music which would be valued not for its picturesque charm but for those enduring and purely musical beauties which have nothing to do with either time or place. And so, with no fear of losing his Czech inheritance he studied the works of the great masters and made himself a man of the musical world. For Smetana, nationalism was always a starting point, not a stopping place. He set out to create the best possible music, and because he was both a sincere artist and an ardent patriot that music became, inevitably, the best possible Bohemian music.

My Country is a cycle of six symphonic poems beginning with *Vysehrad*, picturing that ancient citadel at Prague which seems to symbolize the glorious

Czech past. Then comes *Vltava (The Moldau)*, in which the poet follows the course of the river from its source in the Sumava forest to Prague, where it widens into a majestic stream. *Sarka*, the title of the third poem, recalls the legend of Sarka, the wildest and loveliest of the Bohemian Amazons. *From Bohemian Fields and Groves* is a joyous pastoral inspired by the beautiful Czech countryside. Quite different in mood are the last two poems. *Tabor* honors those famous Hussite fighters who in the dark days of Bohemia's religious wars drove the crusading armies far beyond the frontiers. The Taborites were Smetana's ideal of Czech courage, and he expresses this ideal in valiant music. *Blanik*, which ends the cycle, takes its name from the mountain within whose rocky fastness there sleeps an army of Bohemia's glorious dead, and, says the legend, on the Day of Judgment that shining company will sally forth and lead the Czechs to final victory. At the end of *Blanik*, Smetana brings back the motif of *Vysehrad*, thus linking Bohemia's past and future glory.

My Country is a patriot's creed more convincingly stated than if Smetana had said, "I love my country for her natural beauties and the spirit of her people. I glory in her past, dedicate heart and hand to her present, and declare my faith in her future!" For these are but words, while the music gives the feeling of tenderness, courage, and triumph.

These tone poems do more than satisfy the listener's love of the picturesque and the artist's demand for musical values. They convince. Their almost compelling sincerity is doubtless due to the fact that Smetana does not depend upon some other man's poems for the background of his music. *My Country* pictures scenes and events which belong to Smetana as a Czech. He creates his own poems, using tones instead of words, and this is perhaps why they are among the most musical as well as the most convincing of all program works.

On the cover page of each score, the composer gives a brief program, doubtless in deference to us "outlanders," since surely no Czech would need one! This is his preface to *Vltava* [*The Moldau*]:

> In the shadows of the Bohemian forests two springs arise, the one, warm and bubbling, the other, cool and quiet. Trickling down the rocks they unite and chatter gaily together in the morning sunlight. Soon this hurrying brook becomes a little river which, flowing farther and farther through the land of the Czechs, swells to a mighty stream, the Vltava. It passes through deep forests where the sound of the chase and the huntsman's horn rings clear; it glides through rich meadows and lowlands where with noisy song and dance a peasant wedding is being celebrated. At night, nymphs and naiads play in its moonlit waters. Its gleaming surface mirrors many a grim old castle, mute witness of the days of knighthood and the glorious deeds of vanished warriors. At St. John's Rapids the stream bursts through rocky walls in a wild cataract and goes foaming on its way. Then, broadening out, it flows past Prague where it is welcomed by the ancient fortress, Vysehrad, and then sweeps splendidly into the far distance beyond the poet's eye.
>
> *Translation*—L.L.B.

A single flute accompanied by scattered, spray-like notes from the harp and violins, introduces the first, the bubbling spring:

The second spring, the cool, quiet one, joins it:

and flute and clarinet ripple along together in delightful fashion. Smetana loved the clarinet, "the national instrument of Bohemia," and used it effectively and constantly.

Soon the hurrying brooklet broadens with a wavelike figure in the strings and deepens with a long soft horn tone until it becomes the river Vltava. And now above the rippling water we hear the song of the river:

a simple, happy song voicing the beauty and contentment of the land of the Czechs.

It passes through the deep forest, where a clear call:

the rhythm of galloping hoofs:

and the winding horn:

suggest the hunt.

Then, leaving the huntsmen far behind, it glides into rich farmlands and we hear the merry sounds of a village wedding. It is a gay dance tune they are playing:

with clever orchestral suggestions of a country fiddler, energetically scraping, and of wheezing bagpipes and the clump, clump of heavy peasant boots.

The scene changes. Twilight falls in dim woodwind harmonies. The river sparkles in the moonlight, and a high, sweet song floats through the night:

as nymphs and naiads trip their wreathing dance.

Then, mingling with the murmur of the stream and the song of the nymphs comes the ghost of martial music:

as some grim old castle with its memories of the days of knighthood is reflected in the water. But this, too, passes, and only the sound of the water breaks the stillness of the night.

On flows the river, singing its happy song, until it reaches the Rapids of St. John. Here, with a wild pounding of brass and woodwinds and eddying, foaming strings, the stream battles with the rocks that would hold it back. Then having forced its way through, the Vltava sings again. It is the old song, heard in the beginning but now transformed by major harmonies and lilting rhythm into a hymn of victory.

Now at its widest part it flows past the ancient fortress and we hear the motif of the *Vysehrad*, symbol of Bohemia's glorious past:

With increasing strength the great river sweeps jubilantly on and vanishes in the distance "beyond the poet's vision."

What valiant, joyous music it is! And when we remember that it was written in those first tragically silent months of sudden, total deafness, then, indeed, *My Country* becomes not only a magnificent cycle of symphonic poems but an even more magnificent monument of human courage worthy of a place beside the Milton sonnet "On His Blindness" and the Beethoven Ninth symphony.

Dimitri Shostakovich

Nationalistic sentiment has influenced the music of Shostakovich in rather unusual fashion. Born in St. Petersburg, now Leningrad, in 1906, he saw the overthrow of the czar and the success of the Bolshevist revolution when a boy of eleven. He later studied music at the Leningrad Conservatory under the Communist regime; all his life he has had to compose under restrictions imposed by a Communist dictatorship. The painter, poet, novelist and composer all lose much of their creative freedom when they try to work in a controlled society like the Soviet Union today. In such a society music must serve mainly practical purposes. The composer is not free to follow the demands of his art but must submit his work to the judgment of those whose chief interests are not esthetic but political and social.

It is not surprising that in this situation Shostakovich has had a varied career, one which illustrates clearly the difficulties of creative achievement in a totalitarian society. His early opera The Nose *(1928-1929), a caricature of the Old Regime in Russia, was praised by Soviet authorities but is no longer in the repertory. Another opera,* Lady Macbeth *(1934), highly praised at first in Russia as well as in the United States, was later denounced in Russia as bourgeois, unhealthy, and unintelligible. In 1935 a Shostakovich ballet was also denounced in Moscow. During World War II, however, he became something of a national hero. His Symphony No. 7 was composed in 1941 during the siege of Leningrad by the Nazis. When the government was moved from Moscow to Kuibyshev in October 1941, Shostakovich went along and finished the symphony in the new Volga capital, where it was first played in 1942. Its success in this situation was enormous and its score, photographed, was flown to the United States, where our best conductors competed for the honor of introducing it to the American public. The premiere was given by Toscanini and the NBC Symphony Orchestra in July 1942. Since then it has been widely performed. Because of the occasion of its composition this symphony is known as the Leningrad Symphony.*

Denounced again in 1948 for "decadent journalism" Shostakovich nevertheless received the Stalin prize in 1949. He has produced a large volume of music—operas, ballets, film music, and choral, vocal, orchestral, band, and solo works—and is one of the most distinguished contemporary composers. From the viewpoint of critics, both Russian and Western, however, Shostakovich has alternated between work of marked distinction and rather ordinary pieces. The selection we reprint from Masterworks of the Orchestral Repertoire *by Donald N. Ferguson throws further light upon the career of Shostakovich and contains an analysis of the Fifth as well as the Seventh Symphony.*

SHOSTAKOVICH:

Symphony No. 5, Op. 47

THE OFFICIAL opinion of the Soviet State upon art works of all sorts is loosely comparable to the authoritative opinions of the Académie Française. That institution, established in 1635 to ensure the purity of the French language and literature, has exerted since that time an influence upon almost every field of French thought. Its value has been variously estimated. Apostles of perfection in style like Matthew Arnold have praised it as a bulwark of educated opinion, and as the very fount and origin of sound criticism. Others have pointed to the fact that great literary figures like Balzac, Flaubert, Gautier, and Zola have failed of election to that august company. But the judgments of the Academy have neither issued from nor directly supported any political theorems.

It is otherwise in Soviet Russia. The Soviet republics not only recognize that literature and the other arts are significant contributions to culture; they have discovered criteria by which art works may be judged as supporting or weakening the precious consciousness of Soviet solidarity. These criteria remain, however, apparently a close governmental secret. Thus it is hard for the uninitiated—and for the composer himself—to imagine the state of mind in which an artist must work if he is to live up to those standards.

His recorded experiences suggest that these perplexities are not unknown to Shostakovich. First displaying musical talent at the age of nine, he pursued his studies under the banner—and sometimes under the ban—of the Soviet esthetic. While he was in favor, in 1931, he thus expressed his understanding of that esthetic (in a letter to *The New York Times*):

> I am a Soviet composer, and I see our epoch as something heroic, spirited, and joyous. Music cannot help having a political basis—an idea that the *bourgeoisie* are slow to comprehend. There can be no music without ideology. [One wonders whether he has forgotten Beethoven's Ninth or Wagner's *Ring*.] The old composers . . . most of them . . . were bolstering the rule of the upper classes. We as revolutionists have a different conception. . . . Lenin himself said that "music is a means of unifying great masses of people." . . . Good music lifts and heartens, and lightens people for work and effort. It may be tragic, but it must be strong. It is no longer an end in itself, but a vital weapon in the struggle.

His Second and Third symphonies (*October*, and *May-day*) were accordingly provided with or were based on explicitly revolutionary themes or programs. But in 1936 *Pravda* sharply reproved the young composer for his "formalistic ideas founded on bourgeois musical conceptions." His opera *Lady Macbeth of the Mzensk District*, a rather lurid tale of adultery and murder in the provinces, was condemned, even though it had been performed with much applause not only in Russia but in New York; and a new ballet, *Limpid Stream*, although it depicted scenes on a communal farm, was dismounted almost as soon as it had been produced. Alarmed, the composer withdrew his new Fourth Symphony from performance by the Leningrad Philharmonic, even though it had been accepted in the face of this storm of criticism.

The Fifth, possibly composed with the sting of that criticism in mind, and performed in celebration of the twentieth anniversary of the Soviet State, apparently reinstated him in official as well as in popular favor. "The fetters of musical formalism which held this composer captive for so long, and have prevented him from creating works profound in conception, have been torn off. He must follow up his new trend in his work. He must turn more boldly toward Soviet reality. He must understand it more profoundly and find in it a new stimulus for his work." (Thus a critic in the *Moscow Daily News*.)

The Fifth Symphony, in contrast to the Second and Third, has no program. It is thus doubly difficult for us who lack insight into the Soviet esthetic to decide wherein this music accords with that theory, while the Second and Third do not. But it has won considerable acclaim among those who do not live in the sunshine of that theory.

If we compare it with the First, we shall find a considerable deepening of the composer's perceptions and a certain clarifying of his technique. The novelty of the orchestra as a fascinating instrument on which to play has somewhat worn off. So also has disappeared some of the naïveté that was there so engaging. But he has by no means become the slave of any particular modernistic idiom, and apparently has no special desire to appear "advanced." The alarming longwindedness which will characterize both the Seventh and the Eighth symphonies—perhaps the product of a too superficial study of the essential principles of rhetoric—is not yet in evidence; and there is still apparent the desire to write music which men of any race may understand.

The symphony has the usual four movements, and these correspond in many features to the classical symphonic scheme. The first and last movements attain to climax by the familiar device of a gradual increase in speed, here indicated metronomically. The movement which corresponds to the Scherzo stands second in order. But these are hardly novelties of structure, and the thematic substances, as well as the harmonies that result from their manipulation, seldom appear distorted or bizarre.

In the first movement the somewhat angular principal theme is announced at the outset antiphonally between the lower and the higher strings. The second subject (this terminology is justified by the form) is lyrical, in extended strains. The quickening extends throughout the development period, the rhythmic accentuations becoming more incisive and the colors bolder. The peak of the development is attained in a passage dominated by the brass. After that the original slow tempo recurs, the principal theme being sounded by the whole orchestra *largamente.* The woodwinds, sparingly used hitherto, provide the close.

The Scherzo (it is not so entitled, but is in that character) smacks a little of the *Ländler* of Schubert's day. The conventional form (Scherzo, Trio, Scherzo *da capo*) is readily recognizable, and there are approximations to the usual repetitions in each of the sections.

The slow movement is neither portentous in length nor pretentious in structure. Its main theme somewhat resembles that of the first movement. It seems to expand, by its own intrinsic energies, out of the tentative beginnings in the strings.

The Finale is a readily recognizable Rondo whose principal theme is a march tune, obviously intended to invigorate the spirit. It is thus clearly in accord with that general principle of composition announced by the composer; but it is not known to have produced any converts to communism among its hearers in America. The subordinate themes offer interesting but hardly striking or dramatic contrast with the main theme, and the whole movement is easy to follow.

SHOSTAKOVICH:

Symphony No. 7, Op. 60

The genesis of this symphony was described as follows by the composer, as reported in the Boston *Herald:*

On that peaceful summer morning of June 22, 1941, I was on my way to the Leningrad Stadium to see my favorite Sunday soccer game. Molotov's radio address announcing Hitler's invasion of Russia found me hurrying down the street for fear I should miss the opening quarter. . . . Peacetime plans, the manuscript of a symphonic work I had just started—all these things I put aside to start on an entirely new epoch of life and work. . . . I served as a fire-fighter. I had already applied for volunteer service, but . . . I wasn't called for duty. Instead, I worked with the People's Voluntary Army theater. . . . Meanwhile I started work on my seventh symphony, conceived as a broad musical embodiment of majestic ideas of the patriotic war. . . . By October 1st I had already completed three movements and most of the fourth. I finished the symphony in Kuibyshev a few months later. . . . I would like to have my symphony heard in all the United Nations as a symbol of friendship between our countries; as a symbol that we are brothers in arms, in culture, and in fraternity in the struggle for a better world.

The music itself was also described by the composer for Ralph Parker of *The New York Times*, from whose report the following is culled:

The first movement (*Allegro moderato*) opens with a theme intended to describe the existence of

ordinary people—people not distinguished by any special features or talents—just good, quiet people, going about their daily life. After this preliminary theme I introduce the main theme, which was inspired by the transformation of these ordinary people into heroes by the outbreak of the war. This builds up into a requiem for those of them who are perishing in the performance of their duty. In the first movement's final passages I introduce something very intimate, like a mother's tears over her lost children. It is tragic, but finally becomes transparently clear.

The scherzo and adagio movements are of an intermediate character, in which I am moved by the idea that war doesn't necessarily mean destruction of cultural values. The fourth movement can be described by one word, victory. But my idea of victory isn't something brutal; it's better explained as the victory of light over darkness, of humanity over barbarism, of reason over reaction.

And the following comment, from the pen of Carl Sandburg, was read by Raymond Massey for a radio performance of the symphony by the Cleveland Orchestra:

It begins with the good earth, and with plains and valleys naked for the toil of a man seeking crops and bread. . . .

It goes on with touches like people in peace time having a chance to hunt for themselves, their personal birds of happiness to listen to. . . .

Then come drums and guns and evermore drums and guns and the war is on and the test of a nation and people—and an ordeal for the whole family of man. . . .

The music marches and fights, it struggles and kills, it stands up and says there are a thousand terrible deaths, it is better to die than to let the Nazis take over your homeland and tell you how you must live. . . .

What you say sometimes, Dimitri Shostakovich, is the same as the message MacArthur sent by radio to Stalin: "Magnificent! Matchless!"

Jean Sibelius

Jean Sibelius belongs to Finland in a unique way. His ideal was to create music that expressed not only his own patriotic feelings but also the culture of his native land, and in this undertaking he was remarkably successful. He was only thirty-two when the Finnish government awarded him an annual grant in order that he might devote himself entirely to musical composition. In the last ten years of the nineteenth century Finland was suffering from Russian oppression and national feeling was strong. To contribute to the spirit of national freedom Sibelius composed his first truly Finnish music, a five-movement symphonic poem called Kullervo. *It was a tremendous success when it was first played in Helsingfors in 1892, and from that moment Sibelius was accepted as the national composer.*

Until his death in 1958 at the age of ninety-two, he was the musical voice of Finland, recognized as a national hero and a patriotic symbol.

Sibelius was born in 1865 in Tavastehus, the son of a well-known physician. He early showed musical talent but received a classical education and was sent to Helsingfors (now Helsinki) University to study law. He had already begun to play the violin and to learn musical theory, harmony, and counterpoint, however, and after a year, he enrolled in the Helsingfors Conservatory. Later he was awarded a scholarship for study in Germany and from there he went to Vienna for a period. But in 1891 he returned to his native land, and from that time on his independence and strong individuality have been his most striking characteristics.

He taught for a few years at the conservatory in Helsingfors but upon receiving the government grant that made him financially independent, he and his wife established their home in a beautiful villa near a small town in the forests north of the capital. From then on his life was relatively uneventful, punctuated only by journeys to the United States, which he visited in 1914, and to other European countries, where he conducted his own compositions. In America Yale University conferred on him an honorary Doctor of Music, and everywhere he was recognized as one of the great composers of the time. After 1924 he went into complete retirement and about 1929 he stopped composing. Little is known about him during the last ten or fifteen years of his life.

Sibelius' music is not nationalistic in the narrow sense. Even in the popular Finlandia *he did not use a folk theme but one entirely original with him. His melodies are all his own, but they are profoundly Finnish in feeling and spirit. The Second Symphony, which is discussed in the selection that follows, cannot be considered national music in the sense in which Smetana's* Moldau *represents Czech music or Copland's* Appalachian Spring *represents the folk songs of the American southern highlands. But critics have always felt that it expresses the somber wildness of the northern woods and the intensity of the Finnish revolt against oppression.*

SIBELIUS:

Symphony No. 2 in D Major, Op. 43

IN THE Second Symphony, Sibelius makes a definite break with the influences and derivations that can be marked in the First; he establishes himself here as a composer of distinct individuality, with a style and idiom uniquely his own. Here also we can observe the two most characteristic features of Sibelius' music—its strongly national character and the amazing economy and effectiveness of its orchestration. This is the real Sibelius, terse, powerful, and convincing; devoid of the factitious and the unnecessary, naked and pulsating and enormously vital.

This may be, as some commentators assert, Sibelius' "pastoral" symphony, but it is scarcely more descriptive of his native land than others of his musical works. The spirit of Finnish folk music is always strong in Sibelius; images and atmosphere of fiord and crag and gray unfriendly seas, of sparsely covered meadows and acrid salt marshes, are always evoked by it. In this particular work, however, we can feel something more powerful; something of the aroused patriotism of *Finlandia*, as well as the laconic finality exhibited so wonderfully in the Fourth Symphony.

First Movement

The uncanny certainty with which the composer selects the one most effective voice through which his melodies shall be projected is beautifully revealed throughout this music. It has been said that Sibelius conceives a melody and its instrumental expression simultaneously; that he is incapable of dissociating melody and instrument. If so, he has developed this valuable faculty to the point of papal infallibility, for when a melody sings out from the orchestra of Sibelius, we somehow feel that *that* is the one inevitable voice through which the given melody could be proclaimed.

The first movement is filled with the subdued light of a Finnish landscape. At once the foundation of the movement is laid—a markedly rhythmic figure in the strings which is at once an intimation of a musical thought presently to be expressed and a dominating idea in the symphony. The first theme itself is given out, briefly, by oboes and clarinets; the accompaniment of the throbbing strings continues. Both ideas are developed freely and at some length, but the orchestration remains superbly simple. An atmosphere of severity rather than of gloom, of a harsh relentless vitality asserting itself with quiet strength rather than with bombastic proclamations, colors the whole movement. New thematic material, presented by woodwind in octaves, above the pulsing figure heard from the first in strings, reveals the picture in another aspect and in new colors, but does not alter its outlines. At the end the mesmerizing throbbing of the strings, having wrought its charm and created its mood, sounds less assertively.

Second Movement

The stubborn and sometimes gloomy patriotism of his fellow countrymen seems to be the moving spirit of this strange music. In it are outlined grim forebodings, and the realization of them; sturdy opposition, tragic defeats, and a kind of wild and suppressed nobility. The timpani, pregnant with thunders, give out threatening rumblings; then the low strings, pizzicato, sketch the melodic line of the movement. The weirdest voice in the orchestra—that of the bassoon—sings sadly of sorrows and tears and terrors, and there is menace in the dull roar of the great drums that sound below. Such an atmosphere rarely endures for long in the music of Sibelius; presently it is dissipated in a stormy climax that evokes the orchestra's fullest powers.

The folk-song influence is distinctly felt in the presentation of the second principal theme. It must be remembered here, as always in the music of Sibelius, that the composer does not borrow his melodies from the folk music of Finland; but so intensely feels and loves the native music that his own melodies quite naturally adopt its characteristic outlines.

The strings, divided, present the poignant melody, and at the same time accompany themselves; later added color is given by woodwinds. The palette is reversed, after a few moments, with the theme in the woodwind and accompaniment by strings. There is a distinct lightening of the gloom that has heretofore pervaded the movement, and with each succeeding climactic wave the feeling of strength and assertiveness and hope grows stronger. Though there are frequent disjointed remembrances of thematic fragments scattered throughout the movement, its unity and power and vitality are maintained, even though its dynamics are temporarily held in restraint. The final climax is of crushing power and vehemence.

Third Movement

If there were a program for this symphony, the third movement would undoubtedly be regarded as the "call to arms," the "awakening of national pride and spirit," the taking up of a struggle against oppression. The movement springs into agitated life with the very first note. The violins have a lightfooted figure, which not only establishes the mood of the scherzo, but also supplies a rhythmic basis against which other thematic elements are projected. A curious combination of glitter and shadow—flute and bassoon—utters the second chief subject, still animated and nervous like the first.

The trio, or middle section of the scherzo, is in marked contrast to the first. Here the piercing tones of the oboe are arranged in a simple and appealing melody, its thinness and sharpness relieved by the warm and softly sonorous accompaniment of bassoon and horn. The strings are momentarily invoked, but during its brief moments this part of the movement maintains a calm and pastoral atmosphere. The elastic rhythms of the opening section return, and after a final reference to the quiet melody of the trio, a long crescendo begins, and leads with ever-developing power directly into the

Fourth Movement

Here the blazing and imperious proclamations of this music sound a mighty song of triumph. This is the Sibelius of *Finlandia;* this is boldness and spaciousness and powerful uncomplicated assertiveness. The main theme is brief, strong, and simple. The strings, down to and including

cellos, pronounce it with vigor. Woodwinds present a second, and strongly rhythmical, idea, and the two are developed in a series of climaxes piled upon one another like mountains.* Yet there is here, as in most of Sibelius' moments of excitement or grandeur, something of godlike passionless detachment; as if some remote being handled mighty intractable forces with unerring firm hands, and, inexorable and unperturbed, molded them to his will. It is curious that this music, that can be so moving and so mighty, can at the same moment be so cold. It has the beat and the breath of life, but its life stream moves deliberately, inevitably, fatefully, and never passionately. That the music of this composer rarely has in it the quality we call sensuousness is one of the many apparent contradictions we find in it, for though it seems to omit this quality, it is the very character of the sounds Sibelius makes the orchestra produce that most fascinates our ears and most powerfully calls forth our response to this music.

* 

Aaron Copland

During the last hundred years, in America as well as in Europe, there has been considerable interest in folk materials in both literature and music. Although there is not the cultural unity in the United States that there is in most European countries, and although we have no genuine peasant class from which folk music would naturally arise, yet mountain ballads, cowboy songs, Negro spirituals, American-Indian dances, and other music of this kind have flourished here.

Among contemporary American composers using these native materials, Aaron Copland is one of the best known. Copland was born in Brooklyn in 1900 of Russian parents. After graduation from high school he went to Paris, where he became the first American pupil of Nadia Boulanger, an unusual teacher and organist. His early compositions were in a dissonant modern style; later in the 1920s he made a vigorous attempt to adapt jazz techniques to serious music. Both these practices aroused the hostility of audiences when his music was played. By 1934, however, Copland had become seriously concerned with the problem of narrowing the gap between the composer and his public. "I began to feel an increasing dissatisfaction with the relations of the music loving public and the living composer," he writes. "It seemed to me that composers were in danger of working in a vacuum. Moreover an entirely new public for music had grown up around the radio and phonograph. It made no sense to ignore them and continue writing as if they did not exist. I felt that it was worth the effort to see if I couldn't say what I had to say in the simplest terms."

To this end Copland introduced more obvious melodies in his compositions and for these he frequently turned to folk music. He has used these folk themes with great skill and they have no doubt helped to produce a lyricism which now gives his music a wide appeal. He has likewise given considerable time and thought to what is known as "functional" music. In 1937 he composed a school opera Second Hurricane *and in 1939 music for a puppet show. He has done music for the ballet, film, and radio, including such things as* Our Town *(1940),* Of Mice and Men *(1939), and a documentary film* The City, *for which Lewis Mumford did the narrative.* Appalachian Spring *was originally produced as a ballet, and his other ballet scores,* Billy the Kid *(1939) and* Rodeo *(1942), both emphasize distinctively American themes. His books,* What to Listen for in Music *(1939),* Our New Music *(1941), and* Music and Appreciation *(1952), are all directed to the general reader, and their purpose is to provide increased understanding for the laymen interested in music.*

In the selections included here are more detailed analyses of three of Copland's popular compositions, Appalachian Spring, Lincoln Portrait, *and* El Salón México, *by well-known music critics.*

APPALACHIAN SPRING

Ballet (1945)

Appalachian Spring was composed for Martha Graham on a commission from the Elizabeth Sprague Coolidge Foundation. Miss Graham introduced it at the Library of Congress in Washington, D.C., on October 30, 1944. In the spring of 1945, Copland arranged some of the best passages into an orchestral suite which has enjoyed numerous performances throughout the country. In 1945 *Appalachian Spring* won a Pulitzer prize and the award of the New York Music Critics Circle.

The composer has provided us with a history of this, one of his most successful works:

> The music of the ballet takes as its point of departure the personality of Martha Graham. I have long been an admirer of Miss Graham's work. She, in turn, must have felt a certain affinity for my music, because in 1931 she chose my *Piano Variations* as background for a dance composition entitled *Dithyramb*. . . . Ever since then, at long intervals, Miss Graham and I planned to collaborate on a stage work. Nothing might have come of our intention if it were not for the lucky chance that brought Mrs. Elizabeth Sprague Coolidge to a Graham performance for the first time early in 1942. With typical energy, Mrs. Coolidge translated her enthusiasms into action. She invited Martha Graham to create three new ballets for the 1943 annual fall festival of the Coolidge Foundation in Washington, and commissioned three composers—Paul Hindemith, Darius Milhaud, and myself—to compose scores especially for the occasion.
>
> After considerable delay, Miss Graham sent me an untitled script. I suggested certain changes, to which she made no serious objections. I began work on the music of the ballet in Hollywood in June 1943, but didn't complete it until a year later, in June 1944, in Cambridge, Massachusetts.
>
> The title, *Appalachian Spring*, was chosen by Miss Graham. She borrowed it from the heading of one of Hart Crane's poems, though the ballet bears no relation to the text of the poem itself.

The première of the ballet took place in October 1944. The setting was designed by Isamu Noguchi, and Edith Guilford supplied the costumes.

The orchestral suite from the ballet score includes eight sections, played without interruption:

I. Very Slowly—The Introduction of the Characters.

II. Sudden Burst of Unison Strings, marking the beginning of the action. The sentiment here expressed combines elation with religious feeling.

III. Moderate (Duo for the Bride and Her Intended), a tender and passionate scene.

IV. Quite Fast (The Revivalist and His Flock). The feeling is folklike, with echoes of country fiddlers and suggestions of square dances.

V. Still Faster (Solo Dance of the Bride). The extremes of joy and fear are here voiced.

VI. Very Slowly (as at first). This is a transition scene in which the music brings up recollections of the introduction.

VII. Calm and Flowing (Scenes of Daily Activity for the Bride and Her Farmer-Husband). A Shaker theme is heard, followed by five variations. The theme (solo clarinet) is derived from an actual Shaker melody entitled *Simple Gifts*.

VIII. Moderate (Coda). The married couple are left alone in their new home. Music that is almost reverent is intoned by muted strings. The final measures recall the opening pages.

LINCOLN PORTRAIT

The *Lincoln Portrait* is one of the results of a three-part commission offered in 1942 by André Kostelanetz, well-known conductor of popular broadcasts and records, to

[From *The Victor Book of Overtures, Tone Poems and Other Orchestral Works*, by Charles O'Connell. Copyright, 1934, 1950, by Simon and Schuster, Inc. Reprinted by permission of Simon and Schuster, Inc.]

three noted American composers, Aaron Copland, Jerome Kern, and Virgil Thomson. Mr. Kostelanetz conceived the idea of attempting to portray in music three inspiring leaders who, through the emotional suggestiveness of music, might be held up before war-harassed Americans as symbols of the courage and strength and will to victory that the country needed. Mr. Copland preferred to do a "portrait" of Walt Whitman, but was persuaded that a statesman and wartime leader would be perhaps a better choice under the circumstances, and he therefore chose to portray Lincoln. Mr. Kern produced his *Portrait for Orchestra* of Mark Twain, and Mr. Thomson chose as his subject the late Fiorello H. LaGuardia, one-time army flier, member of Congress, and vigorous, colorful mayor of New York. The first performance of *Lincoln Portrait* was given at a concert of the Cincinnati Symphony Orchestra, May 14, 1942. It was conducted by André Kostelanetz, to whom the work is dedicated.

The composer tells that he entertained some doubts, which were not modified after a discussion with his colleague, Virgil Thomson, that he could write music of sufficient importance to justify in itself the title *Lincoln Portrait*. He felt, however, that by bringing Lincoln himself into the picture through the device of quoting some of Lincoln's own words he might be successful. He therefore interpolated excerpts from various papers and speeches of Lincoln, and had the good judgment and the fortitude to confine his quotations for the most part to the lesser-known utterances of the Great Emancipator, the last quotation only being from a familiar Lincoln speech. In the score Mr. Copland also adverts to certain American tunes, though he does not use any of them literally. The two conspicuous fragments he employed are from the well-known *Camptown Races* and from a ballad first published in 1840 under the title *The Pesky Sarpent* but later known as *Springfield Mountain* [as illustrated in the figure below].*

In this music the composer seeks to suggest, in the first division of the score, something of the "mysterious sense of fatality that surrounds Lincoln's personality." Too, toward the end of this section he wants us to feel something of Lincoln's warm, simple, and human qualities, his sympathy with his fellow man, and perhaps his determination to accomplish something for the improvement of the condition of the downtrodden.

The middle section of the work is intended to give us a picture of the times in which Lincoln lived. All this leads to the third section and—background and framework now more clearly perceived—we are prepared for the very words of Lincoln himself, which are closely synchronized with the music. The excerpts from Lincoln's papers and speeches, together with some connective material which are delivered by a speaker against the background of the orchestra, follow.

"*Fellow citizens, we cannot escape history.*"
That is what he said,
That is what Abraham Lincoln said:
"*Fellow citizens, we cannot escape history. We of this Congress and this administration will be remembered in spite of ourselves. No personal significance or insignificance can spare one or another of us. The fiery trial through*

which we pass will light us down, in honor or dishonor, to the latest generation. We—even we here—hold the power and bear the responsibility."
He was born in Kentucky, raised in Indiana, and lived in Illinois.
And this is what he said,
This is what Abe Lincoln said:
"The dogmas of the quiet past are inadequate to the stormy present. The occasion is piled high with difficulty, and we must rise with the occasion. As our case is new, so must we think anew and act anew. We must disenthrall ourselves, then we shall save our country."
When standing erect he was six feet four inches tall.
And this is what he said,
He said:
"It is the eternal struggle between two principles—right and wrong throughout the world. . . . It is the same spirit that says, 'You toil and work and earn bread and I'll eat it.' No matter in what shape it comes, whether from the mouth of a king who bestrides the people of his own nation and lives by the fruit of their labor, or from one race of men as an apology for enslaving another race, it is the same tyrannical principle."
Lincoln was a quiet man.
Abe Lincoln was a quiet and a melancholy man.
But when he spoke of democracy,
This is what he said,
He said:
"As I would not be a slave, so I would not be a master. This expresses my idea of democracy. Whatever differs from this, to the extent of the difference, is no democracy."
Abraham Lincoln, sixteenth President of these United States is loved by all his countrymen.
For on the battlefield at Gettysburg, this is what he said,
He said:
" . . . that from these honored dead we take increased devotion to that cause for which they gave the last full measure of devotion: that we here highly resolve that these dead shall not have died in vain; that this nation, under God, shall have a new birth of freedom: and that government of the people, by the people, for the people, shall not perish from the earth."

EL SALÓN MÉXICO

This fascinating music certainly comes under the head of "modern composition." To label it so, however, is perhaps to frighten, if not to antagonize, many a music lover who would find it completely fascinating. It is true that much modern music is

[From *The Victor Book of Overtures, Tone Poems and Other Orchestral Works*, by Charles O'Connell. Copyright, 1934, 1950, by Simon and Schuster, Inc. Reprinted by permission of Simon and Schuster, Inc.]

self-conscious, cerebral rather than emotional or spiritual, and devised more for the exploitation of theory than for the exploration of human feeling.

But if a symphony orchestra playing contemporary music has any terrors for anyone, here is music that will dispel them. It is difficult to believe that anyone with red blood, whether it be the kind that is agitated by Beethoven or the type that moves faster to the goings on of Benny Goodman, will fail to respond, and respond with active pleasure, to this extraordinary music. To be sure it has its dissonances—but no dissonances that the scholar, the theorist, or the jitterbug need reject. It is light, even vulgar, but it is alive, it is vivid, and it reflects a picture in which the action is forthright and the colors raw, crude, and recklessly applied. This music has the quality of universal appeal, which is certainly an essential of all true art; and the proof of its universal effectiveness is established by its equal success in Mexico City, London, Boston, Cincinnati, or Brooklyn. It is amusing to find the Boston *Herald*, for example, comment that "Mr. Copland has been wasting his time all these years and should have been sunning himself and keeping his ears open in the cafés of Latin America. The public will care little that he ruin his health so long as he produces exotic and exciting scores like this."

El Salón México is the Mexican version of the Roseland Ballroom of New York, or the cheaper dance halls of any large city. It is one of the famous hot spots of Mexico City and Mr. Copland, attracted by the typically Mexican flavor of the place, decided to write music descriptive of it. The temperature of the atmosphere of the music and the dancers quite fascinated him, as did many other details. "Where else in the world," he asks, "could you find a sign on a dance-hall wall which says: 'Please don't throw lighted butts on the floor so the ladies don't burn their feet'?"

The fact is that though centering his attention primarily on *El Salón México*, Mr. Copland condensed and crystallized the life, the feeling, and the color of all Mexico. In this music, which superficially seems so jazzy, there are flashes of purest Spanish fire as well as fragments of the most vulgar dance music of today, not to mention certain attractive Mexican folk dances which, as he said, he has taken and strung together like the beads of a string. Mr. Copland writes, "Other tourists will pull out their snapshots to show you what a country looks like, but a composer wants you to know what a country sounds like." One feels the composer has been eminently successful in his project.

"I follow no general rule," he adds, "in the use of the themes that I treated. Almost all of them come from the *Cancionero Mexicano* by Frances Toor, or from the erudite work by Ruben M. Campos, *El Folklore y la Musica Mexicana*. To both authors I owe thanks. Probably the most direct quotation of a complete melody is that of *El Mosco* (No. 84 in the book by Campos), which is presented twice, immediately after the introductory measures (in which may be found fragments of *El Palo Verde*, and of *La Jesusita*)." [See below.]

This music actually pants with excite-

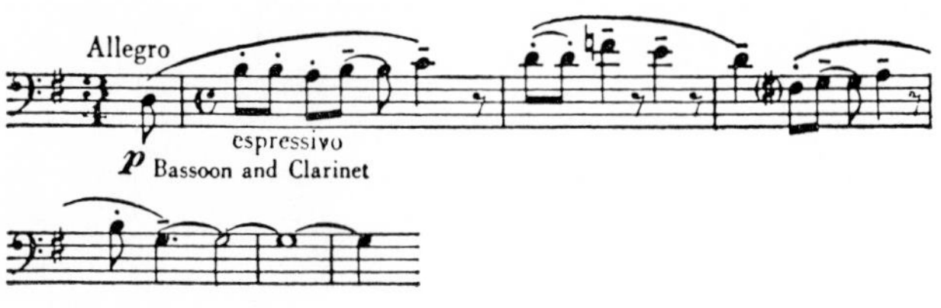

ment and occasionally even staggers with emotional exhaustion. The precise and compelling rhythms, while jazzy enough, might extend even the best dance band beyond its physical powers, but the ecstatic shudders and squeals of the clarinet would be a most welcome invitation to the best possible jitterbug virtuoso. The use of percussion instruments, both those which are standard in the symphony orchestra and several exotic ones, is of exceptional interest, and various instrumentalists in addition to the percussion player, and especially the solo trumpet and solo clarinet, have parts that might stagger many a virtuoso, but can often be realized by players in our better symphony orchestras.

Many alleged experts feel that a symphony player cannot grasp, much less execute, jazz music. Performances of this work by various orchestras, and particularly by the Boston Symphony Orchestra, completely refute any such notion. Here is what might be called subtropical jazz, infinitely elaborated and clarified, bristling with difficulties of all kinds, yet played with conviction, enthusiasm, and expertness by orchestra men who might scowl on a popular fox trot.

Part Two

THE IMPACT OF SCIENTIFIC THOUGHT

1. *Religion and the Scientific Spirit*
2. *Science and the Moral Life*
3. *Logical Positivism*
4. *Architecture: The International Style*
5. *Painting: Impressionism, Postimpressionism, and Cubism*
6. *Literature: Naturalism and Realism*
7. *Music: Contemporary Neoclassicism*

THE POINT OF VIEW

THE INFLUENCE of modern science upon contemporary life and thought has been tremendous. Without exaggeration we might say that this is the most striking feature of the past hundred years—roughly since the publication of Darwin's *Origin of Species* in 1859, an event which in itself has become a landmark. During this period modern science and technology have revolutionized the kind of world in which we live. We accept as normal today occurrences that would have been dismissed by any sane person as fantastic less than a hundred years ago; many of the changes we take for granted without being aware of their significance. Ours is an urban and industrial society, a world of large cities—there are a dozen cities in the world with as many as three or four million people (150 years ago New York City had a population of only sixty thousand). The mass production of automobiles, which requires ever-expanding systems of highways and superhighways, makes us a mobile society; it also brings into daily life the constant irritation of finding a place to park one's car. Our way of life is increasingly being transformed by jet planes, nuclear energy, hydrogen bombs, and earth satellites, with talk of trips to outer space that can no longer be dismissed as "science fiction"—not to mention such familiar things as radio and television, or the metropolitan newspaper, which provide us with a full account of newsworthy events everywhere in the world almost as soon as they occur.

Science and the Humanities

As significant as are these material and physical changes, there are also other more pervasive if less obvious social, moral, religious, and intellectual changes that have accompanied them. Today we frequently emphasize differences between the sciences and the humanities. As humanists we bemoan the fact that in times of war or national crisis so much more time and money is given to the sciences than to the humanities—when it is quite obvious, to us at least, that the reverse should be the case. But the essential relationships between science and the humanities are certainly as significant as are their differences. During the past hundred years every area of the humanities has felt the effect of scientific achievements and the scientific point of view—so much so that it has seemed desirable here to deal directly and in some detail with the impact of science upon the humanities.

Life in the city, for example, is not the kind of life in which our traditional moral convictions and religious faith developed. In the urban and industrial society that modern science has made possible many new and perplexing moral problems have arisen. The "scientific point of view" likewise has come to have an immense prestige, much greater than that of the church in most cases. The scientist has frequently spoken with authority on all subjects simply because of the authority that came from his scientific achievement. And with our growing concern over the great strides being made by scientists in Russia, we are now witnessing a renewed emphasis upon science in this country that gives it a prestige as great perhaps as it has ever enjoyed. Until quite recently indeed to be "unscientific" in one's approach to any significant problem was enough to make the undertaking suspect, if not downright unacceptable to the more enlightened of our age. To meet this demand of the modern mind we find influential efforts during the past several decades to develop not only a strictly scientific philosophy but also a scientific morality and even a "scientific religion," if this is not a contradiction in terms.

The Scientific Point of View

In a meaningful sense it is possible, we believe, to speak of "the scientific point of view" as a view of human life and the universe appreciably different from other contemporary points of view. Our concern here is not so much to *define* this view of man and the world with "scientific" exactness, but rather to illustrate its meaning with fullness and concreteness as it is expressed by some of its ablest exponents in areas with which we in the humanities are most directly concerned.

Outstanding contemporary thinkers like Bertrand Russell and Alfred North Whitehead have written frequently of the impact of modern science upon philosophy and religion. John Dewey, perhaps the most influential American philosopher of our generation, was much concerned with the influence of scientific method on philosophy. Dewey, Russell, and Max Otto have all pointed to significant changes in morals produced by the impact of science. Charles Sanders Peirce is being recognized today as one of the first American philosophers to understand the scientific point of view and to see clearly its implications. In logical positivism, we see an influential contemporary effort to identify philosophy with scientific analysis. Able and thoughtful journalists like Walter Lippmann and Lincoln Barnett have been discussing in more popular fashion the way in which the impact of science has affected the philosophy, religion and morals of ordinary men and women. And Albert Einstein represents for us the supreme example in our day of the scientific spirit and scientific achievement.

In the thought of men like these, the scientific point of view becomes meaningful and easy to distinguish. We see the major principles upon which those who accept this point of view can agree, as well as the kind of differences one may expect to find in their views. Likewise the implications of scientific thought for those areas of life and thought that concern us more intimately—for morals and social institutions, for religious faiths and the church—become apparent.

Science and the Arts

In such areas as literature, painting, music, and architecture, the impact of science is not so obvious nor so easily dealt with. But in these areas also the influence of scientific thought and achievement has been pervasive and inescapable. After consideration of the scientific point of view, we turn more directly to a discussion of the arts as they have been modified and shaped by the impact of science during the past hundred years. Our primary concern in this discussion is to provide a better understanding of contemporary painting, literature, architecture, and music. But we believe that such insight is best achieved by the average student, not through a study of the arts in isolation from the rest of life and thought—that is, by a consideration of esthetic principles and techniques alone—but rather through a consideration of these artistic principles and techniques as they are modified by the larger influences at work in the life and world of the artist.

As already suggested, among such influences during the past century none has been stronger than the scientific. We will not be surprised to find, therefore, that the work of such great architects of our day as Le Corbusier or Walter Gropius is dominated by the achievements of the engineer, by the vision of the mathematician. Nor will it be difficult to point out that the revolutionary developments in painting during the past generation or two reflect the influence of scientific thought as definitely as they do the genius of the great artists immediately involved in them. This is as true, for example, of the work of the French impressionists (men like Monet and Pissarro) and Cézanne, that great forerunner of contemporary painting, as it is of Picasso whose cubism so disturbed the traditional complacency in art early in the present century.

In literature and music the influence of scientific thought is less obvious but by no means absent. As one discerning critic has put it, "naturalism tries—rather awkwardly—to apply the methods of science to literature, and to its special field, the novel." In literature, this has come to mean observing the behavior of the human animal in a cool, detached, and objective spirit, and reporting it with scrupulous honesty and clarity. The naturalistic writer remains aloof and uninvolved, as anxious to depict the truth, no matter how unpleasant it may be, as is the scientist in his laboratory. If this attitude hardly seems to exhibit a "humanistic" spirit, still great nineteenth century French writers like Emile Zola and Guy de Maupassant, as well as Americans like Stephen Crane, Theodore Dreiser, and in the twentieth century, Ernest Hemingway, show the important influence of such naturalism upon contemporary literature. And if our own taste in literature has shifted somewhat today, the influence of recent developments in science upon our view of man and human life is still clearly reflected in excellent short stories like that by Stephen Vincent Benét included here.

In music contemporary neo-classicism may well be seen as a development of a somewhat comparable sort. We include here selections dealing with the music of such recent composers as Stravinsky, Prokofieff, Hindemith, and Bartók in which the major characteristics of neo-classicism are discussed and its general significance analyzed.

Charles Sanders Peirce

Not until some years after his death in 1914 was Charles Sanders Peirce recognized as a writer of exceptional ability, yet today he is ranked among the ablest and most influential American philosophers. Born in Cambridge, Massachusetts, in 1839, he was the son of a distinguished mathematician who encouraged the boy's early interests in mathematics and science and likewise, if the stories are reliable, planted in his mind a growing skepticism of the accepted philosophies of his day. Peirce was educated at Harvard, where he moved in a small circle of intellectual friends, and later worked for some years for the Geodetic Survey of the federal government. He never received while he was alive the academic recognition that his intellectual ability merited. In an essay called Concerning the Author *(the first part of the selection included here), Peirce tells of his extensive education. He explains that he is qualified to write about science since he had been trained in physics, chemistry, and mathematics. And he carefully adds that he has also studied logic and philosophy quite thoroughly, lest one think that when he speaks somewhat slightingly of philosophers he is talking from ignorance or prejudice.*

The two essays reprinted here provide an excellent description of the scientific point of view as Peirce knew it at first hand. They are a wholesome, refreshing reply to amateur scientists who talk of the "certainty" of their knowledge and to amateur philosophers who denounce science as if they themselves had attained final truth. The sense of "humility" of the genuine scientists, his diligent inquiry into truth for its own sake, the importance of the creative imagination on the one hand, of devotion to fact on the other—these things stand out clearly in the scientific spirit as Peirce ably portrays it.

An original thinker, Peirce suggested many ideas that today are widely held and have been influential in shaping contemporary scientific thought. In the 1930s the logical positivists, at present the most influential advocates of a thoroughly scientific philosophy, hailed Peirce as the great forerunner of the their position. Thirty years earlier William James, who was soon to be recognized as America's first great philosopher, borrowed from Peirce the idea of pragmatism which James then made the most popular philosophy in the country. Indeed, James had a great admiration for Peirce and was one of the few men who recognized his stature during Peirce's lifetime.

Peirce published only one book during his life. In the present selection, when he speaks delightedly of a forthcoming work, he is talking about a great hope that never materialized. Some twenty years after his death, however, admiring editors produced six volumes of his Collected Papers *(1931-1935). The two essays included here were published even more recently in* The Philosophy of Peirce: Selected Writings *(1940).*

THE SCIENTIFIC ATTITUDE AND FALLIBILISM

I

Concerning the Author

THE READER has a right to know how the author's opinions were formed. Not, of course, that he is expected to accept any conclusions which are not borne out by argument. But in discussions of extreme

[From *The Philosophy of Peirce: Selected Writings*, edited by Justus Buchler. Copyright, 1940. Routledge & Kegan Paul, Ltd., London. Reprinted by permission of the publishers.]

difficulty, like these, when good judgment is a factor, and pure ratiocination is not everything, it is prudent to take every element into consideration. From the moment when I could think at all, until now, about forty years, I have been diligently and incessantly occupied with the study of methods [of] * inquiry, both those which have been and are pursued and those which ought to be pursued. For ten years before this study began, I had been in training in the chemical laboratory. I was thoroughly grounded not only in all that was then known of physics and chemistry, but also in the way in which those who were successfully advancing knowledge proceeded. I have paid the most attention to the methods of the most exact sciences, have intimately communed with some of the greatest minds of our times in physical science, and have myself made positive contributions—none of them of any very great importance, perhaps—in mathematics, gravitation, optics, chemistry, astronomy, etc. I am saturated, through and through, with the spirit of the physical sciences. I have been a great student of logic, having read everything of any importance on the subject, devoting a great deal of time to medieval thought, without neglecting the works of the Greeks, the English, the Germans, the French, etc., and have produced systems of my own both in deductive and inductive logic. In metaphysics my training has been less systematic; yet I have read and deeply pondered upon all the main systems, never being satisfied until I was able to think about them as their own advocates thought.

The first strictly philosophical books that I read were of the classical German schools; and I became so deeply imbued with many of their ways of thinking that I have never been able to disabuse myself of them. Yet my attitude was always that of a dweller in a laboratory, eager only to learn what I did not yet know, and not that of philosophers bred in theological seminaries, whose ruling impulse is to teach what they hold to be infallibly true. I devoted two hours a day to the study of Kant's *Critic of the Pure Reason* for more than three years until I almost knew the whole book by heart, and had critically examined every section of it. For about two years, I had long and almost daily discussions with Chauncey Wright, one of the most acute of the followers of J. S. Mill.

Thus, in brief, my philosophy may be described as the attempt of a physicist to make such conjecture as to the constitution of the universe as the methods of science may permit, with the aid of all that has been done by previous philosophers. I shall support my propositions by such arguments as I can. Demonstrative proof is not to be thought of. The demonstrations of the metaphysicians are all moonshine. The best that can be done is to supply a hypothesis, not devoid of all likelihood, in the general line of growth of scientific ideas, and capable of being verified or refuted by future observers.

Religious infallibilism, caught in the current of the times, shows symptoms of declaring itself to be only practically speaking infallible; and when it has thus once confessed itself subject to gradations, there will remain over no relic of the good old tenth-century infallibilism, except that of the infallible scientists, under which head I include, not merely the kind of characters that manufacture scientific catechisms and homilies, churches and creeds, and who are indeed "born missionaries," but all those respectable and cultivated persons who, having acquired their notions of science from reading, and not from research, have the idea that "science" means knowledge, while

* Words enclosed in brackets have been inserted by the editor of the above volume (Justus Buchler) in the unpublished manuscripts of Peirce.

the truth is, it is a misnomer applied to the pursuit of those who are devoured by a desire to find things out.

Though infallibility in scientific matters seems to me irresistibly comical, I should be in a sad way if I could not retain a high respect for those who lay claim to it, for they comprise the greater part of the people who have any conversation at all. When I say they lay claim to it, I mean they assume the functions of it quite naturally and unconsciously. The full meaning of the adage *Humanum est errare,* they have never waked up to. In those sciences of measurement which are the least subject to error—metrology, geodesy, and metrical astronomy—no man of self-respect ever now states his result, without affixing to it its *probable error;* and if this practice is not followed in other sciences it is because in those the probable errors are too vast to be estimated.

Only once, as far as I remember, in all my lifetime have I experienced the pleasure of praise—not for what it might bring but in itself. That pleasure was beatific; and the praise that conferred it was meant for blame. It was that a critic said of me that I did not seem to be *absolutely sure of my own conclusions.* Never, if I can help it, shall that critic's eye ever rest on what I am now writing; for I owe a great pleasure to him; and, such was his evident animus, that should he find that out, I fear the fires of hell would be fed with new fuel in his breast.

My book will have no instruction to impart to anybody. Like a mathematical treatise, it will suggest certain ideas and certain reasons for holding them true; but then, if you accept them, it must be because you like my reasons, and the responsibility lies with you. Man is essentially a social animal: but to be social is one thing, to be gregarious is another. I decline to serve as bellwether. My book is meant for people who *want to find out;* and people who want philosophy ladled out to them can go elsewhere. There are philosophical soup shops at every corner, thank God!

The development of my ideas has been the industry of thirty years. I did not know as I ever should get to publish them, their ripening seemed so slow. But the harvest time has come, at last, and to me that harvest seems a wild one, but of course it is not I who have to pass judgment. It is not not quite you, either, individual reader; it is experience and history.

For years in the course of this ripening process, I used for myself to collect my ideas under the designation *fallibilism;* and indeed the first step toward *finding out* is to acknowledge you do not satisfactorily know already; so that no blight can so surely arrest all intellectual growth as the blight of cocksureness; and ninety-nine out of every hundred good heads are reduced to impotence by that malady—of whose inroads they are most strangely unaware!

Indeed, out of a contrite fallibilism, combined with a high faith in the reality of knowledge, and an intense desire to find things out, all my philosophy has always seemed to me to grow.

II

If we endeavor to form our conceptions upon history and life, we remark three classes of men. The first consists of those for whom the chief thing is the qualities of feelings. These men create art. The second consists of the practical men, who carry on the business of the world. They respect nothing but power, and respect power only so far as it [is] exercised. The third class consists of men to whom nothing seems great but reason. If force interests them, it is not in its exertion, but in that it has a reason and a law. For men of the first class, nature is a picture; for men of the second class, it is an opportunity; for men of the third class, it is a cosmos, so admirable, that to penetrate to its ways seems to them the only thing that makes life worth living. These are the men whom we see possessed by a passion to learn, just as other men have a passion to teach and to disseminate their influence. If they do not give themselves over completely to their passion to learn, it is because they exercise self-control. Those are the natural scientific men, and they are the only men that have any real success in scientific research.

If we are to define science, not in the sense of stuffing it into an artificial pigeonhole where it may be found again by some insignificant mark, but in the sense of characterizing it as a living historic entity, we must conceive it as that about which such men as I have described busy themselves. As such, it does not consist so much in *knowing*, nor even in "organized knowledge," as it does in diligent inquiry into truth for truth's sake, without any sort of axe to grind, nor for the sake of the delight of contemplating it, but from an impulse to penetrate into the reason of things. This is the sense in which this book is entitled a History of *Science*. Science and philosophy seem to have been changed in their cradles. For it is not knowing, but the love of learning, that characterizes the scientific man; while the "philosopher" is a man with a system which he thinks embodies all that is best worth knowing. If a man burns to learn and sets himself to comparing his ideas with experimental results in order that he may correct those ideas, every scientific man will recognize him as a brother, no matter how small his knowledge may be.

But if a man occupies himself with investigating the truth of some question for some ulterior purpose, such as to make money, or to amend his life, or to benefit his fellows, he may be ever so much better than a scientific man, if you will—to discuss that would be aside from the question—but he is not a scientific man. For example, there are numbers of chemists who occupy themselves exclusively with the study of dyestuffs. They discover facts that are useful to scientific chemistry; but they do not rank as genuine scientific men. The genuine scientific chemist cares just as much to learn about erbium—the extreme rarity of which renders it commercially unimportant—as he does about iron. He is more eager to learn about erbium if the knowledge of it would do more to complete his conception of the Periodic Law, which expresses the mutual relations of the elements.

When a man desires ardently to know the truth, his first effort will be to imagine what that truth can be. He cannot prosecute his pursuit long without finding that imagination unbridled is sure to carry him off the track. Yet nevertheless, it remains true that there is, after all, nothing but imagination that can ever supply him an inkling of the truth. He can stare stupidly at phenomena; but in the absence of imagination they will not connect themselves together in any rational way. Just as for Peter Bell a cowslip was nothing but a cowslip, so for thousands of men a falling apple was nothing but a falling apple; and to compare it to the moon would by them be deemed "fanciful."

It is not too much to say that next after the passion to learn there is no quality so indispensable to the successful prosecution of science as imagination. Find me a people whose early medicine is not mixed up with magic and incantations, and I will find you a people devoid of all scientific ability. There is no magic in the medical Papyrus Ebers. The stolid Egyptian saw nothing in disease but derangement of the affected organ. There never was any true Egyptian science.

There are, no doubt, kinds of imagination of no value in science, mere artistic imagination, mere dreaming of opportunities for gain. The scientific imagination dreams of explanations and laws.

III

The last fifty years have taught the lesson of not trifling with facts and not trusting to principles and methods which are not logically founded upon facts and which serve only to exclude testimony from consideration.

Such, for example, was the dictum of Claude Bernard that a disease is not an entity—a purely metaphysical doctrine. But the observation of facts has taught us that a disease is in many, if not most, serious cases, just as much an entity as a human family consisting of father, mother, and children.

Such was the dictum of the old psychology which identified the soul with the ego, declared its absolute simplicity, and held that its faculties were mere names for logical divisions of human activity. This was all unadulterated fancy. The observation of facts has now taught us that the ego is a mere wave in the soul, a superficial and small feature, that the soul may contain several personalities and is as complex as the brain itself, and that the faculties, while not exactly definable and not absolutely fixed, are as real as are the different convolutions of the cortex.

Such were the dicta by means of which the internal criticism of historical documents was carried to such a height that it often amounted to the rejection of all the testimony that has come down to us, and the substitution for it of a dream spun out of the critic's brain. But archeological researchers have shown that ancient testimony ought to be trusted in the main, with a small allowance for the changes in the meanings of words. When we are told that Pythagoras had a golden thigh, we are to remember that to the ancients gold did not mean a chemical element of atomic weight 197.5 and specific gravity 19.3, melting at 1045° C and forming saline compounds of the types AuX and AuX_3. It means something of metallic luster, warmer in color than electrum and cooler than copper. Dr. Schliemann's discoveries were the first socdolager that "higher criticism" received. It has since got many others.

Such were the dicta by which everything of the nature of extraordinary powers connected with psychological states of which the hypnotic trance is an example were set down as tricks. At present, while the existence of telepathy cannot be said to be established, all scientific men are obliged by observed facts to admit that it presents at least a very serious problem requiring respectful treatment.

Persons who know science chiefly by its results—that is to say, have no acquaintance with it at all as a living inquiry—are apt to acquire the notion that the universe is now entirely explained in all its leading features; and that it is only here and there that the fabric of scientific knowledge betrays any rents.

But in point of fact, notwithstanding all that has been discovered since Newton's time, his saying that we are little children picking up pretty pebbles on the beach while the whole ocean lies before us unexplored remains substantially as true as ever, and will do so though we shovel up the pebbles by steam shovels and carry them off in car loads. An infinitesimal ratio may be multiplied indefinitely and remain infinitesimal still.

It is a great mistake to suppose that the mind of the active scientist is filled with propositions which, if not proved beyond all reasonable cavil, are at least extremely probable. On the contrary, he entertains hypotheses which are almost wildly incredible, and treats them with respect for the time being. Why does he do this? Simply because any scientific proposition whatever is always liable to be refuted and dropped at short notice. A hypothesis is something which looks as if it might be true and were true, and which is capable of verification or refutation by comparison with facts. The best hypothesis, in the sense of the one most recommending itself to the inquirer, is the one which can be the most readily refuted if it is false. This far outweighs the trifling merit of being likely. For after all, what is a *likely* hypothesis? It is one which falls in with our preconceived ideas. But these may be wrong. Their errors are just what the scientific man is out gunning for more particularly. But if a hypothesis can quickly and easily be cleared away so as to go toward leaving the field free for the main struggle, this is an immense advantage.

IV

Upon this first, and in one sense this sole, rule of reason, that in order to learn you must desire to learn, and in so desiring not to be satisfied with what you already incline to think, there follows one corollary which itself deserves to be inscribed upon every wall of the city of philosophy:

Do not block the way of inquiry.

Although it is better to be methodical in our investigations, and to consider the economics of research, yet there is no positive sin against logic in *trying* any theory which may come into our heads, so long as it is adopted in such a sense as to permit the investigation to go on unimpeded and undiscouraged. On the other hand, to set up a philosophy which barricades the road of further advance toward the truth is the one unpardonable offense in reasoning, as it is also the one to which metaphysicians have in all ages shown themselves the most addicted.

Let me call your attention to four familiar shapes in which this venemous error assails our knowledge.

The first is the shape of absolute assertion. That we can be sure of nothing in science is an ancient truth. The Academy taught it. Yet science has been infested with overconfident assertion, especially on the part of the third-rate and fourth-rate men, who have been more concerned with teaching than with learning, at all times. No doubt some of the geometries still teach as a self-evident truth the proposition that if two straight lines in one plane meet a third straight line so as to make the sum of the internal angles on the one side less than two right angles those two lines will meet on that side if sufficiently prolonged. Euclid, whose logic was more careful, only reckoned this proposition as a *Postulate*, or arbitrary Hypothesis. Yet even he places among his axioms the proposition that a part is less than its whole, and falls into several conflicts with our most modern geometry in consequence. But why need we stop to consider cases where some subtilty of thought is required to see that the assertion is not warranted when every book which applies philosophy to the conduct of life lays down as positive certainty propositions which it is quite as easy to doubt as to believe?

The second bar which philosophers often set up across the roadway of inquiry lies in maintaining that this, that, and the other never can be known. When Auguste Comte was pressed to specify any matter of positive fact to the knowledge of which no man could by any possibility attain, he instanced the knowledge of the chemical composition of the fixed stars; and you may see his answer set down in the *Philosophie positive*. But the ink was scarcely dry upon the printed page before the spectroscope was discovered and that which he had deemed absolutely unknowable was well on the way of getting ascertained. It is easy enough to mention a question the answer to which is not known to me today. But to aver that that answer will not be known tomorrow is somewhat risky; for oftentimes it is precisely the least expected truth which is turned up under the ploughshare of research. And when it comes to positive assertion that the truth never will be found out, that, in the light of the history of our time, seems to me more hazardous than the ventures of Andrée.

The third philosophical stratagem for cutting off inquiry consists in maintaining that this, that, or the other element of science is basic, ultimate, independent of aught else, and utterly inexplicable—not so much from any defect in our knowing as because there is nothing beneath it to know. The only type of reasoning by which such a conclusion could possibly be reached is *retroduction*. Now nothing justifies a retroductive inference except its affording an explanation of the facts. It is, however, no explanation at all of a fact to pronounce it *inexplicable*. That, therefore, is a conclusion which no reasoning can ever justify or excuse.

The last philosophical obstacle to the advance of knowledge which I intend to mention is the holding that this or that law or truth has found its last and perfect formulation—and especially that the ordinary and usual course of nature never can be broken through. "Stones do not fall from heaven," said Laplace, although they had been falling upon inhabited ground every day from the earliest times. But there is no kind of inference which can lend the slightest probability to any such absolute denial of an unusual phenomenon.

All positive reasoning is of the nature of judging the proportion of something in a whole collection by the proportion found in a sample. Accordingly, there are three things to which we can never hope to attain by reasoning, namely, absolute certainty, absolute exactitude, absolute universality. We cannot be absolutely certain that our conclusions are even approximately true; for the sample may be utterly unlike the unsampled part of the collection. We cannot pretend to be even probably exact; because the sample consists of but a finite number of instances and only admits special values of the proportion sought. Finally, even if we could ascertain with absolute certainty and exactness that the ratio of sinful men to all men was as 1 to 1; still among the infinite generations of men there would be room for any finite number of sinless men without violating the proportion. The case is the same with a seven-legged calf.

Now if exactitude, certitude, and universality are not to be attained by reasoning, there is certainly no other means by which they can be reached.

Somebody will suggest *revelation*. There are scientists and people influenced by science who laugh at revelation; and certainly science has taught us to look at testimony in such a light that the whole theological doctrine of the "Evidences" seems pretty weak. However, I do not think it is philosophical to reject the possibility of a revelation. Still, granting that, I declare as a logician that revealed truths—that is, truths which have nothing in their favor but revelations made to a few individuals—constitute by far the most uncertain class of truths there are. There is here no question of universality; for revelation is itself sporadic and miraculous. There is no question of mathematical exactitude; for no revelation makes any pretension to that character. But it does pretend to be *certain*; and against that there are three conclusive objections. First, we never can be absolutely certain that any given deliverance really is inspired; for that can only be established by reasoning. We cannot even prove it with any very high degree of probability. Second, even if it is inspired, we cannot be sure, or nearly sure, that the statement is true. We know that one of the commandments was in one of the Bibles printed with[out] a *not* in it. All inspired matter has been subject to human distortion or coloring. Besides we cannot penetrate the counsels of the most High, or lay down anything as a principle that would govern his conduct. We do not know his inscrutable purposes, nor can we comprehend his plans. We cannot tell but he might see fit to inspire his servants with errors. In the third place, a truth which rests on the authority of inspiration only is of a somewhat incomprehensible nature; and we never can be sure that we rightly comprehend it. As there is no way of evading these difficulties, I say that revelation, far from affording us any certainty, gives results less certain than other sources of information. This would be so even if revelation were much plainer than it is.

But, it will be said, you forget the laws which are known to us *a priori*, the axioms of geometry, the principles of logic, the maxims of *causality*, and the like. Those are absolutely certain, without exception and exact. To this I reply that it seems to me there is the most positive historic proof that innate truths are particularly uncertain and mixed up with error, and therefore *a fortiori*, not without exception. This historical proof is, of course, not infallible; but it is very strong. Therefore, I ask *how do you know* that *a priori* truth is certain, exceptionless, and exact? You cannot know it by *reasoning*. For that would be subject to uncertainty and inexactitude. Then, it must amount to this that you know it *a priori*; that is, you take *a priori* judgments at their own valuation, without criticism or credentials. That is barring the gate of inquiry.

Ah! but it will be said, you forget direct experience. Direct experience is neither certain nor uncertain, because it affirms nothing—it just *is*. There are delusions, hallucinations, dreams. But there is no mistake that such things really do appear, and direct experience means simply the appearance. It involves no error, because it testifies to nothing but its own appearance. For the same reason, it affords no certainty. It is not *exact*, because it leaves much vague; though it is not *inexact* either; that is, it has no false exactitude.

All this is true of direct experience at its first presentation. But when it comes up to be criticized it is past, itself, and is represented by *memory*. Now the deceptions and inexactitude of memory are proverbial. . . . On the whole, then, we cannot in any way reach perfect certitude nor exactitude. We never can be absolutely sure of anything, nor can we with any probability ascertain the exact value of any measure or general ratio.

This is my conclusion, after many years study of the logic of science; and it is the conclusion which others, of very different cast of mind, have come to, likewise. I believe I may say there is no tenable opinion regarding human knowledge which does not legitimately lead to this corollary. Certainly there is nothing new in it; and many of the greatest minds of all time have held it for true.

Indeed, most everybody will admit it until he begins to see what is involved in the admission—and then most people will draw back. It will not be admitted by persons utterly incapable of philosophical reflection. It will not be fully admitted by masterful minds developed exclusively in the direction of action and accustomed to claim practical infallibility in matters of business. These men will admit the incurable fallibility of all opinions readily enough; only, they will always make exception of their own. The doctrine of fallibilism will also be denied by those who fear its consequences for science, for religion, and for morality. But I will take leave to say to these highly conservative gentlemen that however competent they may be to direct the affairs of a church or other corporation, they had better not try to manage science in that way. Conservatism—in the sense of a dread of consequences—is altogether out of place in science—which has on the contrary always been forwarded by radicals and radicalism, in the sense of the eagerness to carry consequences to their extremes. Not the radicalism that is cocksure, however, but the *radicalism that tries experiments*. Indeed, it is precisely among men animated by the spirit of science that the doctrine of fallibilism will find supporters.

Still, even such a man as that may well ask whether I propose to say that it is not quite certain that twice two are four—and that it is even not probably quite exact! But it would be quite misunderstanding the doctrine of fallibilism to suppose that it means that twice two is probably not exactly four. As I have already remarked, it is not my purpose to doubt that people can usually *count* with accuracy. Nor does fallibilism say that men cannot attain a sure knowledge of the creations of their own minds. It neither affirms nor denies that. It only says that people cannot attain absolute certainty concerning questions of fact. Numbers are merely a system of names devised by men for the purpose of counting. It is a matter of real fact to say that in a certain room there are two persons. It is a matter of fact to say that each person has two eyes. It is a matter of fact to say that there are four eyes in the room. But to say that *if* there are two persons and each person has two eyes there *will be* four eyes is not a statement of fact, but a statement about the system of numbers which is our own creation.

Lincoln Barnett on Einstein

In our discussion of the scientific point of view, it will be helpful to have a look at the greatest scientist of our generation, a man whose life and work embody so well the qualities that Peirce takes to be essential in the scientific spirit. Albert Einstein was born in Ulm, Germany, in 1878. Educated in Switzerland, he became a Swiss citizen in 1900 and professor of theoretical physics at the University of Zurich a few years later. In 1905 he published a series of five monographs presenting his Special Theory of Relativity *which brought him immediate renown in the world of science. Ten years later he formulated the* General Theory of Relativity, *and his place among the great scientists of all time was well established. In 1914 he accepted the chair of theoretical physics at the University of Berlin. In 1921 he was awarded the Nobel prize in physics; a few years later he was guest lecturer at Oxford University; and for a time visiting professor at the California Institute of Technology*

In 1933, branded by the Nazi government as an unwanted Jew with a price on his head, Einstein left Germany for America. He made his home in Princeton, New Jersey, where, as the most distinguished resident at the Institute for Advanced Study, he spent the last twenty-two years of his life in scientific research and writing. In 1940 he became an American citizen, remarking that "as long as I have any choice I will stay only in a country where political liberty, toleration and equality of all citizens before the law is the rule."

On his seventy-fourth birthday a new medical school in New York was named in his honor The Albert Einstein College of Medicine. He died in 1955.

It has never been easy, of course, for the layman to comprehend Einstein's scientific theories. At one time there were reputed to be only six men who understood him. But a number of efforts have been made to present his ideas in popular fashion and of these a series of articles in Harper's *by Lincoln Barnett in 1948 is among the best. Barnett is an expert in this difficult field. He has written many popular biographies and articles on science for both* Harper's *and* Life *and was for a time an associate editor of* Life. *In recent years he has done the text of several quite successful features in* Life, *including those on "The World's Great Religions," "The World We Live In," and "The Epic of Man."*

In 1950 Barnett collected his series of articles on Einstein in book form under the title, The Universe and Dr. Einstein. *Our selection, from the revised (1957) edition of this book, deals in the main with the view of the universe that Einstein came to hold some time before his death. This is without question an excellent illustration of the scientific point of view; and if the world-view of the scientist, as Einstein outlines it for us, at times baffles and perplexes the ordinary reader, it also arouses his curiosity and stretches his imagination in desirable fashion.*

THE UNIVERSE AND DR. EINSTEIN

I

CARVED IN THE white walls of the Riverside Church in New York, the figures of six hundred great men of the ages—saints, philosophers, kings—stand in limestone immortality, surveying space and time with blank imperishable eyes. One panel enshrines the geniuses of science, fourteen of them, spanning the centuries from Hippocrates, who died around 370 B.C., to Albert Einstein, who died in 1955. In this whole sculptured gallery of the illustrious dead, Einstein is the only one who shook the world within the memory of most living men.

It is equally noteworthy that of the thousands of people who worship weekly at Manhattan's most spectacular Protestant church, probably 99 percent would be hard pressed to explain why Einstein's image is there. It is there because a generation ago, when the iconography of the church was being planned, Dr. Harry Emerson Fosdick wrote letters to a group of the nation's leading scientists asking them to submit lists of the fourteen greatest names in scientific history. Their ballots varied. Most of them included Archimedes, Euclid, Galileo, and Newton. But on every list appeared the name of Albert Einstein.

The vast gap that has persisted for more than fifty years—since 1905, when the Theory of Special Relativity was first published—between Einstein's scientific eminence and public understanding of it is the measure of a gap in American education. Today most newspaper readers know vaguely that Einstein had something to do with the atomic bomb; beyond that his name is simply a synonym for the abstruse. While his theories form part of the body of modern science, they are not yet part of the modern curriculum. It is not surprising therefore that many a college graduate still thinks of Einstein as a kind of mathematical surrealist rather than as the discoverer of certain cosmic laws of immense importance in man's slow struggle to understand physical reality. He may not realize that Relativity, over and above its scientific import, comprises a major philosophical system which augments and illumines the reflections of the great epistemologists—Locke, Berkeley, and Hume. Consequently he has very little notion of the vast, arcane, and mysteriously ordered universe in which he dwells.

* * *

Dr. Einstein, long professor emeritus at the Institute for Advanced Study at Princeton, spent the last years of his life working on a problem which had baffled him for more than a quarter of a century. This was his Unified Field Theory, which sets forth in one series of mutually consistent equations the physical laws governing the two fundamental forces of the universe, gravitation and electromagnetism. The significance of this task can be appreciated only when one realizes that most of the phenomena of nature seem to be produced by these two primordial forces.

Since the aim of science is to describe and explain the world we live in, such a theory would, by thus defining the manifold of nature within the terms of a single harmonious theory, attain its loftiest goal. The meaning of the word "explain," however, suffers a contraction with man's every step in quest of reality. Science cannot yet really "explain" electricity, magnetism, and gravitation; their effects can be measured and predicted, but of their ultimate nature no more is known to the modern scientist than to Thales of Miletus, who first speculated on the electrification of amber around 585 B.C. Most contemporary physicists reject the notions that man can ever discover what these mysterious forces "really" are. Electricity, Bertrand Russell says, "is not a thing, like St. Paul's Cathedral; it is a way in which things behave. When we have told how things behave when they are electrified, and under what circumstances they are electrified, we have told all there is to tell." Until recently scientists would have scorned such a thesis. Aristotle, whose natural sciences dominated Western thought for two thousand years, believed that man could arrive at an understanding of ultimate reality by reasoning from *self-evident principles*. It is, for example, a self-evident principle that everything in the universe has its proper place, hence one can deduce that objects fall to the ground because that's where they belong, and smoke goes up because that's where *it* belongs. The goal of Aristotelian science was to explain *why* things happen. Modern science was born when Galileo began trying to explain *how* things happen and thus originated the method of controlled experiment which now forms the basis of scientific investigation.

Out of Galileo's discoveries and those of Newton in the next generation there evolved a mechanical universe of forces, pressures, tensions, oscillations, and waves. There seemed to be no process of nature which could not be described in terms of ordinary experience, illustrated by a concrete model or predicted by Newton's amazingly accurate laws of mechanics. But before the turn of the past century, certain deviations from these laws became apparent; and though these deviations were slight, they were of such a fundamental nature that the whole edifice of Newton's machinelike universe began to topple. The certainty that science can explain *how* things happen began to dim about twenty years ago. And right now it is a question whether scientific man is in touch with "reality" at all—or can ever hope to be.

II

The factors that first led physicists to distrust their faith in a smoothly functioning mechanical universe loomed on the inner and outer horizons of knowledge—in the unseen realm of the atom and in the fathomless depths of intergalactic space. To describe these phenomena quantitatively, two great theoretical systems were developed between 1900 and 1927. One was the Quantum Theory, dealing with the fundamental units of matter and energy. The other was Relativity, dealing with space, time, and the structure of the universe as a whole.

Both are now accepted pillars of modern physical thought. Both describe phenomena in their fields in terms of consistent, mathematical relationships. They do not answer the Newtonian "how" any more than Newton's laws answered the Aristotelian "why." They provide equations, for example, that define with great accuracy the laws governing the radiation and propagation of light. But the actual mechanism by which the atom radiates light and by which light is propagated through space remains one of nature's supreme mysteries. Similarly the laws governing the phenomenon of radioactivity enable scientists to predict that in a given quantity of uranium a certain number of atoms will disintegrate in a certain length of time. But just which atoms will decay and how they are selected for doom are questions that man cannot yet answer.

In accepting a mathematical description of nature, physicists have been forced to abandon the ordinary world of our experience, the world of sense perceptions. To understand the significance of this retreat it is necessary to step across the thin line that divides physics from metaphysics. Questions involving the relationship between observer and reality, subject and object, have haunted philosophical thinkers since the dawn of reason. Twenty-three centuries ago the Greek philosopher Democritus wrote: "Sweet and bitter, cold and warm, as well as all the colors, all these things exist but in opinion and not in reality; what really exists are unchangeable particles, atoms, and their motions in empty space." Galileo was also aware of the purely subjective character of sense qualities like color, taste, smell, and sound and pointed out that "they can no more be ascribed to the external objects than can the tickling or the pain caused sometimes by touching such objects."

The English philosopher John Locke tried to penetrate to the "real essence of substances" by drawing a distinction between what he termed the primary and secondary qualities of matter. Thus he considered that shape, motion, solidity, and all geometrical properties were real or primary qualities, inherent in the object itself; while secondary qualities, like colors, sounds, tastes, were simply projections upon the organs of sense. The artificiality of this distinction was obvious to later thinkers.

"I am able to prove," wrote the great German mathematician, Leibnitz, "that not only light, color, heat, and the like, but motion, shape, and extension too are mere apparent qualities." Just as our visual sense, for example, tells us that a golf ball is white, so vision abetted by our sense of touch tells us that it is also round, smooth, and small—qualities that have no more reality, independent of our senses, than the quality which we define by convention as white.

Thus gradually philosophers and scientists arrived at the startling conclusion that since every object is simply the sum of its qualities, and since qualities exist only in the mind, the whole objective universe of matter and energy, atoms and stars, does not exist except as a construction of the consciousness, an edifice of conventional symbols shaped by the senses of man. As Berkeley, the archenemy of materialism, phrased it, "All the choir of heaven and furniture of earth, in a word all those bodies which compose the mighty frame of the world, have not any substance without the mind. . . . So long as they are not actually perceived by men, or do not exist in my mind, or that of any other created spirit, they must either have no existence at all, or else subsist in the mind of some Eternal Spirit." Einstein carried this train of logic to its ultimate limits by showing that even space and time are forms of intuition, which can no more be divorced from consciousness than can our concepts of color, shape, or size. Space has no objective reality except as an order or arrangement of the objects we perceive in it, and time has no independent existence apart from the order of events by which we measure it.

* * *

Realization that our whole knowledge of the universe is simply a residue of impressions clouded by our imperfect senses makes the quest for reality seem hopeless. If nothing has existence save in its being perceived, the world should dissolve into an anarchy of individual perceptions. But a curious order runs through our perceptions, as if indeed there might be an underlayer of objective reality which our senses translate. Although no man can ever know whether his sensation of red or of Middle C is the same as another man's, it is nevertheless possible to act on the assumption that everyone sees colors and hears tones more or less alike.

This functional harmony of nature Berkeley, Descartes, and Spinoza attributed to God. Modern physicists who prefer to solve their problems without recourse to God (although this seems to become more difficult all the time) emphasize that nature mysteriously operates on mathematical principles. It is the mathematical orthodoxy of the universe that enables theorists like Einstein to predict and discover natural laws simply by the solution of equations. But the paradox of physics today is that with every improvement in its mathematical apparatus the gulf between man the observer and the objective world of scientific description becomes more profound.

It is perhaps significant that in terms of simple magnitude man is the mean between macrocosm and microcosm. Stated crudely this means that a supergiant red star (the largest material body in the universe) is just as much bigger than man as an electron (tiniest of physical entities) is smaller. It is not surprising, therefore, that the prime mysteries of nature dwell in those realms farthest removed from sense-imprisoned man, nor that science, unable to describe the extremes of reality in the homely metaphors of classical physics should content itself with noting such mathematical relationships as may be revealed.

III

Cosmologists for the most part maintain silence on the question of ultimate origins, leaving that issue to the philosophers and theology. Yet only the purest empiricists among modern scientists turn their backs on the mystery that underlies physical reality. Einstein, whose philosophy of science has sometimes been criticized as materialistic, once said:

> The most beautiful and most profound emotion we can experience is the sensation of the mystical. It is the sower of all true science. He to whom this emotion is a stranger, who can no longer wonder and stand rapt in awe, is as good as dead. To know that what is impenetrable to us really exists, manifesting itself as the highest wisdom and the most radiant beauty which our dull faculties can comprehend only in their most primitive forms—this knowledge, this feeling is at the center of true religiousness.

And on another occasion he declared, "The cosmic religious experience is the strongest and noblest mainspring of scientific research." Most scientists, when referring to the mysteries of the universe, its vast forces, its origins, and its rationality and harmony, tend to avoid using the word God. Yet Einstein, who has been called an atheist, has no such inhibitions. "My religion," he says, "consists of a humble admiration of the illimitable superior spirit who reveals himself in the slight details we are able to perceive with our frail and feeble minds. That deeply emotional conviction of the presence of a superior reasoning power, which is revealed in the incomprehensible universe, forms my idea of God."

So far as science is concerned, there are at the moment two gateways which offer the promise of closer access to physical reality. One is the great new telescope which now, from Palomar Mountain, California, projects man's vision into deeper abysses of space and time than ever were dreamed by astronomers a generation ago. Until recently the extreme range of telescopic perception was essentially terminated at the faint hurrying galaxies 500 million light years away. But the two-hundred-inch reflector of Palomar doubles that range, enabling man to look upon whatever lies beyond. Already it is revealing new homogeneous oceans of space and new myriads of far galaxies whose antique light has swum to earth through a billion years of terrestrial time. But it may reveal other things—variations in the density of matter or visual evidence of a cosmic curvature from which man can accurately compute the dimensions of the universe in which he so insignificantly dwells.

The other gateway to this knowledge may be opened by further developments or elaboration of the new Unified Field Theory on which Einstein labored for the last quarter century of his life. Today the outer limits of man's knowledge are defined by Relativity, the inner limits by the Quantum Theory. Relativity has shaped all our concepts of space, time, gravitation, and the realities that are too remote and too vast to be perceived. The Quantum Theory has shaped all our concepts of the atom, the basic units of matter and energy, and the realities that are too elusive and too small to be perceived. Yet these two great scientific systems rest on entirely different and unrelated theoretical foundation. They do not, as it were, speak the same language. The purpose of the Unified Field Theory is to construct a bridge between them. Believing in the harmony and uniformity of nature, Einstein has evolved a single edifice of physical laws to encompass both the phenomena of the atom and the phenomena of outer space.

A complete Unified Field Theory touches the "grand aim of all science," which, as Einstein once defined it, is "to cover the greatest number of empirical facts by logical deduction from the smallest possible number of hypotheses or axioms." The urge to consolidate premises, to unify concepts, to penetrate the variety and particularity of the manifest world to the undifferentiated unity that lies beyond is not only the leaven of science; it is the loftiest passion of the human intellect. The philosopher and mystic, as well as the scientist, have always sought through their various disciplines of introspection to arrive at a knowledge of the ultimate immutable essence that undergirds the mutable illusory world. More than twenty-three hundred years ago Plato declared, "The true lover of knowledge is always striving after *being*. . . . He will not rest at those multitudinous phenomena whose existence is appearance only."

* * *

But the irony of man's quest for reality

is that as nature is stripped of its disguises, as order emerges from chaos and unity from diversity, as concepts merge and fundamental laws assume increasingly simpler form, the evolving picture becomes ever more remote from experience—far stranger indeed and less recognizable than the bone structure behind a familiar face. For where the geometry of a skull predestines the outlines of the tissue it supports, there is no likeness between the image of a tree transcribed by our senses and that propounded by wave mechanics, or between a glimpse of the starry sky on a summer night and the four-dimensional continuum that has replaced our perceptual Euclidean space.

In trying to distinguish appearance from reality and lay bare the fundamental structure of the universe, science has had to transcend the "rabble of the senses." But its highest edifices, Einstein has pointed out, have been "purchased at the price of emptiness of content." A theoretical concept is emptied of content to the very degree that it is divorced from sensory experience. For the only world man can truly know is the world created for him by his senses. If he expunges all the impressions which they translate and memory stores, nothing is left. That is what the philosopher Hegel meant by his cryptic remark: "Pure Being and Nothing are the same." A state of existence devoid of associations has no meaning. So paradoxically what the scientist and the philosopher call the world of appearance—the world of light and color, of blue skies and green leaves, of sighing wind and murmuring water, the world designed by the physiology of human sense organs—is the world in which finite man is incarcerated by his essential nature. And what the scientist and the philosopher call the world of reality—the colorless, soundless, impalpable cosmos which lies like an iceberg beneath the plane of man's perceptions—is a skeleton structure of symbols.

In the evolution of scientific thought, one fact has become impressively clear: there is no mystery of the physical world which does not point to a mystery beyond itself. All highroads of the intellect, all byways of theory and conjecture lead ultimately to an abyss that human ingenuity can never span. For man is enchained by the very condition of his being, his finiteness and involvement in nature. The farther he extends his horizons, the more vividly he recognizes the fact that, as the physicist Niels Bohr puts it, "we are both spectators and actors in the great drama of existence." Man is thus his own greatest mystery. He does not understand the vast veiled universe into which he has been cast for the reason that he does not understand himself. He comprehends but little of his organic processes and even less of his unique capacity to perceive the world about him, to reason and to dream. Least of all does he understand his noblest and most mysterious faculty: the ability to transcend himself and perceive himself in the act of perception.

Man's inescapable impasse is that he himself is part of the world he seeks to explore; his body and proud brain are mosaics of the same elemental particles that compose the dark, drifting dust clouds of interstellar space; he is, in the final analysis, merely an ephemeral conformation of the primordial space-time field. Standing midway between macrocosm and microcosm he finds barriers on every side and can perhaps but marvel, as St. Paul did nineteen hundred years ago, that "the world was created by the word of God so that what is seen was made out of things which do not appear."

1

RELIGION AND THE SCIENTIFIC SPIRIT

Walter Lippmann

In 1929 Lippmann published one of his most controversial and widely discussed books, A Preface to Morals. *It is an unusually discerning account of the moral and religious problems raised in the early decades of the twentieth century by the impact of scientific thought on an urban society. Writing neither as a scientist nor as a man of religious faith, but rather as one of America's ablest journalists whose life has been spent in observing and interpreting the course of human affairs,* Lippmann seeks in this volume to examine with some detachment the forces at work in contemporary American life. While not a philosopher by profession, Lippmann is quite familiar with philosophical problems. His interests in this field go back to his college days at Harvard University where, as a member of the famous class of 1910, he majored in philosophy during the years that Josiah Royce, William James, and George Santayana made Harvard the most influential center of philosophy ever known in America.*

What distinguishes our age, Lippmann declares, is its loss of religious certainty. Men and women today are no longer sure of finding God in the Bible or in church; indeed, they are not sure about God at all. "Among those who no longer believe in the religion of their fathers, some are proudly defiant, and many are indifferent. But there are also a few, perhaps an increasing number, who feel that there is a vacancy in their lives. This inquiry deals with their problems. It is not intended to disturb the serenity of those who are unshaken in the faith they hold, and it is not concerned with those who are still exhilarated by their escape from stale orthodoxy. It is concerned with those who are perplexed by the consequences of their own irreligion."

In the selection we reprint from A Preface to Morals *Lippmann points to what seems to him an inescapable conflict between the world view that most scientists accept and the world view of religion that people want because it will give life purpose and meaning. He published this book in 1929 when popular interest in religion seemed more intense than it*

* For a brief biographical sketch of Lippmann see p. 53 above.

is today. At that time newspapers played up heresy trials; pronouncements of scientists on religious questions appeared regularly; and discussions of evolution and the Bible were eagerly read. If today the headlines are about other problems, the ideas that Lippmann writes about so clearly are still alive, and the particular problem he discusses is still an important one.

ON RECONCILING SCIENCE AND RELIGION

MANY REASONS have been adduced to explain why people do not go to church as much as they once did. Surely the most important reason is that they are not so certain that they are going to meet God when they go to church. If they had that certainty they would go. If they really believed that they were being watched by a Supreme Being who is more powerful than all the kings of earth put together, if they really believed that not only their actions but their secret thoughts were known and would be remembered by the creator and ultimate judge of the universe, there would be no complaint whatever about church attendance. The most worldly would be in the front pews, and preachers would not have to resort so often to their rather desperate expedients to attract an audience. If the conviction were there that the creed professed was invincibly true, the modern congregation would not come to church, as they usually do today, to hear the preacher and to listen to the music. They would come to worship God.

Religious professions will not work when they rest merely on a kind of passive assent; or on intricate reasoning, or on fierce exhortation, or on a good-natured conspiracy to be vague and highflown. A man cannot cheat about faith. Either he has it in the marrow of his bones, or in a crisis, when he is distracted and in sorrow, there is no conviction there to support him.

I

The American people, more than any other people, is composed of individuals who have lost association with their old landmarks. They have crossed an ocean, they have spread themselves across a new continent. The American who still lives in his grandfather's house feels almost as if he were living in a museum. There are few Americans who have not moved at least once since their childhood, and even if they have stayed where they were born, the old landmarks themselves have been carted away to make room for progress. That, perhaps, is one reason why we have so much more Americanism than love of America. It takes time to learn to love the new gas station which stands where the wild honeysuckle grew. Moreover, the great majority of Americans have risen in the world. They have moved out of their class, lifting the old folks along with them perhaps, so that together they may sit by the steam pipes, and listen to the crooning of the radio. But more and more of them have moved not only out of their class, but out of their culture; and then they leave the old folks behind, and the continuity of life is broken. For faith grows well only as it is passed on from parents to their children amidst surroundings that bear witness, because nothing changes radically, to a deep permanence in the order of the world. It is true, no doubt, that in this great physical and psychic migration some of the old household gods are carefully packed up and put with the rest of the luggage, and then unpacked and set up on new altars in new places. But what can be taken along is at best no more than the tree which is above the ground. The roots remain in the soil where they first grew.

The sidewalks of a city would in any case be a stony soil in which to transplant religion. Throughout history, as Spengler points out, the large city has bred heresies, new cults, and irreligion. Now when we speak of modern civilization we mean a civilization dominated by the culture of the great metropolitan centers. Our own civilization in America is perhaps the most completely urbanized of all. For even the American farmers, though they live in the country, tend to be suburban rather than rural. I am aware of how dominating a role the population outside the great cities plays in American life. Yet it is in the large cities that the tempo of our civilization is determined, and the tendency of mechanical inventions as well as economic policy is to create an irresistible suction of the country towards the city.

The deep and abiding traditions of religion belong to the countryside. For it is there that man earns his daily bread by submitting to superhuman forces whose behavior he can only partially control. There is not much he can do when he has ploughed the ground and planted his seed except to wait hopefully for sun and rain from the sky. He is obviously part of a scheme that is greater than himself, subject to elements that transcend his powers and surpass his understanding. The city is an acid that dissolves this piety. How different it is from an ancient vineyard where men cultivate what their fathers have planted. In a modern city it is not easy to maintain that "reverent attachment to the sources of his being and the steadying of his life by that attachment." It is not natural to form reverent attachments to an apartment on a two-year lease, and an imitation mahogany desk on the thirty-second floor of an office building. In such an environment, piety becomes absurd, a butt for the facetious, and the pious man looks like a picturesque yokel or a stuffy fool.

Yet without piety, without a patriotism of family and place, without an almost plant-like implication in unchangeable surroundings, there can be no disposition to believe in an external order of things. The omnipotence of God means something to men who submit daily to the cycles of the weather and the mysterious power of nature. But the city man puts his faith in furnaces to keep out the cold, is proudly aware of what bad sewage his ancestors endured, and of how ignorantly they believed that God, who made Adam at 9 A.M. on October 23 in the year 4004 B.C., was concerned with the behavior of Adam's children.

II

The common man is an unconscious pragmatist: he believes because he is satisfied that his beliefs change the course of events. He would not be inspired to worship a god who merely contemplates the universe, or a god who created it once, and then rested, while its destiny unfolds itself inexorably. To the plain people religion is not disinterested speculation but a very practical matter. It is concerned with their well-being in this world and in an equally concrete world hereafter. They have wanted to know the will of God because they had to know it if they were to put themselves right with the king of creation.

Those who professed to know God's will had to demonstrate that they knew it. This was the function of miracles. They were tangible evidence that the religious teacher had a true commission. "Then those men, when they had seen the miracle (of the loaves and the fishes) that Jesus did, said, This is of a truth that prophet that should come into the world." When Jesus raised the dead man at the gate of the city of Nain, "there came a fear on all: and they glorified God, saying, That a great prophet is risen up among us; and, That God hath visited his people." The most authoritative Catholic theologians teach that miracles "are not wrought to show the internal truth of the doctrines, but only to give *manifest* reasons why we should accept the doctrines." They are "essentially an appeal to knowledge," demonstrations, one might almost say divine experiments, by which men are enabled to know the glory and the providence of God.

The Catholic apologists maintain that God can be known by the exercise of reason, but the miracle helps, as it were, to clinch the conviction. The persistent attachment of the Catholic Church to miracles is significant. It has a longer unbroken experience with human nature than any other institution in the western world. It has adapted itself to many circumstances, and under the profession of an unalterable creed it has abandoned and then added much. But it has never ceased to insist upon the need of a physical manifestation of the divine power. For with an unerring instinct for realities, Catholic churchmen have understood that there is a residuum of prosaic, matter-of-factness, of a need to touch and to see, which verbal proofs can never quite satisfy. They have resolutely responded to that need. They have not preached God merely by praising him; they have brought God near to men by revealing him to the senses, as one who is great enough and good enough and sufficiently interested in them to heal the sick and to make the floods recede.

But today scientists are ever so much superior to churchmen at this kind of demonstration. The miracles which are recounted from the pulpit were, after all, few and far between. There are even theologians who teach that miracles ceased with the death of the Apostles. But the miracles of science seem to be inexhaustible. It is not surprising, then, that men of science should have acquired much of the intellectual authority which churchmen once exercised. Scientists do not, of course, speak of their discoveries as miracles. But to the common man, they have much the same character as miracles. They are wonderful, they are inexplicable, they are manifestations of a great power over the forces of nature.

It cannot be said, I think, that the people at large, even the moderately educated minority, understand the difference between scientific method and revelation, or that they have decided upon reflection to trust science. There is at least as much mystery in science for the common man as there ever was in religion; in a sense there is more mystery, for the logic of science is still altogether beyond his understanding, whereas the logic of revelation is the logic of his own feelings. But if men at large do not understand the method of science, they can appreciate some of its more tangible results. And these results are so impressive that scientific men are often embarrassed by the unbounded popular expectations which they have so unintentionally aroused. Their authority in the realm of knowledge has become virtually irresistible. And so when scientists teach one theory and the Bible another, the scientists invariably carry the greater conviction.

The conflicts between scientists and churchmen are sometimes ascribed to a misunderstanding on both sides. But when we examine the proposals for peace, it is plain, I think, that they are in effect proposals for a truce. There is, for example, the suggestion first put out, I believe, in the Seventeenth Century that God made the universe like a clock, and that having started it running he will let it alone till it runs down. By this ingenious metaphor, which can neither be proved nor disproved, it was possible to reconcile for a time the scientific notion of natural law with the older notion of God as creator and as judge. The religious conception was held to be true for the beginning of the world and for the end, the scientific conception was true in between. Later, when the theater of the difficulty was transferred from physics and astronomy to biology and history, a variation was propounded. God, it was said, created the world and governs it; the way he creates and governs is the way described by scientists as "evolution."

Attempts at reconciliations like these are based on a theory that it is feasible somewhere in the field of knowledge to draw a line and say that on one side the methods of science shall prevail, on the other the methods of traditional religion. It is acknowledged that where experiment and observation are possible, the field belongs to the scientists; but it is argued that there is a vast field of great interest to mankind which is beyond the reach of practical scientific inquiry, and that here, touching questions like the ultimate destiny of man, the purpose of life, and immortality, the older method of revelation, inspired and verified by intuition, is still reliable.

In any truce of this sort there is bound to be aggression from both sides. For it is a working policy rather than an inwardly accepted conviction. Scientists cannot really believe that there are fields of possible knowledge which they can never enter. They are bound to enter all fields and to explore everything. And even if they fail, they cannot believe that other scientists must always fail. Their essays, moreover, create disturbance and doubt which orthodox churchmen are forced to resent. For in any division of authority, there must be some ultimate authority to settle questions of jurisdiction. Shall scientists determine what belongs to science, or shall churchmen? The question is insoluble as long as both claim that they have the right to expound the nature of existence.

III

The radical novelty of modern science lies precisely in the rejection of the belief, which is at the heart of all popular religion, that the forces which move the stars and atoms are contingent upon the preferences of the human heart. The science of Aristotle and of the Schoolmen, on the other hand, was a truly popular science. It was in its inspiration the instinctive science of the unscientific man. "They read into the cause and goal of the universe," as Dr. Randall has said, "that which alone justifies it for man, its service of the good." They provided a conception of the universe which was available for the religious needs of ordinary men, and in the *Divine Comedy* we can see the supreme example of what science must be like if it is to satisfy the human need to believe. The purpose of the whole poem, said Dante himself, "is to remove those who are living in this life from the state of wretchedness, and to lead them to the state of blessedness."

This is the great climax which men instinctively expect: the ability to say with perfect assurance that when the truth is fully evident it will be seen that their desire and will are ruled by the love that moves the sun and the other stars. They hope not only to find the will of God in the universe but to know that his will is fundamentally like their own. Only if they could believe that on the basis of scientific investigation would they really feel that science had "explained" the world.

Explanation, in this sense, cannot come from modern science because it is not in this sense that modern science attempts to explain the universe. It is wholly misleading to say, for example, that the scientific picture of the world is mechanical. All that can properly be said is that many scientists have found it satisfying to think about the universe as if it were built on a mechanical model. "If I can make a mechanical model," said Lord Kelvin, "I can understand it. As long as I cannot make a mechanical model all the way through, I cannot understand it." But what does the scientist mean by "understanding it"? He means, says Professor Bridgman, that he has "reduced a situation to elements with which we are so familiar that we accept them as a matter of course so that our curiosity rests." Modern men are familiar with machines. They can take them apart and put them together, so that even though we should all be a little flustered if we had to tell just what we mean by a machine, our curiosity tends to be satisfied if we hear that the phenomenon, say, of electricity or of human behavior, is like a machine.

The man who says that the world is a machine has really advanced no further than to say that he is so well satisfied with this analogy that he is through with searching any further. That is his business, as long as he does not insist that he has reached a clear and ultimate picture of the universe. For obviously he has not. A machine is something in which the parts push and pull each other. But why are they pushing and pulling, and how do *they* work? Do they push and pull because of the action of the electrons in their orbits within the atoms? If that is true, then how does an electron work? Is it, too, a machine? Or is it something quite different from a machine? Shall we attempt to explain machines electrically, or shall we attempt to explain electricity mechanically?

It becomes plain, therefore, that scientific explanation is altogether unlike the explanations to which the common man is accustomed. It does not yield a certain picture of anything which can be taken naively as a representation of reality. And therefore the philosophies which have grown up about science, like mechanism or creative evolution, are in no way guaranteed by science as the account of creation in Genesis is guaranteed by the authority of Scripture. They are nothing but provisional dramatizations which are soon dissolved by the progress of science itself.

That is why nothing is so dead as the scientific religion of yesterday. It is far more completely dead than any revealed religion, because the revealed religion, whatever may be the defects of its cosmology or its history, has some human experience at its core which we can recognize and to which we may respond. But a religion like scientific materialism has nothing in it, except the pretension that it is a true account of the world. Once that pretension is exploded, it is wholly valueless as a religion. It has become a collection of discarded concepts.

IV

It follows from the very nature of scientific explanation, then, that it cannot give man such a clue to a plan of existence as they find in popular religion. For that plan must suppose that existence is explained in terms of human destiny. Now conceivably existence might again be explained, as it was in the Middle Ages, as the drama of human destiny. It does not seem probable to us; yet we cannot say that it is impossible. But even if science worked out such an explanation, it would still be radically different from the explanations which popular religion employs.

For if it were honestly stated, it would be necessary to say first, that it is tentative, and subject to disproof by further experiment; second, that it is relative, in that the same facts seen from some other point and with some other purpose in mind could be explained quite differently; third, that it is not a picture of the world, as God would see it, and as all men must see it, but that it is simply one among many possible creations of the mind into which most of the data of experience can be fitted. When the scientist had finished setting down his qualifications, the essence of the matter as a simple, devout man sees it, would have evaporated. Certainty, as the devout desire it, would be gone; variety, as they understand it, would be gone; objectivity, as they imagine it, would be gone. What would remain would be a highly abstracted, logical fiction, suited to disinterested inquiry, but utterly unsuited to be the vehicle of his salvation.

The difficulty of reconciling popular religion with science is far deeper than that of reconciling Genesis with Darwin, or any statement of fact in the Bible with any discovery by scientists. It is the difficulty of reconciling the human desire for a certain kind of universe with a method of explaining the world which is absolutely neutral in its intention. One can by twisting language sufficiently "reconcile" Genesis with "evolution." But what no one can do is to guarantee that science will not destroy the doctrine of evolution the day after it has been triumphantly proved that Genesis is compatible with the theory of evolution. As a matter of fact, just that has happened. The Darwinian theory, which theologians are busily accepting, is so greatly modified already by science that some of it is almost as obsolete as the Babylonian myth in Genesis. The reconciliation which theologians are attempting is an impossible one, because one of the factors which has to be reconciled—namely, the scientific theory, changes so rapidly that the layman is never sure at any one moment what the theory is which he has to reconcile with religious dogma.

Yet the purpose of these attempts at reconciliation is evident enough. It is to find a solid foundation for human ideals in the facts of existence. Authority based on revelation once provided that foundation. It gave an account of how the world began, of how it is governed, and of how it will end, which made pain and joy, hope and fear, desire and the denial of desire the central motives in the cosmic drama. This account no longer satisfies our curiosity as to the nature of things; the authority which certifies it no longer commands our complete allegiance. The prestige, which once adhered to those who spoke by revelation, has passed to scientists. But science, though it is the most reliable method of knowledge we now possess, does not provide an account of the world in which human destiny is the central theme. Therefore, science, though it has displaced revelation, is not a substitute for it. It yields a radically different kind of knowledge. It explains the facts. But it does not pretend to justify the ways of God to man. It enables us to realize some of our hopes. But it offers no guarantees that they can be fulfilled.

Bertrand Russell

Now in his eighties Bertrand Russell has come to hold a place among the best-known and most influential contemporary philosophers. Born in 1872 into a family long famous in the history of England (his grandfather introduced the great Reform Bill of 1832), Russell was educated at Cambridge University, where he later became a lecturer and fellow. His early work was in the field of mathematics and the philosophy of science, and he is recognized as one of the ablest exponents of the scientific point of view in philosophy. In 1910 he cooperated with Alfred North Whitehead in the publication of a widely known though little read work, entitled Principia Mathematica. Owing to his opposition to World War I, Russell lost his fellowship at Cambridge University and was imprisoned for a short time. In more recent years, however, he supported war against the Nazi government in Germany and has published vehement essays attacking Soviet Russia.*

The early essay reprinted here, "A Free Man's Worship," is one of which Russell himself no longer wholly approves. It is too poetic for his present taste. But this essay nevertheless has become a classic in its field. Instead of saying, "This is the scientific view of the world, and there, opposed to it, is the religious view: which shall I choose?" Russell here accepts the scientific point of view without reservation, discards the religious, and makes the best of what remains. He seeks to do what Walter Lippmann in the preceding selection suggests one cannot do successfully—substitute the insights of science for the faith of religion. The reader must judge for himself how successful Russell has been in the effort.

The word "worship" in the title of this essay is a surprising one for a man who has written a book called, Why I Am Not A Christian, but as Russell has himself confessed, "Those who attempt to make a religion of humanism, which recognizes nothing greater than man, do not satisfy my emotions. And yet I am unable to believe that, in the world as known, there is anything that I can value outside human beings, and, to a much lesser extent, animals. . . . And so my intellect goes with the humanists, though my emotions violently rebel." Something of this paradox is reflected in the bold and arresting drama Russell uses in "A Free Man's Worship" to portray the spiritual dilemma of the uncompromising devoteé of scientific thought.

A FREE MAN'S WORSHIP

I

TO DR. FAUSTUS in his study Mephistopheles told the history of the Creation, saying:

For countless ages the hot nebula whirled aimlessly through space. At length it began to take shape, the central mass threw off planets, the planets cooled, boiling seas and burning mountains heaved and tossed, from black masses of cloud hot sheets of rain deluged the barely solid crust. And now the first germ of life grew in the depths of the ocean, and developed rapidly in the fructifying warmth into vast forest trees, huge ferns springing from the damp mold, sea monsters breeding, fighting, devouring, and passing

* For additional biographical data, see p. 600.

[From Bertrand Russell, *Mysticism and Logic*, Essay III, Abridged.]

away. And from the monsters, as the play unfolded itself, Man was born, with the power of thought, the knowledge of good and evil, and the cruel thirst for worship. And Man saw that all is passing in this mad, monstrous world, that all is struggling to snatch, at any cost, a few brief moments of life before Death's inexorable decree. And Man said: "There is a hidden purpose, could we but fathom it, and the purpose is good; for we must reverence something, and in the visible world there is nothing worthy of reverence." And Man stood aside from the struggle, resolving that God intended harmony to come out of chaos by human efforts. And when he followed the instincts which God had transmitted to him from his ancestry of beasts of prey, he called it Sin, and asked God to forgive him. But he doubted whether he could be justly forgiven, until he invented a divine Plan by which God's wrath was to have been appeased. And seeing the present was bad, he made it yet worse, that thereby the future might be better. And he gave God thanks for the strength that enabled him to forgo even the joys that were possible. And God smiled; and when he saw that Man had become perfect in renunciation and worship, he sent another sun through the sky, which crashed into Man's sun; and all returned again to nebula.

"Yes," he murmured, "it was a good play; I will have it performed again."

II

Such, in outline, but even more purposeless, more void of meaning, is the world which Science presents for our belief. Amid such a world, if anywhere, our ideals henceforward must find a home. That Man is the product of causes which had no prevision of the end they were achieving; that his origin, his growth, his hopes and fears, his loves and his beliefs, are but the outcome of accidental collocations of atoms; that no fire, no heroism, no intensity of thought and feeling, can preserve an individual life beyond the grave; that all the labors of the ages, all the devotion, all the inspiration, all the noonday brightness of human genius, are destined to extinction in the vast death of the solar system, and that the whole temple of Man's achievement must inevitably be buried beneath the debris of a universe in ruins—all these things, if not quite beyond dispute, are yet so nearly certain, that no philosophy which rejects them can hope to stand. Only within the scaffolding of these truths, only on the firm foundation of unyielding despair, can the soul's habitation henceforth be safely built.

How, in such an alien and inhuman world, can so powerless a creature as Man preserve his aspirations untarnished? A strange mystery it is that Nature, omnipotent but blind, in the revolutions of her secular hurryings through the abysses of space, has brought forth at last a child, subject still to her power, but gifted with sight, with knowledge of good and evil, with the capacity of judging all the works of his unthinking Mother. In spite of Death, the mark and seal of the parental control, Man is yet free, during his brief years, to examine, to criticize, to know, and in imagination to create. To him alone, in the world with which he is acquainted, this freedom belongs; and in this lies his superiority to the resistless forces that control his outward life.

The savage, like ourselves, feels the oppression of his impotence before the powers of Nature; but having in himself nothing that he respects more than Power, he is willing to prostrate himself before his gods, without inquiring whether they are worthy of his worship. Pathetic and very terrible is the long history of cruelty and torture, of degradation and human sacrifice, endured in the hope of placating the jealous gods: surely, the trembling believer thinks, when what is most precious has been freely given, their lust for blood must be appeased, and more will not be required. The religion of Moloch—as such creeds may be generically called—is in essence the cringing submission of the slave, who dare not, even in his heart, allow the thought that his master deserves no adulation. Since the independence of ideals is not yet acknowledged, Power may be freely worshiped, and receive an unlimited respect, despite its wanton infliction of pain.

But gradually, as morality grows bolder, the claim of the ideal world begins to be felt; and worship, if it is not to cease, must be given to gods of another kind than those created by the savage. Some, though they feel the demands of the ideal, will still consciously reject them, still urging that naked Power is worthy of worship. Such is the attitude inculcated in God's answer to Job out of the whirlwind: the divine power and knowledge are paraded, but of the divine goodness there is no hint. Such also is the attitude of those who, in our own day, base their morality upon the struggle for survival, maintaining that the survivors are necessarily the fittest. But others, not content with an answer so repugnant to the moral sense, will adopt the position which we have become accustomed to regard as specially religious, maintaining that, in some hidden manner, the world of fact is really harmonious with the world of ideals. Thus Man creates God, all-powerful and all-good, the mystic unity of what is and what should be.

But the world of fact, after all, is not good; and, in submitting our judgment to it, there is an element of slavishness from which our thoughts must be purged. For in all things it is well to exalt the dignity of Man, by freeing him as far as possible from the tyranny of non-human Power. When we have realized that Power is largely bad, that man, with his knowledge of good and evil, is but a helpless atom in a world which has no such knowledge, the choice is again presented to us: Shall we worship Force, or shall we worship Goodness? Shall our God exist and be evil, or shall he be recognized as the creation of our own conscience?

III

The answer to this question is very momentous, and affects profoundly our whole morality. The worship of Force, to which Carlyle and Nietzsche and the creed of Militarism have accustomed us, is the result of failure to maintain our own ideals against a hostile universe: it is itself a prostrate submission to evil, a sacrifice of our best to Moloch. If Power is bad, as it seems to be, let us reject it from our hearts. In this lies Man's true freedom: in determination to worship only the God created by our own love of the good, to respect only the heaven which inspires the insight of our best moments. In action, in desire, we must submit perpetually to the tyranny of outside forces; but in thought, in aspiration, we are free, free from our fellow-men, free from the petty planet on which our bodies impotently crawl, free even, while we live, from the tyranny of death. Let us learn, then, that energy of faith which enables us to live constantly in the vision of the good; and let us descend, in action, into the world of fact, with that vision always before us.

But the vision of beauty is possible only to unfettered contemplation, to thoughts not weighted by the load of eager wishes; and thus Freedom comes only to those who no longer ask of life that it shall yield them any of those personal goods that are subject to the mutations of Time.

There is in resignation a further good element: even real goods, when they are unattainable, ought not to be fretfully desired. To every man comes, sooner or later, the great renunciation. For the young, there is nothing unattainable; a good thing desired with the whole force of a passionate will, and yet impossible, is to them not credible. Yet, by death, by illness, by poverty, or by the voice of duty, we must learn, each one of us, that the world was not made for us, and that, however beautiful may be the things we crave, Fate may nevertheless forbid them. It is the part of courage, when misfortune comes, to bear without repining the ruin of our hopes, to turn away our thoughts from vain regrets. This degree of submission to Power is not only just and right: it is the very gate of wisdom.

When, without the bitterness of impotent rebellion, we have learnt both to resign ourselves to the outward rule of Fate and to recognize that the non-human world is unworthy of our worship, it becomes possible at last so to transform and refashion the unconscious universe, so to transmute it in the crucible of imagination, that a new image of shining gold replaces the old idol of clay. In all the multiform facts of the world—in the visual shapes of trees and mountains and clouds, in the events of the life of man, even in the very omnipotence of Death—the insight of creative idealism can find the reflection of a beauty which its own thoughts first made. In this way mind asserts its subtle mastery over the thoughtless forces of Nature. The more evil the material with which it deals, the more thwarting to untrained desire, the greater is its achievement in inducing the reluctant rock to yield up its hidden treasures, the prouder its victory in compelling the opposing forces to swell the pageant of its triumph.

Of all the arts, Tragedy is the proudest, the most triumphant; for it builds its shining citadel in the very center of the enemy's country, on the very summit of his highest mountain; from its impregnable watch-towers, his camps and arsenals, his columns and forts, are all revealed; within its walls the free life continues, while the legions of Death and Pain and Despair, and all the servile captains of tyrant Fate, afford the burghers of that dauntless city new spectacles of beauty. Happy those sacred ramparts, thrice happy the dwellers on that all-seeing eminence. Honor to those brave warriors who, through countless ages of warfare, have preserved for us the priceless heritage of liberty, and have kept undefiled by sacrilegious invaders the home of the unsubdued.

IV

The life of Man, viewed outwardly, is but a small thing in comparison with the forces of Nature. The slave is doomed to worship Time and Fate and Death, because they are greater than anything he finds in himself, and because all his thoughts are of things which they devour. But, great as they are, to think of them greatly, to feel their passionless splendor, is greater still. And such thought makes us free men; we no longer bow before the inevitable in Oriental subjection, but we absorb it, and make it a part of ourselves. To abandon the struggle for private happiness, to expel all eagerness of temporary desire, to burn with passion for eternal things—this is emancipation, and this is the free man's worship. And this liberation is effected by a contemplation of Fate; for Fate itself is subdued by the mind which leaves nothing to be purged by the purifying fire of Time.

United with his fellow-men by the strongest of all ties, the tie of a common doom, the free man finds that a new vision is with him always, shedding over every daily task the light of love. The life of Man is a long march through the night, surrounded by invisible foes, tortured by weariness and pain, towards a goal that few can hope to reach, and where none may tarry long. One by one, as they march, our comrades vanish from our sight, seized by the silent orders of omnipotent Death. Very brief is the time in which we can help them, in which their happiness or misery is decided. Be it ours to shed sunshine on their path, to lighten their sorrows by the balm of sympathy, to give them the pure joy of a never-tiring affection, to strengthen failing courage, to instill faith in hours of despair. Let us not weigh in grudging scales their merits and demerits, but let us think only of their need—of the sorrows, the difficulties, perhaps the blindnesses, that make the misery of their lives; let us remember that they are fellow-sufferers in the same darkness, actors in the same tragedy with ourselves. And so, when their day is over, when their good and their evil have become eternal by the immortality of the past, be it ours to feel that, where they suffered, where they failed, no deed of ours was the cause; but wherever a spark of the divine fire kindled in their hearts, we were ready with encouragement, with sympathy, with brave words in which high courage glowed.

Brief and powerless is Man's life; on him and all his race the slow, sure doom falls pitiless and dark. Blind to good and evil, reckless of destruction, omnipotent matter rolls on its relentless way; for Man, condemned today to lose his dearest, tomorrow himself to pass through the gate of darkness, it remains only to cherish, ere yet the blow falls, the lofty thoughts that ennoble his little day; disdaining the coward terrors of the slave of Fate, to worship at the shrine that his own hands have built; undismayed by the empire of chance, to preserve a mind free from the wanton tyranny that rules his outward life; proudly defiant of the irresistible forces that tolerate, for a moment, his knowledge and his condemnation, to sustain alone, a weary but unyielding Atlas, the world that his own ideals have fashioned despite the trampling march of unconscious power.

Alfred North Whitehead

For more than twenty years Alfred North Whitehead was a familiar and distinguished figure on the campus of Harvard University. Born in Ramsgate, England, in 1861, he graduated from Cambridge University where he lectured in mathematics until 1911. In that year he moved to the University of London, and from 1914 to 1924 he taught mathematics at the Imperial College of Science and Technology. Then at the age of sixty-three Whitehead began a new phase of his career by going to Harvard University to teach philosophy. It is now generally agreed that his most important work was done in these later years in America. Some of his best-known books, such as Science and the Modern World *(1925),* Process and Reality *(1929), and* Adventures of Ideas *(1933) were published during this period. When he died in 1947 he was generally recognized as one of the ablest metaphysicians of our day.* Dialogues of Alfred North Whitehead *as recorded by Lucien Price* is a delightful introduction to his thought.*

In the essay on "Religion and Science" reprinted here from Science and the Modern World, *we are immediately aware of the balanced, judicious spirit of scientific thought at its best. It is this spirit for which Whitehead is noted in all his philosophical writing—and one cannot but feel that he brings to a discussion highly charged with emotion and misunderstanding a dimension lacking in the essays of Walter Lippmann and Bertrand Russell. In his work as a mathematician and logician Whitehead acquired two ways of reasoning which he uses to good advantage in the present essay. These are extension and generality. Whenever he is confronted with a modern difficulty or dispute he extends the argument*

* Boston: Little, Brown, 1954, and the paperbound edition, New York: New American Library, 1956.

back through history to show that the dispute is not new and that solutions have been found for it in the past. Accordingly, he does not despair in the present situation. He can surprise the reader who begins to say to himself, "Whitehead is all on the side of religion," by showing mistakes that religious people have made in standing too firmly on uncertain grounds. But when a reader feels that Whitehead is being chiefly the scientist in his thinking, he will cite from his wide knowledge of history some deflating example of an overzealous scientist claiming too much for his theories. Thus, his habit of extension saves him from a shortsighted point of view.

When he defines the words "religion" and "god" Whitehead uses the principle of generality, making his definitions so inclusive and so removed from doctrinal formulations that no one can seriously object to them. Whether they are specific enough to satisfy men's souls (as Lippmann expects religion to do) is another question. At least there will be no heresy trials if Whitehead's definitions are accepted.

RELIGION AND SCIENCE

I

THE DIFFICULTY in approaching the question of the relations between Religion and Science is, that its elucidation requires that we have in our minds some clear idea of what we mean by either of the terms, "religion" and "science." Also I wish to speak in the most general way possible, and to keep in the background any comparison of particular creeds, scientific or religious. We have got to understand the type of connection which exists between the two spheres, and then to draw some definite conclusions respecting the existing situation which at present confronts the world.

The *conflict* between religion and science is what naturally occurs to our minds when we think of this subject. It seems as though, during the last half-century, the results of science and the beliefs of religion had come into a position of frank disagreement, from which there can be no escape, except by abandoning either the clear teaching of science, or the clear teaching of religion. This conclusion has been urged by controversialists on either side. Not by all controversialists, of course, but by those trenchant intellects which every controversy calls out into the open.

The distress of sensitive minds, and the zeal for truth, and the sense of the importance of the issues, must command our sincerest sympathy. When we consider what religion is for mankind, and what science is, it is no exaggeration to say that the future course of history depends upon the decision of this generation as to the relations between them. We have here the two strongest general forces (apart from the mere impulse of the various senses) which influence men, and they seem to be set one against the other—the force of our religious intuitions, and the force of our impulse to accurate observation and logical deduction.

A great English statesman once advised his countrymen to use large-scale maps, as a preservative against alarms, panics, and general misunderstanding of the true relations between nations. In the same way in dealing with the clash between permanent elements of human nature, it is well to map our history on a large scale, and to disengage ourselves from our immediate absorption in the present conflicts. When we do this, we immediately discover two great facts. In the first place, there has always been a conflict between religion and science; and in the second place, both religion and science have always been in a state of continual development. In the early days of Christianity, there was a general belief among Christians that the world was coming to an end in the lifetime of people then living. We can make only indirect inferences as to how far this belief was authoritatively proclaimed; but it is certain that it was widely held, and that it formed an impressive part of the popular religious doctrine. The belief proved itself to be mistaken, and Christian doctrine adjusted itself to the change. Again in the early Church individual theologians very confidently deduced from the Bible opinions concerning the nature of the physical universe. In the year A.D. 535, a monk named Cosmas wrote a book which he entitled, *Christian Topography*. He was a traveled man who had visited India and Ethiopia; and finally he lived in a monastery at Alexandria, which was then a great center of culture. In this book, basing himself upon the direct meaning of Biblical texts as construed by him in a literal fashion, he denied the existence of the antipodes, and asserted that the world is a flat parallelogram whose length is double its breadth.

In the seventeenth century the doctrine of the motion of the earth was condemned by a Catholic tribunal. A hundred years ago the extension of time demanded by geological science distressed religious people, Protestant and Catholic. And today the doctrine of evolution is an equal stumbling block. These are only a few instances illustrating a general fact.

But all our ideas will be in a wrong perspective if we think that this recurring perplexity was confined to contradictions between religion and science; and that in these controversies religion was always wrong, and that science was always right. The true facts of the case are very much more complex, and refuse to be summarized in these simple terms.

II

No man of science could subscribe without qualification to Galileo's beliefs, or to Newton's beliefs, or to all his own scientific beliefs of ten years ago. In both regions of thought, additions, distinctions, and modifications have been introduced. So that now, even when the same assertion is made today as was made a thousand, or fifteen hundred years ago, it is made subject to limitations or expansions of meaning, which were not contemplated at the earlier epoch. We are told by logicians that a proposition must be either true or false, and that there is no middle term. But in practice, we may know that a proposition expresses an important truth, but that it is subject to limitations and qualifications which at present remain undiscovered. It is a general feature of our knowledge, that we are insistently aware of important truths; and yet that the only formulations of these truths which we are able to make presuppose a general standpoint of conceptions which may have to be modified. I will give you two illustrations, both from science: Galileo said that the earth moves and that the sun is fixed; the Inquisition said that the earth is fixed and the sun moves; and Newtonian astronomers, adopting an absolute theory of space, said that both the sun and the earth move. But now we say that any one of these three statements is equally true, provided that you have fixed your sense of "rest" and "motion" in the way required by the statement adopted. At the date of Galileo's controversy with the Inquisition, Galileo's way of stating the facts was, beyond question, the fruitful procedure for the sake of scientific research. But in itself it was not more true than the formulation of the Inquisition. But at that time the modern concepts of relative motion were in nobody's mind; so that the statements were made in ignorance of the qualifications required for their more perfect truth. Yet this question of the motions of the earth and the sun expresses a real fact in the universe; and all sides had got hold of important truths concerning it. But with the knowledge of those times, the truths appeared to be inconsistent.

Again I will give you another example taken from the state of modern physical science. Since the time of Newton and Huygens in the seventeenth century there have been two theories as to the physical nature of light. Newton's theory was that a beam of light consists of a stream of very minute particles, or corpuscles, and that we have the sensation of light when these corpuscles strike the retinas of our eyes. Huygens' theory was that light consists of very minute waves of trembling in an all-pervading ether, and that these waves are traveling along a beam of light. The two theories are contradictory. In the eighteenth century Newton's theory was believed, in the nineteenth century Huygens' theory was believed. Today there is one large group of phenomena which can be explained only on the wave theory, and another large group which can be explained only on the corpuscular theory. Scientists have to leave it at that, and wait for the future, in the hope of attaining some wider vision which reconciles both.

We should apply these same principles to the questions in which there is a variance between science and religion. We would believe nothing in either sphere of thought which does not appear to us to be certified by solid reasons based upon the critical research either of ourselves or of competent authorities. But granting that we have honestly taken this precaution, a clash between the two on points of detail where they overlap should not lead us hastily to abandon doctrines for which we have solid evidence. It may be that we are more interested in one set of doctrines than in the other. But, if we have any sense of perspective and of the history of thought, we shall wait and refrain from mutual anathemas.

We should wait: but we should not wait passively, or in despair. The clash is a sign that there are wider truths and finer perspectives within which a reconciliation of a deeper religion and a more subtle science will be found.

In one sense, therefore, the conflict between science and religion is a slight matter which has been unduly emphasized. A mere logical contradiction cannot in itself point to more than the necessity of some readjustments, possibly of a very minor character on both sides. Remember the widely different aspects of events which are dealt with in science and in religion respectively. Science is concerned with the general conditions which are observed to regulate physical phenomena; whereas religion is wholly wrapped up in the contemplation of moral and esthetic values. On the one side there is the law of gravitation, and on the other the contemplation of the beauty of holiness. What one side sees, the other misses; and vice versa.

Consider, for example, the lives of John Wesley and of Saint Francis of Assisi. For physical science you have in these lives merely ordinary examples of the operation of the principles of physiological chemistry, and of the dynamics of nervous reactions: for religion you have lives of the most profound significance in the history of the world. Can you be surprised that, in the absence of a perfect and complete phrasing of the principles of science and of the principles of religion which apply to these specific cases, the accounts of these lives from these divergent standpoints should involve discrepancies? It would be a miracle if it were not so.

It would, however, be missing the point to think that we need not trouble ourselves about the conflict between science and religion. In an intellectual age there can be no active interest which puts aside all hope of a vision of the harmony of truth. To acquiesce in discrepancy is destructive of candor, and of moral cleanliness. It belongs to the self-respect of intellect to pursue every tangle of thought to its final unravelment. If you check that impulse, you will get no religion and no science from an awakened thoughtfulness. The important question is, In what spirit are we going to face the issue? There we come to something absolutely vital.

A clash of doctrines is not a disaster—it is an opportunity. I will explain my meaning by some illustrations from science. The weight of an atom of nitrogen was well known. Also it was an established scientific doctrine that the average weight of such atoms in any considerable mass will be always the same. Two experimenters, the late Lord Rayleigh and the late Sir William Ramsay, found that if they obtained nitrogen by two different methods, each equally effective for that purpose, they always observed a persistent slight difference between the average weights of the atoms in the two cases. Now I ask you, would it have been rational of these men to have despaired because of this conflict between chemical theory and scientific observation? Suppose that for some reason the chemical doctrine had been highly prized throughout some district as the foundation of its social order:—would it have been wise, would it have been candid, would it have been moral, to forbid the disclosure of the fact that the experiments produced discordant results? Or, on the other hand, should Sir William Ramsay and Lord Rayleigh have proclaimed that chemical theory was now a detected delusion? We see at once that either of these ways would have been a method of facing the issue in an entirely wrong spirit. What Rayleigh and Ramsay did was this: They at once perceived that they had hit upon a line of investigation which would disclose some subtlety of chemical theory that had hitherto eluded observation. The discrepancy was not a disaster: it was an opportunity to increase the sweep of chemical knowledge. You all know the end of the story: finally argon was discovered, a new chemical element which had lurked undetected, mixed with the nitrogen. But the story has a sequel which forms my second illustration. This discovery drew attention to the importance of observing accurately minute differences in chemical substances as obtained by different methods. Further researches of the most careful accuracy were undertaken. Finally another physicist, F. W. Aston, working in the Cavendish Laboratory at Cambridge in England, discovered that even the same element might assume two or more distinct forms, termed *isotopes*, and that the law of the constancy of average atomic weight holds for each of these forms, but as between the different isotopes differs slightly. The research has effected a great stride in the power of chemical theory, far transcending in importance the discovery of argon from which it originated. The moral of these stories lies on the surface, and I will leave to you their application to the case of religion and science.

In formal logic, a contradiction is the signal of defeat: but in the evolution of real knowledge it marks the first step in progress towards a victory. This is one great reason for the utmost toleration of variety of opinion. Once and forever, this duty of toleration has been summed up in the words, "Let both grow together until the harvest." The failure of Christians to act up to this precept, of the highest authority, is one of the curiosities of religious history. But we have not yet exhausted the discussion of the moral temper required for the pursuit of truth. There are short cuts leading merely to an illusory success. It is easy enough to find a theory, logically harmonious and with important applications in the region of fact, provided that you are content to disregard half your evidence. Every age produces people with clear logical intellects, and with the most praiseworthy grasp of the importance of some sphere of human experience, who have elaborated, or inherited, a scheme of thought which exactly fits those experiences which claim their interest. Such people are apt resolutely to ignore, or to explain away, all evidence which confuses their scheme with contradictory instances. What they cannot fit in is for them nonsense. An unflinching determination to take the whole evidence into account is the only method of preservation against the fluctuating extremes of fashionable opinion. This advice seems so easy, and is in fact so difficult to follow.

One reason for this difficulty is that we cannot think first and act afterwards. From the moment of birth we are immersed in action, and can only fitfully guide it by taking thought. We have, therefore, in various spheres of experience to adopt those ideas which seem to work within those spheres. It is absolutely necessary to trust to ideas which are generally adequate, even though we know that there are subtleties and distinctions beyond our ken. Also apart from the necessities of action, we cannot even keep before our minds the whole evidence except under the guise of doctrines which are incompletely harmonized. We cannot think in terms of an indefinite multiplicity of detail; our evidence can acquire its proper importance only if it comes before us marshaled by general ideas. These ideas we inherit—they form the tradition of our civilization. Such traditional ideas are never static. They are either fading into meaningless formulae, or are gaining power by the new lights thrown by a more delicate apprehension. They are transformed by the urge of critical reason, by the vivid evidence of emotional experience, and by the cold certainties of scientific perception. One fact is certain, you cannot keep them still. No generation can merely reproduce its ancestors. You may preserve the life in a flux of form, or preserve the form amid an ebb of life. But you cannot permanently enclose the same life in the same mold.

III

The present state of religion among the European races illustrates the statements which I have been making. The phenomena are mixed. There have been reactions and revivals. But on the whole, during many generations, there has been a gradual decay of religious influence in European civilization. Each revival touches a lower peak than its predecessor, and each period of slackness a lower depth. The average curve marks a steady fall in religious tone. In some countries the interest in religion is higher than in others. But in those countries where the interest is relatively high, it still falls as the generations pass. Religion is tending to degenerate into a decent formula wherewith to embellish a comfortable life. A great historical movement on this scale results from the convergence of many causes. I wish to suggest two of them which lie within the scope of this chapter for consideration.

In the first place for over two centuries religion has been on the defensive, and on a weak defensive. The period has been one of unprecedented intellectual progress. In this way a series of novel situations have been produced for thought. Each such occasion has found the religious thinkers unprepared. Something, which has been proclaimed to be vital, has finally, after struggle, distress, and anathema, been modified and otherwise interpreted. The next generation of religious apologists then congratulates the religious world on the deeper insight which has been gained. The result of the continued repetition of this undignified retreat, during many generations, has at last almost entirely destroyed the intellectual authority of religious thinkers. Consider this contrast: when Darwin or Einstein proclaim theories which modify our ideas, it is a triumph for science. We do not go about saying that there is another defeat for science, because its old ideas have been abandoned. We know that another step of scientific insight has been gained.

Religion will not regain its old power until it can face change in the same spirit as does science. Its principles may be eternal, but the expression of those principles requires continual development. This evolution of religion is in the main a disengagement of its own proper ideas from the adventitious notions which have crept into it by reason of the expression of its own ideas in terms of the imaginative picture of the world entertained in previous ages. Such a release of religion from the bonds of imperfect science is all to the good. It stresses its own genuine message. The great point to be kept in mind is that normally an advance in science will show that statements of various religious beliefs require some sort of modification. It may be that they have to be expanded or explained, or indeed entirely restated. If the religion is a sound expression of truth, this modification will only exhibit more adequately the exact point which is of importance. This process is a gain. In so far, therefore, as any religion has any contact with physical facts, it is to be expected that the point of view of those facts must be continually modified as scientific knowledge advances. In this way, the exact relevance of these facts for religious thought will grow more and more clear. The progress of science must result in the unceasing codification of religious thought, to the great advantage of religion.

The religious controversies of the sixteenth and seventeenth centuries put theologians into a most unfortunate state of mind. They were always attacking and defending. They pictured themselves as the garrison of a fort surrounded by hostile forces. All such pictures express half-truths. That is why they are so popular. But they are dangerous. This particular picture fostered a pugnacious party spirit which really expresses an ultimate lack of faith. They dared not modify, because they shirked the task of disengaging their spiritual message from the associations of a particular imagery.

Let me explain myself by an example. In the early medieval times, Heaven was in the sky, and Hell was underground; volcanoes were the jaws of Hell. I do not assert that these beliefs entered into the official formulations: but they did enter into the popular understanding of the general doctrines of Heaven and Hell. These notions were what everyone thought to be implied by the doctrine of the future state. They entered into the explanations of the influential exponents of Christian belief. For example, they occur in the *Dialogues* of Pope Gregory the Great, a man whose high official position is surpassed only by the magnitude of his services to humanity. I am not saying what we ought to believe about the future state. But whatever be the right doctrine, in this instance the clash between religion and science, which has relegated the earth to the position of a second-rate planet attached to a second-rate sun, has been greatly to the benefit of the spirituality of religion by dispersing these medieval fancies.

IV

So far, my point has been this: that religion is the expression of one type of fundamental experiences of mankind: that religious thought develops into an increasing accuracy of expression, disengaged from adventitious imagery: that the interaction between religion and science is one great factor in promoting this development.

I now come to my second reason for the modern fading of interest in religion. This involves the ultimate question which I stated in my opening sentences. We have to know what we mean by religion. The churches, in their presentation of their answers to this query, have put forward aspects of religion which are expressed in terms either suited to the emotional reactions of bygone times or directed to excite modern emotional interests of nonreligious character. What I mean under the first heading is that religious appeal is directed partly to excite that instinctive fear of the wrath of a tyrant which was inbred in the unhappy populations of the arbitrary empires of the ancient world, and in particular to excite that fear of an all-powerful arbitrary tyrant behind the unknown forces of nature. This appeal to the ready instinct of brute fear is losing its force. It lacks any directness of response, because modern science and modern conditions of life have taught us to meet occasions of apprehension by a critical analysis of their causes and conditions. Religion is the reaction of human nature to its search for God. The presentation of God under the aspect of power awakens every modern instinct of critical reaction. This is fatal; for religion collapses unless its main positions command immediacy of assent. In this respect the old phraseology is at variance with the psychology of modern civilizations. This change in psychology is largely due to science, and is one of the chief ways in which the advance of science has weakened the hold of the old religious forms of expression. The nonreligious motive which has entered into modern religious thought is the desire for a comfortable organization of modern society. Religion has been presented as valuable for the ordering of life. Its claims have been rested upon its function as a sanction to right conduct. Also the purpose of right conduct quickly degenerates into the formation of pleasing social relations. We have here a subtle degradation of religious ideas, following upon their gradual purification under the influence of keener ethical intuitions. Conduct is a by-product of religion —an inevitable by-product, but not the main point. Every great religious teacher has revolted against the presentation of religion as a mere sanction of rules of conduct. Saint Paul denounced the Law, and the Puritan divines spoke of the filthy rags of righteousness. The insistence upon rules of conduct marks the ebb of religious fervor. Above and beyond all things, the religious life is not a research after comfort. I must now state, in all diffidence, what I conceive to be the essential character of the religious spirit.

Religion is the vision of something which stands beyond, behind, and within, the passing flux of immediate things; something which is real, and yet waiting to be realized; something which is a remote possibility, and yet the greatest of present facts; something that gives meaning to all that passes, and yet eludes apprehension; something whose possession is the final good, and yet is beyond all reach; something which is the ultimate ideal, and the hopeless quest.

The immediate reaction of human nature to the religious vision is worship. Religion has emerged into human experience mixed with the crudest fancies of barbaric imagination. Gradually, slowly, steadily the vision recurs in history under nobler form and with clearer expression. It is the one element in human experience which persistently shows an upward trend. It fades and then recurs. But when it renews its force, it recurs with an added richness and purity of content. The fact of the religious vision, and its history of persistent expansion, is our one ground for optimism. Apart from it, human life is a flash of occasional enjoyments lighting up a mass of pain and misery, a bagatelle of transient experience.

The vision claims nothing but worship; and worship is a surrrender to the claim for assimilation, urged with the motive force of mutual love. The vision never overrules. It is always there, and it has the power of love presenting the one purpose whose fulfillment is eternal harmony. Such order as we find in nature is never force—it presents itself as the one harmonious adjustment of complex detail. Evil is the brute motive force of fragmentary purpose, disregarding the eternal vision. Evil is overruling, retarding, hurting. The power of God is the worship He inspires. That religion is strong which in its ritual and its modes of thought evokes an apprehension of the commanding vision. The worship of God is not a rule of safety—it is an adventure of the spirit, a flight after the unattainable. The death of religion comes with the repression of the high hope of adventure.

2

SCIENCE AND THE MORAL LIFE

Max C. Otto

Philosophy often seems a forbidding subject to college students. In university courses it has frequently been presented in abstract and technical fashion with little relation to the things that students feel to be important. Especially to those students whose main interest lies in preparing themselves to succeed in business or a profession, the study of philosophy may appear impractical, if not a downright waste of time. However, one of the most stimulating teachers of philosophy we have had in America, Max Otto, undertakes here to show that such an attitude is a serious mistake. The task of philosophy, Otto believes, is to provide ordinary men and women with the wisdom they need to live a full and satisfying life, and nothing could be more important than this. Much influenced by recent scientific thought and committed in his own philosophy to a naturalistic point of view, Otto wants to give philosophy something of the practical and empirical temper of modern science. The impact of science upon our moral and religious convictions has been wholesome and constructive, he argues, for only as morals are infused with the spirit of science and rescued from the narrowness and dogmatism of emotion or prejudice, can we hope to develop a more mature and humane moral life. And this is what philosophy should help us do.

Now Emeritus Professor at the University of Wisconsin after almost forty years on its faculty, Otto came to this country from Germany in 1881 at the age of five. He studied at the universities of Chicago, Heidelberg, and Wisconsin and received his Ph.D. at the latter institution in 1911. Among his best-known books are Things and Ideals *(1924),* Natural Laws and Human Hopes *(1926), and* The Human Enterprise *(1940).*

During his years at Wisconsin Otto "achieved a nationwide reputation as a thinker and teacher whose persistent thesis has been that philosophy is the concern of Everyman rather than of professionals alone. His course Man and Nature *was, for twenty-five years, one of the great educational offerings in the University of Wisconsin's brilliant teaching history. . . . Humane, warm and in the best sense simple, his wisdom is pervaded by a profound sense of dedication to the enrichment of man's intellectual and spiritual life." Thus Frederick Burkhardt, former president of Bennington College, introduces Otto's volume of essays on* Science and the Moral Life *from which our present selections are taken.*

The first selection, entitled "Of What Good Is Philosophy Anyway?," is a practical and nontechnical discussion of the subject which every student should find helpful in clarifying his thinking. The second selection, an essay on "Scientific Humanism," brings together two ideas which are not usually associated—science which suggests laboratories, impersonal experiments, and the like, and humanism which usually is concerned with the emotional and esthetic needs of man. Otto insists, however, upon the necessity of both in a mature life. He goes on to describe in a warmhearted way what science can actually do for people today if they are willing to make more use of the scientific method in dealing with moral problems and to accept in their own working philosophy a little more of the scientist's love of truth and objectivity.

OF WHAT GOOD IS PHILOSOPHY ANYWAY?

I

OF WHAT GOOD is philosophy anyway? That is the question frequently asked, and more often than not it is a purely rhetorical question, amounting to the assertion that philosophy is of no practical use. It is this question which we are to take seriously and try to answer.

Now, there is more to this question than is evident on the surface. The person who asks it implies something he does not say. It is not as though he were asking, "Why do you eat rich food when you are too fat already?" Or "Why do you sleep so late in the morning that you have to rush off without a decent breakfast?" Such questions can be answered by saying, "Very well, I'll stop doing it. I'll eat plainer food," or "I'll get up earlier." But suppose the questions were: "Why eat at all, since you only get hungry again?" or "Why sleep a part of your life away which heaven knows is short enough already?" These questions imply that it is possible to get on without eating or sleeping; and since the best anyone can do is to choose what to eat and how long to sleep, always eating something and always sleeping more or less, they are unreal questions in the sense that they are out of touch with the realities of experience. In this respect the question proposed as regards philosophy is identical with them It, too, is an unreal question in that it implies a state of affairs that has no existence The implication is that a person can have a philosophy or not as he pleases, whereas his having a philosophy is unavoidable. The best he can do is to have one kind or another.

Charles and Mary Beard have made this point excellently at the beginning of their book, *The American Spirit:*

> Every person, whether primitive or highly civilized, has a conception of himself and the universe in which he lives and works or idles. This is his idea of his world—his world-view. His world-view may be dimly formed, barely recognized, even somewhat surreptitiously held. But a world-view is in the mind of every man and every woman
>
> An individual may deny that he has a world view. He may say that he has no interest in th world. He may insist that he is an independent free-swinging person, hedonist or ascetic, choosing his way of life at his own will; but the denial is itself a world-view—something on the basis of which independence is asserted, whether he is aware of it or not.

This representation by two of our foremost scholars is duplicated in principle by an outstanding leader of American business Eric A. Johnston, addressing the graduating class at the University of Virginia. "Philosophy is something more," he told the graduates, "than a course in your school curric

[From *Philosophy in American Education*, Chapter VI. Copyright 1945 by Harper & Brothers. Reprinted by permission of the publishers.]

ulum to be passed and forgotten. It is something each of us has, whether we know it or not. It is the aggregate of our enthusiasms and prejudices. It is the moral code by which we live. It is the equipment we bring to life and the responses we expect from life." And the space between scholar and businessman—quite a large space, at that—could easily be filled in by others who have spoken to the same effect, doctors, lawyers, journalists, and men prominent in politics.

Opinions such as these do not *demonstrate* that a degree and kind of philosophy is practically universal among men, but they do prove that well-qualified observers believe this to be the case. Anyone who questions what they say need only observe a little on his own account, examine himself, and the people he knows or hears about and what he reads, and he will have plenty of evidence that one thing which everyone gains from living, whatever else he may win or lose, is a more or less elaborated theory of life, based upon an idea of human nature and the conditioning natural and social environment.

This widespread general philosophy is of course not invariably of a kind to take pride in. Constituted as it is of bits picked up for the most part accidentally, a belief here, an attitude there, it cannot easily be inwardly coherent or outwardly comprehensive. And it is likely to be vague, ambiguous, equivocal, just where clearness is most needed. Moreover, the chief motivating influence in its construction may be agreeable feeling rather than logic or fact. Yet, though piecemeal and fortuitous, it is the outgrowth of the human urge to make sense of things. It mirrors the effort of individuals and communities to take life in charge and deliberately make the best of it. Untutored as this philosophy may be, it has one quality which professional philosophy often lacks: it is alive with the impulses and ambitions that keep men going. And it does a good deal, even if not so much as the critics may demand, to illuminate those native impulses and ambitions. In some cases, indeed, it rises to such loftiness of aspiration, is so critically intelligent, and so broad in its application, as put professional idealists to shame.

Besides whatever this unstudied philosophy comes to, it is responsible for the choices millions of people make day in and day out, and hence it sets the tone of the human venture for most of us. Gerald Johnson, in an article that appeared in *Life* in 1942, "Whose War Aims?", made this pertinent suggestion: "The President may dictate until he is black in the face, but the terms are going to be enforced by the American people, or they will not be enforced at all." This is as true of life as it is of war aims. Men of letters, college professors, clergymen, and all others who feel it their duty to instruct may complain and dictate until they are black in the face, but it is the life aims put into practice by men and women at large which determine the character of the human venture.

II

Here, then, is the beginning of an answer to anyone who wants to know what philosophy is good for. We have interpreted the question to mean essentially, Why try to understand the conditions under which men exist or why aim to formulate a rational program of conduct? Why attempt to gain knowledge of the world and wisdom of life? And our answer has been something like this: We cannot help it. As human beings we seek information and employ it to meliorate and dignify our lot. Some acquaintance with the surrounding environment, some notion of the sensible thing to do in ordinary situations, even some judgment of relative values is bound to be acquired by everyone, the more so under contemporary conditions when a profusion of reading matter is spread before our eyes and radio broadcasts are everlastingly bombarding our ears. Although the knowledge and the abilities thus gained may in many cases leave much to be desired, some persons are in this manner provided with a theory of life and a program of living, both of a high order of excellence.

Granting all this, is it philosophy? Surely most people would not think so. The word "philosophy" seems to them among the highbrowest of words. But the word "philosophy," like other words, denotes more than one kind of object. It does so even when lay philosophy is referred to, some lay philosophies, as already intimated, being superficial hand-to-mouth schemes of immediate advancement, while others are life plans broadly and generously conceived. And besides lay philosophy there is professional or technical philosophy, which also occurs in variations of depth and scope, all differing from lay philosophies in being the work of trained formulators of world and life views.

Suppose the broader conception is allowed to stand, are the two types, the nonprofessional and the professional, completely independent enterprises, or is the philosophy of philosophers the refinement of what is begun by the layman?

On this point there is no general agreement. And since an adequate discussion of the problem would take us away from the main task, let us tentatively accept the second alternative without argument and discover, if we can, how the nonprofessional philosophy may move in the direction of depth and breadth of insight, and may do so with the help of those for whom philosophy is a profession.

One thing should scarcely need mentioning. The philosopher is expected to think with uncommon intensity and to reach out for the ultimate in wisdom. He is believed to follow up every clue that might possibly help in piecing together a picture of the world in totality, and to travel further and dig deeper than any other thinker in the search for the true criteria of value. This is an idealization, but it is more true than false. The philosopher does belong at the opposite pole from those who rest satisfied with superficial observation and short-range ideals, or who practice the theory that ideas and emotions are self-justifying, so that everyone has a right to believe and feel as he likes, if only he believes and feels sincerely. A narrow, slipshod attitude toward fact and value, however well intentioned, is the very antithesis of the philosophic temper of mind.

Surely this determination to face things as they actually are—things singly and things collectively—is unusual. A businessman will think hard about business problems; a man of science will be keen in setting up and following through laboratory experiments; a military leader will do his best to figure out how to win victory over the enemy; but with respect to the larger issues of life, or even important sections of that life, businessmen, scientists, military leaders, and most of the rest of us tend to give up thinking altogether. We prefer to let someone else do the thinking for us. We do not choose to engage in that kind of mental effort.

Professional philosophers encourage us to make just that kind of mental effort. They want us to be educated persons—an educated person being, in Mildred McAfee's telling phrase, "one who thinks more than is necessary for survival." It is true, there is a species of philosopher who plants a tiny seed of doubt in some susceptible crevice of your mind and nurses it along until a blighting skepticism of life has spread over the whole of your thinking. And there is the kind who pretends to conjure the ultimate of reality from an item of personal experience. And of course there is the more common variety, the one who angles in the quiet waters of speculative meditation for abstract ideas which he can mount and proudly exhibit in disparagement of the wriggling, darting particulars whose habitat is the current of events. Nevertheless, taking them all together, philosophers are the most active and outreaching thinkers in the community. Philosophy at its best might adopt for its slogan the title of a book by Brian Penton, an Australian journalist: *Think—or Be Damned.*

III

It is because the professional philosopher proposes to be intelligent in this rigorous and specific fashion, that any man or woman who goes to him in the hope of refining his nonprofessional outlook, sharpening his ideas, enlarging the pattern of his thinking, and sending its roots deeper into reality, finds the improvement he desires. He may be disconcerted by the task proposed, may even be shocked by the renovation demanded in his views, but few who make the trial will be sorry for having undertaken it. They will recognize that they have become more mature than they were before, more critical of offhand beliefs, more concerned for the quality of the evidence on which opinions are based. William James, in the manuscript of a book left to be published after his death, offers some reasons why professional philosophy does this service. He wrote:

> The principles of explanation that underlie all things without exception, the elements common to gods and men and animals and stones, the first *whence* and the last *whither* of the whole cosmic procession, the conditions of all knowing, and the most general rules of human action—these furnish the problems commonly deemed philosophic *par excellence;* and the philosopher is the man who finds the most to say about them.

One of the consequences is, as he also said, that the study of philosophy "rouses us from our native dogmatic slumber and breaks up our caked prejudices." And since this is one of its consequences, he expressed his faith in philosophy in these words:

> To know the chief rival attitudes toward life, as the history of human thinking has developed them, and to have heard some of the reasons they can give for themselves, ought to be considered an essential part of liberal education. Philosophy, indeed, in one sense of the term is only a compendious name for the spirit in education which the word "college" stands for in America.

Since philosophers start with so much in common, one might expect a considerable unanimity among them as to first principles. This expectation is not realized. The typical philosopher is an intellectual lone wolf. It is his genius to envisage the sum of things with his own eyes and to refuse to depend on the eyes of another. He is at one with his colleagues in the intensity of his gaze, and in the field it embraces, though even this statement cannot be taken as literally true; but he glories in the employment of this intense and rangy vision to report a metaphysical landscape no other ever saw in just that perspective or in just that concatenation of shapes and colors.

Still, it is not impossible to classify philosophies on the basis of similarities in their interpretation of the world and their attitude toward fact and value. At least four interpretations or world views appear in the Platonic dialogues and no doubt could even when they were written summon tradition in their support. These four have persisted or have been revived again and again and are "living hypotheses" today.

There is the atomistic materialism of Democritus, one of the greatest thinkers of antiquity, whom Plato disdains to mention by name. In our own day this is the view usually ascribed to natural science.

There is the moral indifferentism of Thrasymachus, a philosophy of life which Plato endeavors to refute in the human interest. According to Thrasymachus, all the so-called virtues are disguised forms of self-seeking, and a realist will recognize them as such and not allow himself to be fooled. This conception is alive among us as the doctrine that might makes right.

As a third philosophy, there is the relativism of Protagoras, the doctrine: "Man is the measure of all things, of the existence of things that are, and of the nonexistence of things that are not." The contemporary form of this scheme of life is by some identified as pragmatism, which is looked upon as a social hybrid, the result of crossing three theoretical strains; biological evolution, business ambition, and America's reputed infatuation with size.

Finally, there is the immaterialistic philosophy of Plato himself, separated as by a continent from the other three. The spirit of it is detachment from nature in the usual meaning of that term, despair of humankind, and contempt for daily affairs. The philosopher's aim is contemplation of the supersensible, which assures him the best life attainable in this transitory earthly existence, and prepares his soul for its eternal abode in the world to come. For it is, after all, a city in heaven, not on earth, which is discussed at length in Plato's *Republic*.

It may be objected that, in spite of such simplification, the philosophic offering is still too bewildering to be of help to an amateur who wants to improve his nonprofessional outlook. Fortunately there are yet simpler listings. A typical example is one by Henry A. Wallace. That it is the work of a layman should be counted in its favor, since we want to discover what value acquaintance with professional philosophizing may have for ordinary life.

The following paragraph is from Wallace's little book, *The Century of the Common Man:*

> There are three great philosophies in the world today. The first, based on the supremacy of might over right, says that war between nations is inevitable until such time as a single master race dominates the entire world and everyone is assigned his daily task by an arrogant, self-appointed *Fuehrer*. The second—Marxian philosophy—says that class warfare is inevitable until such time as the proletariat comes out on top, everywhere in the world, and can start building a society without classes. The third—which we in this country know as the democratic Christian philosophy—denies that man was made for war, whether it be war between nations or war between classes, and asserts boldly that ultimate peace is inevitable, that all men are brothers, and that God is their Father.

A casual reader of this summary of the great philosophic positions might possibly overlook a qualifying clause of importance. It is, says Wallace, "*we in this country*" who know the third as "the democratic Christian philosophy." But he has not left it at that. He makes his meanings so clear that even the casual reader should get it. "This democratic philosophy," he writes, "pervades not only the hearts and minds of those who live by the Christian religion, both Protestant and Catholic, but of those who draw their inspiration from Mohammedanism, Judaism, Hinduism, Confucianism, and other faiths." That is to say, democratic philosophy occurs in association with diverse religious creeds. It is present in any faith that preaches "the doctrine of the dignity of each individual human soul, the doctrine that God intended man to be a good neighbor to his fellow man, and the doctrine of the essential unity of the entire world. . . ."

IV

In the context of the present discussion the thing of chief significance about Wallace's classification is its basic assumption regarding the nature of philosophy. Philosophy is taken to be primarily an attitude toward life and only incidentally a cosmic theory. This is a telltale assumption. It places the classifier. It indicates that he is interested in *practical* as against *speculative* wisdom. While this is as it should be, since he is a layman, not a professional philosopher, it is well to make the point explicit. Possibly professional philosophy is intrinsically a search for speculative finality and only thereafter for wisdom in practical living. Should this actually be the aim of philosophy, laymen, I think, had better devote themselves to the improvement of lay philosophy and look for no help from philosophic experts.

Consider a typical statement by a most honored philosopher. "Speculative Philosophy," says Alfred North Whitehead, "is the endeavor to frame a coherent, logical, necessary system of general ideas in terms of which every element of our experience can be interpreted." Now doubtless such a "general scheme," when achieved, is an intellectual triumph of the first order, deserving to rank as a creative accomplishment with the supreme generalizations of science or the greatest works of art. And like these it cannot but bring rare satisfaction to the genius in whose mind it originally takes form. Moreover, it will have high value for all those who find these intellectual structures a source of mental stimulation or emotional refreshment.

But how about the general public? A "necessary system of general ideas" will have no significance for the men and women whose life aims must be realized through everyday commitments. However busy they may be with practical matters or however successful in making their way therein, most of them want something more life-filling than economic or social success, more mind-filling than knowledge of the world as they find it spread out before their eyes; but it must be germane to what they are involved in doing and hence of a piece with the world in which they are busy.

Let us consider this matter more closely. Men are to go to professional philosophy for the broadening and deepening of the philosophy picked up in the process of living. If that purpose is to be fulfilled, such help must be forthcoming. Personally I firmly believe that it is forthcoming, but only if professional philosophy bears a certain relation to the obligations of life as plain men and women face them.

Philosophy of the type we have just evaluated does not measure up to this requirement. Its thinking is concentrated upon all-inclusiveness and finality. This objective is beyond human attainment. It is beyond the attainment of the masters in tested inquiry, the physical scientists, not to speak of investigators whose findings, by virtue of their less exacting method, must fall still further short. And this situation holds down the philosopher as it does all other thinkers. There is simply no way whereby a searcher can escape the relative nature of the true or the good or the beautiful of which he may catch sight.

And could a philosopher get around the disability which no other investigator can, plain men and women, who must keep their feet on the earth and their eyes on where they are going, would still have to make their way from the relatively worse to the relatively better. Consequently, a philosopher of absolutes cannot help them. And he, too, would become aware of this fact quickly enough were he less oblivious to the problems involved in the application of his speculative absolutes to the specific circumstances of practical experience.

Furthermore, there is the fact, which John Dewey has pointed out, that wisdom is not an intellectual term. It is a moral term. It does not denote profound, systematic knowledge of the ultimate pattern of things, but an active preference for the best ends and means of life. It is loyalty to the better values, to the goods which are satisfying in the light of reflection; and it implies active interest in bringing those goods into more general and secure enjoyment. So far as can be made out, the earth was not created with the happiness and dignity of mankind in view. We must attain both of them through struggle, in part each one for himself and in part in cooperation one with another. The more successfully we hit upon the best way to go about this the more meaningful and joyous and touched with beauty our existence can be made. Technical philosophy will be useful to laymen in this emergency in proportion as it furthers the attainment of this moral wisdom.

V

Is it possible for philosophy to meet these human specifications and yet measure up to scholarly standards? The answer depends upon whom you ask. My answer is a confident affirmative.

And what will professional philosophy so conceived do for the nonprofessional who makes its acquaintance? My answer is that it will do more for him than any other discipline can.

For one thing, it will work upon him in the same manner that intimate contact with mature philosophy of any kind does. It will break down the walls set up by habitual notions and feelings; will free him from the dominion of immediate appeals, from provincialism of ideas and narrowness of spirit, and thus aid in the emancipation of his mind. Superstitious credulity, dormant in almost all of us and active in the vast majority, will, so far as he is concerned, be recognized for what it is. Occult explanations, which still exercise enormous and harmful power over mankind, will lose the intellectual standing still so widely accorded to them wherever rational insight is weak. He will experience new interest in the value side of experience even as the whole process of evaluation is brought under critical scrutiny. Above all, he will gain in centrality of vision, in striking contrast with the mixture of confused and contradictory attitudes induced by the conflicting demands of present-day society.

To these benefits sure to result from contact with any responsible philosophy, others of a distinctive sort will accrue from the particular philosophy which we are advocating. For this philosophy has taken a distinctive task upon itself and is therefore characterized by attributes which do not belong to the philosophic profession as such. It is from these unique attributes especially that most help is to be gained by the men and women who must continue to do the work of the world. The novel feature of this philosophy is the closeness of its relationship with human affairs. It is an indigenous philosophy, whose ideals are the outgrowth of those affairs rather than exotic rarities sponsored by intellectuals whose ideals are those of the connoisseur.

Among the more essential of these distinctive attributes is the tying up of every meaning to a concrete object or a denotable doing or undergoing. People in everyday life have acted on this principle ever since they have reflected upon conduct. They have become more and more aware in the course of time that the real significance of thoughts and words is to be looked for in some tangible object or some actual deed or something observable going on. It is merely in relation to moral ideals, the "higher life," the "things of the spirit"—all believed to be confined to an area where the natural man's step is unsure—that most men have shown a willingness to accept the experience of emotional elevation, the sense of intellectual achievement, or even a feeling of relief from a burden of guilt, in lieu of an objective reference or an operational test.

The philosophy before us undertakes to move common-sense wisdom toward its full potential orbit. It teaches that not only in practical matters, but everywhere, no word has any other significance than the specific thing to which it points; that every thought, however subtle or fine-spun, and every ideal, however lofty, means the conduct or behavior it is fitted to produce, or the specific experience it is to eventuate in, if it means anything at all. Confucius, Socrates, Jesus, Galileo, Thomas Jefferson, Abraham Lincoln, John Stuart Mill, William James, John Dewey—these are some of the names on the roster of the great ones who have contributed to the advancement of this conception.

SCIENTIFIC HUMANISM

I

ALL HUMANISMS have one thing in common. It is the ideal of realizing mankind's completest development. From here on they diverge. The most far-reaching disagreement turns on the question whether man is or is not absolutely distinct from everything else in the hierarchy of earthly existences. It is at this point that the designation of one humanism as scientific takes on significance.

What does scientific mean in this connection? It means that human beings are viewed naturalistically. They are placed in the natural world along with the lower animals, plants, rocks, minerals, and star clusters. Their intellectual, moral, and esthetic powers, their ideas of decency, their feelings of good will, all they are and aspire to be is looked upon as the consummation of a long evolution from the animal status. Scientific humanism is a form of naturalism.

This is part of the answer. The rest of it is that the scientific humanist is wholeheartedly committed to the use of scientific method. He favors its extension to moral and social problems of every kind, and he believes that a correct understanding of scientific procedure permits this to be done. As a rule this procedure is so narrowly defined that it cannot be applied to human beings in their actuality, to human interests as they are experienced, or even to the world of which human beings are aware. Take Sir Arthur Eddington's example of the elephant sliding down a grassy hillside. From the viewpoint of physics the elephant fades out and is replaced by the reading of the pointer indicating a certain mass. The hillside disappears and its place is taken by the reading of a plumb line against the divisions of a protractor. In the same way the descent becomes a pointer-reading on the seconds' dial of a watch. The result is, says this professor of astronomical physics, that what really slides is a bundle of pointer-readings, and the sliding is a function of space and time measures. There is simply no elephant to slide down a hill and no hill for an elephant to slide down. "The whole subject matter of exact science," as thus conceived, "consists of pointer readings and similar indications."

Ordinarily, when we think of science, it is this kind of science we think of. Our notion of scientific method is our notion of what goes on in physical or chemical laboratories, including what we believe to be the special kind of subject matter dealt with in them. Consequently, we conclude that if man is to be studied scientifically he must be reduced to a mindless, indeed lifeless, concourse of material entities, to atoms, electrons, or even to more abstract elements. And a purely material assemblage or a pattern of abstract entities is certainly anything but human.

Suppose, however, that we broaden our idea of science, as in the end I think we must, to take in every field of knowledge where a sufficiently painstaking effort is made to establish conclusions on a thorough-going examination of relevant fact. In that case the word "scientific" takes on a meaning to correspond. We may then say that a method of investigation is scientific to the extent that it exemplifies the ideal of objective verification. Objective verification is of course a kind of technical shorthand. It has to be broken down into a statement of particulars, and I shall presently attempt to enumerate those particulars.

In line with this revised conception, here are five requirements of objective verification:

(1) Formulation of only such problems as can be solved by an appeal to facts in the external world. (2) Gathering of facts and, as far as possible, all obtainable facts pertinent to the problem. (3) The subjection of facts, inferences, hypotheses, generalizations, to a test admitted to be decisive, publicly applicable, open to the scrutiny of friend or foe. (4) Progressive building up of verification in which different investigators participate. (5) Recognition of the provisional result of even the most exacting demonstration, hence the relativity of all knowledge.

Of these requirements, the one of chief significance is the third. Probably all the others would follow from the appeal to a "publicly applicable" test, rigorously interpreted. Of course, everybody who engages in an investigation worthy of the name appeals to facts and uses criteria to determine what knowledge his facts yield. Not everybody, however, appeals to the kind of facts or uses the kind of criteria of knowledge which can be judged by others than the investigator himself. On the contrary, certain claims to the possession of truth, regarded as the highest truth at that, are frankly declared to rely on criteria which are and must be strictly private. Moreover, there are so-called facts and truths which have logical force providing they can count on a "will to believe." They are powerless to convince a critic who demands to be "shown." In contrast with attitudes like these, scientific method calls for willingness to try conclusions by the application of a test that is recognized as definitive whatever may be the hopes or fears of investigator or critic.

A simple description of scientific procedure by a man of science will make all this clear. It occurs, as it were incidentally, in a discussion by Lewis G. Westgate of a geological problem, and seems to me admirably put:

> Science is a growth, a series of approximations; as it advances some old views are discarded, new views introduced. The discarded views are seen in the light of fuller knowledge to be in error. Inadequate approximations would be a better characterization; they were the best formulation the earlier science could make.

The individual worker

> builds on the work of his predecessors, sometimes on their errors. By his own field work and thought he corrects some of these errors and adds new material. . . . His published results bring the matter out into the open for discussion and criticism by his fellow workers. His errors can be challeneged by other facts unknown to him. His statements may suggest other studies, which may or may not corroborate his views. And so science advances by a process of trial and error, ever working toward a more truthful generalization.

There it is: the collection of data or facts in the outside world; the suggested solution brought out into the open to be tested by critical thinking and active field work; the development of a conclusion supported by cooperative examination and verification; the recognition of the approximate truth of the best established position. Now why should anyone doubt the feasibility of adapting this technique to every field where problems are to be solved? The difficulty of its application grows, to be sure, with the irreducible complexity of certain problems, and with the presence in men of prejudicial habits of thought or feeling which interfere with objective inquiry. But this in no way invalidates the claim that, properly understood, scientific method is applicable to areas from which it is conventionally thought to be barred.

Summarizing this phase of our study we may say that the scientific humanist sees no valid ground for believing men and women to be isolated or insulated creatures in nature. On the contrary, he regards them as strictly integrant to the great complexity of things, living and nonliving, which is commonly spoken of as the world. In conformity with this naturalistic interpretation the scientific humanist rejects both pure Reason and Revelation as sources of light for the understanding of human nature or the art of life. For his part he tries to emulate as best he can in his own field of interest the temper of mind and the workmanship of scientists.

II

We turn now to the other word in the title—humanism. I was just saying that the scientific humanist looks upon man as belonging altogether to the order of nature. I did not say that he thinks man identical with the lower animals, not to speak of lifeless matter. The fact is that no other humanist so consistently exalts man, or looks with equal generosity upon his *humanitas*, upon those attributes which differentiate man from all other living creatures. In a word, the scientific humanist does not lose any of his interest in the human aspect of human nature because he aspires to be scientific in his thinking.

Critics make short work of this avowed dual responsibility. Few of them think it worth while to examine the position. They simply rely upon derogatory names as if these had power to kill. The critics acknowledge that science has a large place in modern life. Sometimes they even advise that education should by all means introduce the student to some knowledge of science. But what do they expect from science? This is their answer: "From scientific investigation we may expect an understanding of scientific knowledge. We are confusing the issue and are demanding what we have no right to ask if we seek to learn from science the goals of human life and of organized society." Rarely do we find anything beyond this bare assertion. Any attempt to extend scientific method beyond the physical substance of things is dubbed "the cult of scientism," a "cult" that "does a disservice to both science and civilization." Perhaps that should kill scientific humanism on the spot, or even better, cause it to crawl off to die in some out-of-the-way corner.

It is, however, an interesting and happy fact that people will try to do, and sometimes succeed in doing, things they are told cannot be done. Either they do not know or do not believe that the things are impossible. The scientific humanist is one of those people. In spite of reiterated arguments purporting to show that the very attempt is irrational, he persists in trying to extend scientific thinking to every kind of individual and social problem. And what is more, he succeeds. Let us consider two or three great human goals or ends, observe how he reinterprets them, and then decide whether his view is as sterile culturally as the opponents charge.

III

Among the great goals of man's long endeavor is truth. In one of his poems Stephen Crane tells of two travelers. The first traveler calls truth a rock, a mighty fortress, and claims that he has often been to it, even to its highest towers. The second traveler likens truth to a phantom, which, though he has long pursued it, has always eluded his grasp. "And I believed the second traveler," says the poet.

This disjunctive proposition—that truth is either absolute or there is no truth at all —puts before us an article of popular theory as widely held, I believe, as any that could be mentioned. Now a little observation of people shows that they hold to this disjunction in a curious manner. If a man feels sure that a belief is true, and another feels as sure that the contrary is true, and neither of them knows of any way to adjudicate the disagreement, both of them will as a rule agree that a thing may be true for one person and untrue for another. In doing so each takes the position that truth is absolute and, at the same time, that there is no truth at all. For surely a type of truth which rests solely upon personal conviction is about as variable as you please. Between such truth and truth as a shadow or a phantom there is nothing to choose.

The scientific humanist refuses to play fast and loose with truth in this manner. He places too high a value on it to let it go at that. Convinced that it is important for men to have *true* ideas, and that *untrue* ideas do them harm, sometimes irreparable harm, he thinks it necessary to reach a better conception of the truth situation. And as he looks about he discovers that the truths men live by are not in either of the classes referred to by Stephen Crane. They are not true in any *absolute* sense, yet are not mere *fantasies*, either. They are as true as the tests by which they are established are reliable; no more true, but also no less true. That is what is meant by calling truth relative; it is dependent truth.

At any rate, the scientific humanist takes the position that when something is spoken of as true it is presumed to measure up to the test by which the true is distinguished from the untrue in some field of operation. He therefore does not spend time trying to make contact with Truth as a spiritual essence which hovers above the earth out of reach of human contamination. He labors to invent and put into practice better and better truth tests, especially in areas of human interest where the need to do this has received and still receives little attention. He does "field work" in the service of social idealism. In his effort to improve truth tests he shows his scientific bent; his humanistic bent is shown in the determination to extend the use of such improved truth tests to all the phases of individual and communal experience where the better potentialities of human beings may either turn out well or come to naught.

This buckling down to the task of furthering the true as against the false in the big and little affairs of everyday, although it is not highly regarded by the devotee of absolute and abstract Truth, happens to be the kind of truth-concern upon which progress in the attainment of truer beliefs, attitudes, and ideas depends. Truth from this point of view is a collective name for a sum of particular truths, as true as they are and no truer. Since the scientific humanist consistently endeavors to improve the standard of the true precisely where there is greatest need that this be done, it should be obvious that truth has a place of unusual honor in scientific humanism.

IV

Another of the great human goals is moral character. In that impressive book, *The Dawn of Conscience*, J. E. Breasted undertakes to show how the idea of right, as distinguished from wrong in the ethical sense, had its origin in Egypt 4000 or more years ago. Early in Occidental history authority in the realm of moral ideas and ideals was taken over by church religion. In the course of time secular life took it away again. But long association with theology left its mark. The belief, not to say illusion, for which this association is responsible, that morality must be defined and vitalized "from on high," is still with us. Likewise the alleged antagonism between character and wants or desires. Innumerable people continue to believe that there is something shameful, if not pathological, about desires. What they spontaneously think of when they hear the word moral or immoral is sex. Sex desire, taken to be the most unruly, leaps to the foreground of the mind because the inherited conception of morality is essentially the mastery of desire by something in man higher than desire.

The scientific humanist does what he can to liberate himself from this prejudice against desires. He accepts with hope the fact that men and women have wants and desires. He believes that the human energies called desires are the only driving power we have to help us toward the good life—the happy life as well as the noble life. The good life involves more than desires: intelligence, knowledge, imagination, and at its best, creativeness of a high order. But desires are the life of the whole business. Not to recognize this openly and frankly has no end of unhappy results. Desires are made to work themselves out surreptitiously, abnormally. Maliciousness, coarseness, brutality can cloak themselves in sanctity. The fanatic gets the opportunity to step forth as moral dictator.

Does the scientific humanist then refuse to divide desires into good and bad? In one sense, yes; in another sense, no. Anything a person wants he wants because it appears good. That is why he wants it. I say "appears," rather than "is," for no better reason than to avoid immediate disagreement. Whether it is wants or needs or obligations he goes out for, he believes them good to have. If he believed them bad to have he would not want them. However, everyone soon finds out, and finds out again and again, that the wanted, the good, can not be isolated from antecedents and consequences. These antecedents and consequences may in certain cases not be wanted at all. And sometimes upon reflection the not-wanted aspect so outweighs the wanted that the offering as a whole fails to appeal and so is not regarded as good. And every person soon finds out that his own wants and the wants of others overlap in ways to further or to thwart each other. It turns out, moreover, that every individual is interested in wants of other individuals, wanting some of them satisfied and some not. Thus the wanted and the not-wanted are frequently tied up in one package.

A desire is morally bad when the desirer insists on having what he wants in disregard of his want's unwanted concomitants. A desire is bad when the desirer insists upon having what he wants no matter what holes he tears in the fabric of human interdependence without which no life can approach all-over satisfactoriness.

This interpretation of character and the good life implies that everybody is desirous of finding life as livable as possible; that the goal of life, to put it in a word, is happiness. Is this a valid assumption? There are those who deny it. Alexander Meiklejohn, for example, contends that the objective is not happiness but a personal quality which he calls "excellence." His moral philosophy is socially conscious, clean and fine-spirited, free from the conceit of learning, high-minded and intentionally austere. I introduce a quotation from his book *What Does America Mean?* in order to sharpen the humanistic argument for the dignity of desires.

In Mr. Meiklejohns' view, "It is not imperative that any individual, or any nation, or even the race itself, should continue to be happy, should even continue to exist. It is imperative that so long as we live, we do so with taste and intelligence, with fineness and generosity." And the reason is this: "Many things are worse than unhappiness. But nothing is worse than being contemptible." The scientific humanist agrees with the college student who, having read Mr. Meiklejohn, made this comment: "Yes, let us include among our desires the desire for taste, intelligence, fineness, generosity, for they are helps in the production of happiness. Many things are worse than being contemptible. But nothing is worse than being unhappy. The worst thing about being contemptible is that it makes you so damn unhappy."

Looking back over this section, it is obvious that the analysis is oversimple. Possibly it is not too simple for the present purpose, which is to spotlight the distinctive element in the moral attitude from the standpoint under review. No desire liveth to itself or dieth to itself. At bottom the difference between the moral and the immoral or nonmoral attitude is the presence in the former, and its absence from the latter, of scrutiny and appraisal of desires with regard to their effect upon what was just called all-over satisfactoriness. Satisfactoriness may of course be envisaged broadly or narrowly; may be restricted to pleasurable excitement, physical convenience, social prominence, the exercise of power, or include appreciation of art, music, literature, religion, philosophy. It may be bounded by the welfare of the self or the family, or be touched by interests as wide as the world. While the practical necessity of acting will inevitably impose limits, the measure of moral personality is sensitiveness to the consequences of desiring what is desired. Naturalistic in outlook as scientific humanism is, and thus at pains to vindicate desires, it is, being also humanistic in outlook, at equal pains to emphasize the need for criticism and discipline. The ideal is that desires shall spring up spontaneously, freely, and differently in response to the richest, most various goods and that this dynamic exuberance shall be matched by well developed habits of critical appraisal and intelligent choice.

We conclude then, that the moral ideal here outlined cannot fairly be described as a cheap, superficially conceived, or easily realized ideal. To commit oneself to it is to undertake a difficult, complicated, often elusive assignment. Even moderate success in it calls for thoughtful application and takes time. One may know at a given moment what it is one wants, but whether it would still be wanted were there a looking before and after, whether the wanted is also, when well considered, the wantable, that is not so easy to be clear about. Still, with some people it becomes second nature to seek a genuinely richer, worthier, happier life-experience, and they show remarkable expertness in discovering the right means and ends. It would be a long step in advance if public education naturally introduced the young to this way of life and prepared them for effectiveness in it. There are teachers who do just that, and some day they may be the majority. Some day, too, the world of affairs may encourage instead of discourage moral progress. And while in some respects each one must define and realize the good life for himself, no one can attain his moral growth except in reciprocal relationship with other human beings, so that there is the additional problem of making our way together toward a social arrangement which provides the indispensable opportunities.

All this is part of the scientific humanist's moral program. It is an ironical fact that the humanist who regards it as essential that all wants be related to disciplined taste, and who is everlastingly stressing the need for informed criticism of the self and of society, should be accused of working against moral idealism and moral integrity.

V

We come to the end of this sketch with whole areas of important endeavor left untouched. Scientific humanistic principles and methods are of course applicable to those omitted areas. Some persons will nevertheless remain unpersuaded. They are sure to complain that scientific humanism is not enough. And the complaint is understandable. Scientific civilization, so widely extolled, still shows glaring faults. Innumerable people get little indeed out of living, and all they are promised in the scheme of life most prominently and alluringly set before them, even could they attain it, is far less than the human spirit craves. Can we take pride in the global strife which scientific civilization has made possible? Are we to enjoy the spectacle of millions of human beings deliberately engaged in killing each other? Is there anything reassuring in a colossal waste of economic goods or in the destruction of the best that artistic genius has achieved through centuries of labor? No, there is nothing unnatural in the conclusion that any view which is allied to scientific civilization is not enough; that to be really adequate a way of life must transcend life, must make good its shortcomings by laying hold upon the realities of a promised experience that is to begin when the earthly experience is over.

The complaint, I repeat, is understandable, but it is a pointless and futile complaint unless a better philosophy can be shown to be available. What if this is a vain hope? What if it is an unrealizable dream? What if scientific humanism, although it does not set before us all that can be imagined, does offer the best we can actually get? "Impostor for impostor," George Bernard Shaw flippantly declares, "I prefer the mystic to the scientist—the man who at least has the decency to call his nonsense a mystery, to him who pretends that it is ascertained, weighed, measured, analyzed fact." Others assert, "There are no atheists in foxholes," as if this were complimentary to God. A gull landing on the head of a man adrift in a rubber boat is supposed to have established theistic cosmology. Well-known theological philosophers urge a return to a time when men are said to have preferred spiritual worth and inner peace to physical comfort and outer power. But Shaw's irresponsible witticism is not quite a philosophy of life. Foxholes are at best temporary domiciles. Gulls are not unfailingly responsive to prayer. The men on the raft with Seaman Izzi called upon God in vain. Two of them finally died of exhaustion, and the three who survived were not picked up in answer to prayer, so far as one can tell. As for returning to the theism of the past, the clock of experience cannot be turned back. It has never been done in human history.

If wishes could make universes we might have the one we want and exactly as we want it. But we have learned a few things in the last three hundred years, and it is just possible that in the light of what we have learned scientific humanism will have to be enough. Super-earthly idealism was once compatible with the best established knowledge of the day. For better, for worse, our ancestors ventured beyond the walls of that knowledge and the gates were shut upon their descendants forever. Truth, goodness, beauty, individual personality, these remain and must always remain among the primary objectives of a life in search of lasting happiness. All of them, however, have had to be sought in a vaster world because our forbears refused to stay at home. And every value of life must henceforth be sought in the strange new world that is shaping itself about us.

One of the foremost educators of our time, Boyd H. Bode, has long been telling college students, prospective teachers, that the supreme contemporary issue is whether the democratic way of life as a moral system can stand on its own feet. The choice, as he sees the situation, is between a naturalistically based democracy or something worse, not something better. Since he began life in Iowa I cannot believe that this is a prejudice to which he was conditioned as a boy. He could scarcely have picked it up during his college days in Michigan or as a graduate student at Cornell. I have not consulted him to find out, but the probabilities are that, trained as he had been in the traditional religious outlook, exposed as he then was to naturalistic modernity, and sensitive to both influences, he grew to appreciate the fact that nothing can in the end save the great ideals of the human spirit but their profound reinterpretation. In setting forth that reinterpretation he became a pioneer of scientific humanism. The persistent theme of his lectures and articles and books has been the many-sided problem of how to increase the meaning and joy in life on earth by making use of the best intellectual and moral tools. In the educational philosophy of this keen, most clear-headed and mature American we have a striking and happy illustration of the kind of high-mindedness and objective-mindedness that can work hand in hand in the world as it has now to be faced.

So it all comes to this. Scientific humanism is not a bleak materialism and it is not a superstitious or an intellectualized spiritualism. The scientific humanist does not pretend that every experience of life can be forced into a test tube or that every interest can be weighed on a scales. He knows that something in everything always escapes the technique of measurement. It must be directly appreciated or go unnoticed. And when he contemplates the whole of things he exclaims as Heraclitus did when philosophy was young: "Nature loves to hide." He says, with Gilbert Murray who belongs to the present age: "The life of man can be divided, like the old maps of the world, into the charted and the uncharted. The charted is finite and the other infinite." But he knows also that there is no way of escaping the new world-order or the new moral and intellectual climate, and that man's aspirational life must adjust itself to these conditions or lose its redemptive power. Scientific humanism is the name for his determination to stand up to the task and the opportunity.

John Dewey

John Dewey, Charles S. Peirce, and William James stand together as the three great American empiricists of our age. Of these three philosophers, Dewey is most directly committed to bringing the spirit and method of science into the moral life. Accepting the pragmatic principle of Peirce that the meaning of an idea is to be found only in the observable consequences in behavior it produces, Dewey insists that our moral convictions as well as our scientific theories must be examined in this concrete and specific fashion. The moral quality of any act, he argues, is determined by its consequences; it is good only if it produces good results. While honesty is usually the best policy, there are obviously many situations in which men do not and perhaps should not tell the truth. It may well be that laziness is more immoral for a college student than drinking. In any case for a man who adopts the scientific attitude, what is right or wrong can only be known by looking at the specific results of an act in the life of the individual.

And intelligence is needed, Dewey points out, both to foresee possible results and to determine what results actually do occur. Thus Dewey's empiricism in morals leads him to a basic agreement with Socrates: before we can be good, we must know what we are doing, we must be intelligent. In the selection we reprint from Reconstruction in Philosophy, *Dewey develops such a moral empiricism, maintaining that morals become more difficult, more demanding—but also more meaningful—when intelligence and scientific method are recognized as essential in the moral life.*

Born in Vermont in 1859, just before the Civil War, Dewey took his Ph.D. in philosophy at Johns Hopkins in 1884. Early in his career he became head of the department of philosophy at the University of Chicago and there set up the experimental or "laboratory" school which had so marked an effect on educational philosophy in America at the turn of the century. In 1905 he joined the faculty of Columbia University where for more than forty-five years he was a distinguished and controversial figure. During these years at Columbia Dewey took an active interest in the causes that he felt might help make American political and social democracy a reality, and was frequently branded a radical by those who disgreed with him. He died in 1952 at the age of ninety-three.

While at Chicago Dewey published, with Edgar Tufts, a text in Ethics *(1908) which was one of the influential books on the subject for a generation. In such later works as* Reconstruction in Philosophy *(1920),* Human Nature and Conduct *(1922), and* The Quest for Certainty *(1929), he developed more fully the empirical and pragmatic approach to morals adopted in that early text and seen in the present selection.*

RECONSTRUCTION IN MORALS

I

THE BLUNT ASSERTION that every moral situation is a unique situation having its own irreplaceable good may seem not merely blunt but preposterous. For the established tradition teaches that it is precisely the irregularity of special cases which makes necessary the guidance of conduct by universals, and that the essence of the virtuous

[From John Dewey, *Reconstruction in Philosophy*, Chapter VII, abridged. Boston: Beacon Press, 1920. Reprinted by permission of the publisher.]

disposition is willingness to subordinate every particular case to adjudication by a fixed principle. It would then follow that submission of a generic end and law to determination by the concrete situation entails complete confusion and unrestrained licentiousness. Let us, however, follow the pragmatic rule, and in order to discover the meaning of the idea ask for its consequences. Then it surprisingly turns out that the primary significance of the unique and morally ultimate character of the concrete situation is to transfer the weight and burden of morality to intelligence. It does not destroy responsibility; it only locates it. A moral situation is one in which judgment and choice are required antecedently to overt action. The practical meaning of the situation—that is to say the action needed to satisfy it—is not self-evident. It has to be searched for. There are conflicting desires and alternative apparent goods. What is needed is to find the right course of action, the right good. Hence, inquiry is exacted: observation of the detailed makeup of the situation; analysis into its diverse factors; clarification of what is obscure; discounting of the more insistent and vivid traits; tracing the consequences of the various modes of action that suggest themselves; regarding the decision reached as hypothetical and tentative until the anticipated or supposed consequences which led to its adoption have been squared with actual consequences. This inquiry is intelligence. Our moral failures go back to some weakness of disposition, some absence of sympathy, some one-sided bias that makes us perform the judgment of the concrete case carelessly or perversely. Wide sympathy, keen sensitiveness, persistence in the face of the disagreeable, balance of interests enabling us to undertake the work of analysis and decision intelligently are the distinctively moral traits—the virtues or moral excellencies.

It is worth noting once more that the underlying issue is, after all, only the same as that which has been already threshed out in physical inquiry. There too it long seemed as if rational assurance and demonstration could be attained only if we began with universal conceptions and subsumed particular cases under them. The men who initiated the methods of inquiry that are now everywhere adopted were denounced in their day (and sincerely) as subverters of truth and foes of science. If they have won in the end, it is because, as has already been pointed out, the method of universals confirmed prejudices and sanctioned ideas that had gained currency irrespective of evidence for them; while placing the initial and final weight upon the individual case, stimulated painstaking inquiry into facts and examination of principles. In the end, loss of eternal truths was more than compensated for in the accession of quotidian facts. After all, then, we are only pleading for the adoption in moral reflection of the logic that has been proved to make for security, stringency and fertility in passing judgments upon physical phenomena. And the reason is the same. The old method in spite of its nominal and esthetic worship of reason discouraged reason, because it hindered the operation of scrupulous and unremitting inquiry.

More definitely, the transfer of the burden of the moral life from following rules or pursuing fixed ends over to the detection of the ills that need remedy in a special case and the formation of plans and methods for dealing with them, eliminates the causes which have kept moral theory controversial, and which have also kept it remote from helpful contact with the exigencies of practice. The theory of fixed ends inevitably leads thought into the bog of disputes that cannot be settled. If there is one *summum bonum*, one supreme end, what is it? To consider this problem is to place ourselves in the midst of controversies that are as acute now as they were two thousand years ago. Suppose we take a seemingly more empirical view, and say that while there is not a single end, there also are not as many as there are specific situations that require amelioration; but there are a number of such natural goods as health, wealth, honor or good name, friendship, esthetic appreciation, learning and such moral goods as justice, temperance, benevolence, etc. What or who is to decide the right of way when these ends conflict with one another, as they are sure to do? Shall we resort to the method that once brought such disrepute upon the whole business of ethics: Casuistry? Or shall we have recourse to what Bentham well called the *ipse dixit* method: the arbitrary preference of this or that person for this or that end? Or shall we be forced to arrange them all in an order of degrees from the highest good down to the least precious? Again we find ourselves in the middle of unreconciled disputes with no indication of the way out.

Meantime, the special moral perplexities where the aid of intelligence is required go unenlightened. We cannot seek or attain health, wealth, learning, justice or kindness in general. Action is always specific, concrete, individualized, unique. And consequently judgments as to acts to be performed must be similarly specific. To say that a man seeks health or justice is only to say that he seeks to live healthily or justly. These things, like truth, are adverbial. They are modifiers of action in special cases. How to live healthily or justly is a matter which differs with every person. It varies with his past experience, his opportunities, his temperamental and acquired weaknesses and abilities. Not man in general but a particular man suffering from some particular disability aims to live healthily, and consequently health cannot mean for him exactly what it means for any other mortal. Healthy living is not something to be attained by itself apart from other ways of living. A man needs to be healthy *in* his life, not apart from it, and what does life mean except the aggregate of his pursuits and activities? A man who aims at health as a distinct end becomes a valetudinarian, or a fanatic, or a mechanical performer of exercises, or an athlete so one-sided that his pursuit of bodily development injures his heart. When the endeavor to realize a so-called end does not temper and color all other activities, life is portioned out into strips and fractions. Certain acts and times are devoted to getting health, others to cultivating religion, others to seeking learning, to being a good citizen, a devotee of fine art and so on. This is the only logical alternative to subordinating all aims to the accomplishment of one alone—fanaticism. This is out of fashion at present, but who can say how much of distraction and dissipation in life, and how much of its hard and narrow rigidity is the outcome of men's failure to realize that each situation has its own unique end and that the whole personality should be concerned with it? Surely, once more, what a man needs is to live healthily, and this result so affects all the activities of his life that it cannot be set up as a separate and independent good.

Nevertheless the general notions of health, disease, justice, artistic culture are of great importance: Not, however, because this or that case may be brought exhaustively under a single head and its specific traits shut out, but because generalized science provides a man as physician and artist and citizen, with questions to ask, investigations to make, and enables him to understand the meaning of what he sees. Just in the degree in which a physician is an artist in his work he uses his science, no matter how extensive and accurate, to furnish him with tools of inquiry into the individual case, and with methods of forecasting a method of dealing with it. Just in the degree in which, no matter how great his learning, he subordinates the individual case to some classification of diseases and some generic rule of treatment, he sinks to the level of the routine mechanic. His intelligence and his action become rigid, dogmatic, instead of free and flexible.

II

Moral goods and ends exist only when something has to be done. The fact that something has to be done proves that there are deficiencies, evils in the existent situation. This ill is just the specific ill that it is. It never is an exact duplicate of anything else. Consequently the good of the situation has to be discovered, projected and attained on the basis of the exact defect and trouble to be rectified. It cannot intelligently be injected into the situation from without. Yet it is the part of wisdom to compare different cases, to gather together the ills from which humanity suffers, and to generalize the corresponding goods into classes. Health, wealth, industry, temperance, amiability, courtesy, learning, esthetic capacity, initiative, courage, patience, enterprise, thoroughness and a multitude of other generalized ends are acknowledged as goods. But the *value* of this systematization is intellectual or analytic. Classifications *suggest* possible traits to be on the lookout for in studying a particular case; they suggest methods of action to be tried in removing the inferred causes of ill. They are tools of insight; their value is in promoting an individualized response in the individual situation.

Morals are not a catalogue of acts nor a set of rules to be applied like drugstore prescriptions or cookbook recipes. The need in morals is for specific methods of inquiry and of contrivance: Methods of inquiry to locate difficulties and evils; methods of contrivance to form plans to be used as working hypotheses in dealing with them. And the pragmatic import of the logic of individualized situations, each having its own irreplaceable good and principle, is to transfer the attention of theory from preoccupation with general conceptions to the problem of developing effective methods of inquiry.

Two ethical consequences of great moment should be remarked. The belief in fixed values has bred a division of ends into intrinsic and instrumental, of those that are really worth while in themselves and those that are of importance only as means to intrinsic goods. Indeed, it is often thought to be the very beginning of wisdom, of moral discrimination, to make this distinction. Dialectically, the distinction is interesting and seems harmless. But carried into practice it has an import that is tragic.

No one can possibly estimate how much of the obnoxious materialism and brutality of our economic life is due to the fact that economic ends have been regarded as *merely* instrumental. When they are recognized to be as intrinsic and final in their place as any others, then it will be seen that they are capable of idealization, and that if life is to be worth while, they must acquire ideal and intrinsic value. Esthetic, religious and other "ideal" ends are now thin and meager or else idle and luxurious because of the separation from "instrumental" or economic ends. Only in connection with the latter can they be woven into the texture of daily life and made substantial and pervasive. The vanity and irresponsibility of values that are merely final and not also in turn means to the enrichment of other occupations of life ought to be obvious. But now the doctrine of "higher" end gives aid, comfort and support to every socially isolated and socially irresponsible scholar, specialist, esthete and religionist. It protects the vanity and irresponsibility of his calling from observation by others and by himself. The moral deficiency of the calling is transformed into a cause of admiration and gratulation.

The other generic change lies in doing away once for all with the traditional distinction between moral goods, like the virtues, and natural goods like health, economic security, art, science and the like. . . . But the experimental logic when carried into morals makes every quality that is judged to be good according as it contributes to amelioration of existing ills. And in so doing, it enforces the moral meaning of natural science.

When all is said and done in criticism of present social deficiencies, one may well wonder whether the root difficulty does not lie in the separation of natural and moral science. When physics, chemistry, biology, medicine, contribute to the detection of concrete human woes and to the development of plans for remedying them and relieving the human estate, they become moral; they become part of the apparatus of moral inquiry or science. The latter then loses its peculiar flavor of the didactic and pedantic; its ultra-moralistic and hortatory tone. It loses its thinness and shrillness as well as its vagueness. It gains agencies that are efficacious. But the gain is not confined to the side of moral science. Natural science loses its divorce from humanity; it becomes itself humanistic in quality. It is something to be pursued not in a technical and specialized way for what is called truth for its own sake, but with the sense of its social bearing, its intellectual indispensableness. It is technical only in the sense that it provides the technique of social and moral engineering.

When the consciousness of science is fully impregnated with the consciousness of human value, the greatest dualism which now weighs humanity down, the split between the material, the mechanical, the scientific and the moral and ideal will be destroyed. Human forces that now waver because of this division will be unified and reinforced. As long as ends are not thought of as individualized according to specific needs and opportunities, the mind will be content with abstractions, and the adequate stimulus to the moral or social use of natural sciences and historical data will be lacking. But when attention is concentrated upon the diversified concretes, recourse to all intellectual materials needed to clear up the special cases will be imperative. At the same time that morals are made to focus in intelligence, things intellectual are moralized. The vexatious and wasteful conflict between naturalism and humanism is terminated.

III

These general considerations may be amplified. First: Inquiry, discovery take the same place in morals that they have come to occupy in sciences of nature. Validation, demonstration become experimental, a matter of consequences. Reason, always an honorific term in ethics, becomes actualized in the methods by which the needs and conditions, the obstacles and resources, of situations are scrutinized in detail, and intelligent plans of improvement are worked out. Remote and abstract generalities promote jumping at conclusions, "anticipations of nature." Bad consequences are then deplored as due to natural perversity and untoward fate. But shifting the issue to analysis of a specific situation makes inquiry obligatory and alert observation of consequences imperative. No past decision nor old principle can ever be wholly relied upon to justify a course of action. No amount of pains taken in forming a purpose in a definite case is final; the consequences of its adoption must be carefully noted, and a purpose held only as a working hypothesis until results confirm its rightness. Mistakes are no longer either mere unavoidable accidents to be mourned or moral sins to be expiated and forgiven. They are lessons in wrong methods of using intelligence and instructions as to a better course in the future. They are indications of the need of revision, development, readjustment. Ends grow, standards of judgment are improved. Man is under just as much obligation to develop his most advanced standards and ideals as to use conscientiously those which he already possesses. Moral life is protected from falling into formalism and rigid repetition. It is rendered flexible, vital, growing.

In the second place, every case where moral action is required becomes of equal moral importance and urgency with every other. If the need and deficiencies of a specific situation indicate improvement of health as the end and good, then for that situation health is the ultimate and supreme good. It is no means to something else. It is a final and intrinsic value. The same thing is true of improvement of economic status, of making a living, of attending to business and family demands—all of the things which under the sanction of fixed ends have been rendered of secondary and merely instrumental value, and so relatively base and unimportant. Anything that in a given situation is an end and good at all is of equal worth, rank and dignity with every other good of any other situation, and deserves the same intelligent attention.

We note thirdly the effect in destroying the roots of Phariseeism. We are so accustomed to thinking of this as deliberate hypocrisy that we overlook its intellectual premises. The conception which looks for the end of action within the circumstances of the actual situation will not have the same measure of judgment for all cases. When one factor of the situation is a person of trained mind and large resources, more will be expected than with a person of backward mind and uncultured experience. The absurdity of applying the same standard of moral judgment to savage peoples that is used with civilized will be apparent. No individual or group will be judged by whether they come up to or fall short of some fixed result, but by the direction in which they are moving. The bad man is the man who no matter how good he *has* been is beginning to deteriorate, to grow less good. The good man is the man who no matter how morally unworthy he *has* been is moving to become better. Such a conception makes one severe in judging himself and humane in judging others. It excludes that arrogance which always accompanies judgment based on degree of approximation to fixed ends.

In the fourth place, the process of growth, of improvement and progress, rather than the static outcome and result, becomes the significant thing. Not health as an end fixed once and for all, but the needed improvement in health—a continual process—is the end and good. The end is no longer a terminus or limit to be reached. It is the active process of transforming the existent situation. Not perfection as a final goal, but the ever-enduring process of perfecting, maturing, refining is the aim in living. Honesty, industry, temperance, justice, like health, wealth, and learning, are not goods to be possessed as they would be if they expressed fixed ends to be attained. They are directions of change in the quality of experience. Growth itself is the only moral "end."

3

LOGICAL POSITIVISM

Rudolf Carnap

Rudolf Carnap is probably the ablest exponent in this country of the philosophical position generally known as logical positivism. This is a vigorous contemporary movement in philosophy—the term itself appeared for the first time in 1930—which derives historically from the interaction between two university groups, the "Vienna Circle" and the Cambridge School of Analysis, during a creative period of about fifteen years. A seminar started in 1922 by Moritz Schlick when he became professor of philosophy at the University of Vienna gradually grew into the Vienna Circle. Its original members were scientists who had become philosophers or practicing scientists with an interest in philosophy. Thoroughly scientific and empirical in spirit, they found the thought of such mathematical logicians as Charles Sanders Peirce and Ernst Schroeder quite congenial but were influenced predominantly by two men at Cambridge University, A. N. Whitehead and Bertrand Russell.

Two aspects of logical positivism should be distinguished: a negative, critical, almost contemptuous attitude toward the traditional disciplines of metaphysics and ethics, and a positive, admiring attitude toward logic and the sciences. Put together these lead to the view that philosophy when properly understood is actually the logic of science. Its major task, according to the Cambridge School of Analysis, is to press forward in the tradition of Russell and Whitehead's Principia Mathematica *and do for other disciplines what that work accomplished so admirably for logic and mathematics.*

Logical positivism or, as its exponents now prefer to call it, "logical empiricism," is thus the clearest and most significant outcome of the impact of scientific thought upon contemporary philosophy; yet it is not easy to find a discussion of its major principles that can be read with profit by one who is relatively unfamiliar with philosophical concepts and terminology. Statements of this position all depend heavily upon closely reasoned argument and a large use of technical terminology. The selection reprinted here from Carnap's Philosophy and Logical Syntax *(1935) is one of the best available for the layman.*

Born in Germany in 1891 and educated at Jena, Carnap came to the University of Vienna in 1927 and participated actively in the discussions of the Vienna Circle. At that time Ludwig Wittgenstein was its outstanding member, and his Tractatus Logico-Philosophicus, *published in 1922, was the most important statement of its philosophy. Very soon the doctrines of logical positivism spread to England and America. Schlick visited the United States in 1929; Wittgenstein moved to England in the same year and became a professor of philosophy at Cambridge University in 1939. Carnap came to the United States in 1936 as professor at the University of Chicago; in 1954 he moved to the University of California in Los Angeles. Trained originally in physics, he is also an accomplished logician, author of more than a dozen scholarly books, and has exerted a powerful influence upon philosophical thought in this country.*

THE REJECTION OF METAPHYSICS

I. *Verifiability*

THE PROBLEMS of philosophy as usually dealt with are of very different kinds. From the point of view which I am here taking we may distinguish mainly three kinds of problems and doctrines in traditional philosophy. For the sake of simplicity we shall call these parts *Metaphysics-Psychology*, and *Logic*. Or, rather, there are not three distinct regions, but three sorts of components which in most theses and questions are combined: a metaphysical, a psychological, and a logical component.

The considerations that follow belong to the third region: we are here carrying out *Logical Analysis*. The function of logical analysis is to analyze all knowledge, all assertions of science and of everyday life, in order to make clear the sense of each such assertion and the connections between them. One of the principal tasks of the logical analysis of a given proposition is to find out the method of verification for that proposition. The question is: What reasons can there be to assert this proposition; or: How can we become certain as to its truth or falsehood? This question is called by the philosophers the epistemological question; epistemology or the philosophical theory of knowledge is nothing other than a special part of logical analysis, usually combined with some psychological questions concerning the process of knowing.

What, then, is the method of verification of a proposition? Here we have to distinguish between two kinds of verification: direct and indirect. If the question is about a proposition which asserts something about a present perception, e.g., "Now I see a red square on a blue ground," then the proposition can be tested directly by my present perception. If at present I do see a red square on a blue ground, the proposition is directly verified by this seeing; if I do not see that, it is disproved. To be sure, there are still some serious problems in connection with direct verification. We will however not touch on them here, but give our attention to the question of *indirect* verification, which is more important for our purposes. A proposition *P* which is not directly verifiable can only be verified by direct verification of propositions deduced from *P* together with other already verified propositions.

Let us take the proposition P_1: "This key is made of iron." There are many ways of verifying this proposition; e.g.: I place the key near a magnet; then I perceive that the key is attracted. Here the deduction is made in this way:

[From Rudolf Carnap, *Philosophy and Logical Syntax*, Chapter I. London: Routledge and Kegan Paul, 1935. Copyright 1935 by C. K. Ogden and reprinted by permission of the Executors of his Estate.]

Premises:

P_1: "This key is made of iron;" the proposition to be examined.

P_2: "If an iron thing is placed near a magnet, it is attracted;" this is a physical law, already verified.

P_3: "This object—a bar—is a magnet;" proposition already verified.

P_4: "The key is placed near the bar;" this is now directly verified by our observation.

From these four premises we can deduce the conclusion:

P_5: "The key will now be attracted by the bar."

This proposition is a prediction which can be examined by observation. If we look, we either observe the attraction or we do not. In the first case we have found a positive instance, an instance of verification of the proposition P_1 under consideration; in the second case we have a negative instance, an instance of disproof of P_1.

In the first case the examination of the proposition P_1 is not finished. We may repeat the examination by means of a magnet, *i.e.* we may deduce other propositions similar to P_5 by the help of the same or similar premises as before. After that, or instead of that, we may make an examination by electrical tests, or by mechanical, chemical, or optical tests, etc. If in these further investigations all instances turn out to be positive, the certainty of the proposition P_1 gradually grows. We may soon come to a degree of certainty sufficient for all practical purposes, but *absolute* certainty we can never attain. The number of instances deducible from P_1 by the help of other propositions already verified or directly verifiable is *infinite*. Therefore there is always a possibility of finding in the future a negative instance, however small its probability may be. Thus the proposition P_1 *can never be completely verified.* For this reason it is called an *hypothesis.*

So far we have considered an individual proposition concerning one single thing. If we take a general proposition concerning all things or events at whatever time and place, a so-called natural *law,* it is still clearer that the number of examinable instances is infinite and so the proposition is an hypothesis.

Every assertion *P* in the wide field of science has this character, that it either asserts something about present perceptions or other experiences, and therefore is verifiable by them, or that propositions about future perceptions are deducible from *P* together with some other already verified propositions. If a scientist should venture to make an assertion from which no perceptive propositions could be deduced, what should we say to that? Suppose, e.g., he asserts that there is not only a gravitational field having an effect on bodies according to the known laws of gravitation, but also a *levitational field,* and on being asked what sort of effect this levitational field has, according to his theory, he answers that there is no observable effect; in other words, he confesses his inability to give rules according to which we could deduce perceptive propositions from his assertion. In that case our reply is: your assertion is no assertion at all; it does not speak about anything; it is nothing but a series of empty words; it is simply without sense.

It is true that he may have images and even feelings connected with his words. This fact may be of psychological importance; logically, it is irrelevant. What gives theoretical meaning to a proposition is not the attendant images and thoughts, but the possibility of deducing from it perceptive propositions, in other words, the possibility of verification. To give sense to a proposition the presence of images is not sufficient; it is not even necessary. We have no actual image of the electro-magnetic field, nor even, I should say, of the gravitational field. Nevertheless the propositions which physicists assert about these fields have a perfect sense, because perceptive propositions are deducible from them. I by no means object to the proposition just mentioned about a levitational field that we do not know how to imagine or conceive such a field. My only objection to that proposition is that we are not told how to verify it.

II. *Metaphysics*

What we have been doing so far is *logical analysis*. Now we are going to apply these considerations not to propositions of physics as before, but to propositions of *metaphysics*. Thus our investigation belongs to *logic*, to the third of the three parts of philosophy spoken about before, but the *objects* of this investigation belong to the first part.

I will call *metaphysical* all those propositions which claim to represent knowledge about something which is over or beyond all experience, *e.g.*, about the real Essence of things, about Things in themselves, the Absolute, and such like. I do not include in metaphysics those theories—sometimes called metaphysical—whose object is to arrange the most general propositions of the various regions of scientific knowledge in a well-ordered system; such theories belong actually to the field of empirical science, not of philosophy, however daring they may be. The sort of propositions I wish to denote as metaphysical may most easily be made clear by some examples: "The Essence and Principle of the world is Water," said Thales; "Fire," said Heraclitus; "the Infinite," said Anaximander; "Number," said Pythagoras. "All things are nothing but shadows of eternal ideas which themselves are in a spaceless and timeless sphere," is a doctrine of Plato. From the Monists we learn: "There is only one principle on which all that is, is founded"; but the Dualists tell us: "There are two principles." The Materialists say: "All that is, is in its essence material," but the Spiritualists say: "All that is, is spiritual." To metaphysics (in our sense of the word) belong the principal doctrines of Spinoza, Schelling, Hegel, and—to give at least one name of the present time—Bergson.

Now let us examine this kind of proposition from the point of view of *verifiability*. It is easy to realize that such propositions are not verifiable. From the proposition: "The Principle of the world is Water" we are not able to deduce any proposition asserting any perceptions or feelings or experiences whatever which may be expected for the future. Therefore the proposition, "The Principle of the world is Water," asserts nothing at all. It is perfectly analogous to the proposition in the fictive example above about the levitational field and therefore it has no more sense than that proposition. The Water-Metaphysician—as we may call him—has no doubt many images connected with his doctrine; but they cannot give sense to the proposition, any more than they could in the case of the levitational field. Metaphysicians cannot avoid making their propositions nonverifiable, because if they made them verifiable, the decision about the truth or falsehood of their doctrines would depend upon experience and therefore belong to the region of empirical science. This consequence they wish to avoid, because they pretend to teach knowledge which is of a higher level than that of empirical science. Thus they are compelled to cut all connection between their propositions and experience; and precisely by this procedure they deprive them of any sense.

III. *Problems of Reality*

So far I have considered only examples of such propositions as are usually called metaphysical. The judgment I have passed on these propositions, namely, that they have no empirical sense, may perhaps appear not very astonishing, and even trivial. But it is to be feared that the reader will experience somewhat more difficulty in agreement when I now proceed to apply that judgment also to philosophical doctrines of the type which is usually called epistemological. I prefer to call them also metaphysical because of their similarity, in the point under consideration, to the propositions usually so called. What I have in mind are the doctrines of Realism, Idealism, Solipsism, Positivism and the like, taken in their traditional form as asserting or denying the Reality of something. The Realist asserts the Reality of the external world; the Idealist denies it. The Realist—usually at least—asserts also the Reality of other minds; the Solipsist—an especially radical Idealist—denies it, and asserts that only his own mind or consciousness is real. Have these assertions sense?

Perhaps it may be said that assertions about the reality or unreality of something occur also in empirical science, where they are examined in an empirical way, and that therefore they have sense. This is quite true. But we have to distinguish between two concepts of reality, one occurring in empirical propositions and the other occurring in the philosophical propositions just mentioned. When a zoologist asserts the reality of kangaroos, his assertion means that there are things of a certain sort which can be found and perceived at certain times and places; in other words that there are objects of a certain sort which are elements of the space-time system of the physical world. This assertion is of course verifiable; by empirical investigation every zoologist arrives at a positive verification, independent of whether he is a Realist or an Idealist. Between the Realist and the Idealist there is full agreement as to the question of the reality of things of such and such sort, *i.e.*, of the possibility of locating elements of such and such sort in the system of the physical world. The disagreement begins only when the question about the Reality of the physical world as a whole is raised. But this question has no sense, because the reality of anything is nothing else than the possibility of its being placed in a certain system, in this case, in the space-time system of the physical world, and such a question has sense only if it concerns elements or parts, not if it concerns the system itself.

The same result is obtained by applying the criterion explained before: the possibility of deducing perceptive propositions. While from the assertion of the reality or the existence of kangaroos we *can* deduce perceptive propositions, from the assertion of the Reality of the physical world this is not possible; neither is it possible from the opposite assertion of the Unreality. Therefore both assertions have no empirical content—no sense at all. Sometimes the views of the *Vienna Circle* have been mistaken for a denial of the Reality of the physical world, but we make no such denial. It is true that we reject the thesis of the Reality of the physical world; but we do not reject it as false, but as having no sense, and its Idealistic *anti*-thesis is subject to exactly the same rejection. We neither assert nor deny these theses, we reject the whole question.

All the considerations which apply to the question of the Reality of the physical world apply also to the other philosophical questions of Reality, e.g., the Reality of other minds, the Reality of the given, the Reality of universals, the Reality of qualities, the Reality of relations, the Reality of numbers, etc. If any philosophical thesis answering any of these questions positively or negatively is added to the system of scientific hypotheses, this system will not in the least become more effective; we shall not be able to make any further prediction as to future experiences. Thus all these philosophical theses are deprived of empirical content, of theoretical sense; they are pseudo-theses.

If I am right in this assertion, the philosophical problems of Reality—as distinguished from the empirical problems of Reality—have the same logical character as the problems (or rather, pseudo-problems) of transcendental metaphysics earlier referred to. For this reason I call those problems of Reality not epistemological problems—as they usually are called—but metaphysical.

Among the metaphysical doctrines that have no theoretical sense I have also mentioned *Positivism,* although the *Vienna Circle* is sometimes designated as Positivistic. It is doubtful whether this designation is quite suitable for us. In any case we do not assert the thesis that only the Given is Real, which is one of the principal theses of traditional Positivism. The name Logical Positivism seems more suitable, but this also can be misunderstood. At any rate it is important to realize that our doctrine is a logical one and has nothing to do with metaphysical theses of the Reality or Unreality of anything whatever.

IV. *Ethics*

One division of philosophy, which by some philosophers is considered the most important, has not been mentioned at all so far, namely, the philosophy of values, with its main branch, moral philosophy or *Ethics.* The word "Ethics" is used in two different senses. Sometimes a certain empirical investigation is called "Ethics," *viz.* psychological and sociological investigations about the actions of human beings, especially regarding the origin of these actions from feelings and volitions and their effects upon other people. Ethics in this sense is an empirical, scientific investigation; it belongs to empirical science rather than to philosophy. Fundamentally different from this is ethics in the second sense, as the philosophy of moral values or moral norms, which one can designate normative ethics. This is not an investigation of facts, but a pretended investigation of what is good and what is evil, what it is right to do and what is is wrong to do. Thus the purpose of this philosophical, or normative, ethics is to state norms for human action or judgments about moral values.

It is easy to see that it is merely a difference of formulation whether we state a norm or a value judgment. A norm or rule has an imperative form, for instance: "Do not kill!" The corresponding value judgment would be: "Killing is evil." This difference of formulation has become practically very important, especially for the development of philosophical thinking. The rule, "Do not kill," has grammatically the imperative form and will therefore not be regarded as an assertion. But the value statement, "Killing is evil" although, like the rule, it is merely an expression of a certain wish, has the grammatical form of an assertive proposition. Most philosophers have been deceived by this form into thinking that a value statement is really an assertive proposition, and must be either true or false. Therefore they give reasons for their own value statements and try to disprove those of their opponents. But actually a value statement is nothing else than a command in a misleading grammatical form. It may have effects upon the actions of men, and these effects may either be in accordance with our wishes or not; but it is neither true nor false. It does not assert anything and can neither be proved nor disproved.

This is revealed as soon as we apply to

such statements our method of logical analysis. From the statement "killing is evil" we cannot deduce any proposition about future experiences. Thus this statement is not verifiable and has no theoretical sense, and the same thing is true of all other value statements.

Perhaps somebody will contend in opposition that the following proposition is deducible: "If a person kills anybody he will have feelings of remorse." But this proposition is in no way deducible from the proposition "killing is evil." It is deducible only from psychological propositions about the character and the emotional reactions of the person. These propositions are indeed verifiable and not without sense. They belong to psychology, not to philosophy; to psychological ethics (if one wishes to use this word), not to philosophical or normative ethics. The propositions of normative ethics, whether they have the form of rules or the form of value statements, have no theoretical sense, are not scientific propositions (taking the word scientific to mean any assertive proposition).

To avoid misunderstanding it must be said that we do not at all deny the possibility and importance of a scientific investigation of value statements as well as of acts of valuation. Both of these are acts of individuals and are, like all other kinds of acts, possible objects of empirical investigation. Historians, psychologists, and sociologists may give analyses and causal explanations of them, and such historical and psychological propositions about acts of valuation and about value statements are indeed meaningful scientific propositions which belong to ethics in the first sense of this word. But the value statements themselves are here only objects of investigation; they are not propositions in these theories, and have, here as elsewhere, no theoretical sense. Therefore we assign them to the realm of metaphysics.

V. *Metaphysics as Expression*

Now we have analyzed the propositions of metaphysics in a wide sense of this word, including not only transcendental metaphysics, but also the problems of philosophical Reality and lastly normative ethics. Perhaps many will agree that the propositions of all these kinds of metaphysics are not verifiable, *i.e.*, that their truth cannot be examined by experience. And perhaps many will even grant that for this reason they have not the character of scientific propositions. But when I say that they are without sense, assent will probably seem more difficult. Someone may object: these propositions in the metaphysical books obviously have an effect upon the reader, and sometimes a very strong effect; therefore they certainly *express* something. That is quite true, they *do* express something, but nevertheless they have no sense, no theoretical content.

We have here to distinguish two functions of language, which we may call the expressive function and the representative function. Almost all the conclusions and unconscious movements of a person, including his linguistic utterances, express something of his feelings, his present mood, his temporary or permanent dispositions to reaction, and the like. Therefore we may take almost all his movements and words as symptoms from which we can infer something about his feelings or his character. That is the expressive function of movements and words. But besides that, a certain portion of linguistic utterances (e.g., "this book is black"), as distinguished from other linguistic utterances and movements, has a second function: these utterances represent a certain state of affairs; they tell us that something is so and so; they assert something, they predicate something, they judge something.

In special cases, this asserted state may be the same as that which is inferred from a certain expressive utterance; but even in such cases we must sharply distinguish between the assertion and the expression. If, for instance, somebody is laughing, we may take this as a symptom of his merry mood; if on the other hand he tells us without laughing: "Now I am merry," we can learn from his words the same thing which we inferred in the first case from his laughing. Nevertheless, there is a fundamental difference between the laughter and the words: "I am merry now." This linguistic utterance *asserts* the merry mood, and therefore it is either true or false. The laughter does not assert the merry mood but *expresses* it. It is neither true nor false, because it does not assert anything, although it may be either genuine or deceptive.

Now many linguistic utterances are analogous to laughing in that they have only an expressive function, no representative function. Examples of this are cries like "Oh, Oh" or, on a higher level, lyrical verses. The aim of a lyrical poem in which occur the words "sunshine" and "clouds" is not to inform us of certain meteorological facts, but to express certain feelings of the poet and to excite similar feelings in us. A lyrical poem has no assertional sense, no theoretical sense, it does not contain knowledge.

The meaning of our anti-metaphysical thesis may now be more clearly explained. This thesis asserts that metaphysical propositions—like lyrical verses—have only an expressive function, but no representative function. Metaphysical propositions are neither true nor false, because they assert nothing, they contain neither knowledge nor error, they lie completely outside the field of knowledge, of theory, outside the discussion of truth or falsehood. But they are, like laughing, lyrics, and music, expressive. They express not so much temporary feelings as permanent emotional or volitional dispositions. Thus, for instance, a Metaphysical system of Monism may be an expression of an even and harmonious mode of life, a Dualistic system may be an expression of the emotional state of someone who takes life as an eternal struggle; an ethical system of Rigorism may be expressive of a strong sense of duty or perhaps of a desire to rule severely. Realism is often a symptom of the type of constitution called by psychologists extroverted, which is characterized by easily forming connections with men and things; Idealism, of an opposite constitution, the so-called introverted type, which has a tendency to withdraw from the unfriendly world and to live within its own thoughts and fancies.

Thus we find a great similarity between metaphysics and lyrics. But there is one decisive difference between them. Both have no representative function, no theoretical content. A metaphysical proposition, however—as distinguished from a lyrical verse—*seems* to have some, and by this not only is the reader deceived, but the metaphysician himself. He believes that in his metaphysical treatise he has asserted something, and is led by this into argument and polemics against the propositions of some other metaphysician. A poet, however, does not assert that the verses of another are wrong or erroneous; he usually contents himself with calling them bad.

The non-theoretical character of metaphysics would not be in itself a defect; all arts have this non-theoretical character without thereby losing their high value for personal as well as for social life. The danger lies in the *deceptive* character of metaphysics; it gives the illusion of knowledge without actually giving any knowledge. This is the reason why we reject it.

4

ARCHITECTURE: THE INTERNATIONAL STYLE

James M. Richards

During the early decades of the present century the scientific point of view naturally had a more direct influence upon developments in philosophy, in morals, and in religion than upon movements in literature, art, or music. But its influence in these latter areas was nonetheless a significant one, and especially in modern architecture the impact of scientific thought and technology has been quite apparent and far reaching. Indeed J. M. Richards (1907-   ), a well-known British journalist and critic, argues that the more important developments in contemporary architecture have grown directly out of and are dependent upon modern scientific achievements. "Architecture," Richards writes, "is a social art related to the life of the people it serves, not an academic exercise in applied ornament. . . . Modern architecture is truly of this age in that it does recognize that machinery and factories are the essence of the age."

Before he turned to a career of writing and lecturing on art and architecture, Richards studied architecture in London and was later employed for some years by an engineering firm with offices in London, Canada, and the United States. As a practicing architect, he learned the architect's problems at first hand. As a professional critic he is familiar with the basic principles of good architecture and knows how contemporary architecture differs from that of the nineteenth century. As a student of the history of architecture he is able to evaluate the accomplishments of great modern architects like Le Corbusier, Gropius, and Frank Lloyd Wright without being unduly disturbed by professional jealousy or hindered by lack of proper historical perspective.

Because of his ability to write about architecture for the general public, Richards was asked by Penguin Books to do their Introduction to Modern Architecture. This was originally published in 1940 and has been reprinted and revised a number of times since. An American edition appeared in 1947 from which the chapter on "Architecture and Machinery" reprinted here is taken. Books on The Bombed Buildings of Britain, The Castles on the Ground, and A Miniature History of the English House present in popular fashion interesting aspects of British architecture, and reflect Richards' interest in providing good homes for men and women today. He now lives in London where he devotes his time to broadcasting and publishing. He is a member also of the Royal Fine Arts Commission and the Council of Industrial Design; he has served as assistant editor of The Architect's Journal *and for a number of years has been an editor of* The Architectural Review.

ARCHITECTURE AND MACHINERY

I

THROUGHOUT history both the general appearance of buildings and their style of ornament have been determined by the knowledge of building technique available, as well as by the materials used and the tools with which they were worked and, of course, as well as by fashion and taste. Roman architecture, for example, developed so far from the Greek model on which it was based because the Romans discovered the use of the round arch and the vault, whereas the Greeks built only with columns and beams.

Modern architecture is conditioned by the same sort of factors. We know more exactly than our ancestors how materials behave in different circumstances, and we have invented or discovered a number of new materials. For both these reasons our range or vocabulary is greater, and for the former reason we have no excuse for building unscientifically. We cannot avoid the obligation to build scientifically. In no age have men built less skillfully than they knew how.

But neither the introduction of these new materials, such as structural steel and reinforced concrete, nor the advent of all the mechanical aids to comfortable living, such as air conditioning and refrigeration, which we are so rich in today—both results of our modern industrial economy—themselves produce a revolution in architecture. They only represent the natural development of traditional architecture. For the architect has always made it part of his job to adapt his methods to suit new materials and mechanical contrivances. And he has successfully assimilated into his practice in the past many innovations more startling than those of the present. The difference between the heating system of the Elizabethan manor with its grouped chimney flues and that of the modern house with its central heating and electrical wiring—or even the modern hospital containing every kind of built-in equipment—is only a difference of degree. The architect may have more complications of this kind to think about—the telephone and radio as well as fresh air and smoke—in the same way that he has more materials at his disposal, but the way he goes about his task of incorporating them all in a building without intruding their presence or interfering with their efficiency remains the same.

One thing, however, that has made modern architecture different in *kind* from the architecture of the past is also connected with modern industry, particularly with its dependence on power production, namely, the factory system. The actual labor of producing the parts of a building is now centered in the factories instead of being left in the hands of the individual workman. At one time the workmen arrived on the site of a proposed building with all their raw materials and the tools to shape them with: stone or timber for the walls, more timber for floors, doors, and windows, lime for plastering the walls; and they constructed the building on the spot, manufacturing as they went along whatever was needed in the way of doors and windows, sometimes even quarrying stone, clay, or sand on the site. Later, for convenience, the doors and window frames were made in the builder's joinery shops, and hinges, bolts and other ironwork were made at the local blacksmith's, but even then they were made as needed especially for the occasion.

The first important example of what we now call "prefabrication"—that is, the manufacture of ready-made building parts—was the brick industry. The earliest bricks may have been molded from clay dug up on the site, but as soon as bricks were in common use (in England by the end of the fifteenth century) brickfields were started to fill a permanent demand, and these were the first building-material factories. Since then, factories having become the normal way of making things, the process has been tremedously accelerated. Today a large proportion of building jobs are usually done in the factory; the windows—probably metal windows—arrive ready-made, so do steel beams and columns, so do doors and sinks, bathtubs and all equipment. The erection of a building is being changed into a process of assembling ready-made parts, and the completely prefabricated house (or school, or hospital or whatever), trucked to the site as factory-made sections that can be put together ready for occupation in a few days, is no longer theory but ubiquitous actuality. Foundation work must still be done on the spot, for concrete has to be poured into the foundation trenches while it is still wet; but even here the practice is growing of having it delivered ready mixed—in those revolving drums mounted on trucks—thereby doing all that can be done in advance.

II

This is how machine production affects building technique. But how does the new building technique—especially prefabrication—affect the appearance of buildings? Or better, since our manufacturers of prefabricated houses frequently go to absurd lengths to give their products a quaintly handwrought appearance, let us put the question another way: how *should* the new technique affect the appearance of buildings? First, of course, directly through the new factory-made materials themselves and the things they can do: span great distances, carry heavy loads, or merely shine in the sun instead of melting into the background. We shall come to that later. But second—and equally important—through the effect on design of the specialization of labor. In fact this is one clue to the fundamental difference, about which we have already spoken, between modern architecture and the architecture of previous centuries: one reason why architecture can never be the same again.

The difference is this: that before this highly industrialized age, each workman was responsible directly for one part of the building, which he could see growing before his eyes. He may only have shaped the rafters for the roof, or he may have carved the ornament round a Gothic door, or molded the plaster ceiling of a Georgian country house; but the building was a direct result of his efforts, and the quality of its design—in many cases its actual nature—depended on his skill. Nowadays, on the other hand, his counterpart is the man who minds a machine in a factory; who is not concerned with the use to which the particular object he is making will be put or the effect it will have on a finished building. The building in which it is to be used has, in fact, probably not yet been thought of. The manufacturer is producing a quantity of whatever it is he makes—metal windows or steel beams or door handles—for an estimated future demand.

It is true that there are workmen employed on the building itself, even in these days of prefabrication; but, as we have already pointed out, they tend more and more to perform partial, mechanically routinized jobs, and are often simply the assemblers of ready-made parts, like the men who work on the assembly line in an automobile factory. The latter cannot be said to be making automobiles themselves. This is being done collectively by the men at the machines that separately turn out the hundreds of different parts.

Now, the whole tradition of craftsmanship on which the architectural style of previous centuries was based, consisted of first the fashioning and then the embellishment of parts of a building by a set of craftsmen who between them imagined and made the whole building. Even when, as during the Renaissance period, there was a controlling mind in the person of the architect, the individual craftsmen knew the building they were working on and their contribution was automatically related to the whole. Always in the past ornament was created as part of the process of making something, wherein an individual gave something of himself in the process. But ornament divorced from handicraft is not the same thing, and nowadays the man who makes things has no longer any say in their design. Much of the value of handicraft ornament, moreover, lay in its virtuosity. It represented an effort of workmanship. It stood for someone's skill and patience. But now that machines can turn out any quantity of ornament with ease there is less virtue in it. At best it is only a sign of wealth—to be able to afford a more complicated machine—which has little to do with architecture.

That is why Victorian machine ornament, when it mechanically imitated hand carving, produced bad architecture; and that is also why modern architecture tends to do without ornament in the sense of carving or applied decoration. It is not because we are puritans nowadays, or because we have not succeeded in thinking out a "modern" style of ornament, or because modern life is too much of a rush, or for any of the nonsensical reasons that are customarily given. Modern buildings are not enriched with conventional ornament because their parts are made by machines, and applied ornament is not the machine's method of beautification.

Complication and richness have their place in modern architecture, but complication by itself is no longer a virtue. It is sometimes mistaken for one, notably by the people who make cheap furniture. If you want simple, well-made furniture, you have to pay for it, as for a luxury, because nearly all mass-produced furniture is covered with nasty machine-made ornament, presumably because either the manufacturer or the trade buyer or the public thinks it an improvement. Though possibly the ornament is stuck on to cover up the cracks.

This misuse of machinery was what William Morris, the famous English theorist and designer, had in mind when he campaigned against mid-Victorian ugliness and insincerity and tried to revive a genuine spirit of craftsmanship. He understood that the vitality had gone from everyday design because the man who designed things no longer made them, and *vice versa;* but he wanted to abolish machines, as being chiefly responsible—which was trying to do the impossible. He and his followers would have done more good by admitting that machinery is only an instrument, to be used well or badly, and campaigning for a more intelligent use of it. William Morris saw man as a creative animal being overwhelmed by the machinery he had produced, the same

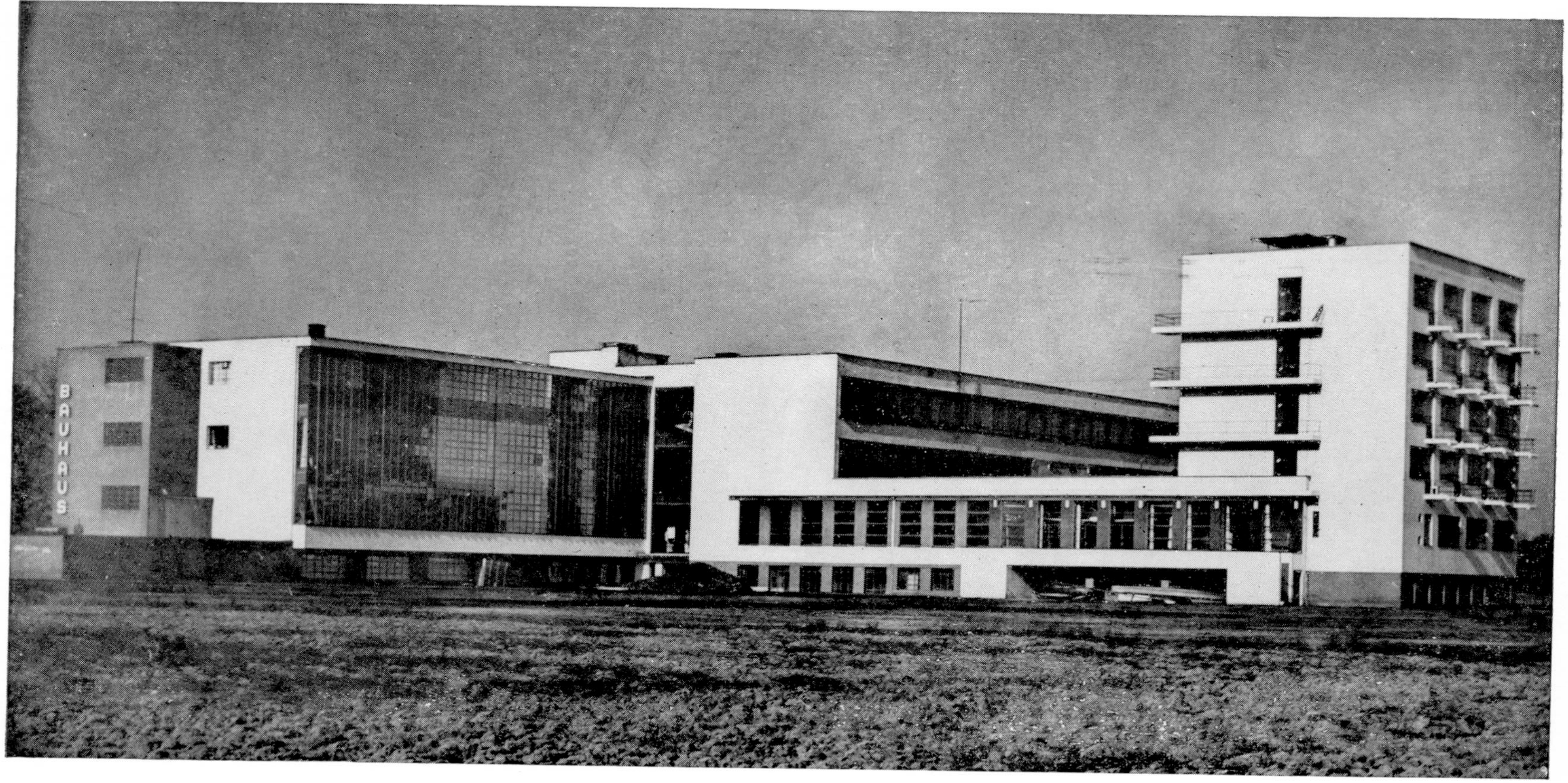

FIG. 20. WALTER GROPIUS: Bauhaus, Dessau, Germany, 1926. Photo Sigfried Giedion.

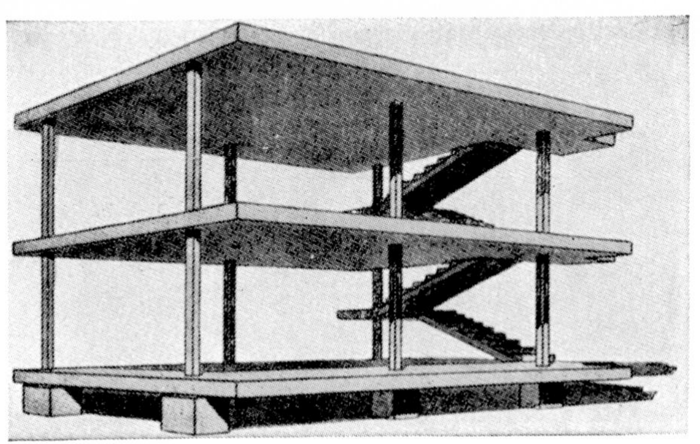

Fig. 21 (*top, left*). LE CORBUSIER: Ferr
crete skeleton for a dwelling house, 1915

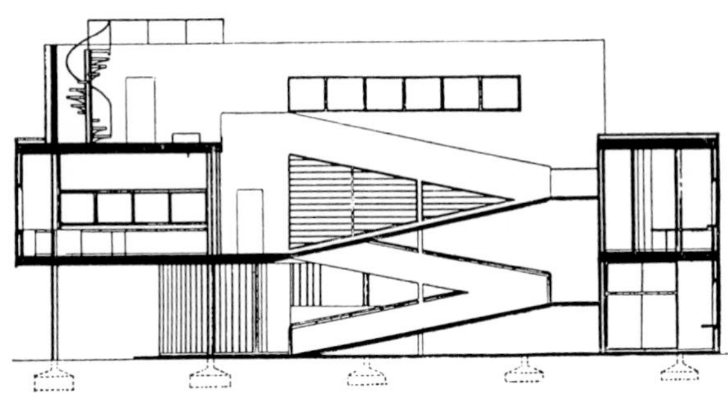

Fig. 22 (*left*). LE CORBUSIER and P.
NERET: Villa Savoye, Poissy-sur-Seine, F
1929-1930, cross section.

Fig. 23 (*below*). LE CORBUSIER and P. JEANNERET: Villa Savoye, Poissy-sur-Seine, France, 192
1930, view from the north. Photo courtesy The Museum of Modern Art, New York.

. 24 (*above*). CLAUDE MONET: *Sailboats at Argenteuil*, 1875. Fogg Art Mu-
m, Cambridge, Mass., Maurice Wertheim Bequest. Photo Durand-Ruel.

FIG. 25 (*below*). CAMILLE PISSARRO: *The Oise River near Pontoise*, 1873. Photo Durand-Ruel.

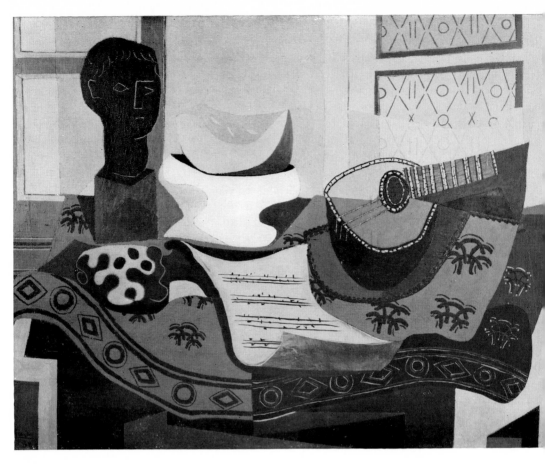

FIG. 26 (*above*). PABLO PICASSO: *The Red Tablecloth*, 1924. Private Collection, New York.

FIG. 27 (*below*). SCHOOL OF PIERO DELLA FRANCESCA: *Perspective*, c. 1470. State Museum of Berlin.

28 (*right*). CLAUDE MONET: *Rouen Cathe-*
West Façade, Sunlight, c. 1894. National
ry of Art, Washington, D. C., Chester Dale
ction.

29 (*below*). PIERRE AUGUSTE RENOIR:
heon of the Boating Party, 1881. Phillips
ction, Washington, D. C.

Fig. 30. paul cézanne: *Mont Sainte-Victoire*, 1885-1887. Phillips Collection, Washington, D.

Fig. 31. paul cézanne
Bridge at Gardanne,
1886. The Museum of
ern Art, New York, Lil
Bliss Collection.

32 (*right*). PABLO PICASSO: *Woman with a lolin*, c. 1910. Private Collection, New York.

33 (*below*). PABLO PICASSO: *Les Demoiselles gnon (Women of Avignon)*, 1907. Col- n The Museum of Modern Art, New York. ired through the Lillie P. Bliss Bequest.

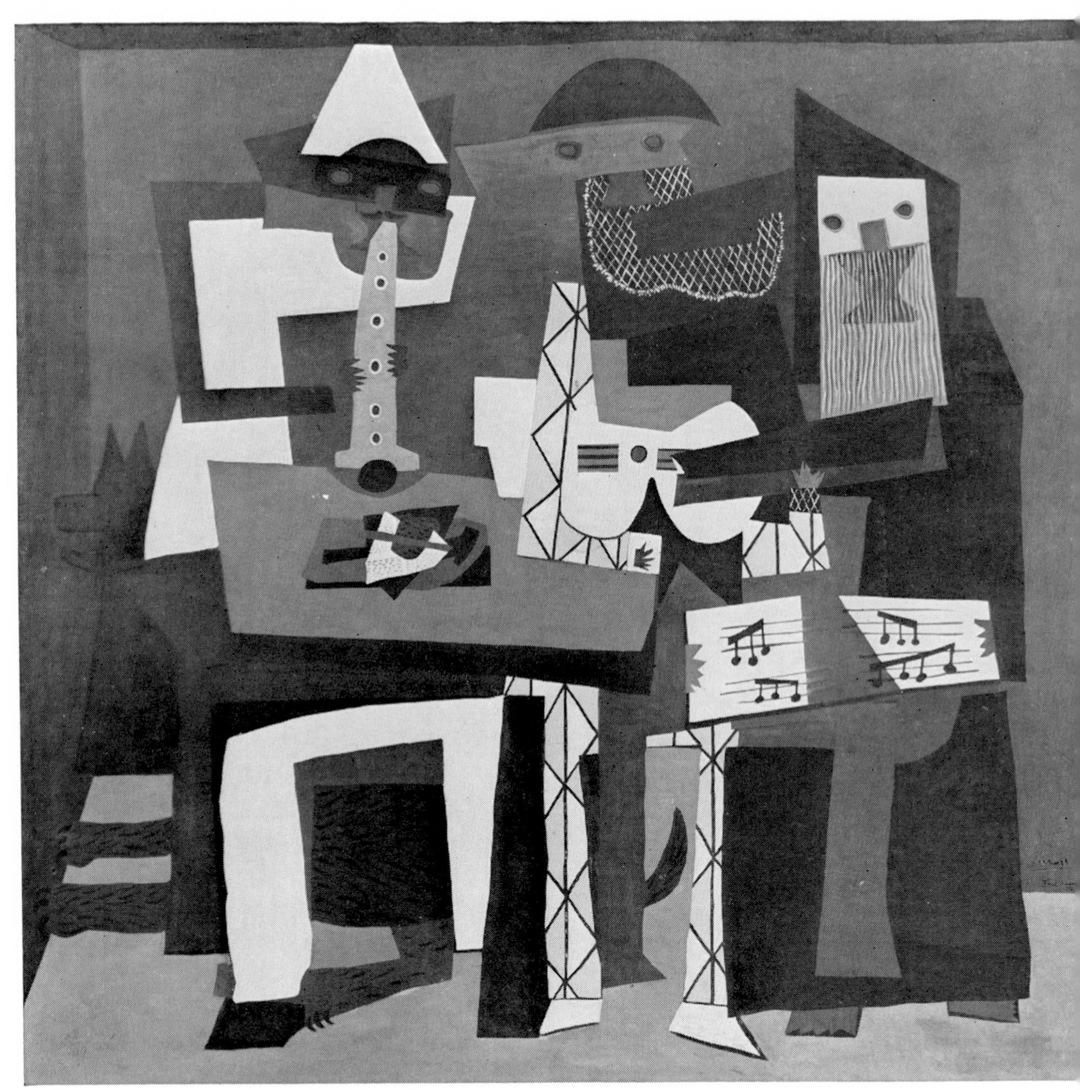

FIG. 34. PABLO PICASSO: *Three Musicians*, 1921. Collection The Museum of Modern Art, N
York, Mrs. Simon Guggenheim Fund.

way that, as a political philosopher, he saw man the individual being submerged in the system of competitive capitalism that he had produced. To his farseeing mind ideas about art were inseparable from ideas about society. Today the machinery he loathed has increased in power and complexity, and art (including architecture) is still suffering from confusion of purpose and ideas, owing to our failure to adapt ourselves to the possession of machinery, and make it provide for us some modern substitute for the direct craft tradition of the medieval period or the code of discipline and taste that the autocracy of the seventeenth and eighteenth centuries provided. Society and art are still indivisible, so it is probable that the reform most needed to put art right with itself is a social reform: some change that would enable the creative designer and the machines he uses to be directly available once more to society as a whole, instead of serving the whims of fashion, money, or snobbery. It has been said before that great architecture is more a product of the times than of personalities.

III

However, such questions are outside the scope of this book. What we are concerned with is not the social results of machinery as reflected in architecture, but the direct effect of machinery on the appearance of architecture itself. And this we can study. For, in spite of our general failure during the past hundred years to adapt ourselves to the new conditions that industrialization has brought, we have in modern architecture a phenomenon of modern life that is remarkable for having done so. Modern architecture is truly of this age in that it does recognize that machinery and factories are the essence of the age. It exploits them esthetically as well as practically, finding new beauties inherent in the products of machinery instead of merely regretting, like Morris and other nineteenth century reformers, that old beauties have passed away.

It is likely to be misleading, however, to define modern architecture as the architecture of the machine age—not because it is untrue but because it suggests that it is thereby of a limited and inhuman kind. There is an idea called "functionalism" that is often associated with modern architecture; in fact even by well-informed people modern architecture is often described as "functionalist." As this description is entirely untrue it may be as well, before we continue our examination of the actual effect of machine production on architectural design, to give some attention to laying this particular bogey.

It is difficult to say when the idea of functionalism first took hold. It is present, with reservations, in many writings about architecture from the Roman Vitruvius onward; but in these cases, of course, the reservations are all important. For architecture, being a practical art, must always depend to some degree on function, a fact that all sensible writers on the subject have recognized. But the idea of absolute functionalism—which can be defined as the idea that good architecture is produced automatically by strict attention to utility, economy and other purely practical considerations—is a more recent phenomenon. It is doubtful, as a matter of fact, whether this theory in its absolute form has ever been seriously held by practicing architects; they would soon have found that it prevented them from exercising their functions at all: but as there is nevertheless a popular belief that the modern kind of architecture is functionalist it is necessary to discuss the theory at some length, if only as a way of showing what modern architecture is by explaining one important thing that it is not.

The confusion arose largely through the

theorizing and propaganda about modern architecture that were current during the first quarter of this century. A new architecture was then emerging from the confusion of the nineteenth century. And the most striking difference between the new architecture and the old was that the former laid stress on the utilitarian basis of architecture that the latter had largely ignored. Modern architects took the opportunity provided by all the new materials and methods that science had made available to rescue architecture from the stagnation of stylistic revivals. They found it necessary, as we have already described, to return to first principles, and one among the first principles of architecture is that it should do the job it has to do as efficiently as possible. It is not surprising, therefore, that when architects and writers tried to explain to the world what the new architecture was all about, they should have stressed this practical side of it as its special virtue. In some instances, moreover, as in the writings of the famous Swiss architect and propagandist Le Corbusier, an extreme functionalist attitude was deliberately taken up as the best way of instilling into the public the importance of being practical first and foremost. His famous pronouncement "*une maison est une machine à habiter*"* served very well as a slogan advertising the simple, but at that time revolutionary, conception of architecture as primarily a matter of shelter. His technique of deliberate oversimplification did succeed in doing a lot to clear away the sentimentalities and prejudices that had come to form so large a proportion of people's views on architecture. That Le Corbusier himself, as an architect, never thought of buildings as being nothing but machines is very clear from the buildings themselves. He is one of the most brilliant architects of the modern movement, whose buildings are remarkable for their freedom from rule-of-thumb designing. He never does anything just because it has been done before or because it is customary, and he therefore fulfills absolutely his ideal of rational design; but he is also one of the most imaginative architects living. His buildings are full of a poetic quality that is pure art and very far from being the product of mechanical thinking.

Le Corbusier also, in his very influential writings about architecture, was one of the first to illustrate an airplane, an automobile, and a turbine in a book about architectural design; and this, too, has led people to suppose that modern architects believe that beautiful buildings can arise automatically from mechanical efficiency.

The difference between these two things, beautiful building and mechanical efficiency, is, of course, the difference between architecture and engineering. It is true that modern architects are influenced by the work of modern engineers. It is natural that this should be so. For all the new shapes and materials that made the unexplored possibilities of modern architecture so exciting arrived in the beginning by way of engineering: steel was used for bridges with thrilling results before it was used in architecture, and many architects first saw the beauty of machine products in the mechanical equipment—the power installations, the kitchen equipment, even the electric light bulbs—that science provided and demanded that they fit into their buildings, even while the latter were still enslaved to the ritual of historical styles. The great engineering works that modern science and industry produced had a breathtaking beauty, and it was easy for the architect, confused by contradictory esthetic creeds, to feel that he would ask nothing better than to have designed a building as directly appealing and as moving as this transmission tower

* A house is a machine for living.

or that enormous floating dock, which were primarily utilitarian; and therefore perhaps architecture would do best to follow the same method. But architecture, as the modern architects now appreciate, goes deeper than engineering. The beauty of the new structures that engineering has introduced into the landscape is genuine enough, and one's emotional reaction to them is natural, but this appeal is not really an architectural one. It is the appeal of size, simplicity, clearness, and honesty—in fact of all the qualities that nineteenth century academic architecture lacked. It is the appeal of a new world, inevitably stimulating to people who are becoming conscious that they live surrounded by the leavings of an old one, but it is not the *art* of a new world. One can admire things that possess some of the qualities that modern architecture should have, without taking them for modern architecture itself. One can also learn from them; and the important thing that modern architecture has learned from engineering and machine design—from docks, transmission towers, and airplanes—is first, the technique of using new materials, second, simplicity of line and honesty of expression, and third, the overwhelming grandeur of the fundamental architectural qualities, rhythm, scale, and contrast, which engineering used anonymously and as if by chance. These qualities could instructively be compared with the pettiness of personal mannerism and individual expression that architecture was still wasting so much of its time on.

Even after we have said that it is engineering that is functional and architecture that is something more, it is often difficult to decide where one begins and the other ends. The "something more" means that architectural design includes decisions or preferences made for nonutilitarian reasons, but we find that in all but the very simplest engineering problems room is also left for taste or preference to enter: choosing between certain alternatives or consciously varying the result within certain limits. Even engineering itself, that is to say, is seldom truly functional. The explanation of this difficulty is of course that the distinction between engineering and architecture is entirely an artificial one. It is only a hundred years old, having come about when the academic architects became primarily engrossed in styles early in the nineteenth century; when they came to regard the language of architecture as an end in itself instead of as the means to an end. We now recognize the works of the great English engineers of this period—the bridges, harbors, railway works, and the like of such men as Thomas Telford, I. K. Brunel, Robert Stephenson, and Joseph Paxton—which were designed with real creative imagination, as being among the best architecture of the early nineteenth century; and the Roeblings' magnificent Brooklyn Bridge takes a proud place in the world as one of the few architectural masterpieces of the latter part of that century.

The harm that resulted from the splitting of the architect's functions is obvious. It put the architect in the position of being only the decorator of buildings designed by engineers, as though art was something that could be applied after the utilitarian side of the buildings was finished. Today it is part of the creed of the modern architect that the processes of constructing and designing a building are inseparable.

Modern architecture then, although it is dependent on machinery in many ways, remains as *an art* fundamentally a matter of the architect's discernment and imagination. He is free to use his imagination within the limits of utility. But if utility and art are properly coordinated one does not impose limits on the other. On the contrary, the utilitarian aspect of architecture provides a basis on which the architect's artistic sense can build something of more than utilitarian value. This of course is true of all good architecture; the difference being that nowadays the architect's material is largely machine-produced and machine-finished, which strongly influences his esthetic ideals.

From machines themselves he has learned the charm of simplicity and precision. He has learned the value of eliminating everything unnecessary, not so much for reasons of economy as because the process of elimination brings out the essential character of structure. Much of the beauty of a transmission tower, as of a Gothic spire, lies in its spare economy of means, indicating its designer's complete mastery over the material of which it is constructed. Secondly, machines, as we have seen, have lessened the virtue in elaborate ornament because they have abolished the point of doing something because it is difficult. This does not mean that richness has gone from architecture. Machine-produced shapes and textures lend themselves to infinite complication. The modern equivalent of applied ornament, however, largely lies in the natural qualities of materials themselves: in the grain and surface of beautiful woods, in the sheen of new metal alloys and in the contrasting texture of fabrics; all used with the exactness of finish that machines have introduced into architecture. Indeed, the eventual result of the precision with which machinery works may be an increase in our own awareness of the subtleties produced by precision. Our perceptions in the past have been blunted by the vulgarities of architectural clichés: by the meaningless masses of material hung on to architecture; but the new architecture gives us a chance to develop a more subtle appreciation of proportion and rhythm such as set the standards of eighteenth century taste. One can foresee a new connoisseurship coming into play, developing out of our acceptance of modern architecture's mechanistic basis.

One other thing that tends to reduce the high standards we might otherwise have, apart from the quantity of *vague* architecture we see every day around us, is the fact that so many of us live in surroundings that are only adapted, not designed, for their purpose: large old-fashioned houses converted into apartments, for example, and houses not originally wired for electricity, so that the cables run all over the walls instead of being neatly concealed. We get accustomed to accepting as a matter of habit, in converted buildings, shifts and approximations that the ideals of modern architecture would never tolerate. And the standards we demand follow suit, for you cannot train your perceptions to judge things according to two standards of finish simultaneously.

Any discussion of the influence machinery has had on architecture must not omit the important part played by standardization. We have already discussed the growth of mass production of building parts in factories, beginning with the first brickfields and ending in complete prefabrication. But the fact of standardization—which results from mass production—has a strong influence on design as well as on technique. It puts great responsibility on the industrial designer: the man who invents the object that the machine merely copies an infinite number of times. Complete prefabrication, of course, would simply bring the architect into the factory as designer; but this degree of prefabrication could only apply to types of building in which the needs are more or less standardized. In more complex buildings their varying needs and the problems of planning in relation to other buildings will always demand a specially thought-out solution. So the architect's job is not becoming a less responsible one, but under present-day conditions he is also dependent on the industrial designer for the quality of the standard parts he uses so much. The latter must take some of the responsibility of making the most of the architectural opportunities offered by modern building technique; for a good type of metal window, sensible and good-looking wash basins, well-designed door handles, and many more such details—besides furniture and fabrics—all play a big part in the final quality of the whole. And the production of such things as these in factories, according to standard patterns, should bring about a high quality of design, because it enables the collective experience of designers to be pooled. Instead of each individual craftsman having to start from the beginning, making his own experiments and mistakes, each new design can build on the experience of previous ones. It is by this process of gradual improvement that the design of airplanes and automobiles is perfected, and this is what architecture can adapt from their example.

IV

To represent the developments characteristic of the nineteen-twenties and early nineteen-thirties—a most important formative period—it should be sufficient to say something about the work of two architects, not only because they are the two greatest that modern European architecture has produced, but because they personify two tendencies in which the trend of modern architecture between the wars can be summed up.

These two are Walter Gropius and Le Corbusier. Gropius may be said to be the senior of the two as his earliest works date from about 1911, whereas Le Corbusier is entirely a post-1918 figure. Gropius's earlier works were industrial; but his great opportunity came soon after the war of 1914-1918 when Germany, his native country, was undergoing internal reconstruction on a scale that needed the service of architects with farseeing ideas and the ability to plan for actual social needs, not architects who regarded buildings merely as isolated occasions for putting into practice their personal talent for invention. In the early twenties under the German Republic many enormous housing schemes were planned, following the example of those erected by the Socialist Municipality of Vienna. They consisted of huge colonies, known as *Siedlungen*, usually complete with schools and shopping centers, the residential part consisting of blocks of flats well spaced apart—quite different from the old-fashioned dark courtyard plan—and carefully aligned to make the most of the sun.

Gropius himself designed several of these housing schemes, but his fame rests chiefly on another achievement: the celebrated *Bauhaus* which was a sort of university of design. In 1919 Gropius was given the opportunity of remodeling the school according to plans of his own. In 1925 the school was moved to Dessau, where Gropius was invited by the Town Council to design a great group of buildings including the school itself, with all necessary living accommodations, a labor exchange, and a housing colony. Here it flourished until the advent of the Nazi regime in 1933, when it was closed down. At the same time Gropius, who had resigned from the *Bauhaus* in 1928 to concentrate on his own housing work, left the country.

The *Bauhaus* acquired wide influence, not only because designs that it produced were adopted for mass production by industrial concerns, but also because it became the intellectual center and fount of inspiration for the whole new architectural movement that was spreading fast through central Europe. The unanswerable logic of Gropius's own ideas was supplemented by the actual work of students and teaching staff, who included some of the best artists and designers in Germany, many of whom the reputation of the *Bauhaus* had brought from other countries.

Gropius's own architecture, as exemplified in the *Bauhaus* buildings (see Fig. 20), is rational to the point of extreme—almost forbidding—severity; but so thoroughly and rhythmically planned, with every part in perfect coordination, as to give the whole a sort of nobility that a more fanciful style seldom achieves.

This quality of rectitude is in striking contrast to the romantic poetic quality we find in the work of Le Corbusier. Le Corbusier is Swiss and his real name is Charles Édouard Jeanneret; but he has lived so long in Paris and such a large proportion of his work has been done in France that he may reasonably be regarded as a French architect. The real nature of his work is the subject of much confusion, as his character as a propagandist so often seems to differ from his character as an architect. His name, because of his writings, is the one most closely associated with the idea of "functionalism," yet his buildings are much less functionalist than those of Gropius. Although he is always true to his enthusiasm for modern technique, it has been aptly said that Le Corbusier designs rather than builds. His best work shows a poetic and imaginative use of geometrical forms, inspired originally by Cubism. One of his early masterpieces is illustrated in Figure 23.

Another contrast that illustrates still further the conflicting yet complementary tendencies which emerged as modern architecture established itself simultaneously in different parts of the world, is the contrast between the work of Le Corbusier and that of Frank Lloyd Wright, the American architect who had long been fighting a solitary battle in his own country. Wright builds consciously in sympathy with nature; Le Corbusier in defiance of it. He exploits the surprising, and at first sight unnatural, things modern construction will do. Unlike Wright, whose buildings lie close to the ground, Le Corbusier's often stand up on pillars as near as possible floating in the air, dissociated from the earth. Further, the contrasting nature of their work illustrates the two dangers that modern architecture tends to be led into. Le Corbusier's romantic geometry, disciplined by Cubism, tends to exhaust itself in sterile abstraction of form, or in a renewal of academic formulae. It has this tendency in common with the more doctrinaire modernism of the *Bauhaus* School. In contrast, Wright's more "natural" architecture tends to escape from technical and social problems into art-and-crafty idealism. The ideal of course is a fusion of these two tendencies: an architecture that is free and natural without being unworldly and in tune with the mechanical world without being inhumanly exclusive.

Le Corbusier

A contemporary architect whose work illustrates to most people the direct impact of scientific thought and invention upon architecture is the French architect, Le Corbusier. Le Corbusier designs his buildings for an efficient urbanized way of life. His designs reflect a pure intelligence; they are constructed on geometric rather than organic principles and make direct use of contemporary scientific thought. In his opinion people deserve homes as well made and efficient as airplanes or Pullman cars or ships. He first published his theories in Towards A New Architecture *(1923), presenting his views with all the enthusiasm of a young reformer. Since 1923 he has written a dozen other books interpreting his work and supporting his theories; today he is ranked among the three or four most important figures in the development of modern architecture. The influence of his ideas has been so great indeed that his architecture is widely known as the International Style.*

Born in Switzerland in 1887 and christened Charles Édouard Jeanneret, Le Corbusier had a wide and varied experience as a student of art and architecture. He studied medieval art in Italy, industrial art in Berlin, and classical architecture in Asia Minor, Greece, and Rome. For several years he was employed as an interior designer in Switzerland. During World War I he worked in France, largely in the field of city planning. In 1921, at the age of thirty-four, he finally became a practicing architect. Adopting his maternal grandfather's name (Le Corbusier) as his architectural pseudonym, he reserved the name Jeanneret for his work as an artist. Among important early designs are those for the Palace of the League of Nations in Geneva (1927) and his Moscow buildings (1928-1930). "Radiant City," a housing project for 1600 people in Marseille, is one of his most exciting and controversial accomplishments. He has been a consultant on housing projects in Antwerp, Stockholm, Barcelona, Algiers, and South America, and assisted with the design of the United Nations headquarters in New York City. Since 1950 he has spent much of his time in India where he has designed an entire city to be the new capital of East Punjab.

In the selection reprinted here from Towards A New Architecture, *Le Corbusier writes as simply as he can. He uses italics to attract attention; he talks directly to his readers, and he insists repeatedly that houses should be fitted to man's needs, instead of man being forced to adapt himself to traditional houses. When Le Corbusier uses the phrase he made famous—"a house is a machine for living"—he is careful to indicate that a house is much more than this; it can be a work of art through the harmony of its various parts. Being a great artist himself, he knows that mere usefulness is not enough.*

TOWARDS A NEW ARCHITECTURE

The airplane is the product of close selection.

The lesson of the airplane lies in the logic which governed the statement of the problem and its realization.

The problem of the house has not yet been stated.

Nevertheless there do exist standards for the dwelling house.

Machinery contains in itself the factor of economy, which makes for selection.

The house is a machine for living in.

THE AIRPLANE is indubitably one of the products of the most intense selection in the range of modern industry.

The War was an insatiable "client," never satisfied, always demanding better. The orders were to succeed at all costs and death followed a mistake remorselessly. We may then affirm that the airplane mobilized invention, intelligence and daring: *imagination* and *cold reason*. It is the same spirit that built the Parthenon.

Let us look at things from the point of view of architecture, but in the state of mind of the inventor of airplanes.

The lesson of the airplane is not pri-

[From *Towards a New Architecture* by Le Corbusier. The Architectural Press, Ltd., London, 1946. Reprinted by permission of the publishers and of Frederick A. Praeger, Inc.]

marily in the forms it has created, and above all we must learn to see in an airplane not a bird or a dragon-fly, but a machine for flying; the lesson of the airplane lies in the logic which governed the enunciation of the problem and which led to its successful realization. When a problem is properly stated, in our epoch, it inevitably finds its solution.

The problem of the house has not yet been stated.

One commonplace among Architects (the younger ones): *the construction must be shown.*

Another commonplace amongst them: *when a thing responds to a need, it is beautiful.*

But. . . . To show the construction is all very well for an Arts and Crafts student who is anxious to prove his ability. The Almighty has clearly shown our wrists and our ankles, but there remains all the rest!

When a thing responds to a need, it is not beautiful; it satisfies all one part of our mind, the primary part, without which there is no possibility of richer satisfactions; let us recover the right order of events.

Architecture has another meaning and other ends to pursue than showing construction and responding to needs (and by "needs" I mean utility, comfort and practical arrangement).

ARCHITECTURE is the art above all others which achieves a state of platonic grandeur, mathematical order, speculation, the perception of the harmony which lies in emotional relationships. This is the AIM of architecture.

But let us return to our chronology.

If we feel the need of a new architecture, a clear and settled organism, it is because, as things are, the sensation of mathematical order cannot touch us since *things no longer respond to a need,* and because there is no longer real construction in architecture. An extreme confusion reigns. Architecture as practiced provides no solution to the present-day problem of the dwelling house and has no comprehension of the structure of things. It does not fulfill the very first conditions and so it is not possible that the higher factors of harmony and beauty should enter in.

The architecture of today does not fulfill the necessary and sufficient conditions of the problem.

The reason is that the problem has not been stated as regards architecture. There has been no salutary war as in the case of the airplane.

But you will say, the Peace has set the problem in the reconstruction of the North of France. But then, we are totally disarmed, we do not know how to build in a modern way—materials, systems of construction, THE CONCEPTION OF THE DWELLING, all are lacking. Engineers have been busy with barrages, with bridges, with Atlantic liners, with mines, with railways. Architects have been asleep.

The airplane shows us that a problem well stated finds its solution. To wish to fly like a bird is to state the problem badly, and Ader's "Bat" never left the ground. To invent a flying machine having in mind nothing alien to pure mechanics, that is to say, to search for a means of suspension in the air and a means of propulsion, was to put the problem properly: in less than ten years the whole world could fly.

Let Us State the Problem

Let us shut our eyes to what exists.

A house: a shelter against heat, cold, rain, thieves, and the inquisitive. A receptacle for light and sun. A certain number of cells appropriated to cooking, work, and personal life.

A *room:* a surface over which one can walk at ease, a bed on which to stretch yourself, a chair in which to rest or work, a work table, receptacles in which each thing can be put at once in its right place.

The number of rooms: one for cooking and one for eating. One for work, one to wash yourself in, and one for sleep.

Such are the standards of the dwelling.

Then why do we have the enormous and useless roofs on pretty suburban villas? Why the scanty windows with their little panes; why large houses with so many rooms locked up? Why the mirrored wardrobes, the washstands, the commodes? And then, why the elaborate bookcases? the consoles, the china cabinets, the dressers, the sideboards? Why the enormous glass chandeliers? The mantelpieces? Why the draped curtains? Why the damasked wallpapers thick with color, with their motley design?

Daylight hardly enters your home. Your windows are difficult to open. There are no ventilators for changing the air such as we get in any dining car. Your chandeliers hurt the eyes. Your imitation stone stucco and your wallpapers are an impertinence, and no good modern picture could ever be hung on your walls, for it would be lost in the welter of your furnishings.

Why do you not demand from your landlord:

1. Fittings to take underclothing, suits, and dresses in your bedroom, all of one depth, of a comfortable height and as practical as an "Innovation" trunk;

2. In your dining room fittings to take china, silver, and glass, shutting tightly and with a sufficiency of drawers in order that "clearing away" can be done in an instant, and all these fittings "built in" so that round your chairs and table you have room enough to move and that feeling of space which will give you the calm necessary to good digestion;

3. In your living-room *fittings to hold your books and protect them from dust and to hold your collection of paintings and works of art.* And in such a way that the walls of your room are unencumbered. You could then bring out your pictures one at a time when you want them.

As for your dressers, and your mirrored wardrobes, you can sell all these to one of those young nations which have lately appeared on the map. There *Progress* rages, and they are dropping the traditional home (with its fittings, etc.) to live in an up-to-date house à *l'européenne* with its imitation stone stucco and its mantelpieces.

Let us repeat some fundamental axioms:

(a) *Chairs are made to sit in.* There are rush-seated church chairs at 5s., luxuriously upholstered armchairs at £20, and adjustable chairs with a movable reading desk, a shelf for your coffee cup, an extending footrest, a back that raises and lowers with a handle and gives you the very best position either for work or a nap, in a healthy, comfortable, and right way. Your *bergères*, your Louis XVI *causeuses*, bulging through their tapestry covers, are these machines for sitting in? Between ourselves, you are more comfortable at your club, your bank, or your office.

(b) *Electricity gives light.* We can have concealed lighting, or we can have diffused and projected lighting. One can see as clearly as in broad daylight without ever hurting one's eyes.

A hundred-candle-power lamp weighs less than two ounces, but there are chandeliers weighing nearly two hundredweight with elaborations in bronze or wood, and so huge that they fill up all the middle of the room; the upkeep of these horrors is a terrible task because of the flies. These chandeliers are also very bad for the eyes at night.

(c) *Windows serve to admit light, "a little, much, or not at all," and to see outside.* There are windows in sleeping cars which close hermetically or can be opened at will; there are the great windows of modern cafés which close hermetically or can be entirely opened by means of a handle which causes them to disappear below ground; there are the windows in dining cars which have little louvers opening to admit air "a little, much, or not at all," there is modern plate glass which has replaced bottle glass and small panes; there are roll shutters which can be lowered gradually and will keep out the light at will according to the spacing of their slats. But architects still use only windows like those at Versailles or Compiègne, Louis X, Y, or Z which shut badly, have tiny panes, are difficult to open, and have their shutters outside; if it rains in the evening one gets wet through in trying to close them.

(d) *Pictures are made to be looked at and meditated on.* In order to see a picture to advantage, it must be hung suitably and in the proper atmosphere. The true collector of pictures arranges them in a cabinet and hangs on the wall the particular painting he wants to look at; but your walls are a riot of all manner of things.

(e) *A house is made for living in.*—"No!"—"But of course!"—"Then you are a Utopian!"

Truth to tell, the modern man is bored to tears in his home; so he goes to his club. The modern woman is bored outside her boudoir; she goes to tea parties. The modern man and woman are bored at home; they go to nightclubs. But lesser folk who have no clubs gather together in the evening under the chandelier and hardly dare to walk through the labyrinth of their furniture which takes up the whole room and is all their fortune and their pride.

The existing plan of the dwelling house takes no account of man and is conceived as a furniture store. This scheme of things, favorable enough to the trade of Tottenham Court Road, is of ill omen for society. It kills the spirit of the family, of the home; there are no homes, no families, and no children, for living is much too difficult a business.

The temperance societies and the anti-Malthusians should address an urgent appeal to architects; they should have the MANUAL OF THE DWELLING printed and distributed to mothers of families and should demand the resignation of all the professors in the architectural schools.

The Manual of the Dwelling

Demand a bathroom looking south, one of the largest rooms in the house or flat, the old drawing-room for instance. One wall to be entirely glazed, opening if possible on to a balcony for sun baths; the most up-to-date fittings with a shower bath and gymnastic appliances.

An adjoining room to be a dressing room in which you can dress and undress. Never undress in your bedroom. It is not a clean thing to do and makes the room horribly untidy. In this room demand fitments for your linen and clothing, not more than 5 feet in height, with drawers, hangers, etc.

Demand one really large living room instead of a number of small ones.

Demand bare walls in your bedroom, your living room, and your dining room. Built-in fittings to take the place of much of the furniture, which is expensive to buy, takes up too much room and needs looking after.

If you can, put the kitchen at the top of the house to avoid smells.

Demand concealed or diffused lighting.

Demand a vacuum cleaner.

Buy only practical furniture and never buy decorative "pieces." If you want to see bad taste, go into the houses of the rich. Put only a few pictures on your walls and none but good ones.

Keep your odds and ends in drawers or cabinets.

The gramaphone or the pianola or wireless will give you exact interpretations of first-rate music, and you will avoid catching cold in the concert hall, and the frenzy of the virtuoso.

Demand ventilating panes to the windows in every room.

Teach your children that a house is only habitable when it is full of light and air, and when the floors and walls are clear. To keep your floors in order eliminate heavy furniture and thick carpets.

Demand a separate garage to your dwelling.

Demand that the maid's room should not be an attic. Do not park your servants under the roof.

Take a flat which is one size smaller than what your parents accustomed you to. Bear in mind economy in your actions, in your household management, and in your thoughts.

Conclusion. Every modern man has the mechanical sense. The feeling for mechanics exists and is justified by our daily activities. This feeling in regard to machinery is one of respect, gratitude, and esteem.

Machinery includes economy as an essential factor leading to minute selection. There is a moral sentiment in the feeling for mechanics.

The man who is intelligent, cold, and calm has grown wings to himself.

Men—intelligent, cold, and calm—are needed to build the house and to lay out the town.

Sigfried Giedion

If we were to judge an author by the number of copies his books have sold, Sigfried Giedion (1888-) is one of the most popular and most successful critics of architecture now writing. He is a Swiss professor of architecture who has had a great success in this country. While he was Norton Professor at Harvard University he published, in 1941, Space, Time and Architecture *which has been reprinted frequently. Its success is due largely to Professor Giedion's enormous enthusiasm for the best in architecture and city planning since the time of the Renaissance.*

He appeals to Americans because he speaks with such admiration of architects like Sullivan and Wright, and seems to know so much about the anonymous architecture of this country. He has often lamented the fact that though America has a fine native tradition in tool making, in constructing houses, and in designing towns, we have destroyed most of the records concerning this work.

In writing about contemporary architecture he is especially interested in the relation between the art of painting and that of architecture. He thinks no high civilization has existed, or indeed is possible, in the absence of close cooperation between the two arts. In Le Corbusier he has a happy subject, since Le Corbusier is both painter and architect.

LE CORBUSIER AND THE MEANS OF ARCHITECTONIC EXPRESSION

I

LE CORBUSIER (Charles Édouard Jeanneret) was born at La Chaux-de-Fonds, in the French part of Switzerland. His family, the Jeannerets, had been painters and engravers for generations. Le Corbusier himself learned to engrave watches.

Le Corbusier's spirit was never ground to a smooth specialization at a university. He showed the instinctive prescience of genius by turning up wherever new things were being done, or wherever a stimulating relationship to a bygone era could be established. From 1909 to 1910 he was in Paris, learning to use ferroconcrete in Perret's atelier. At Berlin he worked in the studio of Peter Behrens. His first published book —an examination and criticism of the German industrial art movement—was a product of this experience. He saw Vienna and the Wiener *Werkstätte*, but made his excuses when Josef Hoffmann (Otto Wagner's best-known pupil) asked him to come and work with him.

Instead, Le Corbusier set out—with empty pockets—to visit Athens and the Near East. St. Peter's in Rome, the Acropolis, the white houses indigenous to Mediterranean culture everywhere—from all these things he derived just the kind of assistance that was needed for the work of today.

Another influence must be mentioned: Le Corbusier's contact with (and share in) modern painting. Contemporary painting was at the high point of its development in 1917, the year Le Corbusier finally returned to Paris. He had the advantage not merely of living there at this time but of being himself a painter.

Our specialized period rarely produces a combination of painter and architect in the same person. Le Corbusier is one of the exceptions; in his scheme of daily work the morning is devoted to painting, the afternoon to architecture. Architectural creations come easily to him, but for twenty years he has been struggling with painting. The foundation of his work in both fields is his conception of space. Architecture and painting are merely two different instruments through which he expresses the same conception.

Around 1910 Picasso and Braque, as the consequence of a new conception of space, exhibited the interiors and exteriors of objects simultaneously. In architecture Le Corbusier developed, on the same principle, the interpenetration of inner and outer space. We have already observed gropings toward such an interpenetration in the seventeenth-century buildings of Francisco Borromini. But this interpenetration of space at large and space-particles could have further development only in an age whose science and art both perceived space as essentially many-sided and relational.

Le Corbusier takes ferroconcrete as the instrument for the expression in architecture of his ideas. In this he joins the French tradition, continues the work of Perret and Tony Gernier. It was only in France that architects could use ferroconcrete unrestrictedly and without hesitation. Building legislators in Germany and England distrusted elegant constructions in reinforced concrete and insisted upon an unnecessary bulkiness. The French had always sought for lightness and precision in their buildings, and they made corresponding laws.

The real starting point of Le Corbusier's career is a drawing dated 1915 (Fig. 21). It shows nothing but six reinforced concrete pillars and three horizontal slabs which are connected by a mere hint of a staircase. Le Corbusier was able—as no one before him had been—to transmute the concrete skeleton developed by the engineer into a means of architectonic expression. He knew how to bring out the secret affinity that existed between ferroconcrete construction and the human needs and cravings that were just coming to the surface.

To create houses of unprecedented lightness and to carry still farther the kind of "open planning" which Frank Lloyd Wright had begun, Le Corbusier used those properties of the supporting framework of reinforced concrete which make the disposition of the inner walls a matter of choice. This new interpretation of the concrete skeleton is the significant part of Le Corbusier's work.

The problem of the dwelling is the unequivocal center of Le Corbusier's activity, both theoretical and practical. His first house, built in the Swiss Jura in 1916, is externally of conventional form. It already shows, however, the reinforced concrete skeleton which appears in all its successors. The skeleton is actually turned to the purposes of housing.

Le Corbusier has laid down five points of liaison between contemporary architecture and contemporary construction:

1. *The pillar*, which is to be left free to rise through the open space of a dwelling.

Such a use of the pillar had been made early in the nineteenth century by John Nash. Henri Labrouste in 1843 had also used a free-standing cast-iron pillar in one of the rooms of his Bibliothèque Sainte-Geneviève. Le Corbusier uses the free pillar with a difference, however: through the girders of the framework it takes up all the load in the structure and leaves the walls with nothing to support. This leads directly to Le Corbusier's second principle.

2. *The functional independence of skeleton and wall*, in the case not only of the outer walls but of the inner partitions also.

William Le Baron Jenney, in the first true skeleton construction, his Leiter Building of 1889 (Chicago), also took advantage of the complete freedom this type of framework building permitted in the disposition of the nonsupporting inner walls.

3. *Le plan libre.* Le Corbusier converted the ferroconcrete skeleton from a technical device into an esthetic means. Le Corbusier uses the partition walls to model the interior space of the house in the most varied manner, employing curved staircases and curving or flat partition walls for both functional and expressive purposes. The same means allow him to hollow out large portions of the house, and to bring about interpenetrations of outer and inner space which are unfamiliar and daring.

This whole treatment, the completely free and individualized organization of separate stories, is what is meant by "open planning" or *le plan libre.* By now the difference between the open planning of Frank Lloyd Wright and that of European architects should be apparent. The work of the latter is based upon the new conception of space as essentially many-sided which grew out of cubism.

4. *The free façade*, which is a direct consequence of skeleton construction.

5. *The roof garden.* Frank Lloyd Wright's houses demand that we go around them if we wish to understand their formation. Now a house can also be looked at from above or below; in a sense it presents a

surface that opens on the sky. The flat roof is a recognition of that additional space-relation in the dwelling—although the flat roof can, of course, be used with many different intentions. Its employment by contemporary architects—often in conjunction with flat slabs that form free-standing dividing walls or hovering partial coverings—does not serve practical ends alone. Such treatments express the sense of space of our period.

Since 1922, when he first began to build regularly, Le Corbusier has made use of and developed these five principles. The experience gained in the construction of several private homes has enabled him to use them in his work in more and more clarified form. They appear at their purest, perhaps, in his Villa Savoye, built at Poissy in 1928-1930 (Fig. 23).

All Le Corbusier's houses attack the same problem. He is always endeavoring to open up the house, to create new possibilities for connections between its interior and exterior and within the interior itself. We want rooms which can be thrown open or enclosed at will, rooms whose outer partitions fall away when we wish. Briefly, it is a question of achieving dwellings of a sort which, up to the present, have been beyond the reach of conception and execution alike. The armature construction is here in secret alliance with our half-realized desires; it anticipates them, in fact.

Previously to this, Le Corbusier's houses had been built on rather cramped plots, in more or less close proximity to their neighbors. The site of the Savoye house, on the contrary, was completely isolated.

The problem involved here was one which affects every man when he leaves his work and seeks to regain contact with nature, with growing things, the countryside, and the sky. This attempt to renew our connections with nature raises the same fundamental questions wherever we build, by the seashore, in the mountains, or—as in this case—on the undulating expanses of the Seine valley just outside Paris.

At one period in his development Frank Lloyd Wright used to employ the smallest crevices in the rocks to help bind his houses still more closely to the earth. In the Savoye house Le Corbusier does exactly the opposite. The city dweller for whom it was designed wanted to look out over the countryside rather than to be set down among trees and shrubbery. He wanted to enjoy the view, the breezes, and the sun—to experience that unhurried natural freedom which his work deprived him of. This is another instance of two eternally opposed responses to nature: a contemporary reflection of the difference between the Greek temple, sharply outlined against its background, and the medieval town, attached like a plant to the site on which it stands.

This house is a cube elevated on pillars. The cube part is not a solid mass; it is hollowed out on both the southeast and southwest sides so that when the sun comes up the light floods the whole interior instead of merely skimming the outer wall.

The entrance hall is on the northwest, but in coming in from the road one has to go all around the south side of the house to reach it. Of course there is really no façade and no back or front, since the house is open on every side.

The living room—five meters by fourteen—has horizontally sliding windows on two sides. The third wall (facing onto the terrace) is glass from floor to ceiling for some two thirds of its length. Half of this glass partition can be slid back by an easily manipulated lever. As a result, the room can be arranged quite freely, while the occupant is brought into connection with both the interior and the outdoors. The surrounding landscape, however, never appears in its full sweep. It is always shown in segments—framed, as it were—not only in the interior rooms but also on the terrace.

Since his La Roche house at Auteuil (1923-1924), Le Corbusier has been preoccupied by the problem of the ramp in the interior of the house. When there is room enough, the elimination of the staircase permits an almost insensible transition from one level in the house to another. The ramp in the Savoye house is in two sections (Fig. 22): one wing is inside; the other wing continues along an outer wall to the roof garden. Besides the ramp, there is a spiral staircase which leads from the ground to the roof.

It is impossible to comprehend the Savoye house by a view from a single point; quite literally, it is a construction in space-time. The body of the house has been hollowed out in every direction: from above and below, within and without. A cross section at any point shows inner and outer space penetrating each other inextricably.

Borromini had been on the verge of achieving the interpenetration of inner and outer space in some of his late baroque churches. This interpenetration was first realized in our period, through the methods of modern engineering, with the Eiffel Tower of 1889. Now, in the late twenties, it had become possible to achieve it in a dwelling. This possibility was latent in the skeleton system of construction, but the skeleton had to be used as Le Corbusier uses it: in the service of a new conception of space. That is what he means when he defines architecture as *construction spirituelle.*

II

In Paris, at about the same time, two large constructions by Le Corbusier appeared in quick succession: the Salvation Army hospice (1929-1933) and the Swiss Pavilion of the University City (1931-1933). Both show additions to Le Corbusier's equipment of esthetic means.

The pavilion of the Swiss dormitory is one of Le Corbusier's freest and most imaginative creations. The whole building is supported by immense ferroconcrete pillars which run deep into the soil to the underlying rock. One side of the building consists of the glass curtain wall of the studios; the other is modeled carefully in a curved wall of rugged stone and smooth slabs.

But what strikes one from the very first as extraordinary is the molding of volumes and space in the entrance hall. Although the room at his disposal was relatively limited, the imagination of the architect has created a space that is living, free, and vast. In the inventiveness it displays it is comparable to the work of the great periods. It is significant that the means employed are apparently very simple: the exact placement of the staircase, the unexpected undulations in the walls (the principle of the *plan libre*), and the use of microphotograph murals, set out checkerboard fashion. The incorporation into modern architecture of such imaginative elements is necessary to maintain its vitality.

Quite different inquiries and quite different solutions are involved in the Salvation Army hospice, the Cité de Refuge. This building—the largest Le Corbusier and his partner have yet built—is on the east side of Paris. Although there was a very limited budget and the building equipment had to be quite primitive, the hospice represents a really daring achievement. It is one of the first many-storied buildings in Europe to attempt a very simplified type of air conditioning.*

But here too the astonishing thing is the impression of grandeur produced by the interrelations between its volumes and space

* Frank Lloyd Wright's Larkin Building, Buffalo (1904) was, according to its architect, "the first air-conditioned office building."

at large. It is such relations that give modern architecture its vitality. Notice how smoothly the entry leads into the semicircular reception room, how smoothly the latter finds its continuation in the main hall, and how smoothly this in turn leads the men and women to their respective quarters. The building is a moving and unaffected assertion of the right of even the most humble to a human and dignified life.

Le Corbusier has two great gifts: he can reduce a complicated problem to astonishingly simple basic elements, and he can summarize these results in formulas of lapidary clearness. But however summary the manner of treatment may be, basic concepts and principles are never lost sight of.

III

Le Corbusier has grown so greatly in his powers and in his outlook that the period between 1938 and 1953 cannot be passed over in silence. In this later development small structures and one-family houses play no important role: Le Corbusier has become more and more the creator of large-scale designs.

These projects coincide with general signs that a new humanization of urban life is on the horizon. Man is no longer satisfied to remain a mere onlooker, whether at a football game or a television screen. His spontaneous relations can be seen in every part of the world during moments in which the passive spectator has become transformed into an active participant. There is a worldwide trend toward creating centers of social activity, and this calls for far more from the architect than just technical capacity. His task today is infinitely more complicated than that of his predecessors at the time when Versailles was built. They had but to give concrete form to an exact program placed before them by a clearly stratified society. Today the architect has to anticipate needs and to solve problems that exist only half consciously in the crowd. This involves a great responsibility. The architect has to have the rare gift of a peculiar sensitivity that we would like to term *social imagination.*

This is the aspect of Le Corbusier's later work which will here be evaluated.

Le Corbusier has cast the net of his vision over the chaos of the contemporary metropolis. In his plans he has cut thoroughfares through vested interests, demolishing whole quarters and raising them anew. Reality does not easily permit the realization of such radical operations, yet many of these plans—such as the second master plan for Algiers, 1942—will have more significance for future planners than the usual piecemeal rehabilitation.

Three landmarks stand out from Le Corbusier's work between 1938 and 1952. All of them are related to farsighted plans: The Core of St. Dié, 1945, the Unité d'Habitation, Marseille, 1947-1952, and the Capitol of Chandigarh, India, 1951.

The civic center of St. Dié displays in a masterly way a new kind of spatial relationship. The different buildings are designed and placed in such a way that each emanates its own spatial atmosphere and yet bears a close relationship to the whole core. The area is perforated by volumes of widely different shape that continually fill in or hollow out the space like contemporary sculptures.

People walking around or sitting in the cafe that forms a corner of the square would have a continuously changing spatial experience. Theater, museum, administration center, all are freely placed in space, and the eye can even glimpse the distant old cathedral and on the opposite bank of the river green-girdled factories, *les usines vertes*, as Le Corbusier calls them. Medieval Italy knew how to place volumes in space: in the Piazza del Duomo in Pisa the cathedral, baptistry, campanile, and *camposanto* give an exciting display of volumes in space. The modest unrealized scheme of St. Dié develops a different spatial conception. The relationship in the Gothic period was the relationship of formally closed volumes. Today we are moving toward a more dynamic conception of space, created by solids and voids.

The whole area of the core of St. Dié is reserved exclusively for pedestrians and this, but not only this, relates it to the Greek Agora. St. Dié, for the first time in our period, would have presented a crystallization of community life which could have equaled the Greek meeting place. All political parties of the small French city of St. Dié, including those of the extreme left, incited by the academicians, shouted so effectively against the scheme that Le Corbusier's core was condemned to remain on paper.

Architecture cannot be confined to those buildings that have been erected. Architecture is a part of life and architecture is a part of art. As a part of life it is more dependent than any other form of art upon the will of the public; upon their desire to see or not to see a scheme come into being. In architecture the standard of values of the client is as important as the standards of the builder.

If in the time of the Parthenon, the Pantheon, Chartres, or St. Peter's the taste of those who had power to order the erection of public buildings had been as weak and debased as it is today, none of them would ever have been built. They were daring experiments, all of them.

One of the few instances where social imagination has been given three dimensional expression is the "Unité d'Habitation," 1947-1952—the residential unit—on the Boulevard Michelet in the outskirts of Marseille. The Marseillais call it simply "Maison Le Corbusier." That this daring building could be successfully completed during five difficult postwar years is due to the courage of M. Claudius Petit, the French minister of reconstruction, who defended it to the very last against violent attacks.

The housing problem begins to take on a wider meaning. Both, architect and planner, are now working to rebuild the broken relationship between the individual and the collective spheres.

The boldness of the Unité d'Habitation does not consist in housing some 1600 people under one roof or even in providing twenty-three different types for its 337 apartments varying from one room up to dwellings for "families with eight children." Its boldness consists in its social implementation. The most interesting experiment in this residental unit was to take the shopping center from the ground and from the street and to place it on the central floor of the building itself. From outside, this central shopping street—*la rue marchande*—can be immediately identified by its two-story louvers. These, together with the vertical rows of square staircase windows in the middle of the block, vitalize and give scale to the whole front. The shopping street includes shops for groceries, vegetables, meat and fish, laundry and cleaning services, hairdresser and beautyshop, newspaper-stand, post-office, cafeteria, and hotel rooms. On the seventeenth floor is placed the nursery for 150 children. A ramp leads directly to the roof terrace with its rest room on pilotis, its shallow pool, and some charming installations for the children, who are encouraged to decorate the walls with their own murals.

The other part of the 24 x 165 meter roof terrace is designed for social activities of the adults. There is an area for gymnastics, partly open and partly covered, and, at the north end of the building, a large slab which acts as a protection against the strong north wind—the *Mistral*—and also as a background for open-air theatrical performances. On July 26th, 1953, when CIAM* celebrated its twenty-fifth anniversary on the roof terrace of the Unité d'Habitation, it looked like a painting of Paolo Veronese, for all the different levels were filled with people, and architecture was vibrant with life.

Strong, pure colors are used in this building, but Le Corbusier, the painter, has refrained from using any colors directly upon the façade. He paints the side walls of the balconies red, green, yellow, but not the front. In this way they are made to gleam like vivid colors through gauze. Bright color is also used in all the artificially lit *rue-intérieures* and serves to lighten the dimness of these long corridors.

The Unité d'Habitation rises beside the road which leads to the Riviera and faces east and west. Each two-story apartment looks to both sides. To the east their view embraces an arena of the limestone mountains that can be found everywhere in Provence. To the west lie the blue waters of the Mediterranean; while directly below the eye can rest on tree tops interspersed with red-tiled southern roofs. If Cézanne was able to seize the soul of Provence in his pictures, Le Corbusier has known how to capture it within an architectural frame.

Le Corbusier, as well as everybody else, knew that the Unité d'Habitation was a daring experiment both in the plastic sense and even more in the sphere of social imagination. Even after its successful opening in the fall of 1952 the French government remains skeptical and dares not even to take the risk of renting the apartments and shops but demands that they be sold outright, loading any risk upon the shoulders of the inhabitants and shopkeepers.

Yet there is no longer any doubt that this building will have an enormous influence in shaping the mind of the coming generation. It will help to liberate also the mind of the architect and planner from the conception of housing as a simple addition of single units and expand it to the wider frame of the human habitat.

* *Congrès internationaux d'architecture moderne.*

IV

The foundation of new towns is a sign of vitality and of an enterprising courage. New towns are often related to higher living standards or to the promise of them. This was the case during the Gothic period, when new towns suddenly sprang up in central and western Europe. The same phenomenon occurred during the last century in the United States, foreshadowing its industrial hegemony.

Toward the middle of the twentieth century we are witnessing the decentralization of western culture. New energy radiates from its former fringes: Finland, Brazil, Colombia, Venezuela, Canada, the African Gold Coast, to name only some areas of the centers of a new vitality. The Middle East is now also going ahead with an astonishing speed. Countries which have long been slumbering in their own lethargy or under oppression begin to awake and to become active participants in an evolution which is encompassing the entire world. In this process spirits of East and West are meeting together.

In the foreword to the Japanese translation of this book we tried to give some hint of this development:

> Western civilization is actually in a state of transition. Experience is slowly showing us that the rationalist and exclusively materialistic attitude upon which the latest phase of western civilization has been grounded is insufficient. Full realization of this fact lead us slowly towards a new hybrid development.

This meeting of East and West may explain why India—through the understanding of its leader Pandit Nehru—could choose a western architect for the new Capitol of Chandigarh. Yet there is also another reason. This is an inherent trend in contemporary architecture toward satisfying cosmic and terrestrial conditions and the habits which have developed naturally out of them. This explains why the forms of Brazilian architecture and Aalto's work in Finland, though so different, are both imbued with the spirit of the age. Both are regional contributions to a universal architectural conception. This attempt to meet cosmic, terrestrial, and regional conditions may be termed the new regional approach. This is the method of the best contemporary architects and is fully developed in Le Corbusier's boldest architectural adventure: the Capitol of Chandigarh.

When the Punjab was divided in 1947 between Pakistan and India, the ancient capital of Lahore was attached to Pakistan. A new capital became necessary for the East Punjab with its twelve and a half million inhabitants. On a sloping plateau at the foot of the Himalayas a superb site was discovered in 1950 through airplane reconnaissance by E. L. Varma, an eminent Indian government engineer.

The new capital city was called Chandigarh after a village on the site. When complete, it will house half a million people. The first section, now largely constructed, is for a population of 150,000. Neighborhood planning, housing, and schools are under the direction of Pierre Jeanneret and of Maxwell Fry and Jane Drew (whose building activities on the Gold Coast have been recognized) in cooperation with an entirely Indian staff of architects and engineers. The Capitol itself was entrusted to Le Corbusier, who has also been responsible for the final master plan of the whole city.

A town planner, an architect, an artist, a sculptor, and a man with the grasp of a poet are surveying a wide empty space at the foot of the Himalayas. These five are united in one person. This is the spot where the Capitol of Chandigarh is to stand. There is nothing more thrilling for the truly creative mind than to turn a dream into reality here on this myth-soaked soil. To achieve this, it may be worthwhile to have accepted a lifetime of humiliations.

We can follow line by line in Le Corbusier's sketchbook how the vision of the new Capitol crystallized, how it became a mighty monument, in which, for the first time, eastern and western thought flowed into each other without a break. Western calculation, shell concrete vaulting, and a butterfly roof of huge size which are normally associated with locomotive sheds and station platform, here change under our very eyes into some dream building of the East.

The program for the Capitol consists of a House of Parliament, a building for the Ministries, the Palace of the Governor, and the High Court of Justice. The most fantastic of these will probably be the Palace of the Governor, designed in April 1952, with its roof terraces, the upper one concave in shape. The Court of Justice, with its seven chambers under construction in 1953, is under the shade of an enormous butterfly roof which provides an umbrella of reinforced concrete against tropical sun and monsoon rains, which last from July to October. The huge sloping eaves stretch far out from the building. Parabolic shell vaults stiffen the structure and span the wide open entrance hall, which reaches up to the full height of the building. In this strange Palace of Justice modern techniques comply with cosmic conditions, with the country and with the habits of its people.

What astonishes the European eye is the large distances between the buildings. Only reality will show whether these are not too grandiose, as has happened in India with government buildings erected under the

British Raj. But there will be no dead surfaces between them. The sculptor in Le Corbusier has taken the opportunity to mold the enormous surface by varying levels, large pools, green lawns, single trees, artificial hills made of surplus material; and also by symbolic representations of the harmonic spiral, the daily path of the sun and other such. A dominant symbol will be the "open hand" which will be seen from everywhere and will "turn on ball bearings like a weathercock." The impress of the human hand placed upon the rock was the first artistic utterance of man. This symbol is still alive in India, and at the marriage feast friends leave the red stamp of their hands—red is the color of good luck—on the white walls of the bridal pair.

A monument in form of an enormous hand can be found earlier in the work of Le Corbusier. It was then an aggressive and menacing hand. Now under an eastern sky it has quieted down like the hand of Buddha.

5

PAINTING: IMPRESSIONISM, POSTIMPRESSIONISM, AND CUBISM

Lionello Venturi

What we now call the modern movement in art grew directly out of ideas and techniques developed by the French Impressionists in the late nineteenth century. The discussion of impressionism by Lionello Venturi, which we reprint, provides a clear picture of the major characteristics of impressionistic painting. Venturi shows how the impressionists' central concern with light influenced not only the new way in which they handled color but also the subjects they chose to paint and the composition of their paintings. Few art critics and historians have the ability to interpret modern art with such sympathy and clarity. Venturi's grasp of the meaning and structure of a painting is unusually keen; his style has been described as "deceptively simple." His detailed analysis of several paintings by Monet and Pissarro, two outstanding French impressionists, should enable students to understand better why these are good paintings—and to see more clearly what qualities distinguish an impressionistic painting from other styles. The influence of scientific thought upon the impressionists is developed more directly in a selection by Maurice Grosser which follows the two by Venturi.

Born in Modena, Italy, in 1885, Venturi ranks today among the most distinguished Italian art critics and historians. He received his Ph.D. in art history in Rome in 1907 and, after serving as director of art galleries in Venice and in Rome, became professor of art history at Turin University in 1915. Dismissed in 1932 by the fascist government of Italy because he would not take the required oath of allegiance to fascist principles, Venturi spent seven years in Paris and then six in America. He was visiting professor at Johns Hopkins University (1940), at the University of California (1941), and at the University of Mexico (1942). In 1945 he was recalled by the democratic government of Italy and appointed professor of the history of modern art at the University of Rome. Among his best-known works are two volumes on modern art, Modern Painters (1947), and Impressionists and Symbolists (1950), and the more popular book on Painting and Painters (1946) from which *our present selections are taken. He has also published studies of Cézanne, Chagall and Botticelli and a three-volume work on Italian painting.*

The selection on Picasso and cubism is to be read after the study of impressionism and Cézanne has been completed. Venturi's intimate acquaintance with Italian painting of the Renaissance makes cubism seem to him a bit cold and intellectual—reflecting an influence of science upon the arts which in his opinion is not entirely desirable—but his clear analysis of Picasso's The Red Tablecloth *(Fig. 26) should prove an especially helpful introduction to contemporary abstract art.*

VITALIZING NATURE: THE IMPRESSIONISTS

I

IN THE years just prior to 1870, three young men, Monet, Renoir, and Pissarro, used to sit on the banks of the Seine and the Oise rivers and paint landscapes. They were realistic painters, greatly interested in rendering the reflection of light on the water, which showed continuous movement and gave a new life to the water. Furthermore, the various colors thus reflected suggested to them the idea of expressing light by opposing colors without using dark tones for shadows. And so they clarified their palette unconsciously, and divided colors, not by following any theory, but only by experience. For some time, they painted water in this new way, and hills, trees, houses, and sky in the old realistic traditional way. However, this resulted in unbalanced canvases. To avoid this mistake, they then tried to portray everything, even human figures, in the same way that they painted water. They saw every image not in abstract form, not in chiaroscuro, but as a reflection of light, either real or imaginary. They had selected only one element from reality—light—to interpret all of nature. But then, light ceased to be an element of reality. It had become a principle of style, and impressionism was born.

Light is the element which reveals the appearance of reality. What impressionists painted and interpreted was not reality but the appearance of reality. They stuck to the appearance of things with a clearer vision than had painters before them. The grasping of appearance is a form of sensation as free from reasoning and will as it can possibly be. Thus impressionists were faithful to their sensations, that is to their impressions of nature, and found a form closer to the first impression of the appearance of nature than previous painters. And it was closer because of their vivid sensibility, whereby they understood the absolute value in art of the appearance of things, nor did they undervalue their impressions since their mind was sufficiently free from the traditional principles of abstract form.

The first step in art is the contact with the appearance of nature. It is the essential condition in art without which there can be no art. Raphael or Rembrandt, for example, realized the appearance of things. Then, through their imaginative process, they went farther in order to reach a physical or moral ideal which was beyond sensation. The impressionists found their physical and moral ideal within the limits of their sensations. They forsook many possible developments of their imagination in order to make sure that the sensible actuality should be perfectly realized.

Impressionists painted simple trees instead of monumental ones; peasant cottages instead of palaces; plain girls instead of great ladies; workingmen instead of noblemen. This was not for the purpose of advancing a political issue, but was the expression of a natural sympathy towards familiar subjects, familiar to their everyday life, the life of poor people and open country. In the old historical landscapes an oak is always a nobleman; an impressionistic poplar is just a common man. This meant the discovery of a new source for art.

II

The composition of impressionist painters was a composition of light, and not of things represented. The arrangement of things in balance, or the representation of space in perspective was lacking in their paintings. Hence they were accused of painting only fragments. This is rather amusing. Where is the painter who can represent the whole of nature? Every artist, of course, represents mere fragments. True, painters concentrate on each fragmentary element their feeling for the whole of nature, which is nature itself. So did the impressionists. They had selected light as one of the many elements of nature. They had endowed their own created light with their artistic quality, and had subordinated all other elements to their light. One can be aware of the totality of their works of art, only if he sees the expression of their composition of light.

The most evident, and the most recognized, quality of the impressionists was that their paintings were brighter than all other paintings since the sixteenth century. This was due above all to the division of colors we spoke of. The bright effect of this division of colors was due to the fact that the fusion of two lights is brighter than the mixture of the two corresponding tints. If, for example, you mix two tints, one blue and the other yellow, you obtain a green with some quantity of gray which lessens the intensity of the original blue and yellow. But if you juxtapose the blue and the yellow, at a certain distance the eye sees a green, resulting from the lights of the blue and the yellow; and this resulting green will be much more intense than if you had mixed the two tints. Impressionists never followed a systematic use of this fusion of lights, but they reached this result through their sense of coloring, the most subtle the history of art has ever known.

This division of colors required an appropriate form. In the original of Figure 24 [Monet, *Sailboat at Argenteuil*] the purple roof of an orange house is reflected in the water: the reflection is a series of tremulous zones of yellow representing light, and of purple representing shade. This division of two colors emphasizes the vibration of the reflection. But through that division the form of the roof is lost; what remains is the form of the vibration. And correctly so; for had the form of the roof been maintained the vibration of the reflection would have disappeared, and the purpose of the painter would have failed. This is the reason why so many painters who adopted impressionistic colors but remained faithful to traditional drawing and to chiaroscuro, lost both form and color. Thus the division of colors is at the very basis of that distortion of form which is typical of modern art and which for many different reasons has been adopted by so many painters, even by those who refused to use any division of colors. Impressionists, for the first time, conceived a distortion of traditional form, as the necessary form for divided colors. Of course, they realized it much more easily in the image of a sky, a river, a sailboat, or a tree, than in the human figure, as we shall see later in these pages. This is one of the reasons why impressionism originated with landscape painting, and was only later applied to human figures.

When the division of colors was adopted, the conception of space had also to be changed. Florentines in the fifteenth century discovered perspective and used space as a void wherein to isolate human figures. With Leonardo and the Venetians of the sixteenth century, aerial perspective was added to linear perspective in order to represent not empty space but a space full of atmosphere. And as the atmosphere was deepened through the effect of color, a three-dimensional effect, full of nuances, less sharp and better related to the surface, was finally realized. Now consider the atmosphere of a picture suggested by the vibrations of divided colors and full of light reflections, and you will soon realize the necessity for the painter to diminish the three-dimensional effect in his painting. The fact that in an impressionistic painting the painted surface prevails over the illusion of space in depth has been one of the charges made against the impressionists—an unjust accusation because there is no law which requires of a picture a three-dimensional effect, and the impressionists in emphasizing the surface of their paintings were perfectly coherent in their use of light through divided colors as the unifying factor of their painting.

Finally, the conception of movement held by the impressionists was also an entirely new one. As their painting had its origin in the reflections of light in water, the whole effect of their pictures was due to a perennial movement, a cosmic vibration. Any static object introduced into that vibration, would have destroyed the whole effect of their art. To visualize a cosmic vibration meant for them to reveal the impression of that energy which is the life of nature. Vibrating light was for them the force which endowed everything in nature with life and vigor. Thus the impressionists brought pictorial form—that is, the form of color—to extreme consequences, undreamed of before them.

III

Figure 24 reproduces *Sailboat at Argenteuil* by Claude Monet (1840-1926), painted in 1875 during the best period of his activity. Both the sky and the water in the picture are dominated by the action of the sunset, with the orange, yellow, and purple tones vibrating with the pagan abandonment of an orgiastic festivity, and yet, withal, somehow calmed by the green and blue into a perfect balance. The sailboat, slightly off center in the picture, done in opaque almost neutral green, is the pivot around which light dances; while in the sky the sun, in its last daily salute to earth, spreads its gemlike treasure of light, and reflects it into the water. But with the suggested calm of the evening approaching, the opacity of the sailboat suggests the lull after the orgy. The excitement with which Monet painted this picture is evident in his divided colors and in his clarified palette, as well as in his furious brush strokes. The painter here seems immersed both in the movement of colors and in the vibration of light. His enthusiasm here is at its height, the wonder of nature completely overpowering him. And yet he is not joyous in this profusion of nature's bounty. He feels the coming end of it all, and it is precisely this pervasive sentiment of melancholy which results both in the balance of colors and the human expression of nature.

The personal accent of Monet is on the wonder of nature, but he balanced it by the variations of his color nuances, so that it might become natural. And since his aspiration was always towards the wonder of nature he invented the impressionistic touches, not only for dividing colors, but also to express directly through them the vibration of nature. This was an innovation in painting as daring as it could possibly be, and was no doubt prompted by an inner necessity to rebel against traditional modes of expression and by a faith in his own mode of expression unequalled among his fellow impressionists. It was indeed Monet who started the offensive for "plein air" in painting—that is, painting directly out of doors from the motif, without in the least caring for the finish of the studio. And because of this he was recognized as the leader of impressionism. This, however, does not mean that Monet was the greatest artist among impressionists, but that he was the leader of that revolution in taste. The greatest artists are perhaps less daring than Monet was; they are less exclusive; they usually fashion their style with a more comprehensive mind, and they seldom stress the unusual wonders of nature.

IV

Figure 25 represents the *Oise River near Pontoise* by Camille Pissarro (1830-1903), painted in 1873. In this picture the flowering earth, the water, the factory buildings, the sky—every bit of this canvas—vibrate with the light Pissarro painted in it. But this vibration is not the only subject matter of the painting, as in Monet's. There is also a very well-defined construction of space in depth from the right foreground to the left middle ground. However, Pissarro does not lose sight of the surface by the emphasis put on the horizon and the ample sky above it. His free touches of light are impressionistic, as is the form of the flowers, of the reflections of light in the water, of the buildings, and of the clouds, in the picture; it is always the form of the effect of light, and not of the things in themselves. This emphasis on the effect of light is more evident in the flowers than in other passages of the picture, because they are in the foreground. But it none the less motivates all other aspects of the painting as well. And in accordance with the impressionistic principles of seeing things, the colors too are as bright and intense as the light. But the contrast between light and shade in Pissarro's painting is more pronounced than in Monet's, so that the form acquires a greater volume, a greater stability, in perfect coherence with the composition. This stability, however, does not lessen the vibration and the vitality of anything in nature; but the vibration is slower and larger, and is thoroughly integrated with the construction of the picture.

Pissarro's eye is less excited and his contemplation of nature is calmer, even if the vibration gives the vision a hint of drama, sufficient for vitalizing nature, but mastered by a deep sense of reality. Pissarro did not seek wonders in nature. He believed that *all* of nature was wonderful and that the most wonderful of all wonders was the everyday life of nature. He is at the same time more, yet less, of a realist than Monet. Pissarro sought to retain in his pictures the freshness of his first impression of nature, but always worked accurately to transform it into a unity of pictorial effect, so that he eventually became more detached from nature than was Monet. Such an attitude was responsible for the accurate construction of his paintings, the volume of his masses of colors, and finally for the preciousness of color itself, which in his best works is unsurpassed.

He has often been accused of being prosaic, and his subject matters are indeed prosaic. But Pissarro's poetry exists, even if it is necessary to find it, not in his subject matter, but in his form, his light, and his colors. No painter so far has surpassed him in his feeling for nature and in endowing it with life. Nature for him was a matter of faith, a moral principle. He believed that the society of his time was corrupt—an evil to be avoided—and found his right to freedom and humanity only in contact with nature. This moral attitude made it possible for him to impress his landscapes with his utter faith in the life of nature.

ABSTRACT ART

Picasso and Cubism

AT THE BEGINNING of our century, a reaction took place against realism and impressionism as trends adhering too faithfully to nature. To find the essence, the truth, the absolute in art, the new painters began to distort the shape of things, and then to invent new shapes which were independent, sometimes absolutely independent, of any natural shape. Such a trend is known as "abstract art."

Today when we speak of *abstract art we* mean cubism and its variations. The painters who invented cubism and the critics who supported it were not well versed in philosophy, and they therefore ignored the new ideas on esthetics concerning the reality of art as consisting of the sensations of the artist. They craved a reaction against nature; yet, while anxious to be free of nature, they thought always, paradoxically, in terms of nature. They therefore created an image of something which was the very opposite of nature without being aware that the opposite of nature is on the same level with nature, and not on the level of art.

To all this must be added that at the beginning of our century a crisis was noted in the conclusions of science, which was no longer sure of its concepts based on pure logic alone, of its mathematical truths. So the new painters felt free to use science for their own purposes and to believe in their own scientific achievements without in the least caring for the skeptical attitude of sound criticism or for the control of logic. Their science was only a starting point for the free play of their imagination. What they wanted was to reach an ideal that would embrace the "infinite universe," but having cut themselves off completely from their experiences of the surrounding world, they eventually ended up in a vacuum, where they had to be contented with their innate power of mystic suggestion, and were forced to admit their objective impotence, their negation of any objective ideal.

This was the program of cubism; and the following summary is an attempt to give an idea of the way it was finally realized in practice: An object has always been represented from only one point of view, but the cubists wanted to represent it from many sides. So they cut it into parts, reduced each part to its simplest form, which is approximately a geometric form, and juxtaposed the other parts like projections of the first one. Then they transposed on the surface of their painting all elements which in their perspective arrangement had represented space in depth. This dissection of an object into parts, and their arrangement on the surface, was an attempt to suggest both the view of the object from all possible sides and the exposition of its parts on the surface. The result, of course, was that human perception of the object utterly failed, and that an interpretation was needed to reconstruct in the imagination the dissected object. The arrangement of the parts of the object, which were partly geometric and partly verisimilar in form, followed the geometric projections only partially, and generally was due to free imagination. If this imagination was arbitrary, that is, detached from the senses, the result was a failure. But if the imaginative arrangement included a pattern, a sense of proportion—a sense of balance, of relation between form and color, of harmony of colors and so on—then the result could reveal the personality of the painter, his interest in life; how, for example, he felt, loved, and hated. Then the result would be a work of art.

Generally speaking, a painter feels his motif, and expresses himself through the motif, going from the concrete to the abstract, that is, from feeling to style. In this, cubist painters made use of a double process: going from the concrete to the abstract and back again to the concrete. But their process of abstracting from the object was not an artistic one. It was a cool, logical calculation, a purely mechanical process. When, however, they found themselves confronted with their artificial abstractions, and, if they were real artists, decided to let their imagination work in a concrete way, then they came down to earth and began to wrestle in earnest with the reality of their feeling, sometimes achieving a real work of art.

Now please look at *The Red Tablecloth* by Picasso (Fig. 26), one of the most renowned, and the easiest to understand, of all his semi-abstract paintings. It is a still-life, representing a table covered by a red cloth, a sheet of music, a guitar, a fruit-dish with a slice of melon on it, a sculptured head, and a large window in the background. The cubistic method is evident in the projections of the guitar and the fruit-dish, in the juxtaposition of the zones of light and shade, like patterns which are independent of the representation of the table, and in the linear features of the head. That is, this still-life has an indirect relation to a natural still-life; it has a unity of lines, forms, and colors, an organism of its own, and a unity of style. The formal relation of the sheet of music, of the fruit-dish and the melon, of the lines of the head and the window, of the decoration of the guitar and the cloth, and so on, contribute to the unity of the scene; while the arrangement of colors accentuates that unity. The upper part of the picture is painted in very bright colors: the window is white, sky-blue, and, a small section of it, very light gray; the melon and bowl are white, with some very transparent green, violet, pink, and yellow; and the sheet of music is white and black. All of these are framed by colors which are very strong and dark, beginning with the black marble head on the brown table, the red-and-black cloth, and the brown-and-black guitar. The dark color zones give the impression of great monumentality, of plastic stability; while the bright color zones express the free flight of the artist's imagination from darkness towards light.

At this point, we may well ask: What is abstract in this painting? And what is the character of this abstraction?

Figure 27 shows a composition of architectonic space in *Perspective* by a follower of Piero della Francesca, painted in the fifteenth century. It is an abstract painting. Its abstraction does not consist in the fact that it does not represent anything. On the contrary, it represents some columns, some houses, a street, and some boats in the background. However, it is abstract because the geometric forms and the perspective lines dominate the representation of the scene to such an extent that nothing is left of the freedom and variety of man and nature. It is a cold rigid architecture, if you will—but still a mathematical scheme of space. Here the painter first made his calculation of perspective, and then covered it with the most appropriate buildings he could design to demonstrate his calculation. All this could very well be a scholastic exercise in geometry, but how could it become art? The painter loved something—empty space in perspective, emphasized by the porch in the foreground, and gave to this empty space something of magic, the sense of things fixed for eternity. His belief or illusion that perspective could impress things with the sense of eternity, of universality, and of absoluteness is the artistic seal of this painting.

If now we leave the follower of Piero della Francesca and go back to Picasso, we shall soon become aware that the latter has no faith at all in science and uses geometric elements capriciously, occasionally only, sticking to arbitrary forms, in relation both to science and nature. Still, there is in Picasso a necessity for abstraction, in order to follow certain rhythms of his own in pattern and color. It is an abstraction born of the imagination, and, as always happens in abstractions, the only possibility in it for art is to induce a vague feeling of contemplation for the eternal, the universal, and the absolute. That is, in the fifteenth as in the twentieth century, abstract painting could realize a contemplative world, without distinctions, without emotions, but still capable of a rarefied life, which is art.

But let us look at the man himself. A Spaniard, Picasso was born in 1881, and since early youth has been drawing with a natural skill for mastering technique rare at any time. He said: "I have difficulty in understanding the meaning of research. I do not seek. I find." This is perfectly true: his facility in achieving what he wants is the result of this exceptional mastery of technique. In fact, he could very easily have become a successful academic painter. But as he is a very serious and faithful artist, he could not waste his great talent on such questionable worldly success. Believing that art is invention, he has during a lifetime of furious activity changed his style of painting many times in obedience to the impulse of the moment to invent something new. He "does not seek," he "finds." But what he finds is always something unexpected and amazing. This is due to the quick workings of his decisive mind in immediate compliance with his impulses. But he never thinks of integrating his new achievements with those of the past, nor even with his own previous achievements. And when inspired by motifs drawn from the past, he changes them so radically that nothing remains of them in his painting but the realization of his ideas held at that particular moment. Picasso is no more moderate as a man than he is as an artist. In fact, he deliberately ignores moderation, and is often contradictory and violent in his opinions as he is in his art. But everything he does he affirms with unshaken assurance, with terrific authority. This is the secret of his artistic success and fame. No painter since the death of Cézanne has had such tremendous influence on other painters as Picasso has had.

All these forceful elements in Picasso's character are no doubt favorable to a conqueror, to an inventor, perhaps to an executive. But are they favorable to an artist? We all know, or should know, that an essential difference exists between the inventor and the creator, and that the artist is, above all, a creator. An inventor may invent or discover some new object or gadget useful to humanity, say the airplane, the radio or the safety razor. A creator, on the other hand, does not discover anything outside himself. What he puts into his painting or his poem must come from within himself. And the artistic value of the object he has made—the canvas painted or the book written—consists exactly in his making the object capable of revealing his own personality or personal values, which are beyond the measuring rod of science or mechanical formulae.

As Gertrude Stein has said, the soul of people does not interest Picasso very much; he is too much occupied with the body to be aware of the soul. Besides, he does not seem interested in the changing trends of thought, feeling, and imagination impinging on man today. He can believe in the eternity of what he sees, because he fails to perceive that humanity is always changing. He reduces almost everything human to a physical level, and his approach to feeling is always cold and intellectual. His painting can be sentimental, because sentimentality gives feeling an intellectual direction towards some practical action, which often startles, but does not move; conquers, but does not attract. Picasso is perhaps more, but in many ways he is less, than an artist.

Maurice Grosser

Maurice Grosser is a successful artist who believes that if the intelligent layman is to understand painting he must know something of a painter's own problems. He has the distinction also of being a painter who can write about the technical aspects of his art. Most of his colleagues, when they talk about their paintings, either omit this aspect of their work, or merely say that a good painting communicates directly to the artist (or the spectator with sensitivity) and that is that. Grosser, on the other hand, in his popular book on modern art, The Painter's Eye *(1951), tried to explain some of the painter's peculiar difficulties to the layman.*

Among the problems that have interested him ever since he studied art in Boston and Paris during the 1930's are why portrait painting no longer attracts the best artists, why abstraction fascinates so many of them, and, in the selection reprinted here from The Painter's Eye, *what chance there is of developing a dependable, really scientific, theory of color. In this discussion Grosser is particularly concerned with what he takes to be the major contribution of the impressionists to modern art—their new understanding and handling of color—and he treats this aspect of impressionism with particular insight.*

Attention should be called to two other aspects of Grosser's thought in the present selection. The first of these is his high estimate of what he calls "the impressionist revolution." While art critics recognize the important influence of impressionism in the history of modern art, they by no means all agree with Grosser that it is "the source of all the painting of the present day." A somewhat different point of view, for example, is presented in the selection by Sir Kenneth Clark which follows. Nevertheless, Grosser does provide the kind of detailed discussion of the way in which modern science influenced the impressionists that makes clear the reason for treating impressionism in this section of the Anthology. His statement—"Indeed the whole originality of the impressionists derives from the scientific progress of their time" [emphasis inserted]—may be a bit uncritical; but his specific analysis of developments in physics and chemistry that largely influenced the painting of the impressionists carries conviction. And his discussion of the way in which photography and painting were related at this time suggests another effect of science upon the arts to which attention might well be given. At these points in particular his essay provides desirable enlargement of the treatment of impressionism in the earlier selection by Venturi.

THE PAINTER'S EYE: COLORS AND COLOR

IT IS the impressionist revolution which is the source of all the painting of the present day. We are accustomed to think of impressionism as the theory of broken color, as a revolt against the brown sauces of the academic painters. But the impressionist revolt was more profound than this. It was a revolt against the anecdote, and even against the planned picture itself. The impressionists threw overboard the whole body of academic tradition. The great scandal of their painting was not that their pictures were bright but that they were unpremeditated.

Improvisatory painting was not entirely new. It had been practiced as early as the middle of the eighteenth century. There is a nude of Fragonard inscribed on the back of the canvas "Frago painted this in an hour." But throughout the eighteenth century the distinctions were maintained. Improvisations were understood to be sketches. Real pictures took planning. But with the impressionists this difference disappeared. The sketch became the picture. And the big picture—which always takes a certain time to paint—became a series of sketches superimposed one on top of the other.

I

The most striking characteristic of the impressionist pictures is perhaps their cool, their blue or violet, general tone. It is partly that the impressionists disdained the orange tinted varnish "soups" the official painters used to give their own work a false age and a museum respectability. But it is chiefly the accidental result of the impressionists' habit of painting out-of-doors. Shadow tones out-of-doors, on the bright days when painters work, are likely to be blue or violet. And it is the color of the shadows, not of the lights, which determines the general color tone of a picture.

The official painters painted indoors, if possible in a studio with windows facing north so that the sun could not enter or the direction of the light on the model change. North light is blue. Even on a cloudy day it is relatively cool. The color of a studio itself is generally warm. That is to say that the color of its walls, floors, hangings, and other furniture is more likely to be in the browns and reds and oranges than in the lilacs, grays, or blues. Consequently a model posed in a studio will be lighted by a cold light; and the shadows, which reflect the warm tones of the room, will be reddish, brown, or orange. Even when such a painter painted out-of-doors, he was more likely than not to execute his picture in the tonality he had been accustomed to use for indoor painting, just as if the landscape had been brought into the studio and lighted with the usual studio lighting of warm shadows and cool lights.

The impressionists, on the other hand, painted out-of-doors on principle. Sunlight is yellow or orange. The blue of the sky gives blue reflections in the shadows of nearby objects, and the blue color of the air gives a blue cast to all distant things, so that the only warm colors in the impressionists' landscapes are the brightly lighted parts of the objects in the foreground. All the rest of the picture is in violets, greens, and blues. Even when the impressionist painted indoors, he was likely to look for, find, and paint, if not warm lights, at any rate blue shadows, and to exaggerate them. Vuillard, of course, worked almost entirely indoors, and consequently used a great deal of brown. But with the other impressionists, a cool tonality and blue or lilac shadows became a trade mark and the easiest way to distinguish their work from the painters of the official schools.

In one respect, all these painters were alike. Different as the color system of the rebel impressionists may have been from that of the official and academic painters, all the post-photographic painters are equally dependent on some aspect of photography. They differ only in the kind of photography each employs. The virtuoso brush-stroke painter manipulates a large, slow, expensive plate camera in a photographer's studio, using time exposures, arranged lighting, and a portrait lens. The impressionist wanders about the woods and fields with the new, fast, portable, inexpensive, daylight-loading, snapshot apparatus. Certain of the impressionists, I have heard, even went to the trouble of having made large camera shutters through which they could look, and by painting only what they could see while the shutter was open, thought to reproduce more exactly the effect of an instantaneous exposure.

The impressionist camera is loaded with color film. In fact, color photography and the impressionists' broken color are both derived from the same source—the new theories of color vision and color mixing which the physicists had just recently formulated. The principles on which the first practical system of color photography was based had already been sketched out by Ducos du Hauron as early as 1868, only six years before the first impressionist exposition. The first successful commercial application of these principles, the Autochrome process (in which the photograph is taken on a plate covered by a mixture of starch grains dyed three primary colors) differs little either in theory or appearance from the paintings of Monet or Pissarro. However, the Autochrome plate did not appear on the market until the first decade of the twentieth century. By this time the public had become accustomed to impressionist painting, and could accept without question the somewhat coarse spottiness which the larger color granulations of the Autochrome process give to the appearance of nature. So that perhaps we have here an example of what in our own time is more common than the influence of photography on painting—a contrariwise example of the influence of the painter on the camera.

II

The impressionist theory, with which we are all familiar, is that the painter is a disinterested spectator. His eye is pure. Like the camera, his eye has no preferences. Each element in the field of its vision is of equal importance in forming the image it sees. The painter aims his eye like a camera at the thing he is to paint and records the variations of light his eye receives in terms of spots of color. For the impressionist, the world he paints is the world of the eye's sensations.

A painter in the classical tradition, on the other hand, considers the primary reality to be the object's solid form, which intercepts the light and casts a shadow. For the traditional painter a light cannot exist without a shadow. The presence of the one implies the other. But for the impressionist, the primary reality is the sensation in his eye. What he is painting is not form but light. One light cannot exist without another. The presence of a light does not imply a shadow. It implies the presence of another, different light. Consequently, his tones of paint do not represent chiaroscuro or light and dark. They represent, all of them, lights—lights of different strengths and colors, but none the less lights. Each tone, even a tone of deepest shadow, stands for a colored light. Each spot of colored light is of equal importance in producing in the painter's eye the sensation of the object he is painting. Since each square centimeter of painted canvas is to represent a light, each square centimeter of the finished picture must have an equal weight and an equal importance. Thus each square centimeter of the canvas must be painted with a similar, a carefully equalized, texture.

An equalized painted surface such as this cannot be got by any of the methods the official painters used. The virtuoso brush stroke which copies the shapes of lights and shadows in thick paint will not achieve it. The sharp edges of the brush strokes interfere. They are too important. The weights and tensions they add to the painted surface cannot be equally distributed. Nor will the laborious system of concealing the marks of the brush and painting with no apparent brush stroke at all do it either. In such painting one part of the picture will invariably be more detailed than another, and the surface of the picture at that point, in consequence, more labored. The impressionists solved the problem and arrived at an equalized surface by adopting a neutral brush stroke, each one approximately the same size and shape, done with small brushes all the same size. The brush stroke never changes sizes or shape or inclination to fit the size of the detail being painted. It never at any time follows the direction of the shape of the painted forms. The painter uses his brush to make an extra pattern superimposed on the pattern of the picture and independent of the objects that are in it. Monet dabs. Pissarro scatters confetti. Seurat plants polka dots. Cézanne, in certain of his periods, adopts a diagonal twill. Thus by stylizing the brush stroke and painting everything in the picture in the same way, the objective clarity of the painter's impression of nature is not obscured by any mannerism of hand or handling.

This painted surface with equal tension in all its parts is the second of the impressionist's great inventions. It was devised to represent more closely the camera's vision. We have taken it over for our own uses. It is to the impressionists and their practices that we owe our present-day esthetic of the equalized surface tension, of continuous surface without accent, on which is based all the good building, painting, design and even music of our time, from jet planes and pictures to soap boxes and swing.

It was the impressionist revolution of 1870, and not the cubist revolution of 1910, which was responsible for modern art. The cubist revolution brought nothing new to the technique of painting. It brought only a new subject matter, already foreseen in the parodies of Manet, and executed in the accepted style of the improvised picture, with the continuous and equalized surface, already developed by the impressionists. It is to impressionism that we owe not only our liberation from a moribund romanticism, but also the invention of the techniques and the establishment of the traditions of the painting of our time.

III

The painter depends on the poet, the chemist, and the physicist a great deal more than he likes to admit. He eagerly adopts the subjects the poets propose, the pigments the chemists invent, and the theories of perspective and light the physicists devise, and turns them to his own uses. The impressionist painters themselves were perhaps less dependent on the poets and literary men than is generally the case. Zola's painter hero in *L'Oeuvre*, for example, who killed himself because he could not finish a picture, aroused only their amused disdain. A real painter, as Cézanne pointed out, would have found it more advantageous to have begun another picture instead. But if the impressionists found little inspiration in poetry itself, the poetry of applied science, on the other hand, they found extremely useful. Indeed the whole originality of the impressionists derives from the scientific progress of their time—from a new theory of color mixing which they made their own, and from the new bright colors they used to expound it—from the most recent findings of physics and chemistry which were ready at hand when the impressionists began to paint.

But with all their bright new colors, the impressionists' pictures were never as bright as the old masters', nor were they, in fact, ever intended to be. They were only meant to be bright and clear. The impressionists' pictures seemed startlingly bright to their contemporaries, not because their colors were bright but because they were unexpected. The impressionists put their bright colors in places where painters had been in the habit of putting no color at all. They painted lavender and green in the shadows where gray or brown had always been used before. They got the effect of black with dark red and green and blue. They put bright blue in the shadows of snow and green in the shadows of hair. They were attempting to represent the effects of light, even to paint light itself. They wished the paint in their pictures to look like light instead of paint. As a consequence, they painted in a very light, pale key, with a great deal of white mixed with all the colors.

The older painters of the sixteenth and seventeenth centuries never considered that they were painting with light. They had few bright colors and preferred to use them in the deeper tonal ranges where these pigments could be shown at their highest intensity and beauty. Their one bright red was vermilion. If a bright red coat was to be painted, the lights and darks of the rest of the picture would be so graded that the vermilion could be used pure. Any touch of black or white thrown in to adjust the pigment's tone would mar its brilliance. If a more scarlet hue than the orange of vermilion was needed for the coat, the painter would add yellow to all the other colors in the picture. Thus the general yellow tone of the rest of the picture would make a red-orange flame of the vermilion seem a scarlet red. A picture with much blue sky would be painted dark enough so that the costly ultramarine could be exhibited at its greatest beauty, as can be seen, for example, in the sky of Titian's *Rape of Europa* in Boston. These older painters considered that their pigments were only substances, with precise character and limited possibilities, and used every trick they knew to set them off to their best advantage. They knew that too many bright colors in a picture neutralized one another. The most brilliant effects were to be had with one or two bright colors set off by duller ones. Their few vivid pigments, used pure and thrown into relief against a neutral background, make their pictures very bright indeed. Look at certain of Velasquez' paintings, apparently executed with only white, black, brown, and vermilion, or the superb Veronese in the Ringling Museum, where the Holy Family, resting under a palm tree, is being tended by hovering angels. The colors in the picture appear astonishingly bright. Actually the only pigment used at its full intensity is the blue in the sky. Tiepolo was especially skillful at this sort of effect, where a robe, apparently a deep rich red, can only be matched as anyone who has tried to copy one of his pictures knows, by a sort of reddish mud.

But the impressionists were not painting

pictures of colored objects. They were interested in a more complicated problem—what colored objects look like under colored light. Their palette was vastly richer than the older painters'. They had what none of the older painters possessed, mauves, violets, bright greens, oranges, and intense yellows. They could allow themselves the liberty of forgetting that their pigments were only substances. They could permit themselves to confuse the paint on their palettes with the light they were attempting to represent. Operating with the new theory of the additive mixture of colors, which was based on the behavior of mixtures of colored lights, the impressionists put down their dots of paint as if they were speckling the canvas with spots of colored light. These dots of paint were as far as possible pure, unmixed colors, nor were they blended on the canvas. They were intended to be mixed in the spectator's eye, where they were to produce the effect, not of a painting, but of an open window.

Sir Kenneth Clark

Born in 1903 of a wealthy British family, Kenneth Clark traveled widely as a boy not only in Europe but also in the Orient, and he early developed a consuming interest in art. At fifteen he determined to make art criticism his profession in life, and he began his first book, a study of the Gothic revival in architecture, when a student at Oxford University. For several years during his student days he also worked in Italy with Bernard Berenson on the art of the Italian Renaissance.

Over a period of twenty years (1931-1951), Clark held important positions in England that gave him a broad experience in the world of art. He was for a time head of the Department of Fine Arts at the Ashmolean Museum at Oxford; at thirty he became director of the National Gallery in London, the outstanding art museum in England; twelve years later he was appointed Slade Professor of Fine Arts at Oxford University, perhaps the top academic position in art in England. He has also been a visiting lecturer at Yale University. More recently he retired from active teaching in order to give full time to writing and lecturing. He is recognized as an authority on a wide range of subjects: Baroque architecture, Chinese painting, and the poetry of Wordsworth as well as nineteenth-century landscape painting.

Among Clark's better known books are The Gothic Revival *(1929),* Leonardo da Vinci *(1939),* Florentine Painting: Fifteenth Century *(1945), and* Landscape into Art *(1949), from which our present selection is taken. In England Clark is known especially for his encouragement of modern art, of which he has made a large private collection, but he brings to this study of contemporary painting a broad historical perspective and a catholic taste.*

The selection reprinted here presents the kind of objective evaluation of impressionism which will appeal to the thoughtful student. Although Clark recognizes the large contribution to modern art made by the impressionists, he does not share Grosser's unrestrained enthusiasm for that movement. He is aware also of the problems that the limited concern of the impressionists (with light and color) inevitably produced; he examines carefully their effort to meet these problems, and he estimates the significance of the impressionist movement in terms of a much broader philosophy of art than either Venturi or Grosser brings to the subject. In our study of the Humanities this larger perspective is, of course, particularly desirable and valuable. Our interest is not merely in art for art's sake but in art as an expression of values and insights that are intimately related to the whole of human life.

THE NATURAL VISION: IMPRESSIONISM

An Evaluation

I

IN THE pictures of Argenteuil by Monet * and Renoir, done between 1871 and 1874, the painting of sensation yielded its most perfect fruits. They show an unquestioning joy in the visible world, and an unquestioning belief that the new technique alone can convey it. This balance between subject, vision, and technique was so complete that it not only captivated sympathetic spirits like Sisley and Pissarro †, but imposed itself on painters to whom it was quite alien. Even Gauguin and van Gogh, who were to destroy impressionism, painted some of their most beautiful pictures in this style.

There are few things more refreshing in art than the sense of delight in a newly acquired mastery. The excitement with which the impressionists conquered the representation of light by the rainbow palette, is like the excitement with which the Florentines of the fifteenth century conquered the representation of movement by the flowing plastic line. But art which depends too much on the joy of discovery inevitably declines when mastery is assured. By the middle of the 1880s the great impressionist moment had passed. At first Renoir and Monet tried to keep up their excitement by choosing more and more brilliant subjects. Renoir painted gardens which gave him the added problem of bright local colors, and Monet painted coast scenes which have the most intense light that can be put on canvas. Later he moved to the French Riviera, and there, in the garish sunshine of that hitherto unpaintable region, not only forms but tones are dissolved in incandescence. It was the crisis of sensational painting and each member of the group responded in a different manner. Renoir, with his fundamentally classical outlook, was inspired by the antique painting at Naples and Raphael's frescoes in the Vatican to recapture the firm outline; and thenceforward gave up naturalistic landscape painting entirely. Pissaro, who had always taken more interest than the others in the architectural composition of his pictures, joined in the return to order. . . . Sisley, who had always been the least intellectual and self-critical of the group, went on painting in the same way with declining confidence. His last pictures are a warning that simple perception of nature is not enough.

It was Monet, the real inventor of impressionism, who alone had the courage to push its doctrines through to their conclusion. Not content with the sparkle of his Riviera scenes, he undertook to prove that the object painted was of no importance, the sensation of light was the only true subject. He said to an American pupil that "he wished he had been born blind and then had suddenly gained his sight so that he would have begun to paint without knowing what the objects were that he saw before him."

Actually Monet's technique made him particularly dependent on the nature of his

* For a Monet example, see *Sailboat at Argenteuil* (1873), Figure 24—THE EDITORS.

† For example, see Pissarro's *Oise River near Pontoise*, Figure 25—THE EDITORS.

subjects; and they were limited. Only sun on water and sun on snow could give full play to the prismatic vision and the sparkling touch. In such pictures Monet has remained without an equal. But in order to prove his point he chose for the subjects of his experiments cathedrals and haystacks. No doubt he did so intentionally in order to show that the most articulate works of man, and the most formless, were pictorially of equal importance to the painter of light. But the choice, especially that of cathedrals, was disastrous, because grey Gothic façades do not sparkle [Fig. 28]. In an attempt to make them vehicles of light Monet painted them now pink, now mauve, now orange; and it is evident that even he, with his marvellous capacity for seeing the complementary colors of a shadow, did not really believe that cathedrals looked like melting ice creams. In these muffled, obstinate pictures impressionism has departed altogether from the natural vision from which it sprang, and has become as much an abstraction as Gilpin's picturesque.

III

Impressionism is a short and limited episode in the history of art. . . . We may therefore survey, with some detachment, the gains and losses of the movement.

There was the gain of the light key. Ever since Leonardo attempted scientifically to achieve relief by dark shadows, pictures have tended to be dark spots on the wall. Those who have visited the Naples Gallery will remember with what relief, after wading through three centuries and about thirty rooms of black pictures, one comes on the rooms of antique painting, still fresh and gay in tone. They are only journeyman's work, far poorer in execution than the great canvases, but they are a delight to the eye. The impressionists recaptured this tone. We are grateful that the pictures on our walls (and that, of course, is where pictures should be, not on the walls of galleries) are not only a pleasure to look into but also a pleasure to look at. This rise in tone was connected with the final liberation of color. To read what was said of color by Ingres and the other great teachers of the nineteenth century, one would suppose that it was some particularly dangerous and disreputable form of vice. This was a rearguard action of idealist philosophy which had maintained that form was a function of the intellect, color of the senses. The belief was philosophically unsound, and had proved a real obstacle to free and sincere expression for centuries. Its removal gained a new liberty for the human spirit.

Then impressionism gave us something which has always been one of the great attainments of art: it enlarged our range of vision. We owe much of our pleasure in looking at the world to the great artists who have looked at it before us. In the eighteenth century, gentlemen carried a device called a Claude glass in order that they might see the landscape with the golden tone of a Claude—or rather of the varnish on a Claude. The impressionists did the exact reverse. They taught us to see the color in shadows. Every day we pause with joy before some effect of light which we should otherwise have passed without notice. Impressionism achieved something more than a technical advance. It expressed a real and valuable ethical position. As the Count of Nieuwenrkerke correctly observed, it was the painting of democrats. Impressionism is the perfect expression of democratic humanism, of the good life which was, till recently, thought to be within the reach of all. What pleasures could be simpler or more eternal than those portrayed in Renoir's *Dejeuner des Canotiers* [*Luncheon of the Boating Party*, Fig. 29]; what images of an earthly paradise more persuasive than the white sails in Monet's estuaries, or the roses in Renoir's garden? These pictures prove that what matters in art is an all-pervading belief and not the circumstances of the individual artist. The men who painted them were miserably poor, and their letters show us that they often did not know where to turn for the next meal. Yet their painting is full of a complete confidence in nature and in human nature. Everything they see exists for their delight, even floods and fog.

Looking back over sixty years, it may seem that this confidence in the physical world was a fundamental weakness. Art is concerned with our whole being—our knowledge, our memories, our associations. To confine painting to purely visual sensations is to touch only the surface of our spirits. This is only a way of saying in pictorial terms that impressionism did not address itself to the imagination. We cannot call it the art of materialism, for that word carried too gross an implication; but we cannot (as many critics have done) call it pagan, for paganism involves the idea of remote country superstition, spring festivals and Dionysiac rites. Paganism has precisely that element of magic which impressionism excludes. That is the price we must pay for the happiness of here and now, on which it is founded.

Sheldon Cheney

Sheldon Cheney has been one of the popular contemporary interpreters of modern art. His books have been widely enough read, as a matter of fact, to cause some concern among professional artists and art historians who are not always in agreement with his point of view. Among Cheney's favorite painters are Cézanne and El Greco, and of these he puts Cézanne first. In his opinion, which in this instance is shared by most art historians, the work of Cézanne has had more influence upon the development of modern art than that of any other painter. In the brief selection reprinted here from A Primer of Modern Art, *Cheney does a fine job of singling out the central feature in the paintings of Cézanne and showing how Cézanne's concern with "significant form" provides the necessary introduction to the cubism of Picasso. This discussion also makes it clear that in the work of Cézanne and Picasso we find another dimension of the impact of scientific thought upon contemporary painting. When he was working on* The Bathers, *Cézanne said to a friend that the painter must "see in nature the cylinder, the sphere, and the cone." His own paintings and those of the cubists develop the implications of this statement in a fashion that is startling at times and indicates the fundamental differences between the postimpressionism of Cézanne and the work of men like Monet, Pissarro, and Renoir.*

Cheney was born in Berkeley, California, in 1886, and was educated at the University of California. His interest in the arts began with the theater. For a number of years he was a drama and art critic for various newspapers and magazines. In 1916 he founded Theater Arts *and for five years was the editor of this magazine; from 1922 to 1925 he was with the Actor's Theater in New York. He has published five books dealing with the theater: the first,* New Movements in the Theater, *in 1914; the last and most important,* The Theater—3000 Years of Drama, Acting and Stagecraft, *published in 1929 and reissued in revised form in 1952.*

Cheney's first book on painting, A Primer of Modern Art, *appeared in 1923;* Expressionism in Art *was published in 1934, and* The Story of Modern Art *in 1941. These three books provide one of the most successful efforts to present modern art to the general public, and to develop a better understanding and appreciation of what the newer movements in art are seeking to do. As the books have appeared in successive editions, Cheney has added interesting and illuminating notes, showing how his own taste has developed in the intervening years. His* World History of Art, *published in 1937 and reissued in a handsome enlarged edition in 1956, provides a fitting climax to his work as an art critic and historian.*

CÉZANNE, PICASSO, AND CUBISM

I

IT IS seldom given to an artist to make history as Cézanne has made it. Even within the century, men before him had hinted at the thing he accomplished. But he in his own work achieved a revolution. Even when he was exhibiting with the impressionists—themselves still considered rebels—he was off seeking a thing diametrically opposed to impressionism. They were busy with the surface—he turned the painter's eye within. They were realists. He put an end to the four centuries reign of imitativeness in painting. Practically all the postimpressionists acknowledge him as a master, the cubists found the basic principle of their formula in his work, the expressionists claim him as their own. Even in the obscurity that hid him and his work from the world through most of his life (1838-1906) a few of the world's most sensitive artists accorded him that sincerest form of compliment, imitation. And today, nine tenths of the painters who count—and the sculptors and etchers—are paying him that compliment more or less directly.

Cézanne is the perfect antithesis to those nine hundred and ninety-nine artists whom I have described as the competent tradesmen of art—the imitative intelligences, the reasonable professionals. He ignored the world, he gave his all to his art. He not only climbed above the limitation of seeing a landscape as ordinary people, or ordinary painters, see it; he gave his whole life to trying to realize in color the emotion he felt at something he divined out of that landscape. He did not make pictures for sale—indeed it is said he more often than not threw the day's canvas into a handy ditch before reaching home. He lived to paint; individual pictures were nothing to him; his progress was marked by increasing achievement of the precious quality of expressive form. And he died despairing because he could not touch yet closer to pure form. So heedless was he of everything except this search that he gained for himself the reputation of being a misanthrope and even a madman, except to a very few.

Even so individual and passionate an artist, in being modern, epitomizes certain things out of the immediate and distant past. Color—he was the intimate of Pissarro, and he could hardly have revolutionized painting had not the impressionists made their advance. But he saw through impressionism, guessed its shallowness, and studied the masters of all times. He is credited with saying that he wanted to make something solid and durable—like museum art—out of impressionism. One can imagine him pausing before El Greco and perhaps Tintoretto out of all the rest, and his mind working furiously at a sort of distortion there apparent, coupled with a rare sort of expression. One sees him packing off to the South of France in middle age, thus equipped, with color, with a vision of something to be realized beyond contemporary practice, beyond nineteenth or eighteenth or seventeenth century achievement.

What was this thing he was after—this new thing, yet old with El Greco? He called it the "realization," thus externalizing it from himself more than do the expressionists; making it less subjective, less of him as an individual, and yet not of outward nature. He spoke much of the motive. He must penetrate nature to find it, not see the static surface but the dynamic essence. He must fix this on canvas, filter it through his passion as an artist and his craftsmanship as painter, until it was realized, as what? *Form*. That again is the only name we have for it—expressive form, significant form, plastic form, esthetic form.

Cézanne, being utterly disinterested in the aspects and attributes of nature, simply found nothing to hold him in the accidental prettiness of a landscape or the facial expression of a model, nothing in the atmosphere of a scene or in the revealing pose of a body. These were merely contributory bits to the larger problem of his art, and as often as not he deformed and distorted them to get the right volume or the right slope or the right organization of color. Mere composition in the flat seemed incomplete. . . . He struck through surface nature and surface composition toward something which we must accept as the nearest approach to the soul of painting: organizational form expressed in color. There, too, he surpassed all who had preceded him, for even El Greco conceived form as separate from color—added objective coloring—whereas Cézanne resolved drawing and coloring into one process. Today practically the whole world of painting recognizes them as inseparable.

The landscape shown here [*Mt. Ste. Victoire*, Fig. 30] is equally innocent both of the objective truth of the early realists and of the emphasized atmospheric fidelity of the impressionists. But it has the voluminous solidity, the poised form, the dynamic movement, that belong most characteristically to Cézanne.

Painters and the more recondite critics have discovered technical advances in Cézanne that seem to go far to explain the means by which he was able to come so near to revelation of form: methods of using and counterweighting line and color, concentric harmonies, stereoscopic vision, etc. But these are not for an introductory and unassuming book, and we may well turn to a brief inquiry regarding Cézanne's contemporaries and his followers.

II

Cubism grew out of the postimpressionism of Cézanne. The invention of cubism is popularly credited to Pablo Picasso, a Spaniard who has been a leader in the French capital for many years. "Leader" is not applied in any loose sense. Picasso is a man of amazing versatility. Cubism marked but one phase of his activity. In each phase —his "blue period," his "red period," his "Negro sculpture period"—he had followers and imitators; but in cubism he instigated a world movement. Building from something out of Cézanne, doubtless with equipment out of the Negro sculpture period to aid, he erected a structure which became a storm center of the modernist movement for many years.

The fundamental idea of cubism is, I think, that it is possible to dissociate the planes of an object seen, and to rearrange them in a picture, so organized that they will give a truer emotional or structural sense than the original "appearance." One sees an object from one side; it is an incomplete vision. A complete vision would show it not only as synthesized visually from all sides and aspects, but as it is from within. Perhaps there is a mathematical equivalent for such vision. In painting it must have to do with planes. Planes must be organized, then, to express the painter's esthetic emotion of it.

In the earlier cubist pictures the planes seemed to be merely flattened out, and the intersections accented. The organization of the accented lines in the picture might be decoratively creative, but in general this was merely a summary and simplified sort of illustration. Then came the phase of disorganizing the planes of reality and rearranging them in an arbitrary order. They were made to intersect and overlap at will, the structural reorganization being what counted. This took cubism out of the category of modified surface representation and put it directly into line with Cézanne's search—in so far as anyone could link with him and renounce color. For most of the dyed-in-the-wool cubists worked in tone, browns and grays, totally overlooking a good half of Cézanne's legacy—the knowledge that color might be made to bend a plane backward or forward, build structurally, be the backbone of esthetic organization.

The illustrations of this chapter show the development graphically from Cézanne to the full-fledged theoreticians of cubism and down to the sterile decadents. The Cézanne watercolor [Fig. 31] indicates how much that artist had to do with inspiring the movement. Then the Picasso reproduction, *Woman with a Mandolin* [Fig. 32], suggests the breaking-in process, the flattening of planes, the accentuation of intersections, and the occasional slight dislocation of objective planes. This was in the intermediate period, before the name "cubism" had come into vogue and before any group or school exhibition.

The second *Woman with a Mandolin* [not shown]* is of the period when the artists have begun to pull apart the planes of nature and reorganize them for structural purposes. Speaking entirely physically, the woman might appear more firmly structural if merely photographed as is, without being decomposed as to her planes; but there can be no doubt that Picasso has achieved some sort of abstract organization in the rearrangement which gives the composition a formal value of its own. And if we do not find the distortion of nature too much of a petty distraction, we are likely to get a true emotional reaction from it. It is worthwhile to note how the overlapping of planes is manipulated, certain other planes brought forward and still others obscured, and the displacement of volumes in the background as well as in the figure.

Picasso achieves something of a synthesis when he starts from an objective model, and his canvases invariably speak some esthetic meaning, perhaps only in a sensuously decorative way, perhaps more deeply. At best his cubistic pictures have undeniable, even profound, form-value. But the great mass of cubist work outside of two or three such creative men, seems shallow and insignificant. When natural forms are broken up arbitrarily, the only excuse for their rearrangement is creative composition, and most of the cubists seem to arrive at only a sterile sort of intellectual puzzle-picture or a flat, rather uninteresting decoration.

Certain tenets of the cubist faith hold much of suggestive value for the general advancement of painting. In declaring himself against the existence of any dead planes in a canvas, the cubist hit upon a principle that will bear extensive study, for its impli-

* The development of cubism, as described in this paragraph, is illustrated by two well-known pictures by Picasso, *Women of Avignon* [Fig. 33] and *Three Musicians* [Fig. 34].—The Editors.

cations of eliminating inessentials and the resultant possibility of multiplying essentials. This should logically lead to that sort of emotional intensification which is a first aim of modernism. There is also a pregnant idea behind the principle of Simultaneity. It is the principle of looking, in memory, at all the outward aspects of an object at once, thus getting a sort of composite or synthetic view of it. Here again is means to intensification. But the cubists in general, instead of letting these principles free their creative powers, made the principles their gods, followed them too logically and ended perilously close to esthetic sterility.

It will be noticed that through the series of illustrations in this chapter we have been working closer and closer to abstraction. That indeed is the logical progression—attempted improvisation in abstract form is a final answer to the cubist desire to disorganize objective nature. And if the average cubist had given himself up to composition of that sort, untrammeled by his code of laws, and with color, he might live more importantly in the history of art.

6

LITERATURE: NATURALISM AND REALISM

Guy de Maupassant

Sometimes called the father of the modern short story, Guy de Maupassant is a recognized master in the art of storytelling. Witty and clever, he is never dull. He does not seek to be profound, but observes without prejudice and reports with scrupulous clarity the behavior of the human animal in life's more amusing predicaments. As a critic has observed, "he is as precise as a lawyer devising an ironclad will; as detached as a chemical formula." The similarity of an attitude such as this and the spirit of scientific investigation is obvious, and for this reason the French called the school of writing to which Maupassant belongs "naturalism." The leader of this school in France, Émile Zola, boasted that he did not create plots, but let his characters behave in a given environment as if they were a part of a chemical experiment. A somewhat unsympathetic critic comments that naturalism is "a deviation of realism, certain tendencies of which it exaggerates. It wishes to see nothing in humanity but ugliness, and it describes people cynically, brutally, without showing the least pity for them. Naturalism tries—rather awkwardly—to apply the methods of science to literature, and its special field is the novel." In this section of the anthology we include stories by two of the foremost naturalistic writers of the turn of the century, one French and the other American.

Guy de Maupassant was born at the Chateau of Miromesnil, in Norman France, on August 5, 1850. Of good but not distinguished parentage, he entered the civil service after a limited secondary school education. Stimulated by his early association with Turgenev and Flaubert, Maupassant soon became a prolific writer of short stories and received what was an excellent income in Paris of the 1880s from the magazines and newspapers in which his stories appeared. In time he was recognized as one of the great figures in the French literary world. He wrote both novels and short stories but his stories are better known. They were widely read in England and the United States as well as in France and have appeared in numerous popular collections in this country and in Europe since his death in 1893.

For the average American reader today, Maupassant can be difficult unless one realizes that his is a French world, created by Frenchmen, and peopled by Frenchmen. His best-known story (too often reprinted) is "The Necklace," a chilling account of how a romantic girl ruined her life by borrowing, then losing, some gems. The present story is "The Necklace" in reverse; it is written with more humor but with the same detached, rather cynical spirit. The reversal at the end of the story, a favorite Maupassant device, is admirably and callously done.

THE FALSE GEMS

M. LANTIN had met the young woman at a *soirée* at the home of the assistant chief of his bureau and at first sight had fallen madly in love with her.

She was the daughter of a country physician who had died some months previously. She had come to live in Paris with her mother, who visited much among her acquaintances, in the hope of making a favorable marriage for her daughter. They were poor and honest, quiet and unaffected.

The young girl was a perfect type of the virtuous woman whom every sensible young man dreams of one day winning for life. Her simple beauty had the charm of angelic modesty, and the imperceptible smile which constantly hovered about her lips seemed to be the reflection of a pure and lovely soul. Her praises resounded on every side. People were never tired of saying: "Happy the man who wins her love! He could not find a better wife."

Now M. Lantin enjoyed a snug little income of seven hundred dollars and, thinking he could safely assume the responsibilities of matrimony, proposed to this model young girl and was accepted.

He was unspeakably happy with her; she governed his household so cleverly and economically that they seemed to live in luxury. She lavished the most delicate attentions on her husband, coaxed and fondled him, and the charm of her presence was so great that six years after their marriage M. Lantin discovered that he loved his wife even more than during the first days of their honeymoon.

He only felt inclined to blame her for two things: her love of the theater and a taste for false jewelry. Her friends (she was acquainted with some officers' wives) frequently procured for her a box at the theater, often for the first representations of the new plays, and her husband was obliged to accompany her, whether he willed or not, to these amusements, though they bored him excessively after a day's labor at the office.

After a time M. Lantin begged his wife to get some lady of her acquaintance to accompany her. She was at first opposed to such an arrangement, but, after much persuasion on his part, she finally consented—to the infinite delight of her husband.

Now with her love for the theater came also the desire to adorn her person. True, her costumes remained as before, simple and in the most correct taste, but she soon began to ornament her ears with huge rhinestones which glittered and sparkled like real diamonds. Around her neck she wore strings of false pearls, and on her arms bracelets of imitation gold.

Her husband frequently remonstrated with her, saying:

"My dear, as you cannot afford to buy

[From *The Complete Short Stories of Guy de Maupassant,* New York: Doubleday, 1955.]

real diamonds, you ought to appear adorned with your beauty and modesty alone, which are the rarest ornaments of your sex."

But she would smile sweetly and say:

"What can I do? I am so fond of jewelry. It is my only weakness. We cannot change our natures."

Then she would roll the pearl necklaces around her fingers and hold up the bright gems for her husband's admiration, gently coaxing him.

"Look! Are they not lovely? One would swear they were real."

M. Lantin would then answer smilingly:

"You have Bohemian tastes, my dear."

Often of an evening, when they were enjoying a tête-a-tête by the fireside, she would place on the tea table the leather box containing the "trash," as M. Lantin called it. She would examine the false gems with a passionate attention, as though they were in some way connected with a deep and secret joy, and she often insisted on passing a necklace around her husband's neck and, laughing heartily, would exclaim: "How droll you look!" Then she would throw herself into his arms and kiss him affectionately.

One evening in winter she attended the opera and on her return was chilled through and through. The next morning she coughed, and eight days later she died of inflammation of the lungs.

M. Lantin's despair was so great that his hair became white in one month. He wept unceasingly; his heart was torn with grief, and his mind was haunted by the remembrance, the smile, the voice—by every charm of his beautiful, dead wife.

Time, the healer, did not assuage his grief. Often during office hours, while his colleagues were discussing the topics of the day, his eyes would suddenly fill with tears, and he would give vent to his grief in heartrending sobs. Everything in his wife's room remained as before her decease, and here he would seclude himself daily and think of her who had been his treasure—the joy of his existence.

But life soon became a struggle. His income, which in the hands of his wife had covered all household expenses, was now no longer sufficient for his own immediate wants, and he wondered how she could have managed to buy such excellent wines and such rare delicacies, things which he could no longer procure with his modest resources.

He incurred some debts and was soon reduced to absolute poverty. One morning, finding himself without a cent in his pocket, he resolved to sell something, and immediately the thought occurred to him of disposing of his wife's paste jewels. He cherished in his heart a sort of rancor against the false gems. They had always irritated him in the past, and the very sight of them spoiled somewhat the memory of his lost darling.

To the last days of her life she had continued to make purchases, bringing home new gems almost every evening. He decided to sell the heavy necklace which she seemed to prefer and which, he thought, ought to be worth about six or seven francs, for although paste it was, nevertheless, of very fine workmanship.

He put it in his pocket and started out in search of a jeweler's shop. He entered the first one he saw, feeling a little ashamed to expose his misery and also to offer such a worthless article for sale.

"Sir," he said to the merchant, "I wish to know what this is worth."

The man took his necklace, examined it, called his clerk and made some remarks in an undertone; then he put the ornament back on the counter and looked at it from a distance to judge of the effect.

M. Lantin was annoyed by all this detail

and was on the point of saying: "Oh! I know well enough it is not worth anything," when the jeweler said: "Sir, that necklace is worth from twelve to fifteen thousand francs, but I could not buy it unless you tell me now whence it comes."

The widower opened his eyes wide and remained gaping, not comprehending the merchant's meaning. Finally he stammered: "You say—are you sure?" The other replied dryly: "You can search elsewhere and see if anyone will offer you more. I consider it worth fifteen thousand at the most. Come back here if you cannot do better."

M. Lantin, beside himself with astonishment, took up the necklace and left the store. He wished time for reflection.

Once outside, he felt inclined to laugh and said to himself: "The fool! Had I only taken him at his word! That jeweler cannot distinguish real diamonds from paste."

A few minutes after, he entered another store in the Rue de la Paix. As soon as the proprietor glanced at the necklace he cried out:

"Ah, *parbleu!* I know it well; it was bought here."

M. Lantin was disturbed and asked:

"How much is it worth?"

"Well, I sold it for twenty thousand francs. I am willing to take it back for eighteen thousand when you inform me, according to our legal formality, how it comes to be in your possession."

This time M. Lantin was dumbfounded. He replied:

"But—but—examine it well. Until this moment I was under the impression that it was paste."

Said the jeweler:

"What is your name, sir?"

"Lantin—I am in the employ of the Minister of the Interior. I live at Number 16 Rue des Martyrs."

The merchant looked through his books, found the entry and said:

"That necklace was sent to Madame Lantin's address, 16 Rue des Martyrs, July 20, 1876."

The two men looked into each other's eyes—the widower speechless with astonishment, the jeweler scenting a thief. The latter broke the silence by saying:

"Will you leave this necklace here for twenty-four hours? I will give you a receipt."

"Certainly," answered M. Lantin hastily. Then, putting the ticket in his pocket, he left the store.

He wandered aimlessly through the streets, his mind in a state of dreadful confusion. He tried to reason, to understand. He could not afford to purchase such a costly ornament. Certainly not. But then it must have been a present!—a present!—a present from whom? Why was it given her?

He stopped and remained standing in the middle of the street. A horrible doubt entered his mind—she? Then all the other gems must have been presents too! The earth seemed to tremble beneath him; the tree before him was falling; throwing up his arms, he fell to the ground, unconscious. He recovered his senses in a pharmacy into which the passers-by had taken him and was then taken to his home. When he arrived he shut himself up in his room and wept until nightfall. Finally, overcome with fatigue, he threw himself on the bed, where he passed an uneasy, restless night.

The following morning he arose and prepared to go to the office. It was hard to work after such a shock. He sent a letter to his employer, requesting to be excused. Then he remembered that he had to return to the jeweler's. He did not like the idea, but he could not leave the necklace with that man. So he dressed and went out.

It was a lovely day; a clear blue sky smiled on the busy city below, and men of leisure were strolling about with their hands in their pockets.

Observing them, M. Lantin said to him

self: "The rich, indeed, are happy. With money it is possible to forget even the deepest sorrow. One can go where one pleases and in travel find that distraction which is the surest cure for grief. Oh, if I were only rich!"

He began to feel hungry, but his pocket was empty. He again remembered the necklace. Eighteen thousand francs! Eighteen thousand francs! What a sum!

He soon arrived in the Rue de la Paix, opposite the jeweler's. Eighteen thousand francs! Twenty times he resolved to go in, but shame kept him back. He was hungry, however, very hungry, and had not a cent in his pocket. He decided quickly, ran across the street in order not to have time for reflection and entered the store.

The proprietor immediately came forward and politely offered him a chair; the clerks glanced at him knowingly.

"I have made inquiries, Monsieur Lantin," said the jeweler, "and if you are still resolved to dispose of the gems I am ready to pay you the price I offered."

"Certainly, sir," stammered M. Lantin.

Whereupon the proprietor took from a drawer eighteen large bills, counted and handed them to M. Lantin, who signed a receipt and with a trembling hand put the money into his pocket.

As he was about to leave the store he turned toward the merchant, who still wore the same knowing smile, and, lowering his eyes, said:

"I have—I have other gems which I have received from the same source. Will you buy them also?"

The merchant bowed: "Certainly, sir."

M. Lantin said gravely: "I will bring them to you." An hour later he returned with the gems.

The large diamond earrings were worth twenty thousand francs; the bracelets, thirty-five thousand; the rings, sixteen thousand; a set of emeralds and sapphires, fourteen thousand; a gold chain with solitaire pendant, forty thousand—making the sum of one hundred and forty-three thousand francs.

The jeweler remarked jokingly:

"There was a person who invested all her earnings in precious stones."

M. Lantin replied seriously:

"It is only another way of investing one's money."

That day he lunched at Voisin's and drank wine worth twenty francs a bottle. Then he hired a carriage and made a tour of the Bois, and as he scanned the various turnouts with a contemptuous air he could hardly refrain from crying out to the occupants:

"I, too, am rich! I am worth two hundred thousand francs."

Suddenly he thought of his employer. He drove up to the office and entered gaily, saying:

"Sir, I have come to resign my position. I have just inherited three hundred thousand francs."

He shook hands with his former colleagues and confided to them some of his projects for the future; then he went off to dine at the Café Anglais.

He seated himself beside a gentleman of aristocratic bearing and during the meal informed the latter confidentially that he had just inherited a fortune of four hundred thousand francs.

For the first time in his life he was not bored at the theater and spent the remainder of the night in a gay frolic.

Six months afterward he married again. His second wife was a very virtuous woman with a violent temper. She caused him much sorrow.

Stephen Crane

Among American writers at the end of the nineteenth century Stephen Crane was the most successful in employing the naturalism that Émile Zola and Guy de Maupassant had made so popular in France. Crane is noted for his ability to tell a brutal story in a cool, detached way, as if all the characters in it were without a sense of comradeship or human pity. Ernest Hemingway, in The Green Hills of Africa, *said to a companion, "The good writers [in America] are Henry James, Stephen Crane, and Mark Twain. . . . Crane wrote two fine stories.* The Open Boat *and* The Blue Hotel. *The last one is the best."*

"The Blue Hotel," which we include here, looks at first like a meaningless story of a drunk who picked a fight with an innocent man and was killed for his pains. But at the very end of the story Crane skillfully exposes its theme, and shows that it is the reader who is responsible for any impression of meaninglessness. Crane's neat conclusion here is one of the best inverted endings in the literature of the short story.

*Stephen Crane was born in Newark, New Jersey, in 1871, and attended Lafayette College and Syracuse University. His story—too often repeated in American literature—is of a writer who had the greatest difficulty in getting his first work published (*Maggie: A Girl of the Streets*), who had to turn to journalism to make a living, and when he finally made a financial success with* The Red Badge of Courage *in 1895, had too little time left in which to enjoy his earnings or to perfect his art. He died of tuberculosis in Germany in 1900.*

THE BLUE HOTEL

I

THE PALACE HOTEL at Fort Romper was painted a light blue, a shade that is on the legs of a kind of heron, causing the bird to declare its position against any background. The Palace Hotel, then, was always screaming and howling in a way that made the dazzling winter landscape of Nebraska seem only a gray swampish hush. It stood alone on the prairie, and when the snow was falling the town two hundred yards away was not visible. But when the traveler alighted at the railway station he was obliged to pass the Palace Hotel before he could come upon the company of low clapboard houses which composed Fort Romper, and it was not to be thought that any traveler could pass the Palace Hotel without looking at it. Pat Scully, the proprietor, had proved himself a master of strategy when he chose his paints. It is true that on clear days, when the great transcontinental expresses, long lines of swaying Pullmans, swept through Fort Romper, passengers were overcome at the sight, and the cult that knows the brown-reds and the subdivisions of the dark greens of the East expressed shame, pity, horror, in a laugh. But to the citizens of this prairie town and to the people who would naturally stop there, Pat Scully had performed a feat. With this opulence and splendor, these creeds, classes, egotisms, that streamed through Romper cn the rails day after day, they had no color in common.

As if the displayed delights of such a blue hotel were not sufficiently enticing, it was Scully's habit to go every morning and evening to meet the leisurely trains that stopped at Romper and work his seductions upon any man that he might see wavering, gripsack in hand.

One morning, when a snow-crusted engine dragged its long string of freight cars and its one passenger coach to the station, Scully performed the marvel of catching three men. One was a shaky and quick-eyed Swede, with a great shining cheap valise; one was tall bronzed cowboy, who was on his way to a ranch near the Dakota line; one was a little silent man from the East, who didn't look it, and didn't announce it. Scully practically made them prisoners. He was so nimble and merry and kindly that each probably felt it would be the height of brutality to try to escape. They trudged off over the creaking board sidewalks in the wake of the eager little Irishman. He wore a heavy fur cap squeezed tightly down on his head. It caused his two red ears to stick out stiffly, as if they were made of tin.

At last, Scully, elaborately, with boisterous hospitality, conducted them through the portals of the blue hotel. The room which they entered was small. It seemed to be merely a proper temple for an enormous stove, which, in the center, was humming with godlike violence. At various points on its surface the iron had become luminous and glowed yellow from the heat. Beside the stove Scully's son Johnnie was playing High-Five with an old farmer who had whiskers both gray and sandy. They were quarreling. Frequently the old farmer turned his face toward a box of sawdust—colored brown from tobacco juice—that was behind the stove, and spat with an air of great impatience and irritation. With a loud flourish of words Scully destroyed the game of cards, and bustled his son upstairs with part of the baggage of the new guests. He himself conducted them to three basins of the coldest water in the world. The cowboy and the Easterner burnished themselves fiery red with this water, until it seemed to be some kind of a metal polish. The Swede, however, merely dipped his fingers gingerly and with trepidation. It was notable that throughout this series of small ceremonies the three travelers were made to feel that Scully was very benevolent. He was conferring great favors upon them. He handed the towel from one to another with an air of philanthropic impulse.

Afterward they went to the first room, and, sitting about the stove, listened to Scully's officious clamor at his daughters, who were preparing the midday meal. They reflected in the silence of experienced men who tread carefully amid new people. Nevertheless, the old farmer, stationary, invincible in his chair near the warmest part of the stove, turned his face from the sawdust-box frequently and addressed a glowing commonplace to the strangers. Usually he was answered in short but adequate sentences by either the cowboy or the Easterner. The Swede said nothing. He seemed to be occupied in making furtive estimates of each man in the room. One might have thought that he had the sense of silly suspicion which comes to guilt. He resembled a badly frightened man.

Later, at dinner, he spoke a little, addressing his conversation entirely to Scully. He volunteered that he had come from New York, where for ten years he had worked as a tailor. These facts seemed to strike Scully as fascinating, and afterward he volunteered that he had lived at Romper for fourteen years. The Swede asked about the crops and the price of labor. He seemed barely to listen to Scully's extended replies. His eyes continued to rove from man to man.

Finally, with a laugh and a wink, he said

that some of these Western communities were very dangerous; and after his statement he straightened his legs under the table, tilted his head, and laughed again, loudly. It was plain that the demonstration had no meaning to the others. They looked at him wondering and in silence.

II

As the men trooped heavily back into the front room, the two little windows presented views of a turmoiling sea of snow. The huge arms of the wind were making attempts—mighty, circular, futile—to embrace the flakes as they sped. A gatepost like a still man with a blanched face stood aghast amid this profligate fury. In a hearty voice Scully announced the presence of a blizzard. The guests of the blue hotel, lighting their pipes, assented with grunts of lazy masculine contentment. No island of the sea could be exempt in the degree of this little room with its humming stove. Johnnie, son of Scully, in a tone which defined his opinion of his ability as a card-player, challenged the old farmer of both gray and sandy whiskers to a game of High-Five. The farmer agreed with a contemptuous and bitter scoff. They sat close to the stove, and squared their knees under a wide board. The cowboy and the Easterner watched the game with interest. The Swede remained near the window, aloof, but with a countenance that showed signs of an inexplicable excitement.

The play of Johnnie and the gray-beard was suddenly ended by another quarrel. The old man arose while casting a look of heated scorn at his adversary. He slowly buttoned his coat, and then stalked with fabulous dignity from the room. In the discreet silence of all the other men the Swede laughed. His laughter rang somehow childish. Men by this time had begun to look at him askance, as if they wished to inquire what ailed him.

A new game was formed jocosely. The cowboy volunteered to become the partner of Johnnie, and they all then turned to ask the Swede to throw in his lot with the little Easterner. He asked some questions about the game, and, learning that it wore many names, and that he had played it when it was under an alias, he accepted the invitation. He strode toward the men nervously, as if he expected to be assaulted. Finally, seated, he gazed from face to face and laughed shrilly. This laugh was so strange that the Easterner looked up quickly, the cowboy sat intent and with his mouth open, and Johnnie paused, holding the cards with still fingers.

Afterward there was a short silence. Then Johnnie said, "Well, let's get at it. Come on now!" They pulled their chairs forward until their knees were bunched under the board. They began to play, and their interest in the game caused the others to forget the manner of the Swede.

The cowboy was a board-whacker. Each time that he held superior cards he whanged them, one by one, with exceeding force, down upon the improvised table, and took the tricks with a glowing air of prowess and pride that sent thrills of indignation into the hearts of his opponents. A game with a board-whacker in it is sure to become intense. The countenances of the Easterner and the Swede were miserable whenever the cowboy thundered down his aces and kings, while Johnnie, his eyes gleaming with joy, chuckled and chuckled.

Because of the absorbing play none considered the strange ways of the Swede. They paid strict heed to the game. Finally, during a lull caused by a new deal, the Swede suddenly addressed Johnnie: "I suppose there have been a good many men killed in this room." The jaws of the others dropped and they looked at him.

"What in hell are you talking about?" said Johnnie.

The Swede laughed again his blatant laugh, full of a kind of false courage and defiance. "Oh, you know what I mean all right," he answered.

"I'm a liar if I do!" Johnnie protested. The card was halted, and the men stared at the Swede. Johnnie evidently felt that as the son of the proprietor he should make a direct inquiry. "Now, what might you be drivin' at mister?" he asked. The Swede winked at him. It was a wink full of cunning. His fingers shook on the edge of the board. "Oh, maybe you think I have been to nowheres. Maybe you think I'm a tenderfoot?"

"I don't know nothin' about you," answered Johnnie, "and I don't give a damn where you've been. All I got to say is that I don't know what you're driving at. There hain't never been nobody killed in this room."

The cowboy, who had been steadily gazing at the Swede, then spoke: "What's wrong with you, mister?"

Apparently it seemed to the Swede that he was formidably menaced. He shivered and turned white near the corners of his mouth. He sent an appealing glance in the direction of the little Easterner. During these moments he did not forget to wear his air of advanced pot-valor. "They say they don't know what I mean," he remarked mockingly to the Easterner.

The latter answered after prolonged and cautious reflection. "I don't understand you," he said, impassively.

The Swede made a movement then which announced that he thought he had encountered treachery from the only quarter where he had expected sympathy, if not help. "Oh, I see you are all against me. I see—"

The cowboy was in a state of deep stupefaction. "Say," he cried, as he tumbled the deck violently down upon the board, "say, what are you gittin' at hey?"

The Swede sprang up with the celerity of a man escaping from a snake on the floor, "I don't want to fight!" he shouted. "I don't want to fight!"

The cowboy stretched his long legs indolently and deliberately. His hands were in his pockets. He spat into the sawdust-box. "Well, who the hell thought you did?" he inquired.

The Swede backed rapidly toward a corner of the room. His hands were out protectingly in front of his chest, but he was making an obvious struggle to control his fright. "Gentlemen," he quavered, "I suppose I am going to be killed before I can leave this house! I suppose I am going to be killed before I can leave this house!" In his eyes was the dying-swan look. Through the windows could be seen the snow turning blue in the shadow of dusk. The wind tore at the house, and some loose thing beat regularly against the clapboards like a spirit tapping.

A door opened, and Scully himself entered. He paused in surprise as he noted the tragic attitude of the Swede. Then he said, "What's the matter here?"

The Swede answered him swiftly and eagerly: "These men are going to kill me."

"Kill you!" ejaculated Scully. "Kill you! What are you talkin'?"

The Swede made the gesture of a martyr.

Scully wheeled sternly upon his son. "What is this, Johnnie?"

The lad had grown sullen. "Damned if I know," he answered. "I can't make no sense to it." He began to shuffle the cards, fluttering them together with an angry snap. "He says a good many men have been killed in this room, or something like that. And he says he's goin' to be killed here too. I don't know what ails him. He's crazy, I shouldn't wonder."

Scully then looked for explanation to the

cowboy, but the cowboy simply shrugged his shoulders.

"Kill you?" said Scully again to the Swede. "Kill you? Man, you're off your nut."

"Oh, I know," burst out the Swede. "I know what will happen. Yes, I'm crazy—yes. Yes, of course, I'm crazy—yes. But I know one thing—" There was a sort of sweat of misery and terror upon his face. "I know I won't get out of here alive."

The cowboy drew a deep breath, as if his mind was passing into the last stages of dissolution. "Well, I'm doggoned," he whispered to himself.

Scully wheeled suddenly and faced his son. "You've been troublin' this man!"

Johnnie's voice was loud with its burden of grievance. "Why, good Gawd, I ain't done nothin' to 'im."

The Swede broke in. "Gentlemen, do not disturb yourselves. I will leave this house, I will go away, because"—he accused them dramatically with his glance—"because I do not want to be killed."

Scully was furious with his son. "Will you tell me what is the matter, you young divil? What's the matter, anyhow? Speak out!"

"Blame it!" cried Johnnie in despair, "don't I tell you I don't know? He—he says we want to kill him, and that's all I know. I can't tell what ails him."

The Swede continued to repeat: "Never mind, Mr. Scully; never mind. I will leave this house. I will go away, because I do not wish to be killed. Yes, of course, I am crazy—yes. But I know one thing! I will go away. I will leave this house. Never mind, Mr. Scully; never mind. I will go away."

"You will not go 'way," said Scully. "You will not go 'way until I hear the reason of this business. If anybody has troubled you I will take care of him. This is my house. You are under my roof, and I will not allow any peaceable man to be troubled here." He cast a terrible eye upon Johnnie, the cowboy, and the Easterner.

"Never mind, Mr. Scully; never mind. I will go away. I do not wish to be killed." The Swede moved toward the door, which opened upon the stairs. It was evidently his intention to go at once for his baggage.

"No, no," shouted Scully peremptorily; but the white-faced man slid by him and disappeared. "Now," said Scully severely, "what does this mane?"

Johnnie and the cowboy cried together: "Why, we didn't do nothin' to 'im!"

Scully's eyes were cold. "No," he said, "you didn't?"

Johnnie swore a deep oath. "Why, this is the wildest loon I ever seen. We didn't do nothin' at all. We were jest sittin' here playin' cards, and he—"

The father suddenly spoke to the Easterner. "Mr. Blanc," he asked, "what has these boys been doin'?"

The Easterner reflected again. "I didn't see anything wrong at all," he said at last, slowly.

Scully began to howl. "But what does it mane?" He stared ferociously at his son. "I have a mind to lather you for this, me boy."

Johnnie was frantic. "Well, what have I done?" he bawled at his father.

III

"I think you are tongue-tied," said Scully finally to his son, the cowboy, and the Easterner; and at the end of this scornful sentence he left the room.

Upstairs the Swede was swiftly fastening the straps of his great valise. Once his back happened to be half turned toward the door, and, hearing a noise there, he wheeled and sprang up, uttering a loud cry. Scully's wrinkled visage showed grimly in the light of the small lamp he carried. This yellow effulgence, streaming upward, colored only his prominent features, and left his eyes, for instance, in mysterious shadow. He resembled a murderer.

"Man! man!" he exclaimed, "have you gone daffy?"

"Oh, no! Oh, no!" rejoined the other. "There are people in this world who know pretty nearly as much as you do—understand?"

For a moment they stood gazing at each other. Upon the Swede's deathly pale cheeks were two spots brightly crimson and sharply edged, as if they had been carefully painted. Scully placed the light on the table and sat himself on the edge of the bed. He spoke ruminatively. "By cracky, I never heard of such a thing in my life. It's a complete muddle. I can't, for the soul of me, think how you ever got this idea into your head." Presently he lifted his eyes and asked: "And did you sure think they were going to kill you?"

The Swede scanned the old man as if he wished to see into his mind. "I did," he said at last. He obviously suspected that this answer might precipitate an outbreak. As he pulled on a strap his whole arm shook, the elbow wavering like a bit of paper.

Scully banged his hand impressively on the footboard of the bed. "Why, man, we're goin' to have a line of ilictric street-cars in this town next spring."

" 'A line of electric street-cars,' " repeated the Swede, stupidly.

"And," said Scully, "there's a new railroad goin' to be built down from Broken Arm to here. Not to mintion the four churches and the smashin' big brick schoolhouse. Then there's the big factory, too. Why, in two years Romper'll be a met-tro-*pol*-is."

Having finished the preparation of his baggage, the Swede straightened himself. "Mr. Scully," he said, with sudden hardihood, "how much do I owe you?"

"You don't owe me anythin'," said the old man, angrily.

"Yes, I do," retorted the Swede. He took seventy-five cents from his pocket and tendered it to Scully; but the latter snapped his fingers in disdainful refusal. However, it happened that they both stood gazing in a strange fashion at three silver pieces on the Swede's open palm.

"I'll not take your money," said Scully at last. "Not after what's been goin' on here." Then a plan seemed to strike him. "Here," he cried, picking up his lamp and moving toward the door. "Here! Come with me a minute."

"No," said the Swede, in overwhelming alarm.

"Yes," urged the old man. "Come on! I want you to come and see a picter—just across the hall—in my room."

The Swede must have concluded that his hour was come. His jaw dropped and his teeth showed like a dead man's. He ultimately followed Scully across the corridor, but he had the step of one hung in chains.

Scully flashed the light high on the wall of his own chamber. There was revealed a ridiculous photograph of a little girl. She was leaning against a balustrade of gorgeous decoration, and the formidable bang to her hair was prominent. The figure was as graceful as an upright sled-stake, and, withal, it was of the hue of lead. "There," said Scully, tenderly, "that's the picter of my little girl that died. Her name was Carrie. She had the purtiest hair you ever saw! I was that fond of her, she—"

Turning then, he saw that the Swede was not contemplating the picture at all, but, instead, was keeping keen watch on the gloom in the rear.

"Look, man!" cried Scully, heartily. "That's the picter of my little gal that died. Her name was Carrie. And then here's the picter of my oldest boy, Michael. He's a lawyer in Lincoln, an' doin' well. I gave that boy a grand eddycation, and I'm glad for it now. He's a fine boy. Look at 'im now.

Ain't he bold as blazes, him there in Lincoln, an honored an' respicted gintleman!" "An honored and respicted gintleman," concluded Scully with a flourish. And, so saying, he smote the Swede jovially on the back.

The Swede faintly smiled.

"Now," said the old man, "there's only one more thing." He dropped suddenly to the floor and thrust his head beneath the bed. The Swede could hear his muffled voice. "I'd keep it under me piller if it wasn't for that boy Johnnie. Then there's the old woman— Where is it now? I never put it twice in the same place. Ah, now come out with you!"

Presently he backed clumsily from under the bed, dragging with him an old coat rolled into a bundle. "I've fetched him," he muttered. Kneeling on the floor, he unrolled the coat and extracted from its heart a large yellow-brown whisky-bottle.

His first maneuver was to hold the bottle up to the light. Reassured, apparently, that nobody had been tampering with it, he thrust it with a generous movement toward the Swede.

The weak-kneed Swede was about to eagerly clutch this element of strength, but he suddenly jerked his hand away and cast a look of horror upon Scully.

"Drink," said the old man affectionately. He had risen to his feet, and now stood facing the Swede.

There was a silence. Then again Scully said: "Drink!"

The Swede laughed wildly. He grabbed the bottle, put it to his mouth; and as his lips curled absurdly around the opening and his throat worked, he kept his glance, burning with hatred, upon the old man's face.

IV

After the departure of Scully the three men, with the cardboard still upon their knees, preserved for a long time an astounded silence. Then Johnnie said: "That's the doddangedest Swede I ever see."

"He ain't no Swede," said the cowboy, scornfully.

"Well, what is he then?" cried Johnnie. "What is he then?"

"It's my opinion," replied the cowboy deliberately, "he's some kind of a Dutchman." It was a venerable custom of the country to entitle as Swedes all light-haired men who spoke with a heavy tongue. In consequence the idea of the cowboy was not without its daring. "Yes, sir," he repeated. "It's my opinion this feller is some kind of a Dutchman."

"Well, he says he's a Swede, anyhow," muttered Johnnie, sulkily. He turned to the Easterner: "What do you think, Mr. Blanc?"

"Oh, I don't know," replied the Easterner.

"Well, what do you think makes him act that way?" asked the cowboy.

"Why, he's frightened." The Easterner knocked his pipe against a rim of the stove. "He's clear frightened out of his boots."

"What at?" cried Johnnie and the cowboy together. The Easterner reflected over his answer.

"What at?" cried the others again.

"Oh, I don't know, but it seems to me this man has been reading dime novels, and he thinks he's right out in the middle of it—the shootin' and stabbin' and all."

"But," said the cowboy, deeply scandalized, "this ain't Wyoming, ner none of them places. This is Nebrasker."

"Yes," added Johnnie, "an' why don't he wait till he gits *out West*?"

The traveled Easterner laughed. "It isn't different there even—not in these days. But he thinks he's right in the middle of hell."

Johnnie and the cowboy mused long.

"Yes," said the cowboy. "This is a queer game. I hope we don't git snowed in, because then we'd have to stand this here man bein' around with us all the time. That wouldn't be no good."

"I wish pop would throw him out," said Johnnie.

Presently they heard a loud stamping on the stairs, accompanied by ringing jokes in the voice of old Scully, and laughter, evidently from the Swede. The men around the stove stared vacantly at each other. "Gosh!" said the cowboy. The door flew open, and old Scully, flushed and anecdotal, came into the room. He was jabbering at the Swede, who followed him, laughing bravely. It was the entry of two roisterers from a banquet hall.

"Come now," said Scully sharply to the three seated men, "move up and give us a chance at the stove." The cowboy and the Easterner obediently sidled their chairs to make room for the newcomers. Johnnie, however, simply arranged himself in a more indolent attitude, and then remained motionless.

"Come! Git over, there," said Scully.

"Plenty of room on the other side of the stove," said Johnnie.

"Do you think we want to sit in the draught?" roared the father.

But the Swede here interposed with a grandeur of confidence. "No, no. Let the boy sit where he likes," he cried in a bullying voice to the father.

"All right! All right!" said Scully, deferentially. The cowboy and the Easterner exchanged glances of wonder.

The five chairs were formed in a crescent about one side of the stove. The Swede began to talk; he talked arrogantly, profanely, angrily. Johnnie, the cowboy, and the Easterner maintained a morose silence, while old Scully appeared to be receptive and eager, breaking in constantly with sympathetic ejaculations.

Finally the Swede announced that he wa thirsty. He moved in his chair, and said tha he would go for a drink of water.

"I'll git it for you," cried Scully at onc

"No," said the Swede, contemptuousl "I'll get it for myself." He arose and stalke with the air of an owner off into the exec tive parts of the hotel.

As soon as the Swede was out of hearin Scully sprang to his feet and whispered i tensely to the others: "Upstairs he though I was tryin' to poison 'im."

"Say," said Johnnie, "this makes me sic Why don't you throw 'im out in the snow?"

"Why, he's all right now," declare Scully. "It was only that he was from th East, and he thought this was a tough plac That's all. He's all right now."

The cowboy looked with admiration upo the Easterner. "You were straight," he sai "You were on to that there Dutchman."

"Well," said Johnnie to his father, "h may be all right now, but I don't see i Other time he was scared, but now he's to fresh."

Scully's speech was always a combinatio of Irish brogue and idiom, Western twan and idiom, and scraps of curiously form diction taken from the storybooks an newspapers. He now hurled a strange mas of language at the head of his son. "Wha do I keep? What do I keep? What do keep?" he demanded, in a voice of thunde He slapped his knee impressively, to ind cate that he himself was going to make re ply, and that all should heed. "I keep hotel," he shouted. "A hotel, do you mind A guest under my roof has sacred privilege He is to be intimidated by none. Not on word shall he hear that would prijudic him in favor of goin' away. I'll not have i There's no place in this here town wher they can say they iver took in a guest c mine because he was afraid to stay here. He wheeled suddenly upon the cowboy an the Easterner. "Am I right?"

"Yes, Mr. Scully," said the cowboy, "I think you're right."

"Yes, Mr. Scully," said the Easterner, "I think you're right."

V

At six-o'clock supper, the Swede fizzed like a fire-wheel. He sometimes seemed on the point of bursting into riotous song, and in all his madness he was encouraged by old Scully. The Easterner was encased in reserve; the cowboy sat in wide-mouthed amazement, forgetting to eat, while Johnnie wrathily demolished great plates of food. The daughters of the house, when they were obliged to replenish the biscuits, approached as warily as Indians, and having succeeded in their purpose, fled with ill-concealed trepidation. The Swede domineered the whole feast, and he gave it the appearance of a cruel bacchanal. He seemed to have grown suddenly taller; he gazed, brutally disdainful, into every face. His voice rang through the room. Once when he jabbed out harpoon-fashion with his fork to pinion a biscuit, the weapon nearly impaled the hand of the Easterner, which had been stretched quietly out for the same biscuit.

After supper, as the men filed toward the other room, the Swede smote Scully ruthlessly on the shoulder. "Well, old boy, that was a good, square meal." Johnnie looked hopefully at his father; he knew that shoulder was tender from an old fall; and, indeed, it appeared for a moment as if Scully was going to flame out over the matter, but in the end he smiled a sickly smile and remained silent. The others understood from his manner that he was admitting his responsibility for the Swede's new viewpoint.

Johnnie, however, addressed his parent in an aside. "Why don't you license somebody to kick you downstairs?" Scully scowled darkly by way of reply.

When they gathered about the stove, the Swede insisted on another game of High-Five. Scully gently deprecated the plan at first, but the Swede turned a wolfish glare upon him. The old man subsided, and the Swede canvassed the others. In his tone there was always a great threat. The cowboy and the Easterner both remarked indifferently that they would play. Scully said that he would presently have to go to meet the 6:58 train, and so the Swede turned menacingly upon Johnnie. For a moment their glances crossed like blades, and then Johnnie smiled and said, "Yes, I'll play."

They formed a square, with the little board on their knees. The Easterner and the Swede were again partners. As the play went on, it was noticeable that the cowboy was not board-whacking as usual. Meanwhile, Scully, near the lamp, had put on his spectacles, and, with an appearance curiously like an old priest, was reading a newspaper. In time he went out to meet the 6:58 train, and, despite his precautions, a gust of polar wind whirled into the room as he opened the door. Besides scattering the cards, it chilled the players to the marrow. The Swede cursed frightfully. When Scully returned, his entrance disturbed a cosy and friendly scene. The Swede again cursed. But presently they were once more intent, their heads bent forward and their hands moving swiftly. The Swede had adopted the fashion of board-whacking.

Scully took up his paper and for a long time remained immersed in matters which were extraordinarily remote from him. The lamp burned badly, and once he stopped to adjust the wick. The newspaper, as he turned from page to page, rustled with a slow and comfortable sound. Then suddenly he heard three terrible words: "You are cheatin'!"

Such scenes often prove that there can be little of dramatic import in environment. Any room can present a tragic front; any room can be comic. This little den was now hideous as a torture-chamber. The new faces of the men themselves had changed it upon the instant. The Swede held a huge fist in front of Johnnie's face, while the latter looked steadily over it into the blazing orbs of his accuser. The Easterner had grown pallid; the cowboy's jaw had dropped in that expression of bovine amazement which was one of his important mannerisms. After the three words, the first sound in the room was made by Scully's paper as it floated forgotten to his feet. His spectacles had also fallen from his nose, but by a clutch he had saved them in air. His hand, grasping the spectacles, now remained poised awkwardly and near his shoulder. He stared at the card players.

Probably the silence was while a second elapsed. Then, if the floor had been suddenly twitched out from under the men they could not have moved quicker. The five had projected themselved headlong toward a common point. It happened that Johnnie, in rising to hurl himself upon the Swede, had stumbled slightly because of his curiously instinctive care for the cards and the board. The loss of the moment allowed time for the arrival of Scully, and also allowed the cowboy time to give the Swede a great push which sent him staggering back. The men found tongue together, and hoarse shouts of rage, appeal, or fear burst from every throat. The cowboy pushed and jostled feverishly at the Swede, and the Easterner and Scully clung wildly to Johnnie; but through the smoky air, above the swaying bodies of the peace-compellers, the eyes of the two warriors ever sought each other in glances of challenge that were at once hot and steely.

Of course the board had been overturned, and now the whole company of cards was scattered over the floor, where the boots of the men trampled the fat and painted kings and queens as they gazed with their silly eyes at the war that was waging above them.

Scully's voice was dominating the yells. "Stop now! Stop, I say! Stop, now—"

Johnnie, as he struggled to burst through the rank formed by Scully and the Easterner, was crying, "Well, he says I cheated! He says I cheated! I won't allow no man to say I cheated! If he says I cheated, he's a —— ——!"

The cowboy was telling the Swede, "Quit, now! Quit, d'ye hear—"

The screams of the Swede never ceased: "He did cheat! I saw him! I saw him—"

As for the Easterner, he was importuning in a voice that was not heeded: "Wait a moment, can't you? Oh, wait a moment. What's the good of a fight over a game of cards? Wait a moment—"

In this tumult no complete sentences were clear. "Cheat"—"Quit"—"He says"—these fragments pierced the uproar and rang out sharply. It was remarkable that, whereas Scully undoubtedly made the most noise, he was the least heard of any of the riotous band.

Then suddenly there was a great cessation. It was as if each man had paused for breath; and although the room was still lighted with the anger of men, it could be seen that there was no danger of immediate conflict, and at once Johnnie, shouldering his way forward, almost succeeded in confronting the Swede. "What did you say I cheated for? What did you say I cheated for? I don't cheat, and I won't let no man say I do!"

The Swede said, "I saw you! I saw you!"

"Well," cried Johnnie, "I'll fight any man what says I cheat!"

"No, you won't," said the cowboy. "Not here."

"Ah, be still, can't you?" said Scully, coming between them.

The quiet was sufficient to allow the

Easterner's voice to be heard. He was repeating, "Oh, wait a moment, can't you? What's the good of a fight over a game of cards? Wait a moment!"

Johnnie, his red face appearing above his father's shoulder, hailed the Swede again. "Did you say I cheated?"

The Swede showed his teeth. "Yes."

"Then," said Johnnie, "we must fight."

"Yes, fight," roared the Swede. He was like a demoniac. "Yes, fight! I'll show you what kind of a man I am! I'll show you who you want to fight! Maybe you think I can't fight! Maybe you think I can't! I'll show you, you skin, you card-sharp! Yes, you cheated! You cheated! You cheated!"

"Well, let's go at it, then, mister," said Johnnie, coolly.

The cowboy's brow was beaded with sweat from his efforts in intercepting all sorts of raids. He turned in despair to Scully. "What are you goin' to do now?"

A change came over the Celtic visage of the old man. He now seemed all eagerness; his eyes glowed.

"We'll let them fight," he answered, stalwartly. "I can't put up with it any longer. I've stood this damned Swede till I'm sick. We'll let them fight."

VI

The men prepared to go out-of-doors. The Easterner was so nervous that he had great difficulty in getting his arms into the sleeves of his new leather coat. As the cowboy drew his fur cap down over his ears his hands trembled. In fact, Johnnie and old Scully were the only ones who displayed no agitation. These preliminaries were conducted without words.

Scully threw open the door. "Well, come on," he said. Instantly a terrific wind caused the flame of the lamp to struggle at its wick, while a puff of black smoke sprang from the chimney-top. The stove was in mid-current of the blast, and its voice swelled to equal the roar of the storm. Some of the scarred and bedabbled cards were caught up from the floor and dashed helplessly against the farther wall. The men lowered their heads and plunged into the tempest as into a sea.

No snow was falling, but great whirls and clouds of flakes, swept up from the ground by the frantic winds, were streaming southward with the speed of bullets. The covered land was blue with the sheen of an unearthly satin, and there was no other hue save where, at the low, black railway station—which seemed incredibly distant—one light gleamed like a tiny jewel. As the men floundered into a thigh-deep drift, it was known that the Swede was bawling out something. Scully went to him, put a hand on his shoulder, and projected an ear. "What's that you say?" he shouted.

"I say," bawled the Swede again, "I won't stand much show against this gang. I know you'll all pitch on me."

Scully smote him reproachfully on the arm. "Tut, man!" he yelled. The wind tore the words from Scully's lips and scattered them far alee.

"You are all a gang of—" boomed the Swede, but the storm also seized the remainder of this sentence.

Immediately turning their backs upon the wind, the men had swung around a corner to the sheltered side of the hotel. It was the function of the little house to preserve here, amid this great devastation of snow, an irregular V-shape of heavily encrusted grass, which crackled beneath the feet. One could imagine the great drifts piled against the windward side. When the party reached the comparative peace of this spot it was found that the Swede was still bellowing.

"Oh, I know what kind of a thing this

is! I know you'll all pitch on me. I can't lick you all!"

Scully turned upon him panther-fashion. "You'll not have to whip all of us. You'll have to whip my son Johnnie. An' the man what troubles you durin' that time will have me to dale with."

The arrangements were swiftly made. The two men faced each other, obedient to the harsh commands of Scully, whose face, in the subtly luminous gloom, could be seen set in the austere impersonal lines that are pictured on the countenances of the Roman veterans. The Easterner's teeth were chattering, and he was hopping up and down like a mechanical toy. The cowboy stood rocklike.

The contestants had not stripped off any clothing. Each was in his ordinary attire. Their fists were up, and they eyed each other in a calm that had the elements of leonine cruelty in it.

During this pause, the Easterner's mind, like a film, took lasting impressions of three men—the iron-nerved master of the ceremony; the Swede, pale, motionless, terrible; and Johnnie, serene yet ferocious, brutish yet heroic. The entire prelude had in it a tragedy greater than the tragedy of action, and this aspect was accentuated by the long, mellow cry of the blizzard, as it sped the tumbling and wailing flakes into the black abyss of the south.

"Now!" said Scully.

The two combatants leaped forward and crashed together like bullocks. There was heard the cushioned sound of blows, and of a curse squeezing out from between the tight teeth of one.

As for the spectators, the Easterner's pent-up breath exploded from him with a pop of relief, absolute relief from the tension of the preliminaries. The cowboy bounded into the air with a yowl. Scully was immovable as from supreme amazement and fear at the fury of the fight which he himself had permitted and arranged.

For a time the encounter in the darkness was such a perplexity of flying arms that it presented no more detail than would a swiftly revolving wheel. Occasionally a face, as if illumined by a flash of light, would shine out, ghastly and marked with pink spots. A moment later, the men might have been known as shadows, if it were not for the involuntary utterance of oaths that came from them in whispers.

Suddenly a holocaust of warlike desire caught the cowboy, and he bolted forward with the speed of a broncho. "Go it, Johnnie! go it! Kill him! Kill him!"

Scully confronted him. "Kape back," he said; and by his glance the cowboy could tell that this man was Johnnie's father.

To the Easterner there was a monotony of unchangeable fighting that was an abomination. This confused mingling was eternal to his sense, which was concentrated in a longing for the end, the priceless end. Once the fighters lurched near him, and as he scrambled hastily backward he heard them breathe like men on the rack.

"Kill him, Johnnie! Kill him! Kill him! Kill him!" The cowboy's face was contorted like one of those agony masks in museums.

"Keep still," said Scully, icily.

Then there was a sudden loud grunt, incomplete, cut short, and Johnnie's body swung away from the Swede and fell with sickening heaviness to the grass. The cowboy was barely in time to prevent the mad Swede from flinging himself upon his prone adversary. "No, you don't," said the cowboy, interposing an arm. "Wait a second."

Scully was at his son's side. "Johnnie! Johnnie, me boy!" His voice had a quality of melancholy tenderness. "Johnnie! Can you go on with it?" He looked anxiously down into the bloody, pulpy face of his son.

There was a moment of silence, and then

Johnnie answered in his ordinary voice, "Yes, I—it—yes."

Assisted by his father he struggled to his feet. "Wait a bit now till you git your wind," said the old man.

A few paces away the cowboy was lecturing the Swede. "No, you don't! Wait a second!"

The Easterner was plucking at Scully's sleeve. "Oh, this is enough," he pleaded. "This is enough! Let it go as it stands. This is enough!"

"Bill," said Scully, "git out of the road." The cowboy stepped aside. "Now." The combatants were actuated by a new caution as they advanced toward collision. They glared at each other, and then the Swede aimed a lightning blow that carried with it his entire weight. Johnnie was evidently half stupid from weakness, but he miraculously dodged, and his fist sent the overbalanced Swede sprawling.

The cowboy, Scully, and the Easterner burst into a cheer that was like a chorus of triumphant soldiery, but before its conclusion the Swede had scuffled agilely to his feet and come in berserk abandon at his foe. There was another perplexity of flying arms and Johnnie's body again swung away and fell, even as a bundle might fall from a roof. The Swede instantly staggered to a little wind-waved tree and leaned upon it, breathing like an engine, while his savage and flame-lit eyes roamed from face to face as the men bent over Johnnie. There was a splendor of isolation in his situation at this time which the Easterner felt once when, lifting his eyes from the man on the ground, he beheld that mysterious and lonely figure, waiting.

"Are you any good yet, Johnnie?" asked Scully in a broken voice.

The son gasped and opened his eyes languidly. After a moment he answered, "No—I ain't–any good—any—more." Then, from shame and bodily ill, he began to weep, the tears furrowing down through the blood-stains on his face. "He was too—too—too heavy for me."

Scully straightened and addressed the waiting figure. "Stranger," he said evenly, "it's all up with our side." Then his voice changed into that vibrant huskiness which is commonly the tone of the most simple and deadly announcements. "Johnnie is whipped."

Without replying, the victor moved off on the route to the front of the hotel.

The cowboy was formulating new and unspellable blasphemies. The Easterner was startled to find that they were out in a wind that seemed to come direct from the shadowed arctic floes. He heard again the wail of the snow as it was flung to its grave in the south. He knew now that all this time the cold had been sinking into him deeper and deeper, and he wondered that he had not perished. He felt indifferent to the condition of the vanquished man.

"Johnnie, can you walk?" asked Scully.

"Did I hurt—hurt him any?" asked the son.

"Can you walk, boy? Can you walk?"

Johnnie's voice was suddenly strong. There was a robust impatience in it. "I asked you whether I hurt him any!"

"Yes, yes, Johnnie," answered the cowboy, consolingly; "he's hurt a good deal."

They raised him from the ground, and as soon as he was on his feet he went tottering off, rebuffing all attempts at assistance. When the party rounded the corner they were fairly blinded by the pelting of the snow. It burned their faces like fire. The cowboy carried Johnnie through the drift to the door. As they entered, some cards again rose from the floor and beat against the wall.

The Easterner rushed to the stove. He was so profoundly chilled that he almost dared to embrace the glowing iron. The Swede was not in the room. Johnnie sank into a chair and, folding his arms on his knees, buried his face in them. Scully, warming one foot and then the other at a rim of the stove, muttered to himself with Celtic mournfulness. The cowboy had removed his fur cap, and with a dazed and rueful air he was running one hand through his tousled locks. From overhead they could hear the creaking of boards, as the Swede tramped here and there in his room.

The sad quiet was broken by the sudden flinging open of a door that led toward the kitchen. It was instantly followed by an inrush of women. They precipitated themselves upon Johnnie amid a chorus of lamentation. Before they carried their prey off to the kitchen, there to be bathed and harangued with that mixture of sympathy and abuse which is a feat of their sex, the mother straightened herself and fixed old Scully with an eye of stern reproach. "Shame be upon you, Patrick Scully!" she cried. "Your own son, too. Shame be upon you!"

"There, now! Be quiet, now!" said the old man, weakly.

"Shame be upon you, Patrick Scully!" The girls rallying to this slogan, sniffed disdainfully in the direction of those trembling accomplices, the cowboy and the Easterner. Presently they bore Johnnie away, and left the three men to dismal reflection.

VII

"I'd like to fight this here Dutchman myself," said the cowboy, breaking a long silence.

Scully wagged his head sadly. "No, that wouldn't do. It wouldn't be right. It wouldn't be right."

"Well, why wouldn't it?" argued the cowboy. "I don't see no harm in it."

"No," answered Scully, with mournful heroism. "It wouldn't be right. It was Johnnie's fight, and now we mustn't whip the man just because he whipped Johnnie."

"Yes, that's true enough," said the cowboy; "but—he better not get fresh with me, because I couldn't stand no more of it."

"You'll not say a word to him," commanded Scully, and even then they heard the tread of the Swede on the stairs. His entrance was made theatric. He swept the door back with a bang and swaggered to the middle of the room. No one looked at him. "Well," he cried, insolently, at Scully, "I s'pose you'll tell me now how much I owe you?"

The old man remained stolid. "You don't owe me nothin'."

"Huh!" said the Swede, "huh! Don't owe 'im nothin'."

The cowboy addressed the Swede. "Stranger, I don't see how you come to be so gay around here."

Old Scully was instantly alert. "Stop!" he shouted, holding his hand forth, fingers upward. "Bill, you shut up!"

The cowboy spat carelessly into the sawdust-box. "I didn't say a word, did I?" he asked.

"Mr. Scully," called the Swede, "how much do I owe you?" It was seen that he was attired for departure, and that he had his valise in his hand.

"You don't owe me nothin'," repeated Scully in the same imperturbable way.

"Huh!" said the Swede. "I guess you're right. I guess if it was any way at all, you'd owe me somethin'. That's what I guess." He turned to the cowboy. " 'Kill him! Kill him! Kill him!' " he mimicked, and then guffawed victoriously. " 'Kill him!' " He was convulsed with ironical humor.

But he might have been jeering the dead. The three men were immovable and silent, staring with glassy eyes at the stove.

The Swede opened the door and passed

into the storm, giving one derisive glance at the still group.

As soon as the door was closed, Scully and the cowboy leaped to their feet and began to curse. They trampled to and fro, waving their arms and smashing into the air with their fists. "Oh, but that was a hard minute!" wailed Scully. "That was a hard minute! Him there leerin' and scoffin'! One bang at his nose was worth forty dollars to me that minute! How did you stand it, Bill?"

"How did I stand it?" cried the cowboy in a quivering voice. "How did I stand it? Oh!"

The old man burst into sudden brogue. "I'd loike to take that Swade," he wailed, "and hould'im down on a shtone flure and bate 'im to a jelly wid a shtick!"

The cowboy groaned in sympathy. "I'd like to git him by the neck and ha-ammer him"—he brought his hand down on a chair with a noise like a pistol-shot—"hammer that there Dutchman until he couldn't tell himself from a dead coyote!"

"I'd bate 'im until he—"

"I'd show *him* some things—"

And then together they raised a yearning, fanatic cry—"Oh-o-oh! if we only could—"

"Yes!"

"Yes!"

"And then I'd—"

"O-o-oh!"

VIII

The Swede, tightly gripping his valise, tacked across the face of the storm as if he carried sails. He was following a line of little naked, gasping trees which, he knew, must mark the way of the road. His face, fresh from the pounding of Johnnie's fists, felt more pleasure than pain in the wind and the driving snow. A number of square shapes loomed upon him finally, and he knew them as the houses of the main body of the town. He found a street and made travel along it, leaning heavily upon the wind whenever, at a corner, a terrific blast caught him.

He might have been in a deserted village. We picture the world as thick with conquering and elate humanity, but here, with the bugles of the tempest pealing, it was hard to imagine a peopled earth. One viewed the existence of man then as a marvel, and conceded a glamor of wonder to these lice which were caused to cling to a whirling, fire-smitten, ice-locked, disease-stricken, space-lost bulb. The conceit of man was explained by this storm to be the very engine of life. One was a coxcomb not to die in it. However, the Swede found a saloon.

In front of it an indomitable red light was burning, and the snowflakes were made blood-color as they flew through the circumscribed territory of the lamp's shining. The Swede pushed open the door of the saloon and entered. A sanded expanse was before him, and at the end of it four men sat about a table drinking. Down one side of the room extended a radiant bar, and its guardian was leaning upon his elbows listening to the talk of the men at the table. The Swede dropped his valise upon the floor and, smiling fraternally upon the barkeeper, said, "Gimme some whiskey, will you?" The man placed a bottle, a whiskey-glass, and a glass of ice-thick water upon the bar. The Swede poured himself an abnormal portion of whiskey and drank it in three gulps. "Pretty bad night," remarked the bartender, indifferently. He was making the pretension of blindness which is usually a distinction of his class; but it could have been seen that he was furtively studying the half-erased blood-stains on the face of the Swede. "Bad night," he said again.

"Oh, it's good enough for me," replied the Swede, hardily, as he poured himself some more whiskey. The barkeeper took his coin and maneuvered it through its reception by the highly nickelled cash-machine. A bell rang; a card labeled "20 cts." had appeared.

"No," continued the Swede, "this isn't too bad weather. It's good enough for me."

"So?" murmured the barkeeper, languidly.

The copious drams made the Swede's eyes swim, and he breathed a trifle heavier. "Yes, I like this weather. I like it. It suits me." It was apparently his design to impart a deep significance to these words.

"So?" murmured the bartender again. He turned to gaze dreamily at the scroll-like birds and bird-like scrolls which had been drawn with soap upon the mirrors back of the bar.

"Well, I guess I'll take another drink," said the Swede, presently. "Have something?"

"No, thanks; I'm not drinkin'," answered the bartender. Afterward he asked, "How did you hurt your face?"

The Swede immediately began to boast loudly. "Why, in a fight. I thumped the soul out of a man down here at Scully's hotel."

The interest of the four men at the table was at last aroused.

"Who was it?" said one.

"Johnnie Scully," blustered the Swede. "Son of the man what runs it. He will be pretty near dead for some weeks, I can tell you. I made a nice thing of him, I did. He couldn't get up. They carried him in the house. Have a drink?"

Instantly the men in some subtle way encased themselves in reserve. "No, thanks," said one. The group was of curious formation. Two were prominent local business men; one was the district attorney; and one was a professional gambler of the kind known as "square." But a scrutiny of the group would not have enabled an observer to pick the gambler from the men of more reputable pursuits. He was, in fact, a man so delicate in manner, when among people of fair class, and so judicious in his choice of victims, that in the strictly masculine part of the town's life he had come to be explicitly trusted and admired. People called him a thoroughbred. The fear and contempt with which his craft was regarded were undoubtedly the reason why his quiet dignity shone conspicuous above the quiet dignity of men who might be merely hatters, billiard-markers, or grocery-clerks. Beyond an occasional unwary traveler who came by rail, this gambler was supposed to prey solely upon reckless and senile farmers who, when flush with good crops, drove into town in all the pride and confidence of an absolutely invulnerable stupidity. Hearing at times in circuitous fashion of the despoilment of such a farmer, the important men of Romper invariably laughed in contempt of the victim, and if they thought of the wolf at all, it was with a kind of pride at the knowledge that he would never dare think of attacking their wisdom and courage. Besides, it was popular that this gambler had a real wife and two real children in a neat cottage in a suburb, where he led an exemplary home life; and when any one even suggested a discrepancy in his character, the crowd immediately vociferated descriptions of this virtuous family circle. Then men who led exemplary home lives, and men who did not lead exemplary home lives, all subsided in a bunch, remarking that there was nothing more to be said.

However, when a restriction was placed upon him—as, for instance, when a strong clique of members of the new Pollywog Club refused to permit him, even as a spectator, to appear in the rooms of the organization—the candor and gentleness with which he accepted the judgment disarmed many of his foes and made his friends more desperately partisan. He invarably distinguished between himself and a respectable Romper man so quickly and frankly that his manner actually appeared to be a continual broadcast compliment.

And one must not forget to declare the fundamental fact of his entire position in Romper. It is irrefutable that in all affairs outside his business, in all matters that occur eternally and commonly between man and man, this thieving card-player was so generous, so just, so moral, that, in a contest, he could have put to flight the consciences of nine tenths of the citizens of Romper.

And so it happened that he was seated in this saloon with the two prominent local merchants and the district attorney.

The Swede continued to drink raw whiskey, meanwhile babbling at the barkeeper and trying to induce him to indulge in potations. "Come on. Have a drink. Come on. What—no? Well, have a little one, then. By gawd, I've whipped a man tonight, and I want to celebrate. I whipped him good, too. Gentlemen," the Swede cried to the men at the table, "have a drink?"

"Ssh!" said the barkeeper.

The group at the table, although furtively attentive, had been pretending to be deep in talk, but now a man lifted his eyes toward the Swede and said, shortly, "Thanks. We don't want any more."

At this reply the Swede ruffled out his chest like a rooster.

"Well," he exploded, "it seems I can't get anybody to drink with me in this town. Seems so, don't it? Well!"

"Ssh!" said the barkeeper.

"Say," snarled the Swede, "don't you try to shut me up. I won't have it. I'm a gentleman, and I want people to drink with me. And I want 'em to drink with me now. Now—do you understand?" He rapped the bar with his knuckles.

Years of experience had calloused the bartender. He merely grew sulky. "I hear you," he answered.

"Well," cried the Swede, "listen hard then. See those men over there? Well, they're going to drink with me, and don't you forget it. Now you watch."

"Hi!" yelled the barkeeper, "this won't do!"

"Why won't it?" demanded the Swede. He stalked over to the table, and by chance laid his hand upon the shoulder of the gambler. "How about this?" he asked wrathfully. "I asked you to drink with me."

The gambler simply twisted his head and spoke over his shoulder. "My friend, I don't know you."

"Oh, hell!" answered the Swede, "come and have a drink."

"Now, my boy," advised the gambler, kindly, "take your hand off my shoulder and go 'way and mind your own business." He was a little, slim man, and it seemed strange to hear him use this tone of heroic patronage to the burly Swede. The other men at the table said nothing.

"What! You won't drink with me, you little dude? I'll make you, then! I'll make you!" The Swede had grasped the gambler frenziedly at the throat, and was dragging him from his chair. The other men sprang up. The barkeeper dashed around the corner of his bar. There was a great tumult, and then was seen a long blade in the hand of the gambler. It shot forward, and a human body, this citadel of virtue, wisdom, power, was pierced as easily as if it had been a melon. The Swede fell with a cry of supreme astonishment.

The prominent merchants and the district attorney must have at once tumbled out of the place backward. The bartender found himself hanging limply to the arm of a chair and gazing into the eyes of a murderer.

"Henry," said the latter, as he wiped his knife on one of the towels that hung beneath the bar rail, "you tell 'em where to find me. I'll be home, waiting for 'em." Then he vanished. A moment afterward the barkeeper was in the street dinning through the storm for help and, moreover, companionship.

The corpse of the Swede, alone in the saloon, had its eyes fixed upon a dreadful legend that dwelt atop of the cash-machine: "This registers the amount of your purchase."

IX

Months later, the cowboy was frying pork over the stove of a little ranch near the Dakota line, when there was a quick thud of hoofs outside, and presently the Easterner entered with the letters and the papers.

"Well," said the Easterner at once, "the chap that killed the Swede has got three years. Wasn't much, was it?"

"He has? Three years?" The cowboy poised his pan of pork, while he ruminated upon the news. "Three years. That ain't much."

"No. It was a light sentence," replied the Easterner as he unbuckled his spurs. "Seems there was a good deal of sympathy for him in Romper."

"If the bartender had been any good," observed the cowboy, thoughtfully, "he would have gone in and cracked that there Dutchman on the head with a bottle in the beginnin' of it and stopped all this here murderin'."

"Yes, a thousand things might have happened," said the Easterner, tartly.

The cowboy returned his pan of pork to the fire, but his philosophy continued. "It's funny, ain't it? If he hadn't said Johnnie was cheatin' he'd be alive this minute. He was an awful fool. Game played for fun, too. Not for money. I believe he was crazy."

"I feel sorry for that gambler," said the Easterner.

"Oh, so do I," said the cowboy. "He don't deserve none of it for killin' who he did."

"The Swede might not have been killed if everything had been square."

"Might not have been killed?" exclaimed the cowboy. "Everythin' square? Why, when he said that Johnnie was cheatin' and acted like such a jackass? And then in the saloon he fairly walked up to git hurt?" With these arguments the cowboy browbeat the Easterner and reduced him to rage.

"You're a fool!" cried the Easterner, viciously. "You're a bigger jackass than the Swede by a million majority. Now let me tell you one thing. Let me tell you something. Listen! Johnnie *was* cheating!"

" 'Johnnie,' " said the cowboy, blankly. There was a minute of silence, and then he said, robustly, "Why, no. The game was only for fun."

"Fun or not," said the Easterner, "Johnnie was cheating. I saw him. I know it. I saw him. And I refused to stand up and be a man. I let the Swede fight it out alone. And you—you were simply puffing around the place and wanting to fight. And then old Scully himself! We are all in it! This poor gambler isn't even a noun. He is kind of an adverb. Every sin is the result of a collaboration. We, five of us, have collaborated in the murder of this Swede. Usually there are from a dozen to forty women really involved in every murder, but in this case it seems to be only five men—you, I, Johnnie, old Scully; and that fool of an unfortunate gambler came merely as a culmination, the apex of a human movement, and gets all the punishment."

The cowboy, injured and rebellious, cried out blindly into this fog of mysterious theory: "Well, I didn't do anythin', did I?"

Stephen Vincent Benét

*Although written more than twenty years ago, Benét's story, "By the Waters of Babylon," has an uncomfortable prophetic ring about it today. This story is about the end of one civilization and the beginning of another: New York is pictured in ruins as the result of several wonderful scientific discoveries, and life and learning have to begin all over again because of the way in which man has used his scientific knowledge. "By the Waters of Babylon" is not science fiction in the usual sense of the term but the title of a collection of stories in which it appears—*Thirteen O'Clock: Stories of Several Worlds*—suggests the different way of looking at the world that scientific thought has brought into contemporary fiction.*

Stephen Vincent Benét was born in Bethlehem, Pennsylvania, in 1898, and was educated at Yale and the Sorbonne. He wrote his best-known book, a long narrative poem called John Brown's Body, *in 1928. This poem won the Pulitzer prize that year but Benét lost the considerable returns from it in the depression. During the thirties he worked hard to recoup his losses, writing reviews and short stories for popular magazines such as the* Saturday Evening Post *where "By the Waters of Babylon" first appeared in 1937. For a time he took a position also as editor in a publishing firm. He died in 1943 before he could finish what might have been his finest work,* Western Star. *Even unfinished, his book was awarded the Pulitzer prize in 1944.*

"By the Waters of Babylon" shows Benét's love of American subjects and his unusual ability to handle fantasy that manages, somehow, to be completely believable. It was written when thoughtful men guessed that war was on its way again, and feared that technological improvements might, this time, really bring civilization to an end. With a scientist's interest in following the results of an odd assumption, Benét asked himself, "If American civilization as we know it disappears, how can it possibly be recovered?"

The title of his story comes from Psalm 137—"By the rivers of Babylon, there we sat down, yea, we wept, when we remembered Zion."

BY THE WATERS OF BABYLON

THE NORTH and the west and the south are good hunting ground, but it is forbidden to go east. It is forbidden to go to any of the Dead Places except to search for metal and then he who touches the metal must be a priest or the son of a priest. Afterwards, both the man and the metal must be purified. These are the rules and the laws; they are well made. It is forbidden to cross the great river and look upon the place that was the Place of the Gods—this is most strictly forbidden. We do not even say its name though we know its name. It is there that spirits live, and demons—it is there that there are the ashes of the Great Burning. These things are forbidden—they have been forbidden since the beginning of time.

My father is a priest; I am the son of a priest. I have been in the Dead Places near us, with my father—at first, I was afraid. When my father went into the house to search for the metal, I stood by the door and my heart felt small and weak. It was a dead man's house, a spirit house. It did not have the smell of man, though there were old bones in a corner. But it is not fitting that a priest's son should show fear. I looked at the bones in the shadow and kept my voice still.

Then my father came out with the metal —a good, strong piece. He looked at me with both eyes but I had not run away. He gave me the metal to hold—I took it and did not die. So he knew that I was truly his son and would be a priest in my time. That was when I was very young—nevertheless, my brothers would not have done it, though they are good hunters. After that, they gave me the good piece of meat and the warm corner by the fire. My father watched over me—he was glad that I should be a priest. But when I boasted or wept without a reason, he punished me more strictly than my brothers. That was right.

After a time, I myself was allowed to go into the dead houses and search for metal. So I learned the ways of those houses—and if I saw bones, I was no longer afraid. The bones are light and old—sometimes they will fall into dust if you touch them. But that is a great sin.

I was taught the chants and the spells—I was taught how to stop the running of blood from a wound and many secrets. A priest must know many secrets—that was what my father said. If the hunters think we do all things by chants and spells, they may believe so—it does not hurt them. I was taught how to read in the old books and how to make the old writings—that was hard and took a long time. My knowledge made me happy—it was like a fire in my heart. Most of all, I liked to hear of the Old Days and the stories of the gods. I asked myself many questions that I could not answer, but it was good to ask them. At night, I would lie awake and listen to the wind—it seemed to me that it was the voice of the gods as they flew through the air.

We are not ignorant like the Forest People—our women spin wool on the wheel, our priests wear a white robe. We do not eat grubs from the tree, we have not forgotten the old writings, although they are hard to understand. Nevertheless, my knowledge and my lack of knowledge burned in me—I wished to know more. When I was a man at last, I came to my father and said, "It is time for me to go on my journey. Give me your leave."

He looked at me for a long time, stroking his beard, then he said at last, "Yes. It is time." That night, in the house of the priesthood, I asked for and received purification. My body hurt but my spirit was a cool stone. It was my father himself who questioned me about my dreams.

He bade me look into the smoke of the fire and see—I saw and told what I saw. It was what I have always seen—a river, and, beyond it, a great Dead Place and in it the gods walking. I have always thought about that. His eyes were stern when I told him—he was no longer my father but a priest. He said, "This is a strong dream."

"It is mine," I said, while the smoke waved and my head felt light. They were singing the Star song in the outer chamber and it was like the buzzing of bees in my head.

He asked me how the gods were dressed and I told him how they were dressed. We know how they were dressed from the book, but I saw them as if they were before me. When I had finished, he threw the sticks three times and studied them as they fell.

"This is a very strong dream," he said. "It may eat you up."

"I am not afraid," I said and looked at

him with both eyes. My voice sounded thin in my ears but that was because of the smoke.

He touched me on the breast and the forehead. He gave me the bow and the three arrows.

"Take them," he said. "It is forbidden to travel east. It is forbidden to cross the river. It is forbidden to go to the Place of the Gods. All these things are forbidden."

"All these things are forbidden," I said, but it was my voice that spoke and not my spirit. He looked at me again.

"My son," he said. "Once I had young dreams. If your dreams do not eat you up, you may be a great priest. If they eat you, you are still my son. Now go on your journey."

I went fasting, as is the law. My body hurt but not my heart. When the dawn came, I was out of sight of the village. I prayed and purified myself, waiting for a sign. The sign was an eagle. It flew east.

Sometimes signs are sent by bad spirits. I waited again on the flat rock, fasting, taking no food. I was very still—I could feel the sky above me and the earth beneath. I waited till the sun was beginning to sink. Then three deer passed in the valley, going east—they did not wind me or see me. There was a white fawn with them—a very great sign.

I followed them, at a distance, waiting for what would happen. My heart was troubled about going east, yet I knew that I must go. My head hummed with my fasting—I did not even see the panther spring upon the white fawn. But, before I knew it, the bow was in my hand. I shouted and the panther lifted his head from the fawn. It is not easy to kill a panther with one arrow but the arrow went through his eye and into his brain. He died as he tried to spring—he rolled over, tearing at the ground. Then I knew I was meant to go east—I knew that was my journey. When the night came, I made my fire and roasted meat.

It is eight suns journey to the east and a man passes by many Dead Places. The Forest People are afraid of them but I am not. Once I made my fire on the edge of a Dead Place at night and, next morning, in the dead house, I found a good knife, little rusted. That was small to what came afterward but it made my heart feel big. Always when I looked for game, it was in front of my arrow, and twice I passed hunting parties of the Forest People without their knowing. So I knew my magic was strong and my journey clean, in spite of the law.

Toward the setting of the eighth sun, I came to the banks of the great river. It was half-a-day's journey after I had left the god-road—we do not use the god-roads now for they are falling apart into great blocks of stone, and the forest is safer going. A long way off, I had seen the water through trees but the trees were thick. At last, I came out upon an open place at the top of a cliff. There was the great river below, like a giant in the sun. It is very long, very wide. It could eat all the streams we know and still be thirsty. Its name is Ou-dis-sun, the Sacred, the Long. No man of my tribe had seen it, not even my father, the priest. It was magic and I prayed.

Then I raised my eyes and looked south. It was there, the Place of the Gods.

How can I tell what it was like—you do not know. It was there, in the red light, and they were too big to be houses. It was there with the red light upon it, mighty and ruined. I knew that in another moment the gods would see me. I covered my eyes with my hands and crept back into the forest.

Surely, that was enough to do, and live. Surely it was enough to spend the night upon the cliff. The Forest People themselves do not come near. Yet, all through the night, I knew that I should have to cross the river and walk in the places of the gods, although the gods ate me up. My magic did not help me at all and yet there was a fire in my bowels, a fire in my mind. When the sun rose, I thought, "My journey has been clean. Now I will go home from my journey." But, even as I thought so, I knew I could not. If I went to the place of the gods, I would surely die, but, if I did not go, I could never be at peace with my spirit again. It is better to lose one's life than one's spirit, if one is a priest and the son of a priest.

Nevertheless, as I made the raft, the tears ran out of my eyes. The Forest People could have killed me without fight, if they had come upon me then, but they did not come. When the raft was made, I said the sayings for the dead and painted myself for death. My heart was cold as a frog and my knees like water, but the burning in my mind would not let me have peace. As I pushed the raft from the shore, I began my death song—I had the right. It was a fine song.

"I am John, son of John," I sang. "My people are the Hill People. They are the men.
I go into the Dead Places but I am not slain.
I take the metal from the Dead Places but I am not blasted.
I travel upon the god-roads and am not afraid. E-yah! I have killed the panther, I have killed the fawn!
E-yah! I have come to the great river. No man has come there before.
It is forbidden to go east, but I have gone, forbidden to go on the great river, but I am there.
Open your hearts, your spirits, and hear my song.
Now I go to the Place of the Gods, I shall not return.
My body is painted for death and my limbs weak, but my heart is big as I go to the Place of the Gods!"

All the same, when I came to the Place of the Gods, I was afraid, afraid. The current of the great river is very strong—it gripped my raft with its hands. That was magic, for the river itself is wide and calm. I could feel evil spirits about me, in the bright morning; I could feel their breath on my neck as I was swept down the stream. Never have I been so much alone—I tried to think of my knowledge, but it was a squirrel's heap of winter nuts. There was no strength in my knowledge any more and I felt small and naked as a new-hatched bird—alone upon the great river, the servant of the gods.

Yet, after a while, my eyes were opened and I saw. I saw both banks of the river—I saw that once there had been god-roads across it, though now they were broken and fallen like broken vines. Very great they were, and wonderful and broken—broken in the time of the Great Burning when the fire fell out of the sky. And always the current took me nearer to the Place of the Gods, and the huge ruins rose before my eyes.

I do not know the customs of rivers—we are the People of the Hills. I tried to guide my raft with the pole but it spun around. I thought the river meant to take me past the Place of the Gods and out into the Bitter Water of the legends. I grew angry then—my heart felt strong. I said aloud, "I am a priest and the son of a priest!" The gods heard me—they showed me how to paddle with the pole on one side of the raft. The current changed itself—I drew near to the Place of the Gods.

When I was very near, my raft struck and turned over. I can swim in our lakes—I swam to the shore. There was a great spike of rusted metal sticking out into the river—I hauled myself up upon it and sat there panting. I had saved my bow and two arrows and the knife I found in the Dead Place but that was all. My raft went whirling downstream toward the Bitter Water. I looked after it, and thought if it had trod me under, at least I would be safely dead.

Nevertheless, when I had dried my bowstring and restrung it, I walked forward to the Place of the Gods.

It felt like ground underfoot; it did not burn me. It is not true what some of the tales say, that the ground there burns forever, for I have been there. Here and there were the marks and stains of the Great Burning, on the ruins, that is true. But they were old marks and old stains. It is not true either, what some of our priests say, that it is an island covered with fogs and enchantments. It is not. It is a great Dead Place—greater than any Dead Place we know. Everywhere in it there are god-roads, though most are cracked and broken. Everywhere there are the ruins of the high towers of the gods.

How shall I tell what I saw? I went carefully, my strung bow in my hand, my skin ready for danger. There should have been the wailings of spirits and the shrieks of demons, but there were not. It was very silent and sunny where I had landed—the wind and the rain and the birds that drop seeds had done their work—the grass grew in the cracks of the broken stone. It is a fair island—no wonder the gods built there. If I had come there, a god, I also would have built.

How shall I tell what I saw? The towers are not all broken—here and there one still stands, like a great tree in a forest, and the birds nest high. But the towers themselves look blind, for the gods are gone. I saw a fish-hawk, catching fish in the river. I saw a little dance of white butterflies over a great heap of broken stones and columns. I went there and looked about me—there was a carved stone with cut-letters, broken in half. I can read letters but I could not understand these. They said UBTREAS. There was also the shattered image of a man or a god. It had been made of white stone and he wore his hair tied back like a woman's. His name was ASHING, as I read on the cracked half of a stone. I thought it wise to pray to ASHING, though I do not know that god.

How shall I tell what I saw? There was no smell of man left, on stone or metal. Nor were there many trees in that wilderness of stone. There are many pigeons, nesting and dropping in the towers—the gods must have loved them, or, perhaps, they used them for sacrifices. There are wild cats that roam the god-roads, green-eyed, unafraid of man. At night they wail like demons but they are not demons. The wild dogs are more dangerous, for they hunt in a pack, but them I did not meet till later. Everywhere there are the carved stones, carved with magical numbers or words.

I went North—I did not try to hide myself. When a god or a demon saw me, then I would die, but meanwhile I was no longer afraid. My hunger for knowledge burned in me—there was so much that I could not understand. After awhile, I knew that my belly was hungry. I could have hunted for my meat, but I did not hunt. It is known that the gods did not hunt as we do—they got their food from enchanted boxes and jars. Sometimes these are still found in the Dead Places—once, when I was a child and foolish, I opened such a jar and tasted it and found the food sweet. But my father found out and punished me for it strictly, for, often, that food is death. Now, though, I had long gone past what was forbidden, and I entered the likeliest towers, looking for the food of the gods.

I found it at last in the ruins of a great temple in the mid-city. A mighty temple it must have been, for the roof was painted like the sky at night with its stars—that much I could see, though the colors were faint and dim. It went down into great caves and tunnels—perhaps they kept their slaves there. But when I started to climb down, I heard the squeaking of rats, so I did not go—rats are unclean, and there must have been many tribes of them, from the squeaking. But near there, I found food, in the heart of a ruin, behind a door that still opened. I ate only the fruits from the jars—they had a very sweet taste. There was drink, too, in bottles of glass—the drink of the gods was strong and made my head swim. After I had eaten and drunk, I slept on the top of a stone, my bow at my side.

When I woke, the sun was low. Looking down from where I lay, I saw a dog sitting on his haunches. His tongue was hanging out of his mouth; he looked as if he were laughing. He was a big dog, with grey-brown coat, as big as a wolf. I sprang up and shouted at him but he did not move—he just sat there as if he were laughing. I did not like that. When I reached for a stone to throw, he moved swiftly out of the way of the stone. He was not afraid of me; he looked at me as if I were meat. No doubt I could have killed him with an arrow, but I did not know if there were others. Moreover, night was falling.

I looked about me—not far away there was a great, broken god-road, leading North. The towers were high enough, but not so high, and while many of the dead-houses were wrecked, there were some that stood. I went toward this god-road, keeping to the heights of the ruins, while the dog followed. When I had reached the god-road, I saw that there were others behind him. If I had slept later, they would have come upon me asleep and torn out my throat. As it was, they were sure enough of me; they did not hurry. When I went into the dead-house, they kept watch at the entrance—doubtless they thought they would have a fine hunt. But a dog cannot open a door and I knew, from the books, that the gods did not like to live on the ground but on high.

I had just found a door I could open when the dogs decided to rush. Ha! They were surprised when I shut the door in their faces—it was a good door, of strong metal. I could hear their foolish baying beyond it but I did not stop to answer them. I was in darkness—I found stairs and climbed. There were many stairs, turning around till my head was dizzy. At the top was another door—I found the knob and opened it. I was in a long small chamber—on one side of it was a bronze door that could not be opened, for it had no handle. Perhaps there was a magic word to open it but I did not have the word. I turned to the door in the opposite side of the wall. The lock of it was broken and I opened it and went in.

Within, there was a place of great riches. The god who lived there must have been a powerful god. The first room was a small ante-room—I waited there for some time, telling the spirits of the place that I came in peace and not as a robber. When it seemed to me that they had had time to hear me, I went on. Ah, what riches! Few, even, of the windows had been broken—it was all as it had been. The great windows that looked over the city had not been broken at all though they were dusty and streaked with many years. There were coverings on the floors, the colors not greatly faded, and the chairs were soft and deep. There were pictures upon the walls, very strange, very wonderful—I remember one of a bunch of flowers in a jar—if you came close to it, you could see nothing but bits of color, but if you stood away from it, the flowers might have been picked yesterday. It made my heart feel strange to look at this picture—and to look at the figure of a bird, in some hard clay, on a table and see it so like our birds. Everywhere there were books and writings, many in tongues that I could not read. The god who lived there must have been a wise god and full of knowledge. I felt I had right there, as I sought knowledge also.

Nevertheless, it was strange. There was a washing-place but no water—perhaps the gods washed in air. There was a cooking-place but no wood, and though there was a machine to cook food, there was no place to put fire in it. Nor were there candles or lamps—there were things that looked like lamps but they had neither oil nor wick. All these things were magic, but I touched them and lived—the magic had gone out of them. Let me tell one thing to show. In the washing-place, a thing said "Hot" but it was not hot to the touch—another thing said "Cold" but it was not cold. This must have been a strong magic but the magic was gone. I do not understand—they had ways—I wish that I knew.

It was close and dry and dusty in their house of the gods. I have said the magic was gone but that is not true—it had gone from the magic things but it had not gone from the place. I felt the spirits about me weighing upon me. Nor had I ever slept in a Dead Place before—and yet, tonight, I must sleep there. When I thought of it, my tongue felt dry in my throat, in spite of my wish for knowledge. Almost I would have gone down again and faced the dogs, but I did not.

I had not gone through all the rooms when the darkness fell. When it fell, I went back to the big room looking over the city and made fire. There was a place to make a fire and a box with wood in it, though I do not think they cooked there. I wrapped myself in a floor-covering and slept in front of the fire—I was very tired.

Now I tell what is very strong magic. I woke in the midst of the night. When I woke, the fire had gone out and I was cold. It seemed to me that all around me there were whisperings and voices. I closed my eyes to shut them out. Some will say that I slept again, but I do not think that I slept. I could feel the spirits drawing my spirit out of my body as a fish is drawn on a line.

Why should I lie about it? I am a priest and the son of a priest. If there are spirits, as they say, in the small Dead Places near us, what spirits must there not be in that great Place of the Gods? And would not they wish to speak? After such long years? I know that I felt myself drawn as a fish is drawn on a line. I had stepped out of my body—I could see my body asleep in front of the cold fire, but it was not I. I was drawn to look out upon the city of the gods.

It should have been dark, for it was night, but it was not dark. Everywhere there were lights—lines of light—circles and blurs of light—ten thousand torches would not have been the same. The sky itself was alight—you could barely see the stars for the glow in the sky. I thought to myself "This is strong magic" and trembled. There was a roaring in my ears like the rushing of rivers. Then my eyes grew used to the light and my ears to the sound. I knew that I was seeing the city as it had been when the gods were alive.

This was a sight indeed—yes, that was a sight: I could not have seen it in the body—my body would have died. Everywhere went the gods, on foot and in chariots—there were gods beyond number and counting and their chariots blocked the streets. They had turned night to day for their pleasure—they did not sleep with the sun. The noise of their coming and going was the noise of many waters. It was magic what they could do—it was magic what they did.

I looked out of another window—the great vines of their bridges were mended and the god-roads went East and West. Restless, restless, were the gods and always in motion! They burrowed tunnels under rivers—they flew in the air. With unbelievable tools they did giant works—no part of the earth was safe from them, for, if they wished for a thing, they summoned it from the other side of the world. And always, as they labored and rested, as they feasted and made love, there was a drum in their ears—the pulse of the giant city, beating and beating like a man's heart.

Were they happy? What is happiness to the gods? They were great, they were mighty, they were wonderful and terrible. As I looked upon them and their magic, I felt like a child—but a little more, it seemed to me, and they would pull down the moon from the sky. I saw them with wisdom beyond wisdom and knowledge beyond knowledge. And yet not all they did was well done—even I could see that—and yet their wisdom could not but grow until all was peace.

Then I saw their fate come upon them and that was terrible past speech. It came upon them as they walked the streets of their city. I have been in the fights with the Forest People—I have seen men die. But this was not like that. When gods war with gods, they use weapons we do not know. It was fire falling out of the sky and a mist that poisoned. It was the time of the Great Burning and the Destruction. They ran about like ants in the streets of their city—poor gods, poor gods! Then the towers began to fall. A few escaped—yes, a few. The legends tell it. But, even after the city had become a Dead Place, for many years the poison was still in the ground. I saw it happen, I saw the last of them die. It was darkness over the broken city and I wept.

All this, I saw. I saw it as I have told it, though not in the body. When I woke in the morning, I was hungry, but I did not think first of my hunger for my heart was perplexed and confused. I knew the reason for the Dead Places but I did not see why it had happened. It seemed to me it should not have happened, with all the magic they had. I went through the house looking for an answer. There was so much in the house I could not understand—and yet I am a priest and the son of a priest. It was like being on one side of the great river, at night, with no light to show the way.

Then I saw the dead god. He was sitting in his chair, by the window, in a room I had not entered before and, for the first moment, I thought that he was alive. Then I saw the skin on the back of his hand—it was like dry leather. The room was shut, hot and dry—no doubt that had kept him as he was. At first I was afraid to approach him—then the fear left me. He was sitting looking out over the city—he was dressed in the clothes of the gods. His age was neither young nor old—I could not tell his age. But there was wisdom in his face and great sadness. You could see that he would have not run away. He had sat at his window, watching his city die—then he himself had died. But it is better to lose one's life than one's spirit—and you could see from the face that his spirit had not been lost. I knew, that, if I touched him, he would fall into dust—and yet, there was something unconquered in the face.

That is all of my story, for then I knew he was a man—I knew then that they had been men, neither gods nor demons. It is a great knowledge, hard to tell and believe. They were men—they went a dark road, but they were men. I had no fear after that—I had no fear going home, though twice I fought off the dogs and once I was hunted for two days by the Forest People. When I saw my father again, I prayed and was purified. He touched my lips and my breast, he said, "You went away a boy. You come back a man and a priest." I said, "Father, they were men! I have been in the Place of the Gods and seen it! Now slay me, if it is the law—but still I know they were men."

He looked at me out of both eyes. He said, "The law is not always the same shape—you have done what you have done. I could not have done it my time, but you come after me. Tell!"

I told and he listened. After that, I wished to tell all the people but he showed me otherwise. He said, "Truth is a hard deer to hunt. If you eat too much truth at once, you may die of the truth. It was not idly that our fathers forbade the Dead Places." He was right—it is better the truth should come little by little. I have learned that, being a priest. Perhaps, in the old days, they ate knowledge too fast.

Nevertheless, we make a beginning. It is not for the metal alone we go to the Dead Places now—there are the books and the writings. They are hard to learn. And the magic tools are broken—but we can look at them and wonder. At least, we make a beginning. And, when I am chief priest we shall go to the Place of the Gods—the place newyork—not one man but a company. We shall look for the images of the gods and find the god ASHING and the others—the gods Lincoln and Biltmore and Moses. But they were men who built the city, not gods or demons. They were men. I remember the dead man's face. They were men who were here before us. We must build again.

7

MUSIC: CONTEMPORARY NEOCLASSICISM

Igor Stravinsky

In literature, painting, sculpture, and architecture the term "neoclassicism" generally means a return to the principles and practices of ancient Greece or perhaps of the Roman empire. Nearly every century since the Renaissance has had its neoclassical phase. In music, however, the eighteenth century is considered the "classical" period, and the term "neoclassicism" denotes a twentieth-century movement that combines the forms of Bach, Mozart, and Italian music of the eighteenth century with entirely modern techniques.

Modern music has been much influenced by Wagner and the kind of romanticism he exemplified, and some composers have continued along the traditional lines of the nineteenth century and extended the principles of Wagner. But what is often called the "new music" of our time is definitely anti-romantic. It began with Debussy's impressionism, which, though anti-Wagnerian, nevertheless was derived from Romanticism and was perhaps its ultimate expression. Following World War I and a period of experimentation with primitive sounds and rhythms, Bach became the magic name, and serious composers were for a while united in their desire to turn back to the eighteenth century for their models. These composers were concerned mainly with the form and spirit of the "classical" music of that century rather than with classical harmonic principles; they felt free to combine in a string quartet, for example, strict sonata form with twentieth-century dissonant techniques. They concentrated upon music for small ensembles, generally without any programme or literary subject matter. The aim was to simplify, to condense, to eliminate the nonessential. This music was, therefore, suitable to a scientific age, with its objectivity, clarity, and absence of emotional display.

Neoclassical music has aroused considerable controversy; conservative critics often consider it a mark of decadence while others find in it one of the most significant developments of our time. Without doubt it has gained a strong foothold in modern music, and some of the most notable contemporary composers have at least gone through a neoclassical phase. The music of four such composers is included here: Stravinsky, Prokofieff, Hindemith, and Bartók.

Although the German-Italian Busoni (1866-1924) has been called the first neoclassicist, the general movement did not begin until 1923, when Igor Stravinsky startled the music world with his Octet for Wind Instruments, a composition written in an eighteenth-century style. The Firebird Suite in 1910 first brought Stravinsky to the attention of the public, and with Petrouchka, presented in Paris in 1911, he was recognized as one of the most original musicians since Debussy. But neither of these ballets was half so original as The Rite of Spring, one of the landmarks of twentieth-century music, produced in Paris in 1913.

Stravinsky was born in Russia in 1882 and lived through the Bolshevik Revolution. Although he was brought up in a musical atmosphere (his father was a bass singer at the Imperial Opera), his parents did not intend for him to be a musician. They gave him an academic education and sent him to the university to study law. But music always attracted him and in 1902 he met Rimsky-Korsakoff who eventually became his teacher and encouraged the performance of his early, rather conventional, compositions. By 1917 he had achieved musical fame through his work with the Russian Ballet. Not in sympathy with the Revolution, he broke permanently with the land of his birth in 1919 and moved to the outskirts of Paris where he intended to live the rest of his life. But in 1939 political events again caused him to pull up his roots. He left Paris and came to America, married a second wife in Bedford, Massachusetts, applied for citizenship, and eventually settled in California. He has continued active and creative, some of his major works having been written since he came to this country.

IGOR STRAVINSKY

LIKE A COLOSSUS, Stravinsky has straddled the world of contemporary music for almost half a century. One foot has been planted in the world of iconoclasm and revolt; the other, in the opposing world of neoclassicism, with its order and symmetry.

The rebel appeared in a series of masterpieces which many still consider among the greatest of Stravinsky's works: *The Firebird*, *Petrouchka*, and *The Rite of Spring*. Though he drew his strength and inspiration from Russian folklore and backgrounds, Stravinsky nevertheless struck a path of his own into new, formerly unexplored regions of musical sound. Orthodox harmony made way for dissonance, traditional tonality for polytonality. A severe, often crude, melodic line brought brutal strength. Rhythm was revitalized through the use of rapidly changing meters and polymeters. The orchestration exploited bizarre, sensational colors. This was a neoprimitive art, at one and the same time elemental and sophisticated.

This was the "music of the future." On the impressionistic and postimpressionistic world of 1912-1914 it descended with shattering impact. It created fierce dissension between those who envisioned its composer as a prophetic voice in music and others who saw only sham and artifice in his tonal audacities. Few works were so violently attacked in their own time as these three scores; and few works have had such a decisive influence on the musical thinking of an entire generation. Consciously or otherwise, composers began imitating this fresh, vital speech. Younger men accepted Stravinsky as the spearhead of their attacks against formalism and tradition. In Italy, the futurist Marinetti paraded the streets with a banner proclaiming: "Down With Wagner! Long Live Stravinsky!"

Then just when these revolutionary works began slowly to gain general acceptance, and when the name of Stravinsky was conveniently identified with the avant-garde of contemporary music, a subtle evolution in style took place in his works. It was a breaking away from the complexity, the dissonance, and the hot blood of his Russian music. Stravinsky, seeking a more objective approach to his art, felt the need of greater clarity and lucidity in his writing, greater economy and simplicity. Indicative of this new attitude was the ballet *Pulcinella*, in which the creator of "the music of the future" was turning to the past by utilizing materials, and adapting the classical style, of Pergolesi! Brevity of forms, transparency of texture, avoidance of emotion in style, economy of instrumentation (with frequent excursions into novel combinations), a predilection for counterpoint—these were now the qualities of Stravinsky's works. From music that tended to be pictorial, Stravinsky turned to music that was abstract, pure, formal.

Once again acrid controversy raged around the personality of Igor Stravinsky, controversy between those who felt that the reservoir of his genius had now run dry and others who insisted that this new phase was a logical, even inevitable, development in the evolution of a great creative personality. To his many critics, Stravinsky insisted with calm self-assurance that just as they had refused to understand him when he wrote his Russian ballets, but later learned to accept him, so they would some day come around to his new way of thinking. "Their attitude certainly cannot make me deviate from my path," he wrote firmly in his autobiography. "I shall assuredly not sacrifice my predilection and my aspirations to the demands of those who, in their blindness, do not realize that they are simply asking me to go backwards. It should be obvious that what they wish for has become obsolete for me, and that I could not follow them without doing violence to myself."

And, it must be added, once again Stravinsky conquered. While not all of his neoclassical works have won full acceptance—some of them are singularly arid and unpalatable—the best of them (the *Symphony of Psalms*, say, or *Oedipus Rex*) have, in recent performances, made a profound impression. They are deeply moving in the intensity of expression and so inevitable in architectonic logic that many critics do not hesitate in referring to them as masterpieces.

In his most recent works a greater warmth and a more personal feeling have entered into this neoclassic writing. There may be, as there has always been with Stravinsky's music, a divergence of opinion as to the greatness of works like his recent symphonies, the ballet *Orpheus*, the Mass, etc.; but there will be few to deny that Stravinsky is still one of the most dynamic personalities in the world of contemporary music.

THE RITE OF SPRING (*Le Sacre Du Printemps*)
BALLET, 1913

SOON AFTER COMPLETING *The Firebird*, Stravinsky had a "vision," as he himself described it. He saw a girl dancing herself to death in a sacrificial pagan rite. He reported this transport to the painter Nicolas Roerich, who, impressed, agreed that this could be elaborated into a new ballet. Roerich helped Stravinsky work out a general outline in which images of pagan Russia were evoked.

The Rite of Spring has no detailed specific program. In abstract terms it portrays a ritual of pagan Russia. Symbolic or anecdotal details are not permitted to intrude. An exquisite orchestral introduction of seventy-five bars sets the mood of springtime: the earth is reborn; life is regenerated. There then takes place the Ballet of the Adolescents, who accompany their uneven stamping on the ground with an incantation. A second ceremonial consists of a kind of community contest, during which the Sage of the tribe appears to consecrate the soil. A pagan night, touched with mystery and sadness, descends. The Mysterious Circle of Adolescents begin a frenetic dance. A victim for the sacrifice is now chosen; and she dances herself to death.

The première performance, at the Théatre de Champs Élysées in Paris on May 29, 1913, created a scandal which has been frequently described. Nijinsky's exotic choreography and Roerich's bizarre settings and costumes were partially responsible. But it was Stravinsky's revolutionary score which, more than any single factor, stirred that first-night audience to dynamic reactions. The performance had not progressed very far when catcalls, shouts, and stamping of feet began to drown out the music. On the one hand, musicians like Maurice Ravel and Debussy arose to exclaim that this was a work of genius; on the other, people like the critic André Capu, the Austrian Ambassador, and the Princess de Pourtalès pronounced it a fake. Blows were exchanged. One woman spat in the face of a demonstrator. Pandemonium followed. Very little of the music could now be heard.

Such was the birth of a musical work which has justifiably been described as one of the epochal landmarks in the music of our generation. More than any other single composition, it has influenced composers throughout the world, setting forth a new trend in musical composition, helping to evolve a new idiom. The dynamism of Stravinsky's rhythmic writing—the rapidly changing meters, the counterpoint of different rhythms—had a devastating kinesthetic appeal; the tension of the music, built up through dissonance and polytonality, had a terrifying effect; the brazen colors produced by unorthodox instrumentation were dazzling; the primitive appeal to the elementary senses of masses of sound and disjointed melodies had overwhelming impact. All this destroyed the complacency not only of a first-night audience but also of an entire musical era.

When *The Rite of Spring* was introduced in London at the Drury Lane Theatre on July 11, 1913, the audience was better mannered than the one which had witnessed the première performance in Paris. But the critics were just as savage. "It has no relation to music at all as most of us understand the word," one of them wrote. Another remarked: "A crowd of savages . . . might have produced such noises."

Appreciation for this powerful and original music did not come suddenly. When the orchestral suite was introduced in this country by Pierre Monteux and the Boston Symphony in 1924, there was still profound antagonism to this music. One wit contributed the following verse to the pages of the Boston *Herald:*

Who wrote this fiendish *Rite of Spring?*
What right had he to write this thing?
Against our helpless ears to fling
Its crash, clash, cling, clang, bing, bang, bing!

If acceptance came slowly, it came inevitably as well. The score is now heard often—more often in the symphony hall than in the theatre—and much of the original surprise is gone. Instead, we now appreciate the incomparable vitality, the richness of speech, the audaciousness of thinking in this music. Indicative that this work is no longer for esoteric ears alone is the fact that it was incorporated in a Walt Disney motion picture, *Fantasia*, which was seen by millions.

The Rite of Spring, as heard in the concert auditorium, is divided into two parts:

I. The Adoration of the Earth. Introduction—Harbingers of Spring—Dance of the Adolescents—Spring Rounds; Games of the Round Cities—the Procession of Wise Men—The Adoration of the Earth—Dance of the Earth.

II. The Sacrifice. Introduction—Mysterious Circle of the Adolescents—Glorification of the Chosen One—Evocation of the Ancestors—The Sacrificial Dance of the Chosen One.

STRAVINSKY: *Capriccio for Piano and Orchestra*

THEORETICALLY, concert-hall virtuosos are always eager for new concertos; but it often happens that if a composer does not perform his own music, it goes a long while unheard. Besides, if a composer fortunately happens also to excel as a performer, he finds his reputation and his livelihood considerably enhanced thereby; and for his personal appearances he needs new music. "I must play some new works," wrote Mozart, getting ready for twenty-two concert appearances in less than six weeks, "and therefore I must compose." Hindemith wrote his *Schwanendreher* because, as he put it, "I played too many times my two other viola concertos." Stravinsky had played his Piano Concerto some forty times in a few years and thought it time "to give the public another work for piano and orchestra." This new piano concerto he called a *Capriccio*.

The reason for the title is set forth by Stravinsky as follows: "I had in mind the definition of a *capriccio* given by Praetorius, the celebrated musical authority of the seventeenth century. He regarded it as a synonym of the *fantasia*, which was a free form made up of fugato instrumental passages. This form enabled me to develop music by the juxtaposition of episodes of various kinds which follow one another and by their very nature give the piece that aspect of caprice from which it takes its name."

Critics have offered this work as evidence of a neoclassic trend in Stravinsky, of a reawakened interest in eighteenth-century music. Nicolas Slonimsky has pointed out, with considerable truth, that in the *Capriccio* "once more Stravinsky reasserted his belief in the perpetually young forms of old music, and once more he filled the old forms with new ideas." The beautiful opening of the slow movement has a fine eighteenth-century flavor, and the entire work is governed by the kind of mannered precision and polish which characterize not only Mozart or Bach, but their minor contemporaries. Stravinsky, of course, is an iconoclast who will not keep the sources of his inspiration straight to please any critic. Contrariwise, he asserts that his creative thought during this period was "dominated by that prince of music, Carl Maria von Weber." Weber was an inveterate romantic, as far removed from the eighteenth century in temperament as Stravinsky is in time.

The *Capriccio* was begun during Christmas 1928 and completed in September the following year. It was first performed at a Paris Symphony Orchestra concert on December 6, 1929, Stravinsky the soloist and Ansermet conducting. Its American première took place December 19, 1930, Jesús María Sanromá at the piano, with Serge Koussevitzky conducting the Boston Symphony Orchestra.

Stravinsky is one of the acknowledged masters of the modern orchestra. He has a penchant for setting unique scoring problems for himself in each successive work, and this *Capriccio* is no exception. Besides a large orchestra and a solo piano, he also employs a secondary solo group comprising a violin, viola, cello, and a double bass. This is a *concertino* unit such as one would expect to find in a *concerto grosso*. However, Stravinsky delights in disappointing reasonable expectations, and this hint of *concerto grosso* scoring is contained in a work which shows no trace of a *concerto grosso* style or form. In point of fact, nearly every instrument in the orchestra has its chance at solo work.

The orchestration, as a whole, is tight and economical. Stravinsky does not believe in doubling instruments unnecessarily. No matter how complex and interwoven the ensemble, each instrument makes a clearly individual contribution to the total effect.

1. Presto *2. Andante rapsodico*
3. Allegro capriccioso

The work opens with a discourse "betwixt the cold bear and the raging lion"; a fierce, leonine outburst, followed by a bleak descent of the solo strings. Once more the orchestra thunders, and the descending answer now passes to the bare and frigid woodwinds. This serves as both an introduction and a conclusion to the first movement. Piano and timpani start a rhythm going, and an English horn responds. Once again the piano-timpani rhythm, and this time rejoinders come in clearly spaced succession from various parts of the orchestra. The melodic material is light, engaging, often dancelike. Flutes start one delicate dance episode; the piano eventually begins another. Oboe and clarinet exchange a ceremonious salutation of trills. Oboe and piccolo do likewise, then clarinet and oboe again. A new episode begins, with the piano returning to its earlier dance while two flutes serenade sweetly. Clarinet, bassoon, horn, and piano make polite and pleasantly inconsequential conversation during the next section. The piano-timpani rhythm returns, marking a new episode. The dramatic introductory dialogue is ultimately resumed, neatly rounding out the movement.

The opening of the slow movement (*andante rapsodico*) is a magnificent recreation, in an idiom entirely modern, of the textures and tensions of an eighteenth-century concerto. Its mood is sober and rhapsodical, its texture contrapuntal, and its figurations are precise. The first episode that breaks in upon this beautiful opening is a reminder that the title *Capriccio* is to be taken literally. It is right out of the days of the silent film when a piano player was employed in the local theater to supply the musical background. Horns and clarinets pump melodramatically, and then the piano does background music for the villain, who arrives on the invisible screen with his mustachios and his mortgage. The next episode is light, sophisticated musicmaking. The opening section returns, leading to a powerful and passionate cadenza.

A note sustained by the flute bridges the gap to the finale (*allegro capriccioso*). Suspense is built up quietly and then climaxed by a fortissimo outburst. Introductory formalities thus quickly dispensed with, piano and orchestra settle to a succession of scintillating and sophisticated episodes mainly dancelike in character. There is a trace of the old dance-hall conception of jazz and a touch of Viennese gaiety. For one strange moment the pianist even flashes the sort of tremolo that used to be thought so clever in the ragtime days. All in all, the movement is charming and accomplished entertainment, the sort that a concerto finale is traditionally expected to provide.

Sergei Prokofieff

Prokofieff was born in 1891 in the Ukraine. His mother, a fine pianist, introduced him to music when he was very young, and at thirteen he entered the St. Petersburg Conservatory, where Rimsky-Korsakoff was one of his teachers. His first compositions were largely imitative and traditional in technique, but he soon began to experiment with dissonance, unconventional chords, and new tonalities. His Second Piano Concerto puzzled and shocked the audience when played at a public concert in 1914 but it won the Rubenstein prize. During World War I he remained in Russia composing music until the Revolution, but in 1917 he took advantage of an opportunity to tour America and left Soviet Russia, eventually to settle in Paris.

In 1933 he decided to return to Russia and identify himself with the Soviet cultural life. Since that time much of his music has been dedicated to propagandizing or interpreting Communist ideology and idealizing Russian culture. His basic style, however, has remained unchanged in spite of this difference in subject matter. Living in a Moscow suburb during World War II, he composed some of his most ambitious works: Symphonic Suite: 1941, the Stalingrad Sonata, the Fifth Symphony, and the opera War and Peace.

Prokofieff, like Shostakovitch, has struggled with the problem of adjusting his music to the demands of the Soviet state. He has alternately yielded and rebelled, and even when he was able to remain in the good graces of the authorities he never abandoned completely his independence and individuality. In 1948, when he was at the height of his fame, considered one of the great cultural figures of the Soviet Union, he became the victim of a new music policy adopted by the General Committee of the Communist party. Along with Shostakovitch, Khatchaturian, and other leading composers he was denounced for "decadent formalism," for his use of atonality and dissonance, and for the influence of Western ideas in his music. Although angry at first, he eventually wrote a detailed and abject apology in which he promised subservience in the future. An oratorio condemning Western warmongers got him back in the good graces of the party. In 1951 he received the Stalin prize but was too ill to attend the special concert given on his sixtieth birthday. He died in Moscow in 1953.

An intellectual strain runs throughout Prokofieff's music, and neoclassicism is one of the primary elements. It is illustrated aptly, though not ambitiously, in the rather playful Classical Symphony, analyzed in the following selection. Along with this modern classicism has gone a search for innovation in harmony, melody, orchestration, and stage technique. An almost mischievous quality also appears frequently in his work. In Peter and the Wolf *it is good humored and gay; in the* Classical Symphony *it is subtle and whimsical. In later political satires a good deal of bitterness is at times apparent and replaces the more appealing mood of his earlier music.*

PROKOFIEFF:

Classical Symphony in D Major, Op. 25

WHEN THIS CENTURY was in its teens, Sergei Prokofieff was regarded as a leader in the trend toward dissonance and artistic iconoclasm. But as early as 1930 he had recanted. Asked by Olin Downes what he had become, he replied:

> I hope, simpler and more melodic. Of course I have used dissonance in my time, but there has been too much dissonance. Bach used dissonance as good salt for his music. Others applied pepper, seasoned the dishes more and more highly until finally the music was nothing but pepper. Society has had enough of that. We want a simpler style for music, with dissonance again relegated to its proper place. Music has reached and passed the greatest degree of discord and complexity that it is practicable for it to attain. Therefore I think the desire which I and many of my fellow composers feel, to attain a more simple and melodic expression, is the inevitable direction for the music of the future. . . . In the field of instrumental or symphonic music, I want nothing better, nothing more flexible or complete than the sonata form, which contains everything necessary to my structural purpose.

One might suppose this dictum of 1930 to be the apologia for the *Classical Symphony*. That work, however, was written in 1917, after the *Scythian Suite* for orchestra and the piano composition *Sarcasms*, both of which were written in 1914 and were highly dissonant. It is evident that in the midst of his most vigorous pursuit of modernism there was at least a moment of nostalgic retrospect.

The themes, the form, and the simple orchestration of the *Classical Symphony* are reminiscent of Mozart. The principal subject of the first movement appears in the third bar, in the violins. It is straightforward in rhythm, clear in key, and as untroubled by any expressive burden as many a theme in the early works of Mozart. The transitional theme, beginning in D, is less active than the first subject. The second theme, instead of striving for lyric warmth, begins with a figure leaping two octaves, in A major, and continues on the arpeggio of F major. The development shows little disposition to escape the restraints imposed upon the exposition. The recapitulation begins, irregularly, in C, but the continuation is so managed that the second subject recurs in the orthodox key of D major. There is a brief Coda.

The second movement (Larghetto, A major, 2-2 time) has but one main theme, a serene melody beginning high in the violins after four introductory measures. With this theme relieved by a variety of interpolated excursions, the form of the movement becomes that of a simple Rondo.

Instead of the Minuet which Mozart

would doubtless have written, we find a Gavotte (D major, 4-4—instead of 2-2—time) whose first section pursues a succession of keys hardly imaginable in a Mozartian dance form. Here, for the first time in the symphony, appears a tinge of that grotesque humor which was so apparent in other works of this early period. The very short first section is followed by a Trio (the classical alternative section of the Gavotte was the Musette, often on a drone bass in imitation of the cornemuse, or bagpipe) which is somewhat longer than the Gavotte itself and is less adventurous in modulation.

The Finale (D major, 2-2 time) is again in sonata form. The main theme, insistently reiterating the arpeggio of D major, is suggestive of the classic manner, although its very insistence seems to go somewhat beyond the usual restraints of that style. The second theme also features a persistently reiterated figure, shunning the lyric mood for one more vital. There follows the usual development and recapitulation.

The orchestra is essentially that of Mozart's day.

Paul Hindemith

The music of Paul Hindemith well illustrates the dominant characteristics of our time. Like other composers, Hindemith has gone through various phases of development. He started with German romanticism, was briefly influenced by impressionism, then found his own individual idiom, which combined the contrapuntal techniques of an earlier age with twentieth-century freedom of tonality. His music is not lacking in feeling but the emotional content is held under strong intellectual control. For this reason the neoclassical current of the 1930s appealed to him. His symphony, Mathis der Maler, composed in 1932, and analyzed in the following selection, shows the influence of earlier polyphonic music, but the composer is already beginning to abandon here the harsh tone and mechanical effect of strict neoclassical music for a more sympathetic and harmonious mood.

Hindemith's career has had two important phases. During the first of these, before he was forced to leave Nazi Germany in 1935 because he would not make his music subservient to the state, he achieved recognition as one of the great modern European composers. Born in Hanau in 1895, he early developed an interest in music. When his parents were unwilling for him to become a professional musician, he ran away from home and earned his living playing in dance bands and cafés while he studied at the conservatory in Frankfort. When his First String Quartet won the Mendelssohn prize, his creative gifts became evident.

From 1915 to 1923 he was concertmaster in the orchestra of the Frankfort Opera. In 1921 he helped organize the Amar String Quartet, in which he was violist, and until 1929 traveled with the quartet through central Europe playing the works of modern composers and propagandizing for modern music. For this quartet he composed his first important chamber music. For a while he taught composition at the Berlin Academy of Music, but his career there was ended in 1935 by the Nazi government. This was a crucial experience which sharply divided his life into two periods. Yet none of the emotional turmoil he must have experienced appears in his music either before or after the changes in country, language, and environment that he was forced to make. After he left Germany Hindemith spent some time in Turkey; then in 1939 he settled in the United States, and in 1942 joined the music faculty at Yale. In 1953 he became professor of music theory at the University of Zurich where he now teaches.

In part perhaps because of his war experiences in Germany, Hindemith felt keenly the need to write music that would be understood and appreciated by a wide audience, not just by an esoteric few, and along with his more complex compositions he has written music intended for mass consumption—for radio, films, the theater, brass bands, children's games, and the like. This Gebrauchsmusik ("workaday music") did not replace more serious works in his own complicated style, but his compositions after 1933 are certainly easier for audiences and critics to understand.

HINDEMITH:
Symphony, *Mathis der Maler (Mathias the Painter)*

IN THE MUSEUM of Colmar there is to be seen a great altarpiece, a polyptych of eleven panels, painted by Mathias Grünewald, who was a disciple of Altdorfer and Dürer. This work was ordered for the monastery church of St. Anthony at Isenheim, in Alsace, and was apparently completed before the Abbot died in 1516. The altar was dismembered after the French Revolution, but while several sculptured figures were lost or destroyed, Grünewald's paintings were kept intact and were later sent to the Colmar museum.

The life of the painter is the theme of an opera composed by Hindemith, and the symphony is a selection of three excerpts from that work. Each of these movements bears a title referring us to one of the panels of the altarpiece as the source of its character; and while there is no attempt at mere illustration or description in the music, the sense of its character is much vivified by reference to its source. The three panels with which the music is concerned are:

"The Concert of the Angels." This, in the scheme of the whole, was a companion to the panel "The Incarnation." In the foreground an angel kneels, playing a bass viol.

Behind him rise two pale-rose marble steps which support a richly decorated, fantastic little tabernacle. The polychrome architecture and sculptural decoration, both of human form and of designs from nature, brightened with gold and different shades of red, are varied and colorful; no less the celestial choir, some of whose members, with brown exotic features and gay feathered headdress, of green, blue, orange, and red, approach the grotesque. The figures of the floating angels become ever smaller as they reach far back to the depths of the chapel or rise to its very top. . . . The brightest spot of all is the figure of Mary kneeling in the smaller opening of the temple, a crown of pointed fragile leaves like tongues of flame upon her head. . . . Behind her the chapel sinks again into the darkness of night.*

"The Entombment" is the footpiece to the central panel, which depicts the crucifixion.

The despairing complaint of the group at the left in the Crucifixion is somewhat subdued in the sense of mourning on the footpiece. Noisy protest here yields to silent tears, stormy emotion to resigned calm, dramatic intensity of the passion to a lyric mood of elegy more befitting the quiet scene of lamentation. The body of Christ is supported under the arms by John. The treatment of the dead body is realistic in detail, with the hands stiff in death, gaping wounds in the

* This and the following descriptions are derived from Arthur Burkhard's *The Isenheim Altar*, as quoted in the program-book of the Boston Symphony Orchestra.

feet, thorns sticking in the flesh, but it is no longer horrible or repellent. The drapery is less disturbed, the hair smoothed, the expression of pain in the pale tear-stained faces of Magdalene and Mary considerably softened. . . . Before the empty tomb lies the crown of thorns, withered and dead. The balanced symbolical landscape is suffused with soft natural evening light, equally distributed over the entire expanse. The different shades of blue, of red, brown, and green are combined in a surprisingly modern manner, making the scene of mourning the most beautiful in coloring of the entire altar.

"The Temptation of St. Anthony" is designed to contrast with the corresponding panel, depicting the conversation of St. Anthony with St. Paul.

One discovers the poor tortured saint, prostrate and apparently helpless before the attack of a veritable chaos of monstrous demons that swarm down upon him from all sides. The devils are imaginary combinations of all kinds and conditions of men and beasts, their parts curiously assembled from different creatures of the entire animal kingdom. . . . A feathered foe with an eagle's head, long birds' legs, and a muscled fleshy human forearm raises a knotty threatening club. A gaping fish mouth seems to belong to a sort of hippopotamus. Other uncanny beasts pull apart the fallen saint's mantle, tear his hair, and lunge forward to strike him with bones and sticks. In the left hand corner squats a horrible creature, human in face and form but with webbed feet, his arms, legs and swollen abdomen covered with loathesome running sores.

The first movement of the symphony begins *(Ruhig bewegt)* with the assertion of the tonality of G major in the horns and in long-held chords in the strings. Against this background a quiet melodic curve rises in clarinets, oboes, and flutes. This is a brief prologue to the main theme, an old church tune, *Es sungen drei Engel* ("Three Angels Were Singing"), softly intoned by the trombones. The key of the entrance is D flat; and the melodic curve of the wind instruments heard in the prologue is now amplified as a background to this theme. The same theme is heard in the horns and lower wood winds, and again in the highest register of the winds; then the intensity subsides. The time changes to a rather animated 2-2 *(Zeimlich lebhafte Halbe)*. There is a principal subject of sturdy rhythmic design in flutes and first violins, accompanied by a few clear contrapuntal lines, and extended to a total length of sixteen measures. The two opening bars present a figure of which much is made in the sequel. After some development a second theme appears, more lyrical and with a kind of singsong chord pattern for accompaniment. These two themes are presently combined, fugue-fashion, in an extended development. The Angels' Song, again in the trombones, is added at the climax and leads back to the mood and tempo of the prologue. A brief Coda brings the movement to a joyous end.

"The Entombment" *(Grablegung)* is but forty-five bars long. Two emotional characteristics are set forth: a funereal tension, in a somber, dead-march rhythm, and a tenderer strain, gently syncopated and still further softened by a fluid triplet. The brevity of the design is striking, yet there is no sense of fragmentariness.

The last movement has by far the most extended design of the three. Its title is amplified by the agonized cry of the saint, *Ubi eras, bone Jhesu ubi eras, quare non affuisti ut senares vulnera mea?* ("Where wert Thou, good Jesus, where wert Thou, why wert Thou not present that Thou mightest heal my wounds?") Although the composer would doubtless repudiate the suggestion that his themes are in any way equivalent to the Wagnerian leading-motives, it is impossible not to associate the Introduction *(Sehr langsam, frei im Zeitmass)* with this outcry. The main movement (*Sehr labhaft*, 9-8 time) must likewise be associated with the hideous struggle depicted by the painter. The main theme is a writhing line in all the strings, accompanied by an insistent but very simple rhythmic figure. A huge climax is followed by a flowing theme, begun in the oboe and continued in the clarinet, against a persistent, repetitive figure in the strings. This is also much developed. The turmoil grows and only begins to clear when the clarinets, and afterward the horn, return to the theme of the string introduction. A sense of victory is suggested in the hymn *Lauda Sion Salvatorem*, high in the winds and in the key of D flat. The close is a mighty *Alleluia*, delivered with utmost power by the brass.

Béla Bartók

All the more important musical styles of the twentieth century find expression in the music of the contemporary Hungarian composer, Béla Bartók. Beginning with a kind of traditional classicism, Bartók went through an expressionistic period around 1921-1922 and then, like many of his contemporaries, he turned back to the stricter forms of the eighteenth century and for a while wrote in a true neoclassical style. In his last works he completed the cycle and returned to a quieter, more serene classicism. His partiality for classical forms—concertos, string quartets, sonatas, and chamber music for various types of ensembles—is at once apparent in a list of his works. Within these forms, however, he embodied most of the traits of Hungarian folk music, which he did not imitate but completely absorbed into his own highly individual style.

According to Bartók himself the most important event of his life took place in 1905, when he heard a servant girl singing as she cleaned his apartment. The tune fascinated and excited him; investigating, he came upon the rich vein of Hungarian folk music and his life's passion. Already a well-known musician and composer at the time, Bartók had given his first public concert some fifteen years earlier when he was only ten. At the Budapest Academy of Music he went through the various phases of late Romantic allegiance, but in 1902 he heard Thus Spake Zarathustra *performed and the music of Richard Strauss overwhelmed him. Strauss and the surging nationalist spirit inspired his first major orchestral composition,* Kossuth, *performed in 1904; his study of Hungarian peasant music during the next few years also brought him into close contact with Kodály whose music abounds in colorful folk themes.*

In 1907 Bartók became a member of the music faculty at the Liszt Academy in Budapest, succeeding his own teacher, Dohnanyi. He began to bring into his music elements from Hungarian folksongs and dances, however, and his work became so complex and so individual that he was unable to gain any sort of wide public approval, although he was everywhere recognized as an important composer. Becoming discouraged and embittered, he withdrew from active concert life and gave himself almost entirely to composition and research.

Gradually his reputation increased outside Hungary and he made a number of concert tours, not only in Western Europe but also in the United States, in Egypt, in Turkey, and in Russia. But the growing influence of the Nazi movement after 1934 made his situation at home more and more difficult, and in the autumn of 1940 he and his wife left for America, where he spent the last years of his life in wretched health, suffering from poverty and neglect. Eventually he was given an honorary position at Columbia University to enable him to carry on his research in folk music. In 1943 he was invited to lecture at Harvard but was unable to do so because of his health. A victim of leukemia, he nevertheless continued to compose until his death in 1945 at the age of sixty-four, and some of his finest works were written during these last years.

BARTÓK: *Concerto for Orchestra*

THE SCORE of this work bears the date October 8, 1943. It was composed for the Koussevitzky Foundation, in memory of Natalia Koussevitzky, and was first performed by the Boston Orchestra on December 1, 1944. For that performance the composer (who had written the music during his convalescence from an illness which had seriously alarmed his friends) offered the following comment:

The general mood of the work represents, apart from the jesting second movement, a gradual transition from the sternness of the first movement and the lugubrious death-song of the third, to the life-assertion of the last one. The title of this symphony-like orchestral work is explained by its tendency to treat the single instruments or instrument groups in a "*concertant*" or soloistic manner. The "virtuoso" treatment appears, for instance, in the fugato sections of the development of the first movement (brass instruments), or in the "*perpetuum mobile*"-like passage of the principal theme in the last movement (strings), and, especially, in the second movement, in which pairs of instruments consecutively appear with brilliant passages.

As for the structure of the work, the first and fifth movements are written in a more or less regular sonata form. The development of the first contains fugato sections for brass; the exposition in the finale is somewhat extended, and its development consists of a fugue built on the last theme of the exposition. Less traditional forms are found in the second and third movements. The main part of the second consists of a chain of independent short sections, by wind instruments consecutively introduced in five pairs (bassoons, oboes, clarinets, flutes, and muted trumpets). Thematically, the five sections have nothing in common. A kind of "trio"—a short chorale for brass instruments and side-drum—follows, after which the five sections are recapitulated in a more elaborate instrumentation. The structure of the fourth movement likewise is chainlike; three themes appear successively. These constitute the core of the movement, which is enframed by a misty texture of rudimentary motifs. Most of the thematic material of this movement derives from the "Introduction" to the first movement. The form of the fourth movement—*Intermezzo interrotto*—could be rendered by the letter symbols "ABA—interruption—BA."

This account is rather severely condensed, and the hearer may be helped by the description of a few salient details. In the *Introduzione* the cellos and basses announce, unharmonized, a theme of somber strength whose intervals are all perfect fourths except for two stepwise progressions. The final note of this theme, prolonged, is clouded by a curious inflation and deflation of sound in the *tremolando* violins and violas, and a little flicker of light comes from the flutes to dissipate the cloud. This general effect is repeated. The theme of fourths, now moving a little more quickly in even quarter-notes, ascends higher than before, and the flute, above the *tremolando* strings, begins to speak articulately. Now the "fourths-theme" becomes a figure of eighth-notes in the lower strings, their several parts in tangled motion one against the other, while the trumpets amplify a figure of four quick notes and a longer one that the flute announced at the beginning of its solo. Slightly broadened, this figure becomes a well-defined theme in the violins. The whole rhythm, gradually accelerated, makes unmistakable and exciting preparation for the main body of the movement, *Allegro vivace*, 3-8 time.

[From Donald N. Ferguson, *Masterworks of the Orchestral Repertoire*.

Both this rhythm and the characteristic interval of the fourth will be found in the principal subject, whose pattern is an upward design for three bars, completed by its inversion (of course, downward) for three more. The matter is much more extendedly dealt with than is usual in the conventional sonata design, but the consistency of the treatment is such that no aberration from that design is felt. It subsides at length into a murmur (somewhat analogous to that which followed the first theme in the Introduction), making obvious preparation for the second subject. The underlying rhythm is here quietly tapped by the violins and 'celli, and the theme itself appears in the oboe—at first a wavering on two adjacent notes of the scale, then a spreading out into a wide upward and downward sweep. The development of this matter is mostly delicate and ingenious, the process being that described by the composer. A striking moment is offered by the clarinet which, in a three-bar rhythm, *tranquillo*, has a new version of the "fourths-theme" of the opening.

The second movement is entitled *Giuoco delle Coppie*—freely translated, Dance of the Happy Couples. (The "couples" are the pairs of instruments mentioned by the composer.) The snare drum gives out a curiously broken rhythm that introduces the theme of the first section—a tune that at first recalls a familiar Haydn piano sonata. The feeling of the folk dance seems to us frankly expressed, in a manner as engaging as Haydn's, but in character definitely Bartók's. The rather loose structure in five independent but linked sections as described by the composer will be apparent. The "kind of trio" is begun by the trumpets, trombones, and tuba, and is continued in the horns. The structure is designedly loose, but is not diffuse.

The third movement is entitled *Elegia*. With no more than a counterpoint in the tympani, the basses first present an inversion of the opening "fourths-theme" of the concerto. The more rapid movement developed therefrom in the first movement ensues; then the harps, *glissandi*, and what might also be called *glissando* figures in the clarinets and flutes, make a background for the emergence of a sinuous line of melody in the oboe. After some fluid swirling in the wood wind the piccolo whistles a strange tune; the perky figure of rhythm given to flute and then to trumpets in the first movement comes back in the violins and clarinets, and there is a new tune in the horn. Then, *poco agitato, mosso*, the violas have a melody in constricted intervals that is soon taken up by the winds. With a return to the original tempo there is a straining, soaring climax, a dwindling, and then a conclusion which recalls at last the characteristic fourths, whose pattern is now largely descending.

The fourth movement, the "Interrupted Intermezzo," moves in *Allegretto* tempo. Four introductory notes present the first theme in the oboe, a tune obsessed by the interval of the augmented fourth. This movement is not long, and the composer's description of its form is sufficient.

The Finale, like most of the other movements, begins with a unison figure—here, a good, sturdy dance-step. Presently pizzicato chords, accelerating for three bars, introduce the persistent sixteenth-note figure which forms the "'*perpetuum mobile*'-like passage." This is accompanied by the chords announced by the strings. There is a kind of second subject, *pp* in the flute, backgrounded by harps and *tremolando* strings. At length the bassoon recalls the opening figure. The conclusion, *piu presto*, is on triplet figures, taken at breakneck speed.

BARTÓK: *Music for Strings, Percussion, and Celesta*

THIS SOMEWHAT abstract experiment in unusual colors and rhythms was composed at Budapest in 1936. The positions of the players on the platform are prescribed by the composer: the strings in two quartets, one at the right and one at the left, with the percussion instruments between and the double basses at the back.

There are four movements. The first is essentially fugal, with the subject introduced by muted violas. The percussion enlivens the conversation, which proceeds in a long crescendo and diminuendo, and in remarkably varied rhythm, throughout.

The second movement (*Allegro*, 2-4 time) has two themes, one from the plucked and one from the bowed strings. There is much variation; then a sort of middle section in uneven rhythm; then a short fugato on the bowed theme.

The third movement has been described by Lawrence Gilman as a "mystical nocturne, elemental and earth-born." The percussion is here treated with extraordinary delicacy and appropriateness to the themes, the most important of which are announced by viola and by celesta and violins.

The last movement *(Allegro molto)* is a vigorous dance in the Lydian mode (an F-scale with B♯ instead of B♭). Two main themes, with some lesser ideas, provide the substance, and the form is in large outline very simple—the first gay dance subsiding into a *molto moderato* section, with a return of the gaiety thereafter.

The percussion instruments demanded by the score are tympani, bass and side drums (some without snare), gong, celesta, harp, piano (four hands), and xylophone.

Part Three

THE WORLD OF INTUITIVE THOUGHT

1. Exploration of the Unconscious
2. Anti-Intellectualism in Philosophy
3. Religious Existentialism
4. Organic Architecture
5. Painting: Expressionism and Abstract Expressionism
6. Literature: Romanticism and Symbolism
7. Music: Romanticism, Impressionism, and Modern Jazz

THE POINT OF VIEW

ALTHOUGH today we are still deeply impressed by the practical achievements of science in such things as air conditioning, television, and space missiles, there is also a reawakened interest in the psychology of human behavior and in our spiritual welfare. The influence upon contemporary thinking of the work of men like Freud, Jung, and Pavlov has been pervasive and lasting; their ideas are now an accepted part of everyday conversation. Indeed, we now are more aware than ever before of the vast, uncharted unconscious forces at work in the human mind, forces which so largely shape our thought and conduct, and we are more anxious to find a satisfying answer to the meaning and purpose of human life.

Man's emotional reactions and his sense of values determine not only his social attitudes but also his use of scientific knowledge. His creative and intuitive capacities are as interesting as the processes of the atom, and quite as significant. At this point in the twentieth century it appears outmoded to accept the popular Darwinian notion of a universe in which there is only the blind interaction of environmental and hereditary forces. The moral responsibility and the creative potentiality of the individual have again assumed a significant place in our concept of man and society.

Intuition and the Humanities

Without the interplay of intuitive insight and imagination human life would lose much of its variety and color. Who could wish the human scene to be reduced to a dull, flat consistency? As Jacques Barzun, distinguished contemporary historian and literary critic, has repeatedly insisted, the intimate and intuitive are the primary concern of the humanities. The scientist tries to discover the uniformities in nature's physical and chemical processes; the social theorist is concerned with broad patterns and typical results of individual and group behavior. By contrast, a student of the humanities tends to look at the unusual or unique manifestations of the human spirit. He values the novelty and unpredictability of man and commends the peculiar potentialities of the individual, the emotional impulses and the intuitive insight that leads man to the summits of moral vision and imaginative creativity.

The genuinely new comes from individual effort; originality arises from a rebellious spirit strong enough to act in accord with his beliefs. In a time of mass conformity and platitudes we need to be reminded of the value of not belonging, of not following every popular trend. Original thinkers and artists, often relying on intuitive insights, are lonely and isolated not because they prefer to be that way but because the public has not yet caught up with their personal understanding of life or with their creative method of portraying this understanding.

Friedrich Nietzsche, an influential German philosopher of the late nineteenth century, is among the most outspoken modern advocates of the superiority of will and intuition over reason and logic in human life. But in our day the "existentialists," perhaps the most popular writers on philosophy, have also developed a theory of human nature based on feeling and instinct. To Jean-Paul Sartre, a leading spokesman of this movement, man exists "only to fulfill himself." He discovers himself, indeed he creates himself, only as his impulses and commitments are given expression in his life.

Emphasis on the importance of feeling and of faith is especially noteworthy in the thought of William James, distinguished American pragmatist at the end of the nineteenth century. Likewise Sören Kierkegaard, a Danish religious writer largely rediscovered in our day, dramatically portrayed the overwhelming emotions of the individual soul trying to come to grips with his moral destiny. Leo Tolstoy, the great Russian novelist and religious leader, became convinced rather late in life that man can achieve spiritual greatness only as he is uncompromisingly loyal to his conscience and his moral ideals. In the work of men such as these, we find a point of view that commands widespread attention and respect in contemporary thought.

Intuition in the Arts

In the arts no better example of originality can be found than the architecture of Frank Lloyd Wright. Although to a large degree architecture is governed by social needs, every Wright structure is marked with his distinctive temperament and sense of values. A good building, he believed, contributes to the psychological well-being of each person who uses it. For Wright every structure was a fresh challenge to create an organic unity of function and effect. Recent painters also tend to emphasize the primary importance of feeling and intuition. From van Gogh to Klee the spirit of "expressionism" runs through their work, its chief distinction being the artist's compulsion to explore and express his innermost responses to life in a personalized language of line and color. More and more directly modern painting reflects the private temperament of each artist.

Individuality of interpretation also characterizes much contemporary literature. In both idea and style recent writers have been apt to revolt against established tradition and to experiment with bold psychological and dramatic effects. Recognition of the worth of the individual, so typical of nineteenth-century romanticism in a Wordsworth or a Shelley, reappears with new emphasis in such later poets as Hopkins and Yeats. Strong emotional reactions distinguish the fiction of Kafka and Faulkner. Both poetry and prose rely heavily on the stimulation of metaphor or symbol to convey the inner qualities of the writers' imagination in a distinctive style. These writers feel that their vision of life requires a unique method of communication.

From Beethoven to contemporary jazz, modern music likewise explores man's complex emotional experiences. Abandoning academic models, the contemporary composer struggles to find inspiration within himself. A variety of musical styles and structures suggest the shifting moods in self-discovery so characteristic of the music of our day. Freedom of treatment characterizes a Beethoven symphony as well as a Debussy prelude, temperamentally unlike as these two composers may be. In symphonic music Brahms probably achieved a mature balance of the new with the old more effectively than any other composer; by contrast the music of Wagner and Tschaikovsky display extreme degrees of intense emotion.

Throughout the arts one finds, then, a primary concern to discover and portray the value of emotion and intuition. The quest of the creative individual has always been to express human dreams and aspirations in the beauty of artistic form. Life and art of a high order result from this labor of self-discovery and self-purification. The artist offers a way of understanding the potential greatness of humanity. To be truly human is to welcome the positive powers of the intuitive spirit of man.

Crane Brinton

Crane Brinton's Ideas and Men, *from which this selection is taken, is a popularly written intellectual history of Western civilization. Prepared originally for the general education program at Harvard University where Brinton is Professor of Ancient and Modern History, this book provides a useful survey of major trends in Western thought and has been widely read in academic circles. As one of the characteristic manifestations of the spirit of our age, Brinton singles out a point of view which, for want of a better term, he calls "anti-intellectualism," and he defines and illustrates largely in terms acceptable to the social scientist. In his work with the history of ideas, however, Brinton seems to be impressed with the fact that, of all the sciences, psychology seems to have had the greatest influence upon popular thinking in the early decades of the twentieth century, just as biology had in the later decades of the nineteenth. Among the more important figures shaping the anti-intellectualism of our day, he identifies such men as Darwin, Freud, and Pavlov, along with Nietzsche, Machiavelli, and Pareto.*

When reading the following selection, one should remember that Brinton's definition of anti-intellectualism is very much his own. He does not use any standard dictionary definition. Nor do literary critics entirely approve of the distinction he makes between "romanticism" and "anti-intellectualism." On the other hand, Brinton does state clearly and specifically the meaning he gives anti-intellectualism; he indicates the difficulty of finding a better term for his purpose, and in support of his position he draws together a wide range of psychological and sociological data that merit careful consideration.

One cannot but be impressed, moreover, by the large measure of agreement with Brinton that we find in the thought of other writers. Not only such psychologists as Freud and Jung but also philosophers like Schopenhauer, Nietzsche, Sartre, and William James and religious writers like Kierkegaard and Tolstoy interpret human nature in similar fashion. The dominant influence of the same point of view in contemporary art and literature is outlined with unusual clarity by William Barrett in his recent book, Irrational Man, A Study in Existential Philosophy. *Selections from the works of these men provide a desirable opportunity for further examination of the issues raised in the following essay.*

For a brief biographical sketch of Brinton, see page 62 above.

CONTEMPORARY ANTI-INTELLECTUALISM

Anti-Intellectualism: A Definition

PERHAPS WHAT WE HERE call anti-intellectualism will to the future historian be no more than one of the strands of our twentieth-century culture, part of the spirit of the age, part of the whole of our attitudes toward life and the universe that is so much more than cumulative knowledge, or science. It seems safer here to treat anti-intellectualism, especially in its bearings on the study of men in society, as simply one

[From Crane Brinton, *Ideas and Men,* pages 503-526 (Abridged). Copyright 1950, by Prentice-Hall, Inc., Englewood Cliffs, N. J. Reprinted by permission of the publishers.]

of the characteristic manifestations of the spirit of our age.

The name is an unfortunate one, especially in its emphasis on negation or opposition, yet there seems at the moment no other that will do as well. For, as should be clear in a moment, any attempt to indicate by a name that this tendency positively values, say, emotion as higher than thinking, the heart as superior to the head, drives, urges, impulses, or, if you wish to be Freudian, the "libido" or the "id" as better than the intellect, would be a bad misrepresentation of its nature. Basically the anti-intellectual, in the sense we here use the term, does not regard the instrument of thought as *bad*, but among most men most of the time as *weak*. The romantic agrees with Thomas Hardy that "thought is a disease of the flesh"; the anti-intellectual notes merely that thought seems often at the mercy of appetites, passions, prejudices, habits, conditioned reflexes, and of a good deal else in human life that is not thinking. There is unfortunately no agreed-upon nomenclature in this matter. The term [*anti-intellectualism*] is widely used, however, to describe something quite different —the *praise* of nonrationality, the exaltation of nonrationality as the really desirable human activity, the denigration of rationality. Such an attitude of dislike for rationality and love for nonrationality we prefer to call *romanticism*, the romanticism of Goethe's "feeling is all." The modern lover of the nonrational, like many of the apologists for Nazism, goes far beyond these first romanticists, but the root of the concept is in romanticism. It is most unfortunate that there is such confusion in a very important problem of terminology. We shall, however, attempt to use the term *anti-intellectual* without praise or blame.

Now the anti-intellectual, though in his opposition to the philosophy of the Enlightenment that universal education would overnight teach everybody to think correctly he often seemed to disparage the instrument of thought, *is in a sense a true heir of the Enlightenment*, is at bottom a believer in the power of thought to make man's life here on earth a better one. Freud himself, whom some tender-minded people quite strongly regard as the apostle of deep, dark, instinctual self-indulgence, believed as firmly as any eighteenth-century *philosophe* in the power of the truth—scientific truth duly established—to promote good conduct on the part of the individual who had succeeded in learning the truth; but—and this is a difference of major importance—the *philosophe* thought that all that stood between the individual and the learning of truth was a rotten shell of decayed institutions, the Catholic Church and the French monarchy; whereas Freud thought that not only a very strong set of institutions but also a strong set of personal habits and inclinations and a strong set of habits established in early infancy stood between the individual and the learning of the truth. Freud, even before his old age of exile and unhappiness, had no hopes that *many* men could win their way through to this sort of truth in a short time.

The tempered hopes for the slow improvement in human relations—an improvement that even the Leftishly inclined among the anti-intellectuals put well short of Utopian perfectibility—comes out in a quotation from Graham Wallas, an English Fabian of the days of Wells, Shaw, and the Webbs, a Progressive member of the London County Council, and the author of a book called *Human Nature in Politics* (London, 1908). Wallas had made a mildly anti-intellectual and "realistic" study of British politics in which he pointed out that voters did not coldly and logically reason things out, did not even very often exercise intelligent self-interest, but were influenced by flattery, by appeals to their prejudices, by the good looks of the candidate, and above all by a candidate's paying them attention as persons, by so small a thing as calling them by name. Wallas was grieved when some of his fellow workers in the Labor party accused him of selling out to the enemy by this anti-intellectualism, and he wrote:

> Thought may be late in evolution, it may be deplorably weak in driving power, but without its guidance no man or organization can find a safe path amid the vast impersonal complexities of the universe as we have learned to see it.

The anti-intellectual insists that man is a complex creature whose behavior must be studied as far as possible without preconceptions concerning the goodness and badness of that behavior. Just as with the place of logical thinking in human life, so with the place of good behavior; the anti-intellectual does not deny the difference between good and bad, does not hesitate to prefer goodness to badness. What he does insist is that, to judge by the evidence to be obtained by observation of what men have done and are doing, there is a great deal of badness about and—this is the important thing—there seems to be no direct and simple causal relation between men's moral ideals and their actions. Therefore the anti-intellectual repeats Bacon's praise of Machiavelli, himself in many ways an early anti-intellectual: "We are much beholden to Machiavel and others that wrote what men do, and not what they ought to do."

To sum up: Most anti-intellectuals accept, by and large, the goals of order, happiness, individual freedom, and all the rest we associate with the Enlightenment, but they hold these goals as only imperfectly and only very slowly attainable on earth; and they believe the best way to attain them is not to preach that they must be attained, *not to pretend they have been attained* (a not uncommon claim among American educators, editors, and preachers with aspirations to mass audiences), but to work patiently at building up a true social science based on the long-tried methods of cumulative knowledge and to hope that this knowledge will be used by men to promote the good rather than the bad.

Contemporary Anti-Intellectualism

We have already noted how such natural scientists as Newton and Darwin gave leads in the social sciences. In our own times the great leads have come from biology and psychology. Probably the two most commanding figures in this respect of influence on the social studies are Pavlov and Freud, both psychologists trained in physiology and the other biological sciences. Note that we are here considering not the meaning of their professional studies within their own nowadays very specialized professions, but their influence on the much more general currents of thought among men of various training concerned with human affairs.

I

Pavlov's is the simpler case. What reached the outside world from the laboratories of this Russian scientist whose independence was respected by both Tsarist and Soviet governments was the well-known phrase "conditioned reflexes." Pavlov's dogs are as familiar as any laboratory animals have ever been. Most of us know how, after being repeatedly fed at a certain signal, such as a bell, they came to water at the mouth in anticipation of food at a mere signal. The natural—that is the untrained—response of watering at the mouth would ordinarily come only when the dog had actual food before him; Pavlov got the same response artificially by a signal that certainly didn't smell or look like food to the dog. The upshot was clear evidence that training (conditioning) could produce automatic responses in the animal that were essentially similar to the kind of automatic responses the animal is born with. Conditioned reflexes like watering at the mouth at a signal were the same as natural reflexes like watering at the mouth when a fine red beefsteak was held before the animal.

Now the cautious social scientist does not, of course, take over Pavlov's conditioned reflexes and apply them uncritically to all human behavior. He does not assume, for instance, that the Vermonter voting the straight Republican ticket is behaving quite like the dog watering at the mouth as an accustomed bell is rung. Even in Vermont, voting Republican is probably not quite a conditioned reflex. But the cautious social scientist will hold that concepts like that of the conditioned reflexes do throw light on a great deal of habit-determined human conduct. For the anti-intellectual, Pavlov's work was further demonstration that a very great deal of our behavior is not determined—nor even greatly influenced—by what goes on in the cerebral cortex.

II

Freud is a much more complex figure than Pavlov—indeed one of the most complex figures in the intellectual history of the West. He was a scientist brought up in the simple craftsman's belief in a material universe from which the supernatural was ruled out, and with the scientist's contempt for all metaphysical ideas but the unavowed, positivist metaphysics of conventional modern science. His total work is a bewildering compound of natural science and rather pessimistic—almost Christian—metaphysics. In a book of this scope we cannot properly examine Freud's complexities; moreover, his work, like that of all great system-making thinkers, looks quite different to outsiders and to true believers. He has created a method of dealing with certain kinds of human disability usually thought of as mental—nervous breakdown, neurosis, and the like. This method is called psychoanalysis, and must be distinguished from conventional handling of mental disease, usually by physicians with special training as neurologists, which is called psychiatry. Freudian psychoanalysis, though as a part of medical science it is in 1950 vastly more reputable among conventional physicians than one would have thought possible only a few decades ago, is still mostly heretical, the belief of an ardent sect. This is especially true when the ideas Freud developed in the treatment of mental disease are extended, as Freud himself extended them in later life, to most of the fields of the social sciences. Finally, the study of Freud is made still more difficult by the fact that he was always revising even his very fundamental ideas, so that to take his system as complete at any one time is dangerous.

Freud gave leads to many in the study of human behavior who knew nothing, or very little, about psychoanalysis and its metaphysical superstructure. Our century is indeed a century in which psychology is the fashionable science, and in which the chatter of the educated makes use of psychological terms much as the habitués of the eighteenth-century salons chattered about the laws of physics and astronomy discovered by Newton. Many of these modern smooth coins of conversation were once sharply minted by Freud himself—libido, Oedipus complex, infantile sexuality, sublimation. Perhaps the smoothest coin of all—inferiority complex—was minted by a disciple, Adler, who later quarreled with the master and set up his own psychological shop.

Here, as has been our practice in this book, we are concerned rather with this phase of Freud's ideas as they circulated among the intellectual classes than with their professional significance in psychology and medicine. For this purpose, a very schematic outline of his basic ideas as of about 1920 should suffice. To Freud, what makes people go is a whole set of "drives" he first called *libido* and associated very closely with sexual desires and later called the *id*, and made a little less clearly sexual. The id in the human being is part of the unconscious; it wishes, pushes the individual into action. But the whole behavior of the human being involves two other parts of the human psyche, the ego and the *super-ego*. Conventional natural scientists are greatly annoyed by the fact that there is no way of locating the id, the ego, and the super-ego in the human brain or anywhere else in the human anatomy; nobody ever "saw" a part of the id, even under a microscope; actually Freud was not in this respect at least sinning against true science —the test of these concepts is not whether they can be apprehended as a part of human receptor experiences aided by instruments, but whether they work, whether their use enables us to understand human behavior better.

The ego is wholly—or almost wholly—part of a man's conscious mental life, but it is not pure logical activity; it is an umpire, or governor, the guardian of the interests of the organism as a whole and the arbitrator of conflicting desires rising out of the id into consciousness. Some of these desires, especially if they seem to the ego of the kind to discredit the person, are suppressed by the ego, but continue hard at work in the unconscious id; some of them are "sublimated," turned from a sexual goal, for instance, into art or poetry or governing men. In the super-ego the notions taught the individual about right and wrong, the "proper" way to behave, the "proper" ideas to hold, come to play on the individual's action. In part, the super-ego is unconscious; its dictates, inculcated from infancy on so that they do not go through the logical process, do not present him with problems of alternative action. The ego is like a somewhat un-Christian individual conscience; the super-ego is like a social or collective conscience working on and in the individual.

In a healthy individual the id, the ego, and the super-ego cooperate to keep him aware of the realities of his environment and to enable him to adjust his conduct in accord with these realities so that he is on the whole a happy man and a good citizen. In the neurotic individual desires balked by the negative of the ego or the super-ego are thereby driven back into the unconscious, where they continue to live and push on as desires must. They make the stuff of a man's dreams. They crop up in disguised (but not genuinely sublimated) form in all sorts of acts that are clearly not in the line of normal sensible conduct—in obsessive fears, in withdrawal from ordinary responsibilities, in worrying and fretting, in all the great variety of conduct, we nowadays label "neurotic." These balked desires are, be it noted, in the unconscious; the neurotic individual does not really know what he wants.

Freud's basic notions of therapy—and it is these that caused us to classify him as a child of the Enlightenment—can be summed up as an elaborate, difficult (and very expensive) way of teaching the patient to know what he really wants. More particularly, Freud held that the original repression, the original driving back into the id of certain desires, was the source of the evil, the *trauma* or wound inflicted in the individual's psyche. Usually, he thought, this trauma went back to infancy and was tied up with the fact that the infant's very early sexual desires are strongly disapproved in our culture, that both his ego and his super-ego are taught rather harshly that they must not allow such conduct. Even if there were no simple single incident of infancy that seemed the origin of a difficulty in later life, Freud believed that the very early years were always of major importance. But how could these forgotten things be dug up by the individual? Only by a long process of "free association," of letting the individual roam back in memory day after day, with the psychoanalyst at his side noting the tiny clues as they came into the flow of memories, and by aid from dreams, recent and recalled.

We cannot of course attempt a detailed account of Freud's methods of therapy. The point should be clear: Freud held that the individual was a bundle of confused thoughts and desires that could only with the greatest difficulty be brought to make sense; but that when after long investigation the analyst could show the individual just *why* he behaved as he did, then the individual would cease to behave badly, unprofitably for himself and for his fellows. Note particularly that Freud did *not* take the old, innocent, Rousseauistic position that since all the trouble came from the original suppression the way to avoid difficulty is to have everybody from infancy on follow all his desires, let the id dictate all his acts. Freud and the Freudians do indeed tend to be "permissive" in child training, tend to sympathize with the ideal of as much individual freedom in society as can be attained. Freud himself seems never to have liked the contents of most of our super-egos, the "higher things" of Western tradition. But the Freudians do not advocate an orgy of lust, they do not want man to be the slave of his cruder appetites, they are not—for the most part—antinomian cranks. They are trained physicians trying to be true to the standards of an exacting profession, trying to see men as they really are.

Freud's contribution to contemporary anti-intellectualism was very great. His work, taken with that of Pavlov and many other psychologists and physiologists, put great emphasis on the proportion of human actions in which the traditional instrument of thought had no part, or little part. Action came to the anti-intellectual to be the result of automatic responses, natural or conditioned, of all sorts of unconscious drives and urges, of traditions, social habits, even theological and metaphysical principles made by early training and conditioning part of the individual's way of responding to the need to make a decision. To the anti-intellectual actual ratiocinative thought in an individual is to the rest of his living even less than the small part of the iceberg visible above water is to the whole mass of the iceberg. The *amount* of reasoning in human life, then, and not the *existence* of reasoning, is the point over which the anti-intellectual and those who oppose anti-intellectualism really differ. The tradition of American moral and political thinking is *not* anti-intellectual. The practice of a good deal of American politics, and of much of American life—advertising is a clear example—is anti-intellectual.

III

The roots and ramifications of this view that the actual, functional, place of the instrument of thought in the sum total of human activity on earth is small—and remember it is not either rejoicing over or bemoaning the smallness of this place—can be traced in many fields of modern thought. Important roots lie in what social thinkers made of Darwin; for it became pretty clear that, if in general one could hold that what gave man such good results in the struggle for life was his brain, in most concrete cases it was by no means the intellectual who did best in the struggle for life.

One of the first, and one of the most interesting of nineteenth-century writers on man as *politique et moraliste* to take up this theme was the Englishman Walter Bagehot, whose *Physics and Politics* (1869) is one of the earliest attempts to follow up Darwinian leads in the study of human affairs. The book should have been entitled *Biology and Politics;* Bagehot was merely using *physics* to stand for *natural science.* Bagehot held that the first stage in building civilization from mere savagery was a state of totalitarian rigidity of law and order—not a personal dictatorship, but the dictatorship of what Bagehot called the "cake of custom." In competition among groups, that group wins, by and large, which has the best discipline, the firmest cake of custom. But in the next stage the inventive mind comes more into play; new ideas are produced that enable one group to cope better than another with the environment; and finally there comes the "government by discussion" that is a mark of the modern age.

All this may sound like the conventional Victorian view of unilinear progress. But Bagehot is careful to insist that even after the breaking of the cake of custom by the new ideas, the successful society will still have a lot of the old nonintellectual traits, or it will go under. Indeed, he found what for his age was a paradoxical, and for us a typical anti-intellectualist, explanation for the success of parliamentary democracy: The great trouble with a civilization made up of *homo sapiens* is that human beings are impatient, unrestrained animals, always wanting to *do something;* the great virtue of government by discussion is that it *postpones* action, takes up time in debate and palaver and so allows time for the healing work of nature. In much the same way, Bagehot decided that the trouble with the French is that they are too intellectual, too interested in ideas to achieve adequate political stability; he found that the English people, on the whole, are able to withstand the temptation to indulge in abstract thinking, that they have the necessary stupidity to make democracy work.

Nietzsche who in one mood appealed to the Superman and wrote in pseudo-Biblical prose about the prophet Zarathustra was in another mood an anti-intellectualist. Nietzsche attempted what he called a "natural history of morals"—that is, a rapid survey of how men actually did behave in relation to how they thought they ought to behave. Like many of the school, he was perhaps too much tempted to paradox by his opposition to the general belief of mankind that their acts follow logically from their beliefs. He was, moreover, unable to carry out his study in a systematic way; all his work is a series of aphorisms, a long and uncommon common-place book. Nevertheless, Nietzsche hit clearly upon another of the main points the anti-intellectualist makes, a point Machiavelli himself had already made. That is the observation that men often gain ends useful to themselves and to society by acting on erroneous ideas.

> The falseness of an opinion is not for us any objection to it; it is here, perhaps, that our new language sounds most strangely. The question is, how far an opinion is life-furthering, life-preserving, species-preserving; perhaps species-rearing; and we are fundamentally inclined to maintain that the falsest opinions are the most indispen-

sable to us; that without a recognition of logical fictions, without a comparison of reality with the purely *imagined* world of the absolute and immutable . . . man could not live—that the renunciation of false opinion would be a renunciation of life, a negation of life. *To recognize untruth as a condition of life*: that is certainly to impugn the traditional ideas of value in a dangerous manner, and a philosophy which ventures to do so, has thereby alone placed itself beyond good and evil.*

IV

By the twentieth century some of anti-intellectualism had begun to catch on with the intellectual classes, and in less obvious forms had begun to seep down into popular consciousness. In its origins a good deal of the point of view we here call anti-intellectualism is that of a self-conscious "superior," a man wise enough to know how little wisdom prevails in the world. It is a point of view that turns easily into a kind of snobbery, the feeling that the masses are the herd and we wise few are, or should be, the masters. This runs all through Nietzsche, who is the clearest example of this strain in the attitude of modern anti-intellectualism. Yet there is also a strain, clear ultimately in Freud, that emphasizes the possibility that ordinary men may learn the truth about themselves, a truth far more complex than the eighteenth-century view of man, and that once having learned it they can themselves make the necessary adjustments to this newly seen reality. Once men realize the really grave difficulties of thinking straight, they will, according to this more democratic view, be well on the road to straight thinking.

Much of modern anti-intellectualism, unpalatable though it is to optimistic democratic taste, is actually widespread in Western culture today. We have all heard about rationalization, propaganda, the ambiguities and other inadequacies of language; we are all reminded daily that to get ahead in this world you must exercise your skill in handling other people, you must deliberately win friends and influence people by arts other than logic. The experts in propaganda know that one of the factors they must reckon with is public awareness and distrust of propaganda, which the French call expressively—and cynically—*bourrage de crâne*, "brain-stuffing."

We are brought squarely up against the problem of the relation of anti-intellectualism to our democratic tradition, way of life, cosmology. Democracy as it ripened in the eighteenth century held out hope of rapid and thorough social change toward universal happiness on earth to be achieved by educating all men to use their natural reason—or at least by entrusting power to an enlightened group of political planners who could devise and run institutions under which all men would be happy. Anti-intellectualism maintains against these democratic beliefs the belief that men are not and cannot under the best educational system be guided by their reason, that the drives, habits, conditioned reflexes that mostly do guide them cannot be changed rapidly, that, in short, there is something in the nature of man that makes him and will continue to make him behave in the immediate future not very differently from the way he has behaved in the past. These two sets of beliefs, the democratic and the anti-intellectual, seem mutually incompatible.

All but the very softest and most idealistic of social scientists in our culture have had to retreat from eighteenth-century rationalism and learn from the anti-intellectuals. And it is difficult for most of us to read Machiavelli, Bacon, La Rochefoucauld,

* From *Beyond Good and Evil*, "Prejudices of Philosophers," §3.

and the other "realists" about human nature and human affairs without feeling that much of what they say is quite true.

We are back, of course, to the eternal contrast, the eternal tension, so strong in Western culture, between this world and the next, the real and the ideal, the practical and the desirable. The anti-intellectuals are pulling democracy over toward the first of these pairs. Yet to emphasize the facts of life, the "spotted actuality," is not necessarily to adopt the conclusion that no improvement in actual conditions is possible. The real and the ideal are not, we have insisted throughout this book, by nature enemies. They belong together. It is only when they are divorced that each, pursued in neglect of the other, is a danger to society. One of the great questions we now face is whether good democrats can accept the reality the anti-intellectuals have brought to their attention without losing their belief in the possibility of improving that reality.

William Barrett

William Barrett, an associate professor of philosophy at New York University and a former editor of the Partisan Review, *has become well known in recent years for his work on existentialism. His volume,* Irrational Man: A Study in Existential Philosophy *(1958), is one of the more illuminating treatments of this somewhat controversial subject. Describing existentialism as "the philosophy of the atomic age," Barrett here examines the position of four major exponents of this point of view—Kierkegaard, Nietzsche, Heidegger, and Sartre—and discusses the important literature and art in which one finds the same sense of futility and lack of rational meaning or purpose in human life that is a major concern of the existentials. Not only does he include such earlier literary figures as Dostoevski and Tolstoy and contemporary writers like Joyce, Kafka, Hemingway, and Faulkner, but he suggests relationships to the romantic poetry of Wordsworth and Coleridge and even analyzes the basic principles of cubism to show that contemporary painting further expresses the same underlying spirit so characteristic of our times.*

A selection on "The Testimony of Modern Art" from this volume of Barrett's is included here. It provides a needed supplement to Brinton's essay on "Contemporary Anti-Intellectualism." Where Brinton writes from the viewpoint of the social sciences, Barrett discusses the contemporary literature and painting that portray the inadequacies and limitations of human reason in its effort to provide an acceptable and satisfying answer to the deeper needs of man in the modern world.

In this connection the title of Barrett's book, Irrational Man, *is also significant. He, like Brinton, is unable to find a term that will satisfactorily describe the dominant mood and point of view of one age; in deciding upon the phrase "irrational man" for this purpose, he adopts a more radical "anti-intellectualism" than that proposed by Brinton. Commenting upon the characteristic outlook of our own country, Barrett writes as follows: "As a teacher of philosophy, a very dubious profession in this country, I am in a position to observe how precarious a hold the intellect has upon American life; and this is not true merely of the great majority of students but of cultured people, of intellectuals, to whom here in America a philosophical idea is an alien and embarrassing thing. In their actual life Americans are not only nonintellectual but an anti-intellectual people. The charm of the American as a new human type, his rough and ready pragmatism, his spontaneity and openness to experience are true of him only because he is unreflective by nature. . . . The fact is a good dose of intellectualism—genuine intellectualism—would be a very helpful thing in American life."*

THE PRESENT AGE

NO AGE has ever been so self-conscious as ours. At any rate, the quantity of journalism the modern age has turned out in the process of its own self-analysis already overflows our archives and, were it not that most of it is doomed to perish, would be a dull burden to hand down to our descendants. The task still goes on, as indeed it must, for the last word has not been spoken, and modern man seems even further from understanding himself than when he first began to question his own identity. Of documentation of external facts we have had enough and to spare; but of the inner facts—of what goes on at the center where the forces of our fate first announce themselves—we are still pretty much in ignorance, and most of the contemporary world is caught up in an unconscious and gigantic conspiracy to run away from these facts. Hence the necessity of returning to a subject that only appears to be well worn. With civilizations, as with individuals, the outer fact is often merely the explosion resulting from accumulated inner tension, the signs of which were plentifully present, though none of the persons concerned chose to heed them.

I. *The Decline of Religion*

The central fact of modern history in the West—by which we mean the long period from the end of the Middle Ages to the present—is unquestionably the decline of religion. No doubt, the churches are still very powerful organizations; there are millions of churchgoers all over the world; and even the purely intellectual possibilities of religious belief look better to churchmen now than in the bleak days of self-confident nineteenth-century materialism. A few years ago there was even considerable talk about a "religious revival," and some popular and patriotic periodicals such as *Life* magazine gave a great deal of space to it; but the talk has by now pretty much died down, the movement, if any, subsided, and the American public buys more automobiles and television sets than ever before. When *Life* magazine promotes a revival of religion, one is only too painfully aware from the nature of this publication that religion is considered as being in the national interest; one could scarcely have a clearer indication of the broader historical fact that in the modern world the nation-state, a thoroughly secular institution, outranks any church.

The decline of religion in modern times means simply that religion is no longer the uncontested center and ruler of man's life, and that the Church is no longer the final and unquestioned home and asylum of his being. The deepest significance of this change does not even appear principally at the purely intellectual level, in loss of belief, though this loss due to the critical inroads of science has been a major historical cause of the decline. The waning of religion is a much more concrete and complex fact than a mere change in conscious outlook; it penetrates the deepest strata of man's total psychic life. It is indeed one of the major stages in man's psychic evolution—as Nietzsche, almost alone among nineteenth-century philosophers, was to see. Religion to medieval man was not so much a theological system as a solid psychological matrix surrounding the individual's life from birth to death, sanctifying and enclosing all its ordinary and extraordinary occasions in sacrament and ritual. The loss of the Church was the loss of a whole system of symbols, images, dogmas, and rites which had the psychological validity of immediate experience, and within which hitherto the whole psychic life of Western man had been safely contained. In losing religion, man lost the concrete connection with a transcendent realm of being; he was set free to deal with this world in all its brute objectivity. But he was bound to feel homeless in such a world, which no longer answered the needs of his spirit. A home is the accepted framework which habitually contains our life. To lose one's psychic container is to be cast adrift, to become a wanderer upon the face of the earth. Henceforth, in seeking his own human completeness man would have to do for himself what he once had done for him, unconsciously, by the Church, through the medium of its sacramental life.

No believer, no matter how sincere, could possibly write the *Divine Comedy* today, even if he possessed a talent equal to Dante's. Visions and symbols do not have the immediate and overwhelming reality for us that they had for the medieval poet. In the *Divine Comedy* the whole of nature is merely a canvas upon which the religious symbol and image are painted. Western man has spent more than five hundred years—half a millennium—in stripping nature of these projections and turning it into a realm of neutral objects which his science may control. Thus it could hardly be expected that the religious image would have the same force for us as it did for Dante. This is simply a psychic fact within human history; psychic facts have just as much historical validity as the facts that we now, unlike the man of Dante's time, travel in airplanes and work in factories regulated by computing machines. A great work of art can never be repeated—the history of art shows us time and again that literal imitation leads to pastiche—because it springs from the human soul, which evolves like everything else in nature. This point must be insisted upon, contrary to the view of some of our more enthusiastic medievalists who picture the psychic containment of medieval man as a situation of human completeness to which we must return. History has never allowed man to return to the past in any total sense. And our psychological problems cannot be solved by a regression to a past state in which they had not yet been brought into being. On the other hand, enlightened and progressive thinkers are equally blind when they fail to recognize that every major step forward by mankind entails some loss, the sacrifice of an older security and the creation and heightening of new tensions. (We should bear this in mind against some of the criticisms of Existentialism as a philosophy that has unbearably heightened human tensions: it did not create those tensions, which were already at work in the soul of modern man, but simply sought to give them philosophic expression, rather than evading them by pretending they were not there.)

At the gateway that leads from the Middle Ages into the modern world stand Science, Protestantism, and Capitalism. Protestantism, like science, helped carry forward that immense project of modern man: the despiritualization of nature, the emptying of it of all the symbolic images projected upon it by the human psyche. With Protestantism begins that long modern struggle, which reaches its culmination in the twentieth century, to strip man naked. To be sure, in all of this the aim was progress, and Protestantism did succeed in raising the religious consciousness to a higher level of individual sincerity, soul-searching, and strenuous inwardness. Man was impoverished in order to come face to face with his God and the severe and inexplicable demands of his faith; but in the process he was stripped of all the mediating rites and dogmas that could make this confrontation less dangerous to his psychic balance. Protestantism achieved a heightening of the religious consciousness, but at the same time severed this consciousness from the deep unconscious life of our total human nature. In this respect, its historical thrust runs parallel to that of the New Science and capitalism, since science was making the mythical and symbolic picture of nature disappear before the success of its own rational explanations, and capitalism was opening up the whole world as a field of operations for rationally planned enterprise.

As the modern world moves onward, it becomes more and more secularized in every department of life; faith consequently becomes more attenuated, and Protestant man begins to look more and more like a gaunt skeleton, a sculpture by Giacometti. A secular civilization leaves him more starkly naked than the iconoclasm of the Reformation had ever dreamed. The more severely he struggles to hold on to the primal face-to-face relation with God, the more tenuous this becomes, until in the end the relation to God Himself threatens to become a relation to Nothingness. In this sense Kierkegaard, in the middle of the nineteenth century, was the reckoning point of the whole Protestant Reformation that began three centuries earlier: He sees faith for the uncompromising and desperate wager it is, if one takes it in all its Protestant strictness; and he cannot say, like his Catholic counterpart Pascal, "Stupefy yourself, take holy water, receive the sacraments, and in the end all shall be well"—for Protestant man has forsworn the sacraments and natural symbols of the soul as the snares and pomp of the devil. Some of Kierkegaard's books, such as *The Sickness unto Death* and *The Concept of Dread*, are still frightening to our contemporaries and so are excused or merely passed over as the personal outpourings of a very melancholy temperament; yet they are the truthful record of what the Protestant soul must experience on the brink of the great Void. Protestant man is the beginning of the West's fateful encounter with Nothingness —an encounter that was long overdue and is perhaps only now in the twentieth century reaching its culmination.

Existential philosophy (like much of modern art) is thus a product of bourgeois society in a state of dissolution. Marxists have labored this point but without really understanding it; nevertheless, it remains true. The dissolution is a fact, but neither Existentialism nor modern art produced it. The individual is thrust out of the sheltered nest that society has provided. He can no longer hide his nakedness by the old disguises. He learns how much of what he has taken for granted was by its own nature neither eternal nor necessary but thoroughly temporal and contingent. He learns that the solitude of the self is an irreducible dimension of human life no matter how completely that self had seemed to be contained in its social milieu. In the end, he sees each man as solitary and unsheltered before his own death. Admittedly, these are painful truths, but the most basic things are always learned with pain, since our inertia and complacent love of comfort prevent us from learning them until they are forced upon us. It appears that man is willing to learn about himself only after some disaster; after war, economic crisis, and political upheaval have taught him how flimsy is that human world in which he thought himself so securely grounded. What he learns has always been there, lying concealed beneath the surface of even the best-functioning societies; it is no less true for having come out of a period of chaos and disaster. But so long as man does not have to face up to such a truth, he will not do so.

II. *The Testimony of Modern Art*

Anyone who attempts to gain a unified understanding of modern art as a whole is bound to suffer the uncomfortable sensation of having fallen into a thicket of brambles. We ourselves are involved in the subject, and we can hardly achieve the detachment of the historian a few centuries hence. Modern art still provokes violent controversy, even after it has been on the scene a good half century and names like Picasso and Joyce have become almost household words. The Philistine still finds it shocking, scandalous, and foolish; and there is always a case to be made for the Philistine, and surely for the Philistine in ourselves without whom we could not carry on the drab business of ordinary living. Indeed, from the point of view we are taking here, the Philistine attitude, particularly in its irritation, may be just as revelatory historically as any other. But it is a case not only of the Philistine; sensitive observers still exist—directors of museums, connoisseurs, and historians—who find in modern art a disastrous falling away from the excellence of the art of the past. In a sense, all this controversy is pointless; so much of it has to do with the eventual historical rating of our own period, which is something we cannot even foresee. The century from Manet to Matisse may figure in future art histories as a period of impoverishment and decline, whose works cannot stand beside those of the old masters; or it may figure as a period of such abundant creativity that it can be matched only by the Renaissance during the fifteenth century. My own personal prejudice is toward the latter judgment, but I have no way of proving it; and such speculation, in any case, does not enter into my own experience of this art. We have simply got to give up the attempt to assess ourselves for posterity; the men of the future will form their own opinions without our help. What we so self-consciously call "modern art," after all, is nothing more nor less than the art of this time, *our* art; there is no other today. If we could have a different art, or a better, we would have it. As it is, we are lucky in this period to have any art at all. In the end the only authentic art is that which has about it the power of inevitability.

Nevertheless, the controversy, irritation, and bafflement to which modern art gives rise does provide us a very effective handle with which to take hold of it. Irritation usually arises when something touches a sore spot in ourselves, which most of the time we would like desperately to hide; rarely if ever does the fault lie totally with the provoking object. Modern art touches a sore spot, or several sore spots, in the ordinary citizen of which he is totally unaware. The more irritated he becomes at modern art the more he betrays the fact that he himself, and his civilization, are implicated in what the artist shows him. The ordinary man is uncomfortable, angry, or derisive before the dislocation of forms in modern art, before its bold distortions, or arbitrary manipulations of objects. The painter puts three or more eyes in the face, or several noses, or twists and elongates the body at the expense of photographic resemblance in order to build up his own inner image. Has the contrary attitude of strict and literal attachment to objects succeeded in resolving all the anxieties of the ordinary man, and has not in fact the rampant extroversion of modern civilization brought it to the brink of the abyss? Finally, the ordinary man—and in this respect the ordinary man is joined by the learned and sensitive traditionalist in art—objects to the content of modern art; it is too bare and bleak, too negative or "nihilistic," too shocking or scandalous; it dishes out unpalatable truths. But have the traditional ideals worked so well in this century that we can afford to neglect the unpalatable truths about human life that those ideals have chosen to ignore? Does the esthete who extols the greatness of the past as an argument against modern art have any idea of how pallid his own response to, say, the Virgin of Chartres appears before the medieval man's response? Or that his own estheticism, however cultured, is in fact a form of sentimentality—since sentimentality, at bottom, is nothing but false feeling, feeling that is untrue to its object, whether by being excessive or watered down?

In a famous passage in *A Farewell to Arms* Ernest Hemingway writes:

> I was always embarrassed by the words sacred, glorious, and sacrifice and the expression in vain. We had heard them, sometimes standing in the rain almost out of earshot, so that only the shouted words came through, and had read them, on proclamations that were slapped up by billposters over other proclamations, now for a long time, and I had seen nothing sacred, and the things that were glorious had no glory and the sacrifices were like the stockyards at Chicago if nothing was done with the meat except to bury it. There were many words that you could not stand to hear and finally only the names of places had dignity. Certain numbers were the same way and certain dates and these with the names of places were all you could say and have them mean anything. Abstract words such as glory, honor, courage, or hallow were obscene beside the concrete names of villages, the numbers of roads, the names of rivers, the numbers of regiments and the dates.

For a whole generation that was the great statement of protest against the butchery of the First World War. But it has a greater historical significance than that; it can be taken as a kind of manifesto of modern art and literature, an incitement to break through empty abstractions of whatever kind, to destroy sentimentality even if the real feelings exposed should appear humble and impoverished—the names of places and dates; and even if in stripping himself naked the artist seems to be left with Nothing. Modern art thus begins, and sometimes ends, as a confession of spiritual poverty. That is its greatness and its triumph, but also the needle it jabs into the Philistine's sore spot, for the last thing he wants to be reminded of is his spiritual poverty. In fact, his greatest poverty is not to know how impoverished he is, and so long as he mouths the empty ideals or religious phrases of the past he is but as tinkling brass. In matters of the spirit, poverty and riches are sometimes closer than identical twins: the man who struts with borrowed feathers may be poor as a church mouse within, while a work that seems stark and bleak can, if genuine, speak with all the inexhaustible richness of the world. The triumph of Hemingway's style is its ability to break through abstractions to see what it is one really senses and feels. When the modern sculptor disdains the pomp of marble and uses industrial materials, steel wire, or bolts, or even rejected materials like old board, rope, or nails, he is perhaps showing himself to be impoverished next to the heroic grandeur of a Michelangelo, but he is also bringing us back to the inexhaustible brute world that surrounds us. Sometimes the confession of poverty takes a violent and aggressive tone, as when the Dadaists drew a mustache on the Mona Lisa. Dada itself, like Hemingway, came out of the revolt against the First World War, and despite its clowning must now be regarded as one of the *valid* eruptions of the irrational in this century. The generation of the First World War could hardly be expected to view Western culture as sacrosanct, since they perceived—and rightly—that it was bound up with the civilization that had ended in that ghastly butchery. Better then to reject the trappings of that culture, even art itself, if that would leave one a little more honest in one's nakedness. To discover one's own spiritual poverty is to achieve a positive conquest by the spirit.

Cubism is the classicism of modern art: that is, the one formally perfected style which modern art has elaborated and from which all modern abstract art that is valid has derived. A great deal of nonsense has been written about the creation of cubism, connecting it with relativity physics, psychoanalysis, and heaven knows how many other complex and remote things. The fact is that the painters who created cubism were creating paintings and nothing else—certainly they were not dealing in ideologies. Cubism evolved in a succession of perfectly logical steps out of previous stages of painting, out of the impressionists and Cézanne, and it raised a series of pictorial problems that had to be solved within the medium of painting and by painters working strictly as painters—that is, upon the visual image as such.

Yet a great formal style in painting has never been created that did not draw upon the depths of the human spirit, and that did not, in its newness, express a fresh mutation of the human spirit. Cubism achieved a radical flattening of space by insisting on the two-dimensional fact of the canvas. This flattening out of space would seem not to be a negligible fact historically if we reflect that when, once before in history, such a development occurred but in the opposite direction—when the flatness of the Gothic or primitive painters passed over into the solidity, perspective, and three-dimensional style of early Renaissance painting—it was a mark that man was turning outward, into space, after the long period of introspection of the Middle Ages. Western man moved out into space in his painting, in the fourteenth century, before he set forth into actual physical space in the age of exploration that was to follow. Thus painting was prophetic of the new turn of the human spirit which was eventually to find expression in the conquest of the whole globe. Have we the right, then, to suggest that the flattening of painting in our century portends a turning inward of the human spirit, or at any rate a turning away from the arena of Western man's extroversion? With cubism begins that process of detachment from the object which has become the hallmark of modern art. Even though cubism is a classical and formal style, the artist nevertheless asserts his own subjectivity by the freedom with which he cuts up and dislocates objects—bottles, pitchers, guitars—as it pleases him for the sake of the picture, which is now no longer held up to us as a representation of those objects but as a visual image with its own independent value alongside that of nature. The subjectivity that is generally present in modern art is a psychological compensation for, sometimes a violent revolt against, the gigantic externalization of life within modern society. The world pictured by the modern artist is, like the world meditated upon by the existential philosopher, a world where man is a stranger.

When mankind no longer lives spontaneously turned toward God or the supersensible world—when, to echo the words of Yeats, the ladder is gone by which we would climb to a higher reality—the artist too must stand face to face with a flat and inexplicable world. This shows itself even in the formal structures of modern art. Where the movement of the spirit is no longer vertical but only horizontal, the climactic elements in art are in general leveled out, flattened. The flattening of pictorial space that is achieved in cubism is not an isolated fact, true only of painting, but is paralleled by similar changes in literary techniques. There is a general process of flattening, three chief aspects of which may be noted:

(1) *The flattening out of all planes* upon the plane of the picture. Near and far we are pushed together. So in certain works of modern literature time, instead of space, is flattened out upon one plane. Past and present are represented as occurring simultaneously, upon a single plane of time. James Joyce's *Ulysses*, T. S. Eliot's *The Waste Land*, and Ezra Pound's *Cantos* are examples; and perhaps the most powerful use of the device was made by Faulkner in his early novel *The Sound and the Fury*.

(2) More important perhaps is *the flattening out of climaxes*, which occurs both in painting and literature. In traditional Western painting there is a central subject, located at or near the center of the picture, and the surrounding space in the picture is subordinate to this. In a portrait the figure is placed near the center, and the background becomes secondary to it, something to be blended as harmoniously as possible with the figure. Cubism abolished this idea of the pictorial climax: the whole space of the picture became of equal importance. Negative spaces (in which there are no objects) are as important as positive spaces (the contours of physical objects). If a human figure is treated, it may be broken up and distributed over various parts of the canvas. Formally speaking, the spirit of this art is anticlimactic.

When we turn to observe this same deflation or flattening of climaxes in literature, the broader human and philosophic questions involved become much clearer. The classical tradition in literature, deriving from Aristotle's *Poetics*, tells us that a drama (and consequently any other literary work) must have a beginning, middle, and end. The action begins at a certain point, rises toward a climax, and then falls to a denouement. One can diagram a classical plot of this kind by means of a triangle whose apex represents the climax with which everything in the play has some logical and necessary connection. The author subordinates himself to the requirements of logic, necessity, probability. His structure must be an intelligible whole in which each part develops logically out of what went before. If our existence itself is never quite like this, no matter; art is a selection from life, and the poet is required to be selective. However, it is important to note that this canon of intelligible literary structure—beginning, middle, and end, with a well-defined climax—arose in a culture in which the universe too was believed to be an ordered structure, a rational and intelligible whole.

What happens if we try to apply this classical Aristotelian canon to a modern work like Joyce's *Ulysses*, 734 pages of power and dullness, beauty and sordidness, comedy and pathos, where the movement is always horizontal, never ascending toward any crisis, and where we detect not the shadow of anything like a climax, in the traditional sense of that term? If Joyce's had been a disordered mind, we could dismiss all this as a sprawling chaos; but he was in fact an artist in superb control of his material, so that the disorder has to be attributed to his material, to life itself. It is, in fact, the banal gritty thing that we live that Joyce gives us, in comparison with which most other fiction is indeed fiction. This world is dense, opaque, unintelligible; that is the datum from which the modern artist always starts. The formal dictates of the well-made play or the well-made novel, which were the logical outcome of thoroughly rational preconceptions about reality, we can no longer hold to when we become attentive "to the things themselves," to the facts, to existence in the mode in which we do exist. If our epoch still held to the idea, as Western man once did, that the whole of reality is a system in which each detail providentially and rationally is subordinated to others and ultimately to the whole itself, we could demand of the artist that his form imitate this idea of reality, and give us coherence, logic, and the picture of a world with no loose ends. But to make such a demand nowadays is worse than an impertinence; it is a travesty upon the historical being of the artist.

Even where the writer has more of a story, in the traditional sense, to tell, he may prefer not to tell it in the traditional way. In *The Sound and the Fury* Faulkner has much more of a novelistic narrative than Joyce in *Ulysses*—the decline of a family, a suicide, the elopement of a girl, and so on—but he chooses not to present these events in the form of the well-made novel. And the choice is wise, for the power of the novel is increased immeasurably thereby. The brute, irrational, given quality of the world comes through so strongly in Faulkner's peculiar technique that he actually shows, and does not merely state, the meaning of the quotation from which his title is derived:

> [Life] is a tale,
> Told by an idiot, full of sound and fury,
> Signifying nothing.

Shakespeare places these lines in the context of a fairly well-made tragedy in which evil is destroyed and good triumphs; but Faulkner shows us the world of which Shakespeare's statement would be true: a world opaque, dense, and irrational, that could not have existed for Shakespeare, close as he was still to medieval Christianity. Even where a purposeful human action is planned, in the novel, and the necessary steps taken to carry it through—as in the section on the day Quentin Compson commits suicide—what really happens has little to do with the traditional order, logic, sequence of events that normally accompany such an action. The day described shows us not the abstraction "Quentin Compson commits suicide" but, as the author turns his own and his reader's eye "to the things themselves," a process far more concrete and contingent: a sparrow chirps at the window, a watch breaks, the hero gets entangled in a perfectly absurd melee with a little runaway girl, there is a fist fight, etc.; and underneath all this is, but never mentioned, the slow blind surge moving forward like an underground river toward the sea, of a man's going to his death. This section, and the book itself, is a masterpiece, perhaps as great as anything yet written by an American; and is to be recommended to anyone who wants to know the concrete feel of that world with which in his thinking the existential philosopher has to deal.

In the course of the brute random flow of detail that is that last day of his life, Quentin Compson breaks the crystal of his watch. He twists off the two hands and thereafter, throughout the day, the watch continues to tick loudly but cannot, with its faceless dial, indicate the time. Faulkner could not have hit on a better image to convey the sense of time which permeates the whole book. The normal reckonable sequence of time—one moment after another—has been broken, has disappeared; but as the watch pounds on, time is all the more urgent and real for Quentin Compson. He cannot escape time, he is in it, it is the time of his fate and his decision; and the watch has no hands to reassure him of that normal, calculable progression of minutes and hours in which our ordinary day-to-day life is passed. Time is no longer a reckonable sequence, then, for him, but an inexhaustible inescapable presence. We are close here to the thought of Heidegger. (Faulkner certainly never read Heidegger; he may never even have heard of him. So much the better; for the testimony of the artist, the poet, is all the more valid when it is not contaminated by any intellectual preconceptions.) Real time, the time that makes up the dramatic substance of our life, is something deeper and more primordial than watches, clocks, and calendars. Time is the dense medium in which Faulkner's characters move about as if dragging their feet through water; it is their substance or Being, as Heidegger would put it. The abolition of clock time does not mean a retreat into the world of the timeless; quite the contrary: the timeless world, the eternal, has disappeared from the horizon of the modern writer as it has from the horizon of modern Existentialists like Sartre and Heidegger, and from the horizon of our own everyday life; and time thereby becomes all the more inexorable and absolute a reality. The temporal is the horizon of modern man, as the eternal was the horizon of the man of the Middle Ages. That modern writers have been so preoccupied with the reality of time, handling it with radically new techniques and from radically new points of view, is evidence that the philosophers in our age who have attempted a new understanding of time are responding to the same hidden historical concerns, and are not merely elaborating some new conceptual novelty out of their heads.

No beginning, middle, end—such is the structureless structure that some modern literary works struggle toward; and analogously in painting, no clearly demarcated foreground, middleground, and background. To the traditionalist, immersed in the classical Western tradition, all this will appear negative, purely destructive. But if we do not keep our gaze narrowly riveted on the tradition of the West (and in any case this classical canon is only one of the traditions that have arisen in the course of the whole history of the West), we find that these requirements of logical and rational form do not hold for other traditions of art in other cultures. Oriental art, for example, is much more formless, organic, and sprawling than classical Western art. It has form, but a different form from that of the West. Why is this? The question is not a trivial one; it is perhaps as profound as any the West can ask these days, for this difference in art is not mere happenstance but the inevitable concomitant of a different attitude toward the world.

One of the best indications of this peculiar (to us) sense of artistic form among Orientals is given by E. M. Forster in his novel *A Passage to India*. A mixed group, English and Indians, are at tea, and Professor Godbole, a Hindu, has been asked to sing, but has let the occasion go by; then, as all are leaving, the Hindu says, "I may sing now," quite unexpectedly. (This unexpectedness is significant, for the song is not to be given a formal setting, but to drop upon their ears as casually and contingently as life itself.) Forster's description of the song makes our point so beautifully that it is worth quoting in its entirety:

> His thin voice rose, and gave out one sound after another. At times there seemed rhythm, at times there was the illusion of a Western melody. But the ear, baffled repeatedly, soon lost any clue, and wandered in a maze of noises, none harsh or unpleasant, none intelligible. It was the song of an unknown bird. Only the servants understood it. They began to whisper to one another. The man who was gathering water chestnuts came naked out of the tank, his lips parted with

delight, disclosing his scarlet tongue. The sounds continued and ceased after a few moments as casually as they had begun—apparently half through a bar, and upon the subdominant.

The song begins, goes on, suddenly stops; but there is not the least trace of an Aristotelian beginning, middle, or end. Compare Godbole's song with the structure of an aria from an Italian opera. In the latter we have a beginning, a development through certain predictable phases toward the inevitable climax of the high note, and then the falling away or denouement, tying up the whole thing in a neat package: here is Aristotelian and rational form in music. But the Oriental song baffles the ear of the Westerner; it appears unintelligible. The reason is that the Westerner demands (or, let us say, used to demand) an intelligibility that the Easterner does not. If the Westerner finds the Oriental music "meaningless," the Oriental might very well reply that this is the meaninglessness of nature itself which goes on endlessly without beginning, middle, or end.

The real reason for the difference between the sense of artistic form in the East and in the West is thus ultimately a difference in philosophic outlook. Since the Greeks, Western man has believed that Being, all Being, is intelligible, that there is a reason for everything (at least, the central tradition that runs from Aristotle through St. Thomas Aquinas into the beginning of the modern period has held this), and that the cosmos is, finally, intelligible. The Oriental, on the other hand, has accepted his existence within a universe that would appear to be meaningless, to the rational Western mind, and has lived with this meaninglessness. Hence the artistic form that seems natural to the Oriental is one that is just as formless or formal, as irrational, as life itself. That the Western artist now finds his own inherited classical form unconvincing and indeed almost intolerable is because of a profound change in his total attitude toward the world—a change that is no less true even when the artist himself has not been able to bring it to conceptual expression. The final intelligibility of the world is no longer accepted. Our existence, as we know it, is no longer transparent and understandable by reason, bound together into a tight, coherent structure. The world that we are shown in the work of the modern painters and writers is opaque and dense. Their vision is not inspired primarily by intellectual premises; it is a spontaneous revelation of the kind of which perhaps only art is capable; it shows us where we stand, whether or not we choose to understand it. If we really open ourselves to the experience of two works of art as widely separated in time as Dante's *Divine Comedy* and Faulkner's *The Sound and the Fury*, the distance that Western man has traveled in the intervening centuries is revealed to us more clearly than through any number of abstract arguments. And the road that has been traveled is irreversible.

(3) The last and most important aspect of what we have called the process of flattening in modern art is *the flattening out of values*. To understand this one can begin at the simplest level in painting, where it means merely that large and small objects are treated as of equal value. Cézanne paints apples with the same passionate concentration as he paints mountains, and each apple is as monumental as a mountain. Indeed, in some of Cézanne's still lifes, if one covers up all of the picture except a certain patch of folded tablecloth, one might very well be looking at the planes and peaks of his *Mont Sainte Victoire* [Fig. 30]. For Cézanne the painting dictates its own values: little and big, high and low, sublime and ordinary outside the painting

are of equal importance if in a given painting they play the same plastic role.

Now all this is quite contrary to the great tradition of Western art, which distinguishes sharply between the sublime and the banal and requires that the highest art treat the most sublime subjects. The mind of the West has always been hierarchical; the cosmos has been understood as a great chain of Being, from highest to lowest, which has at the same time operated as a scale of values, from lowest to highest. Painters were expected to portray the sublime scenes from the Gospel, great battles, or noble personages. The beginning of genre painting in the seventeenth century was the first step toward what we now think of as modern painting, but it was not until the present century that the reversal of Western values was really accomplished. By now, the hierarchical scheme has been abolished altogether. Following Cézanne, the cubists took as subjects for their most monumental paintings ordinary objects like tables, bottles, glasses, guitars. Now the painter dispenses with objects altogether: the colored shape on his canvas is itself an absolute reality, perhaps more so than the imaginary scene, the great battle, which in a traditional canvas it might serve to depict. Thus we arrive at last at *l'art brut* (raw, crude, or brute art), which seeks to abolish not only the ironclad distinction between the sublime and the banal but that between the beautiful and the ugly as well. Says the painter Dubuffet, one of the more interesting cultivators of this style:

> The idea that there are beautiful objects and ugly objects, people endowed with beauty and others who cannot claim it, has surely no other foundation than convention—old poppycock—and I declare that convention unhealthy. . . . People have seen that I intend to sweep away everything we have been taught to consider—without question—as grace and beauty; but have overlooked my work to substitute another and vaster beauty, touching all objects and beings, not excluding the most despised—and because of that, all the more exhilarating. . . . I would like people to look at my work as an enterprise for the rehabilitation of scorned values, and, in any case, make no mistake, a work of ardent celebration. . . .
>
> I am convinced that any table can be for each of us a landscape as inexhaustible as the whole Andes range. . . .
>
> I am struck by the high value, for a man, of a simple permanent fact, like the miserable vista on which the window of his room opens daily, that comes, with the passing of time, to have an important role in his life. I often think that the highest destination at which a painting can aim is to take on that function in someone's life.

The deflation, or flattening out, of values in Western art does not necessarily indicate an ethical nihilism. Quite the contrary; in opening our eyes to the rejected elements of existence, art may lead us to a more complete and less artificial celebration of the world. In literature, again, the crucial example is Joyce's *Ulysses*. It was not a literary critic but a psychologist, C. G. Jung, who perceived that this book was non-Western in spirit; he sees it as Oriental to such an extent that he recommends it as a much-needed bible to the white-skinned races. For *Ulysses* breaks with the whole tradition of Western sensibility and Western esthetics in showing each small object of Bloom's day—even the objects in his pocket, like a cake of soap—as capable at certain moments of taking on a transcendental importance—or in being, at any rate, equal in value to those objects to which men usually attribute transcendental importance. Each grain of sand, Joyce seems to be saying (as the Oriental says), reflects the whole universe—and the Irish writer was not in the least a mystic; he simply takes experience as it comes, in the course of the single day he depicts in the novel. Any such break with tradition, where a serious reversal of values is involved, is of course dangerous, for the artist runs the risk of losing the safeguards that the experience of the past has erected for him. A good deal of modern art has clearly succumbed to this danger, and the result is disorder in the art and the artist; but the danger is the price that must be paid for any step forward by the human spirit.

An epoch, as we have seen, reveals itself in its religion, its social forms, but perhaps most profoundly or, at any rate, lucidly in its art. Through modern art our time reveals itself to itself, or at least to those persons who are willing to look at their own age dispassionately and without the blindness of preconceptions, in the looking glass of its art. In our epoch existential philosophy has appeared as an intellectual expression of the time, and this philosophy exhibits numerous points of contact with modern art. The more closely we examine the two together, the stronger becomes the impression that existential philosophy is the authentic intellectual expression of our time, as modern art is the expression of the time in terms of image and intuition.

Not only do the two treat similar themes, but both start off from the sense of crisis and of a break in the Western tradition. Modern art has discarded the traditional assumptions of rational form. The modern artist sees man not as the rational animal, in the sense handed down to the West by the Greeks, but as something else. Reality, too, reveals itself to the artist not as the Great Chain of Being, which the tradition of Western rationalism has declared intelligible down to its smallest link and in its totality, but as much more refractory: as opaque, dense, concrete, and in the end inexplicable. At the limits of reason one comes face to face with the meaningless; and the artist today shows us the absurd, the inexplicable, the meaningless in our daily life.

This break with the Western tradition imbues both philosophy and art with the sense that everything is questionable, problematic. Our time, said Max Scheler, is the first in which man has become thoroughly and completely problematic to himself. Hence the themes that obsess both modern art and existential philosophy are the alienation and the strangeness of man in his world; the contradictoriness, feebleness, and contingency of human existence; the central and overwhelming reality of time for man who has lost his anchorage in the eternal.

The testimony art brings to these themes is all the more convincing in that it is spontaneous; it does not spring from ideas or from any intellectual program. That modern art which is most successful and powerful moves us because we see in it the artist subordinate (as must always be the case in art) to his vision. And since we recognize that man's being is historical through and through, we must take this vision of modern art as a sign that the image of man which has been at the center of our tradition till now must be reevaluated and recast.

There is a painful irony in the new image of man that is emerging, however fragmentarily, from the art of our time. An observer from another planet might well be struck by the disparity between the enormous power which our age has concentrated in its external life and the inner poverty which our art seeks to expose to view. This is, after all, the age that has discovered and harnessed atomic energy, that has made airplanes that fly faster than the sun, and that will, in a few years (perhaps in a few months), have atomic-powered planes which can fly through outer space and not need to return to mother earth for weeks. What cannot man do! He has greater power now than Prometheus or Icarus or any of those daring mythical heroes who were later to succumb to the disaster of pride. But if an observer from Mars were to turn his attention from these external appurtenances of power to the shape of man as revealed in our novels, plays, painting, and sculpture, he would find there a creature full of holes and gaps, faceless, riddled with doubts and negations, starkly finite.

However disconcerting this violent contrast between power and impoverishment, there is something a little consoling in it for anyone who is intimidated by excessive material power, as there is in learning that a dictator is a drunkard or marked by some other ordinary failing which makes him seem a trifle more human. If we are to redeem any part of our world from the brute march of power, we may have to begin as modern art does by exalting some of the humble and dirty little corners of existence. On another level, however, this violent contrast is frightening, for it represents a dangerous lagging of man behind his own works; and in this lag lies the terror of the atomic bomb which hangs over us like impending night. Here surely the ordinary man begins to catch a fleeting glimpse of that Nothingness which both artist and philosopher have begun in our time to take seriously. The bomb reveals the dreadful and total contingency of human existence. Existentialism is the philosophy of the atomic age.

1

EXPLORATION OF THE UNCONSCIOUS

Sigmund Freud

The theories of Freud have had a profound influence on contemporary thought. Like Darwin and Einstein, Freud is a scientist with whose ideas one must be familiar in order to understand the spirit of our age. When Freud died in 1939 scholars throughout the world testified to his importance. A typical comment is that by Bernard De Voto, distinguished American critic: "In all history few scientists have had as immediate effect on the thought of their time, and probably no scientist has ever had so strong and so widespread an influence upon literature. Long before Freud died the basic principles of his work had become part of the common property of mankind. They are now implicit in the way men habitually think about one another."

Sigmund Freud was born in Moravia in 1856, but most of his life was spent in Vienna, where he studied medicine and received a degree in medicine in 1881. Originally interested in biological research, Freud became more and more fascinated by mental illness. He was influenced by the work of Josef Breuer, who had experimented with hypnosis as a means of curing neuroses, and later he studied under Charcot, the great French neurologist, in Paris. Returning to Vienna, he spent years in clinical work with mental patients and proposed novel theories to account for mental illness. He finally adopted a view of human nature that explained the mind in terms of the importance of the unconscious, the repression of instinctual drives, and the dominant influence of sexuality. Gradually he developed a method of diagnosis and treatment (psychoanalysis) that emphasized the free association of ideas rather than hypnosis. After the union of Austria with Germany under Hitler, Freud became fearful of German anti-Semitism and at the age of eighty-three moved to London where he died in 1939.

A prolific writer, Freud published many books, among which The Interpretation of Dreams, Civilization and Its Discontents, *and* An Outline of Psychoanalysis *are notable. His more significant studies are available in a Modern Library Giant, entitled* Basic Writings of Sigmund Freud. *In his later years he increasingly turned his attention to such subjects as art, history, religion, and biography, interpreting the work of men as diverse as Moses and Leonardo da Vinci in terms of his theory.*

Psychoanalysis is an exceedingly complex subject. A scientific literature of its own has been developed about it, much of which is highly controversial and far beyond the scope of the present volume. We are interested here only in a brief nontechnical introduction to Freud which will enable the thoughtful student to understand ideas that hold so important a place in contemporary literature and philosophy. In one of his more popular books, The Question of Lay Analysis, *Freud has explained the basic tenets of psychoanalysis in simple fashion for the lay reader. We reprint here a generous selection from this work together with brief excerpts from two other volumes in which Freud suggests some broader philosophical and literary implications of his theories.*

PSYCHOANALYSIS AND MAN'S SENSE OF HIS OWN IMPORTANCE

I PROPOSE to describe how the universal narcissism of men, their self-love, has up to the present suffered three severe blows from the researches of science.

(a) In the early stages of his researches, man believed at first that his dwelling place, the earth, was the stationary center of the universe, with the sun, moon, and planets circling round it. In this he was naïvely following the dictates of his sense perceptions, for he felt no movement of the earth, and wherever he had an unimpeded view he found himself in the center of a circle that enclosed the external world. The central position of the earth, moreover, was a token to him of the dominating part played by it in the universe and appeared to fit in very well with his inclination to regard himself as lord of the world.

The destruction of this narcissistic illusion is associated in our minds with the name and work of Copernicus in the sixteenth century. But long before his day the Pythagoreans had already cast doubts on the privileged position of the earth, and in the third century B. C. Aristarchus of Samos had declared that the earth was much smaller than the sun and moved round that celestial body. Even the great discovery of Copernicus, therefore, had already been made before him. When this discovery achieved general recognition, the self-love of mankind suffered its first blow, the *cosmological* one.

(b) In the course of the development of civilization man acquired a dominating position over his fellow-creatures in the animal kingdom. Not content with this supremacy, however, he began to place a gulf between his nature and theirs. He denied the possession of reason to them, and to himself he attributed an immortal soul, and made claims to a divine descent which permitted him to break the bond of community between him and the animal kingdom. Curiously enough, this piece of arrogance is still foreign to children, just as it is to primitive and primeval man. It is the result of a later, more pretentious stage of development. At the level of totemism primitive man had no repugnance to tracing his descent from an animal ancestor. In myths, which contain the precipitate of this ancient attitude of mind, the gods take animal shapes, and in the art of earliest times they are portrayed with animals' heads. A child can see no difference between his own nature and that of animals. He is not astonished at animals thinking and talking in fairy tales; he will transfer an emotion of fear which he feels for his human father

[From *The Standard Edition of the Complete Psychological Works of Sigmund Freud,* Vol. XVII. The Hogarth Press, Ltd., London. By permission of the publishers and The Macmillan Co.]

onto a dog or a horse, without intending any derogation of his father by it. Not until he is grown up does he become so far estranged from animals as to use their names in vilification of human beings.

We all know that little more than half a century ago the researches of Charles Darwin and his collaborators and forerunners put an end to this presumption on the part of man. Man is not a being different from animals or superior to them; he himself is of animal descent, being more closely related to some species and more distantly to others. The acquisitions he has subsequently made have not succeeded in effacing the evidences, both in his physical structure and in his mental dispositions, of his parity with them. This was the second, the *biological* blow to human narcissism.

(c) The third blow, which is psychological in nature, is probably the most wounding.

Although thus humbled in his external relations, man feels himself to be supreme within his own mind. Somewhere in the core of his ego he has developed an organ of observation to keep a watch on his impulses and actions and see whether they harmonize with its demands. If they do not, they are ruthlessly inhibited and withdrawn. His internal perception, consciousness, gives the ego news of all the important occurrences in the mind's working, and the will, directed by these reports, carries out what the ego orders and modifies anything that seeks to accomplish itself spontaneously. For this mind is not a simple thing; on the contrary, it is a hierarchy of superordinated and subordinated agencies, a labyrinth of impulses striving independently of one another towards action, corresponding with the multiplicity of instincts and of relations with the external world, many of which are antagonistic to one another and incompatible. For proper functioning it is necessary that the highest of these agencies should have knowledge of all that is going forward and that its will should penetrate everywhere, so as to exert its influence. And in fact the ego feels secure both as to the completeness and trustworthiness of the reports it receives and as to the openness of the channels through which it enforces its commands.

In certain diseases—including the very neuroses of which we have made special study—things are different. The ego feels uneasy; it comes up against limits to its power in its own house, the mind. Thoughts emerge suddenly without one's knowing where they come from, nor can one do anything to drive them away. These alien guests even seem to be more powerful than those which are at the ego's command. They resist all the well-proved measures of enforcement used by the will, remain unmoved by logical refutation, and are unaffected by the contradictory assertions of reality. Or else impulses appear which seem like those of a stranger, so that the ego disowns them; yet it has to fear them and take precautions against them. The ego says to itself: "This is an illness, a foreign invasion." It increases its vigilance, but cannot understand why it feels so strangely paralyzed.

Psychiatry, it is true, denies that such things mean the intrusion into the mind of evil spirits from without; beyond this, however, it can only say with a shrug: "Degeneracy, hereditary disposition, constitutional inferiority!" Psychoanalysis sets out to explain these uncanny disorders; it engages in careful and laborious investigations, devises hypotheses and scientific constructions, until at length it can speak thus to the ego:—

"Nothing has entered into you from without; a part of the activity of your own mind has been withdrawn from your knowledge and from the command of your will. That, too, is why you are so weak in your defence; you are using one part of your force to fight the other part and you cannot concentrate the whole of your force as you would against an external enemy. And it is not even the worst or least important part of your mental forces that has thus become antagonistic to you and independent of you. The blame, I am bound to say, lies with yourself. You overestimated your strength when you thought you could treat your sexual instincts as you liked and could utterly ignore their intentions. The result is that they have rebelled and have taken their own obscure paths to escape this suppression; they have established their rights in a manner you cannot approve. How they have achieved this, and the paths which they have taken, have not come to your knowledge. All you have learned is the *outcome* of their work—the symptom which you experience as suffering. Thus you do not recognize it as a derivative of your own rejected instincts and do not know that it is a substitutive satisfaction of them.

"The whole process, however, only becomes possible through the single circumstance that you are mistaken in another important point as well. You feel sure that you are informed of all that goes on in your mind if it is of any importance at all, because in that case, you believe, your consciousness gives you news of it. And if you have had no information of something in your mind you confidently assume that it does not exist there. Indeed, you go so far as to regard what is 'mental' as identical with what is 'conscious'—that is, with what is known to you—in spite of the most obvious evidence that a great deal more must constantly be going on in your mind than can be known to your consciousness. Come, let yourself be taught something on this one point! What is in your mind does not coincide with what you are conscious of; whether something is going on in your mind and whether you hear of it, are two different things. In the ordinary way, I will admit, the intelligence which reaches your consciousness is enough for your needs; and you may cherish the illusion that you learn of all the more important things. But in some cases, as in that of an instinctual conflict such as I have described, your intelligence service breaks down and your will then extends no further than your knowledge. In every case, however, the news that reaches your consciousness is incomplete and often not to be relied on. Often enough, too, it happens that you get news of events only when they are over and when you can no longer do anything to change them. Even if you are not ill, who can tell all that is stirring in your mind of which you know nothing or are falsely informed? You behave like an absolute ruler who is content with the information supplied him by his highest officials and never goes among the people to hear their voice. Turn your eyes inward, look into your own depths, learn first to know yourself! Then you will understand why you were bound to fall ill; and perhaps, you will avoid falling ill in future."

It is thus that psychoanalysis has sought to educate the ego. But these two discoveries—that the life of our sexual instincts cannot be wholly tamed, and that mental processes are in themselves unconscious and only reach the ego and come under its control through incomplete and untrustworthy perceptions—these two discoveries amount to a statement that *the ego is not master in its own house*. Together they represent the third blow to man's self-love, what I may call the *psychological* one. No wonder, then, that the ego does not look favorably upon psychoanalysis and obstinately refuses to believe in it.

Probably very few people can have realized the momentous significance for science and life of the recognition of unconscious mental processes. It was not psychoanalysis, however, let us hasten to add, which first took this step. There are famous philosophers who may be cited as forerunners—above all the great thinker Schopenhauer, whose unconscious "Will" is equivalent to the mental instincts of psychoanalysis. It was this same thinker, moreover, who in words of unforgettable impressiveness admonished mankind of the importance, still so greatly underestimated by it, of its sexual craving. Psychoanalysis has this advantage only, that it has not affirmed these two propositions which are so distressing to narcissism—the psychical importance of sexuality and the unconsciousness of mental life—on an *abstract* basis, but has demonstrated them in matters that touch every individual personally and force him to take up some attitude towards these problems. It is just for this reason, however, that it brings on itself the aversion and resistances which still hold back in awe before the great name of the philosopher.

AN INTRODUCTON TO PSYCHOANALYSIS

I

LET US ASSUME that a patient is suffering from attacks of moodiness, which he is unable to control, or else is the victim of a despondency so depressing as to paralyze his energy, causing him to lose all confidence in himself, manifesting extreme self-consciousness when among strangers. Without knowing why, the patient may observe that not only the discharge of his daily duties becomes more and more arduous for him, but also that he experiences difficulties when called upon to make a decision or embark upon some enterprise.

Or—what appears very peculiar to him—his thoughts "wander"; they are no longer subject to his will. They attach themselves to problems which, in reality, do not interest him at all but which he is, nevertheless, unable to dismiss from his mind. He imposes perfectly ludicrous tasks upon himself, such as counting the windows along the street. When attending to simple functions, such as mailing a letter or turning off the gas, doubts harass him a few moments later, as to whether he has really dropped the letter into the mail box and whether he actually turned off the gas.

To take another case—this time of a female patient, who is suffering in an entirely different way, presenting entirely different symptoms. We will assume that she is a pianist, who suddenly experiences cramps in her fingers and discovers herself unable to play. As soon as she thinks of attending a social affair, she immediately feels the necessity of obeying a recurrent natural need, making it impossible for her to leave her house. Thus, she has been forced to give up mingling with her friends, or attending dances, the theater, or concerts.

At the most inopportune moments, she becomes the victim of headaches or other painful sensations. Eventually, after meals, she feels impelled to yield to nausea, a condition which, if prolonged, may become dangerous. Finally, she becomes absolutely

[Reprinted from *The Question of Lay Analysis* by Sigmund Freud. By permission of W. W. Norton & Company, Inc. Copyright 1950 by W. W. Norton & Company, Inc.]

unable to stand any of those little excitements which cannot be eliminated from daily life. Upon such occasion, she readily faints. As these spells are frequently complicated with muscular spasms, such attacks assume the aspect of dreadful afflictions.

Still other patients become subject to disturbances in a sphere where bodily functions coordinate with manifestations of sentiment. They find themselves unable to give physiological expression to those tender urges that induce them to gravitate towards the other sex. On the other hand, all the physiological reactions may be at their command when not aimed at the person they cherish most. Then, there are still other cases, when bonds of sensuality will tie them to persons whom they actually despise and of whom they have the most earnest desire to free themselves. Or their sensuality imposes urges upon them whose fulfillment causes them to shudder.

Sooner or later, all such persons come to consider themselves sick and appeal to physicians, expecting to be cured of their nervous ailments. Physicians have classified these manifestations, diagnosing them differently, according to their own personal point of view. These ailments are listed under such terms as neurasthenia, psychasthenia, phobias and neuroses of different kinds, and that sweeping term hysterics. The parts of the body inducing such disturbances are examined: the heart, the stomach, the intestines, the sex organs, and all are found to be in the best of condition. The physician then advises the patient to change his mode of living, to take a vacation, to exercise. Thus, with perhaps the aid of mild stimulants, the patient's condition may, or may not, be temporarily relieved.

Eventually, the patient is informed that there are certain practitioners who specialize in the treatment of just such ailments, and thus they come to be psychoanalyzed.

II

To all appearances, nothing takes place between patient and psychoanalyst except that they talk with each other. The psychoanalyst does not take recourse to any instruments while examining the patient nor does he write out prescriptions. If it can be arranged, he will not even take the patient out of his usual surroundings, or upset his daily routine in any way, while treating him. Usually the analyst simply makes an appointment with his patient, then lets him talk, listens to him, lets him talk again and listens once more.

Of course, some preparatory work is necessary, but that is easily accomplished in a simple manner. The patient is asked to be absolutely frank with the psychoanalyst, not to withhold intentionally anything that crowds itself into his mind, and to overcome gradually all such influences as may exert themselves to prevent certain of his thoughts or memories from being communicated to the psychoanalyst.

There is not one of us but does not know that there are certain things which we hate to tell anybody else, or which we are utterly unable to express at all. These are the so-called "most intimate" things. We also surmise—and this proves the great progress that has been made in the psychological understanding of our Selves—that there are some other things which we hate to admit to ourselves, which we try to hide from ourselves and which, once they are accidentally touched upon, we immediately endeavor to crowd out of our thoughts.

Doubtless, the root of a very remarkable psychological problem manifests itself in the fact that there are certain of our thoughts which we try to hide from our very own Self! That would seem to indicate that our very own Self is not an indivisible unit, as we have always considered it. Rather, there is a certain something which may rise in opposition to our very own Self. Vaguely, then, we surmise that our own Self and our psychic life may be two different things. If now, the patient submits to the demand of psychoanalysis to express in words every thing that comes to his mind, he comes to believe that an interchange of thoughts, under such extraordinary conditions, is liable to lead to extraordinary results.

III

To make myself perfectly plain to you, it will be necessary for me to acquaint you with certain psychological teachings which are not known beyond the circle of analysts and accordingly, not appreciated beyond this group. On the basis of this theory, it will be easy for you to deduce what we expect of the patient and how we go about obtaining it.

In explaining matters to you, I will allude to our theory dogmatically, as if it already were an accepted doctrine. Nevertheless, I do not want you to assume that our theory, as I shall presently put it before you, came into being as a fully developed, well-rounded out philosophical system. The development of our theory came about only very gradually, little by little, and was built up through continuous observation. Moreover, our theory, in accordance with these observations, was continually modified until it finally evolved in a manner apparently satisfactory for our purposes.

Only so short a time as a few years back, it would have been necessary for me to express this theory in somewhat different terms. And even today, I cannot guarantee that the terms I am using are definitely fixed and will not be modified again. You know very well that scientific truths do not burst upon us with the unexpectedness of a sudden phenomenon. As a rule, any science, long after its early stages, lacks the character of definiteness, unchangeability, and infallibility for which our human way of thinking longs so intensely.

"If I understood you correctly, you were going to speak about the fundamental presumptions underlying the new psychology."*

It was not my intention to start with that. Rather, I intend to tell you what we have learned of the psychic apparatus, in the course of our analytical studies.

This obscure psychic apparatus, which serves as the agent for all psychological processes, is conceived by us as an instrument consisting of several parts. Each of these parts we shall call an agency. There is an individual function attached to each of these agencies, and all of them are correlated to each other in reference to space. Aspects of space like "near" and "far," and "above" and "below," for the time being, only serve to illustrate the regular sequence of the functions allotted to the different agencies of the psychic apparatus—Do you still follow me?

"Hardly! However, I hope I will understand you eventually. At any rate, your explanation appeals to me as a somewhat peculiar description of the anatomy of the soul, which, according to biologists, is nonexistent."

I will grant that what you call my "somewhat peculiar description of the anatomy of the soul," is merely a parallel drawn upon for the purpose of elucidation, as is so often done in sciences. In the early stages of a new science such parallels have always been quite primitive—open to revision, as it were.

However, for argument's sake, let us accept the popular conception and assume that within us there is a physical organization, recording sensations and perceptions of physical wants on one hand, and releas-

* In this essay Freud writes as though he were discussing psychoanalysis with an interested listener.

ing motoric actions on the other. This medium for establishing this definite co-operation we call the ego.

Of course this is nothing new. Each one of us takes this for granted, if he is not a philosopher, and some despite being philosophers. However, our description of the physical apparatus is not by far complete.

Aside from the ego, we perceive another region of the psyche, much more extensive, much more impressive, and much more obscure than the ego, which we designate the *id*.

It is the relation between the ego and id upon which we shall dwell first.

In the realm of psychology, we can only make ourselves understood by taking recourse to comparisons. This, after all, is no special peculiarity of psychology, inasmuch as other sciences also find it necessary to avail themselves of analogous expedients. These comparisons, however, must be modified time and again, as their application generally proves too limited. If you are seeking an explanation of the relation of the ego to the id, it would be well to remember that the ego serves as a foreground to the id. The ego is, as it were, the outer, front layer of the id. We may so much more readily accept this comparison, inasmuch as layers—say, of a tree—owe their peculiar characteristics to the modifying influence of that exterior medium with which they are in contact. Thus, we visualize that the ego, being the outer layer of the psychical apparatus, is the id, modified in accordance with the influence which the outer world exerts upon it.

Here you will perceive how conceptions of space apply to psychoanalysis. To all intents and purposes, the ego is actually the front layer, the obvious, whereas the id is the inner layer, the hidden. To make it even more plain: The ego is inserted between the reality of the outer world and the id, the latter constituting as it were, the main body of psychic life.

"I am not going to inquire how you came to know all this. I should first like to know how this differentiation between the ego and id assists you in your psychoanalytical work, and why you need it."

Your question clearly shows me how to proceed.

It is most important and extremely valuable to know that the ego and the id, in so many instances, greatly differ from each other. As far as the ego is concerned, psychical activations are subject to a different rule from the one applying to the id. The ego has different intentions from the id, availing itself of means other than those resorted to by the id.

Of course, much could be said in this respect, but perhaps it will be best if I give you a new comparison and a new example. Just remember the differences which developed during the late war, between the actual front and the hinterland. We were apparently never surprised to observe that there were certain things going on at the front, utterly different from analogous developments in the hinterland, and that in the hinterland many a thing was permissible which had to be strictly prohibited at the front. In the war, the deciding factor, of course, was the proximity of the enemy. In our physical life, the deciding factor is the proximity of the outer world. Remember that in ancient times "outside," "strange," "hostile," used to be identical conceptions.

And now, the example I promised you: The id is never assailed by any conflicts. Within the id, contradiction and opposition dwell undisturbed in close proximity to each other, frequently equalizing one another by means of compromise. However, while the id thus remains undisturbed, the ego cannot avoid facing conflicts, and the only way for the ego to escape the dilemma is by renouncing some particular intention, or urge, for the benefit of the other.

The ego is controlled by a very remarkable trend toward unification, integration—a characteristic utterly lacking in the id. The latter never manifests such unity of intention, but rather displays a tendency towards dissipation and a diversity of aims, utterly independent of one another, and without regard to each other.

IV

"If there really is such an important hinterland of the mind, how do you explain the fact that it was never discovered before the advent of psychoanalysis?"

By this question, you are leading us back to one of your former inquiries. Let me advise you, then, that orthodox psychology blocked its own way to the id, by holding on tenaciously to a presumption which, in itself, seemed obvious enough but which, nevertheless, cannot be successfully sustained any more. It was presumed that all psychical activities are conscious, that consciousness is the characteristic of any psychological process, and that if there really were unconscious processes of our brain, these processes did not deserve to be termed psychological processes, having nothing at all to do with psychology proper.

"I should say that this is self-evident!"

Of course. That is exactly what all the orthodox psychologists claim. However, it is easy enough to prove that such a view is incorrect, or rather amounts to an impractical separation. Observing ourselves, we easily perceive that many of our thoughts could not have arisen unless they were induced by certain premises. However, of the preparatory stages of these thoughts, which must have been psychical, too, we are unaware, inasmuch as only the complete result enters into our consciousness. Once in a while, it may be possible for us to reconstruct the development of a thought by retrospective contemplation.

"Most probably, our attention had been diverted so that we missed observing the development of the thought in the making, so to speak."

That's just an obvious excuse!—insufficient to obscure the fact that quite frequently psychical activations—and often highly complicated ones, too—may occur in our psychic life without our becoming actually aware of them. Alas, you may be ready to accept the hypothesis that just a little more or less of your "attention" may prove sufficient to transmute a non-psychical action into a psychical one. But why squabble? The existence of unconscious thoughts has been proven in hypnotic experiments, time and again, to the satisfaction of everybody.

"I don't wish to deny that, and I actually believe I am now beginning to understand you at last. What you term the ego is the Conscious while the id describes the so-called Subconscious, which is so much discussed just now. But why, pray, this masquerade of new terms, if I may ask?"

This is no masquerade, inasmuch as other terms cannot be employed here properly. Besides, let me ask you not to substitute literature for science. If somebody refers to the Subconscious, I don't know whether he is alluding to it as a stratum, that is, something dwelling in the soul beneath the Conscious, or whether he refers to it as to quality, that is, another consciousness, a subterranean one, so to say. To be sure, the greatest probability seems to be that anybody juggling such terms is himself not at all sure of what he really means. The only permissible differentiation is one between Conscious and Unconscious.

V

"I expect that, on the basis of psychoanalytical theories, you will explain to me how the development of a nervous ailment may be conceived!"

I shall try. For this purpose, however, it is necessary that we study our ego and id from a new point of view. We shall have to look into these two factors for their dynamic values, that is, in regard to the forces active in and between them. You will remember that previously we restricted ourselves to the description of the psychical apparatus.

"I am only hoping that things won't be so impossible to grasp."

I do not think so. As a matter of fact, I believe that you will soon comprehend the whole system. To start with, let us assume that those forces which actuate the psychic apparatus are generated by the different organs of our system, as the result of important needs of our body. Don't forget what the poet-philosopher Schiller once said:

> Until philosophy sublime,
> Supremely rules the course of time,
> The world in oldest fashion,
> By hunger moves, and passion.

Hunger and Passion are two very powerful agents!

The needs of our body which stimulate the mind into action we call instinctual drives.

It is these instinctual drives which fill the id. All energies generated by the id were conceived by these instinctual drives. The powers of the ego have no other origin either, inasmuch as they are derived from the id.

What, now, do these instinctual drives want?

They want to be satisfied, that is, they endeavor to create those situations whereby the needs of our body are gratified.

As soon as any tension, created by our instinctual drives, slackens simultaneously with the satisfied cravings of our body, our Consciousness experiences a pleasurable sensation, whereas an intensification of our instinctual drives will soon enough result in decided displeasure. In accordance with these fluctuations of pleasurable and distressing sensations, our psychic apparatus regulates its activity. Thus, the rule of the *Pleasure Principle* manifests itself.

Intolerable conditions develop in case the urges of the id are not satisfied. Experience proves that situations of complete gratification can only be achieved in contact with the outer world. Thus, that part of the id which faces the outer world, i.e., the ego, assumes its functions. While the driving power is produced by the id, it is the ego which then assumes the management, takes the steering wheel in hand, so to speak, without which the coveted goal could never be reached.

It is characteristic of the urges of the id that they are always bent upon immediate, rash gratification without ever attaining their ends, but thus they may expose the human being to serious harm. Therefore, it devolves upon the ego to forestall such failure, by mediating between the reckless claims of the id and the checks of the outer world. Thus, the censorial activity of the ego makes itself felt in two different directions.

On one hand, the ego, assisted by that organ which conveys to it the reactions of an outer world, scans the horizon, as it were, in an attempt to seize upon the most opportune moment for a harmless gratification of the urges prompting it. On the other hand, the ego exerts a restraining influence on the id, controlling its "passions" and inducing its urges to postpone their gratification, or modify them, or renounce them for some compensation, as the case may be.

Restraining the reckless id in such a way, the ego replaces the formerly predominant Pleasure Principle with the so-called *Reality Principle* which, although striving for the same ends as the Pleasure Principle, nevertheless considers such practical necessities as the outer world imposes.

Later on, the ego discovers that there is another way of insuring gratification of urges than adaptation to the outer world. This newly discovered method consists of changing conditions in the outer world in such a way as to bring about circumstances favorable for gratification. This activity of the ego constitutes its supreme achievement. Sufficient discernment to perceive when it is opportune to stifle passions and when it is opportune to either face or fight the realities of the outer world is, after all, the Alpha and Omega of practical wisdom.

VI

"As I understand you, the id is by far the stronger of the two. How, then, is it possible that the id will permit the weaker ego to hold sway over it?"

The ego is well in a position to exert such influence over the id, provided its organization and efficiency are in no way hampered. There is no inherent opposition between the ego and id, both belonging together. In cases of normal health, it is practically impossible to distinguish between the two. As long as the ego discharges its duties fully, and its relations to the id are maintained in a satisfactory manner, no nervous disturbances will develop. However, disturbances are liable to arise at some unsuspected spot. Even in such living beings as later on develop an efficient ego-organization, this ego is quite weak in the years of childhood and only slightly different from the id.

And now, I ask you to visualize what would happen in the event this powerless ego is actuated by an urge arising from the id—an urge which the weak ego would like to resist, because it feels that a gratification of this urge may involve danger, may result in a traumatic situation, a collision with the outer world with which it is not strong enough to deal.

"Then what?"

Then, the ego deals with the danger, arising from an id-inspired urge, in exactly the same way that an exterior danger would have to be faced. The ego makes an attempt at flight, deserting this specific part of the id and leaving it to its fate. We refer to such a case as a repression of instinctual drives by the ego.

For the time being, danger is thus parried, but to confound inner and outer world is certain to invite punishment. Running away from oneself is a thing that cannot be done! In a case of repression, the ego succumbs to the Pleasure Principle which it otherwise strives to correct. Thus, it is the ego upon which damage is inflicted in such cases of repression. This damage consists of the ego experiencing a lasting restriction in its own sphere of rule The repressed drive is now isolated, left to itself, unapproachable, and cannot be influenced. The repressed drive now goes its own way. Frequently, even after the ego has attained power, it proves impossible to release this repression. With its integrative function impaired, a part of the id remains forbidden ground to the ego.

The isolated impulse does not remain idle, however. Because normal gratification was denied it, it contrives to compensate itself by engendering psychical derivates which take its place and, connecting with other psychical activations, estrange them from the ego. Finally, in the form of an unrecognizable substitute, the isolated impulse penetrates to the ego and to consciousness, presenting itself as what is known as a "symptom."

We now become aware of what a nervous disturbance is. We see an ego hampered in its integrative power, unable to exert any influence on certain parts of the id. In addition, the ego must renounce some of its inherent activities, to avoid new collisions with the repressed urge. We perceive an ego exhausting itself in mostly unavailing defensive measures against symptoms that are nothing other than results of the repression. Moreover, it becomes evident now that in the id some urges have assumed independence. They aim at their own gratification without any concern for the whole, subject only to such primitive psychology as reigns in the lowermost depths of the id.

Observing such a state of affairs, we face the quite simple situation in which the ego, attempting to oppress certain parts of the id, proceeded *in an utterly unsuitable manner*. Consequently, the ego has failed in its intention and now the id is taking revenge on the ego. This revenge of the id on the ego resulted in nothing less than a neurosis.

Accordingly, a neurosis is the result of a conflict between the ego and the id, a conflict—as investigations will show—forced upon the ego, because the latter insisted on maintaining its state of pliability, in reference to an outer world. The conflict, in fact, is one between the id and the outer world. However, because the ego, faithful and true, takes sides with the outer world, it becomes entangled in this conflict of the id with the outer world.

Note that the condition of nervous disturbances is not induced by the conflict between the ego and the id but rather by the fact that the ego, for the purpose of settling this conflict, availed itself of the unsuitable agent of repression. As a rule, conflicts between reality and the id are unavoidable, and it is a routine task for the ego to act as a mediator in such cases. That in the case of this specific conflict which we have under observation just now, the ego took recourse to repression as agent, is due to the fact that at this time the ego was powerless and immature. After all, repressions of lasting importance occur exclusively during early childhood!

VII

"But, pray, tell me what advice your theory offers for the treatment of neurotic conditions?"

It is quite simple to describe our therapeutic goal:

We aim at restituting the ego and liberating it from its restrictions, restoring to the ego once more the sovereignty over the id which it lost, on account of early repressions. Psychoanalysis, in general, aims at this goal; our whole technique strives for this end. It is up to us to discover those repressions, to induce the ego to correct them with our assistance, and to settle conflicts more satisfactorily than by a mere flight. Inasmuch as these repressions are part of our early childhood, psychoanalysis must needs go back to those years of our life.

The way to those mostly forgotten conflict situations, which we must revive in the memory of our "cases," is pointed out to us by symptoms, dreams, and "free associations" of the patient. Of course, all these hints must first be interpreted, translated, as it were, because these symptoms and dreams, under the influence of the psychology of the id, have assumed various disguises which it is our purpose to penetrate.

If a patient communicates to us certain ideas, thoughts and memories after long hesitation only, we feel safe in assuming that they have some connection with his early repressions, or are, at least, derivates of such. By encouraging the patient to conquer his hesitancy when talking to us, we are training his ego to overcome its tendency to "run away" and rather to face that early repression. At the end, after we have been successful in reproducing the situation which originally induced his repression, the pliancy of the patient is splendidly rewarded. The number of years that have meanwhile elapsed prove to be all in favor of the patient. What once scared his immature ego and threw it into panic and flight, appears to the adult-strengthened ego as nothing more than a childish bugaboo.

VIII

We have discovered that sexual tendencies permeate life from very birth. We also ascertained that it is to combat these drives that the infantile ego resorts to repressions.

The most remarkable thing in the sex life of the child, to my mind, is the fact that its whole, extensive development is completed in the course of the first five years of life. From then, until the beginning of puberty, there is a time when sex remains latent, a time during which—normally—sexuality is not progressing but rather losing in intensity.

It is during this period after the first bloom of sex life has withered, that such conceptions of the ego develop as shame, disgust, morality, destined to serve as support later on, in the storm and stress of puberty, and to direct newly awakened sexual tendencies. This new, second phase of sex life plays a very important part in the inception of nervous disturbances. Apparently, it is only in man that this twofold onset of sex life prevails. It is, perhaps, this which is one of the contributing factors to the truly human prerogative to indulge in neuroses.

Before the advent of psychoanalysis, the early period of sex life had been overlooked, just as had the unconscious background of conscious psychic life. If you should now suspect that both belong together, you have guessed correctly.

It is obvious enough that the child never surmises the real facts as to the actual physical relations of the sexes, but this ignorance is compensated by impressions and experiences deduced from his own observations. Usually, a child's desires culminate in the wish to give birth to a baby, or beget one, in some vague manner.

Even the little boy, in his ignorance, has this desire to give birth to a child.

Such manifestations, in their entirety, are termed in accordance with Greek mythology, *Oedipus Complex*.

Normally, an *Oedipus Complex* should be abandoned or thoroughly changed simultaneously with the termination of early sex life. The results of this transformation of the *Oedipus Complex* are destined to bring about great achievements, to play a big part in later psychic life.

As a rule, this transformation is not thorough enough. Therefore, during the period of puberty, the *Oedipus Complex* may be revived, in which case it is liable to induce dire results.

IX

When I explained to you the relations between the ego and the id, I withheld from you an important part of the psychic apparatus. You see, within the ego itself, there persists a particular faction which we call the super-ego.

This super-ego enjoys a privileged position between the ego and the id. It belongs to the ego, sharing with it its intricate psychological make-up. On the other hand, it entertains very close relations with the id. The super-ego is in reality the record of first impressions as conceived by the id; it is the heir of the dissolved *Oedipus Complex*.

This super-ego, as a matter of fact, is able

to oppose the ego, act towards it as if it were something inferior and, in general, treat it almost with contempt. For the ego it is just as important to remain in agreement with the super-ego as with the id. Disagreement between the super-ego and the ego is of far-reaching consequences for the soul life.

Doubtless, you have already surmised that the super-ego is the agent of that phenomenon which we call our conscience.

For the maintenance of sound mental life, it is very important that the super-ego develop normally, that is, become sufficiently impersonal. It is just this development which is insufficient in the neurotic, because his *Oedipus Complex* was not properly transformed. His super-ego, in regard to the ego, still assumes the role of the strict father to the child, with the morality of the ego manifesting itself in a primitive manner by meekly submitting to punishment, meted out by the super-ego. Sickness is resorted to, as the means of this "self-punishment." The neurotic, behaving as if under a burden of guilt, accepts sickness as a punishment to assuage this feeling of delinquency.

All those forces which oppose the recuperation of a patient, we term the "resistances" of the patient. While gain from the disease is the source of such resistances, the "unconscious feeling of guilt" represents the resistance of the super-ego of which, as the strongest factor, we are in the most fear.

But there are other manifestations of resistance which become evident in the process of treatment. If the ego, at an early period, was induced through fear, to take recourse to a repression, this fear still persists, manifesting itself now as a resistance, as soon as the ego approaches that which was repressed.

The battle against all these resistances is our main work during the analytical treatment, in comparison with which the task of interpretation almost fades into insignificance. But by this battle and the ensuing defeat of resistances, the ego of the patient is so transformed and strengthened that his future behavior, after the termination of the treatment, may be regarded with complete confidence.

On the other hand, you will understand now why our treatment is so protracted. Remember that the same course, which in times of peace, may be traveled in a few hours by railroad, may take an army, during wartime, weeks and weeks, because the resistance of the enemy must first be overcome. Battles to overcome resistance require time in psychic life also. I am sorry to say that, up to now, all exertions to shorten the duration of analytical treatments to any appreciable degree have proved unavailing. It seems that the best way to shorten the length of the treatment, is simply to apply it as correctly as possible.

THE INTERPRETATION OF DREAMS

I

IN MY EXPERIENCE, which is already extensive, the chief part in the mental lives of all children who later become psychoneurotics is played by their parents. Being in

[From Sigmund Freud, *The Interpretation of Dreams*. English translation by James Strachey. Copyright 1955 by Basic Books, Inc., New York, N. Y. Reprinted by permission of the publishers.]

love with the one parent and hating the other are among the essential constituents of the stock of physical impulses which is formed at that time and which is of such importance in determining the symptoms of the later neurosis. It is not my belief, however, that psychoneurotics differ sharply in this respect from other human beings who remain normal—that they are able, that is, to create something absolutely new and peculiar to themselves. It is far more probable—and this is confirmed by occasional observations on normal children—that they are only distinguished by exhibiting on a magnified scale feelings of love and hatred to their parents which occur less obviously and less intensely in the minds of most children.

This discovery is confirmed by a legend that has come down to us from classical antiquity: a legend whose profound and universal power to move can only be understood if the hypothesis I have put forward in regard to the psychology of children has an equally universal validity. What I have in mind is the legend of King Oedipus and Sophocles' drama which bears his name.

Oedipus, son of Laius, King of Thebes, and of Jocasta, was exposed as an infant because an oracle had warned Laius that the still unborn child would be his father's murderer. The child was rescued, and grew up as a prince in an alien court, until, in doubts as to his origin, he too questioned the oracle and was warned to avoid his home since he was destined to murder his father and take his mother in marriage. On the road leading away from what he believed was his home, he met King Laius and slew him in a sudden quarrel. He came next to Thebes and solved the riddle set him by the Sphinx who barred his way. Out of gratitude the Thebans made him their king and gave him Jocasta's hand in marriage. He reigned long in peace and honor, and she who, unknown to him, was his mother bore him two sons and two daughters. Then at last a plague broke out and the Thebans made enquiry once more of the oracle. It is at this point that Sophocles' tragedy opens. The messengers bring back the reply that the plague will cease when the murderer of Laius has been driven from the land.

> But he, where is he? Where shall now be read
> The fading record of this ancient guilt?

The action of the play consists in nothing other than the process of revealing, with cunning delays and ever-mounting excitement—a process that can be likened to the work of a psychoanalysis—that Oedipus himself is the murderer of Laius, but further that he is the son of the murdered man and of Jocasta. Appalled at the abomination which he has unwittingly perpetrated, Oedipus blinds himself and forsakes his home. The oracle has been fulfilled.

Oedipus Rex is what is known as a tragedy of destiny. Its tragic effect is said to lie in the contrast between the supreme will of the gods and the vain attempts of mankind to escape the evil that threatens them. The lesson which, it is said, the deeply moved spectator should learn from the tragedy is submission to the divine will and realization of his own impotence. Modern dramatists have accordingly tried to achieve a similar tragic effect by weaving the same contrast into a plot invented by themselves.

If *Oedipus Rex* moves a modern audience no less than it did the contemporary Greek one, the explanation can only be that its effect does not lie in the contrast between destiny and human will, but is to be looked for in the particular nature of the material on which that contrast is exemplified. There must be something which makes a voice within us ready to recognize the compelling force of destiny in the *Oedipus*, while we can dismiss as merely arbitrary such dispositions as are laid down in the modern tragedies of destiny. And a factor of this kind is in fact involved in the story of King Oedipus. His destiny moves us only because it might have been ours—because the oracle laid the same curse upon us before our birth as upon him. It is the fate of all of us, perhaps, to direct our first sexual impulse towards our mother and our first hatred and our first murderous wish against our father. Our dreams convince us that that is so. King Oedipus, who slew his father Laius and married his mother Jocasta, merely shows us the fulfilment of our own childhood wishes. But, more fortunate than he, we have meanwhile succeeded, in so far as we have not become psychoneurotics, in detaching our sexual impulses from our mothers and in forgetting our jealousy of our fathers. Here is one in whom these primeval wishes of our childhood have been fulfilled, and we shrink back from him with the whole force of the repression by which those wishes have since that time been held down within us. While the poet, as he unravels the past, brings to light the guilt of Oedipus, he is at the same time compelling us to recognize our own inner minds, in which those same impulses, though suppressed, are still to be found. The contrast with which the closing Chorus leaves us confronted—

> Fix on Oedipus your eyes,
> Who resolved the dark enigma,
> noblest champion, and most wise.
> Like a star his envied fortune
> mounted beaming far and wide:
> Now he sinks in seas of anguish,
> whelmed beneath a raging tide. . . .

—strikes as a warning at ourselves and our pride, at us who since our childhood have grown so wise and so mighty in our own eyes. Like Oedipus, we live in ignorance of these wishes, repugnant to morality, which have been forced upon us by Nature, and after their revelation we may all of us well seek to close our eyes to the scenes of our childhood.*

There is an unmistakable indication in the text of Sophocles' tragedy itself that the legend of Oedipus sprang from some primeval dream-material which had as its content the distressing disturbance of a child's relation to his parents owing to the first stirrings of sexuality. At a point when Oedipus, though he is not yet enlightened, has begun to feel troubled by his recollection of the oracle, Jocasta consoles him by referring to a dream which many people dream, though, as she thinks, it has no meaning:

> Many a man ere now in dreams hath lain
> With her who bare him. He hath least annoy
> Who with such omens troubleth not his mind.

II

Another of the great creations of tragic poetry, Shakespeare's *Hamlet*, has its roots in the same soil as *Oedipus Rex*. But the changed treatment of the same material reveals the whole difference in the mental life of these two widely separated epochs of civilization: the secular advance of repression in the emotional life of mankind. In the *Oedipus* the child's wishful fantasy

* [Footnote added 1914:] None of the findings of psychoanalytic research has provoked such embittered denials, such fierce opposition—or such amusing contortions—on the part of critics as this indication of the childhood impulses toward incest which persist in the unconscious. An attempt has even been made recently to make out, in the face of all experience, that the incest should only be taken as "symbolic."—Ferenczi (1912) has proposed an ingenious "over-interpretation" of the Oedipus myth, based on a passage in one of Schopenhauer's letters.—[Added 1919:] Later studies have shown that the "Oedipus complex," which was touched upon for the first time in the above paragraphs in the *Interpretation of Dreams*, throws a light of undreamt-of importance on the history of the human race and the evolution of religion and morality. (See my *Totem and Taboo*, 1912-13 [Essay IV].).

that underlies it is brought into the open and realized as it would be in a dream. In *Hamlet* it remains repressed; and—just as in the case of a neurosis—we only learn of its existence from its inhibiting consequences. Strangely enough, the overwhelming effect produced by the more modern tragedy has turned out to be compatible with the fact that people have remained completely in the dark as to the hero's character. The play is built up on Hamlet's hesitations over fulfilling the task of revenge that is assigned to him; but its text offers no reasons or motives for these hesitations and an immense variety of attempts at interpreting them have failed to produce a result. According to the view which was originated by Goethe and is still the prevailing one today, Hamlet represents the type of man whose power of direct action is paralyzed by an excessive development of his intellect. (He is "sicklied o'er with the pale cast of thought.") According to another view, the dramatist has tried to portray a pathologically irresolute character which might be classed as neurasthenic. The plot of the drama shows us, however, that Hamlet is far from being represented as a person incapable of taking any action. We see him doing so on two occasions: first in a sudden outburst of temper, when he runs his sword through the eavesdropper behind the arras, and secondly in a premeditated and even crafty fashion, when, with all the callousness of a Renaissance prince, he sends the two courtiers to the death that had been planned for himself.

What is it, then, that inhibits him in fulfilling the task set him by his father's ghost? The answer, once again, is that it is the peculiar nature of the task. Hamlet is able to do anything—except take vengeance on the man who did away with his father and took that father's place with his mother, the man who shows him the repressed wishes of his own childhood realized. Thus the loathing which should drive him on to revenge is replaced in him by self-reproaches, by scruples of conscience, which remind him that he himself is literally no better than the sinner whom he is to punish. Here I have translated into conscious terms what was bound to remain unconscious in Hamlet's mind; and if anyone is inclined to call him a hysteric, I can only accept the fact as one that is implied by my interpretation. The distaste for sexuality expressed by Hamlet in his conversation with Ophelia fits in very well with this: the same distaste which was destined to take possession of the poet's mind more and more during the years that followed, and which reached its extreme expression in *Timon of Athens*. For it can of course only be the poet's own mind which confronts us in Hamlet. I observe in a book on Shakespeare by Georg Brandes (1896) a statement that *Hamlet* was written immediately after the death of Shakespeare's father (in 1601), that is, under the immediate impact of his bereavement and, as we may well assume, while his childhood feelings about his father had been freshly revived. It is known, too, that Shakespeare's own son who died at an early age bore the name of "Hamnet," which is identical with "Hamlet." Just as *Hamlet* deals with the relation of a son to his parents, so *Macbeth* (written at approximately the same period) is concerned with the subject of childlessness. But just as all neurotic symptoms, and, for that matter, dreams, are capable of being "over-interpreted" and indeed need to be, if they are to be fully understood, so all genuinely creative writings are the product of more than a single motive and more than a single impulse in the poet's mind, and are open to more than a single interpretation. In what I have written I have only attempted to interpret the deepest layer of impulses in the mind of the creative writer.

Carl Gustav Jung

In the minds of many people the theories of Freud are taken to be the only reputable ones in the field of psychiatry. Actually, two of his ablest disciples, Adler and Jung, broke with Freud because of his insistence upon the dominant place of sexuality in human nature and developed influential positions of their own. The ideas of Jung have proved particularly appealing to many who feel that Freud failed to do justice to man's basic moral and spiritual resources. In human nature Jung recognizes not only biological drives and passions repressed by social convention but also religious impulses and creative energies seeking expression in the complete human being. Indeed, to Jung the need for spiritual harmony seems paramount here, and beyond the personal factors he recognizes a "collective unconscious" that brings into the life of the individual the whole psychological and religious development of the race.

Born in 1875 in a Swiss village on Lake Constance, Jung grew up in Basel where as a precocious youth he was twice almost thrown out of school because it was believed unlikely that he had come by so much knowledge honestly. He studied medicine, specialized in medical psychology in Paris, and became chief psychiatrist first at Burghölzli and then in Zurich. In 1907 he made his now historic pilgrimage to Vienna to meet Freud, who was twenty years his senior, and soon became a leading advocate of the new Freudian ideas. In 1913, however, after six years of assocation with Freud and an exchange of over three hundred letters on problems of psychoanalysis, Jung finally broke with the Freudian position. In recent years, he has lived in his comfortable home on Lake Geneva and devoted himself to writing and to his private patients.

Already famous for novel types of diagnosis, Jung pioneered in the study of the unconscious through a free response to certain key words (free association), and in the measurement of emotional reactions to these words by a galvanometer connected to the patients' hands—the origin of "lie detectors." He developed the now widely current classification of individuals as "introverts" and "extroverts," and recognized the important role of the "inferiority complex" in human life. Today in his eighties he is the most distinguished living figure in the field of psychiatry. In a series of lectures given at Yale and published under the provocative title, Modern Man in Search of a Soul, *Jung drew together in popular fashion the general position developed in his more scientific studies. The following selection from this volume outlines the major points of difference that Jung sees between his own position and that of Freud, and also contains a discerning analysis of the creative work of the artist.*

FREUD AND JUNG—CONTRASTS

THE DIFFERENCE between Freud's views and my own ought really to be dealt with by someone who stands outside the circles of influence of those ideas which go under our respective names. Can I be credited with sufficient impartiality to rise above my own ideas? Can any man do this? I doubt it. If I were told that someone had rivalled Baron Münchausen by accomplishing such a feat, I should feel sure that his ideas were borrowed ones.

It is true that widely accepted ideas are never the personal property of their so-called author; on the contrary, he is the

[From *Modern Man in Search of a Soul* by C. G. Jung. Chapters VI and VIII, abridged. Reprinted by permission of Harcourt, Brace and Company, Inc.]

bond-servant of his ideas. Impressive ideas which are hailed as truths have something peculiar to themselves. Although they come into being at a definite time, they are and have always been timeless; they arise from that realm of procreative psychic life out of which the ephemeral mind of the single human being grows like a plant that blossoms, bears fruit and seed, and then withers and dies. Ideas spring from a source that is not contained within one man's personal life. We do not create them; they create us. To be sure, when we deal in ideas we inevitably make a confession, for they bring to the light of day not only the best that in us lies, but our worst insufficiencies and personal shortcomings as well. This is especially the case with ideas about psychology. Whence should they come except from the most subjective side of life? Can experience with the objective world save us from subjective prejudgments? Is not every experience, even in the best of circumstances, to a large extent subjective interpretation? On the other hand, the subject also is an objective fact, a piece of the world. What issues from it comes, after all, from the universal soil, just as the rarest and strangest organism is none the less supported and nourished by the earth which we all share in common. It is precisely the most subjective ideas which, being closest to nature and to the living being, deserve to be called the truest. But what is truth?

For the purposes of psychology, I think it best to abandon the notion that we are today in anything like a position to make statements about the nature of the psyche that are "true" or "correct." The best that we can achieve is true expression. By true expression I mean an open avowal and a detailed presentation of everything that is subjectively noted. One person will stress the forms into which this material can be worked, and will therefore believe that he has created what he finds within himself. Another will lay most weight upon the fact that he plays the part of an observer; he will be conscious of his receptive attitude, and insist that his subjective material presents itself to him. The truth lies between the two. True expression consists in giving form to what is observed.

I

The psychology we at present possess is the testimony of a few individuals here and there regarding what they have found within themselves. The form in which they have cast it is sometimes adequate and sometimes not. Since each individual conforms more or less to a type, his testimony can be accepted as a fairly valid description of a large number of people. And since those who conform to other types belong none the less to the human species, we may conclude that the description applies, though less fully, to them too. What Freud has to say about sexuality, infantile pleasure, and their conflict with the "principle of reality," as well as what he says about incest and the like, can be taken as the truest expression of his own psychic make-up. He has given adequate form to what he has noted in himself. I am no opponent of Freud's; I am merely presented in that light by his own shortsightedness and that of his pupils. No experienced psychotherapist can deny having met with dozens of cases at least which answer in all essentials to Freud's descriptions. By his avowal of what he has found in himself, Freud has assisted at the birth of a great truth about man. He has devoted his life and his strength to the construction of a psychology which is a formulation of his own being.

Our way of looking at things is conditioned by what we are. And since other people are differently constituted, they see things differently and express themselves differently. Adler, one of Freud's earliest pupils, is a case in point. Working with the same empirical material as Freud, he approached it from a totally different standpoint. His way of looking at things is at least as convincing as Freud's, because he also represents a well-known type. I know that the followers of both schools flatly assert that I am in the wrong, but I may hope that history and all fair-minded persons will bear me out. Both schools, to my way of thinking, deserve reproach for overemphasizing the pathological aspect of life and for interpreting man too exclusively in the light of his defects. A convincing example of this in Freud's case is his inability to understand religious experience, as is clearly shown in his book: *The Future of an Illusion*. For my part, I prefer to look at man in the light of what in him is healthy and sound, and to free the sick man from that point of view which colors every page Freud has written. Freud's teaching is definitely one-sided in that it generalizes from facts that are relevant only to neurotic states of mind; its validity is really confined to those states. Within these limits Freud's teaching is true and valid even when it is in error, for error also belongs to the picture, and carries the truth of a true avowal. In any case, Freud's is not a psychology of the healthy mind.

The morbid symptom in Freud's psychology is this: it is based upon a view of the world that is uncriticized, or even unconscious, and this is apt to narrow the field of human experience and understanding to a considerable extent. It was a great mistake on Freud's part to turn his back on philosophy. Not once does he criticize his premises or even the assumptions that underlie his personal outlook. Yet to do so was necessary, as may be inferred from what I have said above; for had he critically examined his assumptions, he would never have put his peculiar mental disposition naively on view, as he has done in *The Interpretation of Dreams*. At all events, he would have had a taste of the difficulties which I have met with. I have never refused the bitter-sweet drink of philosophical criticism, but have taken it with caution, a little at a time. All too little, my opponents will say; almost too much, my own feeling tells me. All too easily does self-criticism poison one's naiveté, that priceless possession, or rather gift, which no creative man can be without. At any rate, philosophical criticism has helped me to see that every psychology—my own included—has the character of a subjective confession. And yet I must prevent my critical powers from destroying my creativeness. I know well enough that every word I utter carries with it something of myself—of my special and unique self with its particular history and its own particular world. Even when I deal with empirical data, I am necessarily speaking about myself. But it is only by accepting this as inevitable that I can serve the cause of man's knowledge of man—the cause which Freud also wished to serve, and which, in spite of everything, he has served. Knowledge rests not upon truth alone, but upon error also.

It is perhaps here, where the question arises of accepting the fact that every psychological teaching which is the work of one man is subjectively colored, that the line between Freud and myself is most sharply drawn.

A further difference seems to me to consist in this, that I try to free myself from all unconscious and therefore uncriticized assumptions as to the world in general. I say "I try," for who can be sure that he has freed himself from all his unconscious assumptions? I try to save myself at least from the crassest prejudices, and am therefore inclined to recognize all manner of gods provided only that they are active in the human psyche. I do not doubt that the natural instincts or drives are forces of propulsion in human life, whether we call them sexuality or the will to power; but I also do not doubt that these instincts come into collision with the spirit, for they are continually colliding with something, and why should not this something be called spirit? I am far from knowing what spirit is in itself, and equally far from knowing what instincts are. The one is as mysterious to me as the other, yet I am unable to dismiss the one by explaining it in terms of the other. That would be to treat it as a mere misunderstanding. The fact that the earth has only one moon is not a misunderstanding. There are no misunderstandings in nature; they are only to be found in the realms that man calls "understanding." Certainly instinct and spirit are beyond my understanding. They are terms that we allow to stand for powerful forces whose nature we do not know.

II

As may be seen, I attribute a positive value to all religions. In their symbolism I recognize those figures which I have met with in the dreams and fantasies of my patients. In their moral teachings I see efforts that are the same as or similar to those made by my patients, when, guided by their own insight or inspiration, they seek the right way of dealing with the forces of the inner life. Ceremonial, ritual, initiation rites and ascetic practices, in all their forms and variations, interest me profoundly as so many techniques for bringing about a proper relation to these forces. I likewise attribute a positive value to biology, and to the empiricism of natural science in general, in which I see a herculean attempt to understand the human psyche by approaching it from the outer world. I regard the gnostic religions as an equally prodigious undertaking in the opposite direction: as an attempt to draw knowledge of the cosmos from within. In my picture of the world there is a vast outer realm and an equally vast inner realm; between these two stands man, facing now one and now the other, and, according to his mood or disposition, taking the one for the absolute truth by denying or sacrificing the other.

This picture is hypothetical, of course, but it offers a hypothesis which is so valuable that I will not give it up. I consider it heuristically and empirically verified; and what is more, it is supported by the *consensus gentium*. This hypothesis certainly came to me from an inner source, though I might imagine that empirical findings had led to its discovery. Out of it has come my theory of types, and also my reconciliation with views as different from my own as those of Freud.

I see in all happening the play of opposites, and derive from this conception my idea of psychic energy. I hold that psychic energy involves the play of opposites in much the same way as physical energy involves a difference of potential, which is to say, the existence of such opposites as warm and cold, high and low. Freud began by taking sexuality as the only psychic driving power, and only after my break with him did he grant an equal status to other psychic activities as well. For my part, I have subsumed the various psychic drives or forces under the concept of energy in order to avoid the arbitrariness of a psychology that deals with drives or impulses alone. I therefore speak, not of separate drives or forces, but of "value intensities." By what has just been said I do not mean to deny the importance of sexuality in psychic life, though Freud stubbornly maintains that I do deny it. What I seek is to set bounds to the rampant terminology of sex which threatens to vitiate all discussion of the human psyche; I wish to put sexuality itself in its proper place. Common-sense will always return to the fact that sexuality is only one of the life-instincts—only one of the psychophysiological functions—though one that is without doubt very far reaching and important.

Beyond all question, there is a marked disturbance today in the realms of sexual life. It is well known that when we have a bad toothache, we can think of nothing else. The sexuality which Freud describes is unmistakably that sexual obsession which shows itself whenever a patient has reached the point where he needs to be forced or tempted out of a wrong attitude or situation. It is an overemphasized sexuality piled up behind a dam; and it shrinks at once to normal proportions as soon as the way to development is opened. It is being caught in the old resentments against parents and relations and in the boring emotional tangles of the family situation which most often brings about the damming-up of the energies of life. And it is this stoppage which shows itself unfailingly in that kind of sexuality which is called "infantile." It is really not sexuality proper, but an unnatural discharge of tensions that belong to quite another province of life. This being so, what is the use of paddling about in this flooded country? Surely, straight thinking will grant that it is more important to open up drainage canals. We should try to find, in a change of attitude or in new ways of life, that difference of potential which the pent-up energy requires. If this is not achieved a vicious circle is set up, and this is in fact the menace which Freudian psychology appears to offer. It points no way that leads beyond the inexorable cycle of biological events. This hopelessness would drive one to exclaim with Paul: "Wretched man that I am, who will deliver me from the body of this death?" And our man of intellect comes forward, shaking his head, and says in Faust's words: "Thou art conscious only of the single urge," namely of the fleshly bond leading back to father and mother or forward to the children that have sprung from our flesh—"incest" with the past and "incest" with the future, the original sin of the perpetuation of the family situation. There is nothing that can free us from this bond except that opposite urge of life, the spirit. It is not the children of the flesh, but the "children of God" who know freedom. In Ernst Barlach's tragic novel of family life, *Der Tote Tag*, the mother-demon says at the end: "The strange thing is that man will not learn that God is his father." That is what Freud would never learn, and what all those who share his outlook forbid themselves to learn. At least, they never find the key to this knowledge. Theology does not help those who are looking for the key, because theology demands faith, and faith cannot be made: it is in the truest sense a gift of grace. We moderns are faced with the necessity of rediscovering the life of the spirit; we must experience it anew for ourselves. It is the only way in which we can break the spell that binds us to the cycle of biological events.

III

My position on this question is the third point of difference between Freud's views and my own. Because of it I am accused of mysticism. I do not, however, hold myself responsible for the fact that man has, everywhere and always, spontaneously developed religious forms of expression, and that the human psyche from time immemorial has been shot through with religious feelings and ideas. Whoever cannot see this aspect of the human psyche is blind, and whoever chooses to explain it away, or to "enlighten" it away, has no sense of reality. Or should we see in the father complex which shows itself in all the members of the Freudian school, and in its founder as well, convincing evidence of any release worth mentioning from the inexorable family situation? This father complex, fanatically defended with such stubbornness and oversensitivity, is a cloak for religiosity misunderstood; it is a mysticism expressed in terms of biology and the family relation. As for Freud's idea of the "super-ego," it is a furtive attempt to smuggle in his time-honored image of Jehovah in the dress of psychological theory. When one does things like that, it is better to say so openly. For my part, I prefer to call things by the names under which they have always been known. The wheel of history must not be turned back, and man's advance toward a spiritual life, which began with the primitive rites of initiation, must not be denied. It is permissible for science to divide its field of enquiry and to set up limited hypotheses, for science must work in that way; but the human psyche may not be parcelled out. It is a whole which embraces consciousness, and is the mother of consciousness. Scientific thought, being only one of its functions, can never exhaust all the possibilities of life. The psychotherapist must not allow his vision to be colored by the glasses of pathology; he must never allow himself to forget that the ailing mind is a human mind, and that, for all its ailments, it shares in the whole of the psychic life of man. The psychotherapist must even be able to admit that the ego is ill for the very reason that it is cut off from the whole, and has lost its connection with mankind as well as with the spirit. The ego is indeed the "place of fears," as Freud says in *The Ego and the Id*, but only so long as it has not returned to the "father" and "mother." Freud shipwrecks on the question of Nicodemus: "Can a man enter his mother's womb a second time and be born again?" To compare small things with great, we might say that history repeats itself here, for the question once more comes to the front today in a domestic quarrel of modern psychology.

For thousands of years, rites of initiation have been teaching spiritual rebirth; yet, strangely enough, man forgets again and again the meaning of divine procreation. This is surely no evidence of a strong life of the spirit; and yet the penalty of misunderstanding is heavy, for it is nothing less than neurotic decay, embitterment, atrophy, and sterility. It is easy enough to drive the spirit out of the door, but when we have done so the salt of life grows flat—it loses its savor. Fortunately, we have proof that the spirit always renews its strength in the fact that the central teaching of the ancient initiations is handed on from generation to generation. Ever and again human beings arise who understand what is meant by the fact that God is our father. The equal balance of the flesh and the spirit is not lost to the world.

The contrast between Freud and myself goes back to essential differences in our basic assumptions. Assumptions are unavoidable, and this being so, it is wrong to pretend that we have made no assumptions. That is why I have dealt with fundamental questions; with these as a starting point, the manifold and detailed differences between Freud's views and my own can best be understood.

PSYCHOLOGY AND LITERATURE: THE POET

CREATIVENESS, like the freedom of the will, contains a secret. The psychologist can describe both these manifestations as processes, but he can find no solution of the philosophical problems they offer. Creative man is a riddle that we may try to answer in various ways, but always in vain, a truth that has not prevented modern psychology from turning now and again to the question of the artist and his art. Freud thought that he had found a key in his procedure of deriving the work of art from the personal experiences of the artist. It is true that certain possibilities lay in this direction, for it was conceivable that a work of art, no less than a neurosis, might be traced back to those knots in psychic life that we call the complexes. It was Freud's great discovery that neuroses have a causal origin in the psychic realm—that they take their rise from emotional states and from real or imagined childhood experiences. Certain of his followers, like Rank and Stekel, have taken up related lines of enquiry and have achieved important results. It is undeniable that the poet's psychic disposition permeates his work root and branch. Nor is there anything new in the statement that personal factors largely influence the poet's choice and use of his materials. Credit, however, must certainly be given to the Freudian school for showing how far reaching this influence is and in what curious ways it comes to expression.

Freud takes the neurosis as a substitute for a direct means of gratification. He therefore regards it as something inappropriate—a mistake, a dodge, an excuse, a voluntary blindness. To him it is essentially a shortcoming that should never have been. Since a neurosis, to all appearances, is nothing but a disturbance that is all the more irritating because it is without sense or meaning, few people will venture to say a good word for it. And a work of art is brought into questionable proximity with the neurosis when it is taken as something which can be analyzed in terms of the poet's repressions. In a sense it finds itself in good company, for religion and philosophy are regarded in the same light by Freudian psychology. No objection can be raised if it is admitted that this approach amounts to nothing more than the elucidation of those personal determinants without which a work of art is unthinkable. But should the claim be made that such an analysis accounts for the work of art itself, then a categorical denial is called for. The personal idiosyncrasies that creep into a work of art are not essential; in fact, the more we have to cope with these peculiarities, the less is it a question of art. What is essential in a work of art is that it should rise far above the realm of personal life and speak from the spirit and heart of the poet as man to the spirit and heart of mankind. The personal aspect is a limitation—and even a sin—in the realm of art. When a form of "art" is primarily personal it deserves to be treated as if it were a neurosis. There may be some validity in the idea held by the Freudian school that artists without exception are narcissistic—by which is meant that they are undeveloped persons with infantile and auto-erotic traits. The statement is only valid, however, for the artist as a person, and has nothing to do with the man as an artist. In his capacity of artist he is neither auto-erotic, nor hetero-erotic, nor erotic in any sense. He is objective and impersonal—even inhuman—for as an artist he is his work, and not a human being.

Every creative person is a duality or a synthesis of contradictory aptitudes. On the one side he is a human being with a personal life, while on the other side he is an impersonal, creative process. Since as a human being he may be sound or morbid, we must look at his psychic make-up to find the determinants of his personality. But we can only understand him in his capacity of artist by looking at his creative achievement. We should make a sad mistake if we tried to explain the mode of life of an

English gentleman, a Prussian officer, or a cardinal in terms of personal factors. The gentleman, the officer, and the cleric function as such in an impersonal role, and their psychic make-up is qualified by a peculiar objectivity. We must grant that the artist does not function in an official capacity—the very opposite is nearer the truth. He nevertheless resembles the types I have named in one respect, for the specifically artistic disposition involves an overweight of collective psychic life as against the personal. Art is a kind of innate drive that seizes a human being and makes him its instrument. The artist is not a person endowed with free will who seeks his own ends, but one who allows art to realize its purposes through him. As a human being he may have moods and a will and personal aims, but as an artist he is "man" in a higher sense—he is "collective man"—one who carries and shapes the unconscious, psychic life of mankind. To perform this difficult office it is sometimes necessary for him to sacrifice happiness and everything that makes life worth living for the ordinary human being.

All this being so, it is not strange that the artist is an especially interesting case for the psychologist who uses an analytical method. The artist's life cannot be otherwise than full of conflicts, for two forces are at war within him—on the one hand the common human longing for happiness, satisfaction, and security in life, and on the other a ruthless passion for creation which may go so far as to override every personal desire. The lives of artists are as a rule so highly unsatisfactory—not to say tragic—because of their inferiority on the human and personal side, and not because of a sinister dispensation. There are hardly any exceptions to the rule that a person must pay dearly for the divine gift of the creative fire. It is as though each of us were endowed at birth with a certain capital of energy. The strongest force in our make-up will seize and all but monopolize this energy, leaving so little over that nothing of value can come of it. In this way the creative force can drain the human impulses to such a degree that the personal ego must develop all sorts of bad qualities—ruthlessness, selfishness, and vanity (so-called "auto-erotism")—and even every kind of vice, in order to maintain the spark of life and to keep itself from being wholly bereft. The auto-erotism of artists resembles that of illegitimate or neglected children who from their tenderest years must protect themselves from the destructive influence of people who have no love to give them—who develop bad qualities for that very purpose and later maintain an invincible egocentrism by remaining all their lives infantile and helpless or by actively offending against the moral code or the law. How can we doubt that it is his art that explains the artist, and not the insufficiencies and conflicts of his personal life? These are nothing but the regrettable results of the fact that he is an artist—that is to say, a man who from his very birth has been called to a greater task than the ordinary mortal. A special ability means a heavy expenditure of energy in a particular direction, with a consequent drain from some other side of life.

It makes no difference whether the poet knows that his work is begotten, grows, and matures with him, or whether he supposes that by taking thought he produces it out of the void. His opinion of the matter does not change the fact that his own work outgrows him as a child its mother. The creative process has feminine quality, and the creative work arises from unconscious depths—we might say, from the realm of the mothers. Whenever the creative force predominates, human life is ruled and moulded by the unconscious as against the active will, and the conscious ego is swept along on a subterranean current, being nothing more than a helpless observer of events. The work in process becomes the poet's fate and determines his psychic development. It is not Goethe who creates *Faust* but *Faust* which creates Goethe. And what is *Faust* but a symbol? By this I do not mean an allegory that points to something all too familiar, but an expression that stands for something not clearly known and yet profoundly alive. Here it is something that lives in the soul of every German, and that Goethe has helped to bring to birth. Could we conceive of anyone but a German writing *Faust* or *Also sprach Zarathustra?* Both play upon something that reverberates in the German soul—a "primordial image," as Jakob Burckhardt once called it—the figure of a physician or teacher of mankind. The archetypal image of the wise man, the savior or redeemer, lies buried and dormant in man's unconscious since the dawn of culture; it is awakened whenever the times are out of joint and a human society is committed to a serious error. When people go astray they feel the need of a guide or teacher or even of the physician. These primordial images are numerous, but do not appear in the dreams of individuals or in works of art until they are called into being by the waywardness of the general outlook. When conscious life is characterized by one-sidedness and by a false attitude, then they are activated—one might say, "instinctively"—and come to light in the dreams of individuals and the visions of artists and seers, thus restoring the psychic equilibrium of the epoch.

In this way the work of the poet comes to meet the spiritual need of the society in which he lives, and for this reason his work means more to him than his personal fate, whether he is aware of this or not. Being essentially the instrument for his work, he is subordinate to it, and we have no reason for expecting him to interpret it for us. He has done the best that in him lies in giving it form, and he must leave the interpretation to others and to the future. To grasp its meaning, we must allow it to shape us as it once shaped him. Then we understand the nature of his experience. We see that he has drawn upon the healing and redeeming forces of the collective psyche that underlies consciousness with its isolation and its painful errors; that he has penetrated to that matrix of life in which all men are embedded, which imparts a common rhythm to all human existence, and allows the individual to communicate his feeling and his striving to mankind as a whole.

The secret of artistic creation and of the effectiveness of art is to be found in a return to the state of *participation mystique*—to that level of experience at which it is man who lives, and not the individual, and at which the weal or woe of the single human being does not count, but only human existence. This is why every great work of art is objective and impersonal, but none the less profoundly moves us each and all. And this is also why the personal life of the poet cannot be held essential to his art—but at most a help or a hindrance to his creative task. He may go the way of a Philistine, a good citizen, a neurotic, a fool, or a criminal. His personal career may be inevitable and interesting, but it does not explain the poet.

2

ANTI-INTELLECTUALISM IN PHILOSOPHY

Friedrich Nietzsche

In the philosophy of Friedrich Nietzsche (1844-1900), the logic of Darwinian evolution finds clear and uncompromising expression. If life is a struggle for existence in which the strong alone survive, then strength becomes the only virtue and weakness the greatest sin. What we need in the battle of life is not unselfishness or altruism but unrestrained egoism, not humility but pride, not goodness in the traditional sense but strength and power. Equality and democracy are contrary to the spirit of natural selection and the survival of the fittest; the goal of evolution is not the welfare of the masses but the creation of genius and a gifted aristocracy. It is by power, not by reason, that the destiny of men and nations is determined, and our social philosophy must be restated to recognize these facts. So Nietzsche argued in terms that strike us as surprisingly contemporary although he died more than fifty years ago.

Born in 1844 in a small village in Prussia where his father was the Lutheran minister, Nietzsche later studied at the University of Leipzig and was considered one of the university's most promising students. One afternoon at Leipzig he ran across Schopenhauer's The World as Will and Idea. *Taking the book home, he read it with increasing excitement and soon proclaimed himself a disciple of the great pessimist. From this early pessimism he was eventually rescued, however, by his contact with Darwin and the idea of evolution. When only twenty-four Nietzsche was appointed professor of classical philology at the University of Basel in Switzerland, but ten years later he retired from his professorship to devote himself entirely to writing. On August 25, 1900, he died in Weimar.*

Thus Spake Zarathustra *(1885) is Nietzsche's best-known book. It is an enigmatic work, however, a collection of parables, sermons, and poems purporting to be the gospel of the old Persian prophet whom we know in English as Zoroaster. Nietzsche's next two books,* Beyond Good and Evil *(1886) and* The Genealogy of Morals *(1887), are the clearest statements of his philosophy. These books contain some of the most discerning comment upon human nature and conduct to be found in the literature of philosophy, and it is upon the insight expressed here that Nietzsche's significance as a philosopher actually rests. We reprint several selections from* Beyond Good and Evil *which make clear the relevance of Nietzsche's thought to the age in which we live and reveal him as an uncompromising anti-intellectual. He challenges all the moral assumptions that our democratic and Christian civilization has taken for granted and adopts a forthright distrust of reason as one of his major principles.*

BEYOND GOOD AND EVIL

Prejudices of Philosophers

1

THE WILL TO TRUTH, which is to tempt us to many a hazardous enterprise, the famous Truthfulness of which all philosophers have hitherto spoken with respect, what questions has this Will to Truth not laid before us! What strange, perplexing, questionable questions! It is already a long story; yet it seems as if it were hardly commenced. Is it any wonder if we at last grow distrustful, lose patience, and turn impatiently away? *What* really is this "Will to Truth" in us? In fact we made a long halt at the question as to the origin of this Will—until at last we came to an absolute standstill before a yet more fundamental question. We inquired about the *value* of this Will. Granted that we want the truth: *why not rather* untruth? And uncertainty? Even ignorance? The problem of the value of truth presented itself before us—or was it we who presented ourselves before the problem? And could it be believed that it at last seems to us as if the problem had never been propounded before, as if we were the first to discern it, get a sight of it, and *risk raising it.* For there is risk in raising it, perhaps there is no greater risk.

2

Having kept a sharp eye on philosophers, and having read between their lines long enough, I now say to myself that the greater part of conscious thinking must be counted amongst the instinctive functions, and it is so even in the case of philosophical thinking; one has here to learn anew, as one learned anew about heredity and "innateness." As little as the act of birth comes into consideration in the whole process and procedure of heredity, just as little is "being-conscious" *opposed* to the instinctive in any decisive sense; the greater part of the conscious thinking of a philosopher is secretly influenced by his instincts, and forced into definite channels. And behind all logic and its seeming sovereignty of movement, there are valuations, or to speak more plainly, physiological demands, for the maintenance of a definite mode of life. For example, that the certain is worth more than the uncertain, that illusion is less valuable than "truth": such valuations, in spite of their regulative importance for us, might notwithstanding be only superficial valuations, special kinds of *niaiserie,* such as may be necessary for the maintenance of beings such as ourselves. Supposing, in effect, that man is not just the "measure of things."...

3

The falseness of an opinion is not for us any objection to it: it is here, perhaps, that our new language sounds most strangely. The question is, how far an opinion is life-furthering, life-preserving, species-preserving, perhaps species-rearing; and we are fundamentally inclined to maintain that the falsest opinions (to which the synthetic judgments *a priori* belong) are the most indispensable to us; that without a recognition of logical fictions, without a comparison of reality with the purely *imagined* world of the absolute and immutable, without a constant counterfeiting of the world by means of numbers, man could not live—that the renunciation of false opinions would be a renunciation of life, a negation of life. *To recognize untruth as a condition of life:* that is certainly to impugn the traditional ideas of value in a dangerous manner, and a philosophy which ventures to do so, has thereby alone placed itself beyond good and evil.

4

That which causes philosophers to be regarded half-distrustfully and half-mockingly is not the oft-repeated discovery how innocent they are—how often and easily they make mistakes and lose their way, in short, how childish and childlike they are—but that there is not enough honest dealing with them, whereas they all raise a loud and virtuous outcry when the problem of truthfulness is even hinted at in the remotest manner. They all pose as though their real opinions had been discovered and attained through the self-evolving of a cold, pure, divinely indifferent dialectic (in contrast to all sorts of mystics, who, fairer and foolisher, talk of "inspiration"); whereas, in fact, a prejudiced proposition, idea, or "suggestion," which is generally their heart's desire abstracted and refined, is defended by them with arguments sought out after the event. They are all advocates who do not wish to be regarded as such, generally astute defenders, also, of their prejudices, which they dub "truths"—and *very* far from having the conscience which bravely admits this to itself; very far from having the good taste of the courage which goes so far as to let this be understood, perhaps to warn friend or foe, or in cheerful confidence and self-ridicule.

5

It has gradually become clear to me what every great philosophy up till now has consisted of—namely, the confession of its originator, and a species of involuntary and unconscious autobiography; and moreover that the moral (or immoral) purpose in every philosophy has constituted the true vital germ out of which the entire plant has always grown. Indeed, to understand how the abstrusest metaphysical assertions of a philosopher have been arrived at, it is always well (and wise) to first ask oneself: "What morality do they (or does he) aim at?" Accordingly, I do not believe that an "impulse to knowledge" is the father of philosophy; but that another impulse, here as elsewhere, has only made use of knowledge (and mistaken knowledge!) as an instrument. For every impulse is imperious, and as *such,* attempts to philosophize. To be sure, in the case of scholars, in the case of really scientific men, it may be otherwise—"better," if you will; there there may really be such a thing as an "impulse to knowledge," some kind of small, independent clockwork, which, when well wound up, works away industriously to that end, *without* the rest of the scholarly impulses taking any material part therein. The actual "interests" of the scholar, therefore, are generally in quite another direction—in the family, perhaps, or in money-making, or in politics; it is, in fact, almost indifferent at what point of research his little machine is placed, and whether the hopeful young worker becomes a good philologist, a mushroom specialist, or a chemist; he is not *characterized* by becoming this or that. In the philosopher, on the contrary, there is absolutely nothing impersonal; and above all, his morality furnishes a decided and decisive testimony as to *who he is*—that is to say, in what order the deepest impulses of his nature stand to each other.

6

Psychologists should bethink themselves before putting down the instinct of self-preservation as the cardinal instinct of an organic being. A living thing seeks above all to *discharge* its strength—life itself is *Will to Power;* self-preservation is only one of the indirect and most frequent *results* thereof. In short, here, as everywhere else, let us beware of *superfluous* teleological principles!—one of which is the instinct of self-preservation (we owe it to Spinoza's inconsistency).

7

All psychology hitherto has run aground on moral prejudices and timidities, it has not dared to launch out into the depths. In so far as it is allowable to recognize in that which has hitherto been written, evidence of that which has hitherto been kept silent, it seems as if nobody had yet harbored the notion of psychology as the Morphology and *Development-doctrine of the Will to Power,* as I conceive of it. The power of moral prejudices has penetrated deeply into the most intellectual world, the world apparently most indifferent and unprejudiced, and has obviously operated in an injurious, obstructive, blinding, and distorting manner. A proper physiopsychology has to contend with unconscious antagonism in the heart of the investigator, it has "the heart" against it; even a doctrine of the reciprocal conditionalness of the "good" and the "bad" impulses, causes distress and aversion in a still strong and manly conscience—still more so, a doctrine of the derivation of all good impulses from bad ones. If, however, a person should regard even the emotions of hatred, envy, covetousness, and imperiousness as life-conditioning emotions, as factors which must be present, fundamentally and essentially, in the general economy of life (which must, therefore, be further developed if life is to be further developed), he will suffer from such a view of things as from seasickness. And yet this hypothesis is far from being the strangest and most painful in this immense and almost new domain of dangerous knowledge; and there are in fact a hundred good reasons why every one should keep away from it who *can* do so! On the other hand, if one has once drifted hither with one's bark, well! very good! now let us set our teeth firmly! let us open our eyes and keep our hand fast on the helm! We sail away right *over* morality, we crush out, we destroy perhaps the remains of our own morality by daring to make our voyage thither—but what do *we* matter! Never yet did a profounder world of insight reveal itself to daring travelers and adventurers, and the psychologist who thus "makes a sacrifice" will at least be entitled to demand in return that psychology shall once more be recognized as the queen of the sciences, for whose service and equipment the other sciences exist. For psychology is once more the path to the fundamental problems.

The Meaning of Nobility

1

Every elevation of "man" as a type has hitherto been the work of an aristocratic society and so it will always be—a society believing in a long scale of gradations of rank and differences of worth among human beings, and requiring slavery in some form or other. One must not give oneself to any humanitarian illusions about the history of the origin of an aristocratic society (that is to say, of the preliminary condition for the elevation of the type "man"): the truth is hard. Let us acknowledge unprejudicedly how every higher civilization hitherto has *originated!* Men still with a "natural" nature, barbarians in every terrible sense of the word, men of prey, still in possession of unbroken strength of will and desire for power, threw themselves upon weaker, more moral, more peaceful races (perhaps trading or cattle-rearing communities), or upon old mellow civilizations in which the final vital force was flickering out in brilliant fireworks of wit and depravity. In the beginning, the noble caste was always the barbarian caste; their superiority did not consist first of all in their physical, but in their psychical power—they were more *complete* men (which at every point also implies "more complete beasts").

2

The essential thing in a good and healthy aristocracy is that it should *not* regard itself as a function either of the kingship or the commonwealth, but as the *significance* and highest justification thereof—that it should therefore accept with a good conscience the sacrifice of a legion of individuals, who, *for its sake*, must be suppressed and reduced to imperfect men, to slaves and instruments. Its fundamental belief must be precisely that society is *not* allowed to exist for its own sake, but only as a foundation and scaffolding, by means of which a select class of beings may be able to elevate themselves to their highest duties, and in general to a higher *existence:* like those sun-seeking climbing plants in Java—they are called *Sipo Matador*—which encircle an oak so long and so often with their arms, until at last, high above it, but supported by it, they can unfold their tops in the open light, and exhibit their happiness.

3

To refrain mutually from injury, from violence, from exploitation, and put one's will on a par with that of others: this may result in a certain rough sense in good conduct among individuals when the necessary conditions are given (namely, the actual similarity of the individuals in amount of force and degree of worth, and their co-relation within one organization). As soon, however, as one takes this principle more generally, and if possible even as *the fundamental principle of society,* it immediately discloses what it really is—namely, a Will to the *denial* of life, a principle of dissolution and decay. Here one must think profoundly to the very basis and resist all sentimental weakness: life itself is *essentially* appropriation, injury, conquest of the strange and weak, suppression, severity, obtrusion of peculiar forms, incorporation, and at the least, putting it mildest, exploitation;—but why should one for ever use precisely these words on which for ages a disparaging purpose has been stamped? Even the organization within which, as was previously supposed, the individuals treat each other as equal—it takes place in every healthy aristocracy—must itself, if it be a living and not a dying organization, do all that towards other bodies, which the individuals within it refrain from doing to each other: it will have to be the incarnated Will to Power, it will endeavor to grow, to gain ground, attract to itself and acquire ascendency—not owing to any morality or immorality, but because it *lives,* and because life is precisely Will to Power. On no point, however, is the ordinary consciousness of Europeans more unwilling to be corrected than on this matter; people now rave everywhere, even under the guise of science, about coming conditions of society in which "the exploiting character" is to be absent:—that sounds to my ears as if they promised to invent a mode of life which should refrain from all organic functions. "Exploitation" does not belong to a depraved, or imperfect and primitive society: it belongs to the *nature* of the living being as a primary organic function; it is a consequence of the intrinsic Will to Power, which is precisely the Will to Life.—Granting that as a theory this is a novelty—as a reality it is the *fundamental fact* of all history: let us be so far honest toward ourselves!

4

In a tour through the many finer and coarser moralities which have hitherto prevailed or still prevail on the earth, I found certain traits recurring regularly together, and connected with one another, until finally two primary types revealed themselves to me, and a radical distinction was brought to light. There is *master-morality* and *slave-morality*. The distinctions of moral values have either originated in a ruling caste, pleasantly conscious of being different from the ruled—or among the ruled class, the slaves and dependents of all sorts.

In the first case, when it is the rulers who determine the conception "good," it is the exalted, proud disposition which is regarded as the distinguishing feature, and that which determines the order of rank. The noble type of man separates from himself the beings in whom the opposite of this exalted, proud disposition displays itself: he despises them. Let it at once be noted that in this first kind of morality the antithesis "good" and "bad" means practically the same as "noble" and "despicable";—the antithesis "good" and "*evil*" is of a different origin. The cowardly, the timid, the insignificant, and those thinking merely of narrow utility are despised; moreover, also, the distrustful with their constrained glances, the self-abasing, the dog-like kind of men who let themselves be abused, the mendicant flatterers, and above all the liars:—it is a fundamental belief of all aristocrats that the common people are untruthful. "We truthful ones"—the nobility in ancient Greece called themselves. It is obvious that everywhere the designations of moral value were at first applied to *men*, and were only derivatively and at a later period applied to *actions*.

The noble type of man regards *himself* as a determiner of values; he does not require to be approved of; he passes the judgment: "What is injurious to me is injurious in itself"; he knows that it is he himself only who confers honor on things; he is a *creator of values*. He honors whatever he recognizes in himself: such morality is self-glorification. In the foreground there is the feeling of plentitude, of power, which seeks to overflow, the happiness of high tension, the consciousness of a wealth which would fain give and bestow:—the noble man also helps the unfortunate, but not—or scarcely—out of pity, but rather from an impulse generated by the superabundance of power. The noble man honors in himself the powerful one, him also who has power over himself, who knows how to speak and how to keep silence, who takes pleasure in subjecting himself to severity and hardness, and has reverence for all that is severe and hard. "Wotan placed a hard heart in my breast," says an old Scandinavian Saga: it is thus rightly expressed from the soul of a proud Viking. Such a type of man is even proud of *not* being made for sympathy; the hero of the Saga therefore adds warningly: "He who has not a hard heart when young, will never have one." The noble and brave who think thus are the furthest removed from the morality which sees precisely in sympathy, or in acting for the good of others, or in *désintéressement*, the characteristic of the moral; faith in oneself, pride in oneself, a radical enmity and irony towards "selflessness," belong as definitely to noble morality as do a careless scorn and precaution in presence of sympathy and the "warm heart."

It is the powerful who *know* how to honor, it is their art, their domain for invention. The profound reverence for age and for tradition—all law rests on this double reverence—the belief and prejudice in favor of ancestors and unfavorable to newcomers, is typical in the morality of the powerful; and if, reversely, men of "modern ideas" believe almost instinctively in "progress" and the "future," and are more and more lacking in respect for old age, the ignoble origin of these "ideas" has complacently betrayed itself thereby. A morality of the ruling class, however, is more especially foreign and irritating to present-day taste in the sternness of its principle that one has duties only to one's equals; that one may act toward beings of a lower rank, toward all that is foreign, just as seems good to one, or "as the heart desires," and in any case "beyond good and evil"; it is here that sympathy and similar sentiments can have a place. The ability and obligation to exercise prolonged gratitude and prolonged revenge—both only within the circle of equals—artfulness in retaliation, *raffinement* of the idea in friendship, a certain necessity to have enemies (as outlets for the emotions of envy, quarrelsomeness, arrogance—in fact in order to be a good *friend*): all these are typical characteristics of the noble morality, which, as has been pointed out, is not the morality of "modern ideas," and is therefore at present difficult to realize, and also to unearth and disclose.

It is otherwise with the second type of morality, *slave-morality*. Supposing that the abused, the oppressed, the suffering, the unemancipated, the weary, and those uncertain of themselves, should moralize, what will be the common element in their moral estimates? Probably a pessimistic suspicion with regard to the entire situation of man will find expression, perhaps a condemnation of man, together with his situation. The slave has an unfavorable eye for the virtues of the powerful; he has a scepticism and distrust, a *refinement* of distrust of everything "good" that is there honored—he would fain persuade himself that the very happiness there is not genuine. On the other hand, *those* qualities which serve to alleviate the existence of sufferers are brought into prominence and flooded with light; it is here that sympathy, the kind, helping hand, the warm heart, patience, diligence, humility, and friendliness attain to honor; for here these are the most useful qualities, and almost the only means of supporting the burden of existence. Slave-morality is essentially the morality of utility.

Here is the seat of the origin of the famous antithesis "good" and "evil":—power and dangerousness are assumed to reside in the evil, a certain dreadfulness, subtlety, and strength, which do not admit of being despised. According to slave-morality, therefore, the "evil" man arouses fear; according to master-morality, it is precisely the "good" man who arouses fear and seeks to arouse it, while the bad man is regarded as the despicable being. The contrast attains its maximum when, in accordance with the logical consequences of slave-morality, a shade of depreciation—it may be slight and well intentioned—at last attaches itself to the "good" man of this morality; because, according to the servile mode of thought, the good man must in any case be the *safe* man: he is good-natured, easily deceived, perhaps a little stupid, *un bonhomme*. Everywhere that slave-morality gains the ascendency, language shows a tendency to approximate the significations of the words "good" and "stupid."—A last fundamental difference: the desire for *freedom*, the instinct for happiness and the refinements of the feeling of liberty belong as necessarily to slave-morals and morality, as artifice and enthusiasm in reverence and devotion are the regular symptoms of an aristocratic mode of thinking and estimating.

Our Virtues

1

Our Virtues?—It is probable that we, too, have still our virtues, although naturally they are not those sincere and massive virtues on account of which we hold our grandfathers in esteem and also at a little distance from us. We Europeans of the day after tomorrow, we firstlings of the twentieth century—with all our dangerous curiosity, our multifariousness and art of disguising, our mellow and seemingly sweetened cruelty in sense and spirit—we shall presumably, *if* we must have virtues, have those only which have come to agreement with our most secret and heartfelt inclinations, with our most ardent requirements: well, then, let us look for them in our labyrinths!—where, as we know, so many things lose themselves, so many things get quite lost! And is there anything finer than to *search* for one's own virtues? Is it not almost to *believe* in one's own virtues? But this "believing in one's own virtues"—is it not practically the same as what was formerly called one's "good conscience," that long, respectable pigtail of an idea, which our grandfathers used to hang behind their heads, and often enough also behind their understandings?

2

In these later ages, which may be proud of their humanity, there still remains so much fear of the "cruel wild beast," the mastering of which constitutes the very pride of these humaner ages—that even obvious truths have long remained unuttered, because they have the appearance of helping the finally slain wild beast back to life again.

One ought to learn anew about cruelty, and open one's eyes; one ought at last to learn impatience, in order that such immodest gross errors—as, for instance, have been fostered by ancient and modern philosophers with regard to tragedy—may no longer wander about virtuously and boldly. Almost everything that we call "higher culture" is based upon the spiritualizing and intensifying of *cruelty*—this is my thesis; the "wild beast" has not been slain at all, it lives, it flourishes, it has only been—transfigured. That which constitutes the painful delight of tragedy is cruelty; that which operates agreeably in so-called tragic sympathy, and at the basis even of everything sublime, up to the highest and most delicate thrills of metaphysics, obtains its sweetness solely from the intermingled ingredient of cruelty. What the Roman enjoys in the arena, the Christian in the ecstasies of the cross, the Spaniard at the sight of the faggot and stake, or of the bull fight, the present-day Japanese who presses his way to the tragedy, the workman of the Parisian suburbs who has a homesickness for bloody revolutions, the Wagnerienne who, with unhinged will, "undergoes" the performance of *Tristan and Isolde*—what all these enjoy, and strive with mysterious ardor to drink in, is "cruelty." Here, to be sure, we must put aside entirely the blundering psychology of former times, which could only teach with regard to cruelty that it originated at the sight of the suffering of *others:* there is an abundant, superabundant enjoyment even in one's own suffering, in causing one's own suffering—and wherever man has allowed himself to be persuaded to self-denial in the *religious* sense, or to self-mutilation, as among the Phoenicians and ascetics, or in general, to desensualization, decarnalization, and contrition, to Puritanical repentance spasms, to vivisection of conscience and to Pascal-like *sacrifizia dell' intelleto,* he is secretly allured and impelled forward by his cruelty, by the dangerous thrill of cruelty *toward himself.*

Finally, let us consider that even the seeker of knowledge operates as an artist and glorifier of cruelty, in that he compels his spirit to perceive *against* his own inclination, and often enough against the wishes of his heart:—he forces it to say Nay, where he would like to affirm, love, and adore; indeed, every instance of taking a thing profoundly and fundamentally, is a violation, an intentional injuring of the fundamental will of the spirit, which instinctively aims at appearance and superficiality—even in every desire for knowledge there is a drop of cruelty.

3

To be mistaken in the fundamental problem of "man and woman," to deny here the profoundest antagonism and the necessity for an eternally hostile tension, to dream here perhaps of equal rights, equal training, equal claims and obligations: that is a *typical* sign of shallow-mindedness; and a thinker who has proved himself shallow at this dangerous spot—shallow in instinct!—may generally be regarded as suspicious, nay more, as betrayed, as discovered; he will probably prove too "short" for all fundamental questions of life, future as well as present, and will be unable to descend into *any* of the depths. On the other hand, a man who has depth of spirit as well as of desires, and has also the depth of benevolence which is capable of severity and harshness, and easily confounded with them, can only think of women as *Orientals* do: he must conceive of her as a possession, as confinable property, as a being predestined for service and accomplishing her mission therein—he must take his stand in this matter upon the immense rationality of Asia, upon the superiority of the instinct of Asia, as the Greeks did formerly; those best heirs and scholars of Asia—who, as is well known, with their *increasing* culture and amplitude of power, from Homer to the time of Pericles, became gradually stricter toward woman, in short, more oriental. *How* necessary, *how* logical, even *how* humanely desirable this was, let us consider for ourselves!

4

The weaker sex has in no previous age been treated with so much respect by men as at present—this belongs to the tendency and fundamental taste of democracy, in the same way as disrespectfulness to old age—what wonder is it that abuse should be immediately made of this respect? They want more, they learn to make claims, the tribute of respect is at last felt to be well-nigh galling; rivalry for rights, indeed actual strife itself, would be preferred: in a word, woman is losing modesty. And let us immediately add that she is also losing taste. She is unlearning to *fear* man: but the woman who "unlearns to fear" sacrifices her most womanly instincts. That woman should venture forward when the fear-inspiring quality in man—or more definitely, the *man* in man—is no longer either desired or fully developed, is reasonable enough and also intelligible enough; what is more difficult to understand is that precisely thereby—woman deteriorates.

This is what is happening nowadays: let us not deceive ourselves about it! Wherever the industrial spirit has triumphed over the military and aristocratic spirit, woman strives for the economic and legal independence of a clerk: "woman as clerkess" is inscribed on the portal of the modern society which is in course of formation. While she thus appropriates new rights, aspires to be "master," and inscribes "progress" of woman on her flags and banners, the very opposite realizes itself with terrible obviousness: *woman retrogrades*. Since the French Revolution the influence of woman in Europe has *declined* in proportion as she has increased her rights and claims; and the "emancipation of woman," in so far as it is desired and demanded by women themselves (and not only by masculine shallowpates), thus proves to be a remarkable symptom of the increased weakening and deadening of the most womanly instincts. There is *stupidity* in this movement, an almost masculine stupidity, of which a well-reared woman—who is always a sensible woman—might be heartily ashamed. To lose the intuition as to the ground upon which she can most surely achieve victory; to neglect exercise in the use of her proper weapons; to let herself go before man, perhaps even "to the book," where formerly she kept herself in control and in refined, artful humility; to neutralize with her virtuous audacity man's faith in a *veiled*, fundamentally different ideal in woman, something eternally, necessarily feminine; to emphatically and loquaciously dissuade man from the idea that woman must be preserved, cared for, protected, and indulged, like some delicate, strangely wild, and often pleasant domestic animal; the clumsy and indignant collection of everything in the nature of servitude and bondage which the position of woman in the hitherto existing order of society has entailed and still entails (as though slavery were a counterargument, and not rather a condition of every higher culture, of every elevation of culture):—what does all this betoken, if not a disintegration of womanly instincts, a defeminizing?

That which inspires respect in woman, and often enough fear also, is her *nature*, which is more "natural" than that of man, her genuine, carnivora-like, cunning flexibility, her tiger claws beneath the glove, her *naiveté* in egoism, her untrainableness and innate wildness, the incomprehensibleness, extent and deviation of her desires and virtues. . . . That which, in spite of fear, excites one's sympathy for the dangerous and beautiful cat, "woman," is that she seems more afflicted, more vulnerable, more necessitous of love and more condemned to disillusionment than any other creature. Fear and sympathy: it is with these feelings that man has hitherto stood in the presence of woman, always with one foot already in tragedy, which rends while it delights.—What?—And all that is now to be at an end? And the *disenchantment* of woman is in progress? The tediousness of woman is slowly evolving? Oh Europe! Europe!

Jean-Paul Sartre

Sartre is a philosopher in the French tradition that has so often produced men who stand on the borderline between philosophy and literature. Voltaire, Rousseau, and Pascal come to mind as important examples. Like them, Sartre is distinguished by a remarkable versatility; he is as well known for his short stories, essays, plays, and literary criticism as for his philosophy. In temperament and point of view, however, Sartre is closer perhaps to Nietzsche than to his French predecessors, and the source of many of his ideas can be seen in Nietzsche's philosophy. But the thought of Sartre also bears the stamp of his own experience. In World War II he was captured by the Nazis, but he escaped and returned to Paris to fight in the French resistance forces. Out of the experiences of those years his existential philosophy was born, and his comments on commitment and decision, dread and death are charged with personal meaning.

Sartre's decision after World War II to make common cause with the Communists because to him they alone seemed serious in trying to do something about the state of affairs in France (and the world) perplexed some critics. He insisted, however, that he was not a Communist and did not accept party doctrines. Apparently a deep and genuine sense of social responsibility sometimes finds surprising expression in this action. More recently he has been openly critical of Communist behavior. Until the last few years Sartre was widely considered a mere littérateur and it was fashionable to treat him as an imaginative essayist rather than a serious thinker. Today he is recognized as one of the foremost advocates of existentialism, and existentialism is regarded one of the more significant movements in contemporary philosophy. In the English-speaking world the lecture Existentialism and Humanism (1945) is probably the best-known statement of Sartre's philosophy. His more systematic work, Being and Nothingness (1944), is much too abstract to have wide popular appeal; but his short stories are well known and often reprinted.

Two types of existentialism can be distinguished, the religious and the secular. Sartre belongs, of course, to the latter group, and insists upon atheism as one of the significant aspects of his own existential point of view. The essays by William James and Kierkegaard, included in the next section, suggest some aspects of religious existentialism. Sartre's essay, Existentialism and Humanism, partly reprinted here, presents in brief compass the central ideas in contemporary secular existentialism. It is a statement to which exception has been taken by some writers, for even among themselves the existentialists do not agree. For our purposes this essay contains a more useful introduction to the subject than anything available in the writings of other well-known exponents of existentialism such as Heidegger, Jaspers, or Marcel.

EXISTENTIALISM AND HUMANISM

I

MY PURPOSE HERE is to offer a defence of existentialism against several reproaches that have been laid against it.

First, it has been reproached as an invitation to people to dwell in quietism of despair. For if every way to a solution is barred, one would have to regard any action in this world as entirely ineffective, and one would arrive finally at a contemplative philosophy. Moreover, since contemplation is a luxury, this would be only another bourgeois philosophy. This is, especially, the reproach made by the Communists.

From another quarter we are reproached for having underlined all that is ignominious in the human situation, for depicting what is mean, sordid, or base to the neglect of certain things that possess charm and beauty and belong to the brighter side of human nature: for example, according to

[From *L'Existentialisme Est Un Humanisme*, Les Editions Nagel, Paris, 1946. English translation by Philip Mairet, Methuen & Co., Ltd., London (abridged). By permission of the publishers.]

the Catholic critic, Mlle. Mercier, we forget how an infant smiles. Both from this side and from the other we are also reproached for leaving out of account the solidarity of mankind and considering man in isolation. And this, say the Communists, is because we base our doctrine upon pure subjectivity—upon the Cartesian "I think"; which is the moment in which solitary man attains to himself; a position from which it is impossible to regain solidarity with other men who exist outside of the self.

From the Christian side, we are reproached as people who deny the reality and seriousness of human affairs. For since we ignore the commandments of God and all values prescribed as eternal, nothing remains but what is strictly voluntary. Everyone can do what he likes, and will be incapable, from such a point of view, of condemning either the point of view or the action of anyone else.

It is to these various reproaches that I shall endeavor to reply today; that is why I have entitled this brief exposition "Existentialism and Humanism." Many may be surprised at the mention of humanism in this connection, but we shall try to see in what sense we understand it. In any case, we can begin by saying that existentialism, in our sense of the word, is a doctrine that does render human life possible; a doctrine, also, which affirms that every truth and every action imply both an environment and a human subjectivity. The essential charge laid against us is, of course, that of overemphasis upon the evil side of human life. I have lately been told of a lady who, whenever she lets slip a vulgar expression in a moment of nervousness, excuses herself by exclaiming, "I believe I am becoming an existentialist." So it appears that ugliness is being identified with existentialism. That is why some people say we are "naturalistic," and if we are, it is strange to see how much we scandalize and horrify them, for no one seems to be much frightened or humiliated nowadays by what is properly called naturalism. Those who can quite well keep down a novel by Zola such as *La Terre* are sickened as soon as they read an existentialist novel. Those who appeal to the wisdom of the people—which is a sad wisdom—find ours sadder still. Indeed their excessive protests make me suspect that what is annoying them is not so much our pessimism, but, much more likely, our optimism. For at bottom, what is alarming in the doctrine that I am about to try to explain to you is—is it not?—that it confronts man with a possibility of choice. To verify this, let us review the whole question upon the strictly philosophic level. What, then, is this that we call existentialism?

Most of those who are making use of this word would be highly confused if required to explain its meaning. For since it has become fashionable, people cheerfully declare that this musician or that painter is "existentialist." A columnist in *Clartés* signs himself "The Existentialist," and, indeed the word is now so loosely applied to so many things that it no longer means anything at all. It would appear that, for the lack of any novel doctrine such as that of surrealism, all those who are eager to join in the latest scandal or movement now seize upon this philosophy in which, however, they can find nothing to their purpose. For in truth this is of all teachings the least scandalous and the most austere: it is intended strictly for experts and philosophers. All the same, it can easily be defined.

The question is only complicated because there are two kinds of existentialists. There are, on the one hand, the Christians, amongst whom I shall name Jaspers and Gabriel Marcel, both professed Catholics, and on the other the existential atheists, amongst whom we must place Heidegger as well as the French existentialists and myself. What they have in common is simply the fact that they believe that *existence* comes before *essence*—or, if you will, that we must begin from the subjective. What exactly do we mean by that?

If one considers an article of manufacture—as, for example, a book or a paper knife—one sees that it has been made by an artisan who had a conception of it; and he has paid attention, equally, to the conception of a paper knife and to the pre-existent technique of production which is a part of that conception and is, at bottom, a formula. Thus the paper knife is at the same time an article producible in a certain manner and one which, on the other hand, serves a definite purpose, for one cannot suppose that a man would produce a paper knife without knowing what it was for. Let us say, then, of the paper knife that its essence—that is to say, the sum of the formulas and the qualities which made its production and its definition possible—precedes its existence. The presence of such-and-such a paper knife or book is thus determined before my eyes. Here, then, we are viewing the world from a technical standpoint, and we can say that production precedes existence.

When we think of God as the creator, we are thinking of him most of the time, as a supernal artisan. . . . So that when God creates he knows precisely what he is creating. Thus, the conception of man in the mind of God is comparable to that of the paper knife in the mind of the artisan: God makes man according to a procedure and a conception, exactly as the artisan manufactures a paper knife, following a definition and a formula. Thus each individual man is the realization of a certain conception which dwells in the divine understanding. In the philosophic atheism of the eighteenth century, the notion of God is suppressed, but not, for all that, the idea that essence is prior to existence; something of that idea we still find everywhere, in Diderot, in Voltaire, and even in Kant. Man possesses a human nature; that "human nature," which is the conception of human being, is found in every man; which means that each man is a particular example of a universal conception, the conception of Man. Here again, the essence of man precedes that historic existence which we confront in experience.

Atheistic existentialism, of which I am a representative, declares with greater consistency that if God does not exist there is at least one being whose existence comes before its essence, a being which exists before it can be defined by any conception of it. That being is man or, as Heidegger has it, the human reality. What do we mean by saying that existence precedes essence? We mean that man first of all exists, encounters himself, surges up in the world—and defines himself afterwards. If man as the existentialist sees him is not definable, it is because to begin with he is nothing. He will not be anything until later, and then he will be what he makes of himself. Thus, there is no human nature, because there is no God to have a conception of it. Man simply is. Not that he is simply what he conceives himself to be, but he is what he wills, and as he conceives himself after already existing—as he wills to be after that leap towards existence. Man is nothing else but that which he makes of himself. That is the first principle of existentialism. And this is what people call its "subjectivity," using the word as a reproach against us. But what do we mean to say by this, but that man is of a greater dignity than a stone or a table? For we mean to say that man primarily exists—that man is, before all else, something which propels itself towards a future and is aware that it is doing so. Man is, indeed, a project which possesses a subjective life, instead of being a kind of moss, or a fungus, or a cauliflower. Before that projection of the self nothing exists; not even in the heaven of intelligence: man will only attain existence when he is what he purposes to be. Not, however, what he may wish to be. For what we usually understand by wishing or willing is a conscious decision taken—much more often than not—after we have made ourselves what we are. I may wish to join a party, to write a book, or to marry—but in such a case what is usually called my will is probably a manifestation of a prior and more spontaneous decision. If, however, it is true that existence is prior to essence, man is responsible for what he is. Thus, the first effect of existentialism is that it puts every man in possession of himself as he is, and places the entire responsibility for his existence squarely upon his own shoulders. And when we say that man is responsible for himself, we do not mean that he is responsible only for his own individuality, but that he is responsible for all men.

The word "subjectivism" is to be understood in two senses, and our adversaries play upon only one of them. Subjectivism means, on the one hand, the freedom of the individual subject and, on the other, that man cannot pass beyond human subjectivity. It is the latter which is the deeper meaning of existentialism. When we say that man chooses himself, we do mean that every one of us must choose himself; but by that we also mean that in choosing for himself he chooses for all men. For in effect, of all the actions a man may take in order to create himself as he wills to be, there is not one which is not creative, at the same time, of an image of man such as he believes he ought to be. To choose between this or that is at the same time to affirm the value of that which is chosen; for we are unable ever to choose the worse. What we choose is always the better; and nothing can be better for us unless it is better for all. If, moreover, existence precedes essence and we will to exist at the same time as we fashion our image, that image is valid for all and for the entire epoch in which we find ourselves. Our responsibility is thus much greater than we had supposed, for it concerns mankind as a whole. If I am a worker, for instance, I may choose to join a Christian rather than a Communist trade union. And if, by that membership, I choose to signify that resignation is, after all, the attitude that best becomes a man, that man's kingdom is not upon this earth, I do not commit myself alone to that view. Resignation is my will for everyone, and my action is, in consequence, a commitment on behalf of all mankind. Or if, to take a more personal case, I decide to marry and to have children, even though this decision proceeds simply from my situation, from my passion or my desire, I am thereby committing not only myself but humanity as a whole, to the practice of monogamy. I am thus responsible for myself and for all men, and I am creating a certain image of man as I would have him to be. In fashioning myself I fashion man.

II

This may enable us to understand what is meant by such terms—perhaps a little grandiloquent—as anguish, abandonment, and despair. As you will soon see, it is very simple. First, what do we mean by anguish? The existentialist frankly states that man is in anguish. His meaning is as follows—When a man commits himself to anything, fully realizing that he is not only choosing what he will be, but is thereby at the same time a legislator deciding for the whole of mankind—in such a moment a man cannot escape from the sense of complete and profound responsibility. There are many, indeed, who show no such anxiety. But we affirm that they are merely disguising their anguish or are in flight from it. Certainly, many people think that in what they are doing they commit no one but themselves to anything: and if you ask them, "What would happen if everyone did so?" they shrug their shoulders and reply, "Everyone does not do so." But in truth, one ought always to ask oneself what would happen if everyone did as one is doing; nor can one escape from that disturbing thought except by a kind of self-deception. The man who lies in self-excuse, by saying "Everyone will not do it" must be ill at ease in his conscience, for the act of lying implies the universal value which it denies. By its very disguise his anguish reveals itself. This is the anguish that Kierkegaard called "the anguish of Abraham." You know the story: An angel commanded Abraham to sacrifice his son: and obedience was obligatory, if it really was an angel who had appeared and said, "Thou, Abraham, shalt sacrifice thy son." But anyone in such a case would wonder, first, whether it was indeed an angel and secondly, whether I am really Abraham. Where are the proofs?

I shall never find any proof whatever; there will be no sign to convince me of it. If a voice speaks to me, it is still I myself who must decide whether the voice is or is not that of an angel. If I regard a certain course of action as good, it is only I who choose to say that it is good and not bad. There is nothing to show that I am Abraham; nevertheless, I also am obliged at every instant to perform actions which are examples. Everything happens to every man as though the whole human race had its eyes fixed upon what he is doing and regulated its conduct accordingly. So every man ought to say, "Am I really a man who has the right to act in such a manner that humanity regulates itself by what I do?" If a man does not say that, he is dissembling his anguish. Clearly, the anguish with which we are concerned here is not one that could lead to quietism or inaction. It is anguish pure and simple, of the kind well known to all those who have borne responsibilities. When, for instance, a military leader takes upon himself the responsibility for an attack and sends a number of men to their death, he chooses to do it and at bottom he alone chooses. No doubt he acts under a higher command, but its orders, which are more general, require interpretation by him and upon that interpretation depends the life of ten, fourteen, or twenty men. In making the decision, he cannot but feel a certain anguish. All leaders know that anguish. It does not prevent their acting, on the contrary it is the very condition of their action, for the action presupposes that there is a plurality of possibilities, and in choosing one of these, they realize that it has value only because it is chosen. Now it is anguish of that kind which existentialism describes, and moreover, as we shall see, makes explicit through direct responsibility towards other men who are concerned. Far from being a screen which could separate us from action, it is a condition of action itself.

And when we speak of "abandonment"—a favorite word of Heidegger—we only mean to say that God does not exist, and that it is necessary to draw the consequences of his absence right to the end. The existentialist is strongly opposed to a certain type of secular moralism which seeks to suppress God at the least possible expense. Toward 1880, when the French professors endeavored to formulate a secular morality, they said something like this:—God is a useless and costly hypothesis, so we will do without it. However, if we are to have morality, a society, and a law-abiding world, it is essential that certain values should be taken seriously; they must have an *a priori* existence ascribed to them. It must be considered obligatory *a priori* to be honest, not to lie, not to beat one's wife, to bring up children, and so forth; so we are going to do a little work on this subject, which will enable us to show that these values exist all the same, inscribed in an intelligible heaven although, of course, there is no God. In other words—and this is, I believe, the purport of all that we in France call radicalism—nothing will be changed if God does not exist; we shall rediscover the same norms of honesty, progress, and humanity, and we shall have disposed of God as an out-of-date hypothesis which will die away quietly of itself.

The existentialist, on the contrary, finds it extremely embarrassing that God does not exist, for there disappears with Him all possibility of finding values in an intelligible heaven. There can no longer be any good *a priori,* since there is no infinite and perfect consciousness to think it. It is nowhere written that "the good" exists, that one must be honest or must not lie, since we are now upon the plane where there are only men. Dostoevski once wrote, "If God did not exist, everything would be permitted"; and that, for existentialism, is the starting point. Everything is indeed permitted if God does not exist, and man is in consequence forlorn, for he cannot find anything to depend upon either within or outside himself. He discovers forthwith that he is without excuse. For if indeed existence precedes essence, one will never be able to explain one's action by reference to a given and specific human nature; in other words, there is no determinism—man is free, man *is* freedom.

Thus we have neither behind us, nor before us in a luminous realm of values, any means of justification or excuse. We are left alone, without excuse. That is what I mean when I say that man is condemned to be free. Condemned, because he did not create himself, yet is nevertheless at liberty, and from the moment that he is thrown into this world he is responsible for everything he does. The existentialist does not believe in the power of passion. He will never regard a grand passion as a destructive torrent, upon which a man is swept into certain actions as by fate, and which, therefore, is an excuse for them. He thinks that man is responsible for his passion. Neither will an existentialist think that a man can find help through some sign being vouchsafed upon earth for his orientation: for he thinks that the man himself interprets the sign as he chooses. He thinks that every man, without any support or help whatever, is condemned at every instant to invent man. As Ponge has written in a very fine article, "Man is the future of man." That is exactly true. Only, if one took this to mean that the future is laid up in Heaven, that God knows that it is, it would be false, for then it would no longer even be a future. If, however, it means that, whatever man may now appear to be, there is a future to be fashioned, a virgin future that awaits him—then it is a true saying. But in the present one is forsaken.

As an example by which you may the better understand this state of abandonment, I will refer to the case of a pupil of mine, who sought me out in the following circumstances. His father was quarreling with his mother and was also inclined to be a "collaborator"; his elder brother had been killed in the German offensive of 1940 and this young man, with a sentiment somewhat primitive but generous, burned to avenge him. His mother was living alone with him, deeply afflicted by the semitreason of his father and by the death of her eldest son, and her one consolation was in this young man. But he, at this moment, had the choice between going to England to join the Free French Forces or of staying near his mother and helping her to live. He fully realized that this woman lived only for him and that his disappearance—or perhaps his death—would plunge her into despair. He also realized that, concretely and in fact, every action he performed on his mother's behalf would be sure of effect in the sense of aiding her to live, whereas anything he did in order to go and fight would be an ambiguous action which might vanish like water into sand and serve no purpose. For instance, to set out for England, he would have to wait indefinitely in a Spanish camp on the way through Spain; or, on arriving in England or in Algiers, he might be put into an office to fill up forms. Consequently, he found himself confronted by two very different modes of action; the one concrete, immediate, but directed toward only one individual; and the other an action addressed to an end infinitely greater, a national collectivity, but for that very reason ambiguous—and it might be frustrated on the way.

At the same time, he was hesitating between two kinds of morality; on the one side the morality of sympathy, of personal devotion, and, on the other side, a morality of wider scope but of more debatable validity. He had to choose between those two. What could help him to choose? Could the Christian doctrine? No. Christian doctrine says: Act with charity, love your neighbor, deny yourself for others, choose the way which is hardest, and so forth. But which is the harder road? To whom does one owe the more brotherly love, the patriot or the mother? Which is the more useful aim, the general one of fighting in and for the whole community, or the precise aim of helping one particular person to live? Who can give an answer to that *a priori?* No one. Nor is it given in any ethical scripture. The Kantian ethic says, Never regard another as a means, but always as an end. Very well; if I remain with my mother, I shall be regarding her as the end and not as a means: but by the same token I am in danger of treating as means those who are fighting on my behalf; and the converse is also true, that if I go to the aid of the combatants I shall be treating them as the end at the risk of treating my mother as a means.

If values are uncertain, if they are still too abstract to determine the particular, concrete case under consideration, nothing remains but to trust in our instincts. That is what this young man tried to do; and when I saw him he said, "In the end, it is feeling that counts; the direction in which it is really pushing me is the one I ought to choose. If I feel that I love my mother enough to sacrifice everything else for her—my will to be avenged, all my longings for action and adventure—then I stay with her. If, on the contrary, I feel that my love for her is not enough, I go." But how does one estimate the strength of a feeling? The value of his feeling for his mother was determined precisely by the fact that he was standing by her. I may say that I love a certain friend enough to sacrifice such or such a sum of money for him, but I cannot prove that unless I have done it. I may say, "I love my mother enough to remain with her," if actually I have remained with her. I can only estimate the strength of this affection if I have performed an action by which it is defined and ratified. But if I then appeal to this affection to justify my action, I find myself drawn into a vicious circle.

In other words, feeling is formed by the deeds that one does; therefore I cannot consult it as a guide to action. And that is to say that I can neither seek within myself for an authentic impulse to action, nor can I expect, from some ethic, formulas that will enable me to act. You may say that the youth did, at least, go to a professor to ask for advice. But if you seek counsel—from a priest, for example—you have selected that priest; and at bottom you already knew, more or less, what he would advise. In other words, to choose an adviser is nevertheless to commit oneself by that choice. If you are a Christian, you will say, "Consult a priest"; but there are collaborationists, priests who are resisters, and priests who wait for the tide to turn: which will you choose? Had this young man chosen a priest of the resistance, or one of the collaboration, he would have decided beforehand the kind of advice he was to receive. Similarly, in coming to me, he knew what advice I should give him, and I had but one reply to make. You are free, therefore choose—that is to say, invent. No rule of general morality can show you what you ought to do: no signs are vouchsafed in this world. That is what "abandonment" implies, that we ourselves decide our being. And with this abandonment goes anguish.

As for "despair," the meaning of this expression is extremely simple. It merely means that we limit ourselves to a reliance upon that which is within our wills, or within the sum of the probabilities which render our action feasible. Whenever one wills anything, there are always these elements of probability. If I am counting upon a visit from a friend, who may be coming by train or by tram, I presuppose that the train will arrive at the appointed time, or that the tram will not be derailed. I remain in the realm of possibilities; but one does not rely upon any possibilities beyond those that are strictly concerned in one's action. Beyond the point at which the possibilities under consideration cease to affect my action, I ought to disinterest myself. For there is no God and no prevenient design, which can adapt the world and all its possibilities to my will. When Descartes said, "Conquer yourself rather than the world," what he meant was, at bottom, the same—that we should act without hope.

III

In the light of all this, what people reproach us with is not, after all, our pessimism but the sternness of our optimism. If people condemn our works of fiction, in which we describe characters that are base, weak, cowardly, and sometimes even frankly evil, it is not only because those characters are base, weak, cowardly or evil. For suppose that, like Zola, we showed that the behavior of these characters was caused by their heredity, or by the action of their environment upon them, or by determining factors, psychic or organic. People would be reassured, they would say, "You see, that is what we are like, no one can do anything about it." But the existentialist, when he portrays a coward, shows him as responsible for his cowardice. He is not like that on account of a cowardly heart or lungs or cerebrum, he has not become like that because he has made himself into a coward by his actions. There is no such thing as a cowardly temperament. There are nervous temperaments; there is what is called impoverished blood, and there are also rich temperaments. But the man whose blood is poor is not a coward for all that, for what produces cowardice is the act of giving up or giving way; and a temperament is not an action. A coward is defined by the deed that he has done. What people feel obscurely, and with horror, is that the coward as we present him is guilty of being a coward. What people would prefer would be to be born either a coward or a hero. One of the charges most often laid against the *Chemins de la Liberté* is something like this—"But, after all, these people being so base, how can you make them into heroes?" That objection is really rather comic, for it implies that people are born heroes: and that is, at bottom, what such people would like to think. If you are born cowards, you can be quite content. You can do nothing about it and you will be cowards all your lives whatever you do; and if you are born heroes you can again be quite content; you will be heroes all your lives, eating and drinking heroically. Whereas, the existentialist says that the coward makes himself cowardly, the hero makes himself heroic; and that there is always a possibility for the coward to give up cowardice and for the hero to stop being a hero. What counts is the total commitment, and it is not by a particular case or particular action that you are committed altogether.

We have now, I think, dealt with a certain number of the reproaches against existentialism. You have seen that it cannot be regarded as a philosophy of quietism since it defines man by his action; nor as a pessimistic description of man, for no doctrine is more optimistic, the destiny of man is placed within himself. Nor is it an attempt to discourage man from action since it tells him that there is no hope except in his action, and that the one thing which permits him to have life is the deed. Upon this level therefore, what we are considering is an ethic of action and self-commitment.

In our view, man finds himself in an organized situation in which he is himself involved: his choice involves mankind in its entirety, and he cannot avoid choosing. Either he must remain single, or he must marry without having children, or he must marry and have children. In any case, and whichever he may choose, it is impossible for him, in respect of this situation, not to take complete responsibility. Doubtless he chooses without reference to any pre-established values, but it is unjust to tax him with caprice. Rather let us say that the moral choice is comparable to the construction of a work of art.

I mention the work of art only by way of comparison. That being understood, does anyone reproach an artist, when he paints a picture, for not following rules established *a priori?* Does one ever ask what is the picture that he ought to paint? As everyone knows, there is no predefined picture for him to make; the artist applies himself to the composition of a picture, and the picture that ought to be made is precisely that which he will have made. As everyone knows, there are no esthetic values *a priori,* but there are values which will appear in due course in the coherence of the picture, in the relation between the will to create and the finished work. No one can tell what the painting of tomorrow will be like; one cannot judge a painting until it is done. What has that to do with morality? We are in the same creative situation. We never speak of a work of art as irresponsible; when we are discussing a canvas by Picasso, we understand very well that the composition became what it is at the time when he was painting it, and that his works are part and parcel of his entire life.

It is the same upon the plane of morality. There is this in common between art and morality, that in both we have to do with creation and invention. We cannot decide *a priori* what it is that should be done. I think it was made sufficiently clear to you in the case of that student who came to see me, that to whatever ethical system he might appeal, the Kantian or any other, he could find no sort of guidance whatever; he was obliged to invent the law for himself. Certainly we cannot say that this man, in choosing to remain with his mother—that is, in taking sentiment, personal devotion and concrete charity as his moral foundations—would be making an irresponsible choice, nor could we do so if he preferred the sacrifice of going away to England. Man makes himself; he is not found ready-made; he makes himself by the choice of his morality, and he cannot but choose a morality, such is the pressure of circumstances upon him. We define man only in relation to his commitments; it is therefore absurd to reproach us for irresponsibility in our choice.

We have to take things as they are. And moreover, to say that we invent values means neither more nor less than this; that there is no sense in life *a priori.* Life is nothing until it is lived; but it is yours to make sense of, and the value of it is nothing else but the sense that you choose. Therefore, you can see that there is a possibility of creating a human community. I have been reproached for suggesting that existentialism is a form of humanism: people have said to me, "But you have written in your *Nausée* that the humanists are wrong, you have even ridiculed a certain type of humanism, why do you now go back upon that?" In reality, the word humanism has two very different meanings. One may understand by humanism a theory which upholds man as the end-in-itself and as the supreme value. Humanism in this sense appears, for instance, in Cocteau's story *Round the World in 80 Hours,* in which one of the characters declares, because he is flying over mountains in an airplane, "Man is magnificent!" This signifies that although I, personally, have not built airplanes, I have the benefit of those particular inventions and that I personally, being a man, can consider myself responsible for, and honored by, achievements that are peculiar to some men. It is to assume that we can ascribe value to man according to the most distinguished deeds of certain men. That kind of humanism is absurd, for only the dog or the horse would be in a position to pronounce a general judgment upon man and declare that he is magnificent, which they have never been such fools as to do—at least, not as far as I know. But neither is it admissible that a man should pronounce judgment upon Man. Existentialism dispenses with any judgment of this sort: an existentialist will never take man as the end, since man is still to be determined. And we have no right to believe that humanity is something to which we could set up a cult, after the manner of Auguste Comte. We do not want a humanism like that.

But there is another sense of the word, of which the fundamental meaning is this: Man is all the time outside of himself: it is in projecting and losing himself beyond himself that he makes man to exist; and, on the other hand, it is by pursuing transcendent aims that he himself is able to exist. Since man is thus self-surpassing, and can grasp objects only in relation to his self-surpassing, he is himself the heart and center of his transcendence. There is no other universe except the human universe, the universe of human subjectivity. This relation of transcendence as constitutive of man (not in the sense that God is transcendent, but in the sense of self-surpassing) with subjectivity (in such a sense that man is not shut up in himself but forever present in a human universe)—it is this that we call existential humanism. This is humanism, because we remind man that there is no legislator but himself; that he himself, thus abandoned, must decide for himself; also because we show that it is not by turning back upon himself, but always by seeking, beyond himself, an aim which is one of liberation or of some particular realization, that man can realize himself as truly human.

3

RELIGIOUS EXISTENTIALISM

William James

William James was the first great American philosopher, the first American to develop a philosophy that attracted enthusiastic disciples in Europe and became one of the important systems of thought in the Western world. Although the pragmatism of James is essentially American in spirit, it gave clear, forceful expression to the spirit of the age in which he lived and achieved a prestige and influence for its author such as no American had known before.

Throughout his life James had a lively interest in religion. In the experience of a wide variety of people, he found that religion worked constructively for a deeply satisfying life. From the pragmatic point of view, as he insisted repeatedly: "The whole defense of religious faith hinges upon action." In The Varieties of Religious Experience, from which our present selection is taken, James describes with rare psychological insight the part played by religion in the crises of life where a man's personal destiny is determined, where he discovers a meaning and purpose that alone makes life worthwhile, and where he finds a faith that meets needs of the human spirit which reason cannot satisfy. These are aspects of experience emphasized in contemporary existentialism and James' discussion provides an excellent introduction to religious existentialism.

Born in New York City in 1842, James enrolled at Harvard University when he was about twenty and for the next forty-six years was connected with that institution. His interest in experimental physiology and psychology led him to the study of medicine and, after a winter at the University of Berlin, he took a degree in medicine at Harvard and was appointed instructor in physiology there. Gradually but surely he began working his way from physiology through psychology to philosophy.

In 1890 James published an influential two-volume work on The Principles of Psychology, and in 1897, when he was fifty-five, his first book in philosophy, The Will to Believe and Other Essays in Popular Philosophy. Several years later he delivered the Gifford Lectures in Edinburgh (a signal distinction among philosophers) which were published under the title The Varieties of Religious Experience. Like his earlier work on psychology, this volume has been widely read by layman as well as scholars. By the time his lectures on Pragmatism were given (in 1906) James was a well-known and influential figure. In 1910 he was elected to the French Academy of Moral and Political Sciences; he died in 1912. Among numerous philosophers influenced by James in this country, John Dewey was the ablest and shared with him the leadership of the strong group of American pragmatists.

THE SIGNIFICANCE OF RELIGIOUS EXPERIENCE

Conclusions

I

THE PIVOT ROUND which the religious life, as we have traced it, revolves, is the interest of the individual in his private personal destiny. Religion, in short, is a monumental chapter in the history of human egotism. The gods believed in—whether by crude savages or by men disciplined intellectually—agree with each other in recognizing personal calls. Religious thought is carried on in terms of personality, this being, in the world of religion, the one fundamental fact. Today, quite as much as at any previous age, the religious individual tells you that the divine meets him on the basis of his personal concerns.

Science, on the other hand, has ended by utterly repudiating the personal point of view. She catalogues her elements and records her laws indifferent as to what purpose may be shown forth by them, and constructs her theories quite careless of their bearing on human anxieties and fates. Though the scientist may individually nourish a religion, and be a theist in his irresponsible hours, the days are over when it could be said that for Science herself the heavens declare the glory of God and the firmament showeth his handiwork. Our solar system, with its harmonies, is seen now as but one passing case of a certain sort of moving equilibrium in the heavens, realized by a local accident in an appalling wilderness of worlds where no life can exist. In a span of time which as a cosmic interval will count but as an hour, it will have ceased to be. The Darwinian notion of chance production, and subsequent destruction, speedy or deferred, applies to the largest as well as to the smallest facts. It is impossible, in the present temper of the scientific imagination, to find in the driftings of the cosmic atoms, whether they work on the universal or on the particular scale, anything but a kind of aimless weather, doing and undoing, achieving no proper history, and leaving no result. Nature has no one distinguishable ultimate tendency with which it is possible to feel a sympathy. In the vast rhythm of her processes, as the scientific mind now follows them, she appears to cancel herself. The books of natural theology which satisfied the intellects of our grandfathers seem to us quite grotesque, representing, as they did, a God who conformed the largest things of nature to the paltriest of our private wants. The God whom science recognizes must be a God of universal laws exclusively, a God who does a wholesale, not a retail business. He cannot accommodate his processes to the convenience of individuals. The bubbles on the foam which coats a stormy sea are floating episodes, made and unmade by the forces of the wind and water. Our private selves are like those bubbles, their destinies weigh nothing and determine nothing in the world's irremediable currents of events.

In spite of the appeal which this impersonality of the scientific attitude makes to a certain magnanimity of temper, I believe it to be shallow, and I can now state my reason in comparatively few words. That reason is that so long as we deal with the cosmic and the general, we deal only with the symbols of reality, but *as soon as we deal with private and personal phenomena as such, we deal with realities in the completest sense of the term.* I think I can easily make clear what I mean by these words.

The world of our experience consists at all times of two parts, an objective and a subjective part, of which the former may be incalculably more extensive than the latter, and yet the latter can never be omitted or suppressed. The objective part is the sum total of whatsoever at any given time we may be thinking of, the subjective part is the inner "state" in which the thinking comes to pass. What we think of may be enormous—the cosmic times and spaces, for example—whereas the inner state may be the most fugitive and paltry activity of mind. Yet the cosmic objects, so far as the experience yields them, are but ideal pictures of something whose existence we do not inwardly possess but only point at outwardly, while the inner state is our very experience itself; its reality and that of our experience are one. A conscious field *plus* its object as felt or thought of *plus* an attitude towards the object *plus* the sense of a self to whom the attitude belongs—such a concrete bit of personal experience may be a small bit, but it is a solid bit so long as it lasts; not hollow, not a mere abstract element of experience, such as the "object" is when taken all alone. It is a *full* fact, even though it be an insignificant fact; it is of the *kind* to which all realities whatsoever must belong; the motor currents of the world run through the like of it; it is on the line connecting real events with real events. That unsharable feeling which each one of us has of the pinch of his individual destiny as he privately feels it rolling out on fortune's wheel may be disparaged for its egotism, may be sneered at as unscientific, but it is the one thing that fills up the measure of our concrete actuality, and any would-be existent that should lack such a feeling, or its analogue, would be a piece of reality only half made up.

If this be true, it is absurd for science to say that the egotistic elements of experience should be suppressed. The axis of reality runs solely through the egotistic places—they are strung upon it like so many beads. To describe the world with all the various feelings of the individual pinch of destiny, all the various spiritual attitudes, left out from the description—they being as describable as anything else—would be something like offering a printed bill of fare as the equivalent for a solid meal. Religion makes no such blunder. The individual's religion may be egotistic, and those private realities which it keeps in touch with may be narrow enough; but at any rate it always remains infinitely less hollow and abstract, as far as it goes, than a science which prides itself on taking no account of anything private at all.

A bill of fare with one real raisin on it instead of the word "raisin," with one real egg instead of the word "egg," might be an inadequate meal, but it would at least be a commencement of reality. I think, therefore, that however particular questions connected with our individual destinies may be answered, it is only by acknowledging them as genuine questions, and living in the sphere of thought which they open up, that we become profound. But to live thus is to be religious; so I unhesitatingly repudiate the survival-theory of religion,* as being founded on an egregious mistake. It does not follow, because our ancestors made

* The notion that religion is probably only an anachronism, a case of "survival," a relapse into a mode of thought which humanity as it becomes more enlightened has outgrown. [ED.]

so many errors of fact and mixed them with their religion, that we should therefore leave off being religious at all. By being religious we establish ourselves in possession of ultimate reality at the only points at which reality is given us to guard. Our responsible concern is with our private destiny, after all.

You see now why I have been so individualistic throughout these lectures, and why I have seemed so bent on rehabilitating the element of feeling in religion and subordinating its intellectual part. Individuality is founded in feeling; and the recesses of feeling, the darker, blinder strata of character, are the only places in the world in which we catch real fact in the making, and directly perceive how events happen, and how work is actually done. Compared with this world of living individualized feelings, the world of generalized objects which the intellect contemplates is without solidity or life. As in stereoscopic or kinetoscopic pictures seen outside the instrument, the third dimension, the movement, the vital element, are not there. We get a beautiful picture of an express train supposed to be moving, but where in the picture, as I have heard a friend say, is the energy or the fifty miles an hour?

II

Let us agree, then, that Religion, occupying herself with personal destinies and keeping thus in contact with the only absolute realities which we know, must necessarily play an eternal part in human history. The next thing to decide is what she reveals about those destinies, or whether indeed she reveals anything distinct enough to be considered a general message to mankind.

Both thought and feeling are determinants of conduct, and the same conduct may be determined either by feeling or by thought. When we survey the whole field of religion, we find a great variety in the thoughts that have prevailed there; but the feelings on the one hand and the conduct on the other are almost always the same, for Stoic, Christian, and Buddhist saints are practically indistinguishable in their lives. The theories which Religion generates, being thus variable, are secondary; and if you wish to grasp her essence, you must look to the feelings and the conduct as being the more constant elements. It is between these two elements that the short circuit exists on which she carries on her principal business, while the ideas and symbols and other institutions form loop-lines which may be perfections and improvements, and may even some day all be united into one harmonious system, but which are not to be regarded as organs with an indispensable function, necessary at all times for religious life to go on. This seems to me the first conclusion which we are entitled to draw from the phenomena we have passed in review.

The next step is to characterize the feelings. To what psychological order do they belong?

The warring gods and formulas of the various religions do indeed cancel each other, but there is a certain uniform deliverance in which religions all appear to meet. It consists of two parts:—

1. An uneasiness; and
2. Its solution.

1. The uneasiness, reduced to its simplest terms, is a sense that there is *something wrong about us* as we naturally stand.

2. The solution is a sense that *we are saved from the wrongness* by making proper connection with the higher powers.

In those more developed minds which alone we are studying, the wrongness takes a moral character, and the salvation takes a mystical tinge. I think we shall keep well within the limits of what is common to all such minds if we formulate the essence of their religious experience in terms like these:—

The individual, so far as he suffers from his wrongness and criticizes it, is to that extent consciously beyond it, and in at least possible touch with something higher, if anything higher exist. Along with the wrong part there is thus a better part of him, even though it may be but a most helpless germ. With which part he should identify his real being is by no means obvious at this stage; but when stage 2 (the stage of solution or salvation) arrives,* the man identifies his real being with the germinal higher part of himself; and does so in the following way. *He becomes conscious that this higher part is conterminous and continuous with a MORE of the same quality, which is operative in the universe outside of him, and which he can keep in working touch with, and in a fashion get on board of and save himself when all his lower being has gone to pieces in the wreck.*

It seems to me that all the phenomena are accurately describable in these very simple general terms. There is probably no autobiographic document, among all those which I have quoted, to which the description will not well apply. One need only add such specific details as will adapt it to various theologies and various personal temperaments, and one will then have the various experiences reconstructed in their individual forms.

So far, however, as this analysis goes, the experiences are only psychological phenomena. They possess, it is true, enormous biological worth. Spiritual strength really increases in the subject when he has them, a new life opens for him, and they seem to him a place of conflux where the forces of two universes meet; and yet this may be nothing but his subjective way of feeling things, a mood of his own fancy, in spite of the effects produced. I now turn to my second question: What is the objective "truth" of their content?

The part of the content concerning which the question of truth most pertinently arises is that "MORE of the same quality" with which our own higher self appears in the experience to come into harmonious working relation. Is such a "more" merely our own notion, or does it really exist? If so, in what shape does it exist? Does it act, as well as exist? And in what form should we conceive of that "union" with it of which religious geniuses are so convinced?

It is in answering these questions that the various theologies perform their theoretic work, and that their divergencies most come to light. They all agree that the "more" really exists; though some of them hold it to exist in the shape of a personal god or gods, while others are satisfied to conceive it as a stream of ideal tendency embedded in the eternal structure of the world. They all agree, moreover, that it acts as well as exists, and that something really is effected for the better when you throw your life into its hands.

Disregarding the over-beliefs, and confining ourselves to what is common and generic, we have in *the fact that the conscious person is continuous with a wider self through which saving experiences come*, a positive content of religious experience which, it seems to me, is literally and objectively true as far as it goes. If I now proceed to state my own hypothesis about the farther limits of this extension of our personality, I shall be offering my own over-belief—though I know it will appear a sorry under-belief to some of you—for which I can only bespeak the same indulgence which in a converse case I should accord to yours.

The further limits of our being plunge,

* Remember that for some men it arrives suddenly, for others gradually, whilst others again practically enjoy it all their life.

it seems to me, into an altogether other dimension of existence from the sensible and merely "understandable" world. Name it the mystical region, or the supernatural region, whichever you choose. So far as our ideal impulses originate in this region (and most of them do originate in it, for we find them possessing us in a way for which we cannot articulately account), we belong to it in a more intimate sense than that in which we belong to the visible world, for we belong in the most intimate sense wherever our ideals belong. Yet the unseen region in question is not merely ideal, for it produces effects in this world. When we commune with it, work is actually done upon our finite personality, for we are turned into new men, and consequences in the way of conduct follow in the natural world upon our regenerative change. But that which produces effects within another reality must be termed a reality itself, so I feel as if we had no philosophic excuse for calling the unseen or mystical world unreal.

God is the natural appellation, for us Christians at least, for the supreme reality, so I will call this higher part of the universe by the name of God. We and God have business with each other; and in opening ourselves to his influence our deepest destiny is fulfilled. The universe, at those parts of it which our personal being constitutes, takes a turn genuinely for the worse or for the better in proportion as each one of us fulfills or evades God's demands. As far as this goes I probably have you with me, for I only translate into schematic language what I may call the instinctive belief of mankind: God is real since he produces real effects.

The real effects in question, so far as I have as yet admitted them, are exerted on the personal centers of energy of the various subjects, but the spontaneous faith of most of the subjects is that they embrace a wider sphere than this. Most religious men believe (or "know," if they be mystical) that not only they themselves, but the whole universe of beings to whom the God is present, are secure in his parental hands. There is a sense, a dimension, they are sure, in which we are *all* saved, in spite of the gates of hell and all adverse terrestrial appearances. God's existence is the guarantee of an ideal order that shall be permanently preserved. This world may indeed, as science assures us, some day burn up or freeze; but if it is part of his order, the old ideals are sure to be brought elsewhere to fruition, so that where God is, tragedy is only provisional and partial, and shipwreck and dissolution are not the absolutely final things. Only when this farther step of faith concerning God is taken, and remote objective consequences are predicted, does religion, as it seems to me, get wholly free from the first immediate subjective experience, and bring a *real hypothesis* into play. A good hypothesis in science must have other properties than those of the phenomenon it is immediately invoked to explain, otherwise it is not prolific enough. God, meaning only what enters into the religious man's experience of union, falls short of being an hypothesis of this more useful order. He needs to enter into wider cosmic relations in order to justify the subject's absolute confidence and peace.

That the God with whom, starting from the hither side of our own extra-marginal self, we come at its remoter margin into commerce should be the absolute world ruler, is of course a very considerable over-belief. Over-belief as it is, though, it is an article of almost every one's religion. Most of us pretend in some way to prop it upon our philosophy, but the philosophy itself is really propped upon this faith. What is this but to say that Religion, in her fullest exercise of function, is not a mere illumination of facts already elsewhere given, not a mere passion like love, which views things in a rosier light. It is indeed that, as we have seen abundantly. But it is something more, namely, a postulator of new *facts* as well. The world interpreted religiously is not the materialistic world over again, with an altered expression; it must have, over and above the altered expression *a natural constitution* different at some point from that which a materialistic world would have. It must be such that different events can be expected in it, different conduct must be required.

This thoroughly "pragmatic" view of religion has usually been taken as a matter of course by common men. They have interpolated divine miracles into the field of nature, they have built a heaven out beyond the grave. I believe the pragmatic way of taking religion to be the deeper way. It gives it body as well as soul, it makes it claim, as everything real must claim, some characteristic realm of fact as its very own. What the more characteristically divine facts are, apart from the actual inflow of energy in the faith-state and the prayer-state, I know not. But the over-belief on which I am ready to make my personal venture is that they exist. The whole drift of my education goes to persuade me that the world of our present consciousness is only one out of many worlds of consciousness that exist, and that those other worlds must contain experiences which have a meaning for our life also; and that although in the main their experiences and those of this world keep discrete, yet the two become continuous at certain points, and higher energies filter in.

By being faithful in my poor measure to this over-belief, I seem to myself to keep more sane and true. I *can*, of course, put myself into the sectarian scientist's attitude, and imagine vividly that the world of sensations and of scientific laws and objects may be all. But whenever I do this, I hear that inward monitor of which W. K. Clifford once wrote, whispering the word "bosh"! Humbug is humbug, even though it bear the scientific name, and the total expression of human experience, as I view it objectively, invincibly urges me beyond the narrow "scientific" bounds. Assuredly, the real world is of a different temperament—more intricately built than physical science allows. So my objective and my subjective conscience both hold me to the over-belief which I express. Who knows whether the faithfulness of individuals here below to their own poor over-beliefs may not actually help God in turn to be more effectively faithful to his own greater tasks?

Sören Kierkegaard

Although he died a hundred years ago and although until recently his books were almost unknown outside his native Denmark, Sören Kierkegaard is today one of the influential and controversial figures in the field of religious thought. During six years from 1842 to 1848, Kierkegaard produced a body of creative work that has earned him the title of the Danish Pascal. He is generally regarded as the man to whom contemporary religious existentialism owes the greatest debt, and even the secular existentialists recognize the importance of his thought. Not to be familiar with Kierkegaard in sophisticated literary and philosophical circles today is almost like confessing one's lack of intellectual competence.

Kierkegaard was born in Copenhagen in 1813 and died in 1855. Throughout his life he was a man in revolt. He attacked the popular Christianity prevalent in his day and con-

demned the church for its failure to deal realistically with the basic problems of human existence. Even more rigorously he rejected the theoretical philosophy of Hegel, who at that time was the outstanding figure in European philosophy. The crucial decisions that shape a man's destiny must be our central concern, Kierkegaard insists—and faith is a more significant and trustworthy guide in making these decisions than is reason. But Kierkegaard has in mind no superficial, shallow, or hypocritical faith. He returns repeatedly to the faith that enabled Abraham to sacrifice his beloved son, Isaac, as an excellent example of both what genuine faith is like and of the kind of crucial decisions with which a man is at times confronted.

In recent years, after a century of neglect, most of Kierkegaard's work has been translated into English. Among his more important books are Either-or, Stages on Life's Way, The Concluding Unscientific Postscript, Fear and Trembling, *and* Purity of Heart. *Loneliness and pathos pervade these books; Kierkegaard was so deeply involved in his search for the divine that he cut himself off almost completely from all human companionship and sympathy.*

It is not easy to select a brief passage that portrays his thought without misrepresentation but his meditation on the faith of Abraham in Fear and Trembling, *reprinted here in part, is such a passage—and it also provides a fine example of the kind of experience with which contemporary existentialism is concerned. During the period when he was writing* Fear and Trembling, *Kierkegaard was struggling to renounce his hope of happiness in marriage with the woman he loved. Abraham's sacrifice of Isaac—the thing he held dearest in life—seemed to him a comparable experience, and he describes Abraham's experience with all the intensity and heart searching that he knew so well in his own life.*

FEAR AND TREMBLING

Prelude

ONCE UPON A TIME there was a man who as a child had heard the beautiful story [Genesis, Ch. 22] about how God tempted Abraham, and how he endured temptation, kept the faith, and a second time received again a son contrary to expectation. When the child became older he read the same story with even greater admiration, for life had separated what was united in the pious simplicity of the child. The older he became, the more frequently his mind reverted to that story, his enthusiasm became greater and greater, and yet he was less and less able to understand the story. At last in his interest for that he forgot everything else; his soul had only one wish, to see Abraham, one longing, to have been witness to that event. His desire was not to behold the beautiful countries of the Orient, or the earthly glory of the Promised Land, or that godfearing couple whose old age God had blessed, or the venerable figure of the aged patriarch, or the vigorous young manhood of Isaac whom God had bestowed upon Abraham—he saw no reason why the same thing might not have taken place on a barren heath in Denmark. His yearning was to accompany them on the three days' journey when Abraham rode with sorrow before him and with Isaac by his side. His only wish was to be present at the time when Abraham lifted up his eyes and saw Mount Moriah afar off, at the time when he left the asses behind and went alone with Isaac up unto the mountain; for what his mind was intent upon was not the ingenious web of imagination but the shudder of thought.

That man was not a thinker, he felt no need of getting beyond faith; he deemed it the most glorious thing to be remembered as the father of it, an enviable lot to possess it, even though no one else were to know it.

That man was not a learned exegete, he didn't know Hebrew; if he had known Hebrew, he perhaps would easily have understood the story and Abraham.

I

And God tempted Abraham and said unto him, Take Isaac, thine only son, whom thou lovest, and get thee into the land of Moriah, and offer him there for a burnt offering upon the mountain which I will show thee.

It was early in the morning, Abraham arose betimes, he had the asses saddled, left his tent, and Isaac with him, but Sarah looked out of the window after them until they had passed down the valley and she could see them no more. They rode in silence for three days. On the morning of the fourth day Abraham said never a word, but he lifted up his eyes and saw Mount Moriah afar off. He left the young men behind and went on alone with Isaac beside him up to the mountain. But Abraham said to himself, "I will not conceal from Isaac whither this course leads him." He stood still, he laid his hand upon the head of Isaac in benediction, and Isaac bowed to receive the blessing. And Abraham's face was fatherliness, his look was mild, his speech encouraging. But Isaac was unable to understand him, his soul could not be exalted; he embraced Abraham's knees, he fell at his feet imploringly, he begged for his young life, for the fair hope of his future, he called to mind the joy in Abraham's house, he called to mind the sorrow and loneliness. Then Abraham lifted up the boy, he walked with him by his side, and his talk was full of comfort and exhortation. But Isaac could not understand him. He climbed Mount Moriah, but Isaac understood him not. Then for an instant he turned away from him, and when Isaac again saw Abraham's face it was changed, his glance was wild, his form was horror. He seized Isaac by the throat, threw him on the ground, and said, "Stupid boy, dost thou then suppose that I am thy father? I am an idolater. Dost thou suppose that this is God's bidding? No, it is my desire." Then Isaac trembled and cried out in his terror, "O God in heaven, have compassion upon me. God of Abraham, have compassion upon me. If I have no father upon earth, be Thou my father!" But Abraham in a low voice said to himself, "O Lord in heaven, I thank Thee. After all it is better for him to believe that I am a monster, rather than that he should lose faith in Thee."

When the child must be weaned, the mother blackens her breast, it would indeed be a shame that the breast should look delicious when the child must not have it. So the child believes that the breast has changed, but the mother is the same, her glance is as loving and tender as ever. Happy the person who had no need of more dreadful expedients for weaning the child!

II

It was early in the morning, Abraham arose betimes, he embraced Sarah, the bride of his old age, and Sarah kissed Isaac, who had taken away her reproach, who was her pride, her hope for all time. So they rode on in silence along the way, and Abraham's glance was fixed upon the ground until the fourth day when he lifted up his eyes and saw afar off Mount Moriah, but his glance turned again to the ground. Silently he laid the wood in order, he bound Isaac, in silence he drew the knife—then he saw the ram which God had prepared. Then he offered that and returned home. . . . From that time on Abraham became old, he could not forget that God had required this of him. Isaac throve as before, but Abraham's eyes were darkened, and he knew joy no more.

When the child has grown big and must be weaned, the mother virginally hides her breast, so the child has no more a mother. Happy the child which did not in another way lose its mother.

III

It was early in the morning, Abraham arose betimes, he kissed Sarah, the young mother, and Sarah kissed Isaac, her delight, her joy at all times. And Abraham rode pensively along the way, he thought of Hagar and of the son whom he drove out into the wilderness, he climbed Mount Moriah, he drew the knife.

It was a quiet evening when Abraham rode out alone, and he rode to Mount Moriah; he threw himself upon his face, he prayed God to forgive him his sin, that he had been willing to offer Isaac, that the father had forgotten his duty toward the son. Often he rode his lonely way, but he found no rest. He could not comprehend that it was a sin to be willing to offer to God the best thing he possessed, that for which he would many times have given his life; and if it was a sin, if he had not loved Isaac as he did, then he could not understand that it might be forgiven. For what sin could be more dreadful?

When the child must be weaned, the mother too is not without sorrow at the thought that she and the child are separated more and more, that the child which first lay under her heart and later reposed upon her breast will be so near to her no more. So they mourn together for the brief period of mourning. Happy the person who has kept the child as near and needed not to sorrow any more!

IV

It was early in the morning, everything was prepared for the journey in Abraham's house. He bade Sarah farewell, and Eleazar, the faithful servant, followed him along the way, until he turned back. They rode together in harmony, Abraham and Isaac, until they came to Mount Moriah. But Abraham prepared everything for the sacrifice, calmly and quietly, but when he turned and drew the knife, Isaac saw that his left hand was clenched in despair, that a tremor passed through his body—but Abraham drew the knife.

Then they returned again home, and Sarah hastened to meet them, but Isaac had lost his faith. No word of this had ever been spoken in the world, and Isaac never talked to anyone about what he had seen, and Abraham did not suspect that anyone had seen it.

When the child must be weaned, the mother has stronger food in readiness, lest the child should perish. Happy the person who has stronger food in readiness!

Thus and in many like ways that man of whom we are speaking thought concerning this event. Every time he returned home after wandering to Mount Moriah, he sank down with weariness, he folded his hands and said, "No one is so great as Abraham! Who is capable of understanding him?"

Preliminary Analysis

I

An old proverb fetched from the outward aspect of the visible world says: "Only the man that works gets the bread." Strangely enough this proverb does not aptly apply in that world to which it expressly belongs. For the outward world is subjected to the law of imperfection, and again and again the experience is repeated that he too who does not work gets the bread, and that he who sleeps gets it more abundantly than the man who works.

It is different in the world of spirit. Here an eternal divine order prevails, here it does not rain both upon the just and upon the unjust, here the sun does not shine both upon the good and upon the evil, here it holds good that only he who works gets the bread, only he who was in anguish finds repose, only he who descends into the underworld rescues the beloved, only he who draws the knife gets Isaac.

There is a knowledge which would presumptuously introduce into the world of spirit the same law of indifference under which the external world sighs. It counts it enough to think the great—other work is not necessary. But therefore it doesn't get the bread, it perishes of hunger, while everything is transformed into gold. And what does it really know? There were many thousands of Greek contemporaries, and countless numbers in subsequent generations, who knew all the triumphs of Miltiades, but only one [Themistocles] was made sleepless by them. There were countless generations which knew by rote, word for word, the story of Abraham—how many were made sleepless by it?

Now the story of Abraham has the remarkable property that it is always glorious, however poorly one may understand it; yet here again the proverb applies, that all depends upon whether one is willing to labor and be heavy laden. But they will not labor, and yet they would understand the story. They exalt Abraham—but how? They express the whole thing in perfectly general terms: "The great thing was that he loved God so much that he was willing to sacrifice to Him the best." That is very true, but "the best" is an indefinite expression. In case that rich young man whom Christ encountered on the road had sold all his goods and given to the poor, we should extol him, as we do all that is great, though without labor we would not understand him—and yet he would not have become an Abraham, in spite of the fact that he offered his best.

What they leave out of Abraham's history is dread; for to money I have no ethical obligation, but to the son the father has the highest and most sacred obligation. Dread, however, is a perilous thing for effeminate natures, hence they forget it, and in spite of that they want to talk about Abraham. So they talk—in the course of the oration they use indifferently the two terms, Isaac and "the best." All goes famously. However, if it chanced that among the auditors there was one who suffered from insomnia—then the most dreadful, the profoundest tragic and comic misunderstanding lies very close. He went home, he would do as Abraham did, for the son is indeed "the best." If the orator got to know of it, he perhaps went to him, he summoned all his clerical dignity, he shouted, "O abominable man, offscouring of society, what devil possessed thee to want to murder thy son?" In case the same orator had a little superabundance of reason which might be lost, I think he would have lost it if the sinner were to say calmly and with dignity, "That in fact is what you yourself preached on Sunday."

How is one to explain the contradiction illustrated by that orator? Is it because Abraham had a prescriptive right to be a great man, so that what he did is great, and when another does the same it is sin, a heinous sin? In that case I do not wish to participate in such thoughtless eulogy. If faith does not make it a holy act to be willing to murder one's son, then let the same condemnation be pronounced upon Abraham as upon every other man. If a man perhaps lacks courage to carry his thought through, and to say that Abraham was a murderer, then it is surely better to acquire this courage, rather than waste time upon undeserved eulogies. The ethical expression for what Abraham did is, that he would murder Isaac; the religious expression is, that he would sacrifice Isaac; but precisely in this contradiction consists the dread which can well make a man sleepless, and yet Abraham is not what he is without this dread. Or perhaps he did not do at all what is related, but something altogether different, which is accounted for by the circumstances of his times—then let us forget him, for it is not worth while to remember *that* past which cannot become a present.

II

Can one then speak plainly about Abraham without incurring the danger that an individual might in bewilderment go ahead and do likewise? If I do not dare to speak freely, I will be completely silent about Abraham, above all I will not disparage him in such a way that precisely thereby he becomes a pitfall for the weak. For if one makes faith everything, that is, makes it what it is, then, according to my way of thinking, one may speak of it without danger in our age, which hardly extravagates in the matter of faith, and it is only by faith one attains likeness to Abraham, not by murder. If one makes love a transistory mood, a voluptuous emotion in a man, then one only lays pitfalls for the weak when one would talk about the exploits of love. Transient emotions every man surely has, but if as a consequence of such emotions one would do the terrible thing which love has sanctified as an immortal exploit, then all is lost, including the exploit and the bewildered doer of it.

After all, in the poets love has its priests, and sometimes one hears a voice which knows how to defend it; but of faith one hears never a word. Who speaks in honor of this passion? Philosophy goes further. Theology sits rouged at the window and courts its favor, offering to sell her charms to philosophy. It is supposed to be difficult to understand Hegel, but to understand Abraham is a trifle. To go beyond Hegel is a miracle, but to get beyond Abraham is the easiest thing of all. I for my part have devoted a good deal of time to understanding of the Hegelian philosophy, I believe also that I understand it tolerably well, but when in spite of the trouble I have taken there are certain passages I cannot understand, I am foolhardy enough to think that he himself has not been quite clear. All this I do easily and naturally, my head does not suffer from it. But on the other hand, when I have to think of Abraham, I am as though annihilated. I catch sight every moment of that enormous paradox which is the substance of Abraham's life, every moment I am repelled, and my thought in spite of all its passion cannot get a hairsbreadth further. I strain every muscle to get a view of it—that very instant I am paralyzed.

I am not unacquainted with what has been admired as great and noble in the world, my soul feels affinity with it, being convinced in all humility that it was in my cause the hero contended, and the instant I contemplate his deed I cry out to myself, *jam tua res agitur.** I *think* myself *into* the

* It's your affair when a neighbor's house is afire.

hero, but into Abraham I cannot think myself; when I reach the height I fall down, for what I encounter there is the paradox. I do not however mean in any sense to say that faith is something lowly, but on the contrary that it is the highest thing, and that it is dishonest of philosophy to give something else instead of it and to make light of faith. Philosophy cannot and should not give faith but it should understand itself and know what it has to offer and take nothing away, and least of all should fool people out of something as if it were nothing.

Generally people are of the opinion that what faith produces is not a work of art, that it is coarse and common work, only for the more clumsy natures; but in fact this is far from the truth. The dialectic of faith is the finest and most remarkable of all; it possesses an elevation, of which indeed I can form a conception, but nothing more. I am able to make from the springboard the great leap whereby I pass into infinity, my back is like that of a tightrope dancer, having been twisted in my childhood, hence I find this easy; with a one-two-three! I can walk about existence on my head; but the next thing I cannot do, for I cannot perform the miraculous, but can only be astonished by it. Yes, if Abraham the instant he swung his leg over the ass's back had said to himself, "Now, since Isaac is lost, I might just as well sacrifice him here at home, rather than ride the long way to Moriah"—then I should have no need of Abraham, whereas now I bow seven times before his name and seventy times before his deed. For this indeed he did not do, as I can prove by the fact that he was glad at receiving Isaac, heartily glad, that he needed no preparation, no time to concentrate upon the finite and its joy. If this had not been the case with Abraham, then perhaps he might have loved God but not believed; for he who loves God without faith reflects upon himself, he who loves God believingly reflects upon God.

Abraham I cannot understand; in a certain sense there is nothing I can learn from him but astonishment. If people fancy that by considering the outcome of this story they might let themselves be moved to believe, they deceive themselves and want to swindle God out of the first movement of faith, the infinite resignation. They would suck worldly wisdom out of the paradox. Perhaps one or another may succeed in that, for our age is not willing to stop with faith, with its miracle of turning water into wine, it goes further, it turns wine into water.

III

Would it not be better to stop with faith, and is it not revolting that everybody wants to go further? When in our age (as indeed is proclaimed in various ways) they will not stop with love, where then are they going? To earthly wisdom, to petty calculation, to paltriness and wretchedness, to everything which can make man's divine origin doubtful. Would it not be better that they should stand still at faith, and that he who stands should take heed lest he fall? For the movements of faith must constantly be made by virtue of the absurd, yet in such a way, be it observed, that one does not lose the finite but gains it every inch.

For my part, I can well describe the movements of faith, but I cannot make them. When one would learn to make the motions of swimming one can let oneself be hung by a swimming belt from the ceiling and go through the motions (describe them, so to speak, as we speak of describing a circle), but one is not swimming. In that way I can describe the movements of faith, but when I am thrown into the water, I swim, it is true (for I don't belong to the beachwaders), but I make other movements, I make the movements of infinity, whereas faith does the opposite: after having made the movements of infinity, it makes those of finiteness. Hail to him who can make those movements, he performs the marvelous, and I shall never grow tired of admiring him, whether he be Abraham or a slave in Abraham's house, whether he be a professor of philosophy or a servant girl, I look only at the movements. But at them I do look, and do not let myself be fooled, either by myself or by any other man. The knights of the infinite resignation are easily recognized: their gait is gliding and assured. Those on the other hand who carry the jewel of faith are likely to be delusive, because their outward appearance bears a striking resemblance to that which both the infinite resignation and faith profoundly despise—to Philistinism.

I candidly admit that in my practice I have not found any reliable example of the knight of faith, though I would not therefore deny that every second man may be such an example. I have been trying, however, for several years to get on the track of this, and all in vain. People commonly travel around the world to see rivers and mountains, new stars, birds of rare plumage, queerly deformed fishes, ridiculous breeds of men—they abandon themselves to the bestial stupor which gapes at existence, and they think they have seen something. This does not interest me. But if I knew where there was such a knight of faith, I would make a pilgrimage to him on foot, for this prodigy interests me absolutely. I would not let go of him for an instant, every moment I would watch to see how he managed to make the movements, I would regard myself as secured for life, and would divide my time between looking at him and practicing the exercises myself, and thus would spend all my time admiring him.

As was said, I have not found any such person, but I can well think him. Here he is. Acquaintance made, I am introduced to him. The moment I set eyes on him I instantly push him from me, I myself leap backwards, I clasp my hands and say half aloud, "Good Lord, is this the man? Is it really he? Why, he looks like a tax collector!" However, it is the man after all. I draw closer to him, watching his least movements to see whether there might not be visible a little heterogeneous fractional telegraphic message from the infinite, a glance, a look, a gesture, a note of sadness, a smile, which betrayed the infinite in its heterogeneity with the finite. No! I examine his figure from tip to toe to see if there might not be a cranny through which the infinite was peeping. No! He is solid through and through. His tread? It is vigorous, belonging entirely to finiteness; no smartly dressed townsman who walks out to Fresberg on a Sunday afternoon treads the ground more firmly, he belongs entirely to the world, no Philistine more so. One can discover nothing of that aloof and superior nature whereby one recognizes the knight of the infinite. He takes delight in everything, and whenever one sees him taking part in a particular pleasure, he does it with the persistence which is the mark of the earthly man whose soul is absorbed in such things. He tends to his work. So when one looks at him one might suppose that he was a clerk who had lost his soul in an intricate system of bookkeeping, so precise is he. He takes a holiday on Sunday. He goes to church. No heavenly glance or any other token of the incommensurable betrays him; if one did not know him, it would be impossible to distinguish him from the rest of the congregation, for his healthy and vigorous hymn singing proves at the most that he has a good chest. In the afternoon he walks to the forest. He takes delight in everything he sees, in the human swarm, in the new omnibuses, in the water of the Sound; when one meets him on the Beach Road one might suppose he was a shopkeeper taking his fling, that's just the way he disports himself, for he is not a poet, and I have sought in vain to detect in him the poetic incommensurability. Toward evening he walks home, his gait is as indefatigable as that of the postman. On his way he reflects that his wife has surely a special little warm dish prepared for him, e.g., a calf's head roasted, garnished with vegetables. If he were to meet a man like-minded, he could continue as far as East Gate to discourse with him about that dish, with a passion befitting a hotel chef. As it happens, he hasn't four pence to his name, and yet he fully and firmly believes that his wife has that dainty dish for him. If she had it, it would then be an invidious sight for superior people and an inspiring one for the plain man, to see him eat; for his appetite is greater than Esau's. His wife hasn't it—strangely enough, it is quite the same to him.

In the evening he smokes his pipe; to look at him one would swear that it was the grocer over the way vegetating in the twilight. He lives as carefree as a ne'er-do-well, and yet he buys up the acceptable time at the dearest price, for he does not do the least thing except by virtue of the absurd. And yet, and yet I could become furious over it—for envy, if for no other reason—because the man has made and every instant is making the movements of infinity. With infinite resignation he has drained the cup of life's profound sadness, he knows the bliss of the infinite, he senses the pain of renouncing everything, the dearest things he possesses in the world, and yet finiteness tastes to him just as good as to one who never knew anything higher, for his continuance in the finite did not bear a trace of the cowed and fearful spirit produced by the process of training; and yet he has this sense of security in enjoying it, as though the finite life were the surest thing of all. And yet, and yet the whole earthly form he exhibits is a new creation by virtue of the absurd. He resigned everything infinitely, and then he grasped everything again by virtue of the absurd. He constantly makes the movements of infinity, but he does this with such correctness and assurance that he constantly gets the finite out of it, and there is not a second when one has a notion of anything else.

It is supposed to be the most difficult task for a dancer to leap into a definite posture in such a way that there is not a second when he is grasping after the posture, but by the leap itself he stands fixed in that posture. Perhaps no dancer can do it—that is what this knight does. Most people live dejectedly in worldly sorrow and joy; they are the ones who sit along the wall and do not join in the dance. The knights of infinity are dancers and possess elevation. They make the movements upward, and fall down again; and this too is no mean pastime, nor ungraceful to behold.

One need not look at them when they are up in the air, but only the instant they touch or have touched the ground—then one recognizes them. But to be able to fall down in such a way that the same second it looks as if one were standing and walking, to transform the leap of life into a walk, absolutely to express the sublime and the pedestrian—that only these knights can do—and this is the one and only prodigy.

IV

In the infinite resignation there is peace and rest; every man who will, who has not abased himself by scorning himself (which is still more dreadful than being proud), can train himself to make these movements.

Infinite resignation is that shirt we read about in the old fable. The thread is spun under tears, the cloth bleached with tears, the shirt sewn with tears, but then too it is a better protection than iron and steel. The imperfection in the fable is that a third party can manufacture this shirt. The secret in life is that everyone must sew it for himself, and the astonishing thing is that a man can sew it fully as well as a woman. In the infinite resignation there is peace and rest and comfort in sorrow—that is, if the movement is made normally. It would not be difficult for me, however, to write a whole book, were I to examine the various misunderstandings, the preposterous attitudes, the deceptive movements, which I have encountered in my brief practice.

The infinite resignation is the last stage prior to faith, so that one who has not made this movement has not faith; for only in the infinite resignation do I become clear to myself with respect to my eternal validity, and only then can there be any question of grasping existence by virtue of faith.

Faith, therefore, is not an esthetic emotion but something far higher, precisely because it has resignation as its presupposition; it is not an immediate instinct of the heart, but is the paradox of life and existence. So when in spite of all difficulties a young girl still remains convinced that her wish will surely be fulfilled, this conviction is not the assurance of faith, even if she was brought up by Christian parents, and for a whole year perhaps has been catechized by the parson. She is convinced in all her childish naiveté and innocence, this conviction also ennobles her nature and imparts to her a preternatural greatness, so that like a thaumaturge she is able to conjure the finite powers of existence and make the very stones weep, while on the other hand in her flurry she may just as well run to Herod as to Pilate and move the whole world by her tears. Her conviction is very lovable, and one can learn much from her, but one thing is not to be learned from her, one does not learn the movements, for her conviction does not dare in the pain of resignation to face the impossibility.

So I can perceive that it requires strength and energy and freedom of spirit to make the infinite movements of resignation. I can also perceive that it is feasible. But the next thing astonishes me, it makes my head swim, for after having made the movement of resignation, then by virtue of the absurd to get everything, to get the wish whole and uncurtailed—that is beyond human power, it is a prodigy. But this I can perceive, that the young girl's conviction is mere levity in comparison with the firmness faith displays notwithstanding it has perceived the impossibility. Whenever I essay to make this movement, I turn giddy, the very instant I am admiring it absolutely a prodigious dread grips my soul—for what is it to tempt God? And yet this movement is the movement of faith and remains such, even though philosophy, in order to confuse the concepts, would make us believe that it has faith, and even though theology would sell out faith at a bargain price.

By faith I make renunciation of nothing, on the contrary, by faith I acquire everything, precisely in the sense in which it is said that he who has faith like a grain of mustard can remove mountains. A purely human courage is required to renounce the whole of the temporal to gain the eternal; but this I gain, and to all eternity I cannot renounce it, that is a self-contradiction; but a paradox enters in and a humble courage is required to grasp the whole of the temporal by virtue of the absurd, and this is the courage of faith. By faith Abraham did not renounce his claim upon Isaac, but by faith he got Isaac. By virtue of resignation that rich young man should have given away everything, but then when he had done that, the knight of faith should have said to him, "By virtue of the absurd thou shalt get every penny back again. Canst thou believe that?" And this speech ought by no means to have been indifferent to the aforesaid rich young man, for in case he gave away his goods because he was tired of them, his resignation was not much to boast of.

V

People construe the story of Abraham in another way. They extol God's grace in bestowing Isaac upon him again—the whole thing was only a trial. A trial—that word may say much or little, and yet the whole thing is over as quickly as it is said. One mounts a winged horse, the same instant one is at Mount Moriah, the same instant one sees the ram; one forgets that Abraham rode only upon an ass, which walks slowly along the road, that he had a journey of three days, that he needed some time to cleave the wood, to bind Isaac, and to sharpen the knife.

And yet they extol Abraham. He who is to deliver the discourse can very well sleep till a quarter of an hour before he has to preach, the auditor can well take a nap during the discourse, for all goes smoothly, without the least trouble from any quarter. If there was a man present who suffered from insomnia, perhaps he then went home and sat in a corner and thought: "It's an affair of a moment, this whole thing; if only you wait a minute, you see the ram, and the trial is over."

Let us then either consign Abraham to oblivion, or let us learn to be dismayed by the tremendous paradox which constitutes the significance of Abraham's life, that we may understand that our age, like every age, can be joyful if it has faith. In case Abraham is not a nullity, a phantom, a show one employs for a pastime, then the fault can never consist in the fact that the sinner wants to do likewise, but the point is to see how great a thing it was that Abraham did, in order that man may judge for himself whether he has the call and the courage to be subjected to such a test. The comic contradiction in the behavior of the orator is that he reduced Abraham to an insignificance, and yet would admonish the other to behave in the same way.

Should not one dare then to talk about Abraham? I think one should. If I were to talk about him, I would first depict the pain of his trial. To that end I would like a leech suck all the dread and distress and torture out of a father's sufferings, so that I might describe what Abraham suffered, whereas all the while he nevertheless believed. I would remind the audience that the journey lasted three days and a good part of the fourth, yea, that these three and a half days were infinitely longer than the few thousand years which separate me from Abraham. Then I would remind them that, in my opinion, every man dare still turn around ere he begins such an undertaking, and every instant he can repentantly turn back. If the hearer does this, I fear no danger, nor am I afraid of awakening in people an inclination to be tried like Abraham. But if one would dispose of a cheap edition of Abraham, and yet admonish everyone to do likewise, then it is ludicrous.

It is my intention to draw out from the story of Abraham the dialectical consequences inherent in it, in order to see what a tremendous paradox faith is, a paradox which is capable of transforming a murder into a holy act well pleasing to God, a paradox which gives Isaac back to Abraham, which no thought can master, because faith begins precisely there where thinking leaves off.

Leo Tolstoy

In two popular works, My Confession *and* My Religion, *Count Leo Tolstoy (1828-1910), famous Russian novelist and religious writer, examines with unusual insight and frankness the spiritual need that led him to religion, the inadequacies he found in the traditional Russian Orthodox faith of his own day, and the guidance that he gained at last from the Sermon on the Mount. Then, with devastating consistency, he points out what it means to follow without compromise the ethical implications of the Christian gospel of brotherhood and good will. While not thinking of himself as an existentialist—the term was not yet current—Tolstoy describes with fine literary and psychological skill his own spiritual crisis, his desperate search for meaning in life, and the act of commitment by which this meaning was found—all essential concerns of religious existentialism today.*

In his spiritual autobiography, Tolstoy is quite critical of one important achievement in his life—the fact that he wrote some of the world's greatest fiction. Reading the selections we reprint from his Confession *one would think he had written purely for cash and notoriety. It is true that writing fiction was easy for him and for that reason perhaps, as well as because of his later religious convictions, he did not regard it too highly. Actually, Tolstoy ranks among the greatest writers of all time. His best novels are* War and Peace, Anna Karenina, *and* Resurrection; *his most most famous short story is "The Death of Ivan Ilyitch."*

Among other aspects of his life not dealt with in our selections are Tolstoy's birth to a noble family and his marriage to Sophia Behrs. Theirs was a happy marriage at first and a desperately unhappy one toward the end. Countess Tolstoy could never understand why her husband would rather give his royalties to peasants than to his family; and she was spiritually unfit to live with a man who eventually became something of a saint. For few men have made so determined an effort as Tolstoy to interpret Christianity based upon the ethical teachings of Jesus as a way of life and to put this theory into practice. And few religious teachers in the modern world have had such great influence. During the last years of his long life, Tolstoy became almost a legendary figure. People from all over the world made pilgrimages just to see the famous old man. Among the large number of those influenced by his teaching, probably the most outstanding was Mahatma Gandhi, religious leader of India, who was more successful than any of Tolstoy's Christian disciples in demonstrating the practical effectiveness of the nonresistance which Tolstoy took to be essential in the Christian spirit of love.

MY CONFESSION

I

I WAS christened and educated in the Orthodox Christian Faith; I was taught it in my childhood, and in my boyhood and youth. Nevertheless, when, at eighteen years of age, I left the university in the second year, I had discarded all belief in anything I had been taught.

To judge by what I can now remember,

[From *My Confession: My Religion: The Gospel in Brief* by Leo Tolstoy. Abridged. Copyright 1899, 1927. Reprinted by permission of the publisher, Thomas Y. Crowell Company, New York.]

I never had a serious belief; I merely trusted in what my elders made their profession of faith, but even this trust was very precarious.

I remember once in my twelfth year, a boy, now long since dead, Volodinka M——, a pupil in the gymnasium, spent a Sunday with us, and brought us the news of the last discovery in the gymnasium. This discovery was that there was no God, and that all we were taught on the subject was a mere invention (this was in 1838). I remember well how interested my elder brothers were in this news; I was admitted to their deliberations, and we all eagerly accepted the theory as something particularly attractive, and possibly quite true.

Thus it happens that now, as formerly, the influence of early religious teaching, accepted merely on trust and upheld by authority, gradually fades away under the knowledge and practical experience of life, which is opposed to all its principles, and that a man often believes for years that his early faith is still intact, while all the time not a trace of it remains in him.

The belief instilled from childhood in me, as in so many others, gradually disappeared, but with this difference; that as from fifteen years of age I had begun to read philosophical works, I became very early conscious of my own disbelief. From the age of sixteen I ceased to pray, and ceased, from conviction to attend the services of the church and to fast. I no longer accepted the faith of my childhood, but I believed in something, though I could not exactly explain in what. I believed in a God —or rather, I did not deny the existence of a God—but what kind of God I could not have told; I denied neither Christ nor His teaching, but in what that teaching consisted I could not have said.

This estrangement from all belief went on in me, as it does now, and always has done, in those of the same social position and culture. This falling off, as it seems to me, for the most part goes on thus: people live as others live, and their lives are guided, not by the principles of the faith that is taught them, but by their very opposite; belief has no influence on life, nor on the relations among men—it is relegated to some other sphere apart from life and independent of it; if the two ever come into contact at all, belief is only one of the outward phenomena, and not one of the constituent parts of life.

By a man's life, by his acts, it was then, as it is now, impossible to know whether he was a believer or not. If there be a difference between one who openly professes the doctrines of the Orthodox Church, and one who denies them, the difference is to the advantage of the former. Then, as now, the open profession of the Orthodox doctrines was found mostly among dull, stern, immoral men, and those who think much of their own importance. *Intellect, honor, frankness, good nature, and morality are oftener met with among those who call themselves disbelievers.*

The schoolboy is taught his catechism and sent to church; *chinovniks*, or functionaries, are required to show a certificate of having taken the holy communion. But the man belonging to our class, who is done with school and does not enter the public service, may now live a dozen years—still more was this the case formerly—without being once reminded of the fact that he lives among Christians, and is reckoned as a member of the Orthodox Christian Church.

Now, when I think over that time, I see clearly that all the faith I had, the only belief which, apart from mere animal instinct, swayed my life, was a belief in the possibility of perfection, though what it was in itself, or what would be its results, I could not have said.

At first, of course, moral perfection seemed to me the main end, but I soon found myself contemplating in its stead an idea of general perfectibility; in other words, I wished to be better, not in my own eyes nor in God's, but in the sight of other men. And very soon this "striving to be better in the sight of men" feeling again changed into another—the desire to have more power than others, to secure for myself a greater share of fame, of social distinction, and of wealth.

II

Such was my life during ten years.

During that time I began to write, out of vanity, love of gain, and pride. I followed as a writer the same path which I had chosen as a man. In order to obtain the fame and the money for which I wrote, I was obliged to hide what was good and to say what was evil. Thus I did. How often while writing have I cudgeled my brains to conceal under the mask of indifference or pleasantry those yearnings for something better which formed the real thought of my life. I succeeded in this also, and was praised.

At twenty-six years of age I came to Petersburg and made the acquaintance of the authors of the day. I met with a hearty reception and much flattery.

Before I had time to look around, the prejudices and views of life common to the writers of the class with which I associated became my own, and completely put an end to all my former struggles after a better life.

The view of life taken by these fellow-writers was that life is a development, and the principal part in that development is played by ourselves, the thinkers, while among the thinkers the chief influence is again due to us, the artists, the poets. Our vocation is to teach men.

I was myself considered a marvelous artist and poet, and I therefore very naturally adopted this theory. I, an artist and poet, wrote and taught I knew not what. For doing this I received money; I kept a splendid table, had excellent lodgings, women, society; I had fame. Naturally what I taught was very good. I long remained in this belief.

But in the second and especially in the third year of this way of life, I began to doubt the infallibility of the doctrine, and to examine it more closely. What first led me to doubt was the fact that I began to notice the priests of this belief did not agree among themselves. They disputed, quarreled, abused, deceived, and cheated one another. Moreover, there were many among us who, quite indifferent to the questions who was right or who was wrong, advanced only their own private interests by the aid of our activity. All this forced on me doubts as to the truth of our belief.

I grew disgusted with mankind and with myself, and I understood that this belief was a delusion. The strangest thing in all this was that, though I soon saw the falseness of this belief and renounced it, I did not renounce the rank given me by these men—the rank of artist, poet, teacher. I was simple enough to imagine that I was a poet and artist, and could teach all men without knowing what I was teaching. But so I did.

III

I lived in this senseless manner another six years; up to the time of my marriage. During this time I went abroad. My life in Europe, and my acquaintance with many eminent and learned foreigners, confirmed my belief in the doctrine of general perfectibility, as I found the same theory prevailed among them. This belief took the form which is common among most of the cultivated men of our day. This belief was expressed in the word "progress." It then appeared to me this word had a real meaning. I did not as yet understand that, tormented like every other man by the question, "How was I to live better?" when I answered that I must live for progress, I was only repeating the answer of a man carried away in a boat by the waves and the wind, who to the one important question for him, "Where are we to steer?" should answer, "We are being carried somewhere."

I did not see this then; only at rare intervals my feelings, and not my reason, were roused against the common superstition of our age, which leads men to ignore their own ignorance of life.

After I returned I married. The new circumstances of a happy family life completely led me away from the search after the meaning of life as a whole. My life was concentrated at this time in my family, my wife and children, and consequently in the care for increasing the means of life. The effort to effect my own individual perfection, already replaced by the striving after general progress, was again changed into an effort to secure the particular happiness of my family.

In this way fifteen years passed.

Notwithstanding that during these fifteen years I looked upon the craft of authorship as a very trifling thing, I continued all the time to write. I had experienced the seductions of authorship, the temptations of an enormous pecuniary reward and of great applause for valueless work, and gave myself up to it as a means of improving my material position, and of stifling in my soul all questions regarding my own life and life in general. In my writings I taught what for me was the only truth—that the object of life should be our highest happiness and that of our family.

Thus I lived; but, five years ago, a strange state of mind began to grow upon me: I had moments of perplexity, of a stoppage, as it were, of life, as if I did not know how I was to live, what I was to do, and I began to wander, and was a victim to low spirits. But this passed, and I continued to live as before. Later, these periods of perplexity began to return more and more frequently, and invariably took the same form. These stoppages of life always presented themselves to me with the same questions: "Why?" and "What after?"

At first it seemed to me that these were aimless unmeaning questions; it seemed to me that all they asked about was well known, and that if at any time when I wished to find answers to them I could do so without much trouble—that just at that time I could not be bothered with this, but whenever I should stop to think them over I should find an answer. But these questions presented themselves to my mind with ever increasing frequency, demanding an answer with still greater and greater persistence, and like dots grouped themselves into one black spot.

It was with me as it happens in the case of every mortal internal ailment—at first appear the insignificant symptoms of indisposition, disregarded by the patient; then these symptoms are repeated more and more frequently, till they merge in uninterrupted suffering. The sufferings increase, and the patient, before he has time to look around, is confronted with the fact that what he took for a mere indisposition has become more important to him than anything else on earth, that it is death!

This is exactly what happened to me. I became aware that this was not a chance indisposition, but something very serious, and that if all these questions continued to recur, I should have to find an answer to them. And I tried to answer them. The questions seemed so foolish, so simple, so childish; but no sooner had I taken hold of them and attempted to decide them than I was convinced, first, that they were neither childish nor silly, but were concerned with the deepest problems of life; and, in the second place, that I could not decide them —could not decide them, however I put my mind upon them.

Before occupying myself with my Samara estate, with the education of my son, with the writing of books, I was bound to know why I did these things. As long as I do not know the reason "why" I cannot do anything, I cannot live. While thinking about the management of my household and estate, which in these days occupied much of my time, suddenly this question came into my head:—

"Well and good, I have now six thousand desyatins * in the government of Samara, and three hundred horses—what then?"

I was perfectly disconcerted, and knew not what to think. Another time, dwelling on the thought of how I should educate my children, I asked myself, "*Why?*" Again, when considering by what means the well-being of the people might best be promoted, I suddenly exclaimed, "But what concern have I with it?" When I thought of the fame which my works were gaining me, I said to myself:—

"Well, what if I should be more famous than Gogol, Pushkin, Shakespeare, Molière —than all the writers of the world—well, and what then?". . .

I could find no reply. Such questions will not wait: they demand an immediate answer; without one it is impossible to live; but answer there was none.

I felt that the ground on which I stood was crumbling, that there was nothing for me to stand on, that what I had been living for was nothing, that I had no reason for living.

* A desyatin is 2.7 acres.

IV

My life had come to a stop. I was able to breathe, to eat, to drink, to sleep, and I could not help breathing, eating, drinking, sleeping; but there was no real life in me because I had not a single desire, the fulfilment of which I could feel to be reasonable. If I wished for anything, I knew beforehand that, were I to satisfy the wish, or were I not to satisfy it, nothing would come of it. Had a fairy appeared and offered me all I desired, I should not have known what to say. If I had, in moments of excitement, I will not say wishes, but the habits of former wishes, at calmer moments I knew that it was a delusion, that I really wished for nothing. I could not even wish to know the truth, because I guessed in what it consisted.

The truth was that life was meaningless. Every day of life, every step in it, brought me, as it were, nearer the precipice, and I saw clearly that before me there was nothing but ruin. And to stop was impossible; to go back was impossible; and it was impossible to shut my eyes so as not to see that there was nothing before me but suffering and actual death, absolute annihilation.

Thus I, a healthy and a happy man, was brought to feel that I could live no longer— some irresistible force was dragging me onward to escape from life. The force that drew me away from life was stronger, fuller, and more universal than any wish; it was a force like that of my previous attachment to life, only in a contrary direction. With all my force I struggled away from life. The idea of suicide came as naturally to me as formerly that of bettering my life. This thought was so attractive to me that I was compelled to practice upon myself a species of self-deception in order to avoid carrying it out too hastily. I was unwilling to act hastily, only because I wanted to employ all my powers in clearing away the confusion of my thoughts; if I should not clear them away, I could at any time kill myself. And here was I, a man fortunately situated, hiding away a cord, to avoid being tempted to hang myself by it to the transom between the closets of my room, where I undressed alone every evening; and I ceased to go hunting with a gun because it offered too easy a way of getting rid of life. I knew not what I wanted; I was afraid of life; I struggled to get away from it, and yet there *was* something I hoped for from it.

Such was the condition I had to come to, at a time when all the circumstances of my life were pre-eminently happy ones, and when I had not reached my fiftieth year. I had a good, loving, and beloved wife, good children, and a large estate, which, without much trouble on my part, was growing and increasing; I was more than ever respected by my friends and acquaintances; I was praised by strangers, and could lay claim to having made my name famous without much self-deception. Moreover, I was not mad or in an unhealthy mental state; on the contrary, I enjoyed a mental and physical strength which I have seldom found in men of my class and pursuits; I could keep up with a peasant in mowing, and could continue mental labor for eight or ten hours at a stretch, without any evil consequences. And in this state of things it came to this—that I could not live, and as I feared death I was obliged to employ ruses against myself so as not to put an end to my life.

The mental state in which I then was seemed to me summed up in the following: My life was a foolish and wicked joke played on me by some one. Notwithstanding the fact that I did not recognize a "Some one," who may have created me, this conclusion that some one had wickedly and foolishly made a joke of me in bringing me into the world seemed to me the most natural of all conclusions.

I could not help reasoning that *there*, somewhere, is some one who is now diverting himself at my expense, as he watches me, as after from thirty to forty years of a life of study and development, of mental and bodily growth, with all my powers matured and having reached that summit of life from which it is seen in its completeness, I stand like a fool on this height, understanding clearly that there is nothing in life, that there never was anything, and never will be. To him it must seem ridiculous.

V

In every branch of human knowledge I sought an explanation of the questions that tormented me; I sought that explanation painfully and long, not out of mere curiosity; I did not seek it indolently, but painfully, obstinately, day and night: I sought it as a perishing man seeks safety, and I found nothing.

I sought in all directions, and thanks to a life spent in study, and also to my connections with the learned world, the most accomplished scholars in all the various branches of knowledge were accessible to me, and they did not refuse to open to me all the sources of knowledge both in books and through personal intercourse. I knew all that learning could answer to the question, "What is life?"

It was long before I could believe that human learning had no clear answer to this question. For a long time it seemed to me, as I listened to the gravity and seriousness of tone wherewith Science affirmed its positions on matters unconnected with the problem of life, that I must have misunderstood something. I fancied that the insufficiency of the answers which I received was owing to my own gross ignorance; but this thing was not a joke or pastime with me, and I was at last forced, willy-nilly, to the conclusion that these questions of mine were the only legitimate questions underlying all knowledge, and that it was not I that was in fault in putting them, but science in pretending to have an answer to them.

When I turned to one branch of human science, I obtained an endless number of exact answers to questions I had not asked: about the chemical elements of the stars, about the movement of the sun toward the constellation Hercules, on the origin of species and of man, about the infinitely small and imponderable particles of ether; but the only answer to my question as to the meaning of my life was this:—

"You are what you call your life; that is, a temporary and accidental agglomeration of particles. The mutual action and reaction of these particles on one another has produced what you call your life. This agglomeration will continue during a certain time, then the reciprocal action of these particles will cease, and with it will end what you call your life, and with it will end all your questions as well. You are an accidentally combined lump of something. The lump undergoes decomposition, this decomposition men call life; the lump falls asunder, decomposition ceases, and with it all doubting."

This is the answer from the clear and positive side of human knowledge, and if true to its own principles it can give no other.

Whenever speculative science is exact, where philosophy is true to itself, and wherever the philosopher does not overlook the greatest question of all, the answer is always the same, the answer given by Socrates, Schopenhauer, Solomon, and Buddha.

Here we have the only direct answer which human wisdom can give to the problem of life.

"The life of the body is evil and a lie, and so the annihilation of that life is a good for which we ought to wish," says Socrates.

"Life is what it ought not to be, an evil; and a passage from it into nothingness is the only good in life," says Schopenhauer.

"Everything in the world, both folly and wisdom, both riches and poverty, rejoicing and grief—all is vanity and worthless. Man dies and nothing is left of him, and this again is vanity," says Solomon.*

"To live, knowing that sufferings, illness, old age, and death are inevitable, is not possible; we must get rid of life, get rid of the possibility of living," says Buddha.

And what these powerful intellects have said, millions on millions of men have thought and felt. I also have thought and felt the same.

Thus my wanderings over the fields of knowledge not only failed to cure me of my despair, but increased it. One branch of knowledge gave no answer at all to the problem of life; another gave a direct answer which confirmed my despair, and showed that the state to which I had come was not the result of my going astray, of any mental disorder, but, on the contrary, it assured me that I was thinking rightly, that I was in agreement with the conclusions of the most powerful intellects among mankind.

I could not be deceived. All is vanity. A misfortune to be born. Death is better than life; life's burden must be got rid of.

* From the Book of Ecclesiastes which is accepted by Tolstoy as an expression of the views of Solomon.

VI

Having failed to find an explanation in knowledge, I began to seek it in life itself, hoping to find it in the men who surrounded me; and I began to watch men like myself, to observe how they lived, and how they practically treated the question that had brought me to despair.

And this is what I found among those of the same social position and culture as myself.

I found that for the people of my class there were four means of escape from the terrible state in which we all were.

The first means of escape is through ignorance. It consists in not perceiving and understanding that life is an evil and an absurdity. People of this class—for the greater part women, or very young or very stupid men—have not understood the problem of life as it presented itself to Schopenhauer, to Solomon, and to Buddha. They see neither the dragon awaiting them, nor the mice eating through the plant to which they cling, and they lick the drops of honey. But they only lick the honey for a time; something directs their attention to the dragon and the mice, and then there is an end to their tasting. From these I could learn nothing: we cannot unknow what we do know.

The second means of escape is the Epicurean. It consists, even while we know the hopelessness of taking advantage of every good there is in life, in avoiding the sight of the dragon and mice, and in the meantime in seeking the honey as best we can, especially wherever there is most of it.

Thus most of the people of our circle maintain the possibility of living. The conditions in which they are placed cause them to know more of the good than the evil of life, and their moral obtuseness enables them to forget that all the advantages of their position are accidental, and that not all men can have harems and palaces, like Solomon; that for one man who has a thousand wives, there are a thousand men who have none, and for each palace there must be thousands of men to build it in the sweat of their brow, and that the same chance which has made me a Solomon today may make me Solomon's slave tomorrow. The dullness of their imagination enables these men to forget what destroyed the peace of Buddha, the inevitable sickness, old age, and death, which if not today, then tomorrow, must be the end of all their pleasures.

The third means of escape is through strength and energy. It consists in destroying life when we have perceived that it is an evil and an absurdity. Only the rare men, strong and logical, act thus. Understanding all the stupidity of the joke that is played on us, and understanding that the happiness of the dead is more than the happiness of the living, and that it is better not to be, they thus act and put an end at once to the stupid joke, using any means of doing it—a rope round the neck, water, a knife in the heart, or a railway train. The number of those in my own class acting thus continually increases, and those that do this are for the most part in the very prime of life, with their intellectual powers in their flower, and with but few of the habits that undermine man's reason as yet formed.

I saw that this means of escape was the worthiest, and wished to make use of it.

The fourth means of escape is through weakness. It consists, though the evil and absurdity of life are well known, in continuing to drag it out, though aware that nothing can come of it. People of this class know that death is better than life, but have not the strength of character to act as their reason dictates, to have done with deceit and kill themselves; they seem to be waiting for something to happen. . . . To this class of men I myself belonged.

VII

I long lived in this state of mental aberration, which, though not always openly expressed in words, is not the less common among the most learned and most liberal men. But whether, owing to my strange kind of instinctive affection for the laboring classes, which impelled me to understand them, and to see that they are not so stupid as we think, or owing to the sincerity of my conviction that I could know nothing beyond the advisability of hanging myself, I felt that, if I wished to live and understand the meaning of life, I must seek it not amongst those who have lost the meaning of life but amongst the milliards of the living and the dead on whom now rests the burden of our life and their own.

I began to draw nearer to the believers among the poor, the simple, and the ignorant, the pilgrims, the monks, the *raskolniks,* and the peasants. The doctrines of these men of the people, like those of the pretended believers of my own class, were Christian. Here also much that was superstitious was mingled with the truths of Christianity, but with this difference, that the superstition of the believers of our class was entirely unnecessary to them, and never influenced their lives beyond serving as a kind of Epicurean distraction; while the superstition of the believing laboring class was so interwoven with their lives that it was impossible to conceive them without it—it was a necessary condition of their living at all. The whole life of the believers of our class was in flat contradiction with their faith, and the whole life of the believers of the people was a confirmation of the meaning of life which their faith gave them.

Thus I began to study the lives and the doctrines of the people, and the more I studied the more I became convinced that a true faith was among them, that their faith was for them a necessary thing, and alone gave them a meaning in life and a possibility of living. In direct opposition to what I saw in our circle—where life without faith was possible, and where not one in a thousand professed himself a believer—amongst the people there was not a single unbeliever in a thousand. In direct opposition to what I saw in our circle—where a whole life is spent in idleness, amusement, and dissatisfaction with life—I saw among the people whole lives passed in heavy labor and unrepining content. In direct opposition to what I saw in our circle—men resisting and indignant with the privations and sufferings of their lot—the people unhesitatingly and unresistingly accepting illness and sorrow, in the quiet and firm conviction that all these must be and could not be otherwise, that all was for the best. In contradiction to the theory that the less learned we are the less we understand the meaning of life, and see in our sufferings and death but an evil joke, these men of the people live, suffer, and draw near to death, in quiet confidence and oftenest with joy. In contradiction to the fact that an easy death, without terror or despair, is a rare exception in our class, a death which is uneasy, rebellious, and sorrowful is among the people the rarest exception of all.

I began to grow attached to these men. The more I learned of their lives, the more I liked them, and the easier I felt it so to live. I lived in this way during two years, and then there came a change which had long been preparing in me, and the symptoms of which I had always dimly felt: the life of our circle of rich and learned men, not only became repulsive, but lost all meaning. All our actions, our reasoning, our science and art, all appeared to me in a new light. I understood that it was all child's play, that it was useless to seek a meaning in it. The life of the working-classes, of the whole of mankind, of those that create life, appeared to me in its true significance. I understood that this was life itself, and that the meaning given to this life was true, and I accepted it.

The bird is so constituted that it must fly, pick up its food, build its nest, and when I see the bird doing this I rejoice in its joy. The goat, the hare, the wolf, are so constituted that they must feed and multiply, and bring up their young; and when they do this, I have a firm conviction that they are happy, and that their life is reasonable.

What, then, must man do? He also must gain his living like the animals, but with this difference, that he will perish if he attempt it alone; he must labor, not for himself, but for all. And when he does so, I am firmly convinced he is happy, and his life is reasonable.

What had I done during my thirty years of conscious life? I had not only not helped the life of others, I had done nothing for my own. I had lived the life of a parasite, and when I asked myself why I lived at all I received the answer, "There is no reason why." If the meaning of the life of man lies in his having to work out his life himself, how could I, who during thirty years had done my best to ruin my own life and that of others, expect to receive any other answer than this—that my life was an evil and an absurdity? . . .

It was an evil, an absurdity.

VIII

I renounced the life of our class, for I had come to confess that it was not life, but only the semblance of life, that its superfluous luxuries prevent the possibility of understanding life, and that in order to understand life, I must understand not the life of exceptional people, the parasites, but the life of the simple working-classes, the life that fashions life, and gives it the meaning which the working-classes accept. The simple laboring men around me were the Russian people, and I turned to this people and to the meaning which it gives to life.

This meaning, if it can be expressed, was as follows—

Every man has come into this world by the will of God, and God has so created man that every man is able to ruin or to save his soul. The problem of man's life being to save his soul, in order to save his soul, he must live after God's word; to live after God's word, he must renounce all the pleasures of life, must labor, be humble, endure, and be meek. This, to the people, is the meaning of the whole system of faith, as it has come down to them through, and is now given them by, the pastors of their Church and the traditions which exist among them.

The position which I occupied with relation to questions of faith had become quite different to what it once was. Formerly, life itself had seemed to me full of meaning, and faith an arbitrary assertion of certain useless and unreasonable propositions which had no direct bearing on life. I had tried to find out their meaning; and once convinced they had none, had thrown them aside. Now, on the contrary, I knew for certain that my life had not and could not have any meaning, and that the propositions of faith not only appeared no longer useless to me, but had been shown beyond dispute by my own experience to be that which alone gave a meaning to life. Formerly I looked on them as a worthless, illegible scrawl; but now if I did not understand them, still I knew that they had a meaning, and I said to myself that I must learn to understand them.

MY RELIGION

I HAVE LIVED in the world fifty-five years, and after the fourteen or fifteen years of my childhood, for thirty-five years of my life I was, in the proper acceptation of the word, a nihilist—not a socialist and revolutionist, as is generally understood by that word, but a nihilist in the sense of one who believed in nothing. Five years ago I came to believe in the doctrine of Christ, and my whole life underwent a sudden transformation. What I had once wished for I wished for no longer. What had once appeared to me good now became evil, and the evil of the past I beheld as good.

My condition was like that of a man who goes forth on some errand, and suddenly on the way decides that the matter is of no importance, and returns home. What was at first on his right hand is now on his left, and what was at his left hand is now on his right; his former desire to be as far as possible from home has changed into a desire to be as near to it as possible. The direction of my life and my desires were completely changed; good and evil had changed places. All this resulted from the fact that I understood the doctrine of Christ in a different way from that in which I had understood it before.

I do not care to expound the doctrine of Christ; I wish only to tell how it was that I came to understand what in this doctrine is most simple, clear, evident, indisputable, and appeals most to all men, and how this understanding refreshed my soul and gave me happiness and peace.

All the Christian Churches have always maintained that all men, however unequal in education and intellect—the wise and the foolish—are equal before God; that divine truth is accessible to every one. Christ has even declared it to be the will of God that what is concealed from the wise shall be revealed to the simple.

Not every one is able to understand the mysteries of dogmatics, homiletics, patristics, liturgics, hermeneutics, apologetics; but every one is able and ought to understand what Christ said to the millions of simple and ignorant people who have lived, and who are living today. Now, the things that Christ said to all these simple people, who could not avail themselves of the comments of Paul, of Clement, of Chrysostom, and of others, are just what I did not understand, and which now that I have come to understand them, I wish to make plain to all.

The thief on the cross believed in Christ, and was saved. Would it have been bad or injurious to any one if the thief had not died on the cross, but had descended from it, and told all men how he believed in Christ?

Like the thief on the cross, I believed in the doctrine of Christ, and was saved. This is not a vain comparison, but a most accurate expression of my spiritual condition of horror and despair in the presence of life and death, in which I found myself formerly, and of that condition of happiness and peace in which I find myself now.

Like the thief, I knew that my past and present life was vile; I saw that the majority of men about me lived in the same way. I knew, like the thief, that I was wretched

[From *My Confession: My Religion: The Gospel in Brief* by Leo Tolstoy. Abridged. Copyright 1899, 1927. Reprinted by permission of the publisher, Thomas Y. Crowell Company, New York.]

and suffering, that all those about me suffered and were wretched; and I saw before me no escape from this condition, but in death. As the thief was nailed to his cross, so was I nailed to this life of suffering and evil by an incomprehensible power. And as the thief saw before him, after the senseless and evil sufferings of life, the horrible shadows of death, so did I behold the same prospect.

In all this I was absolutely like the thief. But there was a difference in our conditions; he was about to die, and I was still alive. The thief might believe that his salvation would be beyond the grave, while I had not only that before me, but also life this side of the grave. I understood nothing of this life, it seemed to me frightful; and then suddenly I heard the words of Christ, and understood them; life and death ceased to seem evil, and instead of despair I tasted the joy and happiness that death could not take away.

Can it be harmful to any one, then, if I tell how this came about?

I

Almost from the first period of my childhood, when I began to read the New Testament, I was touched and stirred most of all by that portion of the doctrine of Christ which inculcates love, humility, self-denial, and the duty of returning good for evil. This, to me, has always been the substance of Christianity; it was what I loved in it with all my heart, it was that in the name of which, after despair and disbelief, caused me to accept as true the meaning found in the Christian life by the working people, and in the name of which I submitted myself to those doctrines professed by these same working people—in other words, the Orthodox Church.

But in making my submission to the Church, I soon saw that I should not find in its creed the confirmation, the explanation of those principles of Christianity which seemed to me essential; I observed that the essence of Christianity, dear though it was to me, did not constitute the chief element in the doctrine of the Church. I observed that what seemed to me essential in Christ's teaching was not recognized by the Church as most important. Something else was regarded by the Church as most important. At first I did not appreciate the significance of this peculiarity of the Church teaching. "Well now,"—I thought—"the Church sees in Christianity, aside from its inner meaning of love, humility, and self-denial, an outer, dogmatic meaning. This meaning is strange and even repulsive to me, but it is not in itself pernicious."

But the longer I continued to live in submission to the doctrine of the Church, the more clearly I saw this particular point was not so unimportant as it had seemed to me at first. I was driven from the Church by the strangeness of its dogmas, and the approval and the support which it gave to persecutions, to the death penalty, to wars, and by the intolerance common to all sects; but my faith was chiefly shattered by the indifference of the Church to what seemed to me essential in the teachings of Jesus, and by its avidity for what seemed to me not essential. I felt that something was wrong; but I could not discover what was wrong. I could not discover, because the doctrine of the Church did not deny what seemed to me essential in the doctrine of Christ; it fully recognized it, yet recognized it in such a way that what was chief in the teaching of Christ was not given the first place. I could not blame the Church because she denied the essence of the doctrine of Jesus, but because she recognized it in a way which did not satisfy me. The Church did not give me what I expected from her.

I had passed from nihilism to the Church simply because I felt it to be impossible to live without religion, without a knowledge of good and evil beyond the animal instincts. I hoped to find this knowledge in Christianity; but Christianity, as it then presented itself to me, was only a very indeterminate spiritual tendency, from which it was impossible to deduce any clear and obligatory principles of life. For these rules I turned to the Church. The Church offered me certain rules, but they not only did not attract me to the Christian dispensation now so dear to me, but rather repelled me from it. I could not follow the Church. A life based on Christian truth was precious and indispensable to me, and the Church offered me rules completely at variance with the truth I loved. The rules of the Church touching belief in dogmas, the observance of the sacrament, fasts, prayers, were not necessary to me, and did not seem to be based on Christian truth. Moreover, the rules of the Church weakened and sometimes destroyed the desire for Christian truth which alone gave meaning to my life.

I was troubled most by the fact that all human evil, the habit of judging private persons, of judging whole nations, of judging other religions, and the wars and massacres that were the consequence of such judgments, all went on with the approbation of the Church. Christ's teaching—judge not, be humble, forgive offenses, deny self, love—this doctrine was extolled by the Church in words, but at the same time the Church approved what was incompatible with the doctrine. Was it possible that Christ's teaching admitted of such contradiction? I could not believe so.

Moreover, it always seemed to me astonishing that, as far as I knew the Gospels, the passages on which the Church based affirmation of its dogmas were those that were most obscure, while the passages from which came the fulfilment of its teaching were the most clear and precise. And yet the dogmas and the obligations depending on them were definitely formulated by the Church, while the recommendation to obey the moral law was put in the most obscure, vague, and mystical terms. Was this the intention of Jesus in teaching His doctrine? A resolution of my doubts I could find only in the Gospels, and I read them, and reread them.

Of everything in the Gospels, the Sermon on the Mount always had for me an exceptional importance. I now read it more frequently than ever. Nowhere else does Christ speak with so great solemnity as in these passages, nowhere else does He give so many clear and comprehensible moral laws, appealing to every man's heart; nowhere else does He address Himself to a larger multitude of the common people. If there are any clear and precise Christian principles, one ought to find them here. I therefore sought the solution of my doubts in these three chapters of Matthew.* I read the Sermon on the Mount many, many times, and I always experienced the same feelings of enthusiasm and emotion, as I read the verses that exhort the hearer to turn the other cheek, to give up his cloak, to be at peace with all men, to love his enemies—but each time with the same disappointment. The divine words—addressed to all men—were not clear. They exhorted to an absolute renunciation of everything, such as entirely stifled life, as I understood it; to renounce everything, therefore, could not, it seemed to me, be an absolute condition of salvation. But the moment this ceased to be an absolute condition, clearness and precision were at an end.

I read not only the Sermon on the Mount; I read all the Gospels, and all the theological commentaries on them. I was not satisfied with the declarations of the theologians that the Sermon on the Mount was only an indication of the degree of perfection to which man should aspire; but

* Chapters V, VI, and VII.

that fallen man, weighed down by sin, could not reach such an ideal; and that the salvation of humanity was in faith and prayer and grace.

I could not admit the truth of these propositions, because it seemed to me strange that Christ, knowing beforehand that it was impossible for man, with his own powers, to carry his teaching into practice, should propound rules so clear and admirable, addressed to the understanding of every one. But as I read these maxims it always seemed to me that they applied directly to me, that their fulfilment was demanded of me. As I read these maxims I was filled with the joyous assurance that I might that very hour, that very moment, begin to practice them. I desired to do so, I tried to do so, but as soon as I began to enter upon the struggle I could not help remembering the teaching of the Church—*Man is weak, and to this he cannot attain*—and my strength failed. I was told, "You must pray, and God will give you faith; this faith will inspire prayer, which in turn will invoke faith that will inspire more prayer, and so on, indefinitely."

But reason and experience alike convinced me that such methods were useless. It seemed to me that the only true way was for me to try to follow the teaching of Christ.

And so, after all this fruitless search, study of all that had been written for and against the divinity of this doctrine, after all this doubt and suffering, I remained alone with my heart and with the mysterious book before me. I could not give to it the meanings that others gave, neither could I discover what I sought nor could I get away from it. Only after I had gone through alike all the interpretations of the wise critics and all the interpretations of the wise theologians and had rejected them all according to the words of Jesus, "*Except ye . . . become as little children, ye shall not enter into the kingdom of heaven*"—I suddenly understood what I had not understood before. I understood, not because I made any artificial combination of texts, or any profound and ingenious misinterpretations; on the contrary, I understood everything because I put all commentaries out of my mind. The passage that gave me the key to the whole was from the fifth chapter of Matthew, verses thirty-eight and thirty-nine:—

"*It has been said unto you, An eye for an eye, and a tooth for a tooth: But I say unto you, That you resist not evil.*"

Suddenly, for the first time, I understood the exact and simple meaning of those words; I understood that Jesus meant exactly what he said. Immediately—not that I saw anything new; only the veil that had hidden the truth from me fell away, and the truth was revealed in all its significance.

"*It has been said unto you, An eye for an eye, and a tooth for a tooth: But I say unto you, That you resist not evil.*"

Those words suddenly appeared to me absolutely new, as if I had never read them before. Always before, when I had read this passage, I had, singularly enough, allowed certain words to escape me, "*But I say unto you, that you resist not evil.*" To me it had always been as if the words just quoted had never existed, or had never possessed a definite meaning.

Later on, as I talked with many Christians familiar with the Gospel, I noticed frequently the same blindness with regard to these words. No one remembered them, and often, in speaking of this passage, Christians took up the Gospel to see for themselves if the words were really there. Through a similar neglect of these words I had failed to understand the words that follow:—

"*But whosoever shall smite thee on thy right cheek, turn to him the other also,*" etc.

Always these words had seemed to me to demand long-suffering and privation contrary to human nature. These words touched me; I felt that it would be noble to follow them, but I also felt that I should never have the strength to put them into practice, only to put them into practice so as to suffer. I said to myself, "If I turn the other cheek, I shall get another blow; if I give, all that I have will be taken away. Life would be an impossibility. Since life is given to me, why should I deprive myself of it? Christ cannot demand that." Thus I reasoned, persuaded that Christ in these words exalted suffering and deprivation, and in exalting them, made use of exaggerated terms lacking in clearness and precision; but when I understood the words "*Resist not evil*," it became clear to me that Jesus did not exaggerate, that He did not demand suffering for suffering, but that He said with great clearness and precision exactly what He wished to say.

He said "*Resist not evil*, and if you do so you will know beforehand that you may meet with those who, when they have struck you on one cheek and met with no resistance, will strike you on the other; who having taken away your coat, will take away your cloak also; who, having profited by your labor, will force you to labor still more without reward. And, yet, though all this should happen to you, '*Resist not evil*'; do good to them that injure you."

When I understood these words as they were said, all that had been obscure became clear to me, and what had seemed exaggerated I saw to be perfectly reasonable. For the first time I saw that the center of gravity of the whole idea lay in the words "Resist not evil"; and that what followed was only a development of this command; I saw that Jesus did not exhort us to turn the other cheek and give up the cloak that we might endure suffering, but that his exhortation was, "*Resist not evil*," and that he afterward declared suffering to be the possible consequence of the practice of this maxim.

These words, "*Resist not evil or the evil man*," understood in their direct significance, were to me truly the key that opened all the rest. And I began to be astonished that I could have miscomprehended words so clear and precise.

"*It has been said unto you, An eye for an eye, and a tooth for a tooth: but I say unto you, That you resist not evil or the evil man*."

Whatever injury the evil-disposed may inflict upon you, bear it, give all that you have, but resist not evil or the evil one. Could anything be more clear, more definite, more intelligible than that? I had only to grasp the simple and exact meaning of these words, just as they were spoken, when the whole teaching of Christ, not only as set forth in the Sermon on the Mount, but in the entire Gospels, became clear to me; what had seemed contradictory was now in harmony; above all, what had seemed superfluous was now indispensable. Each portion fell into harmonious unison and filled its proper part, like the fragments of a broken statue when put together as they should be. In the Sermon on the Mount, as well as throughout the whole Gospel, I found everywhere affirmation of the same doctrine, "*Resist not evil*."

In the Sermon on the Mount, as well as in all other places, Christ presents Himself to His disciples, in other words, to those that observe the rule of non-resistance to evil, as turning the other cheek, giving up their cloaks, persecuted, used despitefully, and in want. Elsewhere many times Christ says that he who does not take up his cross, who does not renounce worldly advantage, he who is not ready to bear all the consequences of the commandment, "*Resist not evil*," cannot become His disciple.

To His disciples Jesus says, Choose to be

poor; be ready to bear persecution, suffering, and death, without resistance to evil.

He himself was ready to bear suffering and death rather than resist evil, and He reproved Peter for wishing to avenge Him, and He died forbidding His followers to resist, nor did He make any modification in His doctrine. All His early disciples observed this rule, and passed their lives in poverty and persecution, and never rendered evil for evil.

Christ must have meant what He said. We may declare the universal practice of such a rule is very difficult; we may deny that he who follows it will find happiness; we may say with the unbelievers that it is stupid, that Christ was a dreamer, an idealist who propounded impracticable maxims which His disciples followed out of sheer stupidity; but it is impossible not to admit that Christ expressed in a manner at once clear and precise what He wished to say; that is, that according to His doctrine a man must not resist evil, and, consequently, that whoever adopts His doctrine cannot resist evil. And yet neither believers nor unbelievers will admit this simple and clear interpretation of Christ's words.

II

When I understood that the words "*Resist not evil,*" meant *resist not evil,* my whole former conception of Christ's teaching suddenly changed; and I was horrified, not that I had failed to understand it before, but that I had misunderstood it so strangely. I knew, as we all know, that the true significance of the Christian doctrine was comprised in the injunction to love one's neighbor. When we say, "*Turn the other cheek,*" "*Love your enemies,*" we express the very essence of Christianity. I knew all that from my childhood; but why had I failed to understand aright these simple words? Why had I always sought for some ulterior meaning? "*Resist not evil*" means never resist, never oppose violence; or, in other words, never do anything contrary to the law of love. If any one takes advantage of this disposition and affronts you, bear the affront, and do not, above all, have recourse to violence. Christ said this in words so clear and simple that it would be impossible to express the idea more clearly. How was it, then, that believing or trying to believe that He who said this was God, I still maintain that it is beyond my power to obey them? If my master says to me, "Go; cut some wood," and I reply, "I cannot do this: it is beyond my strength," I say one of two things: either I do not believe what my master says, or I do not wish to do what my master commands. Should I, without having made the slightest effort of my own to obey, then say of God's commandment that I could not obey it without the aid of a supernatural power? Should I say this of a commandment which He gave us to obey, concerning which He said that whoever obeyed it and taught it should be called great, concerning which He declared that only those that obey it shall have light, which He Himself obeyed, and which He expressed so clearly and simply that it leaves no room for doubt as to its meaning!

From my childhood I had been taught that Christ was God, and that His doctrine was divine, but at the same time, I was taught to respect the institutions that protected me from violence and evil, and to regard them as sacred. I was taught to resist evil; I was inspired with the idea that it was humiliating to submit to evil, and that resistance to it was praiseworthy. I was taught to judge, and to inflict punishment. Then I was taught the soldier's trade, that is, to resist evil by homicide; the army to which I belonged was called "The Christophile Army," and it was sent forth with a Christian benediction. Moreover, from infancy to manhood I learned to venerate what was in direct contradiction to Christ's law—to meet an aggressor with his own weapons, to avenge myself by violence for all offenses against my person, my family, or my people. Not only was I not blamed for this, but I was led to regard it as fine, and not contrary to Christ's law.

All that surrounded me, my comfort, my personal security, and that of my family and my property, depended then on a law which Christ repudiated—the law of "a tooth for a tooth."

My Church instructors taught me that Christ's teaching was divine, but, because of human weakness, impossible of practice, and that the grace of Christ alone could aid us to follow its precepts. My secular teachers and the whole organization of life agreed in calling Christ's teaching impracticable and visionary, and by words and deeds taught what was opposed to it. I was so thoroughly possessed with this idea of the impracticability of the divine doctrine, it had gradually become such a habit with me, the idea conformed so well with my desires, that I had never noticed the contradiction in which I had become involved. I did not see how impossible it was to confess Christ as God, the basis of whose teaching is the law of the non-resistance of evil, and at the same time deliberately to assist in the organization of property, of tribunals, of the government, of the army; to arrange my life in a manner entirely contrary to the doctrine of Jesus, and at the same time to pray to this same Christ to help us to obey His commands, to forgive our sins, and to aid us that we resist not evil. It did not enter my head, clear as it is to me now, how much more simple it would be to arrange and organize life conformably to Christ's law, and then to pray for tribunals, and massacres, and wars, if these things are so indispensable to our happiness.

Thus I came to understand how my error arose. It arose from my confessing Christ in words and rejecting Him in reality.

The position concerning the resistance of evil is a position which unites the whole teaching into one whole, nor only because it is not a mere verbal affirmation; it is a rule the practice of which is obligatory, since it is a law.

It is exactly like a key which opens everything, but only when the key is thrust into the lock. When we regard it as a verbal affirmation impossible of performance without supernatural aid, it amounts to the nullification of the entire doctrine. Why should not a doctrine seem impracticable, when we have suppressed its fundamental proposition? Unbelievers look on it as totally absurd—they cannot look on it in any other way. To set up an engine, to heat the boiler, to start it, but not to attach the belt—that is what is done with Christ's teaching when it is taught that one may be a Christian without observing the commandment, "*Resist not evil.*"

III

I now understood what Christ meant when he said "*Ye have heard that it hath been said, An eye for an eye, and a tooth for a tooth: but I say unto you, That ye resist not evil, but endure it.*"

Christ says: "You have thought that you were acting in a reasonable manner in defending yourself by violence against evil, in tearing out an eye for an eye, by establishing criminal tribunals, guardians of the peace, armies; by resisting your enemies; but I say unto you: Do no violence; have no share in violence; do harm to no one, not even to those that you consider your enemies."

I understood now that on the ground Christ took with regard to the non-resistance of evil, He not only told us what would result from the observance of this rule, but established a new basis for society conformable to His doctrine, and opposed to the social basis established by the law of Moses, by Roman law, and by the different codes in force today. He formulated a new law, the effect of which would be to deliver humanity from the evil which it has brought on itself.

He said: "You believe that your laws correct evil; as a matter of fact, they only increase it. There is only one way to suppress evil, and that is to return good for evil, without distinction. For thousands of years you have tried that method; now try mine, try the reverse."

Christ's doctrine is understood in a hundred different ways, but never in the simple and direct way which harmonizes with the inevitable meaning of His words.

We have arranged our entire social fabric on the very principles that Jesus repudiated; we do not wish to understand His doctrine in its simple and direct acceptation, and yet we assure ourselves and others, either that we follow His doctrine, or else that His doctrine is not expedient for us.

So-called believers believe that Christ-God, the second person of the Trinity, descended upon earth to teach men by His example how to live; they go through the most elaborate ceremonies for the consummation of the sacraments, the building of churches, the sending out of missionaries, the establishment of priesthoods, for parochial administration, for the performance of rituals; but they forget one little detail—to do what He said.

Unbelievers endeavor in every possible way to organize their existence independent of the Christ's law, having decided that this law is not expedient for them. But to endeavor to put His teachings in practice, this no one wishes to do; and moreover, without any attempt to put them in practice, both believers and unbelievers have decided in advance that it is impossible.

He said, simply and clearly, this law of resistance to evil by violence, which you have made the basis of your life, is false and wrong; and He gave another basis, that of non-resistance to evil, a law which, according to His doctrine, would deliver man from evil. He says:—

"You believe that your laws, which resort to violence, correct evil; they only augment it. For thousands of years you have tried to destroy evil by evil, and you have not destroyed it; you have only augmented it. Do as I command you, as I do, and you will know that this is true."

Not only in words, but by His whole life and by His death, did He carry out His doctrine of the non-resistance of evil.

The prophet Elijah, a fugitive from men, took refuge in a cave, and was told that God would appear to him. There came a great wind—the trees were uprooted. Elijah thought that this was God, and he looked, but the Lord was not in the wind. After the wind came tempest; the thunder and the lightning were terrific and Elijah went to see if God was there; but God was not there. Then came an earthquake: the earth belched forth fire, the rocks were shattered, the mountains were rent; Elijah looked for the Lord, but God was not in the earthquake. Then it became calm; a gentle breeze came to the prophet, bearing the freshness of the fields; and Elijah looked, and God was there. Such are these simple words of God—"*Resist not evil.*"

They are very simple, but, nevertheless, they express God's law and man's law, one and eternal. This law is to such a degree eternal that if there has been in history a progressive movement for the suppression of evil, it is due to the men who understood the doctrine of Jesus—who endured evil and resisted not evil by violence. The advance of humanity toward righteousness is due, not to tyrants, but to the martyrs. As fire cannot extinguish fire, so evil cannot suppress evil. Only good, confronting evil and resisting its contagion, can overcome evil. And in the inner world of the human soul, the law is as absolute as was even the law of Galileo, more absolute, more clear, more immutable. Men may turn aside from it, they may hide its truth from others; but the progress of humanity toward righteousness can be attained only in this way. Every forward step must be taken only in the name of the non-resistance of evil. A disciple of Christ may say now, with greater assurance than did Galileo, in spite of misfortunes and threats: "And yet it is not violence, but good, that overcomes evil."

IV

I believe in Christ's teaching, and this is my faith:—

I believe that my happiness is possible on earth only when all men fulfil Christ's teaching.

I believe that the fulfilment of this teaching is possible, easy, and pleasant.

I believe that even now, when this teaching is not fulfilled, if I should be the only one among all those that do not fulfil it, there is, nevertheless, nothing else for me to do for the salvation of my life from the certainty of eternal loss but to fulfil this teaching, just as a man in a burning house, if he find a door of safety, must go out.

I believe that my life according to the teaching of the world has been a torment, and that a life according to Christ's teaching can alone give me in this world the happiness for which I was destined by the Father of Life.

I believe that this teaching will give welfare to all humanity, will save me from inevitable destruction, and will give me in this world the greatest happiness. Consequently, I cannot help fulfilling it.

4

ORGANIC ARCHITECTURE

Frank Lloyd Wright

Frank Lloyd Wright is America's best-known architect. Early in life he caught the independent, pioneering spirit of the Midwest and became enthusiastic about the future of American democracy. His work as an architect is distinguished by this social concern, the desire to build in the authentic spirit of America as he understands it, and by a bold experimentation. Wright always insisted that every architectural problem is unique and therefore must be solved in an original way; yesterday's solutions will not meet our needs today. Beyond the practical purposes of any building he was deeply interested in designs that seemed natural and fitted into their surroundings—the term by which he preferred to describe his architecture is "organic." His emphasis upon this aspect of architecture went so far indeed that many critics labeled his work "romantic" in spirit rather than functional. In his best buildings, however, he combined the practical and the imaginative with unusual vision and success.

Born in Wisconsin in 1869, Wright was the recognized leader of the modern movement in architecture in this country until his death in 1959. From the time of his association with Louis Sullivan in Chicago during the 1890s, he constantly experimented with improved designs. His prairie houses in the Middle West gave to American architecture at the turn of the century a new concept in home building, and his later work was equally influential. He was widely honored not only in Europe but throughout much of the rest of the world for his outstanding achievements, and his buildings are still the subject of heated controversy. He wrote numerous books explaining and defending his ideas, including Modern Architecture (1931), When Democracy Builds (1946), and his Autobiography (1943). He also established a school of his own, The Taliesin Fellowship, to train young architects and helped produce a generation of American architects who believe a building must not only serve its purpose well but must go beyond mere practicality to express the spirit of our land and our people.

Wright was most fully himself when he described the countryside he had loved from his childhood—Wisconsin—and the homes he put there to fit its landscape. In the selection on Taliesin, reprinted here from his Autobiography, he writes much as Thoreau did about Walden Pond, in the same free-thinking, free-speaking, pioneer American tradition, and shows clearly the romantic spirit in his philosophy. The descriptions (also from his Autobiography) of his prairie houses, built in the Midwest at the turn of the century, and of

Unity Temple, built in Chicago in 1906, illustrate clearly the major principles of his organic architecture, outlined by Wright himself in an early article in the Architectural Record *which is also reprinted. (Figures 35-38 depict buildings discussed here.)*

ORGANIC ARCHITECTURE

IN 1894, with this text from Carlyle—"The Ideal is within thyself, thy condition is but the stuff thou art to shape that same Ideal out of"—I formulated the following "propositions." I set them down here much as they were written then, although in the light of experience they might be stated more completely and succinctly.

I. Simplicity and Repose are qualities that measure the true value of any work of art.

But simplicity is not in itself an end nor is it a matter of the side of a barn but rather an entity with a graceful beauty in its integrity from which discord, and all that is meaningless, has been eliminated. A wild flower is truly simple. Therefore:

1. A building should contain as few rooms as will meet the conditions which give it rise and under which we live, and which the architect should strive continually to simplify; then the ensemble of the rooms should be carefully considered that comfort and utility may go hand in hand with beauty. Beside the entry and necessary work rooms there need be but three rooms on the ground floor of any house, living room, dining room, and kitchen, with the possible addition of a "social office"; really there need be but one room, the living room, with requirements otherwise sequestered from it or screened within it by means of architectural contrivances.

2. Openings should occur as integral features of the structure and form, if possible, its natural ornamentation.

3. An excessive love of detail has ruined more fine things from the standpoint of fine art or fine living than any one human shortcoming—it is hopelessly vulgar. Too many houses, when they are not little stage settings or scene paintings, are mere notion stores, bazaars, or junkshops. Decoration is dangerous unless you understand it thoroughly and are satisfied that it means something good in the scheme as a whole, for the present you are usually better off without it. Merely that it "looks rich" is no justification for the use of ornament.

4. Appliances or fixtures as such are undesirable. Assimilate them together with all appurtenances into the design of the structure.

5. Pictures deface walls oftener than they decorate them. Pictures should be decorative and incorporated in the general scheme as decoration.

6. The most truly satisfactory apartments are those in which most or all of the furniture is built in as a part of the original scheme considering the whole as an integral unit.

II. There should be as many kinds (styles) of houses as there are kinds (styles) of people and as many differentiations as there are different individuals. A man who has individuality (and what man lacks it?) has a right to its expression in his own environment.

III. A building should appear to grow easily from its site and be shaped to harmonize with its surroundings if Nature is manifest there, and if not try to make it

[Reprinted from *The Architectural Record*, March 1908. By permission of Frank Lloyd Wright.]

as quiet, substantial and organic as She would have been were the opportunity Hers.

We of the Middle West are living on the prairie. The prairie has a beauty of its own and we should recognize and accentuate this natural beauty, its quiet level. Hence, gently sloping roofs, low proportions, quiet sky lines, suppressed heavy-set chimneys and sheltering overhangs, low terraces and out-reaching walls sequestering private gardens.

IV. Colors require the same conventionalizing process to make them fit to live with that natural forms do; so go to the woods and fields for color schemes. Use the soft, warm, optimistic tones of earths and autumn leaves in preference to the pessimistic blues, purples, or cold greens and grays of the ribbon counter; they are more wholesome and better adapted in most cases to good decoration.

V. Bring out the nature of the materials, let their nature intimately into your scheme. Strip the wood of varnish and let it alone—stain it. Develop the natural texture of the plastering and stain it. Reveal the nature of the wood, plaster, brick, or stone in your designs; they are all by nature friendly and beautiful. No treatment can be really a matter of fine art when these natural characteristics are outraged or neglected.

VI. A house that has character stands a good chance of growing more valuable as it grows older while a house in the prevailing mode, whatever that mode may be, is soon out of fashion, stale, and unprofitable.

Buildings like people must first be sincere, must be true and then withal as gracious and lovable as may be.

Above all, integrity. The machine is the normal tool of our civilization, give it work that it can do well—nothing is of greater importance. To do this will be to formulate new industrial ideals, sadly needed.

THE PRAIRIE HOUSES

AS I HAD regularly gone to and fro between Oak Park and my work with Adler and Sullivan in Chicago, here at hand was the typical American dwelling, the "monogoria" of earlier days, standing about on the Chicago prairie. That dwelling got there somehow and became typical. But by any faith in nature, implicit or explicit, it did not belong there. I had seen that far in the light of the conception of architecture as natural. And ideas had naturally begun to come to me as to a more natural house. Each house I built I longed for the chance to build another. And I soon got the chance. I was not the only one sick of hypocrisy and hungry for reality around there, I found.

I

What was the matter with the kind of house I found on the prairie? Well—let me tell you in more detail.

Just for a beginning, let's say that house *lied* about everything. It had no sense of Unity at all nor any such sense of space as should belong to a free man among a free people in a free country. It was stuck up and stuck on, however it might be done. Wherever it happened to be. To take any one of those so-called "homes" away would have improved the landscape and cleared the atmosphere. It was a box, too, cut full of holes to let in light and air, an especially ugly one to get in and out of. Or else it

[From *An Autobiography* by Frank Lloyd Wright. Duell, Sloan & Pearce, Inc., New York.]

was a clumsy gabled chunk of roofed masonry similarly treated. Otherwise joinery reigned supreme; you know—"Carpenter and Joiner," it used to read on the signs. Floors were the only part of the house left plain and the housewife covered those with a tangled rug-collection, because otherwise the floors were "bare"—bare, I suppose, only because one could not very well walk on jig-sawing or turned spindles, or plaster-ornament.

It is not too much to say that as an architect my lot in Oak Park was cast with an inebriate lot of sinners hardened by habit against every human significance except one—and why mention "the one touch of nature that makes the whole world kin"? I will venture to say that the aggregation was the worst the world ever saw—at the lowest esthetic level in all history. Steam heat, plumbing, and electric light were coming in as its only redeeming features.

My first feeling therefore had been a yearning for simplicity. A new sense of simplicity as "organic." This had barely begun to take shape in my mind when the Winslow house was planned. But now it began in practice. Organic simplicity might be seen producing significant character in the harmonious order we call nature. Beauty in growing things. None were insignificant.

I loved the prairie by instinct as a great simplicity—the trees, flowers, sky itself, thrilling by contrast.

I saw that a little height on the prairie was enough to look like much more—every detail as to height becoming intensely significant, breadths all falling short. Here was tremendous spaciousness but all sacrificed needlessly. All space was cut up crosswise and cut up lengthwise into the fifty-foot lot—or would you have twenty-five feet less or twenty-five feet more? Salesmanship cut and parceled it out, sold it with no restrictions. In a great, new, free country there was, then, everywhere a characteristic tendency to huddle and in consequence a mean tendency to tip everything in the way of human habitation up edgewise instead of letting it lie comfortably and naturally flat with the ground. Nor has this changed much since automobilization made it stupid as an economic measure and criminal as a social habit. I had an idea that the horizontal planes in building, those planes parallel to earth, identify themselves with the ground—make the building belong to the ground. I began putting this idea to work.

The buildings standing around there on the Chicago prairies were all tall and all tight. Chimneys were lean and taller still—sooty fingers threatening the sky. And beside them, sticking up almost as high, were the dormers. Dormers were elaborate devices—cunning little buildings complete in themselves—stuck on to the main roof—slopes to let the help poke their heads out of the attic for air. Invariably the damp, sticky clay of the prairie was dug out for a basement under the whole house and the rubble stone walls of this dank basement always stuck above the ground a foot or so—and blinked through half-windows.

So the universal "cellar" showed itself above ground as a bank of some kind of masonry running round the whole, for the house to sit up on—like a chair. The lean upper house walls of the usual two floors above this stone or brick basement were wood and were set up on top of this masonry chair. Preferably house walls were both sided and shingled, mixed up and down or crosswise, together or with moldings. These overdressed wood house walls had cut in them, or cut out of them to be precise, big holes for the big cat and little holes for the little cat to get in or get out of for ulterior purposes of light and air. These house walls were be-corniced or fancy bracketed up at the top into the tall, purposely, profusely complicated roof. Dormers plus. The whole roof was ridged and tipped, swanked and gabled to madness before they would allow it to be either watershed or shelter. The whole exterior was bedeviled, that is to say, mixed to puzzle pieces with corner boards, panel boards, window frames, corner blocks, plinth blocks, rosettes, fantails, and jigger-work in general. This was the only way "they" seemed to have then of putting on style. The wood butchery of scroll saw and turning lathe were at that moment the honest means to this fashionable and unholy but entirely moral end as things were.

Unless the householder of the period were poor indeed, usually the ingenious corner tower as seen in monogoria, eventuated into a candle-snuffer dome, a spire, an inverted rutabaga, radish or onion. Always elaborate bay windows and fancy porches rallied around this imaginatively unimaginative corner fetich—ring around a rosie. And all this the builders of the period could do nearly as well in brick as in stone. It was an impartial society. All materials looked pretty much alike to it in that day and do today.

Simplicity was as far from this scrap-pile as the pandemonium of the barnyard is far from music. But easy enough for the architect. Oh yes. All he had to do was call, "Boy, take down No. 37, and put a bay window on it for the lady."

II

First thing in building the new house, get rid of the attic, therefore the dormer. Get rid of the useless false heights below it. Next, get rid of the unwholesome basement, yes absolutely—in any house built on the prairie. Instead of lean, brick chimneys bristling up everywhere to hint at Judgment, I could see necessity for one chimney only. A broad generous one, or at most two. These kept low-down on gently sloping roofs or perhaps flat roofs. The big fireplace in the house below became now a place for a real fire. A real fireplace at that time was extraordinary. There were mantels instead. A mantel was a marble frame for a few coals in a grate. Or it was a piece of wooden furniture with tile stuck in it around the grate, the whole set slam up against the plastered, papered wall. Insult to comfort. So the *integral* fireplace became an important part of the building itself in the houses I was allowed to build out there on the prairie.

It comforted me to see the fire burning deep in the solid masonry of the house itself. A feeling that came to stay.

Taking a human being for my scale, I brought the whole house down in height to fit a normal one—ergo, 5′ 8½″ tall, say. This is my own height. Believing in no other scale than the human being I broadened the mass out all I possibly could to bring it down into spaciousness. It had been said that were I three inches taller than 5′ 8½″ all my houses would have been quite different in proportion. Probably.

House walls were now started at the ground on a cement or stone water table that looked like a low platform under the building, and usually was. But the house walls were stopped at the second-story windowsill level to let the bedrooms come through above in a continuous window series below the broad eaves of a gently sloping, overhanging roof. In this new house the wall was beginning to go as an impediment to outside light and air and beauty. Walls had been the great fact about the box in which holes had to be punched. It was still this conception of a wall-building which was with me when I designed the Winslow house. But after that my conception began to change.

My sense of "wall" was no longer the side of a box. It was enclosure of space affording protection against storm or heat only when needed. But it was also to bring the outside world into the house and let the inside of the house go outside. In this sense I was working away at the wall as a wall and bringing it towards the function of a screen, a means of opening up space which, as control of building-materials improved, would finally permit the free use of the whole space without affecting the soundness of the structure.

The climate being what it was, violent in extremes of heat and cold, damp and dry, dark and bright, I gave broad protecting roof shelter to the whole, getting back to the purpose for which the cornice was originally designed. The underside of roof projections was flat and usually light in color to create a glow of reflected light that softly brightened the upper rooms. Overhangs had double value: shelter and preservation for the walls of the house, as well as this diffusion of reflected light for the upper story through the "light screens" that took the place of the walls and were now often the windows in long series.

And at this time I saw a house, primarily, as livable interior space under ample shelter. I liked the *sense of shelter* in the look of the building. I still like it. The house began to associate with the ground and become natural to its prairie site.

III

What I have just described was on the *outside* of the house. But it was all there, chiefly because of what had happened *inside*.

Dwellings of that period were cut up, advisedly and completely, with the grim determination that should go with any cutting process. The interiors consisted of boxes beside boxes or inside boxes, called *rooms*. All boxes were inside a complicated outside boxing. Each domestic function was properly box to box.

I could see little sense in this inhibition, this cellular sequestration that implied ancestors familiar with penal institutions, except for the privacy of bedrooms on the upper floor. They were perhaps all right as sleeping boxes. So I declared the whole lower floor as one room, cutting off the kitchen as a laboratory, putting the servants' sleeping and living quarters next to the kitchen but semidetached, on the ground floor. Then I screened various portions of the big room for certain domestic purposes like dining, reading, receiving callers.

There were no plans in existence like these at the time. But my clients were all pushed toward these ideas as helpful to a solution of the vexed servant problem. Scores of unnecessary doors disappeared and no end of partition. Both clients and servants liked the new freedom. The house became more free as space and more livable too. Interior spaciousness began to dawn.

Thus came an end to the cluttered house. Fewer doors; fewer window holes though much greater window area; windows and doors lowered to convenient human heights. These changes once made, the ceilings of the rooms could be brought down over on to the walls by way of the horizontal broad bands of plaster on the walls themselves above the windows and colored the same as the room ceilings. This would bring ceiling surface and color down to the very window tops. Ceilings thus expanded by way of the wall band above the windows gave generous overhead even to small rooms. The sense of the whole broadened, made plastic by this means.

Here entered the important new element of plasticity—as I saw it. And I saw it as an indispensable element to the successful use of the machine. The windows would sometimes be wrapped around the building corners as inside emphasis of plasticity and to increase the sense of interior space. I fought for outswinging windows because the casement window associated house with the out-of-doors gave free openings outward. In other words, the so-called casement was not only simple but more human in use and effect. So more natural. If it had not existed I should have invented it. But it was not used at the time in the United States so I lost many clients because I insisted upon it. The client usually wanted the double-hung (the guillotine window) in use then, although it was neither simple nor human. It was only expedient. I used it once, in the Winslow house, and rejected it forever thereafter. Nor at that time did I entirely eliminate the wooden trim. I did make the "trim" plastic, that is to say, light and continuously flowing instead of the prevailing heavy "cut and butt" carpenter work. No longer did trim, so-called, look like carpenter work. The machine could do it all perfectly well as I laid it out, in this search for quiet. This plastic trim enabled poor workmanship to be concealed. There was need of that much trim then to conceal much in the way of craftsmanship because the battle between the machines and the Union had already begun to demoralize workmen.

Machine resources of this period were so little understood that extensive drawings had to be made merely to show the mill-man what to leave off. Not alone in the trim but in numerous ways too tedious to describe in words, this revolutionary sense of the *plastic* whole began to work more and more intelligently and have fascinating unforeseen consequences. Nearly everyone had endured the house of the period as long as possible, judging by the appreciation of the change. Here was an ideal of organic simplicity put to work, with historical consequences not only in this country but especially in the thought of the civilized world.

DESIGNING UNITY TEMPLE

LET US TAKE Unity Temple to pieces in the thought of its architect and see how it came to be the Unity Temple you now see.

Had Doctor Johonnot, the Universalist pastor of Unity Church [in Oak Park, Illinois], been Fra Junipero the style of Unity Temple would have been predetermined—"Mission." Had he been Father Latour it would have been Midi-Romanesque. Yes, and perhaps being what he was, he was entitled to the only tradition he knew—that of the little white New England church, lean spire pointing to heaven—"back East." If sentimentality were sense this might be so.

But the pastor was out of luck. Circumstances brought him to yield himself up in the cause of architecture. And to that cause everyone who undertakes to read what follows is called upon to yield a little.

I

Our building committee were all good men and true. One of them, Charles E. Roberts, the mechanical engineer and inventor I have mentioned, was himself enlightened in creation. One, enlightened, is leaven enough in any Usonian committee lump. The struggle began. It is always a struggle in architecture for the architect where good men and true are concerned.

[From *An Autobiography* by Frank Lloyd Wright. Duell, Sloan & Pearce, Inc., New York.

First came the philosophy of the building in my own mind.

I said, let us abolish, in the art and craft of architecture, literature in any symbolic form whatsoever. The sense of inner rhythm deep planted in human sensibility lives far above all other considerations in art. Then why the steeple of the little white church? Why *point* to heaven?

I told the committee a story. Did they not know the tale of the holy man who, yearning to see God, climbed up and up the highest mountain—climbed to the highest relic of a tree there was on the mountain? There, ragged and worn, he lifted up his eager perspiring face to heaven and called upon God. He heard a voice bidding him get down . . . go back!

Would he really see God's face? Then he should go back, go down there in the valley below where his own people were—there only could *he* look upon God's countenance. . . .

Why not, then, build a temple, not to God in that way—more sentimental than sense—but build a temple to man, appropriate to his uses as a meeting place, in which to study man himself for his God's sake? A modern meeting house and a good-time place.

The pastor was a liberal. His liberality was thus challenged, his reason was piqued, and the curiosity of all was aroused. What would such a building look like? They said they could imagine no such thing.

"That's what you came to me for," I ventured. "I can imagine it and I will help you create it." Promising the building committee something tangible to look at soon—I sent them away.

The first idea was to keep a noble room for worship in mind, and let that sense of the great room shape the whole edifice. Let the room inside be the architecture outside.

What shape? Well, the answer lay in the material. There was only one material to choose—as the church funds were $45,000—to "church" 400 people in 1906. Concrete was cheap.

Why not make the wooden boxes or forms so the concrete could be cast in them as separate blocks and masses, these grouped about an interior space in some such way as to preserve this sense of the interior space, the great room, in the appearance of the whole building? And the block masses might be left as themselves with no facing at all? That would be cheap and permanent and not ugly either.

What roof? What had concrete to offer as a cover shelter? The concrete slab—of course. The reinforced slab. Nothing else if the building was to be thoroughbred, meaning built in character out of one material.

Too monumental, all this? Too forthright for my committee I feared. Would a statement so positive as that final slab over the whole seem irreligious to them? Profane in their eyes? Why? But the flat slab was cheap and direct. It would be nobly simple. The wooden forms or molds in which concrete buildings must at that time be cast were always the chief item of expense, so to repeat the use of a single form as often as possible was necessary. Therefore a building, all four sides alike, looked like the thing. This, reduced to simplest terms, meant a building square in plan. That would make their temple a cube—a noble form in masonry.

The slab, too, belonged to the cube by nature. "*Credo simplicitatem.*" That form is most imaginative and happy that is most radiant with the aura or overtone of superform. Integrity.

Then the Temple itself—still in my mind—began to take shape. The site was noisy, by the Lake Street car tracks. Therefore it seemed best to keep the building closed on the three front sides and enter it from a court to the rear at the center of the lot. Unity Temple itself, with the thoughts in mind I have just expressed, arrived easily enough, but there was a secular side to Universalist church activities—entertainment often, Sunday school, feasts, and so on.

To embody these with the temple would spoil the simplicity of the room—the noble Room in the service of man for the worship of God. So I finally put the secular space designated as "Unity House," a long free space to the rear of the lot, as a separate building to be subdivided by movable screens for Sunday school or on occasion. It thus became a separate building but harmonious with the Temple—the entrance to both to be the connecting link between them. That was that.

And why not put the pulpit at the entrance side at the rear of the square Temple, and bring the congregation into the room at the sides on a lower level so those entering would be imperceptible to the audience? This would preserve the quiet and dignity of the room itself. Out of that thought came the depressed foyer or cloister corridor on either side, leading from the main lobby at the center to the stairs in the near and far corners of the room. Those entering the room in this way could see into the big room but not be seen by those already seated within it.

And, important to the pastor, when the congregation rose to disperse, here was opportunity to move forward toward their pastor and by swinging wide doors open beside the pulpit allow the entire flock to pass out by him and find themselves directly in the entrance loggia from which they had first come in. They had gone into the depressed entrances at the sides from this same entrance to the big room. But it seemed more respectful to let them go out thus toward the pulpit than turn their backs upon their minister as is usual in most churches.

So this was done.

The room itself—size determined by comfortable seats with leg room for four hundred people—was built with four interior free standing posts to carry the overhead structure. These concrete posts were hollow and became free-standing ducts to insure economic and uniform distribution of heat. The large supporting posts were so set in plan as to form a double tier of alcoves on four sides of the room. I flooded these side-alcoves with light from above to get a sense of a happy cloudless day into the room. And with this feeling for light the center ceiling between the four great posts became skylight, daylight sifting through between the intersecting concrete beams, filtering through amber glass ceiling lights. Thus managed the light would, rain or shine, have the warmth of sunlight. Artificial lighting took place there at night as well. This scheme of lighting was integral, gave diffusion and kept the room-space clear.

Now for proportion—for the concrete expression of concrete in this natural arrangement—the idea of an organic whole well in mind. And we have arrived at the question of *style*. For observe, so far, what has actually taken place is only reasoned *arrangement*. The "plan" with an eye to an exterior in the realm of ideas but meantime "felt" in imagination as a whole.

First came the general philosophy of the thing as repeated in the little story to the trustees. All artistic creation has its own philosophy. It is the first condition of creation. However, some would smile and say, "the result of it."

Second there was the general purpose of the whole to consider in each part: a matter of reasoned arrangement. This arrangement must be made with a sense of the yet-unborn-whole in the mind, to be blocked out as appropriate to concrete masses cast in wooden boxes. Holding all this diversity together in a preconceived direction is really no light matter but is the condition of creation. Imagination conceives here the Plan suitable to the material and the purpose of the whole, seeing the probable possible form clearer all the time.

Imagination reigns supreme, until now the form the whole will naturally take must be seen.

But if all this preliminary planning has been well conceived that question in the main is settled. This matter of style is organic now.

We do not choose the style. No. Style is what is coming now and it will be what we *are* in all this. A thrilling moment in any architect's experience. He is about to see the countenance of something he is invoking with intense concentration. Out of this inner sense of order and love of the beauty of life something is to be born—maybe to live long as a message of hope and be a joy or a curse to his kind. *His* message he feels. None the less it will be "theirs," and rather more. And it is out of love and understanding that any building is born to bless or curse those it is built to serve. Bless them if they will see, understand and aid. Curse them as it will be cursed by them if either they or the architect fail to understand each other. This is the faith and the fear in the architect as he makes ready—to draw his design.

In all artists it is somewhat the same fear and the same faith.

II

Now regard this pure white sheet of paper! It is ready for recording the logic of the plan.

T-square, triangle, scale—seductive invitation lying upon the spotless surface. Temptation!

"Boy! Go tell Black Kelly to make a blaze there in the work-room fireplace! Ask Brown Sadie if it's too late to have Baked Bermudas for supper! Then go ask your Mother—I shall hear her in here—to play something—Bach preferred, or Beethoven if she prefers."

Now comes to brood—to suffer doubt, hesitate yet burn with eagerness. To test bearings—and prove ground already assumed by putting all together in definite scale on paper. Preferably small scale study at first. Then larger. Finally still larger scale detail studies of parts.

An aid to creative effort, the open fire. What a friend to the laboring artist the poetic baked-onion! Real encouragement to him is great music. Yes, and what a poor creature, after all, creation comes singing through. About like catgut and horsehair in the hands of a Sarasate.

Night labor at the draughting board is best for intense creation. It may continue uninterrupted.

Meantime glancing side reflections are passing in the mind—"design is abstraction of nature-elements in purely geometric terms"—that is what we ought to call pure design? . . . This cube—this square—proportion. But—nature-pattern and nature-texture in materials themselves often approach conventionalization, or the abstract, to such a degree as to be superlative means ready to the designer's hand to qualify, stimulate, and enrich his own efforts. . . . What texture this concrete mass? Why not its own gravel? How to bring the gravel clean on the surface? . . . I knew. Here was reality. Yes, the "fine thing" is always reality. Always reality? . . . Realism, the subgeometric, however, is the abuse of this fine feeling. . . . Keep the straight lines clean and keep all significant of the idea—the flat plane expressive and always clean cut. But let texture come into them to qualify them in sunlight.

Reality is spirit—the essence brooding just behind all aspect. Seize it! And—after all you will see that the pattern of reality *is* supergeometric, casting a spell or a charm over any geometry, and is such a spell in itself.

Yes, so it seems to me as I draw with T-square, triangle and scale. That is what it means to be an artist—to seize this essence brooding everywhere in everything, just behind aspect. These questionings arising each with its own train of thought by the way, as the architect sits at his work.

Suddenly it is morning. To bed for a while.

III

But returning to the drawing board, here we see penciled upon a sheet of paper, the plan, section, and elevation in the main—all except the exterior of Unity House, as the room for secular recreation is to be called. To establish harmony between these buildings of separate function proved difficult, utterly exasperating.

Another series of concentrations—lasting hours at a time for several days. How to keep the noble scale of the temple in the design of the subordinate mass of the secular hall and not falsify the function of that secular mass? The ideal of an organic architecture is often terribly severe discipline for the imagination. I came to know that full well. And, always, some minor concordance takes more time, taxes concentration more than all besides. Any minor element may become a major problem to vex the architect. How many schemes I have thrown away because some one minor feature would not come true to form!

Thirty-four studies were necessary to arrive at this concordance as it is now seen. Unfortunately the studies are lost with thousands of others of many other buildings: the fruit of similar struggles to coordinate and perfect them as organic entities—I wish I had kept them. Unity House looks easy enough now, for it is right enough. But it was not.

Finally, see the sense of the room not only preserved—*it may be seen as the soul of the design*. Instead of being built into the heart of a block of sculptured building material, out of sight, the sacrosanct space for worship is merely screened in . . . does it come through as the living "motif" of the architecture?

Many studies in detail as a matter of course yet remain to be made, in order to determine what further may be left out to protect the design. These studies never seem to end and in this sense no organic building may ever be "finished." The complete goal of the ideal of organic architecture is never reached. Nor need be. What worthwhile ideal is ever reached?

Unity Temple is a complete building on paper, already. There is no "sketch" and there never has been one. There seldom is in a thought-built building.

The hardest of an architect's trials is to show his work for the first time to anyone not entirely competent or perhaps unsympathetic.

Already the architect begins to fear for the fate of his design. If it is to be changed much he prefers to throw it all away and begin all over again. Not much hope in the committee except Mr. Roberts. Why not ask him to see the design and explain it to him first? This is done. He is delighted. He *understands!* He is himself an inventor. And every project in architecture needs this one intimate friend in order to proceed. Mr. Roberts suggests a model. Without it nothing can be done. So the model is soon made.

All right; let the committee come now. They do come—all curious. Soon confounded—taking the "show me" attitude. At this moment the creative architect is distinctly at a disadvantage as compared with his obsequious brother of the "styles," he who can show his patternbook, speak glibly of St. Mark's at Venice or Capella Palatine, impress the no less craven clients by brave show of erudite authorities.

But the architect with the ideal of an organic architecture at stake can talk only principle and sense. His only appeal is fresh and must be made to the independent thought and judgment of his client such as it is. The client, too, must know how to think a little or follow from generals to particulars. How rare it is for an architect to go into any court where that quality of mind is on the bench! This architect has learned to dread the personal idiosyncrasy—offered him three times out of five—as a substitute for the needed, hoped-for intelligence.

But hoping, we try. And we use all our resources, we two—the inventor and I—and we win a third member of the committee at the first meeting. Including the pastor, there are now four only left in doubt. One of the four openly hostile—Mr. Skillin. Dr. Johonnot, the pastor, is himself impressed but cautious—oh, very—but tactful. He really has a glimpse of a new world. There is hope, distinctly hope, when he makes four as he soon does and the balance of power is with us. We need three more but the architect's work is done now. The four will get the others. The pastor is convinced. He will work! Doubts and fears are finally put to sleep—all but Mr. Skillin's. Mr. Skillin is sure the room will be dark—sure the acoustics will be bad. Finally the commission to go ahead is formally given over his dissent and warnings. Usually there is a Mr. Skillin on every modern building project in Usonia.

Now, who will build the Temple? After weeks of prospecting, no one can be found who wants to try it. Simple enough—yes—that's the trouble. So simple there is nothing at all to gauge it by. Requires too much imagination and initiative to be safe. The only bids available came in double, or more, our utmost limit. No one really wanted to touch it. Contractors are naturally gamblers but they usually bet on a sure thing—as they see the thing.

Now Paul Mueller comes to the rescue, reads the scheme like easy print. Will build it for only a little over their appropriation—and does it. He takes it easily along for nearly a year but he does it. Doesn't lose much on it in the end. It is exciting to him to rescue ideas, to participate in creation. And together we overcame difficulty after difficulty in the field, where an architect's education is never finished.

This building, however, is finished and the Sunday for dedication arrives.

I do not want to go. Stay at home.

When the church was opened the phone began to ring. Happy contented voices are heard in congratulation. Finally weary, I take little Francie by the hand to go out into the air to get away from it all. Enough.

But just as my hat goes on my head, another ring, a prosaic voice, Mr. Skillin's: "Take back all I said. . . . Light everywhere—all pleased."

"Hear well?"

"Yes, see and hear fine—see it all now."

"I'm glad."

"Goodbye." At last the doubting member, sincere in praise, a good sport besides.

Francie got tossed in the air. She came down with a squeal of delight.

And that is how it was and is and will be as often as a building is born.

Now, even though you are interested in architecture this story is more or less tedious and partly meaningless to you, as you were fairly warned at the beginning it would be. Without close study of the plans and photographs as it is read it must bore you. I have undertaken here, for once, to indicate the process of building on principle to insure character and achieve style, as near as

I can indicate it by taking Unity Temple to pieces. Perhaps I am not the one to try it. It really would be a literary feat and feast were it well done.

TALIESIN

I

TALIESIN was the name of a Welsh poet, a druid-bard who sang to Wales the glories of fine art. Many legends cling to that beloved reverend name in Wales.

Richard Hovey's charming masque, "Taliesin," had just made me acquainted with his image of the historic bard. Since all my relatives had Welsh names for their places, why not Taliesin for mine? . . . Literally the Welsh word means "shining brow."

This hill on which Taliesin now stands as "brow" was one of my favorite places when as a boy looking for pasque flowers I went there in March sun while snow still streaked the hillsides. When you are on the low hill crown you are out in mid-air as though swinging in a plane, the Valley and two others dropping away from you leaving the tree-tops standing below all about you. And "Romeo and Juliet" still stood in plain view over to the southeast. The Hillside Home School was just over the ridge.

As a boy I had learned to know the ground plan of the region in every line and feature. For me now its elevation is the modeling of the hills, the weaving and the fabric that clings to them, the look of it all in tender green or covered with snow or in full flow of summer that burst into the glorious blaze of autumn. I still feel myself as much a part of it as the trees and birds and bees are, and the red barns. Or as the animals are, for that matter.

When family life in Oak Park that spring of 1909 conspired against the freedom to which I had come to feel every soul was entitled, I had no choice, would I keep my self-respect, but go out a voluntary exile into the uncharted and unknown. Deprived of legal protection, I got my back against the wall in this way. I meant to live if I could an unconventional life. I turned to this hill in the Valley as my Grandfather before me had turned to America—as a hope and haven. But I was forgetful, for the time being, of Grandfather's Isaiah. His smiting and punishment.

And architecture by now was quite mine. It had come to me by actual experience and meant something out of this ground we call America. Architecture was something in league with the stones of the field, in sympathy with "the flower that fadeth and the grass that withereth." It had something of the prayerful consideration for the lilies of the field that was my gentle grandmother's: something natural to the great change that was America herself.

It was unthinkable to me, at least unbearable, that any house should be put *on* that beloved hill.

I knew well that no house should ever be *on* a hill or *on* anything. It should be *of* the hill. Belonging to it. Hill and house should live together each the happier for the other. That was the way everything found round about was naturally managed except when man did something. When he added his mite he became imitative and ugly. Why? Was there no natural house?

I felt I had proved there was. Now I wanted a *natural* house to live in myself. I scanned the hills of the region where the rock came cropping out in strata to suggest buildings. How quiet and strong the rock-ledge masses looked with the dark red cedars and white birches, there, above the green slopes. They were all part of the countenance of southern Wisconsin.

I wished to be part of my beloved southern Wisconsin, too. I did not want to put my small part of it out of countenance. Architecture, after all, I have learned—or before all, I should say—is no less a weaving and a fabric than the trees are. And as anyone might see, a beech tree is a beech tree. It isn't trying to be an oak. Nor is a pine trying to be a birch, although each makes the other more beautiful when seen together.

The world had had appropriate buildings before—why not appropriate buildings now, more so than ever before? There must be some kind of house that would belong to that hill, as trees and the ledges of rock did; as Grandfather and Mother had belonged to it in their sense of it all.

There must be a natural house, not natural as caves and log cabins were natural, but native in spirit and the making, having itself all that architecture had meant whenever it was alive in times past. Nothing at all I had ever seen would do. This country had changed all that old building into something inappropriate. Grandfather and Grandmother were something splendid in themselves that I couldn't imagine living in any period houses I had ever seen or the ugly ones around there. Yes, there was a house that hill might marry and live happily with ever after. I fully intended to find it. I even saw for myself what it might be like. And I began to build it as the brow of that hill.

It was still a very young faith that undertook to build that house. It was the same faith, though, that plants twigs for orchards, vineslips for vineyards, and small whips to become beneficent shade trees. And it planted them all about!

I saw the hill-crown back of the house as one mass of apple trees in bloom, perfume drifting down the Valley, later the boughs bending to the ground with red and white and yellow spheres that make the apple tree no less beautiful than the orange tree. I saw plum trees, fragrant drifts of snow-white in the spring, loaded in August with blue and red and yellow plums, scattering them over the ground at a shake of the hand. I saw the rows on rows of berry bushes, necklaces of pink and green gooseberries hanging to the under side of the green branches. I saw thickly pendent clusters of rubies like tassels in the dark leaves of the currant bushes. I remembered the rich odor of black currants and looked forward to them in quantity.

Black cherries? White cherries? Those too.

There were to be strawberry beds, white, scarlet and green over the covering of clean wheat-straw.

And I saw abundant asparagus in rows and a stretch of great sumptuous rhubarb that would always be enough. I saw the vineyard now on the south slope of the hill, opulent vines loaded with purple, green and yellow grapes. Boys and girls coming in with baskets filled to overflowing to set about the rooms, like flowers. Melons lying thick in the trailing green on the hill slope. Bees humming over all, storing up honey in the white rows of hives beside the chicken yard.

And the herd that I would have! The gentle Holsteins and a monarch of a bull—a sleek glittering decoration of the fields and meadows as they moved about, grazing. The sheep grazing too on the upland slopes and hills, the plaintive bleat of little white lambs in spring.

Those grunting sows to turn all waste into solid gold.

I saw the spirited, well-schooled horses, black horses and chestnut mares with glossy coats and splendid strides, being saddled and led to the mounting block for rides about the place and along the country lanes I loved—the best of companionship alongside. I saw sturdy teams ploughing in the fields. There would be the changing colors of the slopes, from seeding time to harvest. I saw the scarlet comb of the rooster and his hundreds of hens—their white eggs and the ducks upon the pond. Geese, too, and swans floating upon the water in the shadow of the trees.

I looked forward to peacocks Javanese and white on the low roofs of the buildings or calling from the walls of the courts. And from the vegetable gardens I walked into a deep cavern in the hill—modern equivalent of the rootcellar of my grandfather. I saw its wide sand floor planted with celery, piled high with squash and turnips, potatoes, carrots, onions, parsnips. Cabbages wrapped in paper and hanging from the roof. Apples, pears, and grapes stored in wooden crates walled the cellar from floor to roof. And cream! All the cream the boy had been denied. Thick—so lifting it in a spoon it would float like an egg on the fragrant morning cup of coffee or ride on the scarlet strawberries.

Yes, Taliesin should be a garden and a farm behind a real workshop and a good home.

I saw it all, and planted it all and laid the foundation of the herd, flocks, stable, and fowl as I laid the foundation of the house.

All these items of livelihood came back—improved from boyhood.

And so began a "shining brow" for the hill, the hill rising unbroken above it to crown the exuberance of life in all these rural riches.

There was a stone quarry on another hill a mile away, where the yellow sand limestone uncovered lay in strata like outcropping ledges in the façades of the hills. The look of it was what I wanted for such masses as would rise from these native slopes. The teams of neighboring farmers soon began hauling the stone over to the hill, doubling the teams to get it to the top. Long cords of this native stone, five hundred or more from first to last, got up there ready to hand, as Father Larson, the old Norse stone mason working in the quarry beyond, blasted and quarried it out in great flakes. The slabs of stone went down for pavements of terraces and courts. Stone was sent along the slopes into great walls. Stone stepped up like ledges on to the hill and flung long arms in any direction that brought the house to the ground. The ground! My Grandfather's ground. It was lovingly felt as intimate in all this.

Finally it was not so easy to tell where pavements and walls left off and ground began. Especially on the hill-crown, which became a low-walled garden above the surrounding courts, reached by stone steps walled into the slopes. A clump of fine oaks that grew on the hilltop stood untouched on one side above the court. A great curved stone-walled seat enclosed the space just beneath them, and stone pavement stepped down to a spring or fountain that welled up into a pool at the center of the circle. Each court had its fountain and the winding stream below had a great dam. A thick stone wall was thrown across it, to make a pond at the very foot of the hill and raise the water in the valley to within sight from Taliesin. The water below the falls thus made was sent by hydraulic ram up to a big stone reservoir built into the higher hill, just behind and above the hilltop garden, to come down again into the fountains and go on down to the vegetable gardens on the slopes below the house.

Taliesin, of course, was to be an architect's workshop, a dwelling as well, for young workers who could come to assist. And it was a farm cottage for the farm help. Around a rear court were to be farm buildings, for Taliesin was to be a complete living unit genuine in point of comfort and beauty, yes, from pig to proprietor. The place was to be self-sustaining if not self-sufficient, and with its domain of two hundred acres was to be shelter, food, clothing and even entertainment within itself. It had to be its own light-plant, fuelyard, transportation and water system.

Taliesin was to be recreation ground for my children and their children, perhaps for many generations more. This modest human program in terms of rural Wisconsin arranged itself around the hilltop in a series of four varied courts leading one into the other, the courts all together forming a sort of drive along the hillside flanked by low buildings on one side and by flower gardens against the stone walls that retained the hill-crown on the other.

The hill-crown was thus saved and the buildings became a brow for the hill itself. The strata of fundamental stonework kept reaching around and on into the four courts, and made them. Then stone, stratified, went into the lower house walls and up from the ground itself into the broad chimneys. This native stone prepared the way for the lighter plastered construction of the upper wood-walls. Taliesin was to be an abstract combination of stone and wood as they naturally met in the aspect of the hills around about. And the lines of the hills were the lines of the roofs, the slopes of the hills their slopes, the plastered surfaces of the light wood-walls, set back into shade beneath broad eaves, were like the flat stretches of sand in the river below and the same in color, for that is where the material that covered them came from.

The finished wood outside was the color of gray tree trunks in violet light.

The shingles of the roof surfaces were left to weather silver-gray like the tree branches spreading below them.

The chimneys of the great stone fireplaces rose heavily through all, wherever there was a gathering place within, and there were many such places. They showed great rock faces over deep openings inside.

Outside they were strong, quiet, rectangular rock masses bespeaking strength and comfort within.

Country masons laid all the stone with the stone quarry for a pattern and the architect for a teacher. The masons learned to lay the walls in the long, thin, flat ledges natural to the quarry, natural edges out. As often as they laid a stone they would stand back to judge the effect. They were soon as interested as sculptors fashioning a statue; one might imagine they were as they stepped back head cocked one side, to get the general effect. Having arrived at some conclusion they would step forward and shove the stone more to their liking, seeming never to tire of this discrimination. Many of them were artistic for the first time, and liked it. There were many masons from first to last, all good. Perhaps old Dad Signola, in his youth a Czech, was the best of them until Philip Volk came. Philip worked away five years at the place as it grew from year to year—for it will never be finished. And with not much inharmonious discrepancy, one may see each mason's individuality in his work at Taliesin to this day. I frequently recall the man as I see his work.

At that time, to get this mass of material to the hilltop meant organizing man and horse-power. Trucks came along years later. Main strength and awkwardness, directed by commanding intelligence, got the better of the law of gravitation by the ton as sand, stone, gravel, and timber went up into appointed places. Ben Davis was commander of these forces at this time. Ben was a creative cusser. He had to be. To listen to Ben back of all this movement was to take off your hat to a virtuoso. Men have cussed between every word, but Ben split the words and artistically worked in an oath between every syllable. One day Ben with five of his men was moving a big rock that suddenly got away from its edge and fell over flat, catching Ben's big toe. I shuddered for that rock as, hobbling slowly back and forth around it, Ben hissed and glared at it, threatening, eyeing, and cussing it. He rose to such heights, plunged to such depths of vengeance as I had never suspected, even in Ben. No Marseillaise nor any damnation in the mouth of a Mosaic prophet ever exceeded Ben at this high spot in his career as a cusser. William Blake says exuberance is beauty. It would be profane perhaps to say that Ben at this moment was sublime. But he was.

And in Spring Green (the names in the region are mostly simple like Black Earth, Blue Mounds, Cross Plains, Lone Rock, Silver Creek) I found a carpenter. William Weston was a natural carpenter. He was a carpenter such as architects like to stand and watch work. I never saw him make a false or unnecessary movement. His hammer, extra light with a handle fashioned by himself, flashed to the right spot every time like the rapier of an expert swordsman. He with his nimble intelligence and swift sure hand was a gift to any architect. That William stayed with and by Taliesin through trials and tribulations the better part of fourteen years. America turns up a good mechanic around in country places every so often. Billy was one of them.

Winter came. A bitter one. The roof was on, plastering done, windows in, men working now inside. Evenings the men grouped around the open fireplaces, throwing cord wood into them to keep warm as the cold wind came up through the floor boards. All came to work from surrounding towns and had to be fed and bedded down on the place somewhere during the week. Saturday nights they went home with money for the week's work in pocket, or its equivalent in groceries and fixings from the village. Their reactions were picturesque. There was Johnnie Vaughn who was, I guess, a genius. I got him because he had gone into some kind of concrete business with another Irishman for a partner, and failed. Johnnie said, "We didn't fail sooner because we didn't have more business." I overheard this lank genius, he was looking after the carpenters, nagging Billy Little, who had been foreman of several jobs in the city for me. Said Johnnie, "I built this place off a shingle." "Huh," said Billy, "that ain't nothin'. I built them places in Oak Park right off'n the air." No one ever got even a little over the ratlike perspicacity of that little Billy Little.

Workmen never have enough drawings or explanations no matter how many they get—but this is the sort of slander an architect needs to hear occasionally.

The workmen took the work as a sort of adventure. It was adventure. In every realm. Especially in the financial realm. I kept working all the while to make the money come. It did. And we kept on inside with plenty of clean soft wood that could be left alone pretty much in plain surfaces. The stone, too, strong and protective inside, spoke for itself in certain piers and walls.

Inside floors, like outside floors, were stone-paved or if not were laid with wide, dark-streaked cypress boards. The plaster in the walls was mixed with raw sienna in the box, went onto the walls natural, drying out tawny gold. Outside, the plastered walls were the same but grayer with cement. But in the *constitution* of the whole, in the way the walls rose from the plan and spaces were roofed over, was the chief interest of the whole house. The whole was supremely natural. The rooms went up into the roof, tentlike, and were ribanded overhead with marking strips of waxed, soft wood. The house was set so sun came through the openings into every room sometime during the day. Walls opened everywhere to views as the windows swung out above the tree tops, the tops of red, white and black oaks and wild cherry trees festooned with wild grapevines. In spring, the perfume of the blossoms came full through the windows, the birds singing there the while, from sunrise to sunset—all but the several white months of winter.

I wanted a home where icicles by invitation might beautify the eaves. So there were no gutters. And when the snow piled deep on the roofs and lay drifted in the courts, icicles came to hang staccato from the eaves. Prismatic crystal pendants sometimes six feet long, glittered between the landscape and the eyes inside. Taliesin in winter was a frosted palace roofed and walled with snow, hung with iridescent fringes, the plate-glass of the windows shone bright and warm through it all as the light of the huge fireplaces lit them from the firesides within, and streams of wood-smoke from a dozen such places went straight up toward the stars.

The furnishings inside were simple and temperate. Thin tan-colored flax rugs covered the floors, later abandoned for the severer simplicity of the stone pavements and wide boards. Doors and windows were hung with modest, brown checkered fabrics. The furniture was homemade of the same wood as the trim, and mostly fitted into the trim. I got a compliment on this from old Dan Davis, a rich and "savin' " Welsh neighbor who saw we had made it ourselves. "Gosh-dang it, Frank," he said, "Ye're savin' too, ain't ye?" Although Mother Williams, another neighbor, who came to work for me, said, "Savin'? He's nothin' of the sort. He could 'ave got it most as cheap readymade from that Sears and Roebuck . . . I know."

A house of the North. The whole was low, wide and snug, a broad shelter seeking fellowship with its surroundings. A house that could open to the breezes of summer and become like an open camp if need be. With spring came music on the roofs, for there were few dead roofspaces overhead, and the broad eaves so sheltered the windows that they were safely left open to the sweeping, soft air of the rain. Taliesin was grateful for care. Took what grooming it got with gratitude and repaid it all with interest.

Taliesin's order was such that when all was clean and in place its countenance beamed, wore a happy smile of well-being and welcome for all.

It was intensely human, I believe.

Although, thanks to "bigger and better publicity" among those who besieged it Saturdays and Sundays from near and far, came several characteristic ladies whose unusual enterprise got them as far as the upper half of the Dutch door, standing open to the living room. They couldn't see me. I was lying on a long walled-seat just inside. They poked in their heads and looked about with Oh's and Ah's. A pause. In the nasal twang of the more aggressive one, "I wonder . . . I wonder, now, if I'd like living in a regular home?"

The studio, lit by a bank of tall windows to the north, really was a group of four studies, one large, three small. And in their midst stood a stone fire-proof vault for treasures. The plans, private papers, and such money as there was, took chances anywhere outside it. But the Taliesin library of Genroku embroidery and antique colored wood-block prints all stayed safely inside. As work and sojourn overseas continued, Chinese pottery and sculpture and Momoyama screens overflowed into the rooms where, in a few years, every single object used for decorative accent became an "antique" of rare quality.

If the eye rested on some ornament it could be sure of worthy entertainment. Hovering over these messengers to Taliesin from other civilizations and thousands of years ago, must have been spirits of peace and good will? Their figures seemed to shed fraternal sense of kinship from their places in the stone or from the broad ledges where they rested.

Yes. It all actually happened as I have described it. It is all there now.

II

But the story of Taliesin, after all, is old: old as the human spirit. These ancient figures were traces of that spirit, left behind in the human procession as Time went on its way. They now came forward to rest and feel at home, that's all. So it seemed as you looked at them. But they were only the story within the story: ancient comment on the New.

The New lived for itself for their sake, as long ago they had lived, for its sake.

The storms of the north broke over the low-sweeping roofs that now sheltered a life in which hope purposefully lived at earnest work. The lightning in this region, always so crushing and severe, crashed; (Isaiah) and Taliesin smiled. Taliesin was minding its own business, living up to its own obligations and to the past it could well understand. But the New, failing to recognize it as its own, still pursued and besieged, traduced and insulted it. Taliesin raged, wanted to talk back—and smiled. Taliesin was a "story" and therefore it and all in it had to run the gauntlet. But steadily it made its way through storm and stress, enduring all threats and slanderous curiosity for more than three years, and smiled—always. No one entering and feeling the repose of its spirit could ever believe in the storm of publicity that kept breaking outside because a kindred spirit—a woman—had taken refuge there for life.

5

PAINTING: EXPRESSIONISM AND ABSTRACT EXPRESSIONISM

Vincent van Gogh

Vincent van Gogh is probably the most dynamic painter of the nineteenth century, and, if we can judge by the interest shown today in reproductions and exhibitions of his work, he has become one of the most popular. Few painters have stated as clearly as van Gogh what they wanted to do when painting a picture. Most great artists of the past simply left their pictures to speak for themselves. But van Gogh was not able to sell his pictures, and he felt compelled to explain this fact, and the pictures themselves, to himself and to his brother Theo, who was supporting him and trying to sell the pictures for him. Before Vincent sent a picture to Theo, a letter had to be written about it, explaining his emotions when he was looking at a certain landscape and the extent to which he had succeeded in conveying his feeling through his painting. These letters are really explanations not only of a new way of looking at the world but also of a new method of painting—van Gogh's personal style and technique.

Some of his earlier pictures are clearly impressionistic in spirit and technique, but van Gogh's own deep feeling soon led him beyond the limits of impressionism. If he belongs to any school, it is to that later known as "expressionism": he made little effort to copy the objects he saw, but rather he sought to express through his pictures his own powerful emotions about the world and about men and their souls. He did this by means of a novel use of color. Van Gogh himself said it best when he wrote: "I am always in hope of making a discovery, to express the love of two lovers by a marriage of two complementary colors, their mingling and their opposition, the mysterious vibrations of kindred tones; . . . to express hope by some star, the eagerness of a soul by a sunset radiance." Few artists have tried so deliberately to make a canvas move the beholder to such strong emotion. But these paintings were not in the conventional style and people would not buy them. In 1890 van Gogh sold his first picture; in that same year, only thirty-seven years old but ill and discouraged, he killed himself.

We include here selections from van Gogh's letters to his brother which describe clearly and directly the spirit and intention of his work. They also indicate the extent to which, as an artist, he turned from the conventional "realistic" approach to art and put his trust in his own deep feelings and intuition to provide not an objective recording but an intensely personal interpretation of man and nature. An essay on van Gogh by Lionello Venturi precedes the letters to Theo. It contains a detailed analysis of two of van Gogh's well-known paintings, together with helpful comment upon the important features of the new style in painting that he introduced.

For a brief biographical sketch of Venturi, *see page 293 above.*

VINCENT VAN GOGH

VINCENT VAN GOGH (1853-1890) was born in Holland, the son of a Protestant minister from whom he inherited his great desire to preach, in everything he attempted; in business, religion, social reform, and even his private life, as well as in his art. This reforming zeal was, no doubt, the reason for the great difference between van Gogh's style and the French art of his day—whose lack of preaching is not its least charming quality. Preaching in art is always a sign of bad taste, but van Gogh's infinite energy and humility overcame all his shortcomings. He had the spirit of self-sacrifice and adoration—an adoration for everything he loved, peasants, trees, as well as his masters. Sometimes his scrupulousness in drawing resulted in his paying too much attention to details; his feeling was exaggerated rather than delicate; and his sentimentality often resulted in turbulent expression, but the turbulent expression at last gave way to free imagination. At that moment he found his serenity in forms and colors which would have been arbitrary had they not been impregnated with his excessive emotions.

So long as van Gogh remained within the limits of his Dutch training, which was traditional and academic, his emotions did not, or could not, find perfect artistic expression. But after settling in Paris in 1886, four years before his death, he soon learned what the meaning of impressionism was, how to use colors, and how to find a form adapted to the effect of color. Thereafter he abandoned his preaching in paintings about social problems, and reduced his subject matters to motifs, the motifs of his vision. But after a year of research in the impressionistic world, he went farther. He sympathized with Gauguin's trend towards a simplification of form and the reduction of light effects to a composition of color zones. The simplification was called "symbolism." Forms and colors were no longer imagined as portraying an impression of nature, but as expressing a state of mind. They became the symbols of generalized emotions. A symbol is always an abbreviation or representation excluding all details, and can become a work of art only when the artist impresses on it a concentrated emotion. Van Gogh's emotions were of heroic stature, and so his simplification of form and color meant a concentration of expression. Besides, he loved pure, intense colors, with such a sensuous faith that his expression gained in evidence and striking force thereby. In his later years, such concentration of expression thoroughly absorbed his Christian and humanitarian feelings, thus resulting in a form of extreme vitality precisely because in his every touch of the brush his whole credo is contained.

Hence his greatness, which is distinct

from that of any of his contemporaries. In his art he lacked the balance which favored the lovable naturalness of Renoir or the intellectual power of Cézanne, but he brought the trends of impressionism and symbolism to such extreme consequences that he discovered a new world for art. Of course, his works generally achieve a modern moral beauty rather than a physical beauty. But in Figure 42 [*L'Arlésienne*] one can see that van Gogh realized also a kind of physical beauty. It is a beauty very different from that of Raphael, even more remote than that of Renoir or of Toulouse-Lautrec. But it has neither the pagan attractiveness of Renoir nor the fanciful note of Lautrec. Without being a Madonna or a female saint, this beauty has none the less a Christian feeling. This derives from the fact that it is neither a nude nor a clown, but a peasant woman in her peasant costume, from the town of Arles. She is seated at a table, simply posing for her portrait. The motif is a natural one, belonging to the everyday life of a peasant and to the love for humble beings, which is essentially Christian.

Van Gogh's vision was more abstract than that of any artist before him. Neither plastic relief nor color-volumes interested him; only flat zones of color. Their relation to light and shade is only indirect. Their harmony is based on the contrast of colors, and this contrast lies essentially in the blues of the dress and the hair against the yellow background. Such harmony of colors without light and shade had been dismissed in painting since the fifteenth century. It is necessary to go back to Simone Martini to find a harmony of the qualities of colors without regard to the effect of light. However, the latter's work has a gold background, symbol of Paradise. Van Gogh uses a yellow which can be painted on a wall, thus remaining within the limits of the experience of reality. Furthermore, it is true that the qualities of his colors are harmonized without regard to the effect of light, but the age-old experience of light and shade is not ignored by van Gogh, while Simone Martini did not dream of it. That is, van Gogh's qualities of color are distributed in those places where they have a symbolic function of light and shade. The white blouse and the blue dress of *The Arlesienne* have such function.

The beauty of this portrait of a woman from Arles, with its form in the shape of color zones, consists in its colors. Yet this abstract vision of color zones thoroughly realizes a natural image and it convinces us that both natural image and artistic vision were born together. The artist has created a new vision of reality, different from what we see in reality, but as convincing as reality itself, and coinciding with it in the infinite. This is the physical beauty of the image, and its value as pure art.

Figure 43 reproduces *Bedroom at Arles*, a still-life by van Gogh, which was described by the artist himself as being: "Just simply my bedroom, only here color is to do everything, and, giving by its simplification a grander style to things, is to be suggestive here of *rest* or of sleep in general. In a word, to look at the picture ought to rest the brain or rather the imagination. The walls are pale violet. The ground is of red tiles. The wood of the bed and chairs is the yellow of fresh butter, the sheets and the pillows very light greenish lemon. The coverlet scarlet. The window green. The dressing table orange. The basin blue. The doors lilac. And that is all—there is nothing in the room with closed shutters. The broad lines of the furniture again must express inviolable rest. Portraits on the walls and a mirror and a towel and some clothes. This by way of revenge for the enforced rest I was obliged to take. I shall work at it all day, but you see how simple the conception is. The light and the shadows thrown are suppressed; it is painted in free flat washes like the Japanese prints."

The color is very intense, without shadows, with some colors symbolizing shadow and others symbolizing light. This simplification of the effect of light and shade to pure symbols is suggestive of strong emotional power. The form too is simplified, to such a point that the impression is merely summarily perceived. The form is only a shape, what corresponds to the light and shade being only flat colors. Thus the perfect unity of form and color.

The subject matter is van Gogh's bedroom in Arles. It is a still-life—but van Gogh himself knew how to distinguish between his subject matter and his motif. He says that it suggests: *rest* and *sleep*. This is his motif. He had been ill and obliged to remain there. "By way of revenge for the enforced rest" he painted this picture. He sees a poor sunny room, and he feels that the things themselves are asleep. The room itself emanates a feeling of loneliness excluding any suggestion of the presence either of van Gogh or of any other human being. But the things in the room express something more than sleep—they were abandoned. And they were abandoned in such a careless state as to give the suggestion of disorder. Hence a magic value of something real, felt, and yet immaterial, as of eternal abandonment, departure, or death—a hint of tragedy.

At that time van Gogh was sad and discouraged, still passionately attached to his work, and longing for salvation. He wanted to portray sleep, but he could not. The approaching tragedy of a mind becoming unbalanced thwarted his rest and sleep. In the abandoned room there is calm, but a calm without hope, and without surcease. The colors are brilliant and intense, but they do not suggest joy, only sadness. So that this "rest" born of distress and these sunny colors born of sadness give the mood a sweetness, an innocence, and a grace which are religious in import. They express the intimate state of mind of the painter, in spite of himself. In his letters he is not aware of it. And because he is not aware of it, he achieves a form where all his hope and good nature are evident. Thus the expression is not immediate and direct, but mediate and indirect. In passing from the feeling to the expression something has been found: the form of rest and sunny colors. And it is this form which gives to the expression of feeling the value of art. It is this form which may be called the moral beauty of van Gogh's art.

DEAR THEO

I

IT IS AUTUMN now in the woods. There is sometimes a soft melancholy in the falling leaves, in the tempered light, in the haziness of things, in the elegance of the slender stems. But also I love the sturdier rude side—those strong light effects, for instance, on a man who stands digging and perspiring in the midday sun. At this time of the year it is doubly beautiful at the beach. There is in the view of the sea a light, tender effect, and in the wood there is a gloomier, more serious tone. I am glad both exist in life.

There are effects of color which I but

[From *Dear Theo, The Letters of Vincent van Gogh*, edited by Irving Stone. Copyright 1937 by Irving Stone. Reprinted by permission of Doubleday and Co., Inc.]

rarely find painted in the Dutch pictures. Yesterday evening I was busy painting a rather sloping ground in the wood, covered with moldered and dry beech leaves. You cannot imagine any carpet so splendid as that deep brownish-red, in the glow of an autumn evening sun, tempered by the trees. The question was—and I found it very difficult—how to get the depth of color, the enormous force and solidness of that ground. And while painting it I perceived for the first time how much light there was in that darkness; how was one to keep that light and at the same time retain the glow and depth of that rich color? From that ground young beech trees spring up which catch light on one side and are sparkling green there, while their shadowy side is warm, deep black-green.

Behind those saplings, behind that brownish-red soil, is a sky very delicate, bluish gray, warm, hardly blue, all aglow. A few figures of wood-gatherers are wandering around like dark masses of mysterious shadows. The white cap of a woman who is bending to reach a dry branch stands out all of a sudden against the deep red-brown of the ground; a skirt catches the light; the dark silhouette of a man appears above the underbrush; a white bonnet, a cap, a shoulder, the bust of a woman molds itself against the sky. Those figures, they are large and full of poetry—in the twilight of that deep, shadowy tone they appear as enormous *terres cuites* in molding in a studio.

I describe nature to you; in how far I have rendered the effect in my sketch, I do not know myself; but this I know, that I was struck by the harmony of green, red, black, yellow, blue, brown, gray.

While painting it I said to myself: I must not go away before there is something of an autumn evening feeling in the painting, something mysterious, something serious. But as this effect does not stay, I must paint quickly. So the figures are painted in at once by a few strong strokes. It struck me how firmly those little stems were rooted in the ground. I began them with a brush, but because the painted ground was already so sticky—a brush stroke was lost in it—I squeezed the roots and trunks in from the tube, and modeled them a little with the brush.

Yes, now they stand there rising from the ground, strongly rooted in it. In a certain way I am glad I have not *learned* painting, because then I might have learned to pass by such effects as this. Now I say: No, this is just what I want; if it is impossible, it is impossible; I will try it, though I do not know how it must be done. How I paint it *I do not know myself.* I sit down with a white board before the spot that strikes me, I look at what is before me, I say to myself that that white board must become something; I come back dissatisfied; I put it away, and when I have rested a little, I go to look at it with a kind of fear. Then I am still dissatisfied, because I have still too clearly in my mind that splendid scene of nature.

But after all I find in my work an echo of what struck me. I see that nature has told me something, has spoken to me, and that I have put it down in shorthand. In my shorthand there may be words that cannot be deciphered. There may be mistakes or gaps, but there is something in it of what wood or beech or figure has told me, and it is not a tame or conventional language that proceeds not from nature itself but from a studied manner or a system.

Now I feel myself on the high seas; the painting must be continued with all the strength I can give to it. I know for sure that I have an instinct for color, and that it will come to me more and more; that painting is in the very bone and marrow of me.

I feel in myself such a creative power that I am conscious the time will arrive when, so to speak, I shall daily and regularly make something good. I should not be at all surprised if it happened some day. But very rarely a day passes that I do not make something.

II

This week I started a composition of peasants around a dish of potatoes in the evening. I just came home from this cottage, and have been working at it by lamplight. I have been on it for three days continually, from morning till night; Saturday night the paint got into a condition which forbade all further work until it had become quite dry.

. . . As far as I have got now, however, I see a chance of giving a true impression of what I see; not always literally exact, rather never exact, for one sees nature through one's own temperament. And what I am trying to acquire is not to draw a *hand*, but the gesture; not with mathematical correctness a head, but the *expression*—for example, when a digger looks up and sniffs the wind or speaks. In short, *life*.

I am working at *The Potato Eaters* [Fig. 47] again. I have painted new studies of the heads, and especially the hands are greatly altered. . . . Though the actual picture has been painted in a relatively short time, it has taken a whole winter of painting study heads and hands. And as to the few days in which I have painted it, it has been a regular battle, but one for which I feel great animation.

I have tried to make it clear how these people, eating their potatoes under the lamplight, have dug the earth with those very hands they put in the dish; and so the painting speaks of manual labor, and how they have honestly earned their food. I wanted to give the impression of quite a different way of living than that of us civilized people. Therefore I am not at all anxious for everyone to like it or to admire it at once.

All winter long I have had in hand the threads of this fabric, and have searched for a definite pattern; and though it has taken on a rough, coarse aspect, nevertheless the threads have been selected carefully and according to certain rules. And it may prove to be a real *peasant picture. I know it is.*

But he who prefers to see the peasants in their Sunday best may do as he likes. I for my part am convinced that I get better results by painting them in their roughness than by giving them a conventional charm. I think a peasant girl is beautiful in her dusty and patched blue petticoat and bodice, which gets the most delicate hues from weather, wind, and sun. But if she puts on a lady's dress she loses her typical charm. A peasant in his fustian clothes in the fields is more typical than when he goes to church on Sunday in a kind of dress coat.

In the same way it would be wrong, I think, to give a peasant picture a certain conventional smoothness. If a peasant picture smells of bacon smoke, potato steam, all right, that's not unhealthy; if a stable smells of dung, that belongs to a stable; if the field has an odor of ripe corn or potatoes, or of guano or manure, that's healthy, especially for people from the city. Such pictures may *teach* them something. To paint peasant life is a serious thing, and I should reproach myself if I did not try to make pictures which raise serious thoughts in those who think seriously about art and about life. I see in the Salon number so many pictures which as to technique are faultlessly drawn and painted, if you like, yet bore me terribly because they give me food neither for the heart nor for the mind.

III

Today I am probably going to begin the interior of the *café* where I eat, by gaslight, in the evening. It is what they call here a *café de nuit*, staying open all night. Night prowlers can take refuge there when they have no money to pay for a lodging, or are too tight to be taken to one.

In my picture of the *Night Café* [Fig. 48] I have tried to express the idea that the *café* is a place where one can ruin oneself, run mad, or commit a crime. I have tried to express the terrible passions of humanity by means of red and green. The room is blood-red and dark yellow, with a green billiard table in the middle; there are four lemon-yellow lamps with a glow of orange and green. Everywhere there is a clash and contrast of the most alien reds and greens in the figures of little sleeping hooligans in the empty dreary room, in violet and blue. The white coat of the *patron*, on vigil in a corner, turns lemon-yellow, or pale luminous green.

So I have tried to express, as it were, the powers of darkness in a low wine shop, and all this in an atmosphere like a devil's furnace of pale sulphur—all under an appearance of Japanese gaiety and the good nature of Tartarin.

But what would Monsieur Tersteeg say about the *Night Café*, when he said before a Sisley—Sisley, the most discreet and gentle of the impressionists—"I cannot help thinking that the artist who painted that was a bit tipsy"? If he saw my picture, he would say that it was delirium tremens in full career.

Exaggerated studies such as the *Sower* and the *Night Café* usually seem to me atrociously ugly and bad. The picture of the *Night Café* is one of the ugliest I have done. It is the equivalent, though different, of *The Potato Eaters*. But when I am moved by something, as now by a little article on Dostoievski, these are the only ones which appear to have any deep meaning.

The second [canvas] represents the outside of a *café*, with a terrace lit up by a big gas lamp in the blue night, and a corner of starry blue sky [Fig. 48]. I often think that the night is more alive and more richly colored than the day.

The third is a portrait of myself, *almost colorless*, in gray tones against a background of pale malachite [Fig. 46]. I had bought of set purpose a mirror good enough for me to be able to work from myself in default of a model; because if I can manage to paint the coloring of my own head, which is not to be done without some difficulty, I shall likewise be able to paint the heads of other good souls, men and women. So this week I have done absolutely nothing but paint and sleep and take my meals. That means sittings of twelve hours, of six hours, and a sleep of twelve hours at a time.

IV

I want to get my drawing more spontaneous. I'm trying now to exaggerate the essential, and, of set purpose, to leave the obvious vague. What Pissarro says is true: You must boldly exaggerate the effects either of harmony or discord which colors produce; exact drawing, exact color, is not the essential thing because the reflection of reality in a mirror, if it could be caught, color and all, would not be a picture at all, no better than a photograph.

One night I went for a walk by the sea along the empty shore. It was not gay, but neither was it sad; it was—beautiful. The deep blue sky was flecked with clouds of a blue deeper than the fundamental blue of intense cobalt, and others of a clearer blue, like the blue whiteness of the Milky Way. On the blue depth the stars were sparkling, greenish, yellow, white, rose, brighter, flashing more like jewels than they do even in Paris. The sea was a very deep ultramarine.

I have never had such a chance; nature here is so extraordinarily beautiful. Everywhere and over all the vault of the sky is a marvelous blue, and the sun sheds a radiance of pale sulphur that is soft and lovely. What a country!

I cannot paint it as lovely, but it absorbs me so much that I let myself go, never thinking of a single rule; I have no doubts, no hesitation in attacking things.

I do not know whether anyone before me has talked about suggesting color. Delacroix and Monticelli, without talking about it, did it, and it is true that I see in impressionism the resurrection of Eugene Delacroix, but the interpretations of it are so divergent and in a way so irreconcilable that it will not be impressionism that will give us the final doctrine. I myself remain among the impressionists because it binds you to nothing, and as one of the crowd I have not to declare my formula. At the same time I think it is right to see in the impressionist movement a tendency towards great things, and not *only* a school which would confine itself to optical experiment. And after all, our own personal future we know nothing really about, but we feel that impressionism will last.

V

I have a view of the Rhone—the iron bridge at Trinquetaille, in which the sky and the river are the color of absinthe, the quays a shade of lilac, the figures leaning on their elbows on the parapet blackish, the iron bridge an intense blue, with a note of vivid orange in the blue background, and a note of intense malachite green. Another very rough effort, and yet I am trying to get at something utterly heartbroken and therefore utterly heartbreaking.

I must warn you that everyone will think I work too fast. Don't you believe a word of it. Is it not emotion, the sincerity of one's feeling for nature, that draws us? And if the emotions are sometimes so strong that one works without knowing one works, when sometimes the strokes come with a sequence and a coherence like words in a speech or a letter, one must remember that it has not always been so, and that in the time to come there will again be heavy days, empty of inspiration.

What a mistake Parisians make in not having a palate for crude things! But there, what I learnt in Paris is leaving me, and I am returning to the ideas I had in the country before I knew the impressionists. And I should not be surprised if the impressionists find fault with my way of working, for it has been fertilized by the ideas of Delacroix rather than by theirs. I use color more arbitrarily so as to express myself forcibly. Well, let that be as far as theory goes, but I am going to give you an example of what I mean.

I should like to paint the portrait of an artist friend, a man who dreams great dreams, who works as the nightingale sings, because it is in his nature. He'll be a fair man. I want to put into my picture my appreciation, the love that I have for him. So I paint him as he is, as faithfully as I can.

But the picture is not finished yet. To finish it I am now going to be the arbitrary colorist. I exaggerate the fairness of the hair; I come even to orange tones, chromes, and pale lemon-yellow. Beyond the head, instead of painting the ordinary wall of the mean room, I paint infinity, a plain background of the richest, intensest blue that I can contrive, and by this simple combination of the bright head against the rich blue background I get a mysterious effect, like a star in the depths of an azure sky.

These colors give me extraordinary exaltation. I have no thought of fatigue; I shall do another picture this very night; and I shall bring it off. I have a terrible lucidity at moments when nature is so beautiful; I am not conscious of myself any more, and the pictures come to me as in a dream.

I believe that a new school of *colorists* will take root in the South, as I see more and more that those in the North rely on ability with the brush, and the so-called "picturesque," rather than on the desire to express something by color itself. Here, under a stronger sun, I have found true what Pissarro said, and what Gauguin wrote to me as well: "The simplicity, the gravity of great sunlight effect. Never in the North do you come near suspecting it."

And the painter of the future will be *such a colorist as has never yet been*. Manet was working towards it, but the impressionists have already got stronger color than Manet. I think I am right in feeling that we must work as we can to that end, without doubting and without wavering.

Yesterday and today we have had the mistral again. I have done two still-lifes for this week.

The first shows a coffee pot in blue enamel, a cup on the left, royal blue and gold, a milk jug in squares of pale blue and white; a cup on the right of white with a blue-and-orange pattern, on an earthen plate of grayish-yellow; a jug in earthenware, or majolica, blue with a pattern in reds, greens, and browns; and lastly two oranges and three lemons. The table is covered with a blue cloth, the background greenish-yellow, so that there are six different blues, and four or five yellows and oranges. This canvas absolutely kills all the others; it is only a still-life, but it stands quite by itself—no doubt because of the drawing.

VI

Keep the three hundred Hokusai views of the holy mountain as well as the pictures of Japanese life; there is an attic at Bing's house with millions of prints piled up, landscapes and figures. Let me commend to you that attic of Bing's. I learnt there myself, and I made Anquetin and Bernard learn there too. That manager is a very nice fellow, and decent to anybody who is genuinely interested.

I have lost rather than gained in my business with Bing as far as money goes, but it has given me a chance to look at a lot of Japanese stuff long and steadily. All my work is in a way founded on Japanese art, and we do not know enough about Japanese prints. In decadence in its own country, pigeonholed in collections, already impossible to find in Japan itself, Japanese art is taking root again among the French impressionist artists. Fortunately we know more about the Japanese of France.

What I am sure of is that to make a picture which will be really of the South, it is not enough to have a certain cleverness. It is looking at things for a long time that ripens you and gives you a deeper understanding. If we study Japanese art, we see an artist who is wise, philosophic, and intelligent, who spends his time—how? In studying the distance between the earth and the moon? No. In studying the policy of Bismarck? No. He studies a single blade of grass. But this blade of grass leads him to draw the plant, and then the seasons, the wide aspects of the countryside, the animals, then the human figures. So he passes his life.

Come, now, isn't it almost an actual religion which these simple Japanese teach us, who live in nature as though they them-

FIG. 35. FRANK LLOYD WRIGHT: Robie House, Chicago, 1908. Photo from Sigfried Giedion.

Fig. 36 (*above*). FRANK LLOYD WRIGHT: Unity Church, Oak Park, Illinois, 1906. Photo Giln
Lane.

Fig. 37 (*below*). FRANK LLOYD WRIGHT: Unity Church, Oak Park, Illinois, 1906, plan. Ph
Gilman Lane.

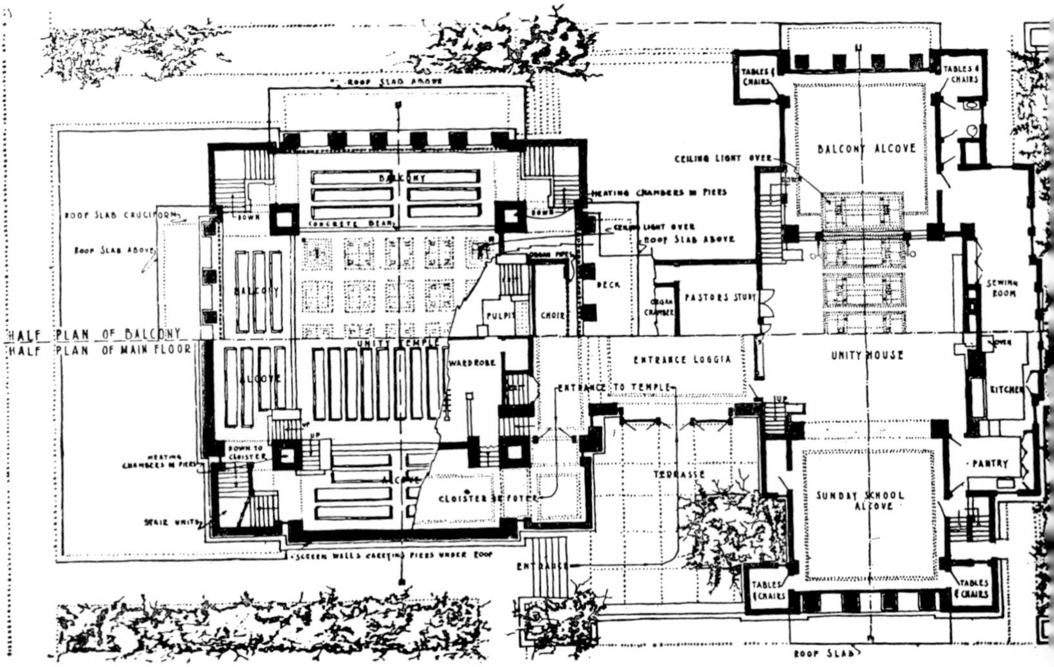

;. 38 (*above*). FRANK LLOYD WRIGHT: Taliesin I, Spring Green, Wisconsin, 1911. Photo Gilman
ne.

;. 39 (*below*). FRANK LLOYD WRIGHT: Taliesin West, Phoenix, Arizona, 1938-1940. Photo © Ezra
ller.

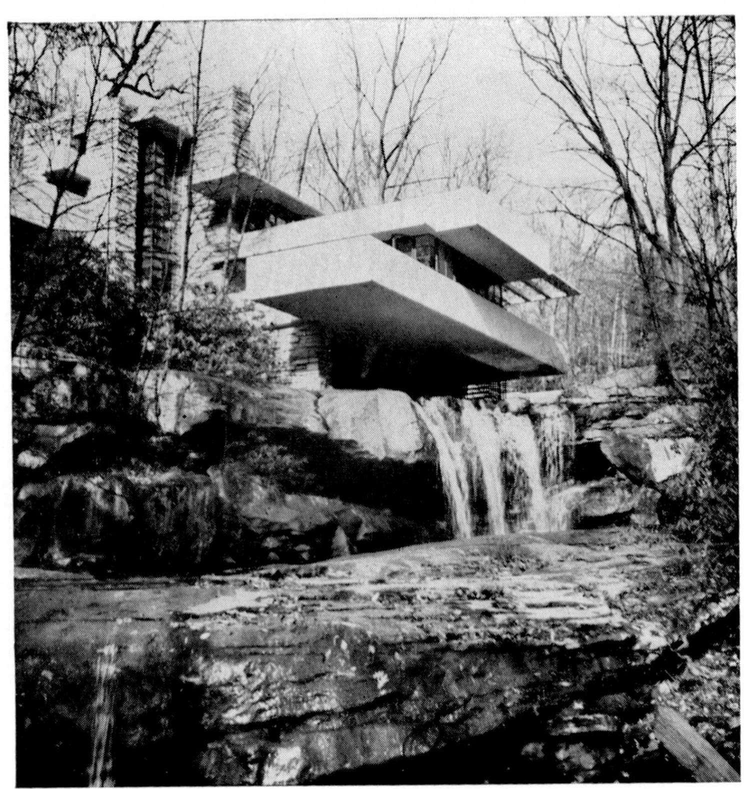

FIG. 40. FRANK LLOYD WRIGHT: Kaufmann House (Falling Water), Bear Run, Pennsylvania, 1930.

FIG. 41. FRANK LLOYD WRIGHT: Price House, Phoenix, Arizona, 1955. Photo Maynard L. Park for *House Beautiful*.

42 (*right*). VINCENT VAN GOGH: *L'Arlésienne* *ame Ginoux)*, 1887. Courtesy of The Met-itan Museum of Art, Bequest of Samuel A. ohn, 1951.

43 (*below*). VINCENT VAN GOGH: *Bedroom* *les*, 1888. Courtesy of The Art Institute of go, Helen Birch Barlett Memorial Collection.

Fig. 44 (*left*). GEORGES ROUAULT: *The Old Clo*
1917. Collection of Mr. and Mrs. Stavros N
chos, Paris.

Fig. 45 (*right*). GEORGES ROUAULT: *Crucifixion,* 1918. Collection Henry P. McIlhenny, Philadelphia.

46 (*right*). VINCENT VAN GOGH: *Portrait*, 1888. Fogg Museum of Cambridge, Mass., Maurice theim Collection.

47 (*below*). VINCENT VAN GOGH: *Potato Eaters*, 1885. Municipal eum, Amsterdam, V. W. van h Collection.

FIG. 48 (*above*). VINCENT VAN GOGH: *Night Café*, 1888. The Museum of Modern Art, New York, Collection Stephen C. Clark.

FIG. 49 (*below*). VINCENT VAN GOGH: *Starry Night*, 1889. Collection The Museum of Modern Art, New York. Acquired through the Lillie P. Bliss Bequest.

IG. 50. WASSILY KANDINSKY: *Composition No. 2*, 1910. The Solomon R. Guggenheim Museum, Iew York.

FIG. 51 (*above*). WASSILY
DINSKY: *Troika*, 1911. A
Jerome Eddy Collection,
Art Institute of Chicago.

FIG. 52 (*left*). WASSILY
DINSKY: *Improvisation No*
1913. Arthur Jerome Eddy
lection, The Art Institu
Chicago.

FIG. 53. WASSILY KANDINSKY: *On the Green Line*. Gift of Mr. and Mrs. Hans von der Marwitz, The Art Institute of Chicago.

FIG. 54. PAUL KLEE: *Around the Fish (Um den Fisch)*, 1926. Collection The Museum of Modern Art, New York, Mrs. John D. Rockefeller, Jr., Fund.

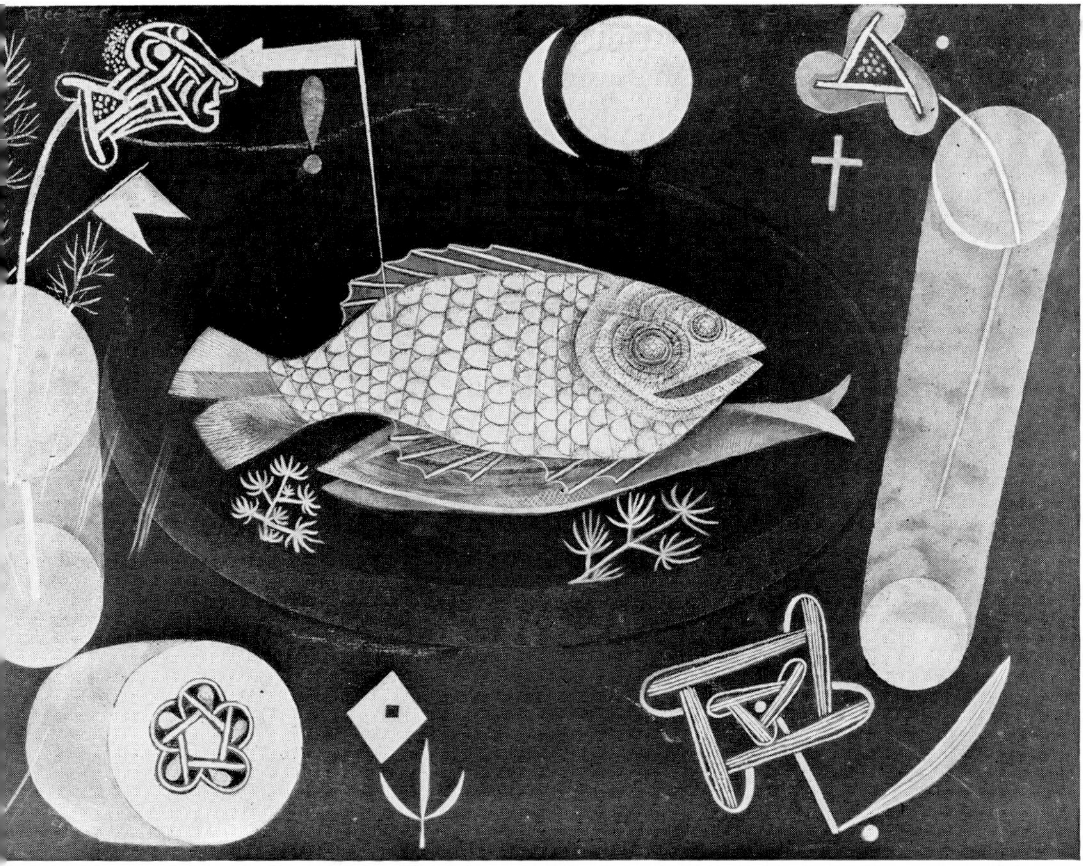

Fig. 55 (*left*). PAUL KLEE: *Dying Plants* (
bende Pflanzen), 1922. Collection The Mus
of Modern Art, New York, Philip L. Goo
Bequest.

Fig. 56 (*right*). PAUL KLEE: *Insects*, 1919. Collection The Museum of Modern Art, New York, Purchase Fund.

selves were flowers? We must return to nature in spite of our education and our work in a world of convention. And you cannot study Japanese art without becoming gayer and happier.

I envy the Japanese the extreme clearness which everything has in their work. Their work is as simple as breathing, and they do a figure in a few strokes with ease. Oh! I must manage some day that in a few strokes the figure of a man, a youngster, a horse, shall have head, body, legs, all in keeping.

VII

Painters—to take them only—dead and buried, speak to the next generation or to several succeeding generations in their work. Is that all, or is there more besides? In a painter's life death is not perhaps the hardest thing there is.

My dear boy, sometimes I know so well what I want. I can do without God both in my life and in my painting, but I cannot, ill as I am, do without something which is greater than I, which is my life—the power to create. And if, defrauded of the power to create physically, a man tries to create thoughts in place of children, he is still part of humanity.

In a picture I want to say something comforting, as music is comforting. I want to paint men and women with that something of the eternal which the halo used to symbolize, and which we seek to give by the actual radiance and vibration of our colorings.

Ah! portraiture, portraiture with the thought, the soul of the model in it, that is what I think must come.

So I am always in one of two currents of thought: first, the material difficulties, turning round and round to make a living; and second, the study of color. I am always in hope of making a discovery there, to express the love of two lovers by a marriage of two complementary colors, their mingling and their opposition, the mysterious vibrations of kindred tones; to express the thought of a brow by the radiance of a light tone against a somber background; to express hope by some star, the eagerness of a soul by a sunset radiance. Certainly there is nothing in that of stereoscopic realism, but is it not something that actually exists?

For my own part, I declare I know nothing whatever about it; but to look at the stars always makes me dream as simply as I dream over the black dots of a map representing towns and villages. Why, I ask myself, should the shining dots of the sky not be as accessible as the black dots on the map of France? If we take the train to get to Tarascon or Rouen, we take death to reach a star. One thing undoubtedly true in this reasoning is this: that while we are alive we cannot get to a star any more than when we are dead we can take the train, so it seems to me possible that cholera, gravel, phthisis, and cancer are the celestial means of locomotion, just as steamboats, omnibuses, and railways are the terrestrial means. To die quietly of old age would be to go there on foot.

I feel more and more that we must not judge God on the basis of this world; it's a study that didn't come off. What can you do, in a study that has gone wrong, if you are fond of the artist? You do not find much to criticize; you hold your tongue. But you have a right to ask for something better. It is only a master who can make such a muddle, and perhaps that is the best consolation we have out of it, since then we have a right to hope that we'll see the same creative hand get even with itself. And this life of ours, so much criticized, and for such good and even exalted reasons—we must not take it for anything but what it is, and go on hoping that in some other life we'll see a better thing than this.

That does not prevent my having a terrible need of—shall I say the word?—religion. That Benedictine father you tell of must have been very interesting. I only wish that they would manage to prove us something that would tranquilize and console us, so that we might stop feeling guilty and wretched, and could go on just as we are without losing ourselves in solitude and nothingness.

There is a book of Tolstoy's called *My Religion*. He does not seem to believe in a resurrection either of the body or the soul. Above all he seems not to believe in heaven—he reasons just as a nihilist reasons, but he attaches great importance to doing whatever you are doing, since probably it is all there is in you. And if he does not believe in the resurrection, he seems to believe in the equivalent—the continuance of life, the progress of humanity—the man and his work almost infallibly continued by humanity in the next generation. Himself a nobleman, he turned laborer, could make boots and frying pans, guide the plough. I can do nothing of that, but I can respect a human soul vigorous enough to mold itself anew.

Good God! we must not complain of living in an age of nothing but slackers when we are side by side with such specimens of mortality as this, and with no great faith in heaven at that. Tolstoy believes in a peaceful revolution caused by the need of love and religion, which must appear among men as a reaction to scepticism, and to that desperate suffering that makes one despair.

Georges Rouault

Because of his distinctive style and his concern with portraying the inner spirit of the subjects he painted, Georges Rouault is usually classed with the "expressionists" who follow the path explored by van Gogh. Although Rouault temperamentally preferred the sharp color effects associated with the paintings of the group of young men who gathered around Matisse in Paris between 1905 and 1910 (the "fauves"), his spirit is distinctly religious instead of secular. At a time when religion seemed out of place in artistic circles, Rouault created work suffused with a sense of mysticism and from his Catholic faith produced stirring interpretations of religious subjects. "I hope," he said, "to paint a Christ so moving that those who see Him will be converted." All of the subjects Rouault used, religious or secular, are imbued with his sympathy for erring humanity. He can paint sin in a prostitute or purity in Christ. The eyes of his clowns are filled with despair; the faces of his judges disclose their dishonesty. With tremendous artistic conscience he often struggled for years over a painting to reveal through his heavy, glowing colors, sharpened by black outlines, the intense emotion he was driven to express.

Although his work is now widely recognized, Rouault lived in poverty until his middle age. He was born at Paris in 1871 and his early apprenticeship to a stained-glass maker obviously affected his forceful style when as a student at the Beaux-Arts he later turned to religious subjects. Persisting in his work despite its neglect, Rouault finally accepted a contract with Vollard, the art dealer, to give him all the paintings from his studio for ten thousand dollars. When Vollard died in 1939 Rouault recovered about seven hundred of his canvases, but he destroyed nearly half of them as unworthy of his aims. It seems significant that his last paintings are filled with much brighter colors than the earlier somber ones. The greens and yellows of his later work appear to declare the joy of salvation and faith.

Generally regarded as one of the leading contemporary painters and surrounded with unfinished canvases, Rouault died at his Paris home in 1958.

In the selection we reprint from Painting and Painters *by Lionello Venturi, the major features of Rouault's work are described and two of his better-known paintings are analyzed in some detail.*

(For a biographical sketch of Venturi see page 293 above.)

GEORGES ROUAULT

GEORGES ROUAULT (born in 1871) has attained in his painting a moral beauty so opposite to any physical beauty that no other painter in modern times has been able even remotely to approach him. To understand why this has happened it is necessary to go back to Goya, Daumier, Cézanne, and van Gogh in order to remember that in the nineteenth century moral beauty was identified with the lot of the common people as a reaction against physical beauty, which had by tradition been identified with the upper classes. This finding of the salvation of the soul in the lower classes, in the simplicity of life, in a subverted sublime, was the claim of nineteenth-century painting, one of the greatest contributions to art of all time. This love for poor people, this ability to feel in them absolute moral values, was essentially Christian, and gave birth to the only really religious art of that time, even if it was not recognized as such by the Catholic Church. At the end of the nineteenth century and at the beginning of this present one, a new revival of religious feeling took place in France, and certain writers as well as painters were even more deeply concerned with religion than with social problems. The common man was considered the real creature of God, but, what was even more significant, the actual goal of these painters and writers was God Himself. No modern painter has manifested such strong religious impulses as has Rouault in his art. He is the only modern exponent of a great art which is at the same time a religious art. In comparison with the art of the preceding century, which extolled the virtues of the common people, Rouault's art has less social meaning, but attains to values which have a universal religious significance.

Rouault flatly refuses to demean himself by painting refined figures of seraphim, angels, and Madonnas acceptable to the Church. He sees the world around him as it actually is, and he is too honest with himself and toward his art to conceal his natural reactions. Seeing ugliness and crime all around him, he condemns the world he lives in, and puts into his condemnation such grandeur, strength, and violence—such a universal meaning—that it becomes a religious condemnation. To do this it was necessary for Rouault to be free of any dogmatic limitation. As a man he is far from being a rebel. On the contrary, he is a faithful observant of Catholic doctrine, but all the power and sincerity of his reaction to the world about him is in his painting. Thus he goes back to the original sources of religious faith, to rediscover faith at whatever risk to the present world, to recognize a God anterior to the idea of Satan. His faith is not mere enlightened choice; it is a force of nature.

In 1937 he wrote: "I am obedient, but it is within the province of everyone to revolt; it is more difficult to obey silently certain inner urges and to pass one's life searching for sincere and appropriate means of expression for our temperament and our talent, if we have any." Rouault is a keen psychologist with a deep insight into human nature and a very subtle discernment for all that is hypocritical, pharisaical, and false, awakening in him a very deep and violent repugnance. Another strong tendency of his is to fling himself "into the heart of the fray" and to sacrifice himself, not for some long-cherished ideal, but for some powerful instinctive impulsion of the moment. Thus, after having pried open all the secrets of the best academic training, he instinctively chose a new direction which came from an "urgent inner impulse, from a . . . penetrating vision and from the need to approach religious subjects in a manner free of hypocritical convention."

Thus, as an act of destiny he became a rebel in art. And when he finally saw his pictures hung in exhibitions he found them "frightening," while the public found them "outrageous." Evidently he believed that the academic manner he had been taught was as false as the world he condemned. Finish, beauty, subtle outline, chiaroscuro, nuance, illusion of space, everything was false and hypocritical. He studied Degas, Lautrec, Cézanne, but rejected for himself everything he had studied. He went straight to the images born of his imagination—images which seem as though belonging to another planet. And by disregarding all rules of painting and anterior experiences of life, he became a primitive master. A painting of his seems sketched in a few minutes, whereas in actuality it might have been reworked scores of times over a period of years.

The Old Clown [Fig. 44] is a good example of the artistic form of Rouault. The nose, the mouth, the eyes are roughly painted; but any refinement would have destroyed the form of the whole. The face and cap have a completely oval shape, but that shape is alive because of its rough features and the sharp interruptions of shadows: without them, it would be a conventional painting; with them, it is as powerful in plasticity as it is original in expression. The shadows are often zones of black tints, being not only shadows but functioning also as sharp contrasts to the intense colors, which function as light. Thus lights and shadows serve both as depth for plasticity and as surface for coloring. Such simplification of means is carried to its extreme, not for the sake of simplification, as in the case of a "primitivist," but for the purpose of intensifying the expression, as with a genuine primitive master. Clowns have been the lifelong dream of Rouault, who has loved them since early youth because of their poverty and sadness, and because they too are artists in their own way, and transcend the misery of their private lives to attain the free fancy of the artist. Moreover, he envies their wandering about the world, while he feels pinned down to his static job of painting, like a peasant to his field. He has painted clowns scores of times, always emphasizing their sadness as well as their ornaments and fanciful colors, thus expressing their humanity not only as men but also as clowns. Their being clowns makes possible their participation in art, and Rouault finds in their art an indirect way to express their humanity. Thus the image of a clown becomes an image of piety, of religious piety. With some slight changes in his features, this clown could easily become an image of the suffering Christ. The fact is that in almost any of Rouault's images the expression is the same: human sympathy for universal suffering.

And it is this sympathy, this participation, this generosity which gives form to the suffering.

Rouault's *Crucifixion* [Fig. 45] expresses his religious feeling directly through the image of God. The sorrow of St. John at right and of the Madonna at left are powerfully represented. Yet theirs are hardly human faces: it is their general attitudes toward the sacred figure on the cross, emblazoned by big black lines under the chin, which are responsible for the expression. The form can hardly be more abstract. But the abstract lines are so impressed with the artist's tremendous emotional intensity that their power is inescapable. Of course, the despair of Rouault's image is neither analyzed nor specified; it is despair in general, but this does not diminish its force. Charged with despair, the Christ on the cross is not an image of piety but of reverence. Hence, grandeur and monumentality. Old masters elevated the cross in their paintings in order to emphasize the monumentality of the image. Not Rouault; his Christ is erected on the ground: it is the ample chest and the erect head which give a feeling of monumentality to the whole image. He is the King, the Savior, and His arms seem thrown open for the protection of the faithful, rather than nailed to the cross.

Thus, the extreme simplicity of Rouault's artistic form reveals the extreme intensity of his feeling—of his emotional participation in the universal sorrow of mankind and in man's reverence for God. Such simplicity is the result of a great revolt against a sophisticated world as well as against a sophisticated tradition of art. Rouault's rebellion against both social and artistic traditions was at the root of his discovery of a new form. Hence, the extraordinary value of his form of moral beauty.

Wassily Kandinsky

At the time of his death in 1944 Wassily Kandinsky was a recognized leader of contemporary abstract expressionism. Divorcing his pictures from any specific objective reference, Kandinsky simply obeyed the voice of intuition and tried to achieve form through a kind of internal necessity. To him logical processes were inadequate for creating a picture. "Never was I able to contrive a form; any consciously planned form was repellent to me," he wrote. This releasing of subjective impulses helped, he believed, to express unexpected spiritual qualities of his art.

Born in Moscow in 1866, Kandinsky attended the University of Moscow, where he specialized in law and political economy, but at the age of thirty he decided to study painting under Franz von Stuck in Munich. In 1902 he opened his own painting school. After traveling in Europe and Africa, he returned to Munich in 1908 and, breaking from conservative representational techniques, did his first nonfigurative painting in 1910. Two years later he founded with Franz Marc The Blue Rider, a group of revolutionary artists who attempted to discover the essence of painting in primary experiences with color and form.

Returning to Moscow in 1914, Kandinsky became a professor in the Academy of Fine Arts and director of the Museum of Pictorial Culture in that city. Eight years later, however, he left Russia and joined the Bauhaus, a university of design directed by the architect Walter Gropius at Weimar, Germany. Here Kandinsky spent some of his most productive years, and with Paul Klee he helped offset the rather rigid functionalism being taught at this school. His settings for Moussorgsky's Pictures at an Exhibition, *done in 1928, were a noteworthy accomplishment. With the coming of Nazism in 1933 Kandinsky decided to leave Germany and spent the last eleven years of his life in Paris. Among his writings are his autobiography,* Concerning the Spiritual in Art *(1912), which explores the abstract language of form and color, and* The Blue Rider *(1912-1916), a symposium edited in Munich by Kandinsky and Marc. He also published expressionistic poems and plays.*

In addition to the selection reprinted from Kandinsky's autobiography, we also include a brief essay by Sheldon Cheney that discusses Kandinsky's theory of art in terms of the three major types of paintings done during his later years: the Impression, the Improvisation, and the Composition.

For a biographical sketch of Cheney, see page 309 above.

AUTOBIOGRAPHY

I

THE FIRST colors which ever impressed me were—a light juicy-green, white, black, carmine-red, and yellow ocher. These impressions first began in the third year of my life, and I would see them on many different objects that stood or passed before my eyes, but never with the vividness of the colors themselves.

Sometimes someone would cut and strip slender spirals of bark off a thin branch—first the outer layer, then the second, deeper one. These strips would become to me as little horses of three colors: a strip of brown (which I disliked and would have gladly exchanged for another color), a strip of tender green—my favorite, and which, even faded, retained much of its enchantment—and, finally, a white one, which was the naked, ivorylike core of the twig itself. When fresh, this last was strongly fragrant, so that you wanted to lick it, only to find it very, very bitter.

At the age of three, shortly before my parents took me to Italy, I remember once standing in the new apartment of my mother's parents. They were about to move in, but the whole place was still empty, devoid of furniture and people. Quite alone, I lingered in a fair-sized room, bare but for a clock hanging on the wall, and gazed with rapture at the white dial and the deep purple red of a rose that was painted on it.

My memories of Italy are spoilt by two dark impressions: One—I am with my mother in a black carriage, crossing over a bridge that spans a stretch of drab, dirt-yellow water. I am being taken to a children's garden in Florence. Two—I am descending steps that plunge ever down to black, lackluster water. On it, floats a long black boat with a terrible, square black box in the middle. We are about to get into a gondola at night.

A great, unforgettable influence in my early life was my mother's eldest sister, Elizabeth Ivanovna Tikheyeva, an enlightened soul never to be forgotten by all who knew her. To her I owe the beginning of my love for music, fairy tales, and, later, Russian literature, and my appreciation and understanding of the Russian nature. One of the memories of my childhood connected with Aunt Elizabeth was a little tin horse I used to play with. It was a bay, with an ocher body and a tail and mane of yellow. And many years later, on my arrival in Munich (where I went at the age of thirty, discarding all the long work of previous years in order to study painting), I saw during the very first days, in the streets, a bay horse that was the exact counterpart of my little tin horse. It invariably appears year after year as soon as the water carts first make their appearance. In the winter months it mysteriously vanishes, only to reappear again next spring—it never changes, nor grows older—I think it is immortal! It has brought me a half-felt, yet clear and joyful premonition and promise. It made my little tin horse live again, and, stretching far back through the years, tied Munich and my new life forever to the memories of my childhood.

I will always remember the time I took somebody's happy advice and made a trip to Rothenburg o.T.* That was an unforgettable trip of many trains and changes. From the mighty express first, to a slower train, and then to the tiny local of a rural branch line. Behind its long-necked little engine, with its shrill, reedy voice, it meandered along the countryside, down grass-grown tracks, the wheels rumbling and clattering sleepily. On it I met an old peasant, resplendent in his velvet vest adorned with large, silver-filigree buttons. A talkative soul, who, for some strange reason, persisted in talking to me about Paris. Unfortunately, I could not understand half of what he said. It was a strange voyage, with an unreal, dreamlike quality about it. It seemed to me, as if some magic power, contrary to all the laws of nature, was thrusting me farther and farther, century after century, back into the distant past.

I got off at a little station, as unreal as the train that left me there, and from there I went through some meadows and under an ancient gateway. Then came more and more gates, moats, a huddle of tall narrow houses, their heads leaning close, as if staring deep in each others' eyes. Then, at last, the massive doorway of the inn, opening directly onto the somber vastness of the dining hall, from which a dark, ponderous oaken stairway led up to the guest room.

Mine was a narrow room, with an equally tall, narrow window, beyond which stretched a frozen, unmoving sea of vividly red slanting tiles.

During my stay, the weather was constantly gray and sad. Large, round raindrops would settle on my palette. Trembling and shaking, they would pause, then suddenly stretch towards each other, run forward and mingle into thin, agile threads that trickled hither and thither amongst my colors, or would suddenly jump down my sleeve.

Only once in the whole week, and then for not more than half an hour, did the sun break through the clouds. The sketches I made all got lost or put away, nobody knows where. Only one picture did I bring back from that trip, and that I did from memory already after my return to Munich. It is *The Ancient Town* and is filled with sunshine, while the roofs are of the most vividly flaming red I could achieve.

What I was really trying to seize in this picture was the well-remembered hour that is, and always will be, the most splendid and sublime of the whole Moscow day. It comes when the sun is already low and has reached, through the striving and expectancy of a whole day, the apex of its power. This moment is but shortlived—a few minutes later the sunshine becomes reddish in tone, as if flushed after so great an exertion. Redder and ever redder it grows, at first with a cold luster, then warmer-toned and darkening. It fuses all Moscow into one solid piece, resounding to a single mighty note that shakes your very soul with its power.

But the beauty of that hour lies not in the all-embracing burst of scarlet alone. This is but the final chord of a symphony

* Rothenburg ob der Tauber, in Bavaria, Germany. [Ed.]

which carries to its utmost pitch the essence of each tone and to which all Moscow responds like the "*fortissimo*" of a gigantic orchestra. Houses—rose, lilac, white, azure, blue, flame-red, pistachio-hued; churches—each alive like a separate bright song; the green madness of the grass, the murmurous humming of trees; and, in winter, the thousand-voiced song of the snow; the brisk *allegretto* of bare branches; the hard-red, unshakable, and silent ring of the Kremlin walls; and over all, soaring like a triumphant and unearthly hallelujah, the slender-white, gracefully devout, and serious bell tower of Ivan the Great. And crowning the long white neck, stretched heavenwards as if in eternal yearning, the resplendent golden heat—the very sun of Moscow—amidst the crowding stars, multihued, gold and silver. To paint this scene appeared to me in my youth as the highest and most unachievable happiness for an artist.

Every sunny day I saw this scene repeat itself. It brought me infinite deep joy and yet, at the same time, tormented me—for art in general, and my own gifts in particular, seemed very puny indeed, when confronted with the mighty power and beauty of nature.

Many years were to pass before I reached, both intuitively and intellectually, the simple solution—that the goal, the aims of nature (and, therefore, also the means at her disposal) are essentially and basically different from those of art. Also that both are equally great and, therefore, equally strong.

This solution—so simple and naturally admirable—now guides my work. It has freed me forever from the many tormenting doubts that had long possessed me. Freed of these, my joy in art and nature both, could rise within me unshackled to ever new and splendid heights.

To this joy was added a feeling of intense gratitude—for I could now envisage new worlds and wider horizons. All things previously despised quivered and suddenly came to life. All things were revealed to me: not only the oft sung flowers and woods, the stars and the moon, but many, many more —a cigarette butt, stiff and frozen on an ashtray, the blankly patient, round button peeping from a puddle, the unresisting sliver of bark, carried through the grass in the strong jaws of the ant, the leaf of a wall calendar, awaiting the unsparing hand that will yank it from amongst its fellow-leaves. All these opened to me their inner essence and image, their secret meaning, which are mostly silent and unobserved.

This new understanding was sufficient to make me grasp fully, with my whole being, the meaning, the possibilities and the reality of the art which is now called "nonobjective" to distinguish it from the "objective."

II

But in my far-off student days, when I could only devote my free hours to the pursuit of art, I strove mightily after the seemingly unattainable aim of reproducing on the canvas the—what I then called—"Choir of Colors" which nature had so painfully thrust into my very soul. I tried desperately to capture its inner note, the very essence of it—but all in vain.

It was around that time that two events took place, both of which were to influence me strongly in my future life. The first was the exhibition of French impressionists that was held in Moscow, one of the pictures being *The Stack of Hay* by Claude Monet. The second was the production of Wagner's *Lohengrin* at the Grand Theatre.

Up to this time I was familiar with the realistic school of painting, and—at that—chiefly with the work of the Russian painters. As a child, I was much impressed by the famous picture *They did not wait* and a few years later I had repeatedly studied the hand of Franz Liszt in Repine's picture. I have many times copied from memory Polenoff's *Christ*, been enchanted by *The Oar* by Levitan and by many others of the same kind.

And then suddenly, for the first time in my life, I found myself looking at a real painting. It seemed to me, that, without a catalogue in my hand, it would have been impossible to recognize what the painting was meant to represent. This irked me, and I kept thinking that no artist has the right to paint in such a manner. But at the same time, and to my surprise and confusion, I discovered that it captivated and troubled me, imprinting itself indelibly on my mind and memory down to its smallest detail. But, on the whole, I could make neither head nor tail of it, and was, therefore, quite incapable of arriving at the conclusions which later appeared so simple.

But what did become clear to me, was the previously unimagined, unrevealed, and all-surpassing power of the palette. Painting showed itself to me in all its fantasy and enchantment. And deep inside of me, there was born the first faint doubt as to the importance of an "object" as the necessary element in a painting. But, on the whole, I felt that at last a part of my Moscow of the fairy tales was taking shape and living on canvas.

It was in *Lohengrin* that I felt the supreme incarnation and interpretation of this vision through music. The violins, deep basses, and most of all, the wind instruments, created for me the full image and power of the evening hour.

I could see all my colors, as they came to life before my eyes. Madly, in raging profusion they drew themselves in my mind. I did not dare admit to myself that Wagner had musically drawn "my hour." But it became totally clear to me that art in general possessed a far greater power than I ever had imagined. I also realized that painting possessed the same power as music. It was then that the impossibility to devote myself to the seeking of these powers became an ever greater torment. The temptation to do so was overwhelming, and I must admit that I did not always have the will power and strength of character to subordinate my wishes to the call of duty. I did not in this case, and finally succumbed. And just then, one of the most formidable obstacles on the way to the realization of my wishes, crumbled and vanished by itself, all thanks to a purely scientific event. This was the disintegration of the atom.

This discovery struck me with terrific impact, comparable to that of the end of the world. In the twinkling of an eye, the mighty arches of science lay shattered before me. All things became flimsy, with no strength or certainty. I would hardly have been surprised, if the stones would have risen in the air and disappeared. To me, science had been destroyed. In its place—a mere delusion, guesswork by the scientists, who, instead of erecting, stone by stone, a divine and unshakable edifice, had—or so it then seemed to me—gropingly, as if in the dark, fumbled for the scientific verities, often—in their blindness—mistaking one thing for another.

At that time, I was working very strenuously, often until late at night, and to the point of dizziness. The rare days when I was unable to work seemed to me lost, irresponsibly and witlessly squandered. Weather permitting, I would sketch in the old Schwabing, at that time not yet completely absorbed by the town.

On days when my studio work and ventures in composition disappointed me, I would sketch passionately and with abandon. When I tackled the landscapes, it was with a feeling of advancing in battle against a foe. A foe, I may add, that usually, and in the end, gained the upper hand, for it was rare that my sketches satisfied me completely, even if, once in a while, I did try to squeeze a painting out of them.

But however exciting these wanderings with a sketch pad in my hand and a hunter's joy in my heart, more important and serious were my ventures in painting, which even then, sometimes consciously, sometimes unconsciously, dealt chiefly with composition.

Composition—the word itself used to arouse in me a deep inner vibration. To draw a composition later became the chief aim of my life. They would arise before me in my reveries—visions, gossamer and intangible, sometimes terrifying in their audacity. Sometimes, in my dreams I would see complete paintings, finished and perfect, but alas, only the vaguest detail, a mere trace, would remain on awakening. Once when I was sick with typhoid fever, I was visited by a visionary painting of quite extraordinary clarity and perfection. But the fever once gone, that vanished with the rest.

In the course of a few years I painted the *Arrival of the Merchants*, *The Multi-Colored Life*, and, later, *Composition No. 2* [Fig. 50]. In the latter, I succeeded in expressing the essence of my fever-inspired vision, but this I only recently realized.

From the very beginning the word "composition" had for me the same sound and implications as the word "palette." It filled me with reverence and to this day I often grieve at the frivolity with which some people treat this matter.

When sketching, I would give my will free rein and let myself follow the many whims and fancies of my inner promptings. With the spatula I would lay on the colors in broad slaps and dashes, worrying but little about the exact detail of form of the object, but stressing the tonality and expression of the individual colors. Loud and insistent would rise in me the memory of Moscow in the unspeakable beauty of the early evening hour, and before my eyes, tremendous, lovely, and deeply resounding, there would unfold the full scale of mighty colors that is Munich.

III

It was while traveling in unusual, faraway places, that I first became aware of a certain phenomenon, a miraculous realization that was to play an important part in my future work. Here I first learned not to look at a picture only from the outside, but to "enter" it, to move around in it, and mingle with its very life. It happened to me on entering a certain room, and I still remember how I stood spellbound on the threshold, gazing in. Before me stood a table, benches, a vast and magnificent stove. The cupboards and dressers were alive with multicolored and sprawling decoration. All over the walls hung peasant prints, telling vividly of battles, of a legendary knight-at-arms, of a song, rendered in colors. One corner was rich with dark-gleaming icons, in front of which, devoutly and whisperingly humble, yet proud and starlike, warmly glimmered a hanging image lamp. When I finally crossed the threshold, it was like entering into a painting and becoming a part of it. This sensation had visited me before in some of the Moscow churches, most of all in the Uspensky cathedral and the church of Basil the Blessed, but it had been subconscious and undefined. Now, for the first time, I fully realized it. On my return to Moscow I experienced it again, this time fully, in many of the much-ornamented churches, and later still, was to feel it anew, with the variations imposed by the difference in style and architecture, in Tyrolese and Bavarian chapels.

Many times I used to paint these ornamented church scenes, not going into any detail, but applying the colors with such force, that everything was submerged by their vivid pattern. In this and many other ways I strived to capture my inner impressions, to define and incorporate them in my art. And for quite a few years I strove mightily to find the means, the medium to draw the spectator into the painting itself, so that he would mingle with it and become part of it. Sometimes I would succeed, for I could judge by the expression of the face of those standing before the painting.

Using the tendency of a painted object to lose much of its form and identity to the general composition of a picture, I gradually acquired the gift of no longer noticing the given object, or, at least, of overlooking it. Much later, in Munich, I was once deeply enchanted by an unexpected sight that met my eye on returning to the studio. Twilight was drawing in. I was returning, immersed in thought, from my sketching, when, on opening the studio door, I was suddenly confronted by a picture of indescribable and incandescent loveliness. Bewildered I stopped; staring at it. The painting lacked all subject, depicted no identifiable object and was entirely composed of bright color patches. Finally I approached closer and, only then, recognized it for what it really was—my own painting, standing on its side on the easel.

My attempts, the next day, to evoke the same effects by daylight, were not wholly successful. Even with the painting again on its side, I could still easily discern the various objects depicted in it. The still lackluster gloss of twilight was also missing, but one thing became very clear to me—that objectiveness, the depiction of objects, need have no place in my paintings, and was indeed harmful to them.

The intense gravity and responsibility of such a decision raised many important questions. Most important of all—if all objectivity be discarded, what was to take its place! I well knew the dangers of overornamentation, and the pseudo-life of styled forms was repellent to me.

Many a time since then, I have tried to close my eyes to these all-important questions, for it has seemed to me that they were pushing me along a dangerous path. And it has only been after many years of intense work, and through an ever clearer succession of new, often unconscious or semiconscious, but always more realized emotions, that I have finally arrived, through a heightened faculty for inner expression, to the pure and nonobjective artistic forms that now govern my work, and to which I hope to give an ever more perfect shape. It has, indeed, taken me a long time to answer that question—What must take the place of the pictorial object in a painting?

Often, on looking back, I despair at the long succession of years that it took me to reach a true decision and course. There is but one consolation—and that is my lifelong inability to apply to my art such forms as arose in me through logical thought or feeling. As far as I can look back, all and any forms I have ever used, come to me, as it were, by themselves. They either appeared before my eyes, complete and ready to be copied, or would form themselves gradually, during the hours of work. Sometimes they would prove obstinate, and then I would have to wait patiently, often with fear in my heart, until such times as they chose to reveal themselves to me.

These inner revelations cannot be described. They are mysterious and are born of many hidden reasons. Their approach is heralded by, as it were, a ripple on the soul's surface, an increasing undefined turmoil, a tautening and intensifying of some deep-set force. They stay, sometimes for an instant, sometimes for days at a stretch. I think that this visionary birth must closely resemble the conception and bearing of man. Maybe firmaments are born in a like manner.

But these "moments of exaltation" are very diverse—both as to quality and degree of tension. Experience alone can teach their correct use. In order to direct these forces I had to train myself in complete self-control and not to surrender blindly to my feelings. In time I realized that work does not benefit from feverishly beating heart, contraction of the chest (accompanied by a corresponding pain in the ribs), and general tension of the entire body. After such exalted moments, during which one's analytical control disappears completely, there follows a period of deep emotional lassitude. For they can last, because of their very intensity, for only a short while, sufficing but for some short work—a sketch, or, what I call, an "improvization," but do not last the span of a longer creative period, which requires an evenly sustained pitch of inner emotional uplift, sometimes lasting for days. A horse may carry its rider with magnificent impetus, but it is the latter who must direct the course. Likewise, a painter must guide the talent that sweeps him along the road of creation. And even if he is capable of calling forth rare, fragmentary moments of self-willed exaltation, it is, nevertheless, given him to qualify its character, as also of those that arise in him independently of his will. Long experience teaches one how to suppress when necessary these moments, and keep them in abeyance, but alive, until a later time.

But, naturally, no certain calculation is here possible. Nevertheless, experience and knowledge in this matter are some of the elements of "consciousness" and "calculation" in work. Undoubtedly, an artist should possess deep and detailed knowledge of his own talent, and, like a good merchant, should not allow any part of it to be wasted or run to seed. Every particle should be cared for, sharpened, and polished, and used to the limit of such capacity as has been allowed him.

I have heard that a famous painter (I do not remember exactly who) once said—"When you paint, you should give half a glance to the palette, one to the canvas, and ten to nature." Though very prettily expressed, I personally, would put it somewhat differently. To me, the right equation should be—ten glances at canvas, to one at the palette, to half a glance at nature, if at all—

It was thus that I learned to combat the stubborn hostility of a canvas, and, finally, to force it into submission. I learned to ignore the persistent white and inimic blankness of the untouched canvas, and see, instead, the tones and colors that are to take its place. In this way—slowly and gradually—I came to learn sometimes one thing, sometimes another.

Painting is the vast, thunderous clash of many worlds, destined, through a mighty struggle, to erupt into a totally new world, which is creation. And the Birth of a creation is much akin to that of the Cosmos. There is the same vast and cataclysmic quality belonging to that mighty symphony—the Music of the Spheres.

The impression of colors strewn over the palette: of colors—alive, waiting, as yet unseen and hidden in their little tubes—all this acquired for me an inner spiritual life and meaning.

These impressions helped to crystallize the thought and ideas which had lain in me for the last fifteen years. I used to jot them down as they came to me, but only later noticed the connection between them all. Ever more strongly I realized that the center of gravity in art did not lie in its "formal expression," but in the inner impulse (subject) that dominates the former. It was not easy to renounce the habitual attitude towards the predominant importance of style, epoch, and formal theories, and to admit to myself that the quality in a work of art depended not on the formal spirit of an epoch, not on the exact conformation to some presumably infallible set of rules, but on the quality and force of the inner impulse of the painter and the degree and quality of his chosen—and personally, to him, important—forms. It became clear to me that the "Spirit of the Age" in regard to questions of artistic forms, is invariably created by those high-sounded painters, those "personalities" in the world of art, who succeed, not only in persuading the more superficially gifted of their contemporaries, but also generations of painters to come.

One more step in my artistic development, a step that took me a grievously long time to achieve, was the conclusion that the essential meaning of art can be realized only on the basis of an inner necessity, urgent and powerful enough to capsize all the existing theoretical laws and boundaries.

It is the spirit that rules over matter, and not the other way around. The inexperienced eye is easily fascinated, but this enchantment soon ends, and the soul, swiftly undeceived, turns away.

This yardstick which I offer has one weakness—it cannot be proven. Especially to those who lack the active, creative, and even passive inner qualities; to those that are destined to remain on the surface and are incapable of penetrating to the inner depth of the subject. But history, which in its inexorable course, divides the grain from the chaff, will be the last, incorruptible judge in this matter.

Thus it came about, that gradually, step by step, the world of art separated itself in me from the world of nature, both acquiring an independent, mutually unrelated existence.

IV

The exclusion of all objectivity in art, naturally imposes some very exacting demands on the ability to inwardly experience a purely artistic form. It becomes necessary for the spectator to develop in feeling and appreciation along these lines. Thus come into existence new conditions which serve to create a new atmosphere—all of which will, in the distant future, form that kind of absolutely pure art, which we can now discern only as an indescribably lovely and elusive vision.

With the passing of time I understood that my ever-growing tolerance towards the work of others was not only harmless but even beneficial to me in my work and strivings. I use, therefore, a somewhat modified version of the well-known dictum—"An artist should be onesided (or single-minded) in creation." The faculty to grasp the work of others (a work inevitably personal to its creator) makes my own soul more receptive, more capable of vibration, widens and sharpens its powers, thus making it more capable of reaching its ultimate goal. The understanding of the working of other people's minds is comparable in a sense to the understanding of the workings of nature. Being neither deaf nor blind, the artist should fully use both great gifts, and seeing the innumerable ways and means being pursued and used (be it rightly or wrongly) in the exercise of art, should apply himself to his own work with a gladder heart and ever-growing enthusiasm.

What concerns me personally, I am in love with any art form that is born or partakes of the spirit. On the other hand, those that don't, are abhorrent to me. I think that all future philosophy will devote itself not only to the essence of things, but also to their spirit. It will then become possible to feel, if only subconsciously, the spirit of all things, in the same way as now is felt the outward essence, a feeling which explains the pleasure derived from purely objective art. With growing realization of the spiritual, it will be easier for man to comprehend—first, the spiritual meaning of material things, and later, that of abstraction in phenomena.

And through this new aptitude, which is "of the spirit," there shall be born the joy in the purely Absolute Art.

My book about the spiritual in art, and also *The Blue Rider* have as their main objective, the future, awakening of the realization and understanding of the spiritual essence in all things. The desire to hasten this awakening was my main aim in publishing both these works. They have often been, and still are considered by many as a species of program apologia by their author, an artist perishing and lost in the wilderness of theories and endless cerebration. But that is not so, for I have always turned to reason and the intellect least of all. That would be premature at this time. What faces the artist is but an all-important and inevitable aim—the next step to be taken.

The spirit, strong and unshakeable, its roots firmly planted in the ground, need have no fear of the so-called "dangerous" participation of reason and the intellect in art, or even of the preponderance of it over the intuitive, maybe even to the final exclusion of all inspiration.

My father was born in Nertchinsk, where, according to a family tradition, his ancestors had been sent for political reasons from Western Siberia. He received his education in Moscow and loved it no less than his home town. In his deep humanity, he was able to understand the Moscow "spirit" which is so strongly impressed in every little detail of that city.

My mother is Moscow-born, striking in appearance, of a beauty profoundly serious and severe. She has much natural simplicity and unbounded energy, in which are strangely interwoven a nervous restlessness together with the most unshakable calm and self-control.

In fact, she combines in herself all those traits and qualities, which, in my opinion, form the true essence of Moscow.

Moscow, with its duality, complexity, its fluid, eternal mobility; the clash and struggle and confusion of its different external elements, which, in the last instance, are all part of the same extraordinary and incomparable entity. The same marvelous variety characterizes its inner life (often confusing foreigners and being the cause of many contrasting and different reports and descriptions), but in the end, here also, all fuses into one unique and wonderful being.

This Moscow, both inner and external, I consider to be the inspiration and starting point of all my endeavors. I could best call it the "metronome of my life," and I think it has always been so, and that whenever I achieved new external forms in my work, I was still drawing from the same source, and it was only the outward interpretation that changed and acquired new significance and expression.

The detours, which occasionally happened on the most straightforward road of my life; the "dead" moments, during which I felt myself powerless and helpless, and which seemed to me, at the moment, to be the end of everything—these were not really harmful to me, but, instead, turned out to be new starting points, pauses to get my breath and collect my inner strength for each new step which would carry me to the next move in my development.

Munich, June-October 1913
Moscow, September 1918

THE SWING TOWARD ABSTRACTION

ABSTRACTION in art may best be defined negatively, as the lack of representative form. It involves absolute composition (as in music)—composition which neither imitates nor suggests objective forms. Abstract painting or sculpture never provides a transcription. It is the negation of the concrete, the material, the outwardly real.

It is almost impossible to state any theory of the abstract in art without recourse to the terminology and the parallel of music. For music is a wholly nonrepresentative art based in its physical aspect on certain widely understood phenomena. The goal of the abstract painters is an art of color as free from associative and objective interest as is this other art of sound. There is no more reason, argue the abstractionists, why painting should be dependent upon the depiction or suggestion of natural objects than there is for music to be dependent upon likeness to natural sounds. Painting must be stripped of the trivial and extraneous elements that give rise to the pleasures typical of drama, anecdote, photography, etc.

Many artists have felt this truth, and the timid experiments have been myriad. But the story of abstraction in modern painting is popularly and legitimately centered in the lifework of one man: Wassily Kandinsky. He is today the world's foremost practitioner of a visual art wholly divorced from material actuality, and the most lucid theorist of the movement. His theory, to be sure, is shaped by an extraneous religious outlook on life, for he is a theosophist. It is limited to a spiritual vision which seems to some of us to ignore certain physical facts of art creation. But he is the greatest figure of the pioneer swing toward abstraction.

Kandinsky was born in Moscow, and was Russian trained. Later he went to Munich to study, and has ever since been associated with the modernist movement in German art. From his early German days we hear echoes of his obsession with composition, with color orchestration, with memory-painting, although his work up to 1908 was marked by nothing more radical than a posteresque simplification.

In 1910 there was published Kandinsky's book *On the Spiritual Element in Art* (published in an English translation in 1914). His theory of painting had already set definitely toward abstract means, although he hesitated to commit himself wholly.

Kandinsky argues the case for his sort of abstraction as follows: Painting has become materialistic, and the great mass of contemporary painters are merely opportunists. Art should, however, be nothing more than an expression of the spirituality in man. Cézanne showed the beginning of a new way. Matisse followed it but got lost in the seductiveness of color, the French love for color decoration; Picasso was important too, but he got lost in a scholar's search for form. Kandinsky feels that color and form are physical means and only incidental—the expression of the artist's inner life is the thing.

Not only color and form, but the third, combining element, composition, "must be decided only by a corresponding vibration in the human soul." There is so much stressing of this "vibration in the human soul" in the book, that one marks that as Kandinsky's major source of creation. It determines certain "combinations of veiled and fully expressed appeals," which presumably are improvised from a multiplicity of colors and forms:

> The adaptability of forms, their organic but inward variations, their motion in the picture, their inclination to material or abstract, their mutual relations, either individually or as parts of a whole; further, the concord or discord of the various elements of a picture, the handling of groups, the combinations of veiled and openly expressed appeals, the use of rhythmical or unrhythmical, of geometrical or non-geometrical forms, their contiguity or separation—all these things are material for counterpoint in painting. . . .
>
> Painting is an art, and art is not vague production, transitory and isolated, but a power which must be directed to the improvement and refinement of the human soul—to, in fact, the raising of the spiritual triangle. . . . *that is beautiful which is produced by the inner need, which springs from the soul.*

The implication is clear: art must be cleansed of what is material. There is no talk of an absolute esthetic quality which is the essential thing sought by the artist. Kadinsky does not renounce imitativeness for that search. When he mentions an element of "pure artistry" (beyond personality and style), it is only to repeat that that too must arise out of "the inner need." Always it is the inner need that is the source of all good art. Out of it one must develop his melodic and symphonic compositions as carefully as one must order his deeds, thoughts and feelings in life—to do otherwise would be to make bad "karma."

Such an approach to art, sincere and purified though it is, leads to the substitution of a certain amount of mystery, mysticism and mood for those hard, simple, definite qualities which most significant modern artists have sought. Thus we find that Kandinsky works largely with what may be called the "mood values" of color. "Blue is the typical Heavenly color." It stands for rest; blue-black for grief, and violet for the echo of grief. White is a pregnant silence, black a dead silence. "Green is the *Bourgeoisie*—self-satisfied, immovable, narrow." And so on. This is a reversion to symbolism—interesting enough in itself, but not on the high road to creation. The artist finds, of course, a musical equivalent for each of these color values.

In his paintings there is a softness that belongs essentially to mood composition. His early pictures had titles. By 1910 he had adopted a system of dividing his canvases into three groups: Impressions, Improvisations, and Compositions. He has not adhered strictly and exclusively to this classification, but it has served to label the great bulk of his paintings. The picture at the head of the chapter [Fig. 51] is an "Impression." The representative element is fairly definite still, although it is obvious that the artist is more interested in form-composition. The next reproduction [Fig. 52] is an "Improvisation." Representation has almost disappeared. The picture opposite is a "Composition." Representation has been completely renounced [Fig. 50].

Kandinsky has written of his three methods of work:

> They represent three different sources of inspiration: (1) A direct impression of outward nature, expressed in purely artistic form. This I call an "Impression." (2) A largely unconscious spontaneous expression of inner character, the non-material nature. This I call an "Improvisation." (3) An expression of a slowly formed inner feeling, which comes to utterance only after long maturing. This I call a "Composition." In this, reason, consciousness, purpose, play an overwhelming part. But of the calculation nothing appears, only the feeling.

The *Impression* shown is clearly representative in origin. The *Improvisation No. 30*, like many another in this group, exhibits somewhere imitative values. This is so true that Kandinsky himself has called it informally "the cannon picture." He wrote to the owner, the late Arthur Jerome Eddy:

> The designation "Cannons" selected by me *for my own use*, is not to be conceived as indicating the "contents" of the picture. These contents are indeed what the spectator *lives* or *feels* while under the effect of the *form and color combinations* of the picture. This picture is nearly in the shape of a cross. . . . The presence of the cannons in the picture could probably be explained by the constant war talk that had been going on throughout the year. . . .

Later he writes, "The observer must learn to look at a picture as a graphic representation of a *mood* and not as a representation of *objects*."

Here there is clearly representative means. The painter has not evaded them, but he tries to explain them away as subconscious on his part, and as something which the spectator should overlook. But the third picture, the *Composition No. 5** has in it no object that we can name. One might make a game of finding approximate representative forms there, but the eye that is not overtrained to seek imitation first will not be seduced so shallowly. The question then is, do these purely abstract pictures give rise to deeper esthetic pleasure than the partly representative pictures?

Judging only from Kandinsky's own work, I should say that they do not. In general there is a wandering, soft, unstructural quality about them which seems to me to be a denial of something important to painting. They may be pure transcriptions of spiritual meanderings, and perhaps we shall find that such things speak to us as we grow more spiritual. But at present I feel that this does not appeal to me (outside its color charm) as anything else than a vague transcription of human mood, to which I must be personally attuned at the moment of seeing the painting. If I happen to be in a veiled Maeterlinckian mood, I am charmed; on other days I have no more than a passing interest.*

* *On the Green Line*, Fig. 53, illustrates this aspect of Kandinsky's painting.

* The opinions set down in this chapter no longer (in 1939) fully express my convictions about abstract art. But since the material and the treatment represent a stage passed through, on the way to fuller understanding and enjoyment, I think it better to make only incidental corrections.

As a matter of fact—I am adding this further note in 1945—I am shocked that I should have so failed in appreciation of Kandinsky's paintings at the time I wrote the lines above. Kandinsky should, I believe, be ranked in a high place among those who produced paintings rich in formal values. Nor has any other abstractionist set down theories quite so suggestive. Since 1935 the current of interest in "absolute" painting has widened and deepened. There are even two camps of American abstractionists. The richly endowed Solomon R. Guggenheim Foundation in New York maintains a museum wholly devoted to nonobjective paintings. It insists upon the distinction between "nonobjective art" and "abstraction" making the point that an abstraction may be "taken from" an object in nature; the highest form of art being, in the foundation's view, an exercise of the spiritual or intellectual faculties independent of objective nature. There is a notable collection of abstract paintings, formed by A. E. Gallatin, at the Philadelphia Museum. There is also an active organization known as the American Abstract Artists.

Paul Klee

Like Kandinsky, Paul Klee adopted a theory of art based upon intuitive imagination rather than on conscious thought or experience. The painting of Kandinsky and of Klee must be understood as spontaneous and springing from impulse; it depends on freedom of treatment.

Born near Bern, Switzerland, in 1879, Klee first turned to music as a means of expression and, when he was still a boy, played the violin in an orchestra his father conducted. After much indecision, however, he took up drawing and studied in Munich with Franz von Stuck, with whom Kandinsky also worked. The bizarre subjects and imaginative originality of Stuck's paintings early suggested to Klee a direction he was to take. Although he visited Paris, he was not immediately attracted by the postimpressionists, but he was drawn to some of Goya's fantasies and the subjective visions of Blake. After moving to Munich in 1906, he became acquainted with the work of van Gogh and Cézanne, but it was especially Matisse who stirred him to experiment with the expressive potentialities of color. More and more completely Klee moved away from a realistic or representational type of painting.

With Kandinsky and Marc he formed the nucleus of The Blue Rider, *the group now famous for its revolt against the academic methods of the time. It was their writing and painting, emphasizing intuitive freedom, that made the term "expressionism" widely known. At the end of World War I, Klee accepted the invitation of Gropius to join the group of artists at the Bauhaus. With Kandinsky and the American Feininger, he helped to balance the technological, utilitarian study of architecture, furniture, and industrial arts at the school. In 1929 he left the Bauhaus to become a professor at the Düsseldorf Academy; but with the coming of the Nazis in 1933 he left Germany and made his home in Switzerland, where he died seven years later.*

By the time of his death Klee was admired throughout the world for the gaiety, humor, and mockery of his painting together with its intricate ingenuity. He had become a supremely sensitive artist, with an unusual gift for making external the intrinsic emotions of life. Dealing with the inside, rather than the outside, world, his painting seems to create the shadowy reality of a dream. His art is, in a way, a kind of self-revealing monologue—original, exciting, even at times tricky. Klee's province is the startling world of subjective fantasy. The brief selection reprinted here is from a lecture of Klee's on "Modern Art" that was published in English after his death. Figures 54, 55 and 56 illustrate paintings of the sort Klee discusses in this lecture.

ON MODERN ART

I

SPEAKING here in the presence of my work, which should really express itself in its own language, I feel a little anxious as to whether I am justified in doing so and whether I shall be able to find the right approach.

For, while as a painter I feel that I have in my possession the means of moving others in the direction in which I myself am driven, I doubt whether I can give the same sure lead by the use of words alone.

But I comfort myself with the thought that my words do not address themselves to you in isolation, but will complement and bring into focus the impressions, perhaps still a little hazy, which you have already received from my pictures.

If I should, in some measure, succeed in giving this lead, I should be content and should feel that I had found the justification which I had required.

Further, in order to avoid the reproach "Don't talk, painter, paint," I shall confine myself largely to throwing some light on those elements of the creative process which, during the growth of a work of art, take place in the subconscious. To my

[From Paul Klee, *On Modern Art*. Translated by Paul Findlay. Copyright 1948, Faber and Faber, Ltd., London. Reprinted by permission of the publisher.]

mind, the real justification for the use of words by a painter would be to shift the emphasis by stimulating a new angle of approach; to relieve the formal element of some of the conscious emphasis which is given and place more stress on content.

This is the kind of readjustment which I should find pleasure in making and which might easily tempt me to embark on a dialectical analysis.

But this would mean that I should be following too closely my own inclinations and forgetting the fact that most of you are much more familiar with content than with form. I shall, therefore, not be able to avoid saying something about form.

I shall try to give you a glimpse of the painter's workshop, and I think we shall eventually arrive at some mutual understanding.

For there is bound to be some common ground between layman and artist where a mutual approach is possible and whence the artist no longer appears as a being totally apart.

But, as a being, who like you, has been brought, unasked, into this world of variety, and where, like you, he must find his way for better or for worse.

A being who differs from you only in that he is able to master life by the use of his own specific gifts; a being perhaps happier than the man who has no means of creative expression and no chance of release through the creation of form.

This modest advantage should be readily granted the artist. He has difficulties enough in other respects.

May I use a simile, the simile of the tree? The artist has studied this world of variety and has, we may suppose, unobtrusively found his way in. His sense of direction has brought order into the passing stream of image and experience. This sense of direction in nature and life, this branching and spreading array, I shall compare with the root of the tree.

From the root the sap flows to the artist, flows through him, flows to his eye.

Thus he stands as the trunk of the tree.

Battered and stirred by the strength of the flow, he molds his vision into his work.

As, in full view of the world, the crown of the tree unfolds and spreads in time and in space, so with his work.

Nobody would affirm that the tree grows its crown in the image of its root. Between above and below can be no mirrored reflection. It is obvious that different functions expanding in different elements must produce vital divergences.

But it is just the artist who at times is denied those departures from nature which his art demands. He has even been charged with incompetence and deliberate distortion.

And yet, standing at his appointed place, the trunk of the tree, he does nothing other than gather and pass on what comes to him from the depths. He neither serves nor rules—he transmits.

His position is humble. And the beauty at the crown is not his own. He is merely a channel.

II

I would like now to examine the dimensions of the object in a new light and so try to show how it is that the artist frequently arrives at what appears to be such an arbitrary "deformation" of natural forms.

First, he does not attach such intense importance to natural form as do so many realist critics, because, for him, these final forms are not the real stuff of the process of natural creation. For he places more value on the powers which do the forming than on the final forms themselves.

He is, perhaps unintentionally, a philosopher, and if he does not, with the optimists, hold this world to be the best of all possible worlds, nor to be so bad that it is unfit to serve as a model, yet he says:

"In its present shape it is not the only possible world."

Thus he surveys with penetrating eye the finished forms which nature places before him.

The deeper he looks, the more readily he can extend his view from the present to the past, the more deeply he is impressed by the one essential image of creation itself, as Genesis, rather than by the image of nature, the finished product.

Then he permits himself the thought that the process of creation can today hardly be complete and he sees the act of world creation stretching from the past to the future. Genesis eternal!

He goes still further!

He says to himself, thinking of life around him: this world at one time looked different and, in the future, will look different again.

Then, flying off to the infinite, he thinks: it is very probable that, on other stars, creation has produced a completely different result.

Such mobility of thought on the process of natural creation is good training for creative work.

It has the power to move the artist fundamentally, and since he is himself mobile, he may be relied upon to maintain freedom of development of his own creative methods.

This being so, the artist must be forgiven if he regards the present state of outward appearances in his own particular world as accidentally fixed in time and space. And as altogether inadequate compared with his penetrating vision and intense depth of feeling.

And is it not true that even the small step of a glimpse through the microscope reveals to us images which we should deem fantastic and overimaginative if we were to see them somewhere accidentally, and lacked the sense to understand them?

Your realist, however, coming across such an illustration in a sensational magazine, would exclaim in great indignation: "Is that supposed to be nature? I call it bad drawing."

Does then the artist concern himself with microscopy? History? Paleontology?

Only for purposes of comparison, only in the exercise of his mobility of mind. And not to provide a scientific check on the truth of nature.

Only in the sense of freedom. In the sense of a freedom, which does not lead to fixed phases of development, representing exactly what nature once was, or will be, or could be on another star (as perhaps may one day be proved).

But in the sense of a freedom which merely demands its rights, the right to develop, as great Nature herself develops.

From type to prototype.

Presumptuous is the artist who does not follow his road through to the end. But chosen are those artists who penetrate to the region of that secret place where primeval power nurtures all evolution.

There, where the power-house of all time and space—call it brain or heart of creation—activates every function; who is the artist who would not dwell there?

In the womb of nature, at the source of creation, where the secret key to all lies guarded.

But not all can enter. Each should follow where the pulse of his own heart leads.

So, in their time, the impressionists—our opposites of yesterday—had every right to dwell within the matted undergrowth of everyday vision.

But our pounding heart drives us down, deep down to the source of all.

What springs from this source, whatever it may be called, dream, idea or phantasy—must be taken seriously only if it unites with the proper creative means to form a work of art.

Then those curiosities become realities—realities of art which help to lift life out of its mediocrity.

For not only do they, to some extent, add more spirit to the seen, but they also make secret visions visible.

I said "with the proper creative means." For at this stage is decided whether pictures or something different will be born. At this stage, also, is decided the kind of the pictures.

These unsettled times have brought chaos and confusion (or so it seems, if we are not too near to judge).

But among artists, even among the youngest of them, one urge seems to be gradually gaining ground: The urge to the culture of these creative means, to their pure cultivation, to their pure use.

The legend of the childishness of my drawing must have originated from those linear compositions of mine in which I tried to combine a concrete image, say that of a man, with the pure representation of the linear element.

Had I wished to present the man "as he is," then I should have had to use such a bewildering confusion of line that pure elementary representation would have been out of the question. The result would have been vagueness beyond recognition.

And anyway, I do not wish to represent the man as he is, but only as he might be.

And thus I could arrive at a happy association between my vision of life (*Weltanschauung*) and pure artistic craftsmanship.

And so it is over the whole field of use of the formal means: in all things, even in colors, must all trace of vagueness be avoided.

This then is what is called the untrue coloring in modern art.

As you can see from this example of "childishness" I concern myself with work on the partial processes of art. I am also a draughtsman.

I have tried pure drawing, I have tried painting in pure tone values. In color, I have tried all partial methods to which I have been led by my sense of direction in the color circle. As a result, I have worked out methods of painting in colored tone values, in complementary colors, in multicolors and methods of total color painting.

Always combined with the more subconscious dimensions of the picture.

Then I tried all possible syntheses of two methods. Combining and again combining, but, of course, always preserving the culture of the pure element.

Sometimes I dream of a work of really great breadth, ranging through the whole region of element, object, meaning, and style.

This, I fear, will remain a dream, but it is a good thing even now to bear the possibility occasionally in mind.

Nothing can be rushed. It must grow, it should grow of itself, and if the time ever comes for that work—then so much the better!

6

LITERATURE: ROMANTICISM AND SYMBOLISM

William Wordsworth

The imagination of William Wordsworth (1770-1850) was profoundly stirred by his sympathy with nature or with persons living close to nature. From his boyhood, when he attended school at the village of Hawkshead in the heart of the beautiful English lake country, he constantly absorbed the scenery into his sensitive spirit. As he says in "Boy of Winander," the voice of the mountain streams, the solemn imagery of rocks, woods, sky, and lake passed unawares into his mind. The French Revolution also had a powerful effect on him during his travels in Europe after graduation from Cambridge. Especially fond of children, he was deeply moved by the poverty of French peasant youngsters. Like many other idealists, he was disillusioned when the Revolution degenerated into bloodshed and anarchy, but he never entirely lost the faith in social and political liberty for all mankind which was engendered here.

Poetry for Wordsworth was a "spontaneous overflow of powerful feelings." Although the love of nature has primary importance to him, there grew from it a sincere regard for ordinary men and women living close to nature. He not only valued the joy he found in natural creation, but he also respected the worth of each individual. From his youthful idealism he created a personal view of the world in which nature and man live in harmony since they are only varying expressions of the benevolent spirit of God. Taken together these aspects of Wordsworth's poetry provide one of the classic expressions of romanticism.

Wordsworth composed some of his finest poetry during his walks in the out-of-doors. The lines reprinted here on nature around Tintern Abbey were inspired by a walking tour with his sister Dorothy through the lovely countryside where he had tramped some years before with a college friend. The vacation walk lasted about four days. On the way back from the country to the town of Bristol, Wordsworth began the poem and finished it as he was entering the town. Like "Tintern Abbey" his earlier poems also disclose the joy that one of his temperament can feel in a comforting relation between the individual and the world of nature. Men may be cruel to each other and nature may at times seem to be indifferent to suffering, but Wordsworth felt keenly that the powers of the universe are not devoid of sympathy with human life, and a spirit of love for all creatures of earth is humanity's highest ideal.

LINES COMPOSED A FEW MILES ABOVE TINTERN ABBEY,

On Revisiting the Banks of the Wye during a Tour.

Five years have past; five summers, with the length
Of five long winters! and again I hear
These waters, rolling from their mountain-springs
With a soft inland murmur.—Once again
Do I behold these steep and lofty cliffs,
That on a wild secluded scene impress
Thoughts of more deep seclusion; and connect
The landscape with the quiet of the sky.
The day is come when I again repose
Here, under this dark sycamore, and view
These plots of cottage-ground, these orchard-tufts,
Which at this season, with their unripe fruits,
Are clad in one green hue, and lose themselves
'Mid groves and copses. Once again I see
These hedge-rows, hardly hedge-rows, little lines
Of sportive wood run wild: these pastoral farms,
Green to the very door; and wreaths of smoke
Sent up, in silence, from among the trees!
With some uncertain notice, as might seem
Of vagrant dwellers in the houseless woods,
Or of some Hermit's cave, where by his fire
The Hermit sits alone.
These beauteous forms,
Through a long absence, have not been to me
As is a landscape to a blind man's eye:
But oft, in lonely rooms, and 'mid the din
Of towns and cities, I have owed to them
In hours of weariness, sensations sweet,
Felt in the blood, and felt along the heart;
And passing even into my purer mind,
With tranquil restoration:—feelings too

[From *The Poetical Works of Wordsworth.* London, Oxford University Press, 1904.]

Of unremembered pleasure: such, perhaps,
As have no slight or trivial influence
On that best portion of a good man's life,
His little, nameless, unremembered acts
Of kindness and of love. Nor less, I trust,
To them I may have owed another gift,
Of aspect more sublime; that blessed mood,
In which the burthen of the mystery,
In which the heavy and the weary weight
Of all this unintelligible world,
Is lightened:—that serene and blessed mood,
In which the affections gently lead us on,—
Until, the breath of this corporeal frame
And even the motion of our human blood
Almost suspended, we are laid asleep
In body, and become a living soul:
While with an eye made quiet by the power
Of harmony, and the deep power of joy,
We see into the life of things.
                                                    If this
Be but a vain belief, yet, oh! how oft—
In darkness and amid the many shapes
Of joyless daylight; when the fretful stir
Unprofitable, and the fever of the world,
Have hung upon the beatings of my heart—
How oft, in spirit, have I turned to thee,
O sylvan Wye! thou wanderer thro' the woods,
How often has my spirit turned to thee!

And now, with gleams of half-extinguished thought,
With many recognitions dim and faint,
And somewhat of a sad perplexity,
The picture of the mind revives again:
While here I stand, not only with the sense
Of present pleasure, but with pleasing thoughts
That in this moment there is life and food
For future years. And so I dare to hope,
Though changed, no doubt, from what I was when first
I came among these hills; when like a roe
I bounded o'er the mountains, by the sides
Of the deep rivers, and the lonely streams,
Wherever nature led: more like a man
Flying from something that he dreads, than one
Who sought the thing he loved. For nature then

(The coarser pleasures of my boyish days,
And their glad animal movements all gone by)
To me was all in all.—I cannot paint
What then I was. The sounding cataract
Haunted me like a passion: the tall rock,
The mountain, and the deep and gloomy wood,
Their colors and their forms, were then to me
An appetite; a feeling and a love,
That had no need of a remoter charm,
By thought supplied, nor any interest
Unborrowed from the eye.—That time is past,
And all its aching joys are now no more,
And all its dizzy raptures. Not for this
Faint I, nor mourn nor murmur; other gifts
Have followed; for such loss, I would believe,
Abundant recompense. For I have learned
To look on nature, not as in the hour
Of thoughtless youth; but hearing oftentimes
The still, sad music of humanity,
Nor harsh nor grating, though of ample power
To chasten and subdue. And I have felt
A presence that disturbs me with the joy
Of elevated thoughts; a sense sublime
Of something far more deeply interfused,
Whose dwelling is the light of setting suns,
And the round ocean and the living air,
And the blue sky, and in the mind of man;
A motion and a spirit, that impels
All thinking things, all objects of all thought,
And rolls through all things. Therefore am I still
A lover of the meadows and the woods,
And mountains; and of all that we behold
From this green earth; of all the mighty world
Of eye, and ear,—both what they half create,
And what perceive; well pleased to recognize
In nature and the language of the sense,
The anchor of my purest thoughts, the nurse,
The guide, the guardian of my heart, and soul
Of all my moral being.
Nor perchance,
If I were not thus taught, should I the more
Suffer my genial spirits to decay:
For thou art with me here upon the banks
Of this fair river; thou my dearest Friend,
My dear, dear Friend; and in thy voice I catch

The language of my former heart, and read
My former pleasures in the shooting lights
Of thy wild eyes. Oh! yet a little while
May I behold in thee what I was once,
My dear, dear Sister! and this prayer I make,
Knowing that Nature never did betray
The heart that loved her; 'tis her privilege,
Through all the years of this our life, to lead
From joy to joy: for she can so inform
The mind that is within us, so impress
With quietness and beauty, and so feed
With lofty thoughts, that neither evil tongues,
Rash judgments, nor the sneers of selfish men,
Nor greetings where no kindness is, nor all
The dreary intercourse of daily life,
Shall e'er prevail against us, or disturb
Our cheerful faith, that all which we behold
Is full of blessings. Therefore let the moon
Shine on thee in thy solitary walk;
And let the misty mountain-winds be free
To blow against thee: and, in after years,
When these wild ecstasies shall be matured
Into a sober pleasure; when thy mind
Shall be a mansion for all lovely forms,
Thy memory be as a dwelling-place
For all sweet sounds and harmonies; oh! then,
If solitude, or fear, or pain, or grief,
Should be thy portion, with what healing thoughts
Of tender joy wilt thou remember me,
And these my exhortations! Nor, perchance—
If I should be where I no more can hear
Thy voice, nor catch from thy wild eyes these gleams
Of past existence—wilt thou then forget
That on the banks of this delightful stream
We stood together; and that I, so long
A worshipper of Nature, hither came
Unwearied in that service: rather say
With warmer love—oh! with far deeper zeal
Of holier love. Nor wilt thou then forget,
That after many wanderings, many years
Of absence, these steep woods and lofty cliffs,
And this green pastoral landscape, were to me
More dear, both for themselves and for thy sake!

1798

Percy Bysshe Shelley

The most ardent of revolutionary spirits, Percy Bysshe Shelley based his romanticism on the power of love to reform the world. His leading themes are ideal democracy and ideal love. To accomplish his dreams, Shelley could be exceedingly independent, even reckless. Although he was born to a wealthy family, at Field Place, England, in 1792, he succeeded through the extreme acts of his youth in alienating his family and forfeiting his inheritance. When Shelley believed in a cause, he seldom hesitated to act. He was the "true" idealist who believed that ideas are the most real thing in life. From boyhood he resisted oppression in any form: at Eton it was the tyranny of the school bullies and at Oxford the tyranny of the church over the freedom of thought. He recorded his hatred of authority in a pamphlet, The Necessity of Atheism, *for which he was expelled from Oxford. He soon afterward married Harriet Westbrook, a girl of sixteen, to rescue her from her father who wanted her to return to school, then later deserted her for Mary Godwin, a woman more his intellectual equal. Shelley's outspoken denunciations of almost all established traditions in government, religion, and marriage so alienated him from the public that he left England in 1818 for Italy, where he spent the remaining four years of his life.*

Prometheus Unbound *(1820), a poetic drama glorifying the ideals of the French Revolution, is Shelley's most impressive attempt to show the salvation of mankind through the spirit of brotherhood. In this drama he makes clear how much he abhors all conservative compromises. Where Wordsworth tended to move toward preserving the existing order of society as he lost sympathy with violent upheaval, Shelley developed increasingly rebellious ideas through a life of intellectual ferment.*

The varieties of Shelley's intense moods can be seen in the two poems reprinted here: "To a Skylark" *(1820), where his emotion soars upward in ecstatic joy, and* "Ode to the West Wind" *(1820), in which he longs for a power as strong as that of the wind to spread his ideas through the world. Although the latter poem passes from despondency over his failures to a clear faith in ultimate triumph, it also effectively portrays through the desolate autumn imagery the weight of life's mystery and pain of which Shelley was then acutely conscious.*

ODE TO THE WEST WIND

I

O, wild West Wind, thou breath of Autumn's being,
Thou, from whose unseen presence the leaves dead
Are driven, like ghosts from an enchanter fleeing,

Yellow, and black, and pale, and hectic red,
Pestilence-stricken multitudes: O thou,
Who chariotest to their dark wintry bed

[From *The Complete Poetical Works of Shelley*. Oxford, The Clarendon Press, 1904.]

The wingèd seeds, where they lie cold and low,
Each like a corpse within its grave, until
Thine azure sister of the Spring shall blow

Her clarion o'er the dreaming earth, and fill
(Driving sweet buds like flocks to feed in air)
With living hues and odors plain and hill:

Wild Spirit, which art moving everywhere;
Destroyer and preserver; hear, oh, hear!

II

Thou on whose stream, 'mid the steep sky's commotion,
Loose clouds like earth's decaying leaves are shed,
Shook from the tangled boughs of Heaven and Ocean,

Angels of rain and lightning: there are spread
On the blue surface of thine aëry surge,
Like the bright hair uplifted from the head

Of some fierce Maenad, even from the dim verge
Of the horizon to the zenith's height,
The locks of the approaching storm. Thou dirge

Of the dying year, to which this closing night
Will be the dome of a vast sepulchre,
Vaulted with all thy congregated might

Of vapours, from whose solid atmosphere
Black rain, and fire, and hail will burst: oh, hear!

III

Thou who didst waken from his summer dreams
The blue Mediterranean, where he lay,
Lulled by the coil of his crystalline streams,

Beside a pumice isle on Baiae's bay,
And saw in sleep old palaces and towers
Quivering within the wave's intenser day,

All overgrown with azure moss and flowers
So sweet, the sense faints picturing them! Thou
For whose path the Atlantic's level powers

Cleave themselves into chasms, while far below
The sea-blooms and the oozy woods which wear
The sapless foliage of the ocean, know

Thy voice, and suddenly grow gray with fear,
And tremble and despoil themselves: oh, hear!

IV

If I were a dead leaf thou mightest bear;
If I were a swift cloud to fly with thee;
A wave to pant beneath thy power, and share

The impulse of thy strength, only less free
Than thou, O uncontrollable! If even
I were as in my boyhood, and could be

The comrade of thy wanderings over Heaven,
As then, when to outstrip thy skiey speed
Scarce seemed a vision; I would ne'er have striven

As thus with thee in prayer in my sore need.
Oh, lift me as a wave, a leaf, a cloud!
I fall upon the thorns of life! I bleed!

A heavy weight of hours has chained and bowed
One too like thee: tameless, and swift, and proud.

V

Make me thy lyre, even as the forest is:
What if my leaves are falling like its own!
The tumult of thy mighty harmonies

Will take from both a deep, autumnal tone,
Sweet though in sadness. Be thou, Spirit fierce,
My spirit! Be thou me, impetuous one!

Drive my dead thoughts over the universe
Like withered leaves to quicken a new birth!
And, by the incantation of this verse,

Scatter, as from an unextinguished hearth
Ashes and sparks, my words among mankind!
Be through my lips to unawakened earth

The trumpet of a prophecy! O, Wind,
If Winter comes, can Spring be far behind? *1819, 1820*

TO A SKYLARK

Hail to thee, blithe Spirit!
Bird thou never wert,
That from Heaven, or near it,
Pourest thy full heart
In profuse strains of unpremeditated art.

Higher still and higher
From the earth thou springest
Like a cloud of fire;
The blue deep thou wingest,
And singing still dost soar, and soaring ever singest.

In the golden lightning
Of the sunken sun,
O'er which clouds are bright'ning,
Thou dost float and run;
Like an unbodied joy whose race is just begun.

The pale purple even
Melts around thy flight;
Like a star of Heaven,
In the broad daylight
Thou art unseen, but yet I hear thy shrill delight,

Keen as are the arrows
Of that silver sphere,
Whose intense lamp narrows
In the white dawn clear
Until we hardly see—we feel that it is there.

All the earth and air
With thy voice is loud,
As, when night is bare,
From one lonely cloud
The moon rains out her beams, and Heaven is overflowed.

What thou art we know not;
What is most like thee?
From rainbow clouds there flow not
Drops so bright to see
As from thy presence showers a rain of melody.

Like a Poet hidden
In the light of thought,
Singing hymns unbidden,
Till the world is wrought
To sympathy with hopes and fears it heeded not:

Like a high-born maiden
In a palace-tower,
Soothing her love-laden
Soul in secret hour
With music sweet as love, which overflows her bower:

Like a glow-worm golden
In a dell of dew,
Scattering unbeholden
Its aëreal hue
Among the flowers and grass, which screen it from the view!

Like a rose embowered
In its own green leaves,
By warm winds deflowered,
Till the scent it gives
Makes faint with too much sweet those heavy-wingèd thieves:

[From *The Complete Poetical Works of Shelley*. Oxford, The Clarendon Press, 1904.]

Sound of vernal showers
On the twinkling grass,
Rain-awakened flowers,
All that ever was
Joyous, and clear, and fresh, thy music doth surpass.

Teach us, Sprite or Bird,
What sweet thoughts are thine:
I have never heard
Praise of love or wine
That panted forth a flood of rapture so divine.

Chorus Hymeneal,
Or triumphal chant,
Matched with thine, would be all
But an empty vaunt,
A thing wherein we feel there is some hidden want.

What objects are the fountains
Of thy happy strain?
What fields, or waves, or mountains?
What shapes of sky or plain?
What love of thine own kind? what ignorance of pain?

With thy clear keen joyance
Languor cannot be:
Shadow of annoyance
Never came near thee:
Thou lovest—but ne'er knew love's sad satiety.

Waking or asleep,
Thou of death must deem
Things more true and deep
Than we mortals dream,
Or how could thy notes flow in such a crystal stream?

We look before and after,
And pine for what is not:
Our sincerest laughter
With some pain is fraught;
Our sweetest songs are those that tell of saddest thought.

Yet if we could scorn
Hate, and pride, and fear;
If we were things born
Not to shed a tear,
I know not how thy joy we ever should come near.

Better than all measures
Of delightful sound,
Better than all treasures
That in books are found,
Thy skill to poet were, thou scorner of the ground!

Teach me half the gladness
That thy brain must know,
Such harmonious madness
From my lips would flow
The world should listen then—as I am listening now.

1820

Samuel Taylor Coleridge

Unlike Wordsworth or Shelley, Samuel Taylor Coleridge customarily wrote about the world of pure fantasy. He was a man of intense imagination, a dreamer, and essentially impractical. The unusual and the weird held a strong attraction for him. He believed that poetry should be so sensuous that it would "by its imagery elicit truth at a flash." His poems move in the mysterious realm of the imagination; their verbal magic is especially effective in suggesting the supernatural. Coleridge wrote "Kubla Khan," which we reprint here, upon awaking from an opium dream; it is a remarkable example of intuitive vision.

Born in 1772 at Ottery St. Mary, Devonshire, Coleridge was the thirteenth child of an Anglican clergyman. Preferring reading to children's games, he finished the Arabian Nights before he was five years old, and at an early age he developed his habits of reflection and dreaming. Upon the death of his father, Coleridge, then only ten years old, was sent to Christ's Hospital, a home for children in London. Here his frail constitution suffered from the poor food and from his unwillingness to take physical exercise. At eighteen he entered Cambridge University, where he may have first sought relief from his pains and fevers by taking opium. Plagued by debts and despondent moods, he left the university and enlisted in the Fifteenth Dragoons. This experience merely proved how ill-suited he was for military life and his brother James, a captain, rescued him by obtaining his discharge. Although he returned to Cambridge for a time, he left in 1794 without having obtained a degree.

Fired with the revolutionary fervor of his age, Coleridge joined Robert Southey, another poet and visionary, in planning an ideal society on the banks of the Susquehanna River in Pennsylvania. To initiate this social experiment twelve able young men were to marry twelve robust young women and emigrate to America. In 1795 Coleridge married Sarah Fricker and Southey married Sarah's sister, but their proposed scheme collapsed when they were unable to raise passage money for the voyage. The same year (1795) Coleridge met Wordsworth, with whom he collaborated on a volume of Lyrical Ballads, published in 1798. At about this time he accompanied Wordsworth and his sister to Germany where he studied philosophy for a brief period. During his few productive years Coleridge wrote some of the most imaginative modern poetry. In fact, in a little over a year he wrote most of the poems for which he is now famous. The remainder of his life was spent either on the Continent or in England in a vain attempt to recover his health. He died in 1834.

KUBLA KHAN*

In Xanadu did Kubla Khan
A stately pleasure-dome decree:
Where Alph, the sacred river, ran
Through caverns measureless to man
    Down to a sunless sea.
So twice five miles of fertile ground
With walls and towers were girdled round:
And here were gardens bright with sinuous rills,
Where blossomed many an incense-bearing tree;
And here were forests ancient as the hills,
Enfolding sunny spots of greenery.

* A Mongol emperor of the thirteenth century who conquered China, founded the Yüan dynasty and made Buddhism the state religion.

[From *The Complete Poetical Works of Samuel Taylor Coleridge*. Oxford, The Clarendon Press, 1912.]

But oh! that deep romantic chasm which slanted
Down the green hill athwart a cedarn cover!
A savage place! as holy and enchanted
As e'er beneath a waning moon was haunted
By woman wailing for her demon-lover!
And from this chasm, with ceaseless turmoil seething,
As if this earth in fast thick pants were breathing,
A mighty fountain momently was forced:
Amid whose swift half-intermitted burst
Huge fragments vaulted like rebounding hail,
Or chaffy grain beneath the thresher's flail:
And 'mid these dancing rocks at once and ever
It flung up momently the sacred river.
Five miles meandering with a mazy motion
Through wood and dale the sacred river ran,
Then reached the caverns measureless to man,
And sank in tumult to a lifeless ocean:
And 'mid this tumult Kubla heard from far
Ancestral voices prophesying war!

The shadow of the dome of pleasure
Floated midway on the waves;
Where was heard the mingled measure
From the fountain and the caves.
It was a miracle of rare device,
A sunny pleasure-dome with caves of ice!

A damsel with a dulcimer
In a vision once I saw:
It was an Abyssinian maid,
And on her dulcimer she played,
Singing of Mount Abora.

Could I revive within me
Her symphony and song,
To such a deep delight 'twould win me,
That with music loud and long,
I would build that dome in air,
That sunny dome! those caves of ice!
And all who heard should see them there,
And all should cry, Beware! Beware!
His flashing eyes, his floating hair!
Weave a circle round him thrice,
And close your eyes with holy dread,
For he on honey-dew hath fed,
And drunk the milk of Paradise.

John Keats

There is a special quality about the romantic idealism of Keats. Although he struggled with the passions of youth, he seldom allowed his emotions to carry him too far from the world of actuality. He did not yield to the temptation to confuse the ideal with the real, and he refused to accept a sentimental compromise with the facts of life, cruel as they seemed to be.

Keats was not a social reformer; the stirring political and social issues that occupied so much of Shelley's attention are absent from his poetry. Before the day of Freud and Jung, he wrote a sensitive record of his inner life, depicting with fine insight his intimate emotional experiences. The impulse to create is beyond conscious control; it comes, he believed, from hidden springs working intuitively. The poet is in its power. But Keats was convinced that such poetic expression is at the center of human life. It not only arises from a powerful flow of feeling but grows as naturally "as the leaves to a tree." Because its basic intuitions are common to all men, poetry "should strike the reader as a wording of his own highest thoughts."

Keats' short life was filled with poverty, illness, and the abusive treatment of literary critics. He was born in 1795 at the Swan and Hoop Inn near London where his father was the keeper of the stables and his mother the daughter of the innkeeper; he died in Rome in 1821 at the age of twenty-five. His active career as a poet covered no more than five years. Soon after he published his first book of poems in 1817, he fell deeply in love with Fanny Brawne whom he met at the home of a mutual friend. From this new happiness came some of Keats' most appealing poetry, but in a few years his health began to fail. Although Fanny nursed him devotedly, he realized that he could not survive another winter in London. Leaving England to seek recovery in Italy, he died a few months later in Rome.

The two poems reprinted here are among his best known. In the "Ode to a Nightingale" Keats permits his imagination to wander freely with the light-winged bird that sings of summer and knows nothing of the weariness and fever that Keats experienced. In the "Ode on a Grecian Urn," he marvelously captures the emotions and fantasy suggested by the figures on the urn without becoming blind to the actual limitations of human life. The distinction of Keats' romanticism is found in its mature ability to contemplate intense joy and beauty while recognizing that they are usually beyond complete fulfillment in an imperfect world.

ODE TO A NIGHTINGALE

My heart aches, and a drowsy numbness pains
    My sense, as though of hemlock I had drunk,
Or emptied some dull opiate to the drains
    One minute past, and Lethe-wards had sunk:
'Tis not through envy of thy happy lot,
    But being too happy in thine happiness,—
        That thou, light-winged Dryad of the trees,
            In some melodious plot

[From *The Poetical Works of John Keats*. Oxford, The Clarendon Press, 1939.]

Of beechen green, and shadows numberless,
Singest of summer in full-throated ease.

O, for a draught of vintage! that hath been
Cool'd a long age in the deep-delved earth,
Tasting of Flora and the country-green,
Dance, and Provençal song, and sun-burnt mirth!
O for a beaker full of the warm South,
Full of the true, the blushful Hippocrene,
With beaded bubbles winking at the brim,
And purple-stained mouth;
That I might drink, and leave the world unseen,
And with thee fade away into the forest dim:

Fade far away, dissolve, and quite forget
What thou among the leaves hast never known,
The weariness, the fever, and the fret
Here, where men sit and hear each other groan;
Where palsy shakes a few, sad, last grey hairs,
Where youth grows pale, and spectre-thin, and dies;
Where but to think is to be full of sorrow
And leaden-ey'd despairs;
Where beauty cannot keep her lustrous eyes,
Or new Love pine at them beyond to-morrow.

Away! away! for I will fly to thee,
Not charioted by Bacchus and his pards,
But on the viewless wings of Poesy,
Though the dull brain perplexes and retards:
Already with thee! tender is the night,
And haply the Queen-Moon is on her throne,
Cluster'd around by all her starry Fays;
But here there is no light,
Save what from heaven is with the breezes blown
Through verdurous glooms and winding mossy ways.

I cannot see what flowers are at my feet,
Nor what soft incense hangs upon the boughs,
But, in embalmed darkness, guess each sweet
Wherewith the seasonable month endows
The grass, the thicket, and the fruit-tree wild;
White hawthorn, and the pastoral eglantine;
Fast-fading violets cover'd up in leaves;
And mid-May's eldest child,
The coming musk-rose, full of dewy wine,
The murmurous haunt of flies on summer eves.

Darkling I listen; and for many a time
I have been half in love with easeful Death,
Call'd him soft names in many a mused rhyme,
To take into the air my quiet breath;
Now more than ever seems it rich to die,
To cease upon the midnight with no pain,
While thou art pouring forth thy soul abroad
In such an ecstasy!
Still wouldst thou sing, and I have ears in vain—
To thy high requiem become a sod.

Thou wast not born for death, immortal Bird!
No hungry generations tread thee down;
The voice I hear this passing night was heard
In ancient days by emperor and clown;
Perhaps the self-same song that found a path
Through the sad heart of Ruth, when, sick for home,
She stood in tears amid the alien corn;
The same that oft-times hath
Charm'd magic casements, opening on the foam
Of perilous seas, in faery lands forlorn.

Forlorn! the very word is like a bell
To toll me back from thee to my sole self.
Adieu! the fancy cannot cheat so well
As she is fam'd to do, deceiving elf.
Adieu! Adieu! thy plaintive anthem fades
Past the near meadows, over the still stream,
Up the hill-side; and now 'tis buried deep
In the next valley-glades:
Was it a vision, or a waking dream?
Fled is that music:—do I wake or sleep?

ODE ON A GRECIAN URN

Thou still unravish'd bride of quietness,
Thou foster-child of silence and slow time,
Sylvan historian, who canst thus express
A flowery tale more sweetly than our rhyme:
What leaf-fringed legend haunts about thy shape
Of deities or mortals, or of both,
In Tempe or the dales of Arcady?
What men or gods are these? What maidens loth?

[From *The Poetical Works of John Keats*. Oxford, The Clarendon Press. 1939.]

What mad pursuit? What struggle to escape?
What pipes and timbrels? What wild ecstasy?

Heard melodies are sweet, but those unheard
Are sweeter; therefore, ye soft pipes, play on;
Not to the sensual ear, but, more endear'd,
Pipe to the spirit ditties of no tone;
Fair youth, beneath the trees, thou canst not leave
Thy song, nor ever can those trees be bare;
Bold Lover, never, never canst thou kiss,
Though winning near the goal—yet, do not grieve;
She cannot fade, though thou hast not thy bliss,
For ever wilt thou love, and she be fair!

Ah, happy, happy boughs! that cannot shed
Your leaves, not ever bid the Spring adieu;
And, happy melodist, unwearied,
For ever piping songs for ever new;
More happy love! more happy, happy love!
For ever warm and still to be enjoy'd,
For ever panting and for ever young;
All breathing human passion far above,
That leaves a heart high sorrowful and cloy'd,
A burning forehead, and a parching tongue.

Who are these coming to the sacrifice?
To what green altar, O mysterious priest,
Lead'st thou that heifer lowing at the skies,
And all her silken flanks with garlands drest?
What little town by river or sea-shore,
Or mountain-built with peaceful citadel,
Is emptied of its folk, this pious morn?
And, little town, thy streets for evermore
Will silent be; and not a soul to tell
Why thou are desolate, can e'er return.

O Attic shape! Fair attitude! with brede
Of marble men and maidens overwrought,
With forest branches and the trodden weed;
Thou, silent form, dost tease us out of thought
As doth eternity: Cold Pastoral!
When old age shall this generation waste,
Thou shalt remain, in midst of other woe
Than ours, a friend to man, to whom thou say'st,
'Beauty is truth, truth beauty,'—that is all
Ye know on earth, and all ye need to know.

Gerard Manley Hopkins

Born in 1844 at Stratford, Essex, Gerard Manley Hopkins was educated at Highgate Grammar School and Oxford University. Like many other undergraduates at Oxford, Hopkins was greatly influenced by Walter Pater's essays on art and literature and by the liberal thinking of Benjamin Jowett, the classical scholar. While at Oxford, Hopkins also decided to join the Roman Catholic Church. A year after his graduation he entered the Jesuit order, burning most of his youthful poems and resolving to write no more verses. After serving parishes in Liverpool and Oxford, he was appointed professor of Greek in the Catholic University at Dublin in 1884. Some years earlier on the encouragement of his superiors he had returned to the writing of poetry. When he died in 1888 his manuscripts went to a close friend since Oxford days, Robert Bridges.

The rhythmic patterns and striking imagery of Hopkins' poetry anticipate the experiments of contemporary English and American poets like Dylan Thomas and E. E. Cummings. Hopkins called his metrical plan "sprung rhythm," by which he meant that in any line the accented syllables may follow each other without interruption or they may be separated by any number of unaccented syllables, according to the psychological intent. This system, found in Anglo-Saxon poetry, is supported by Hopkins' use of another old device, alliteration. In his own view Hopkins' musical use of rhythm and rhyme support the emotional sensations produced by the sharply drawn images, or "inscapes," as he termed them. To intensify the effect of the imagery, he condensed his language, using mainly nouns and verbs, and avoiding pronouns, particles, and other parts of speech that did not contribute directly to the imaginative power of the line. To be understood, his poetry must be read aloud, Hopkins said, so that its metrical qualities can fully strengthen the images.

The originality of Hopkins' writing was appreciated during his lifetime only by a few friends. His poems were not published until thirty years after his death. In comparison with his style, Hopkins' religious ideas are much less striking. The spiritual qualities of his poetry appear most clearly in the delicate imaginative touches of "Heaven-Haven" and the tender warmth of "God's Grandeur," poems which are reprinted here. Hopkins associated religious faith with nature's primitive charm, but in a poem like "Pied Beauty" the sensuous attraction of nature is sublimated to his conviction of the changeless reality of God. Above all, like St. Francis and Wordsworth, Hopkins combines a deep humanity with the insights of the mystic. The tender beauty of childhood, the grandeur of the virtuous life, the pathos of death—all these are given poignant expression as they are seen in and through the love of God.

HEAVEN-HAVEN

A Nun Takes the Veil

I have desired to go
Where springs not fail,
To fields where flies no sharp and sided hail
And a few lilies blow.

And I have asked to be
Where no storms come,
Where the green swell is in the havens dumb,
And out of the swing of the sea.

GOD'S GRANDEUR

The world is charged with the grandeur of God.
It will flame out, like shining from shook foil;
It gathers to a greatness, like the ooze of oil
Crushed. Why do men then now not reck his rod?
Generations have trod, have trod, have trod;
And all is seared with trade; bleared, smeared with toil;
And wears man's smudge and shares man's smell: the soil
Is bare now, nor can foot feel, being shod.

And for all this, nature is never spent;
There lives the dearest freshness deep down things;
And though the last lights off the black West went
Oh, morning, at the brown brink eastward, springs—
Because the Holy Ghost over the bent
World broods with warm breast and with ah! bright wings.

PIED BEAUTY

Glory be to God for dappled things—
For skies of couple-colour as a brinded cow;
For rose-moles all in stipple upon trout that swim;
Fresh-firecoal chestnut-falls; finches' wings;
Landscape plotted and pieced—fold, fallow, and plough;
And áll trádes, their gear and tackle and trim.

All things counter, original, spare, strange;
Whatever is fickle, freckled (who knows how?)
With swift, slow; sweet, sour; adazzle, dim;
He fathers-forth whose beauty is past change:
Praise him.

Emily Dickinson

Emily Dickinson spent most of her life in the house at Amherst, Massachusetts, where she was born in 1830. Although her life outwardly contained little adventure, it was marked by vivid internal drama. Her preference for the contemplative life was doubtless determined in part by her New England inheritance of intellectual and moral independence. As a girl she showed her strength of character by returning home from the South Hadley Female Seminary when she could no longer take its strict discipline. At the age of twenty-three she visited Washington for a few weeks with her father, then a member of Congress, whom she adored. On the trip home she stayed for a time in Philadelphia, where she became acquainted with the Reverend Charles Wadsworth. Other close friends were George Gould and Benjamin F. Newton, a young lawyer, whose early death saddened her. Always reticent about her private life, she never disclosed the degree of her affection for these men.

From 1856 to her death in 1886, she led a retired and somewhat eccentric life in the family house. She wrote many letters, which she preferred others to address for her; she wore only white dresses, which her sister had to try on for her; and she liked to give presents of cookies accompanied by enigmatic verses. During these secluded years she often wrote poems on brown paper bags, margins of newspapers, or backs of envelopes and hid them in bureau drawers and boxes since she disliked having her emotions made public. After her death these scraps of poetry were collected and published, and her place as one of America's more sensitive poets was securely established.

Emily Dickinson's verses seem wholly spontaneous although we know she often added lists of alternate words and phrases in her manuscripts. Yet for the reader the impression created by the condensed movement, the sudden rhythmic shifts, and the unexpected leaps from image to image is the work of a quick mind inevitably impelled to lyric expression. We discover the special turn of her thought in frequent associations between the spiritual and the earthly. The juxtaposing of the trivial and the sublime suggests the incongruities she saw in human experience and reveals how keenly aware she was of the ironic contrast between the real and the ideal. She is always curious about man and God although she often found it difficult to reconcile God's ways to man. In the end, she seems to have passed through disillusioned agony to detached peace. With saucy objectivity she could jest even with God. Emily Dickinson is a mystic who did not lose her identity in the Divine but maintained her own critical independence. Something of this spirit is reflected in the seven short poems reprinted here.

POEMS

I

I taste a liquor never brewed,
From tankards scooped in pearl;
Not all the vats upon the Rhine
Yield such an alcohol!

Inebriate of air am I,
And debauchee of dew,
Reeling, through endless summer days,
From inns of molten blue.

When landlords turn the drunken bee
Out of the foxglove's door,
When butterflies renounce their drams,
I shall but drink the more!

Till seraphs swing their snowy hats,
And saints to windows run,
To see the little tippler
Leaning against the sun!

II

Some keep the Sabbath going to church;
I keep it staying at home,
With a bobolink for a chorister,
And an orchard for a dome.

Some keep the Sabbath in surplice;
I just wear my wings,
And instead of tolling the bell for church,
Our little sexton sings.

God preaches,—a noted clergyman,—
And the sermon is never long;
So instead of getting to heaven at last,
I'm going all along!

III

The bustle in a house
The morning after death
Is solemnest of industries
Enacted upon earth,—

The sweeping up the heart,
And putting love away
We shall not want to use again
Until eternity.

IV

Success is counted sweetest
By those who ne'er succeed.
To comprehend a nectar
Requires sorest need.

Not one of all the purple host
Who took the flag to-day
Can tell the definition,
So clear, of victory,

As he, defeated, dying,
On whose forbidden ear
The distant strains of triumph
Break, agonized and clear.

V

Lightly stepped a yellow star
To its lofty place,
Loosed the Moon her silver hat
From her lustral face.

All of evening softly lit
As an astral hall—
"Father," I observed to Heaven,
"You are punctual."

VI

I never saw a moor,
I never saw the sea;
Yet I know how the heather looks,
And what a wave must be.

I never spoke with God,
Nor visited in heaven;
Yet certain am I of the spot
As if the chart were given.

VII

My life closed twice before its close;
It yet remains to see
If Immortality unveil
A third event to me,

So huge, so hopeless to conceive,
As these that twice befell.
Parting is all we know of heaven,
And all we need of hell.

William Butler Yeats

William Butler Yeats is the greatest lyric poet Ireland has produced. Although born in Dublin (in 1865), Yeats spent much of his boyhood at his mother's home in Sligo, a town in a wild district of Ireland, where the mountains and lakes made an indelible impression on his mind. Here he became familiar with the fanciful folk tales of the Celtic spirits "who lived in souls of passionate men." Irish folklore and history form an important source of his literary inspiration and help account for his tendency toward mystical expression. In the years he spent in London Yeats was influenced by French symbolist poetry and the pre-Raphaelite group of writers and artists who were trying to achieve in their poetry and painting greater individuality, more immediate impressions of nature, and a direct style. Keats was their favorite author. The mood of Yeats' poetry from about 1890 to 1900 was one of longing for escape from civilization into the world of impassioned imagination.

Although he had written some poetic plays before his meeting in 1898 with Lady Gregory, leader of the Irish theater movement, Yeats from then on became interested in writing drama adapted to the modern stage. With Lady Gregory he founded the Irish National Theater in 1899. Among his poetic plays successfully produced at the Abbey Theater were The Countess Cathleen *(1892) and* Deirdre *(1907), based on the Gaelic folk legend of tragic young love. Increasingly drawn into Irish politics, Yeats was one of the first senators of the Irish Free State, holding a seat in the Irish Senate from 1922 to 1928. He had also become a leader of the intellectual life of Ireland and aided its cultural renaissance by founding the Irish Literary Society. In 1923 he received the Nobel Prize for Literature, awarded for "his consistently emotional poetry, which in the strictest form expresses a people's spirit." He died in 1939.*

In his later poetry, after 1928, Yeats wrote more passionately than ever. Impressed by the transistory quality of human feeling, he sought to recapture the intensity of every emotion and to decry every defeat of the happy union of heart and soul. He often reflected on the life unfulfilled by love since he believed it had lost its chance for immortality. His poetic drama Purgatory, *reprinted here, discloses the torment of unhappy souls. To compensate in old age for the weakness of the flesh, the mature person, Yeats felt, must seek within himself the springs of imaginative beauty and spiritual wisdom. These themes are brilliantly explored in poems like "Sailing to Byzantium" (1926) and "Among School Children" (1927).*

PURGATORY

PERSONS IN THE PLAY.

A Boy
An Old Man

SCENE.—*A ruined house and a bare tree in the background.*

Boy

Half-door, hall door,
Hither and thither day and night,
Hill or hollow, shouldering this pack,
Hearing you talk.

Old Man

Study that house.

I think about its jokes and stories;
I try to remember what the butler
Said to a drunken gamekeeper
In mid-October, but I cannot.
If I cannot, none living can.
Where are the jokes and stories of a house,
Its threshold gone to patch a pig-stye?

Boy

So you have come this path before?

Old Man

The moonlight falls upon the path,
The shadow of a cloud upon the house,
And that's symbolical; study that tree,
What is it like?

Boy

A silly old man.

Old Man

It's like—no matter what it's like.
I saw it a year ago stripped bare as now,
So I chose a better trade.
I saw it fifty years ago
Before the thunder-bolt had riven it,
Green leaves, ripe leaves, leaves thick as butter,
Fat, greasy life. Stand there and look,
Because there is somebody in that house.

The Boy puts down pack and stands in the doorway.

Boy

There's nobody here.

Old Man

There's somebody there.

Boy

The floor is gone, the windows gone,
And where there should be roof there's sky,
And here's a bit of an egg-shell thrown
Out of a jackdaw's nest.

Old Man

But there are some
That do not care what's gone, what's left:
The souls in Purgatory that come back
To habitations and familiar spots.

Boy

Your wits are out again.

Old Man

Re-live
Their transgressions, and that not once
But many times; they know at last
The consequence of those transgressions
Whether upon others or upon themselves;
Upon others, others may bring help,
For when the consequence is at an end
The dream must end; upon themselves,
There is no help but in themselves
And in the mercy of God.

Boy

I have had enough!
Talk to the jackdaws, if talk you must.

Old Man

Stop! Sit there upon that stone.
That is the house where I was born.

Boy

The big old house that was burnt down?

Old Man

My mother that was your grand-dam owned it,
This scenery and this countryside,
Kennel and stable, horse and hound—
She had a horse at the Curragh, and there met
My father, a groom in a training stable,
Looked at him and married him.
Her mother never spoke to her again,
And she did right.

Boy

What's right and wrong?
My grand-dad got the girl and the money.

Old Man

Looked at him and married him,
And he squandered everything she had.
She never knew the worst, because
She died in giving birth to me,
But now she knows it all, being dead.
Great people lived and died in this house;
Magistrates, colonels, members of Parliament,
Captains and Governors, and long ago
Men that had fought at Aughrim and the Boyne.
Some that had gone on Government work
To London or to India came home to die,
Or came from London every spring
To look at the may-blossom in the park.
They had loved the trees that he cut down
To pay what he had lost at cards
Or spent on horses, drink and women;
Had loved the house, had loved all
The intricate passages of the house,
But he killed the house; to kill a house
Where great men grew up, married, died,
I here declare a capital offence.

Boy

My God, but you had luck! Grand clothes,
And maybe a grand horse to ride.

Old Man

That he might keep me upon his level
He never sent me to school, but some
Half-loved me for my half of her:
A gamekeeper's wife taught me to read,
A Catholic curate taught me Latin.
There were old books and books made fine
By eighteenth-century French binding, books
Modern and ancient, books by the ton.

Boy

What education have you given me?

Old Man

I gave the education that befits
A bastard that a pedlar got
Upon a tinker's daughter in a ditch.
When I had come to sixteen years old
My father burned down the house when drunk.

Boy

But that is my age, sixteen years old,
At the Puck Fair.

Old Man

And everything was burnt;
Books, library, all were burnt.

Boy

Is what I have heard upon the road the truth,
That you killed him in the burning house?

Old Man

There's nobody here but our two selves?

Boy

Nobody, Father.

Old Man

I struck him with a knife,
That knife that cuts my dinner now,
And after that I left him in the fire.
They dragged him out, somebody saw
The knife-wound but could not be certain
Because the body was all black and charred.
Then some that were his drunken friends
Swore they would put me upon trial,
Spoke of quarrels, a threat I had made.
The gamekeeper gave me some old clothes,
I ran away, worked here and there
Till I became a pedlar on the roads,

No good trade, but good enough
Because I am my father's son,
Because of what I did or may do.
Listen to the hoof-beats! Listen, listen!

Boy

I cannot hear a sound.

Old Man

Beat! Beat!
This night is the anniversary
Of my mother's wedding night,
Or of the night wherein I was begotten.
My father is riding from the public-house,
A whiskey-bottle under his arm.
A window is lit showing a young girl.
Look at the window; she stands there
Listening, the servants are all in bed,
She is alone, he has stayed late
Bragging and drinking in the public-house.

Boy

There's nothing but an empty gap in the wall.
You have made it up. No, you are mad!
You are getting madder every day.

Old Man

It's louder now because he rides
Upon a gravelled avenue
All grass to-day. The hoof-beat stops,
He has gone to the other side of the house,
Gone to the stable, put the horse up.
She has gone down to open the door.
This night she is no better than her man
And does not mind that he is half drunk,
She is mad about him. They mount the stairs.
She brings him into her own chamber.
And that is the marriage-chamber now.
The window is dimly lit again.

Do not let him touch you! It is not true
That drunken men cannot beget,
And if he touch he must beget
And you must bear his murderer.
Deaf! Both deaf! If I should throw
A stick or a stone they would not hear;
And that's a proof my wits are out.
But there's a problem: she must live
Through everything in exact detail,
Driven to it by remorse, and yet
Can she renew the sexual act
And find no pleasure in it, and if not,
If pleasure and remorse must both be there,
Which is the greater?
I lack schooling.
Go fetch Tertullian; he and I
Will ravel all that problem out
Whilst those two lie upon the mattress
Begetting me.
Come back! Come back!
And so you thought to slip away,
My bag of money between your fingers,
And that I could not talk and see!
You have been rummaging in the pack.
The light in the window has faded out.

Boy

You never gave me my right share.

Old Man

And had I given it, young as you are,
You would have spent it upon drink.

Boy

What if I did? I had a right
To get it and spend it as I chose.

Old Man

Give me that bag and no more words.

Boy

I will not.

Old Man

I will break your fingers.
They struggle for the bag. In the strug-

gle it drops, scattering the money. The Old Man staggers but does not fall. They stand looking at each other. The window is lit up. A man is seen pouring whiskey into a glass.

Boy

What if I killed you? You killed my granddad,
Because you were young and he was old.
Now I am young and you are old.

Old Man [*staring at window*]
Better-looking, those sixteen years—

Boy

What are you muttering?

Old Man

Younger—and yet
She should have known he was not her kind.

Boy

What are you saying? Out with it!
Old Man points to window.
My God! The window is lit up
And somebody stands there, although
The floor-boards are all burnt away.

Old Man

The window is lit up because my father
Has come to find a glass for his whiskey
He leans there like some tired beast.

Boy

A dead, living, murdered man!

Old Man

'Then the bride-sleep fell upon Adam':
Where did I read those words?
And yet
There's nothing leaning in the window
But the impression upon my mother's mind;
Being dead she is alone in her remorse.

Boy

A body that was a bundle of old bones
Before I was born. Horrible! Horrible!
He covers his eyes.

Old Man

That beast there would know nothing, being nothing,
If I should kill a man under the window
He would not even turn his head.
He stabs the boy.
My father and my son on the same jack-knife!
That finishes—there—there—there—
He stabs again and again. The window grows dark.
'Hush-a-bye baby, thy father's a knight,
Thy mother a lady, lovely and bright.'
No, that is something that I read in a book,
And if I sing it must be to my mother,
And I lack rhyme.
The stage has grown dark except where the tree stands in white light.
Study that tree.
It stands there like a purified soul,
All cold, sweet, glistening light.
Dear mother, the window is dark again,
But you are in the light because
I finished all that consequence.
I killed that lad because he had grown up,
He would have struck a woman's fancy,
Begot, and passed pollution on.
I am a wretched foul old man
And therefore harmless. When I have stuck
This old jack-knife into a sod
And pulled it out all bright again,
And picked up all the money that he dropped,
I'll to a distant place, and there
Tell my old jokes among new men.
He cleans the knife and begins to pick up money.

Hoof-beats! Dear God,
How quickly it returns—beat—beat—!

Her mind cannot hold up that dream.
Twice a murderer and all for nothing,
And she must animate that dead night
Not once but many times!
O God,
Release my mother's soul from its dream!
Mankind can do no more. Appease
The misery of the living and the remorse
of the dead.

Franz Kafka

Highly original and personal in spirit, Frank Kafka's fiction suggests the weird visions of Dante more than the world of everyday observation. His manner of writing is expressionistic, not realistic, and his stories create a kind of allegory of the tormented mind of man harassed by a sense of undefined guilt. A vague force of doom hovers over all he wrote. The typical Kafka hero is a forlorn, frustrated man lost in a universe whose meaning he cannot grasp. God, vastly removed from human life, hardly cares whether humanity even aspires to a knowledge of the divine. Man is a frail creature, helplessly groping to understand himself in a universe where he is condemned without knowing how he has offended.

Since this feeling about life was intuitive and largely unconscious in Kafka, he never made clear its exact meaning, and the reader is free to interpret Kafka as he thinks best. The reader who accepts a psychoanalytic approach may find Freud useful, while one who prefers a religious point of view will be reminded of Kierkegaard, whose writings Kafka knew. Thus "The Hunter Gracchus," which is included here, has been interpreted in both ways. The peculiar fascination of Kafka's fiction results from the precise, though restrained, style by which he conveyed his fantasies.

Born in Prague of Jewish parents in 1883, Kafka studied law at the University of Prague. For a brief period he worked as an official in a government insurance bureau where he was impressed by the power of a bureaucratic organization to stifle the self. During his student years Kafka had become a friend of Max Brod, a promising young writer, and Brod later encouraged him to turn to literature even though his father strongly disapproved. Kafka's decision to write intensified the conflict between him and his father, which had begun in his boyhood days—he had deeply resented his father's intolerance of other people's opinions, yet desperately wanted his father's approval. The image of a resentful father haunted Kafka all his life.

The first collection of Kafka's writings, Observations, *was published in 1913. Two years later his story "The Stoker" won the Fontane prize. From this story he developed his novel* Amerika. *During most of his life Kafka suffered from poor health and was tormented by a sense of inadequacy. He lived in Berlin during the difficult days of World War I and later returned to Prague where he wrote some of his most striking short stories before he died there in 1924. In the last ten years of his life Kafka wrote a great deal of fiction, but he destroyed over half of his work and left orders that at his death the rest should be burned. None of his novels were published during his lifetime. Max Brod, after a struggle with his conscience, disregarded Kafka's instructions and arranged for the publication of* The Trial *(1925),* The Castle *(1926), and* Amerika *(1927).*

Like much of Kafka's writing, "The Hunter Gracchus" is a story embodying great human symbols, symbols concerned with birth, the meaning of life, human suffering, punishment, and death. Kafka presents them here through the pictorial images of a journey by water, a corpse, a hunter, a government official, and the like. Some interpreters find in the story a point of view that is basically Christian in spirit.

THE HUNTER GRACCHUS

TWO BOYS were sitting on the harbor wall playing with dice. A man was reading a newspaper on the steps of the monument, resting in the shadow of a hero who was flourishing his sword on high. A girl was filling her bucket at the fountain. A fruit seller was lying beside his scales, staring out to sea. Through the vacant window and door openings of a café one could see two men quite at the back drinking their wine. The proprietor was sitting at a table in front dozing. A bark was silently making for the little harbor, as if borne by invisible means over the water. A man in a blue blouse climbed ashore and drew the rope through a ring. Behind the boatman two other men in dark coats with silver buttons carried a bier, on which, beneath a great flower-patterned tasseled silk cloth, a man was apparently lying.

Nobody on the quay troubled about the newcomers: even when they lowered the bier to wait for the boatman, who was still occupied with his rope, nobody went nearer, nobody asked them a question, nobody accorded them an inquisitive glance.

The pilot was still further detained by a woman who, a child at her breast, now appeared with loosened hair on the deck of the boat. Then he advanced and indicated a yellowish two-storeyed house that rose abruptly on the left beside the sea: the bearers took up their burden and bore it to the low but gracefully pillared door. A little boy opened a window just in time to see the party vanishing into the house, then hastily shut the window again. The door too was now shut; it was of black oak, and very strongly made. A flock of doves which had been flying around the belfry alighted in the street before the house. As if their food were stored within, they assembled in front of the door. One of them flew up to the first storey and pecked at the windowpane. They were bright-hued, well-tended, beautiful birds. The woman on the boat flung grain to them in a wide sweep; they ate it up and flew across to the woman.

A man in a top hat tied with a band of crepe now descended one of the narrow and very steep lanes that led to the harbor. He glanced round vigilantly, everything seemed to displease him, his mouth twisted at the sight of some offal in a corner. Fruit skins were lying on the steps of the monument; he swept them off in passing with his stick. He rapped at the house door, at the same time taking his top hat from his head with his black gloved hand. The door was opened at once, and some fifty little boys appeared in two rows in a long entry hall, and bowed to him.

The boatman descended the stairs, greeted the gentleman in black, conducted him up to the first storey, led him round the bright and elegant loggia which encircled the courtyard, and both of them entered, while the boys pressed after them at a respectful distance, a cool spacious room looking towards the back, from whose window no habitation, but only a bare, blackish gray rocky wall was to be seen. The bearers were busied in setting up and lighting several long candles at the head of the bier, yet these did not give light, but only scared away the shadows which had been immobile till then, and made them flicker over the walls. The cloth covering the bier had been thrown back. Lying on it was a man with wildly matted hair, who looked somewhat like a hunter. He lay without motion and, it seemed, without breathing, his eyes closed; yet only his trappings indicated that this man was probably dead.

The gentleman stepped up to the bier, laid his hand on the brow of the man lying upon it, then kneeled down and prayed. The boatman made a sign to the bearers to leave the room; they went out, drove away the boys who had gathered outside, and shut the door. But even that did not seem to satisfy the gentleman; he glanced at the boatman; the boatman understood, and vanished through a side door into the next room. At once the man on the bier opened his eyes, turned his face painfully towards the gentleman, and said: "Who are you?" Without any mark of surprise the gentleman rose from his kneeling posture and answered: "The Burgomaster of Riva."

The man on the bier nodded, indicated a chair with a feeble movement of his arm, and said, after the Burgomaster had accepted his invitation: "I knew that, of course, Burgomaster, but in the first moments of returning consciousness I always forget, everything goes round before my eyes, and it is best to ask about anything even if I know. You too probably know that I am the hunter Gracchus."

"Certainly," said the Burgomaster. "Your arrival was announced to me during the night. We had been asleep for a good while. Then towards midnight my wife cried: 'Salvatore'—that's my name—'look at that dove at the window.' It was really a dove, but as big as a cock. It flew over me and said in my ear: 'Tomorrow the dead hunter Gracchus is coming; receive him in the name of the city.' "

The hunter nodded and licked his lips with the tip of his tongue: "Yes, the doves flew here before me. But do you believe, Burgomaster, that I shall remain in Riva?"

"I cannot say that yet," replied the Burgomaster. "Are you dead?"

"Yes," said the hunter, "as you see. Many years ago, yes, it must be a great many years ago, I fell from a precipice in the Black Forest—that is in Germany—when I was hunting a chamois. Since then I have been dead."

"But you are alive too," said the Burgomaster.

"In a certain sense," said the hunter, "in a certain sense I am alive too. My death ship lost its way; a wrong turn of the wheel, a moment's absence of mind on the pilot's part, a longing to turn aside towards my lovely native country, I cannot tell what it was; I only know this, that I remained on earth and that ever since my ship has sailed earthly waters. So I, who asked for nothing better than to live among my mountains, travel after my death through all the lands of the earth."

"And you have no part in the other world?" asked the Burgomaster, knitting his brow.

"I am forever," replied the hunter, "on the great stair that leads up to it. On that infinitely wide and spacious stair I clamber about, sometimes up, sometimes down, sometimes on the right, sometimes on the left, always in motion. The hunter has been turned into a butterfly. Do not laugh."

"I am not laughing," said the Burgomaster in self-defense.

"That is very good of you," said the hunter. "I am always in motion. But when I make a supreme flight and see the gate actually shining before me I awaken presently on my old ship, still stranded forlornly in some earthly sea or other. The fundamental error of my one-time death grins at me as I lie in my cabin. Julia, the wife of the pilot, knocks at the door and brings me on my bier the morning drink of the land whose coasts we chance to be passing. I lie on a wooden pallet, I wear—it cannot be a pleasure to look at me—a filthy winding sheet, my hair and beard, black tinged with gray, have grown together inextricably, my limbs are covered with a great flower-patterned woman's shawl with long fringes. A sacramental candle stands at my head and lights me. On the wall opposite me is a little picture, evidently of a Bushman who is aiming his spear at me and taking cover as best he can behind a beautifully painted shield. On shipboard one is often a prey to stupid imaginations, but that is the stupidest of them all. Otherwise my wooden case is quite empty. Through a hole in the side wall come in the warm airs of the southern night, and I hear the water slapping against the old boat.

"I have lain here ever since the time when, as the hunter Gracchus living in the Black Forest, I followed a chamois and fell from a precipice. Everything happened in good order. I pursued, I fell, bled to death in a ravine, died, and this ship should have conveyed me to the next world. I can still remember how gladly I stretched myself out on this pallet for the first time. Never did the mountains listen to such songs from me as these shadowy walls did then.

"I had been glad to live and I was glad to die. Before I stepped aboard, I joyfully flung away my wretched load of ammunition, my knapsack, my hunting rifle that I had always been proud to carry, and I slipped into my winding sheet like a girl into her marriage dress. I lay and waited. Then came the mishap."

"A terrible fate," said the Burgomaster, raising his hand defensively. "And you bear no blame for it?"

"None," said the hunter. "I was a hunter; was there any sin in that? I followed my calling as a hunter in the Black Forest, where there were still wolves in those days. I lay in ambush, shot, hit my mark, flayed the skins from my victims: was there any sin in that? My labors were blessed. 'The great hunter of the Black Forest' was the name I was given. Was there any sin in that?"

"I am not called upon to decide that," said the Burgomaster, "but to me also there seems to be no sin in such things. But, then, whose is the guilt?"

"The boatman's," said the hunter. "Nobody will read what I say here, no one will come to help me; even if all the people were commanded to help me, every door and window would remain shut, everybody would take to bed and draw the bedclothes over his head, the whole earth would become an inn for the night. And there is sense in that, for nobody knows of me, and if anyone knew he would not know where I could be found, and if he knew where I could be found, he would not know how to deal with me, he would not know how to help me. The thought of helping me is an illness that has to be cured by taking to one's bed.

"I know that, and so I do not shout to summon help, even though at moments—when I lose control over myself, as I have done just now, for instance—I think seriously of it. But to drive out such thoughts I need only look round me and verify where I am, and—I can safely assert—have been for hundreds of years."

"Extraordinary," said the Burgomaster, "extraordinary.—And now do you think of staying here in Riva with us?"

"I think now," said the hunter with a smile, and, to excuse himself, he laid his hand on the Burgomaster's knee. "I am here, more than that I do not know, further than that I cannot go. My ship has no rudder, and it is driven by the wind that blows in the undermost regions of death."

William Faulkner

In his fiction William Faulkner has created a distinctly personal saga of the South. He is intensely involved in the life of his home state, Mississippi, where he was born in New Albany in 1897. During World War I he served in the Canadian Air Force; he then worked in New York and lived for a time in New Orleans with a group of other young writers, but most of his life has been spent at the family home in Oxford, Mississippi. From his deep roots in his native region he has gradually produced a body of novels and short stories that has won him the reputation in Europe of being America's leading contemporary writer.

Superficially his fiction appears to resemble literary naturalism since it uses so often the sordid subjects of perverted passion and deliberate cruelty; but for Faulkner these themes symbolically represent the eclipse of the values of the Old South, to which he is still deeply loyal. It would be contrary to his temperament to portray the decay of southern tradition with the impersonal eye of a strict naturalist. On the contrary, the strong subjective feeling he imparts to his interpretation of his homeland marks Faulkner as a modern romantic. Most typically, his emotions lose themselves in a melancholy mood over the destruction of values he holds dear. The conflicts in Faulkner's fictional characters are psychological; their problems are moral: the best qualities of the ante-bellum South—gallantry, refinement, sensitivity—are found in the Sartoris family; its worst qualities—selfishness, greed, cruelty—are found in the Snopes clan. The degree of his involvement with these characters, who seem to haunt his imagination, becomes impressively clear in Faulkner's nervous, impassioned style.

Faulkner's view of life is saved from pessimism by his belief that, in spite of the bitter social conflict being waged in the South today, the integrity and enlightened moral sympathy of the intelligent white southerner will respect the vigor and innate spiritual capacity of the Negro. Faulkner admires most the strength of the Negro to endure the injustice of an inhospitable society. Novels like The Sound and the Fury *(1929),* Light in August *(1932), and* Absalom, Absalom! *(1936) disclose the development of his moral vision. The story included here, "Go Down, Moses" (1942), vividly presents the instinctive sympathy of the southern lawyer for the old Negro grandmother whose deepest wish is to have the amenities of tradition afforded the young man who had been "sold in Egypt."*

GO DOWN, MOSES

I

THE FACE was black, smooth, impenetrable; the eyes had seen too much. The negroid hair had been treated so that it covered the skull like a cap, in a single neat-ridged sweep, with the appearance of having been lacquered, the part trimmed out with a razor, so that the head resembled a bronze head, imperishable and enduring. He wore one of those sports costumes called ensembles in the men's shop advertisements, shirt and trousers matching and cut from the same fawn-colored flannel, and they had cost too much and were draped too much, with too many pleats; and he half lay on the steel cot in the steel cubicle just outside which an armed guard had stood for twenty hours now, smoking cigarettes and answering in a voice which was anything under the sun but a southern voice or even a negro voice, the questions of the spectacled young white man sitting with a broad census-taker's portfolio on the steel stool opposite:

"Samuel Worsham Beauchamp. Twenty-six. Born in the country near Jefferson, Mississippi. No family. No—"

"Wait." The census-taker wrote rapidly. "That's not the name you were sen– lived under in Chicago."

The other snapped the ash from the cigarette. "No. It was another guy killed the cop."

"All right. Occupation–

"Getting rich too fast.

—none." The census-taker wrote rapidly. "Parents."

"Sure. Two. I dont remember them. My grandmother raised me."

"What's her name? Is she still living?"

"I dont know. Mollie Worsham Beauchamp. If she is, she's on Carothers Edmonds' farm seventeen miles from Jefferson, Mississippi. That all?"

The census-taker closed the portfolio and stood up. He was a year or two younger than the other. "If they dont know who you are here, how will they know—how do you expect to get home?"

The other snapped the ash from the cigarette, lying on the steel cot in the fine Hollywood clothes and a pair of shoes better than the census-taker would ever own. "What will that matter to me?" he said.

So the census-taker departed; the guard locked the steel door again. And the other lay on the steel cot smoking until after a while they came and slit the expensive trousers and shaved the expensive coiffure and led him out of the cell.

2

On that same hot, bright July morning the same hot bright wind which shook the mulberry leaves just outside Gavin Stevens' window blew into the office too, contriving a semblance of coolness from what was merely motion. It fluttered among the county-attorney business on the desk and blew in the wild shock of prematurely white hair of the man who sat behind it—a thin, intelligent, unstable face, a rumpled linen suit from whose lapel a Phi Beta Kappa key dangled on a watch chain—Gavin Stevens, Phi Beta Kappa, Harvard, Ph.D., Heidelberg, whose office was his hobby, although it made his living for him, and whose serious vocation was a twenty-two-year-old unfinished translation of the Old Testament back into classic Greek. Only his caller seemed impervious to it, though by appearance she should have owned in that breeze no more of weight and solidity than the intact ash of a scrap of burned paper—a little old negro woman with a shrunken, incredibly old face beneath a white headcloth and a black straw hat which would have fitted a child.

"Beauchamp?" Stevens said. "You live on Mr. Carothers Edmonds' place."

"I done left," she said. "I come to find my boy." Then, sitting on the hard chair opposite him and without moving, she began to chant. "Roth Edmonds sold my Benjamin. Sold him in Egypt. Pharaoh got him—"

"Wait," Stevens said. "Wait, Aunty." Because memory, recollection, was about to mesh and click. "If you dont know where your grandson is, how do you know he's in trouble? Do you mean that Mr. Edmonds has refused to help you find him?"

"It was Roth Edmonds sold him," she said. "Sold him in Egypt. I dont know whar he is. I just knows Pharaoh got him. And you the Law. I wants to find my boy."

"All right," Stevens said. "I'll try to find him. If you're not going back home, where will you stay in town? It may take some time, if you dont know where he went and you haven't heard from him in five years."

"I be staying with Hamp Worsham. He my brother."

"All right," Stevens said. He was not surprised. He had known Hamp Worsham all his life, though he had never seen the old Negress before. But even if he had, he still would not have been surprised. They were like that. You could know two of them for years; they might even have worked for you for years, bearing different names. Then suddenly you learn by pure chance that they are brothers or sisters.

He sat in the hot motion which was not breeze and listened to her toiling slowly down the steep outside stairs, remembering the grandson. The papers of that business had passed across his desk before going to the District Attorney five or six years ago—Butch Beauchamp, as the youth had been known during the single year he had spent in and out of the city jail: the old Negress' daughter's child, orphaned of his mother at birth and deserted by his father, whom the grandmother had taken and raised, or tried to. Because at nineteen he had quit the country and come to town and spent a year in and out of jail for gambling and fighting, to come at last under serious indictment for breaking and entering a store.

Caught red-handed, whereupon he had struck with a piece of iron pipe at the officer who surprised him and then lay on the ground where the officer had felled him with a pistol-butt, cursing through his broken mouth, his teeth fixed into something like furious laughter through the blood. Then two nights later he broke out of jail and was seen no more—a youth not yet twenty-one, with something in him from the father who begot and deserted him and who was now in the State Penitentiary for manslaughter—some seed not only violent but dangerous and bad.

And that's who I am to find, save, Stevens thought. Because he did not for one moment doubt the old Negress' instinct. If she had also been able to divine where the boy was and what his trouble was, he would not have been surprised, and it was only later that he thought to be surprised at how quickly he did find where the boy was and what was wrong.

His first thought was to telephone Carothers Edmonds, on whose farm the old Negress' husband had been a tenant for years. But then, according to her, Edmonds had already refused to have anything to do with it. Then he sat perfectly still while the hot wind blew in his wild white mane. Now he comprehended what the old Negress had meant. He remembered now that it was Edmonds who had actually sent the boy to Jefferson in the first place: he had caught the boy breaking into his commissary store and had ordered him off the place and had forbidden him ever to return. *And not the sheriff, the police,* he thought. *Something broader, quicker in scope. . . .* He rose and took his old fine worn panama and descended the outside stairs and crossed the empty square in the hot suspension of noon's beginning, to the office of the county newspaper. The editor was in—an older man but with hair less white than Stevens', in a black string tie and an old-fashioned boiled shirt and tremendously fat.

"An old nigger woman named Mollie Beauchamp," Stevens said. "She and her husband live on the Edmonds place. It's her grandson. You remember him—Butch Beauchamp, about five or six years ago, who spent a year in town, mostly in jail, until they finally caught him breaking into Rouncewell's store one night? Well, he's in worse trouble than that now. I dont doubt her at all. I just hope, for her sake as well as that of the great public whom I represent, that his present trouble is very bad and maybe final too—"

"Wait," the editor said. He didn't even need to leave his desk. He took the press association flimsy from its spike and handed it to Stevens. It was datelined from Joliet, Illinois, this morning:

Mississippi negro, on eve of execution for murder of Chicago policeman, exposes alias by completing census questionnaire. Samuel Worsham Beauchamp—

Five minutes later Stevens was crossing again the empty square in which noon's hot suspension was that much nearer. He had thought that he was going home to his boarding house for the noon meal, but he found that he was not. *'Besides, I didn't lock my office door,'* he thought. Only, how under the sun she could have got to town from those seventeen miles. She may even have walked. "So it seems I didn't mean what I said I hoped," he said aloud, mounting the outside stairs again, out of the hazy and now windless sunglare, and entered his office. He stopped. Then he said,

"Good morning, Miss Worsham."

She was quite old too—thin, erect, with a neat, old-time piling of white hair beneath a faded hat of thirty years ago, in rusty black, with a frayed umbrella faded now until it was green instead of black. He had known her too all his life. She lived alone in the decaying house her father had left her, where she gave lessons in china-painting and, with the help of Hamp Worsham, descendant of one of her father's slaves, and his wife, raised chickens and vegetables for market.

"I came about Mollie," she said. "Mollie Beauchamp. She said that you—"

He told her while she watched him, erect on the hard chair where the old Negress had sat, the rusty umbrella leaning against her knee. On her lap, beneath her folded hands, lay an old-fashioned beaded reticule almost as big as a suitcase. "He is to be executed tonight."

"Can nothing be done? Mollie's and Hamp's parents belonged to my grandfather. Mollie and I were born in the same month. We grew up together as sisters would."

"I telephoned," Stevens said. "I talked to the Warden at Joliet, and to the District Attorney in Chicago. He had a fair trial, a good lawyer—of that sort. He had money. He was in a business called numbers, that people like him make money in." She watched him, erect and motionless. "He is a murderer, Miss Worsham. He shot that policeman in the back. A bad son of a bad father. He admitted, confessed it afterward."

"I know," she said. Then he realized that she was not looking at him, not seeing him at least. "It's terrible."

"So is murder terrible," Stevens said. "It's better this way." Then she was looking at him again.

"I wasn't thinking of him. I was thinking of Mollie. She mustn't know."

"Yes," Stevens said. "I have already talked with Mr. Wilmoth at the paper. He has agreed not to print anything. I will telephone the Memphis paper, but it's probably too late for that. . . . If we could just persuade her to go on back home this afternoon, before the Memphis paper . . . Out there, where the only white person she ever sees is Mr. Edmonds, and I will telephone him; and even if the other darkies should hear about it, I'm sure they wouldn't. And then maybe in about two or three months I could go out there and tell her he is dead and buried somewhere in the North. . . ." This time she was watching him with such an expression that he ceased talking; she sat there, erect on the hard chair, watching him until he had ceased.

"She will want to take him back home

with her," she said.

"Him?" Stevens said. "The body?" She watched him. The expression was neither shocked nor disapproving. It merely embodied some old, timeless, female affinity for blood and grief. Stevens thought: *She has walked to town in this heat. Unless Hamp brought her in the buggy he peddles eggs and vegetables from.*

"He is the only child of her oldest daughter, her own dead first child. He must come home."

"He must come home," Stevens said as quietly. "I'll attend to it at once. I'll telephone at once."

"You are kind." For the first time she stirred, moved. He watched her hands draw the reticule toward her, clasping it. "I will defray the expenses. Can you give me some idea—?"

He looked her straight in the face. He told the lie without batting an eye, quickly and easily. "Ten or twelve dollars will cover it. They will furnish a box and there will be only the transportation."

"A box?" Again she was looking at him with that expression curious and detached, as though he were a child. "He is her grandson, Mr. Stevens. When she took him to raise, she gave him my father's name—Samuel Worsham. Not just a box, Mr. Stevens. I understand that can be done by paying so much a month."

"Not just a box," Stevens said. He said it in exactly the same tone in which he had said He must come home. "Mr. Edmonds will want to help, I know. And I understand that old Luke Beauchamp has some money in the bank. And if you will permit me—"

"That will not be necessary," she said. He watched her open the reticule; he watched her count onto the desk twenty-five dollars in frayed bills and coins ranging down to nickels and dimes and pennies. "That will take care of the immediate expenses. I will tell her—You are sure there is no hope?"

"I am sure. He will die tonight."

"I will tell her this afternoon that he is dead then."

"Would you like for me to tell her?"

"I will tell her," she said.

"Would you like for me to come out and see her, then, talk to her?"

"It would be kind of you." Then she was gone, erect, her feet crisp and light, almost brisk, on the stairs, ceasing. He telephoned again, to the Illinois warden, then to an undertaker in Joliet. Then once more he crossed the hot, empty square. He had only to wait a short while for the editor to return from dinner.

"We're bringing him home," he said. "Miss Worsham and you and me and some others. It will cost—"

"Wait," the editor said. "What others?"

"I dont know yet. It will cost about two hundred. I'm not counting the telephones; I'll take care of them myself. I'll get something out of Carothers Edmonds the first time I catch him; I dont know how much, but something. And maybe fifty around the square. But the rest of it is you and me, because she insisted on leaving twenty-five with me, which is just twice what I tried to persuade her it would cost and just exactly four times what she can afford to pay—"

"Wait," the editor said. "Wait."

"And he will come in on Number Four the day after tomorrow and we will meet it, Miss Worsham and his grandmother, the old nigger, in my car and you and me in yours. Miss Worsham and the old woman will take him back home, back where he was born. Or where the old woman raised him. Or where she tried to. And the hearse out there will be fifteen more, not counting the flowers—"

"Flowers?" the editor cried.

"Flowers," Stevens said. "Call the whole

thing two hundred and twenty-five. And it will probably be mostly you and me. All right?"

"No it aint all right," the editor said. "But it dont look like I can help myself. By Jupiter," he said, "even if I could help myself, the novelty will be almost worth it. It will be the first time in my life I ever paid money for copy I had already promised before hand I wont print."

"Have already promised before hand you will not print," Stevens said. And during the remainder of that hot and now windless afternoon, while officials from the city hall, and justices of the peace and bailiffs come fifteen and twenty miles from the ends of the county, mounted the stairs to the empty office and called his name and cooled their heels a while and then went away and returned and sat again, fuming, Stevens passed from store to store and office to office about the square—merchant and clerk, proprietor and employee, doctor dentist lawyer and barber—with his set and rapid speech: "It's to bring a dead nigger home. It's for Miss Worsham. Never mind about a paper to sign: just give me a dollar. Or a half a dollar then. Or a quarter then."

And that night after supper he walked through the breathless and star-filled darkness to Miss Worsham's house on the edge of town and knocked on the paintless front door. Hamp Worsham admitted him—an old man, belly bloated from the vegetables on which he and his wife and Miss Worsham all three mostly lived, with blurred old eyes and a fringe of white hair about the head and face of a Roman general.

"She expecting you," he said. "She say to kindly step up to the chamber."

"Is that where Aunt Mollie is?" Stevens said.

"We all dar," Worsham said.

So Stevens crossed the lamplit hall (he knew that the entire house was still lighted with oil lamps and there was no running water in it) and preceded the Negro up the clean, paintless stairs beside the faded wallpaper, and followed the old Negro along the hall and into the clean, spare bedroom with its unmistakable faint odor of old maidens. They were all there, as Worsham had said—his wife, a tremendous light-colored woman in a bright turban leaning in the door, Miss Worsham erect again on a hard straight chair, the old Negress sitting in the only rocking chair beside the hearth on which even tonight a few ashes smoldered faintly.

She held a reed-stemmed clay pipe but she was not smoking it, the ash dead and white in the stained bowl; and actually looking at her for the first time, Stevens thought: *Good Lord, she's not as big as a ten-year-old child.* Then he sat too, so that the four of them—himself, Miss Worsham, the old Negress and her brother—made a circle about the brick hearth on which the ancient symbol of human coherence and solidarity smoldered.

"He'll be home the day after tomorrow, Aunt Mollie," he said. The old Negress didn't even look at him; she never had looked at him.

"He dead," she said. "Pharaoh got him."

"Oh yes, Lord," Worsham said. "Pharaoh got him."

"Done sold my Benjamin," the old Negress said. "Sold him in Egypt." She began to sway faintly back and forth in the chair.

"Oh yes, Lord," Worsham said.

"Hush," Miss Worsham said. "Hush, Hamp."

"I telephoned Mr. Edmonds," Stevens said. "He will have everything ready when you get there."

"Roth Edmonds sold him," the old Negress said. She swayed back and forth in the chair. "Sold my Benjamin."

"Hush," Miss Worsham said. "Hush, Mollie. Hush now."

"No," Stevens said. "No he didn't, Aunt

Mollie. It wasn't Mr. Edmonds. Mr. Edmonds didn't—" *But she cant hear me,* he thought. She was not even looking at him. She never had looked at him.

"Sold my Benjamin," she said. "Sold him in Egypt."

"Sold him in Egypt," Worsham said.

"Roth Edmonds sold my Benjamin."

"Sold him to Pharaoh."

"Sold him to Pharaoh and now he dead."

"I'd better go," Stevens said. He rose quickly. Miss Worsham rose too, but he did not wait for her to precede him. He went down the hall fast, almost running; he did not even know whether she was following him or not. *Soon I will be outside,* he thought. *Then there will be air, space, breath.* Then he could hear her behind him—the crisp, light, brisk yet unhurried feet as he had heard them descending the stairs from his office, and beyond them the voices:

"Sold my Benjamin. Sold him in Egypt."

"Sold him in Egypt. Oh yes, Lord."

He descended the stairs, almost running. It was not far now; now he could smell and feel it: the breathing and simple dark, and now he could manner himself to pause and wait, turning at the door, watching Miss Worsham as she followed him to the door—the high, white, erect, old-time head approaching through the old-time lamplight. Now he could hear the third voice, which would be that of Hamp's wife—a true constant soprano which ran without words beneath the strophe and antistrophe of the brother and sister:

"Sold him in Egypt and now he dead."

"Oh yes, Lord. Sold him in Egypt."

"Sold him in Egypt."

"And now he dead."

"Sold him to Pharaoh."

"And now he dead."

"I'm sorry," Stevens said. "I ask you to forgive me. I should have known. I shouldn't have come."

"It's all right," Miss Worsham said. "It's our grief."

And on the next bright hot day but one the hearse and the two cars were waiting when the southbound train came it. There were more than a dozen cars, but it was not until the train came in that Stevens and the editor began to notice the number of people, Negroes and whites both. Then, with the idle white men and youths and small boys and probably half a hundred Negroes, men and women too, watching quietly, the Negro undertaker's men lifted the gray-and-silver casket from the train and carried it to the hearse and snatched the wreaths and floral symbols of man's ultimate and inevitable end briskly out and slid the casket in and flung the flowers back and clapped-to the door.

Then, with Miss Worsham and the old Negress in Stevens' car with the driver he had hired and himself and the editor in the editor's, they followed the hearse as it swung into the long hill up from the station, going fast in a whining lower gear until it reached the crest, going pretty fast still but with an unctuous, an almost bishoplike purr until it slowed into the square, crossing it, circling the Confederate monument and the courthouse while the merchants and clerks and barbers and professional men who had given Stevens the dollars and half-dollars and quarters and the ones who had not, watched quietly from doors and upstairs windows, swinging then into the street which at the edge of town would become the country road leading to the destination seventeen miles away, already picking up speed again and followed still by the two cars containing the four people—the high-headed erect white woman, the old Negress, the designated paladin of justice and truth and right, the Heidelberg Ph.D.—in formal component complement to the Negro murderer's catafalque: the slain wolf.

When they reached the edge of town the hearse was going quite fast. Now they flashed past the metal sign which said Jefferson. Corporate Limit. and the pavement vanished, slanting away into another long hill, becoming gravel. Stevens reached over and cut the switch, so that the editor's car coasted, slowing as he began to brake it, the hearse and the other car drawing rapidly away now as though in flight, the light and unrained summer dust spurting from beneath the fleeing wheels; soon they were gone. The editor turned his car clumsily, grinding the gears, sawing and filling until it was back in the road facing town again. Then he sat for a moment, his foot on the clutch.

"Do you know what she asked me this morning, back there at the station?" he said.

"Probably not," Stevens said.

"She said, 'Is you gonter put hit in de paper?' "

"What?"

"That's what I said," the editor said. "And she said it again: 'Is you gonter put hit in de paper? I wants hit all in de paper. All of hit.' And I wanted to say, 'If I should happen to know how he really died, do you want that in too?' And by Jupiter, if I had and if she had known what we know even, I believe she would have said yes. But I didn't say it. I just said, 'Why, you couldn't read it, Aunty.' And she said, 'Miss Belle will show me whar to look and I can look at hit. You put hit in de paper. All of hit.' "

"Oh," Stevens said. Yes, he thought. *It doesn't matter to her now. Since it had to be and she couldn't stop it, and now that it's all over and done and finished, she doesn't care how he died. She just wanted him home, but she wanted him to come home right. She wanted that casket and those flowers and the hearse and she wanted to ride through town behind it in a car.* "Come on," he said. "Let's get back to town. I haven't seen my desk in two days."

7

MUSIC: ROMANTICISM, IMPRESSIONISM, AND MODERN JAZZ

Ludwig van Beethoven

Beethoven is generally regarded as one of the three or four greatest composers of all time. His symphonies are among the standard works played by every orchestra of any stature; his sonatas and string quartets are equally outstanding. His later works, moreover, provide a transition from the great eighteenth-century classical composers, Haydn and Mozart, to the romantic music of the nineteenth century. To give adequate expression to his spiritual development, Beethoven gradually modified the traditional music forms that he had used with great success in his earlier work. While not abandoning completely the rules of classical structure, he respected more fully the rights of creative impulse. He recognized that a work of art must create its own form, so he sought to find new and more congenial ways of expression. His later music shows its emotional intensity and psychological concentration by a continuous flow without sharp divisions, an intricate interplay of melodies imaginatively associated, a free use of rhythm and melody, and a remarkable artistic unity. It thus marks the transition from the classical to the romantic, from the concern with form and structure to the expression of personal feeling and spiritual insight.

Beethoven was born on December 16, 1770, in Bonn. His father, thinking he could make a child prodigy of Ludwig, disciplined him severely. At eight, he played the violin well, and at eleven he had mastered Bach's Well-Tempered Clavier *on the piano. In 1787 his musical extemporizing amazed Mozart who gave him a few lessons. The local archbishop sent Beethoven to Vienna to study with Haydn, but Beethoven felt Haydn neglected him and failed to appreciate the boldness of his compositions. Although disappointed in his teacher, Beethoven was persuaded to make Vienna his home and gradually established a place for himself in the aristocratic circles there. In time his music became popular and his reputation world-wide. In 1814 his fame reached a peak with the performance of his* Symphony No. 7 *at a concert for the Congress of Vienna. From then on, however, his increasing deafness prevented him from appearing in public, and he lost some of his popularity. Still, ten years later, when his* Ninth Symphony *was performed with Beethoven on the platform to indicate the timing to the conductor, the audience broke out in tremendous applause.*

Beethoven's later music especially represents a triumph of character over adversity. The deafness that gradually overtook him was the tragedy of his life. His famous Heiligenstadt Testament, *written for his brothers in 1802 when he realized that complete deafness was inevitable, reveals the suffering this affliction had cost him, cutting him off from normal social life and producing a dread of the future as far as his work was concerned. But no misfortune could wholly divert Beethoven from his music. His dynamic personality, finding in life little outlet for affection, gives overwhelming power to his music in which many listeners discover a rich mingling of the comic and tragic reminiscent of Shakespeare. Beethoven's music seems to possess the fullness of life itself, filled as it is with elevated drama and heroic emotion. The sonatas and string quartets composed during the later years of his life are Beethoven's most strongly romantic music. He likened the famous Appassionata Sonata to* The Tempest *in its emotional intensity. During these years, however, Beethoven was working under severe emotional strain. Plagued by family discord and misfortune, and his own incurable malady, he fell ill after overexposure and exhaustion on a trip from his brother's home and died in Vienna in 1827.*

The approach adopted by J. W. N. Sullivan in his popular work on Beethoven, *provides a helpful introduction to the "romantic" aspect of Beethoven's later work. "I am concerned with Beethoven's music solely as a record of his spiritual development," Sullivan writes in his Preface. "I believe that in his greatest music Beethoven was primarily concerned to express his personal vision of life. This vision was, of course, the product of his character and his experience." The selection we reprint from Sullivan's book deals primarily with the Third Symphony, the* Eroica.

THE HERO

IT IS USUAL to find that the *Eroica* Symphony marks a definite turning point in Beethoven's music. We believe this point of view to be entirely justified. Beethoven's music, up to the time that he wrote the *Heiligenstadt Testament*, is chiefly a music that expresses *qualities*. This is probably what many people mean by "pure" music. Music of this kind is the very opposite of programme music. It need make very little, if any, reference to experience. Elegance, neatness, economy are the sort of terms that can be applied to the productions of an infant prodigy.

Music of this kind reveals, as it were, the actual nature of the composer. It reveals the qualities with which he will face life, the qualities that will condition his experience and his presentation of it. In most of Beethoven's early music his experiences of life enter, not as a mastered and synthetic whole, but as moods. He may be somber, melancholy, gay, or anything else, but these alternations in a composition have no organic connection. We are not, when listening to an early Beethoven quartet, for instance, becoming acquainted with the elements of one unified spiritual experience. Movements could be interchanged or very different ones substituted, without harming the composition. The only criteria that would have to be observed are those of esthetic variety and unity, that a quick movement should follow the slow movement and so on and, perhaps, that certain key relationships should be preserved. In this, his early music resembles the vast bulk of music written by Haydn and Mozart. There are also, of course, technical resemblances, although too much stress can be laid on them.

When we say that music expresses qualities we are not, of course, describing the content of the music any more than, in describing *Candide* as witty, we are describing the content of *Candide*. But the music we are speaking of does not possess what we have called a "spiritual content," although it expresses spiritual qualities. We may liken it to a mathematical memoir which exhibits elegance, inventive power, imagination, and even wit, but which has no "external" reference whatever.

Particularly unambiguous examples of this purely qualitative music are to be found in some "composed" music in Beethoven's early work. He said himself, for instance, of the *Adagio affetuoso ed appassionato* of the early F major quartet, that he had in mind the tomb scene in *Romeo and Juliet*. The creative process involved here is not the same as that of a dramatist who records his reactions to an imagined situation that he has himself invented. It is, on the contrary, the same process as is involved in writing opera music, and is subject to the same danger, the danger of losing the note of authenticity that belongs to the experience. The more usual the experience to be depicted, the more likely to be shared by all men, the more likely, of course, that it can secure an adequate musical representation. Most operas deal with stock emotions and experiences, for that is the ground on which the poet and the composer can be most assured of understanding one another. The parting of lovers is certainly a stock situation, and the young Beethoven could treat it adequately. Such stock situations were present, we may suspect, on more than one occasion in his early work. The early music expresses individual qualities, individual moods, and the young composer's conception of a few stock poetic situations.

The first piece of music he composed that has really profound and important spiritual content is the *Eroica* Symphony. Indeed, the difference from the earlier music is so startling that it points to an almost catastrophic change, or extremely rapid acceleration, in his spiritual development. We have found that such a change is witnessed to by the *Heiligenstadt Testament*, and we shall see that the *Eroica* Symphony is an amazingly realized and coordinated expression of the spiritual experiences that underlay that document.

The ostensible occasion of the symphony appears to have been the career of Napoleon Bonaparte, but no amount of brooding over Napoleon's career could have given Beethoven his realization of what we may call the life history of heroic achievement as exemplified in the *Eroica*. This is obviously a transcription of personal experience. He may have thought Napoleon a hero, but his conception of the heroic he had earned for himself. It has been objected to the symphony that the Funeral March is in the wrong place and that it should follow the Scherzo. But this objection entirely misses the organic connection of the whole work. The most profound experience that Beethoven had yet passed through was when his courage and defiance of his fate had been followed by despair. He was expressing what he knew when he made the courage and heroism of the first movement succeeded by the black night of the second. And he was again speaking of what he knew when he made this to be succeeded by the indomitable uprising of creative energy in the Scherzo. Beethoven was here speaking of what was perhaps the cardinal experience of his life, that when, with all his strength and courage, he had been reduced to despair, that when the conscious strong man had tasted very death, there came this turbulent, irrepressible, deathless creative energy surging up from depths he had not suspected. The whole work is a miraculously realized expression of a supremely important experience, and is justly regarded as a turning point in Beethoven's music. The last movement is based on what we know to have been Beethoven's "Prometheus" theme. Having survived death and despair the artist turns to creation. By adopting the variation form Beethoven has been able to indicate the variety of achievement that is now open to his "Promethean" energy. The whole work is a most closeknit psychological unit. Never before in music has so important, manifold, and completely coherent an experience been communicated.

Although the *Eroica* Symphony is based on a profound personal experience Beethoven was not yet able to express a subjective state in music in a perfectly direct manner. Indeed, it was only towards the end of his life, and principally in the late quartets, that his music became the perfectly direct expression of his inner state. The dramatist may use characters and incidents as symbols, as carriers of the state of consciousness he wishes to communicate—as Shakespeare obviously does in *Macbeth*—but the musician, although not so bound to the external world, may also achieve a certain degree of "objectification." There are certain musical forms which are recognized vehicles for certain restricted classes of emotions. Of these forms the funeral march is one. In the Funeral March of the *Eroica* Beethoven expressed a personal experience, but only to the extent that the form could accommodate it. By using the form he did, to some extent, depersonalize his experience. In this expression it becomes vaguer and also broader, being linked up with the general human experience of death and with the general human foreboding of the darkness beyond. The root content of the movement is Beethoven's personal experience of despair, transformed, by the form adopted, into a representation of a vaguer and more general human experience. Thus it might be supposed to represent the death of Napoleon or Abercrombie or Nelson or of anybody else whose characteristics could be supposed to support comparison with those depicted in the first movement.

It is for this reason that the Funeral March, magnificent as it is, seems a little too prominent among the other movements of the symphony. There is a little too much display about it, it is a little too suggestive of some great public occasion. The whole symphony is certainly on extremely bold lines, but the other movements are relatively personal and authentic in a way that the Funeral March is not. It is probable that only the Beethoven of the last quartets could have invented a form that should have embodied his experience directly and yet on a sufficiently large scale. To the young Beethoven, who had not yet attained the profound and utter loyalty to his own experience that characterized the music of his later years, there was also the attraction of "great subjects," the triumphant satisfaction of surpassing all other musicians in the treatment of recognized "lofty" themes. The fact, also, that sketches for the Funeral March go back to a period preceding the *Heiligenstadt Testament* shows that the form chosen was not dictated wholly by the experience that actually inspires it.

We need not imagine that the organic unity of the *Eroica* Symphony, or of any other of his greater compositions, was due to considerations that were consciously present in the mind of Beethoven. In an organic work of art the succession of its constituents is not ordered in accordance with any consciously held criterion. The feeling that a certain sequence is "right" is nearly always due to causes the artist could not analyse. In suggesting that the *Eroica* Symphony in its content and sequence, is the musical expression of the experiences that underlay the *Heiligenstadt Testament*, we are not suggesting that Beethoven consciously intended this representation. The initial idea of an "heroic" symphony may indeed have been suggested by the career of Napoleon or Abercrombie or anybody else, but in the process of creation Beethoven had to fall back upon his inner resources, the product of his qualities and his experiences. And the criterion of rightness he employed in the development of his composition was supplied by the order his experience had taken on in the depths of his mind. As a consequence of his own experience the concept of heroism was related, in his mind, within a certain context, largely unconscious, and the conception could only be realized within this context.

This explains why the symphony, which makes so great an impression of organic unity, nevertheless defies all attempts to interpret it as representing any particular hero's career. This difficulty has led a recent writer to suppose that the three great movements represent three entirely different heroes, and that the Scherzo is a sort of intermezzo put where it is, either because Beethoven was timid of further outraging popular taste or because he did not fully perceive the connection of the elements of his own work. Such unconvincing shifts are made necessary merely through attaching too great importance to whatever external occasions may be conjectured to have prompted the work. For works of art of the magnitude that we are considering the external occasion is never more than what psychologists call a "tripper" incident, releasing energies and contexts that have been formed in entire independence of it.

Johannes Brahms

Johannes Brahms was a romanticist who, like Beethoven, also fully explored the forms of classical music. Brahms slowly gained recognition during the latter part of the nineteenth century when the rage for Wagner's music was at its height, but he admired Wagner and never felt himself a rival since he composed in an entirely different vein. His music is without superficial color or glitter; it can best be described perhaps as a massive architecture of sound that combines the tender, imaginative, humorous, and dignified in an original style. Brahms' genius is clearly seen in the polyphony of intricate melodic interweaving that he brings into the already complex structure of the symphony as Beethoven had developed it. His rhythmic devices of syncopation, shifting accents, and irregular phrasings suggest twentieth-century experiments. It is difficult to find elsewhere in musical composition so complete a fusion of intellect and emotion.

Brahms was born in Hamburg, Germany, in 1833, and died in Vienna in 1897. In his youth he was a brilliant pianist and was hailed by Schumann as a composer of great promise. He soon departed from the romanticism that Schumann and Liszt expected of him, however, and his first publications and performances were failures. Brahms pursued his independent way nevertheless, composing, conducting, and making concert tours, and gradually achieved a commanding position in the world of music. In 1881 he was awarded the degree of Doctor of Philosophy by the University of Breslau, a recognition suggesting the best in academic circles that valued both the traditional and the original. Compositions that gained Brahms a secure place in music were his German Requiem, given originally in the Bremen cathedral in April 1868, and his First Symphony, a product of ten years' work, which created a sensation when it was first played in 1876. The spiritual depth of his music is immediately felt in the sense of mournful fate pervading the First Symphony and in the religious devotion so evident in "How Lovely Is Thy Dwelling-Place" from the Requiem. His Second Symphony, though not so impressive as the First, provides a better introduction to Brahms. It is analyzed in some detail in the following selection.

SYMPHONY NO. 2 IN D MAJOR

THE EPIC breadth and grandeur of the C minor Symphony (the First) was never again approached in the four works composed by Brahms in this form. Well might he have exhausted himself of heroic utterance in that matchless music; and so, in succeeding works, other moods, not less impressive or attractive, engross him. Therefore, in the four symphonies, we have more variety of intent and content than can be found in any other group of symphonies by any one composer.

The Second Symphony is perhaps the best introduction to the orchestral music of Brahms. Its content is full and rich enough for the most exigent, but its structure is very clear, its moods not too subtle or exacting. Though not without moments of somberness, it is generally lyric and sunny, occasionally even playful. Melodies in profusion sing through these measures and remain unforgettably in mind, while to satisfy those for whom music must produce a thrill by rhythmic and dynamic power, there is the brilliant fourth movement.

The symphony was performed for the first time by the Vienna Philharmonic Orchestra, December 30, 1877, under the direction of Hans Richter. Brahms had tantalized his musical friends with obscure or misleading information about the character of the music, and with his customary modesty had even denied the work the name of "symphony" in his jesting comment on it. The very day before the performance he wrote that "the orchestra . . . play my new symphony with crepe on their sleeves" . . . and added ironically, "It is to be printed with a black border, too!" How relieved must have been his admirers to hear this glowing and happy music!

First Movement

Over the shadowed figure of the basses the horn romantically dreams upon the first theme. Presently violins suggest a swaying melody, not of profound thematic importance, but leading eventually to the yearning song of the cellos which is to be developed as the second basic idea of the movement. Woodwinds (flutes) are attracted to this flowing melody, and present their own version in answer to the strings. Upon the basis of the melody the composer develops a firm and sonorous tonal fabric, through which runs always the bright strand woven by violins, cellos, and basses, en-

livened by occasionally irregular conflicting rhythmic impulses.

The structural lines of the movement, in spite of the descending transitional phrase which now appears in the flute, are tending upward; and it is possible to visualize the music as forming itself into a strongly defined, a sturdy, and symmetrical pyramid. The apex is reached in the development of the principal theme, which is now elaborated in a series of colorful derivations, increasing always in interest and animation, and gradually drawing upon more and more of the orchestral resources. Yet always there is a beautiful and fascinating clarity, the progress of each instrumental voice somehow seeming independent, yet vitally related to that of its fellows. Alternately powerful and gentle utterances presage a return of the underlying theme in its explicit form, and the music, guided by the wandering horn, gradually descends from the peak of its powers into a placid valley, filled with sunshine and contentment.

Second Movement

It is curious to discover that Brahms, though we know him to have been a dissembler of his inmost thoughts and feelings except in music, regarded himself as "not at all a sensitive person" and "absolutely without nerves or sympathy." It requires only a single hearing of the restrained yet passionate song of the cellos and the violins, in the first few measures of this movement, to convince us otherwise. The music

is grave, but warmed and intensified by a tenderness and intimacy, and by suggestions of secret pain; and it speaks with a directness and shrewd poignancy that few sensitive listeners can resist. This is the utterance, not of a confirmed and neurotic and hypochondriac sufferer, but of one who from a calm yet not remote philosophical eminence observes the woes of humanity, little and great, and grieves for them. Other slow movements in the Brahms symphonies are tender and touching, but nowhere else does Brahms reach so surely into the vast profound of human feeling.

Detaching oneself momentarily from the emotional significance of this music, it is interesting to note the beautifully formed contours and development of the music. After the presentation of the first theme, it is given in a kind of imitation, by horn, oboe, and flute; and a second idea is brought forward by the strings, and later elaborated in woodwind with still another melody moving against it through the cellos and violas. The melodic possibilities of this material having been thoroughly explored, the movement, remembering for a moment the theme that brought it into being, closes in serenity.

Third Movement

The journeyings into the profounder depths of the human soul are too recent for Brahms to burst forth, immediately, into a classical scherzo; so he introduces, at the beginning of the movement, rhythmic and melodic ideas occupying a happy middle ground between the pathos of the preceding movement and the playfulness that is presently to come. The oboe has a bewitching little song, half wistful and half gay, accompanied by cellos pizzicati. Other woodwinds likewise discourse upon this

theme, and it establishes a mood at once questioning and hopeful.

With a sudden change of tempo the strings, in a crisp and elastic rhythm, are given the delightful presto. All questionings are at once answered, all doubts resolved; here is delicate merriment, here is frolic, here is joy. There are interludes of thoughtfulness, and of reflection, as when the woodwinds suggest a serious moment, and the oboe insinuates its pristine pensiveness. The reply is a sturdier assertion of the motive of the presto.

But there is a sudden appearance of darker orchestral colors, and the idea of the presto, which seemed about to be developed as the dominating spirit of the movement, is ultimately discarded for a return to the first plaintive theme. Violins and flutes and oboes are attracted to it, and in this mood the movement closes.

Fourth Movement

The finale of the First Symphony, after its awesome and portentous introduction, brings us into a mood which asserts a profound, a vigorous, and vital optimism.

The present movement is concerned with joy, too; but with a lighter and more brilliant, a more vivacious and unreasoning gladness. The headlong rush of the violins ushers in a period of what seems, emotionally, a period of complete abandon; yet one can observe that Brahms achieves this freedom within the confines of strict form.

Hanslick, the noted Viennese critic, concedes that this movement is "always agreeable," and suggests that "Mozartian blood flows in its veins." One would rather believe that the life fluid which courses through this music is thicker and stronger stuff than any that ever circulated in the delicate tissues of Mozart's music. In its formal finish it can be compared with the work of the older master; but scarcely otherwise.

The development of the chief themes, both of which are first projected by the strings, is highly elaborated, yet the spirit of the music is never lost in these tangles of academic form; on the contrary, it seems to grow in power and emphasis as the music moves along. The concluding section reaches new peaks of exaltation, of almost frantic high spirits; powerful chords, underlined by syncopation, bring new powers to bear; brilliant brasses lend point to the orchestra's declamations, and resounding chords establish a triumph at the end.

Richard Wagner

Richard Wagner was the first composer to achieve an organic unity of drama and music. The great creative artist, Wagner maintained, must be able to combine music, poetry, painting, sculpture, and architecture, each of which had exhausted its possibilities as a separate art. Although this idea was originally his own, he later tried to credit Beethoven with its discovery because in the last movement of his Ninth Symphony Beethoven made use of the singing voice and of Schiller's "Ode to Joy." Actually Wagner's interests were quite different from Beethoven's. While Beethoven probably used the human voice to gain depth and color for his music, Wagner protested against music tyrannizing over poetry and he wanted his music to interpret the lyric or dramatic qualities of poetic literature, not to dominate the work. A poet as well as a musician, he wrote the words for his operas, and combined music and drama in the leitmotiv, a typical melody or a characteristic harmony that suggests the intellectual or emotional attributes of the important characters. Often in a Wagnerian opera the audience can almost tell what is happening on the stage by simply listening to the orchestral music.

Born in Leipzig in 1813, Wagner early showed his taste for literature by translating twelve books of the Odyssey *and, at the age of fourteen, writing a bombastic Shakespearean tragedy. In his early twenties he began composing operas to his own librettos. On a trip by sea to Paris he was caught in a storm; the adventure inspired his opera,* The Flying Dutchman, *a great advance in operatic music. His first operas, however, were rejected with scorn by the critics because they did not fit the accepted formulas of the day. In spite of strong opposition,* Tannhäuser *was successfully produced at Dresden in 1845, but when* Lohengrin *was finished in 1848 no one would risk producing it. His enemies continued to be so bitter that Wagner left Germany and settled in Lucerne where he wrote many of his later operas. In 1872 the cornerstone was laid for the Bayreuth Theater and there his greatest successes in music drama were achieved.* The Ring of the Nibelung *was performed in Bayreuth in 1876 and* Parsifal *in 1882. Wagner's fame was now at last well established, but the exertion of directing so many performances caused his health to decline rapidly. He died in February 1883 and was buried at Bayreuth, which became an international shrine for his enthusiastic followers.*

In Tristan and Isolde *the romanticism of Wagner finds its most direct and unrestrained expression. Leopold Stokowski's arrangement of familiar music from this opera makes its romantic spirit unusually clear, and in the following selection the Stokowski arrangement is discussed in some detail.*

TRISTAN AND ISOLDE

WAGNER made of the music of *Tristan und Isolde* the mightiest paean of love and passion, of suffering and death through love, that mortal ears have ever heard. The legend of the Irish princess, Isolde of the White Hands, and Tristan, knight of ancient Cornwall, antedates the Wagnerian opera by several centuries; stripped of detail and the circumstances of time and place, it is ageless as humanity. The musician does not always know what he means nor what he says, when he writes, for often

[From *The Victor Book of Overtures, Tone Poems, and Other Orchestral Works* by Charles O'Connell.]

he is but a channel for a stream of thought and emotion that transcends articulate meanings, and he speaks a mystical language that finds its understanding and responses only in some remote and secret recess of the human soul. *Tristan* is a rather long opera, with most of the faults and virtues inherent in that hybrid form of art. Yet its music, quite apart from the action, and reduced to its mordant and fiery distillate, becomes the mightiest and saddest and fiercest utterance of human passion that music can pronounce.

On symphony programs, but two excerpts are commonly played—the Prelude and Isolde's "Song of Love and Death." They are usually given without pause. We prefer to discuss here the "symphonic synthesis" arranged by Leopold Stokowski, because it includes not only the Prelude and the *Liebestod,* but the indescribable love music from the second act, together with passages taken from the first and third acts. In the Stokowski arrangement, though it includes in complete form the Prelude and the *Liebestod* of Isolde, the music is presented as a symphonic poem, a single, unified rhapsodic utterance. It is not to be regarded as "excerpts" from the opera, but as a distinct musical work with a climactic scheme of its own, built of the synthesized elements of the music without regard to their sequence in the stage performance. In this form, and according to its mood, the music can be roughly divided into three sections, the Prelude, the "*Liebesnacht*" (Night of Love), and the "*Liebestod*" (Isolde's Death through Love).

I

Prelude

The Prelude is filled with awe and yearning and dreadful portents. Within the few minutes of its length, it traverses the entire emotional range of the opera—from the cellos' breathless whisper that so swiftly grows into a cry of fiercest longing to climaxes of such unimaginable intensity, and of such tragic implication, that the heart is shaken and the spirit moved and troubled with this potent music. The long, slow phrase, that seems at once agonizingly repressed and indescribably eloquent, is but half uttered by the cellos when it is joined by another, briefer sentence of the woodwinds—the avowal of love, and the kindling of desire.

Presently comes the poignant motive, powerfully sung by the orchestra, that suggests the burning yet enigmatic glance that the "wild and amorous Irish maid" turns upon Tristan; a little later, deep in the strings, the rich smooth fragment of melody suggesting the sweet and deadly philter—the distillation of love and death so innocently and so bravely shared by Isolde and Tristan. These eloquent orchestral utterances compound within themselves the elements of the fateful, fatal love of knight and princess, and in their derivations and development through the Prelude foreshadow in climaxes of wordless vehemence the terror and conflict and tragedy by which that love was encompassed—and ended.

It is beautifully significant that, after all the storms of the Prelude, the theme of love's avowal and passion's birth persists to the end, and is the last we hear before the long phrases, disappearing in the darkness of bass strings softly bowed, and the ominous strokes upon the timpani, usher in an atmosphere of dreadful expectancy. Here the conventional concert performance of the Prelude ends, and here, in the opera, the curtain rises.

II

Liebesnacht

The ultimate, and the only complete meeting and union of man and woman is in the embrace of love. The poet and the sentimentalist sing of united spirits—but they are never, in this world, united; for the thoughts and feelings, the mental processes, the emotions in both kind and degree, the approach to a common decision and the action upon it, the very interpretation of words and significance of deeds are inevitably different between man and woman.

Love is the union of two wills. In it the very differences in mind and heart and body, that in everything else combine to hold man and woman apart as individual beings, compose for once to bring them into intimate and perfect oneness. It is the desire for such unity, and the implacable force with which that desire seeks its fulfillment, that is the basis of the tragedy of Tristan and Isolde.

It is no disembodied love, immaterial, spiritualized, and denatured, that Wagner celebrates here. No such incandescent ecstasies were ever born of meetings of the spirit. Here is love that is fierce and exigent and consuming and insatiable; love which at a look, a word, a touch, races through the blood like flames; love which laughs at barriers, forgets enemies, and knows no loyalty but to itself; love which is normal and carnal and human.

Now through the long night that passes, Tristan, all dour scruples done away, all knightly vows forgotten under magic and the spell of love, holds the white loveliness of Isolde in his arms. Now the young girl, the innocent, the beautiful princess of Ireland, becomes heiress overnight to the ageless stratagems and arts of womankind. Now are celebrated the immemorial rites of love, the lovers heedless, careless, forgetful of all but the night, and their own hearts beating close, one upon the other. Death waits without the door, but Isolde has put out the light, that she may see no face but Tristan's; Death paces close, but hearts beat louder than his pacing; Death comes with the day, but the lovers hear no dreadful warning, only broken words of love.

Now with the esurient senses appeased come interludes of exquisite lethargy, sweet warm magical languors, mystical moments when the heart eases itself of burdens and confidences, of secret hopes and longings.

Now as the lovers reflect upon their plight, they despair and long for death; now remembered ecstasy again besieges them. The handmaiden Brangäne warns in vain of approaching day; the henchman Kurvenal bursts into the bower but a step before envious Melot and the outraged king. Tristan, his heart in Isolde's body, defends himself without hope or despair or fury, and takes a not unwelcome mortal wound.

Only music, vibrating in the invisible air, could dramatize such a moment. And what shall one say of such music as this? What magic is there, in wood and wind and brass, that can make this deathless song? What man is this who in his music evokes so surely and so terribly the longings and sorrows and passion of all the lovers of all the world? Answer there is none, for music speaks from heart to heart; to reason with it is to slay it. Only listen to the soothing loveliness of the strings as they sing of love's contentment; hear the echoes of rekindled passion, of piteous questioning and wild despair, in the terrible poignancy of the answering woodwind; feel this music, and you will feel heart's ease and heart hunger and heartbreak. Hear it—and "consider, and bow the head."

III

Liebestod

We love Death, even while we fear it. For Death is the answer to all questions; a negation of all torments and bitter truths, an affirmation of the intolerableness of passion and of life. Self-wrought, it can be a magnificent gesture of contempt or indifference—or of indomitable determination to follow into nothingness the thing that makes life—Life.

Isolde, finally, was not Death's victim. Rather, Death was her servant and her friend. She was not slain by despair; rather, she determined to die. Her spirit was not broken when for the last time the face of Tristan, bloodied and chill, lay upon her breast; but her fierce will drove her to ecstasies of love and grief she knew her frail loveliness would not withstand. Her song, at its outset, is full of ominous purpose. The dark orchestral voice (clarinet) which

supports Isolde's allows no accent of weakness or of despair. Swiftly she pursues Death with ever wilder passion, and with passion bends Death to her will. Tristan is slain; slain she will be also. But no dagger shall mar the loveliness he loved, nor spill the blood that leaped so joyously for him. She will die, and go to him in ecstasy once more; go to him where he lies in silence and cold impersonal calm.

The music grows in terrible beauty as it mounts from Isolde's first quiet words into whirling delirious passion. You feel it forcing itself to new and more powerful utterance . . . never resting, never resolving into perfect and satisfying harmony, mounting again until the awful climax bursts from the straining orchestra.

There is a fading of orchestral glory. Isolde has left the loathed light of day, and has sent her soul to join her lover. Her body sinks down upon his heart, and for the last time, now resolving into peace, the orchestra sings the motive of Desire.

Pëtr Ilích Tchaíkovsky

Pëtr Ilich Tchaikovsky is probably the most popular romantic composer of the nineteenth century. A large number of his works are performed every year in concerts throughout the world. Tchaikovsky's music is popular because of its easily recognizable melodic line, its forthright emotionalism, and its colorful orchestration. He believed that music must come from the heart and capture the listener's interest above all else. The compositions of Brahms, he felt, displayed too much intellectual technique. Less interested in abstract form than in intimate dramatic expression, Tchaikovsky expanded the symphonic structure as a vehicle for revealing emotional experiences. Seldom has a composer created music that echoes so many shifting moods; the dominant effect of his music, however, is pessimistic. Probably his special achievement lies in developing a striking pattern for the symphonic tone poem.

Tchaikovsky was born in Russia in 1840. His early career showed no unusual distinction; in fact he studied law for a while before he turned seriously to music at the age of twenty-two. For twelve years he taught at the Moscow Conservatory, wrote textbooks, and slowly made a name for himself as a composer. A marriage of short duration in 1878 brought on a nervous breakdown and Tchaikovsky went to convalesce in Switzerland, where he concentrated on composition. During this time he wrote long letters to his friend and benefactress, Mme. Nadejda von Meck. In these letters, from which our present selection is taken, Tchaikovsky expressed his innermost feelings and ideas on composition. Although his native country was slow in appreciating his music, he gained recognition abroad. His concert tours won many friends for his music in England and in America, where he conducted his own compositions at the opening of Carnegie Hall in New York in 1891. He died in 1893 shortly after returning from this tour of America.

Of Tchaikovsky's symphonies, the Fifth and Sixth (Pathétique) *are perhaps the best known. His piano concerto in B flat minor and his violin concerto in D have long been favorites. Among his other works, the* Romeo and Juliet Overture, *the* 1812 Overture, *the* Nutcracker Suite, *and the ballet music to* Sleeping Beauty *and* Swan Lake *are heard most frequently.*

THE CREATIVE PROCESS

I

IN YOUR LETTER there is only one thing with which I will never agree—your opinion of music. I dislike especially your comparing music with intoxication. I do not think such comparison possible. A person takes wine to fool himself, to give himself an illusion of satisfaction and happiness. And he gets that illusion in an expensive way. The reaction is terrible. Wine, it is true, gives momentary forgetfulness—but momentary only. Is it so with music? Music is not illusion, but revelation. And she is victorious because she reveals to us elements of beauty, otherwise inaccessible, to experience which is no transitory thing but means permanent reconciliation with life. Music is a lucid and happy thing. It is very difficult to analyze the experience of musical delight, but it has nothing in common with intoxication. It is not a physical thing. Certainly the nerves, and consequently the physical organs, take part in the reception of musical impressions, and in that sense, music pleases the body. But a definite line between the material and spiritual side of man is, as we all know, very difficult to draw. Thought is a physical process because it is one of the functions of the brain. After all, this is only a quarrel of terminology. No matter how differently you and I define musical experience, one thing is clear: we both love music with equal depth; in both our lives it plays an equal part. For my part it is enough to have you love so warmly, and call divine, the art to which I have devoted my life.

II

Your letter today gave me such joy, my priceless Nadejda Philaretovna! How immeasurably happy I am that the symphony pleased you, that my music entered your heart and you experienced the feelings that filled me in writing it!

You ask if the symphony * has a definite program. Ordinarily, when asked that question concerning a symphonic work, I answer, "No, none whatever." And in truth it is not an easy question. How can one express those vague feelings which pass through one during the writing of an instrumental work which in itself has no definite subject? It is a purely lyrical process, a musical confession of the soul that, filled with the experiences of a lifetime, pours itself out through sound, just as the lyric poet pours himself out in verse. The difference is that music is an incomparably more delicate and powerful language in which to express the thousand varicolored moments of the spiritual life. Usually the seed of a future musical creation germinates instantaneously and most unexpectedly. If the soil is eager, if there is a disposition to work, that seed takes root with amazing power and speed, appears above ground as a little stalk which puts forth leaves and branches and finally, flowers. This simile is as near as I can come to a description of the creative process. If the seed appears at a favorable moment, the main difficulty is past. The rest grows of itself.

Words are vain to tell you the boundless joy that comes over me when a new idea is conceived and begins to take definite shape. One forgets everything; one is a madman, trembling and quivering in every organ, with scarcely time to outline the sketches, so rapidly does one idea pursue another. Sometimes in the midst of this magic process an outside shock wakes one from the state of somnambulism. The bell rings, the servant enters, the clock strikes, reminding one that the business of the day must be attended to. These interruptions are inexpressibly trying. Sometimes, inspiration takes flight, one has to seek it again—often in vain. Frequently one must rely here upon a quite cold, deliberate technical process of work. Perhaps such moments are responsible, in the works of the Great Masters, for those places where the organic coherence fails and where one can trace artificial coherence, seams and patches. But this is unavoidable. If that spiritual condition of the artist called inspiration, which I have tried to describe, should continue uninterrupted, the artist could not survive a single day. The strings would snap and the instrument fly to pieces. One thing however is indispensable: the main idea of the piece, together with a general outline of the separate parts, must not be found through searching but must simply appear —a result of that supernatural, incomprehensible and never-analyzed power called inspiration.

But I digress from your question. Our

* References are to the Fourth Symphony.

symphony has a program definite enough to be expressed in words; to you alone I want to tell—and can tell—the meaning of the work as a whole and in part. You will understand I attempt to do so only along general lines. The Introduction is the germ of the entire symphony, the idea upon which all else depends (Fig. 1):

This is "Fatum," the inexorable force that prevents our hopes of happiness from being realized, that watches jealously lest our felicity should become full and unclouded—it is Damocles' sword, hanging over the head in constant, unremitting spiritual torment. It is unconquerable, inescapable. Nothing remains but to submit to what seems useless unhappiness (Fig. 2):

Despair and discontent grow stronger, sharper. Would it not be wiser to turn from reality and sink into dreams? (Fig. 3)

Oh, joy, at last the sweet and tender dream appears! Some bright clear human image passes, beckoning me on (Fig. 4):

How delicious and how remote, now, the distressing first theme of the Allegro. Little by little, dream possesses the soul. Forgotten is sadness and despair. Happiness is here! But no, this was only a dream, and "Fatum" awakes us (Fig. 5):

So life itself is a persistent alternation of hard reality with evanescent dreams and clutchings at happiness. There is no haven. Sail on that sea until it encompass you and drown you in its depths. This, approximately, is the program of the First Movement.

The Second Movement expresses another phase of suffering. It is the melancholy that comes in the evening when we sit alone, and weary of work, we try to

read, but the book falls from our hand. Memories crowd upon us. How sweet these recollections of youth, yet how sad to realize they are gone forever. One regrets the past, yet one would not begin life anew, one is too weary. It is easier to be passive and to look back. One remembers many things—happy moments when the young blood ran hot and life fulfilled all our desire. There were hard times too, irreparable losses, but they are very far away. It is sad and somehow sweet to sink thus into the past.

The Third Movement expresses no definite feelings, rather it is a succession of capricious arabesques, those intangible images that pass through the mind when one has drunk wine and feels the first touch of intoxication. The soul is neither gay nor sad. The mind is empty, the imagination has free rein and has begun, one knows not why, to draw strange designs. Suddenly comes to mind the picture of a drunken peasant, a brief street song is heard. Far off, a military procession passes. The pictures are disconnected, like those which float through the mind when one is falling asleep. They are out of touch with reality; they are wild and strange.

The Fourth Movement: If you truly find no joy within yourself, look for it in others. Go to the people. See—they know how to make the best of their time, how to give themselves up to pleasure! A peasant festival is depicted. No sooner do you forget yourself in this spectacle of others' joy, than the merciless Fatum reappears to remind you of yourself. But the others are indifferent to you; they do not so much as turn their heads toward your loneliness and sadness. Oh, how gay they are! And how fortunate to be ruled by such simple, immediate feelings! Here one sees the existence of simple, deep joys; enter into them and life will be bearable.

This, dear friend, is all I can tell you about the symphony. Of course what I have said is neither clear nor complete. This follows from the very nature of instrumental music, which does not submit to detailed analysis. "Where words cease, there music begins," as Heine said.

It is late. I shall not stop to write about Florence except to say that I shall keep the most agreeable memories. At the end of next week I think of going to Switzerland to stay quietly through March and work upon a number of short pieces.

P. S. Just now, putting my letter into the envelope, I reread it and was horrified at the muddy and slipshod program I am sending you. This is the first time in my life I have tried to transpose musical ideas and images into words, and I have certainly not been successful. All last winter while writing the symphony, I was suffering from terrible hypochondria; it is a true echo of the way I felt. But it is no more than an echo. How then can I translate it into clear and definite words?

Already I have forgotten many things about that time, I have only a general recollection of the horror and intensity of what I felt. It will be very, very interesting to know what my Moscow friends think of my work.

III

TO NADEJDA PHILARETOVNA

Clarens, Mar. 17, 1878

I have your letter, by beloved friend, and read it with the greatest pleasure. Let me answer your questions in order. It is very pleasant to talk with you about my method of creation. I have never before revealed these mysterious manifestations of the spirit —partly because not many have requested it, partly because those that asked did not inspire me with the desire to answer. But it is very good to describe the process of composition to you because you are unusually sensitive to my music. Never has anyone, except perhaps my brothers, made me as happy as you with your sympathy. If you only knew how precious that sympathy is to me, and how little I am spoiled by it!

Do not believe those who tried to persuade you that musical creation is a cold, purely mental exercise. Only the music that pours from the depths of an artistic soul, moved by inspiration, can touch and take possession of the hearer. There is no doubt that even the greatest musical genius has sometimes worked unwarmed by inspiration. It is a guest that does not come on first invitation. In the meantime one must work, and an honest artist cannot sit with his hands crossed because he is not inclined to compose. If one waits for inclination instead of advancing to meet it, one easily drifts into laziness and apathy. One must hold fast and have faith, and inspiration will come.

This happened to me only today. I wrote you that I had been working regularly, but without enthusiasm. If I had given way to a lack of inclination, I would surely not have accomplished anything for a long time. But faith and patience never desert me, and today, ever since morning I have been possessed by the inexplicable, mysterious fire of inspiration of which I told you, thanks to which I know that all that I wrote today will enter and affect people's hearts.

I don't think you will accuse me of self-praise when I tell you that the apathy of which I spoke comes very rarely. I believe this is because I have patience and have trained myself not to surrender to inertia. I know how to conquer myself. I am glad I have not gone the way of my Russian brothers,* who, suffering lack of self-confidence and self-control, lay their work aside at the smallest difficulty. That is why, in spite of great talent, they write so little and with so amateurish a result.

You ask how I work in regard to orchestration. I never compose in the abstract—never does the musical idea come to me except with suitable exterior form. So I find the musical thought simultaneously with the orchestration. When I wrote the Scherzo of our symphony, I imagined it just as you heard it. It is impossible if not performed *pizzicato*. If played with the bow it would lose everything. It would be a soul without a body and all its charm would disappear.

As to the Russian element in my compositions, it is true that I often begin to write with the intention of using one or another popular song. Sometimes (as in the Finale of our symphony) this happens of itself, quite unexpectedly. As to the Russian element in general in my music—the relation to the popular songs in melody and harmony—I grew up in a peaceful spot, saturated from earliest childhood with the miraculous beauty of Russian popular song, so that I love to the point of passion every expression of the Russian spirit. In short, I am a Russian through and through.

IV

TO NADEJDA PHILARETOVNA

Kamenka, July 6, 1878

You want to know my methods of composing? My friend, that is a rather difficult question, because the circumstances under which new compositions are born vary extremely. Yet I shall try to tell you in a general way how I work, and in order to explain the process of composition, I must first divide my compositions into two categories: (1) The ones I write on my own initiative because of sudden inclination and urgent inner need. (2) Compositions inspired from outside, such as the request of

* The Five in Petersburg—Borodin, Moussorgsky, etc.

a friend or publisher, or commissions, like my *Cantata* written for the Polytechnic Exhibition or the *Marche Slav*, written for the Red Cross concert.

I hasten to explain here that experience proves the value of a work does not depend upon which of these categories it belongs to. Very often a piece that was artificially engendered turns out quite successfully, while pieces invented wholly on my own inspiration are sometimes less successful for various incidental reasons. The circumstances surrounding the composer at the time of writing, upon which his state of mind depends, are very important. When he is creating, the artist must have calm. In this sense, creative activity is always objective, even musical creation, and those are mistaken who believe the artist can use his talent to relieve himself of specific feelings of the moment. The sad or happy emotions which he expresses are always and invariably retrospective. With no special reason for rejoicing, I can experience a happy creative mood, and conversely among the happiest surroundings I may write music suffused with darkness and despair. In brief, the artist lives a double life, an everyday human one and an artistic one, and these two lives do not always coincide. Anyway I repeat that for composition, the important thing is to rid oneself temporarily of the troubles of everyday existence, and give oneself unconditionally to the artistic life.

For compositions belonging to the first, or inspired-from-within category, not even the least effort of will is necessary. It is enough to submit to one's inner voice, and if the everyday life does not rise up to crush the artistic life, then work proceeds with the strangest ease. One forgets everything, the spirit quivers with sweet excitement, and before one has time to follow the swift flight to its end, time has gone by unperceived. In this state is something somnambulistic, "*on ne s'entend pas vivre.*" It is impossible to explain these moments. Whatever emerges from the pen at such times, or simply remains in the head, is always of value, and if not interrupted from outside, will be the artist's best work.

For commissioned work one must sometimes create one's own inspiration. Very often one must first conquer laziness and lack of inclination. Then different impediments arise. Sometimes victory comes easily, sometimes inspiration evades entirely. But I believe it the duty of an artist never to submit, because laziness is a strong human trait, and nothing is more harmful to an artist than to let laziness get the better of him. One cannot afford to sit waiting for inspiration; she is a guest that does not visit the lazy, but comes to those who call her. Perhaps there is a foundation to the charge that the Russian nation lacks creative activity, that the Russian is terribly lazy. He loves to postpone things, he has natural talent but has also a natural lack of self-discipline. One must acquire this, one must conquer oneself and not fall into dilettantism, from which even so colossal a talent as Glinka's suffered. That man, dowered with great original power of creation, lived to a mature age, yet wrote amazingly little. Read his memoirs and you will see that he worked only as a dilettante, at leisure, when the mood came. We are proud of Glinka, yet we must admit that he did not fulfill the task his genius put upon him.

Both his operas, in spite of marvelous and quite original beauty, suffer from striking inequality of style. Pure and gracious beauty is followed by childish naiveté and insipidity. What would have happened had Glinka been born to another stratum of society, and had lived under different conditions, if he had worked as an artist who, recognizing his power, feels it a duty to perfect his talent to its very limit, rather than composing music as a dilettante, simply because he had nothing else to do?

I hope, my friend, you will not suspect me of self-praise when I tell you that my appeal to inspiration is never vain. I can only say that this power, which I have called a capricious guest, has long ago become so accustomed to me that we live inseparable, and she leaves me only when she feels herself superfluous because my everyday human life has temporarily intruded.

But always the cloud dissolves and she reappears. So I may say that in my normal state of mind I compose music always, anywhere, at every moment of the day. Sometimes I watch with curiosity this busy flow of creation which, quite by itself, apart from any converse I may be having at the moment, apart from the people I am with at the time, goes on in that section of my brain that is given over to music. Sometimes it is the elaboration, the melodious detail of some little work planned beforehand, another time a quite fresh, original musical idea appears and I try to retain it in my memory. From whence it comes is a mystery.

Two o'clock.

I write my sketches on the first piece of paper that comes to hand, sometimes a scrap of notepaper, and I write in very abbreviated form. The melody never appears in my head without its attendant harmony. In general, these two musical elements, together with the rhythm, cannot be conceived separately; every melodic idea carries its own inevitable harmony and rhythm. If the harmonies are very complicated, one must indicate the voice parts in the sketch. If the harmony is very simple, I often jot down the bass, or write out a figured bass; at other times I don't need even that. It stays in my mind. Concerning instrumentation, if one is composing for orchestra, the musical idea carries with it the proper instrument for its expression. Yet one often changes the instrumentation later. Words must never be written after the music, because it is the text that calls out the suitable musical expression. One can of course adapt the words to a little melody, but for a serious composition such a procedure is impossible. So what you tell me about the *Life of the Tsar* cannot be true. Nor can one write a symphony and then find a program for it, because here again, each episode of a chosen program evokes its own musical illustration. The preliminary sketch of a work is extremely agreeable to do; sometimes it affords a quite inexpressible delight, but it also means anxiety and nervous excitement. One sleeps badly and often quite forgets to eat. But the actual execution of the project is done very calmly and quietly. To instrument a composition that is already ripe, having been worked out in one's head to the last detail, is a very jolly business. One cannot, however, say as much for the composition of piano pieces or songs or little pieces in general. These are annoying to work on; just now I am busy with such work.

You ask if I stick to established forms. Yes and no. In certain compositions, such as a symphony, the form is taken for granted and I keep to it—but only as to the large outline and proper sequence of movements. The details can be manipulated as freely as one chooses, according to the natural development of the musical idea. For instance, the first movement of our symphony is handled very freely. The second theme, which tradition places in a related major key, is here minor and unrelated. In the recapitulation (same movement) the second theme appears only in part, etc. The Finale also deviates from conventional form. In vocal music, where everything depends on the text, and in fantasias (like *The Tempest and Francesca da Rimini*), one can create one's own form.

V

TO NADEJDA

Komenka, July 1, 1878

Talking with you yesterday about the process of composing, I did not express myself clearly concerning the work that follows the first sketch. This phase is especially important: what has been written with passion must now be looked upon critically, corrected, extended, and most important of all, condensed to fit the requirements of the form. One must sometimes go against the grain in this, be merciless, and destroy things that were written with love and inspiration. Although I cannot complain of poor inventive powers or imagination, I have always suffered from lack of skill in the management of form. Only persistent labor has at last permitted me to achieve a form that in some degree corresponds to the content. In the past I was careless. I did not realize the extreme importance of this critical examination of the preliminary sketch. For this reason, the succeeding episodes were loosely held together and seams were always visible. That was a serious defect, and it was years before I began to correct it, yet my compositions will never be good examples of form because I can only correct what is wrong with my musical nature—I cannot change it intrinsically. I know also that I am very far from achieving the full maturity of my talent. But I see with joy that I am progressing slowly, and I ardently desire to take myself as far along this road to perfection as I can go. Therefore, I was inaccurate when I said I wrote out my compositions unhesitatingly from the first sketches. It is more than a copy, it is a detailed, critical examination of the first plan, corrected, rarely added to, and very often cut.

Claude Debussy

The music of Claude Debussy (1862-1918) marks a reaction against the sort of late romanticism in which massive effects, the direct display of emotion, and at times even the bombastic had become dominant. Debussy creates instead by indirection and suggestion. The music in a Debussy tone poem or prelude follows no conventional pattern but exposes the moods motivating the music with remarkable skill. Yet his music shows its relation to romantic musical forms by its use of the tone poem, the free expression of feeling as developed by Liszt, and the prelude, an independent piece in the mood of improvisation, which Chopin used to advantage.

Debussy's most characteristic compositions are found in his piano music. He developed the possibilities of the piano more profoundly than any composer since Chopin, exploring so thoroughly the opportunities for unsuspected effects in handling this instrument and achieving such delicacy of impression that he started a new era in music. Because of some broad similarities to the painting of the French impressionists, which were widely discussed at the time, the compositions of Debussy became known as musical impressionism. His work can be as well interpreted, however, as the final phase of nineteenth-century romanticism. By temperament Debussy was drawn to the intangible aspects of feeling; the free play of imagination transfigures his original impressions. As he said of his tone poem La Mer (The Sea)*: "I have an endless store of memories [of the ocean] and, to my mind, they are worth more than the reality, whose beauty often deadens thought."*

Although Debussy is one of the distinctly original modern composers, he received a thorough academic training at the Paris Conservatory, where he won the Grand Prix de

Rome with an early cantata. His unusual talents soon became apparent, however, in the compositions which he wrote in Rome as part of the conditions for winning the prize. The judges condemned his symphonic suite, Printemps, *for its lack of orthodox form, and denied his other pieces public performance. From 1880 to 1882 Debussy lived in Russia, where he became familiar with the unconventional music of Moussorgsky, whose influence helped establish his own musical independence.*

Gradually public recognition was won. In 1894 his string quartet and The Afternoon of a Faun, *one of his most remarkable compositions, were performed. Debussy's originality was now established in the public mind and his unusual piano works, which appeared in two volumes of preludes, were widely played. His only opera,* Pelléas et Mélisande, *was heard at the Opéra Comique in 1902. The music of this opera, like his preludes, succeeds in capturing the rapidly shifting feelings of the characters by following with great delicacy every nuance of the words. By the time he died in 1918, Debussy was generally acclaimed as one of the most distinguished modern composers.*

L'APRÈS-MIDI D'UN FAUNE

(The Afternoon of a Faun)

DEBUSSY began his work as music columnist for the *Revue Blanche* with this statement: "I shall endeavor to trace in a musical work the many different emotions which have helped to give it birth, also to demonstrate its inner life; this will surely be accounted of greater interest than the game which consists in dissecting it as if it were a curious timepiece." In this critic's creed he has given us the key to the study and enjoyment of his own works. Dissecting Debussy's music is as uselessly cruel as pulling a rose to pieces to find its perfume—"*un crime de lèse-mystère*," he would call it. Debussy's music must be enjoyed as a whole and as the expression of the "many different emotions which have helped to give it birth."

L'Après-midi d'un faune is easy to enjoy, for it is simply a music picture, a moving picture, in which there is no plot demanding attention, no human problem enlisting sympathy, nothing but the shifting light and color of a summer afternoon and the hazy, lazy half-thoughts of an antique nature god.

Debussy called it a prelude, not in the musical sense of a prelude as a short movement introducing a longer and more important work, but rather as a musical forerunner to the poem which inspired it. The poem was Mallarmé's famous "Eclogue" and this is the picture it suggests:

In a grove on the sunlit slopes of ancient Etna, a faun, a quaint snub-nosed creature, half goat, half man, wakes at daybreak and tries to recall a delicious experience of the previous afternoon. Had he really seen nymphs, lovely white and gold forest sprites, or had it been but a dream? With all his dull faun brain he tries to solve the mystery. It is no use. The bright sunlight streaming into his eyes has scattered all his visions.

Yet surely there were, surely there still are, graceful white figures moving there among the brown reeds of the lake! Could it be swans? Perhaps if he had one of the tall white lilies from behind the rose trellis it might help to bring back the vision. Often he has held the memory of amber-colored grapes by blowing out their empty skins and watching the sunlight glint through them. But no, the effort is too great! Why struggle to separate dreams from reality?

Vaguer and vaguer grow his thoughts. Drowsiness steals over him and he curls up again in the soft, fragrant grass. Nymphs, swans, white lilies in the sun—were they real or were they but the dreams of a summer afternoon? Who knows—who cares?

Debussy's music is a literal—or one might better say, a tonal—translation of Mallarmé's poem. Its melodies are as fragmentary, its rhythms as wandering as the faun's thoughts. Its harmonies hold all the hypnotic charm of August sunshine.

A flute, languorous and a bit wistful, suggests the faun trying to recall his vision:

His questionings are echoed by the horns:

his desire by oboes and clarinets, while the harp and muted strings suggest the shimmering light, the warmth and the drowsiness of midday.

Again and again he questions. Fully awake now, he searches among his muddled memories:

For a lovely moment the vision seems so near, so real that a feeling of desire satisfied sings through the music:

But it is of no use. Nymphs or fauns? He cannot be sure. The old questioning returns, intensified by higher pitch and longer notes:

And even as the flute entreats, shadowy figures slip through the strings of the harp and melt into mist before the eyes.

The questioning becomes but the repetitious murmur of one on the borderland between sleeping and waking. Faint notes from a tiny antique cymbal only seem to push it farther from a real and waking world. Then with an unforgettable passage for muted horns and strings, a three-part echo of the principal theme, sound sinks into silence. The faun yields to the spell of the summer afternoon, and we ask ourselves, was the music real or was it, too, but a waking dream?

L'Après-midi d'un faune makes a curious first impression on the listener. Many people have confessed that, on first hearing it, they could not recall a single note. The music seems to reduce even the best music memories to the happy, hazy state of the bewildered faun. And it is doubtful if even one who memorized the score could ever think of *L'Après-midi d'un faune* as anything but a bit of magic which a conductor manages to conjure out of an orchestra. Ink, paper, scales, chords, rules of composition—nonsense! This is the stuff of which dreams are made!

Nocturnes

Six years after he had surprised and delighted the musical world with *L'Après-midi d'un faune,* Debussy brought out *Nocturnes,* three "decorative panels" which definitely established his reputation as a composer. "The title *Nocturnes,*" he explains, "is to be interpreted here in a general and more particularly, in a decorative sense. Therefore, it is not meant to designate the usual form of the nocturne (literally a 'night piece' of subdued, poetic mood), but rather all the various impressions and the special effects of light that the word suggests."

Debussy's *Nocturnes* and those of Whistler are as nearly alike in spirit as it is possible for music and painting to be. Both artists sought to express the atmosphere or feeling of tone rather than the physical likeness of a subject, and both sacrificed definite outline and detail to "harmonies in blue and silver" or strange tonal colorings taken from old modes and irregular scales.

Nuages, Fêtes, and *Sirènes* are the titles of the Debussy *Nocturnes. Sirènes,* to which the composer added the tone coloring of a wordless choir of women's voices, portrays "the sea and its countless rhythms, and presently amongst the waves silvered by moonlight is heard the mysterious song of the Sirens as they laugh and pass on."

Nuages (Clouds)

Have you ever watched the clouds—not self-consciously, wondering whether they may spill a picnic-spoiling shower or whether they seem like suds to some speck of an airplane—but *really* watched them for their own sake and beauty, thinking of them as the architecture of the sky, pillared temples, enchanted castles, galleon fleets soundlessly taking shape before the eyes? If you have, why, then you know that cloud gazing is a limitless, timeless process. You know that one can look and look until one ceases to see in the ordinary conscious sense, and strange feelings, too high and wide for words, come over one! It is as if these feelings were the reflections in one's own mind of those towering mist castles and slow-drifting galleons.

It is these cloud feelings, reflections rather than sky pictures, that Debussy has expressed in his music. *Clouds,* he says, speaking of his first *Nocturne,* expresses the slow, solemn movement of clouds dissolving in gray tints "lightly touched with white."

Slowly and, one might almost say, soundlessly, the cloud procession starts across an empty sky:

These clouds are not driven. No wind harries them on their course. They drift in level lines frayed here and there as a wisp:

a fragment:

is plucked off by the ghost of a breeze.

There is no color—just soft grays, "lightly touched with white":

but effective as a sift of snow on a gray twig. And there is no accent, no emphasis in this music—nothing to break one's contemplation.

There is a moment of slight animation:

a mere whispered promise of motion and color. But the promise is not kept. Slowly and more slowly the gray mist forms drift by, and, as one watches them dissolve into a mysterious sky, one is conscious of a strange shadowy beating, as if through the high stillness of clouds one felt the pulse of the universe.

Fêtes *(Festivals)*

Festivals is yet another impression of air and sky. On the score Debussy has written, "The restless dancing rhythm of the atmosphere with sudden flashes of light. There is also a procession (a dazzling, fantastic vision) passing through the festive scene and mingling with it. But the background remains dust particles taking part in the rhythm of creation."

Who but Debussy would have attempted a dance of luminous dust particles, a festival of atoms! Away they whirl in a lively triplet figure:

to an accompaniment of airy fifths in the strings.

One cannot follow them physically or mentally, for, as a despairing Paris critic of the day remarked, the term, "to defy analysis," seems to have been invented for Debussy's music! But one cannot help following these dancing notes in feeling. As they frolic:

and sway:

tossing the tones about in every conceivable key and meter, it seems as if all the old-world rhythms that ever had been danced—courantes, rigaudons, gavottes, gigues—mingle to make an infectious gaiety.

In the midst of the revelry comes a sudden *pianissimo*. Then to the sound of harp and timbal the phantom procession approaches:

Cymbals and military drum add to the excitement, and the music grows boisterous and strangely un-Debussylike.

But the marchers cannot resist the festival mood. Gradually the procession is lost in the maze of the dance, then all is lost. To low-plucked strings, muffled trumpets, and faint-sounding timbals and cymbals, the fête of atoms vanishes into the thin air from which it came.

André Hodeír

Jazz came to prominence in America in the 1920s when Dixieland jazz, starting in New Orleans, worked its way north to Chicago. The standard Dixieland jazz band was made up of trombone, clarinet, trumpet, piano, and drums. The heart of the jazz it played lay in its lyric impulse. Solo improvisation became increasingly important as individual players decorated the melody they were playing; collective improvisation occurred when several players extemporized simultaneously. Typical tricks of the jazz band were shifting accent from the strong to the weak beat and weaving patterns of melody. The rhythm created the basic scaffolding on which the other instruments built the colors and undulations of melody. The rhythmic basis was further complicated as various instruments constructed a pattern of rhythms within rhythms. Freedom to toy with accent and to modify melodic phrases produces the stimulating excitement of jazz. It expresses the joy of living and creates by fine surprise.

The first jazz period was followed by the age of swing from the 1930s to World War II. Swing was dressed-up jazz designed for dancing and played by big bands of as many as forty pieces. The swing band played from arranged passages and featured "hot" solos. The music was carefully rehearsed down to the last detail. The swing era was fostered by managers, agents, wide publicity, and constant repetition on radio and jukebox. While the early jazz was folk music of the twentieth-century Negro, swing was limited to no single group of people and was a stereotyped commercial product.

The contemporary style in jazz is known as "progressive." In this type of jazz, musicians may start with a selection from Chopin or Beethoven and work their variations on the theme. The players compose as they play; melody and tempo are varied according to the feelings of the musicians. The nuances of subtle interpretation are heightened especially by the offbeat beat—classic yet individualistic. The jazz men simply let themselves go.

Americans are often slow to recognize their own cultural achievements. Robert Frost and Frank Lloyd Wright were first appreciated abroad. The best interpretation of American jazz, Jazz, Its Evolution and Essence *(1955), is written by a Frenchman, André Hodeir. Hodeir brings French clarity to the emotional subtleties of jazz. His study is also the first serious discussion of jazz written by an expert musicologist. At the Paris Conservatory Hodeir has won prizes in harmony, fugue, and musical history. His book brings together articles originally done for the magazine* Jazz-hot, *when he was its editor from 1947 to 1950. The selection reprinted from Hodeir's book provides not only a general interpretation of jazz but also a careful analysis of one of the concertos which Hodeir rates among the top jazz compositions.*

THE WORLD OF JAZZ

I

SINCE the Second World War, jazz has spread appreciably and has become considerably better known. The day is past when this music was symbolized for Europeans by the names of Paul Whiteman, George Gershwin, Ted Lewis, Jack Hylton,

Jean Wiener, and Clément Doucet, and when the colored star of *The Jazz Singer* turned out to be a white man, Al Jolson, made up in blackface for local color. By now it has become evident that jazz is the Negro's art and that almost all the great jazz musicians are Negroes. People are now acquainted with Louis Armstrong, Duke Ellington, Sidney Bechet, and Dizzy Gillespie; they have been applauded throughout France, in the same concert halls as Gieseking and Menuhin. It is no longer possible, as it was fifteen or twenty years ago, for an alert, reasonably well-informed person to confuse authentic jazz with cheap dance music or pretentious pieces like *Rhapsody in Blue*. In many cases jazz is still difficult to get at, but it can be found.

How strange have been the fortunes of this music, which seemed destined to remain confined to the banks of the lower Mississippi! What contemporary observer would have guessed that the folk music of a small group would become the language of an entire people fifteen or twenty years later and, in a few more years, a world-wide phenomenon, with jazz bands existing simultaneously in Melbourne, Tokyo, and Stockholm? What does this success mean? It has been said that jazz is the most fully alive form of dance music of our time; this is true, but jazz is much more than dance music. The importance of the movement it has given rise to may be judged by the number of books and magazines on the subject published all over the world. Nothing is stranger, and nothing more reassuring for humanity, than the universal diffusion of this message first launched by a people numbering ten million.

We must not delude ourselves, however. Jazz has found followers everywhere, but these followers are always in the minority. Everyone remembers the waves of protest that jazz aroused in the greater part of the French public only recently. By now, such protest seems to have given way to a fashionable indifference. People no longer become indignant when they hear Louis Armstrong sing, they smile politely. A very small number of the newspapers and magazines concerned with the arts feel it their duty to carry a jazz column. This reticence in the face of such success and these limitations on an expansion that has been so great in other respects present a problem we cannot avoid. What are the causes of these apparent contradictions?

At first, it might seem that jazz is incapable of touching the masses and is suited only to an élite. This hypothesis would explain its limited success, but unfortunately it is contradicted by the facts. On the contrary, jazz seems to be accepted only with the greatest reservations by those regularly referred to as the élite—that is to say, the small part of the public that is capable of fully appreciating both classical and modern artistic masterpieces. There is a simple explanation for this cultured public's aloofness. Anyone who tries to place jazz in the perspective of European culture without first revising his traditional artistic habits has scarcely any chance of understanding it. He can see only its defects; jazz appears to him in its negative aspects, which are rendered even more striking by being compared with European art. He is thus led to reject this music "which is not thought out, not worked over, not constructed, which has no architecture, whose harmony is dull and sugar-coated, whose melody lacks nobility and breadth, whose form and rhythm are stereotyped," this anti-intellectual music "whose themes are mostly popular ditties and whose creators are trumpet and saxophone players."

Such is the conclusion—severe but in many respects well-founded—reached by the music lover who expects from jazz the same satisfactions he receives from classical masterpieces. But isn't there something nonsensical about this attitude? Would jazz have the slightest interest if its function were only to bring back to life, in its own way—and hence, necessarily, with less force and purity—the very same musical emotions that European art cultivates? Obviously, our music lover is only showing how hard it is for him to enlarge his horizon. Certain listening habits are so strong that not everyone can free himself from them. In that case, our man has the right to retort that he can do without jazz; the rich European musical universe is diversified enough to take up a lifetime by itself.

When an art involves the most elaborate forms of a culture, often only the most highly educated minds can grasp it. When an art is foreign to a culture, it seems, on the contrary, that greater educational conditioning can retard or even prevent an understanding of it. This observation kept me persuaded for a long time that the only way to appreciate jazz was to "acquire a way of feeling like the Negro's." Today I see clearly how illusory such an idea is. Whatever the American Negro's way of feeling is determined by and regardless of whether heredity or environment plays the preponderant role in its formation, it is impossible for a European to identify himself with the Negro, except in a very superficial way. Even if it could be done, the price would be a total renunciation of what is best in European culture. Michelangelo, Vermeer, Bach, Baudelaire, and Kafka have left too profound a mark on us to permit such a monstrous rejection. As great as the merits of jazz may be, this would be too high a price to pay in order to assimilate an art which is not ours by origin.

However, an intermediate position is possible. For us Europeans, the only reasonable solution is to take jazz as a complement to our culture, not as an antidote to the "poisons of intellectualism." What does this music bring to us? Isn't it precisely the kind of music "that can be listened to without burying one's forehead in one's hands," which is what Jean Cocteau called for after the first war? In jazz, "sensorial interests" greatly outweigh "intellectual passion," the simple charm of existence is exalted without much reflection, a sharpened sensuality takes the place of loftiness and the fusion of individualities takes the place of architecture. Consequently, the attitude required of the listener by jazz is completely different from that generally required by classical masterpieces. But whoever knows how to listen to it with the right kind of ear is always paid for his effort. In our time, when the most advanced European art is becoming more and more abstract (Mondrian, Boulez), leaving room for feeling but only in a highly sublimated form, jazz brings an element of balance that may be necessary and is almost surely beneficial.

II

We have seen that the educated man who cannot triumph over his own culture is not well equipped to appreciate the beauty of jazz. To what type of man, then, does Armstrong's trumpet or Hawkins' saxophone speak meaningfully? Who is the jazz fan? Is it the opera subscriber who never fails to shed a tear over the endlessly repeated misfortunes of Manon or Tosca? Is it the matron to whom waltzes bring back fond recollections of her youth, or the shopgirl who swoons when she hears such popular singers as Georges Guétary or Tino Rossi on the radio? Obviously, the jazz fan is not any of these. To be understood, jazz seems to require a fresh, still unsatisfied sensibility (which may explain why it rarely takes hold of someone who has already assimilated the beauty of great European music), a kind of person who is overflowing with energy and searching for an outlet.

Obviously, the adolescent is the one who meets these conditions best. There is therefore nothing surprising in the fact that the young people of both sexes—but particularly boys rather than girls—have in a way made jazz their own.

Of course, there is another explanation of this fact. Since the popularity of jazz is a relatively recent thing, at least in France, it is logical that only the youngest part of the public should have discovered its beauty. It can be easily verified that, past the age of thirty, not everyone is capable of the effort required to assimilate a new way of thinking or feeling. This explanation, however, is only partly satisfactory. It ignores a fact to which all the jazz fans of my generation can testify. Before the war, we all had a few friends who were dominated by their passion for jazz and who used to spend most of their pocket money for Louis Armstrong's and Fats Waller's records. How many of them have kept the faith? Has more than one out of ten of these "frivolous fans" enlarged or even kept his record collection? For the most part, they have succumbed to the routine of bourgeois existence, which leaves little room for artistic satisfactions; their love of jazz has not been strong enough or solidly enough motivated to stand up. They have let others take their place, and there is every reason to believe that these newcomers will act in the same way.

The explanation is that young people's passion for jazz is based less on a real feeling for music than on another quality which is characteristic of adolescence—enthusiasm. I certainly have no intention of belittling the value of enthusiasm; many great things can be accomplished only through it. But, except in persons of unusual quality, enthusiasm is short-lived. Enthusiasm is the element surrounding the young man who has set out to discover jazz and who can't wait to hear the latest Art Tatum record and to discuss with his friends the most recently published book or the opinion of the critic who is willing to exchange comments with him about the latest issue of the magazine he subscribes to. It is enthusiasm, finally, which transforms the love of jazz into a kind of metaphysical crisis in extreme cases and makes Jelly Roll Morton and Tommy Ladnier be regarded as legendary heroes or saints. But when this enthusiasm dies down, everything collapses in a very short time. The torch is passed on to younger hands; and from year to year, the faces change but the average age of people who go to jazz concerts and read jazz magazines remains the same.

Nevertheless, this description is too general to be accepted literally. As I have said, there are few fans whose infatuation with jazz resists the test of time. Still, there are some, and their existence shows that jazz can bring to a man satisfactions that are not superficial, but profound and in a sense necessary. Although I am not fond of generalizing, I should like to sketch the portrait of such a fan. He is between thirty and forty—rarely older, for jazz has penetrated Europe too recently for there to be more than a handful of real oldtimers. His erudition (by which I mean his knowledge of recordings) is solid, and so are his opinions. In the past, he may have regarded the Greats with religious awe; but his present attitude is marked by a familiarity that is much less respectful. When Cozy Cole and Lester Young play in the city where he lives, he has a drink with one and invites the other to dinner.

III

Some pieces of music grow old; others stay young. At times we can hardly believe it possible that once we actually enjoyed listening to a page of music or a chorus that now seems overwhelmingly long on faults and short on merits. To make up for this, some works seem more and more attractive to us as time goes by. For one thing, we are more difficult to please at thirty than we were at twenty. Instead of liking a hundred records, we no longer like more than five or six; but perhaps we like them better. Judging by my own experience, there can be no doubt that the test of time has favored Ellington's *Concerto For Cootie*—more, perhaps, than any other work, and this is a sure sign of merit. It has become clear to me that this piece is one of the high points in Ellington's output, which has been vast and rich in flashes of genius, but unequal and occasionally disappointing. I would even say that it offers a striking epitome of certain essential aspects of his work.

The concerto formula—that is, a composition centered around a single soloist accompanied by large orchestra—is widely used these days. There is almost no repertory that does not include a certain number of arrangements conceived with an eye toward the possibilities, the style, and the ambitions of such and such a popular soloist. In 1940, even though it wasn't exceptional, the *Concerto* was rarer. It was only four years before then that Ellington had recorded his first concertos, one of which, *Echoes of Harlem*, had already been designed for Cootie Williams. Admittedly, the appearance of these compositions did not constitute an innovation in the form. Before Ellington, Armstrong had recorded solos that had all the concerto's appearances. But the Ellington style of *Concerto*, from the very beginning, not only introduced a markedly different musical climate but also laid the foundation for an infinitely richer conception. In it, far from merely serving to set off the soloist as in Armstrong's records, the orchestra worked in close collaboration with him. Naturally, it would be impossible to state positively that Duke Ellington and his group grasped from the beginning all the possibilities that this kind of composition offered, but it seems probable all the same. In any case, the fact is that, after several years of varyingly successful experiments (the detestable *Trumpet in Spades*, in which Rex trumpeted to such poor advantage, comes to mind), the orchestra recorded, on March 15, 1940, this *Concerto For Cootie*, which still strikes us, a decade and a half later, as the masterpiece of jazz concertos and as being along with *Ko-Ko*, the most important composition that Duke Ellington has turned out.

Concerto For Cootie is a masterpiece because everything in it is pure; because it doesn't have that slight touch of softness which is enough to make so many other deserving records insipid. *Concerto For Cootie* is a masterpiece because the arranger and the soloist have refused in it any temptation to achieve an easy effect, and because the musical substance of it is so rich that not for one instant does the listener have an impression of monotony. *Concerto For Cootie* is a masterpiece because it shows the game being played for all it is worth, without anything's being held back, and because the game is won. We have here a real concerto in which the orchestra is not a simple background, in which the soloist doesn't waste his time in technical acrobatics or in gratuitous effects. Both have something to say, they say it well, and what they say is beautiful. Finally, *Concerto For Cootie* is a masterpiece because what the orchestra says is the indispensable complement to what the soloist says; because nothing is out of place or superflous in it; and because the composition thus attains unity.

Concerto For Cootie should not be considered as an ordinary arrangement. Its unusual structure, the polish of its composition, the liberties with certain well-established rules that are taken in it, the refusal to improvise—these characteristics are enough to place it rather on the level of original composition as this term is understood by artists of classical training. *Concerto For Cootie* is not derived from any earlier melody. True, *Do Nothin' Till You Hear From Me* uses the same melodic figure; but this song, composed by Ellington, is several years later than the orchestral work. There can be no doubt that it was adapted from it. *Do Nothin'* is in a way the commercial version of the guiding idea behind *Concerto For Cootie*. Indeed, it retains only the initial phrase. We wouldn't even have mentioned the song here but for the fact that this phrase had to be revised to conform to the traditional framework of the thirty-two-bar song. We shall be able to appreciate the original better by comparing it with this popularized version.

PLAN OF *CONCERTO FOR COOTIE*

Introduction	8 bars
I. *Exposition* (F major)	
Theme A	10 bars
followed by A′	10 bars
followed by B	8 bars
followed by A″	10 bars
followed by a modulatory transition	2 bars
II. *Middle Section* (D♭ major)	
Theme C	16 bars
followed by a modulatory transition	2 bars
III. *Re-exposition and Coda* (F major)	
A‴	6 bars
Coda	10 bars

The harmonic language of *Concerto For Cootie* is, on the whole, extremely simple. Apart from the introduction, the general climate of the piece is as resolutely consonant as *Ko-Ko*, Ellington's other masterpiece of that period, was the opposite. In the *Concerto*, dissonance plays a secondary role; it does not constitute the foundation of the harmony. It does not serve to create a feeling of tension, but operates as a means of adding color. Nonetheless, the many dissonances to be found in the work are not there for nothing: there can be no doubt that their suppression would weaken it considerably. It is they, certainly, that by contrast make the consonances sound so bright and fresh. This over-all harmonic simplicity doesn't rule out subtlety of detail. Certain passages have presented problems to the best-trained ears. The little phrase in contrary motion in the seventh and eighth measures of the coda, which is harmonically a real gem, would provide a test in musical dictation for the greatest specialists in this ticklish sport; but I want to call attention merely to its musical beauty, which I like to think any listener will appreciate.

Another exceptional passage is the measure just before the exposition of theme C. I doubt that there are many examples of modulations more striking than this one, not only in jazz but in all music. On paper, it seems extremely simple, and no doubt it actually is. Listening to it, one has to admire the abruptness and rigor of this turning; and its effect is all the more astonishing because Ellington has put before it a two-beat rest that constitutes—taking into consideration the completely inconclusive phrase just preceding it—the most effective break you could ask for between one part of a piece and another that you would have expected to follow without any break at all. To call this a stroke of genius is, for once, not to misuse the phrase.

It would be possible to mention a number of other harmonic finds. In spite of its ambiguous character and a certain acidity that does not lack charm, the introduction is not the most successful part of the composition. I prefer certain details in the purely accompanying part: the saxes' dissonances behind phrase A′ or a complementary phrase like the one in the eighth measure of C, which has a melodic, harmonic, and instrumental savor that is truly penetrating. Attention should also be called to the occasional use of blue notes in some of the trombones' punctuation of phrases A and A″. Although, basically, *Concerto For Cootie* has no more connection with the blues than Hawkins' *Body and Soul,* these blue notes are by no means out of place; the faint touch of the blues that they introduce fits into the atmosphere of the piece perfectly.

There remains the added-sixth chord, which is put to considerable use here. This harmonic combination, which generally raises my hackles, fills me with joy in the *Concerto.* It is true that Ellington sometimes uses it in a regrettably Gershwin-like way, but that certainly is not the case here. Why? I couldn't say for sure; that sort of thing is more easily felt than explained. Perhaps the consonant climate of the piece accounts for a large part of it; perhaps the general feeling and the orchestration itself play a decisive role. What must be remembered is that no chord, however flaccid, is inherently ugly; the only thing that counts is the use made of it.

Part Four

THE SEARCH FOR VALUES IN CONTEMPORARY LIFE

1. *The Point of View of History*
2. *The Point of View of Philosophy*
3. *The Point of View of Religion*
4. *The Point of View of Creative Imagination*

TOWARD A SYNTHESIS

Samuel Johnson once finished a philosophical novel with a chapter entitled, "The Conclusion in Which Nothing Is Concluded." By far the most difficult and perplexing problem in dealing with contemporary life is to find enduring values and convictions by which we can guide life and give it significance. The writers represented in this anthology have almost all opposed dogmatism and the demand for final answers; they have instead provided a thoughtful analysis of the kind of issues that perplex and disturb us in this generation. Ours is certainly a confused generation, and in our extremity there is always the danger that we will turn to dogmas that have proved unacceptable in the past or grasp at shadows that have no substance in the present.

It has seemed desirable, therefore, to bring together in the concluding section of this anthology selections from six outstanding thinkers, all of whom are making a significant contribution to man's search for values in contemporary life. Their points of view are quite varied; the disciplines they represent are not the same. But each of these authors has faced the kind of problems with which we have been concerned here, and each has found what he believes to be a workable and constructive synthesis upon which to base his own life and philosophy.

Our first author, Herbert J. Muller, writes from the point of view of history. *The Uses of the Past,* from which our selection is taken, has been a popular and widely read discussion of what we can learn from history. Much of the spirit of John Dewey and Max Otto is reflected in the "scientific humanism" that Muller adopts. He argues strongly for the continued use of human reason and the scientific method as our only hope in meeting the present crisis in Western civilization.

Writing more directly from the viewpoint of philosophy, Bertrand Russell and Charles Morris develop somewhat more fully the implications of this faith in human reason and science, especially as it throws light upon man's own nature and potentialities. Albert Schweitzer, one of the great spiritual and moral inspirations of our age, also puts the weight of his strong faith and long experience behind much the same position. Religion can make a greater contribution to human life, Schweitzer believes, if it works in harmony with reason rather than in opposition to it. But Reinhold Niebuhr, who stands among the leaders of religious thought in America, is not willing to accept this point of view without important qualifications. Our selection from his recent book, *The Self and the Dramas of History,* provides a strong argument for a more independent religious view of the human spirit that recognizes man's freedom from the domination of science and history as an essential element in our thinking. A final selection from *Philosophy in a New Key* by

Susanne Langer introduces the contemporary emphasis upon symbolism and shows how this may provide the key to enduring values in all aspects of human experience.

In one way or another each of these writers is a bit dubious about our present world. Schweitzer puts this most bluntly when he says, "With the spirit of the age I am in complete disagreement." But all of them have great confidence in human nature at its best and all have hope for the future. This underlying optimism is reflected in their thoughtful suggestions for using more fully the values they discover in contemporary life.

1

THE POINT OF VIEW OF HISTORY

*Herbert J. Muller**

THE USES OF THE PAST

The Philosophy of History

"HAPPY is the people that is without a history," wrote Christopher Dawson, "and thrice happy is the people without a sociology, for as long as we possess a living culture we are unconscious of it, and it is only when we are in danger of losing it or when it is already dead that we begin to realize its existence and to study it scientifically." There are still such happy people among us, on farms, in business offices, and in congressional chambers. But those who are cursed by consciousness cannot become unconscious by an effort of will, and many have grown unhappier because they know too little history and sociology. A little consciousness is the most dangerous thing. And so we had better strive to become clearly and fully conscious, of who we are, where we are, and how we got this way.

From the outset, we are faced with the striking contradictions of the modern world. Our age is notorious for its want of piety or sense of the past; up-to-date men have been too busy making gadgets, automobiles, depressions, and wars to care much about anything older than the minutes of the last meeting. Our age is nevertheless more historically minded than any previous age, and has a much longer, wider, clearer view of the past. Its contributions to historical knowledge, over the last hundred years, are among its most honorable achievements. In studying the past scientifically, unearthing

* For a brief biographical sketch of Herbert Muller, see page 86 above.

its monuments, recovering its vanished life, historians have performed a work of unprecedented piety. For despite their deep sense of the past, the ancients had little understanding of it. Thucydides, the most objective of ancient historians, began his history of the Peloponnesian War by stating that nothing of great importance had happened before his time; and in his ignorance of all that lay behind his age he could not realize the unique glory of Athens, which for us makes the Peloponnesian War even more momentous and more tragic than he felt it to be. Modern historians are far better acquainted with the early history of the Greeks, as of the Egyptians, the Hebrews, and the Romans, than were these "pious" people themselves.

The triumphs of this historical research involve further ironies. They have been triumphs of the scientific spirit and method. Hence they fostered the illusion that often inspired them—the illusion that history is or should be an exact science, free from all taint of art or philosophy. "Do not applaud me," Fustel de Coulanges told his rapt students. "It is not I who address you, but history that speaks through my mouth." This claim of utter impersonality encouraged the monumental unimaginativeness of German scholarship, which still awes American universities and dehumanizes the humanities. It implied that the significance of human history was to be discovered by a systematic avoidance of significant generalization or judgment. It was based, Carl Becker remarked, on the strange philosophical assumption that by not taking thought a historian could add a cubit to his stature. "Hoping to find something, without looking for it, expecting to obtain final answers to life's riddles by resolutely refusing to ask questions—it was surely the most romantic species of realism yet invented, the oddest attempt ever made to get something for nothing!"

Now this naive faith was understandable, and up to a point quite laudable. Historians of the last century were striving to make their subject intellectually respectable in an age of science. (As late as 1880 there were only eleven professors of history in American colleges.) They had to combat the common tendencies to entertain and edify, to exploit the dramatic and spectacular, to teach political and religious lessons, or to leap to grandiose philosophies of history. These tendencies are still so popular that we can scarcely afford to ridicule any aspiration to objectivity and exactitude. Nevertheless the "scientific" historians had a shallow conception of science, art, and philosophy. They thought of the true scientist as one who deals in plain, unvarnished facts, never making assumptions and never being harried by doubt and dispute over fundamentals. They thought of art as the antithesis of science, as if imagination deals only with the imaginary and can be indulged only when knowledge fails. They thought of philosophy as metaphysical speculation, another inferior substitute for knowledge or threat to it. They failed to see that science itself is an imaginative interpretation of reality, based on philosophical assumptions.

Their very ideal of objectivity and exactitude, in other words, calls for a more exact idea of the nature of historical knowledge, and the limits of its objectivity. The aim of history, said Ranke, is simply to state "what has actually happened," but this is far from being a simple business, even apart from the fact that we can never hope to know all that has actually happened. If we did know all, we should have to forget almost everything before we could understand anything—just as our memory is an aid only because we remember no more than a minute fraction of our past experience. As it is, the main problem is not so much to fill in the many gaps of our factual knowledge as to make sense out of the vast deal that we do know. For a historical fact never speaks for itself. We begin by singling out the "important" happenings; we then try to determine their causes and effects, or their connections with other happenings that we decide are relevant and important; we finally try to determine their significance, their connection with our own purposes. And in this whole process of selecting, interpreting, and evaluating the facts, attempting to answer the unavoidable questions, how, why, and what of it, we are unavoidably committed to questionable assumptions about the nature of man and the world, and about his possible or his proper destiny. We cannot help having some philosophy of history, however vague or unconscious. So we might try to have a clear, conscious, coherent one.

This book is based on the ancient conception of history as "philosophy teaching by experience." It is also based on the "new history," the contribution of this century, which ultimately involves new philosophies of history. More specifically, it is based on the following assumptions:

1. That the ideal of history, in the words of Morris Cohen, is "an imaginative reconstruction of the past which is scientific in its determinations and artistic in its formulation";

2. That history is more genuinely scientific in spirit as it takes into account the reasons why it cannot be utterly objective or strictly scientific in method;

3. That among these reasons is the necessity of dealing with a complex of factors—physical, biological, psychological, cultural—that cannot be measured, isolated in controlled experiments, or reduced to a single cause;

4. That among these factors is the force of human will—of mind and character, ideas and ideals;

5. That this force makes it necessary to pass ethical judgments on history, and that such judgments are in fact implicit in the works of the most resolutely amoral historians;

6. That our scientific, esthetic, and moral interests alike call for a world view, a kind of anthropological study of civilizations, as a perspective on our own civilization;

7. That in this perspective we can make out universals or underlying uniformities but cannot claim possession of the absolute truth about man and the universe, cannot hope for complete certainty about beginnings and ends; and

8. That this is not simply a depressing conclusion.

Though most of these propositions may seem elementary or harmless, all are controversial. All are contested by eminent thinkers, in practice when not in theory, and have still more controversial implications. I therefore propose to amplify them somewhat before beginning my survey of the drama itself.

The Premises of Inquiry

Although the practical value of a knowledge of history is commonly exaggerated, since men do not appear to learn readily from the mistakes of their ancestors, and historians themselves are not always conspicuous for their wisdom, I suppose that few would deny the practical necessity of this knowledge. When Henry Ford, in the good old boom days, said that "history is bunk," he merely illustrated the ignorance of the hard-headed industrial leaders who were leading the country straight to a crash. History has also been described as a series of messes, but only by a historical analysis can we determine how we got into the latest mess, and how we might get out of it. The very idea that we are in a mess involves assumptions about the "natural" course of affairs, as do all policies for dealing with it. In any event, we are forever drawing upon the past. It not only constitutes all the "experience" by which we have learned: it is the source of our major interests, our claims, our rights, and our duties. It is the source of our very identity.

"History is neither written nor made without love or hate," Mommsen wrote. The historian is inevitably an artist of a kind as he composes his narrative, selecting, shaping, coloring. The greater historians, from Herodotus to Toynbee, have generally been distinguished for their imaginative reach and grasp, not necessarily the soundness of their conclusions. Gibbon remains one of the greatest, despite his apparent prejudice and his untrustworthiness in detail, because of his artistic mastery of an epic theme.

Up to a point, all this implies something like Croce's principle, that true history is always contemporary history—history "for the occasion," of what is alive for us. The past has no meaningful existence except as it exists for us, as it is given meaning by us. In piety and justice we try to see it as it was, or as it seemed to the men who lived it, but even this poetic interest is not disinterested; in our contemplation of the drama we see what is most pertinent for our own hopes and fears. Hence the past keeps changing with the present. Every age has to rewrite its history, re-create the past; in every age a different Christ dies on the Cross, and is resurrected to a different end. Today the Peloponnesian War and the decline of the Roman Empire have a special significance for us that they could not have had for the Middle Ages or the Renaissance; by the same token they will have a different significance for a Hindu or Chinese than for a Western historian. Our task is to create a "usable past" for our own living purposes.

Yet this admission of relativity does not permit us to create whatever we have a mind to, make over the past to suit ourselves. Old Testament and early Christian historians could freely tamper with the facts because they knew the divine plan of history; the only important use of facts was to illustrate the all-important religious truth. We cannot simply stick to the facts, but we cannot disregard them either, and must derive our meanings from them in the knowledge that they are both stubborn and ambiguous. Our distinctive interests and beliefs make it possible for history to be relatively disinterested and impartial. Through Marx, Freud, Sumner, Pareto, Boas, Spengler, and many others, we have become aware of the inveterate habit of rationalization and the sources of bias—the class interests, the *mores*, the conditioned reflexes of culture, the unconscious assumptions, the "climate of opinion." Although we can never entirely escape or control our climate, never attain a God's-eye view, we can more freely discount and supplement—at least when we read the other fellow's history.

But I should at once add that the admission of *ultimate* uncertainty does not mean *complete* uncertainty. Hence a refusal on principle to say the last word about human history is not a refusal to say any word, or to pass any firm judgment. Rather, it defines the conditions of judgment. Say that our most cherished beliefs are matters of opinion and it is then our business to get sound opinions, based on honest thought and the best available knowledge; only a fool will say that any opinion is as good as any other opinion—and even a fool is apt to seek expert opinion when he gets sick. Say that our final preferences are matters of taste and it is then our business to cultivate good taste; cultivated men may dispute the relative merits of Donne and Shelley, but they can and do agree that both are better poets than Eddie Guest. Because of the flagrant disagreement among the wise men, we are apt to forget the very general agreement on who were the gerat men—and to overlook the implication of this agreement, the tacit admission that there are diverse forms of goodness and greatness. As for history, we are confronted by societies embodying radically different ways of life, but it remains our business to judge the historical consequences of those ways. We can hope to make more intelligent judgments if we are aware of the many ways, and do not take for granted that our own is necessarily superior to all others.

Here, it seems to me, is the basic problem of thoughtful men today. We do not know the final truth about God and the world; the most certain knowledge we do have about the history of man belies all pretense to absolute certainty. We must nevertheless have principles, standards, faiths; many men have been demoralized by a shallow relativism that denies us the right to judge anyone or anything, while we perforce keep judging. The problem, then, is to maintain principle and morale in the face of ultimate uncertainty, on grounds that permit both the faith and the tolerance required by the pursuit of truth and goodness; just as the problem for statesmen is to compromise and reconcile without a cynical indifference to principle, in order to accommodate fundamentally different ways of life in a world order. The immediate objection to all partisans of absolute truth is that they evade the given terms of this problem.

I am therefore led to my final assumption, that the admission of a principle of relativity and uncertainty should not be simply depressing. It does not destroy all possibility of knowledge and judgment. Rather, it is the outcome of comprehensive knowledge, and the means to further knowledge of man's history. It enables a higher objectivity, a fuller understanding of present and past. It enables wiser choices among the possibilities open to us—among goods that are no less real because they are relative, and that are more relevant than arbitrary absolutes. Above all, this principle encourages a positive faith in positive values; of liberality, breadth of spirit, hospitality to new ideas, willingness to adventure, humility in admitting one's own fallibility and the limitations of the human mind—of the tolerance that is indispensable for the pursuit of truth, for social harmony, and for simple humanity. If these are not the highest values, none are more essential to the hopes of world order and peace.

The Challenge Today

I am not optimistic about our immediate prospects. As I write, we have to live in two worlds, both more or less obsolete. Neither side really believes in the doctrine of coexistence that is the only hope of peace. If there is a world war, only the most naive patriots can believe that the victor will bring lasting peace and good will to the world; and such patriots are not apt to be good peacemakers. Neither am I optimistic about the saving power of historical knowledge. What history teaches, Hegel remarked, is that men have never learned anything from it; or at least their knowledge has not availed against the ancient enemy. Although the learned have often been blind, simple men have always been aware of this enemy, which is selfishness—the egotism of nations as of individuals. Allied with it are the ageless forces of ignorance and stupidity, greed and envy, fear and hate. Today these forces are as active as ever, and more terribly armed. As the old adage has it, most men want peace but do not know or want the things that make for peace. The odds favor catastrophe again.

Yet as we live we must continue to bet on education, on thought, as our only possible chance. We must bet on it even though as individuals we are apt to feel more helpless than ever before, since the fateful decisions involving life or death for hundreds of millions are still made by a few men, even in the democracies. We must bet because we all nevertheless are involved, and have our own decisions to make. In any event, there is logic as well as art in the convention that calls for a book on history to have a Conclusion, even if history itself doesn't. Although it is not my business to predict or plan the future, a book about the past inevitably contains a reference to the future. Our understanding of recent events comes down to ideas about their probable consequences; our interpretation of the remote past is still colored by ideas about what kind of future is possible, and what kind desirable. The effort to be objective, to ground hope and aspiration on the best available knowledge, is itself a bet on the method of intelligence, or education.

At least the immediate terms of our problem seem clear enough. All would agree, I suppose, that the major practical task of our civilization is to establish some kind of world order strong enough to maintain peace. Our technology has made such an order necessary by giving us terrific power—power that we may regret having, but that we will not and cannot do away with. Technology has also made a world order possible, as it was not in Roman times; ancient empires were always unwieldy because of slow, uncertain communication. The obvious trouble remains that men have not kept pace with their machines. The world has been brought together too suddenly and forcibly to be a good neighborhood; the unaccustomed intimacy has intensified the differences between peoples, multiplied the possibilities of friction. Technology has likewise made possible total, universal war.

Given the long series of empires, history might suggest that a likely outcome is a world order dominated by a single power. Russia appears to have imperial ambitions, while many American internationalists call for a tough kind of "world leadership" that to the rest of the world looks like domination. Given the invariable fate of empire, however, history suggests no reason for welcoming such an outcome. A Russian world dictatorship might achieve order but only by a tyranny that would crush the spirit of most Western peoples; if it endured it would probably mean a creeping death for most civilized values. (One portent is the degeneration of Soviet painting, literature, and philosophy, which have already lost much of the fresh ardor that once compensated for their addiction to crude stereotypes.) An American world dictatorship might be more generous but would almost certainly be disorderly and short-lived; Americans have little mind or stomach for such responsibilities. Nor can a detached observer be hopeful about the further possibility that the pride of both Russia and America may be humbled by some new power, such as China. Only the arrogant can believe that any one people has enough wit and virtue to rule the world.

I therefore reach the commonplace conclusion that the best hope for the future is some kind of world federation on a democratic basis. The ideal role of America, given the leadership that has been thrust upon it willy-nilly because of its wealth and power, would be to lead the way to such a federation. This is the avowed goal of its statesmen and at least the vague aspiration of most of its citizens. The aspiration is in keeping with the major historic achievement of America as a melting pot, a new land in which many diverse people have come to form a community and live in liberty under law. The question remains whether the nation is up to this new role.

It has been slow to realize that its vaunted wealth and power are by no means great enough to master a world. Its friends and allies are not too confident of its wisdom and virtue. Nor of their own. Ultimately, the question is whether the ideal values of Western civilization are more vital than they have appeared to be in this century.

Again I cannot be certain of the answer. I still do believe, however, that these values deserve to live, and that the liberal faith offers the only real hope for a decent future. So I propose to recapitulate the main articles of this faith.

A Credo

"What kind of people do they think we are?" exclaimed Winston Churchill during the last war. A major cause of Hitler's undoing was that the British proved to be a much sturdier people than he thought. Even so he had reason to think poorly of them, judging by the mediocrity of their leaders before Churchill, and by the gloominess of many of their intellectuals. The behavior of the British points to simplicities that thinkers are prone to forget. Before we get solemn about the ultimate issues we might take a hard look at these simplicities.

Thus it is a commonplace that American soldiers in the last war had a dim idea of what they were fighting for. Presumably they have no clearer idea of why they went to Korea, and certainly they have no passion for dying for any cause. Nevertheless they have fought sturdily, sweating it out, grumbling it through to the end. As ordinary men they have a toughness of spirit that carries them through crises while clear-eyed intellectuals indulge in despair. In one aspect this is insensitiveness or simple coarseness. In another it is simple loyalty to the company—the chance unit of buddies. The "cause" comes down to such common sentiments as fellow-feeling, pride in workmanship, and self-respect. Our religions, our philosophies, and our histories too seldom take adequate account of these rudiments of human idealism. A philosophy of history might well begin and end with a report I have heard on the French underground that took care of Allied airmen and escaped prisoners in the last war. The report was that the most effective workers in this underground were priests and prostitutes.

In this unphilosophical, unspiritual view we may better understand why democracy has not degenerated into the anarchy and tyranny predicted by its critics, from Plato down—why, on the contrary, it has been able to mobilize its resources for mighty national efforts, and to emerge from two world wars without loss of its basic civil liberties. The very limitations of ordinary men may be sources of strength. The depressing conventionality of Americans, for example, has contributed to their unusual cohesiveness and stability. Their favorite national myth, the success story, has strengthened their faith in themselves and helped to maintain the habits of enterprise and self-reliance. Their spiritual slackness, or incapacity for flaming idealism, is at least in part a saving realism and modesty. The chances for world order and peace are better because they no longer expect wars to end war, and have little sense of manifest destiny, little zeal for making the world safe for democracy at any cost. In a period of deep confusion they can carry on the democratic tradition because they carry much of it unconsciously, in sentiments of equality and fair play learned in kindergarten, habits of tolerance and compromise engrained by everyday give and take. "A very great deal of the Western way of life," writes Crane Brinton, "is thus embedded somewhere in quite ordinary Americans, not in their cerebral cortexes, probably, but in a much safer place which the physiologist hasn't quite located—we used to say, in the heart."

Yet such realism also forbids us to be complacent about these homely virtues, or about any faith learned by heart. Much paltry sentiment and belief have been learned in the same way. Embedded still deeper are the primitive instincts of fear and rage, which now give desperate overtones to the tribal chant of the nation's might and right. Conventional patriotism, oratory, heroics, the fervor of hatred and fear—the conditioned reflexes of national life might still carry us through the present emergency; but they could not make a world order. For the long run we need more sober, lucid, responsible convictions about the kind of people we have been, and will have to be. For wherever the democratic faith is embedded in ordinary Americans, it was not born there and did not settle there by chance. It was engendered by conscious thought; it was propagated by conscious effort. In a revolutionary world it cannot survive indefinitely as mere habit.

And so with Western civilization as a whole. The familiar refrains about its "breakdown" may obscure the extraordinary unflagging creativeness that has made it the richest, most dramatic spectacle in history. It has maintained a high level of creative activity over a longer period of time than have previous societies, which rested on their oars after bursts of great achievement. In particular, as Whitehead observed, thought has been more creative. Whereas in other societies thought served chiefly to explain and conserve, Western man embarked on an endless "adventure of ideas" and put the ideas to work. He has thrived on the continuous disagreement and disharmony from which he has suffered; his life has always been charged with high tension. Since the dawn of the Middle Ages Europe has known the sense of crisis—the symptoms diagnosed by the specialists in "breakdowns." During its most complacent periods, such as the *ancien régime* and the Victorian age, revolutionary forces were agitating the more sensitive spirits and engendering further crises.

Hence I should stress first of all, in very general terms, our continued need of an adventurous spirit—of still more creative thought, bold, imaginative, experimental, self-reliant, critical of all "infallible" authority. This stress may seem unnecessary in an age notorious for its skepticism and irreverence, and at a moment when revolutionaries are the apparent menace. Nevertheless these revolutionaries are much less bold and independent than they appear, what with their childish faith in guaranteed totalitarian solutions. Our conservatives are even less enterprising than they appear; the frequent violence of their tactics masks a fearful timidity and unimaginativeness in their basic strategy, when not a downright panic. And we all have to be wary of another contradiction in our heritage. While the spirit of adventure has been the genius of Western thought, at its heart has remained the venerable assumption of a static, finished world, in which truth is timeless, standards are absolute and fixed, and human nature is always and everywhere the same. Our religion, our ethics, our poetry, our political and economic theory, our proverbs and maxims for daily life—our idealism and our common sense alike are steeped in this assumption, which is at variance both with our scientific knowledge of human history in an evolving world, and with the conditions of life in a revolutionary world.

All along I have been identifying the adventurous spirit with humanism, liberalism, rationalism, the scientific spirit, the ideals of freedom, individualism, and the "open society." Since these have constituted the distinctive faith of our secular civilization,

I appear to be calling for business as usual, at the same old stand—the kind of business that has brought on the present crisis. I should therefore repeat that the adventure in freedom is inevitably precarious. Yet I deny that this faith is the main source of our folly and evil. In the world of affairs the obvious menace is the inveterate self-interest, individual and national, upon which all faiths have foundered. In the world of thought the chief menaces are the various forms of authoritarianism and irrationalism. The worst folly of liberals has been a facile optimism that blinked at both the ancient evils and the new complexities.

Today they are apt to echo the common charge that "scientific philosophy" is the root of our evils. Science has indisputably inspired much narrow, harsh philosophy, and much pseudo-science; its disciples have often been inhuman. As inhuman, however, is the fashion of branding all the efforts of intelligence as sinful pride, and all the works of science as mere materialism. It appears that to study meteorology and scientific agriculture is to be materialistic, whereas to pray for rain and good crops is to be spiritual. Actually, both procedures have utilitarian motives; the immediate choice is between more or less intelligent, efficacious means of attaining human ends; and as for "higher" values, pure science is a more disinterested, more genuinely spiritual activity than ordinary prayer or worship. At least science cannot be charged with the nationalism and imperialism that now threaten catastrophe. No war has ever been fought over scientific causes. No nation—least of all Soviet Russia—has proposed its aims or resolved its issues in a scientific spirit. Science has had very little to do, indeed, with the administration of our economic and political life. It remains the author of our major problem, in its gift of tremendous power that has been terribly abused; but for the wise use of this power we need more, not less, of the objective, dispassionate scientific spirit. For our philosophical purposes we need more of its integrity and its basic humility, its respect at once for fact and for mystery.

Many men now take a strange pleasure in emphasizing the limits of scientific knowledge, as if the validity of poetic, metaphysical, or religious claims to higher truth were thereby automatically proved, and ignorance were not merely bliss but wisdom. Many are attacking the claims of reason itself, in the name of faith, intuition, instinct, the heart, the voice of the blood. In the world of affairs such attitudes are translated into the kind of common sense that scorns all "theory," ridicules "braintrusts," and identifies learning with absent-mindedness. The way is thus cleared for the positive irrationalism of the dictators, the brutal contempt of mind exhibited in their policy when not their creed. We may then realize that a denial of the claims of reason naturally leads to a denial of the claims of the heart too, and that if its powers are as inadequate as many seem pleased to think, there can be no hope of avoiding catastrophe.

If we must make these imprecise, invidious distinctions, we had better try to keep our heads. Scientific knowledge is no less useful because of ultimate uncertainty; it serves the quite sufficient purpose of enabling us to go about our business in a world whose metaphysical 'reality' we do not absolutely need to know. Reliable knowledge is not enough by itself but nothing can take its place—no arbitary assertion of higher truths and goods. Whatever higher faculties man may have—of feeling, intuition, or imagination, in vision, trance, or ecstasy—can be trusted only after they have been interpreted and judged by reason. Otherwise anything goes: the visions of Buddha, Christ, Mohammed, Marx, Whitman, Nietzsche, and Hitler are on the same footing; and what goes best is apt to be blind unreason or brute force. No product of social intercourse is more precious than reasonableness, or more essential to attaining and sharing the goods of life; for love itself is a partial sentiment that often goes wrong, leading to division, jealousy, and hatred.

In this spirit reason must then add that love and hatred remain more elemental. Its claims need to be qualified by modest ideas of its functions and its powers; its ideal product is not pure rationality but reasonableness. Traditional rationalism has taken too supercilious an attitude toward the instinctive, spontaneous life, the sentiment and passion that alone can give force to its ideals. In this century many social scientists have displayed an incredibly naive confidence in the power of intelligence to control the "behavior patterns" with which they play, talking as if social conflict could be handled in the same way as infectious disease. Liberals generally have set their sights too high, overestimating the rationality and virtue of free men. Yet it is still reason that warns us against such unreasonable expectations. In its most mournful judgments of its frail powers it still proves its necessity, its responsibility, and its power.

To live intelligently, in short, we must recognize that man is not simply a "rational animal." To live decently we must also recognize that this definition of him is more adequate than such popular definitions as a beast of prey, an illusioned robot, or an imprisoned soul. He shares his basic drives and reflexes with other animals; and he may or may not have an immortal soul; what most plainly and positively distinguishes him from other animals is the power of conscious thought and responsible behavior. If we respect him at all we must treat him as if he were rational, and enlist his free consent in joint enterprises. The whole argument for liberty and democracy ultimately rests on Pascal's dictum that thought makes the whole dignity of man, and that the endeavor to think well is the basic morality. "The chief virtue of democracy," concluded Carl Becker, "and in the long run the whole reason for cherishing it, is that with all its defects it still provides the most favorable conditions for the maintenance of that dignity and the practice of that morality."

This is also the reason for cherishing the individual, as the essential carrier of that dignity and agent of that morality. In his newly won freedom to think and act for himself he has indeed done himself much harm. He has identified his cause with a gospel of economic individualism that meant slavery to a profit system, a loss of dignity for the many and a warped, impoverished humanity even for the successful. He has tended to forget that the sense of community is indispensable even to full self-realization. His excesses have therefore called out an extreme revulsion. Social scientists have referred to the individual as a "discredited hypothesis," defining him as a mere cell of the social organism, while dictators have discredited him in fact or put him in cells. Yet there is no doing away with him, or without him. The great creative individual, as John Stuart Mill said, not only personifies but initiates all the wise and noble things that the race has done. In everyday life we are as dependent on free relations with the ordinary decent person. We may best appreciate him in time of crisis, for he is capable of more wisdom and virtue than collective man ever can be. He is often superior to the best institutions—the great States and Churches—which repeatedly fall short of the integrity and the decency we can count on in private life.

2

THE POINT OF VIEW OF PHILOSOPHY

Bertrand Russell

One of the most prolific and distinguished writers of English prose, Russell has published more than sixty books covering a wide range of subjects. In his later life, he has become increasingly interested in political philosophy and in morals, rather than in scientific thought. His unconventional life and his hatred of tyranny in every form are matters of common knowledge. In 1953 he published a book of short stories called Satan in the Suburbs. Portraits from Memory *(1946) is a brief but entertaining autobiography. His* History of Western Philosophy *(1945) is a popular but frankly biased introduction to this subject. In 1950 he won the Nobel prize for literature.*

Russell writes with such clarity and integrity, even on highly controversial subjects, that his ideas have had wide circulation. His Conquest of Happiness, *now available in an inexpensive paperback, presents in interesting fashion the synthesis of hedonism and stoicism that he finds most acceptable as a philosophy of living. In the essay included here, "Philosophy for Laymen," Russell explains in nontechnical language what philosophy tries to do and why it is important. Not every philosopher, it is true, will agree with the distinctions that Russell makes between science and philosophy, on the one hand, and religion and philosophy, on the other, but no one can quarrel with his fine statement of the practical values of the study of philosophy itself.*

See page 226 above for additional biographical data.

PHILOSOPHY FOR LAYMEN

MANKIND, ever since there have been civilized communities, have been confronted with problems of two different kinds. On the one hand there has been the problem of mastering natural forces, of acquiring the knowledge and the skill required to produce tools and weapons and to encourage Nature in the production of useful animals and plants. This problem, in the modern world, is dealt with by science and scientific technique, and experience has shown that in order to deal with it adequately it is necessary to train a large number of rather narrow specialists.

But there is a second problem, less precise, and by some mistakenly regarded as unimportant—I mean the problem of how best to utilize our command over the forces of nature. This includes such burning issues as democracy versus dictatorship, capitalism versus socialism, international government versus international anarchy, free speculation versus authoritarian dogma. On such issues the laboratory can give no decisive guidance. The kind of knowledge that gives most help in solving such problems is a wide survey of human life, in the past as well as in the present, and an appreciation of the sources of misery or contentment as they appear in history. It will be found that increase of skill has not, of itself, insured any increase of human happiness or well-being. When men first learned to cultivate the soil, they used their knowledge to establish a cruel cult of human sacrifice. The men who first tamed the horse employed him to pillage and enslave peaceable populations. When, in the infancy of the industrial revolution, men discovered how to make cotton goods by machinery, the results were horrible: Jefferson's movement for the emancipation of slaves in America, which had been on the point of success, was killed dead; child labor in England was developed to a point of appalling cruelty; and ruthless imperialism in Africa was stimulated in the hope that black men could be induced to clothe themselves in cotton goods. In our own day a combination of scientific genius and technical skill has produced the atomic bomb, but having produced it we are all terrified, and do not know what to do with it. These instances, from widely different periods of history, show that something more than skill is required, something which may perhaps be called "wisdom." This is something that must be learned, if it can be learned, by means of other studies than those required for scientific technique. And it is something more needed now than ever before, because the rapid growth of technique has made ancient habits of thought and action more inadequate than in any earlier time.

"Philosophy" means "love of wisdom," and philosophy in this sense is what men must acquire if the new powers invented by technicians, and handed over by them to be wielded by ordinary men and women, are not to plunge mankind into an appalling cataclysm. But the philosophy that should be a part of general education is not the same thing as the philosophy of specialists. Not only in philosophy, but in all branches of academic study, there is a distinction between what has cultural value and what is only of professional interest. Historians may debate what happened to Sennacherib's unsuccessful expedition of 698 B. C., but those who are not historians need not know the difference between it and his successful expedition three years earlier. Professional Grecians may usefully discuss a disputed reading in a play of Aeschylus, but such matters are not for the man who wishes, in spite of a busy life, to acquire some knowledge of what the Greeks achieved. Similarly the men who devote their lives to philosophy must consider questions that the general educated public does right to ignore, such as the differences between the theory of universals in Aquinas and in Duns Scotus, or the characteristics that a language must have if it is to be able, without falling into nonsense, to say things about itself. Such questions belong to the technical aspects of philosophy, and their discussion cannot form part of its contribution to general culture.

Academic education should aim at giving, as a corrective of the specialization which increase of knowledge has made unavoidable, as much as time will permit of what has cultural value in such studies as history, literature, and philosophy. It should be made easy for a young man who knows no Greek to acquire through translations some understanding, however inadequate, of what the Greeks accomplished. Instead of studying the Anglo-Saxon kings over and over again at school, some attempt should be made to give a conspectus of world history, bringing the problems of our own day into relation with those of Egyptian priests, Babylonian kings, and Athenian reformers, as well as with all the hopes and despairs of the intervening centuries. But it is only of philosophy, treated from a similar point of view, that I wish to write.

I

Philosophy has had from its earliest days two different objects which were believed to be closely interrelated. On the one hand, it aimed at a theoretical understanding of the structure of the world; on the other hand, it tried to discover and inculcate the best possible way of life. From Heraclitus to Hegel, or even to Marx, it consistently kept both ends in view; it was neither purely theoretical nor purely practical, but sought a theory of the universe upon which to base a practical ethic.

Philosophy has thus been closely related to science on the one hand, and to religion on the other. Let us consider first the relation to science. Until the eighteenth century science was included in what was commonly called "philosophy," but since that time the word "philosophy" has been confined, on its theoretical side, to what is most speculative and general in the topics with which science deals. It is often said that philosophy is unprogressive, but this is largely a verbal matter: as soon as a way is found of arriving at definite knowledge on some ancient question, the new knowledge is counted as belonging to "science," and "philosophy" is deprived of the credit. In Greek times, and down to the time of Newton, planetary theory belonged to "philosophy," because it was uncertain and speculative, but Newton took the subject out of the realm of the free play of hypothesis, and made it one requiring a different type of skill from that which it had required when it was still open to fundamental doubts. Anaximander, in the six century B. C., had a theory of evolution, and maintained that men descended from fishes. This was philosophy because it was a speculation unsupported by detailed evidence, but Darwin's theory of evolution was science, because it was based on the succession of forms of life as found in fossils, and upon the distribution of animals and plants in many parts of the world. A man might say, with enough truth to justify a joke: "Science is what we know, and philosophy is what we don't know." But it should be added that philosophical speculation as to what we do not yet know has shown itself a valuable preliminary to exact scientific knowledge. The guesses of the Pythagoreans in astronomy, of Anaximander and Empedocles in biological evolution, and of Democritus as to the atomic constitution of matter, provided the men of science in later times with hypotheses which, but for the philosophers, might never have entered their heads. We may say that, on its theoretical side, philosophy consists, at least in part, in the framing of large general hypotheses which science is not yet in a position to test; but when it becomes possible to test the hypotheses they become, if verified, a part of science, and cease to count as "philosophy."

The utility of philosophy, on the theoretical side, is not confined to speculations which we may hope to see confirmed or confuted by science within a measurable time. Some men are so impressed by what science knows that they forget what it does not know; others are so much more interested in what it does not know than in what it does that they belittle its achievements. Those who think that science is everything become complacent and cocksure, and decry all interest in problems not having the circumscribed definiteness that is necessary for scientific treatment. In practical matters they tend to think that skill can take the place of wisdom, and that to kill each other by means of the latest technique is more "progressive," and therefore better, than to keep each other alive by old-fashioned methods. On the other hand, those who pooh-pooh science revert, as a rule, to some ancient and pernicious superstition, and refuse to admit the immense increase of human happiness which scientific technique, if wisely used, would make possible. Both these attitudes are to be deplored, and it is philosophy that shows the right attitude, by making clear at once the scope and the limitations of scientific knowledge.

Leaving aside, for the moment, all questions that have to do with ethics or with values, there are a number of purely theoretical questions, of perennial and passionate interest, which science is unable to answer, at any rate at present. Do we survive death in any sense, and if so, do we survive for a time or forever? Can mind dominate matter, or does matter completely dominate mind, or has each, perhaps, a certain limited independence? Has the universe a purpose? Or is it driven by blind necessity? Or is it a mere chaos and jumble, in which the natural laws that we think we find are only a fantasy generated by our own love of order? If there is a cosmic scheme, has life more importance in it than astronomy would lead us to suppose, or is our emphasis upon life mere parochialism and self-importance? I do not know the answer to these questions, and I do not believe that anybody else does, but I think human life would be impoverished if they were forgotten, or if definite answers were accepted without adequate evidence. To keep alive the interest in such questions, and to scrutinize suggested answers, is one of the functions of philosophy.

Those who have a passion for quick returns and for an exact balance sheet of effort and reward may feel impatient of a study which cannot, in the present state of our knowledge, arrive at certainties, and which encourages what may be thought the time-wasting occupation of inconclusive meditation on insoluble problems. To this view I cannot in any degree subscribe. Some kind of philosophy is a necessity to all but the most thoughtless, and in the absence of knowledge it is almost sure to be a silly philosophy. The result of this is that the human race becomes divided into rival groups of fanatics, each group firmly persuaded that its own brand of nonsense is sacred truth, while the other side's is damnable heresy. Arians and Catholics, Crusaders and Moslems, Protestants and adherents of the Pope, Communists and Fascists, have filled large parts of the last 1600 years with futile strife, when a little philosophy would have shown both sides in all these disputes that neither had any good reason to believe itself in the right. Dogmatism is an enemy to peace, and an insuperable barrier to democracy. In the present age, at least as much as in former times, it is the greatest of the mental obstacles to human happiness.

The demand for certainty is one which is natural to man, but is nevertheless an intellectual vice. If you take your children for a picnic on a doubtful day, they will demand a dogmatic answer as to whether it will be fine or wet, and be disappointed in you when you cannot be sure. The same sort of assurance is demanded, in later life, of those who undertake to lead populations into the Promised Land. "Liquidate the capitalists and the survivors will enjoy eternal bliss." "Exterminate the Jews and everyone will be virtuous." "Kill the Croats and let the Serbs reign." "Kill the Serbs and let the Croats reign." These are samples of the slogans that have won wide popular acceptance in our time. Even a modicum of philosophy would make it impossible to accept such bloodthirsty nonsense. But so long as men are not trained to withhold judgment in the absence of evidence, they will be led astray by cocksure prophets, and it is likely that their leaders will be either ignorant fanatics or dishonest charlatans. To endure uncertainty is difficult, but so are most of the other virtues. For the learning of every virtue there is an appropriate discipline, and for the learning of suspended judgment the best discipline is philosophy.

But if philosophy is to serve a positive purpose, it must not teach mere skepticism, for, while the dogmatist is harmful, the skeptic is useless. Dogmatism and skepticism are both, in a sense, absolute philosophies; one is certain of knowing, the other of not knowing. What philosophy should dissipate is *certainty*, whether of knowledge or of ignorance. Knowledge is not so precise a concept as is commonly thought. Instead of saying "I know this," we ought to say "I more or less know something more or less like this." It is true that this proviso is hardly necessary as regards the multiplication table, but knowledge in practical affairs has not the certainty or the precision of arithmetic. Suppose I say "democracy is a good thing": I must admit, first, that I am less sure of this than I am that two and two are four, and secondly, that "democracy" is a somewhat vague term which I cannot define precisely. We ought to say therefore: "I am fairly certain that it is a good thing if a government has something of the characteristics that are common to the British and American constitutions," or something of this sort. And one of the aims of education ought to be to make such a statement more effective from a platform than the usual type of political slogan.

For it is not enough to recognize that all our knowledge is, in a greater or less degree, uncertain and vague; it is necessary, at the same time, to learn to act upon the best hypothesis without dogmatically believing it. To revert to the picnic: even though you admit that it may rain, you start out if you think fine weather probable, but you allow for the opposite possibility by taking mackintoshes. If you were a dogmatist you would leave the mackintoshes at home. The same principles apply to more important issues. One may say broadly: all that passes for knowledge can be arranged in a hierarchy of degrees of certainty, with arithmetic and the facts of perception at the top. That two and two are four, and that I am sitting in my room writing, are statements as to which any serious doubt on my part would be pathological. I am nearly as certain that yesterday was a fine day, but not quite, because memory does sometimes play odd tricks. More distant memories are more doubtful, particularly if there is some strong emotional reason for remembering falsely, such, for instance, as made George IV remember being at the battle of Waterloo. Scientific laws may be very nearly certain, or only slightly probable, according to the state of the evidence.

When you act upon a hypothesis which you know to be uncertain, your action should be such as will not have very harmful results if your hypothesis is false. In the matter of the picnic, you may risk a wetting if all your party are robust, but not if one of them is so delicate as to run a risk of pneumonia. Or suppose you meet a Muggletonian, you will be justified in arguing with him, because not much harm will have been done if Mr. Muggleton was in fact as great a man as his disciples suppose, but you will not be justified in burning him at the stake, because the evil of being burned alive is more certain than any proposition of theology. Of course if the Muggletonians were so numerous and so fanatical that either you or they must be killed the question would grow more difficult, but the general principle remains, that an uncertain hypothesis cannot justify a certain evil unless an equal evil is equally certain on the opposite hypothesis.

II

Philosophy, we said, has both a theoretical and a practical aim. It is now time to consider the latter.

Among most of the philosophers of antiquity there was a close connection between a view of the universe and a doctrine as to the best way of life. Some of them founded fraternities which had a certain resemblance to the monastic orders of later times. Socrates and Plato were shocked by the sophists because they had no religious aims. If philosophy is to play a serious part in the lives of men who are not specialists, it must not cease to advocate some way of life. In doing this it is seeking to do something of what religion has done, but with certain differences. The greatest difference is that there is no appeal to authority, whether that of tradition or that of a sacred book. The second important difference is that a philosopher should not attempt to establish a church; Auguste Comte tried, but failed, as he deserved to do. The third is that more stress should be laid on the intellectual virtues than has been customary since the decay of Hellenic civilization.

There is one important difference between the ethical teachings of ancient philosophers and those appropriate to our own day. The ancient philosophers appealed to gentlemen of leisure, who could live as seemed good to them, and could even, if they chose, found an independent city having laws that embodied the master's doctrines. The immense majority of modern educated men have no such freedom; they have to earn their living within the existing framework of society, and they cannot make important changes in their own way of life unless they can first secure important changes in political and economic organization. The consequence is that a man's ethical convictions have to be expressed more in political advocacy, and less in his private behavior, than was the case in antiquity. And a conception of a good way of life has to be a social rather than an individual conception. Even among the ancients, it was so conceived by Plato in the *Republic*, but many of them had a more individualistic conception of the ends of life.

With this proviso, let us see what philosophy has to say on the subject of ethics.

To begin with the intellectual virtues: The pursuit of philosophy is founded on the belief that knowledge is good, even if what is known is painful. A man imbued with the philosophic spirit, whether a professional philosopher or not, will wish his beliefs to be as true as he can make them, and will, in equal measure, love to know, and hate to be in error. This principle has a wider scope than may be apparent at first sight. Our beliefs spring from a great variety of causes: what we were told in youth by parents and schoolteachers, what powerful organizations tell us in order to make us act as they wish, what either embodies or allays our fears, what ministers to our self-esteem, and so on. Any one of these causes may happen to lead us to true beliefs, but is more likely to lead us in the opposite direction. Intellectual sobriety, therefore, will lead us to scrutinize our beliefs closely, with a view to discovering which of them there is any reason to believe true. If we are wise, we shall apply solvent criticism especially to the beliefs that we find it most painful to doubt, and to those most likely to involve us in violent conflict with men who hold opposite but equally groundless beliefs. If this attitude could become common, the gain in diminishing the acerbity of disputes would be incalculable.

There is another intellectual virtue, which is that of generality or impartiality. I recommend the following exercise: When, in a sentence expressing political opinion, there are words that arouse powerful but different emotions in different readers, try replacing them by symbols, *A*, *B*, *C*, and so on, and forgetting the particular significance of the symbols. Suppose *A* is England, *B* is Germany, and *C* is Russia. As long as you remember what the letters mean, most of the things you will believe will depend upon whether you are English, German or Russian, which is logically irrelevant. When, in elementary algebra, you do problems about *A*, *B*, and *C* going up a mountain, you have no emotional interest in the gentlemen concerned, and you do your best to work out the solution with impersonal correctness. But if you thought that *A* was yourself, *B* your hated rival, and *C* the schoolmaster who set the problem, your calculations would go askew, and you would be sure to find that *A* was first and *C* was last. In thinking about political problems this kind of emotional bias is bound to be present, and only care and practice can enable you to think as objectively as you do in the algebraic problem.

Thinking in abstract terms is of course not the only way to achieve ethical generality; it can be achieved as well, or perhaps even better, if you can feel generalized emotions. But to most people this is difficult. If you are hungry, you will make great exertions, if necessary, to get food; if your children are hungry, you may feel an even greater urgency. If a friend is starving, you will probably exert yourself to relieve his distress. But if you hear that some millions of Indians or Chinese are in danger of death from malnutrition, the problem is so vast and so distant that unless you have some official responsibility you probably soon forget all about it. Nevertheless, if you have the emotional capacity to feel distant evils acutely, you can achieve ethical generality through feeling. If you have not this rather rare gift, the habit of viewing practical problems abstractly as well as concretely is the best available substitute.

The interrelation of logical and emotional generality in ethics is an interesting subject. "Thou shalt love thy neighbor as thyself" inculcates emotional generality; "ethical statements should not contain proper names" inculcates logical generality. The two precepts *sound* very different, but when they are examined it will be found that they are scarcely distinguishable in practical import. Benevolent men will prefer the traditional form; logicians may prefer the other. I hardly know which class of men is the smaller. Either form of statement, if accepted by statesmen and tolerated by the populations whom they represent, would quickly lead to the millennium. Jews and Arabs would come together and say "Let us see how to get the greatest amount of good for both together, without inquiring too closely how it is distributed among us." Obviously each group would get far more of what makes for the happiness of both than either can at present. The same would be true of Hindus and Moslems, Chinese Communists and adherents of Chiang Kai-shek, Italians and Yugoslavs, Russians and Western democrats. But alas! neither logic nor benevolence is to be expected on either side in any of these disputes.

III

It is not to be supposed that young men and women who are busy acquiring valuable specialized knowledge can spare a great deal of time for the study of philosophy, but even in the time that can easily be spared without injury to the learning of technical skills, philosophy can give certain things that will greatly increase the student's value as a human being and as a citizen. It can give a habit of exact and careful thought, not only in mathematics and science, but in questions of large practical import. It can give an impersonal breadth and scope to the conception of the ends of life. It can give to the individual a just measure of himself in relation to society, of man in the present to man in the past and in the future, and of the whole history of man in relation to the astronomical cosmos. By enlarging the objects of his thoughts it supplies an antidote to the anxieties and anguish of the present, and makes possible the nearest approach to serenity that is available to a sensitive mind in our tortured and uncertain world.

Charles Morris

An able contemporary philosopher, Charles Morris has made distinguished contributions to three related but rather different areas. In the field of philosophy proper his books Six Theories of Mind *(1932) and* Signs, Language and Behavior *(1946) are well known. Likewise, he has given as much direct attention perhaps as any other living philosopher to the problem of values in contemporary life. His books,* Paths of Life *(1942) and* The Open Self *(1948), present in popular fashion for the intelligent layman, perplexed by the conflicts and confusion of our age, clear and helpful suggestions about human nature and the good life. More directly than any other writer in this field, however, Morris has based these suggestions on careful scientific and empirical investigation. His* Varieties of Human Value *(1956) contains the details of this extensive study.*

Born in Denver, Colorado, in 1901, Professor Morris was educated at the University of Wisconsin, Northwestern University, and the University of Chicago, receiving his Ph.D. from Chicago in 1925. He has taught philosophy at Rice, the University of Chicago, and Harvard, and in 1958 was appointed Research Professor of Philosophy at the University of Florida. In recognition of his achievements, he has been made a Fellow of the American Academy of Arts and Sciences and The American Association for the Advancement of Science. He was awarded a Guggenheim fellowship in 1942 and a Rockefeller fellowship in 1943 to enable him to carry on his research in the area of human values, and in 1956-1957 spent a year as a Fellow at the Center for Advanced Study in the Behavioral Sciences in California. He is on the board of editors of Philosophy East and West, *and is an editor of the* International Encyclopedia of Unified Sciences *and of George H. Mead's* Mind, Self and Society *and* The Philosophy of the Act.

Professor Morris combines a scientific and theoretical interest in language, signs, and symbols, of the sort that produced Susanne Langer's Philosophy in a New Key, *with a concern for the more popular presentation of human values such as that in* The Open Self, *from which our selection is taken. In this work he deals directly with those aspects of contemporary life and thought which we have discussed in this anthology, and he undertakes with unusual insight and success to combine the best achievements of scientific thought with high human ideals in a realistic philosophy for an age such as ours.*

MAN AS HIS OWN MAKER

IT IS halfway between midnight and dawn. The last two lighted windows on the street have just been darkened. The last pair of laughing celebrants has passed by to silence. And I begin a book.

Morning was to be the time of beginning. But the words started to say themselves, and they would not remain pillowed. So I write in a little room in this city where Whitman and Melville wrote of the colors and the shadows of this America, beginning a book halfway between midnight and dawn.

New York City. Early autumn. 3 A.M. Musing three remarks. One from a man of wealth with a New York City home and a Long Island estate. He has played the praised and accepted game of power and has won its rewards. But he said a few days ago, "If I were God I would put my thumb down on this city and wipe it out!" And as he spoke he pressed his thumb on the mahogany table top and twisted it around as if annihilating an insect.

A smartly dressed girl, fresh from sailing on the Sound, spoke in a more current idiom: "I would like to ride in the plane that would atom-bomb Western culture."

The third remark completes the triangle. At his desk in a Fifth Avenue office the head of one of the many foundations in this region ended the late afternoon with this question: "How can we keep America young?" And the intentness of his voice underlined the fact that his words, though in the form of a question, uttered a deep but anxious hope.

Too much is not to be made of these three remarks. New Yorkers, like other people, seldom talk this way. A word count on the subway or Times Square or any beach would show that such extreme language is "statistically infrequent." And all persons at times overtalk, magnifying a personal dilemma into the Last Age of Man and the élan of a drink into the onset of an Utterly New World. Those who like semantic cleanliness believe in neither.

Nevertheless, as symptoms, these three remarks are revealing. They match in a homely way the fear of H. G. Wells, expressed in his last work, *Mind at the End of Its Tether*, that there is no hope for modern man—an "Implacable Opponent" is stamping him out. They project on a small screen the strange mixture of midnight and dawn which constitutes contemporary men and women. They exaggerate for illustration the unspoken current of dissatisfaction which lies beneath the polite surfaces of many lives today. They disclose the unrecognized wish for annihilation which at times secretly welcomes current possibilities of destruction. They reveal an uneasy confession that modern man somehow must make of himself a new man fit for a new age—lest he in truth prove obsolete.

It is such thoughts that chose this hour to begin this book. Thoughts about the night forces which work in everyone and in every society. Forces which unceasingly threaten each person and each society with frustration, closure, sterility, destruction. Forces which have made it possible today for one person out of ten to be in danger of serious personality derangements sometime in his or her life, and for many more than one person out of ten to be anxious, discontented, stalemated, uncreative. Forces which have raised concern whether America is losing its vitality, becoming Old America in a new world. Forces which have made serious persons wonder whether Western civilization as a whole is not bent on its own self-destruction.

It is good at night to recognize these black powers. It is good before dawn to recognize that they alone do not have complete dominion over man. For man is the being that continually remakes himself, the selfmaker, the artisan that is himself the material for his own creation. This frontier of life-making is the one frontier at which man always stands; the human frontier, the frontier of man's next making of himself.

To live is to stand before alternatives. Man now stands before large alternatives. He endures early stages of a new epoch. Never before has he had to act with the problems of the earth as a whole pressing so insistently upon him. Never before has he had such vast powers over man and nature under his control. Never before has he been confronted with so momentous a choice between massed slavery and unplumbed freedom. It is no wonder that he is hesitant, confused, afraid, awkward. It is no wonder that he seeks for ideas and ideals to direct him in his gropings on today's frontier.

New Selves for Old

Our crisis is a strange one. We are as children playing with high explosives. And we know this. But since we know it we are unlike children. We are afraid of ourselves, afraid that we will be inadequate, afraid to assume the responsibilities that might give us back the joy of innocence. If an "implacable opponent" is destroying man, that opponent is man himself. We sense acutely the dark powers in ourselves.

We are equally aware that we have great reserves of inner strength. The feeling that a new age is beginning is as insistent as the realization that an old one ends. We have already called it the atomic age. But we do not yet know how to unlock our human resources. We have not yet devised a psychological bomb more powerful than the atomic bomb. We can release gigantic physical power by atomic fission. How can we produce a fission within the locked forces of ourselves that will release correspondingly great human power?

This is our problem. We have new engines, new fabrics, new buildings, new headaches. *We need new selves. And new relationships between selves.* We must bring ourselves up to date. We can subordinate impersonal forces to human ends only if we recover the standpoint of the personal. We must become person-centered in order to construct a person-centered society. Men and women must again become the focus of our attention and our concern. We have made over the material environment, and now we cannot evade remaking ourselves. If the bogeyman gets us, it will be our own fault, for the bogeyman is in us. Our crisis is a human crisis.

To shock ourselves into creativity we must know ourselves. We need to know the sources of our motivations and our frustrations. We need to know the techniques of self-making, and its pitfalls. Contemporary students of man have much to tell us about ourselves. We shall endeavor to tap this knowledge for our purposes, even to add to it. But our purpose remains personal. Our task is to decide what we want to do with our lives while we still have them. Our hope is to unlock energies in ourselves sufficient to blast apart our stalemates and our frustrations. "The experience of each new age requires a new confession." We must dare this new confession. "Safer the center of peril," Melville tells us, "than the circumference."

What is man now to make of man? What are we going to make of ourselves? Such is our theme and our problem.

But these are dawn words that set work for the day.

Stocktaking

Fortunately the day is sober. A proper day to think about ourselves. It occasions neither the somber moodiness of rain nor the outgoing praisefulness of the sun. It is a sturdy day for honest thought. The night is too large and the dawn too expectant for the hard work that must be done. The most difficult task we face is to be honest about ourselves, honest with ourselves. It is easier for man to praise himself than to condemn himself, and easier for him to condemn himself than to know himself. A sober day makes for honest thought.

In this mood we at once find ourselves in doubt concerning the night's delivery that man is the maker of himself.

Man makes many things, to be sure, but does he really make himself? Did we not give the case away when we said that a sober day makes for honest thought? For this suggests that our thoughts are influenced even by the physical environment. And this doubt which our own words awaken is reinforced by doctrines widely current among us, doctrines that our physiques determine what we are, or that the society in which we live molds us into the personalities which we are. Environment, physique, society—are not these the clothes which make the man?

They are indeed mighty agencies. And the doctrines which celebrate their might have almost become the major dogmas of our time. It is not dogma to recognize that the human personality has as its core a biological organism whose growth and fruition takes place only within a society inhabiting a physical environment. It is not dogma to recognize that the human personality carries with it into every future its entire past. The emerging science of man has established these matters beyond legitimate doubt. The recognition of the role of physical environment, physique, and society in the making of man becomes questionable only when their power is made all-inclusive, when they are used to deny that man is unique among all living beings in the degree to which he makes himself and his history.

It is obvious enough that man has greatly modified his physical environment, controlling temperature and humidity in his homes, planting crops and raising cattle, closing and opening the access of the seas and rivers to chosen spots of land. It is less obvious but no less true that man has worked on his body and will in the future work much more. In his capacity as physician he doctors himself into something at least a little different from what he otherwise would have been; his choice of mates determines to some degree the kinds of bodies future men and women will have; he can, if he wishes, consciously select and breed the persons who are to inhabit the earth. And, finally, it is now recognized by some anthropologists that man himself has built through his own choices the various patterns of channeled activity which are the cultures. The cultures of the world are human creations, patterns for living together which persons have constructed, and will continue to construct in unforeseeable ways. Geography, heredity, society set the conditions for human creativity, supply it with the materials upon which it must work, hinder it or enhance it. But to admit that life-making works always within specific conditions cannot be twisted into a denial that man is a major agency in the making of himself.

At this point sober reflection becomes uneasy at so much talk of man. Instead of discourse about man it suggests that we talk of individual men and women, and justly. For it is individual men and women, each unique, each different, who are making their lives. And the history of man is the history of their many specific and diverse careers. In this history different individuals play different roles of hero, villain, minor character, chorus. The richness of the human play resides in this multiplicity of different players. We are only now beginning to see how different various persons really are. To understand these differences will be one of our central tasks. Here merely the fact of difference is underscored, and its importance. For it allows us to recognize that self-making is a matter of degree. There are persons who flow along through life like a river in a meadow, following effortlessly the contours and the channels marked out by the things and people in the social countryside. There are other persons whose lives resemble a rushing waterfall which breaks barriers and carves into new forms the mountain of social history. It is only a few individuals who affect in a momentous manner the course of mankind. Most persons play a humbler role, adopting the ideas, the inventions, the manners of life which others have constructed. Yet the difference remains one of degree, for even to adopt as one's own something built by others is to choose to admit it into one's self; and such admission involves at least some minimum of scrutiny and appraisal, some element, in short, of the self determining what it is to be. Without such acceptance the innovations of those who have more largely made themselves remain only personal achievements. The history of mankind is a history of all men's self-makings, small and great.

The day's sober thoughts impose a third caution. Is not "making" too strong a word and too strenuous a theme? Does it not suggest that all men and women are or should be athletic mountain climbers, continually daring strenuous ascents of the self's Himalayas, extroverted and restless doers? If it does, this suggestion should immediately be erased. For a life with such emphasis is inappropriate for many persons, inappropriate and frustrating. The ways of self-making must be many to answer to human differences. We must champion the right to be different. The current stress in our culture on power has, for instance, devastating effects on many individuals; it destroys their confidence in themselves, and drives them in large numbers through the gates of our asylums. To the list of the many kinds of minorities which we must protect, we need to add a new item: the protection of psychological minorities.

The ways of self-making must be many if human potentialities and human differences are to be respected. There are demands in the self for receptivity and enjoyment, for affection and support, for meditation and truth seeking, for dependence and for detachment, as well as for power and domination. These demands differ in their strength in individuals and all are legitimate. Our theme is the technique of self-making, to be sure, but the stress is on its varieties. In the matter of life-making each of us must remain faithful to our needs and our resources. We wish, in the words of Louis MacNiece, a world of persons "equal in difference, interchangeably sovereign."

With these daytime restrictions and amplifications, the doctrine that man is uniquely the maker of himself loses the grandiose character which the meditations of large night imposed. But not its grandeur. Men live in a physical world mightier than themselves and in societies that channel and transform in various ways their biological urgencies. The artisan must always work where he is and on the materials at hand. These materials are obdurate and set conditions which his work must respect. Not everything can be made with all materials, and what can be made takes skill and time. Creation is nowhere unconditioned. And it does not always reach fruition. The artisan may bungle, may turn in rage against the obdurate stuff on which he works.

Evasion of Responsibility: Irrationalism

Men make themselves by their thoughts—by their ideas and their ideals. Men choose their future insofar as they think. And in no other way.

An idea is something signified. An ideal is something that when signified is found so attractive that one is lured to its attainment. Because men could talk about the earth and about round things, they could talk about the earth as round. When this idea of a round earth had appeared, and was believed, the possibility of sailing around the earth could be entertained. And when this possibility acted as a lure to the urgencies for wealth and power and adventure, the idea of circumnavigating the globe had become an ideal.

The essential moments in the career of man-making are the moments when new ideas and new ideals appear. For these are the moments when the stream of human life takes a fresh direction. The construction of basic ideas marks the turning points of science and philosophy, and the framing of ideals around such ideas marks the creative heights of religion, art, and social organization.

We talk ourselves into new ideas and ideals. The child walks before it talks. In choosing our future selves we must talk before we walk. But talk is cheap and walking in new directions is a hard responsibility. So we talk ourselves out of the burden which ideals impose. There are three Big Words by which modern men and women attempt to evade the responsibility for doing anything drastic about themselves: Irrationalism, Determinism, Sin. We are irrational creatures; we have no freedom; we are sinful—these are the favored masks of our irresponsibility. Half-true talk that needs unmasking, lest it cut the slender nerve of human resolution.

The half-truth of irrationalism protects us against a distorted and sentimental view of rationality, and it is well that it has been stated so vigorously and so often in the last decades. One half of this half-truth is the affirmation of the existence and the importance of non-rational factors in the make-up of the human self—the menagerie of drives, passions, hates, joys, hopes, insights, and anxieties which we are.

To be rational is simply to accept ideas and ideals after critical reflection, after a careful consideration of what would follow from the acceptance of a given idea or ideal. A rational person is a reasoning person, one who advances by pushing out before him the antennas of signs, exploring the terrain of self and surrounding world before committing himself on how to act or how henceforth to be. To renounce rationality in the sense of reasoning is to renounce the making of oneself, to reject one's humanness.

It does not follow that a rational person is or should be always reasoning. For it is the urgency of life in some precarious situation that motivates thinking, controls it, terminates it. To attempt to think endlessly would be to end oneself and thinking. Thought is an agency in the construction of life, and life is lived in an insistent present. Ideas are teased into being in strange and devious ways, by relaxation and receptivity as often as by athletic inference. Once in being they may be elaborated, brought into relation with other ideas, their consequences traced, the evidence for their truth scrutinized. But the pressure of a present urgency always motivates and terminates this process. Even as thinker the self must continually accept or reject the ideas it entertains, favoring one to another, committing itself to belief on the basis of a given amount of evidence. It is the whole self that thinks, and the problems of the self are temporal and not timeless. Decisions must be made or thinking itself becomes vacuous, without eventuation, uneventful.

Ideals differ from ideas precisely in the fact that we now prefer what is signified. This increment of preference stems from the urgencies of the self as it is at the moment. The act of acceptance of one ideal rather than another may be for a while delayed. The presumed consequences for oneself and for other selves may be considered. The self may stall, hesitate, vacillate. But its urgencies are insistent, and it must extend the hand of acceptance to one possible alternative rather than to others. Reasoning airs preferences, holds before the self alternative possibilities of liking and disliking, and in the process the self transforms itself and its allegiances. Even Aristotle admitted that the good is what is *preferred* after deliberation. *The act of preference remains, and to prefer is more than to reason.* To live is to be for some things and against others. Neutrality is a moment in which preferences are being formed. The only persistently neutral self is a dead self.

The other half of the half-truth of irrationalism is the recognition that there are genuinely antirational forces in the self, forces which actively oppose the self's deliberate reconstruction of itself. It is to the interest of the self at certain stages of its development to protect what it has so far attained, and to hide from itself forces which it does not yet feel strong enough to handle. The person who has been able to build some fair picture of himself hugs this fair image. He is loath to admit in himself desires and thoughts and actions which would jar with this bright vision. Evidence which attests these dark colors in himself is ignored, glossed over, minimized; to admit such evidence would be to jeopardize the self-esteem he has precariously attained, to awaken the anxieties he has appeased. Contrariwise, any evidence that confirms his high opinion of himself is eagerly accepted, exhibited, maximized. In this way he can attribute to himself the traits he wishes to have and believes himself to have. The traits in himself which he rejects he attributes to other persons, and the difficulties he encounters he blames on others, and on "the world." So does the self protect itself against the thrust of more truthful ideas, and against the unsettling challenge of the ideal's enlargement and reconstruction.

This process is an intensely active process. And it occurs in everyone. In the insane we merely meet it in its extreme forms. It is wisdom to recognize the presence and power of the forces by which the self actively opposes its own further development. For then we are protected against both the facile optimism that it is easy to think straight and the despair which comes when to think straight is found to be difficult.

In its recognition of nonrational factors in the self and the antirational factors which hinder the reformation of the self, irrationalism is on safe ground, and a friend. It is an error and a danger when it becomes the cult of irrationality.

Evasion of Responsibility: Determinism

The second Big Word by which the self attempts to evade responsibility is Determinism. The reasoning appropriate to our age goes by the name of science. It is an ironic commentary on the state of our confusion that science, the major instrument of human freedom, should so often be feared as an enemy of this very freedom. Science, the theme runs, is deterministic, and determinism means that man has no say as to what will occur. This is a comfortable half-truth, for it relieves us of the difficult task of choice. Such determinism is in fact a form of antirationalism, a device by which reason tries to prevent the extension of reasoning to the dusty corners of the self and society. It is a seductive hide-out of verbal uncleanliness which at once allows us to glory in our dirtiness and to do nothing about it. It is fear that motivates the cult of determinism, not science.

For science is simply a stubborn and resolute search for reliable knowledge. It is an instrument which men have built against great resistance and through incredible labor for the liberation of ideas and for their certification. It is a superb illustration of the extent to which man does make himself. For the scientist is the specialist in knowing, one kind of self that man has made of himself, not the only kind or the only good kind, but an important and unique achievement. For if ideals are ideas clothed with preference, then it is of the greatest importance to have a technique that favors the emergence of new ideas and is able to sort out the more reliable ideas from the less reliable ones. Science is this technique. To oppose science in the name of ideals is in fact to oppose the main human activity by which old ideals are inspected and the basis for new ideals is laid. Such opposition rests on the fear of science; it is supported by anxious selves unsure at heart of what they claim to uphold. The argument that science is hostile to human freedom and dignity because it is deterministic cannot stand up under inquiry. It is not supported by science nor by valid argument. It is a confusion nourished by fear.

Science does not eventuate in determinism. The half-truth of the cult of determinism is that science is mechanistic in the harmless sense that it seeks for mechanisms. It is concerned with the conditions under which something is what it is. Its laws when carefully analyzed always state that if something is so, then something else will be so with such and such probability. If phosphorus exists in dry air, then it is highly likely that it will burst into flame; if a body is raised above the ground and support taken from under it, then it is highly likely that it will fall to the earth in a specifiable time. Science does not say that under these conditions the flame or the fall "must" occur, since its statements are qualified in terms of the evidence which supports them. And more important, science does not say that any given set of initial conditions must occur, but only if they do what else is likely to happen. Men may see to it that phosphorus is kept in water, and that the raised body is given wings and motor so that it will fly. Knowledge of the mechanisms of phosphorus and falling bodies were means by which men learned more about the control of fire and about what they must do if they wished to fly.

Each scientific statement is simply one more factor entering into the process of self-making. But a very important factor. For a scientific statement is a reliable sign, a reliable idea. And without reliable signs we cannot predict, and if we cannot predict we cannot plan. In an utterly chaotic world we would have no leverage for the construction of our lives. We would simply be part of the chaos. Only if we can know what is likely to occur under what conditions are we in a position to attempt to control these conditions or control our attitudes to what will appear in case the conditions are beyond our control. It is the task of science —the sole task of science—to give us reliable knowledge. That is the contribution of science to our freedom. We are free only to the extent that we can find stabilities, and science is the instrument we have built to find such stabilities. The more it can succeed, the better it is for our freedom. We expect science to tell us the details of our purposive behavior, even the conditions of our freedom. For if we wish to enhance our freedom we must know how and when freedom appears, what favors its extension, what thwarts its increase.

This is to say that even in the knowledge of ourselves the indefinite extension of science is not only to be welcomed, but is necessary. The age of man needs a science of man. Such a science is under way. Studies of persons' physical constitutions, the dynamics of their goal-seeking, the role that societies play in molding their characters, the impact of other specific individuals on their development, the way signs operate in their lives:—these studies are not only under way but are converging toward a genuine science of man. And this knowledge is becoming a powerful instrument which persons can use in their own development. By knowing about themselves men and women will increase their freedom.

The self can fly only if it knows the conditions of psychological gravitation under which it tends to fall. To fly well requires reliable instruments of navigation. The science of man must provide such instruments for flight in the celestial regions of modern selfhood.

But as in the case of all scientific statements, the statements of a scientific psychology will be merely additional factors to be used in the construction of our lives. In this construction the focus must of necessity be personal, for it is one's own unique self that one is forming. One must of necessity listen to one's urges, probe the various possibilities of advance, meditate, choose, reject. We must and can use all the knowledge of the material upon which we work—our own selves—that we can get. *Scientific knowledge is not determinism but a lever for freedom's grip.* A science of man is not man, but one more tool for the making of men. As scientists our question is: "What am I entitled to believe?" As persons our problem is: "What do I choose to become?"

Evasion of Responsibility: Sin

At this point, as the defenses of our irresponsibility threaten to collapse, we may succumb to the current temptation to fall back upon a far older defense: our sinfulness. We are evil. Irredeemably petty, inadequate, shortsighted, inconsiderate, cruel, corrupt, and selfish. We are nauseated at ourselves. We want to be saved somehow by somebody. But we cannot do the job ourselves. We are lost in sin. No exit. We are just too bad.

This way of talking to ourselves has a hard core of truth. Sin is indeed a Big Word. On all of us some of the time, and on a lot of us a lot of the time, the list of adjectives from "petty" straight through to "selfish" fits like a glove. To recognize this is to penetrate the hard crust of our pretences, to admit our need of help, to become humble about our attainments, to gain the insight that we continually stand in the way of our own advance. In this there is sanity and wisdom. For life continually tends to stagnation, acquiescence, complacency. The pride in achievement blocks greater achievement. What we have produced in our activities may threaten even our continued existence. This is why we have sanitation systems and fire departments and wrecking crews. That is why we change the water in the goldfish bowl.

But beyond this the doctrine of sinfulness becomes evasive strategy. Why do we take such delight in talking in its terms to ourselves about ourselves? When we luxuriate in the words of sinfulness are we not pretending to be bigger than we really are—to be big at least in evil? Most of our evils are so small they are not worth recording; few of us are as big in badness as we pretend to be. Is not this reiterative talk of our sinfulness itself a sin? For it allows us to indulge our vices on the ground that we are too sinful to correct them. Many a self has smacked its lips in professing nausea at its rottenness. The doctrine of the depravity of man is strategy for the evasion of responsibility.

Nothing is good or bad in itself. To call something good or bad is to view it as satisfying or frustrating some unquestioned urgency or some accepted ideal. The swoop of the bird that catches a fish is good for the bird and bad for the fish. The sexual drive that is repudiated by the ascetic is the welcome agency by which lovers may know joy. The house that is just right for a small family becomes cramping as the family grows. Man is sinful only to the degree that what he does prevents him from becoming what he would like to be. Urgencies are not sinful in themselves but in relation to other urgencies.

But this is not the whole of our worries. For any urgency that has become an accepted ideal encounters obstacles, obstacles in the world and obstacles in the self. These obstacles are the dark powers, the forces of evil. Since they exist in relation to an ideal, they will always exist as long as there are ideals. The fight for the actualization of the ideal is a real fight, and with no final round.

Return to Responsibility

The danger of America is not senility but sterility. Our dilemma lies not in a paucity of human resources but in our failure to use courageously our variegated human abundance. It is not our tradition which has failed us but the betrayers and plunderers of our tradition. The issue we need to fear is that of leaving unachieved what we have so proudly and so greatly begun.

It is not that the whole future of mankind depends on us. We are big—but so were the dinosaurs. Arnold Toynbee, in *A Study of History*, has filled his pages with examples of great cultures that have spent themselves in a creative act, failed to arise in a new crisis to new creation, and destroyed themselves through their inflexible possessiveness. It is of course possible that we, as the spearhead of Western man's adventure, have reached the limit of our thrust. Perhaps the West of which we are a part has so specialized itself on power that it will destroy itself by the power it has produced but cannot control. If so we will join the museum of cultural dinosaurs. This would not be the end of man. The Orient is again prophetic, and might well draw back into its diversified human basin the power techniques gained by a West that humanly failed. There are still many cards in mankind's deck, and we of the West do not hold all the aces.

But it is premature to celebrate our own death. That is not an American custom. We are much more responsive to the warrior words: "We haven't begun to fight!" If we have reared a power technology, we have also sung the new songs of man with nimble center, circumference elastic, and of a society open to all selves. We have not talked power alone, and our anxiety in the face of wealth and social status is evidence that there is more to us than we have privately admitted. Perhaps we have not yet had time to harness our physical power to our human ideal. Perhaps if we shake ourselves out of our coma we will find that we still command the nerve, the verve, the courage, and the inventiveness to carry through what we as a nation have begun.

The new American frontier is human rather than geographical. It lies wherever an American meets another person, young or old, white or yellow or brown or black, inside our borders or beyond them. Pioneering on the domestic frontier and on the international frontier are now inextricably linked. To lose either campaign is to lose them both. We cannot stand before the world as the champion of freedom and slay it at home. We cannot renounce domestic social reconstruction without undermining our efforts to aid other cultures in their own forms of advance.

The new American frontier marks our responsibility and our opportunity. On the domestic frontier our responsibility is to oppose every force which makes for the closed society and to create with fresh inventiveness the cultural conditions which sustain and extend the open self. Our most urgent necessity is to distinguish between the social agencies necessary to further the liberation of individuals and those which in the name of freedom lead to impoverishment of individuality. Both will invoke democratic slogans, but one will encourage and the other obstruct the growth of persons. To keep free the agencies of mass communication so that free trade in ideas is possible, to control food so that hunger cannot be made a political weapon—regulations of this sort are agencies of a person-centered society just as their opposites are agencies of a person-exploitative society. Only foresight, inventiveness, action can keep our society open. Each of our major institutions—business, labor, the farmers, the schools, the churches, and the government—must assume responsibility for such foresight, inventiveness, and action. Those who today fail to see this point or refuse to see it, or label as un-American those who do see it, stab the American tradition in its heart—even though they punctuate every sentence they utter with the words "democracy" and "liberty."

On the international frontier problems of population, the world food supply, health, the development of backward areas of the earth demand, and are leading to, the invention of new international agencies. It is possible for different cultures to keep their uniqueness and yet to cooperate on their common problems. A diversified mankind can find unity in the integration and the celebration of its cultural differences. Men will yet live at home and be citizens of the earth.

At the present threshold of the new epoch, the prevention of total war is the central problem. Modern scientific war has become too humanly destructive to be tolerated. For those who choose fighting for its own sake we might set aside annually a large region for an annual war—a real war, to the death! But for modern man in general, modern war is a cancerous growth which saps the blood of free men and free societies.

Einstein and his fellow-scientists have banded together to warn us that modern warfare is fatal to modern culture, and the military men acknowledge this truth. General Dwight D. Eisenhower's words should be emphatic enough: "The governments of the world will find some way to substitute the council table for the battlefield or within the measurable future civilization as we know it will cease to exist." Hysteria, self-righteousness, and calling names will not save us. Nor the atom bomb. Nor the enjoyment of the bees and butterflies of our individual selves. *Our social inventiveness must embrace and outpace our physical inventions.* If it does not, the people of other continents may still have a chance to do better.

Summons to Create!

If we can with courage and inventiveness break the crust of our anxious stalemate by a bold reconstruction of our individual selves and by a bold attack on our national problems we can be to the world an example of the open society at work. If we support the forces which make for openness in other cultures, they will in their own ways rally to openness. If we overcome the fear of being our larger selves we shall have nothing to fear from others. Cold, hungry, anxious persons inevitably prefer economic security to psychological freedom. If we show men and women by our example and by our help that they need not make this choice, that they can have—increasingly—both security and freedom, and in their own ways, they will choose inevitably to have both. No nation will long be able to keep this double abundance from its people if they know that it can be theirs. Do we Americans mean what we have said we meant? Do we dare to be as forward-looking as we have said we are? Are we big in creativity—or only a dinosaur? Not human history, but the next decades of human history depend on our action's answer.

An exciting unplumbed epoch opens before us. Our inventors and scientists and philosophers and prophets have not let us down. The technology which we have humanly mishandled can serve human ends. The science of man can give us the knowledge of ourselves which we need to build ourselves. We are equipped with the instruments to enter upon the epoch of deliberate man-making. We have individually our own personal ideal of open selfhood. We have in common the social ideal of an open society. Our task is not to predict the future of mankind but to join in making it.

The New Integrity

We are in the early stages of a new epoch. That epoch needs time to unfold. It will take forms we cannot envisage. New selves are needed, selves adequate to endure and to form this epoch. It is our responsibility to become such persons. For our own sake and for the sake of mankind.

It is a time of peril. We are in danger of stalemate, in danger of failing to carry through what we have begun, in danger of selling out. We as individuals are the center of peril. The dark powers of the night are in ourselves. But also in ourselves are the powers that can carry us into the dawn.

We will regain integrity. We will blast apart our stalemate. We will use our scientists. We will use our artists and our prophets. We will think in terms of the whole earth. We will reform our ideals. We will resume the responsibility for man-making. We will not sell out. We will carry through what we have begun.

This is the new confession we dare to make.

3

THE POINT OF VIEW OF RELIGION

Albert Schweitzer

Recognized as one of the great moral leaders of our age, Albert Schweitzer (1875-) has had distinguished careers in three different fields. Although as a young man Schweitzer was already well known as an authority on Bach and an accomplished musician, his major interest at that time lay in theology and New Testament criticism. Appointed in 1902 to the Theological Faculty at the University of Strasbourg, he published two highly controversial volumes that put him in the forefront of New Testament scholarship: The Quest of the Historical Jesus *(1902) and* The Mysticism of Paul the Apostle *(1930). During the same period he published an interesting essay on* The Art of Organ Building and Organ Playing *(1906) and an authoritative study of Bach (1908).*

At the age of thirty, after many years of soul searching, Schweitzer decided to give up his position at Strasbourg in order to work in Equatorial Africa as a missionary doctor. Despite understandable expostulations from his European friends and colleagues, he went through an arduous period of medical study only to find that the Paris Missionary Society, whose appeal for assistance in its Congo Mission had led him to make his final decision, would not accept him because of his very liberal theological views. After raising the necessary money himself to finance a hospital in the African jungle and promising that he would work only as a doctor and do no preaching or religious teaching at all, Schweitzer was finally able to persuade the Missionary Society to allow him to establish the hospital at Lambaréné in French Equatorial Africa in 1913.

In several widely read books he has described the almost incredible difficulties he faced in operating this hospital. On the Edge of the Primeval Forest *(1921) was written to help finance his return to Africa after World War I had temporarily forced him to give up his work there. At the same time he lectured at major universities in Continental Europe and Great Britain to raise additional funds. During later trips to Europe and America his work was everywhere acclaimed and he was given honorary degrees by almost all the great universities. Schweitzer's influence in the field of philosophy rests largely upon* Civilization and Ethics *(1923), the book in which he develops his ethical theory of "reverence for life." His* Indian Thought and Its Development *(1934) is also well known. But his most popular book today is the autobiographical volume* Out of My Life and Thought *(1933, 1949), from which we reprint the Epilogue. It is of particular interest to find a man with Schweitzer's deep religious commitment defending here in such vigorous fashion the reasonableness of Christian faith and rejecting so uncompromisingly the anti-intellectualism of our day.*

OUT OF MY LIFE AND THOUGHT

TWO PERCEPTIONS cast their shadows over my existence. One consists in my realization that the world is inexplicably mysterious and full of suffering; the other in the fact that I have been born into a period of spiritual decadence in mankind. I have become familiar with and ready to deal with each, through the thinking which has led me to the ethical and affirmative position of Reverence for Life. In that principle my life has found a firm footing and a clear path to follow.

I therefore stand and work in the world as one who aims at making men less shallow and morally better by making them think.

With the spirit of the age I am in complete disagreement, because it is filled with disdain for thinking. That such is its attitude is, to some extent, to be explained by the fact that thought has never yet reached the goal which it must set before itself. Time after time it was convinced that it had clearly established an attitude toward life which was in accordance with knowledge and ethically satisfactory. But time after time the truth came out that it had not succeeded.

Doubts, therefore, could well arise as to whether thinking would ever be capable of answering current questions about the world and our relation to it in such a way that we could give a meaning and a content to our lives.

But today in addition to that neglect of thought there is also prevalent a mistrust of it. The organized political, social, and religious associations of our time are at work to induce the individual man not to arrive at his convictions by his own thinking but to make his own such convictions as they keep ready-made for him. Any man who thinks for himself and at the same time is spiritually free is to them something inconvenient and even uncanny. He does not offer sufficient guarantee that he will merge himself in their organization in the way they wish. All corporate bodies look today for their strength not so much to the spiritual worth of the ideas which they represent and to that of the people who belong to them, as to the attainment of the highest possible degree of unity and exclusiveness. It is in this that they expect to find their strongest power for offense and defense.

Hence the spirit of the age rejoices, instead of lamenting, that thinking seems to be unequal to its task, and gives it no credit for what, in spite of imperfections, it has already accomplished. It refuses to admit, what is nevertheless the fact, that all spiritual progress up to today has come about through the achievement of thought, or to reflect that thinking may still be able in the future to accomplish what it has not succeeded in accomplishing as yet. Of such considerations the spirit of the age takes no account. Its only concern is to discredit individual thinking in every possible way, and it deals with that on the lines of the saying: "Whosoever hath not, from him shall be taken away even that which he hath."

Thus, his whole life long, the man of today is exposed to influences which are bent on robbing him of all confidence in his own thinking. The spirit of spiritual dependence to which he is called on to surrender is in everything that he hears or reads; it is in the people whom he meets every day; it is in the parties and associations which have claimed him as their own; it pervades all the circumstances of his life.

From every side and in the most varied ways it is dinned into him that the truths and convictions which he needs for life must be taken by him from the associations which have rights over him. The spirit of the age never lets him come to himself. Over and over again convictions are forced upon him in the same way as, by means of the electric advertisements which flare in the streets of every large town, any company which has sufficient capital to get itself securely established, exercises pressure on him at every step he takes to induce him to buy their boot polish or their soup tablets.

By the spirit of the age, then, the man of today is forced into skepticism about his own thinking, in order to make him receptive to truth which comes to him from authority. To all this constant influence he cannot make the resistance that is desirable because he is an overworked and distracted being without power to concentrate. Moreover, the manifold material trammels which are his lot work upon his mentality in such a way that he comes at last to believe himself unqualified even to make any claim to thoughts of his own.

His self-confidence is also diminished through the pressure exercised upon him by the huge and daily increasing mass of knowledge. He is no longer in a position to take in as something which he has grasped all the new discoveries that are constantly announced; he has to accept them as fact although he does not understand them. This being his relation to scientific truth he is tempted to acquiesce in the idea that in matter of thought also his judgment cannot be trusted.

Thus do the circumstances of the age do their best to deliver us up to the spirit of the age.

The seed of skepticism has germinated. In fact, the modern man has no longer any spiritual self-confidence at all. Behind a self-confident exterior he conceals a great inward lack of confidence. In spite of his great capacity in material matters he is an altogether stunted being, because he makes no use of his capacity for thinking. It will ever remain incomprehensible that our generation, which has shown itself so great by its achievements in discovery and invention, could fall so low spiritually as to give up thinking.

I

In a period which regards as absurd and little worth, as antiquated and long ago left far behind, whatever it feels to be in any way akin to rationalism or free thought, and which even mocks at the vindication of unalienable human rights which was secured in the eighteenth century, I acknowledge myself to be one who places all his confidence in rational thinking. I venture to say to our generation that it must not think it has done with rationalism because the rationalism of the past had to give first place to romanticism, and then to a *Realpolitik* which is coming to dominate the spiritual sphere as well as the material. When it has run the gauntlet of the follies of this universal *Realpolitik* and has thereby got itself into deeper and deeper misery, both spiritual and material, it will discover at last that there is nothing for it to do but trust itself to a new rationalism, deeper and more efficient than the old, and in that seek its salvation.

Renunciation of thinking is a declaration of spiritual bankruptcy. Where there is no longer a conviction that men can get to know the truth by their own thinking, skepticism begins. Those who work to make our age skeptical in this way, do so in the expectation that, as a result of denouncing all hope of self-discovered truth, men will end by accepting as truth what is forced upon them with authority and by propaganda.

But their calculations are wrong. No one who opens the sluices to let a flood of skepticism pour itself over the land must expect to be able to bring it back within its proper bounds. Of those who let themselves get too disheartened to try any longer to discover truth by their own thinking, only a few find a substitute for it in truth taken from others. The mass of people remain skeptical. They lose all feeling for truth, and all sense of need for it as well, finding themselves quite comfortable in a life without thought driven now here, now there, from one opinion to another.

But the acceptance of authoritative truth, even if that truth has both spiritual and ethical content, does not bring skepticism to an end; it merely covers it up. Man's unnatural condition of not believing that any truth is discoverable by himself, continues, and produces its natural results. The city of truth cannot be built on the swampy ground of skepticism. Our spiritual life is rotten throughout because it is permeated through and through with skepticism, and we live in consequence in a world which in every respect is full of falsehood. We are not far from shipwreck on the rock of wanting to have even truth organized.

Truth taken over by skepticism which has become believing has not the spiritual qualities of that which originated in thinking. It has been externalized and rendered torpid. It does obtain influence over a man, but it is not capable of uniting itself with him to the very marrow of his being. Living truth is that alone which has its origin in thinking.

Just as a tree bears year after year the same fruit and yet fruit which is each year new, so must all permanently valuable ideas be continually born again in thought. But our age is bent on trying to make the barren tree of skepticism fruitful by tying fruits of truth on its branches.

It is only by confidence in our ability to reach truth by our own individual thinking, that we are capable of accepting truth from outside. Unfettered thought, provided it be deep, never degenerates into subjectivity. With its own ideas it stirs those within itself which enjoy any traditional credit for being true, and exerts itself to be able to possess them as knowledge.

Not less strong than the will to truth must be the will to sincerity. Only an age which can show the courage of sincerity can possess truth which works as a spiritual force within it.

Sincerity is the foundation of the spiritual life.

With its depreciation of thinking our generation has lost its feeling for sincerity and with it that for truth as well. It can therefore be helped only by its being brought once more on to the road of thinking.

Because I have this certainty I oppose the spirit of the age, and take upon myself with confidence the responsibility of taking my part in the rekindling of the fire of thought.

II

Thought on the lines of Reverence for

Life is by its very nature peculiarly qualified to take up the struggle against skepticism. It is elemental.

Elemental thinking is that which starts from the fundamental questions about the relations of man to the universe, about the meaning of life, and about the nature of goodness. It stands in the most immediate connection with the thinking which impulse stirs in everyone. It enters into that thinking, widening and deepening it.

Such elemental thinking we find in Stoicism. When as a student I began going through the history of philosophy I found it difficult to tear myself away from Stoicism, and to pursue my way through the utterly different thinking which succeeded it. It is true that the results produced by Stoic thought were far from satisfying me, but I had the feeling that this simple kind of philosophizing was the right one, and I could not understand how people had come to abandon it.

Stoicism seemed to me great in that it goes straight for its goal; that it is universally intelligible, and is at the same time profound; that it makes the best of the truth which it recognizes as such, even if it is unsatisfying; that it puts life into such truth by the earnestness with which it devotes itself to it; that it possesses the spirit of sincerity; that it urges men to collect their thoughts, and to become more inward; and that it arouses in them the sense of responsibility. I felt, too, that the fundamental thought of Stoicism is true, namely that man must bring himself into a spiritual relation with the world, and become one with it.

To make men thinking beings once more, then, means to make them resort to their own way of thinking that they may try to secure that knowledge which they need for living. In the thinking which starts from Reverence for Life there is to be found a renewal of elemental thinking. The stream which has been flowing for a long distance underground comes again to the surface.

The idea of Reverence for Life offers itself as the realistic answer to the realistic question of how man and the world are related to each other. Of the world man knows only that everything which exists is, like himself, a manifestation of the Will-to-Live. With this world he stands in a relation of passivity and of activity. On the one hand he is subordinate to the course of events which is given in this totality of life; on the other hand he is capable of affecting the life which comes within his reach by hampering or promoting it, by destroying or maintaining it.

The one possible way of giving means to his existence is that of raising his natural relation to the world to a spiritual one. As a being in a passive relation to the world he comes into a spiritual relation to it by resignation. True resignation consists in this: that man, feeling his subordination to the course of world happenings, wins his way to inward freedom from the fortunes which shape the outside of his existence. Inward freedom means that he finds strength to deal with everything that is hard in his lot, in such a way that it all helps to make him a deeper and more inward person, to purify him, and to keep him calm and peaceful. Resignation, therefore, is the spiritual and ethical affirmation of one's own existence. Only he who has gone through the stage of resignation is capable of accepting the world.

As a being in an active relation to the world he comes into a spiritual relation with it by not living for himself alone, but feeling himself one with all life that comes within his reach. He will feel all that life experiences as his own, he will give it all the help that he possibly can, and will feel all the saving and promotion of life that he has been able to effect as the deepest happiness that can ever fall to his lot.

Let a man once begin to think about the mystery of his life and the links which connect him with the life that fills the world, and he cannot but bring to bear upon his own life and all other life that comes within his reach the principle of Reverence for Life, and manifest this principle by ethical affirmation of life. Existence will thereby become harder for him in every respect than it would be if he lived for himself, but at the same time it will be richer, more beautiful, and happier. It will become, instead of mere living, a real experience of life.

Reverence for Life contains in itself resignation, an affirmative attitude toward the world, and ethics—the three essential elements in a philosophy of life, as mutually interrelated results of thinking.

Up to now there have been systems of thought based on resignation, others based on an affirmative view of the world and still others that sought to satisfy ethics. Not one has there been, however, which has been able to combine the three elements. That is possible only on condition that all three are conceived as essentially products of the universal conviction of Reverence for Life, and are recognized as being one and contained in it. Resignation and an affirmative view of the world have no separate existence of their own by the side of ethics; they are its lower octaves.

Having its origin in realistic thinking, the ethic of Reverence for Life is realistic, and brings man to a realistic and steady facing of reality.

It may seem, at first glance, as if Reverence for Life were something too general and too lifeless to provide the content of a living ethic. But thinking has no need to trouble as to whether its expressions sound living enough, so long as they hit the mark and have life in them. Anyone who comes under the influence of the ethic of Reverence for Life will very soon be able to detect, thanks to what that ethic demands from him, what fire glows in the lifeless expression. The ethic of Reverence for Life is the ethic of Love widened into universality. It is the ethic of Jesus, now recognized as a logical consequence of thought.

Objection is made to this ethic that it sets too high a value on natural life. To this it can retort that the mistake made by all previous systems of ethics has been the failure to recognize that life as such is the mysterious value with which they have to deal. All spiritual life meets us within natural life. Reverence for Life, therefore, is applied to natural life and spiritual life alike. In the parable of Jesus, the shepherd saves not merely the soul of the lost sheep but the whole animal. The stronger the reverence for natural life, the stronger grows also that for spiritual life.

The ethic of Reverence for Life is found particularly strange because it establishes no dividing line between higher and lower, between more valuable and less valuable life. For this omission it has its reasons.

To undertake to lay down universally valid distinctions of value between different kinds of life will end in judging them by the greater or lesser distance at which they seem to stand from us human beings—as we ourselves judge. But that is a purely subjective criterion. Who among us knows what significance any other kind of life has in itself, and as a part of the universe?

Following on such a distinction there comes next the view that there can be life which is worthless, injury to which or destruction of which does not matter. Then in the category of worthless life we come to include, according to circumstances, different kinds of insects, or primitive peoples.

To the man who is truly ethical all life is sacred, including that which from the human point of view seems lower in the scale. He makes distinctions only as each case comes before him, and under the pressure of necessity, as, for example, when it falls to him to decide which of two lives he must sacrifice in order to preserve the other. But all through this series of decisions he is conscious of acting on subjective grounds and arbitrarily, and knows that he bears the responsibility for the life which is sacrificed.

I rejoice over the new remedies for sleeping sickness, which enable me to preserve life, whereas I had previously to watch a painful disease. But every time I have under the microscope the germs which cause the disease, I cannot but reflect that I have to sacrifice this life in order to save other life.

I buy from natives a young fish eagle, which they have caught on a sandbank, in order to rescue it from their cruel hands. But now I have to decide whether I shall let it starve, or kill every day a number of small fishes, in order to keep it alive. I decide on the latter course, but every day I feel it hard that this life must be sacrificed for the other on my responsibility.

Standing, as he does, with the whole body of living creatures under the law of this dilemma in the will-to-live, man comes again and again into the position of being able to preserve his own life and life generally only at the cost of other life. If he has been touched by the ethic of Reverence for Life, he injures and destroys life only under a necessity which he cannot avoid, and never from thoughtlessness. So far as he is a free man he uses every opportunity of tasting the blessedness of being able to assist life and avert from it suffering and destruction.

The ethic, then, which originates in thinking is not "according to reason," but nonrational and enthusiastic. It marks off no skillfully defined circle of duties, but lays upon each individual the responsibility for all life within his reach, and compels him to devote himself to helping it.

In the world the infinite will-to-live reveals itself to us as will-to-create, and this is full of dark and painful riddles for us; in ourselves it is revealed as will-to-love, which will through us remove the dilemma of the will-to-live.

The concept of Reverence for Life has, therefore, a religious character. The man who avows his beliefs in it, and acts upon the belief, shows a piety which is elemental.

III

Through the active ethic of love with its religious character, and through its inwardness, the world view of Reverence for Life is essentially related to that of Christianity. Hence there is a possibility that Christianity and thought may now meet in a new relation to each other which will do more than the present one to promote spiritual life.

Christianity once entered into a connection with thought, namely during the period of Rationalism in the eighteenth century. It did so because thought met it with an enthusiastic ethic which was religious in character. As a matter of fact, however, thought had not produced this ethic itself, but had, without knowing it, taken it over from Christianity. When, later on, it had to depend solely upon its own ethic, this latter proved to have in it so little life and so little religion that it had not much in common with Christian ethics. Then the bonds between Christianity and active thought were loosened, and the situation today is that Christianity has completely withdrawn into itself, and is concerned only with the propagation of its own ideas, as such. It no longer sees any use in proving them to be in agreement with thought, but prefers that they be regarded as something altogether outside it, and occupying a superior position. It loses, however, thereby its connection with the spiritual life of the time and the possibility of exercising any real influence upon it.

To make up to itself for the fact that it does so little to prove the reality of its spiritual and ethical nature, the Christianity of today cheats itself with the delusion that it is making its position as a Church stronger year by year. It is accommodating itself to the spirit of the age by adopting a kind of modern worldliness. Like other organized bodies it is at work to make good, by ever stronger and more uniform organization, its claim to be a body justified by history and practical success. But just in proportion as it gains in external power, it loses in spiritual.

Christianity cannot take the place of thinking, but it must be founded on it.

In and by itself it is not capable of mastering lack of thought and skepticism. The only age which can be receptive for the imperishable elements in its own thoughts is one animated by an elemental piety which springs from thinking.

Just as a stream is preserved from gradually leaking away, because it flows along above subsoil water, so does Christianity need the subsoil water of elemental piety which is the fruit of thinking. It can only attain to real spiritual power when men find the road from thought to religion no longer barred.

I know that I myself owe it to thinking that I was able to retain my faith in religion and Christianity.

The man who thinks stands up freer in the face of traditional religious truth than the man who does not, but the profound and imperishable elements contained in it he assimilates with much more effect than the latter.

The essential element in Christianity as it was preached by Jesus, and as it is comprehended by thought, is this, that it is only through love that we can attain to communion with God. All living knowledge of God rests upon this foundation: that we experience Him in our lives as Will-to-Love.

Anyone who has recognized that the idea of Love is the spiritual beam of light which reaches us from the Infinite, ceases to demand from religion that it shall offer him complete knowledge of the suprasensible. He ponders, indeed, on the great questions: what the meaning is of the evil in the world; how in God, the great First Cause, the will-to-create and the will-to-love are one; in what relation the spiritual and the material life stand to one another, and in what way our existence is transistory and yet eternal. But he is able to leave these questions on one side, however painful it may be to give up all hope of answers to them. In the knowledge of spiritual existence in God through love he possesses the one thing needful.

Because I am devoted to Christianity in deep affection, I am trying to serve it with loyalty and sincerity. In no wise do I undertake to enter the lists on its behalf with the crooked and fragile thinking of Christian apologetics, but I call on it to set itself right in the spirit of sincerity with its past and with thought in order that it may thereby become conscious of its true nature.

My hope is that the emergence of an elemental mode of thought which must lead us to the ethico-religious idea of Reverence for Life, may contribute to the bringing of Christianity and thought closer to each other.

IV

To the question whether I am a pessimist or an optimist, I answer that my knowledge is pessimistic, but my willing and hoping are optimistic.

I am pessimistic in that I experience in its full weight what we conceive to be the absence of purpose in the course of world happenings. Only at quite rare moments have I felt really glad to be alive. I could not but feel with a sympathy full of regret all the pain that I saw around me, not only that of men but that of the whole creation. From this community of suffering I have never tried to withdraw myself. It seemed to me a matter of course that we should all take our share of the burden of pain which lies upon the world. Even while I was a boy at school it was clear to me that no explanation of the evil in the world could ever satisfy me; all explanations, I felt, ended in sophistries, and at bottom had no other object than to make it possible for men to share in the misery around them, with less keen feelings. That a thinker like Leibnitz could reach the miserable conclusion that though this world is, indeed, not good, it is the best that was possible, I have never been able to understand.

But however much concerned I was at the problem of the misery in the world, I never let myself get lost in broodings over it; I always held firmly to the thought that each one of us can do a little to bring some portion of it to an end. Thus I came gradually to rest content in the knowledge that there is only one thing we can understand about the problem, and that is that each of us has to go his own way, but as one who means to help to bring about deliverance.

In my judgment, too, of the situation in which mankind finds itself at the present time I am pessimistic. I cannot make myself believe that that situation is not so bad as it seems to be, but I am inwardly conscious that we are on a road which, if we continue to tread it, will bring us into "Middle Ages" of a new character. The spiritual and material misery to which mankind of today is delivering itself through its renunciation of thinking and of the ideals which spring therefrom, I picture to myself in its utmost compass. And yet I remain optimistic. One belief of my childhood I have preserved with the certainty that I can never lose it: belief in truth. I am confident that the spirit generated by truth is stronger than the force of circumstances. In my view no other destiny awaits mankind than that which, through its mental and spiritual disposition, it prepares for itself. Therefore I do not believe that it will have to tread the road to ruin right to the end.

If men can be found who revolt against the spirit of thoughtlessness, and who are personalities sound enough and profound enough to let the ideals of ethical progress radiate from them as a force, there will start an activity of the spirit which will be strong enough to evoke a new mental and spiritual disposition in mankind.

Because I have confidence in the power of truth and of the spirit, I believe in the future of mankind. Ethical acceptance of the world contains within itself an optimistic willing and hoping which can never be lost. It is, therefore, never afraid to face the dismal reality, and to see it as it really is.

In my own life anxiety, trouble, and sorrow have been allotted to me at times in such abundant measure that had my nerves not been so strong, I must have broken down under the weight. Heavy is the burden of fatigue and responsibility which has lain upon me without a break for years. I have not much of my life for myself, not even the hours I should like to devote to my wife and child.

But I have had blessings too: that I am allowed to work in the service of mercy; that my work has been successful; that I receive from other people affection and kindness in abundance; that I have loyal helpers, who identify themselves with my activity; that I enjoy a health which allows me to undertake most exhausting work; that I have a well-balanced temperament which varies little, and an energy which exerts itself with calmness and deliberation; and, finally, that I can recognize as such whatever happiness falls to my lot, accepting it also as a thing for which some thank offering is due from me.

I feel it deeply that I can work as a free man at a time when an oppressive lack of freedom is the lot of so many, as also that though my immediate work is material, yet I have at the same time opportunities of occupying myself in the sphere of the spiritual and intellectual.

That the circumstances of my life provide in such varied ways favorable conditions for my work, I accept as something of which I would fain prove myself worthy.

How much of the work which I have planned and have in mind shall I be able to complete?

My hair is beginning to turn. My body is beginning to show traces of the exertions I have demanded of it, and of the passage of the years.

I look back with thankfulness to the time when, without needing to husband my strength, I could get through an uninterrupted course of bodily and mental work. With calmness and humility I look forward to the future, so that I may not be unprepared for renunciation if it be required of me. Whether we be workers or sufferers, it is assuredly our duty to conserve our powers, as being men who have won their way through to the peace which passeth all understanding.

Reinhold Niebuhr

Reinhold Niebuhr is one of the outstanding figures in America today. A religious leader who ranks with the ablest contemporary philosophers both in sheer intellectual power and in capacity to deal realistically with the vital issues of our age, his influence upon religious thought both in Europe and in our own country during the past two or three decades has been widespread.

Born in 1892 in a small Missouri community Niebuhr attended several Lutheran schools in the Midwest and then did graduate work in religion at Yale University. For thirteen years he was pastor of a Lutheran church in Detroit where he slowly and painfully worked out his own interpretation of Christianity in that rapidly growing industrial community. By the time he left the church in Detroit (in 1928) to become professor of Applied Christian Ethics at Union Theological Seminary in New York, Niebuhr was recognized as one of the ablest and most courageous Christian thinkers in the country. During his thirty years in New York City he has established himself as a leading exponent of the neo-orthodox theology which finds in the traditional Christian faith a more penetrating and trustworthy understanding of human nature than that provided by the humanistic scientific philosophy of our age.

Niebuhr has been a prolific writer. Author of a dozen or more volumes, he has produced several which rank among the more significant books of our time. Such works as Moral Man and Immoral Society *(1932),* An Interpretation of Christian Ethics *(1935), and the series of Gifford lectures at Edinburgh on* The Nature and Destiny of Man *(1941-1943) are notable. In the fields of history and politics Niebuhr's insights have been equally illuminating and provocative. For many years he has edited a biweekly journal,* Christianity and Crisis, *and he has published such influential books as* Christianity and Power Politics, Christian Realism and Political Problems, The Irony of American History, *and* Faith in History.

In The Self and the Dramas of History *(1955), from which our selection is taken, Niebuhr undertakes a penetrating analysis of the uniqueness, freedom, and creativity of the human self. This discussion will appeal to thoughtful students who are conscious of the inadequacies of Freudian psychology and are perplexed by scientific determinism but are unwilling to accept a position that fails to recognize the important place of reason in human life. Niebuhr provides the same sort of able and illuminating defense of the insights of religion that Herbert Muller gives us for the insights of rational humanism.*

THE SELF AND ITS SEARCH FOR ULTIMATE MEANING

The Uniqueness of the Human Self

MAN is obviously distinguished from the other creatures by some marked capabilities and qualities. In the Western tradition, composed of Hebraic and Hellenic components, Hebraism supplied the poetic metaphor to designate human uniqueness. In the Bible it is affirmed that God made man "after his image and in his likeness." This assertion of the divine element in human nature was however not elaborated, except by implication. It was left to the Greek philosophers to define the uniquely human more precisely. They did so by equating the divine element in man with his "reason." Aristotle further defined the rational capacity as the ability to conceive universals, in short, the capacity for making conceptual images. But reason also meant for Aristotle, and for all of Western thought since his day, the logical and analytical faculties of the mind. With these man distinguishes things from each other, traces the causal sequences in which they are chained and, having separated distinctive things, tries to bring them into some kind of coherence. Obviously the rational faculty is a very significant part of the unique capacity which is indicated by the metaphor "image of God."

The question is whether any of these classical definitions adequately describe the unique capacity for freedom of the human person. Conceptual tools are no doubt necessary for the self's freedom over the flux of natural events and for projecting ends beyond those set by natural appetites and desires. The self must even use concepts to make itself, as the world, the object of its attention. It uses memory, a force of "reason" which neither Plato nor Aristotle completely understood, to transcend its movement through time and be aware of its self-identity in this temporal flux. Plato and Aristotle did not quite understand memory because they equated "recollection" with the conceptual and mathematical forms which the mind used in mastering the rough stuff of its perception. But the significant power of memory lies in its capacity to retain unique events whether they fit into a conceptual mold or not.

Let us define the uniqueness of the human self by emphasizing the three dialogues in which it is involved according to the Hebraic rather than the Hellenic description of its reality. The implications of these three dialogues may give more accurate content to the original metaphor "image of God" than the Greek emphasis on reason. The self is a creature which is in constant dialogue with itself, with its neighbors, and with God, according to the Biblical viewpoint.

(A) The dialogue of the self with itself

is an empiric fact in the sense that every astute person must admit that such a dialogue goes on in the internal life of the self, though there are no external evidences of this dialogue. This internal dialogue is a more significant testimony of the self's freedom over nature than its endowments with conceptual capacities, though these are frequent instruments of the self in the dialogue.

(B) The self is in constant dialogue with various neighbors. This may be a quality which Aristotle was partly describing by defining the self as a *zoon politicon* (political animal). But that definition would not necessarily do justice to the endless nuances and levels of the dialogue of the self with others. It is not merely dependent upon others for its sustenance and security. It is dependent upon them for the image which it has of itself and for the spiritual security which is as necessary to the self as its social security.

(C) The self is in dialogue with God. Perhaps this assertion will immediately prejudice our analysis in the eyes of those who have drawn heavily upon either naturalistic or idealistic versions of the Greek tradition. The assertion that the self is in dialogue with God takes the inquiry immediately beyond the limits of empirical verification. It would seem so much safer to follow Aristotle and define the uniqueness of the self as its reason, a definition which is capable of empirical verification. Let us therefore make some at least preliminary concessions to the spirit of contemporary empiricism and say merely that the self imagines itself in an encounter with the divine. For surely the persistence of this imagination is an empirical datum about the self. Perhaps we can be even more moderate and declare that the self distinguishes itself by a yearning for the ultimate. For if we omit this characteristic we have failed to define the total anatomy of human selfhood. We must leave the more exact definition of what this may mean to a later consideration. It is sufficient now merely to call attention to the fact that any datum which illumines the indeterminate character of the self's capacity for transcending itself, its history and its world is necessary for an adequate conception of the anatomy of human selfhood.

The Internal Dialogue of the Self

We may safely say that the human animal is the only creature which talks to itself. It maintains a rather constant internal dialogue in which it approves or disapproves its actions, or even itself. Its accusations and defences of itself are quite different from those in which it engages in its external dialogues. The self pities and glorifies itself as well as accuses and excuses itself. It could not carry on this dialogue without using its "reason"; for the dialogue means that the self in one of its aspects is making the self, in another of its aspects, its object of thought. It uses conceptual images for this procedure.

But it is important to note that the self which is doing the judging and excusing, the pitying and glorifying, is not necessarily the "rational" or the "intelligible" self in contrast to the "sensible" self. It was the primary mistake of the philosophers from classical days to this day to equate the self as subject with mind; and the self as object with either the body, or the body-soul unity, or with some other aspect of the self as creature. The fact is that there are not two distinct selves in this internal dialogue. There are merely two foci of the same self. We do, of course, know of a pathological condition in which the self becomes separated into two warring and comparatively discrete entities. This is known as "schizophrenia." There are pathological states which border on this internal division. But the healthy self is always one self, no matter how much it engages in a perpetual internal dialogue.

The dialogue within the self proceeds on many levels. Sometimes it is a dialogue between the self as engaged in its various responsibilities and affections and the self which observes these engagements. Sometimes the dialogue is between the self in the grip of its immediate necessities and biological urges, and the self as an organization of long-range purposes and ends. Sometimes the dialogue is between the self in the context of one set of loyalties and the self in the grip of contrasting claims and responsibilities.

When artists try to depict a character in a novel or drama, they frequently resort to the record of this internal dialogue because it may be more revealing than the self's external dialogue or dramatic action. With artistic license they claim to be privy to the secrets of this dialogue, though it is by its very nature secret; and the self which entertains ambitions and desires is subject to temptations and considers alternative modes of action about which even the most intimate friend may know nothing. Only the victorious, and not the vanquished, forces are known to the outside world. The self remains such a mystery even to its friends because so little is known about the stratagems which produced the victory of the one over the other force.

An interesting witness to the reality of the self's inner dialogue, and more particularly of the phenomenon of the self as spectator of its actions and attitudes, is furnished by Lucy Sprague Mitchell in her biography of her husband and her own autobiography, entitled *Two Lives*. Speaking of her adolescence, she writes:

> It was at this time that I became aware of the complexity of one's make-up. When I acted in our stable-theater I seemed to be two people: one making up dramatic lines and rendering them in fine action, and the other listening, approving or disapproving. I was actor and critic at the same time. I found that this was disturbingly true, whatever I did. When I talked with father or helped mother with household arrangements, I always heard and saw myself doing these things. I must be hopelessly insincere, I always thought. But the sense of guilt did not change me one bit. So vivid this inlooker self became, that I called it "the thing in the corner." Among my old papers I find a curious document, written in my fourteenth year and beginning: 'Tis seldom that one personality speaks to another. Even more rare is it that one's other personality speaks to another personality. Too seldom alas, for more often than not they speak another language.

Obviously this is a very significant memory of a vivid experience of childhood, and throws a bright light on the anatomy of selfhood which is superior to the analyses of many learned men.

The analyses of Freud and of subsequent "depth psychology" into the inner tensions of the human psyche have both illumined and obscured this inner dialogue. They have illumined it insofar as the analyses proved conclusively that the old "body-mind" separation was mistaken; and that the inner organization of the self is much more intricate than was supposed.

The Freudian division of the self into "id," "ego," and "super-ego" indicates at least two levels of the dialogue, that between the self in the grip of its immediate necessities and the self in its more inclusive and coherent organization; and that between the self as concerned with itself and the self in its relations to the community. It also proves that the dialogue may leave many scars. The therapeutic efficacy of depth psychology rests largely upon the discovery that a part of the "unconscious element in the ego" is but the repressed portions of a preconscious desire. Freud, in fact, denied the freedom of the will, partly because he was so preoccupied with the limiting forces upon the will by neurotic anxieties, which he attributed to the baneful effect of repression. Sometimes Freud pictured the task of analysis to be that of freeing the "ego" from the limits placed upon it by the "id" and the "super-ego." The task of psychoanalysts is, he declares, "to strengthen the ego, to make it more independent of the super-ego, to widen its vision and extend its field of organization so that it can take over portions of the id. Where the id is, there shall the ego be." *

For all of the therapeutic skill of Freudian psychology, and its wisdom in exploring the labyrinths of the self, it has confused the realities of the internal dialogue in some degree by obscuring the fact that the self is really in both the "id" and the "super-ego." The "id" is defined as a cauldron of "seething excitement." But it obviously has the guile of a real self in trying to evade the guard of the "ego's" "censor." Sometimes Freud pictures the tension between the "ego" and the "repressed" portions of the self. Inasmuch as neuroses are due to these repressions, it is important to bring this repressed material into the open consciousness. The tool of emancipation is the recollection of the experiences in which the repressions took place. Freud notes that the resistance to this process of recollection is offered by the conscious self. "There is no doubt," he declares, "that the conscious and preconscious ego subserves the pleasure principle. It is trying to avoid the pain which would be aroused by a release of the repressed material." Thus the self is in this dialogue between the "coherent ego" and the "id" more than it would at first appear.

The presence of the self in the dialogue between the "ego" and the "super-ego" is even more mistakenly obscured. This is obviously a debate between the self as engaged and obligated to its various communities and the self concerned with its own ends. But the Freudian psychology moves within the limits of a rigid naturalism; and this second level of transcendence is not conceivable within those limits. The "super-ego" is therefore no more than the pressure of society upon the "ego"; and it does not occur to Freud that the self has both the power to defy the community for the sake of its interests and for the sake of interests more inclusive than those of a given community.

* *New Introductory Essays on Psychoanalysis*, p. 112.

The Dialogue between the Will and Conscience

The relation of the conscience to the will of the self is certainly one aspect of the self's internal dialogue. Will and conscience are two levels of the transcendence of the self over itself. More accurately, the will is the result of the self's transcendence over the complex of its impulses and desires. The will is in fact the self organized for the attainment of either a short-range or long-range purpose. This organization requires a rational analysis of the ends in view, a comparison of the relative merits of those ends either from the standpoint of the self's total ends or from the standpoint of some more inclusive system of value. The will is operative on all levels. A young man may, for instance, will to be a lawyer; will to take a college education in pursuit of this ultimate end; and will to join the football squad. He may will the latter course either in pursuit of the ultimate end, or because it is an ancillary end which is deemed by him not to be in conflict with his ultimate end. On all these levels of willing reason is the self's instrument in judging the goals of action. Yet the consistency with which a self pursues its immediate ends and subordinates them to an ultimate end is not an intellectual achievement. Consistency is the achievement of the self rather than of its reason, because there is no power in reason as such to compel consistency though it may have the power to detect inconsistency in the pursuit of goals.

The self's capacity to view itself, and to judge either its short-range or its long-range purposes, gives rise to a reality in its life which is usually termed "conscience." Conscience, like will, avails itself of rational tools but is not subject to these instruments.

It would seem that any judgment by the self of its own actions and attitudes is an expression of conscience. But this is not so. The self may, when viewing its actions, either accuse or excuse itself; and if it accuses itself, it may do so from its own standpoint. That is, it may view its actions as being too "unselfish" and not sufficiently concerned with its own interests. We will define conscience, provisionally at least, as any aspect of the self's judging its actions and attitudes in which a sense of obligation in contrast to inclination is expressed. Many efforts have been made to deny the reality of such a sense of "ought." Most of these efforts are clearly derived from one-dimensional views of selfhood, usually elaborated within a naturalistic ontology. They try to eliminate the distinction between the desired and the desirable in the view of the self. But they fail to explain why the self is under the necessity of seeking what it desires by proving that the desired is really desirable; or that what the self wants is in accord with some wider system of values than the self's own interest. These hypocrisies are the most telling refutations of one-dimensional views of selfhood. They prove that there is a real distinction between inclination and obligation, between the desires of the self and its conception of a system of value which does not depend upon its inclination or desires. This sense of obligation is powerful enough to allow the self freedom to achieve what it desires only when it is able to persuade itself that what it desires is consonant with this more general system of values.

The "content" of conscience is obviously very relative to time and place. Yet the minimal terms of our obligations to our neighbors, incorporated, for instance, in the prohibition of murder, theft, and adultery, are fairly universal. Hume rightly observed that the "preference for benevolence over self regard" was universal, certainly more universal than actual benevolence. Perhaps it would be correct to surmise that the universalities of the "moral law" are derived from intuitions of the self about the essential nature of its selfhood. To this essential nature belong, on the one hand, its biological structure, and, on the other hand, its social nature. Yet the content of conscience is much more relative than the proponents of the idea of "moral intuitions" realize. These relativities point to the social derivation of the moral law. Man is both an historical and social creature. He does not make his moral judgments in a vacuum. The community in which he lives sets the standards by which he judges himself. There is at least that modicum of truth in the moral relativism propounded by modern anthropologists. That this is not the whole truth of the matter is proved by the frequency with which "conscience" expresses itself in defiance of the community. The modern martyrs who have given their life to defy communities which sought to make total claims upon the individual have vividly refuted all theories, whether psychological, sociological or anthropological, which sought to reduce the sense of moral obligation to a purely sociological phenomenon. More particularly they refuted the Freudian theory of the "super-ego" which was no more than the pressure of the community upon the "ego."

It is worth nothing, however, that consistently "liberal" or "bourgeois" notions of conscience as purely individual do not do justice to the fact that the individual is best able to defy a community when his conscience is informed and reinforced by another community, whether religious or political. Perhaps the final paradox of the social and individual dimension of the moral sense is revealed by the fact that the individual may defy a community which directly impinges upon his life and threatens his liberty by its coercions; but his defiance is usually undertaken in the name of another, more inclusive or more worthy, community even though that community makes no overt claims upon him and may exist only in his imagination.

The Self and Its Body

The self is not a particular self merely because it is in a particular body. It can take a partially objective view of its body just as it can of its mind. But it has an internal relation to its body as to its consciousness which makes the idea of "my body" different from the idea of "my property." There is an organic unity in every animal organism which is usually described as its "soul." The self is "soul" insofar as it has an experience of the unity. But it is more than soul insofar as it can think of its body as an object even while it is an inner experience of the bodily organic unity.

In Charles Lindbergh's account of his memorable flight across the Atlantic two decades ago,* he gives an admirable account of the unity and the difference between the self and its body and its mind. The statement occurs in his description of his effort to master physical fatigue after thirty hours of flying across the Atlantic. He writes:

For immeasurable periods I seemed divorced from my body as though I were an awareness, spreading through space, over the earth and into the heavens, unhampered by time and substance, free from the gravitation that binds men to heavy human problems of the world. My body requires no attention. It's not cold. It's not hungry. It's resigned to being left undisturbed. Why have I troubled to bring it here? I might better have left it back at Long Island or St. Louis, while this weightless element that has lived within it flashes through the skies and views the planets. This essential consciousness needs no body for its travels. It needs no plane, no instruments, no engine. Only the release from flesh, which the circumstances I have gone through make possible. Then what am I? The body substance which I can feel with my hands and see with my eyes? Or am I this greater understanding and greater realization which dwells within it and extends to the universe outside; a part of all existence, powerless but without need of power; immersed in solitude yet in contact with all creation? There are moments when the two appear inseparable and others when they can be cut apart with the mere flash of light.

While my hand is on the stick, feet on the rudder and my eyes on the compass, this consciousness, like a winged messenger, goes out to visit the waves below, testing the warmth of the water, the speed of the wind and the thickness of the overhanging clouds. It goes north to the glacial coast of Greenland, over the horizon to the coast of Ireland, England, and the whole of Europe, away through space to the moon and stars, always returning unwillingly to the mortal duty of seeing that the limbs and muscles have done their duty while it was gone.

There could hardly be a more perceptive analysis of the essential aspatial nature of the self, combined with its intimate relation to a body in a given space. Mr. Lindbergh goes on to describe the conflict between the fatigued body and the resolute will:

With the faint trace of day an uncontrollable desire to sleep falls over me in quilted layers. I've been staving it off with difficulty during the hours of moonlight. Now it looms all but unsurmountable. This is the hour I've been dreading; the hour against which I've tried to steel myself. I know it is the beginning of my greatest test. . . . I've lost command of my eyelids. When they start to close I can't restrain them. . . . My body has revolted against the rule of the mind. . . . Every cell in my body is in revolt, sulking in protest claiming that nothing, nothing in the

* From *The Spirit of St. Louis*, by Charles A. Lindbergh. Copyright 1953 by Charles Scribner's Sons, and used by permission.

world could be worth such effort; that man's tissues were never meant for such abuse. . . . I've got to muster all my reserves, all the tricks I've learned, all the remaining strength of mind, for the conflict. . . . I've got to find some way to keep alert. There's no alternative but death and failure, I keep repeating, using the thought too as a whip for my lagging mind, trying to make my senses realize the importance of what I am saying. . . . I set my mind on the sunrise and try to think about that. It will be better when the full light of day has broken. The desire for sleep will give way to the waking habits of the day. . . . shaking my body and stamping my feet no longer has any effect. I'll have to try something else. . . . My eyes close and open and close again. I'm beginning to understand that a new factor has come to my assistance. It seems I'm made of three personalities, three elements, each partly dependent and partly independent of the other. There is my body which knows that what it wants most in the world is sleep. There is my mind constantly making decisions, that my body refuses to comply with. And there is something else, which seems to become stronger rather than weaker with fatigue, an element of spirit, a directive force which has taken control of both mind and body. It seems to guard them as a wise father guards his children . . . when my body cries out that it must sleep the third element replies that it may get what relaxation it can but that sleep is not to be had. When my mind demands that my body stay awake it is informed that alertness is too much to expect under these circumstances. . . . But while it must not expect alertness on the body's part, it can be confident that there will be no sleep.

This is as illuminating an account of the constant inner dialogue in the self as we have in modern literature. It is to be noticed that "my" body is at one time an object among other objects, and in another mode it is different from all other bodies because of its internal connection with the self. It participates in the inner dialogue, or rather it influences a part of the self in the debate, for the body as body obviously lacks an organ for participation. Most interesting is Mr. Lindbergh's suggestion that there must be a "third factor" which he defines as "spirit." This is a significant admission that the division within the self is more complex than the body-mind division. This is the more important in view of the fact that Lindbergh has attributed the power of decision to the "mind" yet he feels that a third element which he tentatively defines as "spirit" is over both body and mind. This tri-partite division of the self falls into a traditional pattern. It is the more significant because Lindbergh has obviously made no academic study of these mysteries. But in common with the scholars he defines as "spirit" what is really the self itself in its awareness of its freedom over its functions. Usually the will, one of the functions of the self, or rather the self in its organization of its impulses and desires, is thought of as more intimate to the self than either its mind or body. But Lindbergh assigns to the self not merely the will which overrules the immediate impulses but also the capacity to reassure the "anxious mind," that is, the anxious self in its immediate consciousness of danger. He has, in short, given us a very accurate description of the complexity of the internal dialogue within the self and of the transcendent unity and freedom of the self in spite of this dialogue. What he defines as "spirit" might be regarded as the ultimate freedom of the self over its inner divisions. This capacity of freedom in Lindbergh's analysis contains elements of will and resolution but also something which seems superior to the anxieties of "mind." It is, in short, the self standing above its functions and capacities and yet proving its relation to them.

The Dialogue between the Self and Others

The self is engaged in a perpetual dialogue with other selves in which its dependence upon others becomes apparent but which also proves its independence over all relationships. These dialogues create dramatic actions of various kinds which must be considered presently. The dialogues may be prompted by casual, or by permanent, relationships with others. While these dialogues represent a dimension of selfhood which is usually intended by the definition of the self as a "social animal," they are not in the category of social life as usually defined. They move above the level of social cohesion which may be observed objectively. They are dramatic elaborations of these social cohesions.

The self, in its dialogue with others, confronts certain invariable conditions of self-fulfillment and self-giving which may be enumerated as follows:

(A) The self faces the other self as a mystery which can never be fully penetrated. It can surmise about the internal life of the other self by way of analogy with its own internal dialogue. But these analogies are usually misleading because the dialogues, while very similar in form, may be very dissimilar in content. The self makes many errors by relying too much on analogy.

(B) The self sees the other as an instrument for its purposes and as a completion for its incompleteness. The sexual relation is the most vivid form of one self seeking completion in another self. The self is completed in the lives and services of a whole community of persons, but these completions do not concern us for the moment. We are considering only those completions which involve dialogic relation between persons who recognize in each other the mystery of similarity and uniqueness.

The most obvious solution of the self's dependence upon others is a relation of mutual dependence which satisfies each self without making one the mere instrument of the other.

(C) Even an ideal relation of mutual helpfulness can not satisfy one condition in such a dialogue. The self can not be truly fulfilled if it is not drawn out of itself into the life of the other. Mutual love seems to be a satisfactory solution for this problem, but insofar as mutual love may involve only cool calculations of reciprocal advantages of the kind Aristotle describes in his analysis of *Philia*, it is always in danger of degenerating into a relation of mere calculation. If so, it will ultimately be corrupted by resentments about the lack of reciprocity in the relationship. For even if Aristotle's elaborate formulae for apportioning "honor" and "profit" in varying proportions to the "superior" and to the "inferior" partner, there can never be perfect recipocity in any relationship because of the uniqueness of the gifts of the persons in the relationship.

Even a mutual partnership therefore requires something more than calculated mutuality to initiate it and to preserve it. Nature has provided the madness and heedlessness of what is called "falling in love" for the initiation of the most intimate and reciprocal of all relationships. One of the problems is to supply some force more permanent than this original madness to preserve what has been initiated. This fact gives social relevance to what would otherwise seem to be a socially irrelevant form of love, defined in the New Testament as *agape*. This dimension of the dialogue between selves clearly transcends all canons of prudence; and reveals how the dialogue is enriched and sustained by viewpoints which are not directly derived from the ordinary level of mutuality.

The paradox that "whosoever seeketh to gain his life will lose it but whoso loseth his life will find it" accurately and succinctly states the issue encountered in the dialogue between persons when each person is too intent to complete his life in the other in calculated mutuality. If this dimension is not recognized, the paradox will seem to be a contradiction. Thus Gardner Murphy worries about this seeming contradiction: "Psychology can not very well admit," he declares, "without in some way adjusting the paradox that human nature is really capable of effective functioning only under conditions of individualistic fulfillment and at the same time claim that it is the nature of man, so to lose himself in others as to care little or nothing for the enhancement of the self. . . . Christianity extols both ideals and leaves us in confusion."

The confusion is rather in Mr. Murphy's mind; and in the mind of all who would reduce human relations to simple canons of prudence. It is an obvious fact, which may be "empirically" observed, that the self does not fulfill itself most fully when self-realization is its conscious aim. In the same way happiness and virtue elude conscious striving. In any event, prudent calculation is not powerful enough to draw the self from itself as the center of its existence and to find a center beyond itself. That is why sacrificial love is such a "scandal" in any system of prudential ethics, but is so relevant to a full consideration of the problem of human togetherness.

(D) The self recognizes the other as the limit of its expansiveness. It is the "other"; and the otherness includes a final mystery which even the most imaginative love can not penetrate. It is an independent and unique life which, ultimately considered, can not be fitted into any, even common, purpose or project. There must therefore be an element of reservation and reverence for the other in even the most mutual relations.

(E) The uniqueness of the individuals which enter into any dialogic relation makes each one of these relations highly unique, however general may be the natural basis of the relation. Thus each marriage relation takes place upon the common ground of heterosexuality. But each such partnership is a unique and distinctive drama of mutual adjustment which exhibits some unrepeatable elements. It becomes a moral and artistic achievement rather than a scientific one, though science must master many of the common and general elements at its foundation, such as common problems of sexual adjustment.

The Self as Creator and Creature in Historical Drama

It is obvious that the self's freedom over natural process enables it to be a creator of historical events. Both its memory of past events and its capacity to project goals transcending the necessities of nature enable it to create the new level of reality which we know as human history. But the self is not simply a creator of this new dimension, for it is also a creature of the web of events, in the creation of which it participates.

This double relationship naturally causes great perplexities and gives rise to some rather simple contradictory theories which emphasize either the one, or the other, role of creator or creature. The tendency to equate history with nature and to confuse the "laws of nature" with those of history has given rise, since the French Enlightenment, to a determinism which minimizes the creative role of man. The most consistent application of this determinism is the economics of *laissez faire*, drawn from physiocratic theory, and warning men from interference with the "natural" processes and "natural" balances of history.

But the tendency to equate history with nature can also prompt a contradictory voluntaristic theory according to which man is called upon to use scientific technics to manage history, as he has managed nature. Many modern social scientists have been influenced by this voluntarism since Comte; and have naively insisted on the possibility of transferring the "scientific method," learned in the natural sciences, to the management of human affairs. Aldous Huxley has satirized the dreams of such voluntarists in his *Brave New World*.

This interesting combination of determinism and voluntarism usually presupposes a vaguely defined élite of scientists who have the omniscience to manage the events in which ordinary mortals are merely creatures. Modern communism presents us with a much more dangerous combination of such determinism and voluntarism. It has a self-appointed élite, the Communist party, who, by reason of being the only ones who are privy to the logic, which supposedly determines historical events, are able to intervene at the crucial moments to further the logic and finally to take the heroic step which will insure not only the victory of the "proletariat," but change the whole human situation by making man the unambiguous master of historical destiny rather than merely both creature and creator.

It remained for some modern cultural anthropologist to correct the absurdities of these combinations of voluntarism and determinism which underestimated the freedom of the man who is to be managed, and the finiteness of the man who is to do the managing, by projecting an even more absurdly consistent determinism, according to which all men are the prisoners of their respective cultures with no opportunity to exhibit characteristically universal human traits.

The freedom of man beyond the limits of the historical situation in which his art and life is formed does not necessarily reveal itself in those elements of his art which rise to the height of universally valid insights. It may manifest itself in highly individual insights, transcending the conventions of his society. As an instance: the culture of France, in the period of the Empire, nurtured three great novelists, Balzac, Flaubert, and George Sand. Their novels were characterized by a common unconventional attitude toward sexual relations, characteristic of that period. But one of them, George Sand, also expressed a highly individual attitude within the general standards of the period. Her novels left the reader uncertain whether she intended to glorify wantonness or wished to expound the thesis that sexual relations, whether inside or outside of marriage, were intolerable without love. This attitude expressed neither the convention of her period nor some universally valid standard.

The freedom of men above their status as creatures of the historical drama does not necessarily express itself in conscious efforts to determine historical destiny. That ambition may be reserved for a few great statesmen; and the illusion of such creativity is held only by a few dreamers. Actually the creativity which may, or may not, affect historical destiny is open to every man even in the humblest walks of life when he comes to terms with his unique problems partly in terms which his culture supplies, and partly according to his unique gifts and inclinations. Whether his unique response "makes" history or not is largely out of his hands, for only the future can determine whether his unique response is to be the basis of a new historical pattern or is to be stored in the store house of history as merely another proof of the endless variety of human responses.

We might speculate endlessly upon such mysteries as the source of the unique moral courage which a man like General Rommel exhibited in his final defiance of Hitler and how it was related to his previous Nazi creed and could be compared with the courage of other generals who had the advantage of non-Nazi background but were not able to show a like courage. We will also have to wait upon history to find whether Churchill's obvious relish in the heroism of this gallant foe restored some of the dignity of gallantry into modern national combats or was merely the last flicker of light from a more romantic age in an age which has no use for such romantic candles in its neon-lighted modernity.

The Self and Its Search for Ultimate Meaning

In analyzing the various dimensions of human selfhood, we have thus far concerned ourselves with the presuppositions of the inquiry only insofar as we have called attention to the fact that the tendency to identify the self with its mind is as erroneous as it is persistent. The error obscures the freedom of the self over its rational faculties.

If we now proceed to inquire more rigorously into the dimension and character of that freedom, it will become apparent that the religious inclination of men is derived from that freedom. The freedom makes it impossible for them to consider systems of rational intelligibility, whether conceived in idealistic or naturalistic terms, as a solution for the problem of the meaning of their life. They discern a mystery and meaning above and beyond their rational faculties in themselves; and they also surmise that the chain of causes, whether conceived in terms of efficient or final cause, that is, whether in terms of idealistic or naturalistic metaphysics, points beyond itself to a mystery of creativity. This is true because any previous event is an intelligible, but not a sufficient, cause for the succeeding event.

The task of penetrating the ultimate mystery prompts many responses, but they could all be placed into three general categories: (A) The first category embraces all religious responses in which the self seeks to break through a universal rational system in order to assert its significance ultimately. It may seek to do this individually, as in modern romantic and existentialist thought; or it may be so conscious of its finiteness as an individual that it finds no opportunity to assert the ultimate significance of itself in history except by asserting the significance of the collective self.

Until a recent day this idolatry, in which the individual self finds the ultimate source of its meaning in the history of the collective self so much more imposing though also so much closer to the flux of nature, was thought to be a phase of history which was overcome by the rise of the rigorously monotheistic religions and monistic philosophies. But the recrudescence of religious nationalism and the pseudo-universalistic Messianism of communism have instructed us that this idolatry, this worship of the collective self as if it were ultimate and not finite, is not merely due to the limits of a primitive imagination. It corresponds to a perennial desire in the human heart to eat one's cake and have it, too; to subordinate the finite self to something greater than itself but not so great that the self may not participate in the exaltation of the finite value. Naturally this idolatrous religion must have baneful effects, not only because it complicates the problem of group relations by exaggerating the claims of contingent historical forces in competition with each other, but because the unconditioned commitment of the self to the collective self must rob it of its freedom; for the collective self is, though more imposing and more long-lived than the individual self, also so much more bound to nature and its necessities, so defective in organs of self-transcendence and therefore so much farther removed from the ultimate source of meaning, that the self debases itself by this uncritical devotion.

(B) The second alternative to explicit religious response has been defined by Aldous Huxley as "The Perennial Philosophy." He is right in asserting that it is a fairly universal response, but wrong in concluding that this universality guarantees its validity. This response, generally defined as "mysticism," stands at the opposite pole of idolatry. It is in fact an heroic effort to transcend all finite values and systems of meaning, including the self as particular existence, and to arrive at universality and "unconditioned" being. The persistence of this mystic tendency in the religions of the world is a telling proof of the ability of the self, in the ultimate reaches of its freedom and self-awareness, to discern some affinity between the mystery within itself and the mystery behind the observable phenomena and to find the key to universality in the joining of these two mysteries. This "perennial philosophy" embraces not only the systems, stemming from the thought of Plotinus, in the Western world but practically all religions of the Orient. It is expressed in the Brahman overtones of Hindu polytheism; in the Sufist tradition of Mohammedanism; in the Taoist tradition of Chinese culture and, most classically, in Buddhism. Here the search for undifferentiated being reaches the height of asserting a type of being as the goal of existence about which one can not be certain whether it is the fullness or the absence of being. It is certainly being bereft of all relationships and meanings.

(C) The third alternative, an explicitly religious answer to the self's search for the ultimate, embraces the two Biblical faiths of Judaism and Christianity. These faiths interpret the self's experience with the ultimate in the final reaches of its self-awareness as a dialogue with God. The idea of a dialogue between the self and God assumes the personality of God, an assumption which both rationalists and mystics find untenable, but to which Biblical faith clings stubbornly. Selfhood or personality is supposedly not attributable to God because the idea of personality is loaded with connotations of finiteness and therefore casts a suspicion of "anthropomorphism" upon Biblical faith. But it is significant that both mystics and rationalists have as much difficulty in ascribing personality to man as to God. This fact suggests that it is not the connotations of finiteness which create the difficulty but rather the fact that personality is characterized by both a basic structure and a freedom beyond structure. The rationalists can comprehend the structure within a system of rational cohesion; and the mystics are able to interpret the freedom as part of a system of undifferentiated potentiality. But neither is able to comprehend the total fact of personality within its system.

The dialogue between the self and God results in the conviction of the self, but not for reason of its finiteness. It is convicted rather of its pretension or "sin"; of claiming too much for its finiteness, and for the virtue and wisdom, which it achieves in its finiteness. The idea of such an encounter therefore permits the Biblical faiths both to affirm the life of the self in history and to challenge its achievements in any particular instance. "Enter not into judgment with thy servant, for in thy sight is no man living justified," declares the Psalmist. Kierkegaard sums up this theme of Biblical religions with the affirmation that "before God all men are in the wrong." The fact that the self is judged for every inclination which affronts God's "majesty" by pride or lust for power is the religious dimension of sin. The prophets are however equally conscious of the social dimension which is the inclination of the self to take advantage of its fellow men. This "injustice" is never speculatively defined, as in Greek philosophy, but rigorously defined by reactions to injustice in particular situations.

The "severity" of God's judgment is matched by the "goodness" of His mercy. The problem of how the mercy of God is related to His justice is a perpetual problem in the Old Testament. The new Biblical faith of Christianity enters into history with the affirmation that the drama of Christ's life is in fact a final revelation, in which this problem is clarified by the assurance that God takes the demand of His justice upon Himself through Christ's suffering love and therefore "God was in Christ reconciling the world unto Himself."

Thus the encounter of the self with God is defined in Biblical faith in terms of a norm which has been set by an historical "revelation." And this revelation is an historical event or series of events which are not essentially miraculous (miracles such as the "virgin birth" are afterthoughts) but are events in history which are discerned by faith to have revelatory power into the ultimate mystery. Both Biblical religions are covenant faiths, which organize covenant communities upon the basis of a common commitment of faith in the divine significance of these events. In this connection it is necessary to observe that the discernment of ultimate significance of an historic event makes the Biblical religions seem primitive and unsophisticated in the eyes of both rationalists and mystics, who look for the ultimate or "unconditioned" in either the permanent structures of existence or in an undifferentiated ground of being. They may fail to note, however, that the Biblical presupposition is the only one of the three alternatives which asserts a discontinuity between the self and God. This discontinuity makes explicit faith indispensable in the ultimate dialogue; but it also prevents the self either from usurping the place of the divine for itself or from imagining itself merged with the divine.

4

THE POINT OF VIEW OF CREATIVE IMAGINATION

Susanne K. Langer

Born in New York City of German parents in 1895, Susanne Langer was educated at Radcliffe College, where she received both her A.B. and Ph.D. degrees and also taught for fifteen years in the department of philosophy. After five years on the faculty of Columbia University, and another five years as visiting lecturer at Northwestern, Ohio State, the University of Washington, and the University of Michigan, she became professor of philosophy at Connecticut College in 1954.

According to Mrs. Langer, the most important aspect of her philosophical education beyond the undergraduate level consisted of ten years' enthusiastic study of symbolic logic, and the influence of this study upon her own mature point of view is quite apparent. Author of a number of books, The Practice of Philosophy *(1930),* Introduction to Symbolic Logic *(1937),* Philosophy in a New Key *(1942), and* Feeling and Form *(1953), Mrs. Langer caught the attention of philosophical circles in this country with the publication of* Philosophy in a New Key. *This book was provocative enough to lead the Rockefeller Foundation to give Mrs. Langer a grant that would enable her to develop more fully the esthetic philosophy suggested there. This fuller statement is found in* Feeling and Form.

The "new key" in philosophy for Mrs. Langer is supplied by the essential role of symbolism in human life and thought—not only in art, religion, and literature, but in science, logic, and depth psychology as well. Because we in this generation have lost contact with the life symbols that gave spiritual support to our forefathers, we find it increasingly difficult to discover meaning and purpose in life, she points out. Around the discovery that meaning is stated not only in language, but also necessarily in "symbolic modes," a re-orientation in philosophy is taking place in our age. "The new key in philosophy is not one which I have struck," Mrs. Langer writes. "Other people have struck it quite clearly and repeatedly. This book purports only to demonstrate the unrecognized fact that it is a new key, and to show how the main themes of our thought tend to be transposed into it."

Our two selections from Philosophy in a New Key *suggest its central emphasis and indicate the significance of this point of view for an understanding of the arts.*

PHILOSOPHY IN A NEW KEY

I

EVERY AGE in the history of philosophy has its own preoccupation. Its problems are peculiar to it, not for obvious practical reasons—political or social—but for deeper reasons of intellectual growth. If we look back on the slow formation and accumulation of doctrines which mark that history, we may see certain groupings of ideas within it, not by subject matter, but by a subtler common factor which may be called their "technique." It is the mode of handling problems, rather than what they are about, that assigns them to an age. Their subject matter may be fortuitous, and depend on conquests, discoveries, plagues, or governments; their treatment derives from a steadier source.

The "technique," or treatment, of a problem begins with its first expression as a question. The way a question is asked limits and disposes the ways in which any answer to it—right or wrong—may be given. If we are asked: "Who made the world?" we may answer: "God made it," "Chance made it," "Love and hate made it," or what you will. We may be right or we may be wrong. But if we reply: "Nobody made it," we will be accused of trying to be cryptic, smart, or "unsympathetic." For in this last instance, we have only seemingly given an answer; in reality we have *rejected the question*. The questioner feels called upon to repeat his problem. "Then how did the world become as it is?" If now we answer: "It has not 'become' at all," he will be really disturbed. This "answer" clearly repudiates the very framework of his thinking, the orientation of his mind, the basic assumptions he has always entertained as common-sense notions about things in general. Everything has become what it is; everything has a cause; every change must be to some end; the world is a thing, and must have been made by some agency, out of some original stuff, for some reason. These are natural ways of thinking. Such implicit "ways" are not avowed by the average man, but simply followed. He is not conscious of assuming any basic principles. They are what a German would call his "*Weltanschauung*," his attitude of mind, rather than specific articles of faith. They constitute his outlook; they are deeper than facts he may note or propositions he may moot.

But, though they are not stated, they find expression in the *forms of his questions*. A question is really an ambiguous proposition; the answer is its determination. There can be only a certain number of alternatives that will complete its sense. In this way the intellectual treatment of any datum, any experience, any subject, is determined by the nature of our questions, and only carried out in the answers.

In philosophy this disposition of problems is the most important thing that a school, a movement, or an age contributes. This is the "genius" of a great philosophy; in its light, systems arise and rule and die. Therefore a philosophy is characterized more by the *formulation* of its problems than by its solution of them. Its answers establish an edifice of facts; but its questions make the frame in which its picture of facts is plotted. They make more than the frame; they give the angle of perspective, the palette, the style in which the picture is drawn—everything except the subject. In our questions lie our *principles of analysis*, and our answers may express whatever those principles are able to yield.

There is a passage in Whitehead's *Science and the Modern World*, setting forth this predetermination of thought, which is at once its scaffolding and its limit. "When you are criticizing the philosophy of an epoch," Professor Whitehead says, "do not chiefly direct your attention to those intellectual positions which its exponents feel it necessary explicitly to defend. There will be some fundamental assumptions which adherents of all the variant systems within the epoch unconsciously presuppose. Such assumptions appear so obvious that people do not know what they are assuming because no other way of putting things has ever occurred to them. With these assumptions a certain limited number of types of philosophic systems are possible, and this group of systems constitutes the philosophy of the epoch."

Some years ago, Professor C. D. Burns published an excellent little article called "The Sense of the Horizon," in which he made a somewhat wider application of the same principle; for here he pointed out that every civilization has its limits of knowledge —of perceptions, reactions, feeling, and ideas. To quote his own words,

> The experience of any moment has its horizon. Today's experience, which is not tomorrow's, has in it some hints and implications which are tomorrow on the horizon of today. Each man's experience may be added to by the experience of other men, who are living in his day or have lived before; and so a common world of experience, larger than that of his own observation, can be lived in by each man. But however wide it may be, that common world also has its horizon; and on that horizon new experience is always appearing. . . .
>
> Philosophers in every age have attempted to give an account of as much experience as they could. Some have indeed pretended that what they could not explain did not exist; but all the great philosophers have allowed for more than they could explain, and have, therefore, signed beforehand, if not dated, the death warrant of their philosophies.

II

The end of a philosophical epoch comes with the exhaustion of its motive concepts. When all answerable questions that can be formulated in its terms have been exploited, we are left with only those problems that are sometimes called "metaphysical" in a slurring sense—insoluble problems whose very statement harbors a paradox. The peculiarity of such pseudo-questions is that they are capable of two or more equally good answers, which defeat each other. An answer once propounded wins a certain number of adherents who subscribe to it despite the fact that other people have shown conclusively how wrong or inadequate it is; since its rival solutions suffer from the same defect, a choice among them really rests on temperamental grounds. They are not intellectual discoveries, like good answers to appropriate questions, but *doctrines*. At this point philosophy becomes academic; its watchword henceforth is Refutation, its life is argument rather than private thinking, fair-mindedness is deemed more important than single-mindedness, and the whole center of gravity shifts from actual philosophical issues to peripheral subjects—methodology, mental progress, the philosopher's place in society, and apologetics.

The springs of philosophical thought have run dry once more. For fifty years at least, we have witnessed all the characteristic symptoms that mark the end of an epoch—the incorporation of thought in more and more variegated "isms," the clamor of their respective adherents to be heard and judged side by side, the defense of philosophy as a respectable and important pursuit, the increase of congresses and symposia, and a flood of text criticism, surveys, popularizations, and collaborative studies. The educated layman does not pounce upon a new philosophy book as people pounced upon *Leviathan* or the great *Critiques* or even *The World as Will and Idea.* He does not expect enough intellectual news from a college professor. What he expects is, rather, to be argued into accepting idealism or realism, pragmatism or irrationalism, as his own belief. We have arrived once more at that counsel of despair, to find a reasoned faith.

But the average person who has any faith does not really care whether it is reasoned or not. He uses reason only to satisfy his curiosity—and philosophy, at present, does not even arouse, let alone satisfy, his curiosity. It only confuses him with impractical puzzles. The reason is not that he is dull, or really too busy (as he says he is) to enjoy philosophy. It is simply that the generative ideas of the seventeenth century—"the century of genius," Professor Whitehead calls it—have served their term. The difficulties inherent in their constitutive concepts balk us now; their paradoxes clog our thinking. If we would have new knowledge, we must get us a whole world of new questions.

Meanwhile, the dying philosophical epoch is eclipsed by a tremendously active age of science and technology. The roots of our scientific thinking reach far back, through the whole period of subjective philosophy, further back than any explicit empiricism, to the brilliant, extravert genius of the Renaissance. Despite the objections of philosophical thinkers, despite the outcry of moralists and theologians against the "crass materialism" and "sensationalism" of the scientists, physical science grew like Jack's beanstalk and overshadowed everything else that human thought produced to rival it. A passion for observation displaced the scholarly love of learned dispute, and quickly developed the experimental technique that kept humanity supplied thrice over with facts. Practical applications of the new mechanical knowledge soon popularized and established it beyond the universities. Here the traditional interests of philosophy could not follow it any more; for they had become definitely relegated to that haven of unpopular lore, the schoolroom. No one really cared much about consistency or definition of terms, about precise conceptions, or formal deduction. The senses, long despised and attributed to the interesting but improper domain of the devil, were recognized as man's most valuable servants, and were rescued from their classical disgrace to wait on him in his new venture. They were so efficient that they not only supplied the human mind with an incredible amount of food for thought, but seemed presently to have most of its cognitive business in hand. Knowledge from sensory experience was deemed the only knowledge that carried any affidavit of truth; for truth became identified, for all vigorous modern minds, with empirical fact.

No one observed, amid the first passion of empirical fact-finding, that the ancient science of mathematics still went its undisturbed way of pure reason. It fell in so nicely with the needs of scientific thought, it fitted the observed world of fact so neatly, that those who learned and used it never stopped to accuse those who had invented and evolved it of being mere reasoners, and lacking tangible data. Yet the few conscientious empiricists who thought that *factual* bases must be established for mathematics made a notoriously poor job of it. Few mathematicians have really held that numbers were discovered by observation, or even that geometrical relationships are known to us by inductive reasoning from many observed instances. Physicists may think of certain facts in place of constants and variables, but the same constants and variables will serve somewhere else to calculate other facts, and the mathematicians themselves give no set of data their preference. They deal only with items whose sensory qualities are quite irrelevant: their "data" are arbitrary sounds or marks called *symbols*.

Behind these symbols lie the boldest, purest coolest abstractions mankind has ever made. No schoolman speculating on essences and attributes ever approached anything like the abstractness of algebra. Yet those same scientists who prided themselves on their concrete factual knowledge, who claimed to reject every proof except empirical evidence, never hesitated to accept the demonstrations and calculations, the bodiless, sometimes avowedly "fictitious" entities of the mathematicians. Zero and infinity, square roots of negative numbers, incommensurable lengths and fourth dimensions, all found unquestioned welcome in the laboratory, when the average thoughtful laymen, who could still take an invisible soul substance on faith, doubted their logical respectibility.

What is the secret power of mathematics, to win hardheaded empiricists, against their most ardent beliefs, to its purely rational speculations and intangible "facts"? Mathematicians are rarely practical people, or good observers of events. They are apt to be cloistered souls, like philosophers and theologians. Why are their abstractions taken not only seriously, but as indispensable, fundamental facts, by men who observe the stars or experiment with chemical compounds?

The secret lies in the fact that a mathematician does not profess to say anything about the existence, really, or efficacy of things at all. His concern is the possibility of *symbolizing things*, and of symbolizing the relations into which they might enter with each other. His "entities" are not "data," but *concepts*. That is why such elements as "imaginary numbers" and "infinite decimals" are tolerated by scientists to whom invisible agents, powers, and "principles" are anathema. Mathematical constructions are only symbols; they have meanings in terms of relationships, not substance; something in reality answers to them, but they are not supposed to be items in that reality. It is entirely at the discretion of the scientists to say, "Let x mean this, let y mean that." All that mathematics determines is that *then* x and y must be related thus and thus. But no mathematician in his professional capacity will ever tell us that *this is* x, and has therefore such and such properties.

The faith of scientists in the power and truth of mathematics is so implicit that their work has gradually become less and less observation, and more and more calculation. The promiscuous collection and tabulation of data have given way to a process of assigning possible meanings, merely supposed real entities, to mathematical terms, working out the logical results, and then staging certain crucial experiments to check the hypothesis against the actual, empirical results. But the facts which are accepted by virtue of these tests are not actually *observed* at all. With the advance of mathematical technique in physics, the tangible results of experiment have become less and less spectacular; on the other hand, their *significance* has grown in inverse proportion. The men in the laboratory have departed so far from the old forms of experimentation—typified by Galileo's weights and Franklin's kite—that they cannot be said to observe the actual objects of their curiosity at all; instead, they are watching index needles, revolving drums, and sensitive plates. No psychology of "association" of sense experiences can relate these data to the objects they signify, for in most cases the objects have never been experienced. Observation has become almost entirely indirect; and *readings* take the place of genuine witness. The sense data on which the propositions of modern science rest are, for the most part, little photographic spots and blurs, or inky curved lines on paper. These data are empirical enough, but of course they are not themselves the phenomena in question; the actual phenomena stand behind them as their supposed causes. Instead of watching the process that interests us, that is to be verified—say, a course of celestial events, or the behavior of such objects as molecules and ether waves—we really see only the fluctuations of a tiny arrow, the trailing path of a stylus, or the appearance of a speck of light, and *calculate to the "facts" of our science.* What is directly observable is only a sign of the "physical fact"; it requires interpretation to yield scientific propositions. Not simply seeing is believing, but *seeing and calculating, seeing and translating.*

This is bad, of course, for a thoroughgoing empiricism. Sense data certainly do not make up the whole, or even the major part of a scientist's material. The events that are given for his inspection could be "faked" in a dozen ways—that is, the same visible events could be made to occur, but with a different significance. We may at any time be wrong about their significance, even where no one is duping us; we may be nature's fools. Yet if we did not attribute an elaborate, purely reasoned, and hypothetical history of causes to the little shivers and wiggles of our apparatus, we really could not record them as momentous results of experiment. The problem of observation is all but eclipsed by the problem of *meaning*. And the triumph of empiricism in science is jeopardized by the surprising truth that our *sense-data are primarily symbols.*

Here, suddenly, it becomes apparent that the age of science has begotten a new philosophical issue, inestimably more profound than its original empiricism: for in all quietness, along purely rational lines, mathematics has developed just as brilliantly and vitally as any experimental technique, and, step by step, has kept abreast of discovery and observation; and all at once, the edifice of human knowledge stands before us, not as a vast collection of sense reports, but as a structure of *facts that are symbols* and *laws that are their meanings.* A new philosophical theme has been set forth to a coming age: an epistemological theme, the comprehension of science. The power of symbolism is its cue, as the finality of sense data was the cue of a former epoch.

But it is not only in philosophy proper that the new keynote has been struck. There are at least two limited and technical fields, which have suddenly been developed beyond all prediction, by the discovery of the all-importance of symbol using or symbol reading. They are widely separate fields, and their problems and procedures do not seem to belong together in any way at all: one is modern psychology, the other modern logic.

In the former we are disturbed—thrilled, or irritated, according to our temperaments—by the advent of psychoanalysis. In the latter we witness the rise of a new technique known as symbolic logic. The coincidence of these two pursuits seems entirely fortuitous; one stems from medicine and the other from mathematics, and there is nothing whatever on which they would care to compare notes or hold debate. Yet I believe they both embody the same generative idea, which is to preoccupy and inspire our philosophical age; for each in its own fashion has discovered the power of symbolization.

They have different conceptions of symbolism and its functions. Symbolic logic is not "symbolic" in the sense of Freudian psychology, and *The Analysis of Dreams* makes no contribution to logical syntax. The emphasis on symbolism derives from entirely different interests, in their respective contexts. As yet, the cautious critic may well regard the one as a fantastic experiment of "mental philosophy," and the other as a mere fashion in logic and epistemology. . . . Yet in both we have a central theme: the human response, as a constructive, not a passive thing. Epistemologists and psychologists agree that symbolization is the key to that constructive process, though they may be ready to kill each other over the issue of what a symbol is and how it functions. One studies the structure of science, the other of dreams; each has his own assumptions—that is all they are—regarding the nature of symbolism itself. Assumptions, generative ideas, are what we fight for. Our conclusions we are usually content to demonstrate by peaceable means. Yet the assumptions are philosophically our most interesting stock-in-trade.

In the fundamental notion of symbolization—mystical, practical, or mathematical, it makes no difference—we have the keynote of all humanistic problems. In it lies a new conception of "mentality," that may illumine questions of life and consciousness, instead of obscuring them as traditional "scientific methods" have done. If it is indeed a generative idea, it will beget tangible methods of its own, to free the deadlocked paradoxes of mind and body, reason and impulse, autonomy and law, and will overcome the checkmated arguments of an earlier age by discarding their very idiom and shaping their equivalents in more significant phrase. The philosophical study of symbols is not a technique borrowed from other disciplines, not even from mathematics; it has arisen in the fields that the great advance of learning has left fallow. Perhaps it holds the seed of a new intellectual harvest, to be reaped in the next season of the human understanding.

ON SIGNIFICANCE IN THE ARTS

I

THERE IS a strong tendency today to treat art as a significant phenomenon rather than as a pleasurable experience, a gratification of the senses. This is probably due to the free use of dissonance and so-called "ugliness" by our leading artists in all fields—in literature, music, and the plastic arts. It may also be due in some measure to the striking indifference of the uneducated masses to artistic values. In past ages, these masses had no access to great works of art; music and painting and even books were the pleasures of the wealthy; it could be assumed that the poor and vulgar would enjoy art if they could have it. But now, since everybody can read, visit museums, and hear great music at least over the radio, the judgment of the masses on these things has become a reality, and has made it quite obvious that *great art is not* a direct sensuous pleasure. If it were, it would appeal—like cake or cocktails—to the untutored as well as to the cultured taste. This fact, together with the intrinsic "unpleasantness" of much contemporary art, would naturally weaken any theory that treated art as pure pleasure. Add to this the current logical and psychological interest in symbolism, in expressive media and the articulation of ideas, and we need not look far afield for a new philosophy of art, based upon the concept of "significant form."

But if forms in and of themselves be significant, and indeed must be so to be classed as artistic, then certainly the kind of significance that belongs to them constitutes a very special problem in semantics. What is artistic significance? What sort of meaning do "expressive forms" express?

Clearly they do not convey propositions, as literal symbols do. We all know that a seascape (say) represents water and rocks, boats and fish piers; that a still life represents oranges and apples, a vase of flowers, dead game or fish, etc. But such a content is not what makes the paint patterns on the canvas "expressive forms." The mere notion of rabbits, grapes, or even boats at sunset is not the "idea" that inspires a painting. The artistic idea is always a "deeper" conception.

Several psychologists have ventured to unmask this "deeper" significance by interpreting pictures, poems, and even musical compositions as symbols of loved objects, mainly, of course, of a forbidden nature. Artistic activity according to the psychoanalysts who have given it their attention, is an expression of primitive dynamisms, of unconscious wishes, and uses the objects or scenes represented to embody the secret fantasies of the artist.

This explanation has much to recommend it. It accounts for the fact that we are inclined to credit works of art with *significance*, although (by reason of the moral censorship which distorts the appearance of basic desires) we can never say what they signify. It does justice to the emotional interest, the seriousness with which we receive artistic experience. Above all, it brings this baffling department of human activity into the compass of a general psychological system—the so-called "dynamic psychology," based on the recognition of certain fundamental human needs, of the conflicts resulting from their mutual interference, and of the mechanism whereby they assert, disguise, and finally realize themselves. The starting-point of this psychology is the discovery of a previously unrecognized *symbolic mode*, typified in dream, and perfectly traceable in all works of fantasy. To assimilate art to the imaginative life in general is surely not a forced procedure. It seems, moreover, to bring the problem of esthetic experience into the symbol-centered philosophy that constitutes the theme of this book.

These are strong recommendations for the psychoanalytic theory of esthetics. But despite them all, I do not think this theory (though probably valid) throws any real light on those issues which confront artists and critics and constitute the philosophical problem of art. For the Freudian interpretation, no matter how far it be carried, never offers even the rudest citerion of *artistic* excellence. It may explain why a poem was written, why it is popular, what human features it hides under its fanciful imagery; what secret ideas a picture combines, and why Leonardo's women smile mysteriously. But *it makes no distinction between good and bad art*. The features to which it attributes the importance and significance of a great masterpiece may all be found just as well in an obscure work of some quite incompetent painter or poet. Wilhelm Stekel, one of the leading Freudian psychologists interested in artistic productions as a field for analysis, has stated this fact explicitly: "I want to point out at once," he says, "that it is irrelevant to our purpose whether the poet in question is a great, universally acknowledged poet, or whether we are dealing with a little poetaster. For, after all, we are investigating only the impulse which drives people to create."

An analysis to which the artistic merit of a work is irrelevant can hardly be regarded as a promising technique of art criticism, for it can look only to a hidden content of the work, and not to what every artist knows as the real problem—the *perfection of form*, which makes this form "significant" in the artistic sense. We cannot evaluate this perfection by finding more and more obscure objects represented or suggested by the form.

Interest in represented objects and interest in the visual or verbal structures that depict them are always getting hopelessly entangled. Yet I believe "artistic meaning" belongs to the sensuous construct as such; this alone is beautiful, and contains all that contributes to its beauty.

The most obvious approach to the formal aspect of art would be, of course, through the study of pure design. But in poetry pure design is nonexistent, and in the plastic arts it has played but a minor role until very recent times. It is carried to considerable heights in textiles, and occurs as decoration in conjunction with architecture and ceramics. But the world's greatest artists have rarely worked in these media; sculptures and paintings are their high achievements. If we would really restrict ourselves to pure perceptible forms, the plastic arts offer but a sparse field for research, and not a central one.

Music, on the other hand, is preeminently nonrepresentative even in its classical productions, its highest attainments. It exhibits pure form not as an embellishment, but as its very essence; we can take it in its flower—for instance, German music from Bach to Beethoven—and have practically nothing but tonal structures before us: no scene, no object, no fact. That is a great aid to our chosen preoccupation with form. There is no obvious, literal content in our way. If the meaning of art belongs to the sensuous percept itself apart from what it ostensibly represents, then such purely artistic meaning should be most accessible through musical works.

Because the forms of human feeling are much more congruent with musical forms than with the forms of language, music can *reveal* the nature of feelings with a detail and truth that language cannot approach. This peculiar articulateness of music as a semantic of vital and emotional facts was discovered nearly two centuries ago by one of the contributors to Marpurg's famous *Beiträge zur Musik*. This writer says:

> There are feelings . . . which are so constantly suppressed by the tumult of our passions, that they can reveal themselves but timidly, and are practically unknown to us. . . . Note, however, what response a certain kind of music evokes in our hearts: we are attentive, it is charming; it does not aim to arouse either sorrow or joy, pity or anger, and yet we are moved by it. We are so imperceptibly, so gently moved, that we do not know we are affected, or *rather, that we can give no name to the effect*. . . .
>
> Indeed, it is quite impossible *to name* everything fascinating in music, and bring it under definite headings. Therefore music has fulfilled its mission whenever our hearts are satisfied.

II

The basic unity of all the arts is sometimes argued from the apparent beginning of all artistic ideas in the so-called "esthetic emotion" which is supposed to be their source and therefore (by a slightly slipshod inference) their import.* Anyone who has worked in more than one medium probably can testify to the sameness of the "esthetic emotion" accompanying creation in the various arts. But I suspect that this characteristic excitement, so closely wedded to original conception and inner vision, is not the source, but the effect, of artistic labor, the personal emotive experience of revelation, insight, mental power, which an adventure in "implicit understanding" inspires. It has often been stated that it is the same emotion which overtakes a mathematician as he constructs a convincing and elegant proof; and this is the beatitude which Spinoza, who knew it well, called "the intellectual love of God." Something like it is begotten in appreciation of art, too, though not nearly in the same measure as in producing; but the fact that the difference is one of degree makes it plausible that the emotion springs from the one activity which the artist and the beholder share in unequal parts—the comprehension of an unspoken idea. In the artist this activity must be sustained, complete, and intense; his intellectual excitement is often at fever pitch. The idea is his own, and if he loses his command of it, confused by the material or distracted by pressing irrelevancies, there is no symbol to hold it for him. His mind is apt to be furiously active while an artistic conception takes shape. To the beholder the work is offered as a constant source of an insight he attains gradually, more or less clearly, perhaps never in logical completeness; and although his mental experience also wakens the characteristic emotion, variously called "feeling of beauty," "esthetic emotion," and "esthetic pleasure," he knows nothing like the exhilaration and tense excitement of an artist before his pristine marble or clay, his unmarked canvas or paper, as the new work dawns in his brain.

Perhaps it is inevitable that this emotion which one really *has* in producing or contemplating an artistic composition should become confused with the content of the work, since that content is itself emotive. If there is feeling in the work, and both artist and spectator experience a feeling, and moreover the artist has *more* of a feeling than the spectator, would it not take a very careful thinker to refrain from jumping to the conclusion that the emotion embodied in the form is felt by the artist before he begins his work, is "expressed" in the process of creating as it might be in shouting or weeping, and is sympathetically felt by the audience? Yet I believe the "esthetic emotion" and the emotional content of a work of art are two very different things; the "esthetic emotion" springs from an intellectual triumph, from overcoming barriers of word-bound thought and achieving insight into literally "unspeakable" realities; but the emotive content of the work is apt to be something much deeper than any intellectual experience, more essential, prerational, and vital, something of the life rhythms we share with all growing, hungering, moving, and fearing creatures: the ultimate realities themselves, the central facts of our brief, sentient existence.

"Esthetic pleasure," then, is akin to (though not identical with) the satisfaction of discovering truth. It is the characteristic reaction to a well-known, but usually ill-defined, phenomenon called "artistic truth" —well-known to all artists, creative or

* Cf. Clive Bell: "The starting-point for all systems of esthetics must be the personal experience of a peculiar emotion. . . . This emotion is called the esthetic emotion; and if we can discover some quality common to all and absent from none of the objects that provoke it, we shall have solved what I take to be the central problem of esthetics." (*Art*, p. 6.) Mr. Bell forgets the logical rule that such a discovery would prove nothing, unless the quality in question were also *peculiar* to esthetic objects; any quality common to all objects whatever would fulfil the condition he states.

appreciative, but so ill-defined by most epistemologists that it has become their favorite aversion. Yet truth is so intimately related to symbolism that if we recognize two radically different types of symbolic expression we should logically look for two distinct meanings of truth; and if both symbolic modes are rational enough, both senses of truth should be definable.

Here it must be noted that the distinction between discursive and presentational symbols does not correspond to the difference between literal and artistic meanings. Many presentational symbols are merely proxy for discourse; geometric relations may be rendered in algebraic terms—clumsy terms perhaps, but quite equivalent—and graphs are mere abbreviated descriptions. They express facts for discursive thinking, and their content *can be verbalized*, subjected to the laws of vocabulary and syntax. Artistic symbols, on the other hand, are untranslatable; their sense is bound to the particular form which it has taken. It is always *implicit*, and cannot be explicated by any interpretation. This is true even of poetry, for though the material of poetry is verbal, its import is not the literal assertion made in the words, but *the way the assertion is made*, and this involves the sound, the tempo, the aura of associations of the words, the long or short sequences of ideas, the wealth or poverty of transient imagery that contains them, the sudden arrest of fantasy by pure fact, or of familiar fact by sudden fantasy, the suspense of literal meaning by a sustained ambiguity resolved in a long-awaited key word, and the unifying, all-embracing artifice of rhythm. (The tension which music achieves through dissonance, and the reorientation in each new resolution to harmony, find their equivalents in the suspensions and periodic decisions of propositional sense in poetry. Literal sense, not euphony, is the "harmonic structure" of poetry; word melody in literature is more akin to tone color in music.)

The poem as a whole is the bearer of artistic import, as a painting or a drama is. We may isolate significant lines, as we may isolate beauties in any work, but if their meaning is not determined and supported by their context, the entire work, then that work is a failure despite the germ of excellence it contains. That is why Professor Urban's restatement of T. S. Eliot's cryptic lines:

> And I see the damp souls of the housemaids
> Sprouting disconsolately at area gates,

namely: "That housemaids' souls are damp and sprout," and his demand for a *more adequate rendering* of this assertion by way of philosophical interpretation, seems to me a fundamental misconception of poetic import.* A "more adequate rendering" would be more, not less, poetic; it would be a better poem. "Artistic truth" does *not* belong to statements in the poem or their obvious figurative meanings, but to its figures and meanings *as they are used*, its statements *as they are made*, its framework of word sound and sequence, rhythm and recurrence and rhyme, color and image and the speed of their passage—in short, to the poem as "significant form." The material of poetry is discursive, but the product—the artistic phenomenon—is not; its significance is purely implicit in the poem as a totality, as a form compounded of sound and suggestion, statement and reticence, and no translation can reincarnate that. Poetry may be approximated in other languages and give rise to surprisingly beautiful new versions revealing new possibilities of its skeletal literal ideas and rhetorical

* Urban, *Language and Reality*. To anyone who cannot grasp the poet's meaning and vision here, Professor Urban's "interpretation" certainly would make matters worse rather than better.

devices; but the product *is* new, like an orchestral scoring of an organ fugue, a piano version of a string quartet, or a photograph of a painting.

"Artistic truth," so called, is the truth of a symbol to the forms of feeling—nameless forms, but recognizable when they appear in sensuous replica. Such truth, being bound to certain logical forms of expression, has logical peculiarities that distinguish it from propositional truth: since presentational symbols have no negatives, there is no operation whereby their truth-value is reversed, no *contradiction*. Hence "the possibility of expressing opposites simultaneously," on which Mersmann commented. Falsity here is a complicated failing, not a function of negation. For this reason Professor Reid calls it not falsity but *inexpressiveness;* and Urban, in a moment undisturbed by epistemology, abandons not only the term "falsity," but also "truth," and suggests that artistic forms should rather be designated as *adequate* or *inadequate* to the ideas they embody. Perhaps he did not see that this shift of terminology belies his doctrine that all art makes assertions which must ultimately be paraphrased in language; for assertions are true or false, and their adequacy has to be taken for granted before we can judge them as assertions at all. They are always debatable and may be tested for their truth-values by the nature of their explicable consequences. Art, on the other hand, has no consequences; it gives form to something that is simply there, as the intuitive organizing functions of sense give form to objects and spaces, color and sound. It gives what Bertrand Russell calls "knowledge by acquaintance" of affective experience, below the level of belief, on the deeper level of insight and attitude. And to this mission it is either adequate or inadequate, as images, the primitive symbols of "things," are adequate or inadequate to give us a conception of what things are "like." *

To understand the "idea" in a work of art is therefore more like *having a new experience* than like entertaining a new proposition; and to negotiate this knowledge by acquaintance the work may be adequate *in some degree*. There are no degrees of literal truth, but artistic truth, which is all significance, expressiveness, articulateness, has degrees; therefore works of art may be good or bad, and each must be judged on our experience of its revelations. Standards of art are set by the expectations of people whom long conversance with a certain mode—music, painting, architecture, or what not—has made both sensitive and exacting; there is no immutable law of artistic adequacy, because significance is always *for* a mind as well as *of* a form. But a form, a harmony, even a *timbre*, that is entirely unfamiliar is "meaningless," naturally enough; for we must grasp a *Gestalt* quite definitely before we can perceive an implicit meaning, or even the promise of such a meaning, in it; and such definite grasp requires a certain familiarity. Therefore the most original contemporary music in any period always troubles people's ears. The more pronounced its new idiom, the less they can make of it, unless the impulse which drove the composer to this creation is something of a common experience, of a yet inarticulate *Zeitgeist*, which others, too, have felt. Then they, like him, may be ready to experiment with new expressions, and meet with an open mind what even the best of them cannot really judge. Perhaps some very wonderful music is lost because

* Lord Russell fails to appreciate, I think, the logical, formulative mission of sense, or else he evades it because it has kept company with idealism. But *to see in certain forms* is not to create their contents, though it is a source of that relativistic character of "data" which makes them less final and absolute than his empiricism lets him admit.

it is too extraordinary. It may even be lost to its composer because he cannot really handle his forms, and abandons them as unsuccessful. But intimate acquaintance with all sorts of music does give some versatile minds a power of grasping new sounds; people so inclined and trained will have a "hunch," at least, that they are dealing with true "significant form" though they still hear a good deal of it as noise, and will contemplate it until they comprehend it, for better or worse. It is an old story that Bach, Beethoven, and Wagner were "hard to hear" in their own time. Many people today, who can follow Rimsky-Korsakoff or Debussy as easily as Schumann, cannot hear music in Hindemith or Bartók; yet the more experienced probably know, by certain signs, that it is there.

On the other hand, artistic forms are exhaustible, too. Music that has fulfilled its mission may be outgrown, so that its style, its quality, its whole conception, palls on a generation that is ardently expressing or seeking to express something else. Only very catholic minds can see beauty in many styles even without the aid of historical fancy, of a conscious "self-projection" into other settings or ages. It is probably easiest in music, where typical forms are not further bound down by literal references to things that have a transient and dated character.

To us whose intelligence is bound up with language, whose achievements are physical comforts, machines, medicines, great cities, and the means of their destruction, theory of knowledge means theory of communication, generalization, proof, in short: critique of science. But the limits of language are not the last limits of experience, and things inaccessible to language may have their own forms of conception, that is to say, their own symbolic devices. Such nondiscursive forms, charged with logical possibilities of meaning, underlie the significance of music; and their recognition broadens our epistemology to the point of including not only the semantics of science, but a serious philosophy of art.

INDEX OF AUTHORS, ARTISTS, AND MUSICIANS